MW01014627

Law, Policy, and Higher Education

LexisNexis Law School Publishing Advisory Board

Law, Policy, and Higher Education

Philip T.K. Daniel
William and Marie Flesher Professor of Educational Administration
Adjunct Professor of Law
The Ohio State University

E. Gordon Gee
President
Professor of Law
The Ohio State University

Jeffrey C. Sun
Associate Professor, Department of Educational Leadership
Afilliate Faculty, School of Law
University of North Dakota

Patrick D. Pauken
Vice Provost for Governance and Faculty Relations
Secretary to the Board of Trustees
Associate Professor of Educational Administration and Leadership Studies
Bowling Green State University

Casebook ISBN 978-0-7698-5429-8
Looseleaf ISBN 978-0-7698-5468-7

Library of Congress Cataloging-in-Publication Data

Daniel, Philip T. K.
Law, policy, and higher education / Philip T.K. Daniel, William and Marie Flesher Professor of Educational Administration, Adjunct Professor of Law, The Ohio State University ; E. Gordon Gee, President, The Ohio State University ; Jeffrey C. Sun, Associate Professor, Department of Educational Leadership, University of North Dakota ; Patrick D. Pauken, Vice Provost of Governance and Faculty Relations, Secretary of the Board of Trustees, Associate Professor of Educational Administration and Leadership Studies, Bowling Green State University.
pages cm.
Includes index.
ISBN 978-0-7698-5429-8
1. Education, Higher--Law and legislation--United States. 2. Universities and colleges--Law and legislation--United States. I. Gee, E. Gordon (Elwood Gordon), 1944- II. Pauken, Patrick D. III. Sun, Jeffrey C. IV. Title.
KF4225.D36 2012
344.73'074--dc23
2012034229

NOTE TO USERS
To ensure that you are using the latest materials available in this area, please be sure to periodically check the LexisNexis Law School web site for downloadable updates and supplements at www.lexisnexis.com/lawschool.

Editorial Offices
121 Chanlon Rd., New Providence, NJ 07974 (908) 464-6800
201 Mission St., San Francisco, CA 94105-1831 (415) 908-3200
www.lexisnexis.com

MATTHEW BENDER

(2012–Pub.3366)

Dedication

I dedicate this book to my granddaughter, Maya Naomi Kanai Daniel, who constantly informs me about how to live a smarter and more enjoyable life.

— Professor Daniel

For Rebekah, and her new family, who are bringing light into my life.

— President Gee

For Ruth and Gary Sun, the two people who inspired me to pursue and share knowledge for the greater good

— Professor Sun

To my best and favorite teachers — my parents Patricia and Raymond Pauken — who taught me that education is not only great for the mind, but also great for the heart.

— Professor Pauken

PREFACE

The authors chose to title this textbook, LAW, POLICY, & HIGHER EDUCATION: CASES AND MATERIALS, with purpose. The research contained in the pages herein not only presents primary materials such as cases, statutes, and regulations, but also secondary sources regarding legal issues that colleges and universities, students, faculty, accreditors, and other related entities face. The discourse also examines the interchange between policy and the law such as, for example, how cases impact the treatment of students' rights and responsibilities or how statutes alter university research activities. In our discussions, we have adopted an intentional and carefully delineated approach weighing considerations of societal forces (i.e., political, economic, cultural, and technological) balanced against the institutional core mission of a college or university. For instance, how do technological innovations alter the ownership rights of faculty who teach online courses, which are recorded? To what extent does a state's expectation that public colleges and universities serve as the region's economic engines alter the contractual relationships for faculty and students in university-business partnerships?

The topics chosen, broken down into 13 designated chapters, raise current issues for faculty, students, attorneys, higher education administrators, policymakers, and other participants in the higher education enterprise. The cases that have been highlighted present questions that can be examined from several perspectives. For example, consider a case involving a student assault on campus. As an administrator, how would a court's holding affect the way official institutional policy is formed in regards to on-campus criminal activity? If in the role of an attorney for a student-plaintiff who was attacked in a university residence hall, with what causes of action would you proceed? As a faculty member sitting on the university senate's "Student Safety" committee, how would this case's decision impact recommendations you submit to the committee? Each chapter has been drafted to educate students in a variety of ways, regardless of whether their ultimate desired career is in administration, in-house university counsel, policy-making, general law practice, or a professorship at a higher education institution.

Specifically, the chapters examine the law and policy issues that are on the forefront of higher education, ranging from intercollegiate athletics to individuals with disabilities, academic integrity measures, and intellectual property — particularly in terms of commercialization. For instance, the topic of students with disabilities reflects an area that has grown substantially in the past decade. This occurrence is not surprising when one looks at the raw numbers. During the 1997-1998 school year, there were 428,280 students with disabilities attending U.S. colleges and universities. Slightly more than a decade later, that number grew to 707,000 students during the 2008-2009 school year. With such a dramatic increase in the enrollment of students with disabilities, courts and policymakers were forced to adapt, leading to new case law and policies. In addition, several other indicators suggest that the legal and policy issues pertaining to students with disabilities are expected to grow. In 2008, the Americans with Disabilities Act was significantly modified, and according to a 2011 U.S. Department of Education Report, the college enrollments of students with disabilities is expected to continue to increase. Thus, the topic lends itself to examination and consideration in terms of the laws and policies associated with supporting students with special needs that will undoubtedly aid students in the future. Similar examples also exist for matters addressing intercollegiate athletics (e.g., the financial commitment of college athletics and its alleged treatment of athletes as commodities), academic integrity measures (e.g., academic standards required to compete in a global society and the legal boundaries in which policymakers have to legislate those mandates), and intellectual property (e.g., commercially valued products and services that spur academic innovation, but require university resources). All of these issues have evolved over the past few decades and will continue to do so. Often there is a lag between the pronouncement of new legal standards and the adaptation of policymakers to the newly articulated mandates. Thus, students will find themselves in the midst of two discussions: First, with regard to clearly established doctrine, how has higher education changed for the better or worse in response to the confines of the law? Second, in terms of new, progressive legal initiatives, how will university and college administrators make adjustments in our evolving reality? What correlating policy changes may ensue as a result of not only the changes in legal standards, but also the changes in the economic environment?

Along with groundbreaking case law and research, the textbook also provides students with basic, foundational knowledge that is imperative to succeeding as a professional in the world of higher education. For instance, students will be introduced to the elements of a negligence cause of action, along with a detailed analysis of the different duties often imposed on university administrators and faculty. Students will be exposed to the workings of Institutional Review Boards and the purposes they serve within the university's research protocols. Further, students will confidently be able to articulate the requirements a college or university must meet in order to be granted tax-exempt status as a charitable institution. These legal foundations are just a sampling of the important groundwork set forth in this textbook.

In sum, this compilation fills a gap in the market for casebooks on higher education law, as the materials presented lend themselves to timely and important discussions of both law and policy issues. Chapters 1 and 2 provide an overview of higher education with respect to the laws and policies that shape its roles and responsibilities in society. Chapters 3 and 4 examine the college's employment relationship with faculty and staff. Chapters 5, 6, and 7 explore the rights and responsibilities of students. Chapter 8 addresses how the university affects and is affected by the intercollegiate athletic enterprise. Chapters 9, 10, and 11 present the influence and impact of government regulations as well as higher education's efforts to shape policies that further institutional aims and manage university resources. Chapter 12 addresses issues of intellectual property, especially involving faculty, but with an eye on public/private partnerships, ownership, and commercialization of research. Chapter 13 presents an exposé of persons with special needs, a largely overlooked and underserved population within the university.

The authors extend appreciation for the valuable research assistance of Christopher Montgomery, Jillian Wolosiansky, Rachel Kepley, Seth Chodosh, Geoffrey Saxe and Joel

Lund all former students at The Ohio State University Moritz College of Law. We are equally grateful for the research assistance of Keisha Hunley-Jenkins and Samara Preisler, graduate students in Ohio State's College of Education and Human Ecology. We also wish to thank Gereon Methner, a graduate student in the School of Educational Foundations, Leadership, and Policy at Bowling Green State University for his research assistance. The authors are grateful for the editing assistance of Chinyere Richardson, Section Associate in Educational Administration.

Philip T.K. Daniel
E. Gordon Gee
Jeffrey C. Sun
Patrick D. Pauken

TABLE OF CONTENTS

TABLE OF CONTENTS

TABLE OF CONTENTS

Chapter I

HISTORY OF HIGHER EDUCATION IN THE UNITED STATES

Introduction

Since the first institutions of higher learning were chartered in the American colonies, higher education has evolved into a national industry comprised of a wide network of approximately 4,500 colleges and universities. Higher education institutions in the U.S. are, in many respects, quite diverse relative to other nations' colleges and universities. U.S. institutions are divided into many different categories such as by governance control (i.e., public, private non-profit, private for-profit), superordinate affiliations (e.g., religious colleges), degree level offerings (i.e., two-year, baccalaureate, masters, doctoral), special foci colleges (e.g., seminaries, minority-serving institutions, single-sex institutions), and legislatively devised colleges with a service agenda (i.e., land grant colleges, military academies). The institutional diversity of U.S. higher education has created greater access for individuals to attend a postsecondary school, and the trend is likely to continue. The National Center for Education Statistics (NCES) reported over 20 million students during the 2009–2010 academic year. Nat'l Ctr. for Educ. Statistics, Digest of Education Statistics: 2011 at Table 196 (2012), available at: http://nces.ed.gov/programs/digest/d11/tables/dt11_197.asp. Yet, in 2009, NCES had posed moderate projections of 20 million enrolled college students in the U.S. by the year 2015, which appeared realistic given that the U.S. already had over 15 million students by the year 2000. Nat'l Ctr. for Educ. Statistics, Education Statistics to 2018 at Table 10 (2012), available at: http://nces.ed.gov/programs/digest/d11/tables/dt11_197.asp. The growth and expansion of U.S. higher education provide societal opportunities as American colleges and universities provide a path to better employment, knowledge access through research, and service to surrounding communities.

As the higher education system has grown, so has the substance surrounding its operation. Universities must continually deal with legal concerns that include academic freedom, constitutional rights of students, government regulation, and university liability just to list a few. This chapter examines the historical and legal context in which these policy issues have taken shape.

The principles of federalism established in the United States Constitution helped craft the rapid evolution of higher education in America. Unlike the traditional model of higher learning found in England (where the universities are funded by the state), the American judiciary carved out a place for private universities in the corporate entrepreneurship doctrine that the federal government, over time, has found somewhat difficult to control. *See Trs. of Dartmouth Coll. v. Woodward*, 4 L.

Ed. 629 (1819). Section A of this chapter begins by examining how this federalist approach to early private universities affected the development of higher education in America. Though there is no central law governing the operation of such institutions, the federal and state governments regulate both public and private universities in a variety of ways. By giving universities land grants and funds through legislation like the Morrill Act and the Higher Education Act of 1965 (and subsequent amendments), legislative officials intentionally entangled themselves in the affairs and operation of private and religious institutions. Because of their ties to government funding and regulation, for example, private universities may be viewed as state actors for the purpose of applying constitutional doctrine. The *Craft* case, contained in Section B, provides an example of this principle. *Craft v. Vanderbilt Univ.*, 18 F. Supp. 2d 786 (M.D. Tenn. 1998).

Section C continues this analysis by providing a variety of judicial decisions that attempt to balance the interplay between government legislation and the private university. Government assisted university funding is linked to many institutional obligations in the educational setting, including racial equality in admissions, gender equality in athletics, religious non-discrimination, and public access to meetings and records. *See Bob Jones Univ. v. United States*, 461 U.S. 574 (1983); *Cohen v. Brown Univ.*, 991 F.2d 888 (1st Cir. 1993); *Associated Press v. Crofts*, 89 P.3d 971 (Mont. 2004). The tension created by this funding relationship is explored further in Section D. How far can a public university go in the observance of religious traditions or themes before the Establishment Clause is violated? Similarly, how much funding or support can the federal government provide to a religious university without also violating the Establishment Clause?

Higher educational institutions do not stand alone, isolated from the effects of legal interpretations elsewhere in the broader spectrum of education law. Part E briefly outlines how K-12 law can apply in the higher education setting and how different lower courts cope with the ambiguous line between the levels of education.

Underlying these questions and the issues presented in this book is the role of policy in higher education. Part F provides a theoretical framework of the connection between law, policy, and institutional goals. While reading this chapter, it is important to note how these goals affect policy decisions and the way they are implemented. What is the source of these goals? What determines whether or not a particular mode of policy implementation will be successful?

A. AMERICAN HIGHER EDUCATION: PAST, PRESENT, AND FUTURE

Martin Trow, *Federalism in American Higher Education*, 39–64, *in* Higher Learning in America, 1980–2000 (Arthur Levine ed., 1993)*

Like Germany and Canada, but unlike most other countries in the world, the United States places the primary responsibility for education (including higher education) on the states rather than on the federal government. In the United States this mirrors the deep suspicion of central government reflected in the separation of powers in the Constitution. Moreover, the Tenth Amendment of the Bill of Rights states simply: "The powers not delegated to the United States by the Constitution, nor prohibited by it to the States, are reserved to the States respectively or to the people." Provision of education is one of these powers.

Federalism in the United States can be seen as the major determinant of the governance and finance of the nation's system of higher education. The concept of federalism focuses attention on the role of regional governments — in the case of American higher education, usually the states, although sometimes counties and cities are also relevant — and on their relation to the central authority of the national government. And federalism is also concerned with the role of private, nongovernmental sources of support, which are especially important for many of America's leading academic institutions, both "public" and "private." Thus, federalism in American higher education cannot be separated from the broader issue of how American higher education developed in the curious and unique ways that it has — so large, untidy, uncoordinated from the center, and without national (or even state) standards for the admission of students, the appointment of academic staff, or the awarding of degrees. For that reason, if no other, a discussion of the nature and emergence of American higher education must involve attention to the nature and emergence of federalism in American life.

Aspects of Federalism in Contemporary American Higher Education

. . . .

The size and diversity of the student body in American colleges and universities reflect the number and diversity of the institutions in which they are enrolled. No central law or authority governs or coordinates American higher education. The nearly two thousand private institutions are governed by lay boards that appoint their own members; the 1,560 public institutions (including nearly one thousand public community colleges) are "accountable" in varying degrees to state or local authorities but usually have a lay board of trustees as a buffer against direct state management, preserving a high if variable measure of institutional autonomy.

Differences in the forms of governance and finance among the public institutions

---

* Levine, Arthur, ed. Higher Learning in America, 1980–2000. pp. 39–64.

are very large, both between and within states. For example, the universities of Michigan and California are able to call on state constitutional provisions protecting their autonomy against political intrusion; it is perhaps not coincidental that they are also the two most distinguished public universities in the country. Over the years both have used their freedom to diversify their sources of support . . . (They are perhaps more accurately "state-aided" than "state" universities). Other state institutions, by contrast, suffer constant state interference in their management and policies, interference facilitated by line-item budgeting, close state control over expenditures, and limited discretionary funds.

While an observer can see contrasting patterns in the legal and formal organizational arrangements from state to state, actual relationships between public institutions and state authorities vary also by historical tradition, the strength and character of institutional leaders, and the values and sentiments of governors and key legislators. Variations in the autonomy of public institutions can be seen not only between states, but also between sectors of higher education within states and even between institutions within the same state sector. . . .

Differences in State Coordination and Support

. . . .

As a consequence of its system of educational federalism, the United States is evidently prepared to sustain differences (or inequities) in support for higher education among the several states . . . . This is perhaps one of the most significant and least remarked differences between the American and European systems. Any effort to achieve or approximate equality in America's provision of public services between and among states or regions would require considerable direct intervention by the central government. The federal government has been prepared to intervene strongly in education to defend the civil rights of students and faculty, most notably in connection with the potential for discrimination on the basis of race or gender, and it can also modestly reduce inequalities among states by providing federal funds directly to students and to researchers. With a few exceptions, however, the federal government does not try to stimulate state spending on higher education to compensate for differences in state wealth or effort or give the states unrestricted funds for support of higher education.

. . . .

The Roots of American Federalism in the Colonial Experience

Despite all the changes and transformations of state, society, and economy in modern times, the American system of higher education has its roots in the colonial period, when it developed characteristics distinguishable from all other systems of higher education in the world, notably in its governance patterns, marked by a strong president and lay governing board; its extraordinary diversity of forms and functions; and its marked responsiveness to forces in society as well as in state and church. In one other respect the colonial colleges are familiar to us, and that is in the importance attached to them by the societies and governments of the colonies. At a time when most European universities were not really central to the vitality of their societies and were more or less preoccupied with the preparation of theologians and divines serving an established church or with defining the virtues and polishing the accomplishments of a ruling elite, seventeenth and eighteenth century colonial colleges in America were regarded by their founders and supporters as forces for survival in a hostile environment. They were seen as crucial, indeed indispensable instruments for staving off the threat of reversion to barbarism, the threatened decline into the savagery of the surrounding forest and its Indian inhabitants. They also played a familiar role for early Calvinists in maintaining a learned ministry and a literate laity. Moreover, in the young colonies as on the later frontier, civilization and its institutions could never be assumed to be inherited. It had always to be created and recreated; for this purpose, learning and learned persons and the institutions that engendered them were needed. . . .

The colonial colleges were founded as public bodies. They were established and then chartered by a public authority and were supported in part by public funds, in part by private gifts and endowments, in part by student fees. The mixing of public and private support, functions, and authority has persisted as a central characteristic of American higher education to this day, blurring the distinction between public and private colleges and universities. Americans have tended to regard all of their higher education institutions as having a public dimension, and they also allowed for a private dimension in their public institutions. As Jurgen Herbst argued, one cannot see the colonial colleges as either "public" or "private" institutions, but as "provincial," stressing their function of service to their sponsoring and chartering colony, rather than to their source of support or authority. Although the distinction between "public" and "private" emerged with a certain clarity during the nineteenth century and especially after the Civil War, it is still more appropriate to see the broad spectrum of American colleges and universities as lying along a continuum from fully public to nearly purely private.

. . . .

. . . [T]he power of colonial governments over their colleges derived from three fundamental sources: the power to give or withhold a charter, the continuing powers reserved for government within the charter, and the power of the public purse. Within those constraints the colonies had the experience before the Revolution of having created a group of colleges or "university colleges" similar in certain respects but differing in others — and having created these institutions at the initiative or with the encouragement of public authorities and power private constituencies. Such support stands in marked contrast to the conspicuous lack of such encouragement and, indeed, the stubborn resistance of or deeply divided responses by political and ecclesiastical authorities in England to the creation of new institutions of higher education, especially and particularly those originating outside the Establishment, during the decades before 1830. . . . [T]he many dissenting academies created in England during the second half of the eighteenth century never had the encouragement of central or local government, and their failure to be fully acknowledged or to gain a charter and the right to grant degrees was among the factors leading them to short lives and a dead end, of no real use or inspiration to those who created the new English colleges and universities during the next century. By contrast, America's colonial experience provided training in the arts of establishing institutions of higher education. And the skills and attitudes necessary for the creation of new colleges that were gained during the colonial period, along with the models of governance afforded by the colonial institutions, led (in a more favorable environment than England provided) directly to the proliferation of colleges and universities after the Revolution . . . .

The Effects of the American Revolution

. . . .

The new states, both those that succeeded the old colonies and those carved out of the new lands in the West, did not give a monopoly to any single state college or university, reflecting the quite different relationship between state and societal institutions that emerged from the Revolution. The states granted charters much more readily than had colonies before the Revolution and on decidedly different terms. Herbst told of efforts in 1762 by Congregationalists dissatisfied with the liberal Unitarian tendencies of Harvard to create a Queen's College in western Massachusetts. The nation's oldest college and its overseers opposed the proposal and prevailed, using the argument that Harvard "was a provincial monopoly, funded and supported by the General Court for reasons of state" and "properly the College of the Government." The principle that reserved a monopoly to the "College of the Government," with its attendant rights and privileges, had to be overthrown for American higher education to break out of the restrictive chartering of higher education that had been historical practice. What is astonishing is not that it was subsequently overthrown, but that it was done with such ease as scarcely to occasion comment.

The ease with which new colleges were granted charters after the Revolution and especially after the turn of the century was both symbol and instrument of the triumph of society over the state the Revolution had achieved. Charters were distributed rather promiscuously to any group that seemed prepared to accept responsibility for raising funds for a building and hiring a president. Despite the efforts of the Federalists, central government itself over time came to be not a dominant institution (alongside the churches) but merely a player in social life, and not a very important one at that. By the fifth decade of the nineteenth century, the national government was scarcely visible in American life: no national bank, no military worth mentioning, no taxes that a growing majority of citizens could remember paying its officials. And even state governments, closer to the people and with constitutional responsibility for education, confined their role to serving as the instruments of groups and interests of the society at large, including groups that wanted to create colleges for a whole variety of motives — cultural, religious, and mercenary, in all weights and combinations.

Long-term Federal Policy toward Higher Education since the Revolution

The colonial period taught Americans how to create colleges and gave us diversity among them. The Revolution gave us freedom from central state power and especially from the power of government, both federal and state, to prevent the creation of independent colleges and universities. But these new freedoms were reinforced and given substance through a further set of decisions that together have defined federal policy toward higher education from the founding of the Republic to the present. This policy, never articulated but defined by those decisions, has been to encourage the provision of higher education, broaden access to college and university to ever wider sectors of the population, apply the contribution of higher education to the practical work of society as well as to learning and scholarship — and to do all this without directly impinging on the autonomy of the institutions or on the constitutional responsibility for higher education reposing in the states. This policy paradoxically encouraged an active federal presence in higher education, yet had the effect of driving power in higher education progressively further away from Washington, D.C., down toward the individual states, the institutions, and their individual members, students, and faculty. It became a kind of continuing self-denying ordinance by which the federal government has acted to facilitate decisions made by others, rather than forcing its own decisions on the states, institutions, or members.

Five of these decisions since the Revolution were so significant as to warrant separate discussion:

1. The failure of George Washington and his immediate presidential successors to establish a national university in the District of Columbia;
2. The Supreme Court's decision of 1819 in the Dartmouth College case;
3. The Morrill, or Land Grant Acts of 1862 and 1890 and the Hatch Act of 1887;
4. The Serviceman's Readjustment Act of 1944, better known as the G.I. Bill; and
5. The Education Amendments of 1972, which created the broad spectrum of federal programs of student aid that we have inherited, much expanded and amended.

The Failure to Establish the University of the United States

. . . The defeat of a proposal is a policy decision, and in the case of the failure of the proposed University of the United States, it is perhaps the most momentous in the history of American higher education.

A multiplicity of factors and motives lay behind the establishment of colleges and universities throughout our nation's history. Among these . . . were a variety of religious motives, a fear of relapse into barbarism at the frontier, and the need for various kinds of professionals, as well as state pride and local boosterism, philanthropy, idealism, educational reform, and even speculation in land, in all combinations. But the resulting number and diversity of institutions, competing with one another for students, resources, and teachers, bringing market considerations and market mechanisms right into the heart of an ancient cultural foundation — all of this also required the absence of any central force of authority that could restrain it, that could limit or control the proliferation of institutions in higher education. The states could not be that restraining force; under the pressures of competition and emulation, they have tended throughout our history to create institutions and programs in the numbers and to the standards of their neighbors. Crucially important has been the absence of a federal ministry of education with the power to charter (or to refuse to charter) new institutions and of a single preeminent university that could influence institutions in other ways.

. . . .

A national university would have profoundly affected American higher education. As the preeminent university, it would have had an enormous influence, direct and indirect, on every other college in the country and, through them, on the secondary schools as well. Its standards of entry, its curricula, its educational philosophies, even its forms of instruction, would have been models for every institution that hoped to send some of its graduates to the University in Washington. A federal system of high standard would surely have inhibited the emergence of hundreds of small, half-starved state and denominational colleges that sprang up over the next century. They simply could not have offered to work to the standard that the University of the United States would have set for the baccalaureate degree and demanded of applicants to its own postgraduate studies. In the United States, after the defeat of the University of the United States, no one has challenged the principle of high academic standards across the whole system because no one has proposed it: there have been no common standards, high or otherwise. In that spirit, we have created a multitude of institutions of every sort, offering academic work of every description and at every level of seriousness and standard.

The Dartmouth College Case

Another major event in the early history of the Republic had powerful effects on the shape and character of American higher education as we know it today: the 1819 decision of the Supreme Court in the Dartmouth College case. This was a landmark decision in that it affirmed the principle of the sanctity of contracts between governments and private institutions. In so doing, it gave expression to the Federalist belief that the government should not interfere with private property even for the purpose of benefiting the public welfare. John Marshall, then Chief Justice of the Supreme Court, had written earlier: "I consider the interference of the legislature in the management of our private affairs, whether those affairs are committed to a company or remain under individual direction, as equally dangerous and unwise." That antistatist position today sounds deeply conservative, but from another perspective it is radically libertarian and had broad and liberalizing effects on higher education. Marshall and his colleagues on the Court decided in the Dartmouth College case that a charter of a private college or university was a contract that a state could not retroactively abridge. And that had important repercussions both for the growth of capitalist enterprises and for the future development of higher education in the United States.

. . . .

The failure of the University of the United States and the success of Dartmouth College in its appeal to the Supreme Court were both victories for local initiative and for private entrepreneurship. The first of these set limits on the role of the federal government in shaping the character of the whole of American higher education; the second set even sharper limits on the power of the state over private colleges. Together, these two events constituted a kind of charter for unrestrained individual and group initiative in the creation of colleges of all sizes, shapes, and creeds. Almost any motive or combination of motives and interests could bring a college into being between the Revolution and the Civil War, and thereafter its survival depended largely on its being able to secure support from a church, from wealthy benefactors, from student fees, and even perhaps from the state. The colleges thus created were established relatively easily but without guarantees of survival. As a result, there arose a situation resembling the behavior of living organisms in an ecological system — competitive for resources, highly sensitive to the demands of the environment, and inclined, over time, through the ruthless process of natural selection, to be adaptive to those aspects of their environment that permitted their survival. Their environment also has included other colleges and, later, universities. So we see in this frog pond a set of mechanisms that we usually associate with the behavior of small entrepreneurs in a market: the anxious concern for what the market wants, the readiness to adapt to its apparent preferences, the effort to find a special place in that market though the marginal differentiation of the product, and a readiness to enter into symbiotic or parasitic relationships with other producers for a portion of that market. That is, to this day, the world of American higher education.

The 1862 Morrill Act

The Morrill Act, which created the land-grant colleges and universities, is indeed a landmark in American higher education. It was very far from being the first provision of support for higher education by central government through grants of government-owned land; indeed, under the Articles of Confederation the Northwest Ordinance provided for tracts of land to be set aside for the support of institutions of higher education in the Western Reserve. . . . But the Morrill Act provided support on an altogether different scale; in 1862 the federal government gave land to the states for the support of colleges and universities of an area equal to the whole of Switzerland or the Netherlands, about eleven thousand square miles. And it did this in the most extraordinarily permissive way. The act made no fixed requirements as to the type of institution or, beyond broad designations of fields of study, as to content of instruction. The only positive obligations were to dispose of the land or scrip in a manner or on terms left to state discretion; maintain the fund as a perpetual endowment invested at 5 percent; devote the income to one or more institutions which, while including the traditional college subjects, must provide instruction in agriculture, mechanic arts, and military tactics; and make an annual report on the results.

. . . .

Basically, the federal government put the money — or at least the scrip — on the stump and walked away, partly because there was no federal educational bureaucracy to provide for federal direction and control of state policy and partly because there was no consensus about what these institutions should look like or should be doing. Indeed, very sharp differences developed in Congress and outside it about the relative emphasis to be placed in these new institutions on pure or applied science, on practical experience and manual work, or on the old classical curriculum. The federal government's solution was to allow these contending forces to fight it out in each state. The result, needless to say, was various and messy, marked by ineptitude and corruption in places, confusion almost everywhere, but also by great imagination, creativity, and even genius — as illustrated by the vision of Ezra Cornell and Andrew Dixon White in New York. Some states got fifty cents an acre for their land, others ten times that much, and the variation in educational practice and academic standard was of the same order of magnitude, adding to the already high level of diversity in American higher education.

. . . .

The G.I. Bill of 1944

We now rightly think of the Serviceman's Readjustment Act of 1944 — the original G.I. Bill — as one of the best things that ever happened to American higher education. It enormously broadened the idea of college going, it moved the enrollment rate from 15 percent of the age grade in 1939 toward 50 percent or more currently, and it brought seriousness and maturity to undergraduate classrooms that were not accustomed to them and that have never quite lost them.

. . . .

Two features of the G.I. Bill deserve particular emphasis. First, veterans could take their tuition payments and stipends anywhere they wished, certainly to any accredited college or university that would accept them and to many other nonaccredited postsecondary educational institutions, too. . . .

Second, one crucial provision of the G.I. Bill stipulated that "no department, agency, or officer of the United States, in carrying out the provisions [of this Act] shall exercise any supervision or control, whatsoever, over any State, educational agency . . . or any educational or training institution." Of course, that is in the tradition of our constitutional reservation of responsibility for education to the states. But beyond that, we see here the same self-denying ordinance — sharp separation of financial support from academic influence — that marked earlier federal policy and that became the model and precedent for the Education Amendments of 1972 and thereafter, which provide substantial noncategorical need-based financial aid to students by way of grants and loans.

The Education Amendments of 1972

The federal legislation on education passed in 1972 established higher education as a national priority in its own right. Various agencies of the federal government were already providing support for targeted issues, such as science laboratories and libraries, and for targeted groups of students, as through fellowships for graduate students in certain areas deemed vital to the national security or economic welfare. But during the late sixties and early seventies, broad support developed for greatly expanded federal aid for higher education, both to aid institutions undergoing rapid growth and to encourage further expansion of access, especially by groups historically underrepresented in higher education.

. . . [T]he driving motivation of those in favor of federal support in the form of student aid was the wish to increase the power of the students in the market and thus encourage the responsiveness of the institutions to changing patterns of student demand. The amendments as enacted in fact centered on student aid; while continuing certain earmarked provisions for the institutions (such as support for college libraries and for the construction of certain academic facilities), the largest part of the new program took the form of federal grants and guaranteed loans to students, with special attention to needy or disadvantaged students. But this was no broad-spectrum student aid, not limited to particular fields of study or professions.

That the legislation took the form it did almost certainly enabled it to survive periodic budget cuts and changes of political mood in Washington by creating a large, stable voting constituency of greater weight to politicians than the leadership of the higher education world itself. But closer to the motivations of those who wrote the legislation is the fact that federal support in the form of student aid is the surest way of defending the autonomy of institutions of higher education against the leverage that block grants would have given to the federal government when, in time, it surely would have wanted to exert its influence over those institutions.

. . . .

Stacy Donoso & Perry A. Zirkel, *The Volume of Higher Education Litigation: An Updated Analysis*, 232 Educ. L. Rep. 549, 550–55 (2008)*

[The authors sought to update previous studies of *The Volume of Higher Education Litigation.* The projected totals for the 2000s include actual data for 2000–2007. The litigation is categorized by institution-level lawsuits, employee lawsuits, and student lawsuits. Prior studies documented the meteoric rise in higher education litigation from the 1950s to 1960s (115%) and 1960s to 1970s (300%). Litigation growth in more recent decades has continued, but has leveled off. From the 1990s through the 2000s, for example, higher education litigation increased by 23%.]

Reported College and University Litigation: Overall

	1940s	1950s	1960s	1970s	1980s	1990s	2000s*
Institution-level	81	91	214	620	491	655	(820)
Employee	20	41	33	388	596	700	(956)
Student	11	26	93	352	388	544	(566)
TOTALS	112	158	340	1360	1475	1899	(2342)

* Extrapolations based on data available on 12/7/07 × 1.29.

. . . .

This update. . . . [suggests] . . . and extends the earlier findings of continuing, albeit decelerating growth, in the overall volume of reported higher education court decisions. A major contributing factor to this growth is the expanding and more fruitful base for litigation. Beginning in the 1940s, college enrollment grew exponentially and continues to grow to this day. Every decade, a larger percentage of the population flocks to gain a college degree. Today, not only are higher education institutions greater in number, but target a larger audience by reaching out to different sexes, races, and socio-economic backgrounds.

The findings reveal that the student sector accounts for the largest part of this overall growth. The contributing factors in the student sector are numerous. The demise of the in loco parentis doctrine is one example. More specifically, the time period leading up to the 1960s was a time of in loco parentis, wherein universities remained largely uninvolved in the affairs of their students in order to avoid liability. After the demise of in loco parentis, courts increasingly held higher education institutions liable to their students. With the increased likelihood of a successful claim came a corresponding increase in the amount of litigation. Second, and to a more limited extent, from the 1950s to 1970s, suicide rates increased by 200 percent among young adults and have maintained that level through to the present. An upsurge in suicide rates, coupled with the courts increased willingness to hold universities liable for neglecting to detect suicidal tendencies, would also contribute to a proliferation in litigation. A third example is the increasing prevalence of binge drinking among college students. Binge drinking is often a catalyst for extremely reckless behavior that could open up higher education institutions to liability for neglect that led to physical injury, property damages, and sexual assault, among others.

Finally, the increase in litigation in federal courts is much more pronounced than in the state courts. This differential is likely attributable to more than one factor. For example, the increased tendency for students to attend college out-of-state may have contributed to a higher likelihood of plaintiffs to assert diversity in federal courts. Similarly, the expansion of federal legislation affecting education, including the Family Education Rights and Privacy Act and the various federal civil rights laws, may well have contributed to the increased movement to the federal judicial forum.

The continued extension, albeit not explosion, in higher education litigation suggests that colleges and universities have reason to bolster their efforts at risk management. Moreover, looking within and beyond these bare numbers, most detailed quantitative and qualitative research concerning the specific issues, jurisdictions, and outcomes of higher education litigation is recommended.

NOTES

1. Based on the information provided in any of the studies above, is there any relationship between the relatively freewheeling development of colleges and universities in the United States and the marked increase in higher education litigation in the twentieth and twenty-first centuries? Would a comprehensive federal higher education policy dating to the time of the country's founding be preferable to the piecemeal development of federal higher education policy that has actually occurred?

2. How has the changing nature of postsecondary schools' relationship with students affected the law's increasing influence on higher education? How many functions have today's colleges or universities assumed? For example, postsecondary schools today are, among other things, educators, guardians, trainers, entertainers, businesses, and economic development engines. Is this what George Washington had in mind when he planned to establish a national university?

3. Dartmouth is just one of nine colleges chartered in the colonies before the American Revolution. CHRISTOPHER J. LUCAS, AMERICAN HIGHER EDUCATION: A HISTORY 105–07 (1994). These "colonial colleges" include Dartmouth, Harvard University, Rutgers, The College of William and Mary, Yale University, Princeton University, the University of Pennsylvania, Brown University, and Columbia University. *Id.* at 105. Unlike Dartmouth, the University of Pennsylvania was successfully seized by the state government in 1779 in an effort to control perceived threats to American authority within the university. Steven M. Friedman, *A Brief History of the University of Pennsylvania*, UNIV. OF PENN. ARCHIVES & RECORDS CTR., *available at* http://www.archives.upenn.edu/histy/genlhistory/brief.html. Both Princeton and Rutgers applied to be the state land-grant college of New Jersey; ultimately, Rutgers won out in 1864. *See History Overview*, RUTGERS UNIV., *available at* http://www.rutgers.edu/about-rutgers/brief-history. Is national security a more compelling justification for state regulation of private universities than the arguments made by the state legislature in the *Dartmouth* case? Should the decision to become public be left entirely to the university's governing board? The *Dartmouth* case is presented following these notes.

4. Other major federal acts also helped change the way Americans fund higher education. The shift toward student grants began with the G.I. Bill, and continued in a line of federal legislation. F. King Alexander, *The Decline and Fall of the Wall of Separation Between Church and State and Its Consequences for Funding of Public and Private Institutions of Higher Education*, 10 U. FLA. J.L. & PUB. POL'Y 103, 113 (1998). The G.I. Bill allowed service members to pursue theological degrees at private religious colleges. *Id.* at 114. Essentially, this provided a new, large source of federal funding for private religious institutions through the form of student vouchers. *Id.* at 114. Following this trend, the Higher Education Facilities Act of 1963 provided public funds and tax subsidies that could be used for construction on both public and private university campuses (provided the funds and subsidies weren't used for the construction of buildings for worship or purely religious education). Pub. L. No. 88-204, Dec. 16, 1963, 77 Stat. 363. Only two years later, Congress passed The Higher Education Act of 1965, which provided financial aid to students and also directly to public and private universities. Pub. L. No. 89-329, Nov. 8, 1965, 79 Stat. 1219. Some legal commentators contend that this Act had the effect of increasing tuition costs and making higher education less available to the public. Alexander, *supra*, at 116; M.M. CHAMBERS, HIGHER EDUCATION: WHO PAYS? WHO GAINS? 96–98 (1968). By shifting the burden of college expenses more toward the student (and away from the traditional model of the government and private benefactors), these legislative acts made the private sector of education more powerful and, consequentially, made higher education less attainable for lower income students.

These federal acts and the early reluctance of the judiciary to encroach into the realm of private universities reflected a free market approach to higher education known as "student choice theory." Alexander, *supra*, at 117. Under this model, students dictate the market of higher education with their tuition dollars. Does this model ignore the societal importance of educating lower income students? Do universities effectively consider the demands and needs of *all* potential students? Should education, perceived as a common good, be treated like an economic commodity?

5. Some legislative efforts to curb the rising tide of university litigation have been aimed at lessening the dangers associated with campus life. The Disclosure of Campus Security Policy and Campus Crime Statistics Act of 1990 requires universities to provide crime statistics to prospective and current students. 20 U.S.C. § 1092(f). Further, The Collegiate Initiative to Reduce Binge Drinking and Illegal Alcohol Consumption, codified in 20 U.S.C. § 1011h, requires universities to implement anti-alcohol policies and programs on campus. More recently, a movement has gained momentum in the academic community pushing state legislators to lower the drinking age. The Amethyst Initiative is a proposal, signed by over 100 university presidents, asking legislators to reconsider the effectiveness of the current drinking age limit. *See* AMETHYST INITIATIVE, *available at* www.amethystinitiative.org. The Initiative contends that a 21-year age limit pushes much of college-aged drinking out of the safety of the public eye and underground into a culture that encourages binge drinking and risky behavior. *Id.* Similarly, Choose Responsibility is a non-profit organization aimed at changing the current policies on the drinking age. *See About*, CHOOSE RESPONSIBILITY, *available at* www.chooseresponsibility.org/about/. Choose Responsibility advocates a multi-faceted set of solutions where young adults over the age of 18 can earn a license to drink through education and compliance, which can be revoked for irresponsible behavior. *See Proposal*, CHOOSE RESPONSIBILITY, *available at* www.chooseresponsibility.org/proposal/. Would changing the drinking age impact the problems on campus that give rise to litigation? Or would it merely push these problems outside the sphere of academic life and liability?

6. Are students third-party beneficiaries to a faculty member's employment contract with the university? In *Reardon v. Allegheny College*, 926 A.2d 477, 483 (Pa. Super. 2007), a student argued that her professor failed to adequately follow university procedure after alleging that she had committed plagiarism. *Id.* at 483. The court ultimately rejected the student's claim on grounds that an assertion of mere unfairness or potential bias of one faculty member in a series of disciplinary proceedings was too vague and unsubstantiated to support a valid claim of contractual liability. *Id.* at 484. The court did not, however, explicitly state whether or not a professor owes a student any duty or obligation as a third-party beneficiary. *Id.* at 484. How might such a ruling, pro or con, affect the inner workings of the university classroom?

7. For additional materials on the historical development of higher education in the United States, see BERNARD BAILYN, EDUCATION IN THE FORMING OF AMERICAN SOCIETY (1960); CLARK KERR, *The American Mixture of Higher Education in Perspective: Four Dimensions, in* THE GREAT TRANSFORMATION IN HIGHER EDUCATION, 1960–1980 (1991); Keith OLSON, THE G.I. BILL, THE VETERANS, AND THE COLLEGES (1974); EARLE ROSS, DEMOCRACY'S COLLEGE: THE LAND-GRANT MOVEMENT IN THE FORMATIVE STAGE (1942).

8. For research on how law impacts higher education, and the accompanying increase in responsibilities for postsecondary institutions, see ROBERT D. BICKEL & PETER F. LAKE, THE RIGHTS AND RESPONSIBILITIES OF THE MODERN UNIVERSITY: WHO ASSUMES THE RISKS OF COLLEGE LIFE? (1999); PHILIP T.K. DANIEL, *The Equal Protection Clause of the Fourteenth Amendment*, *in* CONTEMPORARY ISSUES IN HIGHER EDUCATION LAW 385 (2011); Peter F. Lake, *The Rise of Duty and the Fall of In Loco Parentis and Other Protective Tort Doctrines in Higher Education Law*, 64 MO. L. REV. 1 (1999); Estelle A. Fishbein, *New Strings on the Ivory Tower: The Growth of Accountability in Colleges and Universities*, 12 J.C. & U.L. 381 (1985).

B. PUBLIC SCHOOLS, PRIVATE SCHOOLS, AND THE STATE ACTION DOCTRINE

1. The Public School-Private School Distinction

TRUSTEES OF DARTMOUTH COLLEGE v. WOODWARD

17 U.S. 518, 631 (1819)

. . . .

[Dartmouth College was given a charter by the British Crown in 1769. Dartmouth trustees brought an action in trover (suit for wrongful appropriation of property) following an act by the state legislature to amend the college's charter by increasing the number of trustees from 12 to 21, giving the governor appointment power over the expanded trustee positions, and creating a board of overseers that could control the trustees. The lower court ruled against Dartmouth, and the school appealed to the state supreme court. The court applied the Constitution's Contracts Clause, Article I, § 10: "No state shall enter into any treaty, alliance, or confederation; grant letters of marque and reprisal; coin money; emit bills of credit; make anything but gold and silver coin a tender in payment of debts; pass any bill of attainder, ex post facto law, or law impairing the obligation of contracts, or grant any title of nobility."]

[The charter] is plainly a contract to which the donors, the trustees, and the crown, (to whose rights and obligations New-Hampshire succeeds,) were the original parties. It is a contract made on a valuable consideration. It is a contract for the security and disposition of property. It is a contract, on the faith of which, real and personal estate has been conveyed to the corporation. It is then a contract within the letter of the constitution, and within its spirit also, unless the fact, that the property is invested by the donors in trustees for the promotion of religion and education, for the benefit of persons who are perpetually changing, though the objects remain the same, shall create a particular exception, taking this case out of the prohibition contained in the constitution.

It is more than possible, that the preservation of rights of this description was not particularly in the view of the framers of the constitution, when the clause under consideration was introduced into that instrument. It is probable, that interferences of more frequent recurrence, to which the temptation was stronger, and of which the mischief was more extensive, constituted the great motive for imposing this restriction on the State legislatures. But although a particular and a rare case may not, in itself, be of sufficient magnitude to induce a rule, yet it must be governed by the rule, when established, unless some plain and strong reason for excluding it can be given. It is not enough to say, that this particular case was not in the mind of the Convention, when the article was framed, nor of the American people, when it was adopted. It is necessary to go farther, and to say that, had this particular case been suggested, the language would have been so varied, as to exclude it, or it would have been made a special exception. The case being within the words of the rule, must be within its operation likewise, unless there be something in the literal construction so obviously absurd, or mischievous, or repugnant to the general spirit of the instrument, as to justify those who expound the constitution in making it an exception.

On what safe and intelligible ground can this exception stand? There is no expression in the constitution, no sentiment delivered by its contemporaneous expounders, which would justify us in making it. In the absence of all authority of this kind, is there, in the nature and reason of the case itself, that which would sustain a construction of the constitution, not warranted by its words? Are contracts of this description of a character to excite so little interest, that we must exclude them from the provisions of the constitution, as being unworthy of the attention of those who framed the instrument? Or does public policy so imperiously demand their remaining exposed to legislative alteration, as to compel us, or rather permit us to say, that these words, which were introduced to give stability to contracts, and which in their plain import comprehend this contract, must yet be so construed, as to exclude it?

Almost all eleemosynary corporations, those which are created for the promotion of religion, of charity, or of education, are of the same character. The law of this case is the law of all. In every literary or charitable institution, unless the objects of the bounty be themselves incorporated, the whole legal interest is in trustees, and can be asserted only by them. The donors, or claimants of the bounty, if they can appear in Court at all, can appear only to complain of the trustees. In all other situations, they are identified with, and personated by, the trustees; and their rights are to be defended and maintained by them. Religion, Charity, and Education, are, in the law of England, legatees or donees, capable of receiving bequests or donations in this form. They appear in Court, and claim or defend by the corporation. Are they of so little estimation in the United States, that contracts for their benefit must be excluded from the protection of words, which in their natural import include them? Or do such contracts so necessarily require new modelling by the authority of the legislature, that the ordinary rules of construction must be disregarded in order to leave them exposed to legislative alteration?

All feel that these objects are not deemed unimportant in the United States. The interest which this case has excited proves that they are not. The framers of the constitution did not deem them unworthy of its care and protection. They have, though in a different mode, manifested their respect for science, by reserving to the government of the Union the power "to promote the progress of science and useful arts, by securing for limited times, to authors and inventors, the exclusive right to their respective writings and discoveries." They have so far withdrawn science, and the useful arts, from the action of the State governments. Why then should they be supposed so regardless of contracts made for the advancement of literature, as to intend to exclude them from provisions, made for the security of ordinary contracts between man and man? No reason for making this supposition is perceived.

If the insignificance of the object does not require that we should exclude contracts respecting it from the protection of the constitution; neither, as we conceive, is the policy of leaving them subject to legislative alteration so apparent, as to require a forced construction of that instrument in order to effect it. These eleemosynary institutions do not fill the place, which would otherwise be occupied by government, but that which would otherwise remain vacant. They are complete acquisitions to literature. They are donations to education; donations, which any government must be disposed rather to encourage than to discountenance. It requires no very critical examination of the human mind to enable us to determine, that one great inducement to these gifts is the conviction felt by the giver, that the disposition he makes of them is immutable. It is probable, that no man ever was, and that no man ever will be, the founder of a college, believing at the time, that an act of incorporation constitutes no security for the institution; believing, that it is immediately to be deemed a public institution, whose funds are to be governed and applied, not by the will of the donor, but by the will of the legislature. All such gifts are made in the pleasing, perhaps delusive hope, that the charity will flow forever in the channel which the givers have marked out for it. If every man finds in his own bosom strong evidence of the universality of this sentiment, there can be but little reason to imagine, that the framers of our constitution were strangers to it, and that, feeling the necessity and policy of giving permanence and security to contracts, of withdrawing them from the influence of legislative bodies, whose fluctuating policy, and repeated interferences, produced the most perplexing and injurious embarrassments, they still deemed it necessary to leave these contracts subject to those interferences. . . .

. . . .

FARRINGTON v. TOKUSHIGE

273 U.S. 284 (1927)

OPINION

Mr. Justice McReynolds delivered the opinion of the Court.

The Circuit Court of Appeals affirmed an interlocutory decree rendered by the United States District Court of Hawaii July 21, 1925, which granted a temporary injunction forbidding petitioners — Governor, Attorney General and Superintendent of Public Instruction of that Territory — from attempting to enforce the provisions of Act 30, Special Session 1920, Legislature of Hawaii, entitled, "An Act relating to foreign language schools and teachers thereof" . . . and certain regulations adopted by the Department of Public Instruction June 1, 1925. . . . In these circumstances we only consider whether the judicial discretion of the trial court was improperly exercised.

Respondents claimed below and maintain here that enforcement of the challenged Act would deprive them of their liberty and property without due process of law contrary to the Fifth Amendment. Petitioners insist that the entire Act and the regulations adopted thereunder are valid; that they prescribe lawful rules for the conduct of private foreign language schools necessary for the public welfare; also that if any provision of the statute transcends the power of the Legislature it should be disregarded and the remaining ones should be enforced.

If the enactment is subject to the asserted objections it is not here seriously questioned that respondents are entitled to the relief granted.

There are one hundred and sixty-three foreign language schools in the Territory. Nine are conducted in the Korean language, seven in the Chinese and the remainder in the Japanese. Respondents are members of numerous voluntary unincorporated associations conducting foreign language schools for instruction of Japanese children. These are owned, maintained and conducted by upwards of five thousand persons; the property used in connection therewith is worth two hundred and fifty thousand dollars; the enrolled pupils number twenty thousand; and three hundred teachers are employed. These schools receive no aid from public funds. All children residing within the Territory are required to attend some public or equivalent school; and practically all who go to foreign language schools also attend public or such private schools. It is affirmed by counsel for petitioners that Japanese pupils in the public and equivalent private schools increased from one thousand, three hundred and twenty in 1900 to nineteen thousand, three hundred and fifty-four in 1920, and that out of a total of sixty-five thousand, three hundred and sixty-nine pupils of all races on December 31, 1924, thirty thousand, four hundred and eighty-seven were Japanese.

The challenged enactment declares that the term, "foreign language school," as used therein, "shall be construed to mean any school which is conducted in any language other than the English language or Hawaiian language, except Sabbath schools." And, as stated by the Circuit Court of Appeals, the following are its more prominent and questionable features.

"No such school shall be conducted in the territory unless under a written permit therefor from the Department of Public Instruction, nor unless the fee therefor shall have been paid as therein provided, and such permit shall be kept exposed in a prominent place at the school so as to be readily seen and read by visitors thereat.

"The fee prescribed is one dollar per pupil on the estimated average attendance of pupils at the school during the period during which such school was conducted during the next preceding school year, or if such school was not conducted during any part of such preceding school year, then at the same rate at the estimated average attendance during the school year or unexpired part thereof in question, in which latter case the amount shall be adjusted to conform to the estimated average attendance during such year or part thereof.

"The amount of the fee shall be estimated and determined by the department from such information as it may have, and shall be payable by any person, persons or corporation conducting or participating in conducting such school; and all officers, teachers and all members of any committee or governing board of any such school, and in case such school is conducted by or for a corporation or voluntary association or other group of persons, all members or associates of such corporation, association or group shall be deemed to be participants in conducting such school. Provision is then made for the collection of the fees by suit, but that provision is not deemed material here.

"All permits must be renewed annually on the first day of September of each year and a similar fee must be paid, provided the department shall not be required to renew a permit for conducting any foreign language school, in the conducting of which there has been a violation of the terms of the Act.

"All fees collected by the department under the Act shall be paid over to the Treasurer of the Territory and the moneys so paid are appropriated to the department to be expended in enforcing and carrying out its provisions. If at any time the funds at the disposal of the department from fees previously collected or from royalties, commissions or other moneys received in connection with the publication or sale of foreign language school text-books shall make it possible to fully and effectively carry out the provisions of the Act with the permit fees payable by the schools based on a lower rate than one dollar per pupil, the department is authorized to make such a reduction in that rate as it may deem reasonable and expedient.

"Every person conducting a foreign language school shall, not later than June 15, of each year, file with the department on forms prescribed or furnished by it a sworn list of all pupils in attendance at such school during the current school year, showing the name, sex, parents or guardians, place of birth and residence of each child.

"No person shall teach in a foreign language school unless and until he shall have first applied to and obtained a permit so to do from the department and this shall also be construed to include persons exercising or performing administrative powers at any school. No permit to teach in a foreign language school shall be granted unless and until the department is satisfied that the applicant for the same is possessed of the ideals of democracy; knowledge of American history and institutions, and knows how to read, write and speak the English language.

"It is the declared object of the Act to fully and effectively regulate the conducting of foreign language schools and the teaching of foreign languages, in order that the Americanism of the pupils may be promoted, and the department is directed to carry out the provisions of the Act in accordance with its spirit and purpose.

"Before issuing a permit to conduct a foreign language school or to teach in any such school the department shall require the applicant for such permit to sign a pledge that the applicant will, if granted a permit to teach in such a school, abide by and observe the terms of the Act, and the regulations and orders of the department, and will, to the best of his ability, so direct the minds and studies of pupils in such schools as will tend to make them good and loyal American citizens, and will not permit such students to receive instructions in any way inconsistent therewith.

"No foreign language school shall be conducted in the morning before the school hours of the public schools or during the hours while the public schools are in session, nor shall any pupil attend any foreign language school for more than one hour each day, nor exceeding six hours in any one week, nor exceeding thirty-eight weeks in any school year; provided, however, the department may in its discretion and with the approval of the Governor, modify this provision.

"The department shall have full power from time to time to prescribe by regulations the subjects and courses of study of all foreign language schools, and the entrance and attendance prerequisites or qualifications of education, age, school attainment, demonstrated mental capacity, health and otherwise, and the text-books used in any foreign language school.

"Until otherwise provided by the department, the following regulations are in effect: Up to September 1, 1923, every pupil shall have first satisfactorily completed the American public school first grade, or a course equivalent thereto, before attending or being allowed to attend any foreign language school. Beginning September 1, 1923, and thereafter, every pupil shall have satisfactorily completed the American public school first and second grades, or courses equivalent thereto, before attending or being allowed to attend any foreign language school. Beginning September 1, 1923, and thereafter, for grades one, two and three, and beginning September 1, 1924, and thereafter, for grades four and above, all new text-books used in elementary foreign language schools shall be based upon the principle that the pupil's normal medium of expression is English and shall contain, as far as practicable, English equivalents for foreign words and idioms.

"The department is authorized to prepare, or cause to be prepared, or procure or arrange for procuring suitable text-books for the teaching of foreign languages in the foreign language schools and to enter into an agreement or agreements for the publishing and sale of the same.

"All royalties, commissions and moneys received by or on behalf of the department in connection with the publication or sale of such text-books shall be paid over to the treasurer of the territory and shall be appropriated to the department to be expended for the purposes of the Act.

. . . .

"The department has power to appoint one or more inspectors of foreign language schools and to pay the salary and necessary expenses therefor; such inspectors and other duly authorized agents of the department shall have the right freely to visit such foreign language schools and to inspect the buildings, equipment, records and teaching thereof and the text-books used therein.

"If the department shall at any time become satisfied that any holder of a permit to conduct a foreign language school or to teach therein does not possess the qualifications required by the Act, or shall have violated or failed to observe any of the provisions of the Act or of the regulations or orders of the department, the department may then and thereupon revoke the permit theretofore granted and the same shall thereupon be and become null and void.

"Any person who shall conduct or participate in conducting a foreign language school or who shall teach in a foreign language school contrary to the provisions of the Act, or who shall violate or participate in violating any of the provisions thereof, or any of the regulations or orders of the department, shall be guilty of a misdemeanor, and upon conviction thereof shall be punished by a fine not to exceed $25, and each day's violation shall be deemed a separate offense.

. . . .

On June 1, 1925, the Department of Public Instruction adopted, and the Governor approved, certain regulations which undertook to limit the pupils who might attend foreign language schools to those who regularly attended some public school or approved private school, or had completed the eighth grade, or were over fourteen years of age. Also, to designate the text-books which foreign language schools should use in their primary grades.

The affidavit of T. Iwanaga, in support of motion for temporary injunction, states:

"That in the schools referred to in said bill, which are conducted for each grade for one hour for each school day, nothing contrary to American history and American institutions and principles of democracy is taught, the instruction being confined to the speaking, reading and writing of the Japanese language; . . .

"That in the schools represented by plaintiffs there are about twelve thousand four hundred pupils and said schools employ about one hundred ninety-two teachers; that said teachers are paid and said schools are maintained from voluntary contributions and from the fees of the children attending said schools; that the provisions of said Act 152 of the Session Laws of 1925 are so drastic that the parents of children will be afraid to pay tuition fees and other persons will be afraid to contribute to the funds of said schools lest they be subjected to the pains and penalties provided in said Act, and that, therefore, unless immediate relief is afforded by this Honorable Court, the said schools will be unable to pay the teachers' salaries and the expenses of conducting said schools and the property of plaintiffs in said schools will be utterly destroyed."

An affidavit of the Attorney General describes the litigation which has arisen under the legislation concerning foreign language schools. He does not disavow purpose to enforce all provisions of the challenged Act and regulations. An affidavit by the Superintendent of Public Instruction advances the opinion that respondents could pay the prescribed fees, that compliance with the foreign language school laws would not prevent the operation of schools which conduct kindergartens, and that elimination of the kindergartens would not materially affect them. Also, he says —

"That instruction in said Japanese Language Schools is not and cannot be confined to the speaking, reading and writing of the Japanese language, but extends to many subjects and even in so far as it is intended to have for its object the speaking, reading and writing of said language, the teaching of that is and must be largely through the medium of stories whether of history or fiction and in other ways than the mere teaching of letters and words and sentences. . . .

"That, in the opinion of this affiant, the parents of children will not because of the provisions of said Act 152 be afraid to pay tuition fees nor will other persons be afraid to contribute to the funds of such schools and this affiant denies that said schools will, unless immediate relief is afforded by this Honorable Court, be unable to pay the teachers' salaries and the expenses of conducting said schools, and denies that the property of plaintiffs in said schools will be utterly or at all destroyed."

The foregoing statement is enough to show that the school Act and the measures adopted thereunder go far beyond mere regulation of privately-supported schools where children obtain instruction deemed valuable by their parents and which is not obviously in conflict with any public interest. They give affirmative direction concerning the intimate and essential details of such schools, intrust their control to public officers, and deny both owners and patrons reasonable choice and discretion in respect of teachers, curriculum and text-books. Enforcement of the Act probably would destroy most, if not all, of them; and, certainly, it would deprive parents of fair opportunity to procure for their children instruction which they think important and we cannot say is harmful. The Japanese parent has the right to direct the education of his own child without unreasonable restrictions; the Constitution protects him as well as those who speak another tongue.

Upon the record and the arguments presented, we cannot undertake to consider the validity of each separate provision of the Act and decide whether, dissociated from the others, its enforcement would violate respondents' constitutional rights. Apparently all are parts of a deliberate plan to bring foreign language schools under a strict governmental control for which the record discloses no adequate reason. Here, the enactment has been defended as a whole. No effort has been made to discuss the validity of the several provisions. In the trial court the cause proceeded upon the theory that petitioners intended to enforce all of them.

The general doctrine touching rights guaranteed by the Fourteenth Amendment to owners, parents and children in respect of attendance upon schools has been announced in recent opinions. *Meyer v. Nebraska*, 262 U.S. 390; *Bartels v. Iowa* [262 U.S. 404]; *Pierce v. Society of Sisters*, 268 U.S. 510. While that amendment declares that no State shall "deprive any person of life, liberty or property without due process of law," the inhibition of the Fifth Amendment — "no person shall . . . be deprived of life, liberty or property without due process of law" — applies to the federal government and agencies set up by Congress for the government of the Territory. Those fundamental rights of the individual which the cited cases declared were protected by the Fourteenth Amendment from infringement by the States, are guaranteed by the Fifth Amendment against action by the Territorial Legislature or officers.

We of course appreciate the grave problems incident to the large alien population of the Hawaiian Islands. These should be given due weight whenever the validity of any governmental regulation of private schools is under consideration; but the limitations of the Constitution must not be transcended.

. . . .

We find no abuse of the discretion lodged in the trial court. The decree of the Circuit Court of Appeals must be

Affirmed.

NOTES

1. The *Dartmouth* opinion also influenced the way the law deals with corporate entities. The Court found that Dartmouth was a charitable, non-profit corporation that, under the Contracts Clause, had property rights that the government could not touch. *Trs. of Dartmouth Coll. v. Woodward*, 17 U.S. 518, 524–25 (1819). The Court's interpretation of the Contracts Clause expanded the definition of corporations and their right to property and self-government, even to entities outside of the educational context. Elizabeth Brand Monroe, *The Influence of the Dartmouth College Case on the American Law of Educational Charities*, 32 J. S. CT. HIST. 1, 7 (2007). Justice Story's concurrence directly stated that the private contract analysis should also apply to non-charitable corporate entities like banks and factories. *Dartmouth*, 17 U.S. at 669. This decision to define private charitable corporations broadly was an attempt to resolve a very contentious issue during that time period. What exactly is a college and what is its relationship with the state? Should the purpose of an educational institution influence its treatment by legal officials? More importantly, should the university's role of educating the public imply a deeper relationship with the state?

2. *Farrington* was part of a trio of 1920s cases involving secondary schools that served to firmly establish the principle that private schools enjoy more freedom than public schools. The other two decisions were *Meyer v. Nebraska*, 262 U.S. 390 (1923) (holding unconstitutional a state law that forbade the teaching of any language other than English in any private, denominational, parochial or public school, to any child who had not passed the eighth grade); and *Pierce v. Society of Sisters*, 268 U.S. 510 (1925) (holding a state law that required children to attend public schools unconstitutional under the due process clause).

3. Both the *Dartmouth* case and *Farrington* stand for the proposition that the federal government, in certain instances that are close to an institution's mission and touch on constitutional issues, shields private schools from the vagaries of state government. As we will see, however, the federal government can be just as active, if not more so, than state governments in its attempts to shape education policy at public and private schools. While having unique constitutional protections that public schools do not have, private schools are still subject to an array of federal statutes and regulations.

2. The State Action Doctrine

Public postsecondary schools must respect and abide by the individual rights set forth in the U.S. Constitution, while private postsecondary schools generally are not so bound. To determine whether those "individual rights" requirements have been satisfied, courts must first determine whether a particular action by a school is a "state action."

BRENTWOOD ACADEMY v. TENNESSEE SECONDARY SCHOOL ATHLETIC ASSOCIATION

531 U.S. 288 (2001)

JUSTICE SOUTER delivered the opinion of the Court.

The issue is whether a statewide association incorporated to regulate interscholastic athletic competition among public and private secondary schools may be regarded as engaging in state action when it enforces a rule against a member school. The association in question here includes most public schools located within the State, acts through their representatives, draws its officers from them, is largely funded by their dues and income received in their stead, and has historically been seen to regulate in lieu of the State Board of Education's exercise of its own authority. We hold that the association's regulatory activity may and should be treated as state action owing to the pervasive entwinement of state school officials in the structure of the association, there being no offsetting reason to see the association's acts in any other way.

I

Respondent Tennessee Secondary School Athletic Association (Association) is a not-for-profit membership corporation organized to regulate interscholastic sport among the public and private high schools in Tennessee that belong to it. No school is forced to join, but without any other authority actually regulating interscholastic athletics, it enjoys the memberships of almost all the State's public high schools (some 290 of them or 84% of the Association's voting membership), far outnumbering the 55 private schools that belong. A member school's team may play or scrimmage only against the team of another member, absent a dispensation.

The Association's rulemaking arm is its legislative council, while its board of control tends to administration. The voting membership of each of these nine-person committees is limited under the Association's bylaws to high school principals, assistant principals, and superintendents elected by the member schools, and the public school administrators who so serve typically attend meetings during regular school hours. Although the Association's staff members are not paid by the State, they are eligible to join the State's public retirement system for its employees. Member schools pay dues to the Association, though the bulk of its revenue is gate receipts at member teams' football and basketball tournaments, many of them held in public arenas rented by the Association.

The constitution, bylaws, and rules of the Association set standards of school membership and the eligibility of students to play in interscholastic games. Each school, for example, is regulated in awarding financial aid, most coaches must have a Tennessee state teaching license, and players must meet minimum academic standards and hew to limits on student employment. Under the bylaws, "in all matters pertaining to the athletic relations of his school," the principal is responsible to the Association, which has the power "to suspend, to fine, or otherwise penalize any member school for the violation of any of the rules of the Association or for other just cause."

Ever since the Association was incorporated in 1925, Tennessee's State Board of Education (State Board) has . . . acknowledged the corporation's functions "in providing standards, rules and regulations for interscholastic competition in the public schools of Tennessee." More recently, the State Board cited its statutory authority . . . when it adopted language expressing the relationship between the Association and the State Board. Specifically, in 1972, it went so far as to adopt a rule expressly "designat [ing]" the Association as "the organization to supervise and regulate the athletic activities in which the public junior and senior high schools in Tennessee participate on an interscholastic basis." Tennessee State Board of Education, Administrative Rules and Regulations, Rule 0520-1-2-.26 (1972) (later moved to Rule 0520-1-2-.08). The Rule provided that "the authority granted herein shall remain in effect until revoked" and instructed the State Board's chairman to "designate a person or persons to serve in an ex-officio capacity on the [Association's governing bodies]." That same year, the State Board specifically approved the Association's rules and regulations, while reserving the right to review future changes. Thus, on several occasions over the next 20 years, the State Board reviewed, approved, or reaffirmed its approval of the recruiting Rule at issue in this case. In 1996, however, the State Board dropped the original Rule 0520-1-2-.08 expressly designating the Association as regulator; it substituted a statement "recogniz[ing] the value of participation in interscholastic athletics and the role of [the Association] in coordinating interscholastic athletic competition," while "authoriz[ing] the public schools of the state to voluntarily maintain membership in [the Association]."

The action before us responds to a 1997 regulatory enforcement proceeding brought against petitioner, Brentwood Academy, a private parochial high school member of the Association. The Association's board of control found that Brentwood violated a rule prohibiting "undue influence" in recruiting athletes, when it wrote to incoming students and their parents about spring football practice. The Association accordingly placed Brentwood's athletic program on probation for four years, declared its football and boys' basketball teams ineligible to compete in playoffs for two years, and imposed a $3,000 fine. When these penalties were imposed, all the voting members of the board of control and legislative council were public school administrators.

The United States Court of Appeals for the Sixth Circuit reversed. 180 F.3d 758 (1999). It recognized that there is no single test to identify state actions and state actors but applied three criteria derived from *Blum v. Yaretsky*, 457 U.S. 991 (1982), *Lugar v. Edmondson Oil Co.*, 457 U.S. 922 (1982), and *Rendell-Baker v. Kohn*, 457 U.S. 830 (1982), and found no state action under any of them. It said the District Court was mistaken in seeing a symbiotic relationship between the State and the Association, it emphasized that the Association was neither engaging in a traditional and exclusive public function nor responding to state compulsion, and it gave short shrift to the language from Tarkanian on which the District Court relied. We . . . now reverse.

II

A

Our cases try to plot a line between state action subject to Fourteenth Amendment scrutiny and private conduct (however exceptionable) that is not. The judicial obligation is not only to " 'preserv[e] an area of individual freedom by limiting the reach of federal law' and avoi[d] the imposition of responsibility on a State for conduct it could not control," but also to assure that constitutional standards are invoked "when it can be said that the State is responsible for the specific conduct of which the plaintiff complains." If the Fourteenth Amendment is not to be displaced, therefore, its ambit cannot be a simple line between States and people operating outside formally governmental organizations, and the deed of an ostensibly private organization or individual is to be treated sometimes as if a State had caused it to be performed. Thus, we say that state action may be found if, though only if, there is such a "close nexus between the State and the challenged action" that seemingly private behavior "may be fairly treated as that of the State itself."

What is fairly attributable is a matter of normative judgment, and the criteria lack rigid simplicity. From the range of circumstances that could point toward the State behind an individual face, no one fact can function as a necessary condition across the board for finding state action; nor is any set of circumstances absolutely sufficient, for there may be some countervailing reason against attributing activity to the government.

Our cases have identified a host of facts that can bear on the fairness of such an attribution. We have, for example, held that a challenged activity may be state action when it results from the State's exercise of "coercive power," *Blum*, 457 U.S., at 1004, when the State provides "significant encouragement, either overt or covert," or when a private actor operates as a "willful participant in joint activity with the State or its agents." We have treated a nominally private entity as a state actor when it is controlled by an "agency of the State," *Pennsylvania v. Board of Directors of City Trusts of Philadelphia*, 353 U.S. 230, 231 (1957), when it has been delegated a public function by the State, *Edmonson v. Leesville Concrete Co.*, 500 U.S. 614, 627–628 (1991), when it is "entwined with governmental policies," or when government is "entwined in [its] management or control," *Evans v. Newton*, 382 U.S. 296, 299 (1966).

Amidst such variety, examples may be the best teachers, and examples from our cases are unequivocal in showing that the character of a legal entity is determined neither by its expressly private characterization in statutory law, nor by the failure of the law to acknowledge the entity's inseparability from recognized government officials or agencies. . . . *Pennsylvania v. Board of Directors of City Trusts of Philadelphia* held the privately endowed Girard College to be a state actor and enforcement of its private founder's limitation of admission to whites attributable to the State, because, consistent with the terms of the settlor's gift, the college's board of directors was a state agency established by state law. Ostensibly the converse situation occurred in *Evans v. Newton* which held that private trustees to whom a city had transferred a park were nonetheless state actors barred from enforcing racial segregation, since the park served the public purpose of providing community recreation, and "the municipality remain[ed] entwined in [its] management [and] control."

These examples of public entwinement in the management and control of ostensibly separate trusts or corporations foreshadow this case, as this Court itself anticipated in *Tarkanian. Tarkanian* arose when an undoubtedly state actor, the University of Nevada, suspended its basketball coach, Tarkanian, in order to comply with rules and recommendations of the National Collegiate Athletic Association (NCAA). The coach charged the NCAA with state action, arguing that the state university had delegated its own functions to the NCAA, clothing the latter with authority to make and apply the university's rules, the result being joint action making the NCAA a state actor.

To be sure, it is not the strict holding in *Tarkanian* that points to our view of this case, for we found no state action on the part of the NCAA. We could see, on the one hand, that the university had some part in setting the NCAA's rules, and the Supreme Court of Nevada had gone so far as to hold that the NCAA had been delegated the university's traditionally exclusive public authority over personnel. But on the other side, the NCAA's policies were shaped not by the University of Nevada alone, but by several hundred member institutions, most of them having no connection with Nevada, and exhibiting no color of Nevada law. Since it was difficult to see the NCAA, not as a collective membership, but as surrogate for the one State, we held the organization's connection with Nevada too insubstantial to ground a state-action claim.

But dictum in *Tarkanian* pointed to a contrary result on facts like ours, with an organization whose member public schools are all within a single State. "The situation would, of course, be different if the [Association's] membership consisted entirely of institutions located within the same State, many of them public institutions created by the same sovereign."

. . . .

B

[Our foresight] in *Tarkanian*, [to engage] the "necessarily fact-bound inquiry," leads to the conclusion of state action here. The nominally private character of the Association is overborne by the pervasive entwinement of public institutions and public officials in its composition and workings, and there is no substantial reason to claim unfairness in applying constitutional standards to it.

The Association is not an organization of natural persons acting on their own, but of schools, and of public schools to the extent of 84% of the total. Under the Association's bylaws, each member school is represented by its principal or a faculty member, who has a vote in selecting members of the governing legislative council and board of control from eligible principals, assistant principals, and superintendents.

Although the findings and prior opinions in this case include no express conclusion of law that public school officials act within the scope of their duties when they represent their institutions, no other view would be rational, the official nature of their involvement being shown in any number of ways. Interscholastic athletics obviously play an integral part in the public education of Tennessee, where nearly every public high school spends money on competitions among schools. Since a pickup system of interscholastic games would not do, these public teams need some mechanism to produce rules and regulate competition.

In sum, to the extent of 84% of its membership, the Association is an organization of public schools represented by their officials acting in their official capacity to provide an integral element of secondary public schooling. There would be no recognizable Association, legal or tangible, without the public school officials, who do not merely control but overwhelmingly perform all but the purely ministerial acts by which the Association exists and functions in practical terms. Only the 16% minority of private school memberships prevents this entwinement of the Association and the public school system from being total and their identities totally indistinguishable.

To complement the entwinement of public school officials with the Association from the bottom up, the State of Tennessee has provided for entwinement from top down. State Board members are assigned ex officio to serve as members of the board of control and legislative council, and the Association's ministerial employees are treated as state employees to the extent of being eligible for membership in the state retirement system.

. . . .

The entwinement down from the State Board is therefore unmistakable, just as the entwinement up from the member public schools is overwhelming. Entwinement will support a conclusion that an ostensibly private organization ought to be charged with a public character and judged by constitutional standards; entwinement to the degree shown here requires it.

. . . .

The judgment of the Court of Appeals for the Sixth Circuit is reversed, and the case is remanded for further proceedings consistent with this opinion.

It is so ordered.

JUSTICE THOMAS, with whom THE CHIEF JUSTICE, JUSTICE SCALIA, and JUSTICE KENNEDY join, dissenting.

We have never found state action based upon mere "entwinement." Until today, we have found a private organization's acts to constitute state action only when the organization performed a public function; was created, coerced, or encouraged by the government; or acted in a symbiotic relationship with the government. The majority's holding-that the Tennessee Secondary School Athletic Association's (TSSAA) enforcement of its recruiting rule is state action-not only extends state-action doctrine beyond its permissible limits but also encroaches upon the realm of individual freedom that the doctrine was meant to protect. I respectfully dissent.

I

Like the state-action requirement of the Fourteenth Amendment, the state-action element of 42 U.S.C. § 1983 excludes from its coverage "merely private conduct, however discriminatory or wrongful." "Careful adherence to the 'state action' requirement" thus "preserves an area of individual freedom by limiting the reach of federal law and federal judicial power." The state-action doctrine also promotes important values of federalism, "avoid[ing] the imposition of responsibility on a State for conduct it could not control." Although we have used many different tests to identify state action, they all have a common purpose. Our goal in every case is to determine whether an action "can fairly be attributed to the State."

A

Regardless of these various tests for state action, common sense dictates that the TSSAA's actions cannot fairly be attributed to the State, and thus cannot constitute state action. The TSSAA was formed in 1925 as a private corporation to organize interscholastic athletics and to sponsor tournaments among its member schools. Any private or public secondary school may join the TSSAA by signing a contract agreeing to comply with its rules and decisions. Although public schools currently compose 84% of the TSSAA's membership, the TSSAA does not require that public schools constitute a set percentage of its membership, and, indeed, no public school need join the TSSAA. The TSSAA's rules are enforced not by a state agency but by its own board of control, which comprises high school principals, assistant principals, and superintendents, none of whom must work at a public school. Of course, at the time the recruiting rule was enforced in this case, all of the board members happened to be public school officials. However, each board member acts in a representative capacity on behalf of all the private and public schools in his region of Tennessee, and not simply his individual school.

The State of Tennessee did not create the TSSAA. The State does not fund the TSSAA and does not pay its employees. In fact, only 4% of the TSSAA's revenue comes from the dues paid by member schools; the bulk of its operating budget is derived from gate receipts at tournaments it sponsors. The State does not permit the TSSAA to use state-owned facilities for a discounted fee, and it does not exempt the TSSAA from state taxation. No Tennessee law authorizes the State to coordinate interscholastic athletics or empowers another entity to organize interscholastic athletics on behalf of the State. The state pronouncement acknowledging the TSSAA's existence is a rule providing that the State Board of Education permits public schools to maintain membership in the TSSAA if they so choose.

Moreover, the State of Tennessee has never had any involvement in the particular action taken by the TSSAA in this case: the enforcement of the TSSAA's recruiting rule prohibiting members from using "undue influence" on students or their parents or guardians "to secure or to retain a student for athletic purposes." There is no indication that the State has ever had any interest in how schools choose to regulate recruiting. In fact, the TSSAA's authority to enforce its recruiting rule arises solely from the voluntary membership contract that each member school signs, agreeing to conduct its athletics in accordance with the rules and decisions of the TSSAA.

B

Even approaching the issue in terms of any of the Court's specific state-action tests, the conclusion is the same: The TSSAA's enforcement of its recruiting rule against Brentwood Academy is not state action. In applying these tests, courts of course must place the burden of persuasion on the plaintiff, not the defendant, because state action is an element of a § 1983 claim. The TSSAA has not performed a function that has been "traditionally exclusively reserved to the State." The organization of interscholastic sports is neither a traditional nor an exclusive public function of the States. Widespread organization and administration of interscholastic contests by schools did not begin until the 20th century. Certainly, in Tennessee, the State did not even show an interest in interscholastic athletics until 47 years after the TSSAA had been in existence and had been orchestrating athletic contests throughout the State. Even then, the State Board of Education merely acquiesced in the TSSAA's actions and did not assume the role of regulating interscholastic athletics. The TSSAA no doubt serves the public, particularly the public schools, but the mere provision of a service to the public does not render such provision a traditional and exclusive public function.

It is also obvious that the TSSAA is not an entity created and controlled by the government for the purpose of fulfilling a government objective, as was Amtrak in *Lebron v. National Railroad Passenger Corporation*, 513 U.S. 374, 394 (1995). Indeed, no one claims that the State of Tennessee played any role in the creation of the TSSAA as a private corporation in 1925. The TSSAA was designed to fulfill an objective-the organization of interscholastic athletic tournaments-that the government had not contemplated, much less pursued. And although the board of control currently is composed of public school officials, and although public schools currently account for the majority of the TSSAA's membership, this is not required by the TSSAA's constitution.

In addition, the State of Tennessee has not "exercised coercive power or . . . provided such significant encouragement [to the TSSAA], either overt or covert," that the TSSAA's regulatory activities must in law be deemed to be those of the State. The State has not promulgated any regulations of interscholastic sports, and nothing in the record suggests that the State has encouraged or coerced the TSSAA in enforcing its recruiting rule. To be sure, public schools do provide a small portion of the TSSAA's funding through their membership dues, but no one argues that these dues are somehow conditioned on the TSSAA's enactment and enforcement of recruiting rules.

Likewise, even if the TSSAA were dependent on state funding to the extent of 90%, as was the case in *Blum*, instead of less than 4%, mere financial dependence on the State does not convert the TSSAA's actions into acts of the State. Furthermore, there is no evidence of "joint participation," between the State and the TSSAA in the TSSAA's enforcement of its recruiting rule. The TSSAA's board of control enforces its recruiting rule solely in accordance with the authority granted to it under the contract that each member signs.

Finally, there is no "symbiotic relationship" between the State and the TSSAA. Contrary to the majority's assertion, *see ante*, at 932–933, the TSSAA's "fiscal relationship with the State is not different from that of many contractors performing services for the government." The TSSAA provides a service-the organization of athletic tournaments-in exchange for membership dues and gate fees, just as a vendor could contract with public schools to sell refreshments at school events. Certainly the public school could sell its own refreshments, yet the existence of that option does not transform the service performed by the contractor into a state action. Also, there is no suggestion in this case that, as was the case in *Burton*, the State profits from the TSSAA's decision to enforce its recruiting rule.

Because I do not believe that the TSSAA's action of enforcing its recruiting rule is fairly attributable to the State of Tennessee, I would affirm.

II

Although the TSSAA's enforcement activities cannot be considered state action as a matter of common sense or under any of this Court's existing theories of state action, the majority presents a new theory. Under this theory, the majority holds that the combination of factors it identifies evidences "entwinement" of the State with the TSSAA, and that such entwinement converts private action into state action. *Ante*, at 930–931. The majority does not define "entwinement," and the meaning of the term is not altogether clear. But whatever this new "entwinement" theory may entail, it lacks any support in our state-action jurisprudence. Although the majority asserts that there are three examples of entwinement analysis in our cases, there is no case in which we have rested a finding of state action on entwinement alone.

. . . .

Because the majority never defines "entwinement," the scope of its holding is unclear. If we are fortunate, the majority's fact-specific analysis will have little bearing beyond this case. But if the majority's new entwinement test develops in future years, it could affect many organizations that foster activities, enforce rules, and sponsor extracurricular competition among high schools-not just in athletics, but in such diverse areas as agriculture, mathematics, music, marching bands, forensics, and cheerleading. Indeed, this entwinement test may extend to other organizations that are composed of, or controlled by, public officials or public entities, such as firefighters, policemen, teachers, cities, or counties. I am not prepared to say that any private organization that permits public entities and public officials to participate acts as the State in anything or everything it does, and our state-action jurisprudence has never reached that far. The state-action doctrine was developed to reach only those actions that are truly attributable to the State, not to subject private citizens to the control of federal courts hearing § 1983 actions.

I respectfully dissent.

CRAFT v. VANDERBILT UNIVERSITY

18 F. Supp. 2d 786 (1998)

Opinion by: JOHN T. NIXON

MEMORANDUM

. . . .

I. Background

The Plaintiffs in this action were the unconsenting subjects of experiments involving radioactive iron isotopes conducted at Vanderbilt University from September 1945 through at least May 30, 1947. The Defendants, Vanderbilt University and the Rockefeller Foundation, are alleged to be cooperating participants in a program that administered the radioactive iron to pregnant patients at a Vanderbilt clinic from September 1945 through at least May 30, 1947. Plaintiffs include both women who sought prenatal treatment at Vanderbilt University during the relevant period, and their offspring who may have been exposed to the radiation in utero. Both groups seek damages against Vanderbilt University and the Rockefeller Foundation ("RF") (collectively, "Defendants"), under multiple federal and state law theories. Plaintiffs allege that they have sustained harms under 42 U.S.C. §§ 1983 and 1985, the Bivens doctrine, and various state tort theories. Defendants have filed Motions to Dismiss or for Summary Judgment. In these proceedings the Court considers whether Plaintiffs' federal civil rights claims must fail based on a lack of state action and whether Plaintiffs' claims are barred by the applicable statutes of limitations and repose.

The experiments at issue in this litigation were directly administered by the State of Tennessee and Vanderbilt University, under the auspices of the Tennessee-Vanderbilt Nutrition Project (hereinafter, "TVNP"). Plaintiffs allege that the programs of the TVNP were designed and carried out through the "cooperative work" of Vanderbilt, the Tennessee Department of Public Health, the Rockefeller Foundation, and the Nutrition Foundation. The experiments involved the human ingestion of radioactive iron isotopes to facilitate the scientific tracking of iron absorption in pregnant women ("the project" or "Section B of the TVNP"). Plaintiffs assert that they were misled regarding the nature of their involvement in the project. According to the Plaintiffs' allegations, the researchers failed to disclose the radioactive nature of the iron solution that Plaintiffs were fed and instead referred to it as a "cocktail" or "vitamin drink." Plaintiffs also maintain that they were never informed of the risks of study participation and were not given the opportunity to refuse to participate.

The study was particularly unconscionable, Plaintiffs contend, because at the time of the project scientists already knew that radiation posed a danger to health. In the 1960s Vanderbilt conducted a follow-up study to determine the health effects of Plaintiffs' prior radiation exposure. Throughout the follow-up study Vanderbilt concealed from Plaintiffs the fact that they had been involuntarily exposed to radiation. Vanderbilt also neglected to notify Plaintiffs of the results of the follow-up study, which indicated a disproportionately high incidence of cancer among experiment subjects. The RF, according to the Plaintiffs, consulted with the TVNP regularly, and was fully aware of the nature of the pregnancy experiments during the period of their administration.

Defendants reject Plaintiffs' claims and argue that the Court should grant Defendants' Motions for Summary Judgment or to Dismiss based on, among other arguments, the lack of state action, the application of relevant statutes of repose, and the expiration of applicable statutes of limitations.

Upon consideration of the record and the evidentiary hearings conducted with respect to Defendants' Motions, the Court concludes that genuine issues of material fact exist regarding the existence of state action and the expiration of the applicable statutes of limitations. The Court also finds that the statutes of repose invoked by Defendants do not bar Plaintiffs' claims. Accordingly, the Court denies Defendants' Motions to Dismiss or for Summary Judgment.

. . . .

III. Analysis

A. State Action

In order for Defendants to be liable for violating Plaintiffs' rights under 42 U.S.C. §§ 1983 and 1985, Plaintiffs must show that Defendants were state actors. Based on the following analysis, the Court concludes that genuine issues of material fact exist with respect to whether or not Defendants were state actors for the purpose of Plaintiffs' claims.

Case law establishes that where there is a "symbiotic relationship" between a state entity and a private entity such that the two parties are participants in a cooperative or "joint activity," the actions of the private entity may constitute state action and may give rise to civil rights liability.

. . . .

Conduct that is formally private may become so entwined with governmental policies or so impregnated with a government character that it may be regarded as governmental action. In order to determine whether a sufficiently interdependent relationship exists, the Court must examine the particular facts of a given case.

A private entity may be a state actor based on its cooperative work with a state entity even if the state entity is the one which ultimately takes the challenged action. See *National Collegiate Athletic Ass'n v. Tarkanian*, 488 U.S. 179 (1988). Moreover, in *Tarkanian*, the Supreme Court indicated that where a private entity imposes rules on a state entity, and the state follows those rules and is powerless to reject them, the private entity may be deemed a state actor.

Applying these standards to Defendants, the Court concludes that genuine issues of material fact exist with respect to whether Defendants were state actors in this matter.

1. Vanderbilt University

A reasonable jury could conclude that Vanderbilt was a state actor in this matter based on the symbiotic relationship that Vanderbilt shared with the state and the cooperative work in which the two participated.

There is evidence indicating that the TVNP was conceived of and executed as a joint venture. In June 1943, the State Department of Health ("DOH") appears to have submitted a plan for a Tennessee-Vanderbilt nutrition program to the Rockefeller Foundation ("RF") and the Nutrition Foundation ("NF") for approval and funding. The program proposal appears to have resulted from conferences between the DOH and Professors Youmans and Darby of Vanderbilt.

The name of the project itself, the Tennessee-Vanderbilt Nutrition Project, supports the theory that the TVNP was a joint project. W.C. Williams, M.D., then Commissioner of the Tennessee DOH, appears to have submitted the tentative budget under that name to Vanderbilt and the RF on May 26, 1943. Williams proposed that the research section of the TVNP would be funded by RF, NF, and the State, one-third each. The TVNP budget showed that the Director's salary was to be paid from a joint fund, with two-thirds of the salary coming from the State. Vanderbilt does not appear to have contributed to the salary of the TVNP Directors . . . until after June 30, 1946, despite the Directors' status as Vanderbilt professors.

A June 2, 1943 memorandum that Dr. John A. Ferrell of the RF sent to Dr. W.S. Leathers, Dean of the Vanderbilt University Medical School, DOH Commissioner Williams, and Dr. C.G. King of the Nutrition Foundation indicates that according to the project's structure, the Tennessee State Commissioner of Health was to serve as one of four representatives on the TVNP's Executive Board. According to Ferrell's memorandum, the responsibilities of the Executive Board were to include assessing and approving or rejecting the plans, procedures, and activities of the project. Additional project-related notes kept by the RF indicate that the day-to-day leadership of the projects would be on a cooperative basis with Vanderbilt and State representatives working as co-equals and pooling their funds to cover project costs.

Evidence indicates that the State may have had an even larger role in running the experiment in practice than is suggested by Ferrell's memorandum. Plaintiffs allege that in practice decisions were made through the joint authority of just two individuals, the DOH Commissioner and the Director of the TVNP. . . .

There is evidence indicating that State employees attended an initial June 1945 meeting regarding the radioactive iron study. Materials in the record suggest that Dr. Margaret Kaser, a biochemist directly employed by the State of Tennessee DOH, was considered an active participant in the project. Dr. Darby testified that Dr. Kaser was on the "Planning Committee" of the TVNP study that conceived and approved the radioactive iron experiments. Two other state employees, Pauline Jones and Jo Haile Mayberry, were also listed as project staff.

In September of 1945, Dr. Darby, the Director of the TVNP, sent outlines of plans for the radioactive iron study to RF. In Dr. Darby's outline he noted that the existing staff of the project, which included Dr. Darby, whose salary was primarily paid by State funds, as well as State DOH employees Dr. Margaret Kaser, Pauline

Jones, and Jo Haile Mayberry, would conduct the study. Further evidence suggests that Tennessee employees continued to play a substantial role throughout the project. Dr. Kaser appears to have attended all recorded meetings of the project staff. Pauline Jones and Jo Haile Mayberry appear to have assisted in the administration of iron and the recording of iron absorption statistics, respectively.

Additional documentation in the record indicates that State and Vanderbilt personnel jointly published articles regarding the radioactive iron testing. Moreover, the State civil service requirements were applied to all personnel employed by the TVNP.

Evidence indicates that Vanderbilt and state employees shared facilities during the course of the TVNP. The laboratories of the Tennessee Department of Public Health were apparently housed in the Department of Biochemistry of Vanderbilt University School of Medicine for the purpose of the project. Two State employees appear to have worked in project-related positions at Vanderbilt. Also, a memorandum summarizing the formation of the TVNP in 1943 states that "all the personnel listed under Section B, and Dr. Hanlon and his stenographer from Section A, would be housed by Vanderbilt, utilizing substantially the space and facilities that have been in use for the nutrition studies of Dr. Youmans and those of the State Department of Health."

Finally, evidence suggests that Vanderbilt and the State derived mutual benefit from their cooperation in conducting the TVNP. The TVNP supported private research and paid salaries at the University, while at the same time serving the State's interest in examining Tennesseans' nutritional problems. In this way the TVNP served both private and public functions, and generated mutual benefits.

Based on these assertions, the Court concludes that a jury could reasonably find that Vanderbilt was a state actor. Vanderbilt and the state of Tennessee appear to have engaged in a symbiotic relationship . . . . The two parties appear to have cooperatively agreed to combine their respective nutrition study efforts to promote public welfare and avoid conflict or duplication of efforts . . . . Finally, the parties appear to have participated in a "joint activity" which arguably violated Plaintiffs' rights . . . . Accordingly, the Court concludes that summary judgment is not appropriate with respect to the issue of whether Vanderbilt was a state actor.

2. Rockefeller Foundation

The Court concludes that genuine issues of material fact also exist with respect to whether RF was a state actor for the purpose of Plaintiffs' claims. A jury could reasonably find that RF's actions and intentions were sufficiently intertwined with those of the Tennessee Department of Public Health that RF was a state actor with respect to this matter.

Plaintiffs' allegations against RF do not conform to the factual situations typical of "state action" claims against private entities. In the traditional state action case, the private entity, rather than the state, is alleged to have violated the plaintiff's rights. However, there is Supreme Court precedent indicating that a private entity can be deemed a "state actor" where the state, rather than the private entity, carried out the ultimate act of which the plaintiffs complain.

In *Tarkanian*, the final act challenged by the plaintiff, University of Nevada Basketball Coach Jerry Tarkanian — his suspension — was committed by the University of Nevada at Las Vegas ("UNLV"), a state university subject to the Due Process Clause of the Fourteenth Amendment. However, Tarkanian brought suit against the National Collegiate Athletic Association ("NCAA"), arguing that the NCAA had so influenced and intertwined its actions with the UNLV as to render the NCAA's actions "state action."

The Supreme Court noted that "the question is not whether UNLV participated to a critical extent in the NCAA's activities, but whether UNLV's actions in compliance with the NCAA rules and recommendations turned the NCAA's conduct into state action." The Court went on to state that "State action nonetheless might lie if UNLV, by embracing the NCAA's rules, transformed them into state rules and the NCAA into a state actor." The Court in *Tarkanian* further clarified that the NCAA could not be termed a state actor because the UNLV could have rejected the NCAA rules and the University had only a minor role in their formulation.

Here, analogously, the State of Tennessee and Vanderbilt University were more directly involved in carrying out the radiation experiments than RF. The question is thus whether the joint project, clearly involving both the State of Tennessee and Vanderbilt, "embraced" the RF's rules and suggestions, and was subject to the RF's influence to the point that the RF's actions were transformed into state action. The Court finds, as discussed below, that evidence indicates that the TVNP did "embrace" the RF's rules and suggestions, and that the TVNP did not have the option of disregarding the RF's recommendations while maintaining a crucial funding source. Additionally, a reasonable jury might find that as a result of successful RF efforts to place its staff and fellows in leadership positions within the TVNP, and to continue mentorship relationships between RF and TVNP staff, TVNP staff would have been unable to simply disregard the RF's recommendations.

. . . .

Finally, as noted in *Tarkanian*, a delegation of power from the state of Tennessee to the RF would be an indication of state action. In *Tarkanian*, the Supreme Court noted that, "It is, of course, true that a State may delegate authority to a private party and thereby make that party a state actor. Thus, we recently held that a private physician who had contracted with a state prison to attend to the inmates' medical needs was a state actor." Evidence that the RF and the State of Tennessee acted jointly for purposes of the radiation experimentation, that the RF influenced or encouraged the TVNP, or that the state ceded some of its authority over the project to the RF would weigh in favor of finding state action.

. . . [T]his Court finds that Plaintiffs offer sufficient evidence of a symbiotic relationship between the RF and the TVNP to render summary judgment inappropriate.

There is evidence that, beginning early in the project, the State of Tennessee ceded authority over project-related matters to the RF and acted jointly with RF. Project preliminaries were underway by 1943, although the administration of the radioactive iron did not commence until approximately two years later. A May 26, 1943 letter from Tennessee DOH Commissioner Williams reveals that prior discussion about the "cooperative project" budget had taken place between RF staff and the State of Tennessee. From the TVNP's initiation, the State, the RF, and the NF each paid one third of the costs and salaries required for Section B of the TVNP. The RF notes of a conference involving RF staff in May of 1943 indicate that the RF money was sent to the State of Tennessee, which then dispersed it on an as needed basis to Vanderbilt, which in turn pooled TVNP money and issued checks.

Early communications between RF staff and the Director of Section B, Dr. Robinson, indicate RF's collaborative role in developing the TVNP's research plan. . . .

There is evidence to suggest that the RF exerted influence over the TVNP in the hiring of TVNP staff. . . .

. . . .

The TVNP staff, including State of Tennessee actors, continued to consult with the RF and to solicit recommendations from the RF over the course of the project concerning budgeting, and the program of iron absorption experiments. . . .

Evidence indicates that the RF was aware of the experiments during the period in which the radioactive iron absorption studies were taking place. The TVNP prepared and dispatched semiannual summary reports to the State, the RF, and the NF for each relevant period, which discussed the use of radioactive iron as part of the TVNP programs. Further, there is evidence showing that the TVNP communicated regularly with the RF about the experiment.

. . . .

IV. Conclusion

For the forgoing reasons, the Court concludes that genuine issues of material fact exist with respect to whether Defendants were state actors in this matter and whether the statutes of limitations applicable to Plaintiffs' claims have expired. The Court also concludes that the relevant statutes of repose do not bar Plaintiffs' claims. Accordingly, the Court hereby denies Defendants' Motions to Dismiss or for Summary Judgment.

NOTES

1. The reader will note that the *Brentwood* decision established various tests for courts to use in analyzing the "the range of circumstances" that could constitute state action. A federal district court in Illinois, categorized the tests as follows:

> (1) the symbiotic relationship test (satisfied when private and public actors carry out a public function); (2) the state command and encouragement test (satisfied when the state requires the actions of the private actor); (3) the joint participation doctrine (satisfied when the private action is the same as the state action); and (4) the public function test (satisfied when private activity is fairly attributable to the state).

Garner v. Lakeside Community Committee, No. 10-cv-174, 2011 U.S. Dist. LEXIS 62860 (N.D. Ill. June 13, 2011).

2. While a case involving a high school audience, *Brentwood* casts a wide cloak with plaintiffs in conflicts involving the NCAA, mental health facilities, and homeowners associations. *See, e.g., Smith v. N.C.A.A.*, 266 F.3d 152 (3d Cir. 2001); *Benn v. Universal Health Sys.*, 371 F.3d 165 (3d Cir. 2004); *Hutton v. Shamrock Ridge Homeowners Ass'n*, 2009 U.S. Dist. LEXIS 115953 (N.D. Tex. Dec. 14, 2009). In many such cases the various courts distinguished the holding in *Brentwood*, ruling in essence that the decision clarifies the steps to be used in determining state action rather than establishing itself as controlling authority for any particular test.

3. *Rendell-Baker v. Kohn*, 457 U.S. 830 (1982), decided more than a decade before *Craft*, was considered an emphatic statement by the Supreme Court that it was narrowing the state action doctrine after years of expansion. In *Rendell-Baker*, teachers at a private high school brought suit against the institution, arguing that their discharges for opposing school policies violated their federal constitutional rights to free speech and due process. The school, although private, received most of its funding from public sources.

The Court held for the school, reasoning that neither the government funding nor the government regulation was sufficient to make the school's termination of the teachers a "state action." The Court also rejected two of the teachers' other arguments: (1) the school had engaged in state action because it performs a "public function"; and (2) the school had engaged in state action because it had a "symbiotic relationship" with government.

The Justices in *Rendell-Baker* applied three separate analytical tests to determine whether the school's actions constituted "state action": the "nexus" test, the "symbiotic relationship" test, and the "public function" test. At the postsecondary level, no clear trends have emerged to help administrators determine whether a particular action will be state action; but in general, only the nexus and symbiotic relationship tests have had any kind of meaningful impact in the higher education context. How did the *Brentwood* Court use the *Rendell-Baker* analysis? What was the Supreme Court's interpretation of the reach of *Rendell-Baker*?

4. The court in *Craft* found it was likely that a reasonable jury could determine that Vanderbilt was a state actor. But what if the issues had been more closely aligned with the law? What if the state and Vanderbilt did not jointly publish articles? What if the state civil service requirements did not apply to all personnel employed by the Tennessee-Vanderbilt venture? What if Vanderbilt and state employees did not share facilities?

5. Private organizations connected to higher education can also become state actors. The Court in *Craft* referenced *National Collegiate Athletic Ass'n v. Tarkanian*, 488 U.S. 179 (1988) (discussed in full in Chapter VIII), where a majority of Justices found that a private intercollegiate athletic association may be a state actor under certain conditions. *Craft v. Vanderbilt Univ.*, 18 F. Supp. 2d at 793. Although the Supreme Court ultimately found that the NCAA was not a state actor, the case opened the door for potential liability for private intercollegiate associations. *Tarkanian*, 488 U.S. at 194–96. Similarly, accreditation associations can also become state actors through their primary relationship with the operation of universities. The court in *Auburn University v. Southern Ass'n of Colleges and Schools, Inc.* found that the accrediting association at issue was a "quasi-public" entity that was required to honor common law due process rights, despite falling just below the standard for state action. 489 F. Supp. 2d 1362, 1373 (N.D. Ga. 2002).

6. As the final section in this chapter indicates, the study and application of policy considerations is a major focus of this casebook. A case like *Craft* provides a good example of how a legal decision can be used to craft policy and ensure an opposite result. What else could Vanderbilt University officials have done to avoid the state actor designation? If the school was acting purely as a research center, and had little, if any, influence on the direction of the study, could it still be deemed a state actor?

C. GOVERNMENT REGULATION OUTSIDE OF THE FEDERAL CONSTITUTION

Apart from federal constitutional matters, public and private postsecondary schools are subject to extensive government regulation from a variety of sources, including federal statutes and regulations, state constitutions and statutes, and contract and tort theories of law. Consider this sampling of cases demonstrating the breadth and depth of government involvement in American higher education vis-á-vis racial discrimination, property taxation, gender discrimination, and open meetings laws, respectively.

BOB JONES UNIVERSITY v. UNITED STATES
461 U.S. 574 (1983)

The Supreme Court was faced with the task of deciding whether nonprofit private schools that prescribed and enforced racially discriminatory admissions standards on the basis of religious doctrine qualified as tax-exempt organizations under § 501(c)(3) of the Internal Revenue Code. Bob Jones University, a nonprofit corporation located in Greenville, S.C., operated as a postsecondary school with an emphasis on Christian religion and ethics.

The sponsors of the University espoused that the Bible forbids interracial dating and marriage. Accordingly, the school excluded African Americans until 1971. After that, it accepted applications from African Americans who married within their race. In reaching its decision to deny the school tax-exempt status, the Court focused on the country's settled public policy against racial discrimination:

> Few social or political issues in our history have been more vigorously debated and more extensively ventilated than the issue of racial discrimination, particularly in education. Given the stress and anguish of the history of efforts to escape from the shackles of the "separate but equal" doctrine of *Plessy v. Ferguson*, it cannot be said that educational institutions that, for whatever reasons, practice racial discrimination, are institutions exercising "beneficial and stabilizing influences in community life," or should be encouraged by having all taxpayers share in their support by way of special tax status.

> There can thus be no question that the interpretation of . . . the IRS [to deny the school tax-exempt status] in 1970 was correct. That it may be seen as belated does not undermine its soundness. It would be wholly incompatible with the concepts underlying tax exemption to grant the benefit of tax-exempt status to racially discriminatory educational entities, which "[exert] a pervasive influence on the entire educational process." Whatever may be the rationale for such private schools' policies, and however sincere the rationale may be, racial discrimination in education is contrary to public policy. Racially discriminatory educational institutions cannot be viewed as conferring a public benefit within the "charitable" concept [in the Tax Code].

461 U.S. at 595.

NORTHWESTERN UNIVERSITY v. CITY OF EVANSTON

No. 00 C 7309, 2002 U.S. Dist. LEXIS 17104 (N.D. Ill. Sept. 11, 2002)

Northwestern University alleged that the City Council of Evanston, Illinois, where it is located, wrongfully enacted an historic preservation district that encompassed numerous University properties. Northwestern claimed that its exemption from property taxation fueled a long-running dispute with Evanston regarding the University's refusal to make a financial contribution to offset the cost of city services. Northwestern alleged the dispute led the City Council to include University properties within the preserved lands to pressure the University to make such contributions. In considering whether Northwestern had a viable equal protection claim against the city, the federal district court hearing the case had to interpret and apply local zoning and federal equal protection laws.

> The question before us, then, is this: what percentage of members of a legislative body must be moved by a constitutionally impermissible motive before the municipality itself may be held liable under § 1983 for the adoption of a facially neutral ordinance? Having been squarely presented this question, we hold that to establish municipal liability based on the discriminatory motive of a multi-member body, the plaintiff must show that a majority of its members acted with discriminatory intent. This position is consistent with both the logic of municipal liability and the weight of precedent. . . .
>
> To prevail on its vindictive action equal protection claim, then, Northwestern must show a majority of the City Council acted solely out of illegitimate animus toward the University. We believe Northwestern has offered sufficient evidence to survive summary judgment on this question. Although Northwestern has presented direct evidence of illegitimate animus with respect to only four of the six aldermen who voted for the Designation Ordinance, the motives of the remaining two aldermen remain unclear. Nonetheless, the circumstantial evidence suggests that a reasonable jury could find that these two aldermen were also motivated by illegitimate animus. As such, Northwestern has established genuine issues of material fact which preclude summary judgment . . . .

Id. at *30.

COHEN v. BROWN UNIVERSITY

991 F.2d 888 (1st Cir. 1993)

In this case, Brown University appealed a district court's issuance of a preliminary injunction ordering Brown to reinstate its women's gymnastics and volleyball programs to full intercollegiate varsity status pending the resolution of a Title IX claim. Because of financial difficulties, Brown announced that it planned to drop four sports from its intercollegiate varsity athletic roster: women's volleyball and gymnastics, men's golf and water polo.

Before the cuts Brown athletics offered an aggregate of 328 varsity slots for female athletes and 566 varsity slots for male athletes. Thus, women had 36.7% of the athletic opportunities and men 63.3%. Abolishing the four varsity teams did not materially affect the athletic opportunity ratios; women retained 36.6% of the opportunities and men 63.4%. At that time, Brown's student body comprised approximately 52% men and 48% women.

The court applied the Department of Education's policy conceptualization of Title IX to Brown's actions. Under that interpretation, the satisfaction of Title IX depended on:

(1) Whether intercollegiate level participation opportunities for male and female students are provided in numbers substantially proportionate to their respective enrollments; or

(2) Where the members of one sex have been and are underrepresented among intercollegiate athletes, whether the institution can show a history and continuing practice of program expansion which is demonstrably responsive to the developing interest and abilities of the members of that sex; or

(3) Where the members of one sex are underrepresented among intercollegiate athletes, and the institution cannot show a continuing practice of program expansion such as that cited above, whether it can be demonstrated that the interests and abilities of the members of that sex have been fully and effectively accommodated by the present program.

> . . . In an era where the practices of higher education must adjust to stunted revenues, careening costs, and changing demographics, colleges might well be obliged to curb spending on programs, like athletics, that do not lie at the epicenter of their institutional mission. Title IX does not purport to override financial necessity. Yet, the pruning of athletic budgets cannot take place solely in comptrollers' offices, isolated from the legislative and regulatory imperatives that Title IX imposes.
>
> This case aptly illustrates the point. Brown earnestly professes that it has done no more than slash women's and men's athletics by approximately the same degree, and, indeed, the raw numbers lend partial credence to that characterization. But, Brown's claim overlooks the shortcomings that plagued its program before it took blade in hand. If a school, like Brown, eschews the first two benchmarks of the accommodation test, electing to stray from substantial proportionality and failing to march uninterruptedly in the direction of equal athletic opportunity, it must comply with the third

> benchmark. To do so, the school must fully and effectively accommodate the underrepresented gender's interests and abilities, even if that requires it to give the underrepresented gender . . . what amounts to a larger slice of a shrinking athletic-opportunity pie.

991 F.2d at 906.

ASSOCIATED PRESS v. CROFTS

89 P.3d 971 (Mont. 2004)

As Montana's Commissioner of Higher Education, Richard A. Crofts held a number of meetings with a group of upper-level employees (such as University presidents and chancellors) of the state's University System. The first group referred to itself as the Policy Committee and then the Senior Management Group. The meetings were called by Crofts to discuss issues directly related to the operation of the University System. Crofts also used the meetings to seek input from Committee members on proposed actions within the realm of his authority. At one of the meetings, Crofts refused to allow a reporter for the Associated Press to attend the group's discussions. Media companies sued.

Article II, Section 9, of the Montana Constitution, commonly known as the "Right to Know provision, provides:

> No person shall be deprived of the right to examine documents or to observe the deliberations of all public bodies or agencies of state government and its subdivisions, except in cases in which the demand of individual privacy clearly exceeds the merits of public disclosure.

In holding that the group was subject to the "Right to Know" provision, the Montana Supreme Court developed a new test to use to determine whether a meeting should be open to the public:

> We conclude that under Montana's constitution and statutes, which must be liberally interpreted in favor of openness, factors to consider when determining if a particular committee's meetings are required to be open to the public include: (1) whether the committee's members are public employees acting in their official capacity; (2) whether the meetings are paid for with public funds; (3) the frequency of the meetings; (4) whether the committee deliberates rather than simply gathers facts and reports; (5) whether the deliberations concern matters of policy rather than merely ministerial or administrative functions; (6) whether the committee's members have executive authority and experience; and (7) the result of the meetings. This list of factors is not exhaustive, and each factor will not necessarily be present in every instance of a meeting that must be open to the public. A proper consideration of these factors does not mandate that every internal department meeting meet the requirements of the open meeting laws. Meetings where staff report the result of fact gathering efforts would not necessarily be public. Deliberation upon those facts that have been gathered and reported, and the process of reaching decisions would be open to public scrutiny. The guiding principles are those contained in the constitution; that is "no person shall be deprived of the right to examine

> documents or to observe the deliberations of all public bodies or agencies of state government and its subdivisions," and " all meetings of public or governmental bodies . . . supported in whole or in part by public funds . . . must be open to the public." Art. II, Sec .9, Mont. Const.; § 2-3-203(1), MCA (2001).

Id. at 199.

D. THE PERSISTENT TENSION BETWEEN RELIGION AND THE ACADEMY

1. Public Issues

The most common disputes arise when a public institution has incorporated religious activity into a college or university event.

TANFORD v. BRAND

104 F.3d 982 (7th Cir. 1997)

OPINION

CUMMINGS, CIRCUIT JUDGE.

Three individuals brought this suit to enjoin the giving of an invocation and benediction during the May 19, 1995 Commencement Ceremony on the Bloomington campus of Indiana University. Plaintiff Tanford is an Indiana Law School professor at Bloomington and plaintiffs MacDonald and Suess were law students there. After their motion for preliminary injunction concerning the May 6, 1995 Commencement Ceremony was denied, the complaint was amended to add Joseph Anthony Urbanski as a plaintiff. He was an undergraduate student majoring in computer science on the Bloomington campus. The district court denied summary judgment to plaintiffs and entered judgment in favor of the defendants.

On May 5, 1995, the Bloomington commencement activities began at the University President's home. The following day a university-wide Commencement Ceremony took place in the University's football stadium at 10:00 a.m. Special events followed for graduates of the various schools and their families. A committee consisting of faculty, staff and students was responsible for planning the commencement activities.

Thirty thousand to 35,000 people attended the Saturday morning stadium Commencement Ceremony. All graduating students were invited to attend, but attendance is voluntary and no penalty is imposed for non-attendance. Of the 7,400 graduating students in the undergraduate and graduate schools, approximately 5,000 attended.

Five thousand students and 150 University officials and faculty members formed the academic procession to the Commencement Ceremony. These persons proceeded to chairs placed in the football field whereas the 25,000 to 30,000 visitors and guests were seated in the stadium's permanent seats. The ceremony consisted of the national anthem, a nonsectarian invocation, an address by the commencement speaker, the conferral of honorary degrees, the presentation of the graduating classes, student remarks, the charge to the graduating classes, the conferral of degrees, the induction ceremony, the singing of the University's song, and a nonsectarian benediction. Fifteen to fifty-five percent of the students graduating from the law school attend the university-wide Commencement Ceremony.

In 1840, the University commenced having a nonsectarian invocation and benediction to open and close the morning Commencement Ceremony. A religious leader from the Bloomington area is invited to give the invocation and benediction. The prayers usually refer to a deity. A different person is chosen each year and in addition to the invocation that person is invited to give an uplifting and unifying benediction. . . .

University President Brand has explained that this ceremony is not to sponsor any particular religious faith or even to endorse religion but is meant to serve secular objectives by emphasizing the solemnity and dignity of the ceremony.

The four plaintiffs may be described as follows:

1. Professor Tanford is 45 years old and has tenure at the University. . . . He attended only one Commencement Ceremony since 1979 when he commenced teaching law. He attended the 1987 Commencement Ceremony because he was asked to "hood" students there. However, he absented himself when the invocation began, returned for the hooding and left before the benediction. He said that he did not think all 7,000 people who stood during the invocation and benediction believed in the religious message conveyed and that the Commencement Ceremony would not affect the religious beliefs of those in attendance. . . .

2. Third-year law student MacDonald was expected to graduate in May 1995. She had received her Bachelor of Arts degree from Indiana University in May 1992. She stated that she attended the May 1992 Commencement Ceremony when she received her undergraduate degree although she was uncomfortable in participating in a service led by someone of a different faith. She stated that her conscience would be offended if there were an invocation and benediction in 1995. . . .

3. Plaintiff Suess was a first-year law student, expected to graduate from the law school in May 1997. He is of the Jewish faith and stated that he was offended by the giving of a nonsectarian invocation and benediction because it is a form of proselytizing although he said it would not have any effect on his personal religious beliefs. . . .

4. Urbanski was an undergraduate plaintiff and was added after the preliminary injunction was denied. He opposes graduation prayer because he believes there should be a separation between church and state in a public institution. Prayer makes him uncomfortable. However, he agreed with his public high school policy which permitted students to have a moment of silence or a short prayer during commencement speeches. . . .

Thomas Bolyard, Director of University Field Services, said one of his responsibilities is to accommodate persons who have special problems or requests related to the Commencement Ceremony. He said it would be an easy matter to accommodate plaintiff Tanford and others who wished to be seated where they could enter or exit the Ceremony at will. He said that it was common for seated students or faculty members to get up and move around during the ceremony. . . .

In May 1995 the district court denied a preliminary injunction. After filing an amended complaint and answer, plaintiffs filed a motion for summary judgment which was denied . . . We affirm.

In the opinion below, Chief Judge Barker pointed out that under *Lee v. Weisman*, 505 U.S. 577, 586 (involving a prayer delivered by a clergyman at a middle school graduation), the Constitution guarantees that government "may not coerce anyone to support or participate in religion or its exercise" and under *Lemon v. Kurtzman*, 403 U.S. 602, 612–613, the Constitution requires that state actions "have a secular purpose, that they neither advance nor inhibit religion and * * * that they do not produce excessive government entanglement with religion." The district court concluded that plaintiffs were not entitled to relief under either standard.

The district court found *Lee* to be inapplicable because these plaintiffs are adults rather than younger students requiring special solicitude. In this regard, the district court observed that peer pressure is unlikely to dissuade college graduates from protesting, and the opinion below noted that thousands of graduates chose not to attend the stadium morning ceremony and that non-adherents could dissent without being noticed. The opinion also noted that plaintiffs could simply attend the afternoon ceremonies, which do not contain an invocation or benediction, and that in any event the stadium ceremony presented no threat of establishing religion.

The district court also found that the challenged invocation and benediction passed constitutional muster under the *Lemon* test because they served only to solemnize a public ceremony and continue a 155-year-old University tradition and did not dominate the baccalaureate ceremony, nor did they endorse any particular religion or influence religious beliefs. The instruction given to the cleric at the ceremony was merely to "include an uplifting, general message" and involved only a minor contact between the university and local clergy.

. . . .

Unlike *Lee*, here there was no coercion — real or otherwise — to participate. Many students chose not to attend the stadium exercises. Others left during the invocation, then returned and exited before the benediction. Still others sat during both events, as did most stadium attendees. At the afternoon ceremonies, no prayer was involved. Finally, the mature stadium attendees were voluntarily present and free to ignore the cleric's remarks. Most remained seated. Under these facts, in which the special concerns underlying the Supreme Court's decision in *Lee* are absent, the district court correctly determined that *Lee* does not require the challenged practices to be struck down.

Lemon v. Kurtzman, 403 U.S. 602, is plaintiffs' other principal reliance. There Pennsylvania and Rhode Island each gave financial aid to church-related educational institutions, a far cry from the non-denominational invocation and benediction at the Bloomington commencement.

Here the University's practice of having an invocation and benediction at its commencements has prevailed for 155 years and is widespread throughout the nation. Rather than being a violation of the Establishment Clause, it is "simply a tolerable acknowledgment of beliefs widely held among the people of this country." *Marsh v. Chambers*, 463 U.S. 783, 792. As we held in *Sherman v. Community Consolidated School District* 21, 980 F.2d 437 (7th Cir. 1992), Illinois public schools may lead the Pledge of Allegiance, including its reference to God, without violating the Establishment Clause of the First Amendment. Similarly here, the invocation and benediction serve legitimate secular purposes of solemnizing public occasions rather than approving particular religious beliefs. . . . Finally, as the district court correctly determined, the University's inclusion of a brief non-sectarian invocation and benediction does not have a primary effect of endorsing or disapproving religion, and there is no excessive entanglement of church and state by virtue of the University's selection of a cleric or its instruction to the cleric that his or her remarks should be unifying and uplifting. Insofar as there is any advancement of religion or governmental entanglement, it is de minimis at best.

Judgment affirmed.

NOTES

1. Though the *Tanford* opinion focused exclusively on the Establishment Clause, another case challenged similar religious convocations and prayers at universities on grounds that it violated the Free Exercise Clause, with similar success. The same year *Tanford* was decided, the Sixth Circuit Court of Appeals held that there was no violation of the Free Exercise Clause as long as a professor was never required to attend or participate in any religious exercise. *Chaudhuri v. State of Tenn.*, 130 F.3d 232 (6th Cir. 1997). The court ruled that prayers and moments of silence at university events "cast nothing more than shadows of constitutional concern." *Id.* at 240. When does a religious activity or program cross the line from "shadow" into a constitutional violation? Can any kind of prayer be delivered in the university setting?

The dissent in *Chaudhuri* argued that continuing a historical tradition of Christian prayer at a now-public university essentially establishes religion in the state setting. *Id.* at 241. Similarly, the holding in *Tanford* rests on the fact that the prayers at issue are part of the university's historical tradition dating back 155 years. *Tanford*, 104 F.3d at 986. Would it have made a difference if the prayer, or the religion promoting it, was new to the specific university? Does "establishment" of religion ever apply when prayer or religious beliefs have been a part of the institution since its inception?

2. What if a professor, without university approval, introduces religious content into the classroom? Same result? In one lower court case, a professor argued that his state university employer violated both the Free Exercise Clause and the Establishment Clause by ordering him to cease any religious speech or opinions offered during instructional times or in optional class sessions. *Bishop v. Aronov*, 926 F.2d 1066, 1068–69 (11th Cir. 1991). The professor openly stated to his students that he was Christian and this created some level of bias in his presentation of course material (in health sciences) and that students were free to critique him for it. *Id.* at 1068. The court held that the university's order to cease all in-class religious references did not violate any constitutional provisions because the university classroom is not an "open forum" and the public university has a bona fide interest in maintaining the neutrality and secular nature of all classrooms. *Id.* at 1078. Further, the order was narrowly tailored to address only student complaints about religious speech in the classroom and was, accordingly, a reasonable exercise of the university's control over curriculum content. *Id.* at 1078. What, if any, is the difference between religious speech at a university event and a professor's speech in the classroom? Would it aid the classroom environment for educators to discuss their potential or actual biases with students or, by opposite, ignore them?

2. Private Issues

Common conflicts in this area involve government support for religious schools. Such support could constitute a violation of the First Amendment's Establishment Clause. To determine whether such a violation has occurred, the Supreme Court has generally applied a three-part test developed in *Lemon v. Kurtzman*, 403 U.S. 602 (1971): (1) the statute must have a secular legislative purpose; (2) its principal or primary effect must be one that neither advances nor inhibits religion; and (3) the statute must not foster an excessive government entanglement with religion.

Four U.S. Supreme Court cases have applied the *Lemon* test to religious postsecondary schools, and in each case the aid program passed the test. *See Roemer v. Bd. of Public Works*, 426 U.S. 736 (1976); *Tilton v. Richardson*, 403 U.S. 672 (1971); *Hunt v. McNair*, 413 U.S. 734 (1973); *Witters v. Wash. Dept. of Svcs. for the Blind*, 474 U.S. 481 (1986).

ROEMER v. BOARD OF PUBLIC WORKS

426 U.S. 736 (1976)

OPINION

MR. JUSTICE BLACKMUN announced the judgment of the Court and delivered an opinion in which THE CHIEF JUSTICE and MR. JUSTICE POWELL joined.

We are asked once again to police the constitutional boundary between church and state. Maryland, this time, is the alleged trespasser. It has enacted a statute which, as amended, provides for annual noncategorical grants to private colleges, among them religiously affiliated institutions, subject only to the restrictions that the funds not be used for "sectarian purposes." A three-judge District Court, by a divided vote, refused to enjoin the operation of the statute, and a direct appeal has been taken to this Court . . . .

I

The challenged grant program . . . is . . . embodied in Md. Ann. Code, Art. 77A, §§ 65–69 (1975). It provides funding for "any private institution of higher learning within the State of Maryland," provided the institution is accredited by the State

Department of Education, was established in Maryland prior to July 1, 1970, maintains one or more "associate of arts or baccalaureate degree" programs, and refrains from awarding "only seminarian or theological degrees." The aid is in the form of an annual fiscal year subsidy to qualifying colleges and universities. The formula by which each institution's entitlement is computed has been changed several times and is not independently at issue here. It now provides for a qualifying institution to receive, for each full-time student (excluding students enrolled in seminarian or theological academic programs), an amount equal to 15% of the State's per-full-time-pupil appropriation for a student in the state college system. As first enacted, the grants were completely unrestricted. They remain noncategorical in nature, and a recipient institution may put them to whatever use it prefers, with but one exception. In 1972, following this Court's decisions in *Lemon v. Kurtzman*, 403 U.S. 602 (1971), and *Tilton v. Richardson*, 403 U.S. 672 (1971), § 68A was added to the statute by Laws of 1972, c. 534. It provides:

> "None of the moneys payable under this subtitle shall be utilized by the institutions for sectarian purposes."

The administration of the grant program is entrusted to the State's Board of Public Works "assisted by the Maryland Council for Higher Education." These bodies are to adopt "criteria and procedures . . . for the implementation and administration of the aid program." They are specifically authorized to adopt "criteria and procedures" governing the method of application for grants and of their disbursement, the verification of degrees conferred, and the "submission of reports or data concerning the utilization of these moneys by [the aided] institutions." Primary responsibility for the program rests with the Council for Higher Education, an appointed commission which antedates the aid program, which has numerous other responsibilities in the educational field, and which has derived from these a "considerable expertise as to the character and functions of the various private colleges and universities in the State."

The Council performs what the District Court described as a "two-step screening process" to insure compliance with the statutory restrictions on the grants. First, it determines whether an institution applying for aid is eligible at all, or is one "awarding primarily theological or seminary degrees." Several applicants have been disqualified at this stage of the process. Second, the Council requires that those institutions that are eligible for funds not put them to any sectarian use. An application must be accompanied by an affidavit of the institution's chief executive officer stating that the funds will not be used for sectarian purposes, and by a description of the specific nonsectarian uses that are planned. These may be changed only after written notice to the Council. By the end of the fiscal year the institution must file a "Utilization of Funds Report" describing and itemizing the use of the funds. The chief executive officer must certify the report and also file his own "Post-expenditure Affidavit," stating that the funds have not been put to sectarian uses. The recipient institution is further required to segregate state funds in a "special revenue account" and to identify aided nonsectarian expenditures separately in its budget. It must retain "sufficient documentation of the State funds expended to permit verification by the Council that funds were not spent for sectarian purposes." Any question of sectarian use that may arise is to be resolved by the Council, if possible, on the basis of information submitted to it by the institution and without actual examination of its books. Failing that, a "verification or audit" may be undertaken. The District Court found that the audit would be "quick and non-judgmental," taking one day or less.

In 1971, $1.7 million was disbursed to 17 private institutions in Maryland. The disbursements were under the statute as originally enacted, and were therefore not subject to § 68A's specific prohibition on sectarian use. Of the 17 institutions, five were church related, and these received $520,000 of the $1.7 million. A total of $1.8 million was to be awarded to 18 institutions in 1972, the second year of the grant program; of this amount, $603,000 was to go to church-related institutions. Before disbursement, however, this suit, challenging the grants as in violation of the Establishment Clause of the First Amendment, was filed. The $603,000 was placed in escrow and was so held until after the entry of the District Court's judgment on October 21, 1974. These and subsequent awards, therefore, are subject to § 68A and to the Council's procedures for insuring compliance therewith.

Plaintiffs in this suit, appellants here, are four individual Maryland citizens and taxpayers. Their complaint sought a declaration of the statute's invalidity, an order enjoining payments under it to church-affiliated institutions, and a declaration that the State was entitled to recover from such institutions any amounts already disbursed. In addition to the responsible state officials, plaintiff-appellants joined as defendants the five institutions they claimed were constitutionally ineligible for this form of aid: Western Maryland College, College of Notre Dame, Mount Saint Mary's College, Saint Joseph College, and Loyola College. Of these, the last four are affiliated with the Roman Catholic Church; Western Maryland, was a Methodist affiliate. The District Court ruled with respect to all five. Western Maryland, however, has since been dismissed as a defendant-appellee. We are concerned, therefore, only with the four Roman Catholic affiliates.

After carefully assessing the role that the Catholic Church plays in the lives of these institutions, a matter to which we return in greater detail below, and applying the three-part requirement of *Lemon I*, that state aid such as this have a secular purpose, a primary effect other than the advancement of religion, and no tendency to entangle the State excessively in church affairs, the District Court ruled that the amended statute was constitutional and was not to be enjoined. The court considered the original, unamended statute to have been unconstitutional under *Lemon I*, but it refused to order a refund of amounts theretofore paid out, reasoning that any refund was barred by the decision in *Lemon II*.* The District Court therefore denied all relief. This appeal followed. . . .

II

A system of government that makes itself felt as pervasively as ours could hardly be expected never to cross paths with the church. In fact, our State and Federal Governments impose certain burdens upon, and impart certain benefits to, virtually all our activities, and religious activity is not an exception. The Court has enforced a scrupulous neutrality by the State, as among religions, and also as between

---

* *Lemon II* posed the question of the appropriate relief to be ordered in light of *Lemon I*'s invalidation of the Pennsylvania private school aid statute. . . .

religious and other activities, but a hermetic separation of the two is an impossibility it has never required. . . .

And religious institutions need not be quarantined from public benefits that are neutrally available to all. The Court has permitted the State to supply transportation for children to and from church-related as well as public schools. It has done the same with respect to secular textbooks loaned by the State on equal terms to students attending both public and church-related elementary schools. . . .

Neutrality is what is required. The State must confine itself to secular objectives, and neither advance nor impede religious activity. Of course, that principle is more easily stated than applied. The Court has taken the view that a secular purpose and a facial neutrality may not be enough, if in fact the State is lending direct support to a religious activity. The State may not, for example, pay for what is actually a religious education, even though it purports to be paying for a secular one, and even though it makes its aid available to secular and religious institutions alike. The Court also has taken the view that the State's efforts to perform a secular task, and at the same time avoid aiding in the performance of a religious one, may not lead it into such an intimate relationship with religious authority that it appears either to be sponsoring or to be excessively interfering with that authority. . . .

. . . .

III

The first part of *Lemon I*'s three-part test is not in issue; appellants do not challenge the District Court's finding that the purpose of Maryland's aid program is the secular one of supporting private higher education generally, as an economic alternative to a wholly public system. The focus of the debate is on the second and third parts, those concerning the primary effect of advancing religion, and excessive church-state entanglement. We consider them in the same order.

A

While entanglement is essentially a procedural problem, the primary-effect question is the substantive one of what private educational activities, by whatever procedure, may be supported by state funds. [Precedent] requires (1) that no state aid at all go to institutions that are so "pervasively sectarian" that secular activities cannot be separated from sectarian ones, and (2) that if secular activities can be separated out, they alone may be funded.

(1) The District Court's finding in this case was that the appellee colleges are not "pervasively sectarian." This conclusion it supported with a number of subsidiary findings concerning the role of religion on these campuses:

(a) Despite their formal affiliation with the Roman Catholic Church, the colleges are "characterized by a high degree of institutional autonomy." None of the four receives funds from, or makes reports to, the Catholic Church. The Church is represented on their governing boards, but, as with Mount Saint Mary's, "no instance of entry of Church considerations into college decisions was shown."

(b) The colleges employ Roman Catholic chaplains and hold Roman Catholic religious exercises on campus. Attendance at such is not required; the encouragement of spiritual development is only "one secondary objective" of each college; and "at none of these institutions does this encouragement go beyond providing the opportunities or occasions for religious experience." It was the District Court's general finding that "religious indoctrination is not a substantial purpose or activity of any of these defendants."

(c) Mandatory religion or theology courses are taught at each of the colleges, primarily by Roman Catholic clerics, but these only supplement a curriculum covering "the spectrum of a liberal arts program." Nontheology courses are taught in an "atmosphere of intellectual freedom" and without "religious pressures." Each college subscribes to, and abides by, the 1940 Statement of Principles on Academic Freedom of the American Association of University Professors.

(d) Some classes are begun with prayer. The percentage of classes in which this is done varies with the college, from a "minuscule" percentage at Loyola and Mount Saint Mary's, to a majority at Saint Joseph. There is no "actual college policy" of encouraging the practice. "It is treated as a facet of the instructor's academic freedom." Classroom prayers were therefore regarded by the District Court as "peripheral to the subject of religious permeation," as were the facts that some instructors wear clerical garb and some classrooms have religious symbols. The court concluded:

> "None of these facts impairs the clear and convincing evidence that courses at each defendant are taught 'according to the academic requirements intrinsic to the subject matter and the individual teacher's concept of professional standards.' "

In support of this finding the court relied on the fact that a Maryland education department group had monitored the teacher education program at Saint Joseph College, where classroom prayer is most prevalent, and had seen "no evidence of religion entering into any elements of that program."

(e) The District Court found that, apart from the theology departments, faculty hiring decisions are not made on a religious basis. At two of the colleges, Notre Dame and Mount Saint Mary's, no inquiry at all is made into an applicant's religion. Religious preference is to be noted on Loyola's application form, but the purpose is to allow full appreciation of the applicant's background. Loyola also attempts to employ each year two members of a particular religious order which once staffed a college recently merged into Loyola. Budgetary considerations lead the colleges generally to favor members of religious orders, who often receive less than full salary. Still, the District Court found that "academic quality" was the principal hiring criterion, and that any "hiring bias," or "effort by any defendant to stack its faculty with members of a particular religious group," would have been noticed by other faculty members, who had never been heard to complain.

(f) The great majority of students at each of the colleges are Roman Catholic, but the District Court concluded from a "thorough analysis of the student admission and recruiting criteria" that the student bodies "are chosen without regard to religion."

We cannot say that the foregoing findings as to the role of religion in particular aspects of the colleges are clearly erroneous. Appellants ask us to set those findings aside in certain respects. Not surprisingly, they have gleaned from this record of thousands of pages, compiled during several weeks of trial, occasional evidence of a more sectarian character than the District Court ascribes to the colleges. It is not our place, however, to reappraise the evidence, unless it plainly fails to support the findings of the trier of facts. That is certainly not the case here, and it would make no difference even if we were to second-guess the District Court in certain particulars. To answer the question whether an institution is so "pervasively sectarian" that it may receive no direct state aid of any kind, it is necessary to paint a general picture of the institution, composed of many elements. . . .

(2) Having found that the appellee institutions are not "so permeated by religion that the secular side cannot be separated from the sectarian," the District Court proceeded to the next question posed by *Hunt*: whether aid in fact was extended only to "the secular side." This requirement the court regarded as satisfied by the statutory prohibition against sectarian use, and by the administrative enforcement of that prohibition through the Council for Higher Education. We agree. [Precedent] requires only that state funds not be used to support "specifically religious activity." It is clear that fund uses exist that meet this requirement. We have no occasion to elaborate further on what is and is not a "specifically religious activity," for no particular use of the state funds is set out in this statute. Funds are put to the use of the college's choice, provided it is not a sectarian use, of which the college must satisfy the Council. If the question is whether the statute sought to be enjoined authorizes state funds for "specifically religious activity," that question fairly answers itself. The statute in terms forbids the use of funds for "sectarian purposes," and this prohibition appears to be at least as broad as Hunt' s prohibition of the public funding of "specifically religious activity." We must assume that the colleges, and the Council, will exercise their delegated control over use of the funds in compliance with the statutory, and therefore the constitutional, mandate. It is to be expected that they will give a wide berth to "specifically religious activity," and thus minimize constitutional questions. Should such questions arise, the courts will consider them. It has not been the Court's practice, in considering facial challenges to statutes of this kind, to strike them down in anticipation that particular applications may result in unconstitutional use of funds.

B

If the foregoing answer to the "primary effect" question seems easy, it serves to make the "excessive entanglement" problem more difficult. The statute itself clearly denies the use of public funds for "sectarian purposes." It seeks to avert such use, however, through a process of annual interchange — proposal and approval, expenditure and review — between the colleges and the Council. In answering the question whether this will be an "excessively entangling" relationship, we must consider the several relevant factors identified in prior decisions:

(1) First is the character of the aided institutions. This has been fully described above. As the District Court found, the colleges perform "essentially secular educational functions" that are distinct and separable from religious activity. This

finding, which is a prerequisite under the "pervasive sectarianism" test to any state aid at all, is also important for purposes of the entanglement test because it means that secular activities, for the most part, can be taken at face value. There is no danger, or at least only a substantially reduced danger, that an ostensibly secular activity — the study of biology, the learning of a foreign language, an athletic event — will actually be infused with religious content or significance. The need for close surveillance of purportedly secular activities is correspondingly reduced. . . .

(2) As for the form of aid, we have already noted that no particular use of state funds is before us in this case. The process by which aid is disbursed, and a use for it chosen, is before us. We address this as a matter of the "resulting relationship" of secular and religious authority.

(3) As noted, the funding process is an annual one. The subsidies are paid out each year, and they can be put to annually varying uses. The colleges propose particular uses for the Council's approval, and, following expenditure, they report to the Council on the use to which the funds have been put.

The District Court's view was that in light of the character of the aided institutions, and the resulting absence of any need "to investigate the conduct of particular classes," the annual nature of the subsidy was not fatal. . . .

We agree with the District Court that "excessive entanglement" does not necessarily result from the fact that the subsidy is an annual one. . . .

. . . The present statute contemplates annual decisions by the Council as to what is a "sectarian purpose," but, as we have noted, the secular and sectarian activities of the colleges are easily separated. Occasional audits are possible here, but we must accept the District Court's finding that they would be "quick and non-judgmental." They and the other contacts between the Council and the colleges are not likely to be any more entangling than the inspections and audits incident to the normal process of the colleges' accreditations by the State.

. . . .

(4) As for political divisiveness, the District Court recognized that the annual nature of the subsidy, along with its promise of an increasing demand for state funds as the colleges' dependency grew, aggravated the danger of "[p]olitical fragmentation . . . on religious lines." Nonetheless, the District Court found that the program "does not create a substantial danger of political entanglement." Several reasons were given. . . . [T]he danger of political divisiveness is "substantially less" when the aided institution is not an elementary or secondary school, but a college, "whose student constituency is not local but diverse and widely dispersed." [citation omitted] Furthermore, political divisiveness is diminished by the fact that the aid is extended to private colleges generally, more than two-thirds of which have no religious affiliation . . . . Finally, the substantial autonomy of the colleges was thought to mitigate political divisiveness, in that controversies surrounding the aid program are not likely to involve the Catholic Church itself, or even the religious character of the schools, but only their "fiscal responsibility and educational requirements."

The District Court's reasoning seems to us entirely sound. . . .

There is no exact science in gauging the entanglement of church and state. The wording of the test, which speaks of "excessive entanglement," itself makes that clear. The relevant factors we have identified are to be considered "cumulatively" in judging the degree of entanglement. . . . In reaching the conclusion that it did, the District Court gave dominant importance to the character of the aided institutions and to its finding that they are capable of separating secular and religious functions. For the reasons stated above, we cannot say that the emphasis was misplaced or the finding erroneous.

The judgment of the District Court is affirmed.

It is so ordered.

NOTES

1. The Court in *Roemer* remarked that "[t]here is no exact science in gauging the entanglement of church and state." As you consider the delicate interplay between government and religious postsecondary schools and activities, keep in mind the judiciary's role in the relationship: Are courts equipped to consider religious doctrine and its effects on students and faculty of vastly different ages and experiences? What are the pros and cons of a bright-line test in this area of the law versus a balancing test like "excessive entanglement"?

2. Are restrictions on state scholarships that are used to earn religious degrees (regardless of the university) constitutional? In *Locke v. Davey*, the Supreme Court upheld a Washington state statute that prohibited state scholarship funding toward any theological degree. *Locke v. Davey*, 540 U.S. 712, 725 (2004). The essential issue in *Locke* revolved around the constitutional "play in the joints" between the Free Exercise Clause and the Establishment Clause. *Id.* at 719. Ultimately, the Court found that Washington State's refusal to fund theological degrees was a valid exercise of the Establishment Clause and not constitutionally suspect. *Id.* at 725. In his dissent, Justice Scalia argued that the statute created a public benefit which was discriminatory on its face against religious students who desired to earn religious degrees. *Id.* at 727–28. What advantage does the idea of degree-based approach have over an institutional-based approach for analyzing pubic aid in higher education? For a full discussion of *Locke*, see Chapter V.

3. What would happen if a university required students to pay fees that fund activities that go against their religious beliefs? In one lower court case, a group of public university students challenged mandatory student fees which funded, in part, a university health insurance plan covering abortions on grounds that mandatory funding of abortion services violated their religious beliefs. *Goehring v. Brophy*, 94 F.3d 1294, 1298 (9th Cir. 1996). Applying a strict scrutiny analysis, the court held that the fees in question did not place a substantial burden on the free exercise of a central tenet of their religion. *Id.* at 1299–1300. The fees in question were very small, students were not required to have health insurance, and no abortions took place on campus property. *Id.* at 1300. Hence, the restriction on free exercise of religion was limited and narrowly tailored to legitimate university interests in students' health. *Id.* at 1300. Eventually the federal law relied upon in *Goehring*, The Religious Freedom Restoration Act of 1993, was overturned as applied to the states. *See* 42 U.S.C. § 2000bb. Further, the Court of Appeals for the Ninth Circuit stated the following:

> Congress expanded the statutory protection for religious exercise in 2000 by amending RFRA's definition of "exercise of religion." Under the amended definition — "any exercise of religion, whether or not compelled by, or central to, a system of religious belief" — RFRA now protects a broader range of religious conduct than the Supreme Court's interpretation of "exercise of religion" under the First Amendment. To the extent that our RFRA cases prior to RLUIPA [Religious Land Use and Institutionalized Persons Act] depended on a narrower definition of "religious exercise," those cases are no longer good law.

Navajo Nation v. U.S. Forest Serv., 479 F.3d 1024, 1033 (9th Cir. 2007), *on reh'g en banc*, 535 F.3d 1058 (9th Cir. 2008).

The statute and case law raise several important questions about freedom of religion in the public university. How does religious freedom impact mandatory student health insurance or the funding of students desiring abortions? Is it true that anti-abortion sentiment is not a core tenet of any religious doctrine?

4. What if student organizations that receive university funds and access to university facilities discriminate against other students on the basis of religious conviction? This question was addressed in *Christian Legal Society Chapter of the University of California v. Martinez*, 130 S. Ct. 2971 (2010), where the Hastings College of Law declined to continue to recognize the Christian Legal Society (CLS) as an official student organization because its members refused to comply with state and, hence, college policy against discrimination. CLS required its members to declare through written affirmation their Christian beliefs and denied admission to students who would not do so or who held positions promoting homosexuality. A Supreme Court majority led by Justice Ruth Bader Ginsburg held that the anti-discrimination policy was reasonable and viewpoint neutral. The majority opinion further determined that a lesser level of judicial scrutiny was required as the activity occurred in a limited public forum. Justice Samuel Alito joined by three other justices dissented arguing that the Court's decision promoted the principle that there is no constitutional protection for "expression that offends prevailing standards of political correctness in our country's institutions of higher learning." *Id.* at 3000 (Alito, J. dissenting); see also full discussion *infra* in Chapter VI.

E. THE APPLICABILITY OF SECONDARY SCHOOL LAW TO HIGHER EDUCATION CASES

Principles of law developed in cases involving secondary schools are often transferable to the postsecondary arena. But many courts differ on whether, and how, such principles should apply to higher education cases. Consider the U.S. Supreme Court case of *Hazelwood School District v. Kuhlmeier*, 484 U.S. 260 (1988). In *Hazelwood*, the Court validated a high school principal's editorial control over school-sponsored speech in the form of a student newspaper. The Court's opinion identified but did not address the question "whether the same degree of deference [to administrators' judgments] is appropriate with respect to school-sponsored expressive activities at the college and university level."

And lower courts, it turns out, are mixed on the *Hazelwood* question.

KINCAID v. GIBSON

236 F.3d 342 (6th Cir. 2001) (en banc)

In *Kincaid,* the Sixth Circuit decided with virtually no discussion that *Hazelwood* has no applicability to college newspapers, noting that it "deals exclusively with the First Amendment rights of students in a high school setting."

HOSTY v. CARTER

412 F.3d 731 (7th Cir. 2005) (en banc)

In *Hosty,* on the other hand, the Seventh Circuit held that *Hazelwood* is applicable to college newspapers supported by public funds.

> *Hazelwood* provides our starting point. A high school's principal blocked the student newspaper (which was financed by public funds as part of a journalism class) from publishing articles that the principal thought inappropriate for some of the school's younger students and a potential invasion of others' privacy. When evaluating the students' argument that the principal had violated their right to freedom of speech, the Court first asked whether the paper was a public forum. After giving a negative answer based on the school's established policy of supervising the writing and reviewing the content of each issue, the Court observed that the school's subvention of the paper's costs distinguished the situation from one in which students were speaking independently, as in *Tinker v. Des Moines Independent Community School District,* 393 U.S. 503 (1969). When a school regulates speech for which it also pays, the Court held, the appropriate question is whether the "actions are reasonably related to legitimate pedagogical concerns." "Legitimate" concerns, the Court stated, include setting "high standards for the student speech that is disseminated under its auspices — standards that may be higher than those demanded by some newspaper publishers or theatrical producers in the 'real' world — and [the school] may refuse to disseminate student speech that does not meet those standards. In addition, a school must be able to take into account the emotional maturity of the intended audience in determining whether to disseminate student speech on potentially sensitive topics, which might range from the existence of Santa Claus in an elementary school setting to the particulars of teenage sexual activity in a high school setting." Shortly after this passage the Court dropped a footnote: "A number of lower federal courts have similarly recognized that educators' decisions with regard to the content of school-sponsored newspapers, dramatic productions, and other expressive activities are entitled to substantial deference. We need not now decide whether the same degree of deference is appropriate with respect to school-sponsored expressive activities at the college and university level."

Picking up on this footnote, plaintiffs argue, and the district court held, that *Hazelwood* is inapplicable to university newspapers and that post-secondary educators therefore cannot ever insist that student newspapers be submitted for review and approval. Yet this footnote does not even hint at the possibility of an on/off switch: high school papers reviewable, college papers not reviewable. It addresses degrees of deference. Whether some review is possible depends on the answer to the public-forum question, which does not (automatically) vary with the speakers' age. Only when courts need assess the reasonableness of the asserted pedagogical justification in non-public-forum situations does age come into play, and in a way suggested by the passage we have quoted from *Hazelwood*'s text. To the extent that the justification for editorial control depends on the audience's maturity, the difference between high school and university students may be important. (Not that any line could be bright; many high school seniors are older than some college freshmen, and junior colleges are similar to many high schools.) To the extent that the justification depends on other matters — not only the desire to ensure "high standards for the student speech that is disseminated under [the school's] auspices" (the Court particularly mentioned "speech that is . . . ungrammatical, poorly written, inadequately researched, biased or prejudiced, vulgar or profane, or unsuitable for immature audiences.") but also the goal of dissociating the school from "any position other than neutrality on matters of political controversy" — there is no sharp difference between high school and college papers.

The Supreme Court itself has established that age does not control the public-forum question. So much is clear not only from decisions such as Tinker, which held that public school students have a right of non-disruptive personal expression on school premises, but also from the decisions concerning the use of school funds and premises for religious expression. These decisions hold that no public school, of any level — primary, secondary, or post-secondary — may discriminate against religious speech in a public forum (including classrooms made available to extracurricular activities), or withhold funding that would be available to student groups espousing sectarian views. . . .

If private speech in a public forum is off-limits to regulation even when that forum is a classroom of an elementary school then speech at a non-public forum, and underwritten at public expense, may be open to reasonable regulation even at the college level — or later, as *Rust v. Sullivan*, 500 U.S. 173 (1991), shows by holding that the federal government may insist that physicians use grant funds only for the kind of speech required by the granting authority. We hold, therefore, that *Hazelwood*'s framework applies to subsidized student newspapers at colleges as well as elementary and secondary schools.

F. THE LAW-POLICY DISTINCTION

H.K. COLEBATCH, POLICY 49–66 (2002)*

The dominant paradigm: policy as the systematic pursuit of goals

The question 'what is policy for?' is not often asked, perhaps because the answer seems obvious. The dominant paradigm in discussion of policy, by both participants and observers, sees it as the exercise of authority to achieve collective purposes. Policy is the pursuit of goals. The assumption that policy is a purposive course of action underlies the mainstream definitions of policy. Laswell and Kaplan define policy as 'a projected program of goals, values and practices', Bridgman and Davis define policy as 'a course of action by government designed to achieve certain results' and Friedrich puts it bluntly: 'It is essential for the policy concept that there be a goal, objective or purpose.'

The policy process is then represented as a sequence of stages in the development and pursuit of this goal, beginning with the thought, moving through action and ending with the solution. These stages are often presented not as a line, but as a circle, suggesting that there is a natural progression from one stage to the next. . . .

In this perspective, the policy process is seen as a number of successive stages:

1. Determining goals. Authorized leaders determine the objectives they wish to achieve.

2. Choosing courses of action. They then select the courses of action which will realize these goals, preferably from a range of options, and in the light of the relative costs and benefits of each.

3. Implementing these courses of action. Other workers then have to carry out the courses of action that have been chosen, and the rest of the organizational process is described as the implementation of these choices.

4. Evaluating the results. The outcome of the implementation of the decision can (and should) now be evaluated: 'was the decision thoroughly and economically put into effect?' (efficiency evaluation), and 'did the implementation of the decision have the expected impact on the problem to which the policy decision was addressed?' (effectiveness evaluation).

5. Modifying the policy. If necessary, the policy is then amended in the light of the evaluation.

. . . .

Policy as the implementation of goals

In this perspective, policy is about choosing goals, but it is also about choosing the means of accomplishing these goals: if we do a, then b will result. The policy embodies a theory of cause and effect. When the policy-makers' intentions have been carried out, the desired objective should have been achieved: this is 'implementation'. But if what we find on the ground is significantly different from these goals, then the policy has not been implemented. This was the perspective taken in the pioneering book on this subject, Pressman and Wildavsky's Implementation . . . . They asked, 'why was it that the goals articulated by the policy-makers in Washington bore little relation to what could be seen on the ground in Oakland, California?' When the question was put like this, it was immediately and widely recognized to be a general problem: in all the policy fields, there was a 'problem of implementation', in that the outcome was likely to be quite different from the originally stated intentions. So it was not simply a matter of determining the policy goals: they had to be put into effect.

Pressman and Wildavsky explained the lack of implementation in the Oakland case in terms of the large number of participants in the process, and the diversity of goals. Most of the things to be done needed to be 'cleared' at a number of points, involving a range of participants with distinct perspectives of their own and different levels of commitment to the policy objectives. The more the policy depended on such 'clearances', the more likely it was that the original objectives would not be accomplished.

This was also reported in other studies of implementation, which also found a number of other causes for policies not being implemented: the original decision was ambiguous; the policy directive conflicted with other policies; it was not seen as a high priority; there were insufficient resources to carry it out; it provoked conflict with other significant players; the target group proved hard to reach; the things that were done did not have the expected impact etc. Over time, circumstances changed, and attention shifted to other problems, which made the original goals less important. Indeed, the literature is a little depressing, because it seems to be largely about 'implementation failure'.

Whether implementation is a problem, and what sort of problem it is, depends on the perspective being applied. In the vertical perspective, implementation means that authorized decisions at the top coincide exactly with outcomes at the bottom: it is a question of securing compliance. This reflects constitutional models of government and instrumental models of organization: it is seen as self-evident that 'those elected by the public to government should be able to place their policies into action'. [citation omitted]

In the horizontal dimension, implementation is an exercise in collective negotiation: the focus shifts from the desired outcome to the process and the people through which it would be accomplished. It recognizes that policy is an ongoing process, and that the participants have their own agendas and therefore their own distinct perspective on any policy issue. For instance, an employment agency may propose a system of traineeships as a means of getting the young unemployed back into the workforce. The finance department, which is concerned with controlling spending, may see it as a fresh and potentially expanding spending commitment.

The trade unions (whose cooperation is important) may see it as a threat to traditional apprenticeships. And the young unemployed may see it as an allowance for which they may or may not qualify. All of these are realities which are relevant in the pursuit of this policy, and the implementation of policy will involve negotiation between these different realities as the various participants become involved.

This poses a difficulty for implementation as a concept: what is it that is being implemented? In the vertical perspective, there is a tendency to see 'policy' emerging pristine and fully formed from the head of a detached 'policy-maker', but in the horizontal, it is something which emerges in the course of interaction among the relevant participants. It is not that the policy was complete when it first emerged and was then put at risk in the interaction that followed, but that it was this collective process which produced the policy. This changes the question about implementation from execution of a clear objective, to the achievement of collective action which is compatible with the perspectives of all the relevant participants.

It also recognizes the time dimension, i.e., that the process does not begin with a detached 'policy-maker' articulating a new policy and inscribing it on a blank sheet, but that it is part of a continuing game in which a regular cast of participants recognize and respond to policy questions. The game is not fixed — new players seek to be recognized, and there is contest over how policy questions are to be understood — but there is continuity as well as change, and policy initiatives have to take their place in the ongoing process. This leads Sabatier to suggest that the time-frame for the implementation of a new policy should be ten or twenty years.

The concept of implementation frames the action in a particular way. It highlights some things rather than others, and defines people and processes in relation to the policy under consideration. For instance, it defines regional superintendent of education as the implementor of the policy on multicultural education. The superintendent may have had nothing to do with it and may see it as being of marginal importance, but by definition, he or she is the implementor of the policy. The teachers' union may be interested because of its concern that teachers being asked to do extra duties should get extra money — and it may see success as blocking the introduction of any new policy that is not accompanied by extra allowances. The parents' organization may see the new policy as an irrelevance and potential source of overload, and will be concerned to limit its impact on the core curriculum. The implementation of the policy also involves all of these participants, though they would not see themselves as 'implementors'. To describe the process as 'implementation' is to define what the game is about without asking the players.

. . . .

Goals in the vertical and horizontal dimensions

The assumption that policy is concerned with the definition and accomplishment of goals is so grounded in the dominant paradigm of human action as instrumental rationality that it is not closely examined. It is taken for granted that social action is directed to goals, that policy is the pursuit of collective goals and that policy statements indicate what these goals are.

This perspective makes sense of the policy process as the application of authority.

It sees the core as the determination of authorized goals, and explains the rest of the organizational process as the pursuit of these goals, culminating with an assessment of whether those goals have been achieved. It explains the participants' place in the action in terms of their relation to authority: people can act together because authorized leaders have determined the collective purpose, which all participants then work to achieve. These authority figures are then described as the 'decision-makers', the people who choose the goal and the means to achieve it. Other policy workers are described by reference to, and as subordinate to, the decision-makers: they are offering 'policy advice' or providing 'decision support'. And beyond them are the 'implementers', whose role is seen as carrying out the decisions of the authorities, possibly subject to the scrutiny of 'evaluators', who will report back to the decision-makers on whether their goals have been achieved.

Some writers see this as a skewed, 'top-down' perspective on policy, which reflects the particular interests and understanding of managers and gives an inadequate picture of the policy process as a whole. Barrett and Fudge argue that while it is possible to draw a clear distinction between policy and its implementation as concepts, in practice there is a constant interaction between the managers at the top and the operatives at the workplace, and it is quite inaccurate to see the relationship between the two as 'making' and 'implementing' finished policy. Instead, they say, we have to recognize that those who are giving effect to policy are also shaping what it is. So we should think in terms of 'action' and 'response', recognizing that it is a continuing process, and that the initiative does not necessarily come from the top: a 'bottom-up' perspective shows that operatives are also making policy as they turn problems into routines, articulate rationales for them and seek the commitment of organizational resources.

It is also argued that the implementation of policy rarely involves only superiors and subordinates in the one hierarchical organization. It is likely to require the cooperation of other people, who may be in other governmental organizations (which means that they are in other hierarchies) or in organizations but outside government, or who may not be organized at all. Both formulating policy and putting it into practice are likely to involve a range of participants, with their own distinct understanding of what the policy issue is and what they hope to achieve. The 'bottom-up' critics pointed out that, for the practitioner, an important part of policy work consisted of drawing these various participants into a common framework. This makes it unreal (and from the point of view of those involved, quite unhelpful) to see the policy process as the pursuit of clear objectives. They argue that the focus should not be on the policy-makers and their objectives, but on the whole pattern of relationships through which policy is implemented: how do policy participants manage to work together even though they may have different perspectives on the objective? Hjern and Porter suggest that the focus should be not on a single organization, but on the array of actors who are involved. Any given policy question will involve people from a range of organizations — and not whole organizations, but a few individuals in each one. What draws them together is a programme of action to which all of them can contribute, and which makes sense to all of them, though not necessarily for the same reasons: they can agree on what to do without having to agree on why they are doing it. Hjern and Porter refer to these people as an 'implementation structure' — the grouping of participants which shares a commitment to a particular programme. They make up a loose organizational form — some are more cohesive than others — with the members having enough discretion to make commitments about their own organizations' contribution to the programme.

So while presenting policy as the pursuit of goals is 'normal' (and in many contexts, indisputable), in practice there are many participants in the policy process, and they are likely to have distinct and possibly contradictory ideas about goals and priorities. It is not simply that they have different ideas on what to do about the problem: they may have quite distinct views on what the problem is. With public drunkenness, for instance, different functional specialists will interpret it in terms of their own expertise and activities, and generate different ideas of what would be an appropriate policy response. Determining policy goals is therefore not a matter of a context-free group of 'policy-makers' determining what the goal will be for all the participants: there is a range of interested parties who will have their own analysis of the problem, and will be seeking wider support for what they see as the most appropriate course of action.

So there are a number of policy goals in circulation. Even if action is being taken in pursuit of one goal, it may be at variance with another. Action taken in pursuance of the policy goals of opening up labour markets and meeting our international obligations may act against the goals of protecting employment and maintaining our cultural heritage. The pursuit of goals may conflict with other cues for action. The goal of encouraging school children to discuss public issues like HIV/AIDS may be at odds with the principal's goal of not antagonizing significant numbers of parents. So rather than interpreting policy action as the implementation of a goal, we need to ask what the link is between goal statements and action.

. . . .

Goals and the policy process

So while the idea of policy as the pursuit of goals is important in the analysis of policy, the goal statements which we encounter are not independent of the policy process and prior to it, but instead have to be understood as part of the process. Policy does not start with a goal and proceed to action: people seek to make sense of the action, and frame and refine statements of goals. It is a continuing process of interaction between the interpretation and the action to which it relates. Policy, we have seen, is a way of making sense of the action, drawing disparate forms of activity into a common framework. Our question is: how is this done, and what is the significance of goals in the action and in the analysis?

There is a structural tension in the policy process. In the vertical dimension, policy is characterized by clarity of purpose, and the object of evaluation is to ensure that activity is leading to the accomplishment of known purposes. In the horizontal dimension, there is recognition that there is a diversity of players in the game, and therefore scope for divergence over what constitutes worthwhile activity, and hence ambiguity about how it might be evaluated. Since both these elements of the policy process are always present, there is always going to be tension between them. And not all perspectives are equally valid: 'reducing the road toll among young people' commands more support than 'keeping year 10 occupies and interested', which in turn carries more weight than 'turning young people into car-buyers'. This ambiguity, which was important in getting support for the programme in the first place, is challenged by the process of evaluation, which is shaped by the more presentable (and more measurable) goal of reducing the road toll. This may of course be the intention of those who commissioned the evaluation: contesting the impact of these other participants on the programme. But it shows us the importance of recognizing the range of participants in the game, and the effect that this has on evaluation.

Appealing to experts does not solve the problem. It is unlikely that there is a single, clear field of expertise which can be mobilized, and these will define the question in different ways. It the case of forest policy, for instance, it is likely that economists, foresters and ecologists may all have different answers to the question 'what are the goals of our forest policy?', so that it is not simply a matter of the experts versus the authorities.

This reminds us that policy is about process as well as outcome, and about structures and routines and commitment as well as goals. Participants in the policy process try to build support for their activity, and statements of goal facilitate this. But the broader and less specific they are, the more likely it is what they will attract support, so statements of goals tend not to be very precise, and it becomes difficult to interpret the process as a quest to attain them. They have to be understood in terms of their place in the present, as much as in terms of a future state to which policy will lead.

. . . .

NOTES

1. When relevant, this casebook will consider the policy implications of the legal principles and trends discussed. Law and policy are inseparable, and the importance of developing sound institutional policies is increasing as the law intrudes ever more on campus. How does policymaking work in the higher education context? Professor Colebatch provides a general overview in the above excerpt, but how do postsecondary school board members and administrators interact to craft policy? Consider the guidance of the Association of Governing Boards and Universities and Colleges and the Association of College and University Policy Administrators. Below, review their functions in supporting colleges and universities.

Association of Governing Boards of Universities and Colleges

In its self-assessment instrument, the Association identifies 10 areas in which boards function:

1. Clarifying the institution's mission
2. Promulgating long-range plans
3. Developing the physical plant
4. Ensuring financial solvency
5. Selecting board members

6. Establishing an adequate board organization
7. Appointing, supporting, and monitoring presidential performance
8. Developing educational programs
9. Bolstering student relationships
10. Serving as a court of appeal

ASS'N OF GOVERNING BDS. OF UNIVS. AND COLLS., *available at* http://www.agb.org.

The Association of College and University Policy Administrators

The ACUPA sets out the following process:

Predevelopment

- Identify issues
- Conduct analysis

Development

- Draft language
- Get approvals
- Determine distribution/education

Maintenance

- Solicit evaluation and review
- Plan measurement and compliance

Policy Development Process with Best Practices, ACUPA, *available at* http://process.umn.edu/acupa/projects/process/.

2. Trustees and administrators implementing policy are guided, to a great degree, by legal principles. Consider the impact of the milestone decisions regarding campus policy listed below:

RENDELL-BAKER v. KOHN
457 U.S. 830 (1982)

Policy Implications: Trustees and administrators at private postsecondary schools must take into account *Rendell-Baker* and lower-court decisions applying its principles if they wish to avoid having a particular act constitute a "state action." Also, the policymaking process must be guided with an eye on the nexus, symbiotic relationship, public function, and entwinement approaches courts take when determining whether something constitutes state action.

Unresolved Policy Questions: Is there one test that, if satisfied, necessarily means a school has satisfied all of the other tests? Should a school try to craft policy with that one test in mind?

HAZELWOOD SCHOOL DISTRICT v. KUHLMEIER
484 U.S. 260 (1988)

Policy Implications: Trustees and administrators at public postsecondary schools must continue to wrestle with the unsettled nature of the law involving on-campus student speech. *Hazelwood*, a secondary school case, is currently the primary point of reference. When crafting student-speech policies, trustees and administrators must operate against a backdrop of confusion amongst lower courts about whether *postsecondary* administrators deserve the same level of deference when censoring student speech as elementary and secondary school administrators receive.

Unresolved Policy Questions: In jurisdictions that are silent on this question, how are college and university trustees and administrators to respond?

ROEMER v. BOARD OF PUBLIC WORKS
426 U.S. 736 (1976)

Policy Implications: Trustees and administrators at private postsecondary schools must craft policies that avoid making their schools appear "excessively sectarian" if they want to remain eligible for some government funds.

Unresolved Policy Question: Can religious policies and non-religious policies at such schools co-exist?

TITLE IX
(20 U.S.C. § 1681)

Policy Implications: Title IX, which prohibits discrimination on the basis of sex at schools receiving federal assistance, created a sea change in policymaking at postsecondary schools, especially in the area of collegiate athletics.

Unresolved Policy Question: Should policymaking in this area be guided by fully embracing the law or simply trying to satisfy its minimum requirements?

3. As Professor Colebatch makes clear, policy development is often as much about the issues in question as the individuals considering the issues. For the above examples and the policy discussions elsewhere in this book, consider who should be involved in the policymaking process as much as you consider the relevant issues and appropriate outcomes. Only by paying heed to both primary aspects of policymaking is it possible to develop an effective process.

Chapter II

COLLEGE GOVERNANCE AND LIABILITY

Introduction

The primary themes for Chapter II are authority and liability. Part A of the chapter introduces us to the governing authority of both public and private colleges and universities. State statutory law is the primary source for the authority of public boards of trustees: each state that provides for public higher education will grant governing authority to both the local and the state levels. Across the states, though, the balance of that authority varies. Some states will have a statewide board of trustees, with limited power on each campus; others will be more decentralized and have strong local boards of trustees. In all cases, however, state law will define the terms, powers, and duties of public universities' boards of trustees.

Private colleges and universities also receive their authority from state statutory law. Even though private universities may not be subject to constitutional law due to the absence of state action, they are subject to state regulation through nonprofit incorporation laws. Some board authority is delegated to the administrators of the universities, and some is retained by the boards, as discussed in *Silverman v. University of Colorado* and *FDIC v. Providence College.*

Part B of the chapter explores the second theme, institutional liability, in three categories: tort liability (negligence), contract liability, and civil rights liability (Section 1983). A tort is a private or civil wrong or injury, for which courts will provide a remedy in the form of damages. More specifically in the context of the roles of universities and higher education personnel, a tort is a violation of a duty imposed by general law (statutory or judicial) upon a person occupying a certain relationship with the injured party. The purpose of a tort action is to compensate the injured person for injury he or she has suffered to person or property.

The focus here is mainly on the tort of negligence. To state a claim for negligence, a plaintiff must show that the defendant owed a duty of care to the plaintiff, that the defendant breached that duty, and that the defendant's breach was the proximate cause of the resulting injury. This chapter presents several key examples of negligence law: (1) premises liability, where campus officials have a duty to keep premises safe and/or warn of nonobvious dangers; (2) accidents and injuries in on-campus instructional settings; (3) accidents and injuries in non-sponsored activities on or near campus; (4) student suicide; and (5) defamation. As a necessary part of the discussion on tort liability, the chapter also presents the law of immunity: sovereign immunity for public institutions and charitable immunity for private institutions.

The chapter ends with coverage of contract liability where, in similar fashion to the discussion on governance, the discussion returns to notions of express authority, implied authority, and apparent authority; and finally university liability under § 1983 of the Civil Rights Act of 1871. Under § 1983, persons acting under color of law (as "state actors") may be liable for actions that deprive the civil and constitutional rights of people under their charge. Institutional defendants may, however, assert Eleventh Amendment immunity, which protects state agencies from suit in federal court. *See Kashani v. Purdue University*, 813 F.2d 843 (7th Cir. 1987). Additionally, individual defendants may assert a qualified immunity defense, where courts will only find individuals liable if they violate clearly established law.

A. GOVERNING AUTHORITY AND DELEGATION

1. Boards of Trustees

a. Public Boards of Trustees

CALIFORNIA CONSTITUTION ARTICLE IX, § 9

§ 9. University of California

(a) The University of California shall constitute a public trust, to be administered by the existing corporation known as "The Regents of the University of California," with full powers of organization and government, subject only to such legislative control as may be necessary to insure the security of its funds and compliance with the terms of the endowments of the university and such competitive bidding procedures as may be made applicable to the university by statute for the letting of construction contracts, sales of real property, and purchasing of materials, goods, and services. Said corporation shall be in form a board composed of seven ex officio members, which shall be: the Governor, the Lieutenant Governor, the Speaker of the Assembly, the Superintendent of Public Instruction, the president and the vice president of the alumni association of the university and the acting president of the university, and 18 appointive members appointed by the Governor and approved by the Senate, a majority of the membership concurring; provided, however that the present appointive members shall hold office until the expiration of their present terms.

. . . .

(d) Regents shall be able persons broadly reflective of the economic, cultural, and social diversity of the state, including ethnic minorities and women. However, it is not intended that formulas or specific ratios be applied in the selection of regents.

. . . .

(f) The regents of the University of California shall be vested with the legal title and the management and disposition of the property of the university and of property held for its benefit and shall have the power to take and hold, either by purchase or by donation, or gift, testamentary or otherwise, or in any other manner, without restriction, all real and personal property for the benefit of the university or incidentally to its conduct; provided, however, that sales of university real property shall be subject to such competitive bidding procedures as may be provided by statute. Said corporation shall also have all the powers necessary or convenient for the effective administration of its trust, including the power to sue and to be sued, to use a seal, and to delegate to its committees or to the faculty of the university, or to others, such authority or functions as it may deem wise. . . . The university shall be entirely independent of all political or sectarian influence and kept free therefrom in the appointment of its regents and in the administration of its affairs, and no person shall be debarred admission to any department of the university on account of race, religion, ethnic heritage, or sex.

(g) Meetings of the Regents of the University of California shall be public, with exceptions and notice requirements as may be provided by statute.

FLORIDA CONSTITUTION ARTICLE IX, § 7

§ 7. State University System

(a) PURPOSES. — In order to achieve excellence through teaching students, advancing research and providing public service for the benefit of Florida's citizens, their communities and economies, the people hereby establish a system of governance for the state university system of Florida.

(b) STATE UNIVERSITY SYSTEM. — There shall be a single state university system comprised of all public universities. A board of trustees shall administer each public university and a board of governors shall govern the state university system.

(c) LOCAL BOARDS OF TRUSTEES. — Each local constituent university shall be administered by a board of trustees consisting of thirteen members dedicated to the purposes of the state university system. The board of governors shall establish the powers and duties of the boards of trustees. Each board of trustees shall consist of six citizen members appointed by the governor and five citizen members appointed by the board of governors. The appointed members shall be confirmed by the senate and serve staggered terms of five years as provided by law. The chair of the faculty senate, or the equivalent, and the president of the student body of the university shall also be members.

(d) STATEWIDE BOARD OF GOVERNORS. — The board of governors shall be a body corporate consisting of seventeen members. The board shall operate, regulate, control, and be fully responsible for the management of the whole university system. These responsibilities shall include, but not be limited to, defining the distinctive mission of each constituent university and its articulation with free public schools and community colleges, ensuring the well-planned coordination and operation of the system, and avoiding wasteful duplication of facilities or programs. The board's management shall be subject to the powers of the legislature to appropriate for the expenditure of funds, and the board shall account for such expenditures as provided by law. The governor shall appoint to the board fourteen citizens dedicated to the purposes of the state university system. The appointed members shall be confirmed by the senate and serve staggered terms of seven years as provided by law. The commissioner of education, the chair of the advisory council of faculty senates, or the equivalent, and the president of the

Florida student association, or the equivalent, shall also be members of the board.

OHIO REVISED CODE ANNOTATED §§ 3335.02–3335.14 (2009)

§ 3335.02. Appointment of trustees; term

(A) The government of the Ohio state university shall be vested in a board of fourteen trustees in 2005, and seventeen trustees beginning in 2006, who shall be appointed by the governor, with the advice and consent of the senate. Two of the seventeen trustees shall be students at the Ohio state university, and their selection and terms shall be in accordance with division (B) of this section. Except as provided in division (C) of this section and except for the terms of student members, terms of office shall be for nine years, commencing on the fourteenth day of May and ending on the thirteenth day of May. . . .

(B) The student members of the board of trustees of the Ohio state university have no voting power on the board. Student members shall not be considered as members of the board in determining whether a quorum is present. Student members shall not be entitled to attend executive sessions of the board. . . .

§ 3335.03. Style and power of trustees

(A) The trustees and their successors in office shall be styled the "board of trustees of the Ohio state university," with the right as such, of suing and being sued, of contracting and being contracted with, of making and using a common seal, and altering it at their pleasure.

. . . .

§ 3335.04. Officers of board of trustees

The board of trustees of the Ohio state university annually shall elect one of their number chairman, and in the absence of the chairman, elect one of their number temporary chairman. It also may appoint a secretary, treasurer, and librarian, and such other officers as the interests of the college require, who may be members of the board. Such appointees shall hold their offices for such term as the board fixes, subject to removal by it, and shall receive such compensation as the board prescribes.

§ 3335.08. Board may adopt rules and regulations

The board of trustees of the Ohio state university may adopt bylaws, rules, and regulations for the government of the university.

§ 3335.09. Election of president and professors and teachers; course of instruction

The board of trustees of the Ohio state university shall elect, fix the compensation of, and remove, the president and such number of professors, teachers, and other employees as are necessary; but no trustee, or his relation by blood or marriage, shall be eligible to a professorship or position in the university, the compensation for which is payable out of the state treasury or a university fund. The board shall fix and regulate the course of instruction and prescribe the extent and character of experiments to be made at the university.

§ 3335.10. Supervision and control of property and expenses

The board of trustees of the Ohio state university shall have general supervision of all lands, buildings, and other property belonging to the university, and the control of all expenses therefor, but shall not contract a debt not previously authorized by the general assembly.

§ 3335.14. Attorney general the legal adviser of board

The attorney general shall be the legal adviser of the board of trustees of the Ohio state university. He shall institute and prosecute all suits in its behalf.

FIRST EQUITY CORPORATION OF FLORIDA v. UTAH STATE UNIVERSITY

544 P.2d 887 (Utah 1975)

Opinion by: Hyde, District Judge

This is an action brought by a stock broker, First Equity Corporation of Florida, against Utah State University (USU) and Donald A. Catron, formerly the Assistant Vice-President of Finance of Utah State University, for the recovery of commissions and other monies lost by First Equity as a result of USU's refusal to accept and pay for certain shares of common stock which had been ordered by Catron for USU.

First Equity filed a Motion for Summary Judgment and USU filed a Cross-Motion for Summary Judgment based on its affirmative defense that the orders for the purchase of stock which Catron placed on behalf of USU were ultra vires in that USU had no power to purchase stock and, therefore, USU had no obligation to pay for the stock or any commissions.

First Equity appeals from the Trial Court's denial of their Motion and the granting of Summary Judgment to USU. The defendant Catron is not involved in the Motions or this appeal.

USU authorized Catron to purchase securities of any kind through any broker who was a member of any major securities exchange or the National Association of Securities Dealers. Pursuant to this authority, Catron opened a special cash account with First Equity and through that account Catron ordered and USU received and accepted and paid for certain securities. After receiving an opinion from the Attorney General's office that USU should not be investing in stocks, USU refused to accept delivery and pay for the stocks giving rise to this action.

USU revoked Catron's authority prior to the purchase of the stocks in question but apparently neither the resolution granting Catron authority nor the resolution revoking his authority was transmitted to First Equity.

The case of *The University of Utah v. The Board of Examiners of the State of Utah*, 4 Utah 2d 408, 295 P.2d 348, determined the status of the University of Utah would be applicable to Utah State University. USU is a corporation and thus constitutes a legal entity with limited capacity. It was created and exists for the sole purpose of more conveniently governing and conducting the educational institution. It is a state institution, a public corporation not above the power of the Legislature to control and is subject to the laws of this state from time to time enacted relating to its purposes and government.

Utah State Legislature has from time to time exercised control over USU and given USU some power of investment. The direct question presented here is whether or not USU is empowered to invest in common stock with public funds.

It is the position of First Equity and the Amici Brokers that USU had the power to invest in common stock as part of its general power to control and supervise all appropriated and donated funds.

USU was created in 1888 . . . and a governing Board of Trustees was established with the following duties and powers:

> They shall have the general control and supervision of the agricultural college, the farm pertaining thereto, and such lands as may be vested in the college by Territorial legislation, of all appropriations made by the Territory for the support of the same, and also of lands that may hereafter be donated by the Territory . . . or by any person or corporation, in trust for the promotion of agricultural and industrial pursuits . . . .

It is this "general control . . . . of all appropriations" that appellant claims was perpetrated in 1895 by Article X, Section 4, of Utah Constitution, which provides:

> The location and establishment by existing laws of the University of Utah, and the Agricultural College are hereby confirmed, and all rights, immunities, franchises, and endowments heretofore granted or conferred, are hereby perpetuated unto said University and Agricultural College respectively.

In 1929 the Legislature changed the name of the Agricultural College to Utah State Agricultural College and constituted it a "body politic and corporate." In 1957 the Legislature again changed the name, this time to Utah State University of Agricultural and Applied Sciences. The Legislature expressly perpetuated "all rights, immunities, franchises, and endowments heretofore granted or conferred" upon the college. The statute further provided that USU:

> . . . may have and use a corporate seal, may sue and be sued and contract and be contracted with. It may take, hold, lease, sell and convey real and personal property as the interests of the college may require.

The Higher Education Act of 1969 states each university or college . . . . "may do its own purchasing, issue its own payroll, and handle its own financial affairs under the general supervision of the Board as provided by this Act."

. . . .

Nothing in the Constitution or legislative action involving USU specifically grants or denies to USU the power to invest state appropriations in common stock. Appellant and Amici contend that the general control and supervision of all appropriations and the granted power to do its own purchasing, issue its own payroll and handle its own financial affairs are broad, general grants of power and would include the power to invest in common stock in the absence of specific legislative provisions to the contrary.

Whether or not the grant of a "general control" of "all appropriations" and the right to "handle its own financial affairs" grant unrestricted power to invest is answered by *The University of Utah* (supra) case. After quoting Sections 1 and 2 of Article X of the Constitution which mandates the Legislature to provide for the maintenance of the University of Utah and USU, the Court states:

> Would it be contended by the University that under Article X, Section 1, it might compel the Legislature to appropriate money the University considers essential? Is it contended that the demands of the University are not subject to constitutional debt limits? If so, respondent would have the power to destroy the solvency of the State and all other institutions by demands beyond the power of the State to meet.

The Court then quotes in full Sections 5 and 7 of Article X of the Constitution, which provides, respectively, that the proceeds of the sale of land reserved by Congress for the University of Utah shall constitute permanent funds of the State, and that all public school funds shall be guaranteed by the State against loss or diversion. Then the Court concludes:

> It is inconceivable that the framers of the Constitution in light of the provisions of Sections 1, 5 and 7 of Article X and the provision as to debt limitations intended to place the University above the only controls available for the people of this State as to the property, management and government of the University. We are unable to reconcile respondent's position that the University has a blank check as to all its funds with no pre-audit and no restraint under the provisions of the Constitution requiring the State to safely invest and hold the dedicated funds and making the State guarantor of the public school funds against loss or diversion. To hold that respondent has free and uncontrolled custody and use of its property and funds while making the State guarantee said funds against loss or diversion is inconceivable. We believe the framers of the Constitution intended no such result.

. . . .

A general grant to handle its financial affairs does not give authority to invest in common stock. The power to invest is not granted in the absence of legislation to the contrary but the reverse is true. It depends upon a specific authorizing grant of such power.

The only specific Utah statute on the subject of investment of USU would be Section 33-1-1. Section 33-1-1 is a one sentence paragraph containing over 450 words, but the basic structure is: Investments by (named parties) of their own funds or funds in their possession (in specified securities) shall be lawful. The "named parties" include "any private, political or public . . . . corporation or person" and its provisions and meaning would apply to USU as a public corporation as well as private persons and private corporations. The "specified securities" enumerated are all government guaranteed securities such as "bonds and other obligations of . . . . the United States." The stocks in question in this lawsuit do not fall within enumerated securities set forth in that section.

. . . .

Section 33-1-1 is simply a declaration that investments in specified securities are lawful. Without prohibiting any other investments or requiring only the listed investments, the Legislature declared that certain investments were lawful. It is apparent that in enacting Section 33-1-3 the Legislature envisioned situations where the "named parties" mentioned in Section 33-1-1 might be empowered to invest in securities of a type not enumerated in Section 33-1-1. Further, the language of [another section] was worded to include within its meaning any laws which the Legislature might enact thereafter. [T]he Legislature has enacted statutory definitions of what are legal investments for some state agencies and regulated "industries". However, no other statute . . . defines specifically what type of securities USU may legally invest in. It must be concluded, therefore, that USU had no specific designated power from the Constitution or the Legislature to invest its funds in securities outside those declared lawful by 33-1-1 and investments in common stock are ultra vires acts.

. . . .

Although this action was commenced and argued at the lower Court on the basis of breach of contract between the parties, plaintiff and Amici now contend that in any event plaintiff should be entitled to recover because they were acting as the agents of USU. Under the theory of agency, one of two things would occur; either the loss would have to be absorbed by the seller of the stocks who doesn't have the faintest idea that his stock is being purchased by a public corporation or the rules denying recovery on ultra vires contracts of a public corporation would be meaningless. Substantive rights involving public funds should not be determined by the custom of the securities industry in designating the broker as the agent of the buyer or as agent of the buyer and seller. The rules denying recovery of an ultra vires contract are based on the theory that the party actually dealing with the public entity is charged with the knowledge that the contract is ultra vires and unenforceable, and in this case the plaintiff is the party actually dealing with the public entity and this action was filed on that basis — that USU was a customer of First Equity.

USU had no power to enter into an agreement for the purchase of common stock and the agreement to purchase and pay commissions thereon are ultra vires agreements and unenforceable.

The Trial Court's granting of Summary Judgment to USU is affirmed.

NOTES

1. The *First Equity* case turned on a question of authority, and more specifically, the authority of a public university to invest public money in common stock. Ultimately, the Court of Appeals held that the university did not have such authority, despite the language of some state statutory provisions granting "general control of all appropriations" to universities, allowing these universities to "handle [their] own financial affairs." In coming to its conclusion, the court cited to provisions of the state constitution restricting the authority of state universities to invest public money: "The power to invest is not granted in the absence of legislation to the contrary but the reverse is true. It depends upon a specific authorizing grant of such power." So, according to the Utah Supreme Court, express authority was needed and state law had not granted it. What types of expenditure and investment would be authorized by the more general language of "general control" and "handl[ing] . . . financial affairs"?

2. Compare and contrast the statutory provisions covering the governance of public universities in California, Florida, and Ohio, each with representative provisions reproduced above. Each of these states' universities has governing authority at both the local and the state levels, yet the balance of that authority varies. For example, the board of the University of California has 25 members, seven of whom are ex officio members — some elected state officials and some university-level administrators. *See* Cal. Const. Art. IX, § 9. Ohio State University, on the other hand, has a 17-member board with all members appointed by the governor. Finally, consider Florida, which has a statutorily created state university system comprised of all state universities. Fla. Const. Art. IX, § 7. Florida has a statewide Board of Governors, which has the authority to appoint almost half of each university's local trustees. Further, Florida's Board of Governors defines the distinctive mission of each constituent university. Other state systems, like the one in Georgia, have a single state-level governing board. *See* Ga. Code Ann. §§ 20-3-40, 20-3-50.

While Ohio created a "University System of Ohio" in 2007, the system is more decentralized than Florida's: each public university in Ohio has its own set of statutory provisions that establishes a board of trustees, trustee qualifications, and board powers. What are the advantages and disadvantages of centralized and decentralized state systems of public higher education? For more information about Ohio's statewide "university system," see www.ohiohighered.org.

3. Compare also the statutory provision regarding the general control of appropriations and financial affairs at issue in *First Equity*, with a parallel provision in Ohio, governing Ohio State University. The Ohio statute reads: "The board of trustees . . . shall have general supervision of all lands, buildings, and other property belonging to the university, and the control of all expenses therefor, but shall not contract a debt not previously authorized by the general assembly." Ohio Rev. Code Ann. § 3335.10. As a board member, under which state's rules would you prefer to serve?

4. The Board of Trustees for the Ohio State University specifies certain rules for its two student members. *See* Ohio Rev. Code Ann. § 3335.02. In the case of Ohio's public universities, student members do not have voting rights and do not attend executive sessions. What is your opinion on giving student members of a university board of trustees the right to vote? What are the pros and cons of such rights?

5. The court in *First Equity* held, ultimately, that Assistant Vice President Catron did not have legal authority to invest public money as he had done. What are some options the university could pursue against Catron, or other employees who act outside of their official, legal authority? What factors would you apply in determining the particular punishment, if any?

6. It is fairly clear, after a case like *First Equity*, that universities should rely on "express authority" (e.g., determined by plain statutory language) whenever possible, instead of relying on "implied authority." This is, naturally, fine advice for practitioners. But what are the drawbacks to this advice? And what are the benefits of "implied authority," or more generalized authority, for the work of universities?

Should universities generally get the benefit of the doubt? It is widely recognized that courts defer to the substantive, day-to-day decision making of university faculty, staff, and administrators. *See, e.g., Bd. of Curators of the Univ. of Missouri v. Horowitz*, 435 U.S. 78 (1978) (upholding the academic dismissal of a medical student). In *Horowitz*, the Court held that academic decisions are to be made by those with the expertise to make them. Short of particularized legal provisions holding otherwise, should a similar notion of "judicial deference" be extended to financial and other administrative decisions? Should such deference be applied to the situation the court faced in *First Equity*? Or is the direct expenditure of public funds appropriately subject to more external scrutiny than academic decisions made by faculty? Consider these questions as you read the following case.

SAN FRANCISCO LABOR COUNCIL v. REGENTS OF UNIVERSITY OF CALIFORNIA

608 P.2d 277 (Cal. 1980)

Opinion by: CLARK, J.

Plaintiffs petitioned the superior court for writ of mandate to compel the Regents of the University of California to fix minimum salary rates for certain employees at or above the prevailing wage rates in various localities in accordance with Education Code section 92611. The trial court sustained defendants' demurrer without leave to amend on ground the statute conflicts with article IX, section 9 of the California Constitution. Plaintiffs appeal from judgment of dismissal. The judgment must be affirmed.

Education Code section 92611 provides:

> The minimum and maximum salary limits for laborers, workmen, and mechanics employed on an hourly or per diem basis need not be uniform throughout the state, but the regents shall ascertain, as to each such position, the general prevailing rate of such wages in the various localities of the state.
>
> In fixing such minimum and maximum salary limits within the various localities of the state, the regents shall take into account the prevailing rates of wages in the localities in which the employee is to work and other relevant factors, and shall not fix the minimum salary limits below the general prevailing rate so ascertained for the various localities.

Article IX, section 9 provides:

> (a) The University of California shall constitute a public trust, to be administered by the existing corporation known as 'The Regents of the University of California,' with full powers of organization and government,

> subject only to such legislative control as may be necessary to insure the security of its funds and compliance with the terms of the endowments of the university and such competitive bidding procedures as may be made applicable to the university by statute for the letting of construction contracts, sales of real property, and purchasing of materials, goods, and services . . . .

Article IX, section 9, grants the regents broad powers to organize and govern the university and limits the Legislature's power to regulate either the university or the regents. This contrasts with the comprehensive power of regulation the Legislature possesses over other state agencies.

The courts have also recognized the broad powers conferred upon the regents as well as the university's general immunity from legislative regulation. . . .

We recently pointed out "the University is intended to operate as independently of the state as possible." . . . [W]e concluded the university is so autonomous that, unlike other state agencies, it is subject to the usury laws then applicable to private persons and private universities.

It is true the university is not completely free from legislative regulation. In addition to the specific provisions set forth in article IX, section 9, there are three areas of legislative regulation. First, the Legislature is vested with the power of appropriation, preventing the regents from compelling appropriations for salaries.

Second, it is well settled that general police power regulations governing private persons and corporations may be applied to the university. For example, workers' compensation laws applicable to the private sector may be made applicable to the university.

Third, legislation regulating public agency activity not generally applicable to the public may be made applicable to the university when the legislation regulates matters of statewide concern not involving internal university affairs.

Education Code section 92611 cannot be brought within any of the three categories. A provision requiring an employer to pay prevailing wages in the community does not constitute an appropriation bill. Moreover, the Legislature remains free to refuse to appropriate the money necessary to pay prevailing wages.

Nor may section 92611 be construed as a general regulation pursuant to the police power applicable to private individuals and corporations. Prevailing wage regulations are substantially different from minimum wage statutes. A prevailing wage is in the nature of an average wage, and private persons and corporations will pay both above and below the average. Although, as petitioners point out, the Legislature and some local agencies have adopted statutes and ordinances requiring payment of prevailing wages by some governmental agencies and some of their contractors, a number of governmental agencies are not required to pay the prevailing wage. There is no showing that prevailing wage requirements have been made generally applicable to private persons and corporations.

. . . .

The judgment of dismissal is affirmed.

NOTE

In light of the court's decision in *San Francisco Labor Council*, what is your opinion on the level of autonomy that a public university should receive from the state that supports it? What types of decisions should be afforded autonomy and which ones should be more closely monitored? Should a state system of public higher education be centralized at the state level? Or should each state-supported or public university — municipal, regional, national, land grant, etc. — be permitted to enter the "market" just as any other corporate entity might?

In the summer of 2011, Ohio Board of Regents Chancellor Jim Petro introduced the "Enterprise Universities" to the State of Ohio. *See Ohio Board of Regents Chancellor Jim Petro Introduces Enterprise University Plan*, OhioHigherEd.Com, Aug. 11, 2011, *available at* http://www.ohiohighered.org/node/753. According to the plan, Ohio's public universities would be freed from several state mandates that allegedly stifle efficiency and innovation. Among the allowances in "Phase One" of the plan, Boards of Trustees would be permitted to determine the length of term for Board officers and would be permitted to meet by videoconference or other technological means. The Enterprise University plan would also eliminate enrollment limits set by law. Universities would also be permitted to charge students different tuition based on varying factors such as size and facility availability (e.g., offering "discounted" tuition for enrollment in evening and weekend courses where university space is often under-utilized). "Phase Two" of the plan provides a framework for the universities to reach "enterprise" status and receive greater autonomy from the state through further reduction of statutory mandates. As part of this agreement a university would agree to invest a portion of their state share of instruction to a scholarship foundation for top students. These proposed "enterprise universities" are also known as "charter universities."

b. Private Boards of Trustees

MICHIGAN COMPILED LAWS ANNOTATED,
Chapter 390: Universities and Colleges — Albion College

§ 390.703. Board of trustees; powers; course of study; conferring of degrees.

The said trustees shall have power to make bylaws for their own government and for the government of the institution; to elect or appoint the faculty or board of instruction of said college; to prescribe the course of study; to attend the examinations of the classes; to regulate the government and instruction of students and manage the affairs of said corporation in such manner as they think best calculated to promote and carry out the objects contemplated in this act. They shall have power to confer the bachelor's degree upon such persons as shall have completed satisfactorily to the faculty and said trustees the course of study prescribed. They shall have power to confer the master's degree on such graduates of Albion college or of other institutions of similar grade as they shall judge worthy, and they shall have power, also, to confer such honorary degrees as are usually conferred by colleges and universities and shall have all other powers and privileges belonging to colleges according to the laws of this state: Provided always, that the course of study for graduation shall be equal to that which is required in the University of Michigan.

NOTE

The last sentence of the above statute requires Albion College's course of study to be "equal to that which is required in the University of Michigan." What are the implications of such a provision? What are the advantages, disadvantages, and rationale to this requirement?

CORPORATION OF MERCER UNIVERSITY v. SMITH

371 S.E.2d 858 (Ga. 1988)

Opinion by: Hunt, J.

This is an appeal from the trial court's order setting aside the merger between Tift College and Mercer University.

The central issue before us is whether Tift is a charitable trust or a nonprofit corporation. The Corporations of Mercer University and Tift College contend the trial court erred by holding that Tift is a charitable trust. The defendants argue that Tift College was a nonprofit corporation within the meaning of the Georgia Nonprofit Corporation Code. As such, they contend Tift had all the powers of nonprofit corporations, including the power to merge with another nonprofit corporation . . . without court approval.

Tift is a women's college in Forsyth, Georgia, established by an 1849 act of the General Assembly. In recent years, Tift has suffered declining enrollment. In 1986, Mercer University and Tift College entered into a merger agreement which included a provision requiring Mercer to

> [m]ake a good faith effort to operate Tift College of Mercer University on Tift's present Forsyth, Georgia campus; however, the preservation of an entity bearing the Tift name for the education of women in a Christian context is paramount.

In December 1986, Mercer decided to close the women's college in Forsyth and to preserve the Tift entity as part of Mercer University. Subsequently, the plaintiffs (the district attorney of the Flint Judicial Circuit, three former trustees of Tift, a former professor of Tift, an organization called SavTift, Inc., several alumni and donors of Tift College) brought this action to set aside the merger. Named as defendants were the corporate entities of Mercer University and Tift College, their presidents and boards of trustees.

The trial court set aside the merger, holding, inter alia, that Tift College was a charitable trust and, as such, superior court approval — which had not been obtained — was required for the merger; that the Tift trustees failed to exercise proper care in voting for the merger; and that the district attorney had standing to bring this action. In a subsequent order, the trial court appointed a new board of trustees to operate Tift College, and retained jurisdiction of the case for further rulings regarding the operation of Tift College. The defendants appeal.

Both sides in this dispute cite *Miller v. Alderhold*, 228 Ga. 65, 183 S.E.2d 172 (1971), in which the plaintiffs, a group of students enrolled at Atlanta Baptist College, challenged the sale of land owned by the college. This court affirmed the trial court's dismissal of the action. The majority rejected the plaintiff's argument that the college was a charitable trust and held that it was, instead, a private corporation with its primary purpose being the education of the people. . . .

We reaffirm the majority holding in *Miller v. Alderhold* that the actions of the directors of nonprofit colleges such as Tift must be reviewed in light of corporate rather than trust principles. Trust principles require court supervision of numerous detailed operations of a trust. The formalities of trust law are inappropriate to the administration of colleges and universities which, in this era, operate as businesses. These institutions hold a wide variety of assets, and those persons responsible for the operation of the institutions need the administrative flexibility to make the many day-to-day decisions affecting the operation of the institution, including those decisions involving the acquisition and sale of assets.

As we stated in *Miller v. Alderhold*, citing the courts of Ohio and Florida,

> The operation of a private college or university is touched with eleemosynary characteristics. Even though the public has a great interest in seeing these institutions encouraged and supported, they are operated as a private business.

In light of our holding above, we need not reach the appellants' remaining enumerations. Accordingly, the trial court's orders setting aside the merger and appointing new directors of Tift College are reversed, and this case is remanded to the trial court for dismissal.

Judgment reversed.

IN RE ANTIOCH UNIVERSITY

418 A.2d 105 (D.C. 1980)

NEBEKER, JUDGE

This case involves the denial of a preliminary injunction to the plaintiffs in a suit filed in the Superior Court and a partial granting of the defendant's motion for preliminary injunctive relief. Having examined the trial court's findings and conclusions of law in light of the issues presented, we affirm.

I. BACKGROUND

This case arises from a dispute between Antioch University [hereinafter University] and one of its "units," the law school, concerning the control and spending of certain funds. Because of asserted University financial problems, the law school authorities fear that its existence as an accredited institution is threatened if funds paid by its students and grants for education and clinic programs are not administered by the law school officers. The University urges that its accountability as a trustee of all University funds and its ability to administer such funds for the welfare of the entire institution will be severely impaired unless its proper officers have full and unilateral control over all funds coming into the University. This dispute mushroomed into a claim by the Cahns, co-deans of the law school, that the University had contractually relinquished its control over the fiscal and administrative affairs of the law school and that the University was in breach of its fiduciary duties to the students of the law school and clients of its clinic. The University counters that the co-deans of the law school breached their fiduciary obligations to the University by refusing to follow its direction in the handling of the funds. Reasoning that the University could not employ officers who ignored their duties, the University dismissed the co-deans from their posts. . . .

. . . .

On January 11, 1980, Judge Revercomb entered the order which is now before us on appeal [hereinafter Order]. This Order (1) denied the preliminary injunctive relief sought by the appellants; (2) granted the University's motion for a preliminary injunction to the extent that the court ordered the transfer to the University of all funds received in connection with the operation of the law school except restricted funds where the parties agreed that such funds required special handling because of specific conditions imposed by the grantors or donors; (3) dissolved the previously imposed temporary restraining order; and (4) ordered all costs, including transcript costs and legal fees incurred in connection with the hearing on the cross-motions for preliminary injunctions, to be paid by the defendant University. . . .

. . . .

II. CRITERIA FOR PRELIMINARY INJUNCTION

. . . The trial court considered four factors in evaluating whether the injunction should be issued. These factors were whether the moving party had demonstrated: (1) likelihood of irreparable harm in the absence of a preliminary injunction; (2) likelihood of success on the merits of the underlying cause of action; (3) that the "balance of injuries" favors granting an injunction; and (4) that the public interest would be served by granting the injunctive relief sought. . . .

. . . We will review the trial court's analysis of these four factors in its decision of whether to grant a preliminary injunction in this case.

A. Irreparable Harm

. . . .

The appellants have argued that in the absence of preliminary relief, the law school, as it now exists, will cease. Their fears are that the school will lose its A.B.A. accreditation, lose its government grants, lose its present student body to other institutions and be unable to attract quality students for the upcoming term. Despite these allegations, the trial court stated it could not conclude that "the survival of the law school would be more certainly assured by local control of revenues attributable to the law school." We are unable to find error in this regard.

. . . .

Appellants also contest the trial court's conclusion that the University may suffer irreparable harm if it is denied the right to manage and marshall all of its assets which justified the partial granting of the University's cross-motion for preliminary relief. Appellants argue that the court failed to make required factual findings regarding the irreparable harm that the University would suffer in the absence of granting the relief and that the court applied a different standard of the likelihood of harm to the University as opposed to the appellants.

The Order contested in this appeal consists of forty-one pages. The court ably sifted the long, complicated history of the relationship between the various parties and institutions involved in this case. Much time and effort was devoted to describing the financial difficulties of the University and the law school. What was at stake in the University's cross-motion for preliminary relief was the right to manage and marshall all of its assets. Each day that the University was denied this right, the right was irretrievably lost. The consequences that would flow from the loss of this right can only be determined by the future course of events. We think that it is a fair reading of the court's Order that the denial to the University of its right to manage and marshall its funds and assets pendente lite constitutes in and of itself irreparable harm in the circumstances of this case. While the consequences that may flow from the loss of the right may be speculative, the court could reasonably find that the loss of the right for any period of time constitutes serious harm to an institution that admittedly was on the brink of bankruptcy.

B. Likelihood of Success on the Merits

. . . .

2. Legal Theories of Relief

Appellants have been less than clear in framing justification for entitlement to the relief they have sought. Much of the pleadings and briefs relate an unhappy story of administrative and fiscal problems within a University community. The court is asked to intervene and tell everyone how the academic affairs should be ordered for the common good.

After an evidentiary hearing of three weeks, the only legal theory of relief which could be discerned by the trial court was that "the revenues and assets of the Law School are subject to a charitable trust, and that surrender of these assets to the University's central administration will result in a breach of that trust." We hold that the court did not abuse its discretion in concluding that "the evidence at this time is inadequate to support a conclusion that a special charitable trust exists with regard to the law school . . ."; or that the trustees as fiduciaries of the University are aware of their fiduciary obligations to the law school.

On appeal, appellants argue that the evidence presented supported two additional bases for their likely success on the merits. First, they argue that "commitments," which are asserted to be actual contractual agreements between the University and the law school, provide for an independent administration of the law school. They argue that a resolution passed by the Board of Trustees of Antioch University on December 5 and 6, 1975, established the basis for this conclusion. This resolution reaffirmed the Board of Trustees' commitment to a law school "built around a teaching law firm" and established an "*interim governing structure* pending a determination by the Board of Trustees of *ultimate governance* relationship between the School of Law and the College." (Emphasis added.) The resolution goes on to name a Board of Governors of the law school and to delineate its authority. The resolution specifies those matters over which the Board of Trustees of the University specifically reserves authority unto itself. And finally, the resolution "expressly charges the law school Board of Governors to develop recommendations respecting the ultimate structure of relationships between the Law School and the College. . . ." Although the court understandably did not draw a specific legal conclusion concerning this presently asserted contractual basis for relief, the record clearly reflects its rejection of such a rationale.

Upon the basis of this record, we conclude that the trial court was amply justified in impliedly rejecting appellants' contractual argument based upon this resolution. The University is a not-for-profit corporation organized under the law of the state of Ohio. The University, as any corporation, is governed by the statutes of the state of its incorporation, its articles of incorporation and its bylaws. The law school "is not organized as a corporation or other judicial entity." Concededly, it "was established pursuant to a resolution of the Board of Trustees of Antioch College (the predecessor in name to Antioch University) dated December 3 and 4, 1971." Resolutions adopted by the University in accordance with its articles of incorporation and bylaws effectuate the will of the corporation. However, the plain meaning of this resolution bespeaks a delegation of power for the establishment of an "interim governing structure" of the law school as it relates to the University. It cannot be concluded that such a delegation deprived the Board of Trustees of the power given to them in Article III of the University's Articles of Incorporation, to wit: "All of the rights and powers of the corporation and the entire control and management of its College, property and affairs shall be vested in and exercised by a Board of Trustees composed of twenty-five (25) persons." In fact, a contract conveying such plenary power vested by corporation charter in the trustees would be void.

In the alternative, appellants urge us to apply the rationale of estoppel to hold that by the University's acquiescence in autonomous operation of the law school, the University is estopped to deny its autonomy at this time. This doctrine can have no relevance unless the party who seeks to invoke it is an independent entity from the one which is estopped. Thus, to apply the doctrine of estoppel on behalf of the Board of Governors or the law school, the trial court would have been required to find that these bodies are independent legal entities from the University. Appellant has not demonstrated that such was urged upon the trial court and it cannot be said that the record compels such a finding.

C. Assessing the Impact of Injuries

The pivotal factors in favor of denying the appellants' motion for relief were the trial court's conclusions that the appellants were not likely to succeed on the merits and would not suffer irreparable and immediate harm if their motion was denied. At the same time, the court concluded that the University "may suffer serious injury if it is not permitted to exercise control over all assets for which it is responsible." The appellants argued that the University should have to measure up to the standard of certainty of prospective injury before it could be reasoned that the relative injuries favored a partial granting of their cross-motion for preliminary relief. However, the trial court concluded that the University will likely succeed on the merits. In addition, it is the University which seeks to maintain the status quo in the fiscal administration of the law school. As we have previously indicated, we conclude that the trial court implicitly found that in these circumstances each day that the University was denied its right to control and manage its funds, it was irreparably harmed. The actual consequences of this denial were the only matters that were left to speculation. The trial court did not err in concluding that the balance of the equities shifts to the University and warrants granting of its motion and a denial of the appellants'.

D. Public Interest

Finally, the trial court concluded that "[a] discontinuation of the operation of the Antioch School of Law in its present form might well have an adverse impact on the public interest." However, it also stated that the evidence does not support a conclusion that "resumption of control over the revenues attributable to the law school" by the University would "result in termination of the services now rendered. . . ." We hasten to add that although the operation of any private college or university "is touched with eleemosynary characteristics," it does not lose its character as a private corporation. The trustees of the University are vested by its charter of incorporation with the power to conduct its affairs and are not subject to the interference of the state in that control in absence of an abuse of their fiduciary duties.

We are satisfied that the trial court correctly considered the appropriate factors relevant to the granting of preliminary relief. A full and ample record was made. The court has made detailed findings of fact which are supported by the record and its conclusions of law are not erroneous. Accordingly, the trial court Order . . . denying the appellant's motion for preliminary relief and granting in part the appellee's motion is

Affirmed.

NOTE

Perhaps it is not surprising, in *Mercer University v. Smith*, that the court held that the actions of Tift College administrators should be reviewed in light of corporate principles over trust principles. Interestingly, though, the court stated that the administration of colleges and universities, *in this era*, operate as businesses. Again, this statement may not be debatable in fact. But what should be made of the phrase, "in this era"? Such a statement would indicate that, in an earlier era, colleges and universities were not operated as businesses and the judicial result in this case may have been different. Correct? Compare the *Mercer*

University court's reasoning with that of the court in *Antioch*, where the court said that that fact that the operation of the private college is "touched with eleemosynary characteristics" does not take away from the fact that it operates as a private corporation. What are your feelings on this matter? Do you believe the actions of private universities and their leaders should be scrutinized under business principles?

2. Officers and Administrators

UNIVERSITY OF COLORADO v. SILVERMAN
555 P.2d 1155 (Colo. 1976)

Lee, J.

This action arises from an employment contract dispute between petitioners, the University of Colorado and its board of regents and named officials, and respondent, Linda Silverman, a former assistant professor at the University of Colorado. We granted certiorari to review the decision of the court of appeals . . . reversing the trial court's dismissal of the action. On the issues presented for review, we reverse the judgment of the court of appeals.

The university employed respondent to teach for the 1972–1973 academic year. In December 1972, she received a letter from an associate dean, advising that her current employment was for a one-year period and that reappointment was subject to two conditions:

1. The renewal of a grant under which she was hired;

2. Evidence of competence and recommendation from the program area and division faculty peers that she be continued in her present position.

Respondent alleges that various university officials assured her she would be rehired.

Respondent was notified, however, by letter dated February 14, 1973, that she would not be reappointed. She was told that the school desired to open the position to other applicants. The same letter stated, "Your work has been quite satisfactory and [we are] sure the committee would welcome the resubmission of your papers." This notification of nonreappointment complied with the standard set forth in the University of Colorado Faculty Handbook 1970 in effect at the time of this controversy. Respondent then filed a grievance with the faculty committee on privilege and tenure. The committee recommended to the university president that respondent be reappointed. The president did not respond, nor did he submit the recommendation to the board of regents.

Respondent was not rehired. As a result, in December 1973, she commenced an action in Boulder County district court. She alleged five causes of action, three of which are relevant here: breach of contract, estoppel, and deprivation of property without due process of law. Upon petitioners' motion, the trial court dismissed the action. The court of appeals reversed and remanded the cause for trial.

Petitioners allege that the court of appeals erred in holding (1) that the hiring authority of the board of regents is delegable; (2) that estoppel may be invoked against the university; and (3) that the university president's failure to transmit the recommendation of the faculty committee to the board of regents deprived respondent of property without due process of law. We consider these issues in order.

I.

Respondent's contract claim was essentially that a binding contract of reemployment arose when the two conditions prerequisite to reappointment, as set forth in the December 1972 letter from the associate dean, were satisfied; and that the university breached this contract when it advised respondent of her nonreappointment by the February 1973 letter.

The trial court based its dismissal of respondent's contract claim on [a Colorado statute that] provides in part, "The board of regents shall . . . appoint the requisite number of professors and tutors . . . ." The trial court held that absent action by the regents, no contract with the university could arise. We agree.

The court of appeals, however, reversed, holding that this statute does not prohibit the board of regents from delegating its hiring authority, and that whether delegation had actually occurred was a factual question requiring trial.

In so holding, the court of appeals distinguished *Big Sandy Sch. Dist. v. Carroll*, where it was held that a school board's authority to employ teachers is nondelegable. The court of appeals stressed that, unlike the statute defining the board of regents' authority, the governing statute in *Big Sandy*, supra, made it the school board's "duty" to hire teachers.

We do not find the absence of the word "duty" in [the statute at issue in this case] determinative. As we observed in *Big Sandy*, supra:

> ". . . [L]egislative or judicial powers, involving judgment and discretion on the part of the municipal body, which have been vested by statute in a municipal corporation may not be delegated unless such has been expressly authorized by the legislature. . . ."

Undeniably, the power to hire teachers involves considerable judgment and discretion, whether at the university or high school level. Absent legislative authorization, the board of regents' hiring authority cannot be delegated.

The court of appeals characterized the letter concerning the prerequisites for reappointment as an offer of employment by an agent of the board of regents, which ripened into a contract binding the board of regents upon satisfaction of the two conditions. In view of our holding that the hiring authority cannot be delegated, no contract could come into being absent affirmative action by the board of regents itself.

II.

Respondent alleged in the alternative that by reason of the December 1972 letter and other representations made to her by faculty members the university was estopped to deny that there was a contract of reemployment. In dismissing this claim, the trial court held estoppel would be "an inappropriate basis for relief against the University of Colorado and its Board of Regents" because it would divest the board of its statutory hiring power. The trial court added that estoppel is generally not available against a government agency acting in its public capacity.

The court of appeals reinstated respondent's cause of action, pointing out that under our decisions estoppel is applicable against a government agency to prevent manifest injustice.

We note, first, that the doctrine of estoppel is not favored.

In light of this principle and under the facts of this case, we find no "manifest injustice" requiring the invocation of the estoppel doctrine. Respondent received adequate notice of the regents' decision not to retain her. She was, in fact, notified well before the March 1 deadline set by the university's Faculty Handbook 1970. The regents' decision not to rehire her, made within their statutory authority, cannot be considered manifestly unjust.

. . . .

III.

All parties agree that respondent was not a teacher under tenure. Her contract of employment was for one year only and the controversy does not involve her dismissal or the premature termination of the one-year contract under circumstances which reflect upon her professional competence or character. Thus, she had no expectancy or property interest in reappointment constitutionally protected by the due process clause of either the United States or Colorado Constitution.

Respondent's third cause of action, however, alleges deprivation of property without due process of law by the failure of the university president to transmit the faculty committee's recommendation to the regents, as required by the university procedures. The trial court found "no legally sufficient property right or interest which would require formal response. . . ." In essence, the trial court reasoned that since the respondent had no property right to reemployment she had no property right to have the recommendation of reemployment sent to the regents.

The court of appeals disagreed on two bases. First, it reasoned that the respondent's claimed contract of reappointment gave her a sufficient property interest to entitle her to due process protections. Our holdings in parts I and II substantially answer this argument. Secondly, it is asserted that the university was bound by its own procedural regulations.

In this case, the committee's report and recommendation that the respondent be reappointed were based on its mistaken finding that the December letter and the satisfaction of the two conditions therein constituted a binding commitment by the university to rehire the respondent. We have here held as a matter of law to the contrary.

Additionally, the committee gave great weight to the evidence of the respondent's competence and the recommendations of her faculty peers. Her competence was not in dispute and was acknowledged by the university in its February letter of nonreappointment. This consideration, of course, was a sound basis for the recommendation of reappointment, but it does not confer any right thereto and certainly would not foreclose the determination by the university that the position be opened to all interested parties, including the respondent.

In the circumstances of this case, the respondent's right to have the procedural regulations strictly followed is a right without substance, and to remand for the purpose of ordering a transmittal of the committee's recommendation by the president to the board of regents would be an exercise in futility. This is so because the recommendations of the committee on privilege and tenure are advisory only, as they must be in light of the board of regents' exclusive hiring authority under the statute. We therefore find no deprivation of property without due process of law.

The judgment is reversed and the case is returned to the court of appeals for further proceedings consonant with the views herein expressed.

NOTES

1. The court in *Silverman* found no constitutional liberty interest or property right in the decision to not renew the teaching contract. As a result, the court found no due process violation. Readers who are interested in a deeper discussion of the due process rights of university employees are encouraged to see *Board of Regents v. Roth*, 408 U.S. 564 (1972), *Perry v. Sindermann*, 408 U.S. 593 (1972), and the related materials in Chapter IV.

2. The court in *Silverman* held that the hiring authority of the university's board of regents is not delegable, due to the applicable state statute failing to delegate such authority expressly. The court also said that the hiring of teachers requires a high level of judgment and discretion. Surely, judgment and discretion in this regard are better exercised by faculty and administrators, those with the expertise and experience to make such judgments. The court, in fact, noted that the faculty and administrators admired Silverman's competence and substantive contributions. So, if the authority to make hiring decisions is not delegable and remains in the hands of a board of regents or board of trustees, then what is the true nature of the authority that faculty and administrators have in hiring situations? What legal implications are there, then, if a university hires a faculty member in late spring, the faculty member relocates for the job over the summer, and the board of regents rejects the decision to hire at one of its meetings in the meantime? Does the newly hired faculty member have no recourse, despite his reliance on the administrator's decision to hire? Is it wise, then, in jurisdictions with similar state laws, for universities to have provisions in their employment contracts referring to the board's hiring authority and that no hiring decision is final until the board acts on it? *See Barnett v. Univ. of Louisiana Sys.*, 809 So. 2d 184 (La. Ct. App. 2001) (rejecting the detrimental reliance claim of an employee who was ultimately denied a promotion to the athletic director's position because the employee knew that the Board had to approve the hire before it became official).

3. The court rejected Silverman's argument that the doctrine of estoppel should be invoked. What was the prevailing factor in its decision on this matter? Was it because the doctrine of estoppel is simply disfavored in such situations? Did Silverman not present enough evidence of damage, or detrimental reliance, on the decision she thought the university had made in her favor? While the court did not find in favor of Silverman on this matter, university administrators should be watchful of the decisions they make. "Apparent authority" is not actual authority, but it may be used by a plaintiff who believed a decision was made in her favor and relied to her detriment on that decision. Even if the decision itself is not ratified by the board or the entity with actual authority, the university (and perhaps the official who made the initial decision under apparent authority) may be held liable for resulting damages. See the following case.

FDIC v. PROVIDENCE COLLEGE

115 F.3d 136 (2d Cir. 1997)

Jacobs, Circuit Judge:

In 1987, Providence College (the "College" or "Providence") contracted with two construction companies for a major asbestos abatement project on the campus. The construction companies, both owned by the same family, were evidently short of capital and took out a series of loans from Crossland Savings Bank ("Crossland"). When the first loan was made in 1987, Crossland required the companies' principal officer, Bernard Renzi, to obtain from the College a written guaranty of the companies' loan obligation. Renzi presented the form to his friend, Joseph Byron, the College's Vice President for Business Affairs, who signed it. The guaranty recited that the College would cover all obligations of the companies to the bank — including those incurred in the future — up to a total of $621,000.

Crossland commenced this diversity action in the United States District Court for the Eastern District of New York against the construction companies, members of the Renzi family, and the College. The College defended on the grounds that Vice President Byron lacked actual or apparent authority to guarantee the loans on behalf of the College. Judge Nickerson held on summary judgment that Byron lacked actual authority, but that there were issues of fact remaining as to the apparent authority issue. Following a bench trial, the court concluded that Byron had apparent authority to undertake the obligation on the College's behalf and entered judgment against Providence in the amount of $621,000.

This appeal concerns the judgment — premised solely on the Byron guaranty — against the College, the lone appellant. The only issue presented is whether the district court erred in finding that Byron had apparent authority. For the reasons set forth below, we reverse.

BACKGROUND

The Project and Financing. Providence College is a non-profit corporation which maintains and operates an educational institution in Providence, Rhode Island. In 1987, the College undertook a major project to remove asbestos from its buildings. Two companies that had performed various construction-related work for Providence over many years — A R Construction, Inc. and Westminster Construction, Inc. (the "construction companies" or the "Renzi companies") — were the low bidders, and were awarded the contract.

In order to finance the costly abatement project, the construction companies sought and obtained a series of loans from Crossland. The loan proceeds were used primarily to finance the asbestos removal at the College; apparently, however, some of the proceeds were used to finance other construction projects undertaken by the companies, not all of which concerned Providence.

. . . .

The Guaranty at Issue. In connection with the first of the series of loans, Crossland evidently demanded that the borrowers furnish a written loan guaranty from the College. At the June 10, 1987 closing on the first loan, Crossland handed to Bernard Renzi an original and execution copies of a form on which Providence's name was typed as "Guarantor." The terms of the guaranty were that Providence would guarantee all obligations of the Renzi companies "whether now existing or hereafter incurred" up to $621,000.

Soon thereafter, Renzi brought the forms to Joseph Byron, who at the time was the Vice President for Business Affairs at Providence. (Byron and Renzi had been close friends for about nine years.) Though Byron has no specific recollection, it is undisputed that he executed the forms, that they were notarized by an individual working in the Registrar's office at the College, and that Byron gave the forms back to Renzi, who delivered them to Crossland on or after June 16, 1987. Byron's title did not appear on the forms, and he did not add it. The parties agree that there is no evidence in the record that anyone at Crossland was aware of Byron's identity or title at the time that the forms were received by the bank in June 1987.

Appearances of Authority. Because the claim of apparent authority in this case depends upon the conduct of the College vis-a-vis the bank, we recount the communications between those parties in detail. . . .

Prior to the making of the first loan and the delivery of the guaranty form, Crossland had no direct contact with Providence, oral or written. At the time of the second loan . . . the bank loan officer in charge of the account . . . asked his superior whether financial information on Providence was necessary, and was told that it was not because Providence was very strong financially.

On October 27, 1987, Byron wrote to the construction companies, advising that completion of the work that was the subject of the first loan would be delayed by a strike at the College. That letter, signed by Byron as Vice President for Business Affairs, was faxed to Crossland on the day it was received, and was placed in Crossland's loan file. The October 27 letter is the earliest evidence that the bank had learned of Byron's title. A second letter from Byron, also bearing his title and also found in Crossland's loan file, is dated December 31, 1987, and passes along advice from the College's Director of Physical Plant that the work in the last two phases of construction was 75 percent complete.

The Cunningham Guaranties. In the period from January 1988 to June 1989, Crossland received eleven letters from the Director of Physical Plant, James Cunningham, reporting on the status of the asbestos abatement and the completion of various phases of the work.

When the second of the loans was made in February 1988, Crossland sought and received an additional guaranty signed by Cunningham (another close friend of Bernard Renzi), also supposedly on behalf of Providence. This guaranty provided that the College would be liable for all obligations of the Renzi construction companies "whether now existing or hereafter incurred" up to $440,000, the amount of the second loan. In conjunction with the third, fourth, and fifth loans, Cunningham obliged Crossland by executing additional guaranty forms, also covering both the current and future debts of the companies. The guaranty executed by Cunningham in connection with the fourth loan was in the amount of $1,459,500, and the guaranty in connection with the fifth was unlimited in amount. Crossland apparently sought no confirmation of Cunningham's authority to commit the College to this sizable and open-ended liability (which would appear to cover Providence's full endowment, and all its land and buildings), and relied instead on Cunningham's title as Director of Physical Plant.

DISCUSSION

. . . .

The single question presented on this appeal is whether Crossland was entitled to recover on the ground that Byron had apparent authority [under New York law] to sign the loan guaranty on behalf of Providence. . . . To recover on a theory of apparent authority, Crossland must establish two facts: (1) Providence was responsible for the appearance of authority in Byron to sign the guaranty and (2) Crossland's reliance on the appearance of authority in Byron was reasonable.

A. Responsibility for Byron's Appearance of Authority.

The district court concluded that Providence vested Byron with the apparent authority to sign the loan guaranties by giving Byron responsibilities . . . on a par with those of a chief financial officer in a commercial corporation, and by giving Byron a title — Vice President for Business Affairs — commensurate with those responsibilities. We think that this conclusion is adequately supported by the record.

Providence does not dispute that Byron's title could be understood as vesting him with powers comparable to those of a corporate CFO. Rather, Providence argues that Byron's title and responsibilities are beside the point, because Crossland cannot demonstrate that it actually relied (reasonably or otherwise) on Byron's title or role in making the loans. The guaranty itself does not reveal Byron's title; and the record does not reflect that anyone at Crossland knew what his title was at the time the guaranty was received and the first loan was made. Although letters on Byron's letterhead were placed in Crossland's loan file before the second and subsequent loans were made . . . it is stipulated that Crossland can identify no one at the bank who specifically recalls having relied on the Byron letters in the loan file when deciding whether to rely on the Byron guaranty in making the loans.

However, the Crossland Vice President involved in the making of the second through fifth loans testified that he inevitably would have reviewed the entire credit file before authorizing the loans and therefore would have seen one or both of the Byron letters reflecting his signature and title. . . . Therefore, we cannot say that the district court erred in concluding that Crossland relied upon Byron's name and title in concluding that Byron was authorized to execute the guaranty. The question remains, however, whether such reliance was reasonable in light of the nature of the transaction at issue and the circumstances surrounding that transaction.

B. The Duty of Inquiry and Reasonable Reliance.

The general rule in New York is that a third party "who deals with an agent does so at his peril, and must make the necessary effort to discover the actual scope of authority." However, in the apparent authority context, the duty of inquiry arises only when (1) the facts and circumstances are such as to put the third party on inquiry, (2) the transaction is extraordinary, or (3) the novelty of the transaction alerts the third party to a danger of fraud. The duty of inquiry into an agent's apparent authority "amounts to an alternative way of asking whether the third party reasonably relied on the representations of the agent that he possessed authority to bind the principal."

The district court determined that Crossland's reliance on Byron's apparent authority was reasonable and that Crossland's duty of inquiry was not triggered. The court premised this conclusion on a number of findings. First, the loans were guaranteed for an asbestos removal project, obviously an important institutional goal for the College. Second, the guaranty benefitted Providence by assuring that the work on this significant project would be done by the contractor of Providence's choice. Third, Providence enjoys a reputation as a "distinguished and respected educational institution," thought by Crossland to be in sound financial condition. Finally, the district court relied on Providence's expert witness, Robert Martinsen, who testified that a corporate CFO generally has the authority to sign guaranties.

The record supports the district court's findings that Providence is a respected institution, that the asbestos abatement project was important to it, and that the underlying loan transaction was in the College's interest. On the other hand, there is no record evidence that the Renzi companies were Providence's "preferred" contractors — in the sense that Providence would put its credit behind them rather than use other firms — and that Crossland would have known this. The Renzi companies bid on the project, as they had on projects past; and they submitted the lowest bid; there is no basis for assuming that they were selected in lieu of other qualified firms for any other reason.

. . . .

Even if we accept all of the district court's findings, including the College's preference among contractors, we still conclude that the guaranty transaction at issue was novel and extraordinary, and therefore one that put the bank on inquiry notice as to Byron's apparent authority.

The financial and institutional reputation of Providence College is comforting if one is considering whether the College will honor its obligations, but that reputation has little bearing on whether the College has undertaken the obligation or on whether a particular transaction is novel or extraordinary. If a transaction is novel or extraordinary for a particular institution, it raises the eyebrow even if it is entered into for a vital purpose. Ultimately, the question is whether the particular transaction falls within the range of transactions in which Providence or similarly situated institutions normally engage.

Crossland bears the burden of establishing that the transaction was neither extraordinary nor novel. The record evidence in this case establishes that the loan guaranty was an unusual one for a non-profit educational institution, and therefore suspect for purposes of inquiry notice. There is no record evidence that Providence had ever before guaranteed the loans of companies doing work on its campus, or that non-profit educational institutions regularly or even sometimes guarantee such loans. . . .

Crossland argues that there was a pre-existing relationship between the Renzi companies and Providence, relying on Bernard Renzi's deposition testimony that his companies had been doing business with Providence for over thirty years. However, the issue presented is whether the transaction should have put Crossland on inquiry notice. And as to that, there is no evidence that Crossland knew of the prior relationship between Providence and the Renzi companies.

. . . .

We thus conclude that the district court clearly erred in finding that Crossland's reliance was reasonable, and therefore erred in holding that Crossland was entitled to recover on the ground that Byron possessed apparent authority.

CONCLUSION

For the reasons set forth herein, we reverse the judgment of the district court and direct that judgment be entered dismissing Crossland's claims against Providence College.

B. INSTITUTIONAL LIABILITY

1. Tort Liability

a. Theories of Immunity

i. Sovereign Immunity

EX PARTE CRAFT

727 So. 2d 55 (Ala. 1999)

PETITION FOR WRIT OF MANDAMUS

ALMON, J.

The petitioners, Dr. Lynda Craft, former interim president of Ayers State Technical College; Dr. Fred Gainous, chancellor of the Department of Post-Secondary Education; and Ayers State Technical College, are the remaining defendants in a wrongful-termination action filed by Spencer Tracy Trussell in the Calhoun Circuit Court. The circuit court denied these defendants' motions for summary judgment and ordered the parties to proceed with "discovery, settlement negotiations, or any other action necessary to dispose of this proceeding." These defendants petitioned the Court of Civil Appeals for a writ of mandamus directing the circuit court to enter a judgment for them based on their defense of immunity. The Court of Civil Appeals . . . denied the petition, without an opinion. They now have filed a similar petition in this Court.

In May 1992, Dr. Pierce Cain, then president of Ayers State, appointed Trussell as interim dean of instruction. The appointment was approved by Chancellor Gainous. Cain testified that, during his tenure as president, administrative employees and staff members were employed for a specified number of months, not to exceed one year, and that these employment agreements were not reduced to written contracts.

Trussell and Craft were two of the three people who applied for the permanent position of dean of instruction. On April 2, 1993, President Cain appointed Trussell as dean of instruction, effective May 1, 1993. With regard to this appointment, Cain testified that he did not remember entering into a contract with Trussell and that he had no further employment discussions with Trussell. Cain retired in May 1994, and Craft was appointed interim president of Ayers State, effective June 1, 1994. Craft testified that after she was appointed interim president, she had no conversations with Trussell about his employment.

On March 24, 1995, Craft, with the approval of Gainous, wrote the following letter to Trussell: "This is to notify you that your employment at Ayers State Technical College as Dean of Instruction shall not continue beyond April 30, 1995. You are hereby placed on administrative leave with full pay and benefits effective March 27, 1995." Trussell claimed that Craft required him to vacate his office during business hours on a school day, Friday, March 24. This action, according to Trussell, was taken deliberately to humiliate him, because the following Monday was the beginning of spring break and on that date he could have cleared out his office with no students, faculty members, or other persons present.

On March 27, 1995, in compliance with school procedures, Trussell filed a letter of complaint. On April 10, 1995, Craft wrote a second letter to Trussell, in which she stated:

> I am in receipt of your letter of March 27, 1995, regarding the nonrenewal of your employment with Ayers State Technical College. According to college records, your employment at Ayers began on May 1, 1992. Thus, you are a probationary employee. Under State Board of Education Policy Number 619.01, probationary employees are entitled to be given cause for termination and an opportunity for a hearing only when their employment is terminated within the period of a contract. A search of our records reveals the absence of a written contract for your employment. Under Board policy and state law, I am required to provide you with written notice fifteen (15) days prior to the termination of your employment. You have received appropriate notice. There is no appeal, and you are not entitled to a hearing.

. . . .

Trussell, in his amended complaint "for declaratory judgment and additional relief," alleged 1) that he had been wrongfully terminated from his position at Ayers State for personal and political reasons and without just cause; 2) that Craft had deliberately acted to humiliate him; 3) that Craft had acted arbitrarily and capriciously and had exceeded the scope of her authority as interim president of Ayers State; 4) that the defendants had breached an employment contract with him; 5) that he had been deprived of his interest in his employment without an opportunity to be heard before being terminated; and 6) that the defendants were under an affirmative duty to provide him a hearing before terminating his employment.

. . . .

Craft, Gainous, and Ayers State filed motions to dismiss and motions for summary judgment, raising several affirmative defenses, including absolute and qualified immunity. . . .

. . . .

The trial court denied the defendants' motions, and the Court of Civil Appeals denied the defendants' petition for the writ of mandamus.

I. Claims against Ayers State Technical College

[Under the Alabama Constitution, the state and its agencies, including the state's institutions of higher learning, have absolute immunity from suit in any court.]

Ayers State Technical College is a state institution of higher learning and is entitled to absolute immunity; therefore, the trial court erred in denying its motion to dismiss and its motion for summary judgment.

II. Claims against Craft and Gainous

[Under Alabama law, state officials and employees, in their official capacities and individually, are also absolutely immune from suit when the action is, in effect, one against the state. The theory for providing immunity is that exposing certain state officials and employees to liability for decisions they make would hamper the decision-making process and unduly interfere with the operation of government agencies. To determine whether a state official or employee is immune from liability, the court considers — on a case-by-case basis, in light of all attendant circumstances — whether the official exercised discretion in making a decision that would directly affect a contract or property right of the state. An official or employee who exercises such discretion is immune from liability.]

On April 30, 1995, the effective date of Trussell's termination, his period of service at Ayers totaled 2 years and 11 months; thus, Trussell was a probationary employee at the time of his termination [under an Alabama statute].

[Under that statute, a state employer can remove a probationary employee by furnishing said employee written notification at least 15 calendar days prior to the effective date of termination. If a probationary employee under contract is terminated within the period of a contract, the employee is entitled to be given cause and the opportunity for a hearing under hearing procedures adopted by the State Board of Education.]

Trussell claims that he was deprived of a property right without due process of law — the balance of his "contract" with Ayers State which, according to Trussell, was not scheduled to end until August 31, 1995 (the end of the school year at Ayers State). This claim is without merit. Trussell's employment at Ayers State began on May 1, 1992, when he was appointed interim dean of instruction; therefore, each succeeding year of employment at Ayers State ran from May 1 through April 30 of the calendar year. . . . As a probationary employee, Trussell had no valid expectation of continued employment during the probationary period. . . .

Trussell's arguments depend principally upon his assertion that he was under contract and, thus, that his employment could not be terminated before the end of the contract period without cause and a hearing. However, he offers no evidence of a written contract. The defendants presented evidence indicating that Trussell was appointed, by a letter of appointment, to the position of interim dean of instruction effective May 1, 1992, and, by another letter of appointment, to the position of dean of instruction effective May 1, 1993. Neither of these documents constitutes a contract of employment for a specified time, and the parties presented no other evidence of such a contract. Thus, under [the Alabama statute governing probationary employees], Trussell's employment was subject to termination after 15 days' notice. He was given 37 days' notice, more notice than he was entitled to receive.

Trussell also argues that his being placed on administrative leave with pay constituted a disciplinary action, as to which he says he was entitled to a hearing. However, that leave was merely an adjunct of his termination and was ordered with full pay and benefits. The materials before us contain no evidence tending to show that he was placed on leave for any disciplinary reasons.

The materials contain no evidence tending to show that Dr. Craft or Dr. Gainous erroneously interpreted any law or otherwise acted in such a way as to place themselves outside the scope of the immunity they would have as state officials or employees acting in the line and scope of their authority. To terminate Trussell's employment during his probationary period was well within the discretion of these defendants, and they did not carry out his termination in such a way as to fall outside the scope of their immunity.

III. Conclusion

Dr. Craft, Dr. Gainous, and Ayers State were clearly entitled to a judgment in their favor. Their petition for the writ of mandamus is granted.

KERBERSKY v. NORTHERN MICHIGAN UNIVERSITY

582 N.W.2d 828 (Mich. 1998)

TAYLOR, J.

We granted leave to appeal in this case to determine whether the public building exception to governmental immunity[1] applies to injuries suffered by a construction worker who fell off an allegedly defective ladder on the roof of a Northern Michigan University administration building that remained open to members of the public while renovations were being performed. We find that it does, and therefore we reverse the judgments entered by the Court of Appeals and the trial court.

We hold that a member of the public injured as the result of a defect or dangerous condition of a building that is open to members of the public may invoke the public building exception to governmental immunity, even if the person is injured in an area of the building not open for use by members of the general public.

Facts and Proceedings

On August 10, 1990, plaintiff Gerald Kerbersky was injured when he fell from a permanently attached ladder to a building on the NMU campus. Kerbersky had been working as a welder/carpenter on a renovation project of the building, which remained open for use by members of the public during the construction work. A lawsuit was subsequently filed against defendant in the Court of Claims [under negligence/premises liability and nuisance theories]. A gross negligence claim was also asserted against two individual employees of defendant. It was alleged that the ladder was defective because it was attached closer to the wall than allowed by

---

[1] Michigan Compiled Laws 691.1406 provides in pertinent part:

> Governmental agencies have the obligation to repair and maintain public buildings under their control when open for use by members of the public. Governmental agencies are liable for bodily injury and property damage resulting from a dangerous or defective condition of a public building if the governmental agency had actual or constructive knowledge of the defect and, for a reasonable time after acquiring knowledge, failed to remedy the condition or to take action reasonably necessary to protect the public against the condition.

safety codes and because there was a conduit strung underneath the ladder frame. Defendant moved for summary disposition, arguing that plaintiffs' claim was barred by governmental immunity because the roof of the building was not open to the public and that plaintiff was not present as a member of the public when the accident occurred. Plaintiff opposed the motion, arguing that he was a member of the public and that the area of the roof where the fall occurred was in fact open to members of the public.

After the Court of Claims case was consolidated with a related circuit court action, the circuit court granted defendant's motion for summary disposition on the basis that the area where the fall occurred had restricted access and was not designed or intended for use by members of the general public. The Court of Appeals affirmed, in an unpublished peremptory order, stating that even if it assumed the area was accessible to the general public, the public building exception did not apply because the area where the injury occurred was not intended for use by the general public. The Court of Appeals also affirmed the trial court's dismissal of the gross negligence and nuisance counts. We subsequently granted leave to appeal. 456 Mich. 920, 575 N.W.2d 546 (1998).

. . . .

Governmental Immunity Principles

As we recently reiterated in *Horace v City of Pontiac*, 456 Mich. 744, 749 (1998), the term "governmental function" is to be broadly construed, and the statutory exceptions thereto, including the public building exception, are to be narrowly construed. To come within the narrow confines of this exception, a plaintiff must prove that (1) a governmental agency is involved, (2) the public building in question was open for use by members of the public, (3) a dangerous or defective condition of the public building itself exists, (4) the governmental agency had actual or constructive knowledge of the alleged defect, and (5) the governmental agency failed to remedy the alleged defective condition after a reasonable period or failed to take action reasonably necessary to protect the public against the condition after a reasonable period. MCL 691.1406. The issue in the case at bar involves the proper understanding and application of the second element, i.e., whether the public building was open for use by members of the public.

Review of Case Law

[The court concluded that lower-court holdings on the question of the public building exception to sovereign immunity were mixed.]

Analysis

The public building exception applies to public buildings open for use by members of the public and makes governmental agencies liable for injuries sustained for defects or dangerous conditions of a building if an agency failed to remedy such a condition or take action necessary to protect the public against it. MCL 691.1406.

The first thing we observe is that the statute does not apply to all public buildings. Rather, it applies to public buildings that are open for use by members of the public. . . .

We also take this opportunity to clarify that certain cases have caused confusion by erroneously inserting the word "general" in front of the words "members of the public" in describing those buildings that come within the statute. These cases have stated that the building had to be open to members of the general public even though the statute only requires the building to be open to members of the public. The word "general" is not in the statute and therefore should not be read into the statute. . . .

We find that this unfortunate judicial gloss of requiring that buildings be open to the general public has led to an interpretation of the public building exception that is narrower than the statutory language allows. Even though we give the exception a narrow reading, we are not free to read the statute so narrowly that we defeat the purpose of the statute. Neither the letter nor the spirit of the statute suggests that a public building must be open for use by the entire public.

. . . .

Application

As previously indicated, the building in question was in fact open to members of the public during renovations, the fact that Kerbersky was a construction worker did not deprive him of his status as a member of the public. The second element of the public building exception was satisfied.

CONCLUSION

Affirmed in part and reversed in part. We reinstate the public building exception count and affirm dismissal of the gross negligence and nuisance counts.

NOTES

1. In *Craft*, Trussell began his employment as dean of instruction on May 1, 1992, received another appointment to the same position in May 1993, and then received his termination letter on March 24, 1995, almost two years later. Although there was no tradition at Ayers State Technical College of reducing administrative appointments to a contract, there was a practice of specifying the appointments for a certain number of months, not to exceed one year. Under the circumstances, it is clear that Trussell worked in this position for more than a year, meaning he was clearly reappointed by President Cain before Cain retired. Can Trussell make the argument that a contract existed anyway, even without a document in writing? Generally, there are six elements of a traditional contract: (a) offer, (b) acceptance (of the terms of the offer), (c) legal purpose or objective, (d) mutual consent (a meeting of the minds), (e) consideration (mutual exchange of something of value), and (f) competent parties. To make his case that an oral contract is enforceable, Trussell would need to argue, in addition, that there were witnesses to the agreement, that there was an exchange of services over a long period of time, and that the agreement and the work done were credible. *See generally* 17A Am. Jur. 2d Contracts § 19.

As an example, see *Bracco v. Michigan Tech. Univ.*, 588 N.W.2d 467 (Mich. Ct. App. 1998), in which a campus security guard filed suit for breach of contract after he was fired for what the employer called "just cause." The employee claimed that there was no oral contract claim for "just cause" and that the termination violated his due process rights. The court found that there was no mutual assent to a "just cause" contract and, thus, no oral contract existed.

Furthermore, such an agreement may have to withstand the Statute of Frauds, which says that certain contractual agreements must be put to writing, including those agreements to perform work for longer than one year. So in such circumstances, without a written agreement, the defendant in a breach of contract claim can argue that a formal contract did not exist and that there was, therefore, no breach. All states will have a statute of frauds. There are a handful of statute of fraud cases affecting higher education. For example, see *Clampitt v. American University*, 957 A.2d 23 (D.C. Ct. App. 2008), in which a university radio station employee filed suit for breach of contract after she was terminated. She claimed that an oral contract existed that allowed her to work until retirement age. The court disagreed and held that the oral contract claim was barred by the statute of frauds. *See also Alabama A & M Univ. v. Jones*, 895 So. 2d 867 (Ala. 2004) (the second year of a claimed two-year salary increase fell outside of the statute of fraud's requirement that contracts longer than one year must be in writing and, hence, was not valid oral contract); *Massey v. Houston Baptist Univ.*, 902 S.W.2d 81 (Tex. Ct. App. 1995) (even though the president had the authority to enter into contracts with employees, the statute of frauds still applied against oral contracts that last longer than one year).

2. What are the pros and cons of sovereign immunity? What rationale do the courts in *Craft* and *Kerbersky* offer? As a contribution to this discussion, consider the following statement, from *Board of Regents of Universities and State Colleges v. City of Tempe*, 356 P.2d 399 (Ariz. 1960), which speaks to the control a local municipality may or may not have over a state-supported college or university:

> The essential point is that the powers, duties, and responsibilities assigned and delegated to a state agency performing a governmental function must be exercised free of control and supervision by a municipality within whose corporate limits the state agency must act. . . . A central, unified agency, responsible to State officials . . . is essential to the efficient and orderly administration of a system of higher education responsive to the needs of all the people of the State.

Id. at 406–07.

3. Do you agree with the result in *Kerbersky*? Are "member of the public" and "member of the general public" really that different? What argument does the court offer to make this distinction? The court holds that neither the letter nor the spirit of the applicable state statute suggests that a building must be open to the entire public in order for the public building exception to immunity to apply. What are the letter and spirit of the statute that make this so?

4. What is the practical significance of this case? In other words, what practical advice would you offer as a result of *Kerbersky*?

ii. Charitable Immunity

MULLINS v. PINE MANOR COLLEGE
449 N.E.2d 331 (Mass. 1983)

LIACOS, J.J.

The plaintiff, a female student at Pine Manor College (college), was raped on campus by an unidentified assailant who was never apprehended. She commenced this action against the college and its vice president for operations, William P. Person, to recover damages for injuries suffered. The case was tried before a jury in the Superior Court. The jury returned verdicts against the college and Person in the amount of $175,000. Pursuant to G. L. c. 231, § 85K, the trial judge reduced the amount of the judgment against the college to $20,000. The college and Person appeal from the denial of their motions for directed verdicts and for judgments notwithstanding the verdicts. We granted their applications for direct appellate review. We affirm the judgments.

There was evidence of the following facts. Pine Manor College is a four-year college for women located in the Chestnut Hill section of Brookline. In 1977, approximately 400 students attended the school. The campus is surrounded on all sides by a six-foot high chain link fence, except for an area on either side of the main entrance to the campus where the fence stands four feet tall. The college's dormitories are clustered together in three villages. Each village is comprised of a commons building and a number of separate dormitory buildings. The buildings are arranged to form a square. To gain access to a dormitory, a student must enter an enclosed courtyard through either the commons building or one of three exterior gates. Between 5 P.M. and 7 A.M., these gates and the door to the commons building are locked. Students enter their dormitory through locked doors which open directly into the courtyard. Each student had one key which unlocked the doors to her commons building, her dormitory building, and her individual room.

After 8 P.M., all visitors were admitted by a security guard at the main entrance to the campus. The guard would direct them to the appropriate commons building. At the entrance to the commons building, visitors would be stopped by a student on duty and would be registered. The student hostess would be notified and was required to come to the commons building to act as the visitor's escort. No visitors were permitted anywhere on campus unescorted after 1 A.M. on weekends.

At the time of the rape, the college had two guards on duty after midnight. One guard was stationed in an observation post at the main entrance. The second guard was assigned to patrol the campus. He was responsible for making rounds to the villages every fifteen to thirty minutes to check the doors and gates to see that they were locked. The college had no formal system of supervising the guards. Rather, the director of security at the college would make random checks on their work.

Mullins was a first-year student and, as required by the college, she lived on campus. Her dormitory housed thirty women. . . .

On December 11, 1977, Mullins returned to her dormitory at approximately 3 A.M. with two friends. It was a bitter cold night. They entered the village through one of the exterior gates to the courtyard. It was unlocked. They opened the door to their dormitory and proceeded to their rooms. After changing into her night clothes, Mullins, leaving the door to her room open, went to talk with a friend who resided in the room next door. . . . Mullins returned to her room, locked her door, and went to sleep. Between 4 A.M. and 4:30 A.M., she was awakened by an intruder. [The intruder proceeded to march Mullins to another building on campus, where he raped her.]

Pine Manor is located in an area with relatively few reports of violent crime. In the years prior to this attack, there had been no incidents of violent crime on the campus. The record discloses, however, that one year before the attack a burglary had occurred in one of the dormitory buildings. Additionally, the evening before the rape, a young man scaled the outer fence around the campus and walked into the commons building of Mullins's village, which was the first building he saw. The door to the building was open. The college is also located a short distance from bus and subway lines which lead directly to Boston.

. . . .

1. Duty to protect against criminal acts. The defendants argue that they owe no duty to protect students against the criminal acts of third parties. They rely on the general proposition that there is no duty to protect others from the criminal or wrongful activities of third persons. See Restatement (Second) of Torts § 314 (1965). . . . We conclude that this rule has little application to the circumstances of this case.

[The court proceeded to hold that the college owed a duty to protect its students against the criminal acts of third parties, and that the evidence was sufficient to lead a jury to conclude that the college's negligence caused the plaintiff's injuries.]

3. Liability of an officer of a charitable corporation in tort. Person contends that he is entitled to the protection of the charitable immunity doctrine and that he cannot be held liable for mere negligence in the performance of a discretionary function. These questions were not raised below and, if we followed our usual practice, we would not consider them on appeal. However, 'because the questions presented are of some public importance and the result we reach is not changed by our consideration of them, we choose to state our views briefly. *Royal Indem. Co. v. Blakely*, 372 Mass. 86, 88 (1977).

The common law doctrine of charitable immunity provides that charitable institutions are immune from liability for their torts. *McDonald v. Massachusetts Gen. Hosp.*, 120 Mass. 432, 436 (1876). The general rule, however, is that an agent is not entitled to the protection of his principal's immunity even if the agent is acting on behalf of his principal. Restatement (Second) of Agency § 347 (1) (1958). In 1971, the Legislature abolished entirely the defense of charitable immunity from tort liability "if the tort was committed in the course of activities primarily commercial in character even though carried on to obtain revenue to be used for charitable purposes." G. L. c. 231, § 85K, inserted by St. 1971, c. 785, § 1. "[I]f the tort was committed in the course of any activity carried on to accomplish directly the charitable purposes" of a charitable institution, liability may not exceed $20,000. *Id.* This reflects a legislative determination to confine narrowly the doctrine of charitable immunity. We decline to ignore the wishes of the Legislature and expand the doctrine beyond its original boundaries.

We also reject the contention that an officer of a charitable institution may not be held liable for the negligent performance of a discretionary function without evidence of bad faith. Person relies primarily on our decision in *Whitney v. Worcester*, 373 Mass. 208, 217–218, 220–221 (1977), where we said that governmental entities and officials should be immune from liability when the conduct causing the injury involves the exercise of judgment and discretion. Our decision there rested on overriding considerations of public policy affecting the very quality and efficiency of government itself. *Id.* at 218. These considerations are not present in the instant case. *Cf. LaClair v. Silberline Mfg. Co.*, 379 Mass. 21, 28–29 (1979) (corporate officer is not immune from liability for acts and omissions which occur while performing corporate business).

Judgments affirmed.

GILBERT v. SETON HALL UNIVERSITY

332 F.3d 105 (2d Cir. 2003)

JON. O. NEWMAN, CIRCUIT JUDGE.

This appeal concerns choice of law with respect to charitable immunity. The specific issue is whether New York, the forum state, would apply New Jersey law, which preserves charitable immunity, or the law of New York or Connecticut, both of which have abolished such immunity, to a tort claim brought against a New Jersey university by a Connecticut student attending the university who was injured while participating in an extracurricular sporting event in New York. Michael Gilbert appeals from the December 8, 2000, judgment of the District Court for the Eastern District of New York granting Seton Hall University ("Seton Hall") summary judgment on his claims seeking damages for injuries sustained during a rugby match in 1992. The District Court held that Seton Hall was immune from liability under New Jersey's law of charitable immunity. We agree with the District Court that the New York Court of Appeals would apply the charitable immunity law of New Jersey to this case, and we therefore affirm.

Background

I. Facts

Seton Hall and Its Rugby Club. Seton Hall is a nonprofit educational institution located in South Orange, New Jersey. In addition to its intercollegiate athletics program, Seton Hall makes available to its students "club sports," which, according to a Seton Hall manual, are "organized, financed, and run by students with the administrative assistance of the [Department of Recreational Services]." . . .

Rugby at Seton Hall is a club sport. Players participate through the Seton Hall Rugby Club ("Rugby Club"). The Rugby Club's charter states that it is "organized subject to the authority of Seton Hall University . . . and in conjunction with the Metropolitan New York Rugby Union" ("MNYRU").

. . . .

Gilbert's Participation in the Rugby Club. Gilbert, who is domiciled in Connecticut, enrolled in Seton Hall as a full time student in the fall of 1990 after completing one year of study at Long Island University. He lived in New Jersey on or near the Seton Hall campus during the academic years 1990–91 and 1991–92.

Gilbert's first experience with rugby occurred in the spring of 1991, during his second semester at Seton Hall, when he joined the Rugby Club. . . .

When Gilbert returned to Seton Hall for his second year in the fall of 1991, he continued participating in the Rugby Club . . . .

In the spring semester of 1992, Gilbert continued regularly attending practice. He played the first two matches that semester. On both occasions he played wing forward, the same position he had regularly played the previous semester.

St. John's Match. On April 4, 1992, Gilbert and the Rugby Club traveled to Cunningham Park in Queens, New York, to play the third game of the spring season. The opposing team was nominally affiliated with St. John's University. Unknown to Gilbert or his fellow club members, the St. John's team had been banned by authorities of St. John's University in 1986, and the team playing against the Rugby Club on April 4, 1992, was a pick-up team composed in part of St. John's students. The St. John's team had been suspended from the MNYRU.

Gilbert stated in his deposition that the field was not properly lined and lacked goalposts. A keg of beer was available, and some members of the opposing team drank from it. Gilbert did not drink alcohol during the game and saw none of his teammates drinking. No coach or faculty advisor accompanied the Rugby Club for the match. No "certified referee" was present, although there was apparently an individual performing the function of a referee.

Early in the game, on an inbounding play known as a "line out," Gilbert took possession of the ball. As he was trying to pitch the ball to a teammate, he was hit from behind. Several players then fell on top of him. As a result, Gilbert sustained serious injuries that rendered him a quadriplegic. There is no evidence that any unsportsmanlike conduct occurred on the play during which Gilbert was injured.

II. Procedural History

In April 1994, the Plaintiff filed in the District Court a diversity complaint alleging violations of New York law against Seton Hall and St. John's University. He later filed an amended complaint, joining three individual defendants.

The amended complaint alleges, among other things, that Seton Hall was negligent in supervising the team by failing to ensure the active participation of a faculty advisor and/or coach, and that, if Seton Hall had provided adequate supervision, the match would not have taken place because the field was not a properly sanctioned rugby field, there was no certified referee present, members of the opposing team were drinking beer, members of the Rugby Club had drank beer the night before, and the opposing team was not sanctioned by St. John's University and was suspended from the MNYRU.

In November 2000, [a magistrate] granted Seton Hall's motion for summary judgment. The other defendants were dismissed either previously or subsequently. With respect to Seton Hall, the Court concluded that New Jersey's law of charitable immunity was applicable and provided Seton Hall with a complete defense. . . .

Discussion

New Jersey law recognizes the doctrine of "charitable immunity," whereby non-profit corporations and associations organized exclusively for religious, charitable, or educational purposes are immune from negligence liability for injuries caused to a beneficiary of the charitable institution. N.J. Stat. Ann. § 2A:53A-7 (West 2000). Although New York and Connecticut once recognized charitable immunity, both abolished the doctrine long before the events giving rise to this suit.

The parties agree that, if New Jersey law applies, summary judgment was properly granted. Gilbert argues that New York conflicts law requires the law of New York to be applied, defeating Seton Hall's charitable immunity defense.

In diversity cases, federal courts apply the choice of law rules of the forum state, in this case. . . . Thus, "our task is to determine what law New York courts would apply in this situation." *O'Rourke v. Eastern Air Lines, Inc.*, 730 F.2d 842, 847 (2d Cir. 1984), *abrogated on other grounds*, *Salve Regina College v. Russell*, 499 U.S. 225, 230, 111 S. Ct. 1217, 113 L. Ed. 2d 190 (1991).

Where the conflict of law concerns a loss-allocating rule, a rule that "prohibits, assigns, or limits liability after the tort occurs," *Padula v. Lilarn Properties Corp.*, 644 N.E.2d 1001 (1994), New York courts resolve the conflict by employing the methodology set forth in *Neumeier v. Kuehner*, 286 N.E.2d 454 (1972). Charitable immunity is a loss-allocating rule, and therefore we look to *Neumeier*.

In *Neumeier*, the Court of Appeals adopted a framework of three rules for determining the applicable law. The third rule, applicable where the parties reside in different jurisdictions and the allegedly tortious conduct occurs in a third jurisdiction . . . governs this case because Gilbert is a domiciliary of Connecticut . . . Seton Hall is domiciled in New Jersey, and the injury took place in New York. The third *Neumeier* rule directs a court to apply the law of the jurisdiction where the injury occurred unless it can "be shown that displacing that normally applicable rule will advance the relevant substantive law purposes without impairing the smooth working of the multistate system or producing great uncertainty for litigants." *Neumeier*, 31 N.Y.2d at 128 (quoting *Tooker v. Lopez*, 249 N.E.2d 394 (1969).

The substantive law of three states has potential relevance in this case: New York where the injury occurred, New Jersey where the defendant is domiciled, and Connecticut where the plaintiff is domiciled. As to New York's interest, the New York Court of Appeals has made it reasonably clear that the state in which the injury occurs has little interest in seeing its own loss allocation rules applied. . . .

As to New Jersey's interest, the Court of Appeals decision in [*Schultz v. Boy Scouts of America, Inc.*,480 N.E.2d 679 (1985)] identified three factors that supported New Jersey's interest in that case and similarly support its interest in the pending case. One factor was that the plaintiffs had benefitted from New Jersey's law of charitable immunity and the State therefore had a rightful interest in holding them to its burdens as well. *See id.* Although Gilbert is not a domiciliary of New Jersey, he, like the plaintiffs in Schultz, has benefitted from the charitable immunity law of New Jersey by virtue of his voluntary decision to attend a university in that state.

Charitable immunity reduces the cost at which an institution can provide its services, and, because the institution has no profit motive, these savings are presumably passed on to some extent to the institution's beneficiaries; in return, individuals who choose to take advantage of the institution's services bear the risk that any injury they suffer due to the negligence of the charitable institution will not be compensated by the institution. By electing to attend an institution that is protected by and benefits from New Jersey charitable immunity laws, Gilbert has presumably obtained a better value for his (or his parents') money than he would have obtained if Seton Hall did not enjoy charitable immunity. Because Gilbert has indirectly availed himself of the charitable law of New Jersey and benefitted from it, New Jersey has a strong interest in having him bear a related burden. That the dollar value of the burden in this case exceeds the benefit does not alter the relevance of this first Schultz factor.

A second factor identified in Schultz to favor application of New Jersey's charitable immunity law was that the state had an interest in encouraging the work of charities located within its borders. See id. Similarly here, New Jersey has an important interest in having its law applied so that its universities can continue to provide services to all students at lower costs. It is very common today for universities to enroll a significant number of out-of-state students. Indeed, many universities consider that maintaining a geographically diverse student body is desirable and take this into account during their admissions process. New Jersey has an interest in ensuring that its universities can continue to attract out-of-state students and provide them a low cost educational service without being exposed to unpredictable liability vis-a-vis those students.

A third factor identified in Schultz was that while the injury had taken place in New York, most of the relevant contact between the parties in that case had occurred in New Jersey. *See id.* . . .

As in Schultz, it is undisputed that most of the "voluntary association" between Gilbert and Seton Hall occurred not in New York but in New Jersey, and that whatever failures in the supervision of the Rugby Club might be attributed to Seton Hall (such as not to send a coach) originated in New Jersey before the team left to play its match in New York. Because most of Gilbert's rugby-related activity and Seton Hall's alleged rugby-related negligence occurred in New Jersey, it would be consistent with both parties' expectations that the law of New Jersey would govern questions of loss allocation that might arise between them. . . .

A common theme reflected in all these factors is that Gilbert's decision to attend a university in New Jersey greatly increased the appropriateness of applying that state's law regarding charitable immunity with respect to any claim he might bring against Seton Hall. . . .

As to Connecticut's interest, that state is Gilbert's domicile, and, at least as to accidents where the place of the tort is fortuitous, New York has preferred the law of a plaintiff's domicile to the law of the jurisdiction where the tort occurred. . . . However, the locus here was not fortuitous, and we see no indication that New York law generally surrounds a plaintiff with his home state's repeal of charitable immunity in the face of the plaintiff's voluntary relationship to a defendant domiciled in a state that maintains such immunity. . . .

Taking our guidance from the factors identified as relevant by the New York Court of Appeals, we conclude that New York would consider the interests of New Jersey to be paramount in this case, and would apply that state's law of charitable immunity.

. . . .

Conclusion

The judgment of the District Court is affirmed.

NOTES

1. The court in *Mullins* declined to apply a "bad faith" standard to its question of whether an officer of a charitable institution is liable for negligent performance of a discretionary function. Its reasoning was that the case did not involve "overriding considerations of public policy affecting the very quality and efficiency of government itself," but the court did not offer any detail on this reasoning. Why do you believe this particular case did not involve such overriding considerations?

2. The applicability of the charitable immunity doctrine varies state by state. As we see in *Mullins*, the Supreme Court of Massachusetts declined to adopt it. *See also President and Directors of Georgetown College v. Hughes*, 130 F.2d 810 (D.C. Cir. 1942). As we see in *Gilbert*, however, New Jersey does recognize it. *See also Lax v. Princeton Univ.*, 779 A.2d 449 (N.J. Super. Ct. 2001) (plaintiff injured at a university symphony concert; charitable immunity applied); *Orzech v. Farleigh-Dickinson Univ.*, 985 A.2d 189 (N.J. Super. Ct. 2009) (plaintiff died in a residence hall accident; charitable immunity applied).

3. The teaching and research functions of an institution often reinforce the availability of a charitable immunity defense. *See MacArthur et al. v. Univ. of Va. Health Svcs. Found.*, 72 Va. Cir. 322 (Charlottesville Cir. Ct. 2006) (hospital maintained a strong teaching and research mission). Similarly, volunteer work associated with student organizations reinforces the charitable work of universities, making the charitable immunity defense viable. *See Mooring v. Va. Wesleyan Coll.*, 44 Va. Cir. 41 (Norfolk Cir. Ct. 1997).

4. Are there any limitations or exception to charitable immunity? Should there be? According to *Hardwicke v. American Boychoir School*, 902 A.2d 900 (N.J. 2006), charitable immunity will not be an available defense in cases where the government agent has acted within a willful and wanton manner or has been grossly negligent.

5. What if the defendant university is not engaging in the charitable activities that afford it immunity in the first place? For example, if a student's injury is alcohol related and if the plaintiff can show the university was negligent in its enforcement of alcohol conduct policies, should the university lose its charitable immunity status? The court in *Orzech v. Farleigh-Dickinson University*, 985 A.2d 189 (N.J. Super. Ct. 2009), said no. The court held that the student, who died in a fall from a fourth floor residence hall window, was a beneficiary of the university's charitable objectives at the time of his death because she was living in the hall and receiving the benefits of the university's work. The court also held that the plaintiff's comparative negligence was not relevant to the determination of beneficiary status.

6. What factors were used by the court in *Gilbert* to determine that New Jersey law applied over New York and Connecticut law? Are you convinced by the determination? Factors applied in conflict of laws cases tend to vary case to case. In *Estate of Pigorsch v. York College*, 734 F. Supp. 2d 704 (N.D. Iowa 2010), for example, the court found that Iowa law should apply in a case involving an automobile accident that killed a Nebraska college student. Even though the decedent and her parents resided in Nebraska, and Nebraska was home to the college, the court applied Iowa law since the accident occurred in Iowa. In an opposite conclusion, the court in *Hataway v. McKinley*, 830 S.W.2d 53 (Tenn. Sup. Ct. 1992), determined that Tennessee law should apply in a case involving a wrongful death action by the parents of a Tennessee college student who died while scuba diving in Arkansas on a school trip. The court determined that the parties had their most significant relationships with Tennessee, where the family lived and where the university was located. According to the court in *Hataway*, generally courts will apply the law of the jurisdiction where the incident occurs, unless another state has a more significant relationship to the parties and to the occurrence. Finally, consider *Thompson v. Sinnott*, C.A. No. K09C-11-041 JTV, 2011 Del. Super. LEXIS 182 (Del. Super. Ct. Apr. 26, 2011), a case involving a drunk driving accident where the both the driver and passenger were university students in North Carolina and the injured passenger received medical treatment in both North Carolina and New York. The court, however, applied Delaware law, since that was where the driver was licensed and insured.

b. Negligence

i. Premises Liability

BERGERON v. SOUTHEASTERN LOUISIANA UNIVERSITY

610 So. 2d 986 (La. Ct. App. 1992)

CRAIN, J.

Southeastern Louisiana University ("Southeastern") appeals a judgment of the district court which awarded the plaintiff, Ervin Bergeron, $35,000 for damages sustained in a slip and fall accident which occurred in the lobby of his dormitory. We amend and affirm the judgment of the district court.

On appeal the defendant raises five assignments of error concerning the issues of liability and quantum.

The facts, as revealed by the record, are as follows:

On March 23, 1987, Ervin Bergeron, a 26 year old student at Southeastern had arranged to be tutored in mathematics by a fellow student, Suzette Burks.

The plaintiff and Burks each lived in the Holloway Smith Dormitory on the university campus. The building in question is a two story "L" shaped structure with the lobby situated in the center of the "L", and two doors leading to it. The lobby is a room of approximately 40' x 40' in dimension, with a 3 foot raised portion. The lobby floor is comprised of a substance which is akin to marble in hardness. . . .

At approximately 7 p.m., on the night in question, Bergeron had checked into the dormitory and left his identification at the front desk in order that he could enter Ms. Burks' room. The pair studied for approximately an hour and a half. Upon completion of the tutoring session, Bergeron and Burks walked together under the covered walkway to the lobby. Although it was not raining when the plaintiff originally entered the lobby, it had been raining for about an hour by the time the pair left Ms. Burks' room and reentered the lobby. The walkways leading to the lobby were wet. Plaintiff entered the lobby first, followed by Ms. Burks. As he entered the lobby Bergeron, who was wearing rubber thong shoes, slipped, fell on his back, and struck his head on the floor.

At the time of the accident there were no warning signs, no mats on the floor, and no visible mops and buckets. The testimony indicates that generally the procedures were to post signs, place mats on the floor and mop the wet areas during a period of rain.

The incident was witnessed by Ms. Burks and Ed Clites, a personnel assistant on duty that night. These parties came to Bergeron's aid after the accident. Clites retrieved a blanket and pillow for the plaintiff. He also cleared the lobby, locked the doors and summoned the police. He then went to the resident manager's office to complete a report of the incident.

The campus police arrived in about 15 minutes. After their arrival the ambulance was called and it arrived about 20 minutes thereafter. The plaintiff was taken to

Lallie Kemp Hospital where he was x-rayed, treated and released.

Bergeron had pain in his head, elbow, low back and tailbone. He also had headaches and trouble sleeping. He stayed in bed and would attend class with the aid of crutches, when possible. . . .

Liability

The defendant's first three assignments of error concern the issue of liability.

Defendant, in his first assignment of error, argues that the trial court erred in finding the University was negligent.

The trial court, in its reasons for judgment stated its findings on the issue of the defendant's liability as follows:

> . . . defendant Southeastern Louisiana University through its employees was negligent in not maintaining the entrance of its building in a safe condition. Even though it had been raining for some time, the mats which were readily available were not placed at the entrance, nor were safety measures taken.

A reviewing court will not set aside the factual determinations made by the trial court unless they are clearly wrong. *Arceneaux v. Domingue*, 365 So.2d 1330 (La. 1978); *Lirette v. State Farm Ins.*, 563 So.2d 850 (La. 1990).

. . . .

LEGAL PRINCIPLES

Plaintiff brought this suit essentially under negligence and strict liability theories. Although the two theories constitute separate and distinct avenues for relief for damages resulting from a dangerous condition on land, the analysis that courts utilize when applying the two theories is similar. Under either theory, the plaintiff must prove 1) the thing which caused the damage was in the custody of the defendant; 2) the thing contained a 'defect' (i.e., it had a condition that created an unreasonable risk of harm to the plaintiff); and 3) the 'defective' condition of the thing caused the plaintiff's injuries. *Sistler v. Liberty Mutual Insurance Company*, 558 So.2d 1106 (La. 1990). In essence, the only difference between the negligence theory of recovery and the strict liability theory of recovery is that the plaintiff need not prove the defendant was aware of the existence of the 'defect' under a strict liability theory. . . .

In this case there was testimony to the effect that rain had occurred intermittently throughout the day and most recently an hour before this incident. The lobby had been wet earlier in the day. A monitor was stationed in the lobby to protect against just such conditions. At the time of the accident the lobby was free of warning signs. There were no mats on the floor in this well-trafficked, slippery lobby area. Although the mats had previously been used by the school inside and outside the dormitory area; in this instance, the mat had either been resting on the banister railing or fallen on the floor. Moreover, although evidence was presented that it was normal procedure for mopping to occur if any amount of water accumulated on the floor; at this time no mopping took place. As such, in this case the criterion for a finding of negligence has been met. That is, the lobby floor was in the custody of the University. It contained a defect (i.e., rain/water) that created an unreasonable risk of harm to the plaintiff. It was this rain slick surface of the floor that caused plaintiff's injuries. Due to the campus monitor stationed in the lobby area the university knew of or should have known of the dangerous condition, and failed to implement its normal procedure to ward against the dangerous condition.

Under these circumstances the trial court correctly found that the defendant was negligent in not maintaining the entrance of the building in a safe condition. We find no error in this regard.

In Assignments of Error Nos. 2 and 3 the defendant contends that the trial court erred in failing to find [plaintiff] contributorily negligent and failing to find a percentage of fault.

The defendant argues that the actions of the plaintiff in wearing "flip-flops", especially in light of the monitor's admonition, constituted negligence on his part, for which an assessment of fault should have been made. We agree.

The record reflects that on the date in question the plaintiff was wearing rubber "flip-flop" shoes when he slipped on the wet dormitory floor. . . .

Additionally, according to Roland Jackson, the dorm's resident manager, he had twice warned the plaintiff not to wear flip-flops in the lobby. . . .

Moreover, it is clear from the record that the plaintiff was familiar with the dormitory because he resided there and had been a student at the University for two semesters.

Mr. Bergeron also admitted that he knew it had been raining for about an hour before he re-entered the lobby area. . . .

This evidence clearly supports a finding of negligence on the plaintiff's part. The failure of the trial judge to make such a finding in view of the evidence is clearly wrong. For these reasons we find the plaintiff 40% negligent and we amend the judgment accordingly.

. . . .

AMENDED AND AFFIRMED.

NOTES

1. In a negligence context, what is the general duty of care owed by universities to their students? What are some of the specific duties? Do these duties of care change for faculty and staff? Visitors? Visitors who are children?

2. How does the duty of care owed to university students relate to the traditional doctrine of *in loco parentis*, which holds that, in a higher education context, college or university officials stand "in the place of the parent"? Is the *in loco parentis* doctrine applicable to negligence law in higher education? Should it be? Traditionally, *in loco parentis* was applied to shield universities from liability. In other words, courts stayed out of the internal "family" decisions made by college officials. Over time, however, and by the late twentieth century, *in loco parentis* fell out of legal favor on college campuses. There is now a legal duty of care recognized by the courts, and the conduct engaged by university officials is now scrutinized by the courts. *See Bradshaw v. Rawlings*, 612 F.2d 135 (3d Cir. 1979), *cert. denied*, 446 U.S. 909 (1980). This issue is also discussed further in Chapter V.

3. How would this case have been decided in a jurisdiction with an immunity defense?

4. *Bergeron* presents a question of premises liability; in other words, when a landlord, landowner, or possessor owes a duty of care to people on their premises. The level of care owed generally varies, depending on the role played by the visitor: trespasser, licensee, or invitee. A licensee is on premises with the landowner's permission and for the licensee's own purpose or business. Invitees, in contrast, are present at the express invitation of the landlord, landowner, or possessor. It can be argued that university students are invitees although courts often find that universities owe no duty to students. *See, e.g., Pitre v. Louisiana Tech Univ.*, 673 So. 2d 585 (La. 1996).

Regardless of the status of the visitor, it can be argued comfortably that institutions of higher education have a duty to warn and make safe any known artificial conditions on their premises, particularly if those conditions are not obvious and highly dangerous. For licensees and invitees, the duty includes any known natural conditions as well. Finally, for invitees, the college or university owes an additional duty to make reasonable inspections to discover non-obvious and dangerous conditions, and to warn of their danger and make them safe. While a university would not be liable for injuries under these principles in situations where the danger is open and obvious, foreseeability still plays a role. In other words, institutions of higher education remain liable only for foreseeable injuries on their premises.

Often, foreseeability in such cases is measured by the existence of previous events, like injuries that have occurred in the past from students climbing on residence hall roofs, *Robertson v. State of Louisiana*, 747 So. 2d 1276 (La. Ct. App. 1999), *cert. denied*, 755 So. 2d 882 (La. 2000); or allowing a student with a record of sexual assault and harassment to live in a co-educational residence hall, *Nero v. Kansas State Univ.*, 861 P.2d 768 (Kan. 1993). For an example of a case where the dangerous condition is obvious, consider the following case.

SHIMER v. BOWLING GREEN STATE UNIVERSITY

708 N.E.2d 305 (Ohio Ct. Cl. 1999)

FRED J. SHOEMAKER, JUDGE.

In her complaint, plaintiff Shalene Shimer alleges that defendant was negligent in failing to properly cover an open orchestra pit, which thereby caused plaintiff to fall, resulting in bodily injury to her.

This action came to trial on the sole issue of liability. . . .

In 1996, plaintiff was a student at Bowling Green State University ("BGSU"), majoring in music. On the evening of April 27, 1996, plaintiff participated as a chorus member in the last of four performances of a BGSU theater production that was held at the Eva Marie Saint Theater. After the final performance had ended, plaintiff was expected to help in "striking the set," which entailed dismantling and removing all of the scenery, equipment, and props from the stage. Testimony revealed that plaintiff had not participated in a strike prior to the night of the incident and that she was working under the direction of Steven Boone, the technical director for the production. Boone testified that the theater department's policy required all performers to participate in the strike.

At the time of the incident, the theater stage was configured so that a portion of the orchestra pit was filled in with removable platform sections and covered to function as an extension of the stage. . . . Approximately one-third of the orchestra pit remained open for use during the performance.

Defendant filed an illness and injury report that states that plaintiff was injured at approximately 12:45 a.m. on April 28, 1996, when she fell backwards from the stage into the orchestra pit. According to plaintiffs testimony, she responded to a "heads up" call and looked up to watch for hanging scenery that was being lowered while instinctively taking a few steps backward, causing her to fall into the orchestra pit.

Plaintiff's complaint is construed to set forth a single cognizable action, which is one sounding in negligence. In order to prevail upon her claim of negligence, plaintiff must prove by a preponderance of the evidence that defendant owed her a duty, that it breached that duty, and that the breach proximately caused her injuries. *Strother v. Hutchinson* (1981), 67 Ohio St. 2d 282, 21 Ohio Op. 3d 177, 423 N.E.2d 467.

Plaintiff first contends that defendant is negligent per se for failing to comply with the Ohio Basic Building Code ("OBBC"), Ohio Adm.Code 4101:2-3-05 et seq. Specifically, plaintiff asserts that defendant was not in compliance with the requirements for platform construction. However, plaintiff's inadvertent fall from the edge of a theater stage and her resulting injury are unrelated to any issues regarding the materials or design used to construct the stage. Accordingly, the court finds that the provisions of Ohio Adm.Code 4101:2-3-05 have no application to the circumstances which caused plaintiff's injuries. Therefore, plaintiff's claim of negligence per se is without merit.

The duty of care owed to plaintiff as a student of a state university is that of an invitee. *Baldauf v. Kent State Univ.* (1988), 49 Ohio App. 3d 46, 550 N.E.2d 517. [Under Ohio law, therefore, the university owed plaintiff a duty to exercise ordinary and reasonable care to protect her from unreasonable risks of physical harm of which the university knew or had reason to know.]

. . . .

In order to recover from the occupier of premises for personal injuries claimed to have been caused by the condition of those premises, an invitee must allege and prove that the fall was proximately caused by some unreasonably dangerous condition. *Baldauf supra.* However, where an invitee voluntarily exposes herself to a hazard, the owner or occupier of the premises will not be the insurer of her safety, since an invitee is required to exercise some degree of care for her own safety. *Thompson v. Kent State Univ.* (1987), 521 N.E.2d 526. There is no duty to warn an invitee if a danger is so open and obvious that the invitee may reasonably be expected to discover it and protect herself against it. *Sidle v. Humphrey* (1968), 233 N.E.2d 589.

Upon review of the evidence, there is no doubt that the orchestra pit was open and obvious and that plaintiff was aware of its existence. Plaintiff testified that the stage lighting was adequate at the time of the incident and that she was aware of the stage configuration, including the existence of the orchestra pit. Plaintiff further testified that she had been on stage many times during the four weeks prior to her fall.

Plaintiff also contends that defendant was negligent for not covering the pit in an expeditious manner because the orchestra pit presented a foreseeable risk to those working on the stage. However, in *Grabill v. Worthington Industries, Inc.* (1994), 649 N.E.2d 874, 878, the court stated: "Foresight, not retrospect, is the standard of diligence. It is nearly always easy, after an accident has happened, to see how it could have been avoided. But negligence is not a matter to be judged after the occurrence."

Testimony revealed that a logical sequence was followed to strike the stage and that, in any case, the pit sections could not be replaced in the time between the end of the performance and plaintiff's injury. Moreover, regardless of foreseeability, if the owner and invitee "are equally aware of the dangerous condition and the invitee voluntarily exposes himself to the hazard, the owner or occupier will not be liable." *Stinson v. Cleveland Clinic Found.* (1987), 37 Ohio App. 3d 146, 149, 524 N.E.2d 898, 901.

In the present case, plaintiff failed to prove that the open orchestra pit constituted an unreasonably dangerous condition to plaintiff or the other student performers. Therefore, the court finds that defendant did not breach its duty of ordinary care to plaintiff.

. . . .

Judgment for defendant.

NOTES

1. The court in *Shimer* noted that universities do not have a duty to warn of open and obvious dangerous conditions. What rationale is given for such a statement? How does this rationale compare and contrast to the doctrine that liability may attach for foreseeable injuries on university premises. What's the difference between the lack of a duty of care for "open and obvious" dangers and a duty of care to prevent "foreseeable" injuries? How is foreseeability defined? Foreseeability of what? Of conduct? Of harm or injury?

Several other courts speak to the lack of a duty to warn of open and obvious dangers. *See, e.g., Wellhausen v. Univ. of Kansas*, 189 P.3d 1181 (Kan. Ct. App. 2008) (student fell seven floors to his death when he removed a window screen from his residence hall room and climbed out onto a small ledge to smoke a cigarette; students had been directed not to remove screens or enter and exit through windows); *Welden v. Dunn*, 962 P.2d 1273 (Okla. 1998) (court rejected student's claim for damages against a beauty college after she was injured attempting to lift a client from a malfunctioning shampoo chair; the defects were not hidden and were known to her); *Springer v. Univ. of Dayton*, No. 21538, 2006 Ohio App. LEXIS 3089 (Ohio Ct. App. June 23, 2006) (court denied damages to a plaintiff who tripped over a cable in a parking lot after a basketball game; he would have seen the cable if he had been looking directly in front of himself while jogging, rather than looking into the distance); *Anderson v. Principia Coll.*, 202 F. Supp. 2d 950 (E.D. Mo. 2001) (student had been drinking with friends and fell to his death from a remote bluff on campus; court found injury was not foreseeable, and thus no duty to warn or make safe such an open and obvious danger existed); and *Bellezzo v. State of Arizona*, 851 P.2d 847 (Ariz. Ct. App. 1992) (mother of a university baseball player did not recover for injuries she suffered when she was hit with a foul ball while attending one of her son's games).

On the other hand, colleges and universities do have a duty of care to maintain a campus free from foreseeable harms. *See, e.g., McClure v. Fairfield Univ.*, No. CV000159028, 2003 Conn. Super. LEXIS 1778 (Conn. Super. Ct. June 18, 2003) (by offering shuttle service to and from a local beach, the university assumed responsibility to protect students who traveled there for parties); *Shannon v. Washington Univ.*, 575 S.W.2d 235 (Mo. App. 1978) (college liable for injuries resulting from fall on sidewalk on university grounds); *Miller v. State*, 467 N.E.2d 493 (N.Y. 1984) (college liable for rape of student occurring in dorm room).

2. In some cases, university officials' knowledge of prior incidents and/or injuries is a factor evaluated by courts in finding a duty of care. *See Nero v. Kansas State Univ.*, 861 P.2d 768 (Kan. 1993); *Robertson v. State of Louisiana*, 747 So. 2d 1276 (La. Ct. App. 1999), *cert. denied*, 755 So. 2d 882 (La. 2000); *but see Kavanagh v. Trs. of Boston Univ.*, 795 N.E.2d 1170 (Mass. 2003) (finding the university not liable after a basketball player was punched by an opposing player because the player had no prior history of violence that would have given defendants knowledge of his violent tendencies).

How do you feel about the use of prior incidents at the university being used to determine the existence of a duty of care? What can a university do to mitigate the possibility that such a duty of care would attach where it otherwise would not? How much weight would preventive measures carry in such cases? For example, if a particular space on campus were the site for several past injuries for which the university is now on notice, what can or should the university do to prevent these past injuries from being used to establish a duty of care? And would those actions be useful in the university's defense? Would these preventive measures, though, act as an admission or acknowledgment of liability in those past cases?

ii. Liability Related to On-Campus Instruction

GARRETT v. NORTHWEST MISSISSIPPI JUNIOR COLLEGE

674 So. 2d 1 (Miss. 1996)

McRae, Justice, for the Court:

This appeal arises from a May 26, 1992 order of the Tate County Circuit Court granting Northwest Mississippi Junior College's motion for summary judgment in a negligence action. Joseph Garrett brought suit against Northwest after he sustained a severe injury to his right thumb while working on a milling machine in his tool and die class. He alleged that Northwest failed "to provide reasonably safe tools, products and instrumentalities; a reasonably safe place to work and train; as well as other acts of negligence." Finding that there were questions of fact for a jury to determine, we reverse and remand for a trial on the merits.

I.

On April 12, 1985, Joseph Garrett cut off his thumb while working on a horizontal milling machine in his tool and die class at Northwest Mississippi Junior College. Garrett described the milling machine as a rotary blade used to "cut slots." He was "mike-ing" a piece of metal on the machine when the accident occurred; that is, using a micrometer, a device that measures the width of the metal by very small degrees of tolerance. In describing the accident, Garrett stated, "I was mike-ing the metal — I mean the cutoff blade that I was cutting. And . . . [then] . . . I looked on top of the machine and my finger [thumb] was up there."

At the time of the incident, Garrett stated that his instructor, Frank Houck, was in his office at the opposite end of the room from the milling machine. Houck, however, characterized the distance as "a matter of several feet away," and said he had gone to his office to retrieve a drill bit for another student.

Garrett's deposition testimony suggests that this was the first time he had operated the machine on his own, and that he had not received instruction from anyone on its use. He indicated that there was a self-paced, ad hoc system of training on the machines, "You see a machine open, you get on it," and that he never took a safety test on the milling machine.

Houck acknowledged in his deposition that the students did not have to demonstrate any proficiency on the machinery before using it. He stated that he gave students a safety lecture and personal demonstration and "When they operate it, I'm constantly with them." He further stated, "I tell them — ask questions and demand an answer they can understand".

Houck, who indicated that Garrett was somewhat "slow," recalled that at least one time prior to the accident, he had warned him about the proper use of the machine. . . .

II.

Summary judgment is appropriate "if the pleadings, depositions, answers, to interrogatories and admissions on file, together with the affidavits, if any, show that there is no genuine issue as to any material fact and that the moving party is entitled to a matter of law." Miss. R. Civ. P. 56(c). The non-moving party will survive a motion for summary judgment if he can establish a genuine issue of material fact by the means available under the rule. *Spartan Foods Systems v. American National Insurance*, 582 So. 2d 399 (Miss. 1991) (citing *Galloway v. Travelers Insurance Co.*, 515 So. 2d 678, 682 (Miss. 1987)).

. . . [E]videntiary matters — admissions in the pleadings, answers to interrogatories, depositions, affidavits — are viewed in the light most favorable to the non-moving party, who has the benefit of every reasonable doubt.

III.

Garrett contends that the circuit court erred in granting Northwest's motion for summary judgment. Reviewing the evidence in the record before us in a light most favorable to Garrett, we find that there are genuine issues of material fact regarding the extent of the safety and use instruction he received on the milling machine as well as the adequacy of supervision by his teacher that must be resolved before the extent, if any, of Northwest's liability can be determined.

Our review of cases from other jurisdictions suggests that the extent of the duty owed by vocational education teachers and schools to students is framed largely in terms of the degree of safety and use instruction that students receive on the particular machine that is being used when an accident occurs, as well as the extent of teacher supervision at the time of the accident. Where, as in the case sub judice, there are disputed issues of fact regarding such matters, we are convinced that summary judgment is not appropriate.

[The court proceeded to summarize cases from a variety of other jurisdictions.]

Based upon these precedents, we find that a high school vocational teacher has the duty to take those precautions that any ordinarily reasonable and prudent person would take to protect his shop students from the unreasonable risk of injury. The extent of these precautions must be determined with reference to the age and inexperience of the students involved, their less than mature judgment with regard to their conduct, and the inherently dangerous nature of the power driven equipment available for their use in the shop. In order to discharge this duty, it is incumbent upon a teacher, at a minimum, to instruct his students in the safe and proper use of the equipment, to warn the students of known dangers, and to supervise the students to the extent necessary for the enforcement of adequate rules of shop safety.

Once the trial court has determined that the defendant was under a duty to protect the plaintiff against the event that did, in fact, occur, then it must be proven that the defendant's actions or failure to act constituted a breach of this duty. This second element of proof in a negligence case usually requires a factual determination that can only be made upon the unique facts of each case.

. . . .

IV.

Matters of safety and use instruction on specific machinery and the extent of instructor supervision have been outcome determinative in the shop class injury cases from other jurisdictions. Each has been decided according to its own particular factual scenario. In the case sub judice, there are disputed questions of fact on the critical issues of instruction and supervision. Summary judgment, therefore, was not appropriate. Accordingly, we reverse the decision of the circuit court and remand for trial on the merits.

REVERSED AND REMANDED.

NOTES

1. What are the duties of care owed by a university and its faculty to students in the classroom? What are some of the key factors that help to determine the duties of care and ultimate liability? How do these duties compare and contrast to duties of care owed under general premises liability? How might the knowledge and experience of the instructor play a role in the establishment of a duty of care? Should these be essential factors, or should all instructors be held to the same standard in these regards?

Are there any extra or new duties of care when the classes go off-campus (e.g., non-university property, internships, and field experiences)? *See Nova Southeastern Univ. v. Gross*, 758 So. 2d 86 (Fla. 2000) (finding that the university owed a duty of care in the assignment of students to off-campus internship sites). If the physical location of the course does not change the basic duty of reasonable care, then what about the applicability of classroom duties of care in online courses? Or in study abroad programs? For an example involving a study abroad program, albeit one generating a Title IX claim and not a negligence claim, see *Mattingly v. Univ. of Louisville*, No. 3:05CV-393-H, 2006 U.S. Dist. LEXIS 53259 (W.D. Ky. July 28, 2006) (holding that a university student studying abroad does not have a private right of action against a university under Title IX for a sexual assault committed by someone unaffiliated with the university).

2. What was the duty of care owed in *Garrett*? What factors are applied in determining the duty? Why does the court remand the case for trial? What were the fact disputes that led to the remand? What practical advice would you offer to classroom teachers in higher education as a result of this case? How important was it to the court that Garrett had little experience in the subject being taught? For a comparison, consider the following case.

NILES v. BOARD OF REGENTS OF THE UNIVERSITY SYSTEM OF GEORGIA

473 S.E.2d 173 (Ga. Ct. App. 1996)

ANDREWS, JUDGE.

Julian Niles, a doctoral student at Georgia Tech, suffered severe injuries in a laboratory accident. Chemicals he mixed inside a metal canister reacted violently, causing an explosion which sent fragments of the metal into his leg and lower abdomen. He sued Georgia Tech and the Board of Regents, claiming his professor and the University's administration should have provided him with laboratory safety training and should have warned him of the dangers of mixing acetone, ethanol, and nitric acid inside a metal container. . . . [T]he trial court directed a verdict in the University's favor. After carefully reviewing the evidence, including the evidence Niles claims was improperly excluded, we affirm the trial court's judgment.

A trial court may direct a verdict in a party's favor only "if there is no conflict in the evidence as to any material issue and the evidence introduced, with all reasonable deductions therefrom, shall demand a particular verdict. . . ." O.C.G.A. § 9-11-50 (a). We view that evidence in a light most favorable to Niles . . . and consider only those grounds raised in the University's motion for directed verdict. *Nelson v. Polk County Historical Society*, 216 Ga. App. 756 (1) (456 S.E.2d 93) (1995).

In pursuit of a doctorate in physics, Niles was enrolled in a class called "special problems" under Dr. Erbil and was experimenting with methods of producing superconducting crystals. Doctoral students such as Niles have supervision but also spend much time working independently on experiments. This explosion occurred when Niles was cleaning out a metal canister involved in the experiment, using a procedure outlined for him by a former Ph.D. student who had, the previous quarter, been his "mentor" in the lab. The experts who testified believed the explosion was caused by the combination of acetone and ethanol, which are "organic" chemicals, with inorganic nitric acid, inside a metal canister containing residue of titanium isopropoxide.

Before entering this laboratory course, Niles had graduated summa cum laude from the University of the Virgin Islands with a degree in chemistry. He had also obtained a masters' degree in physics from Clark Atlanta University, maintaining a 4.0 grade point average there. He passed his oral comprehensive examinations approximately ten months before the accident. During his scholastic career, Niles had spent "hundreds" of hours in laboratories. He had previously worked with acetone, ethanol, and nitric acid and knew many of the properties of these chemicals.

Niles' studies had also taught him to use reference materials. He was aware there are "a million" organic compounds, and he had learned to look up the nature of any compounds he did not understand. He had previously used a Merck's index to discover the properties of various chemicals, but he did not use that book — or any other reference — to investigate these chemicals before combining them. Neither did Niles ask any questions of Dr. Erbil, although he was familiar with the professor's "open door" policy. Instead, Niles relied on the process described to him by the former student.

1. Neither Georgia Tech nor Dr. Erbil was required to warn Niles of the dangers of mixing these chemicals. "Whether a duty to warn exists depends upon foreseeability of the [danger], the type of danger involved, and the foreseeability of the user's knowledge of the danger." (Citations and punctuation omitted.) *Exxon Corp. v. Jones*, 209 Ga. App. 373, 375 (433 S.E.2d 350) (1993) (discussing duty to warn in products liability context). Although a university student is an invitee to whom the university owes a duty of reasonable care, see *Rawlings v. Angelo State Univ.*, 648 S.W.2d 430, 432 (Tex. App. 1983), college administrators do not stand in loco parentis to adult college students. *Bradshaw v. Rawlings*, 612 F.2d 135 (3rd Cir. 1979).

Dr. Erbil had the right to assume that a physics doctoral student, who had graduated with highest honors in chemistry, would either know the dangers of mixing these chemicals or would perform the research necessary to determine those dangers and take the necessary precautions. Niles' own expert, a chemist, testified acetone, ethanol, and nitric acid are "common" chemicals in labs and that "in all probability," mixing them would produce a reaction like the one resulting in Niles' injury. "Ordinarily, there is no duty to give warning to the members of a profession against generally known risks. There need be no warning to one in a particular trade or profession against a danger generally known to that trade or profession." (Citations and punctuation omitted.) *Brown v. Apollo Indus.*, 199 Ga. App. 260, 263 (2) (b) (404 S.E.2d 447) (1991); *Eyster v. Borg-Warner Corp.*, 131 Ga. App. 702, 705 (2) (206 S.E.2d 668) (1974). Under these circumstances, neither Dr. Erbil nor Georgia Tech had any duty to warn a student with a degree in chemistry of the dangers of mixing these common chemicals.

2. Even if Georgia Tech and Dr. Erbil had a duty to warn Niles of this danger by hand-delivering him copies of "material safety data sheets," by reducing the cleaning procedure to writing, or by giving him a laboratory safety course, as he suggests, no evidence supports a reasonable inference that this action would have prevented the accident. . . .

With the "million" organic compounds and untold numbers of inorganic compounds which might be combined, nothing in the record supports an inference that any laboratory safety course would have covered the mixing of these chemicals. Niles himself testified he simply relied on his former colleague's oral "outline" of the cleaning procedure and did not read any safety materials which might have warned him of danger because he did not think it worth his time to investigate. Unless we were to hold Georgia Tech responsible for standing at Niles' shoulder and overseeing every action this doctoral student takes in the lab, which we will not do, any claim that his injury was proximately caused by the University's failure to provide him with detailed safety information is too speculative as a matter of law.

3. The court also properly directed a verdict in favor of Georgia Tech and the Board of Regents because Niles is deemed, as a matter of law, to have equal knowledge of the dangers of mixing these chemicals. As in *Evans v. Johns Hopkins Univ.*, 224 Md. 234, 167 A.2d 591, 593 (Md. App. 1961), this doctoral student was "far

from being newly initiated in laboratory work," was familiar with the chemicals he mixed, knew ethanol was flammable and that acid on metal would produce hydrogen gas, and had access to information which would tell him more about these chemicals. The bottle of nitric acid he used contained a label encouraging him to read a material safety data sheet about the chemical before using it, but Niles did not read the label. Instead, he "preferred convenience to safety and knowingly took the chance." *Evans, supra* at 594.

. . . .

Judgment affirmed. Pope, P.J., and Smith, J., concur.

NOTE

The court in *Niles* paid particular attention to the plaintiff's preexisting knowledge in chemistry in holding that the university owed no duty to warn the plaintiff of the dangers associated with his experiment. Comparing *Niles* and *Garrett* (presented earlier in the chapter), it seems that such determinations vary case by case. How do we best measure students' preexisting knowledge and experience in situations involving dangerous classroom and laboratory activities?

iii. Student Suicide

JAIN v. STATE OF IOWA

617 N.W.2d 293 (Iowa 2000)

Considered en banc.

Neuman, Justice.

This appeal concerns the tragic death of Sanjay Jain, a freshman at the University of Iowa. Sanjay committed suicide in his dormitory room. His father and administrator of his estate, Uttam Jain, sued the university for wrongful death, claiming it negligently failed to exercise reasonable care and caution for Sanjay's safety. In particular he claimed that if the university had followed its policy of notifying parents of a student's self-destructive behavior, the suicide could have been prevented.

On the university's motion for summary judgment, the district court dismissed Uttam's suit. It concluded the university owed no legal duty to Sanjay Jain to prevent him from harming himself, nor did it breach any legally recognized duty of care by failing to notify his parents of an earlier suicide attempt. For the reasons that follow, we affirm.

I. Background Facts and Proceedings

Sanjay Jain had just celebrated his eighteenth birthday when he enrolled as a freshman at the University of Iowa and moved into an off-campus university dormitory, the Mayflower. Sanjay came to Iowa from Addison, Illinois, the second of three children born to Uttam and Anita Jain. By all accounts they were a close-knit family.

Sanjay had enjoyed a successful academic career in high school and planned to major in biomedical engineering at the university. That course of study proved difficult. By the middle of the first semester his personal life as well as academic performance were showing the strain. He became moody and skipped many classes. He experimented with drugs and alcohol. In early November he was involved in an egg-throwing incident at the dormitory. He was penalized with three hours of compulsory community service. Soon after he was placed on one-year disciplinary probation for smoking marijuana in his room. Beth Merritt, the hall coordinator for the Mayflower dorm, imposed this discipline and ordered him to attend a series of alcohol and drug education classes.

Sanjay's parents and family were unaware of these difficulties. University policy calls for privacy with respect to the university's relationships with its adult students. . . . His frequent phone conversations with his parents were reportedly upbeat. . . .

In the early morning hours of November 20, 1994, resident assistants on duty at the Mayflower were called to a "domestic" dispute outside Sanjay's apartment. When they arrived they observed Sanjay and his girlfriend, Roopa, fighting over a set of keys to Sanjay's moped. Sanjay had moved the motorized cycle into his room. Roopa asserted that Sanjay was preparing to commit suicide by inhaling exhaust fumes and she was merely trying to stop him. Sanjay was interviewed independently. He, too, reported that he was trying to commit suicide. The RAs concluded from their conversation that Sanjay "had a lot of frustrations about family life and academics." After discussing the situation for about an hour, the group disbanded. Sanjay assured the RAs that he would seek counseling after getting a good night's rest.

Beth Merritt met with Sanjay the next day. He was reportedly evasive and refused to admit or deny that he had tried to commit suicide. She encouraged him to seek help at the university counseling service. She also demanded that he remove the moped from his room because storing it there violated university policy. He agreed to do so. Merritt also gave Sanjay her home phone number, urging him to call her "if he thought he was going to hurt himself." Sanjay assured her he would do so. He reportedly claimed that he just really needed to talk to his family and looked forward to doing so during the Thanksgiving break that would start the next day.

In keeping with university protocol, Merritt discussed the Sanjay incident with her supervisor, David Coleman, the assistant director for residence life. She expressed concern that the RA's incident report stated "Sanjay was trying to commit suicide by inhaling fumes of his scooter in an unventilated room" while Sanjay insisted the report "wasn't exactly the truth." She told Coleman that her personal conversation with Sanjay revealed more tiredness on his part than hopelessness or despair. She also advised Coleman that she requested permission to contact Sanjay's parents about the incident, but he refused to consent. Coleman concurred in Merritt's decision to encourage Sanjay to seek counseling. He took no further action on the matter.

Evidently Sanjay's visit with his family at Thanksgiving did not include discussion of the turmoil in his life. . . . Sanjay returned to the university when classes resumed on November 28. Merritt encountered him briefly and inquired about how things were going. Sanjay responded "good." Unbeknownst to Merritt, however, the moped was back in Sanjay's room. In a statement given after Sanjay's death, his roommate, Scott, reported that the vehicle had been stored in Sanjay's room for roughly three weeks. Sanjay reportedly told Scott that "he would kill himself by running the cycle in the room . . . when Scott was not there."

This threat, apparently taken in jest by Scott, played out on December 4. . . .

At approximately 10:30 a.m., one of Sanjay's suite-mates awoke to the smell of something "unusual." . . . When he opened the door to the kitchen a cloud of exhaust smoke appeared there and in the bathroom. . . . He contacted the RA on duty, who unlocked the door and found Sanjay unconscious, the moped still running. Emergency medical personnel were summoned and the dormitory was evacuated. Sanjay was pronounced dead of self-inflicted carbon monoxide poisoning.

The record reveals that an unwritten university policy dealing with self-destructive behavior dictates that, with evidence of a suicide attempt, university officials will contact a student's parents. The decision to do so rests solely with Phillip Jones, the dean of students. The dean bases his decision on information gathered from a variety of sources. In this case, no information concerning Sanjay Jain was transmitted to the dean's office until after his death.

Plaintiff Uttam Jain commenced this wrongful death action against the university in accordance with the "state agency" provisions of the State Tort Claims Act. *See* Iowa Code § 669.2 (1995). The suit claimed that Sanjay's death proximately resulted from university employees' negligent failure to exercise care and caution for his safety. The state generally denied the claims and asserted, by way of affirmative defenses, the doctrine of superseding-intervening cause and the discretionary function exemption to the State's waiver of sovereign immunity. Extensive discovery ensued. By the close of discovery, the only specification of negligence seriously advanced by plaintiff was his claim that Sanjay's death resulted from the university's failure to notify his parents of his earlier suicide attempt.

The State moved for summary judgment. Following hearing, the district court ruled that (1) no special relationship existed between the university and Sanjay that would give rise to an affirmative duty to prevent his suicide, (2) by adopting a policy of notifying parents of a student's suicide attempt, the university did not thereby assume a voluntary duty to prevent Sanjay's self-inflicted death, and (3) the facts, viewed in the light most favorable to the plaintiff, do not establish an exception to the general rule that suicide is an intentional intervening act which supersedes any alleged negligence by the defendant. The court therefore concluded the State was entitled to judgment as a matter of law. This appeal by plaintiff followed.

. . . .

III. Issues on Appeal.

Overview. At the outset plaintiff concedes that the law generally imposes no duty upon an individual to protect another person from self-inflicted harm in the absence of a "special relationship," usually custodial in nature. Restatement (Second) of Torts § 314, at 116 (1965). . . . Plaintiff claims no reliance on the "custody or control" exception here, conceding the university's relationship with its students is not custodial in nature. What plaintiff does claim is that the university's knowledge of Sanjay's "mental condition or emotional state requiring medical care" created a special relationship giving rise to an affirmative duty of care toward him.

Plaintiff's focus is on the Restatement (Second) of Torts section 323. It states:

> One who undertakes, gratuitously or for consideration, to render services to another which he should recognize as necessary for the protection of the other's person or things, is subject to liability to the other for physical harm resulting from his failure to exercise reasonable care to perform his undertaking, if
>
> (a) his failure to exercise such care increases the risk of such harm, or
>
> (b) the harm is suffered because of the other's reliance upon the undertaking.

He posits two possible circumstances that could establish the university's special duty to Sanjay under this record: (1) its adherence to an exception in federal legislation known as the "Buckley Amendment" that otherwise protects the confidentiality of student records, or (2) the university's adoption of a policy to notify parents of a student's self-destructive behavior. Alternatively, Plaintiff asserts that Sanjay's "intervening" act of suicide constituted a significant part of the risk inherent in the university's negligent failure to notify, thereby rendering inapplicable the intervening-superseding cause doctrine relied upon by the district court.

The state counters that plaintiff has not preserved his argument concerning the Buckley Amendment. It then argues that the university's voluntary conduct created no actionable duty under section 323 of the Restatement and, because there existed no legally-recognized special relationship between Sanjay and the university, the superseding-intervening act doctrine absolves the university of liability as a matter of law. . . .

A. Special relationship.

1. Duty arising under the Buckley Amendment. Congress enacted the Family Educational Rights and Privacy Act (FERPA) to ensure access to educational records for students and parents while protecting the privacy of such records from the public. *See generally* 20 U.S.C. § 1232g (1990). . . . At issue here is an exception that permits institutions to disclose otherwise confidential information to "appropriate parties" when an "emergency" makes it necessary "to protect the health or safety of the student or other persons." 20 U.S.C. § 1232g(b)(1)(I). . . .

Jain contends an emergency existed with respect to his son, Sanjay, and it was vitally important for Sanjay's parents to have information concerning the situation so they could intervene on his behalf. He then seems to argue that because the exception to the Buckley Amendment would have authorized revelation of the pertinent facts, the university was duty bound to reveal them. . . .

We entertain serious doubts about the merits of plaintiff's argument. His claim rests, after all, not on a violation of the Act but on an alleged failure to take advantage of a discretionary exception to its requirements. We need not resolve the question, however, because plaintiff has not preserved the issue for our review. . . .

2. Restatement (Second) of Torts § 323. That brings us to the crux of Plaintiff's claim — that the university has voluntarily adopted a policy (consistent with the Buckley Amendment) of notifying parents when a student engages in self-destructive behavior but it negligently failed to act on that policy in the case of Sanjay Jain. By not following its own policy, plaintiff argues, the "university deprived Sanjay of the medical intervention he so desperately needed."

The argument implicates section 323 of the Restatement (Second) of Torts. Although this court has applied section 323 in a variety of settings, we have not before had occasion to consider the rule's application in the context of an allegedly preventable death by suicide. . . .

. . . .

Cases interpreting section 323(a) have made it clear that the increase in the risk of harm required is not simply that which occurs when a person fails to do something that he or she reasonably should have. Obviously, the risk of harm to the beneficiary of a service is always greater when the service is performed without due care. Rather, as the court stated in *Turbe v. Government of Virgin Islands, Virgin Island Water & Power Auth.*, 938 F.2d 427, 432 (3d Cir. 1991):

> [Section] 323(a) applies only when the defendant's actions increased the risk of harm to plaintiff relative to the risk that would have existed had the defendant never provided the services initially. Put another way, the defendant's negligent performance must somehow put the plaintiff in a worse situation than if the defendant had never begun performance. . . . To prevail under a theory of increased harm a plaintiff must "identify the sins of commission rather than sins of omission."

Power, 110 Ohio App. 3d 29, 673 N.E.2d 617, 620 (Ohio Ct. App. 1996) (citations omitted). Likewise with respect to the "reliance" prong of section 323(b), [an Ohio appeals] court noted the general requirement that the plaintiff show "actual or affirmative reliance, i.e., reliance 'based on specific actions or representations which cause a person to forego other alternatives of protecting themselves.'" *Power v. Boles*, 673 N.E.2d 617, 621 (citations omitted); *accord* Restatement (Second) of Torts § 323 cmt. c, at 137.

Plaintiff argues, in essence, that once university employees discovered Sanjay and Roopa fighting over the moped keys, elicited comments suggestive of a suicide threat and referred Sanjay to counseling, they were bound under section 323 to follow through with their undertaking. In this case, plaintiff argues, that meant bringing the matter to the attention of the dean of students for the purpose of notifying Sanjay's parents.

Although, in hindsight, plaintiff's contention carries considerable appeal, the duty he seeks to impose upon the university cannot be squared with section 323(a) or (b). The record, read in the light most favorable to the plaintiff, reveals that Sanjay may have been at risk of harming himself. No affirmative action by the defendant's employees, however, increased that risk of self-harm. To the contrary, it is undisputed that the RAs appropriately intervened in an emotionally-charged situation, offered Sanjay support and encouragement, and referred him to counseling. Beth Merritt likewise counseled Sanjay to talk things over with his parents, seek professional help, and call her at any time . . . . She sought Sanjay's permission to contact his parents but he refused. In short, no action by university personnel prevented Sanjay from taking advantage of the help and encouragement being offered, nor did they do anything to prevent him from seeking help on his own accord.

The record is similarly devoid of any proof that Sanjay relied, to his detriment, on the services gratuitously offered by these same personnel. . . .

. . . .

B. Superseding — intervening act doctrine.

In Iowa and elsewhere, it is the general rule that unless the possibility of accident or innocence can be reasonably determined, the act of suicide is considered a deliberate, intentional and intervening act that precludes another's responsibility for the harm. *Cutler*, 473 N.W.2d at 182; *McLaughlin*, 461 A.2d at 124; *Falkenstein v. City of Bismarck*, 268 N.W.2d 787, 790 (N.D. 1978); W. Page Keeton, Prosser and Keeton on the Law of Torts § 44, at 311 (5th ed. 1984). As already noted earlier in this opinion, an exception to this general rule arises from the existence of a special relationship that imposes upon the defendant the duty to prevent foreseeable harm to the plaintiff. *Cutler*, 473 N.W.2d at 182. In such a case, the doctrine of intervening-superseding act will not relieve a defendant of liability. *Stevens by Stevens v. Des Moines Indep. Community Sch. Dist.*, 528 N.W.2d 117, 119 (Iowa 1995). That is because the intervening act (in this case, suicide) is the very risk the special duty is meant to prevent. . . .

Here, the district court logically concluded that because no legally-recognized special relationship existed between the university and Sanjay, plaintiff could not rely on the exception to the intervening-superseding cause doctrine to counter the university's affirmative defense. We agree. Accordingly we affirm the district court's summary judgment for the State of Iowa.

NOTES

1. The court in *Jain* held that the suicide was an intervening act which negated liability for the university. Do you agree with this finding or do you instead agree with the plaintiff that the suicide was an element of the risk for which the university owed a duty of care? What about a student's destructive and/or criminal behavior toward other people? Is this, too, an intervening act that shields a university and its staff from liability?

Generally, it may be argued that institutions of higher education owe no duty of care to protect a person from the criminal acts of third parties. Why might this be the case? And what exceptions to this general rule exist? Consider first the classic case of *Tarasoff v. Regents of the University of California*, 551 P.2d 334 (Cal. 1976), where the California Supreme Court held, in a divided opinion, that a patient-therapist relationship created a duty of care to warn others of the foreseeable risk a patient (a student at the university) posed to another person. In *Tarasoff*, a university psychotherapist failed to warn the victim of her patient's dangerous tendencies. The patient threatened to kill the victim and carried out the act after telling the counselor he was going to act on the threats. Similar questions of the imposition of a duty of care in such circumstances have arisen in the wake of the shootings at Virginia Tech in 2007 and Northern Illinois University in 2008. Crisis response, risk management, and associated policies and practices have, undoubtedly, been revisited in colleges and universities across the country since these tragedies. Should universities have an affirmative duty to intervene in cases of students with mental illness, especially those who are prone to violent behavior? *See* Oren R. Griffin, *Constructing a Legal and Managerial Paradigm Applicable to the Modern-Day Safety and Security Challenges at Colleges and Universities*, 54 St. Louis L.J. 241 (2009).

In 1990, Congress enacted the Jeanne Clery Disclosure of Campus Security Policy and Campus Crime Statistics Act (The Clery Act), which obligates institutions of higher education who participate in the federal financial aid system to disclose annual information about crime on campus and in the community. The Clery Act is named after Jeanne Clery, a college freshman who was raped and murdered in her residence hall at Lehigh University in 1986 by another student. The required reports under the Act must include crime data from the past three years, detail on campus and community policies on safety and security, information on campus crime prevention programs, and procedures to be followed in investigation of alleged sex offenses. Finally, institutions of higher education are required to offer timely warnings of any recent crimes and threats to campus safety and security. 20 U.S.C. § 1092(f).

2. The court in *Jain* declined to review the plaintiff's claim that the emergency exception to the Family Educational Rights and Privacy Act (FERPA) applied, permitting the university to notify the parents. In doing so, the court noted that the plaintiffs had failed to preserve that claim for review on appeal. According to the applicable provision of FERPA, educational institutions are permitted to disclose otherwise confidential information to "appropriate parties . . . to protect the health or safety of the student or other persons." 20 U.S.C. § 1232g(b)(1)(I). If this issue had been reviewed, how would the court have held? Because such disclosure is only *permitted*, but not required, would a tort-based duty of care attach to a university in such a case?

Consider also 34 C.F.R. § 99.36, which outlines the conditions under which educational institutions may disclose personally identifiable information of students:

> (a) An educational agency or institution may disclose personally identifiable information from an education record to appropriate parties, *including parents of an eligible student*, in connection with an emergency if knowledge of the information is necessary to protect the health or safety of the student or other individuals. (emphasis added)

What is the impact of the language "including parents of an eligible student," added in 2009, presumably in response to the shootings at Virginia Tech University and the reports that the university was aware of the shooter's dangerous propensities? *See* Allison B. Newhart & Barbara F. Lovelace, *FERPA Then and Now: Tipping the Balance in Favor of Disclosure of Mental Health Information Under the Health and Safety Emergency Exception*, U. RISK MGMT. & INS. ASS'N J., 2009, *available at* http://www.saul.com/media/article/1052_PDF_2096.pdf; see also the cases and notes on FERPA in Chapter VI.

3. What are the legal implications of the disclosure requirements in FERPA and the Clery Act? Notification of crimes and warnings of threats, particularly to specifically targeted individuals, clearly have their advantages. In addition to the confidentiality arguments that come up in cases involving therapists and other medical professionals who do not wish to compromise their patient care or their professional ethics by disclosing certain information (see *Tarasoff v. Regents of the University of California*, discussed in Note 1), there are also questions of student records and student reputation. With no surprise, the balance between student privacy and campus safety has seen much discussion in recent years. *See, e.g.*, Katrina Chapman, *A Preventable Tragedy at Virginia Tech: Why Confusion over FERPA's Provisions Prevents Schools from Addressing Student Violence*, 18 B.U. PUB. INT. L.J. 349 (2009); Lynn M Daggett, *FERPA in the Twenty-First Century: Failure to Effectively Regulate Privacy for All Students*, 58 CATH. U.L. REV. 59 (2008); Sarah G. Johnston, *The Mental Health Security for America's Families in Education Act: Helping Colleges and Universities Balance Students' Privacy and Personal Safety*, 46 DUQ. L. REV. 211 (2008).

Outside of privacy interests, students may also file defamation suits. See, e.g., *Havlik v. Johnson & Wales University*, 509 F.3d 25 (1st Cir. 2007), in which a university posted a crime bulletin to the university community about a physical altercation involving a student. The student then filed suit. The court sided with the university, finding that the university had complied with the law and that its communications were protected by a qualified privilege defense. For more on defamation claims, see *Chonich v. Ford* and the related notes later in the chapter.

SCHIESZLER v. FERRUM COLLEGE

236 F. Supp. 2d 602 (W.D. Va. 2002)

MEMORANDUM OPINION

JACKSON L. KISER, SENIOR UNITED STATES DISTRICT JUDGE

I. Background

This wrongful death suit arises out of the suicide of Michael Frentzel. At the time of his death, Frentzel was a freshman at Ferrum College. His first semester at college apparently was not an entirely happy experience. As a result of some undisclosed "disciplinary issues," Ferrum required Frentzel to comply with certain conditions before permitting him to continue his enrollment. Among these was the requirement that Frentzel enroll in anger management counseling before returning for spring semester.

Frentzel apparently complied with these conditions and returned to Ferrum for a second semester. On February 20, 2000. Frentzel had an argument with his girlfriend, Crystal. The campus police and the resident assistant at Frentzel's on-campus dormitory, Odessa Holley, responded and intervened. At around the same time, Frentzel send a note to Crystal in which he indicated that he intended to hang himself with his belt. Holley and the campus police were shown the note. When they responded, they found Frentzel locked in his room. When they managed to get into his room, they found Frentzel with bruises on his head. He told them the bruises were self-inflicted. The campus police informed Ferrum's dean of student affairs, David Newcombe, about the incident. Newcombe responded by requiring Frentzel to sign a statement that he would not hurt himself. Newcombe then left Frentzel alone to go speak with Crystal.

Within the next few days, Frentzel wrote another note to a friend stating "tell Crystal I will always love her." The friend told Crystal who told the defendants. They refused to allow her to return to Frentzel's dormitory room. The defendants took no other action. Soon thereafter, Frentzel wrote yet another note stating "only God can help me now," which Crystal pressed upon the defendants. When the defendants visited Frentzel's room on February 23, 2002, they found that he had hung himself with his belt.

Frentzel's aunt and guardian, LaVerne Schieszler, was named the personal representative of his estate in Illinois. She filed a wrongful death suit against Ferrum College, Newcombe and Holley. The complaint alleges a single count of wrongful death pursuant to Virginia Code §§ 8.01-5 et seq. It avers that the defendants "knew or personally should have known that Frentzel was likely to attempt to hurt himself if not properly supervised," that they were "negligent by failing to take adequate precautions to insure that Frentzel did not hurt himself," and that Frentzel died as a result.

The defendants have jointly moved to dismiss the complaint, arguing that (1) the court lacks subject matter jurisdiction because the complaint does not allege diversity of citizenship between the parties; (2) the representative lacks capacity to sue under Fed. R. Civ. P. 17(b); (3) a claim for wrongful death will not lie because Frentzel's suicide was an unlawful act; (4) the defendants had no legal duty to take steps to prevent Frentzel from killing himself; and (5) the defendants' actions were not the cause of Frentzel's death. In response, Schieszler moved for leave to file an amended complaint that would cure the first ground for dismissal. The defendants objected, arguing that filing the proposed amended complaint would be futile because it fails to state a claim upon which relief can be granted.

II. Discussion

A. Motion for Leave to File an Amended Complaint and Motion to Dismiss for Failure to State a Claim

Federal Rule of Civil Procedure 15(a) states that leave to amend shall be "freely granted when justice so requires." Fed. R. Civ. P. 15(a). . . . "To justify a denial of such leave [to amend], it must appear to the Court that the amendment is futile, offered in bad faith, prejudicial or otherwise contrary to the interests of justice." *Roper v. County of Chesterfield, Virginia*, 807 F. Supp. 1221, 1223 (E.D.Va.1992). The defendants' primary argument against allowing leave to amend is that the amendment will be futile because it fails to state a claim for wrongful death. Thus, the issue of whether the plaintiff has stated a claim for wrongful death will determine whether I accept the amended complaint. I will therefore address that issue first.

1. Dismissal Standard

Rule 12(b)(6) of the Federal Rules of Civil Procedure permits a party to move for dismissal of a claim for "failure to state a claim upon which relief can be granted." Fed. R. Civ. P. 12(b)(6). The function of motions to dismiss is to test the law governing the claims, not the facts which support them. *See Conley v. Gibson*, 355 U.S. 41, 45–46 (1957). Thus, I may only test the plaintiff's amended complaint for any legal deficiency, and must presume that all factual allegations in it are true. *Scheuer v. Rhodes*, 416 U.S. 232 (1974). Furthermore, all reasonable inferences must be made in favor of the non-moving party, in this case, the plaintiff. *See Johnson v. Mueller*, 415 F.2d 354 (4th Cir. 1969). I cannot dismiss any claim unless it appears beyond a doubt that the plaintiff could not recover under any set of facts which could be proven.

2. Stating a Claim for Wrongful Death

a. Duty

In her claim for wrongful death, the plaintiff alleges that the defendants were negligent in failing to take adequate steps to prevent Frentzel from committing suicide. A cause of action for negligence will not lie unless there is a duty recognized by law. *Chesapeake and Potomac Telephone v. Dowdy*, 235 Va. 55, 61 (1988). In order to survive this motion to dismiss, the plaintiff must have alleged facts sufficient to support her claim that the defendants owed a legal duty to assist Frentzel.

Ordinarily, there is no affirmative duty to act to assist or protect another absent unusual circumstances, which justify imposing such an affirmative responsibility. Under Section 314A of the Restatement (Second) of Torts (1965), an affirmative duty to aid or protect will arise when a special relationship exists between the parties. Section 314A identifies a number of special relationships, including the relationship between a common carrier and its passengers, an innkeeper and his guests, a possessor of land and his invitees, and one who takes custody of another thereby depriving him of other assistance. The special relationships listed in the Restatement are not considered exclusive. Restatement (Second) of Torts § 314A cmt. b (1965).

Virginia law similarly recognizes that a special relationship can give rise to a duty to take affirmative action to assist or protect another. *Thompson v. Skate America*, 261 Va. 121, 129 (2001); *Dudas v. Glenwood Golf Club*, 261 Va. 133, 138 (2002); *Wright v. Webb*, 234 Va. 527, 530 (1987). The Virginia Supreme Court has held that a special relationship exists as a matter of law between a common carrier and its passengers, an employer and his employees, an innkeeper and his guests and a business owner and his invitees. *See Thompson v. Skate America*, 261 Va. 121, 129 (2001) (business owner-invitee); *A.H. v. Rockingham Publishing Co.*, 255 Va. 216, 220 (1998) (employer-employee); *Klingbeil Management Group Co. v. Vito*, 233 Va. 445, 448 (1987). . . .

. . . .

In the case most similar to this one, *Commercial Distributors v. Blankenship*, 240 Va. 382, 393 (1990), the Virginia Supreme Court concluded that a residential facility had a duty to protect its mentally disabled residents while they were on the premises. In doing so, the Court did not expressly conclude that a special relationship existed between the facility and its residents. The Court also found that the facility's duty was not as extensive as that of a hospital, nursing home or other custodial institution. *Id.* Nonetheless, the Court indicated that, had the plaintiff's decedent, a resident who committed suicide, been on the premises at the time of his death, and had his suicide been foreseeable, the facility would have had a duty to take steps to assist him. *Id.*

. . . .

I can find no cases in other jurisdictions, and the parties have proffered none, that address whether a special relationship exists under the facts presented in this case. The defendants point to two cases, *Jain v. Iowa*, 617 N.W.2d 293 (2000), and *Bogust v. Iverson*, 10 Wis.2d 129, 102 N.W.2d 228 (1960). Neither of these cases are helpful because they do not address whether a special relationship exists between school and student. Rather, both cases consider liability under Restatement (Second) of Torts § 323 (1965), a theory the plaintiff in this case abandoned at oral argument.

A number of cases in recent years have considered whether colleges and universities have a duty to take steps to protect students who voluntarily become intoxicated. *See Bradshaw v. Rawlings*, 612 F.2d 135 (3d Cir. 1979) (finding no special relationship); *Coghlan v. Beta Theta Pi Fraternity*, 133 Idaho 388, 987 P.2d 300 (1999) (same); *Univ. of Denver v. Whitlock*, 744 P.2d 54 (Colo. 1987) (same); *Beach v. University of Utah*, 726 P.2d 413, 416 (Utah 1986) (same); *see also Furek v. University of Delaware*, 594 A.2d 506, 522 (Del.1991) (finding special relationship giving rise to duty to protect student from hazing injuries). In the vast bulk of these cases, courts have concluded that no special relationship existed. Underlying the analysis in these cases is the conclusion that the school could not have foreseen that the student was in danger. . . . [However,] [i]n *Furek v. University of Delaware*, the court acknowledged that no duty arose merely from the school-student relationship, but concluded that when a college or university knows of the danger to its students, it has a duty to aid or protect them. 594 A.2d 506, 519–520 (Del.1991).

The conclusion that the relationship between a college or university and its students can give rise to a duty to protect students from harms of which the school has knowledge is consistent with the Virginia Supreme Court's analysis in other contexts. In the recently decided *Thompson v. Skate America, Inc.*, 261 Va. 121, 129 (2001), a case involving the duty of landowner to protect his invitees, the Court concluded that special relationships may exist between particular plaintiffs and defendants because of the factual circumstances of a case. In addition, the Court's analysis has placed particular emphasis on the foreseeability of the harm. Under the Court's precedents, the existence of a special relationship will not, standing alone, give rise to a duty; the harm must be foreseeable. *See Dudas v. Glenwood Golf Club*, 261 Va. 133, 138, 540 S.E.2d 129, 132 (2002) (declining to find inherent in special relationship an absolute duty to protect); *Wright v. Webb*, 234 Va. 527, 530, 362 S.E.2d 919, 921, 4 Va. Law Rep. 1389 (1987) (declining to create a duty of care requiring a business invitor to protect his business invitee). . . .

While it is unlikely that Virginia would conclude that a special relationship exists as a matter of law between colleges and universities and their students, it might find that a special relationship exists on the particular facts alleged in this case. Frentzel was a full-time student at Ferrum College. He lived in an on-campus dormitory. The defendants were aware that Frentzel had had emotional problems; they had required him to seek anger management counseling before permitting him to return to school for a second semester. The defendants knew that, within days of his death, Frentzel was found by campus police alone in his room with bruises on his head and that he claimed these bruises were self-inflicted. The defendants knew that, at around the same time, Frentzel had sent a message to his girlfriend, in which he stated that he intended to kill himself. The defendants knew that Frentzel had sent other communications, to his girlfriend and to another friend, suggesting that he intended to kill himself. After Frentzel was found alone in his room with bruises on his head, the defendants required Frentzel to sign a statement that he would not hurt himself. This last fact, more than any other, indicates that the defendants believed Frentzel was likely to harm himself. Based on these alleged facts, a trier of fact could conclude that there was "an imminent probability" that Frentzel would try to hurt himself, and that the defendants had notice of this specific harm. Thus, I find that the plaintiff has alleged sufficient facts to support her claim that a special relationship existed between Frentzel and defendants giving rise to a duty to protect Frentzel from the foreseeable danger that he would hurt himself.

. . . .

The plaintiff also has alleged sufficient facts to support her allegation that defendants Ferrum and Newcombe breached a duty to assist Frentzel. According to the facts alleged in the complaint, after finding Frentzel alone in his room with bruises on his head, Frentzel was left alone. After Frentzel sent the message to his girlfriend suggesting that he might hurt himself, the defendants responded by refusing to permit her to return to his room. According to the complaint, they took no steps to ensure that Frentzel was supervised or to contact his guardian. They failed to obtain counseling for him even though they had previously required him to undergo counseling. They took no other steps. That said, the facts alleged do not indicate that defendant Holley, the resident assistant at Frentzel's dormitory, could have taken any additional steps to aid or protect Frentzel absent some direction from Ferrum or Newcombe. Thus, I find that, under the facts alleged, only Ferrum and Holcombe could have breached their duty to render assistance to Frentzel. The claim against defendant Holley is therefore dismissed.

. . . .

b. Proximate Cause

Next, the defendants contend that the complaint fails to allege facts from which a trier of fact could find that their acts or omissions proximately caused Frentzel's suicide. Negligent breach of a duty is actionable only when it constitutes a proximate cause of the injury. *S & C Co. v. Horne*, 218 Va. 124, 128 (1977). Ordinarily, however, questions of proximate cause are not decided on a motion to dismiss. *Goff v. Jones*, 47 F. Supp.2d 692 (E.D. Va. 1999). They only become a question of law if the facts alleged are susceptible of only one inference. *Poliquin v. Daniels*, 254 Va. 51, 486 S.E.2d 530, 534 (1997); *Hubbard v. Murray*, 173 Va. 448, 3 S.E.2d 397, 402 (1939).

In Virginia, an injury is proximately caused by a defendant's negligence if the injury is the natural and probable consequence of the negligence. *Wyatt v. Chesapeake & Potomac Tel. Co.*, 158 Va. 470, 476 (1932).

Keeping in mind that proximate cause is a question of fact unless the facts alleged are susceptible of only one inference, *Poliquin*, 486 S.E.2d at 534, I cannot find at this early stage of the proceedings that the defendants' alleged failure to take steps to aid Frentzel was not a proximate cause of his death. The plaintiff has alleged that the defendants had been told that Frentzel had more than once threatened to kill himself and that he had already injured himself once. Thus, the facts alleged in the complaint indicate that the risk that Frentzel would in fact take his own life was foreseeable. Although the defendants had at their disposal campus police, the College's counseling services and the resident assistant in Frentzel's dormitory, the plaintiff alleges that they took no steps to ensure that Frentzel was supervised. In addition, according to the plaintiff's amended complaint, the defendants did not contact Frentzel's guardian and refused to permit Frentzel's girlfriend to return to his room after he threatened to injure himself. Instead, the defendants left Frentzel alone. While alone, in his room, Frentzel hung himself. According to the complaint, all of these events occurred within a three-day period.

In view of these alleged facts, I cannot say as a matter of law that Frentzel's suicide was not a foreseeable result of defendants' failure to ensure that Frentzel was supervised.

3. Motion for Leave to File an Amended Complaint

Because I find that the plaintiff has sufficiently alleged duty and proximate cause, I find that the plaintiff has stated a claim for wrongful death resulting from the defendants' negligence. Consequently, the plaintiff's motion for leave to file an amended complaint is not futile. I will therefore grant it. For purposes of deciding the remaining issues raised by the defendants' motion to dismiss, I will consider the facts alleged in the amended complaint already filed by the plaintiff.

. . . .

III. Conclusion

In sum, I find that the plaintiff has succeeded in stating a claim for wrongful death against defendants Ferrum and Holcombe.

NOTES

1. Compare *Jain* and *Schieszler*. What are the primary differences in fact and law here? The plaintiffs in *Jain* argued that Jain's noticeable mental condition and emotional state created a special relationship. The court did not find such a relationship in *Jain*, yet the court in *Schieszler* did. Why? In student suicide cases, the determination whether a university or its officials have a duty of care seems to vary from cases. What are the central factors used to determine whether this duty exists? What is the nature of this duty of care? In other words, what are we expected to do in order to meet a duty of care in a (potential) suicide case? *See also Leary v. Wesleyan Univ.*, No. CV055003943, 2009 Conn. Super. LEXIS 621 (Conn. Super. Ct. Mar. 10, 2009); *Nannay v. Rowan College*, 101 F. Supp.2d 272 (D.N.J. 2000); *and Shin v. Mass. Inst. of Tech.*, 19 Mass. L. Rep. 570 (Mass. Super. Ct. 2005). For recent commentary on student deaths and institutional liability, see Joy Blanchard, *University Tort Liability and Student Suicide: Case Review and Implications for Practice*, 36 J.L. & Educ. 461 (2007); Daryl J. Lapp & Mark R. Vernazza, *College and University Liability for Student Deaths and Injuries: Massachusetts Courts Find a Duty of Care only in Narrowly Limited Circumstances*, 52 Boston B.J. 18 (2008); Ann MacLean Massie, *Suicide on Campus: The Appropriate Legal Responsibility of College Personnel*, 91 Marq. L. Rev. 625 (2008); Karin McAnaney, *Finding the Proper Balance: Protecting Suicidal Students without Harming Universities*, 94 Va. L. Rev. 197 (2008).

2. The court in *Schieszler*, in discussing prior cases where courts had discussed the existence of a special relationship, made reference to *Furek v. University of Delaware*, 594 A.2d 506 (Del. 1991), in which the court found a special relationship existed between a student and his university once the university knew of particular danger to its students. In *Furek*, the court held that the university's policy against hazing constituted an assumed duty and the university had a duty to regulate and supervise foreseeable dangerous activities occurring on its property. See Chapter V for a full presentation and discussion of *Furek.*

iv. Liability for Non-School-Related Activities

UNIVERSITY OF DENVER v. WHITLOCK

744 P.2d 54 (Colo. 1987)

JUSTICE LOHR delivered the Opinion of the Court.

Plaintiff Oscar Whitlock obtained a judgment against defendant University of Denver in the amount of $5,256,000, as a result of a jury trial in Denver District Court, for injuries suffered in a trampoline accident that rendered him a quadriplegic. The trial court ordered certain relief from this judgment based upon the University's motion for judgment notwithstanding the verdict. Whitlock appealed, and the University cross-appealed. The Colorado Court of Appeals rejected the University's argument that it owed no duty to Whitlock, reversed the trial court's order granting relief from the judgment, and directed that the jury's verdict be reinstated. The University then petitioned for certiorari, and we granted that petition.

The principal issue presented by this negligence case is whether the University of Denver owed a duty of care to Whitlock, who was a student at the University and a member of a fraternity, to take reasonable measures to protect him against injury resulting from his use of a trampoline under unsafe conditions when the trampoline was owned by the fraternity and was located on the front lawn of the house that the fraternity leased from the University. We conclude that the University had no such duty. Therefore, we reverse the judgment of the Colorado Court of Appeals, which recognized such a duty, and return the case to that court with directions to remand it to the trial court for dismissal of Whitlock's complaint against the University of Denver.

I.

The essential facts appear from the record of the jury trial in this case. On June 19, 1978, at approximately 10:00 p.m., plaintiff Oscar Whitlock suffered a paralyzing injury while attempting to complete a one-and-three-quarters front flip on a trampoline. The injury rendered him a quadriplegic. The trampoline was owned by the Beta Theta Pi fraternity (the Beta house) and was situated on the front yard of the fraternity premises, located on the University campus. At the time of his injury, Whitlock was twenty years old, attended the University of Denver, and was a member of the Beta house, where he held the office of acting house manager. The property on which the Beta house was located was leased to the local chapter house association of the Beta Theta Pi fraternity by the defendant University of Denver.

. . . .

During the evening of June 18 and early morning of June 19, 1978, Whitlock attended a party at the Beta house, where he drank beer, vodka and scotch until

2:00 a.m. Whitlock then retired and did not awaken until 2:00 p.m. on June 19. He testified that he jumped on the trampoline between 2:00 p.m. and 4:00 p.m., and again at 7:00 p.m. At 10:00 p.m., the time of the injury, there again was a party in progress at the Beta house, and Whitlock was using the trampoline with only the illumination from the windows of the fraternity house, the outside light above the front door of the house, and two street lights in the area. As Whitlock attempted to perform the one-and-three-quarters front flip, he landed on the back of his head, causing his neck to break.

Whitlock brought suit against the manufacturer and seller of the trampoline, the University, the Beta Theta Pi fraternity and its local chapter, and certain individuals in their capacities as representatives of the Beta Theta Pi organizations. Whitlock reached settlements with all of the named defendants except the University, so only the negligence action against the University proceeded to trial. The jury returned a verdict in favor of Whitlock, assessing his total damages at $7,300,000. The jury attributed twenty-eight percent of causal negligence to the conduct of Whitlock and seventy-two percent of causal negligence to the conduct of the University. The trial court accordingly reduced the amount of the award against the University to $5,256,000.

The University moved for judgment notwithstanding the verdict, or, in the alternative, a new trial. The trial court granted the motion for judgment notwithstanding the verdict, holding that as a matter of law, no reasonable jury could have found that the University was more negligent than Whitlock, and that the jury's monetary award was the result of sympathy, passion or prejudice. The trial court alternatively ruled that if the court of appeals should find that the trial court's ruling on the defendant's motion for judgment notwithstanding the verdict was in error, a remittitur would be entered, reducing the jury's award to $4,000,000. As a third alternative, in the event that the court of appeals should also disapprove the remittitur, the trial court ordered a new trial.

A panel of the court of appeals reversed all three rulings by a divided vote. The court of appeals held that the University owed Whitlock a duty of due care to remove the trampoline from the fraternity premises or to supervise its use, and that it was improper for the trial court to order a remittitur or, in the alternative, a new trial. The case was remanded to the trial court with orders to reinstate the verdict and damages as determined by the jury. The University then petitioned for certiorari review, and we granted that petition.

II.

A negligence claim must fail if based on circumstances for which the law imposes no duty of care upon the defendant for the benefit of the plaintiff. *E.g., Jefferson County School District R-1 v. Justus*, 725 P.2d 767, 769 (Colo. 1986). Therefore, if Whitlock's judgment against the University is to be upheld, it must first be determined that the University owed a duty of care to take reasonable measures to protect him against the injury that he sustained.

Whether a particular defendant owes a legal duty to a particular plaintiff is a question of law. *Imperial Distribution Services, Inc. v. Forrest*, 741 P.2d 1251, slip op. at 5–6 (Colo. 1987). . . . In *Smith v. City & County of Denver*, 726 P.2d 1125 (Colo. 1986), we set forth several factors to be considered in determining the existence of duty in a particular case:

> Whether the law should impose a duty requires consideration of many factors including, for example, the risk involved, the foreseeability and likelihood of injury as weighed against the social utility of the actor's conduct, the magnitude of the burden of guarding against injury or harm, and the consequences of placing the burden upon the actor.

Id. at 1127. As the quoted language makes clear, this list was not intended to be exhaustive and does not exclude the consideration of other factors that may become relevant based upon the competing individual, public and social interests implicated in the facts of each case. *See Bradshaw v. Rawlings*, 612 F.2d 135, 138 (3d Cir. 1979). . . . "No one factor is controlling, and the question of whether a duty should be imposed in a particular case is essentially one of fairness under contemporary standards — whether reasonable persons would recognize a duty and agree that it exists." *Taco Bell v. Lannon*, 744 P.2d 43, 46 (Colo. 1987).

We believe that the fact that the University is charged with negligent failure to act rather than negligent affirmative action is a critical factor that strongly militates against imposition of a duty on the University under the facts of this case. In determining whether a defendant owes a duty to a particular plaintiff, the law has long recognized a distinction between action and a failure to act. . . . Liability for nonfeasance was slow to receive recognition in the law. . . . The Restatement (Second) of Torts § 314 (1965) summarizes the law on this point as follows:

> The fact that an actor realizes or should realize that action on his part is necessary for another's aid or protection does not of itself impose upon him a duty to take such action.

Imposition of a duty in all such cases would simply not meet the test of fairness under contemporary standards.

In nonfeasance cases the existence of a duty has been recognized only during the last century in situations involving a limited group of special relationships between parties. . . . Special relationships that have been recognized by various courts for the purpose of imposition of a duty of care include common carrier/passenger, innkeeper/guest, possessor of land/invited entrant, employer/employee, parent/child, and hospital/patient. *See* Restatement (Second) of Torts § 314 A (1965); 3 Harper and James, § 18.6, at 722–23. The authors of the Restatement (Second) of Torts § 314 A, comment b (1965), state that "the law appears . . . . to be working slowly toward a recognition of the duty to aid or protect in any relation of dependence or of mutual dependence."

. . . .

III.

The present case involves the alleged negligent failure to act, rather than negligent action. The plaintiff does not complain of any affirmative action taken by the University, but asserts instead that the University owed to Whitlock the duty to assure that the fraternity's trampoline was used only under supervised conditions comparable to those in a gymnasium class, or in the alternative to cause the trampoline to be removed from the front lawn of the Beta house. It is true that there is evidence in the record from which the jury could have found that the University possessed the authority to regulate the fraternity's use of the trampoline by enacting rules of student conduct. However, mere possession of such authority is not sufficient to establish that the University had the duty to exert such control with respect to the use of trampolines by fraternity members. If such a duty is to be recognized, it must be grounded on a special relationship between the University and Whitlock. According to the evidence, there are only two possible sources of a special relationship out of which such a duty could arise in this case: the status of Whitlock as a student at the University, and the lease between the University and the fraternity of which Whitlock was a member. We first consider the adequacy of the student-university relationship as a possible basis for imposing a duty on the University to control or prohibit the use of the trampoline, and then examine the provisions of the lease for that same purpose.

A.

The student-university relationship has been scrutinized in several jurisdictions, and it is generally agreed that a university is not an insurer of its students' safety. *See Bradshaw*, 612 F.2d at 138; *Beach*, 726 P.2d at 418–19; *Hegel v. Langsam*, 29 Ohio Misc. 147, 273 N.E.2d 351, 352 (Ohio Ct. of Common Pleas 1971). The relationship between a university and its students has experienced important change over the years. At one time, college administrators and faculties stood in loco parentis to their students, which created a special relationship "that imposed a duty on the college to exercise control over student conduct and, reciprocally, gave the students certain rights of protection by the college." *Bradshaw*, 612 F.2d at 139. However, in modern times there has evolved a gradual reapportionment of responsibilities from the universities to the students, and a corresponding departure from the in loco parentis relationship. *Id.* at 139–40. Today, colleges and universities are regarded as educational institutions rather than custodial ones. *Beach*, 726 P.2d at 419 (contrasting colleges and universities with elementary and high schools). "Their purpose is to educate in a manner which will assist the graduate to perform well in the civic, community, family, and professional positions he or she may undertake in the future." *Id.* A university seeks to foster the maturation of its students.

. . . .

In today's society, the college student is considered an adult capable of protecting his or her own interests; students today demand and receive increased autonomy and decreased regulation on and off campus. *See Bradshaw*, 612 F.2d at 139–40. The demise of the doctrine of in loco parentis in this context has been a direct result of changes that have occurred in society's perception of the most beneficial allocation of rights and responsibilities in the university-student relationship. *See id.*; *Baldwin*, 123 Cal. App. 3d at 291, 176 Cal. Rptr. at 818; *Beach*, 726 P.2d at 418–19. By imposing a duty on the University in this case, the University would be encouraged to exercise more control over private student recreational choices, thereby effectively taking away much of the responsibility recently recognized in students for making their own decisions with respect to private entertainment and personal safety. . . .

The evidence demonstrates that only in limited instances has the University attempted to impose regulations or restraints on the private recreational pursuits of its students, and the students have not looked to the University to assure the safety of their recreational choices. Nothing in the University's student handbook, which contains certain regulations concerning student conduct, reflects an effort by the University to control the risk-taking decisions of its students in their private recreation. . . . Aside from advising the Beta house on one occasion to put the trampoline up when not in use, there is no evidence that the University officials attempted to assert control over trampoline use by the fraternity members. We conclude from this record that the University's very limited actions concerning safety of student recreation did not give Whitlock or the other members of campus fraternities or sororities any reason to depend upon the University for evaluation of the safety of trampoline use. . . . Therefore, we conclude that the student-university relationship is not a special relationship of the type giving rise to a duty of the University to take reasonable measures to protect the members of fraternities and sororities from risks of engaging in extra-curricular trampoline jumping.

. . . .

B.

We next examine the lease between the University and the fraternity to determine whether a special relationship between the University and Whitlock can be predicated on that document. The lease was executed in 1929, extends for a ninety-nine year term, and gives the fraternity the option to extend the term for another ninety-nine years. The premises are to be occupied and used by the fraternity "as a fraternity house, clubhouse, dormitory and boarding house, and generally for religious, educational, social and fraternal purposes." Such occupation is to be "under control of the tenant." (Emphasis added.) . . . The University has the obligation to maintain the grounds and make necessary repairs to the building, and the fraternity is to bear the cost of such maintenance and repair. The University has the right to inspect the building. The fraternity agrees that the building will not be used for unlawful or immoral conduct and that the occupants of the building are to "observe the reasonable rules of conduct therein and thereabout imposed from time to time on students of the University of Denver generally by the lessor." . . . The lease is devoid of any other covenants limiting the activities of the fraternity or its members or giving the University the right to direct or control those activities. The University has promulgated no rules of conduct relating to private trampoline use. A lessor's reservation of rights to inspect the premises and make repairs is generally not sufficient control to give rise to liability of the lessor to the tenant or third parties for tort injuries. G. Thompson, The Modern Law of Real Property § 1239, at 222 (1981).

The extent of control actually exerted by the University over the fraternity has been minimal. The University has supervised fire drills in the fraternity house and has required the fraternity to place a grid over one of its window wells because of an accident that had occurred. Also, a University representative once advised the Betas to take the trampoline down when not in use. Other than the suggestion made by the university official, which appears to have been only advisory as the fraternity failed to comply, the University's supervision has related primarily to fire protection, maintenance and repairs.

We conclude that the lease, and the University's actions pursuant to its rights under the lease, provide no basis of dependence by the fraternity members upon which a special relationship can be found to exist between the University and the fraternity members that would give rise to a duty upon the University to take affirmative action to assure that recreational equipment such as a trampoline is not used under unsafe conditions.

IV.

Considering all of the factors presented, we are persuaded that under the facts of this case the University of Denver had no duty to Whitlock to eliminate the private use of trampolines on its campus or to supervise that use. . . .

We reverse the judgment of the court of appeals and return this case to that court with directions to remand it to the trial court for dismissal of Whitlock's complaint against the University.

BOOKER v. LEHIGH UNIVERSITY

800 F. Supp. 234 (E.D. Pa. 1992)

E. Mac Troutman, District Judge

MEMORANDUM

This matter is now before us on defendant Lehigh University's motion for summary judgment. The issue is whether under the law of Pennsylvania a university may be held liable to one of its underage students when, as a result of her own self-indulgent behavior, she becomes inebriated at on-campus fraternity parties and thereafter injuries herself in a fall. We are thus herein deciding the liability of Lehigh University only. . . . . For the reasons which follow, we conclude that Lehigh University is not liable for the plaintiff's injuries.

I. BACKGROUND.

A. The Night of the Incident.

On November 18, 1988, plaintiff was 19 years and 11 months of age, and was a sophomore at Lehigh University ("Lehigh"). Sometime about 6:00 p.m. plaintiff attended a cocktail party at the Alpha Sigma Phi fraternity. She stayed until approximately 8:00 p.m. During these two hours she consumed four or five vodka collins drinks. She then left the party and returned to her sorority room to change for the next party. At this time she already felt "buzzed". At about 9:00 p.m. she drove with some of the older girls from her sorority up "the hill" to a party at Sigma Alpha Mu fraternity. While at this party, plaintiff drank one bottle of beer and two six inch high plastic cups filled with grain punch. She filled the cups herself from a big vat. At neither of these parties was plaintiff asked to show any identification, nor did she observe any Lehigh University or private security guards. She and a group of friends left this party sometime before midnight, and walked about five minutes to attend a party at Kappa Sigma fraternity. Plaintiff stayed at Kappa Sigma only about one half hour and did not drink any alcohol while there. She and a friend then walked to Sigma Chi fraternity, about a five minute walk. She did not consume any alcohol there either and stayed only about ten minutes before leaving to walk back to her room. By this time she felt drunk and left because it was time to go home. . . .

She walked back to her room alone by following the road to a point in front of the Alpha Tau Omega fraternity house. At this point she decided to leave the road and walk down a "trail" to the next level of the campus since it was a short cut to her sorority. To traverse this trail [called Ho Chi Minh Trail by the students], . . . one must walk across rocks, and in addition, the trail does not have any steps, is not lighted, and is, apparently, a student created shortcut. Students normally do not walk down the trail because it is too steep. For this reason, plaintiff herself had never before attempted to walk down the trail.

Plaintiff does not remember anything after she left the road to walk down the trail, but at some point on the trail she must have fallen and struck her head. The next thing plaintiff remembers is finding herself at the bottom of the trail behind a dormitory, brushing the dust off herself. She then managed to go to the dorm to get assistance from persons inside. A boy from the dorm walked with her to her sorority house where a couple of her sorority sisters took her immediately to defendant St. Luke's Hospital since she had a cut above her eye which was very bloody. This was approximately 2:00 a.m.

The next day, Saturday, plaintiff's father came to take her home. For the rest of the weekend plaintiff suffered from blurred vision, headaches, could not walk or sit up, and did not get a sound sleep. Ultimately, on Monday, plaintiff's pain greatly increased whereupon she was given a CAT scan which revealed a hematoma on her brain and she was operated on immediately. Lehigh was not involved in any respect with the treatment of plaintiff's injuries.

B. Lehigh University's Social Policy re: Alcohol.

In the Summer of 1988, Lehigh published a booklet entitled "A Guide to the Social Policy". In this guide, the policy of Lehigh regarding alcohol use is outlined. Under article D, "Social Policy Rules", the first issue addressed is the "Distribution of Alcohol". The Social Policy states "Party hosts are responsible for ensuring that only persons 21 years of age or over are served alcoholic beverages." (emphasis added.) "Party hosts must hire a uniformed security guard to check identification at the entrance to the room where alcoholic beverages are served." (Social Policy § D.1.c.1.) (emphasis added.) "Hosts must ensure that no one under the age of 21 possesses or consumes alcohol at the party." (Social Policy § D.1.d.) (emphasis added.) Under section 3, "Party Registration", the Social Policy states, inter alia,

"Registration of the party does not constitute University approval of such events." (Social Policy § D.3.) This same language also appears in all capital letters on the registration form itself.

John Smeaton, Assistant Vice President for Student Affairs, Lehigh's designated deponent as the person responsible for, inter alia, student social affairs outside the classroom, testified that Lehigh was not blind to the fact that underage drinking occurs on college campuses, with Lehigh being no exception. Recognizing this, Lehigh revised and updated its Social Policy in an attempt to alter the situation. The Social Policy, while outlining additional responsibilities that the students should observe for the sake of the overall campus environment, essentially tracked state law that a person must be 21 to consume alcohol. In addition to revising its Social Policy regarding alcohol to improve the campus environment, Lehigh hired a person to provide counseling and education regarding drug and alcohol use and abuse.

. . . .

As noted above, one of the requirements that students were to observe under the social Policy was to register any parties. Registration of parties was required simply to provide information to the student life office. It also serves the purpose of reminding the students of the rules and regulations attendant to holding parties; it is a check list to remind the students to follow those rules.

Among the points plaintiff raises, she cites that the registration forms for the parties where she drank alcohol are blank at the space for listing the security guard hired to check identification. It was explained by Mr. Smeaton that this was because the forms are due in his office by 4:00 p.m. on the Wednesday before the party. Security guards would not be hired, and thus known to the host, before that time. Lehigh, however, assumed that guards would be in place "because [it] assumed [its] students would follow the rules and regulations" since "it's an expectation that [Lehigh] has for them." Plaintiff also points to the role of Lehigh security guards, as they have the power to enter the fraternities to check on compliance with Lehigh's regulations. Plaintiff argues that these Lehigh security guards, in fact, have such a duty under the Social Policy. Mr. Smeaton testified that the security guards are to assist the party host. The Social Policy affirms that it is the party host who is responsible for compliance with the Social Policy, not Lehigh.

II. STANDARD OF REVIEW FOR SUMMARY JUDGMENT.

Summary judgment shall be granted when there are no genuine issues of material fact in dispute and the movant is entitled to judgment as a matter of law. Fed.R.Civ.P 56(c).

. . . .

III. DISCUSSION.

Plaintiff's argument is that Lehigh is liable since it (1) undertook a duty to protect underage persons like herself when it promulgated the Social Policy, and that it was negligent by failing to ensure, through its own security guards, compliance by the party hosts with the Social Policy, and (2) is the landlord of the fraternities where plaintiff partook in underage drinking, but failed to control the fraternities.

. . . .

Although plaintiff states that the Social Policy establishes a duty upon Lehigh to enforce its provisions, we do not find such a duty. We conclude that the Pennsylvania courts, faced with the current matter, would not hold that the Social Policy created a special relationship between plaintiff and Lehigh University.

Plaintiff's argument, despite her contention that Lehigh is liable under Restatement (2d) Torts § 323 and § 318, is in fact that Lehigh is responsible for the actions of its (underage) students in loco parentis; that the Social Policy is no more than a detailed written promise to act in loco parentis. Plaintiff argues that the Social Policy amounts to a duty on the part of Lehigh to "control these parties through [its] police function and that defendant failed in this undertaking and, thus through this failure is responsible to the plaintiff for injuries suffered." . . . Inserting the matter of the Social Policy makes no difference and we do not believe that a Pennsylvania court would find otherwise. Since plaintiff is in fact arguing for accountability in loco parentis, *Alumni Association v. Sullivan*, 524 Pa. 356, 572 A.2d 1209 (Pa. 1990) and similar cases are controlling.

At this point, we should explain the interrelationship between plaintiff's adult, minor, and underage status. Plaintiff, being over the age of eighteen at the time of the incident, was an adult. For all facets of life, other than purchasing and consuming alcohol, she was an adult. As to purchasing and consuming alcohol, she would be considered by many to be a minor, i.e., she was legally incompetent to participate in such activities. We believe that a better description of this status is to call her "underage". There can be no question that she was competent, legally or otherwise, to decide, inter alia, whether to break the law, e.g., she was competent to make the initial decision whether to drink alcohol. She thus makes such a decision as an adult who is merely under the legal age for consuming alcohol.

The case of *Bradshaw v. Rawlings*, 612 F.2d 135 (3d Cir. 1979) *cert denied* 446 U.S. 909 (1980) is instructive. After characterizing the interests of plaintiff as remaining free from bodily injury and to recover compensation, and of the college "in the nature of its relationship with its adult students, as well as an interest in avoiding responsibilities that it is incapable of performing", *Bradshaw*, 612 F.2d at 138, the court then examined the relationship between American colleges and their students:

> Our beginning point is a recognition that the modern American college is not an insurer of the safety of its students. The authoritarian role of today's college administrations has been notably diluted in recent decades. Trustees, administrators, and faculties have been required to yield to the expanding rights and privileges of their students. . . . College students today are no longer minors; they are now regarded as adults in almost every phase of community life. . . . There was a time when college administrators and faculties assumed a role in loco parentis. Students were committed to their charge because the students were considered minors. A special relationship was created between college and student that imposed

> a duty on the college to exercise control over student conduct and, reciprocally, gave the students certain rights of protection by the college. The campus revolutions of the late sixties and early seventies were a direct attack by the students on rigid controls by the colleges and were an all-pervasive affirmative demand for more student rights. . . . These movements, taking place simultaneously with legislation and case law lowering the age of majority, produced fundamental changes in our society. . . . Regulation by the college of student life on and off campus has become limited. Adult students now demand and receive expanded rights of privacy in the college life. . . . College administrators no longer control the broad arena of general morals. . . . But today students vigorously claim the right to define and regulate their own lives.
>
> . . . .

Bradshaw, 612 F.2d at 138–40 (footnotes omitted).

. . . .

As a federal district court, we are bound by the rulings from the United States Court of Appeals for the Third Circuit Court, even on matters of state law, unless or until the state's highest court has ruled. . . . *Alumni Association* [*supra*] is such a later ruling from the state's highest court . . . .

In *Alumni Association*, the Pennsylvania Supreme Court [agreeing with Third Circuit precedent] wrote

> We believe that [the Third Circuit's] interpretation does not offend our case law but merely restates our position that a social host must have "knowingly furnished" alcoholic beverages to a minor. . . .

Alumni Association, 572 A.2d at 1212–1213 (emphasis in original). The Pennsylvania Supreme Court declined to adopt a "known or should have known" standard since it would result in imposing a duty in loco parentis upon colleges. . . .

In the instant matter, we too, cannot find that Lehigh acted in a manner consistent with imposing social host liability, i.e., Lehigh did not knowingly furnish alcohol, or knowingly aid or assist plaintiff's consumption of alcohol. Moreover, taken one step further as plaintiff argues it should be, even if Lehigh knowingly failed to prevent alcohol consumption, we could not, nor would we, find a duty in loco parentis. If we were to hold that the Social Policy created a duty to prevent Lehigh students from engaging in underage drinking, we would be finding that Lehigh was potentially liable in loco parentis, despite clear decisions from the Pennsylvania Supreme Court that such cannot form the basis for imposing liability upon a college.

We do conclude, however, that Lehigh assumed no such duty as plaintiff construes it. The Social Policy is just that, a policy by which Lehigh hoped all members of its community would abide. By its very terms, responsibility for compliance with it and with state law at social functions falls upon a function's hosts. Plaintiff's assertion that "the University created a system of enforcement of these parties. They took the system away from the fraternity itself and rather set up a University enforcement procedure and then failed to enforce their own rules" . . . is not supported by the record and goes far beyond the established facts. The Social

Policy and the registration forms explicitly state, inter alia, that registration of a party does not constitute Lehigh University's approval of the party, and that the host is responsible for complying with applicable laws.

. . . .

IV. CONCLUSION.

. . . To require Lehigh to supervise its thousands of students would render null and void the freedoms won by adult students and place Lehigh in loco parentis. The Social Policy was not an assumption of such a duty but rather a policy statement that supposedly responsible adult students should be aware of their own behavior. As noted above, Lehigh's position, and rightly so, was to assume that the adult students were responsible enough to make their own decisions. Lehigh, being detached from the events in question, is not responsible for the indiscretions and poor judgment of one of its underage adult students.

. . . IT IS ORDERED that the motion is GRANTED and summary judgment is entered in favor of Defendant Lehigh University, only, and against Plaintiff.

NOTES

1. In *Booker*, what was Lehigh University's policy on parties? What impact does the policy have on the establishment of a duty of care and ultimate liability? Why did the policy not create a duty of care?

2. Compare *Booker* and *Whitlock*. Neither court found a special relationship between the student and the university; therefore, no affirmative duty of care attached to the defendant universities. Now compare the facts and reasoning in each opinion. How are they similar or different? In particular, consider the fact that in *Booker*, Lehigh University had adopted a specific policy on student parties, noting in its defense that college students and alcohol often spend time together. Booker made an argument that Lehigh's affirmative act in implementing the policy established the duty. Yet the court held in favor of the university, in large part due to the policy language that places responsibility squarely on the parties' hosts. Why would Lehigh's action in policymaking not be enough to establish an affirmative duty of care to see that the policy is followed?

The University of Denver, in *Whitlock*, had no applicable policy on fraternities' use of premises. The court, holding that the university had no affirmative duty of care, made a distinction between negligent action and negligent failure to act. How does the court in *Booker* distinguish Lehigh's policymaking act from the affirmative action that is required in a special relationship?

3. The court in *Booker* declined to adopt plaintiff's argument that Lehigh's Social Policy created a duty of care. To do so, in the court's opinion, would be to recognize the doctrine of *in loco parentis* as applicable to the university-student relationship: a position the court refused to take. The court applied the reasoning in the landmark case of *Bradshaw v. Rawlings*, 612 F.2d 135 (3d Cir. 1979), in which the court rejected an argument from a university student who was severely injured in an automobile accident off campus. The driver of the car was an underage student who had become intoxicated at a class picnic sponsored by the college. The court concluded that the college did not have a special relationship with the student; therefore, no duty of care attached. See Chapter V for full presentation of *Bradshaw* and additional discussion of the *in loco parentis* doctrine.

4. The two cases presented in this section of the chapter — *Booker* and *Whitlock* — highlight examples of alleged negligence in non-classroom settings. Both courts found in favor of the defendant university. How important to the respective rulings is the fact that these injuries occurred away from the classroom setting? For example, the plaintiff in *Whitlock* argued that, because the trampoline was located on property leased by the university to the fraternity, the university had a duty to assure that the fraternity's trampoline was used only under supervised conditions comparable to those in a gymnasium class. The court rejected that argument and found no duty of care. Would a duty of care have attached if the accident occurred in a gymnasium class? See also *Garrett v. Northwest Mississippi Jr. College*, 674 So. 2d 1 (Miss. 1996), and *Niles v. Board of Regents of the University System of Georgia*, 473 S.E.2d 173 (Ga. Ct. App. 1996), presented earlier in this chapter. In both of those cases, the clinching fact appeared to be the level of training and knowledge the respective plaintiffs had in the activity that gave rise to the injury.

c. Defamation

CHONICH v. FORD

321 N.W.2d 693 (Mich. Ct. App. 1982)

BRONSON, J.

Plaintiffs commenced this defamation action on September 17, 1980, in the Wayne County Circuit Court. On March 6, 1981, the circuit court granted defendant's motion for summary judgment on the basis that there existed no genuine issue as to any material fact and holding that defendant's statements were entitled to an absolute privilege. From this order, plaintiffs appeal as of right.

According to plaintiffs' original complaint, defendant [a member of the Wayne County Community College Board of Trustees] read from a written statement at an August 27, 1980, meeting of the [trustees], asserting that Dr. Mostafa Afr and three of his subordinates, the plaintiffs, had all received large home mortgages from American Federal Savings on the same day that Afr transferred $7,000,000 of college funds from First Federal Savings to American Federal Savings. Plaintiffs asserted that these statements were false and defamatory and spoken by defendant with reckless disregard for the truth.

. . . .

We are here concerned with the absolute privilege for statements made during the course of legislative proceedings. This privilege has been held to extend to subordinate and quasi-legislative bodies. *See Gidday v. Wakefield*, 90 Mich. App 752, 755–756 (1979), *lv. den.* 407 Mich. 893 (1979), and the cases cited therein.

Plaintiffs, citing the following excerpt from *Gidday*, argue that defendant here is not entitled to an absolute privilege:

> The finding that the proceeding lends itself to application of the doctrine of absolute privilege does not, however, end our inquiry. The fact that a public official is a member of a legislative body and is in attendance at a duly convened proceeding of such body does not afford him an invitation to undertake an unrestricted slanderous campaign against whomever he pleases, concerning whatever he pleases. In addition to being spoken during a legislative or quasi-legislative session, the statements at issue must be made by the public official while in the process of carrying out an official duty.

Id. at 756.

Plaintiffs assert that the making of the statements in issue was "not an essential function of the defendant's position", that defendant's allegations "were not a proper subject for consideration by the board of trustees", and that "defendant was not acting in a . . . quasi-legislative capacity". Each of these claims will be considered in turn.

Plaintiffs' argument that defendant's conduct did not constitute an essential function of her official duty is premised primarily on the basis that her statements were not made during a debate on an agenda item nor in response to the comments of another person. We have no problem in concluding that the administration of the school's financial matters is, indeed, entrusted to the Wayne County Community College Board of Trustees as an official duty or function. . . . As such, any discussion of possible misuse of college funds is related to the school's development, maintenance, operation and security and must be deemed part of defendant's officially sanctioned functions.

Plaintiffs also assert that discussion of the possible misuse of college funds was not an essential part of defendant's duties because an agreement between the board of trustees and various administrators, including plaintiffs, provides for private disciplinary hearings. We agree with defendant, however, that the alleged misuse of millions of dollars of college funds is more than a mere private employment problem but, rather, an important public topic going to the very financial integrity of the school.

In any case, the existence of alternative dispute resolution mechanisms does not necessarily defeat an absolute privilege. . . .

Plaintiffs assert that the allegations were not a proper subject for consideration at a board meeting because the Open Meetings Act, specifically § 8 of the act, being MCL 15.268(a); MSA 4.1800(18)(a), allows a public body to meet in closed session to consider the dismissal, suspension, or disciplining of its employees. We first note that § 8 of the Open Meetings Act merely permits the public body to meet in a closed session, it does not require a closed meeting. As such, the fact that defendant made her statements at a public meeting does not deprive her of the right to claim an absolute privilege.

Even if plaintiffs correctly asserted that a disciplinary hearing must be held in private, defendant's remarks did not call for the disciplining of anybody. Rather, defendant called for further investigation of charges which had been brought in two anonymous letters, alleging misuse of college funds.

. . . .

Absolute privilege applies to matters of public concern in regard to which, as a matter of policy and the general welfare of society, persons should be allowed to express their views boldly and without fear of legal repercussions. Absolute privileges are extended so that the public's right to know will be maximized and the numerous legislative bodies in society cannot operate in the dark, knowing that their activities will not likely be subject to public scrutiny.

Plaintiffs' unduly restrictive vision of the circumstances under which an absolute privilege may be claimed would defeat the policy reasons underlying the recognition of absolute privilege. If members of legislative bodies are not free to speak their minds on those matters within their domain because the subject of their remarks is not officially part of an agenda, a body's majority could stop important information from ever coming before the public eye simply by refusing to place the item on the agenda. Certainly the taxpaying public which supports Wayne County Community College would have the right to know that its tax dollars are being misused for personal gain. It may well be that in this case defendant's statements were recklessly made. However, this is not a matter for our resolution. If only a qualified privilege were recognized for legislative communications, the public's right to know would be hampered as officials with legitimate information would be inhibited from bringing it to the public's attention — not because the information is thought to be arguably inaccurate — but because the officials would know that their comments could entangle them in a legal dispute which almost surely could only be resolved through a full trial.

. . . .

Affirmed.

NOTES

1. The decision in *Chonich* not only offers comfort to public officials who are often called upon to publicly address serious matters of public concern, but also offers a necessary legal lesson on defamation law. Defamation claims are relatively rare in higher education, perhaps due to the strength of absolute privilege. To make a successful defamation claim, several elements must be proven: (1) defamatory language, (2) of or concerning the plaintiff, (3) publication of this language to a third party, and (4) damage to the plaintiff's reputation. WILLIAM PROSSER & W. PAGE KEETON, PROSSER AND KEETON ON TORTS 773 (5th ed. 1984).

Often, of course, the public official is the plaintiff in a defamation case. For example, a member of a board of trustees is harshly criticized in the press, and the trustee believes he or she has been unlawfully defamed. In such cases, the plaintiff must show the first four elements presented above, plus two more elements: (1) falsity in the alleged defamatory language, and (2) fault on the part of the plaintiff, either actual malice or reckless disregard for the truth. *See N.Y. York Times v.*

Sullivan, 376 U.S. 254 (1964). "Public official" status applies to those people who have responsibility and control over the conduct of governmental affairs, such as members of a board of trustees. *See Rosenblatt v. Baer*, 383 U.S. 75 (1966).

These same two additional elements must also be shown by plaintiffs who are public figures. Decided on a case-by-case basis, a public figure attains that status through (1) pervasive fame or notoriety such that he becomes a public figure in all contexts and for all purposes; or (2) the individual's voluntary injection or involuntary draw into a particular public controversy so that he is a public figure for a limited range of issues. *Gertz v. Robert Welch, Inc.*, 418 U.S. 323 (1974). Examples of public figures in higher education might include presidents and other high-ranking administrators, coaches and athletic directors, and others who achieve a measure of notoriety. In *Waterson v. Cleveland State University*, 639 N.E.2d 1236 (Ohio 1994), for example, the court found a university deputy chief of police to be a public official. (He had sued the editor of the student newspaper for defamation stemming from an editorial written about him; the court did not find actual malice and dismissed the claim). Actual malice is difficult to prove, requiring the plaintiff to show that the defendant made false statements with knowledge of their falsity or with reckless disregard for their truth.

2. The defendant in *Chonich* successfully asserted an absolute privilege defense. There are other common defenses in defamation claims as well. First, consent to publication is a defense. *Baker v. Lafayette Coll.*, 504 A.2d 247 (Pa. Super. Ct. 1986). Second, truth (or substantial truth) can be a defense in cases where the plaintiff has the burden to prove falsity. *Wynne v. Loyola Univ. of Chicago*, 741 N.E.2d 669 (Ill. App. Ct. 2000). Finally, in cases where absolute privilege is not a viable defense (i.e., in cases not involving statements made in quasi-legislative or quasi-judicial proceedings like disciplinary hearings), there may be a *qualified* privilege defense.

In order to assert a qualified privilege defense, the defendant must show three elements: (a) performance of acts within their professional duties; (b) release of allegedly defamatory information only to those individuals who have the need and the right to know; and (c) good faith conduct without malice. For examples of how courts interpret and apply these defenses, see *Slack v. Stream*, 988 So. 2d 516 (Ala. 2008); *Anas v. Brown*, 702 N.Y.S.2d 732 (N.Y. App. Div. 2000); *Havlik v. Johnson & Wales Univ.*, 509 F.3d 25 (1st Cir. 2007); *Ostaz v. Med. Coll. of Ohio*, 683 N.E.2d 352 (Ohio Ct. App. 1996); *Washington v. Central State Univ.*, 699 N.E.2d 1016 (Ohio Ct. Cl. 1998).

In *Slack*, a faculty member sued his former department chair for defamation after the former chair sent a letter of reprimand he had written about the faculty member to the faculty member's new chair (at another university). The court ruled in favor of the faculty member, holding that the chair had failed to follow campus policy on investigation of wrongdoing (here, a claim of plagiarism) and that he acted willfully and maliciously when he sent the reprimand to the faculty member's new chair. As a result, no privilege defense was available to the defendant.

3. What about the viability of defamation lawsuits stemming from faculty evaluation of student work or, more controversially perhaps, from letters of recommendation? In *Olsson v. Indiana University Board of Trustees*, 571 N.E.2d

585 (Ind. Ct. App. 1991), a graduate of a teacher education program applied for a teaching job at an elementary school. The school's principal contacted the applicant's major professor and asked her for an assessment of the applicant's student teaching performance. The professor wrote a letter with a marginal evaluation and the applicant did not get the job. She filed suit and the court held for the university. The professor had a qualified privilege in her work, and the letter was not written or delivered with recklessness, ill will, or malice. Nor, the court reasoned, was it widely disseminated.

2. Contract Liability

LINKAGE CORPORATION v. TRUSTEES OF BOSTON UNIVERSITY
679 N.E.2d 191 (Mass. 1997)

Greaney, J.

This dispute arises out of an agreement between Linkage Corporation (Linkage) and Boston University that called for Linkage to create and provide educational, training, and other programs of a technical nature at a satellite facility owned by Boston University. Linkage claims that the agreement was renewed by Boston University and then unlawfully terminated; Boston University claims that the agreement was lawfully terminated and never renewed. Linkage['s] ten-count complaint . . . asserted theories of contract and tort liability . . . Boston University's answer contained nine counterclaims stating various theories of wrongdoing on Linkage's part . . . . The jury . . . found Boston University liable for breaches of contract, defamation, [and] wrongful interference with advantageous relations . . . . The jury rejected all but one part of Boston University's counterclaims. . . . [T]he judge decided several posttrial motions . . . allowing judgment notwithstanding the verdict on some of Linkage's recovery and denying Boston University a new trial on the remainder. Both parties claimed appeals, and we granted Boston University's application for direct appellate review.

We conclude that the jury's findings that the agreement had been renewed were warranted, and the judge should not have granted Boston University judgment notwithstanding the verdict on the renewal claim. . . .

1. *Background.* We recount at some length the facts that could have been found by the jury. Because of the jury findings in favor of Linkage, we base our recitation on the evidence and inferences most favorable to it.

Linkage was founded in 1988 by Philip Harkins to facilitate the creation of corporate training programs for companies and universities. . . .

Boston University became aware of Harkins's plans to start Linkage and expressed an interest in working with Linkage to develop training programs. Boston University had recently acquired the Wang Institute, a facility consisting of an 80,000 square foot building located on 200 acres in Tyngsborough, and had assumed the debt on the facility. Harkins met with J. Joseph Meng, Boston

University's vice-president for external programs, and discussed his ideas for training offerings with Meng. Meng was looking for a way to produce a revenue stream that would offset Boston University's considerable overhead on the new facility, and Linkage's programs presented a possible solution to this revenue problem.

Together with Dennis Hart of Boston University's office of general counsel, Harkins and Meng drafted an agreement that covered the operation of Linkage's training programs at the Wang Institute (base agreement). Under the terms of the base agreement, Linkage's performance was to be measured by revenue produced, and Linkage was to receive bonuses for achieving revenue goals. The base agreement also contained a provision restricting both Linkage and Boston University from hiring each other's employees for a period of one year following the termination of the agreement.

At the time that Linkage and Boston University undertook performance of the base agreement, Meng reported to John Silber, the president of Boston University, and to Jon Westling, executive vice-president and Silber's second in command. Silber reviewed the base agreement in draft form and discussed its provisions with Meng, but Meng understood that he had actual authority to negotiate and sign the agreement with Linkage.

Meng and Harkins executed the base agreement on August 1, 1988. . . . The base agreement was limited to a term of three years, ending August 1, 1991. Under the base agreement, Linkage was to manage and market educational programs and services at the Wang facility, renamed the Boston University Corporate Education Center (BUCEC). Boston University agreed to provide over-all direction and supervision of BUCEC. . . .

. . . .

Another division of Boston University, the Metropolitan College (MET College), ran a training program, professional development seminars (PDS), under contract with another independent training and development company similar to Linkage. When the PDS contract expired at the end of June, 1989, Linkage assumed responsibility for this program. Eventually, Linkage executed a contract with Boston University to run the PDS program (MET College contract). The compensation under the MET College contract differed from Linkage's compensation under the base agreement: under the latter, Boston University received all revenues from the programs and Linkage was paid a fee with incentive bonuses, while under the MET College contract, Linkage received all revenues, paid all expenses, and remitted a 9.15 per cent royalty to Boston University. . . . The MET College contract was executed on February 6, 1990. . . .

In August, 1990, Harkins and Meng began discussing renewal of the base agreement, scheduled to terminate on August 1, 1991. Harkins wanted to begin negotiations early so that, in the event the base agreement was not renewed, Linkage would have time to replace Boston University as a client. In addition to the renewal of the base agreement, Harkins and Meng negotiated the incorporation of the MET College contract into the base agreement.

In March, 1991, Meng and Harkins, under the direction of Hart, agreed to fold the MET College contract into the base agreement, with the result that Linkage would no longer directly incur the expenses for or receive the revenue from the PDS program and instead would receive a fee for management. . . .

. . . .

Assuming that the base agreement would be renewed, Harkins and his management team prepared a business plan for the next three years, which was presented at the April meeting of Boston University's trustees in Scottsdale, Arizona. . . . The Linkage business plan was well received by the assembled senior Boston University officials.

On April 28, 1991, following the presentation of Linkage's business plan at the trustees' meeting, Hart, Meng, and Harkins met, together with Linkage's chief financial officer and the person in charge of financial operations on the Boston University campus. At that meeting, it was agreed that the MET College contract would be folded into the renewal of the base agreement, and new compensation arrangements were reviewed. On May 21, 1991, Meng and Harkins executed an agreement . . . terminating the MET College contract and making it part of the base agreement (May 21 agreement). . . .

. . . .

On May 29, 1991, Silber's chief of staff sent a memorandum on behalf of Silber to Westling, Hart, and Condon, asking about the status of the renewal agreement. Nestling and Meng subsequently joined Silber in Germany [who was there on business]. In his discussions with Meng in Europe, Silber raised no concerns about Linkage, the renewal agreement, or BUCEC. Silber told Meng that he wanted additional information on Linkage. He and Meng agreed that Harkins would repeat the presentation made by Harkins to the trustees for Silber's benefit after he returned from Europe.

On June 24, 1991, Harkins met with Silber, Westling, and Meng. Silber was rude and confrontational during this meeting, and his actions made it impossible for Harkins to present his business plan. Silber abruptly and angrily left the meeting after only twenty-five minutes. . . .

After leaving the meeting, Silber ordered an unannounced internal audit of Linkage. Harkins, notified of the audit by his staff on his arrival at a BUCEC conference in New Jersey, immediately returned to Massachusetts and assisted the auditors in gathering information for the audit.

Unbeknownst to Harkins or Meng, Silber had been in direct contact with various individuals associated with Linkage's operations at BUCEC. Since his return from Germany, Silber had been in contact with James Devlin, his son-in-law and a part-time instructor in some of the BUCEC programs, and Robert Daniels, a Boston University employee who had originally been hired to work on BUCEC projects by Linkage. . . .

On July 1, Silber again met with Harkins, Meng, and Westling. During the course of that meeting, Silber contended that he was free to hire Linkage's employees despite the express no-hire provision in the base agreement and asked which employees were the most valuable. Harkins declined to give him this information and insisted that Silber had no right to hire Linkage's employees under the base agreement. . . . Silber revealed that he was aware of certain complaints about Linkage. At the close of the meeting, in response to a question by Harkins, Silber told him that the May 21 agreement that Harkins had signed with Meng was ineffective.

Meng, Silber, and Harkins met for the final time on July 3, 1991. At this meeting, Silber produced a preliminary audit report, which, he asserted, gave cause to terminate any agreements between the parties. Silber then demanded that Harkins sign a letter, which, in addition to other provisions, waived the no-hire provisions of the base agreement. When Harkins declined, citing his desire to consult with an attorney, Silber withdrew the first letter and handed Harkins a second letter terminating the base agreement between the parties for cause, effective immediately, based on an unfavorable audit and Linkage's failure to cooperate with the auditors. The letter also terminated the MET College contract between the parties.

. . . .

[At a later meeting with Linkage employees], Westling told [them] that Boston University's contract with Linkage had been terminated "for cause." . . . Harkins then met with his employees. Harkins told his employees that he would not seek legal recourse from individual employees if they were offered and accepted employment from Boston University. Harkins indicated that he would seek such recourse from Boston University for violating the no-hire provision of the base agreement.

Boston University officials came to BUCEC with prepared letters offering employment to selected Linkage employees. While Harkins was gathering his belongings, Boston University conducted interviews with Linkage employees and hired twenty-eight of Linkage's thirty-two employees on the spot. . . .

. . . .

After Boston University took over operations at BUCEC, Daniels was hired to head the conference programs at BUCEC, reporting directly to the executive director, and received a raise in pay. . . .

The internal audit of Linkage operations continued after the takeover. Investigations by the Boston University internal audit department and outside auditors employed by Boston University produced evidence of minor errors in Linkage's reporting of financial matters. Boston University alleged after the termination of the base agreement that a Linkage employee had made backup copies of some Linkage files and that these backup copies were missing.

After the takeover, Linkage was unable to replace Boston University as a client, due in part to its reduced staff and to the conditions surrounding the termination of its contractual relationship with Boston University. Although it has rebuilt to some extent in the time since the termination of its contract with Boston University, the company has not been able to regrow its business to the point where it was in July, 1991.

3. *Contract claims.* We next examine the jury's responses to a series of special questions concerning Linkage's claims for violations of pertinent agreements. . . .

(a) Renewal agreement. The jury found that Boston University had entered into the renewal agreement with Linkage and had committed a material breach of that agreement. The jury awarded damages to Linkage, in the amount of $2,148,000 for lost profits and $330,358 for out-of-pocket damages. The judge entered judgment notwithstanding the verdict on these findings, but later partially vacated this order and reinstated the jury's award for out-of-pocket damages. We conclude that the jury's findings on this claim should be upheld in their entirety.

Linkage contended that Boston University became bound to the renewal agreement on May 21, 1991, when Meng and Harkins signed an agreement that (1) terminated the MET College contract effective July 1, 1991, (2) provided that the activities covered by that contract would thereafter be governed by the base agreement, and (3) stated that the "base agreement is being revised and renewed effective July 1, 1991." For Boston University to be bound by Meng's action, the jury had to find, as a fact, that Meng had either actual or apparent authority to enter into the renewal agreement, or that Boston University had acquiesced in, or failed lawfully to disavow, any unauthorized conduct by Meng, and consequently had become bound by that conduct through ratification. The judge carefully instructed the jury on the requirements for establishing a binding agreement under these theories, but the special verdict form submitted to the jury did not include an express question relating to the existence of actual authority. It is not of consequence whether the evidence would have supported a finding of actual authority because the jury found that Boston University was bound by the renewal agreement on the basis of both apparent authority and ratification. There was sufficient evidence to support both of these findings.

(i) *Apparent authority.* "Apparent or ostensible authority 'results from conduct by the principal which causes a third person reasonably to believe that a particular person . . . has authority to enter into negotiations or to make representations as his agent.' . . . If a third person goes on to change his position in reliance on this reasonable belief, the principal is estopped from denying that the agency is authorized." (Citations omitted.) *Hudson v. Massachusetts Prop. Ins. Underwriting Ass'n*, 386 Mass. 450, 457 (1982). We inquire whether conduct of Boston University's executives warranted a finding that Harkins reasonably believed Meng had authority to enter the renewal agreement.

The jury reasonably could have made the following findings. As Boston University's vice-president for external programs, Meng had virtual autonomy in supervising Linkage's programs at BUCEC. He negotiated and signed the base agreement on behalf of Boston University. Meng was responsible for ensuring Linkage's performance under the base agreement and the MET College contract. . . . Throughout negotiations with Linkage for renewal of the base agreement and the incorporation of the MET College contract therein, Meng was Boston University's primary representative. . . . It was therefore reasonable for Harkins to believe that Meng had the authority to sign the May 21 agreement, thereby binding Boston University to the termination of the MET College contract, the "fold-in" of that contract to the base agreement, and the renewal agreement.

. . . .

Based on the evidence, and their assessment of the credibility of the witnesses, the jury properly could have found that Meng had apparent authority to sign the May 21 agreement, and that the execution of that agreement bound Boston University to the renewal of the base agreement on terms that had been agreed to by Meng and Harkins.

(ii) *Ratification.* Where an agent lacks actual authority to agree on behalf of his principal, the principal may still be bound if the principal acquiesces in the agent's action, or fails promptly to disavow the unauthorized conduct after disclosure of material facts. "It is the instant duty of a principal, upon ascertaining the facts, at once to disaffirm an act done in his name by an agent in execution of a power conferred but in a mode not sanctioned by the terms of the agency or in excess or misuse of the authority given." *Boice-Perrine Co. v. Kelley*, 243 Mass. 327, 330–31 (1923). . . . Ratification relates back, and has the same effect, as a prior grant of authority by the principal to the agent. *See Canton v. Bruno*, 361 Mass. 598, 607 n.8 (1972); *White v. Apsley Rubber Co.*, 194 Mass. 97, 100 (1907).

The jury could have found that any deficiency in Meng's authority to execute the May 21 agreement was obviated by subsequent conduct of Boston University officials, especially Westling in his capacity as provost and executive vice-president, whose approval was ostensibly required by the March 5 directive. Meng sent copies of the May 21 agreement to Condon and Westling immediately on its execution. The draft of the renewal agreement was attached to the May 21 agreement, as was a memorandum from Meng explaining the renewal agreement and explicitly asking whether any further review was needed to secure approval. Harkins and Meng met with Westling on May 22 so that Harkins could present his business plan. Westling did not raise any objections to the renewal agreement, nor did he indicate that the agreement required further approval from him or others before it could take effect. Condon never responded to Meng's query as to whether any further action would be needed. Silber also failed to repudiate Meng's action on behalf of the university. When he met with Meng in Europe in late May, Silber told Meng only that he wanted to "get up to speed" on the Linkage operation, and Silber expressed no objection to the agreement or that Meng had been unauthorized to enter into it without any further approval. Thus, neither Silber nor Westling raised any question about the validity of the renewal agreement until the meeting on July 1, when Silber finally told Harkins and Meng that, in Silber's opinion, Boston University was not bound by the renewal agreement.

Based on this sequence of events, the jury reasonably could have found that ratification of Meng's execution of the May 21 agreement by Boston University followed from the informed acquiescence of Westling, Silber, and other Boston University officials, and from their failure promptly to disavow Meng's conduct after learning material facts.

. . . .

7. *Disposition.* It will be easier to vacate the existing judgments and to have the judge then enter a single judgment in keeping with the conclusions reached in this opinion. The judgment entered on March 28, 1995, and the supplemental judgment entered on April 12, 1995, are vacated. The order granting Boston University judgment notwithstanding the verdict on the jury's findings that a renewed agreement was in effect and had been violated is vacated, and the jury's findings on

that claim are reinstated. A new judgment is to enter awarding Linkage damages, together with attorney's fees, costs, and interest, in accordance with this opinion, particularly Part 6. The order denying Boston University's motion for a new trial is affirmed.

NOTE

For purposes of institutional governance and liability, there are several sources of potential legal authority: among them are express authority, implied authority, and apparent authority. Express authority is exactly what it sounds like — an employee, for example, is given express authority to perform a certain function as outlined expressly in an employment contract or institutional policy (e.g., an employee may have express authority to enter into a contract with a service provider). For employment purposes at a university, a Board of Trustees will likely be the entity that has the express authority to approve employment contracts. *See, e.g., Drake v. Medical College of Ohio*, 698 N.E.2d 463 (Ohio Ct. App. 1997). Therefore, reliance by a presumed, but not formally approved, employee may not be enough to win a contract claim, even when that employee's presumptive supervisor has indicated approval. For example, promises of this sort (employment, contract renewal, etc.) cannot generally be made by heads of academic departments. *See, e.g., Marson v. Northwestern State Univ.*, 607 So. 2d 1093 (La. Ct. App. 1992).

Implied authority belongs to employees who have the ability to perform acts that are necessary and appropriate for the position. In other words, implied authority is intentionally granted, but not expressly authorized. For example, in *Williams v. Case Western Reserve University*, No. 87719, 2006 LEXIS 6116 (Ohio Ct. App. Nov. 22, 2006), the court held that despite the specific three-year commitment made to a non-tenure track instructor, the university, as an employer, had implied authority to terminate the instructor for poor performance.

Apparent authority is neither express nor implied, but arises in situations where a third party reasonably infers, usually from one party's conduct, that actual (express or implied) authority existed. Apparent authority, where it exists, protects third parties who rely on the agent's conduct. For example, consider *Earl v. St. Louis University*, 875 S.W.2d 234 (Mo. Ct. App. 1994). Earl worked as the chief financial officer for St. Louis University Hospital. The university eliminated his position and he offered a severance agreement, which the vice president of the hospital signed. The president later rejected the agreement, and Earl sued. The court affirmed a finding in favor of Earl, relying on evidence that the vice president had apparent authority, given past practice at the university, to bind the university to such agreements.

3. § 1983 Liability

KASHANI v. PURDUE UNIVERSITY

813 F.2d 843 (7th Cir. 1987)

Eschbach, Senior Circuit Judge

Hamid R. Kashani sued Purdue University and various of its officials under 42 U.S.C. § 1983, alleging that he was terminated from a doctoral program at Purdue University on the basis of national origin. The trial court held his claims both for damages and for reinstatement barred by the Eleventh Amendment. In this appeal we uphold the conclusion that Purdue University shares in the sovereign immunity of the State of Indiana under the Eleventh Amendment. We hold further, however, that the Eleventh Amendment does not bar suit against the officials for the injunctive relief of reinstatement into the doctoral program.

I

Hamid R. Kashani, an Iranian, was terminated from the doctoral program in electrical engineering at Purdue University in Indiana during the "Hostage Crisis." He filed a section 1983 action, alleging discrimination on the basis of national origin contrary to the Equal Protection Clause. The suit named as defendants Purdue University; the trustees and president of the university, in their official capacities; various graduate school officials and members of the Ph.D. Review committee, in both their official and individual capacities. Kashani sought both monetary damages and reinstatement from all defendants, except for the claims against the officials in their individual capacities, which sought only monetary damages.

The district court dismissed for lack of subject matter jurisdiction the claims for monetary relief against the University and against the various officials in their official capacity on the basis that Purdue was entitled to the protection of the Eleventh Amendment. The court subsequently dismissed all claims for injunctive relief, on the basis of the Eleventh Amendment. To enable appeal, the parties stipulated to dismissal of the remaining claims for monetary relief against officials in their individual capacities. Kashani does not appeal these stipulated dismissals. Kashani thus appeals only the claims against the university and against its officials in their official capacity. Against both, Kashani seeks monetary and injunctive relief. For the reasons stated below, we hold that Purdue is an arm of the state entitled to the protection of the Eleventh Amendment. We thus affirm the dismissal of all claims against the university and all claims against the officials for monetary relief. We hold, however, that the injunctive relief of reinstatement is not barred by the Eleventh Amendment and thus reverse the dismissal of the claims for injunctive relief against the officials in their official capacity.

II

The jurisdictional bar of the Eleventh Amendment protects the state and its agencies; it does not shield political subdivisions. The question here, then, is whether Purdue "is more like a county or city than it is like an arm of the State." *Mount Healthy School District v. Doyle*, 429 U.S. 274, 280 (1977) (local school board not entitled to immunity). The question of sovereign immunity for a state university is not unexplored territory. The vast majority of cases considering the issue have found state universities to be forfended by the Eleventh Amendment. *E.g., Hall v. Medical College of Ohio at Toledo*, 742 F.2d 299 (6th Cir. 1984), *cert. denied*, 469 U.S. 1113 (1985); *Cannon v. University of Health Sciences/The Chicago Medical School*, 710 F.2d 351 (7th Cir. 1983) (Southern Illinois University and University of Illinois); *Jackson v. Hayakawa*, 682 F.2d 1344 (9th Cir. 1982) (San Francisco State College); *United Carolina Bank v. Board of Regents*, 665 F.2d 553, 558 (5th Cir. 1982) (Stephen F. Austin State University); *Ronwin v. Shapiro*, 657 F.2d 1071, 1073 (9th Cir. 1981) (University of Arizona); *Perez v. Rodriguez Bou*, 575 F.2d 21 (1st Cir. 1978) (University of Puerto Rico); *Brennan v. University of Kansas*, 451 F.2d 1287 (10th Cir. 1971). In fact, the parties' briefs and our own research have failed to reveal a single circuit court opinion holding a state university not entitled to Eleventh Amendment immunity. . . .

Although state universities have consistently been found to be entitled to immunity, courts reexamine the issue with regard to the facts of each case "because the states have adopted different schemes, both intra and interstate, in constituting their institutions of higher learning." *United Carolina Bank v. Board of Regents*, 665 F.2d 553, 557 (5th Cir. 1982). . . .

A

Courts have looked to a number of criteria in deciding this issue. The most important factor is the extent of the entity's financial autonomy from the state. . . . Courts consider the extent of state funding, the state's oversight and control of the university's fiscal affairs, the university's ability independently to raise funds, whether the state taxes the university, and whether a judgment against the university would result in the state increasing its appropriations to the university.

Purdue receives approximately one third of its income directly from the state. For example, in the academic year 1982–83, the university received slightly over 36% of its income from state appropriations. Other sources, with approximate percentages, were auxiliary enterprises (17%); student fees (16%); gifts, grants, and contracts (13%); sales and services (7%); student aid (4%); federal appropriations (3%); organized activities (2%); endowment income (.1%).

. . . .

If a judgment were awarded against Purdue, the state treasury would not write out a check to Kashani. But in view of the fact that Purdue is by design dependent on state appropriations, which are evidently carefully geared through close oversight to meet the changing financial needs of the university, it is apparent that the payment would directly affect the state treasury. Indiana has not created an entity with a separate financial basis; it has created one that is dependent upon and functionally integrated with the state treasury. Our examination of the extent of Purdue's fiscal autonomy, then, strongly indicates that Purdue is entitled to Eleventh Amendment immunity.

B

In determining whether Purdue is independent of the state, we must consider, beside Indiana's financial constraints on the university, the general legal status of the university. . . .

. . . .

Very significant in considering whether Purdue has sufficient autonomy from the State of Indiana to be considered more like a county or city than like an arm of the state is the fact that the majority of the members of Purdue's governing council, the Board of Trustees, are selected by the Governor of Indiana. Indiana Statutes Ann. 20-12-37-2 (Burns 1985). . . . The Governor has the right to select seven of the ten Trustees; the Purdue Alumni Association selects the other three. The Governor officially appoints all ten. The Trustees serve terms ranging from one to three years.

The Board has the right to regulate the use of university property and the conduct of persons on that property, to set fees and tuition, to discipline students and faculty, to prescribe admission standards, to establish curricula, to set academic standards, and to award financial aid. Ind. Code § 20-12-1-2. It would seem that the delegation of such powers is necessary to enable the university to function. The Trustees are also authorized to enter into contracts; to sue, be sued, settle lawsuits, and pay judgments; to exercise eminent domain; to engage in construction projects and own land. The various powers granted are an indication of independence. But that is undercut by the fact that the majority of the members of the Board itself are selected by the chief executive officer of the state and serve for a maximum of three years. Thus the independence is circumscribed. Moreover, the legislature expressly retained the power to amend or repeal the duties and powers of the Trustees. Ind. Code § 20-12-36-6. From that perspective, the functions granted the board appear less like the independent powers of a city or county than like the authority delegated to an instrumentality of the state to spare the legislature the need to ratify its every action. Also these powers are granted the university only so that it is able to carry out its primary purpose of education, in contrast to a city or county, whose exercise of such powers, in far more extensive form, is its very raison d'etre.

The Court in Mount Healthy looked not just to whether the entity was formed with independent powers from the state but also to whether it served the state as a whole or only a region. *Mount Healthy School District v. Doyle*, 429 U.S. 274, 280 (1977) Purdue educates students from all parts of the state. The local powers that it has are granted it to enable it to perform that function. Thus, we conclude as did the district court that the Eleventh Amendment shields Purdue.

III

Although the Amendment bars all claims against Purdue and the damages claims against its officials in their official capacities, it does not thwart the claims against the officials in their official capacities for the injunctive relief of reinstatement. Under the doctrine of *Ex parte Young*, 209 U.S. 123 (1908), a suit for prospective injunctive relief is not deemed a suit against the state and thus is not barred by the Eleventh Amendment. *Edelman v. Jordan*, 415 U.S. 651, 664 (1974); *Quern v.*

Jordan, 440 U.S. 332, 337 (1979). We recently held that an injunction ordering reinstatement of a pharmacist "is clearly prospective in effect and thus falls outside the prohibitions of the Eleventh Amendment." *Elliott v. Hinds*, 786 F.2d 298, 302 (7th Cir. 1986). The same result has been reached by the Sixth Circuit regarding reinstatement of a medical student, *Hall v. Medical College of Ohio at Toledo*, 742 F.2d 299, 307 (6th Cir. 1984), *cert. denied*, 469 U.S. 1113 (1985), and by the Second Circuit regarding reinstatement of an employee to the payroll, *Dwyer v. Regan*, 777 F.2d 825, 836 (2nd Cir. 1985). We must thus remand for consideration of the reinstatement claim based on Kashani's allegation that the defendant officials intentionally discriminated against him on the basis of his national origin.

IV

For the foregoing reasons, the dismissal of Kashani's claims against Purdue University and the dismissal of the claims for damages against the defendant officials are AFFIRMED. The dismissal of the claims for injunctive relief against the officials in their official capacity is REVERSED and REMANDED for further proceedings consistent with this opinion.

NOTES

1. The court in *Kashani* held that the Eleventh Amendment barred all claims against the defendant Purdue University and damages claims against the university's officials in their official capacities. The court did not, however, hold so for the claims against the officials in their official capacities for the student's injunctive relief of reinstatement to the program. Why and how did the court make this distinction? How do the differences between claims for monetary relief and injunctive relief play a role in the court's determination?

2. Are community colleges and other government-supported two-year institutions afforded Eleventh Amendment immunity protection as arms of the state? The results are mixed across the country. For example, in *Griner v. Southeast Community College*, 95 F. Supp. 2d 1054 (D. Neb. 2000), the court held that Southeast Community College was not an arm of the state and, thus, not entitled to Eleventh Amendment immunity because it enjoyed significant independence and autonomy from the state with respect to its ability and authority to acquire operating funds from local sources. In contrast, see *Miller v. Guilford Technical Community College*, No. 2:96CV00329, 1998 U.S. Dist. LEXIS 15153 (M.D.N.C. June 15, 1998), where the court held that the community college defendant, as a state-funded institution, was entitled to Eleventh Amendment immunity as an arm of the state.

HALL v. MEDICAL COLLEGE OF OHIO AT TOLEDO

742 F.2d 299 (6th Cir. 1984)

WEICK, SENIOR CIRCUIT JUDGE.

Robert Hall, Plaintiff-Appellant, has appealed to this Court from a summary judgment of the Federal District Court for the Northern District of Ohio, Western Division, dismissing his civil rights complaint which he has filed against the Medical College of Ohio at Toledo (MCO) and its administrative and faculty personnel. In that complaint, Hall sought damages and reinstatement as a medical student of the College, following his dismissal therefrom on June 26, 1978, for academic dishonesty, after notice of the charges and hearing thereon and an administrative appeal. Hall alleged racial discrimination by MCO and its personnel, in violation of 42 U.S.C. §§ 1981, 1983, and 2000d, and a violation of his constitutional due process rights.

Hall filed a motion for partial summary judgment, and MCO and its personnel also filed a motion for summary judgment. The District Court, in a carefully prepared opinion and order, denied Hall's motion for partial summary judgment and granted the defendants' motion for summary judgment. The court held that MCO is an agency, arm and alter ego of the State of Ohio, and that suit against the school and its officers is barred by the Eleventh Amendment to the United States Constitution . . . .

With respect to the school personnel, the court held that they had a complete defense of qualified immunity from personal liability for damages for acts performed within the scope of their official duties. The court then entered judgment dismissing Hall's entire complaint, including his claim for reinstatement.

The appeal has been heard by this Court on the briefs, appendices and arguments of counsel. For the reasons stated, we affirm the judgment of the District Court.

I
Eleventh Amendment

A

A suit by a private party which, for past acts or omissions, seeks to impose legal or equitable liability payable from state funds, is barred in a federal court by the Eleventh Amendment. *Edelman v. Jordan*, 415 U.S. 651 (1974). This is so even when only individual state officials are the nominal defendants but the state is the real, substantial party in interest. *Ford Motor Co. v. Department of Treasury*, 323 U.S. 459, 464 (1945).

When an action is brought against a public agency or institution, and/or the officials thereof, the application of the Eleventh Amendment turns on whether said agency or institution can be characterized as an arm or alter ego of the state, or whether it should be treated instead as a political subdivision of the state. *Mt.*

Healthy City School District Board of Education v. Doyle, 429 U.S. 274, 280 (1977).

. . .

The great majority of cases addressing the question of Eleventh Amendment immunity for public colleges and universities have found such institutions to be arms of their respective state governments and thus immune from suit. [citations omitted]

[The court proceeded to apply the nine-point analysis employed by the Third Circuit in *Blake v. Kline*, 612 F.2d 718 (3d Cir. 1979)]

In *Blake*, Judge Rosenn utilized the following criteria to examine the position of Pennsylvania's Public School Employees' Retirement Board vis-a-vis the Commonwealth itself:

> Local law and decisions defining the status and nature of the agency involved in its relation to the sovereign are factors to be considered, but only one of a number that are of significance. Among the other factors, no one of which is conclusive, perhaps the most important is whether, in the event plaintiff prevails, the payment of the judgment will have to be made out of the state treasury; significant here also is whether the agency has the funds or the power to satisfy the judgment. Other relevant factors are whether the agency is performing a governmental or proprietary function; whether it has been separately incorporated; the degree of autonomy over its operations; whether it has the power to sue and be sued and to enter into contracts; whether its property is immune from state taxation, and whether the sovereign has immunized itself from responsibility for the agency's operations.

612 F.2d at 722. We will now proceed to examine these factors with respect to the Medical College of Ohio.

B

Status and Nature of MCO under Ohio Law?

In 1964, the Ohio General Assembly created the Toledo State College of Medicine (renamed the Medical College of Ohio at Toledo in 1967). 130 Ohio Laws pt. 2, at 183 (1964) (codified at Ohio Rev. Code Ann. §§ 3350.01-.05 (Page 1980)) . . . .

We also see that Ohio considers such colleges and universities to be part of the "State" for purposes of its sovereign immunity. In *Thacker v. Board of Trustees*, 35 Ohio St. 2d 49 (1973), overruled in part on other grounds, *Schenkolewski v. Cleveland Metroparks System*, 67 Ohio St. 2d 31, 36 & n.4 (1981), the state supreme court reaffirmed an earlier holding that Ohio State University and its hospital "are instrumentalities of the state of Ohio and as such are not suable in tort."

. . . It would therefore appear that Ohio considers MCO an "arm of the state," and not merely a political subdivision thereof. . . .

Judgment Payable from State or Independent MCO Funds?

The second and third factors identified by the Third Circuit in Blake are perhaps the most important of all: Would recovery in damages by Hall against MCO and/or Drs. Ruppert and Kemph in their official capacities require the payment of state funds? In this connection, we must again consult the state statutes governing the school.

The Ohio legislature is required to support MCO "by such sums and in such manner as it may provide," but "support may also come from other sources." Ohio Rev. Code Ann. §§ 3350.05 (Page 1980). According to the affidavit of MCO President Ruppert, attached to the defendants' summary judgment motion, this "support . . . from other sources" constituted from 24 percent of the school's total revenues in 1974 to 54 percent in 1979, and overall comprised 36 percent of the total revenues in years 1974 through 1979. . . .

. . . .

Hall makes much of the fact that MCO can avail itself of self-generated income from hospital charges, tuition and the like, and that any judgment rendered against the school or its officers could be paid from funds not appropriated by the Ohio General Assembly. This, however, overlooks the true state of affairs. By statute, the Ohio legislature permits the state colleges and universities to retain such funds, rather than require them to be paid into the treasury and then appropriated back to the schools as needed, but it could just as easily amend that statute to require the converse. Moreover, the declining amount of operating funds appropriated by the legislature indicates that those appropriations are gauged according to the amount of self-generated funds available each year, such that any added expense (e.g., a judgment for Hall in excess of $4,000,000) that could not be met by hospital, tuition or other revenues would have to be covered by an increase in state appropriations.

Such a link between the appropriated and non-appropriated revenues available to MCO (which the record does not show to be kept in segregated accounts) has the effect of making any judgment against the school a liability payable from the state treasury. . . . Creating any distinction between MCO's appropriated and self-generated revenues in the context of Eleventh Amendment immunity would be a pure exercise in elevating form over substance.

Governmental or Proprietary Function?

Providing facilities and opportunities for the pursuit of higher education is a long-recognized governmental function. *See Wolf v. Ohio State University Hospital*, 170 Ohio St. 49, 53 (1959), overruled in part on other grounds, *Schenkolewski v. Cleveland Metroparks System*, 67 Ohio St. 2d 31, 36 & n.4 (1981); *see also Vaughn v. Regents of University of California*, 504 F. Supp. at 1353; *Buckton v. NCAA*, 366 F. Supp. 1152, 1156 (D. Mass. 1973). Therefore, with respect to the expulsion of Mr. Hall as an MCO student on grounds of academic dishonesty, the school was certainly engaged in a traditional state activity.

Corporate Status and Powers?

Revised Code sections 3350.01 through 3350.05, which establish MCO and regulate the organization and powers of its board of trustees, do not confer corporate status, as such, upon the school or its governing board. The trustees are empowered to "do all things necessary for the creation, proper maintenance, and successful and continuous operation of the college," Ohio Rev. Code Ann. § 3350.03 (Page 1980), to "accept donations of lands and moneys for the purposes of such college," *Id.* to "receive and hold in trust, for the use and benefit of the college, any grant or devise of land, and any donation or bequest of money or other personal property, to be applied to the general or special use of the college," *Id.* § 3350.04, and to "make and enter into all contracts and agreements necessary or incidental to the operation of such college," Id.

Some of these powers are perhaps corporate in nature (i.e., those which are ordinary attributes of corporations), but MCO does not enjoy perpetual existence or a conferral of full corporate powers (including express recognition of the power to sue and be sued). . . . Thus, the statutory scheme under which the medical school exists does not support a finding that MCO has a "legal personality" independent from the State of Ohio.

Overall Autonomy from the State?

Under Revised Code section 3350.01, the "government" of MCO is vested in a board of trustees, nine in number, all of whom are appointed by the governor with the advice and consent of the state senate. The statute further provides staggered nine-year terms for the trustees, denies them compensation for their services (but permits reimbursement for expenses), and establishes a quorum of a majority of the board members. Section 3350.02 requires the board to elect a chairman and vice-chairman annually, and the board treasurer must give bond to the state, approved by the Attorney General of Ohio, "for the faithful performance of his duties and the proper accounting for all moneys coming into his care." Thus, the state legislature has exercised considerable control over the organization and functioning of the school's governing body.

. . . .

C

Taking into account the status of state colleges and universities (including the Medical College of Ohio) under Ohio's law of sovereign immunity and the Court of Claims Act, as well as the sources of revenue available to MCO, its performance of a governmental function, its non-corporate nature, and the fiscal and academic restraints imposed upon the school by state law, this Court must conclude that the District Court did not err in finding that MCO lacks operational autonomy from, and is financially dependent on, the State of Ohio, and is consequently an arm of the state entitled to immunity in federal court. Accordingly, to the extent that Hall's complaint seeks any relief against the Medical College of Ohio at Toledo . . . and damages from the president and dean of that institution in their official capacities . . . summary judgment for those defendants was proper under the Eleventh

Amendment. We are still left, however, with the suits for damages against the individual defendants in their individual capacities . . . and for reinstatement by President Ruppert and Dean Kemph in their official capacities . . . .

II
Qualified Immunity

"Government officials performing discretionary functions generally are shielded from liability for civil damages insofar as their conduct does not violate clearly established statutory or constitutional rights of which a reasonable person would have known." *Harlow v. Fitzgerald*, 457 U.S. 800, 818 (1982). . . .

Although Hall initially claimed in this lawsuit that he was denied equal protection of the laws, and subjected to unlawful racial discrimination, he appears to have dropped that theory before this Court. . . . Consequently, we only consider the claimed due process violations.

Hall first asserts that he was denied due process of law when he was prevented from having his attorney present in the formal disciplinary hearing before the defendant faculty members Sodeman, Higgins, Budd, Ross and Gandy. However, just because his expulsion from a state medical school on grounds of academic dishonesty may implicate a liberty interest protected by constitutional due process guarantees, this does not mean that Hall was necessarily entitled to all the incidents of a full-blown judicial trial. We can find no case authority to "clearly establish" that he had the right to counsel in such a hearing in 1978.

As stated by the Supreme Court in *Goss v. Lopez*, " 'once it is determined that due process applies, the question remains what process is due.' " 419 U.S. 565, 577, 95 S. Ct 729, 42 L. Ed. 2d 725 (1975) (quoting *Morrissey v. Brewer*, 408 U.S. 471, 481 (1972)). The Court in *Goss* dealt with the nature of due process required before public high school students could be suspended for up to ten days, and held that only an oral or written notice of the charges and an opportunity by the student to present his side of the story were "due" in those circumstances. Stating that "we stop short of construing the Due Process Clause to require, countrywide, that hearings in connection with short suspensions must afford the student opportunity to secure counsel, to confront and cross-examine witnesses supporting the charge, or to call his own witnesses to verify his version of the incident," *Id.* 419 U.S. at 583, Justice White, writing for the Court, made it clear that they were then addressing only the question of short suspensions, and that "longer suspensions or expulsions . . . may require more formal procedures." *Id.* at 584.

Three years later, and approximately one month before Hall's disciplinary hearing was conducted, the Supreme Court had occasion to address the issue of when such "more formal procedures" might be required. *Board of Curators v. Horowitz*, 435 U.S. 78 (1978). In Horowitz, a divided Court held that a student dismissed for academic deficiencies (not disciplinary reasons) from the University of Missouri-Kansas City Medical School was not entitled to a hearing before the school's decisionmaking body. Justice Rehnquist, in his majority opinion, distinguished disciplinary proceedings, as discussed in *Goss*, from academic evaluations which are, by nature, more subjective than "the typical factual questions presented in the average disciplinary decision." *Id.* at 90.

Thus, the posture of the law in 1978 was such that some kind of formal hearing was apparently required before a student could be expelled for disciplinary causes (such as cheating). But there was no certainty as to what these formalities might entail. Hall, in his memorandum in support of his motion for partial summary judgment in the trial court, cited a number of cases purporting to require the right to have counsel present in school disciplinary hearings. *Norton v. Discipline Committee*, 419 F.2d 195 (6th Cir. 1969) (East Tennessee State University); *Jones v. State Board of Education*, 279 F. Supp. 190 (M.D. Tenn. 1968) (Tennessee A & I State University) [other citations omitted]. A review of these cases shows that [two district courts] did, in fact, hold that there was a right to counsel. However, this Court in *Norton* went no further than to note, in finding that due process had been satisfied in that case, that the students in question had had the opportunity to be represented by counsel at their hearing. 419 F.2d at 200. District Judge Miller in *Jones* (whose opinion this Court adopted) made a similar finding, and did not expressly hold that the right to counsel was a requisite to due process in such circumstances.

Significantly, the late Judge Miller (who later served on this Court) cited to *Dixon v. Alabama State Board of Education*, 294 F.2d 150 (5th Cir. 1961), *cert. denied*, 368 U.S. 930 (1961), as "the leading case involving the application of these basic principles to a disciplinary proceeding conducted by a state supported educational institution." 279 F. Supp. at 197; *see also Goss*, 419 U.S. at 576 n.8 (*Dixon* was a "landmark decision"). In *Dixon*, the Fifth Circuit established the following standards:

> The notice should contain a statement of the specific charges and grounds which, if proven, would justify expulsion under the regulations of the Board of Education. The nature of the hearing should vary depending upon the circumstances of the particular case. The case before us requires something more than an informal interview with an administrative authority of the college. By its nature, a charge of misconduct, as opposed to a failure to meet the scholastic standards of the college, depends upon a collection of the facts concerning the charged misconduct, easily colored by the point of view of the witnesses. In such circumstances, a hearing which gives the Board or the administrative authorities of the college an opportunity to hear both sides in considerable detail is best suited to protect the rights of all involved. This is not to imply that a full dress judicial hearing, with the right to cross-examine witnesses, is required. Such a hearing, with the attending publicity and disturbance of college activities, might be detrimental to the college's educational atmosphere and impractical to carry out. Nevertheless, the rudiments of an adversary proceeding may be preserved without encroaching upon the interests of the college.

294 F.2d at 158–59. When *Norton* and *Jones* are construed in light of *Dixon*, and of the later developments in *Goss* and *Horowitz*, we cannot see any basis for Hall's claim that he was deprived of any right to counsel which was "clearly established" in this Circuit. We do not, however, speak to the issue of whether such a right should exist in this kind of disciplinary proceeding.

Turning to Hall's other allegations of due process violations, we find that he was given timely notice of both of the charges against him, including the fact that his academic record would be considered since his scores on the two exams in question were much higher than his previous performance. . . . He was given a copy of the hearing panel's report, and of the decisions of Dean Kempf and President Ruppert adopting its recommendations. A formal transcript of the hearing was prepared and (presumably) available to Hall, and he was able to point out what he perceived to be the deficiencies in the hearing and the panel's decision during his meeting with the college president. Aside from the question of counsel, it is hard to see what further procedural safeguards could have been provided without turning this hearing process into an exact equivalent of a courtroom trial — something that no court has yet required.

. . . .

III
Reinstatement

The foregoing reasons for affirming the entry of summary judgment against Hall do not, however, resolve the entire case. The District Court erred in sweeping Hall's claim for reinstatement within the scope of the qualified immunity available to the individual defendants. To the contrary, "immunity from damages does not ordinarily bar equitable relief as well." *Wood v. Strickland*, 420 U.S. at 315 n.6; *Jacobson v. Tahoe Regional Planning Agency*, 566 F.2d 1353, 1366 (9th Cir. 1978), *aff'd in part, rev'd in part sub nom.*; *Lake Country Estates v. Tahoe Regional Planning Agency*, 440 U.S. 391 (1979).

We note, though, that there was clear evidence that Hall had improperly consulted an old examination in his student mailbox while he was still taking the locomotor segment test on February 3, 1978. Moreover, there was evidence that he was not a good student, did not get along with his fellow students, and received barely passing grades except on the exams in which he was accused of cheating (and his papers received excellent grades). It was obvious that he would not be a good doctor, assuming that he would have otherwise graduated from medical school and passed the state medical board examination. Therefore we hold, as a matter of law, that MCO had good cause for expelling Hall from medical school, and thus his expulsion was not caused by whatever due process violation might have occurred when he was denied the assistance of legal counsel at his disciplinary hearing. As a result, there is no need to remand for consideration of the claim for reinstatement and the merits of Hall's argument that a right to counsel exists at such a hearing.

NOTES

1. The court in *Kashani* discussed two primary factors in its determination that Purdue University was an arm of the state and not a political subdivision (like a county or a city) and was, thus, entitled to Eleventh Amendment immunity: (1) limited financial autonomy from the state (i.e., the university's dependency on the state for part of its funding); and (2) general legal status of the university (i.e., powers granted to a Board of Trustees, which is appointed by the governor). The

Hall court, in a citation to *Black v. Kline*, 612 F.2d 718 (3d Cir. 1979), made reference to several other factors used in this determination: (1) local law and decisions defining the status and nature of the university in its relationship with the state; (2) whether a judgment against the university would have to be paid out of the state treasury; (3) whether the university has the funds or the power to satisfy the judgment; (4) whether the agency is performing a governmental or proprietary function; (5) whether the university is separately incorporated; (6) the degree of autonomy the university has over its operations; (7) whether it has the power to sue and be sued; (8) whether it is immune from state taxation; and (9) whether the state has immunized itself from responsibility for the university's operation. The court held that each of these factors pointed toward the Medical College of Ohio as an arm of the state. So, while the college has some level of autonomy and exercises some powers that are corporate in nature, the Court of Appeals held that the district court did not err in its finding that MCO was financially and operationally dependent on the state. This analysis is generally followed in most jurisdictions.

What about the trend seen nationwide with state legislatures funding less and less of a university's operating dollars? Would continued decreases over time lead to an opposite result here, eliminating Eleventh Amendment immunity? Likely not, especially considering the strength of the second factor and its related state-based oversight of university operations. With that said, however, state appropriations to public universities are, in fact, diminishing across the country, before and after the federal stimulus dollars were invested. In spring 2011, Indiana state appropriations to Purdue University totaled 27% of the universities general fund, while 60% came from tuition and fees. *See* Alisha Yadav & Kirsten Gibson, *Admins and Senate Discuss Budget Issues*, THE EXPONENT ONLINE, Mar. 29, 2011, *available at* http://www.purdueexponent.org/city/article_e78930dc-5a0e-11e0-81d1-00127992bc8b.html. Similarly, Ohio's state appropriations to public universities are under 30% now. *See also* NCSL Fiscal Affairs Program, *State Funding for Higher Education in FY 2009 and FY 2010*, NAT'L CONFERENCE OF STATE LEGISLATURES, *available at* http://www.ncsl.org/documents/fiscal/HigherEdFundingFINAL.pdf.

2. In addition to its discussion on Eleventh Amendment immunity for the college as a whole, the court in *Hall* also discussed and granted qualified immunity to the college officials for decisions made within the scope of their authority and in compliance with clearly established law. In *Hall*, the college dismissed the student for academic dishonesty. The student claimed his due process rights were violated when the college refused to allow him to have an attorney present at his hearing. The court sided with the college officials and held that, while the law was established that some kind of hearing was required for disciplinary dismissals, it was not clearly established that the accused student has a right to be represented by counsel at such hearings. In this regard, *Hall* joins a set of cases discussing the due process rights of public college and university students who challenge disciplinary and/or academic decisions made by higher education officials. For a deeper discussion of these issues, see Chapter VII.

Chapter III

EMPLOYMENT RELATIONSHIPS

Introduction

According to the State Higher Education Executive Officers report, salaries and benefits for personnel constitute approximately 75 percent of a higher education institution's expenditures. See State Higher Education Executive Officers, State Higher Education Finance: FY 2011 (2012). Given that significant financial resources are dedicated to this group of individuals, it makes sense to pay attention to the legal concerns and policy issues arising from faculty and staff relationships with the institution. The purpose of this chapter is to provide an overview of key legal concepts in the employment arrangements of higher education institutions. The overarching theme for this chapter is presenting legal parameters in which employment relationships within higher education achieve the goal of fairness.

Employment law in higher education contains many of the same principles of employment law in other industries (e.g., medicine, law, hospitality management) and sectors (i.e., private and public). For instance, the at-will doctrine (and other state employment laws that overcome the presumption the at-will doctrine provides) applies equally to a campus chef at a private university as a chef at a privately owned dining facility. Similarly, in many instances, the employment laws for an administrative assistant at a public university also pertain to an administrative assistant employed at another state agency.

While principles of employment law apply generally to the higher education context, throughout this chapter, the reader will encounter selected topics regarding the employment relationship and its application to the *specific* context of higher education. It should be noted, however, that the employment relationship specific to college faculty is explored in Chapter 4.

This chapter is divided into five major sections. In Section A, the chapter explores what is the qualification of an employee and employer. This qualification impacts benefits and potentially implicates legal rights of the individual — depending on classification. Section B examines cases pertaining to authority to hire and negotiate contract terms. Section C discusses contractual relationships that may be formed as well as disclaimed from documents such as employee handbooks. In Section D, the chapter reveals arguments about unemployment benefits for certain employee arrangements. Finally, in Section E, the chapter presents a series of cases and arguments exploring employee civil rights — particularly in terms of discrimination based on speech, race, religion, and sex. It also draws attention to employment retaliation and due process claims. Throughout this chapter, there exists a thorough examination of each party's interests — the employee (or individual arguing employee status) and the employer. The arguments raise organizational and public policy perspectives contributing to the understanding of higher education administrators, faculty, staff, and legal counsel — who may be engaged in these or similar disputes.

A. QUALIFICATION AS AN EMPLOYEE AND EMPLOYER

1. Graduate Student Researcher

CUDDEBACK v. FLORIDA BOARD OF EDUCATION

381 F.3d 1230 (11th Cir. 2004)

DUBINA, CIRCUIT JUDGE.

Appellant Sandy Cuddeback appeals the district court's order granting summary judgment to the Florida Board of Education, the University of South Florida Board of Trustees, and the University of South Florida (collectively the "University") on her gender discrimination claim brought pursuant to Title VII of the Civil Rights Act of 1964. For the reasons that follow, we affirm.

I. BACKGROUND

A. Facts

Cuddeback, a female, was a graduate student at the University of South Florida, conducting cancer research in the laboratory of Dr. Hong Gang Wang, a University professor. Cuddeback's course work obligations required her to complete a rotation in three laboratories. The University provided the equipment and training. However, much of Cuddeback's work in the laboratory was done for the purpose of completing her dissertation and satisfying her program's publishing requirements. She received a stipend and benefits for her work, as well as sick and annual leave. A comprehensive collective bargaining agreement also governed her employment relationship. In her first year at the laboratory, the University's Department of Pharmacology and Therapeutics funded her stipend of $15,000 with a waiver of tuition. After Cuddeback's first year, Dr. Wang's individual faculty research grant funded Cuddeback's work. While Cuddeback received a stipend for her work, the record does not reflect the amount.

Dr. Wang evaluated Cuddeback's performance on a semi-annual basis, and his evaluation was included in her general academic evaluation presented to her by the University. The department faculty gave Cuddeback the highest possible rating in her September 1998, May 1999, and October 1999 evaluations. According to Cuddeback in the fall of 1999, Dr. Wang told her that she was his best student and had the most potential of all the students in the department.

However, Dr. Wang stated that, beginning in late 1999, he informed Cuddeback of his concerns regarding her attendance, lab notebooks, and lack of communication. In his March 10, 2000, evaluation of Cuddeback, Dr. Wang commented on her

"(1) failure to obey necessary instructions, (2) unstable productivity due to changes of mood, (3) argumentative without scientific standpoint, (4) disrespect to colleagues, and (5) lack of focusing on the project." Furthermore, both Michael Lee, another research assistant, and a lab technician, who worked with Cuddeback in Dr. Wang's lab, stated that they observed conflicts between Dr. Wang and Cuddeback.

The University asserts that, in January 2000, Dr. Wang asked Cuddeback to improve in several areas. The University alleges that, after such request, Cuddeback told Dr. Wang that she would leave his lab at the end of the semester. Cuddeback alleges, however, that Dr. Wang informed her in January 2000 that she would be leaving his lab at the end of April. On April 3, 2000, Cuddeback sent a message to a Dr. Polson advising him of a severe hand injury and requesting time off until April 10, 2000. She did not notify Dr. Wang of the injury or request a leave of absence. Dr. Polson then attempted to notify Cuddeback by certified letter that Dr. Wang was unaware of the reasons for her absence and to request that Cuddeback contact Dr. Wang immediately to discuss the matter. Cuddeback did not accept the certified letter containing this request, despite three delivery attempts. Cuddeback testified that she thought that the matter was none of Dr. Wang's concern.

On May 1, 2000, after Cuddeback applied for a full-time job with Hilton Reservations Worldwide, Cuddeback requested a leave of absence from Dr. Krzanowski, acting chair of the University's Department of Pharmacology and Therapeutics, again without informing Dr. Wang. Dr. Krzanowski granted the request through August 1, 2000. However, on May 9, 2000, Dr. Wang wrote Cuddeback informing her that her lack of improvement in the areas identified in her evaluation and her absence from his lab since April 20, without notice to him, would result in the nonrenewal of her appointment. Cuddeback does not dispute that she failed to show up in Dr. Wang's lab after April 20, 2000, but Cuddeback claims that she kept Dr. Wang apprised of her efforts to obtain a medical leave of absence.

After Cuddeback left Dr. Wang's lab, Hirohito Yamaguchi, a male, took over Cuddeback's research duties. Yamaguchi had joined the lab in March 2000 and worked on his own research projects, but then finished Cuddeback's research project after she left the lab for publication of a journal article. Cuddeback alleges that Dr. Wang paid Yamaguchi to finish the research project initiated by Cuddeback from the stipend funds that originally were to be paid to her. The University alleges that none of the money appropriated as Cuddeback's stipend was used to pay Yamaguchi. However, the district court found from the evidence that "Hirohito Yamaguchi took over plaintiff's position in Dr. Wang's lab after she was terminated. Dr. Wang paid Yamaguchi to complete the experiments and research Plaintiff worked on from Dr. Wang's stipend money that was previously allocated to pay the Plaintiff."

B. Procedural History

Cuddeback filed a complaint alleging gender discrimination in violation of Title VII. The University moved for summary judgment arguing that Title VII did not apply because Cuddeback was a student rather than an employee. . . .

In granting the University's motion for summary judgment, the district court found that Cuddeback was an employee for Title VII purposes because the University supervised her, provided the equipment that she used, paid her biweekly, and gave her sick and annual leave. The district court also supported its finding with the additional facts that a comprehensive collective bargaining agreement covered her employment relationship, and that the decision to terminate her was an employment, not an academic decision.. . . .

Cuddeback then perfected this appeal.

II. ISSUE

(1) Whether the district court erred in determining that Cuddeback was an employee for the purposes of Title VII.

. . . .

III. STANDARD OF REVIEW

This court reviews a grant of summary judgment *de novo.*

IV. DISCUSSION

A. A Title VII "Employee"

The University argues that Cuddeback was not an employee for purposes of Title VII. Title VII defines an "employee" as "an individual employed by an employer." This court has not addressed the specific issue of whether a graduate student assistant constitutes an employee for purposes of Title VII. However, generally, this circuit has adopted the "economic realities" test to determine whether a Title VII plaintiff is an employee. Under this test, the term "employee" is "construed in light of general common law concepts" and "should take into account the economic realities of the situation," "viewed in light of the common law principles of agency and the right of the employer to control the employee." Specifically, the court should consider factors such as whether the defendant directed the plaintiff's work and provided or paid for the materials used in the plaintiff's work. Because the question presented is whether Cuddeback, as a graduate research assistant, is an "employee," we conclude that the economic realities test should apply.

Applying the economic realities test, the fact that much of Cuddeback's work in Dr. Wang's lab was done for the purpose of satisfying the lab-work, publication, and dissertation requirements of her graduate program weighs in favor of treating her as a student rather than an employee. However, the following facts weigh in favor of treating Cuddeback as an employee for Title VII purposes: (1) she received a stipend and benefits for her work; (2) she received sick and annual leave; (3) a comprehensive collective bargaining agreement governed her employment relationship with the University; (4) the University provided the equipment and training; and (5) the decision not to renew her appointment was based on employment reasons, such as attendance and communication problems, rather than academic reasons. Although the record does not indicate the amount that she was paid for the year in which she was terminated, the record does demonstrate that she was paid during that year, and was also paid $15,000 in her first year with Dr. Wang.

Courts that have considered whether graduate students constitute employees for the purposes of Title VII have distinguished between their roles as employees and as students, and have typically refused to treat them as "employees" for Title VII purposes only where their academic requirements were truly central to the relationship with the institution. Compare *Stilley v. University of Pittsburgh of the Commonwealth Sys. of Higher Educ.* (finding that a plaintiff was an employee when she was a student researcher); *Ivan v. Kent State Univ.* (finding that a graduate student researcher was an employee where she was under an employment contract, was paid biweekly, and had retirement benefits withheld); with *Jacob-Mua v. Veneman* (concluding that a volunteer graduate student researcher was not an employee because she was not financially compensated for her work); *Pollack v. Rice Univ.* (finding that paid research or instruction by the plaintiff was "attendant to his capacity as a graduate student" because it was a central part of the graduate program and, therefore, the plaintiff's status was that of "student" rather than "employee"). Therefore, even though Cuddeback's course work obligations required her to complete a rotation in three laboratories and much of her work in Dr. Wang's lab was to fulfill the program's requirements, the economic realities of this particular situation lead us to conclude that the district court correctly found that Cuddeback was an employee for Title VII purposes.. . . .

V. CONCLUSION

We hold that the economic realities test should be used to determine whether a person acting as a graduate research assistant is an employee for the purposes of Title VII. Applying that test to this case, we conclude that Cuddeback was an employee.. . . . AFFIRMED.

NOTES

1. Defining who is an employee determines each party's obligations. An employee may be held to the college's employee handbook, eligible for workers' compensation, and subject to other established terms and conditions. Classifying an individual as an employee changes one's legal position in matters such as whether governmental immunity applies, whether employment benefits are available, whether participation in collective bargaining is an option, and whether employment protections may be asserted.

2. How might the outcome of the case have changed if the graduate student, along with others in the department, worked in the lab as a requirement of their doctoral education and received an institutional scholarship?

3. The "economic realities" test is not the only form of judicial examination courts apply when the definition of who qualifies as an "employee" is unclear. Several tests have been used to determine whether an individual is an employee. Initially, the common law test focused on the employer's control over the employee. However, the U.S. Supreme Court suggested another test, the "economic realities" test, since the "right to control" test was operationally too rigid. *See Bartels v. Birmingham*, 332 U.S. 126, 130 (1947). The *Bartels* Court noted that the economic realities test inquired into whether the individual, who might be classified as an employee, is "as a matter of economic reality . . . dependent upon the business to which they render service." *Id.* Accordingly, subsequent courts examined compensation and the working arrangements as factors within the economic realities test.

Today, courts have also turned to another option, returning to the modified, common law test, which incorporates the former "right to control" test and the "economic realities" test. Borrowing from *Community for Creative Non-Violence v. Reid*, 490 U.S. 730 (1989), a case defining the employer-employee relationship under U.S. copyright law, the Court emphasized and adopted common law agency principles. Although no one factor is decisive, and the analysis requires an examination of the totality of the circumstances, the *Reid* Court constructed a list of factors to help determine whether an individual qualifies as an employee: the degree of skill required to perform the task; the source of the instrumentalities and tools used to conduct the work; the location of the work; the duration of the relationship between the parties; whether the hiring party has the right to assign additional projects to the hired party; the extent of the hired party's discretion over when and how long to work; the method of payment; the hired party's role in hiring and paying assistants; whether the work is part of the regular business of the hiring party; whether the hiring party is in business; the provision of employee benefits; and the tax treatment of the hired party. *Id.* at 751–52.

4. Because of the nature of higher education, individuals who perform services on campuses such as students, research consultants, resident advisors, and guest lecturers, may work for a university or college in limited and unique ways that arguably constitute an employee arrangement or some other form of contractual relationship. Consider these multiple arrangements and construct parameters that would argue for and against that individual's status as an employee.

2. Student Worker

UNIVERSITY OF HAWAI'I v. BEFITEL

100 P.3d 55 (Haw. 2004)

Opinion of the Court by Acoba, J.

We hold that, under Hawai'i Revised Statutes (HRS) § 383-7(9)(B) (1993), eligibility of a student-employee for unemployment insurance benefits rests on whether the "primary relationship" the student occupies with respect to the school, college, or university involved is that of student or employee. Under the circumstances of this case, the primary relationship that Appellee Manaiakalani Kalua (Claimant) had to the University of Hawai'i, Hilo Campus (Hilo Campus) while he performed services during the summer, was that of a student of Appellant-Appellee University of Hawai'i (the University). The March 19, 2001 order of the third circuit court (the court) was to that effect, and therefore the said order which reversed the Department of Labor and Industrial Relations (DLIR) Employment Security Appeals Office Decision 0000952 of August 15, 2000, is affirmed.

I.

The facts in this case are undisputed. Claimant enrolled in the Hilo Campus's Hawaiian Language College in the Fall of 1996. Claimant had been a full-time student at the Hilo Campus for the five consecutive academic years (fall and spring semesters) of 1996–97, 1997–98, 1998–99, 1999–2000, and 2000–01.

On or about January 12, 1998, Claimant signed a University Student Employment Work Agreement (the Student Agreement). The Student Agreement was for a peer counselor position at the Hilo Campus's program called "Na Pua No'eau — Center for Gifted and Talented Native Hawaiian Children" (Na Pua No'eau). The Student Agreement required Claimant to satisfy the following minimum requisites: (1) a Hilo Campus student, currently a sophomore or of higher class standing, (2) 2.0 or better cumulative grade point average, (3) experience working with teenagers, (4) "arts/cultural" skills, (5) "leadership/organizational" skills, (6) valid cardiopulmonary resuscitation/first aid certification, (7) completion of an interview, and (8) "interpersonal" skills. Claimant fulfilled the minimum qualifications and was hired during the summer of 1998.

Claimant worked forty hours per week and did not attend summer school. The work Claimant did was not necessary for Claimant's degree, and he did not receive any credits for his work at Na Pua No'eau. Claimant resumed classes at the Hilo Campus in the fall of 1998.

In December 1999, Claimant filed for unemployment insurance benefits with the DLIR — Unemployment Insurance Division (UID) (collectively the department). In this regard, HRS § 383-2(a) (1993) provides in pertinent part that " 'employment' . . . means service . . . performed for wages or under any contract of hire, written or oral, express or implied." HRS § 383-7(9)(B) states, however, that " '[e]mployment' does not include the following service: . . . Service performed in the employ of a school, college, or university, if the service is performed by a student who is enrolled and is regularly attending classes at the school, college, or university."

The department investigated the claim and determined that Claimant had worked for Na Pua No'eau during the summer of 1998, and he "was not enrolled and regularly attending classes at the [Hilo Campus] during the summer session of 1998." The department decided that the services performed by Claimant for the employer, the University, were thus not subject to the exclusion stated in HRS § 383-7(9)(B). The wages earned by Claimant, then, could be considered for the purpose of unemployment benefits.

The University filed an appeal of the department's determination, and a hearing was held on June 15, 2000. The appeals officer, in a June 16, 2000 decision, reversed the department's determination and held that Claimant's services were excluded from employment. As a result of this decision, Claimant's services could not be considered for unemployment benefits purposes.

The department filed a written request for reopening of the decision. The department attached to the request a May 22, 1979 letter to the University of Hawai'i Manoa, Director of the Student Employment Office, from the DLIR — UID administrator clarifying HRS § 383-7(9)(B). In the letter, the DLIR had ruled that under HRS § 383-7(9)(B), a "student during part of the summer period, when she was not enrolled or attending classes on a full-time basis, [was] covered and the wages useable to establish a valid claim for benefits." The appeals officer granted the reopening and allowed the parties an opportunity to file written memoranda.

On August 15, 2000, the appeals officer issued her "reopened" decision which reversed her June 16, 2000 decision. The appeals officer explained that

> [t]he Department's argument . . . that there must nevertheless be some semblance of "enrollment" or "attending classes" is reasonable, such as the continued enrolled status as an ongoing graduate assistant or continued consultations with professors regarding independent work. In the case in hand, no such semblance can be found. *The claimant had completed his spring semester classes and was not expected to return to his academics at the employer's university in any capacity until the fall.*
>
> . . . .
>
> The employer's argument that it is relevant to consider that the work offered to the claimant was in furtherance of his academic pursuits and was conditioned on his student status is also reasonable. The employer's contention, that as a matter of policy, it may need to re-evaluate its ability to offer student employment if it is not excluded from covered employment under Chapter 383, HRS, was also considered. These considerations, however, must be weighed against the statutory requirements contained in Section 383-7(9)(B), HRS. *Based on a finding that the claimant was not enrolled in or attending classes while performing his services for the employer, the claimant's services are not excluded from the term "employment" under* Section 383-7, HRS.

Subsequently, the University filed for a reopening of the August 15, 2000 decision, which was denied.

On October 18, 2000, the University appealed to the court. In a March 19, 2001 order, the court reversed the appeals officer's decision and ruled that Claimant's services were excluded under HRS § 383-7(9)(B). In the order, the court stated that the purpose of HRS § 383-7(9)(B) was to "exclude, from covered employment, services of persons who are essentially student [sic] rather than workers." Additionally, the court applied the "primary relationship test" which "encourages arbiters to look at the student's primary relationship to the university to determine whether a student-claimant is disqualified form benefits[.]" The court thereby concluded that

> Claimant was essentially a student who worked full-time in the summer of 1998 for UH Hilo's student employment program instead of school; the primary relation of Claimant to UH Hilo was that of a student and not a worker. As such, the exception set forth in HRS § 383-7(9)(B) applies in this case and Claimant is not entitled to unemployment benefits for services performed for UH Hilo in the summer of 1998. Decision 0000952 is reversed.

The final judgment was filed on April 19, 2001. The Director timely filed the May 15, 2001 notice of appeal to this court.

II.

On appeal, the Director argues that the court (1) erroneously interpreted the purpose of HRS § 383-7(9)(B); (2) erroneously relied on *Bachrach v. Dep't of Indus. Labor & Human Relations*, for the proposition that a primary relationship test could be used to exclude the services of a student who was not enrolled and not regularly attending classes; (3) erroneously relied on *Pima Cmty. Coll. v. Arizona Dep't of Econ. Sec.*, for the proposition that a primary relationship test could be used to exclude the services of a student who was not enrolled and not regularly attending classes; and (4) erroneously construed HRS § 383-7(9)(B) too broadly.

The University does not address the Director's points directly but, rather, argues in its answering brief that (1) the express language and the purpose of HRS § 383-7(9)(B) support the conclusion that Claimant's services are exempt, (2) the primary relationship test is applicable because (a) the primary relationship test is founded in the federal counterpart of HRS § 383-7(9)(B) and (b) the reasoning in *Bachrach* and *Pima Cmty Coll.* is sound, and (3) the conclusion that Claimant is not entitled to unemployment benefits is supported by an attorney general letter.

. . . .

IV.

Whereas the court interpreted HRS § 383-7(9)(B), certain established principles apply on appeal. "The interpretation of a statute is a question of law reviewable *de novo.*" When construing a statute, this court's "foremost obligation 'is to ascertain and give effect to the intention of the legislature' which 'is to be obtained primarily from the language contained in the statute itself.' " However, "[w]hen there is doubt, doubleness of meaning, or indistinctiveness or uncertainty of an expression used in a statute an ambiguity exists." "If language of the statute is ambiguous, courts look to legislative history for assistance in construing the statute."

V.

The Hawai'i Employment Security Law, HRS chapter 383, "provides a measure of protection against wage loss resulting from temporary unemployment for Hawaii's workers. Benefits paid to unemployed members of the work force are drawn from a trust fund financed by contributions from employers subject to the law." "Every employer in the state for whom service is performed by an employee is obliged to make contributions to the unemployment compensation fund, unless the service is expressly excluded from coverage under the law."

Claimant would be eligible for unemployment insurance benefits if the services he provided Na Pua No'eau did not fall within the exclusion set forth in HRS § 383-7(9)(B). Because the term "enrolled" in HRS § 383-7(9)(B) could mean a student is registered to take classes currently or during the following semester, the term "enrolled" is ambiguous.[9] In light of this ambiguity, legislative history

[9] Although the attorney for the University stipulated that Claimant was "not enrolled in classes in that summer of 1998[,]" this stipulation pertained to the fact that Claimant was not registered for classes

indicates that when amending HRS chapter 383 in 1971, the legislature expressed an intent that the chapter "[c]onform [ ] with federal standards [which] is required as a condition for allowance of credit for contributions . . . under the Federal Unemployment Tax Act [(FUTA)]." Because of this intent, the fact that the language of HRS § 383-7(9)(B) is identical to the FUTA and the Federal Insurance Contributions Act (FICA), and the silence of Hawai'i case law as to the interpretation of the statute, this court may consider federal case law. In *Gold [v. Harrison]*, when interpreting the Hawai'i Rules of Civil Procedure, this court held that "[i]n instances where Hawai'i case law and statutes are silent, this court can look to parallel federal law for guidance."

The FUTA provides that "[f]or purposes of this chapter, the term 'employment' means any service performed prior to 1955 . . . except . . . service performed in the employ of a school, college, or university, if such service is performed (i) by a student who *is enrolled and is regularly attending classes at such school, college, or university* [.]" The Code of Federal Regulations (Federal Regulations) assists in the interpretation and implementation of this part of the FUTA and provides in relevant part that

> [t]he status of the employee as a student performing the services shall be determined on the basis of the relationship of such employee with the organization for which the services are performed. An employee who performs services in the employ of a school, college, or university as an incident to and for the purpose of pursuing a course of study at such school, college, or university has the status of a student in the performance of such services.

The FICA also provides that the term employment "shall not include . . . service performed in the employ of . . . a school, college, or university . . . [i]f such service is performed by a student who *is enrolled and regularly attending classes* at such school, college, or university[.]" The Federal Regulations pertaining to the FICA also interpret this language to mean:

> The status of the employee as a student performing the services shall be determined on the basis of the relationship of such employee with the organization for which the services are performed. An employee who performs services in the employ of a school, college, or university, as an incident to and for the purpose of pursing a course of study at such school, college, or university has the status of a student in the performance of such services.

Consequently, the status of a student pursuant to the FUTA and the FICA is determined by examining the student/employee's "primary relationship" to the school, college, or university. In obtaining the job with Na Pua No'eau, Claimant was required to be "a University of Hawai'i at Hilo student, currently a sophomore or of higher class standing[.]" But for Claimant's status as a student at the Hilo Campus, he would not have been eligible for the position. Therefore, Claimant performed services as an incident to his course of study at the Hilo Campus. Although Claimant was not actually registered for and physically attending classes

---

during the summer and not as to the meaning of "enrolled" in HRS § 383-7(9)(B).

during the summer of 1998, his primary relationship, which qualified him for a job with the Hilo Campus, was that of a student of the institution. Thus, the 1998 summer position was excluded from the term "employment" pursuant to HRS § 383-7(9)(B).

VI.

For the foregoing reasons, the court's March 19, 2001 order reversing the DLIR Employment Security Appeals Office Decision 0000952 is affirmed.

NOTES

1. Because the classification of an individual as an employee establishes legal rights and responsibilities for and against the "employer," a party may argue for an individual's classification as an "employee." Often, the question arises with students and their relationship with the college.

At some institutions of higher education, selected students leaders such as the student body president receive a stipend, office space, and administrative support. How does that arrangement impact the possible argument that those student leaders are employees of the institution? Now, also consider the treatment of resident advisors, who typically receive room and board as part of the position.

2. The classification of individuals as an employee or agent of the institution contains, at times, uniquely framed issues. For instance, in *Kavanagh v. Trustees of Boston University*, 795 N.E.2d 1170 (Mass. 2003), an athlete at one institution sued the opposing institution for acts of one of its players. In that case, Kenneth Kavanagh played on the Manhattan College men's basketball team. In a game with Boston University (BU), a scuffle ensued and Kavanagh sought to break up the altercation. While doing so, Levar Folk, a BU player, punched Kavanagh in the face and broke his nose. Kavanagh argued that "Folk's status as a scholarship athlete playing for the university made him an agent of the university and that the university is therefore vicariously liable for any torts committed by Folk while playing for the university's basketball team" *Id.* at 1174. The Massachusetts high court disagreed. The court held that "providing a scholarship or other financial assistance does not transform the relationship between the academic institution and the student into any form of employment relationship. While scholarships may introduce some element of 'payment' into the relationship, scholarships are not wages" *Id.* at 1175. Thus, the claim failed that the athlete, who received a scholarship to play basketball, was an agent or servant of the university for purposes of *respondeat superior.* A more detailed excerpt and discussion of the *Kavanagh* case is found in Chapter VIII.

3. Similarly, courts have denied student athletes' claims for workers' compensation from injuries sustained from team practice, since the student-athlete did not qualify as an employee. *See, e.g., Coleman v. Western Mich. Univ.*, 336 N.W.2d 224 (Mich. Ct. App. 1983).

3. Medical Residents

MAYO FOUNDATION FOR MEDICAL EDUCATION & RESEARCH v. UNITED STATES

131 S. Ct. 704 (2011)

CHIEF JUSTICE ROBERTS delivered the opinion of the Court.

Nearly all Americans who work for wages pay taxes on those wages under the Federal Insurance Contributions Act (FICA), which Congress enacted to collect funds for Social Security. The question presented in this case is whether doctors who serve as medical residents are properly viewed as "student[s]" whose service Congress has exempted from FICA taxes under 26 U.S.C. § 3121(b)(10).

I

A

Most doctors who graduate from medical school in the United States pursue additional education in a specialty to become board certified to practice in that field. Petitioners Mayo Foundation for Medical Education and Research, Mayo Clinic, and the Regents of the University of Minnesota (collectively Mayo) offer medical residency programs that provide such instruction. Mayo's residency programs, which usually last three to five years, train doctors primarily through hands-on experience. Residents often spend between 50 and 80 hours a week caring for patients, typically examining and diagnosing them, prescribing medication, recommending plans of care, and performing certain procedures. Residents are generally supervised in this work by more senior residents and by faculty members known as attending physicians. In 2005, Mayo paid its residents annual "stipends" ranging between $41,000 and $56,000 and provided them with health insurance, malpractice insurance, and paid vacation time.

Mayo residents also take part in "a formal and structured educational program." Residents are assigned textbooks and journal articles to read and are expected to attend weekly lectures and other conferences. Residents also take written exams and are evaluated by the attending faculty physicians. But the parties do not dispute that the bulk of residents' time is spent caring for patients.

B

Through the Social Security Act and related legislation, Congress has created a comprehensive national insurance system that provides benefits for retired workers, disabled workers, unemployed workers, and their families. Congress funds Social Security by taxing both employers and employees under FICA on the wages employees earn. Congress has defined "wages" broadly, to encompass "all remuneration for employment." The term "employment" has a similarly broad reach, extending to "any service, of whatever nature, performed . . . by an employee for the person employing him."

Congress has, however, exempted certain categories of service and individuals from FICA's demands. As relevant here, Congress has excluded from taxation "service performed in the employ of . . . a school, college, or university . . . if such service is performed by a student who is enrolled and regularly attending classes at such school, college, or university." The Social Security Act, which governs workers' eligibility for benefits, contains a corresponding student exception materially identical to [FICA].

Since 1951, the Treasury Department has applied the student exception to exempt from taxation students who work for their schools "as an incident to and for the purpose of pursuing a course of study" there. Until 2005, the Department determined whether an individual's work was "incident to" his studies by performing a case-by-case analysis. The primary considerations in that analysis were the number of hours worked and the course load taken.

For its part, the Social Security Administration (SSA) also articulated in its regulations a case-by-case approach to the corresponding student exception in the Social Security Act. The SSA has, however, "always held that resident physicians are not students." In 1998, the Court of Appeals for the Eighth Circuit held that the SSA could not categorically exclude residents from student status, given that its regulations provided for a case-by-case approach. Following that decision, the Internal Revenue Service received more than 7,000 claims seeking FICA tax refunds on the ground that medical residents qualified as students under . . . the Internal Revenue Code.

Facing that flood of claims, the Treasury Department "determined that it [wa]s necessary to provide additional clarification of the ter[m]" "student" as used in § 3121(b)(10), particularly with respect to individuals who perform "services that are in the nature of on the job training." The Department proposed an amended rule for comment and held a public hearing on it.

On December 21, 2004, the Department adopted an amended rule prescribing that an employee's service is "incident" to his studies only when "[t]he educational aspect of the relationship between the employer and the employee, as compared to the service aspect of the relationship, [is] predominant." The rule categorically provides that "[t]he services of a full-time employee"-as defined by the employer's policies, but in any event including any employee normally scheduled to work 40 hours or more per week-"are not incident to and for the purpose of pursuing a course of study." The amended provision clarifies that the Department's analysis "is not affected by the fact that the services performed . . . may have an educational, instructional, or training aspect." The rule also includes as an example the case of "Employee E," who is employed by "University V" as a medical resident. Because Employee E's "normal work schedule calls for [him] to perform services 40 or more hours per week," the rule provides that his service is "not incident to and for the purpose of pursuing a course of study," and he accordingly is not an exempt "student" under § 3121(b)(10).

C

After the Department promulgated the full-time employee rule, Mayo filed suit seeking a refund of the money it had withheld and paid on its residents' stipends during the second quarter of 2005. Mayo asserted that its residents were exempt under § 3121(b)(10) and that the Treasury Department's full-time employee rule was invalid.

The District Court granted Mayo's motion for summary judgment. The court held that the full-time employee rule is inconsistent with the unambiguous text of § 3121, which the court understood to dictate that "an employee is a 'student' so long as the educational aspect of his service predominates over the service aspect of the relationship with his employer." The court also determined that the factors governing this Court's analysis of regulations set forth in *National Muffler Dealers Assn., Inc. v. United States* (1979), "indicate that the full-time employee exception is invalid."

The Government appealed, and the Court of Appeals reversed. Applying our opinion in *Chevron U.S.A. Inc. v. Natural Resources Defense Council, Inc.* (1984), the Court of Appeals concluded that "the statute is silent or ambiguous on the question whether a medical resident working for the school full-time is a 'student' " for purposes of § 3121(b)(10), and that the Department's amended regulation "is a permissible interpretation of the statut[e]."

We granted Mayo's petition for certiorari.

II

A

We begin our analysis with the first step of the two-part framework announced in *Chevron*, and ask whether Congress has "directly addressed the precise question at issue." We agree with the Court of Appeals that Congress has not done so. The statute does not define the term "student," and does not otherwise attend to the precise question whether medical residents are subject to FICA.

Mayo nonetheless contends that the Treasury Department's full-time employee rule must be rejected under *Chevron* step one. Mayo argues that the dictionary definition of "student" — one "who engages in 'study' by applying the mind 'to the acquisition of learning, whether by means of books, observation, or experiment' " — plainly encompasses residents. And, Mayo adds, residents are not excluded from that category by the only limitation on students Congress has imposed under the statute-that they "be 'enrolled and regularly attending classes at [a] school.' "

Mayo's reading does not eliminate the statute's ambiguity as applied to working professionals. In its reply brief, Mayo acknowledges that a full-time professor taking evening classes — a person who presumably would satisfy the statute's class-enrollment requirement and apply his mind to learning — could be excluded from the exemption and taxed because he is not " 'predominant[ly]' " a student. Medical residents might likewise be excluded on the same basis; the statute itself does not resolve the ambiguity.

The District Court interpreted § 3121(b)(10) as unambiguously foreclosing the Department's rule by mandating that an employee be deemed "a 'student' so long as the educational aspect of his service predominates over the service aspect of the relationship with his employer." We do not think it possible to glean so much from the little that § 3121 provides. In any event, the statutory text still would offer no insight into how Congress intended predominance to be determined or whether Congress thought that medical residents would satisfy the requirement.

To the extent Congress has specifically addressed medical residents in § 3121, moreover, it has expressly excluded these doctors from exemptions they might otherwise invoke. That choice casts doubt on any claim that Congress specifically intended to insulate medical residents from FICA's reach in the first place.

In sum, neither the plain text of the statute nor the District Court's interpretation of the exemption "speak[s] with the precision necessary to say definitively whether [the statute] applies to" medical residents.

B

In the typical case, such an ambiguity would lead us inexorably to *Chevron* step two, under which we may not disturb an agency rule unless it is "'arbitrary or capricious in substance, or manifestly contrary to the statute.'" In this case, however, the parties disagree over the proper framework for evaluating an ambiguous provision of the Internal Revenue Code.

Mayo asks us to apply the multi-factor analysis we used to review a tax regulation in *National Muffler*. There we explained:

> "A regulation may have particular force if it is a substantially contemporaneous construction of the statute by those presumed to have been aware of congressional intent. If the regulation dates from a later period, the manner in which it evolved merits inquiry. Other relevant considerations are the length of time the regulation has been in effect, the reliance placed on it, the consistency of the Commissioner's interpretation, and the degree of scrutiny Congress has devoted to the regulation during subsequent re-enactments of the statute."

The Government, on the other hand, contends that the *National Muffler* standard has been superseded by *Chevron*. The sole question for the Court at step two under the *Chevron* analysis is "whether the agency's answer is based on a permissible construction of the statute." Since deciding *Chevron*, we have cited both *National Muffler* and *Chevron* in our review of Treasury Department regulations.

Although we have not thus far distinguished between *National Muffler* and *Chevron*, they call for different analyses of an ambiguous statute. Under *National Muffler*, for example, a court might view an agency's interpretation of a statute with heightened skepticism when it has not been consistent over time, when it was promulgated years after the relevant statute was enacted, or because of the way in which the regulation evolved. The District Court in this case cited each of these factors in rejecting the Treasury Department's rule, noting in particular that the regulation had been promulgated after an adverse judicial decision.

Under *Chevron*, in contrast, deference to an agency's interpretation of an ambiguous statute does not turn on such considerations. We have repeatedly held that "[a]gency inconsistency is not a basis for declining to analyze the agency's interpretation under the *Chevron* framework." We have instructed that "neither antiquity nor contemporaneity with [a] statute is a condition of [a regulation's] validity." And we have found it immaterial to our analysis that a "regulation was prompted by litigation." Indeed, in, we expressly invited the Treasury Department to "amend its regulations" if troubled by the consequences of our resolution of the case.

Aside from our past citation of *National Muffler*, Mayo has not advanced any justification for applying a less deferential standard of review to Treasury Department regulations than we apply to the rules of any other agency. In the absence of such justification, we are not inclined to carve out an approach to administrative review good for tax law only. To the contrary, we have expressly "[r]ecogniz[ed] the importance of maintaining a uniform approach to judicial review of administrative action."

The principles underlying our decision in *Chevron* apply with full force in the tax context. *Chevron* recognized that "[t]he power of an administrative agency to administer a congressionally created . . . program necessarily requires the formulation of policy and the making of rules to fill any gap left, implicitly or explicitly, by Congress." It acknowledged that the formulation of that policy might require "more than ordinary knowledge respecting the matters subjected to agency regulations." Filling gaps in the Internal Revenue Code plainly requires the Treasury Department to make interpretive choices for statutory implementation at least as complex as the ones other agencies must make in administering their statutes. We see no reason why our review of tax regulations should not be guided by agency expertise pursuant to *Chevron* to the same extent as our review of other regulations.

As one of Mayo's *amici* points out, however, both the full-time employee rule and the rule at issue in *National Muffler* were promulgated pursuant to the Treasury Department's general authority . . . to "prescribe all needful rules and regulations for the enforcement" [as codified in] the Internal Revenue Code. In two decisions predating *Chevron*, this Court stated that "we owe the [Treasury Department's] interpretation less deference" when it is contained in a rule adopted under that "general authority" than when it is "issued under a specific grant of authority to define a statutory term or prescribe a method of executing a statutory provision."

We have held that *Chevron* deference is appropriate "when it appears that Congress delegated authority to the agency generally to make rules carrying the force of law, and that the agency interpretation claiming deference was promulgated in the exercise of that authority." Our inquiry in that regard does not turn on whether Congress's delegation of authority was general or specific. For example, in *National Cable & Telecommunications Assn.*, we held that the Federal Communications Commission was delegated "the authority to promulgate binding legal rules" entitled to *Chevron* deference under statutes that gave the Commission "the authority to 'execute and enforce,' " and "to 'prescribe such rules and regulations as may be necessary in the public interest to carry out the provisions' of," the Communications Act of 1934.

We believe *Chevron* . . . , rather than *National Muffler* . . . , provide the appropriate framework for evaluating the full-time employee rule. The Department issued the full-time employee rule pursuant to the explicit authorization to "prescribe all needful rules and regulations for the enforcement" of the Internal Revenue Code. We have found such "express congressional authorizations to engage in the process of rulemaking" to be "a very good indicator of delegation meriting *Chevron* treatment." The Department issued the full-time employee rule only after notice-and-comment procedures, again a consideration identified in our precedents as a "significant" sign that a rule merits *Chevron* deference.

We have explained that "the ultimate question is whether Congress would have intended, and expected, courts to treat [the regulation] as within, or outside, its delegation to the agency of 'gap-filling' authority." In the *Long Island Care* case, we found that *Chevron* provided the appropriate standard of review "[w]here an agency rule sets forth important individual rights and duties, where the agency focuses fully and directly upon the issue, where the agency uses full notice-and-comment procedures to promulgate a rule, [and] where the resulting rule falls within the statutory grant of authority." These same considerations point to the same result here. This case falls squarely within the bounds of, and is properly analyzed under, *Chevron* and *Mead.*

C

The full-time employee rule easily satisfies the second step of *Chevron,* which asks whether the Department's rule is a "reasonable interpretation" of the enacted text. To begin, Mayo accepts that "the 'educational aspect of the relationship between the employer and the employee, as compared to the service aspect of the relationship, [must] be predominant' " in order for an individual to qualify for the exemption. Mayo objects, however, to the Department's conclusion that residents who work more than 40 hours per week categorically cannot satisfy that requirement. Because residents' employment is itself educational, Mayo argues, the hours a resident spends working make him "more of a student, not less of one." Mayo contends that the Treasury Department should be required to engage in a case-by-case inquiry into "*what* [each] employee does [in his service] and *why*" he does it. Mayo also objects that the Department has drawn an arbitrary distinction between "hands-on training" and "classroom instruction."

We disagree. Regulation, like legislation, often requires drawing lines. Mayo does not dispute that the Treasury Department reasonably sought a way to distinguish between workers who study and students who work. Focusing on the hours an individual works and the hours he spends in studies is a perfectly sensible way of accomplishing that goal. The Department explained that an individual's service and his "course of study are separate and distinct activities" in "the vast majority of cases," and reasoned that "[e]mployees who are working enough hours to be considered full-time employees . . . have filled the conventional measure of available time with work, and not study." The Department thus did not distinguish classroom education from clinical training but rather education from service. The Department reasonably concluded that its full-time employee rule would "improve administrability," and it thereby "has avoided the wasteful litigation and continuing uncertainty that would inevitably accompany any purely case-by-case approach" like the one Mayo advocates.

As the Treasury Department has explained, moreover, the full-time employee rule has more to recommend it than administrative convenience. The Department reasonably determined that taxing residents under FICA would further the purpose of the Social Security Act and comport with this Court's precedent. As the Treasury Department appreciated, this Court has understood the terms of the Social Security Act to " 'import a breadth of coverage,' " and we have instructed that "exemptions from taxation are to be construed narrowly." Although Mayo contends that medical residents have not yet begun their "working lives" because they are not "fully trained," . . . [T]he Department certainly did not act irrationally in concluding that these doctors-"who work long hours, serve as highly skilled professionals, and typically share some or all of the terms of employment of career employees"-are the kind of workers that Congress intended to both contribute to and benefit from the Social Security system.

The Department's rule takes into account the SSA's concern that exempting residents from FICA would deprive residents and their families of vital disability and survivorship benefits that Social Security provides. Mayo wonders whether the full-time employee rule will result in residents being taxed under FICA but denied coverage by the SSA. The Government informs us, however, that the SSA continues to adhere to its longstanding position that medical residents are not students and thus remain eligible for coverage.

. . . .

We do not doubt that Mayo's residents are engaged in a valuable educational pursuit or that they are students of their craft. The question whether they are "students" for purposes of § 3121, however, is a different matter. Because it is one to which Congress has not directly spoken, and because the Treasury Department's rule is a reasonable construction of what Congress has said, the judgment of the Court of Appeals must be affirmed.

It is so ordered.

NOTES

1. What are Mayo's principle arguments to qualify medical residents as students? What data might you consider as supporting these arguments? What data might be beneficial as counter-arguments for the United States?

2. As the case articulated, courts give deference to agency regulations. Two frameworks have been asserted. Compare and contrast the *Chevron* framework with the *National Muffler* framework. What conditions or circumstances might make one more appropriate than the other?

3. Prior to the Court's ruling, the U.S. Court of Appeals for the Second, Sixth, Seventh, and Eleventh Circuits had applied the FICA "student exception" rule to medical residents. *See United States v. Memorial Sloan-Kettering Cancer Ctr.*, 563 F.3d 19 (2d Cir. 2009); *United States v. Detroit Med. Ctr.*, 557 F.3d 412 (6th Cir. 2009); *Univ. of Chicago Hospitals v. United States*, 545 F.3d 564 (7th Cir. 2008);

United States v. Mount Sinai Med. Ctr. of Fla., 486 F.3d 1248 (11th Cir. 2007).

4. If the court had ruled in favor of the university hospital and determined that medical residents qualified as students, the U.S. would have collected significantly fewer tax revenues. As Jack Stripling of *Inside Higher Ed* reported, "[w]hile the university has been paying the taxes in accordance with Treasury rules since 2005, a ruling in Mayo's favor would have netted $24 million in estimated refunds for residents, officials said. Applied more broadly to other medical schools and universities, the government estimated an adverse decision would result in more than $1 billion in reimbursements." Jack Stripling, *Medical Residents Ruled Employees*, Inside Higher Ed, Jan. 12, 2011.

5. Whether a medical resident qualifies as either an employee or student differs largely by context and applicable statutory provisions. For instance, in California, medical residents qualify as individuals covered under the Higher Education Employer-Employee Relations Act. *Regents of the Univ. of Cal. v. Public Employment Relations Bd.*, 224 Cal. Rptr. 631 (Cal. 1986). Considering the two views of classifying medical residents as either state employees or students motivated by educational objectives, the California Supreme Court ruled consistently with the state labor board that medical residents were employees. The court noted the state labor board's examination of the character of the medical residents' work to conclude that the educational objectives were subordinate to the services performed.

By contrast, in *Ross v. University of Minnesota*, 439 N.W.2d 28 (Minn. Ct. App. 1989), the court held that the medical resident was a student. In that case, the university-defendant dismissed the plaintiff from the psychiatry residency program. The plaintiff sued, asserting multiple claims including breach of contract and substantive and procedural due process violations. The Minnesota appellate court found that the university's "decision to terminate a resident from a hospital-based residency program is the same as any other decision to fail a graduate student for inability to meet academic requirements. Courts have historically deferred to the decisions of academic institutions on the academic achievements or failures of their students." *Id.* at 33. Thus, the circumstances in this case warrant the examination of the medical resident as a student, not employee.

B. AUTHORITY TO HIRE AND NEGOTIATE TERMS

BRUNER v. UNIVERSITY OF SOUTHERN MISSISSIPPI

501 So. 2d 1113 (Miss. 1987)

Griffin, Justice, for the court:

This case, involving the alleged grant of an employment contract by an agent of a public board, comes to the Court from the Circuit Court of the First Judicial District of Hinds County, Mississippi. At trial, the judge granted directed verdicts as to the Board of Trustees of State Institutions of Higher Learning, the University of Southern Mississippi, Dr. Aubrey Lucas, the University's president, and Roland Dale, the University's athletic director. The jury then returned a verdict in favor of the sole remaining defendant, Jim Carmody, the University's head football coach. Here, Jerry Bruner, the plaintiff, appeals the directed verdicts as well as the lower court's denial of his motion for judgment notwithstanding the verdict. We affirm.

This case concerns a colossal misunderstanding between Jerry Bruner, an unemployed assistant coach, who, languishing in the brown waste of West Texas, viewed Hattiesburg, centrally located between his home in Florida and that of his wife in Louisiana, as a veritable Garden of Eden, and Jim Carmody, then recently appointed head football coach of the Golden Eagles, who was searching for a new offensive line coach.

According to Bruner, on February 2, 1982, Carmody called to offer him a job, stating, "So far as I'm concerned, you are the offensive line coach and I will not be looking for another coach, and I expect the same from you." This is consistent with Cathy Bruner's recollection of the conversation, which she overheard on an extension. On February 7, the parties repeated the essential points of this telephone call in a second conversation. Thereafter, Bruner withdrew his name from consideration for other coaching positions.

On February 15, Bruner flew from his home in El Paso, to Hattiesburg, meeting with Carmody over dinner and, thereafter, in his office. The following day, Bruner met Dale, who stated that he was glad Bruner was "coming over." Later, Bruner received the keys to an automobile, listing the University as his employer on the insurance application. He then contacted a local realtor, for whom Mrs. Carmody had worked, spending three hours looking at houses. Carmody also gave Bruner keys to an administrative office.

In the afternoon, Bruner met with Lucas. Their conversation, consisting of small talk about past work experience and mutual acquaintances, lasted approximately twenty minutes, followed by a two-minute conversation between Dale and Lucas, while Bruner waited outside.

On February 17, Dale told Bruner that he was not to appear on the practice field before the Board of Trustees approved Carmody's recommendation; otherwise, reporters would have the story prior to an official announcement. According to Bruner, this was the first mention of any requirement concerning the Board's approval of his appointment. Consequently, he spent the remainder of the day watching game films.

The next day, February 18, Dale told Bruner that he could fly to El Paso for the weekend, returning after the next Board meeting. Leaving his luggage in the trunk of the automobile, Bruner returned home.

Meanwhile, Cathy Bruner, Jerry's wife, had quit her job. On February 17, she received two estimates for the cost of the move, as required by the University. She also received a letter from the realtor, concerning available houses and their neighborhood schools. The children then notified their respective schools about the transfer of transcripts.

On February 23, 1982, the following Monday, Bruner received a call from Dale, informing him that he did not have the job. Dale offered no explanation. The next day, after several unsuccessful attempts to contact Carmody, the head football coach called Bruner to apologize, telling him that Lucas had not liked his appearance during their meeting. For the next five weeks, Bruner searched for another job, finally accepting one as an assistant coach in the Canadian Football League.

Yet, according to Carmody and Dale, called adversely, Bruner was merely one of several individuals considered for the position of offensive line coach. In fact, during their telephone conversations, Carmody only asked Bruner to come for an interview. Upon his arrival, though, Carmody agreed to recommend Bruner for the job, but stated that it was subject to the Board's approval. When asked then about Bruner's receipt of a car and keys to an office, as well as his access to game films, Carmody stated that this was consistent with interviews for other candidates.

Additionally, Dale testified that he told Bruner about other candidates interviewing for the job. Nevertheless, Bruner expressed extreme confidence in his ultimate selection. Moreover, neither Carmody nor Dale possessed any knowledge, relating to Bruner's purchase of automobile insurance.

Finally, Lucas stated that he had received a recommendation from Carmody and Dale for Bruner, but that based at least partially upon Bruner's appearance, he asked Dale to "look further." Lucas denied, however, that he had rejected their recommendation. The Minutes of the Board of Trustees of Institutions of Higher Learning make no mention of any recommendation for or approval of Bruner.

I.

Bruner appeals the grant of a directed verdict as to the University, arguing that Carmody, its agent, possessed the "apparent authority" to extend an employment contract for the position of assistant coach. The directed verdict then improperly removed the University from the suit, despite its liability as Carmody's principal. This, however, simply will not wash.

The University of Southern Mississippi is an agency of the State of Mississippi controlled by a legislative grant of authority to the Board of Trustees of State Institutions of Higher Learning. Specifically, Miss.Code Ann. § 37-101-15(f) reads, in part:

> (f) The board shall have the power and authority to elect the heads of the various institutions of higher learning and to *contract with all deans, professors, and other members of the teaching staff, and all administrative employees of said institutions* for a term of not exceeding four (4) years. The board shall have the power and authority to terminate any such contract at any time for malfeasance, inefficiency, or contumacious conduct, but never for political reasons. *It shall be the policy of the board to permit the executive head of each institution to nominate for election by the board all subordinate employees* of the institution over which he presides. (emphasis added).

Therefore, a valid employment contract exists with the University of Southern Mississippi where the Board of Trustees of State Institutions of Higher Learning approves a nomination of the school's president. Moreover, this is the *only* way to create such a contract: In respect to public contracts "where a particular manner of contracting is prescribed, the manner is the measure of power and must be followed to create a valid contract."

On several previous occasions, the Court has noted that an enforceable contract must appear in the official minutes of a public board further holding that "each person, firm or corporation," so contracting, "is responsible to see that the contract is legal and properly recorded" on such minutes. Though concerning the Board of Supervisors of Tallahatchie County and not the Board of Trustees of State Institutions of Higher Learning, the rationale for the above rule voiced in *Smith v. Board of Supervisors*, is applicable here:

> A board of supervisors can act only as a body, and its act must be evidenced by an entry on its minutes. The minutes of the board of supervisors are the sole and exclusive evidence of what the board did. The individuals composing the board cannot act for the county, nor officially in reference to the county's business, except as authorized by law, and the minutes of the board of supervisors must be the repository and the evidence of their official acts.

It is undisputed that the Minutes of the Board of Trustees are silent as to any nomination for or approval of Jerry Bruner. As the only recognized manner by which the University may contract for employment with an applicant, there is no basis for liability so as to defeat the University's directed verdict. We can only remind the appellant of the legal maxim, which states that a person, dealing with an agent, must know at his peril the extent of the agent's authority to bind his principal.

As to Lucas and Dale, the trial judge was also correct. In fact, there is no evidence in the record to indicate any grounds on which to submit a question to the jury concerning Lucas' liability.

The same is true for Dale. Indeed, Bruner himself testified that Dale both kept him off the practice field and sent him home to El Paso, awaiting the approval of the Board of Trustees.

. . .

Consistent with the above and finding no other error, we affirm.

AFFIRMED.

NOTES

1. According to the case, under what circumstances would administrators at the University of Southern Mississippi have authority to extend contract offers to candidates? Would the outcome of the case have changed if Bruner was a candidate for a different position?

2. What arguments might Bruner have made if Dale had called Bruner and Lucas had conveyed to Bruner plans about the upcoming season? How would the arguments change if the discussion was only with Dale?

3. Post-hire contract renegotiations follow similar legal rules. In *Huyett v. Idaho State University*, 104 P.3d 946 (Idaho 2004), the Idaho Supreme Court also examined a case involving apparent or actual authority. Explaining the differences between actual and apparent authority, the state high court expressed:

> Actual authority may be either express or implied. Express authority occurs when a principal explicitly authorizes an agent to act on the principal's behalf. Implied authority derives from those actions necessary to accomplish an act expressly authorized. Apparent authority occurs when a principal by words or actions voluntarily places an agent in such a position that an ordinary person of business prudence would believe the agent is acting pursuant to existing authority. A court may make a finding of apparent authority to protect third parties but only where the third party was not on notice of the scope of the agent's actual authority.

Id. at 908. In order to provide some context to the court's analysis, consider the facts that gave rise to the situation in *Huyett*:

> Shirley Huyett (Huyett), was hired by Idaho State University acting through Howard Gauthier (ISU) to serve as head coach of the women's basketball team on June 29, 2001. On this day, Gauthier sent Huyett a letter setting forth terms relating to her one-year employment as head coach. Huyett returned a copy of this letter with her signed assent to the terms indicated in this letter. In a telephone call between Huyett and Gauthier later that day, Huyett expressed her desire for a multi-year employment contract. Gauthier made vague references to the possibility of such a contract after Huyett had begun work at the university. Huyett began as head coach of the ISU women's basketball team in July of 2001. Shortly following her employment she was asked to sign a number of forms to complete her payroll paperwork with the university. One of these forms was listed as an "Employment Contract" and contained language indicating that Huyett's employment was subject to the terms and conditions of the Rules and Governing Policies of the Idaho State Board of Education. This document noted that Huyett's duties were subject to reassignment by the university at any time.
>
> During Huyett's one-year employment term, negotiations for a multi-year contract took place between Huyett and ISU. ISU prepared a draft three-year employment contract in October of 2001. Prior to either party signing the contract, ISU rescinded the draft and placed Huyett on administrative leave. Huyett filed suit in district court alleging, among other things, breach of an expressed or implied contract for multi-year employment and a procedural due process violation based on deprivation of her liberty and property interests associated with continued employment. The district court granted ISU's motion for summary judgment, holding that the creation of a multi-year employment contract required prior approval by the Board of Education (Board) and that no such approval was given. The district court also determined that absent a multi-year contract for employment, Huyett did not have a protected liberty or property interest.

> Huyett appealed, arguing that the district court erred in applying [Idaho Administrative Procedures Act] Personnel Rule 08.01.02.103.02.c rather than a Board of Education policy provision to determine whether prior approval by the Board of Education was required to create a multi-year employment contract. She asserts this error led the court to improperly conclude no multi-year contract existed between the parties and that she did not have a liberty or property interest from which to assert due process claims.

Id. at 906–07. As the Idaho Supreme Court indicated, the Idaho Administrative Procedures Act and the State Board of Higher Education policies were in conflict. The court followed the state administrative procedures act as the prevailing law. The administrative procedures indicated that multi-year contracts require State Board of Higher Education approval. Thus, when the negotiated document did not have the Board's approval, it was not recognized as an employment contract.

C. CONTRACTUAL RELATIONSHIP

1. Handbook

FOGEL v. TRUSTEES OF IOWA COLLEGE
446 N.W.2d 451 (Iowa 1989)

NEUMAN, JUSTICE.

This appeal involves plaintiff Warren Fogel's claim of wrongful termination by his employer, Grinnell College. Four of Fogel's claims-physical disability discrimination, retaliatory discharge, breach of employment contract and breach of covenant of good faith and fair dealing-were dismissed by the trial court on Grinnell's motion for summary judgment. Fogel's fifth claim-age discrimination-was rejected by a jury following trial. On Fogel's appeal from these adverse rulings, we affirm the judgment of the district court. [Editorial Note: For purposes of this case excerpt, the breach of contract issue is the only one analyzed here.]

I. Background Facts and Proceedings.

Fogel was employed by Grinnell College as a receiving clerk and custodian in the college's food service department from August 1977 until his dismissal on January 28, 1985. At the time of his hiring, Fogel was fifty-five years of age. Throughout his employment, Fogel's duties were to unload trucks, handle food products, and perform custodial work in student dining halls and kitchen areas.

There was no written employment contract between Fogel and the college. At the time of Fogel's hiring, however, the college gave him a "Grinnell College Staff Handbook" which was later updated specifically for the guidance of food service employees. Pertinent to this appeal are the handbook's terms regarding dismissal from employment:

> DISMISSAL. If termination is necessary for reasons not prejudicial to the employee (reasons unrelated to job performance), he/she may expect to receive notice of not less than one month prior to the termination date. Upon receiving such notice, the employee is free both to seek and to accept other work immediately and to receive any accrued vacation pay. When dismissal is necessary because of unsatisfactory work, as much notice as possible will be given, ordinarily not less than two weeks. However, dismissals occurring during the probationary period require no notice. Dismissals necessitated by dishonesty or misconduct become effective immediately upon determination of facts concerning the offense.

While employed by the college, Fogel suffered a number of minor injuries resulting in medical insurance claims and reimbursement. The only incident of a serious nature occurred in September 1983. At that time, Fogel experienced back pain from lifting chairs and mopping which caused him to miss between five and ten days of work. The medical and chiropractic attention necessitated by this injury was covered by insurance. It was not until August 1985, seven months after the discharge triggering this appeal, that Fogel filed a workers' compensation claim for this back injury.

Although Fogel routinely received satisfactory evaluations with respect to his work performance, he was also the subject of numerous disciplinary actions. All but one related to what the personnel director described as a "chronic hygiene problem." In September 1981, Fogel was admonished concerning proper dress and personal hygiene standards. One month later Fogel received a written warning for reporting to work in a dirty uniform. In December 1981, Fogel was suspended and placed on probation for urinating in a mop bucket while on duty. He was also cited for carelessness in 1983 after he backed a college vehicle into a parked car.

The incident giving rise to the present action occurred in December 1984 while the college was in recess for the holidays. Fogel, who then wore long hair and a beard, was told by his hair stylist that she thought he had head lice. Fogel used a recommended treatment shampoo and that same evening attended the food service employees' holiday party. Six days later, Fogel consulted a physician in Grinnell who confirmed the presence of "nits," or lice larvae, in Fogel's eyebrows. Further treatment was prescribed.

During the semester break, Fogel wrote a letter to his immediate supervisor concerning the lice condition and the action he had taken in regard to it. In the letter, he acknowledged that he had been aware of a problem "for quite a few months and just thought of a nerve condition, causing the problem." He also updated her about the medical attention and bills he had incurred for continuing back pain, and the exercise program that he was required to follow "[w]orking or no working."

When classes resumed and Fogel reported for work in mid-January 1985, he was advised by David McConnell, director of food service, that he could not return to his job without a medical release. Fogel obtained the release and returned to work that day. On January 28, 1985, McConnell sent Fogel a letter informing him that he was discharged immediately because he was "unfit to work in a food service establishment." The letter stated that Fogel had put the entire food service operation "in jeopardy by coming to work with head lice," an act McConnell understood to be in violation of state food service establishment laws. The letter also cited the 1981 mop bucket incident as a breach of sanitation standards.

Fogel unsuccessfully appealed his dismissal to the college's executive vice-president and president. He then filed suit in district court charging the college with age discrimination, disability discrimination, wrongful discharge in violation of public policy, breach of contract, and breach of an implied covenant of good faith and fair dealing. Upon completion of discovery, the college moved for summary judgment on all counts of Fogel's petition. It asserted that no material facts were in dispute regarding any of Fogel's claims and that the college was entitled to judgment as a matter of law.

The district court sustained the college's motion on all but the age discrimination claim. There it noted the existence of a prima facie case of discrimination (plaintiff in a protected age group, qualified for the job, discharged, replaced by a younger person) and concluded that a fact question remained concerning whether the college's proffered reason for termination was authentic or pretextual. The issue was ultimately tried to a jury and resolved in favor of the college. Fogel does not challenge the jury's verdict on this appeal.

. . . [For purposes of this discussion, we examine the effect of the college handbook.] [T]he district court concluded that the college handbook was insufficient, as a matter of law, to create a contract of employment between Fogel and Grinnell that would give rise to an action for its breach. The court concluded that Fogel was an at-will employee, subject to termination "at any time for any reason." It is from these rulings that Fogel has appealed.

II. Scope of Review.

Fogel insists that his "economic life should not be snuffed out without a trial." His assertion highlights our principal inquiry on this appeal: Did the trial court err when it granted Grinnell judgment as a matter of law? Familiar rules guide our inquiry. We review them briefly.

Summary judgment is proper when there appears no genuine issues of material fact and the moving party is entitled to judgment as a matter of law. The burden is upon the moving party to show that no issue of material fact exists. Moreover, the resisting party is afforded every legitimate inference that can be reasonably deduced from the evidence and a fact question is generated if reasonable minds could differ on how the issue should be resolved.

The party resisting summary judgment, however, "may not rest upon the mere allegations or denials of his pleading." The resistance must set forth specific facts which constitute competent evidence showing a *prima facie* claim. By requiring the resister to go beyond generalities, the basic purpose of summary judgment procedure is achieved: to weed out "[p]aper cases and defenses" in order "to make way for litigation which does have something to it." With these principles in mind, we consider the arguments of the parties in the light of the record of pleadings, affidavits, and deposition testimony submitted to the trial court.

III. Arguments on appeal.

. . . .

C. *Breach of contract.* The district court determined that Fogel was an at-will employee whose employment could be terminated at any time, for any lawful reason. This common law doctrine of employment at-will is firmly rooted in Iowa law.

To date, this court has carved out only two narrow exceptions to the employment at-will doctrine. The first, described earlier in this opinion under Fogel's claim of retaliatory discharge, creates liability in tort when the discharge is in clear violation of a "well-recognized and defined public policy of the State." The second exception arises where a contract created by an employer's handbook or policy manual guarantees an employee that discharge will occur only for cause or under certain conditions. These cases hold that an at-will employee discharged in violation of the terms of such a handbook or policy manual may maintain a breach of contract action against an employer.

Fogel contends that Grinnell's staff handbook created a contract of employment under which he could be discharged only for "misconduct." Citing the court's error for having decided the question as a matter of law, Fogel insists (1) that a material fact question exists over whether carrying lice constitutes misconduct, even for a food service employee, and (2) that the contractual status of the employee handbook is strictly a fact question determinable by *his* reasonable expectations. For this latter proposition, Fogel relies heavily on our language in *Cannon* that

> [w]hether the written personnel policies became part of plaintiff's contract is to be determined on the basis of plaintiff's reasonable expectations.

Fogel's reliance on *Cannon* is misplaced. This court has recently recognized that an employee manual may constitute a unilateral contract only if the traditional requirements of contract formation have been met. Thus, an employee handbook may create a unilateral contract if (1) the handbook is sufficiently definite in its terms to create an *offer;* (2) the handbook has been communicated to and accepted by the employee so as to create an *acceptance;* and (3) the employee has continued working, so as to provide *consideration.* Except in the case of ambiguity, whether such a written instrument binds the parties in contract is a question of law.

The starting point of the unilateral contract inquiry is whether the terms of the handbook are sufficiently definite to constitute an offer of continued employment. As we noted in *McBride*, claims premised on unilateral contract theory frequently fail because the handbook's dismissal or disciplinary provisions are too indefinite to meet this standard of definiteness. The reason for requiring such a high threshold of definiteness is two-fold. First, courts are generally reluctant to dismantle an employer's long-standing common-law right to terminate at-will in the absence of an express offer by the employer to do so. Second, the handbook language must be sufficiently definite in its offer of continued employment that a fact finder is not left adjudicating the alleged breach of a "contract" for which the fact finder has supplied its own terms.

On its face, Grinnell's handbook falls short of the definiteness required to constitute an offer of continued employment. The first sentence of the "dismissal" section unambiguously states that an employee may be terminated "for reasons not prejudicial to the employee." Although the handbook goes on to state the notice which the college would strive to provide depending on the circumstances necessitating dismissal, no guarantee of permanent employment is made or even suggested. No restriction to dismissal "for cause" can be found. The handbook is silent on the meaning of "misconduct" giving rise to the college's prerogative of immediate dismissal. Contrary to Fogel's suggestion that this silence creates an ambiguity in the writing entitling him to offer evidence regarding the intent of the parties, we agree with another court that recently found that an employer's unspecific guidelines "merely reflect[ ] the terminable-at-will status of its employees."

We conclude as a matter of law that Grinnell's employment manual was too indefinite to create an enforceable unilateral contract giving rise to a cause of action for its breach. The district court correctly granted summary judgment for Grinnell on this claim.

. . . .

AFFIRMED.

NOTES

1. How might the outcome in *Fogel* have changed if the employee was a temporary employee or an independent contractor? What arguments might a temporary employee or an independent contractor assert to be deemed an employee? How might the employer overcome these arguments?

2. While many states accept the incorporation of an employee manual into the terms of the employment contract, not all states do. In some states, an employee manual does *not* constitute a contract. *See, e.g., Gilbert v. Tulane Univ.*, 909 F.2d 124 (5th Cir. 1990); *Stanton v. Tulane Univ.*, 777 So. 2d 1242 (La. Ct. App. 2001), *writ of appeal denied*,789 So. 2d 597 (La. 2001). Employment manuals are often considered a unilateral contract, an agreement without mutuality of obligation, or not recognized as a contract at all — which may be justified when parties have not demonstrated some manifestation of assent to the terms of the claimed contract. Similarly, these employee manuals may be recognized as primarily informational in nature used mainly for outlining employee conduct, policies, or grievances procedures. *See, e.g., Wall v. Tulane Univ.*, 499 So. 2d 375 (La. Ct. App. 1986) (university's staff handbook, which described benefits and conditions of employment with university, was primarily informational in nature, was not made part of employee's employment agreement, and, therefore, was not binding promise by university to continue indefinitely benefits described in handbook).

Yet another analytical path was taken by a D.C. court in *Clampitt v. American University.*, 957 A.2d 23 (D.C. 2008). In *Clampitt*, the court found that because the manual had not been updated for some time, the manual did not qualify as part of the terms to the employment contract.

2. College Handbook Disclaimer

ELLIOTT v. BOARD OF TRUSTEES OF MONTGOMERY COUNTY COMMUNITY COLLEGE
655 A.2d 46 (Ct. Sp. App. Md. 1995)

CATHELL, JUDGE.

OPINION

Appellant, James Elliott, appeals from the judgment of the Circuit Court for Montgomery County (Cave, J., presiding), granting appellee's, the Board of Trustees of Montgomery County Community College's, Motion for Summary Judgment in this breach of employment contract case. Appellant presents the following questions on appeal:

A. Did Montgomery College's Policies and Procedures Manual create an enforceable employment contract between Montgomery College and its employee, James Elliott[?]

B. Did Montgomery College clearly and conspicuously disclaim any intent to create an enforceable contract by virtue of the Montgomery College Policies and Procedures Manual[?]

C. Did the trial Court err in finding, as a matter of law, that Montgomery College did not breach the contract created by its Employee Handbook[?]

D. Was the Trial Court precluded by the Maryland Administrative Procedures Act from allowing a jury to determine whether Mr. Elliott was terminated for cause[?]

Appellant was hired by Montgomery County Community College (the College) in 1979. He was promoted to a supervisory position in 1988. In 1992, a female employee charged appellant with sexual harassment. As a result, appellant was disciplined, an action that included a demotion and a transfer to the College's Germantown campus. A "last chance letter" was issued to appellant, which provided, in pertinent part:

> It is very important that you understand that these actions are taken in the context of giving you a last chance to remain employed at Montgomery College. Any violation of . . . College . . . policy . . . and procedures will lead to immediate disciplinary action, up to and including dismissal.

In February of 1993, appellant was charged with violating College policy by leaving work early without permission. The College's "Policies/Procedures Manual" (P & P Manual) provides that employees are "[t]o report to work on time and stay until the end of the work day. . . ." It is undisputed that appellant left his shift up to one hour early on four separate occasions. Appellant claimed that his immediate supervisor, John Day, gave him permission to leave work whenever he had completed his duties, even if this occurred before the end of his shift. Day claimed that he only gave appellant permission to do this during the "winter term" and the four occasions on which appellant was charged with leaving early took place after the "winter term" was over.

Day's supervisor filed a recommendation with the Director of Human Resources that appellant's employment be terminated. The Director approved the recommendation and notified appellant that he was terminated, effective April 2, 1993. Appellant filed a Notice of Appeal on March 23, 1993. An appeal hearing was thereafter held before Provost O. Robert Brown on the issue of whether cause existed to discharge appellant. Dr. Brown recommended that the dismissal be upheld and that recommendation was upheld by the Chief Administrative Officer of the College.

Appellant's supervisor gave him a copy of the P & P Manual to read when he first started working at the College in 1979. Appellant was issued his own P & P Manual when he was promoted to his supervisory position in 1988. That same year, the College issued a new P & P Manual. It is not clear when appellant's promotion occurred in relation to the distribution of the new manual. A two-page memorandum accompanied the new manual that provided, in part:

> The new manual, while similar in content to the old one, has been restructured to make it easier to use and update as follows. . . .

It then listed six numbered paragraphs concerning the use of the manual, a paragraph concerning computer access, and then notes that:

> The primary purpose of changing the format of the manual is to make it easier for you to use it as a reference document.

Conspicuously *absent* from the memorandum is any acknowledgement that the manual modification also changed the inherent nature of the employment relationship. No attempt was made to indicate that the new manual provided the following disclaimer in its introduction: "[The manual] does not contain all terms and conditions of employment nor constitute an express or implied employment contract."

After exhausting his remedies at the College, appellant filed this suit in the circuit court, alleging breach of an employment contract. Appellee filed a Motion for Summary Judgment, including with the motion an affidavit that provided that the handbook containing the disclaimer had been distributed to all employees eligible to receive it in 1988 and, thereafter, to each employee that had since become eligible to receive it. In support of his opposition to appellee's Motion for Summary Judgment, appellant provided an affidavit in which he stated that he had never seen the disclaimer. At the hearing held on the motion, appellant argued that the disclaimer might not have been distributed to all the College's employees that were entitled to receive the P & P Manual. The hearing judge reserved ruling on the motion to allow appellant more time for discovery. After appellant failed to provide any evidence that the manual containing the disclaimer had not been distributed as appellee had claimed, the hearing judge granted appellee's Motion for Summary Judgment.

A. & B.

In *Castiglione v. Johns Hopkins Hosp.*, we stated:

> In Maryland, an employment contract of indefinite duration is considered employment "at will" which, with few exceptions, may be terminated without cause by either party at any time. In two limited situations an "at will" employee may not be discharged without cause. First, the rule that employment contracts of indefinite duration can be legally terminated at any time is inapplicable where the employee is discharged for exercising constitutionally protected rights. . . . The second exception [was] adopted by this court in *Staggs v. Blue Cross of Maryland.*

The exception to the employment at will doctrine that we adopted in *Staggs v. Blue Cross of Maryland*, was that an employee handbook may, in some circumstances, become an unilateral contract. In *Staggs*, we stated:

> The question is whether the contracts in dispute here, which are otherwise of indefinite duration, have been so modified by the personnel policy statement as to remove them from the full strictures of the common law rule. . . .
>
> There has been a great deal of litigation in recent years, throughout the country, over the effect of personnel handbooks and other types of policy statements issued by employers on "at will" employment agreements. Although there has yet to develop any uniform rule and the decisions vary somewhat, depending on the type of provision sought to be enforced and the theory pled by the employee, most of the more recent decisions seem to reflect the view that such unilateral pronouncements by an employer may create legally enforceable expectations on the part of its employees.
>
> Perhaps the best exposition of this view is found in *Toussaint v. Blue Cross & Blue Shield of Mich.* The Court there began by confirming the general rule that indefinite hirings are terminable at the will of either party. It noted, however, that,
>
> > "While an employer need not establish personnel policies or practices, where an employer chooses to establish such policies and practices and makes them known to its employees, the employment relationship is presumably enhanced. The employer secures an orderly, cooperative and loyal work force, and the employee the peace of mind associated with job security and the conviction that he will be treated fairly."
>
> From this, the Court concluded that where the employer "had established a company policy to discharge for just cause only, pursuant to certain procedures, had made that policy known to Toussaint, and thereby had committed itself to discharge him only for just cause in compliance with the procedures," a jury could find that "[a]lthough Toussaint's employment was for an indefinite term . . . the relationship was not terminable at the will of Blue Cross."

We adopted the Michigan court's *Toussaint* decision as the law in Maryland, finding support for doing so in *Dahl v. Brunswick Corp.* There, the Court of Appeals stated that an employer's "policy directive with respect to severance pay constituted an offer of a unilateral contract of which the employees were aware and, by continuing to work for Brunswick, accepted." The Court added that "there is abundant support for the proposition that employer policy directives regarding aspects of the employment relation become contractual obligations when, with knowledge of their existence, employees start or continue to work for the employer."

In *Castiglione*, we noted that a disclaimer in an employee handbook may provide an exception to the *Staggs* rule, stating:

> The handbook contained a statement that it "does not constitute an express or implied contract." . . .
>
> . . . We cautioned . . . [in *Staggs*] that "[n]ot every statement made in a personnel handbook or other publication will rise to the level of an enforceable covenant."
>
> The disclaimer language in the policy manual quoted in appellee's pleadings does not indicate any intent to limit the discretion of the appellee to discharge only for cause, as was the case in *Staggs.* Moreover, other portions of the manual quoted in appellee's memorandum actually served to reserve the rights of appellee "to direct and discipline our workforce . . . and to take whatever action is necessary in our judgment to operate [the Defendant Hospital]." Finally, unlike the situation in *Staggs*, in this case the appellee expressly negated, in a clear and conspicuous manner, any contract based upon the handbook for a definite term and reserved the right to discharge its employees at any time. The provisions for review, when viewed in the larger context, were but "general policy statements" not amounting to an offer of employment for a definite term or requiring cause for dismissal.

Not every disclaimer in an employer's employee manual, however, will effectively disclaim contractual liability. In *Haselrig v. Public Storage, Inc.*, we noted that, in order for a disclaimer to be effective in preventing the formation of an employment contract, the disclaimer must be "clear and unequivocal. . . ." In *Haselrig*, the employer relied on two provisions in the employee handbook in support of its contention that it had effectively disclaimed any contractual liability in excess of that under the employment at will doctrine. One provision, under the heading captioned "Employment Relationship," provided:

> The relationship between you and PSI is *predicated* on an at will basis. That is to say that either the Employee or the Company may terminate their employment at their discretion.

The second provision was found in a section pertaining to a probationary period and provided:

> It should be understood that employment and compensation can be terminated, with or without cause and with or without notice at any time, at the option of either the Company or the Employee.

In deciding that these two provisions were not, as a matter of law, adequate to disclaim the employee handbook as an implied contract, we stated:

> If we determine that the language of the provisions is ambiguous-an ambiguity exists when the language in the provision is, to a reasonably prudent layman, susceptible of more than one meaning, or where the placement of the provisions in the handbook has that effect-and/or equivocal, then the issue of appellant's justification in relying on the other provisions is for the fact finder. Where the issue is, as it is here, the justiciability of an employee's reliance on a handbook, we must consider both the placement of the provisions in the handbook and the language of the provisions.

The language of the disclaimer in the case *sub judice* is not ambiguous. Nor does the placement of the disclaimer cause one to question whether it applied to only a portion of the manual; its placement in the new P & P Manual's introduction clearly indicates its application to the manual as a whole.* Nevertheless, appellant proffers two reasons why the disclaimer was not, as a matter of law, sufficient. First, he claims that he never received the disclaimer. With respect to this contention, we note that it is not necessary that an employee actually read a disclaimer in order for it to be valid.

We initially note that an employer is free to modify unilaterally the contractual relationship that it had previously established with its employees as a result of an employee manual. In *Castiglione*, we responded to [the plaintiff's] argument that the manual she was first issued did not claim a disclaimer by stating:

> Even if the review provisions of the manual in effect at appellant's initial hiring constituted an implied contract, . . . the later manual [which did have a disclaimer] would have superseded any earlier editions. By continuing to work for appellee after the new manual's issuance, appellant, by her conduct, impliedly would have assented to a modification of her employment agreement.

The affidavit that appellee included in its Motion for Summary Judgment provided the undisputed fact that the disclaimer was distributed "College-wide in September 1988." The hearing judge provided appellant the opportunity to conduct discovery and submit evidence that this was not true. Appellant failed to submit any such evidence. While no Maryland appellate court has had the opportunity to address the issue of whether each individual employee must actually see the disclaimer, we note the concern the hearing judge expressed over creating such liability, namely, "It does not matter . . . whether he remembers getting it, whether he received it because everyone, then, can come in and say, 'I don't remember seeing it. I never got it.' If it was generally circulated, then that is what becomes the agreement, and the disclaimer is valid." We agree with Judge Cave on this point.

While other jurisdictions appear to be split over this precise issue, we find the rule adopted by the Michigan courts to be persuasive. In *Grow v. General Products,*

* We nevertheless perceive that the better practice might well be to have such disclaimer language in bold print, at the very beginning of the introduction or in some other way *prominently highlighted* within the introduction.

Inc., the court affirmed the granting of a summary disposition, stating that "an employer may unilaterally change its employment termination policy so long as reasonable notice is given. *Reasonable* notification is not necessarily *actual* notification. . . ." In *Transou v. Electronic Data System*, the court granted the employer's motion for summary judgment, stating: "Though plaintiff claims that he does not recall receiving a copy of the handbook, its disclaimer is effective in light of the uniform and reasonable method of distributing the manual throughout the company." In the case *sub judice*, the undisputed evidence indicates that the P & P Manual containing the disclaimer was generally circulated College-wide in 1988. We hold that, in reference to disclaimers in employee handbooks or manuals, reasonable notification, not actual notification, is sufficient to put the employee on notice of the disclaimer. We further hold that a uniform, system wide distribution of a disclaimer will generally constitute reasonable notice thereof.

Appellant also claims that the memorandum that accompanied the new P & P Manual in its dissemination "did nothing to place employees on notice of the dramatic change in their legal rights vis-a-vis their employer" and lulled the employees "into a false sense of security." We agree.

In *Castiglione*, we stated that a disclaimer must be both clear and conspicuous. Had the memorandum in the case at bar not been a part of the general distribution or had the memorandum specifically referenced the importance of the disclaimer language, we would have no problem deciding that the disclaimer at issue here was clear and conspicuous by reason of its placement in the manual, *i.e.*, its language is clear and it is placed in the introduction.

The purpose of a disclaimer is to point out to such an employee that an important change has occurred. The memorandum at issue here, however, mutes the effectiveness of the disclaimer. The memorandum does, and may have been designed to do, just the opposite of directing the attention of the employee to, what may well be, the most important change. Because the effect of the memorandum was to minimize the importance of what was, if not the most important provision in the new manual, at least a very important change, we do not believe, considering the totality of the circumstances, that the disclaimer was sufficiently conspicuous in the case *sub judice*. The memorandum provided that the new manual was "similar in content to the old one" and "[t]he primary purpose of changing the format of the manual is to make it easier to use. . . ."

. . . [W]hen the employer makes an affirmative statement that the manual is similar to a previous one and is designed merely to make it easier to use, the circumstances are such that an employee would not be likely to review the manual to ascertain whether important changes to the very nature of his employment relationship have been made. The disclaimer here changed the very nature of the relationship from an implied continuing contract unless good cause for termination exists to an at will contract. Therefore, because of the memorandum that down played the significance of the new P & P Manual, we hold that the disclaimer was not, as a matter of law, conspicuous and, thus, the issue of whether appellant received notice of the disclaimer was a matter to be determined by the finder of fact in the context of a resolution of whether the employment relationship had changed.

C. & D.

Our holding above does not dispose of this case because the hearing judge found, in the alternative, that, even if an implied contract existed, *i.e.*, even if the disclaimer was ineffective to change the employment relationship, there was no breach of that prior implied contract because appellant received all that he was entitled to under the employment relationship created by implication from the former policy and pre-modified manual.

Appellant was discharged for leaving his shift early without his supervisor's permission. Appellant contends, however, that he, in fact, had his supervisor's permission. Appellee cites *H & R Block, Inc. v. Garland* and *MacGill v. Blue Cross* apparently for the proposition that, once the College determined that it had "cause" to discharge appellant, the courts could not disturb this finding, absent some evidence of bad faith on the part of the College.

The above cited cases stand for the proposition that, if an employer has contracted to do something that requires it to exercise its discretion, then it must exercise that discretion in good faith. In *Garland*, the issue was whether H & R Block had found Garland's performance "satisfactory." The Court held that, since there was no evidence that H & R Block had not acted in good faith, its motion for a directed verdict should have been granted. In *MacGill*, the issue MacGill attempted to raise on appeal was whether he was the "most qualified" so as to have been entitled to the promotion for which he applied. We noted, in response to MacGill's contention:

> Were such allegations accepted as sufficient, the courts would necessarily become involved in the assessment of the propriety and soundness of a company's personnel decisions; the courts would be required to act as super personnel officers, overseeing and second-guessing the company's decisions whenever an unsuccessful applicant perceives him-or herself to have been the most qualified applicant.

We glean from *Garland* and *MacGill* that, absent evidence of bad faith on the part of an employer, courts should be reluctant to overturn an employer's decision to discharge an employee when the employer has complied with its own procedures for resolving matters such as this.

We have exhaustively examined the exhibits contained in the extract, including the complaint, motions, responses, and affidavits. We have found absolutely no allegations below by appellant of "bad faith" on the part of the employer. There is nowhere contained in the affidavits in opposition to the appellee's motion any proffer of any evidential matter that would even pertain to any assertion of "bad faith." The complaint failed to assert bad faith in the first instance. So long as an employer follows its policy stated procedures and acts in good faith in determining what is good cause as to the formulation of its disciplinary measures and then, using the proper procedures, in good faith, applies its standards to the facts presented, there is no actionable wrong.

The potential issue for a jury is not what constitutes good cause. A jury cannot establish a good cause for separation separate and apart from the agreement of the parties-or, in this case, the unilateral policy of the employer. It is for the parties, or, as in this case, for the employer, through policy statements, to establish what is good cause and the procedures to be followed in determining whether good cause (and not some other cause, or lack thereof, perceived to be appropriate or inappropriate by a fact finder independent of the employer's policy) exists.

. . . .

The determination as to whether liability attaches depends upon whether the employer has followed its stated procedures and, where its manual-generated policy requires the employer to act in good faith, has acted in good faith in determining good cause. If it has satisfied those two criteria, no action will lie. Even when there is conflicting evidence, so long as the employer acts in good faith pursuant to its proper procedures, the fact that a different inference from the evidence might be made does not create an issue to be submitted to a judicial fact finder. Only in instances when the employer's policy promises a good faith application, if there are allegations of bad faith in the resolution of the conflicting evidence, or evidence, or evidentiary proffers properly made of such bad faith, would such an issue result in a triable action. To hold otherwise would be to put the courts in the position of making, as we said in *MacGill*, "personnel decisions," acting as a "super personnel officer," or of "second-guessing a company's decisions," even when the company follows its procedures and does so in good faith.

. . . .

Causes of action arising out of employment relationships implied from employee manuals are not actions in which judicial fact finders are free to make determinations as to what constitutes good cause independent of the manuals and the employer's policy. As we have said, such causes of action are to determine primarily whether the employer has, in good faith, complied with the practices and procedures created by the manual and made a good faith resolution supported by sufficient evidence. Only in the presence of a failure to comply with stated or implied practice or procedures, insufficient evidence, or bad faith in the resolution of the matter may a judicial fact finder be substituted for the employer.

Appellee claimed for the first time on appeal that this suit was barred under the doctrine of sovereign immunity. Because we hold the hearing court did not err in granting appellee's Motion for Summary Judgment, we do not find it necessary to resolve this issue.

JUDGMENT AFFIRMED; COSTS TO BE PAID BY APPELLANT.

NOTES

1. A disclaimer that the employee manual is not a contract must be clear and unambiguous. Adoption of new employee manuals falls within the right of an employer — even when made unilaterally; reasonable notification sufficiently places employees on notice.

2. Is the issue of whether an employee handbook is a contract or not a question of law or fact? In what kind of situation, if any, may your answer change as to whether a disclaimer in an employee handbook is determined as a matter of law or fact? According to a D.C. Circuit Court, construction of the disclaimer must contain a clear reservation of rights for the employer to overcome the notion that the employee handbook is a contract, particularly when distinctions are made between temporary or probationary employees and regular appointed employees. *See U.S. ex rel. Yesudian v. Howard University*, 153 F.3d 731 (D.C. Cir. 1998). In *Yesudian*, a federal appellate court indicated that in D.C., the "presumption in the case of an employee[,] . . . who lacks an express employment contract for a specified time[,] is that he is an employee at-will who may be fired at the employer's discretion." *Id.* at 745. The court observes, however, that an employee handbook "overcomes the at-will presumption 'where it set[s] forth a distinction between probationary and permanent employees, providing that the first could be discharged summarily but the latter only. . . . [after] specific preconditions had [been] met.' " *Id.*

3. As institutions rely more on the electronic versions of their employee manuals, these booklets may only exist in electronic format. How does this change the relationship between the employer and employee, in terms of employee reliance, availability, and modifications to the policies?

D. UNEMPLOYMENT BENEFITS

INDIANA STATE UNIVERSITY v. LAFIEF
888 N.E.2d 184 (Ind. 2008)

SHEPARD, CHIEF JUSTICE

The issue is whether a university professor who agreed to a fixed-term employment contract was entitled to unemployment benefits upon the non-renewal of his contract. We hold that the professor was not voluntarily unemployed and is entitled to benefits.

Facts and Procedural History

Indiana State University appointed William LaFief to a position as an assistant professor in accordance with the University's practice of employing assistant professors for one-year probationary terms with annual reviews that result in reappointment or non-reappointment for subsequent terms. LaFief was initially appointed for the 2004–05 academic year and was reappointed for 2005–06. Thereafter, ISU notified LaFief that he would not be reappointed.

LaFief filed for unemployment. An administrative law judge held that he was not entitled to unemployment benefits, reasoning that LaFief was not "discharged" because his employment ended at the expiration of his contract term. The Review Board of the Indiana Department of Workforce Development reversed, finding that ISU's decision not to reappoint LaFief equated to a "discharge."

The Court of Appeals reversed the board, holding that LaFief was not entitled to unemployment benefits because he had voluntarily agreed to a one-year appointment that expired by its own terms and that he was not "discharged" from his employment when he was not reappointed. We granted transfer.

LaFief Was Not Voluntarily Unemployed

The Unemployment Compensation Act (UCA) was enacted to "provide for payment of benefits to persons unemployed through no fault of their own." To be eligible for unemployment benefits, an individual must meet the requirements set forth in Ind.Code ch. 22-4-14-1 and must not be disqualified by any of the various exceptions provided in ch. 22-4-15-1.

The eligibility requirements for unemployment benefits include that an individual must be unemployed, have sufficient wage credits in his base period, be able, available, and actively seeking work, and meet certain registration and reporting requirements. An otherwise eligible individual can be disqualified from receiving benefits if he voluntarily left his employment without good cause, was discharged from employment for just cause, or failed to accept suitable work.

This appeal involves only questions of law. We review conclusions of law made by the Review Board of the Indiana Department of Workforce Development under a *de novo* standard.

The Act does not contain a requirement that the employee be "discharged" from employment to be eligible for benefits, although "discharge for just cause" is a disqualification from benefits. For example, employees can be eligible for benefits if they leave their employment with good cause. Accordingly, in evaluating whether an individual is eligible for unemployment benefits, the question is not whether he was "discharged" from employment but whether he met the eligibility requirements set forth in Ind.Code ch. 22-4-14-1 and was not otherwise disqualified under Ind.Code ch. 22-4-15-1.

In this case, the parties' dispute centers on whether LaFief was disqualified under Ind.Code ch. 22-4-15-1. Indiana State contends that because LaFief agreed to a fixed-term employment contract, he became voluntarily unemployed at the expiration of that contract term. We hold otherwise.

Employment contracts operate to obligate the parties to continue the employment relationship during the contract's term, not to waive the employee's right to receive unemployment benefits. A contractual provision that attempted to waive an employee's right to receive unemployment benefits would be void because the Act expressly disallows such waivers. To hold otherwise could encourage employers to require fixed-term employment contracts for the express purpose of avoiding unemployment compensation liability.

LaFief was employed by Indiana State during the 2005–06 academic year. He was not permitted to continue this employment during the next academic year. The fact that LaFief had warning that his employment could terminate upon the contract's expiration does not change the fact that at the end of the year he became unemployed. The termination of his employment was no more voluntary than the termination of employment of an employee at will, who is presumably on notice that his employment could terminate at any time.

This holding does not alter the general rule that employees who contractually agree to mandatory vacation periods or temporary shut downs are not eligible for unemployment benefits so long as they have reasonable assurance that they will continue to be employed after the mandatory vacation period or temporary shut down ends. *See* Ind.Code Ann. § 22-4-14-7(a) (individuals employed by educational institutions are not entitled to unemployment benefits during the period between two successive academic years if they were employed during one period and there is a reasonable assurance that they will be employed during the successive term); Ind.Code Ann. § 22-4-14-8 (individuals whose employment consists of participating in sports are not entitled to unemployment benefits between seasons if they were employed during one season and there is a reasonable assurance that they will be employed during the successive season); *Pope v. Wabash Valley Human Serv., Inc.* ("Where the employment contract or collective bargaining agreement provides for a shutdown or vacation period, the employees who signed or assented to the contract are not 'unemployed' within the meaning contemplated by the [Unemployment Compensation Act]").

Conclusion

For the above reasons, we affirm the Review Board's decision.

SULLIVAN and BOEHM, JJ., concur.

DICKSON, J., Dissents with separate opinion, in which RUCKER, J., concurs.

DICKSON, JUSTICE, Dissenting.

Unemployment benefits are contingent upon a person being terminated from or leaving employment. In expressly entering into a fixed-term employment contract, Professor LaFief voluntarily agreed that his employment would terminate at the conclusion of the 2005–2006 academic year. His employment with Indiana State University thus ended when the contract expired. After the end of the 2005–06 academic year, there was no employment to leave. Before the contract ended, that is, during the time he was employed, LaFief was not discharged, nor did he leave his employment, and thus he did not become eligible for unemployment benefits.

The majority notes that the Act was enacted to "provide for payment of benefits to persons unemployed through no fault of their own." The majority further finds that a party voluntarily entering a contract calling for a fixed term of employment is not "at fault" upon the expiration of the contract. I disagree. The professor expressly contracted that his employment would expire at the end of its fixed term. He is thus responsible and accountable for his subsequent unemployment.

At one point in its rationale, the majority states that the expiration of this employment contract "was no more voluntary than the termination of the employment of an employee at will." I believe it is mistaken to thus suggest that the discharge from at will employment is volitionally equivalent to the foreseeable unemployment that follows the conclusion of a consensual fixed-term employment contract.

Because I conclude that Professor LaFief had no employment to leave or from which to be discharged, and further that he is personally accountable and responsible for the natural consequences of his agreement to the fixed-term contract, I would reverse the decision of the Review Board.

RUCKER, J., concurs.

NOTES

1. Typically, states adopt an unemployment policy that presumptively precludes college faculty and staff who are not employed the whole calendar year from unemployment compensation. For example, *In re Schwartz*, 68 A.D.3d 1323 (N.Y. App. Div. 2009), states that "a professional employee of an educational institution is precluded from receiving unemployment insurance benefits during the time between two successive academic years where the claimant has received a reasonable assurance of continued employment" *Id.* at 1324.

2. According to the American Association of University Professors (AAUP), the number and percentage of full-time, non-tenure-track faculty appointments have been rising. In a 2003 report, an AAUP committee indicated that

> The number of *full-time* non-tenure-track appointments is growing even faster than the number of *part-time* non-tenure-track appointments. Full-time appointments off the tenure track were almost unknown a generation ago; in 1969, they amounted to 3.3 percent of all fulltime faculty positions. But between 1992 and 1998, the number of full-time non-tenure-track faculty increased by 22.7 percent, from 128,371 to 157,470. During that same period, the number of part-time non-tenure-track faculty increased by only 9.4 percent, from 360,087 to 393,971, and the number of full-time tenure-line faculty increased by less than 1 percent. By 1998, fulltime non-tenure-track faculty comprised 28.1 percent of all full-time faculty and 16 percent of all faculty.

AM. ASS'N OF UNIV. PROFESSORS, CONTINGENT APPOINTMENTS AND THE ACADEMIC PROFESSION (2003),* *available at* http://www.aaup.org/AAUP/pubsres/policydocs/contents/conting-stmt.htm. The data suggests that more faculty do not have an expectation of a renewable contract. With more faculty members subject to *non*renewal, how might the analysis in *LaFief* need to change if faculty are uncertain, semester-to-semester, whether the employing college will renew the faculty's employment?

3. It is also worth noting that college faculty is increasingly becoming part-time employees. In 1975, 24% of college faculty was part-time, but by 2009, part-time college faculty constituted 41.1% of the college teaching staff. *See* AM. ASS'N OF UNIV. PROFESSORS, TRENDS IN INSTRUCTIONAL STAFF EMPLOYMENT STATUS, 1975–2009, *available at* http://www.aaup.org/NR/rdonlyres/7C3039DD-EF79-4E75-A20D-6F75BA01BE84/0/Trends.pdf.

E. COLLEGE EMPLOYEE CIVIL RIGHTS

1. Discrimination of "Protected Speech"

BATTLE v. BOARD OF REGENTS FOR THE STATE OF GEORGIA

468 F.3d 755 (11th Cir. 2006)

PER CURIAM:

Plaintiff Lillie Battle ("Plaintiff") appeals the district court's grant of summary judgment to Defendants Jeanette K. Huff and Oscar L. Prater ("Defendants"), against Plaintiff's First Amendment Retaliation and False Claims Act claims. We affirm.

I. *Background*

Taking the record in the light most favorable to the Plaintiff, these events are the facts as they occurred. Plaintiff worked in the Office of Financial Aid and Veterans Affairs ("OFA") at Fort Valley State University ("FVSU") between 1987 and 1998. In Spring Quarter 1995, while working as a work study supervisor and veterans affairs counselor, Plaintiff began to observe and document what she believed were fraudulent practices in the Federal Work Study Program. Plaintiff took notes and made copies of suspicious documents, which she stored in a safe-deposit box at home. In January 1996, the OFA was reorganized; and Plaintiff's position changed to financial aid counselor. As part of Plaintiff's employment duties, she was required to verify the completion and accuracy of student files as well as report any perceived fraudulent activity. Some student files previously handled by Plaintiff's supervisor, OFA Director Jeanette Huff ("Huff"), were transferred to Plaintiff. In examining these files, Plaintiff discovered "improprieties" pointing to what she believed was "Huff's fraudulent mishandling and mismanagement of Federal financial aid funds."

Plaintiff first confronted Huff about these improprieties in 1996, but Huff was dismissive and made no corrections. In late 1996, "overwhelmed" by the evidence of fraud, Plaintiff met with FVSU President Oscar Prater ("Prater") and told him that Huff was falsifying information, awarding financial aid to ineligible recipients, making excessive awards, and forging documents. Prater said nothing in response to Plaintiff's accusations and took no remedial steps. Plaintiff confronted Huff on other occasions with folders Plaintiff believed contained improprieties, but Huff made no corrections.

In March 1998, Plaintiff received a rating of "Exceeds Expectations" — the second highest available category — on her annual performance evaluation. The evaluation, however, also contained criticisms of Plaintiff's performance.[1] All of

---

[1] The evaluation criticized that (1) Plaintiff "allows student workers too much [sic] liberties and responsibilities," which "contributes largely to client dissatisfaction"; (2) Plaintiff needs "more self-confidence and assertiveness"; and (3) Plaintiffs' "performance has not lived up to her potential."

Plaintiff's prior evaluations had rated her performance as "Exceeds Requirements" or "Outstanding." Despite the high score, Plaintiff was not pleased with her 1998 evaluation.[2]

Plaintiff arranged a meeting with Huff's direct supervisor, FVSU Vice-President of Student Affairs Cynthia Sellers ("Sellers"), during which Plaintiff complained that her performance review was unfairly low. Sellers advised Plaintiff that, based on the score, Plaintiff's evaluation was not bad and that she would likely receive a raise. During the same meeting, Plaintiff told Sellers that "Huff was doing stuff that was going to get our institution in trouble" and awarding students aid for which they were ineligible. Plaintiff warned Sellers that she "was going to tell" unless changes were made. Sellers responded, "Do what you have to do." Plaintiff then scheduled a second meeting with President Prater to discuss her performance evaluation and "to reiterate the improprieties [of which she] had already informed him in prior years." During the meetings with Prater and Sellers, Plaintiff did not identify specific student files that had been mishandled or provide documentary evidence-which Plaintiff began collecting in 1995-to support her allegations of fraud.

On 25 May 1998, Plaintiff received a letter indicating the contract for her position as financial aid counselor would not be renewed effective 30 June 1998. The letter indicated Plaintiff had been approved for transfer to a position in a different FVSU department, but Plaintiff was later informed that no position was available. Plaintiff appealed the non-renewal of her contract through FVSU and the Board of Regents of the University System of Georgia, alleging her contract was not renewed because of her attempts to expose Huff's fraud. A grievance committee investigated, conducted an evidentiary hearing, and upheld the decision not to renew.

Plaintiff never spoke to anyone outside of FVSU about Huff's fraudulent activity until after she received notice that her contract would not be renewed. A month after receiving notice, Plaintiff met with the Department of Education ("DOE") and provided sixty-one pages of documents showing potential fraud and a thirty-two page analysis of student files.

From June 1998 to February 1999, the Georgia Department of Audits conducted an independent annual audit of FVSU that revealed serious noncompliance with federal regulations and risk factors for fraud. The auditors formed no opinion on whether the noncompliance was intentional. Subsequent audits also revealed similar problems. Huff transferred out of the OFA in July 1999 and resigned in May 2000. In April 2002, FVSU reached a $2,167,941 settlement with the DOE to settle questioned costs identified by the state auditors in audits from 1997–2000 and in lieu of further file review.

In June 2004, Plaintiff filed suit in the district court, alleging (1) she was discharged in violation of the First Amendment for reporting her concerns about fraud, and (2) Huff, Sellers, and Prater knowingly submitted false or fraudulent

[2] In a letter dated 25 May 1998, Plaintiff wrote to Huff that she was not surprised she was being transferred due to "the negative, and unfair evaluation [she] received for the 1997–98 period." Plaintiff also wrote in the comment section of her 1998 evaluation that "I feel that I am being treated unfairly." The score on Plaintiff's 1998 evaluation was originally 3.54, but was increased by Huff to 3.7 after Plaintiff complained.

claims to the United States in violation of the False Claims Act ("FCA"). The district court concluded that Defendants were entitled to qualified immunity on Plaintiff's First Amendment claim because the motivation for Plaintiff's speech was unclear and preexisting case law did not give Defendants fair warning that Plaintiff's speech must be treated as "a matter of public concern" under the circumstances. The district court also concluded that Plaintiff's FCA claims were barred by 31 U.S.C. § 3730(e)(4)(A) because they relied on publicly disclosed information for which Plaintiff was not an "original source." The district court granted summary judgment on both claims. Plaintiff originally appealed the grant of summary judgment against Huff, Prater, and Sellers but later dismissed the appeal of claims against Sellers.

II. *Discussion*

We review a district court order granting summary judgment de novo, viewing the evidence and all reasonable inferences drawn from it in the light most favorable to the nonmoving party. Summary judgment is appropriate when the pleadings, depositions, and affidavits submitted by the parties show that no genuine issue of material fact exists and that the movant is entitled to judgment as a matter of law.

A. First Amendment Retaliation Claim

For a public employee to sustain a claim of retaliation for protected speech under the First Amendment, the employee must show by a preponderance of the evidence these things:

> (1) the employee's speech is on a matter of public concern; (2) the employee's First Amendment interest in engaging in the speech outweighs the employer's interest in prohibiting the speech to promote the efficiency of the public services it performs through its employees; and (3) the employee's speech played a "substantial part" in the employer's decision to demote or discharge the employee. Once the employee succeeds in showing the preceding factors, the burden then shifts to the employer to show, by a preponderance of the evidence, that "it would have reached the same decision . . . even in the absence of the protected conduct."

The first two elements are questions of law designed to determine whether the First Amendment protects the employee's speech. The third element and affirmative defense are questions of fact designed to determine whether the adverse employment action was in retaliation for the protected speech.

In determining whether a public employee's speech is entitled to constitutional protection, we must first ask "whether the employee spoke as a citizen on a matter of public concern. If the answer is no, the employee has no First Amendment cause of action based on his or her employer's reaction to the speech." . . . "[W]hen public employees make statements pursuant to their official duties, the employees are not speaking as citizens for First Amendment purposes, and the Constitution does not insulate their communications from employer discipline."

In *Garcetti*, the Supreme Court concluded that a deputy district attorney's speech was not protected by the First Amendment where the attorney testified in court and wrote in a disposition memorandum that he believed the affidavit used to obtain a critical search warrant in a criminal case contained serious misrepresentations. The "controlling factor" in the Court's decision was that the deputy's "expressions were made pursuant to his duties as a calendar deputy."

> When an employee speaks as a citizen addressing a matter of public concern, the First Amendment requires a delicate balancing of the competing interests surrounding the speech and its consequences. When, however, the employee is simply performing his or her job duties, there is no warrant for a similar degree of scrutiny.

The Court rejected the idea that the nature of public employment transforms a public employee's statements into a matter of public concern protected by the First Amendment:

> Restricting speech that owes its existence to a public employee's professional responsibilities does not infringe any liberties the employee might have enjoyed as a private citizen. . . .
>
> . . . Employees who make public statements outside the course of performing their official duties retain some possibility of First Amendment protection because that is the kind of activity engaged in by citizens who do not work for the government. The same goes for writing a letter to a local newspaper, or discussing politics with a co-worker. When a public employee speaks pursuant to employment responsibilities, however, there is no relevant analogue to speech by citizens who are not government employees.

Although the Court acknowledged that "[e]xposing governmental inefficiency and misconduct is a matter of considerable significance," the Court concluded the public interest was protected by other means, including a "powerful network of legislative enactments-such as whistle-blower protection laws and labor codes" - not by permitting First Amendment retaliation claims based on "expressions employees make pursuant to their professional duties."

In this case, Plaintiff admitted that she had a clear employment duty to ensure the accuracy and completeness of student files as well as to report any mismanagement or fraud she encountered in the student financial aid files.[4] In addition, DOE Guidelines require all financial aid workers to report suspected fraud. Plaintiff alleges her contract was not renewed because of her "continuous efforts to expose the fraud within FVSU's Financial Aid Department." These efforts consisted of attempts to disclose to both Prater and Sellers that her supervisor, Huff, was

---

[4] Plaintiff's deposition transcript contains the following exchange between Plaintiff and Defendant Huff's counsel:

> Q: Was it part of your responsibility in taking over the handling of these files to check the files or audit the files to see whether there was any mismanagement or fraud in the files?
>
> A: It was part of my responsibility to make sure it was complete and accurate.
>
> Q: If a file had fraudulent activity in it or what you perceived to be fraudulent activity, was it part of your responsibility to report that?
>
> A: Yes.

making improper financial aid awards and falsifying information in student files. By Plaintiff's own admission and in the light of federal guidelines, Plaintiff's speech to FVSU officials about inaccuracies and signs of fraud in student files was made pursuant to her official employment responsibilities. We conclude that because the First Amendment protects speech on matters of public concern made by a government employee speaking as a citizen, not as an employee fulfilling official responsibilities, Plaintiff's retaliation claim must fail.[7]

B. FCA Claims

The district court dismissed Plaintiff's Federal Claims Act claim based on the following jurisdictional bar:

> No court shall have jurisdiction over [an FCA qui tam action] based upon the public disclosure of allegations or transactions in a criminal, civil, or administrative hearing, in a congressional, administrative, or Government Accounting Office report, hearing, audit, or investigation, or from the news media, unless . . . the person bringing the action is an original source of the information.

This Court uses a three-part inquiry to determine jurisdiction over an FCA claim based on publicly disclosed information: "(1) have the allegations made by the plaintiff been publicly disclosed; (2) if so, is the disclosed information the basis of the plaintiff's suit; (3) if yes, is the plaintiff an 'original source' of that information." The FCA "is most naturally read to preclude suits based in *any part* on publically disclosed information." Therefore, a plaintiff basing an FCA qui tam claim in any part on such publicly disclosed information must demonstrate that the plaintiff is an original source of that information. The FCA defines "original source" as "an individual who has direct and independent knowledge of the information *on which the allegations are based* and has voluntarily provided the information to the Government before filing an action."

In the district court, Plaintiff "refer[red] Defendants to the audits performed by the State of Georgia Department of Audits and Accounts on June 30, 1998 and June 30, 1999" and indicated Plaintiff would "seek all damages allowed under the False Claims Act for these violations." Plaintiff's appellate brief states that "[i]n asserting damages in this case under the False Claims Act, plaintiff relies on the results of the state audits as well as 'accompanying notes already . . . produced by plaintiff.' " Because Plaintiff's FCA claims rely chiefly on information that was publicly disclosed in the 1997–1998 and 1998–1999 state audits, the claims are barred unless Plaintiff qualifies as an original source.

We have commented that the FCA does not impose a strict tracing rule that would require the relator to trace the allegations from the disclosing agency back through the government bureaucracy to the relator. Nonetheless, the FCA mandates that, to qualify as an original source, a plaintiff must have direct and independent knowledge of the information on which the allegations are based. In

---

[7] Because we conclude that Plaintiff has not been deprived of a First Amendment right, we do not reach the issue of qualified immunity.

other words, a plaintiff need not establish herself as *the* original source of the publicly disclosed information but must establish that she is *an* original source of the information in that she had direct and independent knowledge of the information on which she is basing her FCA claim.

Here, Plaintiff's allegations are based chiefly on the 1997–1998 and 1998–1999 state audits; and she failed to provide facts to the district court that might establish herself as an original source of the information contained in the state audits. Although Plaintiff need not trace the flow of information from herself to the DOE to the state audit reports, summary judgment was proper because Plaintiff failed to provide the district court with specific facts showing that she had direct and independent knowledge of the audit findings on which she bases her FCA claims. None of the facts as evidenced by Plaintiff indicate that she participated in the state audits on which she relies or that she disclosed information to the auditors. More important, Plaintiff does not refer to her own research or documentation to prove that she had direct and independent knowledge of the findings contained in the state audits.[8]

We conclude Plaintiff is no original source as defined under the statute because she lacked direct and independent knowledge of the publicly disclosed information on which her claims are based: namely, the state audits. Therefore, the district court properly dismissed Plaintiff's FCA claims as jurisdictionally barred because Plaintiff's allegations substantially rely on information in the publicly disclosed state audit reports for which Plaintiff was no "original source."

Because they are unnecessary to our decision, we do not reach Defendants' alternative arguments that (1) Plaintiff could not qualify as an original source because her job required her to report fraud, arguably making her disclosure involuntary; (2) the $2 million settlement between FVSU and the DOE was an "alternate remedy" under 31 U.S.C. § 3730(c)(5); (3) the settlement was a release or an accord and satisfaction of Plaintiff's *qui tam* claims; (4) Plaintiff presented insufficient evidence that Defendants knowingly submitted false claims; or (5) that Huff could not be held vicariously liable for acts of the employees she supervised.

AFFIRMED.

NOTES

1. What different actions should Battle have taken to address the alleged misdealing with the Federal Work Study Program? What alternative claims should Battle have asserted?

2. What is the rule in *Garcetti*? How might this case's outcome change if the

---

[8] In this appeal, and for the first time, Plaintiff attempts to introduce evidence of a link between her own independent research of improprieties at FVSU and some of the findings of the state auditors on which she bases her claim. Plaintiff's appellate brief asserts that "there was commonality with 11 student files amounting to over $100,000 in misappropriated federal student aid." Because this argument is made for the first time on appeal, we do not consider it here. "If we were to regularly address questions-particularly fact-bound issues-that district[ ] court [s] never had a chance to examine, we would not only waste our resources, but also deviate from the essential nature, purpose, and competence of an appellate court."

Garcetti case was not available? How does the court balance First Amendment interests with employer rights? How does this discussion differ depending on the actors involved?

2. Discrimination: Race

CRAWFORD v. CARROLL

529 F.3d 961 (11th Cir. 2008)

RODGERS, DISTRICT JUDGE:

Jacquelyn R. Crawford appeals the district court's grant of summary judgment in favor of her former employer, the Board of Regents of the University System of Georgia Georgia State University (GSU), and two of her former supervisors, GSU officers Barbara Carroll and Katherine Johnston. After review and oral argument, we reverse and remand for further proceedings, having determined that genuine issues of material fact exist that preclude summary judgment on Crawford's Title VII retaliation and race discrimination claims against GSU and her 42 U.S.C § 1983 race discrimination claim against Carroll. We affirm the district court's grant of summary judgment to Johnston on Crawford's § 1983 race discrimination claim because Johnston is entitled to qualified immunity.

I. *Standard of Review*

We review a district court's grant of summary judgment *de novo.* At summary judgment we consider all evidence and reasonable factual inferences drawn therefrom in a light most favorable to the non-moving party. Summary judgment is appropriate if the pleadings, depositions, answers to interrogatories, and admissions on file, together with the affidavits, if any, show there is no genuine issue as to any material fact and that the moving party is entitled to judgment as a matter of law.

II. *Background*

Crawford, who is African-American, began working in the personnel field in 1987. She holds a masters degree in public administration, with a specialization in human resources management. In 1992 GSU hired Crawford to serve as the wage and salary administrator in its human resources department. Crawford was promoted in December 1997 to the position of manager of classification and compensation, her job at the time the events giving rise to this case occurred. Carroll was GSU's assistant vice president of human resources from March 1999 until August 2004. She supervised Crawford's position as well the higher level positions of director of human resources, director of human resources information systems, and director of payroll. Johnston came to GSU in July 2000 to serve as its vice president of finance and administration. In that capacity she directly supervised Carroll. Johnston was also responsible for overseeing the supervision of approximately eight hundred other GSU employees, including those in the human resources, budget, physical plant, facilities planning, campus master planning, and campus police departments.

Both Carroll and Johnston are Caucasian.

In early 2000 Crawford was absent from work periodically due to her mother's serious illness; her mother died in February 2000. In March 2000 Carroll formally reprimanded Crawford for misuse of the department's leave policy, in particular its bereavement leave policy which Carroll stated permitted only up to three days' absence in connection with the death of a family member. Carroll asserted that Crawford had missed eighteen full or partial days of work prior to and following her mother's death without giving proper notice or obtaining proper authorization. In response, Crawford filed a grievance in which she protested that the reprimand was factually incorrect as well as culturally insensitive. According to Crawford, Carroll did not understand that the funeral practices of African-Americans require more than three days of leave. When Carroll failed to withdraw the reprimand Crawford appealed to GSU's provost and vice president for academic affairs, who reversed the reprimand and instructed that it be removed from Crawford's file, partly on the ground it contained errors of fact. Crawford maintains that subsequent to the reversal of the reprimand Carroll took retaliatory action against her by making new and unreasonable job demands and by sending her an increased number of e-mail messages, many of which Crawford felt were unfairly critical of her work performance.

In April 2001 Crawford wrote to Carroll to make staffing recommendations for the classification and compensation division. Additionally, based on her own analysis of internal and external market data, Crawford asked Carroll to increase her annual salary of $50,960 to the range of $54,565 to $56,202 in order to be commensurate with other positions of similar responsibility. Carroll responded that she would not address Crawford's requests until a new position, that of director of classification and employment, had been filled. This position would be responsible for supervising classification division functions, *i.e.*, those performed by Crawford's department such as assigning pay classifications and developing job descriptions, as well as functions related to the employment division, such as posting vacant positions and accepting and reviewing job applications. Crawford thought she was eligible to receive an "in-place" promotion to the new position because other employees had been given promotions in similar circumstances but the job was not offered to her; instead, the position was advertised in August 2001.[2]

A five-member panel comprised of GSU management and staff was formed to screen the applicants for the new position and recommend a candidate to Johnston, who would interview the candidate. Johnston, with the approval of Linda Nelson-the director of GSU's Office of Affirmative Action and Diversity Programs (OAADP)-would then make the final selection. Crawford applied for the new job and was chosen for an interview. It was conducted by Carroll and the other panel members in the early fall of 2001.

Carroll favored hiring Nancy Strasner, a Caucasian female, for the new position. Mae Okwandu, an Equal Opportunity specialist at GSU who reviewed the qualifi-

[2] An "in place" promotion is one that results from an employee's being reclassified in job title and salary without posting the new position for competitive recruitment. In this appeal Crawford does not challenge the district court's holding that her claim of being wrongly denied an "in-place" promotion is time-barred.

cations of the applicants during the selection process, felt that Crawford was the most qualified applicant. Nelson thought Crawford's and Strasner's qualifications were "somewhat equal," with Crawford having greater experience in the compensation field and less in the employment area, and Strasner's experience being the reverse. Ultimately, Nelson described Crawford as the "best suited" candidate and slightly preferred her because she was already employed by GSU and was familiar with its operations. Johnston testified that she interviewed Strasner, at Carroll's request, but thought Strasner lacked sufficient experience and therefore-to Carroll's displeasure-declined to endorse Strasner for the job. No other candidates were proposed to her so Johnston interviewed none.

In December 2001 Crawford filed an internal complaint of retaliation with the OAADP. In the complaint Crawford alleged that Carroll had subjected her to increased, unfair scrutiny of her job performance and mishandled the recruitment process for the new position of director of classification and employment.

In January 2002 Nelson issued a determination letter announcing that there had been no consensus reached regarding whom to hire for the new position and that the job therefore would not be filled at that time. No other reason was given. In a deposition Nelson stated that Johnston told her that she did not wish to hire anyone given Nelson's view that Crawford rather than Strasner was the best suited candidate, Nelson's concern there was no real need for the new position, and her concern over "other incidents in the past." When asked to identify the past incidents, Nelson responded, "[s]ome of the issues that Ms. Crawford brought up regarding communication that occurred between Ms. Carroll and Ms. Crawford and, you know, those types of things." With the new position unfilled, Carroll temporarily assigned some of its duties to Brennaman, who had been employed at GSU for approximately twenty years and was then earning a salary of approximately $70,000 per year.

In January or February 2002 the position of director of classification and employment was posted for a second time. Crawford again applied but no applicants were selected for interviews.

In April 2002 Carroll wrote, and Johnston approved, a negative evaluation of Crawford's job performance for the period from March 2001 through March 2002. Crawford learned in May 2002 that as a result of the poor evaluation she would not be eligible to receive a merit pay increase due in October 2002.

In May 2002 Crawford submitted a complaint to Johnston alleging that Carroll had retaliated and discriminated against her. Among other matters, Crawford's complaint addressed Carroll's negative performance review (and Crawford's resulting loss of eligibility for a merit pay increase), Crawford's contention that she suffered racially disparate treatment in the terms and conditions of her employment compared with Brennaman and others, and Crawford's nonselection for the new position of director of classification and employment. Johnston met with Crawford in July 2002 for approximately forty-five minutes to discuss the complaint, then later denied it. According to Johnston, she viewed the tension between Crawford and Carroll as essentially a serious personality conflict between two strong-minded women with major disagreements over how the human resources department's work should be performed. As Johnston "was not convinced that [the problems were related to] discrimination and retaliation," she simply counseled Crawford to work towards improving her relationship with Carroll. Johnston also testified that she took no independent action regarding Crawford's allegations because Johnston believed the claims were being investigated independently by the OAADP. Crawford contends Johnston was hostile during their meeting, accusing her of having an attitude problem, being to blame for the friction between Carroll and herself, and accepting Carroll's version of events without addressing Crawford's concerns.

Crawford appealed Johnston's denial of her complaint to GSU president Carl Patton. Crawford also filed a complaint with the OAADP, which hired independent investigator Arthur Rogers to conduct an inquiry into Crawford's allegations. Rogers submitted a final report in October 2002 in which he recommended that "a cause determination be issued indicating a violation of Title VII occurred in regards to race, and retaliation as they pertain to evaluation merit pay, promotion opportunity and disparate treatment." Nelson accepted Rogers' findings and referred Crawford to Johnston for follow-up. Additionally, although the OAADP did not itself formally investigate Crawford's complaints, the issues her complaints raised were discussed internally within the OAADP by Nelson and her staff, as well as with Johnston and perhaps the provost. Nelson concluded there were Caucasian employees in the human resources department, namely Brennaman and another worker, Angela Bourque, who had been moved forward at a faster pace than had African-American employees.

In September 2002 Crawford wrote to Patton again regarding the appeal of her complaint. She requested that she be given a four percent merit increase in salary, that the requirements of her position be outlined in a detailed job description, and that the classification and compensation division be assigned an additional analyst because it was understaffed. Patton responded that a "desk audit" of plaintiff's position, salary, and responsibilities would be performed and that if changes were warranted they would be made.

In October 2002 Carroll posted the new position of director of classification and employment for a third time. Johnston wished to broaden the pool of those engaged in the selection process, so Carroll established a four-member screening committee to evaluate the applicants. The committee consisted of two individuals from GSU's finance and administration division, one from an academic division on campus, and one from a non-academic division. First, a recruiter in the employment office reviewed the résumés of the one hundred ten applicants, narrowing the field to fifty-four candidates, including Crawford. Next, the four screening committee reviewers individually listed the five to eight applicants each thought should be interviewed. After briefly consulting with Johnston, Carroll decided to limit the group of interviewees to the three candidates whom three of the panelists had chosen. Carroll did not inform Johnston of the names of those selected for interviews but rather simply the result of the method employed. Crawford was selected by only two of the screening committee members and thus was not among those included in the final group of three. Two of these candidates agreed to be interviewed for the position, with the committee ultimately recommending that Russell Willis, a Caucasian male, receive the position over the other finalist, an African-American female.

In December 2002 Crawford filed a charge of discrimination with the Equal Employment Opportunity Commission (EEOC). She identified race as the basis of her charge and claimed a starting date in May 2002, which is when she learned she would be denied a merit pay increase. In January 2003 Crawford submitted a written protest to Nelson regarding the selection process for the new position and complaining of continued acts of race discrimination and retaliation by Carroll. In February 2003 Carroll recommended that Willis be offered the position of director of classification and employment. No offer was made to Willis, however, based on Nelson's advice against filling the position while Crawford's race discrimination claims were pending. Crawford amended her EEOC charge in April 2003 to include race discrimination and retaliation based on her nonselection for the new position of director of classification and employment.

In accordance with Patton's instruction, and as recommended by Johnston, an outside consultant was hired to perform a functional assessment of the office of human resources in January 2003. The consultant, Whit Perrin Wright, completed her "desk audit" in March 2003. Wright observed that most universities do not combine the functions of employment and classification in one job, as GSU had. She also indicated that the duties of the new position could instead be handled by other human resources department staff. Wright further noted that Brennaman's position as director of human resources for information systems did not involve as much responsibility as other directors' positions did; her job also appeared to be no greater in depth or scope to a manager's position and did not require that any other employees directly report to her. Wright recommended that the human resources department have a clearer definition of the criteria used to determine titles, pay bands, and pay grades. She also commented that Crawford's position, with a salary of $50,960, seemed to be paid approximately $4000 below the benchmark for manager-level jobs, while at $73,901 Brennaman's director-level job was paid at the median or average level.

In March 2003 Johnston decided to adjust Crawford's pay grade and increase her salary to $54,740 annually. Johnston also eliminated the new position of director of employment and classification; according to Johnston, due to budget constraints, she was under enormous pressure to reduce expenditures in the departments under her supervision. Relying on Nelson's advice as well as Wright's report, Johnston determined that the new position could be abolished without "hurting the organization." Later that month Johnston was relieved of responsibility for supervising the human resources department. In October 2003, Jerry Rackliffe, who had assumed Johnston's duties, advised Crawford by letter that based on Wright's review her position had been reclassified from a pay grade 17 to a pay grade 18, with a salary adjustment to $54,740 annually. Rackliffe also advised Crawford that "[a]s an action to settle your complaint regarding your 2002 Performance Evaluation, we have retroactively adjusted your salary by 4% on top of your classification adjustment. Thus, this adjustment will move your base salary to $56,930, retroactive to October 1, 2002." In 2004 Crawford was promoted to the position of assistant director of human resources, with a salary of $70,000 per year.

Crawford filed this suit in January 2004, asserting claims pursuant to Title VII of the Civil Rights Act of 1964, as amended, 42 U.S.C. § 2000e, et seq., 42 U.S.C. § 1981, and 42 U.S.C. § 1983. The magistrate judge to whom the case was referred recommended the defendants' motion for summary judgment be granted in part and denied in part. The district court modified and adopted the magistrate judge's report, granting the defendants' motion for summary judgment in its entirety and dismissing the complaint with prejudice. This appeal followed.

III. *Discussion*

The district court addressed Crawford's race discrimination and retaliation claims together in connection with three events: "(1) denial of a merit increase in October 2002, (2) discrepancy in pay and responsibilities between Plaintiff and Melissa Brennaman, and (3) denial of promotion to [d]irector, [c]lassification and [e]mployment. . . ." For ease of discussion we do much the same.

A. Denial of Merit Pay Increase

Crawford claims that her April 2002 performance evaluation was retaliatory and racially discriminatory and resulted in her being denied a merit pay increase she otherwise would have received. With respect to this claim, the parties' arguments, and the district court's analysis, center on whether Crawford presented a *prima facie* case of discrimination or retaliation by showing she suffered an adverse employment action.[9]

To make out a *prima facie* case of racial discrimination a plaintiff must show (1) she belongs to a protected class; (2) she was qualified to do the job; (3) she was subjected to adverse employment action; and (4) her employer treated similarly situated employees outside her class more favorably. These elements also apply to a claim of race discrimination under § 1983 because the analysis of disparate

---

[9] In discussing Crawford's allegations that she was denied a merit pay increase, the district court states that Crawford "was notified on March 12, 2003, that her salary would be retroactively increased four percent from May 6, 2002. The question then becomes whether Plaintiff has suffered an adverse employment action because of the time period between May 6, 2002, and March 12, 2003, when she did not have her increase in salary." Under the district court's calculation, Crawford therefore was denied a merit pay increase for approximately ten months, even though she was not due to receive the increase until October 2002.

> Our review of the voluminous record in this case reveals only that Johnston decided on March 13, 2003, to adjust Crawford's pay grade and increase her salary to $54,740 annually. We did not locate a reference to the four percent merit pay increase being awarded in March 2003. Rather, insofar as we have been able to determine, the merit pay increase was not awarded until October 2003, retroactive to October 2002. If these calculations are correct, Crawford actually went without a merit pay increase for approximately twelve months-from October 2002 until October 2003-even though the increase was eventually paid retroactively. Crawford was also aware of her ineligibility to receive the merit pay increase in May 2002, a period of another five months. Additionally, if it is assumed that Crawford was entitled to a pay grade and salary adjustment in April 2001, when she wrote Carroll requesting an increase, Crawford went without a pay grade adjustment for approximately twenty-three months (this increase apparently was first awarded in March 2003 by Johnston, then directed in October 2003 by Rackliffe to be paid retroactively to October 2002).

Fortunately, it is not necessary for us to know the precise number of months involved with respect to either the denial of the merit pay increase or the pay grade adjustment, which is relevant to Crawford's disparate pay claim. The parties do not dispute the ten month period identified by the district court. In any event, recognizing that a significant period of time was involved, perhaps anywhere from five to twenty-three months for each event, is sufficient for the purpose of our analysis here.

treatment claims under § 1983 is identical to the analysis under Title VII where the facts on which the claims rely are the same.

Title VII also prohibits retaliation against an employee "because [s]he has opposed any practice made an unlawful employment practice by [Title VII], or because [s]he has made a charge, testified, assisted, or participated in any manner in an investigation, proceeding, or hearing [thereunder]." A *prima facie* case of retaliation under Title VII requires the plaintiff to show that: (1) she engaged in an activity protected under Title VII; (2) she suffered an adverse employment action; and (3) there was a causal connection between the protected activity and the adverse employment action.

In the past this circuit's standard for both discrimination and retaliation claims has required an employee to establish an "ultimate employment decision" or make some other showing of substantiality in the employment context in order to establish an adverse employment action. We defined ultimate employment decisions as those "such as termination, failure to hire, or demotion." And we required that conduct falling short of an ultimate employment decision must, in some substantial way, "alter[ ] the employee's compensation, terms, conditions, or privileges of employment, deprive him or her of employment opportunities, or adversely affect [ ] his or her status as an employee." More particularly, when defining the level of substantiality required for a Title VII discrimination claim, we required an employee to demonstrate she suffered "a *serious and material* change in the terms, conditions, or privileges of employment" to show an adverse employment action. The "serious and material change" requirement has also been applied in this circuit to Title VII retaliation claims.

The district court in this case found that because GSU had awarded Crawford a merit pay increase, effective retroactively to October 2002, Crawford could not establish an adverse employment action for purposes of either her discrimination or retaliation claims. According to the district court, because Crawford's "job was never in doubt, and she never lost any of her base salary," she did not suffer a materially adverse employment action in connection with the denial of her merit pay increase. The question then is whether the fact that GSU reversed its decision and awarded Crawford her merit pay increase retroactively somehow deprives her of the right to pursue her claims. For the reasons given below, we think the answer to that question is "no."

We first note that our decision in *Gillis v. Georgia Department of Corrections* is directly on point on Crawford's discrimination claims. The district court recognized the relevance of *Gillis* to the instant case but declined to apply that decision because it concluded, as it did in connection with Crawford's retaliation claim, that her successful grievance resulted in her having suffered no loss and thus no adverse employment action.

In *Gillis* the plaintiff, an African-American female, received a "met expectations" performance evaluation, which resulted in her receiving a three percent raise, rather than an "exceeded expectations" evaluation, which would have yielded a five percent raise. The difference between the three percent raise and the five percent raise was less than $1000 annually, and the plaintiff lost no employment benefits as a result of the evaluation. Gillis brought a Title VII action against her employer and former supervisors. The district court held that Gillis' receiving a smaller pay raise than she would have had her performance evaluation been more favorable did not constitute an adverse employment action and granted summary judgment for the defendants. We reversed the district court's judgment on Gillis' race discrimination claim, holding that a poor performance evaluation that directly results in the denial of a pay raise of any significance clearly affects an employee's compensation and thus constitutes an adverse employment action under Title VII.

We perceive no basis for distinguishing the facts of the instant case from those in *Gillis*. As was true for the plaintiff in *Gillis*, the evidence in this case shows that Crawford's poor evaluation and her compensation were "inextricably intertwined." From October 2002 (when Crawford's paycheck did not include the four percent merit pay increase she otherwise would have received absent the poor evaluation she was given in April 2002) until her position was reclassified in March 2003 and salary retroactively increased by four percent in October 2003, Crawford suffered an adverse employment action directly connected to her compensation. Although Crawford received a retroactively awarded merit pay increase, that raise could not alter the fact that she had been denied the increase or erase all injury associated with it, specifically the lost value and use of the funds during the time she was not receiving them. To conclude otherwise would permit employers to escape Title VII liability by correcting their discriminatory and retaliatory acts after the fact. Following the Seventh Circuit's lead, we too decline to hold as a matter of law that a retroactive pay raise can "undo" the harm caused by a discriminatory or retaliatory act because such a decision could permit employers to elude liability for conduct that otherwise is actionable. We therefore find that the district court erred when it held that Crawford's poor performance evaluation, which made her ineligible for a merit pay increase in October 2002, did not constitute an adverse employment action for purposes of her discrimination claims.

The district court relied on our decision in *Stavropoulos v. Firestone* to analyze Crawford's allegations of retaliation. In that case an untenured college assistant professor claimed she was retaliated against in violation of Title VII when, after she complained about a hiring decision involving another professor, the faculty later twice voted not to renew her teaching contract. On both occasions, after the plaintiff successfully challenged the faculty's votes, her contract was renewed before the prior contract had concluded. We affirmed summary judgment in the defendants' favor, noting first that no ultimate employment decisions were involved because the plaintiff "did not lose her job or suffer a lessening of pay, position, or benefits." We also concluded that the complained-of acts did not rise to a sufficient level of substantiality because they ultimately had no effect on the plaintiff's employment status. Further, we decided that any emotional distress or costs incidental to the plaintiff's seeking review of the votes were too insubstantial to be considered an adverse employment action because the plaintiff's challenges ultimately were successful.

Our decision in *Stavropoulos* hinged on whether the employer's actions adversely affected the plaintiff's employment status. As previously discussed, the plaintiff in that case suffered no loss in pay or benefits whatsoever as a result of the faculty votes recommending that she not be rehired. Stavropoulos' contracts in fact were renewed, with no lapse in employment and thus nothing more than an *anticipated* loss. We thus concluded Stavropoulos suffered no tangible harm as a result of an employment decision that never became final.

We think that on the facts of this case the district court misapplied the standard and the holding of *Stavropoulos.* In Crawford's case, the decision that she not be awarded a merit pay increase was a final decision that resulted in her not receiving a merit pay increase. As acknowledged by the district court, "[t]here is no dispute that as a result of the rating Carroll gave to plaintiff on her 2001–2002 evaluation, Plaintiff did not receive an increase in her salary effective 2002." Crawford, unlike Stavropoulos, therefore, realized an *actual* loss. Although the four percent merit pay increase eventually was awarded retroactively in October 2003, as noted, Crawford nevertheless was deprived of the use or value of her merit pay from the time it otherwise would have been awarded in October 2002. In other words, Crawford suffered an adverse employment action directly related to her compensation: the alleged retaliatory performance appraisal deprived her of the tangible employment opportunity of receiving a merit pay increase and thus adversely affected her status as an employee. Again, we think it important to emphasize that an employer cannot undo the harm its actions have caused, and thereby avoid liability, simply by attempting to make the employee whole retroactively. This case is not, as the district court deemed it, simply a matter of "no harm, no foul."

Thus, for the foregoing reasons, with respect to the temporary denial of a merit pay increase, we conclude that under the standards outlined in *Stavropoulos* and *Gupta* Crawford showed that she suffered an adverse employment action for purposes of her race discrimination and retaliation claims. The district court therefore erred in ruling otherwise.

The district court also discussed but chose not to apply the Supreme Court's decision in *Burlington N. & Santa Fe Ry. Co. v. White*, in which the Court announced a new rule which redefines the standard for retaliation claims under Title VII. For the reasons previously discussed, we are convinced that under this circuit's prior standard the district court erred in granting summary judgment on Crawford's retaliation claim. If any doubt remained regarding the incorrectness of the district court's ruling-though we find none does-application of the decidedly more relaxed *Burlington* standard to the facts of this case must emphatically dispel it.

Under the holding of *Burlington*, the type of employer conduct considered actionable has been broadened from that which adversely affects the plaintiff's conditions of employment or employment status to that which has a materially adverse effect on the plaintiff, irrespective of whether it is employment or workplace-related. Thus, the *Burlington* Court effectively rejected the standards applied by this court in both *Stavropoulos* and *Gupta* that required an employee to show either an ultimate employment decision or substantial employment action to establish an adverse employment action for the purpose of a Title VII retaliation claim. Additionally, the Court explained that in the context of a Title VII retaliation claim, a materially adverse action "means it well might have dissuaded a reasonable worker from making or supporting a charge of discrimination."

This more liberal view of what constitutes an adverse employment action accords an employee protection from a wider range of retaliatory conduct than would be available under the standard applied in *Stavropoulos* and *Gupta.* We therefore are persuaded that the adverse employment action standard previously applied in this circuit to Title VII retaliation claims is more stringent than the "materially adverse" standard announced in *Burlington.* In the instant case, we have no doubt but that Crawford suffered a materially adverse action in the form of the unfavorable performance review she received (that affected her eligibility for a merit pay increase) after she complained of racial discrimination. Such conduct by an employer clearly might deter a reasonable employee from pursuing a pending charge of discrimination or making a new one. We therefore conclude that not only was district court's ruling on Crawford's Title VII retaliation claim wrong under our prior, narrower standard, but also that it most certainly is wrong under *Burlington's* more liberal standard.

B. Disparate Treatment in Terms and Conditions of Employment

With respect to Crawford's disparate pay claim, the district court determined that Brennaman was not a proper comparator for purposes of a straight salary comparison. We agree with that conclusion. Not only had Brennaman been employed at GSU for several years longer than Crawford but also Brennaman possessed specialized and highly valued expertise in the information systems field that Crawford does not claim.

The district court noted that Crawford also presented what it termed a "more nuanced pay claim," *i.e.*, that she was not paid at the proper level for her manager position while Caucasian employees in the department, including Brennaman, were paid at the high end of the range for their positions. With respect to this narrower claim the district court apparently accepted, *arguendo*, that Brennaman and the other employees so paid were proper comparators and that Crawford's allegations could constitute adverse employment actions. Again relying on its analysis of *Stavropoulos*, however, the district court reasoned that Crawford's successful grievance, which resulted in an upward adjustment of her salary, resulted in no loss of salary or benefits and thus she had suffered no adverse employment action.

For essentially the same reasons discussed previously regarding Crawford's merit pay increase claim, we conclude that the district court also erred in finding that Crawford failed to show an adverse employment action in connection with her disparate pay claim. Although Crawford's salary eventually was adjusted to $54,740 (without the four percent merit pay increase), she was denied the use or benefit of that pay raise during the time it should have been in effect. Crawford therefore has shown that she was subjected to a serious and material change affecting her compensation that was sufficient to constitute an adverse employment action for purposes of her disparate pay claim.

C. Denial of Promotion

For the purpose of its discussion the district court accepted that Crawford had established a *prima facie* case of discrimination and retaliation for failure to promote and therefore proceeded to an analysis under *McDonnell Douglas Corp. v. Green.* So doing, the court rejected Crawford's contentions that the defendants' proffered reasons for not selecting her and eventually eliminating the position were pretextual.

On any Title VII claim the plaintiff bears "the ultimate burden of proving discriminatory treatment by a preponderance of the evidence." She may satisfy her burden by presenting direct evidence of an intent to discriminate or circumstantial evidence using *McDonnell Douglas's* burden-shifting framework. Under this framework, if the plaintiff establishes a *prima facie* case, the burden shifts to the employer to "articulate some legitimate, nondiscriminatory reason" for the adverse employment action. If the employer does this, the burden shifts back to the plaintiff to show that the employer's stated reason was a pretext for discrimination. The inquiry into pretext requires the court to determine, in view of all the evidence, "whether the plaintiff has cast sufficient doubt on the defendant's proffered nondiscriminatory reasons to permit a reasonable factfinder to conclude that the employer's proffered legitimate reasons were not what actually motivated its conduct." As with claims of substantive discrimination, Title VII retaliation claims require that "[o]nce the plaintiff establishes [a] *prima facie* case, the employer must proffer a legitimate, non-discriminatory reason for the adverse employment action. If the employer offers such legitimate reasons for the employment action, the plaintiff must then demonstrate that the employer's proffered explanation is a pretext for retaliation."

In analyzing Crawford's failure to promote claim, we assume, as did the district court, that Crawford has made out a *prima facie* case of race discrimination and retaliation on this issue. We disagree, however, with the district court's conclusion that no issues of fact remain with respect to whether Crawford has met her burden of showing the defendants' reasons for failing to promote her to the position of director of classification and employment were pretextual. Given the circumstances surrounding the three postings for the position, and the three failures to hire Crawford or otherwise fill the position, we find that Crawford has cast sufficient doubt on the proffered reasons to permit a reasonable factfinder to conclude that the reasons actually were a pretext for discrimination and retaliation. Specifically, a reasonable jury could conclude that a "lack of consensus" was a pretextual reason for failing to hire Crawford the first time the position of director of compensation and employment was advertised: the evidence reflects that Johnston chose not to make a hiring decision at that time given Nelson's assessment that Crawford was the best suited candidate, that Nelson had doubts about the actual need for the new position, and that Nelson had expressed concerns over "other incidents in the past" involving Crawford. As to the second posting, defendants have pointed to no reason whatsoever for failing to offer Crawford the position. With respect to the third time the job was posted, and Crawford again was not promoted, a reasonable jury could question whether the explanation given for not hiring her, indeed for not including her in the interview process, was a pretext for discrimination and retaliation.

Finally, regarding the decision to eliminate the new position, we agree with the district court that defendants have come forward with sufficient evidence, in the form of Wright's consulting report, to show that the reasons for the decision were legitimate and non-discriminatory. We further find that, given the circumstances leading up to the decision-in particular the numerous grievances and complaints Crawford filed-a jury question exists on the issue of whether defendants' reasons for eliminating the job were a pretext for retaliation. Crawford has not, however, come forward with evidence adequate to create a jury question on the issue of whether defendants' proffered explanation for the decision in fact was a pretext for racial discrimination. Crawford has failed to produce evidence sufficient for a reasonable jury to conclude that Johnston's stated reasons for withdrawing the position-which include reliance on Wright's independent report and Nelson's advice, as well as the need to respond to the University's budget demands-were not the actual reasons for her decision but that instead she was motivated by racial bias. Accordingly, with respect to Crawford's failure to promote allegations, the retaliation claim may proceed but the racial discrimination claims may not.

In summary, as to Crawford's allegations concerning the denial of a merit pay increase, disparate pay, and the failure to promote, we conclude that genuine issues of material fact exist that preclude summary judgment. We therefore reverse and remand Crawford's Title VII retaliation and race discrimination claims against GSU and her § 1983 equal protection race discrimination claim against Carroll for further proceedings consistent with this decision.

D. Qualified Immunity

Because we conclude that Johnston is entitled to qualified immunity we affirm the district court as to the judgment entered in her favor on Crawford's § 1983 equal protection race discrimination claim.

Qualified immunity may provide complete protection for public officials sued in their individual capacities. Where, as in this case, there is no dispute as to the discretionary nature of the actions complained of, we proceed to the two-part test established by the Supreme Court for evaluating a claim of qualified immunity. The threshold question is whether, "[t]aken in the light most favorable to the party asserting the injury, do the facts alleged show [that the official's] conduct violated a constitutional right?" If a constitutional right would have been violated under the plaintiff's version of the facts, the court must then determine "whether the right was clearly established." "For the law to be clearly established to the point that qualified immunity does not apply, the law must have earlier been developed in such concrete and factually defined context to make it obvious to all reasonable government actors, in the defendant's place, that what he is doing violates federal law." Qualified immunity affords "protection to all but the plainly incompetent or those who knowingly violate the law." We have noted that "[i]f the law did not put the officer on notice that his conduct would be clearly unlawful, summary judgment based on qualified immunity is appropriate." "The Supreme Court has urged us to apply the affirmative defense of qualified immunity at the earliest possible stage in litigation because the defense is immunity from suit and not from damages only."

Johnston's liability under § 1983 as Carroll's supervisor must be based on something more than the theory of *respondeat superior*. In *Brown v. Crawford*, we observed that:

> Supervisor liability occurs either when the supervisor personally participates in the alleged constitutional violation or when there is a causal connection between actions of the supervising official and the alleged

> constitutional deprivation. The causal connection can be established when a history of widespread abuse puts the responsible supervisor on notice of the need to correct the alleged deprivation, and he fails to do so. The deprivations that constitute widespread abuse sufficient to notify the supervising official must be obvious, flagrant, rampant, and of continued duration, rather than isolated occurrences.

First, the evidence taken in the light most favorable to Crawford reflects that Johnston cursorily approved Carroll's unfavorable performance evaluation of Crawford. The evidence also reflects that during Johnston's forty-five minute meeting with Crawford regarding her complaint alleging retaliation and discrimination Johnston seemed indifferent to Crawford's concerns, and she later issued a rather dismissive written denial of Crawford's complaint. In addition, Johnston was involved in the selection process for the new director position the first time it was posted to the extent she interviewed but declined to endorse one candidate and did not interview any other candidates because she was not asked to do so. Ultimately, Johnston agreed with Nelson-whose approval Johnston testified she needed before hiring a candidate-that the position should not be filled at that time, in part due to concerns over Crawford's pending grievances. There is no evidence that Johnston was involved when the position was posted a second time. With respect to the third posting of the position, Johnston's involvement included telling Carroll to broaden the group of selectors, responding briefly when Carroll informed Johnston that she had narrowed the field of candidates to three unnamed persons, and again acceding to Nelson's advice against filling the position while Crawford's race discrimination claims were pending. None of this evidence of Johnston's involvement in the events of which Crawford complains is sufficient to show that Johnston personally engaged in any conduct that constitutes a violation of the equal protection clause, which ensures the right to be free from intentional discrimination based on race. There is no hint of a racially discriminatory motive in any of Johnston's conduct, the most questionable of which at worst reflects the exercise of poor professional judgment rather than gross incompetence or the intentional commission of constitutional violations. In short, none of the actions in which Johnston was personally involved rises to a level sufficient to divest her of qualified immunity.

Nor does the record support imposing liability against Johnston for Carroll's alleged constitutional violations because she was aware of widespread abuse by Carroll and failed to take corrective action. In this case, even if Johnston's conduct in answering Crawford's complaint was ineffectual, insensitive, or otherwise less responsive than it might have been, it was not constitutionally inadequate for purposes of qualified immunity. Johnston testified that she did not take any independent action regarding Crawford's allegations because she understood, correctly as the evidence shows, that the claims were being independently investigated by the OAADP. Moreover, a comprehensive desk audit of Crawford's position and the entire human resources department, as ordered by Patton with Johnston's encouragement, was subsequently completed by Wright. Thus, as other corrective action was being taken with respect to Crawford's complaints, it was unnecessary, in fact could have been duplicative or counterproductive, for Johnston to act as well at that time. Because there is no evidence of the existence of widespread abuse which Johnston failed to redress, and thus no causal connection between Johnston's actions and the alleged violations of Crawford's constitutional rights, Johnston should not be stripped of the protection of qualified immunity.[21]

IV. *Conclusion*

For the foregoing reasons, we REVERSE the district court's grant of summary judgment to GSU on Crawford's Title VII retaliation and race discrimination claims and to Carroll on Crawford's § 1983 race discrimination claim. We AFFIRM the district court's grant of summary judgment to Johnston. This case is REMANDED to the district court for further proceedings consistent with this opinion.

REVERSED and REMANDED IN PART; AFFIRMED IN PART.

3. Discrimination: Race and National Origin

SAINT FRANCIS COLLEGE v. AL-KHAZRAJI
481 U.S. 604 (1987)

JUSTICE WHITE delivered the opinion of the Court.

Respondent, a citizen of the United States born in Iraq, was an associate professor at St. Francis College, one of the petitioners here. In January 1978, he applied for tenure; the Board of Trustees denied his request on February 23, 1978. He accepted a 1-year, nonrenewable contract and sought administrative reconsideration of the tenure decision, which was denied on February 6, 1979. He worked his last day at the college on May 26, 1979. In June 1979, he filed complaints with the Pennsylvania Human Relations Commission and the Equal Employment Opportunities Commission. The state agency dismissed his claim and the EEOC issued a right-to-sue letter on August 6, 1980.

On October 30, 1980, respondent filed a *pro se* complaint in the District Court alleging a violation of Title VII of the Civil Rights Act of 1964 and claiming discrimination based on national origin, religion, and/or race. . . . The District Court dismissed [selected claims including] the Title VII claims as untimely but held that the § 1981 and 1983 claims were not barred by the Pennsylvania 6-year statute of limitations. The court at that time also ruled that because the complaint alleged

---

[21] As noted, the parties devote little or no attention in this appeal to Johnston's claim of entitlement to qualified immunity. We nevertheless note that Crawford argued below that "cat's paw" liability applied in this case because Johnston merely "rubber stamped" Carroll's allegedly discriminatory conduct. Under a "cat's paw" theory, a non-decisionmaking employee's discriminatory animus may be imputed to a neutral decisionmaker when the decisionmaker has not independently investigated allegations of misconduct. "In such a case, the recommender is using the decisionmaker as a mere conduit, or 'cat's paw' to give effect to the recommender's discriminatory animus. Here, the evidence does not support the contention that Carroll exercised undue influence over Johnston. Rather, contrary to Carroll's wishes, Johnston declined to endorse Strasner for the new position the first time it was posted. Also, following Nelson's advice but against Carroll's recommendation, Johnston declined to extend an offer to Willis on the job's third posting. Finally, because Johnston reviewed Crawford's complaint and met with her to discuss the issues it presented-albeit not to Crawford's satisfaction-Crawford has failed to show a causal connection between Carroll and Johnston's actions pursuant to a "cat's paw" theory of liability.

denial of tenure because respondent was of the Arabian race, an action under § 1981 could be maintained. Defendants' motion for summary judgment came up before a different judge, who construed the pleadings as asserting only discrimination on the basis of national origin and religion, which § 1981 did not cover. Even if racial discrimination was deemed to have been alleged, the District Court ruled that § 1981 does not reach claims of discrimination based on Arabian ancestry.

The Court of Appeals rejected petitioners' claim that the § 1981 claim had not been timely filed. . . .

Reaching the merits, the Court of Appeals held that respondent had alleged discrimination based on race and that although under current racial classifications Arabs are Caucasians, respondent could maintain his § 1981 claim. Congress, when it passed what is now § 1981, had not limited its protections to those who today would be considered members of a race different from the race of the defendant. Rather, the legislative history of the section indicated that Congress intended to enhance "at the least, membership in a group that is ethnically and physiognomically distinctive." Section 1981, "at a minimum," reaches "discrimination directed against an individual because he or she is genetically part of an ethnically and physiognomically distinctive sub-grouping of *homo sapiens.*" Because respondent had not had full discovery and the record was not sufficient to determine whether he had been subjected to the sort of prejudice § 1981 would redress, respondent was to be given the opportunity to prove his case.

We granted certiorari . . . [raising the issue of] whether a person of Arabian ancestry was protected from racial discrimination under § 1981, and now affirm the judgment of the Court of Appeals.

I

We agree with the Court of Appeals that respondent's claim was not time barred.

II

Section 1981 provides:

> All persons within the jurisdiction of the United States shall have the same right in every State and Territory to make and enforce contracts, to sue, be parties, give evidence, and to the full and equal benefit of all laws and proceedings for the security of persons and property as is enjoyed by white citizens, and shall be subject to like punishment, pains, penalties, taxes, licenses, and exactions of every kind, and to no other.

Although § 1981 does not itself use the word "race," the Court has construed the section to forbid all "racial" discrimination in the making of private as well as public contracts. Petitioner college, although a private institution, was therefore subject to this statutory command. There is no disagreement among the parties on these propositions. The issue is whether respondent has alleged *racial* discrimination within the meaning of § 1981.

Petitioners contend that respondent is a Caucasian and cannot allege the kind of discrimination § 1981 forbids. Concededly, *McDonald v. Santa Fe Trail Transportation Co.* held that white persons could maintain a § 1981 suit; but that suit involved alleged discrimination against a white person in favor of a black, and petitioner submits that the section does not encompass claims of discrimination by one Caucasian against another. We are quite sure that the Court of Appeals properly rejected this position.

Petitioner's submission rests on the assumption that all those who might be deemed Caucasians today were thought to be of the same race when § 1981 became law in the 19th century; and it may be that a variety of ethnic groups, including Arabs, are now considered to be within the Caucasian race. The understanding of "race" in the 19th century, however, was different. Plainly, all those who might be deemed Caucasian today were not thought to be of the same race at the time § 1981 became law.

In the middle years of the 19th century, dictionaries commonly referred to race as a "continued series of descendants from a parent who is called the *stock*," "[t]he lineage of a family," or "descendants of a common ancestor." The 1887 edition of Webster's expanded the definition somewhat: "The descendants of a common ancestor; a family, tribe, people or nation, believed or presumed to belong to the same stock." It was not until the 20th century that dictionaries began referring to the Caucasian, Mongolian, and Negro races, or to race as involving divisions of mankind based upon different physical characteristics. Even so, modern dictionaries still include among the definitions of race "a family, tribe, people, or nation belonging to the same stock."

Encyclopedias of the 19th century also described race in terms of ethnic groups, which is a narrower concept of race than petitioners urge. Encyclopedia Americana in 1858, for example, referred to various races such as Finns, gypsies, Basques, and Hebrews. The 1863 version of the New American Cyclopaedia divided the Arabs into a number of subsidiary races, represented the Hebrews as of the Semitic race, and identified numerous other groups as constituting races, including Swedes, Norwegians, Germans, Greeks, Finns, Italians, Spanish, Mongolians, Russians, and the like. The Ninth edition of the Encyclopedia Britannica also referred to Arabs, Jews, and other ethnic groups such as Germans, Hungarians, and Greeks, as separate races.

These dictionary and encyclopedic sources are somewhat diverse, but it is clear that they do not support the claim that for the purposes of § 1981, Arabs, Englishmen, Germans, and certain other ethnic groups are to be considered a single race. We would expect the legislative history of § 1981, which the Court held in *Runyon v. McCrary* had its source in the Civil Rights Act of 1866, as well as the Voting Rights Act of 1870, to reflect this common understanding, which it surely does. The debates are replete with references to the Scandinavian races, as well as the Chinese, Latin, Spanish, and Anglo-Saxon races. Jews, Mexicans, blacks, and Mongolians were similarly categorized. Gypsies were referred to as a race. . . .

Based on the history of § 1981, we have little trouble in concluding that Congress intended to protect from discrimination identifiable classes of persons who are subjected to intentional discrimination solely because of their ancestry or ethnic characteristics. Such discrimination is racial discrimination that Congress intended

§ 1981 to forbid, whether or not it would be classified as racial in terms of modern scientific theory. The Court of Appeals was thus quite right in holding that § 1981, "at a minimum," reaches discrimination against an individual "because he or she is genetically part of an ethnically and physiognomically distinctive sub-grouping of *homo sapiens.*" It is clear from our holding, however, that a distinctive physiognomy is not essential to qualify for § 1981 protection. If respondent on remand can prove that he was subjected to intentional discrimination based on the fact that he was born an Arab, rather than solely on the place or nation of his origin, or his religion, he will have made out a case under § 1981.

The judgment of the Court of Appeals is accordingly affirmed.

It is so ordered.

NOTES

1. Generally speaking, a Title VII discrimination claim requires a filing within 180 days of the discriminatory action or within 300 days if the complainant first files with the state/local agency that has jurisdiction over the matter. In *Delaware State College v. Ricks*, 449 U.S. 250 (1980), the issue raised was when that time begins to accrue. The U.S. Supreme Court described the case facts as follows:

> Columbus Ricks is a black Liberian. In 1970, Ricks joined the faculty at Delaware State College, a state institution attended predominantly by blacks. In February 1973, the Faculty Committee on Promotions and Tenure (the tenure committee) recommended that Ricks not receive a tenured position in the education department. The tenure committee, however, agreed to reconsider its decision the following year. Upon reconsideration, in February 1974, the committee adhered to its earlier recommendation. The following month, the Faculty Senate voted to support the tenure committee's negative recommendation. On March 13, 1974, the College Board of Trustees formally voted to deny tenure to Ricks.
>
> Dissatisfied with the decision, Ricks immediately filed a grievance with the Board's Educational Policy Committee (the grievance committee), which in May 1974 held a hearing and took the matter under submission.[1] During the pendency of the grievance, the College administration continued to plan for Ricks' eventual termination. Like many colleges and universities, Delaware State has a policy of not discharging immediately a junior faculty member who does not receive tenure. Rather, such a person is offered a "terminal" contract to teach one additional year. When that contract expires, the employment relationship ends. Adhering to this policy, the Trustees on June 26, 1974, told Ricks that he would be offered a 1-year "terminal" contract that would expire June 30, 1975. Ricks signed the contract without objection or reservation on September 4, 1974. Shortly thereafter, on September 12, 1974, the Board of Trustees notified Ricks that it had denied his grievance.
>
> Ricks attempted to file an employment discrimination charge with the Equal Employment Opportunity Commission (EEOC) on April 4, 1975.

Id. at 252–54. As stated earlier, the central issue was when the clock started ticking for statute of limitation purposes. Here, the plaintiff argued time started running on September 12, 1974, but the Court determined that the plaintiff had proper notice of the adverse employment action on June 26, 1974, "when the President of the Board notified Ricks that he would be offered a 'terminal' contract for the 1974–1975 school year." *Id.* at 261–62. The Court thus declared that the timing for a Title VII action commences when the employer makes its official position known to the complainant.

The *Ricks* case does not apply to legal challenges that do not explicitly implicate discriminatory action impacting compensation. In 2009, the Lilly Ledbetter Fair Pay Act became law with a retroactive effective date to May 28, 2007. The law redefines the alleged discriminatory occurrence for Title VII, Title I and § 503 of the Americans with Disabilities Act, §§ 501 and 504 of the Rehabilitation Act, and the Age Discrimination in Employment Act. The relevant section states:

> For purposes of this section, an unlawful employment practice occurs, with respect to discrimination in compensation in violation of this title, when a discriminatory compensation decision or other practice is adopted, when an individual becomes subject to a discriminatory compensation decision or other practice, or when an individual is affected by application of a discriminatory compensation decision or other practice, including each time wages, benefits, or other compensation is paid, resulting in whole or in part from such a decision or other practice.

42 U.S.C. § 2000e-5(e)(3)(A) (2012).

The law emerged in reaction to a U.S. Supreme Court case, *Ledbetter v. Goodyear Tire & Rubber Co.*, 550 U.S. 618 (2007). According to a concisely summarized recount from *Voung v. New York Life Insurance Company*, No. 03 Civ. 1075 (TPG) (S.D.N.Y. 2009):

> [The Court in the *Ledbetter* case] held that a claimant alleging discrimination based on a pay-setting decision must file a charge with the EEOC within 180 days, or 300 days, after the discriminatory decision was made. The Court rejected the plaintiffs claim that she could recover based on a later paycheck she received that would have been larger had the prior discrimination not occurred. The plaintiff conceded that there was no discriminatory intent by the personnel involved in issuing the later paychecks. The Court ruled that the continuing effects of a past employment decision, which was adopted with discriminatory intent, do not transform a subsequent employment act, unaccompanied by discriminatory intent, into a present violation.

In response to the case, Congress passed the Lilly Ledbetter Fair Pay Act. Thus, the law superseded the case.

To what extent does a tenure denial for a member of a protected class raise a *Ledbetter* determination of the discriminatory occurrence? In *Gentry v. Jackson State University*, 610 F. Supp. 2d 564 (S.D. Miss. 2009), a federal district court determined that the denial of tenure negatively effects compensation. Thus, the Ledbetter Act applies. However, in *Leach v. Baylor College of Medicine*, Civ. Action

No. H-07-0921, (S.D. Tex. Feb. 17, 2009), a federal district court declined to apply the Ledbetter Act in a racial discrimination case. In *Leach*, the issue raised was whether a medical doctor at Baylor filed in a timely fashion about alleged discriminatory actions regarding disparate job responsibilities. The court did not connect the suit with a compensation matter; hence, the Ledbetter Act did not apply.

4. Discrimination: Religion

SHELTON v. UNIVERSITY OF MEDICINE & DENTISTRY OF NEW JERSEY

223 F.3d 220 (3d Cir. 2000)

OPINION OF THE COURT

Scirica, Circuit Judge.

In this employment discrimination case, the issue on appeal is whether a state hospital reasonably accommodated the religious beliefs and practices of a staff nurse who refused to participate in what she believed to be abortions. The District Court held it had, and we agree. We will affirm.

I. Background

Yvonne Shelton worked as a staff nurse in the Labor and Delivery section of the Hospital at the University of Medicine and Dentistry of New Jersey. The Hospital's Labor and Delivery section provides patients with routine vaginal and cesarean-section deliveries. The Labor and Delivery section does not perform elective abortions. On occasion, Labor and Delivery section patients require emergency procedures that terminate their pregnancies. Labor and Delivery section nurses are required to assist in emergency procedures as part of their job responsibilities.

Shelton is a member of the Pentecostal faith; her faith forbids her from participating "directly or indirectly in ending a life." The proscription includes abortions of live fetuses. Shelton claims she notified the Hospital in writing about her religious beliefs when she first joined the Hospital in 1989, and again in 1994. During this time, the Hospital accommodated Shelton's religious beliefs by allowing her to trade assignments with other nurses rather than participate in emergency procedures involving what Shelton considered to be abortions.

Two events precipitated Shelton's termination. In 1994, Shelton refused to treat a patient. According to the Hospital, the patient was pregnant and suffering from a ruptured membrane (which the Hospital describes as a life-threatening condition). Shelton learned the Hospital planned to induce labor by giving the patient oxytocin. Shelton refused to assist or participate.

After the incident, Shelton's supervisor asked her to provide a note from her pastor about her religious beliefs. Instead, Shelton submitted her own note:

> Before the foundations of the earth, God called me to be Holy. For this cause I must be obedient to the word of God. From his own mouth he said "Thou shalt not kill." Therefore, regardless of the situation, I will not participate directly or indirectly in ending a life. . . .

In November 1995, Shelton refused to treat another emergency patient. This patient-who was "standing in a pool of blood"-was diagnosed with placenta previa. The attending Labor and Delivery section physician determined the situation was life-threatening and ordered an emergency cesarean-section delivery. When Shelton arrived for her shift, she was told to "scrub in" on the procedure. Because the procedure would terminate the pregnancy, Shelton refused to assist or participate. Eventually, another nurse took her place. The Hospital claims Shelton's refusal to assist delayed the emergency procedure for thirty minutes.

Two months later, the Hospital informed Shelton she could no longer work in the Labor and Delivery section because of her refusal to assist in "medical procedures necessary to save the life of the mother and/or child." The Hospital claimed that staffing cuts prevented it from allowing Shelton to continue to trade assignments when situations arose she considered would lead to an abortion. The Hospital believed Shelton's refusals to assist risked patients' safety.

But the Hospital did not terminate Shelton. Instead, it offered her a lateral transfer to a staff nurse position in the Newborn Intensive Care Unit ("Newborn ICU"). The Hospital also invited Shelton to contact its Human Resources Department, which would help her identify other available nursing positions.

Shelton undertook her own investigation of the Newborn ICU position. She claims she spoke with a nurse (whose name she does not remember) in that unit, who said that "extremely compromised" infants who were not expected to survive would be "set aside" and allowed to die. Shelton did not attempt to confirm this information with the Hospital. Nor did she contact the Human Resources Department to investigate other available positions. Shelton claims she believed no other positions would be available.

The Hospital gave Shelton thirty days to accept the position in Newborn ICU, or to apply for another nursing position. Shelton did neither. Instead, on the thirtieth day, she wrote to her supervisor:

> . . . The ultimatum given me however, doesn't align with the response I am functioned to submit. The decision is not ours to make but the Lords'. The Living God is in control of that which concerns my life and job. "Many are the plans in a mans heart but it's Gods plan/purpose that will prevail."

On February 15, 1996, the Hospital terminated Shelton.

II. Proceedings

Shelton sued, claiming violations of Title VII of the Civil Rights Act, 42 U.S.C. § 2000e, et seq. (Count I), the New Jersey Law Against Discrimination, N.J.S.A. 10:5 et seq. (Count II), and the First Amendment (Count III). The District Court granted summary judgment for the Hospital on Shelton's federal claims, concluding the Hospital reasonably accommodated Shelton by offering to transfer her to the

Newborn ICU and by inviting her to work with its Human Resources Department to identify other available positions. The court declined to continue jurisdiction over Shelton's state law claims. Shelton appealed, claiming the District Court erred by ignoring material issues of fact and by failing to consider the New Jersey Conscience Statute.

We have jurisdiction over Shelton's appeal under 28 U.S.C. § 1291. Our review of a summary judgment is plenary. We view all evidence and draw all inferences therefrom in the light most favorable to the non-movant, affirming if no reasonable jury could find for the non-movant.

III. Discussion

A. The Title VII Religious Discrimination Claim

Title VII of the 1964 Civil Rights Act requires employers to make reasonable accommodations for their employees' religious beliefs and practices, unless doing so would result in "undue hardship" to the employer. To establish a prima facie case, the employee must show:

1. she holds a sincere religious belief that conflicts with a job requirement;
2. she informed her employer of the conflict; and
3. she was disciplined for failing to comply with the conflicting requirement.

If the employee establishes a prima facie case, the burden shifts to the employer to show that it made good faith efforts to accommodate, or that the requested accommodation would work an undue hardship.

The approach employed in *Protos* and *Getz* is similar to that employed by many of our sister courts of appeals. Nonetheless, we are mindful that the Supreme Court has declined to accept or reject any particular prima facie case or burden-shifting approach to Title VII religious accommodation cases. In *Philbrook*, the Court reviewed a Title VII religious discrimination case in which the Court of Appeals for the Second Circuit had applied a prima facie case test virtually identical to that we now apply (and previously applied in *Protos* and *Getz*, both decided shortly before *Philbrook*). The Court of Appeals had held the employee established his prima facie case. Then, assuming without discussion the employer's policy constituted a reasonable accommodation, the court held that where the employer and employee both propose a reasonable accommodation, the employer must accept the employee's proposal unless doing so works an undue hardship. On this latter point the Supreme Court reversed, commenting that it found "no basis in either the statute or its legislative history for requiring an employer to choose any particular reasonable accommodation." The Court specifically declined to "establish for religious accommodation claims a proof scheme analogous to that developed in other Title VII contexts, delineating the plaintiff's prima facie case and shifting production burdens." The Court reasoned that because the matter had been tried on the merits, the prima facie case issue was not before it. Thus, absent further guidance from the Supreme Court, we will continue to apply the prima facie test and burden-shifting approach used in *Protos* and *Getz*.

1. Shelton's Prima Facie Case

The District Court held Shelton established a prima facie case. We agree. There is no dispute that Shelton's religious beliefs are sincere, and that the Hospital ultimately terminated Shelton. Although the parties dispute when Shelton first notified the Hospital she would not participate in abortions (Shelton claims she notified the Hospital when she commenced work), they do not dispute the Hospital was on notice by at least 1994. Although the Hospital claims Shelton failed to establish notice because she never provided the requested note from her pastor, we disagree. Under the facts presented, Shelton provided sufficient notice.

2. The Burden Shifts: The Hospital Must Establish A Reasonable Accommodation, or Undue Hardship

Because Shelton established her prima facie case, the burden shifts to the Hospital to show either that it offered Shelton a reasonable accommodation, or that it could not do so because of a resulting undue hardship. The Hospital claims it satisfied the former.

Title VII does not define what is a "reasonable accommodation." But the Supreme Court in *Philbrook* made clear what it need not be: a sufficient religious accommodation need not be the "most" reasonable one (in the employee's view), it need not be the one the employee suggests or prefers, and it need not be the one that least burdens the employee. In short, the employer satisfies its Title VII religious accommodation obligation when it offers any reasonable accommodation.

On this point, *Philbrook* provides some guidance. Philbrook was a high school teacher whose union agreement allowed him to take three "religious days" a year. "Religious days" were not charged against paid personal leave, but paid leave could not be used for extra religious days. Philbrook's religious practices caused him to miss approximately six school days a year. To resolve the issue, Philbrook proposed that he be allowed either to take additional unpaid personal leave, or to pay for a substitute teacher (and receive his own full pay for the day). The school district declined. The district court held Philbrook failed to prove any religious discrimination. On appeal, the Court of Appeals for the Second Circuit reversed, holding when an employer and employee both propose reasonable accommodations, the employee's must be accepted unless shown to work an undue hardship. The Supreme Court reversed, rejecting the view that an employer must adopt any particular proposed accommodation: "[W]here the employer has already reasonably accommodated the employee's religious needs, the statutory inquiry is at an end. The employer need not further show that each of the employee's alternative accommodations would result in undue hardship." As to whether the school district's policy in fact constituted a reasonable accommodation, the Court remanded. The Court explained that although the school district's policy seemed to be reasonable-because it eliminated the religious conflict-it would not be so if interpreted to allow paid leave for all purposes except religious ones. Further fact-finding was ordered.

Against this background we analyze the Hospital's proffered accommodations.

a. The Hospital's Offer to Transfer Shelton to the Newborn ICU Position

Shelton argues there is a fact issue whether the Hospital reasonably accommodated her by offering a transfer to the Newborn ICU. The core of her argument is that the transfer would not have resolved the religious conflict; in the Newborn ICU she would again be asked to undertake religiously untenable nursing actions (or inactions). The Hospital countered Shelton's claim with testimony that infants in Newborn ICU are not denied medical treatment. Carolyn Franklin, the Hospital's Director of Patient Care Services, testified that she had no knowledge that any baby in Newborn ICU had been taken off of life support, or denied nourishment. Furthermore, there is no evidence that if Shelton worked in the unit, she would be asked to deny care to any infant. Indeed, Shelton admitted that her conclusion about what she might be asked to do in the Newborn ICU was self-drawn.

In sum, Shelton has not established she would face a religious conflict in the Newborn ICU. The Hospital's offer of a lateral transfer to that unit thus constituted a reasonable accommodation.

b. The Hospital's Invitation to Shelton to Meet with the Human Resources Department to Identify Other Available Positions

In another attempt to accommodate Shelton's religious conflict, the Hospital invited Shelton to meet with its Human Resources Department to discuss other available nursing positions. Once the Hospital initiated discussions with that proposal, Shelton had a duty to cooperate in determining whether the proposal was a reasonable one. By refusing to meet with Human Resources to investigate available positions, Shelton failed to satisfy her duty.

Shelton does not dispute that at the relevant time, staff nursing positions may have been available in other departments. But she claims her duty to cooperate in finding an accommodation never arose because a transfer to any other department was not a viable option. Not surprisingly, she does not base this claim on any religious conflict. Instead, she claims a transfer to any other department would have required her to "give up eight years of specialized training and education," and to undertake retraining.

The District Court found unconvincing Shelton's claim that a transfer to another staff nurse position would require her to "give up" all of her years of training and education. We agree. Shelton has not come forward with any evidence that a lateral transfer would have affected her salary or benefits. Indeed, Shelton testified that she did not pursue a meeting with Human Resources to identify other lateral transfers because she believed positions were not available. She never expressed a concern that she would be forced to accept a lower salary or benefits. Instead, conceding that a lateral transfer "may have resulted in no immediate economic impact," Shelton offered only the generic speculation that lateral transfers may result in "long-term economic consequences as to the employee's career prospects." Such speculation is insufficient to raise a fact issue precluding summary judgment.

Although there is evidence that Shelton likely would have to undergo some retraining if she took a position outside of the Labor and Delivery section, there is no evidence that she would lose pay or benefits by accepting a new staff nurse position. On this point, the Hospital's Nursing Manager, Edyth Stroud, testified that although a staff nurse who transferred to another nursing unit would need some training, the relocation would not be burdensome. We agree with the District Court that there was no evidence in this case that a lateral transfer would be unreasonable or burdensome.

In sum, Shelton's refusal to cooperate in attempting to find an acceptable religious accommodation was unjustified. Her unwillingness to pursue an acceptable alternative nursing position undermines the cooperative approach to religious accommodation issues that Congress intended to foster.

In a recent case decided by the Court of Appeals for the Seventh Circuit, a police officer refused, on religious grounds, to protect employees of an abortion clinic. The officer-Rodriguez-asked to be exempted from further assignments to guard an abortion clinic from protestors. Although the police department declined formally to exempt him, it did allow informal accommodations: Rodriguez's captain avoided assigning him to clinic duty, and Rodriguez took vacation time on the days when clinic patrol was most likely to be assigned. Eventually, Rodriguez was assigned to clinic patrol. When he again requested exemption, the on-duty sergeant told him he could not refuse an assignment. Rodriguez took the assignment under protest, then sued under Title VII. The district court granted the police department's motion for summary judgment. The Court of Appeals for the Seventh Circuit affirmed, holding the police department had reasonably accommodated Rodriguez by providing him the opportunity, through a collective bargaining agreement, to transfer to another district, at the same pay and benefit levels. The accommodation was not unreasonable simply because it would have required Rodriguez to forfeit the right to stay in his district of choice.

It would seem unremarkable that public protectors such as police and firefighters must be neutral in providing their services. We would include public health care providers among such public protectors. Although we do not interpret Title VII to require a presumption of undue burden, we believe public trust and confidence requires that a public hospital's health care practitioners-with professional ethical obligations to care for the sick and injured-will provide treatment in time of emergency.

Shelton refused the Hospital's efforts to accommodate her religious beliefs and practices. Having done so, she cannot successfully challenge those efforts as legally inadequate.

B. The New Jersey Conscience Statute

Shelton contends her refusals to participate in certain procedures were protected in the first instance by the New Jersey Conscience Statute. That statute provides in part:

> A-1. No person shall be required to perform or assist in the performance of an abortion or sterilization.
>
> . . . .

> A-3. The refusal to perform, assist in the performance of, or provide abortion services or sterilization procedures shall not constitute grounds for civil or criminal liability, disciplinary action or discriminatory treatment.

Shelton claims the Hospital's actions violated the Conscience Statute. But Shelton did not plead that claim in her complaint. Accordingly, that issue was not before the District Court (which made no mention of the statute in its Opinion), and is not now before us.

C. First Amendment Claim

Shelton also alleges the Hospital violated Shelton's First Amendment right to free exercise of religion by engaging in improper viewpoint discrimination. Specifically, she claims the Hospital fired her because its viewpoint on abortion conflicted with hers. In support of this argument Shelton cites [the U.S. Supreme Court case of] *Rosenberger v. Rector and Visitors of Univ. of Virginia.* We fail to see how *Rosenberger*-or Shelton's viewpoint argument-applies here. *Rosenberger* dealt with whether a public university violated students' First Amendment free speech rights by providing funds to non-religious student publications, but denying funds to a religious publication. The alleged viewpoint discrimination comprised the university's different treatment of two student publications that espoused different views. Here, Shelton has not attempted to establish that the Hospital treated her differently from any other staff nurse who refused to participate in procedures. Nor does it appear that she could, for the evidence was to the contrary: one of the Hospital's representatives testified that when nurses developed sensitivities to latex gloves and could not perform work in their unit, the Hospital "was able to accommodate some of those situations." Thus, it appears that the Hospital has dealt consistently with nurses who could not or would not refuse to perform their nursing duties, regardless of reason.

In sum, Shelton has failed to establish that the Hospital was anything but neutral with respect to religion. Thus we see no error in the District Court's grant of summary judgment to the Hospital on Shelton's First Amendment claim.

IV. Conclusion

For the reasons stated, we will affirm the judgment of the District Court.

5. Sex Discrimination and Retaliation

PATANE v. CLARK

508 F.3d 106 (2d Cir. 2007)

PER CURIAM:

Plaintiff-Appellant Eleanora M. Patane appeals from the dismissal of her Complaint in its entirety pursuant to Federal Rule of Civil Procedure ("FRCP") 12(b)(6) by the United States District Court for the Southern District of New York

(Conner, J.). In her Complaint, Plaintiff presses nine claims against each of the five Defendants-Appellees, John Richard Clark, Harry B. Evans, David Stuhr, Georgina Arendacs and Fordham University ("Fordham"), for discriminatory action, creating a hostile work environment, and retaliatory acts following Plaintiff's initial complaints, in violation of Title VII, 42 U.S.C. § 2000e et seq., [and several New York State laws]. Plaintiff does not appeal the district court's dismissal of her Title VII claims against the four individual defendants on the grounds that "individuals are not subject to liability under Title VII." However, Plaintiff appeals the district court's dismissal of her remaining claims for failure to state a claim upon which relief could be granted.

Taking Plaintiff's allegations as true, as we must, we find that her Complaint asserts claims for a hostile work environment and retaliation in violation of both the federal and state statutes against Defendant Fordham University, and in violation of the state statutes against the four individual Defendants. We vacate the district court's judgment with regard to these claims, and remand for further proceedings consistent with this opinion.

BACKGROUND

Plaintiff began working in 1998 as an executive secretary in Fordham's University's Classics Department. One of her supervisors was Defendant John Richard Clark, a professor in the Classics Department who was also, at various times during Plaintiff's tenure, the Department's Chair. Plaintiff alleges that, from the beginning, Clark engaged in inappropriate sexually-charged conduct in their workplace.

For instance, Plaintiff alleges that, in 1998, Clark engaged in the gender-based harassment of a female classics professor, Dr. Sarah Peirce. Then, starting in 1999–2000, Clark spent one to two hours every day viewing "hard core pornographic" videotapes on a TV-VCR in his office. Plaintiff claims she was aware of Clark's habit because the flickering from his TV screen was visible through the glass partition of his office and because she once saw numerous pornographic videotapes scattered on the floor of his office when she knocked on his door to announce a visitor.

Plaintiff also alleges that some of Clark's behavior was specifically directed at her. Once, she discovered "hard core pornographic websites" on her computer. She alleges that Clark used her computer to view these sites during his weekend trips to the office. After discovering the sites, she obtained a password to protect her computer and had all of the offensive material deleted. Moreover, Plaintiff alleges that Clark regularly had videotapes "concerning masochism and sadism" shipped to the office, which, as his secretary, she was responsible for opening and delivering to his mailbox.

Sometime before 2001, Plaintiff showed one of the videotapes delivered to Clark's office to Defendant Georgina Arendacs, the Director of the Equity and Equal Opportunity ("EEO") Department at Fordham's Bronx campus, who was charged with handling discrimination claims. Arendacs took no remedial action beyond reporting Plaintiff's complaint to Defendant David Stuhr, the Associate Vice-President of Academic Affairs at Fordham's Bronx campus. Plaintiff continued to report Clark's behavior to Arendacs and Stuhr throughout 2004-including showing them the collection of thirty-six pornographic videotapes that Clark kept in his office.

Plaintiff alleges that, by 2001, Clark was "clearly aware" that she had reported his behavior and began to retaliate against her. He "removed virtually all of her secretarial functions, kept her entirely out of the departmental information 'loop,' refused to speak to her, and communicated with her only by e-mail." Indeed, Plaintiff alleges that Defendant Harry B. Evans, another professor in the Classics Department and Clark's friend, advised Clark not to "give [Plaintiff] any more work" in order to "make her leave."

In the fall of 2004, Evans became the Chair of the Classics Department and, Plaintiff alleges, he continued Clark's campaign of retaliation. Plaintiff contends that Evans sought to take disciplinary action against her on the pretext that she inaccurately prepared a time sheet; he constantly monitored her whereabouts and picked up her telephone; and he issued a negative performance evaluation, which Plaintiff alleges was materially false.

On November 10, 2004, Plaintiff filed a Charge of Discrimination with the United States Equal Employment Opportunity Commission ("EEOC"). The EEOC issued Plaintiff a Notice of Right to Sue, which she received on September 9, 2005. On December 6, 2005, Plaintiff filed the Complaint which is the subject of the instant appeal. Shortly thereafter, the Defendants moved to dismiss pursuant to FRCP 12(b)(1) and 12(b)(6) and, in the alternative, to strike certain allegations from the Complaint pursuant to FRCP 12(f). On June 21, 2006, the district court (Conner, J.) granted Defendants' motion to dismiss the Complaint in its entirety for failure to state a claim upon which relief could be granted, declined to reach Defendants' 12(b)(1) motion, and found their 12(f) motion to be moot. This appeal followed.

DISCUSSION

Plaintiff now appeals the district court's dismissal of her federal and state claims against Fordham, and of her state claims against the four individual Defendants. She argues that her Complaint states claims for: (1) gender-based discriminatory action . . . ; (2) the creation of a hostile work environment . . . ; and (3) retaliation in violation. . . .

[Editorial Note: For purposes of this case discussion, we will examine the three claims only under Title VII.]

We review de novo a district court's decision to dismiss a complaint for failure to state a claim pursuant to FRCP 12(b)(6). We must accept all well-pleaded facts as true and consider those facts in the light most favorable to the plaintiff.

On a motion to dismiss, the issue is "whether the claimant is entitled to offer evidence to support the claims." In order to withstand a motion to dismiss, a complaint must plead "enough facts to state a claim for relief that is plausible on its face." In assessing the legal sufficiency of a claim, the court may consider those facts alleged in the complaint, as well as "documents that the plaintiffs either possessed or knew about and upon which they relied in bringing the suit."

I

The *sine qua non* of a gender-based discriminatory action claim under Title VII is that "the discrimination must be because of sex." "It is axiomatic that mistreatment at work . . . is actionable under Title VII only when it occurs because of an employee's sex, or other protected characteristic." Moreover, to be actionable under Title VII, the action that is alleged to be gender-based must rise to the level of an "adverse employment . . . action." We have explained that an action must cause a "materially adverse change in the terms and conditions of employment," and not just "mere inconvenience," in order to qualify as "adverse." In the instant case, the district court was correct to conclude that Plaintiff failed to state a claim for discriminatory action in violation of Title VII, 42 U.S.C. § 2000e et seq., because she failed "to plead any facts that would create an inference that any [adverse] action taken by . . . [any] defendant was based upon her gender."

Plaintiff's Complaint does not allege that she was subject to any specific gender-based adverse employment action by Clark or any of the other defendants, nor does it set forth any factual circumstances from which a gender-based motivation for such an action might be inferred. It does not, for instance, allege that Clark (or any of the other defendants) made any remarks that could be viewed as reflecting discriminatory animus. Nor does it allege that any male employees were given preferential treatment when compared to Plaintiff. Indeed, the only specific employment actions that might qualify as "materially adverse"-being stripped of "virtually all of her secretarial functions"-Plaintiff characterizes as retaliatory and not gender-based.

Because "a complaint must include . . . a plain statement of the claim . . . [that] give[s] the defendant fair notice of what the plaintiff's claim is and the grounds upon which it rests" in order to avoid dismissal under FRCP 12(b)(6), and because Plaintiff's Complaint fails to do so with regards to her Title VII discriminatory action claim, that claim was properly dismissed by the district court.. . . .

II

To state a claim for a hostile work environment in violation of Title VII, a plaintiff must plead facts that would tend to show that the complained of conduct: (1) "is objectively severe or pervasive-that is, . . . creates an environment that a reasonable person would find hostile or abusive"; (2) creates an environment "that the plaintiff subjectively perceives as hostile or abusive"; and (3) "creates such an environment because of the plaintiff's sex." Because Plaintiff has pled facts sufficient to satisfy each prong of this test, the district court erred in dismissing her hostile work environment-related claims.

The district court concluded that Plaintiff's Complaint did not assert that the work environment was *objectively* hostile. The Supreme Court has held that a work environment's hostility should be assessed based on the "totality of the circumstances." Factors that a court might consider in assessing the totality of the circumstances include: (1) the frequency of the discriminatory conduct; (2) its severity; (3) whether it is threatening and humiliating, or a mere offensive utterance; and (4) "whether it unreasonably interferes with an employee's work performance." Ultimately, to avoid dismissal under FRCP 12(b)(6), a plaintiff need only plead facts sufficient to support the conclusion that she was faced with "harassment . . . of such quality or quantity that a reasonable employee would find the conditions of her employment altered for the worse," and "we have repeatedly cautioned against setting the bar too high" in this context.

Specifically, the district court concluded that Plaintiff failed to allege that she faced an objectively hostile work environment, "because [she] never saw the videos, witnessed Clark watch the videos, or witnessed Clark performing sexual acts." However, Plaintiff *does* allege that she regularly observed Clark watching pornographic videos. This Court has specifically recognized that the mere presence of pornography in a workplace can alter the "status" of women therein and is relevant to assessing the objective hostility of the environment. Moreover, Plaintiff alleges that she was regularly required to handle pornographic videotapes in the course of performing her employment responsibilities of opening and delivering Clark's mail; and that she once discovered hard core pornographic websites that Clark viewed on *her* workplace computer. Combined with Plaintiff's other allegations regarding Clark's sexually inappropriate behavior in the workplace, including her allegation regarding his earlier harassment of Dr. Peirce, and with Fordham's failure to take any action notwithstanding Plaintiff's numerous complaints, a jury could well conclude that Plaintiff was subject to frequent severely offensive conduct that interfered with her ability to perform her secretarial functions. Though whether a particular work environment is objectively hostile is necessarily a fact-intensive inquiry, we conclude that Plaintiff has alleged sufficient facts to be "entitled to offer evidence to support [her] claim[ ]."

Defendants also argue that Plaintiff has not alleged that the harassing conduct was *aimed at her*-let alone aimed at her *because of her sex*. However, some of the conduct that Plaintiff has alleged was undoubtedly aimed at her-for instance, the hard core pornographic websites on her computer and the pornography-containing mail that Clark knew she was responsible for handling. Moreover, a plaintiff need only allege that she suffered a hostile work environment because of her gender, not that all of the offensive conduct was *specifically* aimed at her. In *Petrosino v. Bell Atlantic*, we recognized that sexually charged conduct in the workplace may create a hostile environment for women notwithstanding the fact that it is also experienced by men. In that case, we endorsed the Fourth Circuit's reasoning in *Ocheltree v. Scollon Products., Inc.*:

> The employer contended that the offensive conduct could not be deemed discriminatory based on sex "because it could have been heard [or seen] by anyone present in the shop and was equally offensive to some of the men." The court disagreed, concluding that a jury could find "[m]uch of the conduct . . . particularly offensive to women and . . . intended to provoke [plaintiff's] reaction as a woman."

As in *Ocheltree*, Plaintiff pleads facts sufficient to allow a jury to find much of Clark's complained of conduct particularly offensive to women and intended to provoke Plaintiff's reaction as a woman.

Because Plaintiff has pled facts sufficient to satisfy all three prongs of the test for a hostile work environment in violation of Title VII, we vacate the district court's dismissal of her claim against Fordham, and remand for proceedings consistent with this opinion. . . .

III

To state a claim for retaliation in violation of Title VII, a plaintiff must plead facts that would tend to show that: (1) she participated in a protected activity known to the defendant; (2) the defendant took an employment action disadvantaging her; and (3) there exists a causal connection between the protected activity and the adverse action. In the instant case, the district court erred in dismissing Plaintiff's retaliation-related claims, because she has sufficiently alleged that: (1) Defendants were aware that she complained to Arendacs, and later Stuhr, about the harassment she faced from Clark and Evans; (2) Clark stripped her of virtually all of her secretarial duties (among other retaliatory actions taken by Clark and Evans); and (3) there was a causal connection between the above two occurrences.

Defendants contend that Plaintiff has not pled facts in support of her claim that Clark knew that she reported his conduct to Arendacs and Stuhr, as required by the first prong. Defendants are wrong. First, Plaintiff does allege facts from which a reasonable inference of Clark's knowledge could be drawn: she complained about Clark's conduct to a Fordham employee whose job it was to investigate and resolve such complaints. It is not inappropriate at this stage in the litigation to assume that in investigating Plaintiff's complaints, Arendacs made Clark aware of their existence. And, second, "[n]either this nor any other circuit has ever held that, to satisfy the knowledge requirement, anything more is necessary than general corporate knowledge that the plaintiff has engaged in a protected activity." In the instant case, Plaintiff has certainly pled facts showing that Fordham was aware of her protected activity, since she alleges that she complained directly to a university employee.

The district court faulted Plaintiff for not specifying the "severity or degree" of Clark's alleged retaliatory reduction of her job responsibilities, and concluded that, as pled, that reduction did not rise to the level of adverse employment action required to satisfy the second prong. The district court's conclusion is flawed for several reasons. First, Plaintiff's allegation that Clark removed "virtually all of her secretarial functions" in response to her reporting his conduct to Arendacs was both specific enough and severe enough to qualify as an adverse employment action at the time the district court issued its opinion. Only a statement of facts so conclusory that it fails to give notice of the basic events and circumstances on which a plaintiff relies should be rejected as legally insufficient under 12(b)(6). There is no question that Plaintiff's factual statement is detailed enough to avoid dismissal under this standard. Moreover, we have specifically recognized "significantly diminished material responsibilities" as the sort of employment action "sufficiently disadvantageous to constitute an adverse employment action" in a Title VII case.

Second, in a decision issued the day after the district court's in the instant case, the Supreme Court held that the scope of Title VII's anti-retaliation provision is broader than that of its discriminatory action provision, and that any action that "could well dissuade a reasonable worker from making or supporting a charge of discrimination" could constitute retaliation. In addition to her allegations about her reduction in job responsibilities, Plaintiff alleges that Clark and Evans specifically conspired to "not give [her] work" in order to "make her leave." These allegations surely meet *Burlington Northern's* standard. Any reasonable employee that believed that her employers would engage in a concerted effort to drive her from her job if she engaged in Title VII protected activity would think twice about doing so. Defendants' argument to the contrary — that because Plaintiff herself was not dissuaded from again reporting Clark's harassment, the complained of conduct could not have been retaliatory under *Burlington Northern* — is entirely unconvincing, since it would require that *no* plaintiff who makes a second complaint about harassment could *ever* have been retaliated against for an earlier complaint.

Finally, Defendants argue that Plaintiff does not adequately allege the sort of causal connection between her protected activity and Defendants' retaliation required by the third prong, because "[w]hile a plaintiff may allege [such] a causal connection . . . through temporal proximity, case law requires that such proximity in time must be 'very close.' " Defendants argue that, in the instant case, Plaintiff fails to allege such proximity because there was a year between when she first reported Clark's conduct to Arendacs in 2000 and Clark's removal of her secretarial functions in 2001. Even setting aside the fact that a date in 2000 may be as proximate to a date in 2001 as one day, Plaintiff's claim of causal connection is not based only — or even primarily — on temporal proximity. Instead, Plaintiff alleges that she specifically overheard Clark and Evans conspiring to drive her out of her job and that Evans issued a negative performance review that specifically complains about her attitude towards Clark.

Because Plaintiff has pled facts sufficient to satisfy all three prongs of the test for retaliation in violation of Title VII, we vacate the district court's dismissal of her claim against Fordham, and remand for proceedings consistent with this opinion.

. . .

CONCLUSION

The judgment of the district court is AFFIRMED in part, REVERSED in part, and REMANDED to the district court for proceedings in accordance with this decision.

NOTES

1. What are the pleading requirements for hostile work environment and retaliation claims? How do these pleadings differ from the *McDonnell Douglas* framework asserted in *Crawford v. Carroll*?

2. Two U.S. Supreme Court cases have tightened the expectations for case pleadings (*see, e.g., Bell Atlantic Corp. v. Twombly*, 550 U.S. 544 (2007) and *Ashcroft v. Iqbal*, 556 U.S. 662 (2009)). In *Twombly*, the Court concluded that the plaintiffs failed to allege sufficient facts supporting a "plausible" antitrust claim. The Court wrote: "Here, in contrast, we do not require heightened fact pleading of specifics, but only enough facts to state a claim to relief that is plausible on its face. Because the plaintiffs here have not nudged their claims across the line from conceivable to plausible, their complaint must be dismissed" (*Id.* at 570). Furthermore, in *Ashcroft v. Iqbal*, 556 U.S. 662 (2009), the U.S. Supreme Court offered more firm statements about pleadings; that is, something more than just alleging discriminatory harm in a discrimination case. The Court expressed: "Where the claim is invidious discrimination in contravention of the First and Fifth Amendments, our decisions make clear that the plaintiff must plead and prove that the defendant acted with discriminatory purpose" (*Id.* at 676).

3. The cases in this section raised disparate treatment claims. The evidentiary requirements and determination of the filing's timing are somewhat different with disparate impact claims. The disparate treatment claims examine discriminatory intent within the limitations period. By contrast, disparate impact claims examine the application or use of a college policy or practice that implicates a civil rights statute (e.g., Title VII).

6. Due Process

GILBERT v. HOMAR
520 U.S. 924 (1997)

JUSTICE SCALIA delivered the opinion of the Court.

This case presents the question whether a State violates the Due Process Clause of the Fourteenth Amendment by failing to provide notice and a hearing before suspending a tenured public employee without pay.

I

Respondent Richard J. Homar was employed as a police officer at East Stroudsburg University (ESU), a branch of Pennsylvania's State System of Higher Education. On August 26, 1992, when respondent was at the home of a family friend, he was arrested by the Pennsylvania State Police in a drug raid. Later that day, the state police filed a criminal complaint charging respondent with possession of marijuana, possession with intent to deliver, and criminal conspiracy to violate the controlled substance law, which is a felony. The state police notified respondent's supervisor, University Police Chief David Marazas, of the arrest and charges. Chief Marazas in turn informed Gerald Levanowitz, ESU's Director of Human Resources, to whom ESU President James Gilbert had delegated authority to discipline ESU employees. Levanowitz suspended respondent without pay effective immediately. Respondent failed to report to work on the day of his arrest, and learned of his suspension the next day, when he called Chief Marazas to inquire whether he had been suspended. That same day, respondent received a letter from Levanowitz confirming that he had been suspended effective August 26 pending an investigation into the criminal charges filed against him. The letter explained that any action taken by ESU would not necessarily coincide with the disposition of the criminal charges.

Although the criminal charges were dismissed on September 1, respondent's suspension remained in effect while ESU continued with its own investigation. On September 18, Levanowitz and Chief Marazas met with respondent in order to give him an opportunity to tell his side of the story. Respondent was informed at the meeting that the state police had given ESU information that was "very serious in nature," but he was not informed that that included a report of an alleged confession he had made on the day of his arrest; he was consequently unable to respond to damaging statements attributed to him in the police report.

In a letter dated September 23, Levanowitz notified respondent that he was being demoted to the position of groundskeeper effective the next day, and that he would receive backpay from the date the suspension took effect at the rate of pay of a groundskeeper. (Respondent eventually received backpay for the period of his suspension at the rate of pay of a university police officer.) The letter maintained that the demotion was being imposed "as a result of admissions made by yourself to the Pennsylvania State Police on August 26, 1992 that you maintained associations with individuals whom you knew were dealing in large quantities of marijuana and that you obtained marijuana from one of those individuals for your own use. Your actions constitute a clear and flagrant violation of Sections 200 and 200.2 of the [ESU] Police Department Manual." Upon receipt of this letter, the president of respondent's union requested a meeting with President Gilbert. The requested meeting took place on September 24, at which point respondent had received and read the police report containing the alleged confession. After providing respondent with an opportunity to respond to the charges, Gilbert sustained the demotion.

Respondent filed this suit under . . . 42 U.S.C. § 1983, in the United States District Court for the Middle District of Pennsylvania against President Gilbert, Chief Marazas, Levanowitz, and a Vice President of ESU, Curtis English, all in both their individual and official capacities. He contended, *inter alia*, that petitioners' failure to provide him with notice and an opportunity to be heard before suspending him without pay violated due process. The District Court entered summary judgment for petitioners. A divided Court of Appeals reversed the District Court's determination that it was permissible for ESU to suspend respondent without pay without first providing a hearing. We granted certiorari.

II

The protections of the Due Process Clause apply to government deprivation of those perquisites of government employment in which the employee has a constitutionally protected "property" interest. Although we have previously held that public employees who can be discharged only for cause have a constitutionally protected property interest in their tenure and cannot be fired without due process, we have not had occasion to decide whether the protections of the Due Process Clause extend to discipline of tenured public employees short of termination. Petitioners, however, do not contest this preliminary point, and so without deciding it we will, like the District Court, "[a]ssum[e] that the suspension infringed a protected property interest," and turn at once to petitioners' contention that respondent received all the process he was due.

A

In *Cleveland Bd. of Ed. v. Loudermill*, we concluded that a public employee dismissable only for cause was entitled to a very limited hearing prior to his termination, to be followed by a more comprehensive post-termination hearing. Stressing that the pretermination hearing "should be an initial check against mistaken decisions-essentially, a determination of whether there are reasonable grounds to believe that the charges against the employee are true and support the proposed action," we held that pretermination process need only include oral or written notice of the charges, an explanation of the employer's evidence, and an opportunity for the employee to tell his side of the story. In the course of our assessment of the governmental interest in immediate termination of a tenured employee, we observed that "in those situations where the employer perceives a significant hazard in keeping the employee on the job, it can avoid the problem by suspending *with pay.*"

Relying on this dictum, which it read as "strongly suggest[ing] that suspension without pay must be preceded by notice and an opportunity to be heard *in all instances*," and determining on its own that such a rule would be "eminently sensible," the Court of Appeals adopted a categorical prohibition: "[A] governmental employer may not suspend an employee without pay unless that suspension is preceded by some kind of pre-suspension hearing, providing the employee with notice and an opportunity to be heard." Respondent (as well as most of his *amici*) makes no attempt to defend this absolute rule, which spans all types of government employment and all types of unpaid suspensions. This is eminently wise, since under our precedents such an absolute rule is indefensible.

It is by now well established that " 'due process,' unlike some legal rules, is not a technical conception with a fixed content unrelated to time, place and circumstances." "[D]ue process is flexible and calls for such procedural protections as the particular situation demands." This Court has recognized, on many occasions, that where a State must act quickly, or where it would be impractical to provide predeprivation process, postdeprivation process satisfies the requirements of the Due Process Clause. Indeed, in *Parratt v. Taylor* (overruled in part on other grounds), we specifically noted that "we have rejected the proposition that [due process] always requires the State to provide a hearing prior to the initial deprivation of property." And in *FDIC v. Mallen*, where we unanimously approved the Federal Deposit Insurance Corporation's (FDIC's) suspension, without prior hearing, of an indicted private bank employee, we said: "An important government interest, accompanied by a substantial assurance that the deprivation is not baseless or unwarranted, may in limited cases demanding prompt action justify postponing the opportunity to be heard until after the initial deprivation."

. . .

B

To determine what process is constitutionally due, we have generally balanced three distinct factors:

> "First, the private interest that will be affected by the official action; second, the risk of an erroneous deprivation of such interest through the procedures used, and the probable value, if any, of additional or substitute procedural safeguards; and finally, the Government's interest."

Respondent contends that he has a significant private interest in the uninterrupted receipt of his paycheck. But while our opinions have recognized the severity of depriving someone of the means of his livelihood, they have also emphasized that in determining what process is due, account must be taken of "the *length* " and "*finality* of the deprivation." Unlike the employee in *Loudermill*, who faced *termination*, respondent faced only a *temporary suspension* without pay. So long as the suspended employee receives a sufficiently prompt postsuspension hearing, the lost income is relatively insubstantial (compared with termination), and fringe benefits such as health and life insurance are often not affected at all.

On the other side of the balance, the State has a significant interest in immediately suspending, when felony charges are filed against them, employees who occupy positions of great public trust and high public visibility, such as police officers. Respondent contends that this interest in maintaining public confidence could have been accommodated by suspending him *with* pay until he had a hearing. We think, however, that the government does not have to give an employee charged with a felony a paid leave at taxpayer expense. If his services to the government are no longer useful once the felony charge has been filed, the Constitution does not require the government to bear the added expense of hiring a replacement while still paying him. ESU's interest in preserving public confidence in its police force is at least as significant as the State's interest in preserving the integrity of the sport of horse racing, an interest we "deemed sufficiently important. . . to justify a brief period of suspension prior to affording the suspended trainer a hearing."

The last factor in the Mathews balancing, and the factor most important to resolution of this case, is the risk of erroneous deprivation and the likely value of any additional procedures. Petitioners argue that any presuspension hearing would have been worthless because pursuant to an Executive Order of the Governor of Pennsylvania a state employee is automatically to be suspended without pay "[a]s soon as practicable after [being] formally charged with . . . a felony." According to petitioners, supervisors have no discretion under this rule, and the mandatory suspension without pay lasts until the criminal charges are finally resolved. If petitioners' interpretation of this order is correct, there is no need for any presuspension process since there would be nothing to consider at the hearing except the independently verifiable fact of whether an employee had indeed been formally charged with a felony. Respondent, however, challenges petitioners' reading of the Code, and contends that in any event an order of the Governor of Pennsylvania is a "mere directiv[e] which do[es] not confer a legally enforceable right." We need not resolve this disputed issue of state law because even assuming the Code is only advisory (or has no application at all), the State had no constitutional obligation to provide respondent with a presuspension hearing. We noted in *Loudermill* that the purpose of a pre-*termination* hearing is to determine "whether there are reasonable grounds to believe that the charges against the employee are true and support the proposed action." By parity of reasoning, the purpose of any pre-*suspension* hearing would be to assure that there are reasonable grounds to support the suspension without pay. But here that has already been assured by the arrest and the filing of charges.

In *Mallen*, we concluded that an "*ex parte* finding of probable cause" such as a grand jury indictment provides adequate assurance that the suspension is not unjustified. The same is true when an employee is arrested and then formally charged with a felony. First, as with an indictment, the arrest and formal charges imposed upon respondent "by an independent body demonstrat[e] that the suspension is not arbitrary." Second, like an indictment, the imposition of felony charges "itself is an objective fact that will in most cases raise serious public concern." It is true, as respondent argues, that there is more reason to believe an employee has committed a felony when he is indicted rather than merely arrested and formally charged; but for present purposes arrest and charge give reason enough. They serve to assure that the state employer's decision to suspend the employee is not "baseless or unwarranted," in that an independent third party has determined that there is probable cause to believe the employee committed a serious crime.

Respondent further contends that since (as we have agreed to assume) Levanowitz had discretion *not* to suspend despite the arrest and filing of charges, he had to be given an opportunity to persuade Levanowitz of his innocence before the decision was made. We disagree. In *Mallen*, despite the fact that the FDIC had *discretion* whether to suspend an indicted bank employee, we nevertheless did not believe that a presuspension hearing was necessary to protect the private interest. Unlike in the case of a termination, where we have recognized that "the only meaningful opportunity to invoke the discretion of the decisionmaker is likely to be before the termination takes effect," in the case of a suspension there will be ample opportunity to invoke discretion later-and a short delay actually benefits the employee by allowing state officials to obtain more accurate information about the arrest and charges. Respondent "has an interest in seeing that a decision concerning his or her continued suspension is not made with excessive haste." If the State is forced to act too quickly, the decisionmaker "may give greater weight to the public interest and leave the suspension in place."

C

Much of respondent's argument is dedicated to the proposition that he had a due process right to a presuspension hearing because the suspension was open-ended and he "theoretically may not have had the opportunity to be heard for weeks, months, or even years after his initial suspension without pay." But, as respondent himself asserts in his attempt to downplay the governmental interest, "[b]ecause the employee is entitled, in any event, to a prompt post-suspension opportunity to be heard, the period of the suspension should be short and the amount of pay during the suspension minimal."

Whether respondent was provided an adequately prompt *post*-suspension hearing in the present case is a separate question. Although the charges against respondent were dropped on September 1 (petitioners apparently learned of this on September 2), he did not receive any sort of hearing until September 18. Once the charges were dropped, the risk of erroneous deprivation increased substantially, and, as petitioners conceded at oral argument, there was likely value in holding a prompt hearing. Because neither the Court of Appeals nor the District Court addressed whether, under the particular facts of this case, petitioners violated due process by failing to provide a sufficiently prompt postsuspension hearing, we will not consider this issue in the first instance, but remand for consideration by the Court of Appeals.

. . .

The judgment of the Court of Appeals is reversed, and the case is remanded for further proceedings consistent with this opinion.

It is so ordered.

NOTES

1. In *Gilbert*, what is the employee's property interest? How did that interest form?

2. According to the Court in *Gilbert*, when is a pre-suspension or post-suspension hearing required? How would the parties' arguments have changed if the case involved a pre-termination versus a post-termination challenge?

3. *Loudermill*, a decision frequently mentioned in *Gilbert*, requires that employees with an expectation of continued employment receive an oral or written notice of the charges. On the surface, this rule seems rather straightforward. However, in *Riggins v. Board of Regents of University of Nebraska*, 790 F.2d 707 (8th Cir. 1986), the Eighth Circuit dealt with the gray area that sometimes accompany the outer boundaries of this rule. In *Riggins*, a member of the custodial staff at a public university was employed under a contract that only permitted dismissals for cause. When the supervisor met with the employee to address the reasons for her termination, he asserted reasons from past work history as the basis for the termination. The employee argued that her supervisor failed to give her proper notice because she was unaware that her past work history would be discussed at the meeting. The court determined that the discussion of the employee's past work history did not play a large role in the termination, and the court ruled that she had received adequate due process. What other arguments might have the employee asserted? What if, at the very instance the supervisor raised her past work history, she had requested additional time to review the information? Would that have changed the adequacy of notice and her due process rights?

Chapter IV

FACULTY RIGHTS AND RESPONSIBILITIES

Introduction

Academic freedom is considered by many as essential to protecting the free flow of ideas and research in educational institutions, and more specifically, for generating new and important breakthroughs in the educational enterprise. The doctrine can be broken down into two important categories: namely those that protect the individual and those that protect the institution.

Individual academic freedom protects faculty members from intrusion into their classrooms and the censorship of speech outside it. Without the protection afforded by the right to academic freedom, professors would run the risk of being intellectually stifled and subjected to the political whims and orthodoxy of educational and/or government officials.

Similarly, institutional academic freedom protects the educational institution's right to decide all matters of procedure and policy within its walls. Because education plays such a key role in shaping the minds of citizens and progressing avenues of research and exploration, the protection of neutrality and intellectual liberty is of utmost importance to continuing public advancement and progression in every field of study. Though some countries created this right by statute or constitutional provision (such as Article 5 of the German Constitution), the United States created academic security within the bundle of implied freedoms contained in the First and Fourteenth Amendments of the United States Constitution. Academic freedom, as a legal right, emanates from a line of cases that began in 1957 with *Sweezy v. New Hampshire.* This decision and those that followed rapidly evolved into a full-fledged legal doctrine protecting the freedoms of both the educator and the college or university.

Part A of this chapter introduces the legal definition of "academic freedom" and its source of constitutional authority by examining case law regarding past laws that attempted to intrude into the personal lives and political associations of educators in the late 1950s and 1960s. In *Sweezy, Shelton v. Tucker*, and *Keyishian v. Board of Regents*, the Supreme Court was forced to balance the political goals of weeding out politically subversive individuals with protecting long standing professional notions of academic freedom for educators in research and in the postsecondary environment.

As you will see, even before this line of cases arose, the 1940 Statement on Principles of Academic Freedom and Tenure, co-authored by the American Association of University Professors (AAUP) and the Association of American Colleges (AAC), set forth a clear definition of professorial protection still widely used by both the judiciary and those in academe. The statement describes academic freedom in terms of professors' rights inside and outside the university setting within certain limitations. While reading this section, it is important to note how these definitions influence each other and where they potentially differ.

Following the exploration of some general rights established in Part A, Part B describes the evolution of laws protecting faculty members' rights to freedom of expression. Here, the judiciary faced a new balancing-of-rights equation: when should a faculty member's right to speak freely without retaliation come before the rights of universities and school boards to manage their own employees?

A faculty member's freedoms are not absolute and are subject to a careful balancing of competing interests. When faculty members may speak on "matters of public concern" and what exactly counts as a "matter of public concern" are worthy of careful observation. Additionally, faculty members' rights have been slowly diminished by a line of cases establishing a more limited right of government employees to freedom of expression. More recently, for example, the United States Supreme Court in *Garcetti v. Ceballos* has declared that the First Amendment does not protect employees from discipline when they make statements regarding matters of public concern pursuant to their official duties. How do these standards harmonize on the one hand and diverge on the other? What factors should be considered in deciding whether or not academic freedom should apply? Also, what factors come into play regarding safeguards for professors in private institutions?

Part C explores how academic freedom has evolved into an *institutional* right that universities and schools possess entirely separate from individual faculty members. In fact, the concept of institutional authority was briefly discussed in early definitions of academic freedom, but not fully distinguished until cases litigated after *Sweezy, Shelton*, and *Keyishian*. Institutional academic freedom encompasses the college or university prerogative to determine how it should be run, what should be taught, and who may be admitted. Based on this position, the educational institution requires some amount of sovereignty in operation and decision making to effectively maintain an efficient, safe educational environment where students and faculty feel free to express their opinions and explore issues of concern.

As a matter of policy, the institution declares itself in the best position to monitor and police its own employees and ensure that its students can learn in a fair and balanced academic environment. This section examines the boundaries of institutional academic freedom and the interests it must compete with. As the law has evolved, institutional authority has gradually expanded and the individual educator's right to academic freedom has become more and more limited. How do these two concepts conflict with each other in the educational setting? Are there different policy reasons for each kind of protection? In reading these sections, it is important to keep in mind that academic freedom was originally created to protect the *public* good. A corollary question may focus on whether that altruistic beginning has subsequently changed and, if so, what forces have influenced the new direction.

Part D addresses issues of faculty Fourteenth Amendment due process rights and Fourth Amendment rights against illegal searches and seizures. Due process is available to all public employees, without regard to status, if their property rights and liberty interests are at stake. Ultimately the context may vary, however, according to employee position and specific factual contexts. An explication of these principles is found in cases such as *Board of Regents v. Roth, Perry v. Sindermann,* and *Cleveland Board of Education v. Loudermill.* The courts in due process cases stipulate that in order for such rights to exist there must be a proven determination of entitlement. Where are such entitlements found? How are they created, especially in the postsecondary environment? Are their opportunities for abuse, and if so, how are these to be overcome when the due process procedures are carried out by faculty peers?

Fourth Amendment rights of college and university faculty involve the extent to which postsecondary personnel may infringe upon faculty or staff constitutional rights in the security of their property and persons. The initial question is whether the Fourth Amendment even applies in a given situation. The ultimate question is whether such activity is governed by the doctrine of "probable cause" (generally requiring a warrant) or whether the legality of a search is dependent upon the concept of "reasonableness." These issues are discussed in the case of *O'Connor v. Ortega.*

In Part E, the cases and notes examine key legal issues pertaining to faculty unionization. Drawing on national data from the National Center for the Study of Collective Bargaining in Higher Education, Professors Jeffrey Sun and Steve Permuth report that "organized representation of college faculty has increased from 256,504 in 1998 to 318,504 in 2006, an increase of 24%." Jeffrey C. Sun & Steve Permuth, *Evaluations of Unionized College and University Faculty: A Review of the Laws*, 19 J. Pers. Eval. Educ. 115 (2007). While current state legislation in various statehouses may limit the growth of public college faculty's collective bargaining activities, the legal challenges and power struggles between faculty and administration will likely persist, sustaining the relevance and importance of this body of law.

For a significant section of Part E, the qualifications of faculty to unionize are presented. As discussed *infra*, the National Labor Relations Act (NLRA) governs the eligibility of faculty at private colleges and universities while a state's public employment labor relations act (PELRAs), if one exists, determines eligibility of faculty at the respective state's colleges and universities. The cases challenging faculty eligibility and collective bargaining have primarily arisen from higher education faculty at different types of private universities such as ones with strong faculty governance, weak faculty governance, and religious affiliated institutions.

For the remaining portion of Part E, the scope of bargaining is examined. Faculty at public colleges and universities typically raise these issues and question whether the subject matter at-hand falls under an employment sphere, which is negotiable, or an educational sphere, which is non-negotiable.

A. ACADEMIC FREEDOM

1. The Legal Meaning of Academic Freedom

SWEEZY v. NEW HAMPSHIRE

354 U.S. 234 (1957)

MR. CHIEF JUSTICE WARREN announced the judgment of the Court and delivered an opinion, in which MR. JUSTICE BLACK, MR. JUSTICE DOUGLAS, and MR. JUSTICE BRENNAN join.

This case . . . brings before us a question concerning the constitutional limits of legislative inquiry. The investigation here was conducted under the aegis of a state legislature . . . . The ultimate question here is whether the investigation deprived Sweezy of due process of law under the Fourteenth Amendment. For the reasons to be set out in this opinion, we conclude that the record in this case does not sustain the power of the State to compel the disclosures that the witness refused to make.

. . . .

The investigation in which petitioner was summoned to testify had its origins in a statute passed by the New Hampshire legislature in 1951. It was a comprehensive scheme of regulation of subversive activities. There was a section defining criminal conduct in the nature of sedition. "Subversive organizations" were declared unlawful and ordered dissolved. "Subversive persons" were made ineligible for employment by the state government. Included in the disability were those employed as teachers or in other capacities by any public educational institution. A loyalty program was instituted to eliminate "subversive persons" among government personnel. All present employees, as well as candidates for elective office in the future, were required to make sworn statements that they were not "subversive persons."

In 1953, the legislature adopted a "Joint Resolution Relating to the Investigation of Subversive Activities." It was resolved:

> That the attorney general is hereby authorized and directed to make full and complete investigation with respect to violations of the subversive activities act of 1951 and to determine whether subversive persons as defined in said act are presently located within this state. The attorney general is authorized to act upon his own motion and upon such information as in his judgment may be reasonable or reliable . . . .
>
> The attorney general is directed to proceed with criminal prosecutions under the subversive activities act whenever evidence presented to him in the course of the investigation indicates violations thereof . . . .

Under state law, this was construed to constitute the Attorney General as a one-man legislative committee. He was given the authority to delegate any part of the investigation to any member of his staff. The legislature conferred upon the Attorney General the further authority to subpoena witnesses or documents. . . .

. . . .

Petitioner was summoned to appear before the Attorney General on two separate occasions. On January 5, 1954, petitioner testified at length upon his past conduct and associations. He denied that he had ever been a member of the Communist Party or that he had ever been part of any program to overthrow the government by force or violence. . . .

During the course of the inquiry, petitioner declined to answer several questions. His reasons for doing so were given in a statement he read to the Committee at the outset of the hearing. He declared he would not answer those questions which were not pertinent to the subject under inquiry as well as those which transgress the limitations of the First Amendment. In keeping with this stand, he refused to disclose his knowledge of the Progressive Party in New Hampshire or of persons with whom he was acquainted in that organization. No action was taken by the Attorney General to compel answers to these questions.

The Attorney General again summoned petitioner to testify on June 3, 1954. There was more interrogation about the witness' prior contacts with Communists. The Attorney General lays great stress upon an article which petitioner had co-authored. It deplored the use of violence by the United States and other capitalist countries in attempting to preserve a social order which the writers thought must inevitably fall. This resistance, the article continued, will be met by violence from the oncoming socialism, violence which is to be less condemned morally than that of capitalism since its purpose is to create a "truly human society." Petitioner affirmed that he styled himself a "classical Marxist" and a "socialist" and that the article expressed his continuing opinion.

Again, at the second hearing, the Attorney General asked, and petitioner refused to answer, questions concerning the Progressive Party, and its predecessor, the Progressive Citizens of America. . . .

. . . .

The Attorney General also turned to a subject which had not yet occurred at the time of the first hearing. On March 22, 1954, petitioner had delivered a lecture to a class of 100 students in the humanities course at the University of New Hampshire. This talk was given at the invitation of the faculty teaching that course. . . . He declined to answer [questions about the subject of his lecture, in which he purportedly stated that socialism was inevitable in the United States].

. . . .

Following the hearings, the Attorney General petitioned the Superior Court of Merrimack County, New Hampshire, setting forth the circumstances of petitioner's appearance before the Committee and his refusal to answer certain questions. The petition prayed that the court propound the questions to the witness. After hearing argument, the court ruled that the questions set out above were pertinent. Petitioner was called as a witness by the court and persisted in his refusal to answer for constitutional reasons. The court adjudged him in contempt and ordered him committed to the county jail until purged of the contempt.

The New Hampshire Supreme Court affirmed. . . .

There is no doubt that legislative investigations, whether on a federal or state level, are capable of encroaching upon the constitutional liberties of individuals. It is particularly important that the exercise of the power of compulsory process be carefully circumscribed when the investigative process tends to impinge upon such highly sensitive areas as freedom of speech or press, freedom of political association, and freedom of communication of ideas, particularly in the academic community. Responsibility for the proper conduct of investigations rests, of course, upon the legislature itself. If that assembly chooses to authorize inquiries on its behalf by a legislatively created committee, that basic responsibility carries forward to include the duty of adequate supervision of the actions of the committee. This safeguard can be nullified when a committee is invested with a broad and ill-defined jurisdiction. . . .

In this case, the investigation is governed by provisions in the New Hampshire Subversive Activities Act of 1951. The Attorney General was instructed by the legislature to look into violations of that Act. In addition, he was given the far more sweeping mandate to find out if there were subversive persons, as defined in that Act, present in New Hampshire. . . .

"Subversive persons" are defined in many gradations of conduct. Our interest is in the minimal requirements of that definition since they will outline its reach. According to the statute, a person is a "subversive person" if he, by any means, aids in the commission of any act intended to assist in the alteration of the constitutional form of government by force or violence. The possible remoteness from armed insurrection of conduct that could satisfy these criteria is obvious from the language. The statute goes well beyond those who are engaged in efforts designed to alter the form of government by force or violence. The statute declares, in effect, that the assistant of an assistant is caught up in the definition. . . .

The statute's definition of "subversive organizations" is also broad. . . . An organization is deemed subversive if it has a purpose to abet, advise or teach activities intended to assist in the alteration of the constitutional form of government by force or violence.

The situation before us is in many respects analogous to that in *Wieman v. Updegraff*, 344 U.S. 183. The Court held there that a loyalty oath prescribed by the State of Oklahoma for all its officers and employees violated the requirements of the Due Process Clause because it entailed sanctions for membership in subversive organizations without scienter. A State cannot, in attempting to bar disloyal individuals from its employ, exclude persons solely on the basis of organizational membership, regardless of their knowledge concerning the organizations to which they belonged. . . .

. . . .

The sanction emanating from legislative investigations is of a different kind than loss of employment. But the stain of the stamp of disloyalty is just as deep. The inhibiting effect in the flow of democratic expression and controversy upon those directly affected and those touched more subtly is equally grave. . . .

. . . .

The New Hampshire [Supreme Court] concluded that the ". . . right to lecture and the right to associate with others for a common purpose, be it political or otherwise, are individual liberties guaranteed to every citizen by the State and Federal Constitutions but are not absolute rights . . . . The inquiries authorized by the Legislature in connection with this investigation concerning the contents of the lecture and the membership, purposes and activities of the Progressive Party undoubtedly interfered with the defendant's free exercise of those liberties." 100 N. H., at 113, 121 A. 2d, at 791–792.

The State Supreme Court thus conceded without extended discussion that petitioner's right to lecture and his right to associate with others were constitutionally protected freedoms which had been abridged through this investigation. These conclusions could not be seriously debated. Merely to summon a witness and compel him, against his will, to disclose the nature of his past expressions and associations is a measure of governmental interference in these matters. . . . We believe that there unquestionably was an invasion of petitioner's liberties in the areas of academic freedom and political expression — areas in which government should be extremely reticent to tread.

The essentiality of freedom in the community of American universities is almost self-evident. No one should underestimate the vital role in a democracy that is played by those who guide and train our youth. To impose any strait jacket upon the intellectual leaders in our colleges and universities would imperil the future of our Nation. No field of education is so thoroughly comprehended by man that new discoveries cannot yet be made. Particularly is that true in the social sciences, where few, if any, principles are accepted as absolutes. Scholarship cannot flourish in an atmosphere of suspicion and distrust. Teachers and students must always remain free to inquire, to study and to evaluate, to gain new maturity and understanding; otherwise our civilization will stagnate and die.

Equally manifest as a fundamental principle of a democratic society is political freedom of the individual. Our form of government is built on the premise that every citizen shall have the right to engage in political expression and association. This right was enshrined in the First Amendment of the Bill of Rights. Exercise of these basic freedoms in America has traditionally been through the media of political associations. Any interference with the freedom of a party is simultaneously an interference with the freedom of its adherents. All political ideas cannot and should not be channeled into the programs of our two major parties. . . .

Notwithstanding the undeniable importance of freedom in the areas, the Supreme Court of New Hampshire did not consider that the abridgment of petitioner's rights under the Constitution vitiated the investigation. In the view of that court, "the answer lies in a determination of whether the object of the legislative investigation under consideration is such as to justify the restriction thereby imposed upon the defendant's liberties." 100 N. H., at 113–114, 121 A. 2d, at 791–792. It found such justification in the legislature's judgment, expressed by its authorizing resolution, that there exists a potential menace from those who would overthrow the government by force and violence. That court concluded that the need for the legislature to be informed on so elemental a subject as the self-preservation of government outweighed the deprivation of constitutional rights that occurred in the process.

We do not now conceive of any circumstance wherein a state interest would justify infringement of rights in these fields. But we do not need to reach such fundamental questions of state power to decide this case. The State Supreme Court itself recognized that there was a weakness in its conclusion that the menace of forcible overthrow of the government justified sacrificing constitutional rights. . . . There was nothing to connect the questioning of petitioner with this fundamental interest of the State. Petitioner had been interrogated by a one-man legislative committee, not by the legislature itself. The relationship of the committee to the full assembly is vital, therefore, as revealing the relationship of the questioning to the state interest.

In light of this, the state court emphasized a factor in the authorizing resolution which confined the inquiries which the Attorney General might undertake to the object of the investigation. That limitation was thought to stem from the authorizing resolution's condition precedent to the institution of any inquiry. The New Hampshire legislature specified that the Attorney General should act only when he had information which ". . . in his judgment may be reasonable or reliable." The state court construed this to mean that the Attorney General must have something like probable cause for conducting a particular investigation. It is not likely that this device would prove an adequate safeguard against unwarranted inquiries. . . .

. . . .

The respective roles of the legislature and the investigator thus revealed are of considerable significance to the issue before us. . . . The Attorney General has been given such a sweeping and uncertain mandate that it is his decision which picks out the subjects that will be pursued, what witnesses will be summoned and what questions will be asked. In this circumstance, it cannot be stated authoritatively that the legislature asked the Attorney General to gather the kind of facts comprised in the subjects upon which petitioner was interrogated.

. . . .

As a result, neither we nor the state courts have any assurance that the questions petitioner refused to answer fall into a category of matters upon which the legislature wanted to be informed when it initiated this inquiry. The judiciary are thus placed in an untenable position. Lacking even the elementary fact that the legislature wants certain questions answered and recognizing that petitioner's constitutional rights are in jeopardy, we are asked to approve or disapprove his incarceration for contempt.

In our view, the answer is clear. No one would deny that the infringement of constitutional rights of individuals would violate the guarantee of due process where no state interest underlies the state action. Thus, if the Attorney General's interrogation of petitioner were in fact wholly unrelated to the object of the legislature in authorizing the inquiry, the Due Process Clause would preclude the endangering of constitutional liberties. We believe that an equivalent situation is presented in this case. The lack of any indications that the legislature wanted the information the Attorney General attempted to elicit from petitioner must be treated as the absence of authority. It follows that the use of the contempt power, notwithstanding the interference with constitutional rights, was not in accordance with the due process requirements of the Fourteenth Amendment.

. . . .

The judgment of the Supreme Court of New Hampshire is

Reversed.

MR. JUSTICE FRANKFURTER, whom MR. JUSTICE HARLAN joins, concurring in the result.

. . . .

The New Hampshire Supreme Court, although recognizing that such inquiries "undoubtedly interfered with the defendant's free exercise" of his constitutionally guaranteed right to lecture, justified the interference on the ground that it would occur "in the limited area in which the legislative committee may reasonably believe that the overthrow of existing government by force and violence is being or has been taught, advocated or planned, an area in which the interest of the State justifies this intrusion upon civil liberties." [citation omitted.]

When weighed against the grave harm resulting from governmental intrusion into the intellectual life of a university, such justification for compelling a witness to discuss the contents of his lecture appears grossly inadequate. Particularly is this so where the witness has sworn that neither in the lecture nor at any other time did he ever advocate overthrowing the Government by force and violence.

Progress in the natural sciences is not remotely confined to findings made in the laboratory. Insights into the mysteries of nature are born of hypothesis and speculation. The more so is this true in the pursuit of understanding in the groping endeavors of what are called the social sciences, the concern of which is man and society. The problems that are the respective preoccupations of anthropology, economics, law, psychology, sociology and related areas of scholarship are merely departmentalized dealing, by way of manageable division of analysis, with interpenetrating aspects of holistic perplexities. For society's good — if understanding be an essential need of society — inquiries into these problems, speculations about them, stimulation in others of reflection upon them, must be left as unfettered as possible. . . .

These pages need not be burdened with proof, based on the testimony of a cloud of impressive witnesses, of the dependence of a free society on free universities. . . . Suffice it to quote the latest expression on this subject. It is also perhaps the most poignant because its plea on behalf of continuing the free spirit of the open universities of South Africa has gone unheeded.

In a university knowledge is its own end, not merely a means to an end. A university ceases to be true to its own nature if it becomes the tool of Church or State or any sectional interest. A university is characterized by the spirit of free inquiry, its ideal being the ideal of Socrates — 'to follow the argument where it leads.' This implies the right to examine, question, modify or reject traditional ideas and beliefs. Dogma and hypothesis are incompatible, and the concept of an immutable doctrine is repugnant to the spirit of a university. The concern of its scholars is not merely to add and revise facts in relation to an accepted framework, but to be ever examining and modifying the framework itself.

. . . .

"Freedom to reason and freedom for disputation on the basis of observation and experiment are the necessary conditions for the advancement of scientific knowledge. A sense of freedom is also necessary for creative work in the arts which, equally with scientific research, is the concern of the university.

. . . .

". . . It is the business of a university to provide that atmosphere which is most conducive to speculation, experiment and creation. It is an atmosphere in which there prevail 'the four essential freedoms' of a university — to determine for itself on academic grounds who may teach, what may be taught, how it shall be taught, and who may be admitted to study." The Open Universities in South Africa 10-12. (A statement of a conference of senior scholars from the University of Cape Town and the University of the Witwatersrand . . . .)

I do not suggest that what New Hampshire has here sanctioned bears any resemblance to the policy against which this South African remonstrance was directed. I do say that in these matters of the spirit inroads on legitimacy must be resisted at their incipiency. This kind of evil grows by what it is allowed to feed on. . . .

. . . .

And so I am compelled to conclude that the judgment of the New Hampshire court must be reversed.

[The dissenting opinion of Justice Clark joined by Justice Burton is omitted.]

NOTES

1. Justice Clark, writing in dissent, noted that Justices Frankfurter and Harlan, who concurred in the result reached by the plurality, agreed with him on one very important point: "[T]hey conclude, as do I, that the internal affairs of the New Hampshire State Government are of no concern to [the Court]." *Id.* at 268 (Harlan, J., dissenting). Justice Clark disagreed with the plurality's conclusion that the Attorney General's mandate was so "sweeping and uncertain" as to render his investigation unconstitutional. The New Hampshire state legislature, Clark wrote, "determined the general subject matter of the investigation, subversive activities [and] the legislature's committee, the Attorney General, properly decided what witnesses should be called and what questions should be asked. My Brothers surely would not have the legislature as a whole make these decisions." Justice Clark argued that the plurality should not have questioned whether the questions asked of Sweezy were of the type requested by the legislature because the state supreme court had already favorably construed the statute for the State. *Id.* The Court, in Clark's view, was "bound by the state court findings." *Id.* at 269. "We have no right to strike down the state action unless we find not only that there has been a deprivation of Sweezy's constitutional rights, but that the interest in protecting those rights is greater than the State's interest in uncovering subversive activities within its confines. The majority has made no such findings." *Id.* "The short of it," Clark concluded, "is that the Court blocks New Hampshire's effort to enforce its law."

Does Justice Clark have a point? By basing its opinion on due process grounds, the plurality opens itself to questions about how, precisely, it would have the legislature craft such a statute. Did the plurality really expect the legislature to spell out in detail the types of questions it wanted to be asked of potential subversive persons? Was the plurality turning a blind eye to the type of legislative delegation to executive agencies that had become, by that time, a hallmark of the legislative process at both the national and state levels?

2. Why was the decision based on due process grounds rather than those of free expression? Justice Frankfurter, writing in concurrence with the plurality's result, agreed with Justice Clark on the dubiousness of the plurality's due process analysis: "It would make the deepest inroads upon our federal system for this Court now to hold that it can determine the appropriate distribution of powers and their delegation within the forty-eight States." *Id.* at 256 (Frankfurter, J., concurring). But the plurality, for its part, thought that it was improper for the Court to engage in a First Amendment balancing analysis, weighing Sweezy's rights against the interest of New Hampshire in protecting itself and its citizens. "We do not now conceive of any circumstance wherein a state interest would justify infringement of rights in these fields," Chief Justice Warren wrote. *Id.* at 251. "But we do not need to reach such fundamental questions of state power to decide this case."

The plurality's line of reasoning prompted this response from Justice Clark in his dissent:

> Since the conclusion of a majority of those reversing is not predicated on the First Amendment questions presented, I see no necessity for discussing them. But since the principal opinion devotes itself largely to these issues I believe it fair to ask why they have been given such an elaborate treatment when the case is decided on an entirely different ground. It is of no avail to quarrel with a straw man.

Id. at 270 (Clark, J., dissenting). Once again, doesn't Justice Clark have a point? Why spend so much time espousing the importance of First Amendment rights when those rights are immaterial to the plurality's holding? Was the plurality simply unwilling to attack the First Amendment issue head-on at this moment in the nation's history, when fear of Communism was at its height?

3. By the time *Sweezy* was decided, the practice known as "McCarthyism," the relentless, malignant pursuit of Communists and other "subversives" during the Cold War, had lost its namesake, Senator Joseph McCarthy of Wisconsin, who was censured by the full Senate for his investigatory practices in 1954. As such, Senator McCarthy lost all remnants of power when Democrats retook both houses of Congress, and died shortly thereafter. As Professor Geoffrey R. Stone noted, however:

> McCarthy's rise and fall spanned five inglorious years, but the era of what we loosely call "McCarthyism" lasted well over a decade. During all that time, in which tens of thousands of innocent individuals had their reputations, their careers, and their personal lives destroyed, most civil libertarians, most lawyers, most public officials, most intellectuals, and most others who should have known better, including the justices of the Supreme Court, dithered over what to do.

Geoffrey R. Stone, *Free Speech in the Age of McCarthy: A Cautionary Tale*, 93 CAL. L. REV. 1387, 1403–04 (2005)*. All of that started to change, according to Stone, when Justice William Brennan was appointed to the Court in 1957. At Brennan's confirmation hearing, Senator McCarthy was the only senator to vote against Brennan's confirmation, saying at one point that he wanted to know " 'if it is true that Justice Brennan, in his public speeches, has referred to congressional investigations of communism . . . as Salem witch-hunts and inquisitions, and has accused congressional committees of barbarism.' " *Id.* at 1406 (internal quotation marks and citation omitted).

To this, Stone noted:

> Ironically, in his own perverse way, Joseph McCarthy may have been the only member of the Senate who saw clearly into the heart and mind of William Brennan, for once Brennan joined the Court, he was an implacable foe of the witch hunts. Before Brennan's confirmation, the Court had consistently upheld almost every effort of the government to prosecute, expose, harass, humiliate, blacklist, and persecute members of the Communist Party and their "fellow travelers." Beginning in June 1957, however, the Court suddenly shifted gears, and Brennan was a central figure in shaping the First Amendment principles that reversed the course of constitutional history. In decisions [including *Sweezy*] the Supreme Court began to dismantle the apparatus and mindset that had so poisoned our national debate. Just as McCarthy had feared, Justice Brennan was the pivotal voice in this process.

Id. Following Stone's argument, the Court may have been too timid to tackle the First Amendment issue in *Sweezy*; but given some prodding by its most junior Justice, it would soon, as we'll see, make that jurisprudential leap.

4. *Sweezy* is most often cited for Frankfurter's description of the "four essential freedoms" of an educational institution contained in the concurrence. *Id.* at 263. In quoting a statement by two South African deans, Frankfurter's concurrence describes academic freedom as the right to determine "who may teach, what may be taught, how it shall be taught, and who may be admitted to study." *Id.* at 263. The case itself only concerns an individual's right to academic freedom. Does this definition of the four essential freedoms imply a much broader right? Does it matter that this language comes from a statement of university deans and administrators, not professors?

SHELTON v. TUCKER
364 U.S. 479 (1960)

Mr. Justice Stewart delivered the opinion of the Court.

An Arkansas statute compels every teacher, as a condition of employment in a state-supported school or college, to file annually an affidavit listing without limitation every organization to which he has belonged or regularly contributed within the preceding five years. At issue in these two cases is the validity of that statute under the Fourteenth Amendment to the Constitution. [One case] is an appeal from the judgment of a three-judge Federal District Court upholding the statute's validity . . . . [The other case] is here on writ of certiorari to the Supreme Court of Arkansas, which also held the statute constitutionally valid.

The statute in question is Act 10 of the Second Extraordinary Session of the Arkansas General Assembly of 1958.

. . . .

[The] provisions [of the Act] must be considered against the existing system of teacher employment required by Arkansas law. Teachers there are hired on a year-to-year basis. They are not covered by a civil service system, and they have no job security beyond the end of each school year. The closest approach to tenure is a statutory provision for the automatic renewal of a teacher's contract if he is not notified within ten days after the end of a school year that the contract has not been renewed. . . .

The plaintiffs in the Federal District Court (appellants here) were B. T. Shelton, a teacher employed in the Little Rock Public School System, suing for himself and others similarly situated, together with the Arkansas Teachers Association and its Executive Secretary, suing for the benefit of members of the Association. Shelton had been employed in the Little Rock Special School District for twenty-five years. In the spring of 1959 he was notified that, before he could be employed for the 1959-1960 school year, he must file the affidavit required by Act 10, listing all his organizational connections over the previous five years. He declined to file the affidavit, and his contract for the ensuing school year was not renewed. At the trial the evidence showed that he was not a member of the Communist Party or of any organization advocating the overthrow of the Government by force, and that he was a member of the National Association for the Advancement of Colored People. The court upheld Act 10, finding the information it required was "relevant" . . . .

The plaintiffs in the state court proceedings (petitioners here) were Max Carr, an associate professor at the University of Arkansas, and Ernest T. Gephardt, a teacher at Central High School in Little Rock, each suing for himself and others similarly situated. Each refused to execute and file the affidavit required by Act 10. Carr executed an affirmation in which he listed his membership in professional organizations, denied ever having been a member of any subversive organization, and offered to answer any questions which the University authorities might constitutionally ask touching upon his qualifications as a teacher. Gephardt filed an affidavit stating that he had never belonged to a subversive organization, disclosing his membership in the Arkansas Education Association and the American Legion, and also offering to answer any questions which the school authorities might constitutionally ask touching upon his qualifications as a teacher. Both were advised that their failure to comply with the requirements of Act 10 would make impossible their re-employment as teachers for the following school year. The Supreme Court of Arkansas upheld the constitutionality of Act 10, on its face and as applied to the petitioners.

I.

It is urged here, as it was unsuccessfully urged throughout the proceedings in both the federal and state courts, that Act 10 deprives teachers in Arkansas of their rights to personal, associational, and academic liberty, protected by the Due Process Clause of the Fourteenth Amendment from invasion by state action. In considering this contention, we deal with two basic postulates.

First. There can be no doubt of the right of a State to investigate the competence and fitness of those whom it hires to teach in its schools, as this Court before now has had occasion to recognize. "A teacher works in a sensitive area in a schoolroom. There he shapes the attitude of young minds towards the society in which they live. In this, the state has a vital concern." *Adler v. Board of Education*, 342 U.S. 485, 493. . . .

Second. It is not disputed that to compel a teacher to disclose his every associational tie is to impair that teacher's right of free association, a right closely allied to freedom of speech and a right which, like free speech, lies at the foundation of a free society. *De Jonge v. Oregon*, 299 U.S. 353, 364; *Bates v. Little Rock, supra*, at 522–523. Such interference with personal freedom is conspicuously accented when the teacher serves at the absolute will of those to whom the disclosure must be made . . . .

The statute does not provide that the information it requires be kept confidential. Each school board is left free to deal with the information as it wishes. The record contains evidence to indicate that fear of public disclosure is neither theoretical nor groundless. Even if there were no disclosure to the general public, the pressure upon a teacher to avoid any ties which might displease those who control his professional destiny would be constant and heavy. . . .

The vigilant protection of constitutional freedoms is nowhere more vital than in the community of American schools. . . .

II.

The question to be decided here is not whether the State of Arkansas can ask certain of its teachers about all their organizational relationships. It is not whether the State can ask all of its teachers about certain of their associational ties. It is not whether teachers can be asked how many organizations they belong to, or how much time they spend in organizational activity. The question is whether the State can ask every one of its teachers to disclose every single organization with which he has been associated over a five-year period. The scope of the inquiry required by Act 10 is completely unlimited. The statute requires a teacher to reveal the church to which he belongs, or to which he has given financial support. It requires him to disclose his political party, and every political organization to which he may have contributed over a five-year period. It requires him to list, without number, every conceivable kind of associational tie — social, professional, political, avocational, or religious. Many such relationships could have no possible bearing upon the teacher's occupational competence or fitness.

In a series of decisions this Court has held that, even though the governmental purpose be legitimate and substantial, that purpose cannot be pursued by means that broadly stifle fundamental personal liberties when the end can be more narrowly achieved. . . .

In *Lovell v. Griffin*, 303 U.S. 444, the Court invalidated an ordinance prohibiting all distribution of literature at any time or place in Griffin, Georgia, without a license, pointing out that so broad an interference was unnecessary to accomplish legitimate municipal aims. In *Schneider v. State*, 308 U.S. 147, the Court dealt with ordinances of four different municipalities which either banned or imposed prior restraints upon the distribution of handbills. In holding the ordinances invalid, the Court noted that where legislative abridgment of "fundamental personal rights and liberties" is asserted, "the courts should be astute to examine the effect of the challenged legislation. Mere legislative preferences or beliefs respecting matters of public convenience may well support regulation directed at other personal activities, but be insufficient to justify such as diminishes the exercise of rights so vital to the maintenance of democratic institutions." 308 U.S., at 161. In *Cantwell v. Connecticut*, 310 U.S. 296, the Court said that "conduct remains subject to regulation for the protection of society," but pointed out that in each case "the power to regulate must be so exercised as not, in attaining a permissible end, unduly to infringe the protected freedom." 310 U.S., at 304. Illustrations of the same constitutional principle are to be found in many other decisions of the Court, among them, *Martin v. Struthers*, 319 U.S. 141; *Saia v. New York*, 334 U.S. 558; and *Kunz v. New York*, 340 U.S. 290.

. . . .

The unlimited and indiscriminate sweep of the statute now before us brings it within the ban of our prior cases. The statute's comprehensive interference with associational freedom goes far beyond what might be justified in the exercise of the State's legitimate inquiry into the fitness and competency of its teachers. The judgments in both cases must be reversed.

It is so ordered.

[The dissenting opinion of Justice Frankfurter is omitted.]

[The dissenting opinion of Justice Harlan joined by Justices Frankfurter, Clark, and Whittaker is omitted.]

KEYISHIAN v. BOARD OF REGENTS

385 U.S. 589 (1967)

MR. JUSTICE BRENNAN delivered the opinion of the Court.

Appellants were members of the faculty of the privately owned and operated University of Buffalo, and became state employees when the University was merged in 1962 into the State University of New York, an institution of higher education owned and operated by the State of New York. As faculty members of the State University their continued employment was conditioned upon their compliance with a New York plan, formulated partly in statutes and partly in administrative regulations, which the State utilizes to prevent the appointment or retention of "subversive" persons in state employment.

Appellants Hochfield and Maud were Assistant Professors of English, appellant Keyishian an instructor in English, and appellant Garver, a lecturer in philosophy. Each of them refused to sign, as regulations then in effect required, a certificate that he was not a Communist, and that if he had ever been a Communist, he had communicated that fact to the President of the State University of New York. Each was notified that his failure to sign the certificate would require his dismissal. Keyishian's one-year-term contract was not renewed because of his failure to sign the certificate. Hochfield and Garver, whose contracts still had time to run, continue to teach, but subject to proceedings for their dismissal if the constitutionality of the New York plan is sustained. Maud has voluntarily resigned and therefore no longer has standing in this suit.

Appellant Starbuck was a nonfaculty library employee and part-time lecturer in English. Personnel in that classification were not required to sign a certificate but were required to answer in writing under oath the question, "Have you ever advised or taught or were you ever a member of any society or group of persons which taught or advocated the doctrine that the Government of the United States or of any political subdivisions thereof should be overthrown or overturned by force, violence or any unlawful means?" Starbuck refused to answer the question and as a result was dismissed.

Appellants brought this action for declaratory and injunctive relief, alleging that the state program violated the Federal Constitution in various respects. A three-judge federal court held that the program was constitutional. . . . We reverse.

I.

. . . [New York's] Feinberg Law was enacted to implement and enforce two earlier statutes. The first was a 1917 law . . . under which "the utterance of any treasonable or seditious word or words or the doing of any treasonable or seditious act" is a ground for dismissal from the public school system. The second was a 1939 law . . . [that] disqualifies from the civil service and from employment in the educational system any person who advocates the overthrow of government by force, violence, or any unlawful means, or publishes material advocating such overthrow or organizes or joins any society or group of persons advocating such doctrine.

The Feinberg Law charged the State Board of Regents with the duty of promulgating rules and regulations providing procedures for the disqualification or removal of persons in the public school system who violate the 1917 law or who are ineligible for appointment to or retention in the public school system under the 1939 law. The Board of Regents was further directed to make a list, after notice and hearing, of "subversive" organizations, defined as organizations which advocate the doctrine of overthrow of government by force, violence, or any unlawful means. Finally, the Board was directed to provide in its rules and regulations that membership in any listed organization should constitute prima facie evidence of disqualification for appointment to or retention in any office or position in the public schools of the State.

. . . .

II.

A 1953 amendment extended the application of the Feinberg Law to personnel of any college or other institution of higher education owned and operated by the State or its subdivisions. In the same year, the Board of Regents, after notice and hearing, listed the Communist Party of the United States and of the State of New York as "subversive organizations." In 1956 each applicant for an appointment or the renewal of an appointment was required to sign the so-called "Feinberg Certificate" declaring that he had read the Regents Rules and understood that the Rules and the statutes constituted terms of employment, and declaring further that he was not a member of the Communist Party, and that if he had ever been a member he had communicated that fact to the President of the State University. This was the certificate that appellants Hochfield, Maud, Keyishian, and Garver refused to sign.

In June 1965, shortly before the trial of this case, the Feinberg Certificate was rescinded and it was announced that no person then employed would be deemed ineligible for continued employment "solely" because he refused to sign the certificate. In lieu of the certificate, it was provided that each applicant be informed before assuming his duties that the statutes, §§ 3021 and 3022 of the Education Law and § 105 of the Civil Service Law, constituted part of his contract. . . .

The change in procedure in no wise moots appellants' constitutional questions raised in the context of their refusal to sign the now abandoned Feinberg Certificate. The substance of the statutory and regulatory complex remains and from the outset appellants' basic claim has been that they are aggrieved by its application.

III.

Section 3021 requires removal for "treasonable or seditious" utterances or acts. The 1958 amendment to § 105 of the Civil Service Law . . . added such utterances or acts as a ground for removal under that law also. The same wording is used in both statutes — that "the utterance of any treasonable or seditious word or words or the doing of any treasonable or seditious act or acts" shall be ground for removal.

But there is a vital difference between the two laws. . . .

Our experience under the Sedition Act of 1798 . . . taught us that dangers fatal to First Amendment freedoms inhere in the word "seditious." *See New York Times Co. v. Sullivan*, 376 U.S. 254, 273–276. And the word "treasonable," if left undefined, is no less dangerously uncertain. . . .

. . . The difficulty centers upon the meaning of "seditious." Subdivision 3 equates the term "seditious" with "criminal anarchy" as defined in the Penal Law. Is the reference only to Penal Law § 160, defining criminal anarchy as "the doctrine that organized government should be overthrown by force or violence, or by assassination of the executive head or of any of the executive officials of government, or by any unlawful means"? But that section ends with the sentence "The advocacy of such doctrine either by word of mouth or writing is a felony." Does that sentence draw into § 105, Penal Law § 161, proscribing "advocacy of criminal anarchy"? If so, the possible scope of "seditious" utterances or acts has virtually no limit. For under Penal Law § 161, one commits the felony of advocating criminal anarchy if he ". . . publicly displays any book . . . containing or advocating, advising or teaching the doctrine that organized government should be overthrown by force, violence or any unlawful means." Does the teacher who carries a copy of the Communist Manifesto on a public street thereby advocate criminal anarchy? It is no answer to say that the statute would not be applied in such a case. We cannot gainsay the potential effect of this obscure wording on "those with a conscientious and scrupulous regard for such undertakings." *Baggett v. Bullitt*, 377 U.S. 360, 374. Even were it certain that the definition referred to in § 105 was solely Penal Law § 160, the scope of § 105 still remains indefinite. . . . The crucial consideration is that no teacher can know just where the line is drawn between "seditious" and nonseditious utterances and acts.

Other provisions of § 105 also have the same defect of vagueness. Subdivision 1 (a) of § 105 bars employment of any person who "by word of mouth or writing wilfully and deliberately advocates, advises or teaches the doctrine" of forceful overthrow of government. This provision is plainly susceptible of sweeping and improper application. It may well prohibit the employment of one who merely advocates the doctrine in the abstract without any attempt to indoctrinate others, or incite others to action in furtherance of unlawful aims. . . . Does the teacher who informs his class about the precepts of Marxism or the Declaration of Independence violate this prohibition?

Similar uncertainty arises as to the application of subdivision 1 (b) of § 105. That subsection requires the disqualification of an employee involved with the distribution of written material "containing or advocating, advising or teaching the doctrine" of forceful overthrow, and who himself "advocates, advises, teaches, or embraces the duty, necessity or propriety of adopting the doctrine contained therein." Here again, mere advocacy of abstract doctrine is apparently included. . . .

We do not have the benefit of a judicial gloss by the New York courts enlightening us as to the scope of this complicated plan. In light of the intricate administrative machinery for its enforcement, this is not surprising. The very intricacy of the plan and the uncertainty as to the scope of its proscriptions make it a highly efficient in terrorem mechanism. It would be a bold teacher who would not stay as far as possible from utterances or acts which might jeopardize his living by enmeshing him in this intricate machinery. . . .

There can be no doubt of the legitimacy of New York's interest in protecting its education system from subversion. But "even though the governmental purpose be legitimate and substantial, that purpose cannot be pursued by means that broadly stifle fundamental personal liberties when the end can be more narrowly achieved." *Shelton v. Tucker*, 364 U.S. 479, 488. . . .

. . . .

Our Nation is deeply committed to safeguarding academic freedom, which is of transcendent value to all of us and not merely to the teachers concerned. That freedom is therefore a special concern of the First Amendment, which does not tolerate laws that cast a pall of orthodoxy over the classroom. . . . .

. . . .

. . . Because First Amendment freedoms need breathing space to survive, government may regulate in the area only with narrow specificity." [*N.A.A.C.P. v. Button*, 371 U.S. 415, 432–433]. New York's complicated and intricate scheme plainly violates that standard. When one must guess what conduct or utterance may lose him his position, one necessarily will "steer far wider of the unlawful zone . . . ." *Speiser v. Randall*, 357 U.S. 513, 526. The danger of that chilling effect upon the exercise of vital First Amendment rights must be guarded against by sensitive tools which clearly inform teachers what is being proscribed.

The regulatory maze created by New York is wholly lacking in "terms susceptible of objective measurement." [citation omitted]. . . . Vagueness of wording is aggravated by prolixity and profusion of statutes, regulations, and administrative machinery, and by manifold cross-references to interrelated enactments and rules.

We therefore hold that § 3021 of the Education Law and subdivisions 1 (a), 1 (b) and 3 of § 105 of the Civil Service Law as implemented by the machinery created pursuant to § 3022 of the Education Law are unconstitutional.

. . . .

The judgment of the District Court is reversed and the case is remanded for further proceedings consistent with this opinion.

Reversed and remanded.

[The dissent of Justice Clark joined by Justices Harlan, Stewart, and White is omitted.]

NOTES

1. Justice Frankfurter wrote in his dissenting opinion in *Shelton*:

> In the present case the Court strikes down an Arkansas statute requiring that teachers disclose to school officials all of their organizational relationships, on the ground that "Many such relationships could have no possible bearing upon the teacher's occupational competence or fitness."

> Granted that a given teacher's membership in the First Street Congregation is, standing alone, of little relevance to what may rightly be expected of a teacher, is that membership equally irrelevant when it is discovered that the teacher is in fact a member of the First Street Congregation and the Second Street Congregation and the Third Street Congregation and the 4-H Club and the 3-H Club and half a dozen other groups? Presumably, a teacher may have so many divers associations, so many divers commitments, that they consume his time and energy and interest at the expense of his work or even of his professional dedication. Unlike wholly individual interests, organizational connections — because they involve obligations undertaken with relation to other persons — may become inescapably demanding and distracting. Surely, a school board is entitled to inquire whether any of its teachers has placed himself, or is placing himself, in a condition where his work may suffer. . . .
>
> If I dissent from the Court's disposition in these cases, it is not that I put a low value on academic freedom. *See Sweezy v. New Hampshire*, 354 U.S. 234, 255 (concurring opinion). It is because that very freedom, in its most creative reaches, is dependent in no small part upon the careful and discriminating selection of teachers. This process of selection is an intricate affair, a matter of fine judgment, and if it is to be informed, it must be based upon a comprehensive range of information. I am unable to say, on the face of this statute, that Arkansas could not reasonably find that the information which the statute requires — and which may not be otherwise acquired than by asking the question which it asks — is germane to that selection. Nor, on this record, can I attribute to the State a purpose to employ the enactment as a device for the accomplishment of what is constitutionally forbidden. Of course, if the information gathered by the required affidavits is used to further a scheme of terminating the employment of teachers solely because of their membership in unpopular organizations, that use will run afoul of the Fourteenth Amendment. It will be time enough, if such use is made, to hold the application of the statute unconstitutional.

Shelton v. Tucker, 364 U.S. at 494–96. How can Justice Frankfurter's dissent in *Shelton* be squared with his full-throated defense of academic freedom in *Sweezy*? What conceptual differences, if any, are there between the information sought, and the use of that information by government officials, in *Sweezy* and *Shelton*? Do you think the Arkansas school officials were interested in the amount of time teachers spent with outside organizational activities, as Justice Frankfurter asserted, or do you think they were primarily interested in the types of organizations to which teachers belonged?

2. Justice Harlan, joined in dissent by Justices Frankfurter, Clark, and Whittaker, wrote:

> Of course this decision has a natural tendency to enlist support, involving as it does an unusual statute that touches constitutional rights whose protection in the context of the racial situation in various parts of the country demands the unremitting vigilance of the courts. Yet that very circumstance also serves to remind of the restraints that attend constitutional

> adjudication. It must be emphasized that neither of these cases actually presents an issue of racial discrimination. The statute on its face applies to all Arkansas teachers irrespective of race, and there is no showing that it has been discriminatorily administered.

Id. at 496–97. Justice Harlan also noted — and on this point he was in agreement with the majority — that the cases of *N.A.A.C.P. v. Alabama*, 357 U.S. 449 (1958) and *Bates v. Little Rock*, 361 U.S. 516 (1960) were inapposite to the case at bar. In *N.A.A.C.P. v. Alabama*, the organization refused to comply with a court order to turn over its membership lists as part of an investigation of the Alabama attorney general who was attempting to oust it from the state. And in *Bates v. Little Rock*, the N.A.A.C.P. refused to turn over its membership lists to local authorities pursuant to identical license tax statutes. In those cases, Harlan argued, again in agreement with the majority, that "the required disclosure [bore] no substantial relevance to a legitimate state interest." *Shelton*, 364 U.S. at 498. The required disclosure in *Shelton*, on the other hand, was related to the state's legitimate interest in selecting qualified teachers to serve in its public schools. *Id.* at 497.

Given the possibilities for abuse of the disclosure statute at issue in *Shelton* because of the incendiary nature of race relations in the South at that time, was it really enough for the majority and dissenters to decide that the statute was constitutional because of the "legitimacy" of the state's interest? Were the states' interests in *N.A.A.C.P.* and *Bates* any less legitimate than the state's interest in *Shelton*? In *Bates*, for example, the licensing statute at issue applied to all organizations, irrespective of race. Doesn't a municipality have a legitimate interest in knowing the identities of individuals and organizations doing business within its borders?

3. In *Sweezy*, the plurality was unwilling to engage in a balancing of the state's interests against Sweezy's First Amendment rights. Why was the Court willing to engage in such a balancing in *Shelton* just three years after *Sweezy* was decided?

4. Justice Brennan, writing for the majority in *Keyishian*, had to wrestle with squaring the *Keyishian* decision and rationale with the case of *Adler v. Board of Education*, 342 U.S. 485 (1952). As Brennan wrote:

> We considered some aspects of the constitutionality of the New York plan 15 years ago in *Adler v. Board of Education*. That litigation arose after New York passed the Feinberg Law . . . .
>
> . . . .
>
> Adler was a declaratory judgment suit in which the Court held, in effect, that there was no constitutional infirmity in former § 12-a or in the Feinberg Law on their faces and that they were capable of constitutional application. But the contention urged in this case that both § 3021 and § 105 are unconstitutionally vague was not heard or decided. Section 3021 of the Education Law was challenged in Adler as unconstitutionally vague, but because the challenge had not been made in the pleadings or in the proceedings in the lower courts, this Court refused to consider it. Nor was any challenge on grounds of vagueness made in Adler as to subdivisions 1 (a) and (b) of § 105 of the Civil Service Law. Subdivision 3 of § 105 was not

added until 1958. Appellants in this case timely asserted below the unconstitutionality of all these sections on grounds of vagueness and that question is now properly before us for decision. Moreover, to the extent that Adler sustained the provision of the Feinberg Law constituting membership in an organization advocating forceful overthrow of government a ground for disqualification, pertinent constitutional doctrines have since rejected the premises upon which that conclusion rested. Adler is therefore not dispositive of the constitutional issues we must decide in this case.

Keyishian v. Board of Regents, 385 U.S. 589, 593–95 (1967).

To this line of reasoning, Justice Clark, writing in dissent, responded:

> It is clear that the Feinberg Law, in which this Court found "no constitutional infirmity" in 1952, has been given its death blow today. Just as the majority here finds that there "can be no doubt of the legitimacy of New York's interest in protecting its education system from subversion" there can also be no doubt that "the be-all and end-all" of New York's effort is here. And, regardless of its correctness, neither New York nor the several States that have followed the teaching of *Adler v. Board of Education* for some 15 years, can ever put the pieces together again. No court has ever reached out so far to destroy so much with so little.
>
> . . . .
>
> This Court has again and again, since at least 1951, approved procedures either identical or at the least similar to the ones the Court condemns today. In *Garner v. Board of Public Works of Los Angeles*[, 341 U.S. 716 (1951)], we held that a public employer was not precluded, simply because it was an agency of the State, "from inquiring of its employees as to matters that may prove relevant to their fitness and suitability for the public service." The oath there used practically the same language as the Starbuck statement here and the affidavit reflects the same type of inquiry as was made in the old certificate condemned here. Then in 1952, in *Adler v. Board of Education*, this Court passed upon the identical statute condemned here. It, too, was a declaratory judgment action — as in this case. However, there the issues were not so abstractly framed. . . .
>
> And again in 1958 the problem was before us in *Beilan v. Board of Education*, [357 U.S. 399 (1958)]. There our late Brother Burton wrote for the Court:
>
> > "By engaging in teaching in the public schools, petitioner did not give up his right to freedom of belief, speech or association. He did, however, undertake obligations of frankness, candor and cooperation in answering inquiries made of him by his employing Board examining into his fitness to serve it as a public school teacher." 357 U.S., at 405.
>
> And on the same day in *Lerner v. Casey*, 357 U.S. 468 [1958], our Brother Harlan again upheld the severance of a public employee for his refusal to

> answer questions concerning his loyalty. And also on the same day my Brother Brennan himself cited *Garner* with approval in *Speiser v. Randall*, 357 U.S. 513 (1958).
>
> Since that time the *Adler* line of cases has been cited again and again with approval: *Shelton v. Tucker*, 364 U.S. 479 (1960), in which both *Adler* and *Beilan* were quoted with approval, and *Garner* and *Lerner* were cited in a like manner; likewise in *Cramp v. Board of Public Instruction*, 368 U.S. 278 (1961), *Adler* was quoted twice with approval; and, in a related field where the employee was discharged for refusal to answer questions as to his loyalty after being ordered to do so, *Nelson v. Los Angeles County*, 362 U.S. 1 (1960), the Court cited with approval all of the cases which today it says have been rejected, *i.e.*, *Garner*, *Adler*, *Beilan* and *Lerner*. Later *Konigsberg v. State Bar*, 366 U.S. 36 (1961), likewise cited with approval both *Beilan* and *Garner*. And in our decision in *In re Anastaplo*, 366 U.S. 82 (1961), *Garner*, *Beilan* and *Lerner* were all referred to. Finally, only three Terms ago my Brother White relied upon *Cramp*, which in turn cited *Adler* with approval twice. *See Baggett v. Bullitt*, 377 U.S. 360 (1964).
>
> In view of this long list of decisions covering over 15 years of this Court's history, in which no opinion of this Court even questioned the validity of the *Adler* line of cases, it is strange to me that the Court now finds that the "constitutional doctrine which has emerged since . . . has rejected [*Adler*'s] major premise." With due respect, as I read them, our cases have done no such thing.

Id. at 622–25. As a matter of stare decisis, is there a counter-argument to Justice Clark's reasoning? When Justice Brennan wrote that "pertinent constitutional doctrines have since rejected the premises upon which [*Adler*'s] conclusion rested," he cited no authority. What "pertinent constitutional doctrines" had changed? Had those doctrines changed, or had the times changed by the time *Keyishian* was decided in 1967?

5. Justice Clark was in the dissent in all three of the cases in this section, which are regarded as among the most important in broadening First Amendment rights in the latter half of the twentieth century. His view of the First Amendment was clearly falling out of favor among his fellow Justices. In his *Keyishian* dissent, he wrote:

> The majority says that the Feinberg Law is bad because it has an "overbroad sweep." I regret to say — and I do so with deference — that the majority has by its broadside swept away one of our most precious rights, namely, the right of self-preservation. Our public educational system is the genius of our democracy. The minds of our youth are developed there and the character of that development will determine the future of our land. Indeed, our very existence depends upon it. The issue here is a very narrow one. It is not freedom of speech, freedom of thought, freedom of press, freedom of assembly, or of association, even in the Communist Party. It is simply this: May the State provide that one who, after a hearing with full judicial review, is found to have wilfully and deliberately advocated, advised, or taught that our Government should be overthrown by force or

> violence or other unlawful means; or to have wilfully and deliberately printed, published, etc., any book or paper that so advocated and to have personally advocated such doctrine himself; or to have wilfully and deliberately become a member of an organization that advocates such doctrine, is prima facie disqualified from teaching in its university? My answer, in keeping with all of our cases up until today, is "Yes"!

Id. at 628–29. Two years later, the Court decided *Brandenburg v. Ohio*, 395 U.S. 444 (1969), in which it held:

> [T]he constitutional guarantees of free speech and free press do not permit a State to forbid or proscribe advocacy of the use of force or of law violation except where such advocacy is directed to inciting or producing imminent lawless action and is likely to incite or produce such action.

Id. at 447. With that decision, which remains the Court's official pronouncement on words of incitement, Justice Clark's view of the First Amendment was effectively put to rest. For more on the *Brandenburg* decision, see Chris Montgomery, *Can Brandenburg v. Ohio Survive the Internet and the Age of Terrorism?: The Secret Weakening of a Venerable Doctrine*, 70 OHIO ST. L.J. 141 (2009).

6. In *Keyishian*, the Court specifically recognized the free expression rights of colleges and universities and noted that even government awarding of funds could not overcome those rights based on the existence of vagueness or overbreadth doctrines. Has what was thought to be axiomatic in academic circles become attenuated by more recent decisions of the Supreme Court? *Rust v. Sullivan*, 500 U.S. 173 (1991), a non-education case on its face, could be seen as just such a decision.

Rust concerned a federal statute providing funding for family planning services, but excluded programs where abortion could be used as such a method. Grantees of the funds challenged the regulations as unconstitutional, contending that, among other things, the statute's regulations conditioned the receipt of funds on the weakening of First Amendment rights. They asserted that the regulations discriminated on the basis of viewpoint, also a First Amendment violation. The Supreme Court upheld the regulations, stating that the federal government was free to implement policies in favor of non-abortion related methods of family planning and thus restrict the activities, even the speech activities, of clinics and researchers who receive federal funds.

> Petitioners contend that the regulations violate the First Amendment by impermissibly discriminating based on viewpoint . . . .
>
> . . . .
>
> The Government can, without violating the Constitution, selectively fund a program to encourage certain activities it believes to be in the public interest, without at the same time funding an alternative program which seeks to deal with the problem in another way. In so doing, the Government has not discriminated on the basis of viewpoint; it has merely chosen to fund one activity to the exclusion of the other.

Id. at 192–93. What is the message for teachers in *Rust*? Is it that "government can allocate the public's resources any way the political majority chooses to and it may enforce generally applicable laws regardless of their incidental infringement on constitutionally protected conduct[?]" *See* Charles Freeland, *The Political Process as Final Solution*, 68 Ind. L.J. 525 (1993).

Does the case stand for a new phase in academic expression where government may condition the granting of funds on the abandonment or modification of First Amendment rights?

7. With the cases covered up to this point, is it possible to craft a definition of "academic freedom"? Does academic freedom protect professors and other academics? Does it protect postsecondary institutions themselves? Does it protect both? Consider this:

> The First Amendment protects academic freedom. This simple proposition stands explicit or implicit in numerous judicial opinions, often proclaimed in fervid rhetoric. Attempts to understand the scope and foundation of a constitutional guarantee of academic freedom, however, generally result in paradox or confusion. The cases, shorn of panegyrics, are inconclusive, the promise of their rhetoric reproached by the ambiguous realities of academic life.
>
> The problems are fundamental: There has been no adequate analysis of what academic freedom the Constitution protects or of why it protects it. Lacking definition or guiding principle, the doctrine floats in the law, picking up decisions as a hull does barnacles. . . .

J. Peter Byrne, *Academic Freedom: A "Special Concern of the First Amendment,"* 99 Yale L.J. 251, 252–53 (1989)*. Professor Byrne divides "academic freedom" into two distinct concepts: "constitutional academic freedom," meaning the "traditional legal status of academic institutions" and their treatment by the courts; and "academic freedom," which is "a non-legal term referring to the liberties claimed by professors through professional channels against administrative or political interference with research, teaching, and governance." *Id.* at 254–55. In examining *Sweezy* and *Keyishian*, Byrne writes:

> The anomalies in the Court's rhetorical exposition of the meaning of constitutional academic freedom seem to stem from its incomplete understanding of what academic freedom requires. The Court's rhetoric praises academic freedom as an institutional right to be free from orthodoxy prescribed by the government at large. The focus is on the classroom, viewed metaphorically as the process of institutionalized scholarship and teaching, rather than on the rights of any individual teacher or student; the benefits to democracy flow through a system of education not seriously imperiled by isolated injustices. The "orthodoxies" feared are not those of academics themselves, but those imposed by non-academic officials seeking to advance their views on various policies. These are the only kind of interferences in the "free market" of teaching with which the Court is

> concerned. This focus on the protection of the system from government interference can easily be missed because the term academic freedom had always signified an individual right against any interference by laypersons. The Court's rhetoric, however, is quite unsuitable to this traditional notion.
>
> These two cases exhaust the Supreme Court's development of a university faculty member's right of academic freedom. Despite their analytical shortcomings, *Sweezy* and *Keyishian* contributed substantially to the virtual extinction of overt efforts by non-academic government officials to prescribe political orthodoxy in university teaching and research. Today, few politicians seek political capital by attacking academics for their political opinions, and those who do only provide their victims with lawsuits that usually fortify their academic positions against more subtle or justifiable assault. This does not mean that ideological passion and prejudice now play no part in academic appointments (how could they not?); rather the rules of the game are now those of the academy.

Id. at 298.

Professor Byrne maintains that the "potential for reading *Sweezy* as establishing a right of institutional autonomy" was significantly boosted by Justice Powell's separate but controlling opinion in *Regents of the University of California v. Bakke*, 438 U.S. 265 (1978):

> Powell held that, even though the Fourteenth Amendment and Title VIprohibited any state instrumentality from penalizing any applicant because of his race, the First Amendment right of academic freedom empowered a state university to take race or national origin into account in admitting students when doing so in pursuit of the academic goal of a diverse student body. Powell relied on the fourth of Frankfurter's "four essential freedoms" — the right of the university to determine for itself on academic grounds who may be admitted to study. Powell explicitly connected racial diversity with the grounds on which the Court in *Sweezy* praised academic freedom: "The atmosphere of 'speculation, experiment and creation' — so essential to the quality of higher education — is widely believed to be promoted by a diverse student body." Justice Powell's practical accommodation between constitutional interests in non-discrimination generally and the university's right to create a racially diverse student body in particular led to a rejection of racial quotas in admissions but an acceptance of admissions criteria that make race on factor among many to be taken into account.

Byrne, *supra*, at 313–14. For an interesting take on the impact of the Supreme Court's more recent affirmative action jurisprudence on constitutional academic freedom, see J. Peter Byrne, *Constitutional Academic Freedom After Grutter: Getting Real About the "Four Freedoms" of a University*, 77 U. Colo. L. Rev. 929 (2006).

The American Association of University Professors is considered the keeper of the professional meaning of academic freedom, that is, the meaning of academic freedom as traditionally understood within the academy. Through its initial pronouncement on academic freedom in 1915 and its refinement of key concepts together with the Association of American Colleges in 1940,

> the AAUP concocted a generically American, profession-centered, multi-faceted definition of academic freedom. On these shores, by these lights, academic freedom stood for the freedom of the academic, not for the freedom of the academy. Consequently, a violation of academic freedom was seen as something that happened in a university, not something that happened to a university. In the standard plot of this kind of crime story, a dissident professor was the victim, trustees or regents (and their deputies) were the culprits, the power of dismissal was the favored weapon, and the loss of employment was the awful wound. Holding to this criminology, the organized profession grew wise to the ways of the harsh employer, but it lacked a theory and vocabulary to deal with offenses against academic freedom that were not quintessentially inside jobs.

Walter P. Metzger, *Profession and Constitution: Two Definitions of Academic Freedom in America*, 66 Tex. L. Rev. 1265, 1284–85 (1988)*.

2. The Professional Meaning of Academic Freedom

American Association of University Professors and Association of American Colleges and Universities, 1940 Statement of Principles on Academic Freedom and Tenure (1940)*

The purpose of this statement is to promote public understanding and support of academic freedom and tenure and agreement upon procedures to ensure them in colleges and universities. Institutions of higher education are conducted for the common good and not to further the interest of either the individual teacher or the institution as a whole. The common good depends upon the free search for truth and its free exposition.

Academic freedom is essential to these purposes and applies to both teaching and research. Freedom in research is fundamental to the advancement of truth. Academic freedom in its teaching aspect is fundamental for the protection of the rights of the teacher in teaching and of the student to freedom in learning. It carries with it duties correlative with rights.

Tenure is a means to certain ends; specifically: (1) freedom of teaching and research and of extramural activities, and (2) a sufficient degree of economic security to make the profession attractive to men and women of ability. Freedom and economic security, hence, tenure, are indispensable to the success of an institution in fulfilling its obligations to its students and to society.

Academic Freedom

1. Teachers are entitled to full freedom in research and in the publication of the results, subject to the adequate performance of their other academic duties; but research for pecuniary return should be based upon an understanding with the authorities of the institution.

2. Teachers are entitled to freedom in the classroom in discussing their subject, but they should be careful not to introduce into their teaching controversial matter which has no relation to their subject. Limitations of academic freedom because of religious or other aims of the institution should be clearly stated in writing at the time of the appointment.

3. College and university teachers are citizens, members of a learned profession, and officers of an educational institution. When they speak or write as citizens, they should be free from institutional censorship or discipline, but their special position in the community imposes special obligations. As scholars and educational officers, they should remember that the public may judge their profession and their institution by their utterances. Hence they should at all times be accurate, should exercise appropriate restraint, should show respect for the opinions of others, and should make every effort to indicate that they are not speaking for the institution.

Academic Tenure

After the expiration of a probationary period, teachers or investigators should have permanent or continuous tenure, and their service should be terminated only for adequate cause, except in the case of retirement for age, or under extraordinary circumstances because of financial exigencies.

In the interpretation of this principle it is understood that the following represents acceptable academic practice:

1. The precise terms and conditions of every appointment should be stated in writing and be in the possession of both institution and teacher before the appointment is consummated.

2. Beginning with appointment to the rank of full-time instructor or a higher rank, the probationary period should not exceed seven years, including within this period full-time service in all institutions of higher education; but subject to the proviso that when, after a term of probationary service of more than three years in one or more institutions, a teacher is called to another institution, it may be agreed in writing that the new appointment is for a probationary period of not more than four years, even though thereby the person's total probationary period in the academic profession is extended beyond the normal maximum of seven years. Notice should be given at least one year prior to the expiration of the probationary period if the teacher is not to be continued in service after the expiration of that period.

3. During the probationary period a teacher should have the academic freedom that all other members of the faculty have.

4. Termination for cause of a continuous appointment, or the dismissal for cause of a teacher previous to the expiration of a term appointment, should, if possible, be considered by both a faculty committee and the governing board of the institution. In all cases where the facts are in dispute, the accused teacher should be informed before the hearing in writing of the charges and should have the opportunity to be heard in his or her own defense by all bodies that pass judgment upon the case. The teacher should be permitted to be accompanied by an advisor of his or her own choosing who may act as counsel. There should be a full stenographic record of the hearing available to the parties concerned. In the hearing of charges of incompetence the testimony should include that of teachers and other scholars, either from the teacher's own or from other institutions. Teachers on continuous appointment who are dismissed for reasons not involving moral turpitude should receive their salaries for at least a year from the date of notification of dismissal whether or not they are continued in their duties at the institution.

5. Termination of a continuous appointment because of financial exigency should be demonstrably bona fide.

[The statement and interpretive comments can be found at: http://www.aaup.org/AAUP/pubsres/policydocs/contents/1940statement.htm#4.-eds.]

NOTES

1. The 1940 Statement remains the accepted definition of professional academic freedom. The only material changes to it since its drafting occurred in 1970, when a joint committee of the AAUP and Association of American Colleges (now the Association of American Colleges and Universities) released interpretive comments to take into account developments in the concept of academic freedom in the intervening 30 years.

A large portion of the comments was dedicated to clarifying the duties of academics both inside and outside of their institutions. In particular, the joint committee referenced the AAUP's Statement on Professional Ethics, adopted in 1966. That statement provides:

> 1. Professors, guided by a deep conviction of the worth and dignity of the advancement of knowledge, recognize the special responsibilities placed upon them. Their primary responsibility to their subject is to seek and to state the truth as they see it. To this end professors devote their energies to developing and improving their scholarly competence. They accept the obligation to exercise critical self-discipline and judgment in using, extending, and transmitting knowledge. They practice intellectual honesty. Although professors may follow subsidiary interests, these interests must never seriously hamper or compromise their freedom of inquiry.

2. As teachers, professors encourage the free pursuit of learning in their students. They hold before them the best scholarly and ethical standards of their discipline. Professors demonstrate respect for students as individuals and adhere to their proper roles as intellectual guides and counselors. Professors make every reasonable effort to foster honest academic conduct and to ensure that their evaluations of students reflect each student's true merit. They respect the confidential nature of the relationship between professor and student. They avoid any exploitation, harassment, or discriminatory treatment of students. They acknowledge significant academic or scholarly assistance from them. They protect their academic freedom.

3. As colleagues, professors have obligations that derive from common membership in the community of scholars. Professors do not discriminate against or harass colleagues. They respect and defend the free inquiry of associates, even when it leads to findings and conclusions that differ from their own. Professors acknowledge academic debt and strive to be objective in their professional judgment of colleagues. Professors accept their share of faculty responsibilities for the governance of their institution.

4. As members of an academic institution, professors seek above all to be effective teachers and scholars. Although professors observe the stated regulations of the institution, provided the regulations do not contravene academic freedom, they maintain their right to criticize and seek revision. Professors give due regard to their paramount responsibilities within their institution in determining the amount and character of work done outside it. When considering the interruption or termination of their service, professors recognize the effect of their decision upon the program of the institution and give due notice of their intentions.

5. As members of their community, professors have the rights and obligations of other citizens. Professors measure the urgency of these obligations in the light of their responsibilities to their subject, to their students, to their profession, and to their institution. When they speak or act as private persons, they avoid creating the impression of speaking or acting for their college or university. As citizens engaged in a profession that depends upon freedom for its health and integrity, professors have a particular obligation to promote conditions of free inquiry and to further public understanding of academic freedom.

AM. ASS'N OF UNIV. PROFESSORS, STATEMENT ON PROFESSIONAL ETHICS (1966),* *available at* http://www.aaup.org/AAUP/pubsres/policydocs/contents/statementonprofessionalethics.htm.

2. The joint committee also fleshed out the contours of the academic due process that should be provided to professors suspended or terminated for cause. The committee referenced the *Statement on Procedural Standards in Faculty Dismissal Proceedings*, jointly approved by the two associations in 1958:

> The 1958 Statement provides: "Suspension of the faculty member during the proceedings is justified only if immediate harm to the faculty member or others is threatened by the faculty member's continuance. Unless legal considerations forbid, any such suspension should be with pay." A suspension which is not followed by either reinstatement or the opportunity for a hearing is in effect a summary dismissal in violation of academic due process.
>
> The concept of "moral turpitude" identifies the exceptional case in which the professor may be denied a year's teaching or pay in whole or in part. The statement applies to that kind of behavior which goes beyond simply warranting discharge and is so utterly blameworthy as to make it inappropriate to require the offering of a year's teaching or pay. The standard is not that the moral sensibilities of persons in the particular community have been affronted. The standard is behavior that would evoke condemnation by the academic community generally.

JOINT COMM. OF THE AM. ASS'N OF UNIV. PROFESSORS & THE ASS'N OF AM. COLLS., 1970 INTERPRETIVE COMMENTS TO THE 1940 STATEMENT OF PRINCIPLES ON ACADEMIC FREEDOM AND TENURE (1970),* *available at* http://www.aaup.org/AAUP/pubsres/policydocs/contents/1940statement.htm#4.

3. After reading the cases in the first section and the statement on academic freedom in this section, is it possible to reconcile the constitutional and professional meanings of academic freedom? Do they need to be reconciled?

3. Academic Freedom in Private Colleges and Universities

McENROY v. SAINT MEINRAD SCHOOL OF THEOLOGY
713 N.E.2d 334 (Ind. Ct. App. 1999)

RUCKER, JUDGE

Appellant-Plaintiff Dr. Carmel McEnroy ("Dr. McEnroy") filed an action against St. Meinrad School of Theology, Reverend Timothy Sweeney, and Reverend Eugene Hensell (collectively referred to as "Defendants"), asserting breach of contract, tortious interference with contractual relations and breach of an implied covenant of good faith and fair dealing. Defendants responded by filing a motion to dismiss for lack of subject matter jurisdiction, asserting that resolution of this action would excessively entangle the court in religious matters in violation of the First Amendment. The trial court granted Defendants' motion. . . . We affirm.

The facts giving rise to this appeal are these. Dr. McEnroy was employed as a professor of Catholic theology and doctrine at Saint Meinrad School of Theology ("Saint Meinrad"). Saint Meinrad is a Catholic Seminary which serves to train candidates for the priesthood and other ministries of the Roman Catholic Church. At all times relevant to this action, the archabbot of St. Meinrad Archabbey was

Father Timothy Sweeney ("Archabbot Sweeney"). Father Eugene Hensell ("Father Hensell") was President-Rector of Saint Meinrad.

In the spring of 1994, Pope John Paul II issued an Apostolic Letter declaring the issue of the ordination of women as priests resolved and no longer open to debate. Several months after the statement was issued, Dr. McEnroy joined 1,500 others in signing an open letter opposing the Pope's teachings on the subject. After reading the open letter in the National Catholic Reporter, Archabbot Sweeney determined that Dr. McEnroy had become "seriously deficient" in her duties as a seminary professor by publicly dissenting from the Pope's teachings, and that the Church's canon law required that he remove her from the faculty at Saint Meinrad. Pursuant to his jurisdiction over Saint Meinrad provided by the Statement of Governance and contained in the Faculty Handbook, Archabbot Sweeney directed Father Hensell to so remove Dr. McEnroy. He did so and as a result, Dr. McEnroy filed suit against Defendants, asserting breach of contract, intentional interference with contractual relations, and breach of an implied covenant of good faith and fair dealing. Defendants responded by filing a motion to dismiss . . . . The motion argued that the court lacked subject matter jurisdiction "because [resolution of] these claims would require the Court to decide religious issues regarding the Church's good faith motivation and doctrinal basis for removing her under the canon law." After a hearing, the trial court granted the motion. This appeal ensued in due course.

. . . .

Citing the Supreme Court's decision in Employment Div., *Dep't of Human Resources v. Smith*, Dr. McEnroy contends the trial court could avoid violating the First Amendment's prohibition against excessive entanglement by applying neutral principles of contract law. 494 U.S. 872 (1990) (civil courts do not inhibit the free exercise of religion where neutral principle of law may be applied). Dr. McEnroy premises this contention on the twin assertions that the contract granting her continuing appointment status and the Faculty Constitution provide the exclusive circumstances under which she may be dismissed, and that the issue may be resolved without reference to either church law or doctrine. Saint Meinrad counters that Dr. McEnroy's contract also incorporated the terms of the Faculty Handbook, which included the Statement on Governance. The Statement on Governance in turn "provides that the seminary operates through an hierarchical model in the administration of justice as specified by the Church's canon law and its Program of Priestly Formation ("PPF"), and that the Archabbot retains direct jurisdiction over Saint Meinrad within that model," including the authority to remove a seminary professor who is determined to be seriously deficient.

The Supreme Court has long held that the First Amendment requires civil courts to refrain from interfering in matters of church discipline, faith, practice and religious law. *Watson v. Jones*, 80 U.S. (13 Wall) 679, 727 (1871). Thus, civil courts are precluded from resolving disputes involving churches if "resolution of the disputes cannot be made without extensive inquiry . . . into religious law and polity. . . ." *Serbian Eastern Orthodox Diocese v. Milivojevich*, 426 U.S. 696, 709 (1976). Consequently, the First Amendment proscribes intervention by secular courts into many employment decisions made by religious organizations based on religious doctrines or beliefs. Accordingly, personnel decisions are protected from civil court interference where review by civil courts would require the courts to interpret and apply religious doctrine or ecclesiastical law.

The contract granting Dr. McEnroy continuing appointment stated, in relevant part, "the statements on academic freedom and responsibility, on appointment and dismissal contained in the *Faculty Constitution* are *among* the terms of appointment." (emphasis added). Use of the term "among" here creates an ambiguity made evident upon examination of the arguments raised by the parties. Defendants contend the term implies the existence of additional terms, specifically the Faculty Handbook and Statement on Governance. Dr. McEnroy, on the other hand, argues that the Faculty Constitution provide the sole terms of her contract. At oral argument before this court, Dr. McEnroy stated that the phrase "among the terms of appointment," could not refer to documents not specifically mentioned, and therefore refers to the terms of appointment and dismissal as set forth in the Faculty Constitution. When confronted with an ambiguous contract, this court attempts to determine the intent of the parties at the time of formation as disclosed by the language used to express the parties' respective rights and duties. Where, as here, the ambiguity arises from the language employed rather than because of extrinsic facts, its construction is a question of law to be determined by the court. We will read the contract as a whole and accept an interpretation which harmonizes and gives effect and meaning to the contract's words and phrases.

Applying these principles to the contract before us, we find that by declaring the statement on academic freedom and responsibility contained in the Faculty Constitution to be "among the terms of appointment," the parties intended to signify that additional terms were also to apply. The contract does not state what additional terms were intended to apply or their relation to those contained in the Faculty Constitution. We observe, however, that the parties agreed before the trial court the Faculty Handbook, which includes among other things the Statement on Governance, was also incorporated into the contract at trial. In light of the Statement on Governance, resolution of Dr. McEnroy's claims would require the trial court to interpret and apply religious doctrine and ecclesiastical law. At a minimum, the trial court would have to determine whether: (1) Archabbot Sweeney properly exercised his jurisdiction over Saint Meinrad, (2) Dr. McEnroy's conduct constituted public dissent or caused her to be "seriously deficient," and (3) canon law required Archabbot Sweeney to remove Dr. Sweeney from her teaching position. Because the trial court would be clearly and excessively entangled in religious affairs in violation of the First Amendment, we find no error.

Judgment affirmed.

NOTES

1. It is important to note that First Amendment rights and other constitutional protections generally don't apply to *private* postsecondary institutions. Thus, academic freedom claims in the private context must generally be based on contract law, and not constitutional law. Consider this:

> Theoretical problems with establishing an individual constitutional right of academic freedom arise from the anomalies of the state action doctrine.

Only if administrators can be characterized as exercising state power can the First Amendment limit the internal authority of the university. Despite the general uncertainty about the state action doctrine, a rigid rule of application to universities has developed. Faculty and students at state universities enjoy extensive substantive and procedural constitutional rights against their institutions while faculty and students at private institutions enjoy none. This is so despite the substantially similar functions usually served by state and private institutions; the dean of the University of Virginia Law School does not need to be restrained from instituting an assault against liberty any more than does the dean of the Harvard Law School. More significantly, academic tradition accords largely identical rights of academic freedom to professors regardless of their institutions' governmental affiliations. Thus, the state action doctrine mandates judicial enforcement of constitutional liberties against institutional infringements for half the nation's academics and denies it to the other half for reasons which, if desirable at all, are very far removed from the realities of academic life.

The state action doctrine also may blur the important distinctions for academic freedom between university administrators and nonacademic officials. Department heads, deans, and presidents may penalize a faculty member for the content of her scholarship if they follow the correct procedures, apply academic criteria, and do not usurp the judgment of peers; the state attorney general, the state legislature, and the governor may *never* do so. The state action doctrine does not distinguish between those who are part of the system of academic freedom and those who are not. This may tempt a court to intervene in decisions it ought to respect. Indeed, even fellow faculty exercising peer review could be characterized as state officials. To this extent, Chief Justice Rehnquist is correct in insisting that government as educator is different from government as sovereign.

A final anomaly in the application of the state action doctrine is that constitutional academic freedom is the only constitutional right exercised by state actors. Those universities whose institutional liberties have been recognized by the Supreme Court include the state universities of Michigan, Missouri, and California. A state university is a unique state entity in that it enjoys federal constitutional rights against the state itself.

J. Peter Byrne, *Academic Freedom: A "Special Concern of the First Amendment,"* 99 YALE L.J. 251 (1989).*

2. Should there be any judicial protections available for professors in positions similar to those Dr. McEnroy held? Is there any way for a court to get involved in this kind of dispute without becoming embroiled in religious affairs? *See* Ira C. Lupu, *The Case Against Legislative Codification of Religious Liberty*, 21 CARDOZO L. REV. 565, 575 n.53 (1999).

3. If courts decide to inject themselves into these kinds of disputes, would there be any constitutional ramifications? *See* Scott C. Idleman, *Tort Liability, Religious*

Entities, and the Decline of Constitutional Protection, 75 IND. L.J. 219 (2000).

4. At least one lower court has held that judicial intervention of the administrative decisions of private universities is constitutionally "fair and reasonable." *Ryan v. Hofstra University*, 67 Misc. 2d 651, 653, (N.Y. Sup. 1971). In *Ryan*, the court found that Hofstra University was not really "private" enough to avoid constitutional requirements: the university accepted state grants, followed state degree requirements, used the state dormitory authority for many of its buildings. Further, and most importantly, the court reasoned that the university itself could be considered "a public trust for the rendition of education." *Id.* at 666–67. Accordingly, the university was required to provide some minimal procedural rights to a student before permanently expelling him. *Id.* at 669. Under this framework, could any private or religious university still be considered "private"? What would happen if a university were to be considered both semi-private in nature and highly religious in context?

B. FREEDOM OF EXPRESSION

PICKERING v. BOARD OF EDUCATION
391 U.S. 563 (1968)

MR. JUSTICE MARSHALL delivered the opinion of the Court.

Appellant Marvin L. Pickering, a teacher in Township High School District 205, Will County, Illinois, was dismissed from his position by the appellee Board of Education for sending a letter to a local newspaper in connection with a recently proposed tax increase that was critical of the way in which the Board and the district superintendent of schools had handled past proposals to raise new revenue for the schools. Appellant's dismissal resulted from a determination by the Board, after a full hearing, that the publication of the letter was "detrimental to the efficient operation and administration of the schools of the district" and hence, under the relevant Illinois statute, Ill. Rev. Stat., c. 122, § 10-22.4 (1963), that "interests of the school require[d] [his dismissal]."

Appellant's claim that his writing of the letter was protected by the First and Fourteenth Amendments was rejected. Appellant then sought review of the Board's action in the Circuit Court of Will County, which affirmed his dismissal on the ground that the determination that appellant's letter was detrimental to the interests of the school system was supported by substantial evidence and that the interests of the schools overrode appellant's First Amendment rights. On appeal, the Supreme Court of Illinois . . . affirmed the judgment of the Circuit Court. . . . For the reasons detailed below we agree that appellant's rights to freedom of speech were violated and we reverse.

I.

In February of 1961 the appellee Board of Education asked the voters of the school district to approve a bond issue to raise $4,875,000 to erect two new schools.

The proposal was defeated. Then, in December of 1961, the Board submitted another bond proposal to the voters which called for the raising of $5,500,000 to build two new schools. This second proposal passed and the schools were built with the money raised by the bond sales. In May of 1964 a proposed increase in the tax rate to be used for educational purposes was submitted to the voters by the Board and was defeated. Finally, on September 19, 1964, a second proposal to increase the tax rate was submitted by the Board and was likewise defeated. It was in connection with this last proposal of the School Board that appellant wrote the letter to the editor . . . that resulted in his dismissal.

Prior to the vote on the second tax increase proposal a variety of articles attributed to the District 205 Teachers' Organization appeared in the local paper. These articles urged passage of the tax increase and stated that failure to pass the increase would result in a decline in the quality of education afforded children in the district's schools. A letter from the superintendent of schools making the same point was published in the paper two days before the election and submitted to the voters in mimeographed form the following day. It was in response to the foregoing material, together with the failure of the tax increase to pass, that appellant submitted the letter in question to the editor of the local paper.

The letter constituted, basically, an attack on the School Board's handling of the 1961 bond issue proposals and its subsequent allocation of financial resources between the schools' educational and athletic programs. It also charged the superintendent of schools with attempting to prevent teachers in the district from opposing or criticizing the proposed bond issue.

The Board dismissed Pickering for writing and publishing the letter. Pursuant to Illinois law, the Board was then required to hold a hearing on the dismissal. At the hearing the Board charged that numerous statements in the letter were false and that the publication of the statements unjustifiably impugned the "motives, honesty, integrity, truthfulness, responsibility and competence" of both the Board and the school administration. The Board also charged that the false statements damaged the professional reputations of its members and of the school administrators, would be disruptive of faculty discipline, and would tend to foment "controversy, conflict and dissension" among teachers, administrators, the Board of Education, and the residents of the district. . . .

The Illinois courts reviewed the proceedings solely to determine whether the Board's findings were supported by substantial evidence and whether, on the facts as found, the Board could reasonably conclude that appellant's publication of the letter was "detrimental to the best interests of the schools." Pickering's claim that his letter was protected by the First Amendment was rejected on the ground that his acceptance of a teaching position in the public schools obliged him to refrain from making statements about the operation of the schools "which in the absence of such position he would have an undoubted right to engage in." . . .

II.

To the extent that the Illinois Supreme Court's opinion may be read to suggest that teachers may constitutionally be compelled to relinquish the First Amendment rights they would otherwise enjoy as citizens to comment on matters of public interest in connection with the operation of the public schools in which they work, it proceeds on a premise that has been unequivocally rejected in numerous prior decisions of this Court. E. g., *Wieman v. Updegraff*, 344 U.S. 183 (1952); *Shelton v. Tucker*, 364 U.S. 479 (1960); *Keyishian v. Board of Regents*, 385 U.S. 589 (1967). . . . At the same time it cannot be gainsaid that the State has interests as an employer in regulating the speech of its employees that differ significantly from those it possesses in connection with regulation of the speech of the citizenry in general. The problem in any case is to arrive at a balance between the interests of the teacher, as a citizen, in commenting upon matters of public concern and the interest of the State, as an employer, in promoting the efficiency of the public services it performs through its employees.

III.

. . . .

An examination of the statements in appellant's letter objected to by the Board reveals that they, like the letter as a whole, consist essentially of criticism of the Board's allocation of school funds between educational and athletic programs, and of both the Board's and the superintendent's methods of informing, or preventing the informing of, the district's taxpayers of the real reasons why additional tax revenues were being sought for the schools. The statements are in no way directed towards any person with whom appellant would normally be in contact in the course of his daily work as a teacher. Thus no question of maintaining either discipline by immediate superiors or harmony among coworkers is presented here. Appellant's employment relationships with the Board and, to a somewhat lesser extent, with the superintendent are not the kind of close working relationships for which it can persuasively be claimed that personal loyalty and confidence are necessary to their proper functioning. Accordingly, to the extent that the Board's position here can be taken to suggest that even comments on matters of public concern that are substantially correct . . . may furnish grounds for dismissal if they are sufficiently critical in tone, we unequivocally reject it.

We next consider the statements in appellant's letter which we agree to be false. The Board's original charges included allegations that the publication of the letter damaged the professional reputations of the Board and the superintendent and would foment controversy and conflict among the Board, teachers, administrators, and the residents of the district. However, no evidence to support these allegations was introduced at the hearing. So far as the record reveals, Pickering's letter was greeted by everyone but its main target, the Board, with massive apathy and total disbelief. The Board must, therefore, have decided, perhaps by analogy with the law of libel, that the statements were per se harmful to the operation of the schools.

However, the only way in which the Board could conclude, absent any evidence of the actual effect of the letter, that the statements contained therein were per se detrimental to the interest of the schools was to equate the Board members' own interests with that of the schools. Certainly an accusation that too much money is being spent on athletics by the administrators of the school system . . . cannot reasonably be regarded as per se detrimental to the district's schools. Such an accusation reflects rather a difference of opinion between Pickering and the Board as to the preferable manner of operating the school system, a difference of opinion that clearly concerns an issue of general public interest.

In addition, the fact that particular illustrations of the Board's claimed undesirable emphasis on athletic programs are false would not normally have any necessary impact on the actual operation of the schools, beyond its tendency to anger the Board. . . .

More importantly, the question whether a school system requires additional funds is a matter of legitimate public concern on which the judgment of the school administration, including the School Board, cannot, in a society that leaves such questions to popular vote, be taken as conclusive. On such a question free and open debate is vital to informed decision-making by the electorate. Teachers are, as a class, the members of a community most likely to have informed and definite opinions as to how funds allotted to the operation of the schools should be spent. Accordingly, it is essential that they be able to speak out freely on such questions without fear of retaliatory dismissal.

In addition, the amounts expended on athletics which Pickering reported erroneously were matters of public record on which his position as a teacher in the district did not qualify him to speak with any greater authority than any other taxpayer. The Board could easily have rebutted appellant's errors by publishing the accurate figures itself, either via a letter to the same newspaper or otherwise. We are thus not presented with a situation in which a teacher has carelessly made false statements about matters so closely related to the day-to-day operations of the schools that any harmful impact on the public would be difficult to counter because of the teacher's presumed greater access to the real facts. Accordingly, we have no occasion to consider at this time whether under such circumstances a school board could reasonably require that a teacher make substantial efforts to verify the accuracy of his charges before publishing them.

What we do have before us is a case in which a teacher has made erroneous public statements upon issues then currently the subject of public attention, which are critical of his ultimate employer but which are neither shown nor can be presumed to have in any way either impeded the teacher's proper performance of his daily duties in the classroom or to have interfered with the regular operation of the schools generally. In these circumstances we conclude that the interest of the school administration in limiting teachers' opportunities to contribute to public debate is not significantly greater than its interest in limiting a similar contribution by any member of the general public.

IV.

The public interest in having free and unhindered debate on matters of public importance — the core value of the Free Speech Clause of the First Amendment — is so great that it has been held that a State cannot authorize the recovery of damages by a public official for defamatory statements directed at him except when such statements are shown to have been made either with knowledge of their falsity or with reckless disregard for their truth or falsity. *New York Times Co. v. Sullivan*,

376 U.S. 254 (1964). The same test has been applied to suits for invasion of privacy based on false statements where a "matter of public interest" is involved. *Time, Inc. v. Hill*, 385 U.S. 374 (1967). It is therefore perfectly clear that, were appellant a member of the general public, the State's power to afford the appellee Board of Education or its members any legal right to sue him for writing the letter at issue here would be limited by the requirement that the letter be judged by the standard laid down in *New York Times*.

. . . .

In sum, we hold that, in a case such as this, absent proof of false statements knowingly or recklessly made by him, a teacher's exercise of his right to speak on issues of public importance may not furnish the basis for his dismissal from public employment. Since no such showing has been made in this case regarding appellant's letter . . . his dismissal for writing it cannot be upheld and the judgment of the Illinois Supreme Court must, accordingly, be reversed and the case remanded for further proceedings not inconsistent with this opinion.

[The concurrence of Justice Douglas joined by Justice Black is omitted.]

[The dissent of Justice White is omitted.]

GIVHAN v. WESTERN LINE CONSOLIDATED SCHOOL DISTRICT

439 U.S. 410 (1979)

Mr. Justice Rehnquist delivered the opinion of the Court.

Petitioner Bessie Givhan was dismissed from her employment as a junior high English teacher at the end of the 1970-1971 school year. At the time of petitioner's termination, respondent Western Line Consolidated School District was the subject of a desegregation order entered by the United States District Court for the Northern District of Mississippi. Petitioner filed a complaint in intervention in the desegregation action, seeking reinstatement on the dual grounds that nonrenewal of her contract . . . infringed her right of free speech secured by the First and Fourteenth Amendments of the United States Constitution. In an effort to show that its decision was justified, respondent School District introduced evidence of, among other things, a series of private encounters between petitioner and the school principal in which petitioner allegedly made "petty and unreasonable demands" in a manner variously described by the principal as "insulting," "hostile," "loud," and "arrogant." After a two-day bench trial, the District Court held that petitioner's termination had violated the First Amendment. Finding that petitioner had made "demands" on but two occasions and that those demands "were neither 'petty' nor 'unreasonable,' insomuch as all the complaints in question involved employment policies and practices at [the] school which [petitioner] conceived to be racially discriminatory in purpose or effect," the District Court concluded that "the primary reason for the school district's failure to renew [petitioner's] contract was her criticism of the policies and practices of the school district, especially the school to which she was assigned to teach." Accordingly, the District Court held that the dismissal violated petitioner's First Amendment rights, as enunciated in *Perry v.*

Sindermann, 408 U.S. 593 (1972), and *Pickering v. Board of Education*, 391 U.S. 563 (1968), and ordered her reinstatement.

The Court of Appeals for the Fifth Circuit reversed. Although it found the District Court's findings not clearly erroneous, the Court of Appeals concluded that because petitioner had privately expressed her complaints and opinions to the principal, her expression was not protected under the First Amendment. . . . We are unable to agree that private expression of one's views is beyond constitutional protection, and therefore reverse the Court of Appeals' judgment and remand the case so that it may consider the contentions of the parties freed from this erroneous view of the First Amendment.

This Court's decisions . . . do not support the conclusion that a public employee forfeits his protection against governmental abridgment of freedom of speech if he decides to express his views privately rather than publicly. While those cases each arose in the context of a public employee's public expression, the rule to be derived from them is not dependent on that largely coincidental fact.

. . . .

The First Amendment forbids abridgment of the "freedom of speech." Neither the Amendment itself nor our decisions indicate that this freedom is lost to the public employee who arranges to communicate privately with his employer rather than to spread his views before the public. We decline to adopt such a view of the First Amendment.

. . . .

Accordingly, the judgment of the Court of Appeals is vacated insofar as it relates to petitioner, and the case is remanded for further proceedings consistent with this opinion.

CONNICK v. MYERS
461 U.S. 138 (1983)

JUSTICE WHITE delivered the opinion of the Court.

In *Pickering v. Board of Education*, 391 U.S. 563 (1968), we stated that a public employee does not relinquish First Amendment rights to comment on matters of public interest by virtue of government employment. We also recognized that the State's interests as an employer in regulating the speech of its employees "differ significantly from those it possesses in connection with regulation of the speech of the citizenry in general." *Id.*, at 568. The problem, we thought, was arriving "at a balance between the interests of the [employee], as a citizen, in commenting upon matters of public concern and the interest of the State, as an employer, in promoting the efficiency of the public services it performs through its employees." *Ibid.* We return to this problem today and consider whether the First and Fourteenth Amendments prevent the discharge of a state employee for circulating a questionnaire concerning internal office affairs.

I

The respondent, Sheila Myers, was employed as an Assistant District Attorney in New Orleans for five and a half years. She served at the pleasure of petitioner Harry Connick, the District Attorney for Orleans Parish. During this period Myers competently performed her responsibilities of trying criminal cases.

In the early part of October 1980, Myers was informed that she would be transferred to prosecute cases in a different section of the criminal court. Myers was strongly opposed to the proposed transfer and expressed her view to several of her supervisors, including Connick. Despite her objections, on October 6 Myers was notified that she was being transferred. . . .

That night Myers prepared a questionnaire soliciting the views of her fellow staff members concerning office transfer policy, office morale, the need for a grievance committee, the level of confidence in supervisors, and whether employees felt pressured to work in political campaigns. Early the following morning, Myers typed and copied the questionnaire. She also met with Connick who urged her to accept the transfer. She said she would "consider" it. Connick then left the office. Myers then distributed the questionnaire to 15 Assistant District Attorneys. Shortly after noon, Dennis Waldron learned that Myers was distributing the survey. . . . Connick returned to the office and told Myers that she was being terminated because of her refusal to accept the transfer. She was also told that her distribution of the questionnaire was considered an act of insubordination. Connick particularly objected to the question which inquired whether employees "had confidence in and would rely on the word" of various superiors in the office, and to a question concerning pressure to work in political campaigns which he felt would be damaging if discovered by the press.

Myers filed suit under 42 U. S. C. § 1983, contending that her employment was wrongfully terminated because she had exercised her constitutionally protected right of free speech. The District Court agreed, ordered Myers reinstated, and awarded backpay, damages, and attorney's fees. The District Court found that although Connick informed Myers that she was being fired because of her refusal to accept a transfer, the facts showed that the questionnaire was the real reason for her termination. The court then proceeded to hold that Myers' questionnaire involved matters of public concern and that the State had not "clearly demonstrated" that the survey "substantially interfered" with the operations of the District Attorney's office.

Connick appealed to the United States Court of Appeals for the Fifth Circuit, which affirmed on the basis of the District Court's opinion. Connick then sought review in this Court by way of certiorari, which we granted.

II

For at least 15 years, it has been settled that a State cannot condition public employment on a basis that infringes the employee's constitutionally protected interest in freedom of expression. *Keyishian v. Board of Regents*, 385 U.S. 589, 605–606 (1967); *Pickering v. Board of Education*, 391 U.S. 563 (1968); *Perry v. Sindermann*, 408 U.S. 593, 597 (1972); *Branti v. Finkel*, 445 U.S. 507, 515–516

(1980). Our task, as we defined it in *Pickering*, is to seek "a balance between the interests of the [employee], as a citizen, in commenting upon matters of public concern and the interest of the State, as an employer, in promoting the efficiency of the public services it performs through its employees." 391 U.S., at 568. The District Court, and thus the Court of Appeals as well, misapplied our decision in Pickering and consequently, in our view, erred in striking the balance for respondent.

A

The District Court got off on the wrong foot in this case by initially finding that, "[taken] as a whole, the issues presented in the questionnaire relate to the effective functioning of the District Attorney's Office and are matters of public importance and concern." Connick contends at the outset that no balancing of interests is required in this case because Myers' questionnaire concerned only internal office matters and that such speech is not upon a matter of "public concern," as the term was used in *Pickering.* Although we do not agree that Myers' communication in this case was wholly without First Amendment protection, there is much force to Connick's submission. The repeated emphasis in *Pickering* on the right of a public employee "as a citizen, in commenting upon matters of public concern," was not accidental. This language, reiterated in all of *Pickering*'s progeny, reflects both the historical evolvement of the rights of public employees, and the common-sense realization that government offices could not function if every employment decision became a constitutional matter.

For most of this century, the unchallenged dogma was that a public employee had no right to object to conditions placed upon the terms of employment — including those which restricted the exercise of constitutional rights. . . .

The Court cast new light on the matter in a series of cases arising from the widespread efforts in the 1950's and early 1960's to require public employees, particularly teachers, to swear oaths of loyalty to the State and reveal the groups with which they associated. . . .

In all of these cases, the precedents in which *Pickering* is rooted, the invalidated statutes and actions sought to suppress the rights of public employees to participate in public affairs. The issue was whether government employees could be prevented or "chilled" by the fear of discharge from joining political parties and other associations that certain public officials might find "subversive." . . . [T]he Court has frequently reaffirmed that speech on public issues occupies the " 'highest rung of the hierarchy of First Amendment values,' " and is entitled to special protection. *NAACP v. Claiborne Hardware Co.*, 458 U.S. 886, 913 (1982); *Carey v. Brown*, 447 U.S. 455, 467 (1980).

Pickering v. Board of Education, supra, followed from this understanding of the First Amendment. . . .

. . . .

Pickering, its antecedents, and its progeny lead us to conclude that if Myers' questionnaire cannot be fairly characterized as constituting speech on a matter of public concern, it is unnecessary for us to scrutinize the reasons for her discharge.

When employee expression cannot be fairly considered as relating to any matter of political, social, or other concern to the community, government officials should enjoy wide latitude in managing their offices, without intrusive oversight by the judiciary in the name of the First Amendment. . . .

We do not suggest, however, that Myers' speech, even if not touching upon a matter of public concern, is totally beyond the protection of the First Amendment. . . . We in no sense suggest that speech on private matters falls into one of the narrow and well-defined classes of expression which carries so little social value, such as obscenity, that the State can prohibit and punish such expression by all persons in its jurisdiction. *See Chaplinsky v. New Hampshire*, 315 U.S. 568 (1942); *Roth v. United States, supra; New York v. Ferber*, 458 U.S. 747 (1982). . . . We hold only that when a public employee speaks not as a citizen upon matters of public concern, but instead as an employee upon matters only of personal interest, absent the most unusual circumstances, a federal court is not the appropriate forum in which to review the wisdom of a personnel decision taken by a public agency allegedly in reaction to the employee's behavior. . . .

Whether an employee's speech addresses a matter of public concern must be determined by the content, form, and context of a given statement, as revealed by the whole record. In this case, with but one exception, the questions posed by Myers to her co-workers do not fall under the rubric of matters of "public concern." We view the questions pertaining to the confidence and trust that Myers' co-workers possess in various supervisors, the level of office morale, and the need for a grievance committee as mere extensions of Myers' dispute over her transfer to another section of the criminal court. . . . [W]e do not believe these questions are of public import in evaluating the performance of the District Attorney as an elected official. Myers did not seek to inform the public that the District Attorney's Office was not discharging its governmental responsibilities in the investigation and prosecution of criminal cases. Nor did Myers seek to bring to light actual or potential wrongdoing or breach of public trust on the part of Connick and others. Indeed, the questionnaire, if released to the public, would convey no information at all other than the fact that a single employee is upset with the status quo. . . .

To presume that all matters which transpire within a government office are of public concern would mean that virtually every remark — and certainly every criticism directed at a public official — would plant the seed of a constitutional case. . . .

One question in Myers' questionnaire, however, does touch upon a matter of public concern. Question 11 inquires if assistant district attorneys "ever feel pressured to work in political campaigns on behalf of office supported candidates." . . . [W]e believe it apparent that the issue of whether assistant district attorneys are pressured to work in political campaigns is a matter of interest to the community upon which it is essential that public employees be able to speak out freely without fear of retaliatory dismissal.

B

Because one of the questions in Myers' survey touched upon a matter of public concern and contributed to her discharge, we must determine whether Connick was justified in discharging Myers. . . . *Pickering* . . . states . . . that the State's burden in justifying a particular discharge varies depending upon the nature of the employee's expression. Although such particularized balancing is difficult, the courts must reach the most appropriate possible balance of the competing interests.

C

The *Pickering* balance requires full consideration of the government's interest in the effective and efficient fulfillment of its responsibilities to the public. . . .

We agree with the District Court that there is no demonstration here that the questionnaire impeded Myers' ability to perform her responsibilities. The District Court was also correct to recognize that "it is important to the efficient and successful operation of the District Attorney's office for Assistants to maintain close working relationships with their superiors." 507 F.Supp., at 759. Connick's judgment, and apparently also that of his first assistant Dennis Waldron, who characterized Myers' actions as causing a "mini-insurrection," was that Myers' questionnaire was an act of insubordination which interfered with working relationships. When close working relationships are essential to fulfilling public responsibilities, a wide degree of deference to the employer's judgment is appropriate. . . .

. . . .

Also relevant is the manner, time, and place in which the questionnaire was distributed. . . . Here the questionnaire was prepared and distributed at the office; the manner of distribution required not only Myers to leave her work but others to do the same in order that the questionnaire be completed. Although some latitude in when official work is performed is to be allowed when professional employees are involved, and Myers did not violate announced office policy, the fact that Myers, unlike Pickering, exercised her rights to speech at the office supports Connick's fears that the functioning of his office was endangered.

Finally, the context in which the dispute arose is also significant. This is not a case where an employee, out of purely academic interest, circulated a questionnaire so as to obtain useful research. Myers acknowledges that it is no coincidence that the questionnaire followed upon the heels of the transfer notice. When employee speech concerning office policy arises from an employment dispute concerning the very application of that policy to the speaker, additional weight must be given to the supervisor's view that the employee has threatened the authority of the employer to run the office. . . .

III

Myers' questionnaire touched upon matters of public concern in only a most limited sense; her survey, in our view, is most accurately characterized as an employee grievance concerning internal office policy. The limited First Amendment interest involved here does not require that Connick tolerate action which he reasonably believed would disrupt the office, undermine his authority, and destroy close working relationships. Myers' discharge therefore did not offend the First Amendment. . . .

Our holding today is grounded in our longstanding recognition that the First Amendment's primary aim is the full protection of speech upon issues of public concern, as well as the practical realities involved in the administration of a government office. Although today the balance is struck for the government, this is no defeat for the First Amendment. For it would indeed be a Pyrrhic victory for the great principles of free expression if the Amendment's safeguarding of a public employee's right, as a citizen, to participate in discussions concerning public affairs were confused with the attempt to constitutionalize the employee grievance that we see presented here. The judgment of the Court of Appeals is

Reversed.

WATERS v. CHURCHILL
511 U.S. 661 (1994)

JUSTICE O'CONNOR announced the judgment of the Court and delivered an opinion, in which THE CHIEF JUSTICE, JUSTICE SOUTER, and JUSTICE GINSBERG join.

In *Connick v. Myers*, 461 U.S. 138 (1983), we set forth a test for determining whether speech by a government employee may, consistently with the First Amendment, serve as a basis for disciplining or discharging that employee. In this case, we decide whether the *Connick* test should be applied to what the government employer thought was said, or to what the trier of fact ultimately determines to have been said.

I

This case arises out of a conversation that respondent Cheryl Churchill had on January 16, 1987, with Melanie Perkins-Graham. Both Churchill and Perkins-Graham were nurses working at McDonough District Hospital; Churchill was in the obstetrics department, and Perkins-Graham was considering transferring to that department. The conversation took place at work during a dinner break. Petitioners heard about it and fired Churchill, allegedly because of it. There is, however, a dispute about what Churchill actually said, and therefore about whether petitioners were constitutionally permitted to fire Churchill for her statements.

The conversation was overheard in part by two other nurses, Mary Lou Ballew and Jean Welty, and by Dr. Thomas Koch, the clinical head of obstetrics. A few days later, Ballew told Cynthia Waters, Churchill's supervisor, about the incident. According to Ballew, Churchill took " 'the cross trainee into the kitchen for . . . at least 20 minutes to talk about [Waters] and how bad things are in [obstetrics] in general.' " Ballew said that Churchill's statements led Perkins-Graham to no longer be interested in switching to the department.

Shortly after this, Waters met with Ballew a second time for confirmation of Ballew's initial report. Ballew said that Churchill "was knocking the department" and that "in general [Churchill] was saying what a bad place [obstetrics] is to work." Ballew said she heard Churchill say Waters "was trying to find reasons to fire her." Ballew also said Churchill described a patient complaint for which Waters had supposedly wrongly blamed Churchill.

Waters, together with petitioner Kathleen Davis, the hospital's vice president of nursing, also met with Perkins-Graham, who told them that Churchill "had indeed said unkind and inappropriate negative things about [Waters]." Also, according to Perkins-Graham, Churchill mentioned a negative evaluation that Waters had given Churchill, which arose out of an incident in which Waters had cited Churchill for an insubordinate remark. The evaluation stated that Churchill " 'promotes an unpleasant atmosphere and hinders constructive communication and cooperation,' " and " 'exhibits negative behavior towards [Waters] and [Waters'] leadership through her actions and body language' "; the evaluation said Churchill's work was otherwise satisfactory. Churchill allegedly told Perkins-Graham that she and Waters had discussed the evaluation, and that Waters "wanted to wipe the slate clean . . . but [Churchill thought] this wasn't possible." Churchill also allegedly told Perkins-Graham "that just in general things were not good in OB and hospital administration was responsible." Churchill specifically mentioned Davis, saying Davis "was ruining MDH." Perkins-Graham told Waters that she knew Davis and Waters "could not tolerate that kind of negativism."

Churchill's version of the conversation is different. For several months, Churchill had been concerned about the hospital's "cross-training" policy, under which nurses from one department could work in another when their usual location was overstaffed. Churchill believed this policy threatened patient care because it was designed not to train nurses but to cover staff shortages, and she had complained about this to Davis and Waters. According to Churchill, the conversation with Perkins-Graham primarily concerned the crosstraining policy. Churchill denies that she said some of what Ballew and Perkins-Graham allege she said. She does admit she criticized Davis, saying her staffing policies threatened to "ruin" the hospital because they " 'seemed to be impeding nursing care.' " She claims she actually defended Waters and encouraged Perkins-Graham to transfer to obstetrics.

Koch's and Welty's recollections of the conversation match Churchill's. Davis and Waters, however, never talked to Koch or Welty about this, and they did not talk to Churchill until the time they told her she was fired. Moreover, Churchill claims, Ballew was biased against Churchill because of an incident in which Ballew apparently made an error and Churchill had to cover for her.

After she was discharged, Churchill filed an internal grievance. The president of the hospital, petitioner Stephen Hopper, met with Churchill in regard to this and heard her side of the story. He then reviewed Waters' and Davis' written reports of their conversations with Ballew and Perkins-Graham, and had Bernice Magin, the hospital's vice president of human resources, interview Ballew one more time. After considering all this, Hopper rejected Churchill's grievance.

Churchill then sued under Rev. Stat. § 1979, 42 U.S.C. § 1983, claiming that the firing violated her First Amendment rights because her speech was protected under *Connick v. Myers*, 461 U.S. 138 (1983). In May 1991, the United States District Court for the Central District of Illinois granted summary judgment to petitioners.

The court held that neither version of the conversation was protected under *Connick*: Regardless of whose story was accepted, the speech was not on a matter of public concern, and even if it was on a matter of public concern, its potential for disruption nonetheless stripped it of First Amendment protection. Therefore, the court held, management could fire Churchill for the conversation with impunity.

The United States Court of Appeals for the Seventh Circuit reversed. The court held that Churchill's speech, viewed in the light most favorable to her, was protected speech under the *Connick* test: It was on a matter of public concern — "the hospital's [alleged] violation of state nursing regulations as well as the quality and level of nursing care it provides its patients" — and it was not disruptive.

The court also concluded that the inquiry must turn on what the speech actually was, not on what the employer thought it was. "If the employer chooses to discharge the employee without sufficient knowledge of her protected speech as a result of an inadequate investigation into the employee's conduct," the court held, "the employer runs the risk of eventually being required to remedy any wrongdoing whether it was deliberate or accidental."

We granted certiorari to resolve a conflict among the Circuits on this issue.

II

A

There is no dispute in this case about when speech by a government employee is protected by the First Amendment: To be protected, the speech must be on a matter of public concern, and the employee's interest in expressing herself on this matter must not be outweighed by any injury the speech could cause to " 'the interest of the State, as an employer, in promoting the efficiency of the public services it performs through its employees.' " *Connick, supra*, 461 U.S. at 142 (quoting *Pickering v. Board of Ed. of Township High School Dist. 205, Will Cty.*, 391 U.S. 563, 568(1968)). It is also agreed that it is the court's task to apply the *Connick* test to the facts.

The dispute is over how the factual basis for applying the test — what the speech was, in what tone it was delivered, what the listener's reactions were — is to be determined. Should the court apply the *Connick* test to the speech as the government employer found it to be, or should it ask the jury to determine the facts for itself? The Court of Appeals held that the employer's factual conclusions were irrelevant, and that the jury should engage in its own factfinding. Petitioners argue that the employer's factual conclusions should be dispositive. Respondents take a middle course: They suggest that the court should accept the employer's factual conclusions, but only if those conclusions were arrived at reasonably something they say did not happen here.

We agree that it is important to ensure not only that the substantive First Amendment standards are sound, but also that they are applied through reliable procedures. . . .

. . . .

We have never set forth a general test to determine when a procedural safeguard is required by the First Amendment — just as we have never set forth a general test to determine what constitutes a compelling state interest, or what categories of speech are so lacking in value that they fall outside the protection of the First Amendment, or many other matters — and we do not purport to do so now. . . .

Accordingly, all we say today is that the propriety of a proposed procedure must turn on the particular context in which the question arises — on the cost of the procedure and the relative magnitude and constitutional significance of the risks it would decrease and increase. And to evaluate these factors here we have to return to the issue we dealt with in *Connick* and in the cases that came before it: What is it about the government's role as employer that gives it a freer hand in regulating the speech of its employees than it has in regulating the speech of the public at large?

B

We have never explicitly answered this question, though we have always assumed that its premise is correct — that the government as employer indeed has far broader powers than does the government as sovereign. *See, e. g., Pickering*, 391 U.S. at 568; *Connick*, 461 U.S. at 147.

. . . .

Government employee speech must be treated differently with regard to procedural requirements as well. For example, speech restrictions must generally precisely define the speech they target. Yet surely a public employer may, consistently with the First Amendment, prohibit its employees from being "rude to customers," a standard almost certainly too vague when applied to the public at large.

Likewise, we have consistently given greater deference to government predictions of harm used to justify restriction of employee speech than to predictions of harm used to justify restrictions on the speech of the public at large. . . . [W]e have given substantial weight to government employers' reasonable predictions of disruption, even when the speech involved is on a matter of public concern, and even though when the government is acting as sovereign our review of legislative predictions of harm is considerably less deferential. . . .

. . . .

The key to First Amendment analysis of government employment decisions, then, is this: The government's interest in achieving its goals as effectively and efficiently as possible is elevated from a relatively subordinate interest when it acts as sovereign to a significant one when it acts as employer. The government cannot restrict the speech of the public at large just in the name of efficiency. But where the government is employing someone for the very purpose of effectively achieving its goals, such restrictions may well be appropriate.

C

1

The Court of Appeals' decision, we believe, gives insufficient weight to the government's interest in efficient employment decisionmaking. In other First Amendment contexts the need to safeguard possibly protected speech may indeed outweigh the government's efficiency interests. But where the government is acting as employer, its efficiency concerns should, as we discussed above, be assigned a greater value.

The problem with the Court of Appeals' approach — under which the facts to which the *Connick* test is applied are determined by the judicial factfinder — is that it would force the government employer to come to its factual conclusions through procedures that substantially mirror the evidentiary rules used in court. The government manager would have to ask not what conclusions she, as an experienced professional, can draw from the circumstances, but rather what conclusions a jury would later draw. If she relies on hearsay, or on what she knows about the accused employee's character, she must be aware that this evidence might not be usable in court. If she knows one party is, in her personal experience, more credible than another, she must realize that the jury will not share that personal experience. If she thinks the alleged offense is so egregious that it is proper to discipline the accused employee even though the evidence is ambiguous, she must consider that a jury might decide the other way.

But employers, public and private, often do rely on hearsay, on past similar conduct, on their personal knowledge of people's credibility, and on other factors that the judicial process ignores. . . . What works best in a judicial proceeding may not be appropriate in the employment context. . . .

It is true that these practices involve some risk of erroneously punishing protected speech. The government may certainly choose to adopt other practices, by law or by contract. But we do not believe that the First Amendment requires it to do so. Government employers should be allowed to use personnel procedures that differ from the evidentiary rules used by courts, without fear that these differences will lead to liability.

2

On the other hand, we do not believe that the court must apply the *Connick* test only to the facts as the employer thought them to be, without considering the reasonableness of the employer's conclusions. . . . It is necessary that the decisionmaker reach its conclusion about what was said in good faith, rather than as a pretext; but it does not follow that good faith is sufficient. . . .

We think employer decisionmaking will not be unduly burdened by having courts look to the facts as the employer reasonably found them to be. It may be unreasonable, for example, for the employer to come to a conclusion based on no evidence at all. Likewise, it may be unreasonable for an employer to act based on extremely weak evidence when strong evidence is clearly available . . . .

. . . .

Of course, there will often be situations in which reasonable employers would disagree about who is to be believed, or how much investigation needs to be done, or how much evidence is needed to come to a particular conclusion. In those situations, many different courses of action will necessarily be reasonable. Only procedures outside the range of what a reasonable manager would use may be condemned as unreasonable.

. . . .

III

Applying the foregoing to this case, it is clear that if petitioners really did believe Perkins-Graham's and Ballew's story, and fired Churchill because of it, they must win. Their belief, based on the investigation they conducted, would have been entirely reasonable. After getting the initial report from Ballew, who overheard the conversation, Waters and Davis approached and interviewed Perkins-Graham, and then interviewed Ballew again for confirmation. In response to Churchill's grievance, Hopper met directly with Churchill to hear her side of the story, and instructed Magin to interview Ballew one more time. Management can spend only so much of their time on any one employment decision. . . .

And under the Connick test, Churchill's speech as reported by Perkins-Graham and Ballew was unprotected. Even if Churchill's criticism of cross-training reported by Perkins-Graham and Ballew was speech on a matter of public concern — something we need not decide — the potential disruptiveness of the speech as reported was enough to outweigh whatever First Amendment value it might have had. . . .

. . . .

Nonetheless, we agree with the Court of Appeals that the District Court erred in granting summary judgment in petitioners' favor. Though Davis and Waters would have been justified in firing Churchill for the statements outlined above, there remains the question whether Churchill was actually fired because of those statements, or because of something else.

Churchill has produced enough evidence to create a material issue of disputed fact about petitioners' actual motivation. Churchill had criticized the cross-training policy in the past; management had exhibited some sensitivity about the criticisms; Churchill pointed to some other conduct by hospital management that, if viewed in the light most favorable to her, would show that they were hostile to her because of her criticisms. A reasonable factfinder might therefore, on this record, conclude that petitioners actually fired Churchill not because of the disruptive things she said to Perkins-Graham, but because of nondisruptive statements about cross-training that they thought she may have made in the same conversation, or because of other statements she may have made earlier. If this is so, then the court will have to determine whether those statements were protected speech, a different matter than the one before us now.

. . . [W]e vacate the judgment of the Court of Appeals and remand the case for further proceedings consistent with this opinion.

GARCETTI v. CEBALLOS
547 U.S. 410 (2006)

Justice Kennedy delivered the opinion of the Court.

It is well settled that "a State cannot condition public employment on a basis that infringes the employee's constitutionally protected interest in freedom of expression." *Connick v. Myers*, 461 U.S. 138, 142 (1983). The question presented by the instant case is whether the First Amendment protects a government employee from discipline based on speech made pursuant to the employee's official duties.

I

Respondent Richard Ceballos has been employed since 1989 as a deputy district attorney for the Los Angeles County District Attorney's Office. During the period relevant to this case, Ceballos was a calendar deputy in the office's Pomona branch, and in this capacity he exercised certain supervisory responsibilities over other lawyers. In February 2000, a defense attorney contacted Ceballos about a pending criminal case. The defense attorney said there were inaccuracies in an affidavit used to obtain a critical search warrant. The attorney informed Ceballos that he had filed a motion to traverse, or challenge, the warrant, but he also wanted Ceballos to review the case. According to Ceballos, it was not unusual for defense attorneys to ask calendar deputies to investigate aspects of pending cases.

After examining the affidavit and visiting the location it described, Ceballos determined the affidavit contained serious misrepresentations. The affidavit called a long driveway what Ceballos thought should have been referred to as a separate roadway. Ceballos also questioned the affidavit's statement that tire tracks led from a stripped-down truck to the premises covered by the warrant. His doubts arose from his conclusion that the roadway's composition in some places made it difficult or impossible to leave visible tire tracks.

Ceballos spoke on the telephone to the warrant affiant, a deputy sheriff from the Los Angeles County Sheriff's Department, but he did not receive a satisfactory explanation for the perceived inaccuracies. He relayed his findings to his supervisors, petitioners Carol Najera and Frank Sundstedt, and followed up by preparing a disposition memorandum. The memo explained Ceballos' concerns and recommended dismissal of the case. On March 2, 2000, Ceballos submitted the memo to Sundstedt for his review. A few days later, Ceballos presented Sundstedt with another memo, this one describing a second telephone conversation between Ceballos and the warrant affiant.

Based on Ceballos' statements, a meeting was held to discuss the affidavit. Attendees included Ceballos, Sundstedt, and Najera, as well as the warrant affiant and other employees from the sheriff's department. The meeting allegedly became heated, with one lieutenant sharply criticizing Ceballos for his handling of the case.

Despite Ceballos' concerns, Sundstedt decided to proceed with the prosecution, pending disposition of the defense motion to traverse. The trial court held a hearing on the motion. Ceballos was called by the defense and recounted his observations about the affidavit, but the trial court rejected the challenge to the warrant.

Ceballos claims that in the aftermath of these events he was subjected to a series of retaliatory employment actions. The actions included reassignment from his calendar deputy position to a trial deputy position, transfer to another courthouse, and denial of a promotion. Ceballos initiated an employment grievance, but the grievance was denied based on a finding that he had not suffered any retaliation. Unsatisfied, Ceballos sued in the United States District Court for the Central District of California, asserting, as relevant here, a claim under Rev. Stat. § 1979, 42 U.S.C. § 1983. He alleged petitioners violated the First and Fourteenth Amendments by retaliating against him based on his memo of March 2.

Petitioners responded that no retaliatory actions were taken against Ceballos and that all the actions of which he complained were explained by legitimate reasons such as staffing needs. They further contended that, in any event, Ceballos' memo was not protected speech under the First Amendment. Petitioners moved for summary judgment, and the District Court granted their motion. Noting that Ceballos wrote his memo pursuant to his employment duties, the court concluded he was not entitled to First Amendment protection for the memo's contents.

The Court of Appeals for the Ninth Circuit reversed, holding that "Ceballos's allegations of wrongdoing in the memorandum constitute protected speech under the First Amendment." In reaching its conclusion the court looked to the First Amendment analysis set forth in *Pickering v. Board of Educ.*, 391 U.S. 563 (1968), and Connick, supra. Connick instructs courts to begin by considering whether the expressions in question were made by the speaker "as a citizen upon matters of public concern." *See id.*, at 146–147. The Court of Appeals determined that Ceballos' memo, which recited what he thought to be governmental misconduct, was "inherently a matter of public concern." . . .

Having concluded that Ceballos' memo satisfied the public-concern requirement, the Court of Appeals proceeded to balance Ceballos' interest in his speech against his supervisors' interest in responding to it. *See Pickering, supra*, at 568. The court struck the balance in Ceballos' favor, noting that petitioners "failed even to suggest disruption or inefficiency in the workings of the District Attorney's Office" as a result of the memo. The court further concluded that Ceballos' First Amendment rights were clearly established and that petitioners' actions were not objectively reasonable.

. . . .

We granted certiorari and we now reverse.

II

. . . .

Pickering and the cases decided in its wake identify two inquiries to guide interpretation of the constitutional protections accorded to public employee speech. The first requires determining whether the employee spoke as a citizen on a matter of public concern. If the answer is no, the employee has no First Amendment cause of action based on his or her employer's reaction to the speech. *See Connick, supra*, at 147. If the answer is yes, then the possibility of a First Amendment claim arises. The question becomes whether the relevant government entity had an adequate justification for treating the employee differently from any other member of the general public. *See Pickering*, 391 U.S., at 568. This consideration reflects the importance of the relationship between the speaker's expressions and employment. A government entity has broader discretion to restrict speech when it acts in its role as employer, but the restrictions it imposes must be directed at speech that has some potential to affect the entity's operations.

. . . .

The Court's decisions, then, have sought both to promote the individual and societal interests that are served when employees speak as citizens on matters of public concern and to respect the needs of government employers attempting to perform their important public functions. Underlying our cases has been the premise that while the First Amendment invests public employees with certain rights, it does not empower them to "constitutionalize the employee grievance." *Connick*, 461 U.S., at 154.

III

With these principles in mind we turn to the instant case. Respondent Ceballos believed the affidavit used to obtain a search warrant contained serious misrepresentations. He conveyed his opinion and recommendation in a memo to his supervisor. That Ceballos expressed his views inside his office, rather than publicly, is not dispositive. Employees in some cases may receive First Amendment protection for expressions made at work. *See, e.g., Givhan v. Western Line Consol. School Dist.*, 439 U.S. 410, 414. . . .

The memo concerned the subject matter of Ceballos' employment, but this, too, is nondispositive. The First Amendment protects some expressions related to the speaker's job. *See, e.g., Givhan, supra*, at 414. . . .

The controlling factor in Ceballos' case is that his expressions were made pursuant to his duties as a calendar deputy. That consideration — the fact that Ceballos spoke as a prosecutor fulfilling a responsibility to advise his supervisor about how best to proceed with a pending case — distinguishes Ceballos' case from those in which the First Amendment provides protection against discipline. We hold that when public employees make statements pursuant to their official duties, the employees are not speaking as citizens for First Amendment purposes, and the Constitution does not insulate their communications from employer discipline.

Ceballos wrote his disposition memo because that is part of what he, as a calendar deputy, was employed to do. It is immaterial whether he experienced some personal gratification from writing the memo; his First Amendment rights do not depend on his job satisfaction. The significant point is that the memo was written pursuant to Ceballos' official duties. Restricting speech that owes its existence to a public employee's professional responsibilities does not infringe any liberties the employee might have enjoyed as a private citizen. It simply reflects the exercise of employer control over what the employer itself has commissioned or created. Contrast, for example, the expressions made by the speaker in Pickering, whose letter to the newspaper had no official significance and bore similarities to letters submitted by numerous citizens every day.

Ceballos did not act as a citizen when he went about conducting his daily professional activities, such as supervising attorneys, investigating charges, and preparing filings. In the same way he did not speak as a citizen by writing a memo that addressed the proper disposition of a pending criminal case. When he went to work and performed the tasks he was paid to perform, Ceballos acted as a government employee. . . .

This result is consistent with our precedents' attention to the potential societal value of employee speech. Refusing to recognize First Amendment claims based on government employees' work product does not prevent them from participating in public debate. The employees retain the prospect of constitutional protection for their contributions to the civic discourse. This prospect of protection, however, does not invest them with a right to perform their jobs however they see fit.

Our holding likewise is supported by the emphasis of our precedents on affording government employers sufficient discretion to manage their operations. Employers have heightened interests in controlling speech made by an employee in his or her professional capacity. Official communications have official consequences, creating a need for substantive consistency and clarity. . . . Ceballos' memo is illustrative. It demanded the attention of his supervisors and led to a heated meeting with employees from the sheriff's department. If Ceballos' superiors thought his memo was inflammatory or misguided, they had the authority to take proper corrective action.

Ceballos' proposed contrary rule, adopted by the Court of Appeals, would commit state and federal courts to a new, permanent, and intrusive role, mandating judicial oversight of communications between and among government employees and their superiors in the course of official business. This displacement of managerial discretion by judicial supervision finds no support in our precedents. . . .

. . . .

Proper application of our precedents thus leads to the conclusion that the First Amendment does not prohibit managerial discipline based on an employee's expressions made pursuant to official responsibilities. Because Ceballos' memo falls into this category, his allegation of unconstitutional retaliation must fail.

. . . .

Second, Justice Souter [writing in dissent] suggests today's decision may have important ramifications for academic freedom, at least as a constitutional value. There is some argument that expression related to academic scholarship or classroom instruction implicates additional constitutional interests that are not fully accounted for by this Court's customary employee-speech jurisprudence. We need not, and for that reason do not, decide whether the analysis we conduct today would apply in the same manner to a case involving speech related to scholarship or teaching.

IV

. . . .

The judgment of the Court of Appeals is reversed, and the case is remanded for proceedings consistent with this opinion.

JUSTICE SOUTER, with whom JUSTICE STEVENS and JUSTICE GINSBURG join, dissenting.

. . . .

This ostensible domain [of speech] beyond the pale of the First Amendment [created by the majority] is spacious enough to include even the teaching of a public university professor, and I have to hope that today's majority does not mean to imperil First Amendment protection of academic freedom in public colleges and universities, whose teachers necessarily speak and write "pursuant to . . . official duties." *See Grutter v. Bollinger*, 539 U.S. 306, 329 (2003) ("We have long recognized that, given the important purpose of public education and the expansive freedoms of speech and thought associated with the university environment, universities occupy a special niche in our constitutional tradition"); *Keyishian v. Board of Regents of Univ. of State of N. Y.*, 385 U.S. 589, 603 (1967) ("Our Nation is deeply committed to safeguarding academic freedom, which is of transcendent value to all of us and not merely to the teachers concerned. That freedom is therefore a special concern of the First Amendment, which does not tolerate laws that cast a pall of orthodoxy over the classroom. 'The vigilant protection of constitutional freedoms is nowhere more vital than in the community of American schools' " (quoting *Shelton v. Tucker*, 364 U.S. 479, 487 (1960))); *Sweezy v. New Hampshire*, 354 U.S. 234, 250 (1957) (a governmental enquiry into the contents of a scholar's lectures at a state university "unquestionably was an invasion of [his] liberties in the areas of academic freedom and political expression — areas in which government should be extremely reticent to tread").

. . . .

NOTES

1. Justice Souter, writing in dissent, saw no reason to create a new distinction in the *Pickering* line of cases for a set of facts like those in *Garcetti*:

> The difference between a case like *Givhan* and this one is that the subject of Ceballos's speech fell within the scope of his job responsibilities, whereas choosing personnel was not what the teacher was hired to do. The effect of the majority's constitutional line between these two cases, then, is that a *Givhan* schoolteacher is protected when complaining to the principal about hiring policy, but a school personnel officer would not be if he protested that the principal disapproved of hiring minority job applicants. This is an odd place to draw a distinction, and while necessary judicial line-drawing sometimes looks arbitrary, any distinction obliges a court to justify its choice. Here, there is no adequate justification for the majority's

> line categorically denying *Pickering* protection to any speech uttered "pursuant to . . . official duties."
>
> As all agree, the qualified speech protection embodied in *Pickering* balancing resolves the tension between individual and public interests in the speech, on the one hand, and the government's interest in operating efficiently without distraction or embarrassment by talkative or headline-grabbing employees. The need for a balance hardly disappears when an employee speaks on matters his job requires him to address; rather, it seems obvious that the individual and public value of such speech is no less, and may well be greater, when the employee speaks pursuant to his duties in addressing a subject he knows intimately for the very reason that it falls within his duties.

Garcetti, 547 U.S. at 430–31. Instead, Souter thought a slight adjustment to the *Pickering* balancing test would suffice in *Garcetti*-like cases.

> Two reasons in particular make me think an adjustment using the basic *Pickering* balancing scheme is perfectly feasible here. First, the extent of the government's legitimate authority over subjects of speech required by a public job can be recognized in advance by setting in effect a minimum heft for comments with any claim to outweigh it. Thus, the risks to the government are great enough for us to hold from the outset that an employee commenting on subjects in the course of duties should not prevail on balance unless he speaks on a matter of unusual importance and satisfies high standards of responsibility in the way he does it. The examples I have already given indicate the eligible subject matter, and it is fair to say that only comment on official dishonesty, deliberately unconstitutional action, other serious wrongdoing, or threats to health and safety can weigh out in an employee's favor. If promulgation of this standard should fail to discourage meritless actions premised on 42 U.S.C. § 1983 . . . before they get filed, the standard itself would sift them out at the summary-judgment stage.

Id. at 434–35.

Does Justice Souter underestimate the ability of government employees to disrupt the workplace if granted protection for statements made pursuant to "official duties"?

2. Concern that Justice Souter's standard was too lenient led Justice Breyer to write his own dissent, in which he shared the majority's conviction "that the Constitution does not seek to displac[e] . . . managerial discretion by judicial supervision." *Id.* at 446 (internal quotations marks and citation omitted).

> Nonetheless, there may well be circumstances with special demand for constitutional protection of the speech at issue, where governmental justifications may be limited, and where administrable standards seem readily available — to the point where the majority's fears of department management by lawsuit are misplaced. In such an instance, I believe that courts should apply the *Pickering* standard, even though the government

> employee speaks upon matters of public concern in the course of his ordinary duties.
>
> This is such a case. . . . The facts present two special circumstances that together justify First Amendment review.
>
> First, the speech at issue is professional speech — the speech of a lawyer. Such speech is subject to independent regulation by canons of the profession. Those canons provide an obligation to speak in certain instances. And where that is so, the government's own interest in forbidding that speech is diminished. . . . The objective specificity and public availability of the profession's canons also help to diminish the risk that the courts will improperly interfere with the government's necessary authority to manage its work.
>
> Second, the Constitution itself here imposes speech obligations upon the government's professional employee. A prosecutor has a constitutional obligation to learn of, to preserve, and to communicate with the defense about exculpatory and impeachment evidence in the government's possession. . . .
>
> Where professional and special constitutional obligations are both present, the need to protect the employee's speech is augmented, the need for broad government authority to control that speech is likely diminished, and administrable standards are quite likely available. Hence, I would find that the Constitution mandates special protection of employee speech in such circumstances. Thus I would apply the *Pickering* balancing test here.

Id. at 446–47. Are the standards enunciated by Justices Souter and Breyer workable for government employers? Are most managers equipped with the ability to gauge and weigh employee speech in the ways these Justices recommend?

3. The *Garcetti* opinion unleashed a wave of commentary, much of it negative, and most of it raising the specter of the opinion's potentially disastrous effects on academic freedom. At the root of the problem, according to one line of criticism, was the Court's use of categorical balancing to upset the analytical framework established in the *Pickering* line of cases.

> In ruling that the job-required speech of public employees is not protected from employer discipline by the First Amendment, the Court used what has evolved into a conventional approach: categorical balancing. Categorical balancing, as distinct from the ad hoc balancing of the *Pickering-Connick* test, has been used by the Court to deny First Amendment protection to certain categories of speech, e.g., fighting words, obscenity, and child pornography, all of which are considered outside the scope of the First Amendment. On the other hand, categorical balancing has also been used to expand the protection of the First Amendment to include speech previously considered to be outside its scope, e.g., subversive advocacy, defamation, and commercial speech. . . .
>
> What the Court does when it balances categorically is weigh what it considers to be the relevant interests, social and individual, at a fairly high

level of generality, and then by balancing those interests, arrive at a generally applicable rule to be applied in later cases without further balancing. Categorical balancing is thought to have the advantages of predictability (through rules), as well as the flexibility inherent in the balancing process.

The recent trend in the Court, with the unique exception of child pornography, has been to use categorical balancing to expand First Amendment-protected speech. *Garcetti* is an obvious departure from this trend, but it is also a departure in another way. When the Supreme Court determines that certain categories of speech are unprotected by the First Amendment, a crucial aspect of its categorical balancing is its determination that the affected speech has little or no intrinsic First Amendment value. In marked contrast, *Garcetti* did not question the First Amendment value of job-required public employee speech because the speech was highly valuable and relevant to self-government. The *Garcetti* Court did, however, assert that the First Amendment value of job-related speech is trumped because of the government's overwhelming interest in workplace efficiency as employer. To put this another way, even job-required speech that is clearly a matter of public concern and that is required professionally — perhaps constitutionally — is not protected from employer discipline by the First Amendment because it is not considered the speech of a citizen.

Garcetti thus resembles [the Court's] categorical approach to child pornography. Child pornography may indeed have serious social, artistic, or medical value. Nevertheless, this First Amendment value is significantly outweighed by the adverse impact child pornography has on children. Similarly, job-required public employee speech often deals with matters of public concern and has serious First Amendment value because it implicates self-government. Yet the government interest in the efficient operation of the government workplace, which according to *Garcetti* includes both minimizing the displacement of managerial discretion by judicial intervention that applies ad hoc balancing and promoting federalism and separation of powers, is thought to significantly outweigh any First Amendment value.

. . . .

Garcetti described the theoretical underpinning of *Pickering-Connick* as the distinction between the speech of a citizen (who happens to be a public employee) on a matter of public concern, and all other public employee speech. Pickering itself is a good example of a case in which it was relatively easy to conclude that the public employee spoke as a citizen because he wrote a letter to a newspaper.

On the other hand, sometimes the content, form, and context of a public employee's speech indicate that it is speech on a matter of private rather than public concern, in which case the First Amendment is inapplicable to employer discipline. *Connick* is a good example of such a case because the public employee complained about her own employment situation. In *Garcetti*, the Court used this distinction to reach its conclusion that

> job-required public employee speech is by definition not the speech of a citizen, and therefore not protected by the First Amendment from employer discipline, even if it addresses a matter of public concern.
>
> *Garcetti's* reasoning thereby turned the *Pickering-Connick* test on its head by privileging employment status over the subject matter of public employee speech. What was previously crucial for First Amendment protection was not the status of the public employee as a citizen, but rather the subject matter of the speech and its promotion of self-government.

Sheldon H. Nahmod, *Public Employee Speech, Categorical Balancing and § 1983: A Critique of Garcetti v. Ceballos*, 42 U. Rich. L. Rev. 561, 569–74 (2008).*

The implications of the majority's reasoning in *Garcetti* on professors at public postsecondary institutions could be profound.

> This possibility of an overbroad application of the government speech doctrine in the public employee speech setting is intimately connected to the issue of academic freedom. Because public elementary, secondary, and higher education teachers are public employees who are paid to speak, *Garcetti* could be read for the proposition that little if any speech uttered in the classroom by a public school teacher or professor is protected from employer discipline by the First Amendment. This reading, however, calls into question prior statements by the Supreme Court that academic freedom is protected by the First Amendment, particularly at the university level.
>
> The Court's unsurprising response to this possible reading is to avoid the subject, because as it correctly observes, the facts in *Garcetti* do not expressly raise the issue of academic freedom. . . . However, the very difficult open question, which cannot be avoided by the Court for very long, is how to square *Garcetti's* categorical balancing approach insulating job-required public employee speech with First Amendment protection of academic freedom.

Id. at 583–84.

4. Perhaps, however, concern about *Garcetti's* impact on academic freedom are overdrawn. Consider this:

> The academic speech context seems unique for several reasons. Most obvious among them is Justice Kennedy's explicit reservation of that issue in his *Garcetti* opinion. . . .
>
> The Court's declared rationale for deferring that issue in fact sharply understates the importance of its prior treatment of academic speech. Time and again, in cases involving legislative inquiries, loyalty oaths, challenges to admissions actions, and the myriad other government constraints and intrusions, the justices have consistently recognized the distinctive (indeed unique) nature of the university setting and have paid unusual deference to

---

the faculties who govern the policies of institutions of higher learning.

> If academic judgments on such matters as these are entitled to an exceptional level of judicial deference, as clearly they are, then the case for protecting [professorial] speech . . . seems even more clear, in substantial part for the very reasons the *Garcetti* majority invoked in diluting the protections available to the general run of government workers. When it comes, for example, to "official duties," the clarity with which a court can determine the responsibilities of an assistant district attorney . . . simply does not apply to college professors.
>
> Sources for so basic a distinction are not hard to find. When the Supreme Court ruled in 1980 that the National Labor Relations Board lacked jurisdiction over faculties at research universities, it reminded us how fundamentally different are the roles and responsibilities of that group from those of the rest of the workforce. In fact, the *Yeshiva* opinion noted that "the faculty . . . exercise authority which in any other context unquestionably would be managerial," adding that "their authority in academic matters is absolute."
>
> To the extent that an industrial analogy helped at all, said the *Yeshiva* majority, "the faculty determines within each school the product to be produced, the terms upon which it will be offered, and the customers who will be served." Other contexts provide reinforcing statements. To cite just one very different example, a Sixth Circuit ruling that upheld against administrative sanction a state university professor's autonomy with respect to the evaluation and grading of student performance conveyed comparable recognition of the uniqueness of the professorial role. In such a setting, any effort to define the "official duties" of a college teacher seems perilous at best and meaningless at worst.

Robert M. O'Neil, *Academic Speech in the Post-*Garcetti *Environment*, 7 FIRST AMEND. L. REV. 1, 17–18 (2008).* Given the rather amorphous language in the Court's opinions regarding academic freedom and the role of academics in society, is it an overstatement to argue that *Garcetti* simply does not apply to academic speech?

5. The American Association of University Professors, for its part, has expressed grave concerns about *Garcetti*'s potential impact on academic freedom. The organization has gone so far as to establish an "awareness and action campaign" called "Speak Up, Speak Out: Protect the Faculty Voice." *See Speak Up, Speak Out: Protect the Faculty Voice*, AM. ASS'N OF UNIV. PROFS., *available at* http://www.aaup.org/AAUP/programs/protectvoice/. As part of the campaign, the AAUP drafted a report on *Garcetti*. The executive summary reads in part:

> The subcommittee report notes the irony that, based on the broad definition of "official duties" employed in these post-*Garcetti* rulings, only faculty speech on topics beyond the speaker's expertise may be constitu-

> tionally protected and that there now may exist a "negative or inverse correlation between the scope of a professor's (or a faculty's) role in shared governance and the breadth of potential protection for expressive activity. . . . In brief, as the cases stand now, one could argue that the less of a stake you have in your institution's shared governance, the freer you are (as a First Amendment matter) to criticize how it is governed, and vice versa."

AM. ASS'N OF UNIV. PROFS., PROTECTING AN INDEPENDENT FACULTY VOICE: ACADEMIC FREEDOM AFTER *GARCETTI V. CEBALLOS* (2009),* *available at* http://www.aaup.org/AAUP/comm/rep/A/postgarcettireport.htm.

The AAUP is particularly alarmed by three lower-court rulings that followed *Garcetti.* In *Hong v. Grant*, 516 F. Supp. 2d 1158 (C.D. Cal. 2007), Juan Hong, a tenured professor at the University of California-Irvine, criticized administrators for a number of personnel decisions. He was subsequently denied a merit raise, and he filed suit, arguing that administrators had violated his First Amendment rights. The district court, relying on *Garcetti*, ruled against him, holding that Hong made the statements pursuant to his "official duties." The case is on appeal to the Ninth Circuit. In *Renken v. Gregory*, 541 F.3d 769 (7th Cir. 2008), Kevin Renken, a tenured engineering professor at the University of Wisconsin-Milwaukee, criticized his dean over the use of a National Science Foundation grant. When the university returned the grant money, Renken sued, arguing that the administration had retaliated against him for his critical remarks. The Seventh Circuit, relying on *Garcetti*, ruled against Renken, holding that the remarks were made pursuant to his "official duties," and thus were not protected by the First Amendment. The Third Circuit reached a similar conclusion in *Gorum v. Sessoms*, 561 F.3d 179 (3d Cir. 2009).

6. To help stem the perceived erosion in academic freedom, the AAUP has a list of policy recommendations for faculty senates and other groups. Among the highlights:

- Carefully assess the adequacy and coverage of existing institutional policies that affect faculty speech or expressive activity. These can be found in faculty handbooks, university policies or regulations, collective bargaining agreements, and occasionally state laws or regulations. Where the policies are insufficient, advocate for change!
- Gather support from as broad a range of faculty and faculty groups as possible, on campus or across multi-campus systems, to work with administrations and governing boards in enacting policy changes.
- For those faculties represented by a collective bargaining agent, incorporate language protecting academic freedom in the next negotiated agreement between faculty and governing boards.
- Where existing institutional policy meets recognized needs, or could be so adapted with minor revisions, continue to raise awareness and make protections standard practice.

- Publicize the issue in campus-based media and to local news outlets to raise awareness within the community. To highlight faculty's contribution to the public good, supply examples of faculty speaking on issues of importance to the community.
- Notify AAUP and other national faculty and free speech groups about the activity on your campus. Report all litigation involving issues of academic freedom and faculty speech rights so that the AAUP and others can consider offering support at an early stage. Sharing your experiences as broadly as possible can bring support to your efforts and help others in theirs.

As a practical matter, are institution-specific guidelines enough to hold the line against a judiciary that appears increasingly hostile to academic freedom? Or is the AAUP making too much of the *Garcetti* decision? The majority specifically left for another day the academic freedom implications. So why the uproar?

7. The AAUP, in its report on *Garcetti*, indicated its shock at the outcome of the case:

> Even close observers had some reason to be startled by the curious turn of events in the *Garcetti* case. Every federal court of appeals that had recently considered the issue had ruled that speech within a public employee's official duties could claim *Pickering* protection as a "matter of public concern." Such was the unanimous view of the Fifth, Sixth, Seventh, Eighth, Tenth, and Eleventh Circuits. Even the Fourth Circuit, which seemingly implied a contrary view in *Urofsky*, rejoined the chorus in its two later public employee speech cases.

AM. ASS'N OF UNIV. PROFS., PROTECTING AN INDEPENDENT FACULTY VOICE: ACADEMIC FREEDOM AFTER *GARCETTI V. CEBALLOS* (2009), *available at* http://www.aaup.org/NR/rdonlyres/B3991F98-98D5-4CC0-9102-ED26A7AA2892/0/Garcetti.pdf.

The aforementioned *Urofsky* case involved public university professors challenging a Virginia state law restricting state employees from accessing sexually explicit material on computers owned or leased by the state. The district court granted summary judgment in favor of the professors. The Fourth Circuit, on appeal, reversed the district court's decision. The court held that the activity in question, accessing sexually explicit material on the Internet, did not impact professors' ability to speak as private citizens on matters of public concern, and thus did not violate their First Amendment rights. *Urofsky v. Gilmore*, 216 F.3d 401 (4th Cir. 2000) (en banc). *Urofsky* is presented in full later in this Chapter.

Subsequent to *Urofsky*, however, the AAUP report noted the Fourth Circuit "conferred the same degree of presumptive protection as had all the sister circuits" in two cases: *Mansoor v. Trank*, 319 F.3d 133 (4th Cir. 2003); and *Kariotis v. Glendening*, 2000 U.S. App. LEXIS 22506 (4th Cir. Sept. 6, 2000) (observing that a faculty member's "vocal and public opposition to the college's announced plan to eliminate all full-time faculty and to employ only adjunct faculty members" might have involved a matter of public concern and his termination therefore might have violated his First Amendment rights). *See* AM. ASS'N OF UNIV. PROFS., *supra*.

Reading the materials included up to this point, do you think there is a challenge afoot to academic freedom? Can these cases be read in isolation, ignoring any kind of combinative effect they may have? What is the impact of *Garcetti* on postsecondary institutions where faculty is represented by collective bargaining organizations? Is this the real fear of the AAUP?

8. At least one court has determined that the reach of the *Garcetti* decision does not extend to the academic expression of faculty in colleges and universities. In *Adams v. Trustees of the University of North Carolina-Wilmington*, 640 F.3d 550 (4th Cir. 2011), a faculty member claimed his application for promotion to full professor was refused because of his strong ideologically conservative views. Such views were expressed on radio and television broadcasts as well as in a published book representing a collection of previously published columns on an internet blog. University officials claimed of having to field complaints from other faculty, the general public, and from the institution's Board of Trustees about the faculty member. The petition for promotion was refused partly on the grounds that Adams' speech, originally viewed as garnering First Amendment protection, converted to unprotected speech because of the perspective later given to the expression by school personnel that the speech had a negative impact upon the reputation of the institution. In addressing the question of employee-protected speech in colleges and universities, the Fourth Circuit Court of Appeals found there was no focus in *Garcetti* for when such expression is made. More importantly, the court determined that "the plain language of *Garcetti* . . . explicitly left open the question of whether its principles apply in the academic genre where issues of 'scholarship and teaching are in play." *Id.* at 563. Hence, the analysis found in the *Pickering-Connick* standard apply to such cases, that is, whether the faculty member is speaking as a citizen on a matter of public concern. The court found, hence, that a professor's comments outside the institution do not necessarily morph into "statements made pursuant to [his/her] official duties." *Id.* at 564 (quoting *Garcetti v. Ceballos*, 547 U.S 410, 421 (2006)).

9. The court in *Adams* quoted *Garcetti* for the following:

> There is some argument that expression related to academic scholarship or classroom instruction implicates additional constitutional interests that are not fully accounted for by this Court's customary employee-speech jurisprudence. We need not, and for that reason do not, decide whether the analysis we conduct today would apply in the same manner to a case involving speech related to scholarship or teaching.

Id. at 563 (quoting *Garcetti*, 547 U.S. at 425). However, in the case of *Jefferies v. Harleston*, 52 F.3d 9 (2d Cir. 1995), the Second Circuit held that a professor's speech given hundreds of miles away, and not on university business, could reasonably be expected to have a disruptive influence on the university because it has a negative effect on the sensibilities of elected officials, the administration, students, faculty, and alumni. *Id.* at 9. The *Jefferies* decision was originally rendered by the Second Circuit on the *Pickering-Connick* standard where the court reasoned that public employees have a right to "speak on political or social matters without fear of retribution by the government." *Jefferies v. Harleston*, 21 F.3d 1238, 1244 (2d Cir. 1994). The university appealed to the United States Supreme Court. The Court vacated the initial Second Circuit decision and remanded the case in light of its opinion in *Waters v. Churchill*, 511 U.S. 661 (1994), *supra*.

On remand the Second Circuit used *Waters'* "reasonable predictability of harm" test and held that the faculty member's speech could reasonably have a disruptive impact on the university. Importantly, the court indicated that in applying *Waters*, actual disruption to the university no longer had to be demonstrated. How does the *Garcetti* decision square with that of *Waters*? Relatedly, how will the speech of postsecondary personnel, outside of the institution, be evaluated, that is, on a *Waters* or a *Garcetti* standard? Can you find any judicial compatibility between the decisions in *Adams* and *Jefferies*?

10. How can a school administrator protect themselves from letters or statements which may intrude into an educator's academic freedom? Merely adding language that says the statement/letter was not meant to infringe academic freedom is not enough to avoid liability, nor is the removal of any statements from an educator's personnel file. *See Mahoney v. Hankin*, 593 F. Supp. 1171, 1173 (D.C.N.Y. 1984). Further, there is no academic freedom protection for language abusive to students and staff or generally disruptive to a proper school environment; conduct/speech must relate to some pedagogical concern. *See Mills v. W. Wash. Univ.*, 150 Wash. App. 260, 274 (Wash. App. Div. 1. 2009), *rev'd on other grounds, Mills v. W. Wash. Univ.*, 246 P.3d 1254 (Wash. 2011). By establishing content-neutral written policies that are meant to catch only that speech and activity without any pedagogical concern or merit, administrators are likely to prevail on any academic freedom challenges to their actions.

11. For more on the *Garcetti* decision, see Martha M. McCarthy & Suzanne E. Eckes, *Silence in the Hallways: The Impact of Garcetti v. Ceballos on Public School Educators*, 17 B.U. PUB. INT. L.J. 209 (2008); Elizabeth Dale, *Employee Speech & Management Rights: A Counterintuitive Reading of Garcetti v. Ceballos*, 29 BERKELEY J. EMP. & LAB. L. 175 (2008); Susan P. Stuart, *Citizen Teacher: Damned If You Do, Damned If You Don't*, 76 U. CIN. L. REV. 1281 (2008); Helen Norton, *Constraining Public Employee Speech: Government's Control of Its Workers' Speech to Protect Its Own Expression*, 59 DUKE L.J. 1 (2009); Cynthia Estlund, *Harmonizing Work and Citizenship: A Due Process Solution to a First Amendment Problem*, 2006 SUP. CT. REV. 115 (2006).

C. INSTITUTIONAL ACADEMIC FREEDOM

HEALY v. JAMES

408 U.S. 169 (1972)

MR. JUSTICE POWELL delivered the opinion of the Court.

This case, arising out of a denial by a state college of official recognition to a group of students who desired to form a local chapter of Students for a Democratic Society (SDS), presents this Court with questions requiring the application of well-established First Amendment principles. . . . .

I

We mention briefly at the outset the setting in 1969-1970. A climate of unrest prevailed on many college campuses in this country. There had been widespread civil disobedience on some campuses, accompanied by the seizure of buildings, vandalism, and arson. Some colleges had been shut down altogether, while at others files were looted and manuscripts destroyed. SDS chapters on some of those campuses had been a catalytic force during this period. Although the causes of campus disruption were many and complex, one of the prime consequences of such activities was the denial of the lawful exercise of First Amendment rights to the majority of students by the few. . . .

Petitioners are students attending Central Connecticut State College (CCSC), a state-supported institution of higher learning. In September 1969 they undertook to organize what they then referred to as a "local chapter" of SDS. Pursuant to procedures established by the College, petitioners filed a request for official recognition as a campus organization with the Student Affairs Committee, a committee composed of four students, three faculty members, and the Dean of Student Affairs. The request specified three purposes for the proposed organization's existence. It would provide "a forum of discussion and self-education for students developing an analysis of American society"; it would serve as "an agency for integrating thought with action so as to bring about constructive changes"; and it would endeavor to provide "a coordinating body for relating the problems of leftist students" with other interested groups on campus and in the community. The Committee, while satisfied that the statement of purposes was clear and unobjectionable on its face, exhibited concern over the relationship between the proposed local group and the National SDS organization. In response to inquiries, representatives of the proposed organization stated that they would not affiliate with any national organization and that their group would remain "completely independent."

. . . .

With this information before it, the Committee requested an additional filing by the applicants, including a formal statement regarding affiliations. The amended application filed in response stated flatly that "CCSC Students for a Democratic Society are not under the dictates of any National organization." . . .

By a vote of six to two the Committee ultimately approved the application and recommended to the President of the College, Dr. James, that the organization be accorded official recognition. In approving the application, the majority indicated that its decision was premised on the belief that varying viewpoints should be represented on campus and that since the Young Americans for Freedom, the Young Democrats, the Young Republicans, and the Liberal Party all enjoyed recognized status, a group should be available with which "left wing" students might identify. The majority also noted and relied on the organization's claim of independence. Finally, it admonished the organization that immediate suspension would be considered if the group's activities proved incompatible with the school's policies against interference with the privacy of other students or destruction of property. . . .

Several days later, the President rejected the Committee's recommendation, and issued a statement indicating that petitioners' organization was not to be accorded the benefits of official campus recognition. . . . He found that the organization's philosophy was antithetical to the school's policies, and that the group's independence was doubtful. He concluded that approval should not be granted to any group that "openly repudiates" the College's dedication to academic freedom.

Denial of official recognition posed serious problems for the organization's existence and growth. Its members were deprived of the opportunity to place announcements regarding meetings, rallies, or other activities in the student newspaper; they were precluded from using various campus bulletin boards; and — most importantly — nonrecognition barred them from using campus facilities for holding meetings. . . .

Their efforts to gain recognition having proved ultimately unsuccessful, and having been made to feel the burden of nonrecognition, petitioners resorted to the courts. They filed a suit in the United States District Court for the District of Connecticut, seeking declaratory and injunctive relief against the President of the College, other administrators, and the State Board of Trustees. Petitioners' primary complaint centered on the denial of First Amendment rights of expression and association arising from denial of campus recognition. . . . [T]he judge ruled that petitioners had been denied procedural due process because the President had based his decision on conclusions regarding the applicant's affiliation which were outside the record before him. . . . While retaining jurisdiction over the case, the District Court ordered respondents to hold a hearing in order to clarify the several ambiguities surrounding the President's decision. One of the matters to be explored was whether the local organization, true to its repeated affirmations, was in fact independent of the National SDS. . . .

. . . .

Upon reviewing the hearing transcript and exhibits, the President reaffirmed his prior decision to deny petitioners recognition as a campus organization. The reasons stated, closely paralleling his initial reasons, were that the group would be a "disruptive influence" at CCSC and that recognition would be "contrary to the orderly process of change" on the campus.

After the President's second statement issued, the case then returned to the District Court, where it was ordered dismissed. The court concluded, first, that the formal requisites of procedural due process had been complied with, second, that petitioners had failed to meet their burden of showing that they could function free from the National organization, and, third, that the College's refusal to place its stamp of approval on an organization whose conduct it found "likely to cause violent acts of disruption" did not violate petitioners' associational rights.

Petitioners appealed to the Court of Appeals for the Second Circuit where . . . the District Court's judgment was affirmed. . . .

II

At the outset we note that state colleges and universities are not enclaves immune from the sweep of the First Amendment. . . . . *Tinker v. Des Moines*

Independent School District, 393 U.S. 503, 506 (1969). Of course, as Mr. Justice Fortas made clear in Tinker, First Amendment rights must always be applied "in light of the special characteristics of the . . . environment" in the particular case. *Ibid.* And, where state-operated educational institutions are involved, this Court has long recognized "the need for affirming the comprehensive authority of the States and of school officials, consistent with fundamental constitutional safeguards, to prescribe and control conduct in the schools." *Id.*, at 507. Yet, the precedents of this Court leave no room for the view that, because of the acknowledged need for order, First Amendment protections should apply with less force on college campuses than in the community at large. Quite to the contrary, "the vigilant protection of constitutional freedoms is nowhere more vital than in the community of American schools." *Shelton v. Tucker*, 364 U.S. 479, 487 (1960). The college classroom with its surrounding environs is peculiarly the " 'marketplace of ideas,' " and we break no new constitutional ground in reaffirming this Nation's dedication to safeguarding academic freedom.

Among the rights protected by the First Amendment is the right of individuals to associate to further their personal beliefs. . . . There can be no doubt that denial of official recognition, without justification, to college organizations burdens or abridges that associational right. The primary impediment to free association flowing from nonrecognition is the denial of use of campus facilities for meetings and other appropriate purposes. . . .

Petitioners' associational interests also were circumscribed by the denial of the use of campus bulletin boards and the school newspaper. If an organization is to remain a viable entity in a campus community in which new students enter on a regular basis, it must possess the means of communicating with these students. Moreover, the organization's ability to participate in the intellectual give and take of campus debate, and to pursue its stated purposes, is limited by denial of access to the customary media for communicating with the administration, faculty members, and other students. Such impediments cannot be viewed as insubstantial.

Respondents and the courts below appear to have taken the view that denial of official recognition in this case abridged no constitutional rights. . . .

. . . .

We do not agree with the characterization by the courts below of the consequences of nonrecognition. We may concede, as did Mr. Justice Harlan in his opinion for a unanimous Court in *NAACP v. Alabama ex rel. Patterson*, 357 U.S., at 461, that the administration "has taken no direct action . . . to restrict the rights of [petitioners] to associate freely. . . ." But the Constitution's protection is not limited to direct interference with fundamental rights. The requirement in Patterson that the NAACP disclose its membership lists was found to be an impermissible, though indirect, infringement of the members' associational rights. Likewise, in this case, the group's possible ability to exist outside the campus community does not ameliorate significantly the disabilities imposed by the President's action. We are not free to disregard the practical realities. . . .

The opinions below also assumed that petitioners had the burden of showing entitlement to recognition by the College. While petitioners have not challenged the procedural requirement that they file an application in conformity with the rules of the College, they do question the view of the courts below that final rejection could rest on their failure to convince the administration that their organization was unaffiliated with the National SDS. For reasons to be stated later in this opinion, we do not consider the issue of affiliation to be a controlling one. But, apart from any particular issue, once petitioners had filed an application in conformity with the requirements, the burden was upon the College administration to justify its decision of rejection. . . .

III

These fundamental errors — discounting the existence of a cognizable First Amendment interest and misplacing the burden of proof — require that the judgments below be reversed. But we are unable to conclude that no basis exists upon which nonrecognition might be appropriate. Indeed, based on a reasonable reading of the ambiguous facts of this case, there appears to be at least one potentially acceptable ground for a denial of recognition. Because of this ambiguous state of the record we conclude that the case should be remanded, and, in an effort to provide guidance to the lower courts upon reconsideration, it is appropriate to discuss the several bases of President James' decision. Four possible justifications for nonrecognition, all closely related, might be derived from the record and his statements. Three of those grounds are inadequate to substantiate his decision: a fourth, however, has merit.

A

From the outset the controversy in this case has centered in large measure around the relationship, if any, between petitioners' group and the National SDS. . . .

Although this precise issue has not come before the Court heretofore, the Court has consistently disapproved governmental action imposing criminal sanctions or denying rights and privileges solely because of a citizen's association with an unpopular organization. *See, e. g., United States v. Robel*, 389 U.S. 258 (1967); *Keyishian v. Board of Regents*, 385 U.S., at 605–610; *Elfbrandt v. Russell*, 384 U.S. 11 (1966); *Scales v. United States*, 367 U.S. 203 (1961). . . . The government has the burden of establishing a knowing affiliation with an organization possessing unlawful aims and goals, and a specific intent to further those illegal aims.

Students for a Democratic Society, as conceded by the College and the lower courts, is loosely organized, having various factions and promoting a number of diverse social and political views, only some of which call for unlawful action. Not only did petitioners proclaim their complete independence from this organization, but they also indicated that they shared only some of the beliefs its leaders have expressed. On this record it is clear that the relationship was not an adequate ground for the denial of recognition.

B

Having concluded that petitioners were affiliated with, or at least retained an affinity for, National SDS, President James attributed what he believed to be the philosophy of that organization to the local group. He characterized the petitioning group as adhering to "some of the major tenets of the national organization," including a philosophy of violence and disruption. . . .

The mere disagreement of the President with the group's philosophy affords no reason to deny it recognition. As repugnant as these views may have been, especially to one with President James' responsibility, the mere expression of them would not justify the denial of First Amendment rights. . . . The College, acting here as the instrumentality of the State, may not restrict speech or association simply because it finds the views expressed by any group to be abhorrent. . . .

. . . .

C

As the litigation progressed in the District Court, a third rationale for President James' decision — beyond the questions of affiliation and philosophy — began to emerge. His second statement, issued after the court-ordered hearing, indicates that he based rejection on a conclusion that this particular group would be a "disruptive influence at CCSC." . . .

If this reason, directed at the organization's activities rather than its philosophy, were factually supported by the record, this Court's prior decisions would provide a basis for considering the propriety of nonrecognition. The critical line heretofore drawn for determining the permissibility of regulation is the line between mere advocacy and advocacy "directed to inciting or producing imminent lawless action and . . . likely to incite or produce such action." *Brandenburg v. Ohio*, 395 U.S. 444, 447 (1969) (unanimous per curiam opinion). In the context of the "special characteristics of the school environment," the power of the government to prohibit "lawless action" is not limited to acts of a criminal nature. Also prohibitable are actions which "materially and substantially disrupt the work and discipline of the school." *Tinker v. Des Moines Independent School District*, 393 U.S., at 513. Associational activities need not be tolerated where they infringe reasonable campus rules, interrupt classes, or substantially interfere with the opportunity of other students to obtain an education.

. . . [I]f there were an evidential basis to support the conclusion that CCSC-SDS posed a substantial threat of material disruption in violation of that command the President's decision should be affirmed.

The record, however, offers no substantial basis for that conclusion. The only support for the view expressed by the President, other than the reputed affiliation with National SDS, is to be found in the ambivalent responses offered by the group's representatives at the Student Affairs Committee hearing, during which they stated that they did not know whether they might respond to "issues of violence" in the same manner that other SDS chapters had on other campuses. Nor would they state unequivocally that they could never "envision . . . interrupting a class." . . .

. . . .

. . . [T]here was no substantial evidence that these particular individuals acting together would constitute a disruptive force on campus. Therefore, insofar as nonrecognition flowed from such fears, it constituted little more than the sort of "undifferentiated fear or apprehension of disturbance [which] is not enough to overcome the right to freedom of expression." *Tinker v. Des Moines Independent School District*, 393 U.S., at 508.

D

These same references in the record to the group's equivocation regarding how it might respond to "issues of violence" and whether it could ever "envision . . . interrupting a class," suggest a fourth possible reason why recognition might have been denied to these petitioners. These remarks might well have been read as announcing petitioners' unwillingness to be bound by reasonable school rules governing conduct. The College's Statement of Rights, Freedoms, and Responsibilities of Students contains . . . an explicit statement with respect to campus disruption. The regulation, carefully differentiating between advocacy and action, is a reasonable one, and petitioners have not questioned it directly. Yet their statements raise considerable question whether they intend to abide by the prohibitions contained therein.

. . . .

Just as in the community at large, reasonable regulations with respect to the time, the place, and the manner in which student groups conduct their speech-related activities must be respected. A college administration may impose a requirement, such as may have been imposed in this case, that a group seeking official recognition affirm in advance its willingness to adhere to reasonable campus law. Such a requirement does not impose an impermissible condition on the students' associational rights. Their freedom to speak out, to assemble, or to petition for changes in school rules is in no sense infringed. It merely constitutes an agreement to conform with reasonable standards respecting conduct. This is a minimal requirement, in the interest of the entire academic community, of any group seeking the privilege of official recognition.

Petitioners have not challenged in this litigation the procedural or substantive aspects of the College's requirements governing applications for official recognition. Although the record is unclear on this point, CCSC may have, among its requirements for recognition, a rule that prospective groups affirm that they intend to comply with reasonable campus regulations. Upon remand it should first be determined whether the College recognition procedures contemplate any such requirement. If so, it should then be ascertained whether petitioners intend to comply. . . . Assuming the existence of a valid rule . . . we . . . conclude that the benefits of participation in the internal life of the college community may be denied to any group that reserves the right to violate any valid campus rules with which it disagrees.

IV

. . . Because respondents failed to accord due recognition to First Amendment principles, the judgments below approving respondents' denial of recognition must be reversed. Since we cannot conclude from this record that petitioners were willing to abide by reasonable campus rules and regulations, we order the case remanded for reconsideration. . . .

HAZELWOOD SCHOOL DISTRICT v. KUHLMEIER

484 U.S. 260 (1988)

Justice White delivered the opinion of the Court.

This case concerns the extent to which educators may exercise editorial control over the contents of a high school newspaper produced as part of the school's journalism curriculum.

I

Petitioners are the Hazelwood School District in St. Louis County, Missouri; various school officials; Robert Eugene Reynolds, the principal of Hazelwood East High School; and Howard Emerson, a teacher in the school district. Respondents are three former Hazelwood East students who were staff members of Spectrum, the school newspaper. They contend that school officials violated their First Amendment rights by deleting two pages of articles from the May 13, 1983, issue of Spectrum.

Spectrum was written and edited by the Journalism II class at Hazelwood East. The newspaper was published every three weeks or so during the 1982-1983 school year. More than 4,500 copies of the newspaper were distributed during that year to students, school personnel, and members of the community.

The Board of Education allocated funds from its annual budget for the printing of Spectrum. These funds were supplemented by proceeds from sales of the newspaper. The printing expenses during the 1982-1983 school year totaled $4,668.50; revenue from sales was $1,166.84. The other costs associated with the newspaper — such as supplies, textbooks, and a portion of the journalism teacher's salary — were borne entirely by the Board.

The Journalism II course was taught by Robert Stergos for most of the 1982-1983 academic year. Stergos left Hazelwood East to take a job in private industry on April 29, 1983, when the May 13 edition of Spectrum was nearing completion, and petitioner Emerson took his place as newspaper adviser for the remaining weeks of the term.

The practice at Hazelwood East during the spring 1983 semester was for the journalism teacher to submit page proofs of each Spectrum issue to Principal Reynolds for his review prior to publication. On May 10 . . . Reynolds . . . objected to two of the articles scheduled to appear in that edition. One of the stories described three Hazelwood East students' experiences with pregnancy; the other discussed the impact of divorce on students at the school.

Reynolds was concerned that, although the pregnancy story used false names "to keep the identity of these girls a secret," the pregnant students still might be identifiable from the text. He also believed that the article's references to sexual activity and birth control were inappropriate for some of the younger students at the school. In addition, Reynolds was concerned that a student identified by name in the divorce story had complained that her father "wasn't spending enough time with my mom, my sister and I" prior to the divorce, "was always out of town on business or out late playing cards with the guys," and "always argued about everything" with her mother. Reynolds believed that the student's parents should have been given an opportunity to respond to these remarks or to consent to their publication. . . .

Reynolds believed that there was no time to make the necessary changes in the stories before the scheduled press run and that the newspaper would not appear before the end of the school year if printing were delayed to any significant extent. He concluded that his only options under the circumstances were to publish a four-page newspaper instead of the planned six-page newspaper, eliminating the two pages on which the offending stories appeared, or to publish no newspaper at all. Accordingly, he directed [the withholding of] the two pages containing the stories on pregnancy and divorce. . . .

Respondents subsequently commenced this action in the United States District Court for the Eastern District of Missouri seeking a declaration that their First Amendment rights had been violated, injunctive relief, and monetary damages. After a bench trial, the District Court denied an injunction, holding that no First Amendment violation had occurred.

The District Court concluded that school officials may impose restraints on students' speech in activities that are " 'an integral part of the school's educational function' " — including the publication of a school-sponsored newspaper by a journalism class — so long as their decision has " 'a substantial and reasonable basis.' " [citation omitted]

The Court of Appeals for the Eighth Circuit reversed. The court held at the outset that Spectrum was not only "a part of the school adopted curriculum," but also a public forum, because the newspaper was "intended to be and operated as a conduit for student viewpoint." The court then concluded that Spectrum's status as a public forum precluded school officials from censoring its contents except when " 'necessary to avoid material and substantial interference with school work or discipline . . . or the rights of others.' " [citation omitted]

The Court of Appeals found "no evidence in the record that the principal could have reasonably forecast that the censored articles or any materials in the censored articles would have materially disrupted classwork or given rise to substantial disorder in the school." School officials were entitled to censor the articles on the ground that they invaded the rights of others, according to the court, only if publication of the articles could have resulted in tort liability to the school. The court concluded that no tort action for libel or invasion of privacy could have been maintained against the school by the subjects of the two articles or by their families.

Accordingly, the court held that school officials had violated respondents' First Amendment rights by deleting the two pages of the newspaper.

We granted certiorari, and we now reverse.

II

. . . .

A

We deal first with the question whether Spectrum may appropriately be characterized as a forum for public expression. The public schools do not possess all of the attributes of streets, parks, and other traditional public forums that "time out of mind, have been used for purposes of assembly, communicating thoughts between citizens, and discussing public questions." *Hague v. CIO*, 307 U.S. 496, 515 (1939). Hence, school facilities may be deemed to be public forums only if school authorities have "by policy or by practice" opened those facilities "for indiscriminate use by the general public," *Perry Education Assn. v. Perry Local Educators' Assn.*, 460 U.S. 37, 47 (1983), or by some segment of the public, such as student organizations. If the facilities have instead been reserved for other intended purposes, "communicative or otherwise," then no public forum has been created, and school officials may impose reasonable restrictions on the speech of students, teachers, and other members of the school community. 460 U.S., at 46, n. 7. . . .

The policy of school officials toward Spectrum was reflected in Hazelwood School Board Policy 348.51 and the Hazelwood East Curriculum Guide. Board Policy 348.51 provided that "[s]chool sponsored publications are developed within the adopted curriculum and its educational implications in regular classroom activities." . . . The lessons that were to be learned from the Journalism II course . . . included development of journalistic skills under deadline pressure, "the legal, moral, and ethical restrictions imposed upon journalists within the school community," and "responsibility and acceptance of criticism for articles of opinion." . . .

School officials did not deviate in practice from their policy that production of Spectrum was to be part of the educational curriculum and a "regular classroom activit[y]." The District Court found that Robert Stergos, the journalism teacher during most of the 1982-1983 school year, "both had the authority to exercise and in fact exercised a great deal of control over Spectrum." . . . Respondents' assertion that they had believed that they could publish "practically anything" in Spectrum was therefore dismissed by the District Court as simply "not credible." . . .

The evidence relied upon by the Court of Appeals in finding Spectrum to be a public forum is equivocal at best. . . . One might reasonably infer from the full text of Policy 348.51 that school officials retained ultimate control over what constituted "responsible journalism" in a school-sponsored newspaper. . . . [T]hat students were permitted to exercise some authority over the contents of Spectrum was fully consistent with the Curriculum Guide objective of teaching the Journalism II students "leadership responsibilities as issue and page editors." A decision to teach leadership skills in the context of a classroom activity hardly implies a decision to relinquish school control over that activity. In sum, the evidence relied upon by the Court of Appeals fails to demonstrate the "clear intent to create a public forum" . . . . Accordingly, school officials were entitled to regulate the contents of Spectrum in any reasonable manner. It is this standard, rather than our decision in Tinker, that governs this case.

B

The question whether the First Amendment requires a school to tolerate particular student speech — the question that we addressed in *Tinker* — is different from the question whether the First Amendment requires a school affirmatively to promote particular student speech. The former question addresses educators' ability to silence a student's personal expression that happens to occur on the school premises. The latter question concerns educators' authority over school-sponsored publications, theatrical productions, and other expressive activities that students, parents, and members of the public might reasonably perceive to bear the imprimatur of the school. These activities may fairly be characterized as part of the school curriculum, whether or not they occur in a traditional classroom setting, so long as they are supervised by faculty members and designed to impart particular knowledge or skills to student participants and audiences.

Educators are entitled to exercise greater control over this second form of student expression to assure that participants learn whatever lessons the activity is designed to teach, that readers or listeners are not exposed to material that may be inappropriate for their level of maturity, and that the views of the individual speaker are not erroneously attributed to the school. Hence, a school may in its capacity as publisher of a school newspaper or producer of a school play "disassociate itself," *Fraser*, 478 U.S., at 685, not only from speech that would "substantially interfere with [its] work . . . or impinge upon the rights of other students," *Tinker*, 393 U.S., at 509, but also from speech that is, for example, ungrammatical, poorly written, inadequately researched, biased or prejudiced, vulgar or profane, or unsuitable for immature audiences. . . . A school must also retain the authority to refuse to sponsor student speech that might reasonably be perceived to advocate drug or alcohol use, irresponsible sex, or conduct otherwise inconsistent with "the shared values of a civilized social order," *Fraser, supra*, at 683, or to associate the school with any position other than neutrality on matters of political controversy. Otherwise, the schools would be unduly constrained from fulfilling their role as "a principal instrument in awakening the child to cultural values, in preparing him for later professional training, and in helping him to adjust normally to his environment." *Brown v. Board of Education*, 347 U.S. 483, 493 (1954).

Accordingly, we conclude that the standard articulated in *Tinker* for determining when a school may punish student expression need not also be the standard for determining when a school may refuse to lend its name and resources to the dissemination of student expression. Instead, we hold that educators do not offend the First Amendment by exercising editorial control over the style and content of student speech in school-sponsored expressive activities so long as their actions are reasonably related to legitimate pedagogical concerns.

. . . .

III

We also conclude that Principal Reynolds acted reasonably in requiring the deletion from the May 13 issue of Spectrum of the pregnancy article, the divorce article, and the remaining articles that were to appear on the same pages of the newspaper.

The initial paragraph of the pregnancy article declared that "[a]ll names have been changed to keep the identity of these girls a secret." The principal concluded that the students' anonymity was not adequately protected, however, given the other identifying information in the article and the small number of pregnant students at the school. . . . Reynolds therefore could reasonably have feared that the article violated whatever pledge of anonymity had been given to the pregnant students. In addition, he could reasonably have been concerned that the article was not sufficiently sensitive to the privacy interests of the students' boyfriends and parents, who were discussed in the article but who were given no opportunity to consent to its publication or to offer a response. The article did not contain graphic accounts of sexual activity. The girls did comment in the article, however, concerning their sexual histories and their use or nonuse of birth control. It was not unreasonable for the principal to have concluded that such frank talk was inappropriate in a school-sponsored publication distributed to 14-year-old freshmen and presumably taken home to be read by students' even younger brothers and sisters.

The student who was quoted by name in the version of the divorce article seen by Principal Reynolds made comments sharply critical of her father. The principal could reasonably have concluded that an individual publicly identified as an inattentive parent . . . was entitled to an opportunity to defend himself as a matter of journalistic fairness. . . .

Principal Reynolds testified credibly at trial that, at the time that he reviewed the proofs of the May 13 issue during an extended telephone conversation with Emerson, he believed that there was no time to make any changes in the articles, and that the newspaper had to be printed immediately or not at all. . . . We nonetheless agree with the District Court that the decision to excise the two pages containing the problematic articles was reasonable given the particular circumstances of this case. These circumstances included the very recent replacement of Stergos by Emerson, who may not have been entirely familiar with Spectrum editorial and production procedures, and the pressure felt by Reynolds to make an immediate decision so that students would not be deprived of the newspaper altogether.

In sum, we cannot reject as unreasonable Principal Reynolds' conclusion that neither the pregnancy article nor the divorce article was suitable for publication in Spectrum. . . . [W]e conclude that the principal's decision to delete two pages of Spectrum, rather than to delete only the offending articles or to require that they be modified, was reasonable under the circumstances as he understood them. Accordingly, no violation of First Amendment rights occurred.

The judgment of the Court of Appeals for the Eighth Circuit is therefore

Reversed.

UROFSKY v. GILMORE

216 F.3d 401 (4th Cir. 2001)

WILKINS, CIRCUIT JUDGE:

Appellees, six professors employed by various public colleges and universities in Virginia, brought this action challenging the constitutionality of a Virginia law restricting state employees from accessing sexually explicit material on computers that are owned or leased by the state. *See* Va. Code Ann. §§ 2.1-804 to -806 (Michie Supp. 1999) (the Act). The district court granted summary judgment in favor of Appellees, reasoning that the Act unconstitutionally infringed on state employees' First Amendment rights. . . . A majority of the active circuit judges . . . voted to hear this appeal en banc. We now hold that the regulation of state employees' access to sexually explicit material, in their capacity as employees, on computers owned or leased by the state is consistent with the First Amendment. Accordingly, we reverse the decision of the district court.

I

The central provision of the Act states:

> Except to the extent required in conjunction with a bona fide, agency-approved research project or other agency approved undertaking, no agency employee shall utilize agency-owned or agency-leased computer equipment to access, download, print or store any information infrastructure files or services having sexually explicit content. Such agency approvals shall be given in writing by agency heads, and any such approvals shall be available to the public under the provisions of the Virginia Freedom of Information Act[, Va. Code Ann. §§ 2.1-340.1 to -346.1 (Michie Supp. 1999)].

Va. Code Ann. § 2.1-805. Another section of the Act defines "sexually explicit content." When the district court ruled, and when the panel initially considered this appeal, the Act defined "sexually explicit content" to include:

> (i) any description of or (ii) any picture, photograph, drawing, motion picture film, digital image or similar visual representation depicting sexual bestiality, a lewd exhibition of nudity, as nudity is defined in § 18.2-390, sexual excitement, sexual conduct or sadomasochistic abuse, as also defined in § 18.2-390, coprophilia, urophilia, or fetishism.

Va. Code Ann. § 2.1-804 (Michie Supp. 1998). Following our panel decision, the Virginia General Assembly amended the definition of "sexually explicit content" to add the italicized language:

> *content having as a dominant theme* (i) any *lascivious* description of or (ii) any *lascivious* picture, photograph, drawing, motion picture film, digital image or similar visual representation depicting sexual bestiality, a lewd exhibition of nudity, as nudity is defined in § 18.2-390, sexual excitement, sexual conduct or sadomasochistic abuse, as also defined in § 18.2-390, coprophilia, urophilia, or fetishism.

Va. Code Ann. § 2.1-804 (Michie Supp. 1999) (emphasis added).

. . . [T]he Act does not prohibit all access by state employees to such materials, for a state agency head may give permission for a state employee to access such information on computers owned or leased by the state if the agency head deems such access to be required in connection with a bona fide research project or other undertaking. Further, state employees remain free to access sexually explicit materials from their personal or other computers not owned or leased by the state. . . .

None of the Appellees has requested or been denied permission to access sexually explicit materials pursuant to the Act. . . .

Appellees maintain that the restriction imposed by the Act violates the First Amendment rights of state employees. Appellees do not assert that state employees possess a First Amendment right to access sexually explicit materials on state-owned or leased computers for their personal use; rather, Appellees confine their challenge to the restriction of access to sexually explicit materials for work-related purposes. Appellees' challenge to the Act is twofold: They first maintain that the Act is unconstitutional as to all state employees; failing this, they argue more particularly that the Act violates academic employees' right to academic freedom.

II

It is well settled that citizens do not relinquish all of their First Amendment rights by virtue of accepting public employment. *See United States v. National Treasury Employees Union*, 513 U.S. 454, 465 (1995) [hereinafter *NTEU*]; *Connick v. Myers*, 461 U.S. 138, 142 (1983); *Pickering v. Board of Educ.*, 391 U.S. 563, 568 (1968). Nevertheless, the state, as an employer, undoubtedly possesses greater authority to restrict the speech of its employees than it has as sovereign to restrict the speech of the citizenry as a whole. . . . A determination of whether a restriction imposed on a public employee's speech violates the First Amendment requires "a balance between the interests of the [employee], as a citizen, in commenting upon matters of public concern and the interest of the State, as an employer, in promoting the efficiency of the public services it performs through its employees." *Connick*, 461 U.S. at 142 (alteration in original) (quoting *Pickering*, 391 U.S. at 568). This balancing involves an inquiry first into whether the speech at issue was that of a private citizen speaking on a matter of public concern. If so, the court must next consider whether the employee's interest in First Amendment expression outweighs the public employer's interest in what the employer has determined to be the appropriate operation of the workplace. *See Pickering*, 391 U.S. at 568.

The threshold inquiry thus is whether the Act regulates speech by state employees in their capacity as citizens upon matters of public concern. If a public employee's speech made in his capacity as a private citizen does not touch upon a matter of public concern, the state, as employer, may regulate it without infringing any First Amendment protection. *See Connick*, 461 U.S. at 146 . . . .

. . . Speech involves a matter of public concern when it involves an issue of social, political, or other interest to a community. An inquiry into whether a matter is of public concern does not involve a determination of how interesting or important the subject of an employee's speech is. . . . Further, the place where the speech occurs is irrelevant: An employee may speak as a citizen on a matter of public concern at the workplace, and may speak as an employee away from the workplace. . . .

[I]n its decisions determining speech to be entitled to First Amendment protection the Court has emphasized the unrelatedness of the speech at issue to the speaker's employment duties. . . . Thus, critical to a determination of whether employee speech is entitled to First Amendment protection is whether the speech is "made primarily in the [employee's] role as citizen or primarily in his role as employee." *Terrell* [*v. Univ. of Tex. Sys. Police*], 792 F.2d [1360] at 1362 [(5th Cir. 1986)] . . . .

This focus on the capacity of the speaker recognizes the basic truth that speech by public employees undertaken in the course of their job duties will frequently involve matters of vital concern to the public, without giving those employees a First Amendment right to dictate to the state how they will do their jobs. For example, suppose an assistant district attorney, at the District Attorney's direction, makes a formal statement to the press regarding an upcoming murder trial — a matter that is unquestionably of concern to the public. It cannot seriously be doubted that the assistant does not possess a First Amendment right to challenge his employer's instructions regarding the content of the statement. In contrast, when the same assistant district attorney writes a letter to the editor of the local newspaper to expose a pattern of prosecutorial malfeasance, the speech is entitled to constitutional protection because it is made in the employee's capacity as a private citizen and touches on matters of public concern.

. . . .

The speech at issue here — access to certain materials using computers owned or leased by the state for the purpose of carrying out employment duties — is clearly made in the employee's role as employee. Therefore, the challenged aspect of the Act does not regulate the speech of the citizenry in general, but rather the speech of state employees in their capacity as employees. It cannot be doubted that in order to pursue its legitimate goals effectively, the state must retain the ability to control the manner in which its employees discharge their duties and to direct its employees to undertake the responsibilities of their positions in a specified way. . . . The essence of Appellees' claim is that they are entitled to access sexually explicit material in their capacity as state employees by using equipment owned or leased by the state. Because, as Appellees acknowledge, the challenged aspect of the Act does not affect speech by Appellees in their capacity as private citizens speaking on matters of public concern, it does not infringe the First Amendment rights of state employees.

III

Alternatively, Appellees maintain that even if the Act is valid as to the majority of state employees it violates the First Amendment academic freedom rights of professors at state colleges and universities, and thus is invalid as to them. In essence, Appellees contend that a university professor possesses a constitutional right to determine for himself, without the input of the university (and perhaps even contrary to the university's desires), the subjects of his research, writing, and teaching. Appellees maintain that by requiring professors to obtain university approval before accessing sexually explicit materials on the Internet in connection with their research, the Act infringes this individual right of academic freedom. Our review of the law, however, leads us to conclude that to the extent the Constitution recognizes any right of "academic freedom" above and beyond the First Amendment rights to which every citizen is entitled, the right inheres in the University, not in individual professors, and is not violated by the terms of the Act.

. . . .

[The court reviewed the history of the concept of academic freedom in the United States, citing to several leading authors, including J. Peter Byrne, *Academic Freedom: A "Special Concern of the First Amendment"*, 99 Yale L.J. 251, 253 (1989); Richard Hofstadter & Walter P. Metzger, *The Development of Academic Freedom in the United States* 278-79 (1955); Walter P. Metzger, *Profession and Constitution: Two Definitions of Academic Freedom in America*, 66 Tex. L. Rev. 1265, 1269 (1988); Stuller, *High School Academic Freedom: The Evolution of a Fish Out of Water*, 77 Neb. L. Rev. 301, 302 (1998).]

Appellees' insistence that the Act violates their rights of academic freedom amounts to a claim that the academic freedom of professors is not only a professional norm, but also a constitutional right. We disagree. . . . Despite these accolades, the Supreme Court has never set aside a state regulation on the basis that it infringed a First Amendment right to academic freedom. . . .

. . . .

We begin our examination of the cases with *Sweezy*, in which Appellees claim "the Supreme Court first adopted the principle of academic freedom." *Sweezy* arose from an investigation of "subversive activities" by the New Hampshire Attorney General. Paul Sweezy, a target of the investigation, refused to answer certain questions regarding a guest lecture he had given at the University of New Hampshire. His refusal to answer these and other questions ultimately resulted in his incarceration for contempt. On certiorari review of the decision of the New Hampshire Supreme Court affirming the conviction, a plurality of four justices indicated that the action of the state "unquestionably" infringed Sweezy's "liberties in the areas of academic freedom and political expression." *Sweezy*, 354 U.S. at 250.

> The essentiality of freedom in the community of American universities is almost self-evident. No one should underestimate the vital role in a democracy that is played by those who guide and train our youth. To impose any strait jacket upon the intellectual leaders in our colleges and universities would imperil the future of our Nation. No field of education is so thoroughly comprehended by man that new discoveries cannot yet be made. . . . Scholarship cannot flourish in an atmosphere of suspicion and distrust. Teachers and students must always remain free to inquire, to study and to evaluate, to gain new maturity and understanding; otherwise our civilization will stagnate and die.

Id. This paean to academic freedom notwithstanding, the plurality did not vacate Sweezy's contempt conviction on First Amendment grounds, but rather concluded that because the Attorney General lacked authority to investigate Sweezy, the conviction violated due process. *See id.* at 254-55.

Justice Frankfurter, who along with Justice Harlan provided the votes necessary to reverse, relied explicitly on academic freedom in concluding that Sweezy's contempt conviction offended the Constitution. The right recognized by Justice Frankfurter, however, was not the individual right claimed by Appellees, but rather an institutional right belonging to the University of New Hampshire: "When weighed against the grave harm resulting from governmental intrusion into the intellectual life *of a university*, [the] justification for compelling a wit ness to discuss the contents of his lecture appears grossly inadequate." *Id.* at 261 (Frankfurter, J., concurring in the result) (emphasis added). Justice Frankfurter emphasized "the dependence of a free society on free universities" and concluded by enumerating "the four essential freedoms of a university — to determine for itself on academic grounds who may teach, what may be taught, how it shall be taught, and who may be admitted to study." *Id.* at 262-63 (internal quotation marks omitted). Significantly, at no point in his concurrence does Justice Frankfurter indicate that *individual* academic freedom rights had been infringed; in his view, the constitutional harm fell entirely on the university as an institution.

In light of this review of the actual holding and rationale in *Sweezy*, it is difficult to understand how that case can be viewed as clearly "adopting" any academic freedom right, much less a right of the type claimed by Appellees. . . . And, even if *Sweezy* could be read as creating an individual First Amendment right of academic freedom, such a holding would not advance Appellees' claim of a First Amendment right pertaining to their work as scholars and teachers because *Sweezy* involved only the right of an individual to speak in his capacity as a private citizen. . . .

. . . .

Other cases that have referred to a First Amendment right of academic freedom have done so generally in terms of the institution, not the individual. For example, in *Keyishian* the Court considered a renewed challenge to a New York statute and regulations . . . designed "to prevent the appointment or retention of 'subversive' persons in state employment." *Keyishian*, 385 U.S. at 592. *Keyishian*, like the cases discussed above, involved the right of a professor to speak and associate in his capacity as a private citizen, and thus is not germane to Appellees' claim. . . .

This emphasis on institutional rights is particularly evident in more recent Supreme Court jurisprudence. For example, in *Bakke* Justice Powell discussed academic freedom as it related to a program of admissions quotas established by a medical school. Relying on *Keyishian* and on Justice Frankfurter's concurrence in *Sweezy*, Justice Powell characterized academic freedom as "the freedom of a university to make its own judgments as to education." *Bakke*, 438 U.S. at 312 (opinion of Powell, J.). . . .

Significantly, the Court has never recognized that professors possess a First Amendment right of academic freedom to determine for themselves the content of their courses and scholarship, despite opportunities to do so. For example, in *Epperson v. Arkansas*, 393 U.S. 97 (1968), the Court considered a challenge to a state law that prohibited the teaching of evolution. The Court repeated its admonition in *Keyishian* that "the First Amendment 'does not tolerate laws that cast a pall of orthodoxy over the classroom,'" *Epperson*, 393 U.S. at 105 (quoting *Keyishian*, 385 U.S. at 603), but nevertheless declined to invalidate the statute on the basis that it infringed the teacher's right of academic freedom. Rather, the Court held that the provision violated the Establishment Clause. . . .

Taking all of the cases together, the best that can be said for Appellees' claim that the Constitution protects the academic freedom of an individual professor is that teachers were the first public employees to be afforded the now-universal protection against dismissal for the exercise of First Amendment rights. Nothing in Supreme Court jurisprudence suggests that the "right" claimed by Appellees extends any further. . . .

. . . .

Reversed.

NOTES

1. It can be conceptually difficult to apply court decisions concerning K-12 institutions to postsecondary institutions. However, there are numerous cases that help flesh out the analytical differences. The following notes attempt to highlight some of those cases. As an initial matter, however, what differences are there between the K-12 and postsecondary environments that might lead a court to examine First Amendment questions in those environments differently?

2. In *Clark v. Holmes*, 474 F.2d 928 (7th Cir. 1972), Northern Illinois University did not rehire a non-tenured professor because his teaching methods did not comport with the university's expectations. The school offered to rehire the professor if he refrained from counseling students on his own (and instead referred them to the university's professional counselors), and if he reduced the emphasis on sex in his health survey course.

The court, in ruling against the professor, did not apply the *Pickering* balancing test because the matters of disagreement were not matters of public concern, and because the instructor, in this instance, was acting as a private citizen, and not as an employee. Accordingly, the court held that the university's interest as an employer was superior to the instructor's academic freedom interests.

For other examples of judicial deference to the arguments of postsecondary institutions, see *Webb v. Board of Trustees of Ball State University*, 167 F.3d 1146 (7th Cir. 1999); *Edwards v. California University of Pennsylvania*, 156 F.3d 488 (3d Cir. 1998).

3. There have been notable exceptions to the courts' institutional deference. In *Cohen v. San Bernardino Valley College*, 92 F.3d 968 (9th Cir. 1996), for instance, the court held that the college's new sexual harassment policy was too vague as applied to a professor who had used sexual topics as a teaching tool for years. *See also Hardy v. Jefferson Cmty. Coll.*, 260 F.3d 671 (6th Cir. 2001) (holding that a professor's classroom speech examining the cultural impact of such disparaging words as "nigger" and "bitch" regarded a matter of public concern and that the professor's interest in speaking outweighed the college's interest in serving the public); *Parate v. Isibor*, 868 F.2d 821 (6th Cir. 1989) (holding that a postsecondary institution's attempts to force a professor to change a student's grade violated the professor's First Amendment right to academic freedom and unconstitutionally compelled his speech).

4. For an additional example of a court siding with a postsecondary institution in an academic freedom dispute, see *Clinger v. N.M. Highlands Univ.*, 215 F.3d 1162 (10th Cir. 2000) (holding that a professor's criticism of members of a board of regents were not protected as a matter of public concern). For an example of the same circuit siding with a professor, just three years later, see *Hulen v. Yates*, 322 F.3d 1229 (10th Cir. 2003) (holding that a professor's allegations against another professor regarding plagiarism and other misdeeds constituted speech on a matter of public concern and were thus protected under the First Amendment). These seemingly conflicting judicial interpretations illustrate the court's fact-driven, case-by-case evaluation of the context of the "speech" at issue.

5. Should a court examine First Amendment claims differently if the claims involve, on the one hand, personnel matters (such as grading, evaluations, etc.), and on the other hand, a university's concerns about what a professor said in the classroom?

Most lower courts have expanded the bounds of institutional academic freedom in favor of the university in regard to curricular issues such as grading. *Edwards v. Cal. Univ. of Pa.*, 156 F.3d 488 (3d Cir. 1998) (holding that the university, not the educator, had the right to choose the curriculum and course material). Contrary to the exception described above in *Parate v. Isibor, supra*, Note 3, most other circuits follow the rule that the educational institution has the freedom to change grades handed out by faculty. *See Wozniak v. Conry*, 236 F.3d 888 (7th Cir. 2001) (university had absolute authority to set grading policy despite faculty member's claim that such policy violated his academic freedom); *Brown v. Armenti*, 247 F.3d 69 (3d Cir. 2001); *Lovelace v. S.E. Mass. Univ.*, 793 F.2d 419 (1st Cir. 1986) (educational institution has the right to determine grading policy as part of its constitutional right in performing its educational mission). Further, one lower court recently held that a university can override the final grade faculty give to their students without violating the faculty member's academic freedom. *Stronach v. Virginia State University*, 2008 U.S. Dist. LEXIS 2914 (E.D. Va. Jan. 15, 2008).

6. Is the institutional right of academic freedom superior to the individual right of academic freedom? Consider this:

> The strongest argument against creating genuinely distinct individual academic freedom rights, however, is based on the proposition that granting individual academics enforceable rights against their academic supervisors would inevitably restrict the academic autonomy of the institution itself. As a result, there is no avoiding the conflict between a view of academic freedom that views individual academics as its primary and direct beneficiaries, and a contrasting view that locates the right in academic institutions, even if doing so limits the individual rights of the employees of those institutions. Because this is the basic conflict, it is to the latter part of that conflict that I now turn.

. . . .

Although all of the foregoing is designed to express some tentative and preliminary skepticism about the extent to which individual academics have enforceable constitutional law rights against their academic supervisors, it is not designed to be skeptical about a quite different kind of academic freedom right. On the contrary, I want to suggest that an institutional understanding of academic freedom, even if it comes at the expense of an individual understanding, is both more faithful to the best account of what academic freedom is all about and more compatible with larger and emerging themes in First Amendment doctrine generally.

In speaking of an institutional understanding of academic freedom, I am referring to the putative constitutional right of an academic institution qua institution to have an enforceable right to be protected from external political or bureaucratic interference with its academic judgments. I have argued elsewhere that an institutional account of the First Amendment, in which the primary focus is not on the character of communication taken in isolation but instead on the value of institutional autonomy for certain kinds of institutions that play special roles in the development of ideas and public debate, may be a descriptively accurate account of much of existing First Amendment doctrine while at the same time providing a normatively attractive understanding of what the First Amendment should be. And in the immediate context, it may be that such an institutional account provides the foundation for the best explanation, description, and justification for a right to academic freedom.

Under such an institutional understanding, the right to academic freedom would not — or at least need not — be a right of individual academics against their academic supervisors. Those supervisors, after all, are typically themselves making academic judgments, even if often poorly. Indeed, the key to the institutional account, and the reason why such an account is largely incompatible with an individual account, is that the typical individual academic freedom claim is a claim that a court should not interfere with an academic judgment made by an academic institution, and it is hardly clear a priori that such academic judgments made by academic institutions are further removed from the core concerns of the First Amendment than are the academic judgments of individual faculty members.

Thus, an institutional right to academic freedom is best understood as a right of academic institutions against their political and bureaucratic and administrative supervisors, whether those supervisors be elected legislators or appointed administrators. Descriptively, this right to institutional academic freedom is somewhat like the right, or privilege, that the Supreme Court obliquely acknowledged for academic institutions in both *Regents of the University of California v. Bakke* and *Grutter v. Bollinger*, although in *Bakke* and *Grutter*, the academic freedom privilege was more a privilege against an otherwise applicable constitutional standard — compelling interest, or a compelling interest of a certain magnitude — than

> against an otherwise enforceable legislative or regulatory command. Still, the basic idea in both *Bakke* and *Grutter* is that the academic judgments about admissions made by the University of California and the University of Michigan have a sufficient First Amendment dimension that they ought to have special force in the compelling interest calculus. In other words, it is the institutional judgment that is entitled to First Amendment-inspired deference, and not the decision made by an individual academic or the claim of an individual right.

Frederick Schauer, *What Next for Academic Freedom?: Is There a Right to Academic Freedom?*, 77 U. COLO. L. REV. 907, 919–21 (2006).

Which version of academic freedom are courts best equipped to defend — the institutional version or the individual version? Does it matter on a conceptual level*? Is there something to be said for the institutional version because it would keep courts from becoming embroiled in faculty-institution disputes?

7. What is the impact of the Court's ruling in *Garcetti v. Ceballos*, 547 U.S. 410 (2006), on the analysis and ruling in *Urofsky*? Would the result be the same today? Likely yes, given the strength of *Garcetti*'s "pursuant to official duties" standard. See also the passage in Part II of the *Urofsky* opinion on the "capacity of the speaker." The court in *Urofsky* began its analysis with a presentation of the *Pickering-Connick* balancing test, but focused much of its attention on the role the speaker was playing (here, public university faculty members and not private citizens). The dissenting judge in *Urofsky* argued against the emphasis placed on the capacity of the speaker and, instead, argued that the plaintiffs were speaking on matters of public concern and should have prevailed in the case.

8. At least one legal commentator has suggested that the outcome in *Urofsky* is a result of most courts' reluctance to treat government employees differently merely because one is an educator and the other is not. Lawrence White notes, "*Urofsky*, if nothing else, serves as an exemplar of contemporary judicial hostility to claims by faculty members for special exemption from expectations of behavior that apply to other state employees and other community members." Lawrence White, *50 Years of Academic Freedom Jurisprudence*, 36 J. COLL. & U. L. 791, 832–34 (2010). Doesn't this trend run counter to the public goals expressed in *Sweezy*? Wasn't that case decided on the notion that educators and educational institutions *do* deserve special treatment as a policy matter? Moreover, could this theory explain the evolution of institutional academic freedom discussed in the next section?

9. Can the right to individual academic freedom be voluntarily given away to educational institutions? At least one district court has found that school faculty can give away their rights of academic freedom to a school board by contract. *Cary v. Bd. of Educ. of Adams-Arapahoe Sch. Dist. 28-J, Aurora, Colo.*, 427 F. Supp. 945 (D.C. Colo. 1977). Several teachers, who were all members of their union and party to a collective bargaining agreement, argued they should be allowed to assign and teach books the school board had explicitly banned under a theory of academic freedom. *Id.* at 955. But, the collective bargaining agreement to which all teachers were a party gave final authority over choosing instructional material to the school board, which subsequently banned several books from the classroom. *Id.* at 955. The court upheld the contract provision, but emphasized that without this collective bargaining agreement's designation of authority over instructional material, the plaintiff teachers would have likely won on their claims of academic freedom. *Id.* at 955. Also, administrators can prohibit teachers and professors from running for public office through employment contracts without violating academic freedom. *See Jones v. Bd. of Control*, 131 So. 2d 713, 715–16 (Fla. 1961). Are there certain First Amendment freedoms that can never be contracted away? Can all claims of faculty academic freedom be resolved by merely specifying their limitations ahead of time in employee contracts? More broadly, can institutional academic freedom ever be given away by contract?

A separate issue is whether or not the right of academic freedom is a "bargainable" item in collective bargaining agreements. The American Association of University Professors contend that academic freedom is a bargainable right that should be included in all collective bargaining agreements. In their 1973 Statement on Collective Bargaining, the AAUP said:

> As a national organization that has historically played a major role in formulating and implementing the principles that govern relationships in academic life, the Association promotes collective bargaining to reinforce the best features of higher education. The principles of academic freedom and tenure, fair procedures, faculty participation in governance, and the primary responsibility of the faculty for determining academic policy will thereby be secured. Moreover, collective bargaining gives the faculty an effective voice in decisions that vitally affect its members' professional well-being, such as the allocation of financial resources and determination of faculty salaries and benefits. For these reasons, the Association supports efforts of local chapters to pursue collective bargaining.
>
> Policy for Collective-Bargaining Chapters
>
> 1. When a chapter of the Association enters into collective bargaining, it should seek to
>
> a. protect and promote the professional and economic interests of the faculty as a whole in accordance with the established principles of the Association;
>
> b. maintain and enhance within the institution structures of representative governance that provide full participation by the faculty in accordance with the established principles of the Association;
>
> c. obtain explicit guarantees of academic freedom and tenure in accordance with the principles and stated policies of the Association; and
>
> d. create orderly and clearly defined procedures for prompt consideration of problems and grievances of members of the bargaining unit, to which procedures any affected individual or group shall have access.

AM. ASS'N OF UNIV. PROFESSORS, STATEMENT ON COLLECTIVE BARGAINING (1973),* *available at* http://www.aaup.org/AAUP/pubsres/policydocs/contents/statementcolbargaining.htm. According to the AAUP, over 70 public and private universities currently use collective bargaining agreements. For a list of these institutions, see Collective Bargaining Chapters, AM. ASS'N OF UNIV. PROFESSORS (Aug. 2011), *available at* http://www.aaup.org/AAUP/cbc/colbargainchap.htm. Most of these collective bargaining agreements include at least some reference to a faculty's right of academic freedom within reasonable limits. Should *institutional* academic freedom also be bargainable within these collective bargaining agreements? Would more specific and restrictive limitations on academic freedom also be valid?

10. Can the government, by statute, intrude into the normally protected decisions and procedures of an educational institution? In *Rumsfeld v. Forum for Academic and Institutional Rights*, the Supreme Court determined that in very limited circumstances the university was subject to the mandates of federal statutes despite university procedure. 547 U.S. 47 (2006). (See also Chapter VII for a more in depth discussion of this issue.) An association of law schools and faculty challenged a federal statute conditioning the grant of federal funds on a university allowing military recruiters access to their campus, on grounds that the statute violated their rights to academic freedom. *Id.* at 52. The plaintiffs argued that, given the military's then stance on homosexuality, allowing military officials to enter and recruit on university grounds would force the university to violate established institutional policy against discrimination on the basis of sexual orientation. (The military's Don't Ask Don't Tell policy on gays and lesbians in the military has since been repealed by a bill signed into law by President Barack Obama on December 22, 2010. *Id.* at 52.) In an opinion authored by Chief Justice Roberts, the Court found that allowing military recruiters equal access to campus recruiting events was simply not expressive enough of an act to implicate any First Amendment rights. *Id.* at 70. The Court pointed to the narrow language of the statute itself arguing that it does not require that the military recruiters be made any sort of members of the university, that they speak for university, or that they receive any special accommodation that might imply expressive association or speech. *Id.* at 65. How far could federal statutes go without violating institutional academic freedom?

This holding is not limited just to the reach of the federal government. After the decision in *Rumsfeld*, one lower court held that states could also statutorily intrude into the realm of institutional academic freedom. *Faculty Senate of Fla. Int'l Univ. v. Winn*, 477 F. Supp. 2d 1198 (S.D. Fla. 2007). In *Winn*, a group of university faculty members challenged a Florida state law that prohibited non-state universities from using state-provided funds, or state-run universities from using any funds, related to travel and travel expenses to any country listed on the federal government's terrorist list. *Id.* at 1203. The court found that the statute did not prohibit any education, research, or discussion about the terrorist-list countries, and hence, did not touch any academic freedom concerns. *Id.* at 1207. The opinion rested on the fact that the state did not prohibit anyone from traveling to or learning about the relevant countries; it only addressed the state's responsibility to pay for such related travel. *Id.* at 1207. Should academic freedom extend to activities outside the classroom? Should there be different standards for state and federal laws? Doesn't travel abroad as part of a legitimate course and curriculum approved by a university naturally involve the fundamental rights of academic freedom described in *Sweezy*?

11. Can educational institutions use the right of institutional academic freedom to bar discovery of internal reports and documents? The answer depends on the circumstances of the discovery request. Most lower courts have held that a claim of institutional academic freedom will not bar discovery of internal administrative documents, especially tenure committee reports, when issues of employment discrimination are raised. *See Gray v. Bd. of Higher Educ.*, 692 F.2d 901 (2d Cir. 1982); *In re Dinnan*, 661 F.2d 426 (5th Cir. 1981). When balancing the rights of employees and the rights of the educational institution to academic freedom, most courts agree that the rights of employees to fair and open discovery into relevant confidential material should always win. *See Rollins v. Farris*, 108 F.R.D. 714 (D.C. Ark. 1985). Outside employment discrimination matters, however, institutional academic freedom generally bars discovery into internal confidential documents.

12. Could the federal False Claims Act be used to pierce the veil of institutional academic freedom? A state law version of the False Claims Act has been used in an attempt to compel at least one university to reveal documents and communications that would normally be considered within the ambit of academic freedom. *Cuccinelli v. Rector and Visitors of the Univ. of Va.*, 722 S.E. 2d 626 (Va. 2012). The Attorney General of Virginia wanted to discover all university documents and communications concerning the research of one specific faculty member who had used federal and state funds to conduct research on global warming. *Id.* The Virginia Supreme Court (as well as the district, trial, and appellate state courts) found that the Attorney General did not sufficiently provide evidence of any reason to believe the university had engaged in fraudulent activity and that the Attorney General also failed to adequately specify the nature of the conduct he believed to be fraudulent. *Id.* What outcome would have occurred if a whistleblower within the university could have provided some minimal evidence of potential fraudulent activity? Could a university ever be compelled to reveal academic information through the FCA or its state analogs?

Pursuant to an international treaty between the United States and the United Kingdom, a federal district court ordered Boston College to reveal interview records for an oral history research project investigating the violence in Northern Ireland. *See In re Request from the United Kingdom Pursuant to the Treaty*, 2012 U.S. Dist. LEXIS 6516 (D. Mass. 2012).

D. OTHER CONSTITUTIONAL ISSUES IN ACADEMIC FREEDOM DISPUTES

1. Search and Seizure

O'CONNOR v. ORTEGA

480 U.S. 709 (1987)

JUSTICE O'CONNOR announced the judgment of the Court and delivered an opinion in which THE CHIEF JUSTICE, JUSTICE WHITE, and JUSTICE POWELL join.

This suit under 42 U. S. C. § 1983 presents two issues concerning the Fourth Amendment rights of public employees. First, we must determine whether the respondent, a public employee, had a reasonable expectation of privacy in his office, desk, and file cabinets at his place of work. Second, we must address the appropriate Fourth Amendment standard for a search conducted by a public employer in areas in which a public employee is found to have a reasonable expectation of privacy.

I

Dr. Magno Ortega, a physician and psychiatrist, held the position of Chief of Professional Education at Napa State Hospital (Hospital) for 17 years, until his dismissal from that position in 1981. As Chief of Professional Education, Dr. Ortega had primary responsibility for training young physicians in psychiatric residency programs.

In July 1981, Hospital officials, including Dr. Dennis O'Connor, the Executive Director of the Hospital, became concerned about possible improprieties in Dr. Ortega's management of the residency program. In particular, the Hospital officials were concerned with Dr. Ortega's acquisition of an Apple II computer for use in the residency program. The officials thought that Dr. Ortega may have misled Dr. O'Connor into believing that the computer had been donated, when in fact the computer had been financed by the possibly coerced contributions of residents. Additionally, the Hospital officials were concerned with charges that Dr. Ortega had sexually harassed two female Hospital employees, and had taken inappropriate disciplinary action against a resident.

On July 30, 1981, Dr. O'Connor requested that Dr. Ortega take paid administrative leave during an investigation of these charges. At Dr. Ortega's request, Dr. O'Connor agreed to allow Dr. Ortega to take two weeks' vacation instead of administrative leave. . . . Dr. Ortega remained on administrative leave until the Hospital terminated his employment on September 22, 1981.

Dr. O'Connor selected several Hospital personnel to conduct the investigation . . . . Richard Friday, the Hospital Administrator, led this "investigative team." At some point during the investigation, Mr. Friday made the decision to enter Dr. Ortega's office. The specific reason for the entry into Dr. Ortega's office is unclear from the record. The petitioners claim that the search was conducted to secure state property. . . . Dr. Ortega contends that the purpose of the search was to secure evidence for use against him in administrative disciplinary proceedings.

. . . The investigators entered the office a number of times and seized several items from Dr. Ortega's desk and file cabinets, including a Valentine's Day card, a photograph, and a book of poetry all sent to Dr. Ortega by a former resident physician. These items were later used in a proceeding before a hearing officer of the California State Personnel Board to impeach the credibility of the former resident, who testified on Dr. Ortega's behalf. The investigators also seized billing documentation of one of Dr. Ortega's private patients under the California Medicaid program. . . .

Dr. Ortega commenced this action against petitioners in Federal District Court under 42 U. S. C. § 1983, alleging that the search of his office violated the Fourth Amendment. On cross-motions for summary judgment, the District Court granted petitioners' motion for summary judgment. The District Court . . . concluded that the search was proper because there was a need to secure state property in the office. The Court of Appeals for the Ninth Circuit affirmed in part and reversed in part, concluding that Dr. Ortega had a reasonable expectation of privacy in his office. . . . The Court of Appeals also concluded — albeit without explanation — that the search violated the Fourth Amendment. The Court of Appeals held that the record justified a grant of partial summary judgment for Dr. Ortega on the issue of liability for an unlawful search, and it remanded the case to the District Court for a determination of damages.

We granted certiorari, and now reverse and remand.

II

The strictures of the Fourth Amendment, applied to the States through the Fourteenth Amendment, have been applied to the conduct of governmental officials in various civil activities. . . .

The Fourth Amendment protects the "right of the people to be secure in their persons, houses, papers, and effects, against unreasonable searches and seizures . . . ." Our cases establish that Dr. Ortega's Fourth Amendment rights are implicated only if the conduct of the Hospital officials at issue in this case infringed "an expectation of privacy that society is prepared to consider reasonable." *United States v. Jacobsen*, 466 U.S. 109, 113 (1984). We have no talisman that determines in all cases those privacy expectations that society is prepared to accept as reasonable. Instead, "the Court has given weight to such factors as the intention of the Framers of the Fourth Amendment, the uses to which the individual has put a location, and our societal understanding that certain areas deserve the most scrupulous protection from government invasion." *Oliver v. United States*, 466 U.S. 170, 178 (1984) (citations omitted).

Because the reasonableness of an expectation of privacy, as well as the appropriate standard for a search, is understood to differ according to context, it is essential first to delineate the boundaries of the workplace context. The workplace includes those areas and items that are related to work and are generally within the employer's control. At a hospital, for example, the hallways, cafeteria, offices, desks, and file cabinets, among other areas, are all part of the workplace. These areas remain part of the workplace context even if the employee has placed personal items in them, such as a photograph placed in a desk or a letter posted on an employee bulletin board.

Not everything that passes through the confines of the business address can be considered part of the workplace context, however. An employee may bring closed luggage to the office prior to leaving on a trip, or a handbag or briefcase each workday. While whatever expectation of privacy the employee has in the existence and the outward appearance of the luggage is affected by its presence in the workplace, the employee's expectation of privacy in the contents of the luggage is not affected in the same way. The appropriate standard for a workplace search does not necessarily apply to a piece of closed personal luggage, a handbag, or a briefcase that happens to be within the employer's business address.

Within the workplace context, this Court has recognized that employees may have a reasonable expectation of privacy against intrusions by police. *See Mancusi v. DeForte*, 392 U.S. 364 (1968). . . .

. . . .

Given the societal expectations of privacy in one's place of work . . . we reject the contention made by the Solicitor General and petitioners that public employees can never have a reasonable expectation of privacy in their place of work. Individuals do not lose Fourth Amendment rights merely because they work for the government instead of a private employer. The operational realities of the workplace, however, may make some employees' expectations of privacy unreasonable when an intrusion is by a supervisor rather than a law enforcement official. Public employees' expectations of privacy in their offices, desks, and file cabinets, like similar expectations of employees in the private sector, may be reduced by virtue of actual office practices and procedures, or by legitimate regulation. . . . An office is seldom a private enclave free from entry by supervisors, other employees, and business and personal invitees. . . . Given the great variety of work environments in the public sector, the question whether an employee has a reasonable expectation of privacy must be addressed on a case-by-case basis.

The Court of Appeals concluded that Dr. Ortega had a reasonable expectation of privacy in his office, and five Members of this Court agree with that determination. Because the record does not reveal the extent to which Hospital officials may have had work-related reasons to enter Dr. Ortega's office, we think the Court of Appeals should have remanded the matter to the District Court for its further determination. But regardless of any legitimate right of access the Hospital staff may have had to the office as such, we recognize that the undisputed evidence suggests that Dr. Ortega had a reasonable expectation of privacy in his desk and file cabinets. The undisputed evidence discloses that Dr. Ortega did not share his desk or file cabinets with any other employees. Dr. Ortega had occupied the office for 17 years and he kept materials in his office, which included personal correspondence, medical files, correspondence from private patients unconnected to the Hospital, personal financial records, teaching aids and notes, and personal gifts and mementos. . . . Indeed, the only items found by the investigators were apparently personal items . . . .

On the basis of this undisputed evidence, we accept the conclusion of the Court of Appeals that Dr. Ortega had a reasonable expectation of privacy at least in his desk and file cabinets.

III

Having determined that Dr. Ortega had a reasonable expectation of privacy in his office, the Court of Appeals simply concluded without discussion that the "search . . . was not a reasonable search under the fourth amendment." But as we have stated in *T. L. O.*, "[to] hold that the Fourth Amendment applies to searches conducted by [public employers] is only to begin the inquiry into the standards governing such searches. . . . [What] is reasonable depends on the context within which a search takes place." *New Jersey v. T. L. O.*, 469 U.S., at 337. Thus, we must determine the appropriate standard of reasonableness applicable to the search. A determination of the standard of reasonableness applicable to a particular class of searches requires "[balancing] the nature and quality of the intrusion on the individual's Fourth Amendment interests against the importance of the governmental interests alleged to justify the intrusion." *United States v. Place*, 462 U.S. 696, 703 (1983); *Camara v. Municipal Court*, 387 U.S., at 536–537. In the case of searches conducted by a public employer, we must balance the invasion of the employees' legitimate expectations of privacy against the government's need for supervision, control, and the efficient operation of the workplace.

. . . .

There is surprisingly little case law on the appropriate Fourth Amendment standard of reasonableness for a public employer's work-related search of its employee's offices, desks, or file cabinets. Generally, however, the lower courts have held that any "work-related" search by an employer satisfies the Fourth Amendment reasonableness requirement. . . . The only cases to imply that a warrant should be required involve searches that are not work related . . . or searches for evidence of criminal misconduct . . . .

The legitimate privacy interests of public employees in the private objects they bring to the workplace may be substantial. Against these privacy interests, however, must be balanced the realities of the workplace, which strongly suggest that a warrant requirement would be unworkable. While police, and even administrative enforcement personnel, conduct searches for the primary purpose of obtaining evidence for use in criminal or other enforcement proceedings, employers most frequently need to enter the offices and desks of their employees for legitimate work-related reasons wholly unrelated to illegal conduct. . . . An employer may have need for correspondence, or a file or report available only in an employee's office while the employee is away from the office. . . .

In our view, requiring an employer to obtain a warrant whenever the employer wished to enter an employee's office, desk, or file cabinets for a work-related purpose would seriously disrupt the routine conduct of business and would be unduly burdensome. . . .

Whether probable cause is an inappropriate standard for public employer searches of their employees' offices presents a more difficult issue. For the most part, we have required that a search be based upon probable cause, but as we noted in *New Jersey v. T. L. O.*, "[the] fundamental command of the Fourth Amendment is that searches and seizures be reasonable, and although 'both the concept of probable cause and the requirement of a warrant bear on the reasonableness of a search, . . . in certain limited circumstances neither is required.' " 469 U.S., at 340. . . .

As an initial matter, it is important to recognize the plethora of contexts in which employers will have an occasion to intrude to some extent on an employee's expectation of privacy. Because the parties in this case have alleged that the search was either a noninvestigatory work-related intrusion or an investigatory search for evidence of suspected work-related employee misfeasance, we undertake to determine the appropriate Fourth Amendment standard of reasonableness only for these two types of employer intrusions and leave for another day inquiry into other circumstances.

The governmental interest justifying work-related intrusions by public employers is the efficient and proper operation of the workplace. Government agencies provide myriad services to the public, and the work of these agencies would suffer if employers were required to have probable cause before they entered an employee's desk for the purpose of finding a file or piece of office correspondence. . . . To ensure the efficient and proper operation of the agency, therefore, public employers must be given wide latitude to enter employee offices for work-related, noninvestigatory reasons.

We come to a similar conclusion for searches conducted pursuant to an investigation of work-related employee misconduct. Even when employers conduct an investigation, they have an interest substantially different from "the normal need for law enforcement." *New Jersey v. T. L. O., supra*, at 351 (BLACKMUN, J., concurring in judgment). Public employers have an interest in ensuring that their agencies operate in an effective and efficient manner, and the work of these agencies inevitably suffers from the inefficiency, incompetence, mismanagement, or other work-related misfeasance of its employees. . . . In our view, therefore, a probable cause requirement for searches of the type at issue here would impose intolerable burdens on public employers. The delay in correcting the employee misconduct caused by the need for probable cause rather than reasonable suspicion will be translated into tangible and often irreparable damage to the agency's work, and ultimately to the public interest. . . .

Balanced against the substantial government interests in the efficient and proper operation of the workplace are the privacy interests of government employees in their place of work which, while not insubstantial, are far less than those found at home or in some other contexts. . . . The employee may avoid exposing personal belongings at work by simply leaving them at home.

In sum, we conclude that the "special needs, beyond the normal need for law enforcement make the . . . probable-cause requirement impracticable," 469 U.S., at 351 (BLACKMUN, J., concurring in judgment), for legitimate work-related, noninvestigatory intrusions as well as investigations of work-related misconduct. A standard of reasonableness will neither unduly burden the efforts of government employers to ensure the efficient and proper operation of the workplace, nor authorize arbitrary intrusions upon the privacy of public employees. We hold, therefore, that public employer intrusions on the constitutionally protected privacy interests of government employees for noninvestigatory, work-related purposes, as well as for investigations of work-related misconduct, should be judged by the standard of reasonableness under all the circumstances. Under this reasonableness standard, both the inception and the scope of the intrusion must be reasonable . . . .

Ordinarily, a search of an employee's office by a supervisor will be "justified at its inception" when there are reasonable grounds for suspecting that the search will turn up evidence that the employee is guilty of work-related misconduct, or that the search is necessary for a noninvestigatory work-related purpose such as to retrieve a needed file. Because petitioners had an "individualized suspicion" of misconduct by Dr. Ortega, we need not decide whether individualized suspicion is an essential element of the standard of reasonableness that we adopt today. The search will be permissible in its scope when "the measures adopted are reasonably related to the objectives of the search and not excessively intrusive in light of . . . the nature of the [misconduct]." 469 U.S., at 342.

IV

In the procedural posture of this case, we do not attempt to determine whether the search of Dr. Ortega's office and the seizure of his personal belongings satisfy the standard of reasonableness we have articulated in this case. No evidentiary hearing was held in this case because the District Court acted on cross-motions for summary judgment, and granted petitioners summary judgment. The Court of Appeals, on the other hand, concluded that the record in this case justified granting partial summary judgment on liability to Dr. Ortega.

We believe that both the District Court and the Court of Appeals were in error because summary judgment was inappropriate. The parties were in dispute about the actual justification for the search, and the record was inadequate for a determination on motion for summary judgment of the reasonableness of the search and seizure. . . .

. . . .

On remand, therefore, the District Court must determine the justification for the search and seizure, and evaluate the reasonableness of both the inception of the search and its scope.

Accordingly, the judgment of the Court of Appeals is reversed, and the case is remanded to that court for further proceedings consistent with this opinion.

It is so ordered.

NOTES

1. The *O'Connor* decision is based on a ruling in a case entitled *New Jersey v. T.L.O.*, 469 U.S. 325 (1985), where the United States announced that K-12 students are entitled to the constitutional protections of the Fourth Amendment. The Court noted, though, that those rights are restricted based on the need to maintain order in the schools:

> [W]e conclude[e] that the accommodation of the privacy interests of schoolchildren with the substantial need of teachers and administrators for freedom to maintain order in the schools does not require strict adherence to the requirement that searches be based on probable cause to believe that the subject of the search has violated or is violating the law. Rather, the legality of a search of a student should depend simply on the reasonableness, under all the circumstances, of the search. Determining the reasonableness of any search involves a twofold inquiry: first, one must consider "whether the . . . action was justified at its inception," second, one must determine whether the search as actually conducted "was reasonably related in scope to the circumstances which justified the interference in the first place." Under ordinary circumstances, a search of a student by a teacher or other school official will be "justified at its inception" when there are reasonable grounds for suspecting that the search will turn up evidence that the student has violated or is violating either the law or the rules of the school. Such a search will be permissible in its scope when the measures adopted are reasonably related to the objectives of the search and not excessively intrusive in light of the age and sex of the student and the nature of the infraction.
>
> . . .
>
> This standard will, we trust, neither unduly burden the efforts of school authorities to maintain order in their schools nor authorize unrestrained intrusions upon the privacy of schoolchildren. By focusing attention on the question of reasonableness, the standard will spare teachers and school administrators the necessity of schooling themselves in the niceties of probable cause and permit them to regulate their conduct according to the dictates of reason and common sense. At the same time, the reasonableness standard should ensure that the interests of students will be invaded no more than is necessary to achieve the legitimate end of preserving order in the schools.

Id. at 341–43.

How did both *T.L.O.* and *O'Connor* address the issue of searches regarding personnel, since *T.L.O.* obviously involved a K-12 student? Said differently, should there be differences in the treatment of constitutional rights as regards children and adults in the school atmosphere? Should those differences also relate to colleges and universities versus public schools?

2. The Court in *T.L.O.* distinguishes between the "warrant requirement" of the "probable cause" doctrine and that of "reasonable suspicion." The opinion gives as its rationale for lowering the probable cause burden the need to address school discipline and to do so immediately. Why would such a reason apply to college professors? What are the disciplinary concerns for postsecondary personnel that may deserve an exception to the general Fourth Amendment rule that warrantless searches and seizures are *per se* unreasonable? Does such a ruling give university administrators too much discretion?

3. *O'Connor* involves the search of a physician's office at a public hospital. The actual implicating evidence was uncovered by a lower level hospital administrator who reported it to the executive director of the hospital. How much difference does the identity of the informant make? What if the chain of informants is long and a number of persons are involved before the information is related to an official empowered to address the problem? Would this be sufficient under the *T.L.O.* standard? What of the decision in *O'Connor*?

2. Due Process

BOARD OF REGENTS v. ROTH
408 U.S. 564 (1972)

MR. JUSTICE STEWART delivered the opinion of the Court.

In 1968 the respondent, David Roth, was hired for his first teaching job as assistant professor of political science at Wisconsin State University-Oshkosh. He was hired for a fixed term of one academic year. The notice of his faculty appointment specified that his employment would begin on September 1, 1968, and would end on June 30, 1969. The respondent completed that term. But he was informed that he would not be rehired for the next academic year.

. . . .

The respondent had no tenure rights to continued employment. Under Wisconsin statutory law a state university teacher can acquire tenure as a "permanent" employee only after four years of year-to-year employment. Having acquired tenure, a teacher is entitled to continued employment "during efficiency and good behavior." A relatively new teacher without tenure, however, is under Wisconsin law entitled to nothing beyond his one-year appointment. . . . State law . . . leaves the decision whether to rehire a nontenured teacher for another year to the unfettered discretion of university officials.

The procedural protection afforded a Wisconsin State University teacher before he is separated from the University corresponds to his job security. As a matter of statutory law, a tenured teacher cannot be "discharged except for cause upon written charges" and pursuant to certain procedures. A nontenured teacher, similarly, is protected to some extent during his one-year term. Rules promulgated by the Board of Regents provide that a nontenured teacher "dismissed" before the end of the year may have some opportunity for review of the "dismissal." But the Rules provide no real protection for a nontenured teacher who simply is not re-employed for the next year. He must be informed by February 1 "concerning retention or nonretention for the ensuing year." But "no reason for non-retention need be given. No review or appeal is provided in such case."

In conformance with these Rules, the President of Wisconsin State University-Oshkosh informed the respondent before February 1, 1969, that he would not be rehired for the 1969-1970 academic year. He gave the respondent no reason for the decision and no opportunity to challenge it at any sort of hearing.

The respondent then brought this action in Federal District Court alleging that the decision not to rehire him for the next year infringed his Fourteenth Amendment rights. He attacked the decision both in substance and procedure. First, he alleged that the true reason for the decision was to punish him for certain statements critical of the University administration, and that it therefore violated his right to freedom of speech. Second, he alleged that the failure of University officials to give him notice of any reason for nonretention and an opportunity for a hearing violated his right to procedural due process of law.

The District Court granted summary judgment for the respondent on the procedural issue, ordering the University officials to provide him with reasons and a hearing. The Court of Appeals . . . affirmed this partial summary judgment. We granted certiorari. The only question presented to us at this stage in the case is whether the respondent had a constitutional right to a statement of reasons and a hearing on the University's decision not to rehire him for another year. We hold that he did not.

I

The requirements of procedural due process apply only to the deprivation of interests encompassed by the Fourteenth Amendment's protection of liberty and property. When protected interests are implicated, the right to some kind of prior hearing is paramount. But the range of interests protected by procedural due process is not infinite.

The District Court decided that procedural due process guarantees apply in this case by assessing and balancing the weights of the particular interests involved. It concluded that the respondent's interest in re-employment at Wisconsin State University-Oshkosh outweighed the University's interest in denying him re-employment summarily. Undeniably, the respondent's re-employment prospects were of major concern to him — concern that we surely cannot say was insignificant. And a weighing process has long been a part of any determination of the form of hearing required in particular situations by procedural due process. But, to determine whether due process requirements apply in the first place, we must look not to the "weight" but to the nature of the interest at stake. *See Morrissey v. Brewer, ante*, at 481. We must look to see if the interest is within the Fourteenth Amendment's protection of liberty and property.

"Liberty" and "property" are broad and majestic terms. They are among the "great [constitutional] concepts . . . purposely left to gather meaning from experience. . . . They relate to the whole domain of social and economic fact, and the statesmen who founded this Nation knew too well that only a stagnant society remains unchanged." *National Ins. Co. v. Tidewater Co.*, 337 U.S. 582, 646 (Frankfurter, J., dissenting). . . . The Court has . . . made clear that the property interests protected by procedural due process extend well beyond actual ownership of real estate, chattels, or money. By the same token, the Court has required due process protection for deprivations of liberty beyond the sort of formal constraints imposed by the criminal process.

Yet, while the Court has eschewed rigid or formalistic limitations on the protection of procedural due process, it has at the same time observed certain boundaries. For the words "liberty" and "property" in the Due Process Clause of the Fourteenth Amendment must be given some meaning.

II

"While this Court has not attempted to define with exactness the liberty . . . guaranteed [by the Fourteenth Amendment], the term has received much consideration and some of the included things have been definitely stated. Without doubt, it denotes not merely freedom from bodily restraint but also the right of the individual to contract, to engage in any of the common occupations of life, to acquire useful knowledge, to marry, establish a home and bring up children, to worship God according to the dictates of his own conscience, and generally to enjoy those privileges long recognized . . . as essential to the orderly pursuit of happiness by free men." *Meyer v. Nebraska*, 262 U.S. 390, 399. In a Constitution for a free people, there can be no doubt that the meaning of "liberty" must be broad indeed. *See, e. g., Bolling v. Sharpe*, 347 U.S. 497, 499–500; *Stanley v. Illinois*, 405 U.S. 645.

There might be cases in which a State refused to reemploy a person under such circumstances that interests in liberty would be implicated. But this is not such a case.

The State, in declining to rehire the respondent, did not make any charge against him that might seriously damage his standing and associations in his community. It did not base the nonrenewal of his contract on a charge, for example, that he had been guilty of dishonesty, or immorality. Had it done so, this would be a different case. . . . In such a case, due process would accord an opportunity to refute the charge before University officials. In the present case, however, there is no suggestion whatever that the respondent's "good name, reputation, honor, or integrity" is at stake.

Similarly, there is no suggestion that the State, in declining to re-employ the respondent, imposed on him a stigma or other disability that foreclosed his freedom to take advantage of other employment opportunities. The State, for example, did not invoke any regulations to bar the respondent from all other public employment in state universities. Had it done so, this, again, would be a different case. . . .

To be sure, the respondent has alleged that the nonrenewal of his contract was based on his exercise of his right to freedom of speech. But this allegation is not now before us. The District Court stayed proceedings on this issue, and the respondent has yet to prove that the decision not to rehire him was, in fact, based on his free speech activities.

When a State would directly impinge upon interests in free speech or free press, this Court has on occasion held that opportunity for a fair adversary hearing must precede the action, whether or not the speech or press interest is clearly protected under substantive First Amendment standards. Thus, we have required fair notice and opportunity for an adversary hearing before an injunction is issued against the holding of rallies and public meetings. *Carroll v. Princess Anne*, 393 U.S. 175. Similarly, we have indicated the necessity of procedural safeguards before a State makes a large-scale seizure of a person's allegedly obscene books, magazines, and so forth. *A Quantity of Books v. Kansas*, 378 U.S. 205; *Marcus v. Search Warrant*, 367 U.S. 717. *See Freedman v. Maryland*, 380 U.S. 51; *Bantam Books v. Sullivan*, 372 U.S. 58.

In the respondent's case, however, the State has not directly impinged upon interests in free speech or free press in any way comparable to a seizure of books or an injunction against meetings. Whatever may be a teacher's rights of free speech, the interest in holding a teaching job at a state university, simpliciter, is not itself a free speech interest.

Hence, on the record before us, all that clearly appears is that the respondent was not rehired for one year at one university. It stretches the concept too far to suggest that a person is deprived of "liberty" when he simply is not rehired in one job but remains as free as before to seek another.

III

The Fourteenth Amendment's procedural protection of property is a safeguard of the security of interests that a person has already acquired in specific benefits. These interests — property interests — may take many forms.

Thus, the Court has held that a person receiving welfare benefits under statutory and administrative standards defining eligibility for them has an interest in continued receipt of those benefits that is safeguarded by procedural due process. *Goldberg v. Kelly*, 397 U.S. 254. Similarly, in the area of public employment, the Court has held that a public college professor dismissed from an office held under tenure provisions, *Slochower v. Board of Education*, 350 U.S. 551, and college professors and staff members dismissed during the terms of their contracts, *Wieman v. Updegraff*, 344 U.S. 183, have interests in continued employment that are safeguarded by due process. Only last year, the Court held that this principle "proscribing summary dismissal from public employment without hearing or inquiry required by due process" also applied to a teacher recently hired without tenure or a formal contract, but nonetheless with a clearly implied promise of continued employment. *Connell v. Higginbotham*, 403 U.S. 207, 208.

Certain attributes of "property" interests protected by procedural due process emerge from these decisions. To have a property interest in a benefit, a person clearly must have more than an abstract need or desire for it. He must have more than a unilateral expectation of it. He must, instead, have a legitimate claim of entitlement to it. It is a purpose of the ancient institution of property to protect those claims upon which people rely in their daily lives, reliance that must not be arbitrarily undermined. It is a purpose of the constitutional right to a hearing to provide an opportunity for a person to vindicate those claims.

Property interests, of course, are not created by the Constitution. Rather, they are created and their dimensions are defined by existing rules or understandings that stem from an independent source such as state law — rules or understandings that secure certain benefits and that support claims of entitlement to those benefits. . . .

. . . [T]he respondent's "property" interest in employment at Wisconsin State University-Oshkosh was created and defined by the terms of his appointment. Those terms secured his interest in employment up to June 30, 1969. But the important fact in this case is that they specifically provided that the respondent's employment was to terminate on June 30. They did not provide for contract renewal absent "sufficient cause." Indeed, they made no provision for renewal whatsoever.

Thus, the terms of the respondent's appointment secured absolutely no interest in re-employment for the next year. They supported absolutely no possible claim of entitlement to re-employment. Nor, significantly, was there any state statute or University rule or policy that secured his interest in re-employment or that created any legitimate claim to it. In these circumstances, the respondent surely had an abstract concern in being rehired, but he did not have a property interest sufficient to require the University authorities to give him a hearing when they declined to renew his contract of employment.

IV

Our analysis of the respondent's constitutional rights in this case in no way indicates a view that an opportunity for a hearing or a statement of reasons for nonretention would, or would not, be appropriate or wise in public colleges and universities. For it is a written Constitution that we apply. Our role is confined to interpretation of that Constitution.

We must conclude that the summary judgment for the respondent should not have been granted, since the respondent has not shown that he was deprived of liberty or property protected by the Fourteenth Amendment. The judgment of the Court of Appeals, accordingly, is reversed and the case is remanded for further proceedings consistent with this opinion.

PERRY v. SINDERMANN

408 U.S. 593 (1972)

MR. JUSTICE STEWART delivered the opinion of the Court.

From 1959 to 1969 the respondent, Robert Sindermann, was a teacher in the state college system of the State of Texas. After teaching for two years at the University of Texas and for four years at San Antonio Junior College, he became a professor of Government and Social Science at Odessa Junior College in 1965. He was employed at the college for four successive years, under a series of one-year contracts. He was successful enough to be appointed, for a time, the cochairman of his department.

During the 1968-1969 academic year, however, controversy arose between the respondent and the college administration. The respondent was elected president of the Texas Junior College Teachers Association. In this capacity, he left his teaching duties on several occasions to testify before committees of the Texas Legislature, and he became involved in public disagreements with the policies of the college's Board of Regents. In particular, he aligned himself with a group advocating the elevation of the college to four-year status — a change opposed by the Regents. And, on one occasion, a newspaper advertisement appeared over his name that was highly critical of the Regents.

Finally, in May 1969, the respondent's one-year employment contract terminated and the Board of Regents voted not to offer him a new contract for the next academic year. The Regents issued a press release setting forth allegations of the respondent's insubordination. But they provided him no official statement of the reasons for the nonrenewal of his contract. And they allowed him no opportunity for a hearing to challenge the basis of the nonrenewal.

The respondent then brought this action in Federal District Court. He alleged primarily that the Regents' decision not to rehire him was based on his public criticism of the policies of the college administration and thus infringed his right to freedom of speech. He also alleged that their failure to provide him an opportunity for a hearing violated the Fourteenth Amendment's guarantee of procedural due process. The petitioners — members of the Board of Regents and the president of the college — denied that their decision was made in retaliation for the respondent's public criticism and argued that they had no obligation to provide a hearing. . . . [T]he District Court granted summary judgment for the petitioners. It concluded that the respondent had "no cause of action against the [petitioners] since his contract of employment terminated May 31, 1969, and Odessa Junior College has not adopted the tenure system."

The Court of Appeals reversed the judgment of the District Court. First, it held that, despite the respondent's lack of tenure, the nonrenewal of his contract would violate the Fourteenth Amendment if it in fact was based on his protected free speech. Since the actual reason for the Regents' decision was "in total dispute" in the pleadings, the court remanded the case for a full hearing on this contested issue of fact. Second, the Court of Appeals held that, despite the respondent's lack of tenure, the failure to allow him an opportunity for a hearing would violate the constitutional guarantee of procedural due process if the respondent could show that he had an "expectancy" of re-employment. It, therefore, ordered that this issue of fact also be aired upon remand. We granted a writ of certiorari, and we have considered this case along with *Board of Regents v. Roth*, *ante*, p. 564.

I

The first question presented is whether the respondent's lack of a contractual or tenure right to re-employment, taken alone, defeats his claim that the nonrenewal of his contract violated the First and Fourteenth Amendments. We hold that it does not.

For at least a quarter-century, this Court has made clear that even though a person has no "right" to a valuable governmental benefit and even though the government may deny him the benefit for any number of reasons, there are some reasons upon which the government may not rely. It may not deny a benefit to a person on a basis that infringes his constitutionally protected interests — especially, his interest in freedom of speech. For if the government could deny a benefit to a person because of his constitutionally protected speech or associations, his exercise of those freedoms would in effect be penalized and inhibited. . . .

We have applied this general principle to denials of tax exemptions, unemployment benefits, and welfare payments. But, most often, we have applied the principle to denials of public employment. We have applied the principle regardless of the public employee's contractual or other claim to a job.

Thus, the respondent's lack of a contractual or tenure "right" to re-employment for the 1969-1970 academic year is immaterial to his free speech claim. Indeed, twice before, this Court has specifically held that the nonrenewal of a nontenured public school teacher's one-year contract may not be predicated on his exercise of First and Fourteenth Amendment rights. *Shelton v. Tucker* [, 364 U.S. 479 (1960)]; *Keyishian v. Board of Regents* [, 385 U.S. 589 (1967)].We reaffirm those holdings here.

In this case, of course, the respondent has yet to show that the decision not to renew his contract was, in fact, made in retaliation for his exercise of the constitutional right of free speech. The District Court foreclosed any opportunity to make this showing when it granted summary judgment. Hence, we cannot now hold that the Board of Regents' action was invalid.

But we agree with the Court of Appeals that there is a genuine dispute as to "whether the college refused to renew the teaching contract on an impermissible basis — as a reprisal for the exercise of constitutionally protected rights." The respondent has alleged that his nonretention was based on his testimony before legislative committees and his other public statements critical of the Regents' policies. And he has alleged that this public criticism was within the First and Fourteenth Amendments' protection of freedom of speech. Plainly, these allegations present a bona fide constitutional claim. . . .

For this reason we hold that the grant of summary judgment against the respondent, without full exploration of this issue, was improper.

II

The respondent's lack of formal contractual or tenure security in continued employment at Odessa Junior College, though irrelevant to his free speech claim, is highly relevant to his procedural due process claim. But it may not be entirely dispositive.

We have held today in *Board of Regents v. Roth*, that the Constitution does not require opportunity for a hearing before the nonrenewal of a nontenured teacher's contract, unless he can show that the decision not to rehire him somehow deprived him of an interest in "liberty" or that he had a "property" interest in continued employment, despite the lack of tenure or a formal contract. In *Roth* the teacher had not made a showing on either point to justify summary judgment in his favor.

Similarly, the respondent here has yet to show that he has been deprived of an interest that could invoke procedural due process protection. As in *Roth*, the mere showing that he was not rehired in one particular job, without more, did not amount to a showing of a loss of liberty. Nor did it amount to a showing of a loss of property.

But the respondent's allegations — which we must construe most favorably to the respondent at this stage of the litigation — do raise a genuine issue as to his interest in continued employment at Odessa Junior College. He alleged that this interest, though not secured by a formal contractual tenure provision, was secured by a no less binding understanding fostered by the college administration. In particular, the respondent alleged that the college had a de facto tenure program, and that he had tenure under that program. He claimed that he and others legitimately relied upon an unusual provision that had been in the college's official Faculty Guide for many years:

Teacher Tenure: Odessa College has no tenure system. The Administration of the College wishes the faculty member to feel that he has permanent tenure as long as his teaching services are satisfactory and as long as he displays a cooperative attitude toward his co-workers and his superiors, and as long as he is happy in his work.

Moreover, the respondent claimed legitimate reliance upon guidelines promulgated by the Coordinating Board of the Texas College and University System that provided that a person, like himself, who had been employed as a teacher in the state college and university system for seven years or more has some form of job tenure. . . .

We have made clear in *Roth*, that "property" interests subject to procedural due process protection are not limited by a few rigid, technical forms. Rather, "property" denotes a broad range of interests that are secured by "existing rules or understandings." . . .

A written contract with an explicit tenure provision clearly is evidence of a formal understanding that supports a teacher's claim of entitlement to continued employment unless sufficient "cause" is shown. Yet absence of such an explicit contractual provision may not always foreclose the possibility that a teacher has a "property" interest in re-employment. . . .

A teacher, like the respondent, who has held his position for a number of years, might be able to show from the circumstances of this service — and from other relevant facts — that he has a legitimate claim of entitlement to job tenure. . . . This is particularly likely in a college or university, like Odessa Junior College, that has no explicit tenure system even for senior members of its faculty, but that nonetheless may have created such a system in practice.

In this case, the respondent has alleged the existence of rules and understandings, promulgated and fostered by state officials, that may justify his legitimate claim of entitlement to continued employment absent "sufficient cause." We disagree with the Court of Appeals insofar as it held that a mere subjective "expectancy" is protected by procedural due process, but we agree that the respondent must be given an opportunity to prove the legitimacy of his claim of such entitlement in light of "the policies and practices of the institution." Proof of such a property interest would not, of course, entitle him to reinstatement. But such proof would obligate college officials to grant a hearing at his request, where he could be informed of the grounds for his nonretention and challenge their sufficiency.

Therefore, while we do not wholly agree with the opinion of the Court of Appeals, its judgment remanding this case to the District Court is

Affirmed.

NOTES

1. *Roth* and *Sindermann* remain the foundation cases for due process decisions involving personnel in public employment. Each case signifies that faculty must establish the existence of a protected liberty interest or property right in order to have a valid claim. Property rights can be recognized when faculty demonstrate some legitimate entitlement position through a vested right such as tenure or a contract. Hence, in any discussion of property rights, a distinction must be made between those faculty with permanent or continuing status and those whose contracts are limited or terminal. Liberty interests are generated if the faculty member is stigmatized in some way or has his or her good name and reputation tarnished so as to foreclose opportunities for future employment. Note that Roth did not argue against the existence of state law with definite parameters for property rights. Instead, he claimed a comparison of similarly situated individuals who were given additional time in their faculty positions while he was not. What was the Court's response to this? What did the Court mean by informing Roth that he had no more than an "abstract concern" in being retained?

2. Do probationary faculty have any entitlement and any expectation of due process? See *Cleveland Bd. of Educ. v. Loudermill*, 470 U.S. 532 (1985), where the Supreme Court announced that those on limited or terminal contracts have no entitlement to due process other than notice of nonrenewal.

3. Most states and their public colleges and universities have statutes protecting the personnel records of postsecondary faculty. However, in 1996, Congress enacted the federal Freedom of Information Act, 5 U.S.C. § 552 (1996), to encourage openness in the operation of government agencies and to provide for citizen access to government information. The Act requires federal agencies to publish or make available a wide array of information, including employee records. Even before the federal statute was enacted, the United States Supreme Court had declared that university records regarding activity by members of tenure and promotion committees were not protected. In *University of Pennsylvania v. E.E.O.C.*, 493 U.S 182 (1990), the Equal Employment Opportunity Commission brought action seeking to enforce a subpoena after the university declined to release confidential peer review materials relating to the tenure review of a former faculty member (who was claiming racial and gender discrimination). The Court held that colleges and universities do not enjoy a "special privilege requiring judicial finding of particularized necessity of access . . . before peer review materials pertinent to charges of discrimination in tenure decisions are disclosed to the E.E.O.C." *Id.* at 182.

4. *Roth v. Sindermann*, a case decided in the same term as *Board of Regents v. Roth, supra*, determined that a community college teacher, employed continuously for 10 years, was entitled to due process protections after being dismissed. The Court declared: "A person's interest in a benefit is a 'property' [right] for due process purposes if there are such rules or 'mutual explicit understandings that support his claim.' " 408 U.S. at 601.

What is a "mutual understanding"? The Court also uses the term "custom and usage" to bestow property rights as entitlements under the Due Process Clause. What creates a "custom and usage"?

5. *Roth* and *Sindermann* should also be read in conjunction with *Bishop v. Wood*, 426 U.S. 341 (1976), where the Court refined those opinions to rule that no liberty interest is created if termination charges are communicated *privately*, the truth or falsity of the charges notwithstanding. *Id.* at 348.

E. FACULTY UNIONIZATION

1. Professional Employee or Managerial Exemption: "Mature" University

NATIONAL LABOR RELATIONS BOARD v. YESHIVA UNIVERSITY

444 U.S. 672 (1980)

MR. JUSTICE POWELL delivered the opinion of the Court.

Supervisors and managerial employees are excluded from the categories of employees entitled to the benefits of collective bargaining under the National Labor Relations Act. The question presented is whether the full-time faculty of Yeshiva University fall within those exclusions.

I

Yeshiva is a private university which conducts a broad range of arts and sciences programs at its five undergraduate and eight graduate schools in New York City. On October 30, 1974, the Yeshiva University Faculty Association (Union) filed a representation petition with the National Labor Relations Board (Board). The Union sought certification as bargaining agent for the full-time faculty members. . . . The University opposed the petition on the ground that all of its faculty members are managerial or supervisory personnel and hence not employees within the meaning of the National Labor Relations Act (Act). A Board-appointed hearing officer held hearings over a period of five months, generating a voluminous record.

The evidence at the hearings showed that a central administrative hierarchy serves all of the University's schools. Ultimate authority is vested in a Board of Trustees, whose members (other than the President) hold no administrative positions at the University. The President sits on the Board of Trustees and serves as chief executive officer, assisted by four Vice Presidents who oversee, respectively, medical affairs and science, student affairs, business affairs, and academic affairs. An Executive Council of Deans and administrators makes recommendations to the President on a wide variety of matters.

University-wide policies are formulated by the central administration with the approval of the Board of Trustees, and include general guidelines dealing with teaching loads, salary scales, tenure, sabbaticals, retirement, and fringe benefits. The budget for each school is drafted by its Dean or Director, subject to approval by the President after consultation with a committee of administrators. The faculty participate in University-wide governance through their representatives on an elected student-faculty advisory council. The only University-wide faculty body is the Faculty Review Committee, composed of elected representatives who adjust grievances by informal negotiation and also may make formal recommendations to the Dean of the affected school or to the President. Such recommendations are purely advisory.

The individual schools within the University are substantially autonomous. Each is headed by a Dean or Director, and faculty members at each school meet formally and informally to discuss and decide matters of institutional and professional concern. At four schools, formal meetings are convened regularly pursuant to written bylaws. The remaining faculties meet when convened by the Dean or Director. Most of the schools also have faculty committees concerned with special areas of educational policy. Faculty welfare committees negotiate with administrators concerning salary and conditions of employment. Through these meetings and committees, the faculty at each school effectively determine its curriculum, grading system, admission and matriculation standards, academic calendars, and course schedules.

Faculty power at Yeshiva's schools extends beyond strictly academic concerns. The faculty at each school make recommendations to the Dean or Director in every case of faculty hiring, tenure, sabbaticals, termination and promotion. Although the final decision is reached by the central administration on the advice of the Dean or Director, the overwhelming majority of faculty recommendations are implemented. Even when financial problems in the early 1970's restricted Yeshiva's budget, faculty recommendations still largely controlled personnel decisions made within the constraints imposed by the administration. Indeed, the faculty of one school recently drew up new and binding policies expanding their own role in these matters. In addition, some faculties make final decisions regarding the admission, expulsion, and graduation of individual students. Others have decided questions involving teaching loads, student absence policies, tuition and enrollment levels, and in one case the location of a school.

II

A three-member panel of the Board granted the Union's petition in December 1975, and directed an election in a bargaining unit consisting of all full-time faculty members at the affected schools. The unit included Assistant Deans, senior professors, and department chairmen, as well as associate professors, assistant professors, and instructors. Deans and Directors were excluded. The Board summarily rejected the University's contention that its entire faculty are managerial, viewing the claim as a request for reconsideration of previous Board decisions on the issue. Instead of making findings of fact as to Yeshiva, the Board referred generally to the record and found no "significan[t]" difference between this faculty and others it had considered. The Board concluded that the faculty are professional employees entitled to the protection of the Act because "faculty participation in collegial decision making is on a collective rather than individual basis, it is exercised in the faculty's own interest rather than 'in the interest of the employer,' and final authority rests with the board of trustees."

The Union won the election and was certified by the Board. The University refused to bargain, reasserting its view that the faculty are managerial. In the subsequent unfair labor practice proceeding, the Board refused to reconsider its holding in the representation proceeding and ordered the University to bargain with the Union. When the University still refused to sit down at the negotiating table, the Board sought enforcement in the Court of Appeals for the Second Circuit, which denied the petition.

Since the Board had made no findings of fact, the court examined the record and related the circumstances in considerable detail. It agreed that the faculty are professional employees under § 2(12) of the Act. But the court found that the Board had ignored "the extensive control of Yeshiva's faculty" over academic and personnel decisions as well as the "crucial role of the full-time faculty in determining other central policies of the institution." The court concluded that such power is not an exercise of individual professional expertise. Rather, the faculty are, "in effect, substantially and pervasively operating the enterprise." Accordingly, the court held that the faculty are endowed with "managerial status" sufficient to remove them from the coverage of the Act. We granted certiorari, and now affirm.

III

There is no evidence that Congress has considered whether a university faculty may organize for collective bargaining under the Act. Indeed, when the Wagner and Taft-Hartley Acts were approved, it was thought that congressional power did not extend to university faculties because they were employed by nonprofit institutions which did not "affect commerce." Moreover, the authority structure of a university does not fit neatly within the statutory scheme we are asked to interpret. The Board itself has noted that the concept of collegiality "does not square with the traditional authority structures with which th[e] Act was designed to cope in the typical organizations of the commercial world."

The Act was intended to accommodate the type of management-employee relations that prevail in the pyramidal hierarchies of private industry. In contrast, authority in the typical "mature" private university is divided between a central administration and one or more collegial bodies. This system of "shared authority" evolved from the medieval model of collegial decisionmaking in which guilds of scholars were responsible only to themselves. At early universities, the faculty were the school. Although faculties have been subject to external control in the United States since colonial times, traditions of collegiality continue to play a significant role at many universities, including Yeshiva. For these reasons, the Board has recognized that principles developed for use in the industrial setting cannot be "imposed blindly on the academic world."

The absence of explicit congressional direction, of course, does not preclude the

Board from reaching any particular type of employment. Acting under its responsibility for adapting the broad provisions of the Act to differing workplaces, the Board asserted jurisdiction over a university for the first time in 1970. Within a year it had approved the formation of bargaining units composed of faculty members. The Board reasoned that faculty members are "professional employees" within the meaning of § 2(12) of the Act and therefore are entitled to the benefits of collective bargaining.

Yeshiva does not contend that its faculty are not professionals under the statute. But professionals, like other employees, may be exempted from coverage under the Act's exclusion for "supervisors" who use independent judgment in overseeing other employees in the interest of the employer, or under the judicially implied exclusion for "managerial employees" who are involved in developing and enforcing employer policy. Both exemptions grow out of the same concern: That an employer is entitled to the undivided loyalty of its representatives. Because the Court of Appeals found the faculty to be managerial employees, it did not decide the question of their supervisory status. In view of our agreement with that court's application of the managerial exclusion, we also need not resolve that issue of statutory interpretation.

IV

Managerial employees are defined as those who "formulate and effectuate management policies by expressing and making operative the decisions of their employer." These employees are "much higher in the managerial structure" than those explicitly mentioned by Congress, which "regarded [them] as so clearly outside the Act that no specific exclusionary provision was thought necessary." Managerial employees must exercise discretion within, or even independently of, established employer policy and must be aligned with management. Although the Board has established no firm criteria for determining when an employee is so aligned, normally an employee may be excluded as managerial only if he represents management interests by taking or recommending discretionary actions that effectively control or implement employer policy.

The Board does not contend that the Yeshiva faculty's decisionmaking is too insignificant to be deemed managerial. Nor does it suggest that the role of the faculty is merely advisory and thus not managerial. Instead, it contends that the managerial exclusion cannot be applied in a straightforward fashion to professional employees because those employees often appear to be exercising managerial authority when they are merely performing routine job duties. The status of such employees, in the Board's view, must be determined by reference to the "alignment with management" criterion. The Board argues that the Yeshiva faculty are not aligned with management because they are expected to exercise "independent professional judgment" while participating in academic governance, and because they are neither "expected to conform to management policies [nor] judged according to their effectiveness in carrying out those policies." Because of this independence, the Board contends there is no danger of divided loyalty and no need for the managerial exclusion. In its view, union pressure cannot divert the faculty from adhering to the interests of the university, because the university itself expects its faculty to pursue professional values rather than institutional interests. The Board concludes that application of the managerial exclusion to such employees would frustrate the national labor policy in favor of collective bargaining.

This "independent professional judgment" test was not applied in the decision we are asked to uphold. The Board's opinion relies exclusively on its previous faculty decisions for both legal and factual analysis. But those decisions only dimly foreshadow the reasoning now proffered to the Court. Without explanation, the Board initially announced two different rationales for faculty cases, then quickly transformed them into a litany to be repeated in case after case: (i) faculty authority is collective, (ii) it is exercised in the faculty's own interest rather than in the interest of the university, and (iii) final authority rests with the board of trustees. In their arguments in this case, the Board's lawyers have abandoned the first and third branches of this analysis, which in any event were flatly inconsistent with its precedents, and have transformed the second into a theory that does not appear clearly in any Board opinion.

V

The controlling consideration in this case is that the faculty of Yeshiva University exercise authority which in any other context unquestionably would be managerial. Their authority in academic matters is absolute. They decide what courses will be offered, when they will be scheduled, and to whom they will be taught. They debate and determine teaching methods, grading policies, and matriculation standards. They effectively decide which students will be admitted, retained, and graduated. On Occasion their views have determined the size of the student body, the tuition to be charged, and the location of a school. When one considers the function of a university, it is difficult to imagine decisions more managerial than these. To the extent the industrial analogy applies, the faculty determines within each school the product to be produced, the terms upon which it will be offered, and the customers who will be served.

The Board nevertheless insists that these decisions are not managerial because they require the exercise of independent professional judgment. We are not persuaded by this argument. There may be some tension between the Act's exclusion of managerial employees and its inclusion of professionals, since most professionals in managerial positions continue to draw on their special skills and training. But we have been directed to no authority suggesting that that tension can be resolved by reference to the "independent professional judgment" criterion proposed in this case. Outside the university context, the Board routinely has applied the managerial and supervisory exclusions to professionals in executive positions without inquiring whether their decisions were based on management policy rather than professional expertise. Indeed, the Board has twice implicitly rejected the contention that decisions based on professional judgment cannot be managerial. Since the Board does not suggest that the "independent professional judgment" test is to be limited to university faculty, its new approach would overrule *sub silentio* this body of Board precedent and could result in the indiscriminate recharacterization as covered employees of professionals working in supervisory and managerial capacities.

Moreover, the Board's approach would undermine the goal it purports to serve: To ensure that employees who exercise discretionary authority on behalf of the employer will not divide their loyalty between employer and union. In arguing that a faculty member exercising independent judgment acts primarily in his own interest and therefore does not represent the interest of his employer, the Board assumes that the professional interests of the faculty and the interests of the institution are distinct, separable entities with which a faculty member could not simultaneously be aligned. The Court of Appeals found no justification for this distinction, and we perceive none. In fact, the faculty's professional interests — as applied to governance at a university like Yeshiva — cannot be separated from those of the institution.

In such a university, the predominant policy normally is to operate a quality institution of higher learning that will accomplish broadly defined educational goals within the limits of its financial resources. The "business" of a university is education, and its vitality ultimately must depend on academic policies that largely are formulated and generally are implemented by faculty governance decisions. Faculty members enhance their own standing and fulfill their professional mission by ensuring that the university's objectives are met. But there can be no doubt that the quest for academic excellence and institutional distinction is a "policy" to which the administration expects the faculty to adhere, whether it be defined as a professional or an institutional goal. It is fruitless to ask whether an employee is "expected to conform" to one goal or another when the two are essentially the same.

The problem of divided loyalty is particularly acute for a university like Yeshiva, which depends on the professional judgment of its faculty to formulate and apply crucial policies constrained only by necessarily general institutional goals. The university requires faculty participation in governance because professional expertise is indispensable to the formulation and implementation of academic policy. It may appear, as the Board contends, that the professor performing governance functions is less "accountable" for departures from institutional policy than a middle-level industrial manager whose discretion is more confined. Moreover, traditional systems of collegiality and tenure insulate the professor from some of the sanctions applied to an industrial manager who fails to adhere to company policy. But the analogy of the university to industry need not, and indeed cannot, be complete. It is clear that Yeshiva and like universities must rely on their faculties to participate in the making and implementation of their policies. The large measure of independence enjoyed by faculty members can only increase the danger that divided loyalty will lead to those harms that the Board traditionally has sought to prevent.

We certainly are not suggesting an application of the managerial exclusion that would sweep all professionals outside the Act in derogation of Congress' expressed intent to protect them. The Board has recognized that employees whose decision-making is limited to the routine discharge of professional duties in projects to which they have been assigned cannot be excluded from coverage even if union membership arguably may involve some divided loyalty. Only if an employee's activities fall outside the scope of the duties routinely performed by similarly situated professionals will he be found aligned with management. We think these decisions accurately capture the intent of Congress, and that they provide an appropriate starting point for analysis in cases involving professionals alleged to be managerial.

VI

Finally, the Board contends that the deference due its expertise in these matters requires us to reverse the decision of the Court of Appeals. The question we decide today is a mixed one of fact and law. But the Board's opinion may be searched in vain for relevant findings of fact. The absence of factual analysis apparently reflects the Board's view that the managerial status of particular faculties may be decided on the basis of conclusory rationales rather than examination of the facts of each case. The Court of Appeals took a different view, and determined that the faculty of Yeshiva University, "in effect, substantially and pervasively operat[e] the enterprise." We find no reason to reject this conclusion. As our decisions consistently show, we accord great respect to the expertise of the Board when its conclusions are rationally based on articulated facts and consistent with the Act. In this case, we hold that the Board's decision satisfies neither criterion.

Affirmed.

MR. JUSTICE BRENNAN, with whom MR. JUSTICE WHITE, MR. JUSTICE MARSHALL, and MR. JUSTICE BLACKMUN join, dissenting.

In holding that the full-time faculty members of Yeshiva University are not covered employees under the National Labor Relations Act, but instead fall within the exclusion for supervisors and managerial employees, the Court disagrees with the determination of the National Labor Relations Board. Because I believe that the Board's decision was neither irrational nor inconsistent with the Act, I respectfully dissent.

I

Ten years ago the Board first asserted jurisdiction over private nonprofit institutions of higher education. Since then, the Board has often struggled with the Procrustean task of attempting to implement in the altogether different environment of the academic community the broad directives of a statutory scheme designed for the bureaucratic industrial workplace. Resolution of the particular issue presented in this case — whether full-time faculty members are covered "employees" under the Act — is but one of several challenges confronting the Board in this "unchartered area."

Because at the time of the Act's passage Congress did not contemplate its application to private universities, it is not surprising that the terms of the Act itself provide no answer to the question before us. Indeed, the statute evidences significant tension as to congressional intent in this respect by its explicit inclusion, on the one hand, of "professional employees" under § 2(12), and its exclusion, on the other, of "supervisors" under § 2(11). Similarly, when transplanted to the academic arena, the Act's extension of coverage to professionals under § 2(12) cannot easily be squared with the Board-created exclusion of "managerial employees" in the industrial context.

Primary authority to resolve these conflicts and to adapt the Act to the changing patterns of industrial relations was entrusted to the Board, not to the judiciary. The Court has often admonished that "[t]he ultimate problem is the balancing of the conflicting legitimate interests. The function of striking that balance to effectuate national labor policy is often a difficult and delicate responsibility, which the Congress committed primarily to the National Labor Relations Board, subject to limited judicial review." Through its cumulative experience in dealing with labor-management relations in a variety of industrial and nonindustrial settings, it is the Board that has developed the expertise to determine whether coverage of a particular category of employees would further the objectives of the Act. And through its continuous oversight of industrial conditions, it is the Board that is best able to formulate and adjust national labor policy to conform to the realities of industrial life. Accordingly, the judicial role is limited; a court may not substitute its own judgment for that of the Board. The Board's decision may be reviewed for its rationality and its consistency with the Act, but once these criteria are satisfied, the order must be enforced.

II

In any event, I believe the Board reached the correct result in determining that Yeshiva's full-time faculty is covered under the NLRA. The Court does not dispute that the faculty members are "professional employees" for the purposes of collective bargaining under § 2(12), but nevertheless finds them excluded from coverage under the implied exclusion for managerial employees." The Court explains that "[t]he controlling consideration in this case is that the faculty of Yeshiva University exercise authority which in any other context unquestionably would be managerial." But the academic community is simply not "any other context." The Court purports to recognize that there are fundamental differences between the authority structures of the typical industrial and academic institutions which preclude the blind transplanting of principles developed in one arena onto the other; yet it nevertheless ignores those very differences in concluding that Yeshiva's faculty is excluded from the Act's coverage.

As reflected in the legislative history of the Taft-Hartley Amendments of 1947, the concern behind the exclusion of supervisors under § 2(11) of the Act is twofold. On the one hand, Congress sought to protect the rank-and-file employees from being unduly influenced in their selection of leaders by the presence of management representatives in their union. "If supervisors were members of and active in the union which represented the employees they supervised it could be possible for the supervisors to obtain and retain positions of power in the union by reason of their authority over their fellow union members while working on the job." In addition, Congress wanted to ensure that employers would not be deprived of the undivided loyalty of their supervisory foremen. Congress was concerned that if supervisors were allowed to affiliate with labor organizations that represented the rank and file, they might become accountable to the workers, thus interfering with the supervisors' ability to discipline and control the employees in the interest of the employer.

Identical considerations underlie the exclusion of managerial employees. Although a variety of verbal formulations have received judicial approval over the years, this Court has recently sanctioned a definition of "managerial employee" that comprises those who " 'formulate and effectuate management policies by expressing and making operative the decisions of their employer.' " The touchstone of managerial status is thus an alliance with management, and the pivotal inquiry is whether the employee in performing his duties represents his own interests or those of his employer. If his actions are undertaken for the purpose of implementing the employer's policies, then he is accountable to management and may be subject to conflicting loyalties. But if the employee is acting only on his own behalf and in his own interest, he is covered under the Act and is entitled to the benefits of collective bargaining.

After examining the voluminous record in this case, the Board determined that the faculty at Yeshiva exercised its decisionmaking authority in its own interest rather than "in the interest of the employer." The Court, in contrast, can perceive "no justification for this distinction" and concludes that the faculty's interests "cannot be separated from those of the institution." But the Court's vision is clouded by its failure fully to discern and comprehend the nature of the faculty's role in university governance.

Unlike the purely hierarchical decisionmaking structure that prevails in the typical industrial organization, the bureaucratic foundation of most "mature" universities is characterized by dual authority systems. The primary decisional network is hierarchical in nature: Authority is lodged in the administration, and a formal chain of command runs from a lay governing board down through university officers to individual faculty members and students. At the same time, there exists a parallel professional network, in which formal mechanisms have been created to bring the expertise of the faculty into the decisionmaking process.

What the Board realized — and what the Court fails to apprehend — is that whatever influence the faculty wields in university decisionmaking is attributable solely to its collective expertise as professional educators, and not to any managerial or supervisory prerogatives. Although the administration may look to the faculty for advice on matters of professional and academic concern, the faculty offers its recommendations in order to serve its own independent interest in creating the most effective environment for learning, teaching, and scholarship. And while the administration may attempt to defer to the faculty's competence whenever possible, it must and does apply its own distinct perspective to those recommendations, a perspective that is based on fiscal and other managerial policies which the faculty has no part in developing. The University always retains the ultimate decisionmaking authority, and the administration gives what weight and import to the faculty's collective judgment as it chooses and deems consistent with its own perception of the institution's needs and objectives.

The premise of a finding of managerial status is a determination that the excluded employee is acting on behalf of management and is answerable to a higher authority in the exercise of his responsibilities. The Board has consistently implemented this requirement — both for professional and non-professional employees — by conferring managerial status only upon those employees "whose interests are closely aligned with management *as true representatives of management.*" Only if the employee is expected to conform to management policies and is judged by his effectiveness in executing those policies does the danger of divided loyalties exist.

Yeshiva's faculty, however, is not accountable to the administration in its governance function, nor is any individual faculty member subject to personal sanction or control based on the administration's assessment of the worth of his recommendations. When the faculty, through the schools' advisory committees, participates in university decisionmaking on subjects of academic policy, it does not serve as the "representative of management." Unlike industrial supervisors and managers, university professors are not hired to "make operative" the policies and decisions of their employer. Nor are they retained on the condition that their interests will correspond to those of the university administration. Indeed, the notion that a faculty member's professional competence could depend on his undivided loyalty to management is antithetical to the whole concept of academic freedom. Faculty members are judged by their employer on the quality of their teaching and scholarship, not on the compatibility of their advice with administration policy. Board Member Kennedy aptly concluded in his concurring opinion in *Northeastern University* (1975):

> [T]he influence which the faculty exercises in many areas of academic governance is insufficient to make them 'managerial' employees. Such influence is not exercised 'for management' or 'in the interest of the employer,' but rather is exercised in their own professional interest. The best evidence of this fact is that faculty members are generally not held accountable by or to the administration for their faculty governance functions. Faculty criticism of administration policies, for example, is viewed not as a breach of loyalty, but as an exercise in academic freedom. So, too, intervention by the university administration in faculty deliberations would most likely be considered an infringement upon academic freedoms. Conversely, university administrations rarely consider themselves bound by faculty recommendations.

It is no answer to say, as does the Court, that Yeshiva's faculty and administration are one and the same because their interests tend to coincide. In the first place, the National Labor Relations Act does not condition its coverage on an antagonism of interests between the employer and the employee. The mere coincidence of interests on many issues has never been thought to abrogate the right to collective bargaining on those topics as to which that coincidence is absent. Ultimately, the performance of an employee's duties will always further the interests of the employer, for in no institution do the interests of labor and management totally diverge. Both desire to maintain stable and profitable operations, and both are committed to creating the best possible product within existing financial constraints. Differences of opinion and emphasis may develop, however, on exactly how to devote the institution's resources to achieve those goals. When these disagreements surface, the national labor laws contemplate their resolution through the peaceful process of collective bargaining. And in this regard, Yeshiva University stands on the same footing as any other employer.

Moreover, the congruence of interests in this case ought not to be exaggerated. The university administration has certain economic and fiduciary responsibilities that are not shared by the faculty, whose primary concerns are academic and relate solely to its own professional reputation. The record evinces numerous instances in which the faculty's recommendations have been rejected by the administration on account of fiscal constraints or other managerial policies. Disputes have arisen between Yeshiva's faculty and administration on such fundamental issues as the hiring, tenure, promotion, retirement, and dismissal of faculty members, academic standards and credits, departmental budgets, and even the faculty's choice of its own departmental representative. The very fact that Yeshiva's faculty has voted for the Union to serve as its representative in future negotiations with the administration indicates that the faculty does not perceive its interests to be aligned with those of management. Indeed, on the precise topics which are specified as mandatory subjects of collective bargaining — wages, hours, and other terms and conditions of employment — the interests of teacher and administrator are often diametrically opposed.

Finally, the Court's perception of the Yeshiva faculty's status is distorted by the rose-colored lens through which it views the governance structure of the modern-day university. The Court's conclusion that the faculty's professional interests are indistinguishable from those of the administration is bottomed on an idealized model of collegial decisionmaking that is a vestige of the great medieval university. But the university of today bears little resemblance to the "community of scholars" of yesteryear. Education has become "big business," and the task of operating the university enterprise has been transferred from the faculty to an autonomous administration, which faces the same pressures to cut costs and increase efficiencies that confront any large industrial organization. The past decade of budgetary cutbacks, declining enrollments, reductions in faculty appointments, curtailment of academic programs, and increasing calls for accountability to alumni and other special interest groups has only added to the erosion of the faculty's role in the institution's decisonmaking process.

These economic exigencies have also exacerbated the tensions in university labor relations, as the faculty and administration more and more frequently find themselves advocating conflicting positions not only on issues of compensation, job security, and working conditions, but even on subjects formerly thought to be the faculty's prerogative. In response to this friction, and in an attempt to avoid the strikes and work stoppages that have disrupted several major universities in recent years, many faculties have entered into collective-bargaining relationships with their administrations and governing boards. An even greater number of schools — Yeshiva among them — have endeavored to negotiate and compromise their differences informally, by establishing avenues for faculty input into university decisions on matters of professional concern.

Today's decision, however, threatens to eliminate much of the administration's incentive to resolve its disputes with the faculty through open discussion and mutual agreement. By its overbroad and unwarranted interpretation of the managerial exclusion, the Court denies the faculty the protections of the NLRA and, in so doing, removes whatever deterrent value the Act's availability may offer against unreasonable administrative conduct. Rather than promoting the Act's objective of funneling dissension between employers and employees into collective bargaining, the Court's decision undermines that goal and contributes to the possibility that "recurring disputes [will] fester outside the negotiation process until strikes or other forms of economic warfare occur."

III

In sum, the Board analyzed both the essential purposes underlying the supervisory and managerial exclusions and the nature of the governance structure at Yeshiva University. Relying on three factors that attempt to encapsulate the fine distinction between those professional employees who are entitled to the NLRA's protections and those whose managerial responsibilities require their exclusion, the Board concluded that Yeshiva's full-time faculty qualify as the former rather than the latter. I believe the Board made the correct determination. But even were I to have reservations about the specific result reached by the Board on the facts of this case, I would certainly have to conclude that the Board applied a proper mode of analysis to arrive at a decision well within the zone of reasonableness. Accordingly, in light of the deference due the Board's determination in this complex area, I would reverse the judgment of the Court of Appeals.

NOTES

1. The *Yeshiva* decision was a 5-4 vote. What was the reasoning behind the majority decision? What was the reasoning behind the dissent? What type of organizational and decision making arrangement might have strengthened the argument that the Yeshiva faculty qualified for unionization under the NLRA? What type of organizational and decision making arrangement might have strengthened the reasoning behind the majority's ruling that the Yeshiva faculty did not qualify to unionize under the NLRA? In what ways are college professors similar or different from industrial supervisors?

2. *Yeshiva* concerns a private university. The Supreme Court ruled that faculty were managers and not employees inasmuch as duties such as the determination of salaries, criteria for the admission of students, and the evaluation of faculty promotion and tenure were more often supervisory. Today the decision still applies only to private institutions although some faculty, but not all, in public colleges and universities are protected by the collective bargaining rights ushered in by the *Yeshiva* decision.

3. A provision within the National Labor Relations Act (NLRA) provides a three-part test for determining supervisory status: "Employees are statutory supervisors if (1) they hold the authority to engage in any 1 of the 12 listed supervisory functions, (2) their 'exercise of such authority is not of a merely routine or clerical nature, but requires the use of independent judgment,' and (3) their authority is held 'in the interest of the employer.' " *NLRB v. Ky. River Cmty. Care, Inc.*, 532 U.S. 706, 712–13 (2001). Using a statutory interpretation lens, the dissent argues that the National Labor Relations Board (NLRB) has the expertise to determine employee categories. The argument grants some deference to the NLRB. Should the majority have done the same? What weight should the Court give to the NLRB's decision and why?

In *NLRB v. Kentucky River Community Care*, the U.S. Supreme Court had to decide whether nurses working in a health care facility qualified as employees able to bargain under the NLRA. In a dissenting opinion, Justice Stevens argued (and Justices Souter, Breyer, and Ginsburg, joined) that statutory ambiguity justifies deferring to the NLRB's interpretation of the language. Specifically, he writes:

> The term "independent judgment" is indisputably ambiguous, and it is settled law that the NLRB's interpretation of ambiguous language in the National Labor Relations Act is entitled to deference. *See NLRB v. Health Care and Retirement Corporation*, 511 U.S. 571, 579 (1994); *Auciello Iron Works, Inc. v. NLRB*, 517 U.S. 781, 787–788 (1996); *Curtin Matheson Scientific, Inc.*, 494 U.S. 775, 786–787. Such deference is particularly appropriate when the statutory ambiguity is compounded by the use of one ambiguous term — "independent judgment" — to modify another, equally ambiguous term — namely, "responsibly to direct."
>
> Moreover, since Congress has expressly provided that professional employees are entitled to the protection of the Act, there is good reason to resolve the ambiguities consistently with the Board's interpretation. At the same time that Congress acted to exclude supervisors from the NLRA's protection, it explicitly extended those same protections to professionals, who, by definition, engage in work that involves "the consistent exercise of discretion and judgment in its performance." 29 U.S.C. § 152(12)(a)(ii). As this Court has acknowledged, the inclusion of professional employees and the exclusion of supervisors necessarily gives rise to some tension in the statutory text.

532 U.S. 706, 725–26.

4. Keeping within the tradition of autonomous agents of the university, faculty have historically maintained significantly more freedom to exercise professional discretion and decision making authority. Arthur Sussman, then General Counsel at the University of Chicago, recalled an encounter between a university president and his faculty, which captures the traditional power structures of faculty during the 1950s:

> Dwight Eisenhower early in his brief presidency of Columbia University greeted a group of faculty members expressing his delight at meeting some of the "employees" of Columbia. The resulting silence, as the story continues, was broken by a senior professor who rose and said, "with all due respect, [S]ir, we are not employees of Columbia [U]niversity. We are Columbia University."

Arthur M. Sussman, *University Governance Through a Rose-Colored Lens: NLRB v. Yeshiva*, 1980 SUP. CT. REV. 27, 27 (1980)*. Do faculty appear to have the same rights and privileges as they did in the past? What evidence might support or counter that suggestion? Justice Powell writing for the majority points out that the faculty at *Yeshiva* had advisory roles to decisions that deans, directors, and executive administrators could accept or not. If administrators do not adopt the faculty's recommendations, does their participation satisfy the collegial decision making process or might there be instances in which the faculty and administrators have very different positions about the faculty's terms and conditions of work?

5. How does the *Yeshiva* decision impact academic freedom? What is at-stake for the faculty? How do the implications of *Yeshiva* change as the nature of colleges and universities change? For instance, various researchers of higher education have observed the corporatization of universities. *See, e.g.*, DEREK BOK, UNIVERSITIES IN THE MARKETPLACE: THE COMMERCIALIZATION OF HIGHER EDUCATION (2003); SHEILA SLAUGHTER & GARY RHOADES, ACADEMIC CAPITALISM AND THE NEW ECONOMY: MARKETS, STATE, AND HIGHER EDUCATION (2004); ELLEN SCHRECKER, THE LOST SOUL OF HIGHER EDUCATION: CORPORATIZATION, THE ASSAULT ON ACADEMIC FREEDOM, AND THE END OF THE AMERICAN UNIVERSITY (2010). Risa Lieberwitz describes this corporatization movement as "privatization of public services" such as engaging in for-profit distance education, commercializing genetic research, and adopting corporate employment models that employ more contingent faculty. Risa L. Lieberwitz, *Faculty in the Corporate University: Professional Identity, Law and Collective Action*, 16 CORNELL J.L. & PUB. POL'Y 263. How might these movements to a more business-like model that values commodification of higher education, while still employing faculty committees as advisory bodies, remain consistent or deviate from the conception of university governance in the *Yeshiva* majority and dissent?

2. Professional Employee or Managerial Exemption: Faculty Participation Circumscribed

LORETTO HEIGHTS COLLEGE v. NATIONAL LABOR RELATIONS BOARD

742 F.2d 1245 (10th Cir. 1984)

SEYMOUR, CIRCUIT JUDGE.

This case is before us on the petition of Loretto Heights College to review and set aside an order of the National Labor Relations Board and on the cross-application of the Board for enforcement of its order. The Board found that the College violated sections 8(a)(1) and 8(a)(5) of the National Labor Relations Act (the Act), by withdrawing recognition of and refusing to bargain with the Loretto Heights College/Faculty Education Association (the Association), the certified exclusive bargaining representative of the College's faculty. The College argues that the faculty members are managerial employees within the meaning of *NLRB v. Yeshiva University*, 444 U.S. 672 (1980), and therefore are excluded from the Act's coverage. Based on our review of the record as a whole, we conclude that the Board's decision is consistent with the applicable law and supported by substantial evidence. Accordingly, we grant enforcement of its order.

I. BACKGROUND

Loretto Heights College is a four-year liberal arts college located in Denver, Colorado. The College was established in 1918 by the Sisters of Loretto as a parochial school for women. It became independent in 1968 and coeducational in 1970. At the time of the proceedings below, the College had a student body of approximately 850, a full-time faculty of 60 to 65, a part-time faculty of 30 to 35, and an administrative staff of about 26 or 27.

The faculty began organizing in 1971, and in 1972 the Association was certified as the collective bargaining representative for all regular full and part-time professional employees carrying at least a one-fourth faculty load. The College and the Association thereafter began negotiations and ultimately entered into a series of collective bargaining agreements, the last of which expired in May 1980. A few months before the final contract expired, the College gave notice of its intent to terminate the agreement at the end of its term. It advised the Association that in light of the recent Supreme Court decision in *Yeshiva,* it had some questions concerning its duty to bargain with the Association. After exchanging correspondence, the parties discontinued their discussions. The College withdrew its recognition of the Association and refused to negotiate further, although it continued to adhere to most of the provisions of the expired contract.

The Association subsequently filed an unfair labor practice charge with the NLRB, alleging that the College's actions violated sections 8(a)(1) and 8(a)(5) of the Act. The Board issued a complaint against the College, and the case was tried before an administrative law judge (ALJ) in March 1981. The ALJ found the College in violation of the Act and issued a recommended order requiring inter alia that the College recognize and bargain with the Association. In so ruling, the ALJ rejected the College's argument that the faculty members were managerial employees and therefore excluded from the Act's coverage under *Yeshiva.* On review, the Board affirmed the findings and conclusions of the ALJ, with one qualification, and adopted his recommended order.

II. THE *YESHIVA* DECISION

In *NLRB v. Yeshiva,* the Supreme Court examined the faculty at Yeshiva University and concluded that its members were managerial employees and hence excluded from coverage under the Act. The Court defined "managerial employees" as "those who 'formulate and effectuate management policies by expressing and making operative the decisions of their employers.' " Such employees are excluded from the Act's coverage, the Court explained, in order to ensure that they will not divide their loyalty between their employer and the union. The assumption underlying this rationale is that an employer is entitled to the undivided loyalty of its representatives. Accordingly, for the exclusion to apply, an employee "must exercise discretion within, or even independently of, established employer policy and must be aligned with management." The Court indicated that normally an employee will be considered aligned with management "only if he represents management interests by taking or recommending discretionary actions that effectively control or implement employer policy."

Conversely, "employees whose decision making is limited to the routine discharge of professional duties in projects to which they have been assigned cannot be excluded from coverage even if union membership arguably may involve some divided loyalty." For example, architects and engineers who function as project captains on work being performed by teams of professionals are not considered managerial despite their substantial planning responsibility and authority to direct team members. Similarly, in the health care context, no exclusion will lie where "the decisions alleged to be managerial or supervisory are 'incidental to' or 'in addition to' the treatment of patients." Thus, "[o]nly if an employee's activities fall outside the scope of the duties routinely performed by similarly situated professionals will he be found aligned with management."

In reviewing the role of the faculty at Yeshiva, the Court had no difficulty approving the Second Circuit's conclusion that the faculty members were " 'in effect, substantially and pervasively operating the enterprise.' " The evidence showed that although a central administrative hierarchy headed by the Board of Trustees and the President oversaw Yeshiva's five undergraduate and eight graduate schools, the individual schools were "substantially autonomous." Each was headed by a dean or director, and the faculty members met formally and informally to discuss and decide matters of institutional and professional concern. Most schools also had faculty committees involved with particular areas of educational policy. The Court observed that "[t]hrough these meetings and committees, the faculty at each school effectively determine its curriculum, grading system, admission and matriculation standards, academic calendars, and course schedules."

The faculty at each school also made recommendations to its respective dean or director concerning faculty hiring, tenure, sabbaticals, termination, and promotion. Although the central administration ultimately made such decisions, with the advice of the dean or director involved, faculty recommendations were followed in the "overwhelming majority" of cases. In addition, the faculty at some schools made final decisions regarding the admission, expulsion, and graduation of individual students. Other faculty had decided such matters as teaching loads, student absence policies, tuition, and even the location of a school in one instance. Based on all the above facts, the Court concluded:

> The controlling consideration in this case is that the faculty of Yeshiva University exercise authority which in any other context unquestionably would be managerial. Their authority in academic matters is absolute. They decide what courses will be offered, when they will be scheduled, and to whom they will be taught. They debate and determine teaching methods, grading policies, and matriculation standards. They effectively decide which students will be admitted, retained, and graduated. On occasion their views have determined the size of the student body, the tuition to be charged, and the location of a school. When one considers the function of a university, it is difficult to imagine decisions more managerial than these. To the extent the industrial analogy applies, the faculty determines within each school the product to be produced, the terms upon which it will be offered, and the customers who will be served.

The Court further found that application of the managerial exclusion in this case would well serve the doctrine's underlying purpose. As the Court pointed out, the problem of divided loyalty is "particularly acute" for a university like Yeshiva, "which depends on the professional judgment of its faculty to formulate and apply crucial policies constrained only by necessarily general institutional goals." Such a school necessarily requires faculty participation in governance "because professional expertise is indispensable to the formulation and implementation of academic policy."

III. COLLEGE GOVERNANCE AT LORETTO HEIGHTS

As the Court's opinion makes clear, the faculty at Yeshiva exercised an extraordinary amount of authority in the operation of the university. Indeed, the Board in that case did not contend that the Yeshiva faculty's role in university decision making was too insignificant to be deemed managerial. Rather, the Board's chief argument was that the faculty was not aligned with management because it exercised "independent professional judgment" in its own interest rather than in the interest of the university. Here, by contrast, the significance of the faculty's role in College governance is sharply disputed by the parties and constitutes the heart of the issue before us. In order to determine whether faculty authority at the College is "managerial" within the meaning of *Yeshiva*, we must examine the overall structure of the College and the role of the faculty in the College's operation and governance.

Ultimate authority for the operation of the College is vested in the Board of Trustees which consists of 21 to 25 members. The chief executive officer is the President, who is subordinate in authority only to the Board of Trustees. The President is aided administratively by five division heads, the Academic Dean, the Dean of Campus Life, the Director of Admissions, the Director of Fiscal Operations, and the Vice President for External Affairs. These division heads are responsible to the President, and are assisted by some fourteen additional administrative and staff personnel.

The College's academic program is divided into six regular program areas and a special programs area. The six regular programs are nursing, teacher education, humanities and sciences, fine arts, business, and the University Without Walls. Each area is administered by a program director. Although program directors also teach, they have varying and often reduced course loads and are considered part of the administration. One or two programs also have coordinators, who assist program directors in areas of natural grouping such as social sciences. Program areas are further broken down into disciplines — individual areas of specialized study such as sociology, mathematics, or history.

Faculty participation in College governance occurs largely through committees and other such groups. The largest of these is the Academic Forum, a college-wide self-governing body comprised of all full and part-time faculty, including program directors. The Academic Dean also is a participating member, although he has no voting privilege. The Forum meets regularly and discusses academic policy and other matters of interest. Under its by-laws, it may make recommendations to appropriate committees or administrators on a variety of subjects and it is to "actively share in decision making" in matters that pertain to the philosophy and objectives of the College, curriculum changes affecting existing programs, admission, retention, and graduation policies, the academic calendar, and the College's "Governance Policies" document.

The Faculty Administration Relations Council (FARC) is an advisory council to the College President, headed by the President and including four administrators and four faculty members. The FARC was involved in the development of the College's academic policies, which set forth the criteria for student admission, grading and graduation, and academic practices which students are expected to follow. The FARC periodically reviews these policies with program area faculty and makes changes as necessary.

The Rank Committee, composed of five full-time faculty members, reviews and makes recommendations to the President concerning policies and criteria on faculty rank and, applying approved criteria, makes recommendations to the President concerning promotion of faculty members. In making such determinations, the committee reviews written recommendations from the appropriate program director and the Academic Dean, whose recommendations it never has rejected outright. The President has accepted all of the Rank Committee's recommendations in the past five years.

The Tenure Committee, consisting of five full-time tenured faculty members and two program directors, functions similarly to the Rank Committee, making recommendations to the President on tenure of individual faculty members and tenure policies and procedures generally. The Tenure Committee, like the Rank Committee, receives evaluations of applicants from the applicant himself, students, colleagues, the appropriate program director, and the Academic Dean. In recent years, the committee has not disagreed with any recommendations of the Academic Dean, and the President has followed all of the committee's recommendations.

The Faculty Review Committee, comprised of five full-time faculty members, operates as an optional second stage in the three-step grievance procedure contained in the most recent collective bargaining agreement. The committee makes recommendations concerning the disposition of a grievance to the President, who may accept the recommendation or reject it with written reasons. The record contains only one instance of action by the committee, on a grievance matter relating to tenure. In that case, the committee agreed with the President's decision to deny tenure.

The Affirmative Action Committee is composed of "a representative number of faculty, staff, and students as appointed by the President." Its purpose is to assist and advise the Affirmative Action Officer and the President in the implementation of affirmative action and nondiscrimination policies and procedure, and compliance review.

The Faculty Evaluation Committee, composed of three full-time faculty members and two students, is concerned with the procedures by which faculty are evaluated by students and colleagues. The committee develops and administers the evaluation instruments and procedures, subject to approval by the appropriate division heads, and provides the results to the appropriate division heads, program directors, and, when needed, the rank and tenure committees.

The Academic Review Committee, made up entirely of administrators, deals with student retention matters. Its function is to review the standing of any student who is not making satisfactory academic progress and to determine an appropriate sanction, such as academic probation or dismissal. As noted above, the academic policies against which a student's performance is measured were developed and periodically are modified in consultation with faculty members and the FARC.

The Sabbatical Committee is chaired by the Academic Dean, and includes one program director and two full-time faculty members. A faculty member seeking sabbatical leave first discusses the matter with his program director, who sends the committee a summary of the discussion along with a recommendation. The committee reviews all applications for sabbatical and makes a recommendation to the President. Since its inception, all of the committee's recommendations have been approved.

The Program Review and Recommendation Committee (PRRC) is comprised of five faculty members who are nominated through the Academic Forum and appointed by the College President, the Academic Dean, and the Forum's officers. The PRRC reviews programs to determine whether they are consistent with the goals of the College and whether any overlap exists among the courses offered by the College. The committee also reviews and makes recommendations concerning new course proposals. Before reaching the PRRC, such a proposal must first be approved at the discipline and program levels. After review by the PRRC, the matter is submitted to the Academic Dean for his comment. Both the PRRC and the general faculty, through the Academic Forum, review and make recommendations concerning the introduction of new majors, minors, degrees, and interdisciplinary programs. In addition to discipline and program level approval, changes of this nature must also be approved by the Academic Dean, the President, and except in the case of new minors, the Board of Trustees.

The composition of the Research Committee is not mandated and has varied among faculty members and program directors. The committee reviews faculty applications for research funds and makes recommendations to the Academic Dean concerning allocation of the $1,000 available for research projects. In 1978 the Academic Dean refused to approve a proposal recommended by the committee.

Other than committee work, the participation of faculty members in College governance relates primarily to decision making within or concerning particular program areas. For example, faculty members within a particular discipline or program area participate in the hiring of new full-time faculty members for that area by selecting and interviewing applicants and making recommendations to the Academic Dean. The faculty sometimes recommends a salary level for a position as well, in order to attract and hire a particularly qualified candidate. The Academic Dean has followed faculty hiring recommendations in all cases. Termination decisions, on the other hand, are made by the Academic Dean without faculty participation.

Program directors are selected by the Academic Dean from within the relevant program area on the basis of faculty recommendations. Faculty members also have participated in the selection of College presidents through membership on search teams, which interview prospective candidates and make recommendations to the Board of Trustees. In the case of current President Adele Phelan, the search team consisted of two members of the Board of Trustees, one student, two administrators, and two faculty members. However, according to Dr. Amundson's testimony, the Board appointed Phelan president before the search team had finished making its selections.

Faculty members also play a significant role in curriculum development within their program areas. In conjunction with the program director, program area faculty members determine the content of courses, scheduling of courses, and course requirements for majors.[15] They also decide with the program director whether students will be admitted to a major, although faculty members are not authorized to expel students from a major. Outside of their own disciplines or program areas, faculty participation in curriculum development and like matters is minimal.

Finally, faculty members have a very limited degree of input into the budget process within their particular areas. Program directors annually distribute "budget sheets" to program area faculty who fill in the forms and return them to the program director. These sheets list the approved budget items for the previous year and have space for the faculty to indicate their expected needs, within certain guidelines, for the coming year. The program director collects this data from the faculty, puts together a proposed budget for his or her area, and then meets with the Academic Dean and Director of Fiscal Operations to work up a final operations budget for submission to the President and Board of Trustees. Faculty members generally receive no notice of action taken with regard to the budget unless they specifically request information.

IV. MANAGERIAL STATUS

It is evident from these facts that faculty members at Loretto Heights play a substantial role in College governance, participating in decision making and implementation in a wide range of areas. It is equally clear, however, that the faculty's authority in most aspects of College governance is severely circumscribed. Thus, while faculty members do take part in the formulation and implementation of management policy, their role does not in our view rise to the level of "effective recommendation or control" contemplated in *Yeshiva.*

So far as the extent of faculty authority is concerned, the record reveals a number of areas, particularly outside the academic sphere, in which the faculty plays little if any role. For example, the ALJ found that faculty participation is "all but nonexistent" in the College's "business affairs," including such activities as the lease and sale of real estate, the purchase of supplies and equipment for non-classroom use, and the employment and termination of nonacademic and office personnel. Faculty members also play virtually no role in the admission, retention, and expulsion of students from the College, the size of the student body, awarding honorary degrees, establishing tuition requirements, or making financial aid determinations. Of course, to the extent many of these areas are outside the

[15] Faculty members also are responsible for the classroom conduct of their students, and for their own teaching and grading methods. Although a faculty member may suggest limitations on enrollment in a particular course, the registrar has not always heeded such requests. Additionally, the Academic Dean can require, within certain limits, that a faculty member teach classes outside the normal teaching hours or during student recess.

academic realm, lack of faculty participation is of only limited significance, as the ALJ recognized. Since the " 'business' of a university is education," we must focus our attention on the faculty's role in academic affairs in order to determine the question of managerial status.

Unlike *Yeshiva*, where each school's faculty apparently met and decided most academic matters as a collective body, the faculty at Loretto Heights participates in such matters primarily through its representation on a number of committees. These committees vary widely both in terms of their own significance and in the scope and effect of the role afforded the faculty representatives. Some committee work, for example, is of a minor nature in comparison to the other functions routinely performed by the faculty. The record shows that the Sabbatical Committee, Faculty Review Committee, Tenure Committee, and Rank Committee, among others, have met infrequently and only for short periods of time in performing their functions in past years. Thus, while these committees may in fact perform important functions, the extent of faculty involvement in the committees' work is so limited as to be "only incidental to, or in addition to, their primary function of teaching, research, and writing," rather than truly managerial in nature.

Several other committees, including the Affirmative Action Committee, Faculty Evaluation Committee, and Research Committee, are in themselves relatively ineffective or insignificant in terms of their impact on College governance, notwithstanding the time commitments membership on such committees may require. For example, the Research Committee, which at times has not even included any members of the faculty, makes allocation recommendations regarding a mere $1,000. Similarly, the Faculty Evaluation Committee, which includes both students and faculty, plays a role only in the development of evaluation procedures and does not itself evaluate anyone. On the other hand, the Affirmative Action Committee functions in a significant policy area, but appears to be a fairly ineffective body in terms of its actual impact on the College, and one which the College administration apparently has felt free to ignore repeatedly in the past.

Even in those organizations that carry more weight in the College's academic structure — particularly the Academic Forum, the FARC, and the PRRC — faculty power is more theoretical than actual. For example, although the bylaws of the Academic Forum provide that it shall share in decision making with regard to such areas as College philosophy, curriculum changes, and admission, retention, and graduation policies, these decisions are made largely through the committees and task forces outlined above. The Forum does appoint the faculty membership of many of these groups and, as discussed above, the Forum must approve major curriculum changes, such as the introduction of new majors, minors, and degrees. However, there is little other evidence of direct, meaningful involvement by the Forum in College governance, and any input it has is primarily of an advisory nature.

The FARC is an advisory body which is composed predominantly of administrators. Although it appears from the record that the FARC plays an important role in the development and review of the College's academic policies, against which students' academic standing is measured, effective control of these policies scarcely can be imputed to the faculty when it comprises a minority of the Council. Similarly, although the PRRC is composed solely of faculty and plays a significant role in curriculum development and review, it lacks final decision making authority. Its function is simply to review and recommend. Moreover, in the case of curriculum changes, PRRC review is merely one intermediary step in a long process that requires approval both at the program level prior to PRRC review, and by the Academic Dean after PRRC review.

As these examples make clear, faculty power at the College, whatever its extent on paper, is in practice severely diluted. In light of the infrequent or insignificant nature of some committee work, the mixed membership of many committees, the faculty's limited decision making authority, and the layers of administrative approval required for many decisions, the impact of faculty participation in College governance falls far short of the "effective recommendation or control" contemplated by *Yeshiva.* Outside the committee structure, as in the hiring and budget processes for example, faculty participation is similarly limited in authority and ultimately subject to one or more levels of administrative approval. Under these circumstances, we cannot say that faculty members "effectively control or implement employer policy." Accordingly, we agree with the Board that they are not managerial employees within the meaning of *Yeshiva.*

Moreover, we are convinced that application of the managerial exclusion in this case would in no way further the underlying goal of ensuring that employees who are aligned with management will not divide their loyalty between employer and union. In *Yeshiva*, divided loyalty was a potentially serious problem because the school depended on its faculty for the "professional expertise" that is "indispensable to the formulation and implementation of academic policy." As the ALJ correctly recognized, the administrative staff at Yeshiva was fairly small, at least in relation to the university's overall size, and there was no effective buffer between the faculty and top management. The university was, in effect, "compelled to rely upon the faculty for advice, recommendations, establishment of policies, and implementation of policies." As a result, the Yeshiva faculty was by necessity "aligned with management."

Here, by contrast, the administration is fairly large in relation to the size of the College. More significantly, the College has a "very effective buffer" between top management and the faculty in the form of the program directors. Program directors perform a wide range of administrative duties and are considered part of the College administration. They also teach courses within their particular disciplines and function in many respects like members of the faculty. Indeed, program directors generally are appointed by the Academic Dean from among the faculty of the relevant program area. Thus, program directors plainly possess the "professional expertise" that the Court deemed "indispensable" to the formulation and implementation of academic policy. The availability of this expertise within the ranks of the administration obviates the College's need to rely extensively on the professional judgment of its faculty in determining and implementing academic policy. Under these circumstances, while significant faculty input undoubtedly remains beneficial to the College, it is not necessary that the faculty be "aligned with management" as they were in *Yeshiva.* Accordingly, this case presents no problem of divided loyalty equivalent to that found in *Yeshiva.*

The record demonstrates that the program directors' expertise is in fact used substantially by the College, and that these directors play a major role in the administrative process. As the ALJ observed:

> [Program] directors largely control the budget, serve in key positions on committees and task forces, are administrators rather than instructors (although they carry teaching loads), have office space, have private telephones, have access to secretarial services, and generally are an arm of the president for administrative purposes. Administratively, their weight far exceeds that of faculty members in the day-to-day affairs of [the College].

The Academic Dean likewise plays a major and powerful role in academic affairs. He serves with the faculty on a number of committees and task forces, and he has the final word in many administrative areas. The record shows that the College has vested much reliance in his professional judgment as well, and that insofar as academic matters are concerned, "he, rather than the faculty, is the managerial authority. . . ."

Thus, the record clearly reveals that while the faculty plays a large part in College governance, its input is just one of many factors taken into account by administration officials who in fact make the decisions and take the actions that "formulate and effectuate management policies." We certainly cannot say of the faculty members that they "in effect, substantially and pervasively operat[e] the enterprise," or that "[t]heir authority in academic matters is absolute," as was the case in *Yeshiva*. To the contrary, the administration here has retained both actual and effective control of College policy making and implementation. Based on the record before us, we are convinced that the College faculty members are characterized more accurately as employees who routinely apply their professional expertise in the course of carrying out their regular work duties, than as employees who "formulate and effectuate management policies by expressing and making operative the decisions of their employer." Accordingly, we agree with the Board that the members of the College faculty are not managerial employees within the meaning of *Yeshiva*, and thus are not excluded from protection under the Act.

V. CONCLUSION

In passing upon an order of the NLRB, the scope of our review is limited. We are not free to substitute our judgment for that of the Board simply because we might have decided the matter differently. Rather, we should grant enforcement of the order "if the Board correctly interpreted and applied the law and if its findings are supported by substantial evidence in the record, considered in its entirety." In construing the scope of the Act's coverage, we must accord great respect to the expertise of the Board "when its conclusions are rationally based on articulated facts and consistent with the Act."

After careful review of the record in this case, we perceive no reason to disturb the Board's conclusion that the faculty members at Loretto Heights College are not managerial employees within the meaning of *Yeshiva*. We are persuaded that the Board has properly interpreted and applied the *Yeshiva* decision, and that its findings are adequately supported by the record.

Accordingly, we grant enforcement of the Board's order.

NOTES

1. Compare and contrast the faculty responsibilities, decision making processes, and organizational structures in *Yeshiva* and *Loretto Heights*. How did these differences contribute to the appellate court's decision in *Loretto Heights*?

2. For-profit colleges and universities tend to have a corporate model in which decisions are centrally made, while administrators and faculty service on committees is a minority. Given that structure, would faculty at for-profit colleges and universities likely qualify as employees who can collectively bargain under the NLRA? According to Professor Vicente Lechuga, "[a] system of shared governance, as exemplified at traditional institutions, is non-existent." Vicente M. Lechuga, *Who Are They? And What Do They Do?, in* For-Profit Colleges and Universities: Their Markets, Regulation, Performance, and Place in Higher Education 59 (2010). Further, he observes that "[f]aculty members at for-profit institutions may not necessarily be the most qualified individuals within the organization to make business decisions and therefore are often excluded from the process." *Id.* at 59.

3. With the growing presence of online programs, how might college faculty who teach exclusively online argue for the qualification as employees under the NLRA? What circumstances or factors pertaining to faculty at online schools might alter the analysis of faculty covered under the NLRA?

4. Do adjunct faculty fall under the NLRA? How might adjunct faculty organize and try to unionize under the NLRA? At times, parties with a common interest with the organized group and who share similar positions may affiliate with an existing organized unit based on a "community of interest" argument such as adjunct faculty joining interests and the bargaining unit of full-time faculty. *See, e.g., Kendall Coll. v. NLRB*, 570 F.2d 216 (7th Cir. 1978); *but see Parsons Sch. of Design Div. of New Sch. for Soc. Research*, 793 F.2d 503 (2d Cir. 1986) (where part-time faculty had a sufficient community of interest to form its own bargaining unit separate from the full-time faculty).

3. Professional Employee or Managerial Exemption: Religious Institution

CARROLL COLLEGE, INC. v. N.L.R.B.

558 F.3d 568 (D.C. Cir. 2009)

Griffith, Circuit Judge:

The National Labor Relations Board ordered Carroll College to bargain with the recognized collective bargaining agent of its faculty. In this petition for review, the college argues that its religious educational environment and affiliation with the United Presbyterian Church place it beyond the Board's jurisdiction under *NLRB v. Catholic Bishop of Chicago*, 440 U.S. 490 (1979), and *University of Great Falls v. NLRB*, 278 F.3d 1335 (D.C.Cir. 2002). We agree.

I.

Established in 1846, Carroll College is a private college located in Waukesha, Wisconsin, and affiliated with the Synod of Lakes and Prairies of the United Presbyterian Church of the U.S.A. The college has a school of liberal arts and sciences for undergraduates and a school of graduate and professional studies. Its governance structure is composed of a board of trustees, an administration, and a faculty.

In November 2004, the International Union, United Automobile, Aerospace & Agricultural Implement Workers of America-UAW, filed a petition with the NLRB seeking certification as the collective bargaining representative for Carroll's faculty. Carroll challenged the Board's jurisdiction, arguing that requiring it to bargain with the union would substantially burden its free exercise rights in violation of the Religious Freedom Restoration Act (RFRA). In the alternative, Carroll argued that its faculty members are managerial employees not covered by the National Labor Relations Act (NLRA).

After a hearing to consider the union's petition, the Regional Director for the NLRB rejected both of the college's arguments. On the question of jurisdiction, the Regional Director saw no need to address the college's RFRA argument, interpreting Board precedent to foreclose such a challenge unless a school can show under *Catholic Bishop* that it is "church operated." Carroll's affiliation with the Synod, the Regional Director concluded, was insufficient to meet this requirement. Reaching the merits, the Regional Director concluded that Carroll's faculty members are not managerial employees. Carroll filed a timely request to review the Regional Director's decision on jurisdiction and the merits, but stressed that its argument against NLRB jurisdiction was based solely on RFRA and not *Catholic Bishop*.

The NLRB granted Carroll's request for review on the jurisdictional issue alone and concluded that it was no violation of RFRA to apply the NLRA's duty to bargain to the college. In the wake of the NLRB's decision, the Regional Director certified the union as the exclusive representative of Carroll's faculty. Carroll refused to bargain with the union, which drew an unfair labor practice charge from the General Counsel alleging a violation of sections 8(a)(5) and (1) of the NLRA. In its defense before the Board, Carroll presented once again the RFRA and managerial employee arguments it had first made to the Regional Director.

The NLRB granted the General Counsel's motion for summary judgment and ordered Carroll to recognize and bargain with the union. With respect to Carroll's RFRA challenge, the NLRB repeated its earlier analysis and concluded again that the duty to bargain did not substantially burden the college's free exercise rights. With respect to Carroll's argument that its faculty members are managerial employees, the Board used the Regional Director's earlier analysis and likewise concluded that they are not. Carroll now petitions for review, and the NLRB cross-petitions for enforcement of its order. The union has intervened in support of the Board. . . .

II.

Before us, Carroll abandons the argument that the NLRB cannot, consistent with RFRA, order it to bargain with the union. Instead, Carroll asserts for the first time that the NLRB has no jurisdiction under *Catholic Bishop*. We begin with an explanation of *Catholic Bishop* and its progeny.

In *Catholic Bishop*, the Supreme Court read the NLRA in light of the Religion Clauses of the First Amendment to hold that the NLRB lacks jurisdiction over church-operated schools. Central to the Court's reasoning was a concern that despite the best of intentions, a Board authorized to order collective bargaining at church-operated schools would, in many cases, find itself inquiring "into the good faith of the position asserted by the clergy-administrators and its relationship to the school's religious mission." The First Amendment does not permit such inquiry. "It is not only the conclusions that may be reached by the Board which may impinge on rights guaranteed by the Religion Clauses, *but also the very process of inquiry leading to findings and conclusions.*" (emphasis added). The Court saw "no escape" from these "serious First Amendment questions" if the Board was permitted to exercise jurisdiction over church-operated schools.

But the Court offered no test for determining whether a school is beyond Board jurisdiction. In a series of decisions following *Catholic Bishop*, the NLRB created a framework for analysis that looked to whether a school has a "substantial religious character" to determine if it is exempt from jurisdiction. The Board weighed, inter alia, the involvement of the affiliated religious group in the school's day-to-day affairs, the degree to which the school has a religious mission, and whether religious criteria play a role in faculty appointment and evaluation. The "substantial religious character" test allowed the Board to consider "all aspects of a religious school's organization and function that [it deemed] relevant."

In *Great Falls*, we held that the Board's approach involved just "the sort of intrusive inquiry that *Catholic Bishop* sought to avoid," with "the NLRB trolling through the beliefs of [schools], making determinations about [their] religious mission, and that mission's centrality to the 'primary purpose' of the [school]." Accordingly, we read *Catholic Bishop* to require a much different and less intrusive inquiry. Drawing in large part on then-Judge Breyer's opinion in *Universidad Central de Bayamon v. NLRB*, 793 F.2d 383 (1st Cir.1986) (en banc), we fashioned a three-part inquiry. A school is exempt from NLRB jurisdiction if it (1) " 'holds itself out to students, faculty and the community' as providing a religious educational environment," (2) "is organized as a 'nonprofit,' " and (3) "is affiliated with, or owned, operated, or controlled, directly or indirectly, by a recognized religious organization, or with an entity, membership of which is determined, at least in part, with reference to religion." We intended this test to create a "bright-line" rule for determining jurisdiction "without delving into matters of religious doctrine or motive." *Id.* at 1345. It would ensure that schools claiming a *Catholic Bishop* exemption "are *bona fide* religious institutions," *id.* at 1344, while avoiding Board inquiry into the substance and contours of their religious beliefs and missions.

To determine whether the University of Great Falls held itself out as "providing a religious educational environment," we looked to its course catalogue, mission statement, student bulletin, and other public documents. There was no inquiry into the content of the school's religious beliefs nor skepticism whether those beliefs were followed. Probing into the school's religious views would "needlessly engage in the 'trolling' that . . . *Catholic Bishop* itself sought to avoid." The second and third questions were easily answered. The school operated as a nonprofit and it was undisputed that it was affiliated with a recognized religious institution. There was no need to dig deeper. Doing so would only risk infringing upon the guarantees of the First Amendment's Religion Clauses.

III.

Carroll easily satisfies the *Great Falls* test. The college's charter documents make clear that it holds itself out to students, faculty, and the broader community as providing a religious educational environment. Carroll's Articles of Incorporation describe its relationship with the Synod and provide that the college was incorporated "for the purpose of maintaining and conducting [itself] as a Christian liberal arts college dedicated to God." Carroll's mission statement provides that the school will "demonstrate Christian values by . . . example." The board of trustees has adopted a "Statement of Christian Purpose," which declares it the college's mission to provide "a learning environment devoted to academic excellence and congenial to Christian witness." And Carroll and the Synod are parties to an agreement that commits the board of trustees of the college to "recognize and affirm [Carroll's] origin and heritage in the concern of the Church for the intellectual and spiritual growth of its students, faculty, administration, and staff." These objective indicia easily satisfy the first element of our test.

The Regional Director assumed the college could not challenge the Board's jurisdiction under RFRA unless it was exempt from Board jurisdiction under *Catholic Bishop.* As the NLRB had yet to adopt our *Great Falls* test, the Regional Director applied the NLRB's "substantial religious character" approach to conclude that Carroll is not exempt from the Board's jurisdiction under *Catholic Bishop*, but added a footnote explaining that he would reach the same conclusion under the three-part *Great Falls* inquiry. He found Carroll's "aspirational statements of principle and purpose" insufficient to establish that it holds itself out as a college providing a religious educational environment because there was little accompanying evidence of actual religious influence or control over the college or the education it provides. Not only does this heightened standard require a showing of religious influence far beyond what we found necessary in *Great Falls*, but it involves the type of inquiry *Catholic Bishop* forbids. In determining whether a school is exempt from the NLRA under *Catholic Bishop*, the NLRB may not "ask[ ] how effective the institution is at inculcating its beliefs." To do otherwise and require proof of "actual religious influence or control" as the Regional Director did here, is tantamount to questioning the sincerity of the school's public representations about the significance of its religious affiliation. This neither the Board nor we may do.

As we determined in *Great Falls*, focusing solely on a school's public representations as to its religious educational environment-as opposed to conducting a skeptical inquiry into the actual influence exerted over the school by its affiliated religious institution-is also a more useful way for determining the school's religious bona fides. The Regional Director's worry that Carroll's public statements of religious affiliation are "aspirational" and without practical effect is addressed by the incentives Carroll has to adhere to how it describes itself to the consuming public. "[S]uch public representations serve as a market check." Not all students and faculty are attracted to overtly religious environments, so public representations of religious ties come at a cost to the school claiming a *Catholic Bishop* exemption.

There is no dispute that Carroll meets the second element of *Great Falls.* It is a nonprofit institution. The third element is also satisfied because Carroll is "affiliated with . . . a recognized religious organization," The college's Articles of Incorporation provide that it is "related" to the Synod of Lakes and Prairies of the United Presbyterian Church, and Carroll, pursuant to an agreement with the Synod, is bound to "recognize and affirm its origin and heritage in the concern of the Church." Both the Regional Director and the NLRB acknowledged that Carroll and the Synod are affiliated. The Regional Director determined, however, that because "the Church does not sponsor the College, does not own its campus, and does not have any right of ultimate control over it," the third element was not satisfied. Again, after *Great Falls,* this type of analysis requires too much. Although elements of religious ownership, operation, and control were present in the facts before us in *Great Falls,* our test is met with affiliation alone. As the Board found, Carroll is plainly affiliated with a recognized religious organization.

There remains a complication in this otherwise straightforward application of *Great Falls.* Carroll did not raise the *Catholic Bishop* argument before the Board. Certain jurisdictional challenges, however, need not be raised before the Board to be considered on review. "A court can always invalidate Board action that is patently beyond the Board's jurisdiction, even if the jurisdictional challenge was never presented to the Board." After our decision in *Great Falls,* Carroll is patently beyond the NLRB's jurisdiction. *Great Falls* created a bright-line test of the Board's jurisdiction according to which we ask three questions easily answered with objective criteria. From Carroll's public representations, it is readily apparent that the college holds itself out to all as providing a religious educational environment. That it is a nonprofit affiliated with a Presbyterian synod is beyond dispute. From the Board's own review of Carroll's publicly available documents, it should have known immediately that the college was entitled to a *Catholic Bishop* exemption from the NLRA's collective bargaining requirements. The Board thus had no jurisdiction to order the school to bargain with the union, and we have authority to invalidate the Board's order even though the college did not raise its jurisdictional challenge below.

IV.

Under *Great Falls,* Carroll is exempt from the NLRB's jurisdiction. We thus need not address Carroll's argument that its faculty members are managerial employees who fall outside the protection of the NLRA. We grant Carroll's petition for review, vacate the decision and order of the NLRB, and deny the Board's cross-petition for enforcement.

So ordered.

NOTES

1. According to an article reported in the *Chronicle of Higher Education*, "[f]our controversial tenure denials at Carroll College in Wisconsin have spurred professors there to try to organize a union." Scott Smallwood, *Tenure Denials Lead to Union Organizing at Carroll College*, CHRON. OF HIGHER EDUC., Feb. 6, 2004, at A10. If faculty at Carroll cannot organize, what recourse, if any, might the faculty have to express concerns regarding the College's decisions regarding personnel and other educational matters at the institution?

2. In *N.L.R.B. v. Catholic Bishop of Chicago*, 440 U.S. 490 (1979), school teachers employed within two Catholic dioceses in the Chicago area sued for unfair labor practices when the schools refused to bargain with the faculty unions, which represented lay teachers. Setting the stage for its analysis, the Court emphasized that the "church-teacher relationship in a church-operated school differs from the employment relationship in a public or other nonreligious school. We see no escape from conflicts flowing from the Board's exercise of jurisdiction over teachers in church-operated schools and the consequent serious First Amendment questions that would follow." *Id.* at 504. Rather than outlining a test to examine the constitutional questions surrounding the religious employment setting, the U.S. Supreme Court ruled based on statutory intent, examining the legislative history of the NLRA. Based on that review, the Court concluded that "absence of an 'affirmative intention of the Congress clearly expressed' fortifies our conclusion that Congress did not contemplate that the Board would require church-operated schools to grant recognition to unions as bargaining agents for their teachers." *Id.* at 506.

In its reasoning, the Court briefly mentioned the *Lemon* test and referred to a key phrase from the case, which states, in reference to the entanglement prong, "[t]he substantial religious character of these church-related schools gives rise to entangling church-state relationships of the kind the Religion Clauses sought to avoid." *Id.* at 503 (citing *Lemon v. Kurtzman*, 403 U.S. at 628). The faculty union at Carroll argued for application of the "substantial religious character" test. Why did the appellate court in Carroll College dismiss that inquiry? How does the three-part inquiry from *Great Falls* differ from past frameworks to determine religious freedoms consistent with the First Amendment? Under what basis, if any, might a college founded by a religious group (but maintains a largely secular environment) qualify faculty under the NLRA so the faculty may collectively bargain? An article in *Inside Higher Ed* reported, "[w]hile there are many colleges where the religious roots of an institution are so omnipresent that these institutions would pass the NLRB test, there are many others like Carroll that were founded by religious groups and still identify in some ways with the groups, but where church ties are much less visible." Scott Jaschik, *Loss for Private College Union*, INSIDE HIGHER ED, Mar. 16, 2009, *available at* http://www.insidehighered.com/news/2009/03/16/union.

3. Are there instances in which religious tenets or matters not impacting the religious nature of the institution may still arise between faculty and administrators of a religiously affiliated institution? Should there be a limited negotiable set of factors rather than a summary non-application of the NLRA to religiously affiliated colleges and universities? If so, what test might be operable? After reviewing the

University Education Ass'n v. Regents of the University of Minnesota decision below, revisit these questions.

4. Scope of Collective Bargaining

UNIVERSITY EDUCATION ASS'N v. REGENTS OF THE UNIVERSITY OF MINNESOTA

353 N.W.2d 534 (Minn. 1984)

Heard, considered and decided by the court en banc.

AMDAHL, CHIEF JUSTICE.

Appellants, University Education Association (UEA) and Minnesota Education Association (MEA) are certified exclusive bargaining organizations for faculty members at the University of Minnesota campuses in Waseca and Duluth. The UEA and MEA are affiliated and are employee organizations under [the Minnesota Public Employment Labor Relations Act]. Respondent, the Board of Regents of the University of Minnesota, is a public employer. . . . This appeal concerns issues raised in the negotiation of the first collective bargaining agreement between the two parties.

On February 6, 1981 the parties met, in the first of 22 meetings, to negotiate a collective bargaining agreement. The ensuing negotiations gave rise to the instant action. Negotiation continued during the pendency of this suit, and on January 21, 1983, the Regents approved a collective bargaining agreement governing all aspects of the employment relationship between the parties except those issues presently before this court. The agreement was effective July 1, 1981 through August 31, 1983. Although the initial agreement has expired and the parties are in the process of renegotiating a new contract, the issues before this court remain relevant and affect the new negotiations.

This action was initiated by the UEA and MEA (hereinafter referred to solely as the MEA) on February 22, 1982. MEA alleged that the Regents committed unfair labor practices, violating the Minnesota Public Employment Labor Relations Act (PELRA), through their bargaining conduct. . . . First, the MEA asserts that the Regents committed an unfair labor practice by refusing to meet and negotiate regarding the criteria, weights and review of promotion and tenure decisions. Second, the MEA alleges that the Regents committed an unfair labor practice by refusing to meet and negotiate regarding the criteria, weights and review of faculty evaluations. Finally, the MEA asserts that the Regents committed an unfair labor practice by refusing to meet and negotiate concerning issues relating to the academic calendar. The Regents argue that these issues are "inherent managerial prerogatives" and, therefore, non-negotiable under [PERLA]. . . .

. . . The . . . remaining issues were submitted to the district court in cross motions for summary judgment. The court granted the Regents' motion for summary judgment on the tenure, faculty evaluation and academic calendar issues on March 16, 1983. MEA's motion concerning the Regents' duty to provide certain documents and information to the MEA was granted. The MEA appeals the order relating to the tenure, faculty evaluation and academic calendar issues. We affirm the district court and hold that the Regents' refusal to negotiate the tenure and promotion, faculty evaluations and academic calendar issues was not an unfair labor practice. . . .

MEA asserts that tenure and promotion, faculty evaluations and academic calendar have a significant impact on faculty job security, advancement, compensation and work assignment and are terms and conditions of employment. The Regents assert that these issues are matters of inherent managerial policy.

The July 1, 1981 agreement outlines the agreed upon procedure used in granting indefinite tenure. Under this procedure, either the head of an academic department or a probationary faculty member can initiate the process. After the personnel file of the probationary faculty member is reviewed and other applicable information considered, a written notice and agenda for a departmental meeting is distributed to all tenured members of the department. The tenured members vote and the department head submits a written report to the principal administrator concerning the vote and the department head's recommendation. This report is also supplied to the probationary member, who can review or supplement the report.

The principal administrator, upon receipt of the department head's recommendation, reviews the file and that recommendation. The principal administrator prepares a written recommendation which is forwarded to the Provost. Finally, after the Provost's review and written comments are forwarded to the Vice President for Academic Affairs, the Vice President recommends a course of action to the Regents.

The substantive criteria used to determine whether tenure should be conferred on a probationary member are documented and available to the public. Tenure is based upon the following four criteria:

1. teaching effectiveness and advising of students;
2. distinction in research, writing or artistic production;
3. contributions to the school and/or community; and
4. length of service.

The first two criteria are considered primary although none of the criteria is specifically weighted. Evidence relating to each criterion must be presented and become part of the probationary member's personnel file.

The evaluation of faculty members is multifaceted and occurs annually. Evaluation by students, faculty peers and the faculty member may be placed in the faculty member's personnel file.

Vacation and workload are governed by the July 1, 1981 agreement. Whether the academic calendar is based on the quarter or semester system, however, presently remains a managerial decision.

The Regents and MEA have reached an agreement concerning the procedural aspects of the promotion and tenure process at UMD and UMW. The Regents, however, refuse to negotiate the grievability of whether promotion and tenure is granted and the substantive criteria governing these decisions.

PELRA

The ultimate issue in this case is whether the Regents have committed an unfair labor practice under [PELRA]. . . . [Under the Act,] Section 179.68, subd. 2, provides:

> Public employers, their agents or representatives are prohibited from:
>
> (5) refusing to meet and negotiate in good faith with the exclusive representative of its employees in an appropriate unit;

Under Minn.Stat. § 179.63, subd. 16 (1982), the "meet and negotiate" process contemplates mutual good faith negotiations between the employee organization and the public employer.

PELRA specifically outlines the rights and obligations of public employees and employers. With respect to negotiations, Minn.Stat. § 179.65, subd. 4 (1982) provides:

> Public employees through their certified exclusive representative have the right and obligation to meet and negotiate in good faith with their employer *regarding grievance procedures and the terms and conditions of employment*, but such obligation does not compel the exclusive representative to agree to a proposal or require the making of a concession.

(emphasis added). The rights and obligations of employers relating to negotiations are set forth in Minn.Stat. § 179.66, subd. 1, 2 (1982) which provides in pertinent part as follows:

> Subd. 1. A public employer *is not required to meet and negotiate on matters of inherent managerial policy, which include, but are not limited to, such areas of discretion or policy as the functions and programs of the employer, its overall budget, utilization of technology, the organizational structure and selection and direction and number of personnel.* * * *
>
> Subd. 2. A public employer has an obligation to meet and negotiate in good faith with the exclusive representative of the public employees in an appropriate unit regarding grievance procedures and the terms and conditions of employment, but such obligation does not compel the public employer or its representative to agree to a proposal or require the making of a concession.

(emphasis added).

The negotiations contemplated by Minn.Stat. § 179.63, subd. 16 (1982) require employers and employee representatives to meet and negotiate with respect to terms and conditions of employment. Terms and conditions of employment:

> mean[s] *the hours of employment, the compensation therefor* including fringe benefits except retirement contributions or benefits, and *the employ-*

> *er's personnel policies affecting the working conditions of the employees.* In the case of professional employees the term does not mean educational policies of a school district. The terms in both cases are subject to the provisions of section 179.66 regarding the rights of public employers and the scope of negotiations.

Resolution of this case requires a determination whether the tenure and promotion, faculty evaluation and academic calendar issues are terms and conditions of employment under Minn.Stat. § 179.63, subd. 18 (1982).

This court has repeatedly emphasized that the purpose of PELRA requires "the scope of the mandatory bargaining area to be broadly construed so that the purpose of resolving labor disputes through negotiation could best be served." Our recent decisions, however, recognize also that many inherent managerial policies concomitantly and directly affect the terms and conditions of employment. These recent decisions indicate that the clear distinction intended by the legislature between "terms and conditions of employment" and "matters of inherent managerial policy" has become far from distinct.

This court has recognized that "areas of 'inherent managerial policy' and 'terms and conditions of employment' oftentimes overlap." . . . [In *St. Paul Fire Fighters* (1983), the Minnesota Supreme Court stated:]

> A decision in respect of a matter of inherent managerial policy — a discretionary decision which a public employer is not required to negotiate — may well impinge upon negotiable terms and conditions of employment. The impact upon the terms and conditions of employment of an inherent managerial policy decision does not, however, render the policy decision a subject of mandatory negotiation if the decision and its implementation are so inextricably interwoven that requiring the public employer to meet and negotiate the method of carrying out its decision would require the employer to negotiate the basic policy decision. If, however, the inherent managerial policy decision is severable from its implementation, the effect of implementation on the terms and conditions of employment is negotiable to the extent that negotiation is not likely to hamper the employer's direction of its functions and objectives.

St. Paul Fire Fighters provides a logical analytic framework for cases involving issues that are not clearly identifiable as "terms and conditions of employment." Under *St. Paul Fire Fighters*, the impact a particular policy decision has upon terms and conditions of employment is determined. If the policy does "impinge upon negotiable terms and conditions of employment," then we are required to determine whether the policy and terms and conditions are so "inextricably interwoven" that negotiation of the issue involves negotiation of the policy. Thus, the second prong of *St. Paul Fire Fighters*, entails ascertaining whether the policy and its implementation are separable. If the policy and its implementation are distinct, then negotiation is mandatory with respect to issues relating to the implementation of the policy.

Tenure

1. From the Regents' perspective, tenure policies significantly affect the educational goals of a particular institution. Higher standards concerning degree qualifications and publication, for example, influence the reputation and quality of an institution. Moreover, tenure policies also tend to have an impact on an institution's fixed future costs. In contrast to tenure and promotion decisions which affect certain individuals, the specific substantive criteria, weights and review policies concerning faculty evaluations affect all faculty members. These policies are expressions of the educational standards that the Regents feel necessary to maintain — they are used to measure the quality of work of all faculty members. The Regents have consistently maintained that the criteria, weights and review of faculty evaluations are non-negotiable issues.

Tenure is defined, in the academic setting, as a faculty appointment for an indefinite period of time. A tenured faculty member enjoys substantial job security because tenured faculty members can only be removed for cause; any other removal is through retirement or retrenchment due to financial necessity. In addition, tenured status is accompanied by increased prestige, compensation and freedom.

The tenure and promotion policies of an academic institution pertain to both the educational objectives of the institution and the terms and conditions of employment. *Operating Engineers* (1975) is the only Minnesota case that directly addresses the negotiability of a public employer's promotion policies. *Operating Engineers* also implies that certain facets of an employer's promotion policies are severable from the policies involving inherent managerial discretion.

In *Operating Engineers*, the employee organization sought certain specific information relating to the process used to select employees for promotion. The *Operating Engineers* decision recognized that promotion policies were a mixture of severable managerial policy and terms and conditions of employment.

. . .

Operating Engineers contrasts with *Minneapolis Federation of Teachers* (1977). In *Minneapolis Federation*, we held that the decision to transfer a number of teachers was a managerial decision directly concerning the educational objectives of a school district, but that the "criteria for determining which teachers are to be transferred * * * involves a decision * * * [that is] negotiable." *Minneapolis Federation* is significant because of the dicta recognizing the managerial character of educational objectives. Moreover, there is a crucial distinction between the instant case and *Minneapolis Federation.* In *Minneapolis Federation* we determined that the criteria used to determine whether an employee will be transferred from one working place to another were not irreversibly intertwined with the educational objectives of a school district. The substantive criteria used to determine whether a faculty member should be granted tenure, however, *are* irreversibly intertwined with the educational policies and objectives of the University of Minnesota.

The decision to use a civil service exam in order to determine whether an employee was eligible for promotion was recognized, in *Operating Engineers*, as a matter of inherent managerial policy. The exam presumably tested an employee's knowledge in areas perceived by the employer to be important. In other words, the exam evaluated an employee's competence in subjects the employer deemed as essential; there was no question that the employer's selection of subjects to be tested was a matter of inherent managerial policy. Similarly, the Regent's decision to select certain substantive criteria as controlling eligibility for tenure or promotion are matters of inherent managerial policy.

The subjective criteria used to determine promotion and tenure are direct reflections of the educational policy objectives of the Regents. This inherent managerial policy is severable from its implementation. Hence the Regents have agreed to negotiate the procedures (implementation) used to determine tenure and promotion.

. . .

Faculty Evaluation

2. The MEA argues that the faculty has a direct interest in assuring that evaluations are fair, accurate and properly used. The faculty evaluation issue relates to all faculty and consequently is an issue separate from tenure and promotion.

The substantive criteria, weights and review of faculty evaluations are undoubtedly managerial matters while the application of the evaluations is an issue that may directly affect a faculty member's terms and conditions of employment. The fairness of the application of faculty evaluation standards is ensured by the negotiability of the tenure and promotion procedural process. It is obvious that the quality of work an employer, public or private, expects is a managerial decision.

Academic Calendar

3. The MEA has attempted to negotiate the academic calendar with the Regents. The Regents will only negotiate concerning the issues of holidays and vacations. Whether the academic calendar is based on a quarter or semester system and when the quarter or semester starts are alleged to be matters of inherent managerial discretion by the Regents.

MEA's arguments that the academic calendar is a term and condition of employment as opposed to an inherent managerial decision are not well founded. There is overwhelming support for the Regents' position that the academic calendar is a matter of inherent managerial policy.

When the school year begins and ends is comparable to when a work day begins and ends. The decision is made by management and controlled by the objectives and goals of the particular institution. Although employees are entitled to negotiate the number of hours worked, it does not follow that employees can negotiate *when* an employer deems it necessary to report to work. To allow employees to negotiate such a policy would involve negotiation of the actual objectives and goals of an employer.

In conclusion, the district court's determination that the tenure and promotion, faculty evaluation and academic calendar issues are not terms and conditions of employment under [PERLA] . . . is correct. The Regents, therefore, did not commit an unfair labor practice. . . .

Affirmed.

YETKA, JUSTICE (dissenting).

After a long history of broadly construing the mandatory bargaining area under PELRA in order to serve the purpose of resolving labor disputes through negotiation, this court now narrows the scope of mandatory bargaining. I feel that today's decision is contrary to the purpose of PELRA, and I therefore dissent.

As the majority opinion notes, many inherent managerial policies impinge upon negotiable terms and conditions of employment. The test we have established for determining whether such policies must be negotiated inquiries into the degree to which the managerial policy decision is severable from the implementation of that policy.

For example, the decision to use a civil service exam in order to determine whether an employee is eligible for promotion impinges strongly on the terms and conditions of employment. The decision to use the exam is undoubtedly a matter of inherent managerial policy. The fairness of the particular exam used, however, is a separate issue involving the implementation of that policy and is therefore negotiable. Similarly, the decision to transfer a number of teachers was a managerial decision directly concerning the educational objectives of a school district, but the "criteria for determining which teachers are to be transferred * * * involves a decision * * * [that is] negotiable."

In this case, I have no quarrel with the majority's classification of the criteria used in promotion and tenure decisions as a matter of inherent managerial policy. Certainly these criteria reflect the educational policy objectives of the Regents. However, I disagree with the conclusion that the grievability of individual promotion and tenure decisions is not a mandatory bargaining subject.

There can be no doubt that promotion and tenure directly affect the terms and conditions of employment. The majority has no problems with requiring collective bargaining on the *procedures* surrounding promotion and tenure decisions, concluding that the procedures are a severable implementation of the general promotion and tenure policy. However, the majority does not believe that *grievability* is severable from the policy: "[G]rievability of the ultimate decision would effectively subject the substantive criteria and their application to review * * *."

Clearly, the grievance of a particular promotion and tenure decision would not necessitate review of the criteria established for determining tenure; it would only ensure that the established criteria were rationally and fairly applied. Fair procedures can only go so far in guaranteeing just decisionmaking. Precluding grievance of tenure and promotion decisions renders any negotiated procedural fairness meaningless in cases where the procedures have been satisfied but the criteria have been misapplied or ignored. The grievability of allegedly erroneous decisions is entirely separate from the criteria upon which the University wishes to base those decisions. Because grievability is severable from implementation of the promotion and tenure policy, it is a negotiable term and condition of employment.

I also agree that the criteria, weights and review policies used in faculty evaluations are inherently managerial issues because they are expressions of the educational standards the Regents desire to establish and maintain. The quality of work an employer expects is obviously a managerial decision.

The majority admits that the application of faculty evaluations is an issue that may directly affect a faculty member's terms and conditions of employment. However, the majority asserts that the fairness of the application of the faculty evaluations is ensured by the negotiability of the tenure and promotion process.

As discussed above, there is only a guarantee of *procedural* fairness in the tenure and promotion process. There is no assurance that faculty evaluations will be justly made or fairly applied because the grievability of their conclusions and use is precluded from negotiation. The fairness of the application of faculty evaluation standards should be negotiable in a manner similar to the implementation of tenure and promotion decisions.

Thus, I would reverse the trial court on its determination that faculty evaluations and tenure matters are not negotiable. I do not dissent on the question of the academic calendar because, although employees are entitled to negotiate the number of hours worked, it does not follow that employees can negotiate when an employer deems it necessary to report to work.

[Justices Scott, Todd, and Wahl joined the dissent.]

NOTES

1. Based on this case, which applied the Minnesota Public Employment Labor Relations Act (PELRA), what are negotiable or bargainable terms and conditions of work? What is the legal standard to determine bargainable matters? What makes some of the bargainable terms and conditions permissive or mandatory? What is the legal standard to distinguish between matters that are permissive or mandatory?

2. What is the effect of having a "severable" issue? How might the faculty union argue that severability exists between the process and substance of the tenure and promotion reviews as well as for annual reviews?

3. In contrast to the Minnesota decision, the Supreme Court of Michigan ruled in *Central Michigan University Faculty Ass'n v. Central Michigan University*, 273 N.W.2d 21 (Mich. 1978), that matters involving faculty evaluations fell within the employment sphere, not educational sphere; thus, the matters were negotiable. For a more detailed discussion regarding unionized college faculty evaluations, see Jeffrey C. Sun & Steve Permuth, *Evaluations of Unionized College and University Faculty: A Review of the Laws*, 19 J. PERS. EVAL. EDUC. 115 (2007); Philip T.K. Daniel, *Personnel Evaluations in Education and the Law*, 69 SCH. BUS. AFFAIRS 29 (2003).

4. Collective bargaining, especially for public employees such as public school teachers and faculty and staff in public colleges and universities, is the source of tremendous controversy in state and local government. Much of this is owing to fiscal issues as governments seek to slash spending and address major budgetary shortfalls. Political issues also impact the effort to control public unions which are seen as partners to political parties. States such as Ohio, Wisconsin, and Indiana have engaged in legislative measures to limit the collective bargaining process for public workers — especially as regards negotiation for salary, health care, and other benefits. The following excerpt addresses many of the important concerns to be considered:

> In many states, public sector unions are facing dramatic changes in the laws governing collective bargaining. The ongoing national economic malaise and state budget crises have created pressure on government officials to scale back spending on public sector employees. Legislation seeking to restrict and eliminate collective bargaining has been introduced in statehouses across the country, sparking large protests and a renewed debate about the merits of public sector unions. This legislative approach may rewrite labor law and raises the question of how best to control spiraling state labor costs.
>
> *Balancing Budgets and Priorities*
>
> As the Great Recession continues, governments at all levels have been scrambling to balance their budgets. With the economy struggling and unemployment levels in certain areas approaching record levels, the revenues generated through taxes has been dwindling. While on a federal level new currency can be issued, state and municipal governments do not have that "luxury." With labor costs for public employees making up a significant portion of local and state government budgets, many public sector executives have looked at the overall concept of collective bargaining as the culprit that has their balance sheets in disarray.
>
> . . . .
>
> *Pros and Cons of Limiting or Eliminating Collective Bargaining*
>
> There are strong arguments both for and against limiting collective bargaining rights. The upside of restricting collective bargaining, from the perspective of legislators in favor of such reform, is that states and municipalities will be able to save money by limiting what issues are negotiable between unions and employers. Under a restricted system, employers will have the ability to make quick, cost-conscious decisions regarding matters such as the health care, salaries, and overtime payment available to employees. Rather than providing all public employees with premium benefit plans, for instance, states will have the power to opt for adequate but less expensive alternatives, including those where the employees must contribute to their costs. Additionally, taxpayers will benefit through tax cuts resulting from lower government employee salaries and benefits.
>
> The other side of this issue, however, is the sentiment that legislators cannot change the law regarding collective bargaining without stripping

unionized workers of their fundamental rights. In certain states, such as Florida, the ability of unionized workers to engage in collective bargaining is a recognized constitutional right that cannot be taken away without violating state law. Similarly, for public sector employees, the right to recognize a proprietary interest in a job once the employee has passed a mandated probationary period creates a constitutional right that may not be taken away without violating due process. Finally, many believe that by limiting collective bargaining rights, the government deprives unionized employees of a chance to voice their opinions regarding the very factors that affect them the most, such as working conditions, working hours, and personal benefits. Supporters of collective bargaining fear that, if the government does not opt to protect the rights and voice of unionized employees, they will feel abused and workplace productivity will decline.

Alternatives to Limiting Collective Bargaining Rights

Given the current economic state of the nation, budget control should be prioritized. However, state and government officials may be taking the wrong approach by focusing on changing the *laws*, rather than changing their *approach* to negotiating with the public sector unions. If the country's governors, mayors, and schools chiefs would have approached collective bargaining like many of their counterparts in the private sector, it is very possible, if not likely, that the fiscal woes and crises faced by states and municipalities would be tremendously lessened today. Rather than strip the laws and employees' rights, these chief executives need to learn to "say no" to public sector unions. However, if unions are not willing to give concessions to help the states and municipalities balance their budgets, layoffs should ensue as a means of urging unions to negotiate.

Philip S. Mortensen, *The Impact of Limiting Collective Bargaining Rights: An In-Depth Look at the Pros and Cons of State Efforts to Restrict Collective Bargaining Rights*, 2011 ASPATORE SPECIAL REP. 8 (2011)*.

5. What are the benefits and drawbacks of collective bargaining? Does this employee protection system promote fair employment policies and, hence, better performance in the workplace? On the other hand, does the negotiation process establish an untenable morass of unnecessary obstacles to, and restrictions of, the smooth running of government and government services? What of the criticism that collective bargaining inhibits worker productivity and protects those who do little work at all? What of the protection of the public and the notion of operating in the public good? Are collective bargaining organizations established for that purpose especially since much of the sentiment for unions is based on the statement that the middle class is maintained and supported?

Chapter V

COLLEGE-STUDENT RELATIONSHIP

Introduction

While it can be described in several different ways, depending on the perspective and detail offered, the relationship between the student and the university is primarily a contractual one. As the court in *Steinberg v. Chicago Medical School*, presented later in this chapter, reminds us, "A contract, by ancient definition, is an agreement between competent parties, upon a consideration sufficient in law, to do or not to do a particular thing." Each of the sections, cases, and notes in Chapter V explores the relationship between a student and his or her university. In many instances, traditional contract language is used: for example, offer, acceptance, and consideration. In other examples, the relationship is drawn from affirmative action admissions policies, financial aid and scholarships, and student records. In the end, though, it is all about relationships.

Historically, the legal status of the university, in relation to the students, was one where the university acted *in loco parentis* — in the place of the parent. The opening case in this chapter, *Gott v. Berea College*, is one of only a few reported cases that mark this era. By the 1960s and 1970s, however, the *in loco parentis* doctrine was falling out of favor as the primary way to describe the legal relationship between university and student. *Bradshaw v. Rawlings*, 612 F.2d 135 (3d Cir. 1979), is the leading case that marked the shift from a "parental" relationship to a "contractual" one. From the *Bradshaw* court:

> Our beginning point is a recognition that the modern American college is not an insurer of the safety of its students. Whatever may have been its responsibility in an earlier era, the authoritarian role of today's college administrations has been notably diluted in recent decades. Trustees, administrators, and faculties have been required to yield to the expanding rights and privileges of their students.

Id. at 138.

In the first section of this chapter, a sampling of cases is presented that highlight the modern relationship students have with their universities, including applications and admissions (*Steinberg* and *Mangla*), accommodation of disability and academic decision making (*Doherty*), and the awarding of a diploma (*Olsson*). On perhaps a larger scale, there are also contract-based questions raised when a college or a university either decides to shut down or loses accreditation while students are still enrolled.

While Chapter VI and Chapter VII explore the student-university relationship from a decidedly more constitutional law perspective (i.e., due process, free speech, and search and seizure), students may also raise state-based breach of contract claims in the face of disciplinary (*Schaer*) or academic dismissal (*Bleicher*) charges. Though it sounds self-evident, one of the most important lessons colleges and universities can learn from this case law is to follow the policies and practices they adopt. The argument that a student handbook is a contract between the institution and the individual is not a hollow one. Readers are encouraged to make connections between *Schaer* and *Bleicher* and the cases and materials in Chapters VI and VII.

Part B of this chapter draws the student-institution relationship from the perspective of admissions and affirmative action. This section contains several groundbreaking decisions, both for legal theory and professional practice. Primary among them in the section on race discrimination are the 1978 decision of *Regents of the University of California v. Bakke*, and the 2003 cases of *Grutter v. Bollinger* and *Gratz v. Bollinger.* In *Bakke*, a deeply divided Court struck down a quota system employed at the University of California-Davis. Twenty-five years later, the Court revisited *Bakke* with two companion cases arising from policies implemented at the University of Michigan, *Grutter* and *Gratz.* In *Grutter*, the Court held, in a landmark decision, that diversity of the student body was a "compelling governmental interest" and upheld the law school's holistic admissions policy. In *Gratz*, the Court noted the compelling interest, but found the admissions policy for the College of Literature, Science, and the Arts not narrowly tailored to meet that interest. Part B also includes two Supreme Court opinions involving gender-based challenges to university admissions. Finally, readers are encouraged to consult Note 6 following *United States v. Virginia.* Litigation involving university admissions and undocumented immigrants is sparse; but federal and state legislatures continue to grapple with ideas and plans, with several states offering in-state tuition breaks to undocumented immigrants. Though in late 2010, the United States Congress failed to pass the DREAM Act (Development, Relief, and Education for Alien Minors Act), similar federal and state legislation continue to be a heated topic of debate.

Part C of this chapter discusses three important issues of financial aid. First is the traditional contractual relationship a student has with the university with respect to financial aid eligibility (i.e., grade-point average and progress toward degree), seen in *Revay.* Second are the obligations faced by a university whose students receive benefits under federal financial aid programs (*Grove City*). Third, this section explores issues of non-discrimination and affirmative action in institutional and state-level scholarship programs.

The final section of Chapter V covers the Family Educational Rights and Privacy Act (FERPA). FERPA, in part, prohibits educational institutions from disclosing educational records of their students to third parties without the students' consent. There are several exceptions to this nondisclosure rule, permitting disclosure to people with a legitimate educational need to know, in response to subpoenas and judicial orders, and in cases of health and safety emergencies.

A. GENERAL LEGAL STATUS OF STUDENTS

1. In Loco Parentis

GOTT v. BEREA COLLEGE
161 S.W. 204 (Ky. Ct. App. 1913)

. . . .

The larger question, and the one we are called here to pass upon, is whether the rule forbidding students entering eating houses was a reasonable one, and within the power of the college authorities to enact, and the further question whether, in that event, appellant Gott, will be heard to complain. That the enforcement of the rule worked a great injury to Gott's restaurant business cannot well be denied, but unless he can show that the college authorities have been guilty of a breach of some legal duty which they owe to him, he has no cause of action against them for the injury. One has no right of action against a merchant for refusal to sell goods, nor will an action lie, unless such means are used as of themselves constitute a breach of legal duty, for inducing or causing persons not to trade, deal, or contract with another, and it is a well established principle that when a lawful act is performed in the proper manner, the party performing it is not liable for mere incidental consequences injuriously resulting from it to another. . . .

College authorities stand *in loco parentis* concerning the physical and moral welfare, and mental training of the pupils, and we are unable to see why to that end they may not make any rule or regulation for the government, or betterment of their pupils that a parent could for the same purpose. Whether the rules or regulations are wise, or their aims worthy, is a matter left solely to the discretion of the authorities, or parents as the case may be, and in the exercise of that discretion, the courts are not disposed to interfere, unless the rules and aims are unlawful, or against public policy. . . .

"A college or university may prescribe requirements for admission and rules for the conduct of its students, and one who enters as a student impliedly agrees to conform to such rules of government."

NOTE

Gott v. Berea College is a relatively well-known case from early twentieth century higher education law. It is not alone, however, among the historical cases applying the *in loco parentis* doctrine to colleges and universities. *See Baskett v. Crossfield*, 228 S.W. 673 (Ky. Ct. App. 1920) (student expelled for indecently exposing himself to passersby from his dormitory window; letters written by university president to student's parents were not libelous); *Stetson Univ. v. Hunt*, 102 So. 637 (1924) (student suspended after several disorderly acts in her dormitory; suspension was not malicious).

2. Decline of *In Loco Parentis*

BRADSHAW v. RAWLINGS

612 F.2d 135 (3d Cir. 1979)

The major question . . . is whether a college may be subject to tort liability for injuries sustained by one of its students involved in an automobile accident when the driver of the car was a fellow student who had become intoxicated at a class picnic. . . .

The district court permitted the question of negligence to go to the jury against the college. . . . The plaintiff has filed a conditional cross-appeal.

I.

Donald Bradshaw, an eighteen year old student at Delaware Valley College, was severely injured on April 13, 1975 in Doylestown, Pennsylvania, while a backseat passenger in a[n] automobile driven by a fellow student, Bruce Rawlings. Both were sophomores and had attended their class picnic at a grove owned by the Maennerchor Society on the outskirts of the borough. Returning to the college from the picnic, Rawlings . . . struck a parked vehicle. As a result of the collision Bradshaw suffered a cervical fracture which caused quadriplegia.

The picnic, although not held on college grounds, was an annual activity of the sophomore class. A faculty member who served as sophomore class advisor participated with the class officers in planning the picnic and co-signed a check for class funds that was later used to purchase beer. The advisor did not attend the picnic, nor did he get another faculty member to attend in his place. Flyers announcing the picnic were prominently displayed across the campus. They were mimeographed by the college duplicating facility and featured drawings of beer mugs. Approximately seventy-five students attended the picnic and consumed six or seven half-kegs of beer. The beer was ordered from Marjorie Moyer, trading as Sunny Beverages, by the sophomore class president who was underage.

The legal drinking age in Pennsylvania was, and is, twenty-one years, but the great majority of the students drinking at the picnic were sophomores of either nineteen or twenty years of age. Rawlings had been at the picnic for a number of hours. He testified that he had no recollection of what occurred from the time he left the picnic until after the accident. Bradshaw testified that Rawlings had been drinking and another witness, Warren Wylde, expressed his opinion that Rawlings was under the influence of alcohol when he left the picnic grove. That there was sufficient evidence on the question of Rawlings' intoxication to submit to the jury cannot be seriously questioned.

II.

On appeal, the college argues that Bradshaw failed to present sufficient evidence to establish that it owed him a duty for the breach of which it could be held liable in tort. . . .

. . . .

A.

The college's argument strikes at the heart of tort law because a negligence claim must fail if based on circumstances for which the law imposes no duty of care on the defendant. . . . As Professor Prosser has emphasized, the statement that there is or is not a duty begs the essential question, which is whether the plaintiff's interests are entitled to legal protection against the defendant's conduct. " 'Duty' is not sacrosanct in itself, but only an expression of the sum total of those considerations of policy which lead the law to say that a particular plaintiff is entitled to protection" [W. Prosser, Law of Torts 333 (3d ed. 1964)]. Thus, we may perceive duty simply as an obligation to which the law will give recognition in order to require one person to conform to a particular standard of conduct with respect to another person.

These abstract descriptions of duty cannot be helpful, however, unless they are directly related to the competing individual, public, and social interests implicated in any case. An interest is a social fact, factor, or phenomenon existing independently of the law which is reflected by a claim, demand, or desire that people seek to satisfy and that has been recognized as socially valid by authoritative decision makers in society. Certainly, the plaintiff in this case possessed an important interest in remaining free from bodily injury, and thus the law protects his right to recover compensation from those who negligently cause him injury. The college, on the other hand, has an interest in the nature of its relationship with its adult students, as well as an interest in avoiding responsibilities that it is incapable of performing.

B.

Our beginning point is a recognition that the modern American college is not an insurer of the safety of its students. Whatever may have been its responsibility in an earlier era, the authoritarian role of today's college administrations has been notably diluted in recent decades. . . . [E]ighteen year old students are now identified with an expansive bundle of individual and social interests and possess discrete rights not held by college students from decades past. There was a time when college administrators and faculties assumed a role *in loco parentis*. Students were committed to their charge because the students were considered minors. A special relationship was created between college and student that imposed a duty on the college to exercise control over student conduct and, reciprocally, gave the students certain rights of protection by the college. The campus revolutions of the late sixties and early seventies were a direct attack by the students on rigid controls by the colleges and were an all-pervasive affirmative demand for more student rights. In general, the students succeeded, peaceably and otherwise, in acquiring a new status at colleges throughout the country. . . . College administrators no longer control the broad arena of general morals. . . .

Thus, for purposes of examining fundamental relationships that underlie tort liability, the competing interests of the student and of the institution of higher learning are much different today than they were in the past. At the risk of oversimplification, the change has occurred because society considers the modern college student an adult, not a child of tender years. It could be argued, although we need not decide here, that an educational institution possesses a different pattern of rights and responsibilities and retains more of the traditional custodial responsibilities when its students are all minors, as in an elementary school, or mostly minors, as in a high school. . . . But here, because the circumstances show that the students have reached the age of majority and are capable of protecting their own self interests, we believe that the rule would be different. We conclude, therefore, that in order to ascertain whether a specific duty of care extended from Delaware Valley College to its injured student, we must first identify and assess the competing individual and social interests associated with the parties.

. . . .

III.

A.

In the process of identifying the competing interests implicated in the student-college relationship, we note that the record in this case is not overly generous in identifying the interests possessed by the student, although it was Bradshaw's burden to prove the existence of a duty owed him by the college in order to establish a breach thereof. Bradshaw has concentrated on the school regulation imposing sanctions on the use of alcohol by students. The regulation states: "Possession or consumption of alcohol or malt beverages on the property of the College or at any College sponsored or related affair off campus will result in disciplinary action. The same rule will apply to every student regardless of age." We are not impressed that this regulation, in and of itself, is sufficient to place the college in a custodial relationship with its students for purposes of imposing a duty of protection in this case. We assume that the average student arrives on campus at the age of seventeen or eighteen, and that most students are under twenty-one during the better part of their college careers. A college regulation that essentially tracks a state law and prohibits conduct that to students under twenty-one is already prohibited by state law does not, in our view, indicate that the college voluntarily assumed a custodial relationship with its students so as to make operative the [Restatement provisions pertaining to the College having a duty to the student, who is under the college's custodial care, for the conduct of a third party].

Thus, we predict that the Pennsylvania courts would not hold that by promulgating this regulation the college had voluntarily taken custody of Bradshaw so as to deprive him of his normal power of self-protection or to subject him to association with persons likely to cause him harm. Absent proof of such a relationship, we do not believe that a prima facie case of custodial duty was established in order to submit the case to the jury on this theory.

B.

We next examine the facts adduced at trial to determine whether a special relationship existed as a matter of law, which would impose upon the college either a duty to control the conduct of a student operating a motor vehicle off campus or a duty to extend to a student a right of protection in transportation to and from off campus activities. We conclude that Bradshaw also failed to meet his burden of proving either of these duties. Bradshaw's primary argument is that the college had knowledge that its students would drink beer at the picnic, that this conduct violated a school regulation and state law, that it created a known probability of harm to third persons, and that knowledge by the college of this probable harm imposed a duty on the college either to control Rawling's conduct or to protect Bradshaw from possible harm.

Although we are aware of no Pennsylvania decision that has addressed this precise issue, the supreme court of that state has held that a private host who supplies intoxicants to a visibly intoxicated guest may not be held civilly liable for injuries to third parties caused by the intoxicated guest's negligence. Only licensed persons engaged in the sale of intoxicants have been held civilly liable to injured parties, and the source of this liability derives from the common law, as well as from a violation of Pennsylvania's Dram Shop statute. Because the Pennsylvania Supreme Court has been unwilling to find a special relationship on which to predicate a duty between a private host and his visibly intoxicated guest, we predict that it would be even less willing to find such a relationship between a college and its student under the circumstances of this case.

The centerpiece of Bradshaw's argument is that beer-drinking by underage college students, in itself, creates the special relationship on which to predicate liability and, furthermore, that the college has both the opportunity and the means of exercising control over beer drinking by students at an off campus gathering. These contentions miss the mark, however, because they blur the distinction between establishing the existence of a duty and proving the breach thereof. Bradshaw does not argue that beer drinking is generally regarded as a harm-producing act, for it cannot be seriously controverted that a goodly number of citizens indulge in this activity. Our national public policy, insofar as it is reflected by industry standards or by government regulation of certain types of radio-television advertising, permits advertising of beer at all times of the day and night even though Congress has banned advertisement of cigarettes and the broadcasting industry has agreed to ban the advertisement of liquor. What we know as men and women we must not forget as judges, and this panel of judges is able to bear witness to the fact that beer drinking by college students is a common experience. That this is true is not to suggest that reality always comports with state law and college rules. It does not. But the Pennsylvania law that prohibits sales to, and purchases by, persons under twenty-one years of age, is certainly not a universal practice in other countries, nor even the general rule in North America. Moreover in New Jersey, the bordering state from which the majority of Delaware Valley College students come, the legal drinking age is eighteen. Under these circumstances, we think it would be placing an impossible burden on the college to impose a duty in this case.

. . . .

Therefore, we conclude that Bradshaw failed to establish a prima facie case against the college that it should be charged with a duty of custodial care as a matter of law and that the district court erred by submitting the case to the jury.

. . . .

VII.

[W]e reverse and direct that a judgment in favor of Delaware Valley College be entered.

NOTES

1. The picnic in *Bradshaw* was, admittedly, an off-campus event. It was, however, also an annual event and very well-known and publicized around campus. In *Hartman v. Bethany College*, 778 F. Supp. 286 (N.D. W. Va. 1991), the event at issue — an assault of a 17-year-old freshman — took place off campus and at the hands of two men, neither of whom was a student at the college. Nonetheless, the injured student filed suit against the college, alleging that the college failed to supervise her, failed to advise her of the laws of the State, and failed to warn her of the unlawfulness and dangers of her activities at a local bar, where she met the assailants. The result in the case, especially after *Bradshaw*, is not surprising: the college did not stand *in loco parentis* with the student and did not owe a heightened duty of care to her. The court, however, made a few summarizing statements on the duties owed by a college or a university in an era no longer defined by *in loco parentis*:

> It would not be consistent with the caselaw in this area to impose a duty upon colleges to supervise their students when they leave the college campus for non-curricular activities. It would also not be consistent with the settled expectations of students, parents, or colleges. . . . Bethany cannot be held liable for failing to maintain a safe environment . . . when the only evidence of an unsafe environment is the serving of alcoholic beverages at . . . a facility which Bethany College did not own, lease or control.

Id. at 291–92.

2. In *Bradshaw*, the court rejected the plaintiffs' arguments that a special relationship existed between the college and the student. Nearly all other cases asking the same question have similarly found no special relationship and have declined to apply the *in loco parentis* doctrine in cases of alleged negligence on the part of the college, university, or employees. Putting it, perhaps, more bluntly is the court in *Freeman v. Busch*, 349 F.3d 582 (8th Cir. 2003): "In fact, since the late 1970s, the general rule is that no special relationship exists between a college and its *own* students because a college is not an insurer of the safety of its students." *See also Apffel v. Huddleston*, 50 F. Supp. 2d 1129 (D. Utah 1999); *Baldwin v. Zoradi*, 123 Cal. App. 3d 275, 176 Cal. Rptr. 809 (Cal. Ct. App. 1981); *Beach v. Univ. of Utah*, 726 P.2d 413 (Utah 1986); *Eiseman v. State*, 511 N.E.2d 1128 (N.Y. 1987); *Guest v. Hansen*, No. 06-cv-0500, 2007 U.S. Dist. LEXIS 92780 (N.D.N.Y. Dec. 18, 2007); *Nero v. Kan. St. Univ.*, 861 P.2d 768 (Kan. 1993); *Rabel v. Ill. Wesleyan Univ.*, 514 N.E.2d 552 (Ill. Ct. App. 1987) (holding that the responsibility of a university "is to properly educate" its students, not to act as their custodian). Two additional cases making similar arguments appear in Chapter II: *Booker v. Lehigh Univ.*, 800 F. Supp. 234 (E.D. Pa. 1992); and *Univ. of Denver v. Whitlock*, 744 P.2d 54 (Colo. 1987) (en banc).

3. There are exceptions to the general rule of special relationships (or lack thereof) discussed in *Bradshaw.* In *Kleinknecht v. Gettysburg College*, 989 F.2d 1360 (3d Cir. 1993), a case decided in the same judicial circuit as *Bradshaw*, the court held that there is a distinction between the relationship of a college with its students and the relationship of a college with its student-athletes. Along the same vein, in *Schieszler v. Ferrum College*, 236 F. Supp. 2d 602, 609 (E.D. Va. 2002), the court noted the general statement that no university/student relationship existed, but here, when a college had repeated warnings that a student had emotional problems, had made threats of suicide, and had required the student to sign a statement that "he would no longer hurt himself," a special relationship did exist. See Chapter II for a full presentation and discussion of *Schieszler.*

4. Even when a court declines to apply *in loco parentis*, it may nonetheless find a special relationship between a university and a student. In the noteworthy case on hazing, *Furek v. University of Delaware*, 594 A.2d 506 (Del. 1991), the court held that while the university did not stand *in loco parentis* to its students, the relationship was sufficiently close and direct to impose a duty of care. The court held that the university's policy against hazing constituted an assumed duty and the university had a duty to regulate and supervise foreseeable dangerous activities occurring on its property.

According to StopHazing.org, hazing is defined as "any activity expected of someone joining a group (or to maintain full status in a group) that humiliates, degrades or risks emotional and/or physical harm, regardless of the person's willingness to participate." As of 2010, 44 states have enacted anti-hazing laws that apply to K-12 and higher education institutions. For example, Ohio's law defines hazing as follows: "doing any act or coercing another, including the victim, to do any act of initiation into any student or other organization that causes or creates a substantial risk of causing mental or physical harm to any person." OHIO REV. CODE ANN. § 2903.31 (2010). Ohio's law, like many other states' anti-hazing laws, imposes both criminal and civil liability on offenders (most often other students) and, importantly, also on those administrators, staff members, and faculty members who permit such hazing to occur, either recklessly or negligently. Criminal penalties against those who commit hazing and/or permit it to occur range from low-degree misdemeanors to felonies. For Ohio's legislated civil liability standard, consider the following:

> If the hazing involves students in a primary, secondary, or post-secondary school, university, college, or any other educational institution, an action may also be brought against any administrator, employee, or faculty member of the school, university, college, or other educational institution who knew or reasonably should have known of the hazing and who did not make reasonable attempts to prevent it and against the school, university, college, or other educational institution. If an administrator, employee, or faculty member is found liable in a civil action for hazing, then . . . the

school, university, college, or other educational institution that employed the administrator, employee, or faculty member may also be held liable.

OHIO REV. CODE ANN. § 2307.44 (2010). According to the statute, consent of the victim is not a defense. However, evidence that the educational institution is actively enforcing an anti-hazing policy is an affirmative defense for the institution.

Civil liability, most often in the form of substantial monetary damages, can attach to the institution as a whole, the local and national fraternities or other associated organizations, and to the individuals involved, including the student hazers and university employees, administrators, and faculty members. *See Morrison v. Kappa Alpha Psi Fraternity, Inc.*, 738 So. 2d 1105 (La. Ct. App. 1999). But if university officials have no knowledge of the incidents and the victims deny that they ever occurred, then liability may not be imputed to the university or its leaders, particularly if the university has an active, effective policy against hazing. *See Alton v. Texas A & M Univ.*, 168 F.3d 196 (5th Cir. 1999).

Consider the Texas anti-hazing statute, which establishes criminal liability for those who commit acts of hazing, recklessly permit them to occur, and/or knowingly fail to report hazing. TEX. EDUC. CODE ANN. § 37.152. The provision on the duty to report hazing was challenged for its constitutionality in *Texas v. Boyd*, 38 S.W.3d 155 (Tex. Crim. App. 2001), where criminal defendants moved to dismiss the charges against them, arguing that the provision requiring hazing reports presented the risk of self-incrimination. The court rejected the argument, citing a related statute that grants civil and criminal immunity from prosecution for those who report hazing to administrators. *See* TEX. EDUC. CODE ANN. § 37.155. For a more in-depth discussion of tort liability for colleges and universities, see the cases and materials in Chapter II.

3. Contractual Relationship between Student and University

a. Admissions and Academics

STEINBERG v. CHICAGO MEDICAL SCHOOL
371 N.E.2d 634 (1977)

Opinion by: DOOLEY

Robert Steinberg received a catalog, applied for admission to defendant, Chicago Medical School, for the academic year 1974-75, and paid a $15 fee. He was rejected. Steinberg filed a class action against the school claiming it had failed to evaluate his application and those of other applicants according to the academic criteria in the school's bulletin. According to the complaint, defendant used nonacademic criteria, primarily the ability of the applicant or his family to pledge or make payment of large sums of money to the school.

The 1974-75 bulletin distributed to prospective students contained this statement of standards by which applicants were to be evaluated:

"Students are selected on the basis of scholarship, character, and motivation without regard to race, creed, or sex. The student's potential for the study and practice of medicine will be evaluated on the basis of academic achievement, Medical College Admission Test results, personal appraisals by a pre-professional advisory committee or individual instructors, and the personal interview, if requested by the Committee on Admissions."

. . . Count I of the complaint alleged breach of contract; count II was predicated on the Consumer Fraud and Deceptive Business Practices Act and the Uniform Deceptive Trade Practices Act; count III charged fraud; and count IV alleged unjust enrichment. This was sought to be brought as a class action. Accordingly, there were the customary allegations common to such an action.

The trial court dismissed the complaint for failure to state a cause of action. The appellate court reversed as to count I, the contract action, and permitted it to be maintained as a limited class action. It affirmed the circuit court's dismissal of the remaining counts II, III, and IV.

[The state supreme court affirmed the dismissals of counts II and IV, and proceeded with its discussion of counts I and III.]

The real questions on this appeal are: Can the facts support a charge of breach of contract? Is an action predicated on fraud maintainable? Is this a proper class-action situation?

. Count I alleges Steinberg and members of the class to which he belongs applied to defendant and paid the $15 fee, and that defendant, through its brochure, described the criteria to be employed in evaluating applications, but failed to appraise the applications on the stated criteria. On the contrary, defendant evaluated such applications according to monetary contributions made on behalf of those seeking admission.

A contract, by ancient definition, is "an agreement between competent parties, upon a consideration sufficient in law, to do or not to do a particular thing." *People v. Dummer* (1916), 274 Ill. 637, 640.

An offer, an acceptance, and consideration are basic ingredients of a contract. Steinberg alleges that he and others similarly situated received a brochure describing the criteria that defendant would employ in evaluating applications. He urges that such constituted an invitation for an offer to apply, that the filing of the applications constituted an offer to have their credentials appraised under the terms described by defendant, and that defendant's voluntary reception of the application and fee constituted an acceptance, the final act necessary for the creation of a binding contract.

This situation is similar to that wherein a merchant advertises goods for sale at a fixed price. While the advertisement itself is not an offer to contract, it constitutes an invitation to deal on the terms described in the advertisement. . . .

Here the description in the brochure containing the terms under which an application will be appraised constituted an invitation for an offer. The tender of the application, as well as the payment of the fee pursuant to the terms of the brochure, was an offer to apply. Acceptance of the application and fee constituted acceptance of an offer to apply under the criteria defendant had established.

Consideration is a basic element for the existence of a contract. . . . Any act or promise which is of benefit to one party or disadvantage to the other is a sufficient consideration to support a contract. . . . The application fee was sufficient consideration to support the agreement between the applicant and the school.

Defendant contends that a further requisite for contract formation is a meeting of the minds. But a subjective understanding is not requisite. It suffices that the conduct of the contracting parties indicates an agreement to the terms of the alleged contract. . . .

Here it would appear from the complaint that the conduct of the parties amounted to an agreement that the application would be evaluated according to the criteria described by defendant in its literature.

. . . Steinberg does not seek to compel the school to admit him. The substance of his action is that under the circumstances it was defendant's duty to appraise his application and those of the others on the terms defendant represented.

. . . .

As the appellate court noted in a recent case in which this defendant was a party:

> "A contract between a private institution and a student confers duties upon both parties which cannot be arbitrarily disregarded and may be judicially enforced." *DeMarco v. University of Health Sciences* (1976), 40 Ill. App. 3d 474, 480.

Here our scope of review is exceedingly narrow. Does the complaint set forth facts which could mean that defendant contracted, under the circumstances, to appraise applicants and their applications according to the criteria it described? This is the sole inquiry on this motion to dismiss. We believe the allegations suffice and affirm the appellate court in holding count I stated a cause of action.

Count III alleges that, with intent to deceive and defraud plaintiffs, defendant stated in its catalogs it would use certain criteria to evaluate applications; that these representations were false in that applicants were selected primarily for monetary considerations; that plaintiffs relied on said representations and were each thereby induced to submit their applications and pay $15 to their damage.

These allegations support a cause of action for fraud. Misrepresentation of an existing material fact coupled with scienter, deception, and injury are more than adequate. . . . *Roth v. Roth* (1970), 45 Ill. 2d 19, 23, succinctly stated when a misrepresentation may constitute fraud:

> "A misrepresentation in order to constitute a fraud must consist of a statement of material fact, false and known to be so by the party making it, made to induce the other party to act, and, in acting, the other party must rely on the truth of the statement. . . ."

Plaintiff's allegations meet the test of common law fraud.

. . . .

It is immaterial here that the misrepresentation consisted of a statement in the medical school catalog, referring to future conduct, that "the student's potential for the study and practice of medicine will be evaluated on the basis of academic achievement, Medical College Admission Test results, personal appraisals by a pre-professional advisory committee or individual instructors, and the personal interview, if requested by the Committee on Admissions." We concede the general rule denies recovery for fraud based on a false representation of intention or future conduct, but there is a recognized exception where the false promise or representation of future conduct is alleged to be the scheme employed to accomplish the fraud. Such is the situation here.

Here an action for fraud is consistent with the recognition of a contract action. The law creates obligations "on the ground that they are dictated by reason and justice." (*People v. Dummer* (1916), 274 Ill. 637, 641.) The right to recover on a "constructive contract," although phrased in contract terminology, is not based on an agreement between parties but is an obligation created by law. "Such contracts are contracts merely in the sense that [they] * * * are created and governed by the principles of equity." (*People v. Dummer* (1916), 274 Ill. 637, 642.) So here the facts of this situation mandate that equity imply an obligation by the defendant. We note this since the circumstances before us justify a contract action, as well as a fraud action, or, in the event no contract in fact can be proven, an action on an implied-in-law obligation of the defendant.

. . . .

The appellate court was correct in affirming the dismissal of counts II [i.e., consumer fraud] and IV [i.e., unjust enrichment] of plaintiff's complaint and in reversing the dismissal of count I [i.e., break of contract] of the complaint. It erred in affirming the dismissal of count III [i.e., fraud] and abbreviating the class represented by plaintiff.

. . . .

MANGLA v. BROWN UNIVERSITY

135 F.3d 80 (1st Cir. 1998)

Senior Circuit Judge John R. Gibson

Gaurav Mangla appeals from a judgment as a matter of law entered in favor of Brown University following a trial on his breach of contract and promissory estoppel claims. He argues that the district court erred in granting judgment, as a reasonable jury could have found that Brown breached the contract, acted arbitrarily and in bad faith, and that Brown was estopped from denying him admission to the graduate school. He argues that the court improperly raised certain evidence and overlooked and misconstrued other evidence in reaching this decision. We affirm the judgment of the district court.

Mangla applied for admission to the Brown Graduate School in September 1993, and was admitted as a probationary special student, a category of enrollment that permits the taking of graduate level courses but which is not in itself a degree program. His admission in this capacity was recommended by the Computer Science Department and approved by the graduate council. Associate Dean Joan Lusk met with Mangla at that time and explained to him that his admission was probationary because he lacked the requisite academic background or course work in computer science. Lusk further told Mangla that in order to be admitted to the degree program he would need to successfully complete course work in the Computer Science Department. Mangla claims to have satisfactorily completed seven of the eight courses required for a Master's degree.

After completing such course work, Mangla inquired of Dean Lusk about his probationary status, and she instructed him to obtain a faculty advisor for his Master's Project. In response, Mangla obtained a letter signed by Professor Stanley Zdonik, stating that Mangla "will be working under my supervision for his Master's project." Mangla claims that at the time he believed the letter served as a letter of recommendation for admission into the degree program.

In September 1995, Brown informed Mangla that his special student status was discontinued and that he had not been admitted into the Master's program. Mangla thereafter filed a new, formal application for admission into the Master's program. The Computer Science Department faculty reviewed the new application and voted to recommend that Mangla's application be denied. Mangla then appealed to the Graduate Council which voted unanimously to uphold the department's decision.

Mangla brought this action for breach of contract and promissory estoppel for Brown's refusal to admit him into its Master's program. The action was tried before a jury, but . . . the judge granted judgment as a matter of law to Brown. . . . The district court first decided that there was no breach of contract because Mangla knew that one of the things he had to do in performing his side of the contract was to obtain a favorable recommendation from the Computer Science Department faculty and there was no evidence that any such recommendation was obtained. . . .

The court further found that there was no promissory estoppel because there was no reasonable reliance on any of the alleged representations. There was explicit language in the Graduate School manual that even the department does not have the power to offer admission and that offers of admission have binding force only when made by the Graduate School in writing. . . .

. . . .

II.

Mangla argues that judgment as a matter of law was inappropriate because a reasonable jury could find that Brown University breached a contract with Mangla by refusing to confer regular degree status upon him.

. . . .

The student-college relationship is essentially contractual in nature. The terms of the contract may include statements provided in student manuals and registration materials. *See Lyons* [*v. Salve Regina College*], 565 F.2d [200,] 202 [(1st Cir. 1977)] (construing College Manual and Academic Information booklet as terms of a contract between a student and college). The proper standard for interpreting the contractual terms is that of "reasonable expectation — what meaning the party making the manifestation, the university, should reasonably expect the other party to give it." *Id.*

Mangla maintains that he reasonably expected that if he satisfactorily performed his course work and obtained a sponsor for his master's project he would be admitted as a master's degree candidate in the Computer Science Department. Mangla bases his claim on the alleged statements of Associate Dean Lusk and members of the Computer Science Department faculty. However, Brown University's graduate school catalog specifically provided:

> Caveat. Applicants are asked to take particular notice of the fact that the individual academic departments, while having a major role in evaluating the applications of all candidates, do not have the power to offer admission, and that offers of admission have binding force only when made by the Graduate School in writing over the signature of the Dean of the Graduate School or her representative.

By its terms, this provision divested faculty members of any authority to promise admission or to determine the necessary prerequisites for admission. Because the provision was included in the graduate school catalog, Brown could reasonably expect students to be aware of the policy. Thus, it was reasonable for Brown to expect its students not to rely on oral statements by individual faculty members as binding promises by the university.

Likewise, the statements of Associate Dean Lusk did not give Mangla a right to be admitted. As an apparent representative of the Dean of the Graduate School, Lusk arguably had the authority to offer admission. The caveat, however, restricted the acceptable form of such an offer to a signed writing. Mangla concedes that no such writing exists in this case. Therefore, the language of the graduate school catalog seriously compromises Mangla's claim that Lusk's statements gave him a contractual right to be offered admission.

As Mangla correctly asserts, the graduate school catalog is not a wholly integrated contract but instead is only one part of a more complex contractual relationship between the student and the college. We do not foreclose the possibility that, under certain circumstances, the university could obligate itself through the actions and oral statements of its officials, despite the language of the caveat provision. A reasonable jury, however, could not find that such circumstances exist in this case.

Particularly fatal to Mangla's contract claim in this case was his failure to secure a recommendation from the department faculty. Mangla admitted at trial that he understood that a faculty recommendation was a prerequisite to his admission as a regular degree candidate. Mangla maintains that this requirement was reasonably met by a letter signed by Professor Zdonik, a member of the Computer Science department faculty. The Zdonik letter does not, however, recommend that Mangla be admitted. Rather, the letter, addressed "To whomever it may concern," identifies Mangla as a graduate student working under Zdonik's supervision "for his Master's project" and requests that Mangla be provided with help and the use of resources for his research while living in Princeton, New Jersey. Mangla does not claim to have informed Zdonik of his intent to use the letter as a letter of recommendation. Indeed, Mangla does not even contend the letter was a faculty recommendation, but instead contends that he reasonably believed it was the "equivalent of a recommendation." No reasonable jury could find that the letter signed by Zdonik reasonably fulfilled the prerequisite of a faculty recommendation. As a result, no reasonable jury could conclude that Brown should have reasonably expected Mangla to believe that the university was contractually obligated to admit him.

III.

Mangla argues that a jury could reasonably find that Brown acted arbitrarily or in bad faith in refusing to admit Mangla as a regular degree candidate. Brown responds that Mangla's claim of arbitrariness must fail because the university's decision did not substantially depart from established academic norms.

. . . .

The decision to grant or deny admission to a student is a quintessential matter of academic judgment. Courts have long recognized that matters of academic judgment are generally better left to the educational institutions than to the judiciary and have accorded great deference where such matters are at issue. As the Supreme Court stated in *Regents of University of Michigan v. Ewing*, 474 U.S. 214, 225 (1985), "Plainly, [judges] may not override [the faculty's professional judgment] unless it is such a substantial departure from accepted academic norms as to demonstrate that the person or committee responsible did not actually exercise professional judgment."

Applying the standard of deference enunciated in *Ewing*, we conclude that no reasonable jury could find that Brown acted arbitrarily or in bad faith in refusing to admit Mangla as a regular degree candidate. The Computer Science Department recommended against Mangla's admission on the ground that Mangla did not demonstrate an ability to undertake the research or independent work required for a Master's thesis or project. The department's position was based in part on negative assessments of Mangla's research capabilities provided by professors who had supervised Mangla's previous attempts at a research project.

Mangla argues the department's decision was arbitrary and in bad faith because he was never informed that he would be judged on his ability to do independent research. Mangla, however, was aware that a Master's thesis or project was a necessary component of the Master's program. We believe it is self-evident that a committee evaluating an application for admission into a Master's program would be concerned with the applicant's prospects of successfully completing the degree requirements.

The evidence establishes that Brown judged Mangla according to legitimate criteria and had a sufficient basis for believing that Mangla did not meet those criteria. . . .

IV.

Finally, Mangla argues that a reasonable jury could have found Brown liable on a promissory estoppel theory. We reject his argument.

. . . .

As we have previously discussed, Brown should not have reasonably expected Mangla to rely on the oral statements of Dean Lusk or the individual faculty members as binding promises of admission. Therefore, we uphold the district court's ruling that no reasonable jury could find that Brown was estopped from denying Mangla admission as a Master's degree candidate.

We *affirm* the judgment as a matter of law in favor of Brown University.

NOTES

1. Regarding the written caveat appearing in Brown's graduate catalog stating that students are not admitted until the Graduate School says, in writing, that they are, the court in *Mangla* makes the point that students are expected to be aware of such policies and, in effect, not to rely on oral statements made by faculty, staff, and administrators. What about the expectation that faculty, staff, and administrators accurately articulate graduate catalog policy? Surely, if a faculty, staff, or administrative leader in a program offers advice to a student (or an applicant) along the lines of what we see in *Mangla*, there would be an expectation that the student or applicant follow the advice with the belief that it comports with university policy. Correct? The court in *Mangla* even makes reference to this possibility. Why, according to the court's reasoning, are these expectations not enough for Mangla to make a case for promissory estoppel?

The court in *Mangla* makes particular mention of an "offer" of admission. Effectively, in *Mangla*, oral statements such as those made by the associate dean are not legal offers in light of the provisions of the graduate catalog, which explicitly spell out when an offer of admission has been made. For more discussion of contracts and authority of university officials to enter them, see Chapter II.

2. "When a student is admitted to a university, an implied contract arises between the parties which states that if the student complies with the terms prescribed by the university, he will obtain the degree he seeks." *Vought v. Teachers Coll., Colum. Univ.*, 511 N.Y.S.2d 880, 881 (N.Y. App. Div. 1987). Of course, in some circumstances, there may be some controversy over whether the student was ever admitted in the first place. Despite the fact that *Vought* noted the existence of an implied contract between the university and student upon admission of the student, the applicant in *Vought* had not been admitted to the degree program at issue in the case. As a result, there was no fraud and no breach on the part of the university. His application to the program was just that: an application. In other words, the university made no promise of admission, and it did not ultimately admit him to the program. The court in *Johnson v. Lincoln Christian College*, 501 N.E.2d 1380 (Ill. App. 4 Dist. 1986), spells this distinction out with some additional clarity:

> The elements of a traditional contract are present in the implied contract between a college and a student attending that college and are readily discernible. The student's tender of an application constitutes an offer to apply to the college. By "accepting" an applicant to be a student at the college, the college accepts the applicant's offer. Thereafter, the student pays tuition (which obviously constitutes sufficient consideration), attends classes, completes course work, and takes tests. The school provides the student with facilities and instruction, and upon satisfactory completion of the school's academic requirements (which constitutes performance), the school becomes obligated to issue the student a diploma. . . . [A] college may not act maliciously or in bad faith by arbitrarily and capriciously refusing to award a degree to a student who fulfills its degree requirements.

Id. at 1384 (internal citations omitted). In *Johnson*, a student enrolled in a five-year program to earn a degree in the teaching of sacred music. He had paid all tuition and had completed all degree requirements. In his final semester, a classmate reported to the dean that the student (Johnson) might be homosexual. Thereafter, college officials told Johnson that, in order to graduate, he would have to seek counseling. He sought the counseling, under the threat that failing to do so would result in his expulsion. The counselor reported back to the college that Johnson was "not progressing." The college told Johnson that, unless he attended a hearing to defend against the allegation of his homosexuality, he would be dismissed and his transcript would indicate the reason. Johnson chose to withdraw from the college, feeling that the result of the hearing was predetermined. The court denied the college's motion to dismiss on the contract claim, holding that there was a contractual relationship between Johnson and the college.

3. The court in *Johnson*, explained in the above note, did not issue an order that the college grant Johnson his diploma, as the court was addressing a motion to dismiss. The court in *Healy v. Larsson*, 323 N.Y.S.2d 625 (N.Y. App. Div. 1971), on the other hand, did issue such an order, finding that the student had met all degree requirements and was, therefore entitled to receive the degree. The student in *Healy* enrolled in a community college as a full-time student to secure a degree. He was a transfer student and had attended two colleges prior to enrollment and was given credits for this prior work. The student claimed that he consulted with numerous officials at the college in an effort to establish a course of study to meet the degree requirements. The college claimed that the student failed to take proper credits within the area of concentration leading to a degree. The court held that after the student was admitted, there was an implied contract between the student and the college that if he complied with the college's terms he would receive the degree; therefore, the court concluded that the student had satisfied his end of the contract and was entitled to receive his degree. *See also Slaughter v. Brigham Young Univ.*, 514 F.2d 622 (10th Cir. 1975), *cert. denied*, 423 U.S. 898 (1975); *Carr v. St. John's Univ.*, 231 N.Y.S.2d 410, *aff'd*, 12 N.Y.2d 802, 187 N.E.2d 18 (1962).

4. What does a case like *Healy* say to the nature of advising relationships in colleges and universities? Traditional classroom teaching aside, much conversation about the student-university relationship in higher education centers around advising. *See, e.g.*, Benita Barnes & Ann Austin, *The Role of Doctoral Advisors: A*

Look at Advising from the Advisor's Perspective, 33 INNOVATIVE HIGHER EDUC. 297 (2009); VIRGINIA N. GORDON ET AL., ACADEMIC ADVISING: A COMPREHENSIVE HANDBOOK (2d ed. Jossey-Bass 2008); Libby Morris, *The Intersection of Teaching and Advising*, 33 INNOVATIVE HIGHER EDUC. 281 (2009); Jane E. Pizzolato, *Advisor, Teacher, Partner: Using the Learning Partnerships Model to Reshape Academic Advising*, ABOUT CAMPUS, Mar.–Apr. 2008, at 18; David Yarbrough, *The Engagement Model for Effective Academic Advising with Undergraduate College Students and Student Organizations*, 41 J. OF HUMANISTIC COUNSELING, EDUC. AND DEV. 61 (2002). Admittedly, the conversation is typically about retention and time-to-degree and not contract law. However, do the "terms" of an implied contract go beyond the coursework bulletins and checklists and reach the even less formal aspects of the student-university relationship?

DOHERTY v. SOUTHERN COLLEGE OF OPTOMETRY

862 F.2d 570 (6th Cir. 1988)

KENNEDY, CIRCUIT JUDGE.

[Plaintiff-appellant Doherty suffers "retinitis pigmentosa (RP) and an associated neurological condition" restricting his visual field and motor skills. Plaintiff applied to the Southern College of Optometry (SCO), whose faculty examined the plaintiff and determined his RP should not affect his performance at the school. Plaintiff did not mention his neurological problems in his application or when completing a student health survey].

. . . .

During the plaintiff's first year at SCO, the school began to require that students pass a pathology clinic proficiency requirement in order to qualify for an externship program required for fourth year students. According to the school policy, the plaintiff was subject to the new requirement. The pathology clinical proficiency examination requires the student to perform techniques with various instruments. . . . After the plaintiff failed his "check-out" on these instruments, he appealed the decision to the Admissions Committee, requesting that these requirements be waived. The Committee rejected the appeal. The Board of Trustees also denied his appeal, but granted the plaintiff an additional quarter to practice the techniques. In spite of the extra practice, the plaintiff again failed to demonstrate his proficiency with these instruments.

When SCO refused to confer a degree upon the plaintiff, he filed suit in the United States District Court for the Western District of Tennessee against SCO and two faculty members alleging both a violation of section 504 of the Rehabilitation Act of 1973, and section 1983. Plaintiff also asserted pendent state law claims of breach of contract, misrepresentation, outrageous conduct, and tortious interference with contract. . . . The jury returned a verdict of $225,000 in favor of the plaintiff on the breach of contract claim. . . . SCO cross-appeals from the jury's verdict on the breach of contract claim.

. . . .

III

In its appeal from the jury's verdict for the plaintiff on his breach of contract claim, SCO argues first that no contract existed between the parties. Second, if a contract existed, it included SCO's right to make reasonable and necessary changes to the curriculum, and thus SCO did not breach the contract by adding the clinical proficiency requirement. Third, no proof in the record existed that SCO exercised bad faith in making curriculum changes. Fourth, damages were not proven with specificity and, because of the proof, were necessarily speculative. Last, SCO argues that no proximate causal connection was proven between the alleged breach and the alleged damages. The second and third arguments are persuasive.

. . . .

A

[The court noted the traditional reluctance of courts to question academic facilities' ability to determine their curriculum and mentioned this is the backdrop of the court's analysis].

Since plaintiff asserts a state contract law claim, Tennessee law governs this issue. The parties, however, cite little Tennessee law defining the relationship between the university and the student. Plaintiff relies on *Bales v. Lincoln Memorial University*, slip op. (Tenn. Ct. App. Dec. 31, 1980), for the proposition that the student-university relationship is contractual in nature although courts have rejected a rigid application of contract law in this area. We are inclined to agree. Although the relationship may be analyzed as a contractual one, courts have adopted different standards of review when educators' decisions are based upon disciplinary versus academic criteria — applying a more intrusive analysis of the former and a far more deferential examination of the latter. . . . The Tennessee Supreme Court has endorsed this deferential standard of review for decisions by universities based upon academic criteria.

. . . [W]e believe that the Tennessee Supreme Court, in construing the terms of an implied contract between the university and the student, would adopt the deferential standard of " 'reasonable expectation — what meaning the party making the manifestation, the university, should reasonably expect the other party to give it.' " *Lyons*, 565 F.2d at 202 (quoting *Giles v. Howard Univ.*, 428 F. Supp. 603, 605 (D.D.C. 1977)). Furthermore, we are of the opinion that implicit in the university's general "contract" with its students is a right to change the university's academic degree requirements if such changes are not arbitrary or capricious. . . .

B

For purposes of our analysis we divide plaintiff's contractual claims, which are not very clearly focused, into three types: first, an implied contract between plaintiff and SCO containing terms in common with all other students based on the SCO 1978-79 catalog; second, an implied contract unique to the plaintiff himself and SCO based on the representations of Drs. Ebbers and Vasa in conjunction with the SCO catalog; and, third, an implied contract of good faith and fair dealing.

In view of the disclaimer language on the inside front cover of the catalog, it is difficult to find, as plaintiff asserts, that a binding contract was created promising the SCO class entering in 1978 the right to graduate determined under the standards in the 1978-79 catalog. The plaintiff relies on *Bales.* In that case the appellant, who had a perfect 4.0 grade point average and led his class, learned two days prior to graduation that the administration would require a student to complete a minimum of 92 credit hours at the school before he could graduate with any type of honors. This requirement was first announced to the student body at the appellant's graduation rehearsal, one day prior to the ceremony. The appellant had only 91 credit hours; the school admitted that if not for the minimum hours requirement the appellant would have graduated magna cum laude and as valedictorian. The appellant sued, alleging that the catalog under which he enrolled contractually established the exclusive criteria for graduation honors, and that no minimum hours were set out in the catalog as a requirement. The catalog specifically provided that all school policies were subject to change. Witnesses testified that the policy of requiring a certain number of credit hours had always been unwritten.

The *Bales* court found that:

> . . . [T]he provisions of a contract cannot be modified *after one side has completed performance or without giving the student a reasonable time for compliance after receipt of notification of that intended change in policy.* Mr. Bales did not receive notice of any minimum residence hours credit requirement for honors, including the original unwritten policy of 96 hours, until two days prior to his commencement ceremony, at which time he was unable to take any steps to comply with the requirement because he had completed all his courses.

Slip op. at 4 (emphasis added). Thus according to *Bales*, a contractual relationship exists between the student and the institution with respect to requirements for graduation even though the institution retains the right to change the requirements. This reservation, of the right to make changes in the terms of the contract, was subject to reasonable notice. The case at bar stands in sharp contrast to *Bales* in that the plaintiff had ample notice of the change of requirements; plaintiff does not argue that SCO failed to provide him with reasonable notice.

Applying the "reasonable expectation" standard set out in [the preceding section], we believe it was reasonable for SCO, given the disclaimer printed in the front of its handbook and the practice of prospective application of curriculum changes, to expect the students to anticipate and comply with curriculum changes affecting their remaining years at the school. SCO's modification of the degree requirement to include a clinical proficiency in the four instruments was reasonable . . . .

Plaintiff's second contractual argument is that a special contract, express or implied, existed between SCO and himself that he would be able to successfully complete the program based on the requirements as they stood in the 78-79 catalog and the evaluations of Drs. Ebbers and Vasa. Assuming, *arguendo*, that some form of implied contract could be created based upon Dr. Ebbers' assertions coupled with the 78-79 catalog, if plaintiff is to prevail SCO would have had to impliedly agree that plaintiff would complete the program in spite of his handicap *and*, necessarily, that SCO would make no changes or additions to the program (no matter how necessary) if the effect of such changes would be to prevent plaintiff's receipt of his degree. SCO did not expressly agree to such a contract. Nor would it be reasonable for someone in plaintiff's position to so believe. Dr. Ebbers' report to Ms. Dale did not state that plaintiff *would* graduate but merely opines that his *visual* problems are not so acute as to *prohibit* him from studying at SCO. Furthermore, plaintiff himself admitted at trial that he held no belief that the college undertook to guarantee his graduation. Plaintiff's assertions that SCO impliedly agreed not to change its curriculum if the effect would be to prevent his graduation or that SCO by examining him impliedly guaranteed his ability to graduate are unfounded.

Finally, plaintiff indirectly asserts that SCO acted in bad faith by adopting these requirements and/or by refusing to waive them upon request by plaintiff. . . . [A]ll of plaintiff's witnesses stated that the new requirement was reasonable and desirable. Furthermore, no evidence was introduced nor does plaintiff himself maintain that SCO deliberately introduced the new clinical proficiency requirement to prevent plaintiff's graduation. Lastly, SCO fulfilled its obligation to act in good faith when it provided plaintiff daily assistance in practicing with the instruments for one whole quarter. . . . Plaintiff's claim of lack of good faith is based upon SCO's refusal to award plaintiff his diploma in spite of his inability to pass the new requirements. This action by SCO is not an action taken in bad faith — it is simply the university exercising its right to make a necessary change in its curriculum in light of the changing practice of optometry.

Plaintiff failed to show a breach of contract by SCO. SCO's motion for a directed verdict should have been granted as to plaintiff's contract claim. . . .

. . . .

NOTES

1. What standard of review did the court in *Doherty* adopt with respect to the contract claim? Do you agree with the standard applied? Why or why not? Is the standard applied here one based primarily on contract law or is it based primarily on academic decision making? Why might such a distinction be important? Note that the majority opinion uses *Regents of University of Michigan v. Ewing*, 474 U.S. 214 (1985), and *Board of Curators of University of Missouri v. Horowitz*, 435 U.S. 78 and 89–91 (1978), to make the point that courts regularly defer to the curricular and other academic decisions of universities. (For more information on these two cases, see detailed coverage in Chapter VII.) Should all universities be encouraged to put disclaimers in their catalogs and on their web sites telling applicants, students, parents, and other university community members that curricular requirements are subject to change? Is the decision in *Doherty* more a matter of judicial deference, which seemingly would not require such explicit disclaimers? Or is it a matter of contract, where the disclaimer becomes a contractual term?

2. Today, there is much conversation and concern over the time-to-degree for university students, with a greater emphasis on university initiatives that help students finish undergraduate study in four years. *See* Jennifer Gonzalez, *To Pump up Degree Counts, Colleges Invite Dropouts Back*, 57 CHRON. OF HIGHER EDUC., Oct. 29, 2010, at A1; Daniel F. Sullivan, *The Hidden Costs of Low Four-Year Graduation Rates*, LIBERAL EDUC., Summer 2010, at 24. Do you think such initiatives should weigh heavily in a contractual claim, in cases where university-led changes to curriculum requirements result in students taking longer to complete their degrees?

3. The court in *Doherty* distinguished *Bales* by stating that the changes made to the curriculum in *Bales* were subject to reasonable notice and that the student in *Bales* was not given reasonable notice while Doherty was given ample notice. True as this might be, the court in *Doherty* — in analyzing a very similar contract claim — also emphasized the disclaimer language inserted into SCO's annual catalog that stated the curriculum and associated requirements are subject to change. Note that the disclaimer language did not contain any statement on "reasonable notice" of changes to requirements. In your opinion, which fact weighs more heavily in the court's decision here — the express disclaimer language in the catalog or the ample notice Doherty received?

AMERICAN COMPUTER INSTITUTE, INC. v. STATE OF ALASKA

995 P.2d 647 (Alas. 2000)

FABE, JUSTICE.

I. *INTRODUCTION*

American Computer Institute, a postsecondary school providing career education programs, closed its Anchorage and Fairbanks campuses mid-term without prior notice to its students. The issue now before us is whether ACI must refund tuition to those students who were unable to complete their programs due to the school's unscheduled closures. Because ACI failed to provide promised educational services in Fairbanks and Anchorage, we hold that it must make refunds to those students who could not complete their programs due to the closures.

II. *FACTS*

. . . .

[The Alaska Computer Institute (ACI) informed its students and staff that it was closing its Fairbanks campus the day of the announcement. 19 students were enrolled with school scheduled for another 4 months. 6 students refused to sign a contract f or a "teach-out" program that would allow students to complete their instruction on an accelerated schedule. ACI disputed the refunds due those students. Several months later, ACI closed its Anchorage branch and contacted Charter College to provide instruction for free for the remaining students. Several students could not complete their program at Charter and ACI refused to reimburse their additional expenses incurred in completing their ACI-equivalent programs. Ten other students did not complete their free quarter at Charter and ACI disputed whether they should receive full refunds or refunds for voluntary withdrawal. The superior (trial) court concluded ACI had a duty to these students and ordered ACI to pay full refunds, except for those students who did not complete the Charter program.]

. . . .

ACI moved for relief from the superior court's judgment asserting that it should not pay full reimbursements to students who attended but did not complete the accelerated teach-out in Fairbanks (Bennett, Fix, and Willey). The court denied this portion of ACI's . . . motion.

. . . .

V. *DISCUSSION*

A. *The Superior Court Did Not Err in Concluding that ACI Breached Its Enrollment Contract by Failing to Provide Its Students with Certain Educational Programs.*

The superior court found that ACI's enrollment contract obligated it to provide its students with the programs described in the school catalog. These programs established completion dates and required specific numbers of credits and hours. Each student who enrolled at ACI signed a "binding and enforceable" contract that incorporated the school catalog by reference. Based on this contract, the superior court correctly concluded that "ACI had a contractual obligation to provide to its students the educational courses as described in the school catalog."

When a party has contracted to perform certain duties, as ACI did here, any failure to perform those duties amounts to a breach of contract. Given its abrupt closures in both Fairbanks and Anchorage, we agree with the superior court's conclusion that ACI breached its enrollment contract.

1. *The Fairbanks closure*

ACI argues that its enrollment contract permitted it to conduct an accelerated teach-out as a "schedule change," and that the teach-out was "substantially similar to the original program." ACI relies on two provisions from its catalog to support its contention that the enrollment contract permitted the teach-out. The first states:

> [ACI] reserves the right to make changes in program schedule . . . or programs of study. Such changes will not affect the integrity or continuity of programs offered. . . . All changes will be made within the framework of state laws and regulations.

The second states:

> The school also reserves the right to change, within the framework of state law and regulations, the opening and closing of terms [and] hours of

> instruction . . . as circumstances may require for the success of the school and its students.

But we conclude, as did the superior court, that ACI failed to perform its duties under the enrollment contract in Fairbanks.

First, the teach-out was not a mere "schedule change" permitted under ACI's enrollment contract. The superior court found that the teach-out was accelerated by thirty-three percent over the original program and "followed an unexpected two-week hiatus during which students were uncertain about their options." Moreover, ACI admitted that the medical and accounting programs could "not feasibly be accelerated." ACI's "schedule change" provisions nowhere indicated an intent to cover a school closure, and they did not permit ACI's accelerated teach-out. We therefore agree with the superior court that the teach-out was not a "schedule change" under the contract.

Second, the teach-out was not "substantially similar" to the original ACI programs. When a party offers a substitute performance, it has the burden of showing that the substitute is suitable. Whether that substitute is suitable "depends on all the circumstances, including the similarity of the performance and the times and places that they would be rendered." ([*See* Restatement (Second) of Contracts] § 350 cmt. E) In this case, the teach-out's fast pace made it too difficult for some students to complete. One student, for example, stated that he had "lost confidence in the value of the education" that he was receiving under the accelerated plan. Moreover, ACI's president conceded that the medical and accounting programs were not well suited to an accelerated program. Given the teach-out's accelerated pace and its infeasibility for two ACI programs, we agree with the superior court's findings that the teach-out differed substantially from the original ACI programs. Thus, we affirm the superior court's determination that ACI breached its contract when it closed its Fairbanks campus.

2. *The Anchorage closure*

ACI argues that the students who participated in Charter College's voluntary offer for enrollment at Charter had the opportunity to receive "educational upgrades" and are therefore not entitled to refunds. Although ACI did not arrange for an Anchorage teach-out, nor did it contract with Charter College to assume responsibility for continuing its students' educations, Charter College made an independent and voluntary offer to ACI students. Charter offered one tuition-free quarter at Charter and agreed to accept some transfer credits from ACI. Some ACI students elected to participate in this program and subsequently incurred additional tuition expenses at Charter because they were unable to complete their courses of study in one free quarter. Other students enrolled in the Charter program but did not complete it. Still other students did not participate in the Charter offer at all.

The superior court concluded that the Charter offerings differed substantially from ACI's, thus relieving students of any obligation to enroll in Charter's program. It found that "Charter College provided programs that were more rigorous and demanding than [those at] ACI," and that ACI and Charter College offered "different educational programs." The record supports these findings. Indeed, ACI's counsel observed that comparing the educational programs of Charter and ACI was like comparing "a Cadillac . . . to a Chevrolet," and admitted that the Charter College and ACI programs were "not equivalent." Because ACI closed its campus before students could complete the programs for which they contracted, and because ACI did not provide a substantially similar substitute, the superior court did not err in concluding that ACI breached its contract with respect to its Anchorage students.

B. *The Superior Court Did Not Err in Concluding that ACI's Withdrawal Policy Does Not Limit Its Liability Because Students Had No Duty to Complete the Accelerated Teach-Out or Attend Charter College.*

ACI next argues that the students who did not complete the teach-out or attend Charter College were only entitled to refunds under ACI's withdrawal policy. This policy applies to students who voluntarily withdraw from programs they have contracted to complete and provides that prepaid tuition or fees will be refunded based on the following:

> Tuition is charged from the student's class start date through the last day of attendance. Tuition charges withheld will not exceed a weekly prorata portion of tuition for the training completed, rounded upward to the nearest ten percentile of that period.
>
> *Once the student has completed 60% or more of their program, the school may require the student to remain committed for the entire amount of tuition.*
>
> The prorata refund is arrived at by dividing the total number of weeks that make up the period of enrollment (program length) for which the student has been charged, into the number of weeks the student was in school, based on the last recorded day of attendance.

(Emphasis added.)

Because we agree with the superior court's conclusions that ACI breached its contract in both Fairbanks and Anchorage, and that the students had no duty to complete those alternate programs because they were not substantially similar, we do not consider the students to have "withdrawn" from ACI. Thus, the withdrawal policy does not apply to them. We agree with the superior court's view that "clearly, the situation is different from that of a student's voluntary withdrawal. The risk of loss should fall on the school when the school, not the student, is culpable for the cessation of education." We thus affirm the superior court's conclusion that ACI's withdrawal policy does not limit its liability.

C. *The Superior Court Did Not Err in Ordering ACI to Reimburse Fully the Students Who Could Not Complete Their Programs Due to the Fairbanks and Anchorage Closures.*

Because ACI breached its contract in both Fairbanks and Anchorage, and because the withdrawal policy does not apply, the superior court did not err in requiring ACI to make appropriate refunds to the students who could not complete their programs.

1. *The Fairbanks closure*

. . . .

c. *Robin Bennett, Helena Fix, and Phillip Willey*

. . . .

[ACI failed to produce evidence or provide files to the Alaska Commission on Postsecondary Education (the Commission) concerning three students, Robin Bennett, Helena Fix, and Philip Wiley, at trial. ACI would later move for relief form judgment, arguing these three student withdrew for reasons unrelated to the closure. The superior court denied this motion.]

. . . .

We conclude that the superior court should have given ACI an opportunity to present its defenses. . . . [P]rocedural due process and fundamental fairness establish a civil defendant's right to present its defenses. Because these students' claims for refunds were never presented to the court during trial, ACI did not have an opportunity to argue that these students' failure to continue their programs was unrelated to ACI's closure. Therefore, we conclude that the superior court abused its discretion in denying ACI's motion for relief from judgment with respect to Bennett, Fix, and Willey. We vacate the superior court's order and remand for an evidentiary hearing to determine whether Bennett, Fix, and Willey withdrew from ACI for reasons independent of the school's closure or whether they are entitled to refunds. ACI must bear the burden of proof on these issues on remand.

2. *The Anchorage closure*

a. *Students who could not complete their programs at Charter College within the free quarter*

Charter College offered to allow students to complete their programs during a "free quarter" for which Charter would not charge tuition. Four students transferred to Charter College but could not complete their programs within the free quarter. These students subsequently incurred additional tuition expenses finishing their degrees at Charter. The superior court found that none of these four students could complete their programs within the free quarter and awarded reimbursements for the costs of completion at Charter College. These reimbursements amounted to less than the tuition paid to ACI.

ACI argues that the students are not entitled to reimbursements for the extra time spent at Charter, since they benefitted by receiving "better" educations than they would have at ACI. But, as we have observed, "making the best of a bad situation does not necessarily signify a benefit." These students did not choose to attend Charter College; ACI's closure forced them to enroll at an alternative institution. The students cannot be faulted for the additional time they required to complete Charter College's more rigorous programs. We therefore affirm the superior court's order that ACI reimburse [these students] for the costs of completing the ACI-equivalent programs at Charter College.

. . . .

c. *The nine students who did not complete Charter College's program*

. . . .

These nine students are situated almost identically to the Fairbanks students, Bennett, Fix, and Willey, for whom the superior court ordered refunds. . . . ACI failed to provide the Commission with the files for these nine Anchorage students. . . . [A]lthough ACI should not benefit from its failure to turn over the student files, we have determined that it should have the opportunity to present its defense that the closures were unrelated to the students' failure to complete their programs. Thus, the appropriate remedy for the nine Anchorage students — as it is for the Fairbanks students Bennett, Fix, and Willey — is to remand for an evidentiary hearing on whether these students had reasons wholly independent of ACI's closure for failing to complete their ACI-equivalent programs or whether they are entitled to refunds. Again, ACI must bear the burden of proof on these issues on remand.

D. *The Superior Court Did Not Err in Ordering ACI to Reimburse Third Parties Who Paid Tuition on Behalf of Students.*

ACI also disputes the superior court's order requiring ACI to reimburse third parties who paid tuition on behalf of students. ACI argues that "there is no reason that payment needs to be made to a funding source where the student has no legal liability for such payment." But ACI cannot keep tuition money paid on behalf of students simply because the students themselves did not incur the liability. Public and private funds for postsecondary education exist to make it affordable, and in promoting access to postsecondary education, the Commission has an interest in protecting these funding sources. Because ACI should not benefit from tuition paid by students or on behalf of students, we affirm the superior court's order requiring ACI to reimburse third parties.

. . . .

NOTES

1. Are you surprised by the extent of the decision in the *American Computer Institute* case? As you read, the court ordered reimbursement of student expenses incurred due to the closure of the colleges in Fairbanks and Anchorage. Regarding a few of the plaintiffs, the court also ordered reimbursement of expenses beyond the term in which the colleges were closed. What was the rationale for awarding reimbursement beyond the then-current term? Was it because of the differences between the ACI and Charter programs? Was it because of the nature of the initial contract or promises made? In such a case, how far into the future should reimbursement go? Expenses for completion of just those current registered classes? Completion of only the current quarter or semester? What about a program that goes beyond one semester or quarter remaining? Would the discussion change for a school that has students register for two or more terms in advance? Or is it dependent on the payment of tuition for particular terms? *See Aase v. State, South Dakota Board of Regents*, 400 N.W.2d 269 (S.D. 1987) (where the court's majority held that the only contract formed between a student and a university is formed at the payment of tuition). As a result, a breach of contract action for tuition dollars covers only that particular term of study where the tuition was paid, regardless of whether the student would have finished the program at the end of that term *and* regardless of whether the student's program is available at an alternate location.

2. What of a university, college, or program that shuts down and then seeks alternate arrangements for the affected students. Should such efforts be required, legally? Or would such a requirement unfairly bind the educational institution to contracts beyond the current term and those not yet entered with students? Perhaps such efforts are inspired more by ethics than by law.

Is there a difference in the expectation placed on an educational institution if the entire institution is shut down, compared to a situation where only one of that institution's programs is shut down? In a related matter, see *Beukas v. Board of Trustees of Farleigh-Dickinson University*, 605 A.2d 708 (N.J. Super. Ct. 1992). In *Beukas*, Farleigh-Dickinson closed its dental school after its state financial aid was discontinued. The school arranged for the transfer of the students to other dental schools, and subsidized any differences in tuition. Affected students filed suit against the university, claiming that the university's catalog is an enforceable contract and that the university breached the contract when it shut down the school. The court held for the university. According to the court, even if the university's catalog were an enforceable contract, the university did not breach it because the catalog specifically gave the university the right to cancel classes. Noting the university's efforts in helping the harmed students, the court also held that the university did not violate any implied covenant of good faith and fair dealing because it acted reasonably and humanely.

3. What about a case where the university or the program loses accreditation? In *Behrend v. State of Ohio*, 379 N.E.2d 617 (Ohio Ct. App. 1977), former students of the school of architecture at Ohio University filed suit against the university, its board of trustees, and members of the university administration. The plaintiffs claimed that the university and its agents had misrepresented the status of accreditation of the school. According to the students, the university had continually assured the students that if they attended the school and worked hard, they could obtain an accredited degree in architecture. The school faculty met with the accrediting body, which informed the university that they would recommend a two-year accreditation. Unfortunately, though, enrollment declined and the financial state of affairs led the university to decide to phase out the program. The accrediting body then withdrew its recommendation to re-accredit the program. The trial court granted the defendants' motion to dismiss and the court of appeals reversed:

> It is not unreasonable for one matriculating to an institution of higher learning, which offers course materials and degrees in a certain professional field, to assume that the credits for courses taken at such institution, and any degree thereafter that might be granted, would qualify the student or the graduate for the appropriate state professional examination.
>
> Such is the situation presented here where Ohio University offered courses in architecture which looked to a degree in such professional discipline. Although the college had lost its accreditation in 1969, the staff of the college, as well as the dean, continued to convey the thought to these student plaintiffs that every effort would be made to again be accredited. In fact, the record will show that repeated statements were made by the staff and administration of the School of Architecture that there was no great problem in again being accredited.
>
> Our holding that there was an implied contract by Ohio University with these student plaintiffs that the latter be provided accredited academic training is not saying that the board of trustees was powerless to discontinue certain educational school and departments pursuant to the determination of the board. The board of trustees has the jurisdiction to make the policy determination of the continued existence of the various departments within the university.
>
> However, where a determination is made affecting those with whom the university had contracted, unless there is shown to be an impossibility of performance, the contract must be fulfilled, or damages awarded.

Id. at 620–21. The appellate court then stated that the University did not show impossibility of performance and, instead, went with a defense based on academic decision making authority. Why do you think the University went this direction? Was there impossibility of performance of the contract here, given the loss of accreditation? Even if that were the case, why would that defense have failed here?

4. With no surprise, a college's false claims of accreditation will doom not only the college itself, but could also lead to other significant legal issues, including claims for monetary damages from injured students. In *Gonzalez v. North American College of Louisiana*, 700 F. Supp. 362 (S.D. Tex. 1988), for example, the defendant college deceived the federal government in its application for certification under a national program that offered tuition assistance grants and student loan money. The college received the grants and loans, but never disbursed the money to the students. The granting agency discovered the lack of accreditation and revoked the certification, causing the defendant to close its colleges. The plaintiffs, in turn, did not receive the education promised and were also indebted to the banks for the amount of the loan money sent to defendants. The court denied the defendants' motion to dismiss, holding that the plaintiffs successfully stated a federal RICO claim.

5. For another example of a case in which an institution of higher education made false statements and assurances to its students, consider *American Commercial Colleges, Inc. v. Davis*, 821 S.W.2d 450 (Tex. Ct. App. 1991), where a business school presented promises of qualified teachers, modern equipment, a low teacher to student ratio, and excellent training aids. What the students received, however, were high teacher-to-student ratios (e.g., a class of 42 students who were taking different-level courses simultaneously, taught by the registrar who made the promises initially), outdated teaching aids, and unqualified teachers. One student sued the college for violations of state deceptive trade practices law. The jury found that the college knowingly made false representations and awarded the plaintiff $28,000 in damages. The state court of appeals affirmed, holding that the student had relied to her detriment on the promises made by the defendant college.

OLSSON v. BOARD OF HIGHER EDUCATION OF THE CITY OF NEW YORK

402 N.E.2d 1150 (N.Y. 1980)

Opinion by: Gabrielli

This case presents the novel questions of whether and under what circumstances a court may intervene in the decision of an educational institution to withhold a diploma from one of its students on academic grounds. Specifically, we are asked to determine whether an educational institution may be estopped from asserting that a student has not fulfilled the requirements for graduation where the student's deficiency was caused in part by his reliance upon a professor's misleading statement regarding the institution's grading criteria. Although we find that the facts and circumstances presented in this case did not warrant the extreme remedy of requiring the institution to award a diploma to one whom it deemed unqualified, we nevertheless refrain from holding that the principles of equitable estoppel may never be used to avoid the harsh effects of an arbitrary academic determination.

The petitioner in this case, Eugene Olsson, was a candidate for a Master's degree at the John Jay College of Criminal Justice, a branch of the City University of New York. Having completed the bulk of his studies with an "honors" average, Olsson elected to take a final "comprehensive" examination in lieu of submitting a Master's thesis, as permitted by the school's academic regulations. Since he was told that the examination would test his cumulative knowledge in the field of criminal justice, Olsson decided to enroll in a review course to refresh his memory of his past work in the program.

Toward the end of the semester, one of the professors who was conducting the review course undertook to describe to his class the criteria that would be used in the grading of the upcoming examination. Professor Kim apparently intended to inform his students that, in addition to attaining an over-all average score of 2.8 points on the examination, they would be required to score three out of a possible five points on each of four of the five examination questions answered. In the course of relating this information, however, Professor Kim misspoke, stating: "You must have at least three out of five *questions*" (emphasis supplied). This uncorrected misstatement, according to Olsson, left him and several of his classmates with the impression that they could achieve a passing grade on the examination by scoring at least three points on only three of the five questions. As a consequence, Olsson was unpleasantly surprised when he learned that, although his over-all average score exceeded 2.8, he had nevertheless failed the examination because he had received passing scores on only three rather than four of the five questions he had answered.

Believing that the outcome was unfair, Olsson petitioned the academic appeals committee of the college for a reconsideration of his grade. He thought himself aggrieved because he had budgeted his time during the examination in such a way as to maximize his chances of achieving a passing score on three of the five questions. Had he known that he would be required to perform acceptably on four questions, Olsson asserted, he would have allocated his efforts more evenly and might therefore have passed the examination. The academic appeals committee, however, declined to change Olsson's test score to a "pass", concluding that it would be improper to do so in view of the fact that he had failed the examination under the uniformly applied criteria. Nevertheless, in the interest of fairness, the committee offered to expunge the results of Olsson's examination and permit Olsson to retake it without prejudice to his right to sit for the test a second time [which was the program's regular policy for all students] should he fail again.

Finding this offer to be unacceptable, Olsson commenced the instant . . . proceeding in an effort to compel the college to award him a diploma on the strength of his existing examination score. Since he had relied on Professor Kim's classroom statements in allocating his time during the examination and had "passed" the test under the criteria delineated in those statements, Olsson contended that the college should be estopped from applying the higher standard, which had resulted in his failing grade. Both the trial court and the Appellate Division accepted this argument and ordered the college to award Olsson a diploma in his chosen field *nunc pro tunc.* Both courts stressed that there existed [at the time] no written regulations governing grading criteria at the time that Olsson took the examination, and both courts concluded that the college rather than the individual student should bear the ultimate responsibility for Professor Kim's unfortunate "slip-of-the-tongue". We disagree.

In reversing the determinations below, we are mindful that this case involves more than a simple balancing of equities among various competing commercial interests. While it is true that in the ordinary case, a principal must answer for the misstatements of his agent when the latter is clothed with a mantle of apparent authority, such hornbook rules cannot be applied mechanically where the "principal" is an educational institution and the result would be to override a determination concerning a student's academic qualifications. Because such determinations rest in most cases upon the subjective professional judgment of trained educators, the courts have quite properly exercised the utmost restraint in applying traditional legal rules to disputes within the academic community.

. . . .

This is not, of course, to suggest that the decisions of educators are completely immune from judicial scrutiny. Consistent with the policy of ensuring that academic credentials truly reflect the knowledge and skills of the bearer, the courts have indicated that they will intervene if an institution exercises its discretion in an arbitrary or irrational fashion. . . . In addition, it has been suggested that there exists an "implied contract" between the institution and its students such that "if [the student] complies with the terms prescribed by the [institution], he will obtain the degree which he sought" (*Matter of Carr v St. John's Univ., N. Y.*, 17 AD2d 632, 633, *aff'd*, 12 NY2d 802). The essence of the implied contract is that an academic institution must act in good faith in its dealings with its students.

In this case, John Jay College amply fulfilled its obligation to act in good faith when it offered Eugene Olsson the opportunity to retake his comprehensive examination. Certainly, the college was not obliged to confer a diploma upon Olsson before he demonstrated his competence in accordance with the institution's academic standards. The mere circumstance that Olsson may have been misled by Professor Kim's unfortunate remark cannot serve to enhance the student's position in this regard. Despite Olsson's speculative contention that he might have passed the examination had he not been misinformed about the grading criteria, the fact remains that neither the courts nor the college authorities have any way of knowing whether the outcome of the testing would have been different if Olsson had not "relied" upon Professor Kim's misstatement. Indeed, the fact that 23 of the 35 students enrolled in Professor Kim's review course managed to pass the examination despite the faculty member's "slip-of-the-tongue" serves to demonstrate that there was no necessary connection between Olsson's exposure to the "three out of five" comment and his failure to achieve a passing score. Under these circumstances, requiring the college to award Olsson a diploma on equitable estoppel grounds would be a disservice to society, since the credential would not represent the college's considered judgment that Olsson possessed the requisite qualifications.

We hasten to add that our holding today should not be interpreted as an indication that estoppel will never lie when an educational institution seeks to withhold a diploma from one of its students on academic grounds. To be distinguished from the present case are those situations in which a student has fulfilled all of the academic requirements for graduation, but has neglected some technical prerequisite in reliance upon the assurances of a faculty member. The facts in *Matter of Blank v Board of Higher Educ.* (51 Misc 2d 724) are illustrative in this regard. There, the student had elected to pursue the college's "professional option plan" after consulting with his prelaw adviser at the college. Under the plan, a student who had completed at least three quarters of his studies at the college could become entitled to a baccalaureate degree if he completed one years' full-time work in an approved law school. The only proviso was that the student's course of study had to "constitute, in the opinion of the Dean of Faculty, an acceptable program for the AB degree". Since he lacked four required courses at the time he was preparing to enter law school, the student approached the guidance officer of the college and the chairperson of the applicable academic department in an effort to work out an acceptable program. The student, who was planning to attend an out-of-town law school, was unequivocally advised that he would have to enroll in the required courses at the college, but was told that he could obtain the necessary credits without actually attending classes if the individual instructors agreed. Pursuant to this advice, the student in *Blank* took two of the required courses over the summer "in residence" and then made arrangements with college instructors to take the two remaining courses on a "correspondence" basis. Although he passed the final examinations in each of the last two courses with a grade of "B" and received full course credit from the individual instructors, the student in *Blank* was denied his diploma after the dean determined that he had failed to comply with the college's "in residence" requirement. Under these circumstances, Special Term correctly held that the dean of the college should be estopped from asserting the "in residence" requirement as a ground for withholding the student's diploma, since the requirement had, in effect, been waived by several faculty members, all of whom could be regarded agents of the dean.

The outstanding feature which differentiates *Blank* from the instant case is the unavoidable fact that in *Blank* the student unquestionably had fulfilled the academic requirements for the credential he sought. Unlike the student here, the student in *Blank* had demonstrated his competence in the subject matter to the satisfaction of his professors. Thus, there could be no public policy objection to Special Term's decision to award a "diploma by estoppel" (accord *Matter of Healy v Larsson*, 67 Misc 2d 374, affd 42 AD2d 1051, affd 35 NY2d 653). . . .

In summary, it must be stressed that the judicial awarding of an academic diploma is an extreme remedy which should be reserved for the most egregious of circumstances. In light of the serious policy considerations which militate against judicial intervention in academic disputes, the courts should shun the "diploma by estoppel" doctrine whenever there is some question as to whether the student seeking relief has actually demonstrated his competence in accordance with the standards devised by the appropriate school authorities. . . .

For the foregoing reasons, the order of the Appellate Division should be reversed, without costs, and the petition should be dismissed.

NOTES

1. Do you agree with the decision in *Olsson*? The two lower courts held for the plaintiff, while the state court of appeals reversed. In your opinion, what facts are the most important to the decision here? That only one person made the uncorroborated slip-of-the-tongue remark? That a majority of Olsson's classmates who heard the same misstatement managed to pass the exam? That the one person who made the remark was a classroom instructor and not the administrator of the program? If the speaker who made the mistake had been a department chair, program director, or dean, how might Olsson have reframed his argument? What if the misstatement of policy is, in fact, made by college administrators?

2. Further, what if that misstatement is made in the form of a formal, published action? In *Mendez v. Reynolds*, 248 A.D.2d 62 (N.Y. Sup. Ct. 1998), students at Hostos Community College, one of the colleges in the City University of New York (CUNY) system, who were scheduled to graduate in short order, filed suit against CUNY, alleging that it had adopted a graduation requirement so close to their graduation date as to be arbitrary and capricious. CUNY's Board of Trustees did, in fact, issue a resolution five days before commencement requiring all graduating students to pass a writing assessment exam. Traditionally, passage of this particular exam was required as a prerequisite for enrollment in a required course for all students at all colleges in the CUNY system. Hostos Community College had dispensed with this requirement and had developed its own prerequisite exam. Unfortunately for the student plaintiffs here, Hostos had no legal authority to institute a replacement requirement without CUNY Board approval, which it did not have. The court upheld the CUNY resolution and the required prerequisite exam. The students were awarded tuition-free remedial assistance at Hostos for completion of the system-wide prerequisite exam.

3. What if the stakes weren't so high? If the stakes were the cost of retaking only one course where a misstatement was made versus a misstatement made about the final, high-stakes exam in advance of a diploma, would the result have been different? Or does academic decision-making and the judicial deference retain high weight in all such cases?

b. Student-University Relationship in Student Discipline and Academic Dismissal

SCHAER v. BRANDEIS UNIVERSITY
735 N.E.2d 373 (2000)

Abrams, J. The plaintiff, David Arlen Schaer, a student at Brandeis University (Brandeis), filed a seven-count complaint in the Superior Court against Brandeis, seeking injunctive relief and compensatory damages. One Superior Court judge denied injunctive relief and another dismissed the entire complaint for failing to state a claim for which relief can be granted. . . . Schaer appealed from the dismissal of his complaint. The Appeals Court affirmed for the most part, but reversed on count three of the complaint, which alleged breach of contract. . . . We granted Brandeis's application for further appellate review. We conclude that Schaer has failed to state a claim on which relief may be granted. We affirm the judgment of the Superior Court.

1. *Facts and procedural history.* On March 25, 1996, a female student (complainant) filed a report with the Brandeis student judicial system. In the report, she stated that Schaer came to her dormitory room during the early hours of February 14, after she had spoken with him on the telephone. The complainant alleged that, after they kissed, she told Schaer that she "did not want to have sex." She further alleged that she later awoke from sleep to find Schaer having intercourse with her.

After a hearing on April 24, the university board on student conduct (board) found Schaer to have: (1) engaged in unwanted sexual activity and (2) created a hostile environment. The board suspended Schaer for approximately four months and placed him on disciplinary probation for his remaining time at Brandeis[, including refraining from making any contact with the complainant]. Schaer requested a new hearing before the university appeals board on student conduct. . . . The appeals board denied his request on May 13.

On June 4, Schaer filed his complaint in the Superior Court, alleging that he had been unfairly disciplined. He sought injunctive relief and compensatory damages. A Superior Court judge held a hearing and denied Schaer's request for an injunction. Brandeis then moved to dismiss Schaer's complaint for failure to state a claim for which relief could be granted. A second Superior Court judge granted Brandeis's motion, and Schaer appealed.

The Appeals Court upheld the Superior Court judge's judgment of dismissal except with respect to Schaer's breach of contract count. We agree with the Appeals Court that only the breach of contract claim needs to be analyzed. As to this claim, the Appeals Court reversed the Superior Court, concluding that "Schaer's complaint . . . states a claim that Brandeis did not substantially conform its disciplinary process in Schaer's case to the [contract]." The Appeals Court based its conclusion on Schaer's allegations that Brandeis failed to follow certain procedures outlined in "Rights and Responsibilities" (contract), which is contained within Brandeis's student handbook. . . .

2. . . . [W]e turn to the substance of the motion to dismiss.

. . . .

. . . [T]he parties do not dispute the fact that a contractual relationship exists between Schaer and Brandeis. . . . We therefore review each factual allegation to determine whether Schaer has asserted facts which establish that Brandeis failed to meet his reasonable expectations, thereby violating its contract with Schaer.

a. *Failure to investigate in accordance with procedures established by §§ 16.5 and 17 of the contract.* Schaer contends that Brandeis violated §§ 16.5 and 17 of the contract by failing to investigate the complaint. Schaer asserts that at the time of the investigation, he was not asked to give a statement, to offer evidence, or to provide witnesses. As the Superior Court judge noted, Schaer has failed to state a claim under § 16.5 because that section does not apply to investigations of student misconduct.*

Section 17 provides, in relevant part: "The available facts shall be gathered from the [complainant] and a careful evaluation of these facts, as well as the credibility of the person reporting them, shall be made. If corroboration of the information presented is deemed necessary, further inquiry and investigation shall be undertaken." Nothing in this section requires university officials to obtain an interview from the accused student, to seek evidence from the accused student, or to grant the accused student an opportunity to provide witnesses at the investigatory stage in the proceedings. Thus, Schaer could not assign to the contract the meaning he now claims it has. On the facts alleged, Schaer has not stated a claim for which relief may be granted on the ground that Brandeis violated §§ 16.5 or 17 of the contract.

b. *Failure to employ the standard of proof required by § 19.13.* Schaer alleges that Brandeis violated § 19.13, which requires that the board must base its finding "only upon clear and convincing evidence." His contention that the board failed to use the appropriate standard is a legal conclusion, not a factual allegation. "It is only when . . . conclusions are logically compelled, or at least supported, by the stated facts, that is, when the suggested inference rises to what experience indicates is an acceptable level of probability, that 'conclusions' become 'facts' for pleading purposes." *The Dartmouth Review v. Dartmouth College*, 889 F.2d 13, 16 (1st Cir. 1989). . . . Schaer has not set forth facts specifically supporting this allegation. In the

* Section 16.5 is within a section entitled "Policy on Protection of Privacy" and applies to investigations of reported privacy issue violations, such as when a student's room is inspected by a member of the resident staff without providing the requisite advance notice. . . . Section 16.5 simply is not applicable to investigations of student misconduct.

absence of such facts, we conclude that Schaer has not stated a claim for which relief may be granted.

c. *Failure to use evidence in accordance with the procedures outlined in § 19.13.* Schaer contends that the board violated its contract by excluding testimony from an expert (Schaer's sister) as to the difference between rape and "regretted sex." Instead of admitting this testimony, Schaer asserts, the board used its own experience to reach its finding. Schaer concludes that this violated § 19.13, which provides, in relevant part: "Decisions shall be based solely upon evidence and testimony introduced at the hearing." As the Superior Court judge noted: "This claim does not state a violation of [§] 19.13. While that rule prohibits the board from evaluating *evidence* not introduced at the hearing, it does not preclude members of the [board] from using their own common sense and expertise." Schaer has not stated a claim for a violation of § 19.13.

d. *Failure to make a record, as required by § 19.14.* Schaer also alleges that Brandeis violated § 19.4, which requires a record of the proceedings. Schaer does not dispute that a record was made, but contends that the record is insufficient. Specifically, he contends that the " 'record' does not contain a summary of the testimony, in direct contravention of the language of the rule." Further, he contends that the brief record is inadequate documentation of thirteen witnesses who presented conflicting testimony over more than five hours.

Section 19.14 provides, in relevant part: "A record of each hearing, comprised of a summary of the testimony and evidence presented, and of the decision rendered, shall be made by the adviser to the board." The section does not require that the testimony of each witness be summarized. It does not require the record to be any minimum length. We note that the report was extremely brief. The better practice would have been to produce a more complete report. Nevertheless, nothing in the contract suggests that disciplinary proceedings will be conducted as though they were judicial proceedings. We conclude that Schaer may not properly claim that the record here failed to meet his reasonable expectations.

3. In addition to reviewing the allegations of breach of contract, "we . . . examine the hearing to ensure that it was conducted with basic fairness." *Cloud v. Trustees of Boston Univ.*, [720 F.2d 721,] 725 [(1st Cir. 1983)]. . . .

The complaint includes allegations of violation of basic fairness due to the improper admission of testimony from four witnesses. Although these statements would be excluded from a courtroom under the rules of evidence, a university is not required to abide by the same rules. . . . It is not the business of lawyers and judges to tell universities what statements they may consider and what statements they must reject.

. . . .

4. We adhere to the principle that "courts are chary about interfering with academic and disciplinary decisions made by private colleges and universities." . . . A university is not required to adhere to the standards of due process guaranteed to criminal defendants or to abide by rules of evidence adopted by courts. "A college must have broad discretion in determining appropriate sanctions for violations of its policies." See *Woods v. Simpson*, [146 Md. 547, 551, 126 A. 882 (1924)]. . . .

While a university should follow its own rules, Schaer's allegations, even if true, do not establish breaches of contract by Brandeis. Thus, Schaer has failed to state a claim for which relief can be granted. We affirm the judgment of dismissal entered by the Superior Court.

So ordered.

IRELAND, J. (dissenting, with whom COWIN, J., joins). I write separately because I believe the court, while correctly assuming that a contract exists between Brandeis and its students regarding the university's disciplinary procedures, fails to interpret the provisions of the disciplinary code in a commonsense way, or in a manner consistent with the standard rules of contract interpretation. . . . Brandeis should be required to follow its own internal rules when imposing serious disciplinary sanctions on a student. . . .

. . . .

The contours of this "relaxed" contractual relationship, which also may be derived from associational rights, are that in exchange for tuition and the student's compliance with university rules, the university will not act "arbitrarily or capriciously" in disciplining a student. To me, it appears that this prohibition of arbitrary and capricious action would also include the university's obligation to follow the rules and procedures that it has itself put forth in regard to disciplinary proceedings. . . .

The court, however, goes on to analyze the provisions in the "Rights and Responsibilities" section in a manner inconsistent with the standard principles of contract interpretation. The handbook was issued by Brandeis unilaterally. As such, any ambiguities in the contract should be construed against the drafter, especially, as here, where there is no opportunity for meaningful negotiation of any of the terms. . . . However, even interpreting the contract under the standard articulated by the court, that would adopt the meaning of the terms that the university would expect the other party to give it, I still do not understand how the court can read the terms of the contract in the way that it does.

. . . .

In short, if the university puts forth rules of procedure to be followed in disciplinary hearings, the university should be legally obligated to follow those rules. To do otherwise would allow Brandeis to make promises to its students that are nothing more than a "meaningless mouthing of words." *Tedeschi v. Wagner College*, [49 N.Y.2d 652,] 662 [(N.Y. 1980)]. . . .

. . . .

NOTES

1. Schaer formed his complaint as a breach of contract action, using specific provisions of the student handbook to prove the claim. However, many of his complaints are procedural in nature. How might a complaint of "due process" have been made here — that is, deprivation of liberty or property interests in the suspension and probation? Brandeis University is a private institution and is not subject to the Fourteenth Amendment due process clause. If this incident had taken place at a public university, with decisions made by "state actors" under federal and state due process clauses, would the case have been stronger for Schaer? What does the majority in *Schaer* say with respect to due process and fairness claims? See Chapter VII for a discussion of due process in disciplinary decisions at public universities. In particular, readers are encouraged to consult *Dixon v. Alabama State Board of Education*, 294 F.2d 150 (5th Cir. 1961), *cert. denied*, 368 U.S. 930 (1961), and *Goss v. Lopez*, 419 U.S. 565 (1975), in Part [B][1] of that Chapter for a discussion of due process rights for students in public education. See also the excerpt from Lisa Tenerowicz, *Student Misconduct at Private Universities: A Roadmap for "Fundamental Fairness" in Disciplinary Proceedings*, 42 B.C. L. Rev. 653 (2001), in Part [B][3].

2. Justice Ireland's dissenting opinion argues that Brandeis failed to follow its own internal rules and, therefore, was liable in breach of contract. What evidence does Justice Ireland offer? Is this not the standard applied by the majority, as well, with simply a different conclusion? In other words, is the difference between the majority and dissenting opinions in *Schaer* merely *factual*, where there is merely a difference of opinion on how the facts apply to contract law? What *legal* differences exist, if any, in the arguments made? What about Justice Ireland's arguments of unilateral policymaking on the part of Brandeis, making the handbook a one-sided contract where the ambiguous terms are to be interpreted in favor of the nondrafting party, the students? On the other hand, is it better in cases regarding student discipline to interpret the handbook provisions with the judicial deference offered to a university's academic decision making?

3. Note Justice Ireland's comment that students are consumers, especially in times when tuition is increasing so rapidly. So, are the customers always right? What about academic discretion? The student code is interpreted as a full contract here, but surely there is a rightfully "uneven playing (bargaining) field" when it comes to academic and disciplinary decision making. Right?

4. The court in *Schaer* addressed the issue of whether a university appropriately followed its own disciplinary rules as a matter of contract. Consider the following case, which asks a similar question with respect to academic rules and the dismissal of a student.

BLEICHER v. UNIVERSITY OF CINCINNATI COLLEGE OF MEDICINE

604 N.E.2d 783 (1992)

Opinion by: Bowman

In August 1984, appellant, Raymond Robert Bleicher, was dismissed from the University of Cincinnati College of Medicine ("the college") for poor scholarship. In 1986, after college review of his dismissal failed to result in his readmission, appellant initiated a breach of contract action against the college in the Court of Claims, seeking both reinstatement and monetary damages.

After a trial, the Court of Claims rejected appellant's argument that the college had failed to abide by its own educational guidelines, thus breaching its contract with appellant. Appellant now appeals to this court. . . .

. . . .

Appellant's cause arises out of his having earned a failing grade in pharmacology, one of the required courses for graduation from the college. . . .

During the spring quarter of 1984, appellant was a student in pharmacology when personal problems interfered with his scholastic performance. Appellant informed his pharmacology professor, Dr. Ronald Millard, of the situation and sought an excused absence from the final examination with an opportunity to take a make-up examination. He was told a make-up examination was not possible because the final was a "shelf examination" for which no make-up examination was available. Appellant was permitted, however, to substitute his raw score from the pharmacology subsection of the National Board of Medical Examiners ("NBME") examination, to be taken in June 1984, for the final examination in the course, although the parties dispute whether appellant or the college suggested this option and whether the college represented the use of the NBME score as appellant's sole alternative for obtaining a final grade in the course.

Appellant was also aware of a remedial pharmacology course offered during the summer of 1984 for students who failed the spring semester pharmacology course. Appellant knew that the NBME scores would not be released until midsummer, and that he could take the remedial course as a back-up in the event that his NBME pharmacology score was insufficient to allow him to pass the course. Nevertheless, appellant did not enroll in the remedial course.

Appellant received his NBME scores in July 1984. Appellant's score on the pharmacology subsection was fifty-seven percent, which, combined with the other grades earned during the course, did not result in a passing grade. Appellant thus failed pharmacology.

Appellant sought to remedy his failure by sitting for the final examination in the summer remedial course, even though he had not enrolled in nor attended that class. Appellant was informed that he could pass pharmacology only if he took and passed both the midterm and the final examination for the remedial course within the three hours allotted other students for the final examination. During the examination, the instructor apparently gave all students, including appellant, an extra hour. Appellant received a fifty-five percent score on the two examinations, which was less than the sixty percent required to pass the remedial course. Thus, appellant failed the remedial course.

In August 1984, appellant's three years for successfully completing the first two years of medical school curriculum expired and, since he had failed pharmacology, appellant was dismissed from the college.

. . . .

Appellant's first assignment of error is based upon his assertion that the college breached its contract with him, and essentially argues that the trial court's decision was against the manifest weight of the evidence.

It is axiomatic that "* * * when a student enrolls in a college or university, pays his or her tuition and fees, and attends such school, the resulting relationship may reasonably be construed as being contractual in nature." *Behrend v. State* (1977), 55 Ohio App.2d 135, 139, 9 O.O.3d 280, 282, 379 N.E.2d 617, 620. In addressing the issue of whether such contract has been breached, the trier of fact appropriately looks to the terms of the contract as found in the college guidelines supplied to students. . . . However, where the contract permits, the parties may alter its terms by mutual agreement, and any additional terms will supersede the original terms to the extent the two are contradictory. In interpreting the contract, the trial court was required to "* * * attempt to harmonize all the provisions rather than produce conflict in them. * * *" *Ottery* [*v. Bland* (1987), 42 Ohio App.3d 85, 87, 536 N.E.2d 651, 654-655].

In addition to these considerations, the trial court was required to defer to academic decisions of the college unless it perceived "* * * such a substantial departure from accepted academic norms as to demonstrate that the person or committee responsible did not actually exercise professional judgment. * * *" *Regents of the Univ. of Mich. v. Ewing* (1985), 474 U.S. 214, 225. The standard of review is not merely whether the court would have decided the matter differently but, rather, whether the faculty action was arbitrary and capricious.

. . . .

Appellant first argues that the trial court's conclusion that appellant agreed to the use of the NBME score in place of his final examination for the pharmacology course was inconsistent with the court's findings of fact on this issue. Indeed, the trial court concluded that appellant "* * * had no option other than to substitute the NBME pharmacology subsection in place of his final pharmacology examination * * *[,]" which does appear to conflict with the court's conclusion that "* * * plaintiff agreed to the use of the pharmacology component of the NMBE [*sic*], and he can now hardly complain that he was permitted to use such exam that he elected not to take." Inasmuch as the trial court's conclusion was facially inconsistent with its finding of fact, the trial court erred.

Nevertheless, appellant has failed to demonstrate how this error resulted in prejudice to him, since the trial court's decision indicates that this issue was not dispositive. The more pertinent question addressed by the trial court for purposes of determining the breach-of-contract claim was whether the use of the NBME score violated the college guidelines. Section V(E)(3) of the college's Academic Performance Standards and Guidelines provides that the "[p]assing of an NBME Part I or II subtest in the same subject as that requiring remediation cannot be counted or substituted for passage of any part or an entire course. * * *" However, Section V(A)(3) states that "[w]hile a department may have available various options for remediation, it reserves the right to identify the method of remediation required for each student on an individual basis. * * *" The trial court found, based upon the evidence, that substitution of the NBME score for the final examination grade did not violate college guidelines, presumably because appellant and his professor had entered into an agreement which altered the terms of the original contract, something the college had reserved the right to permit.

. . . Whether or not it found appellant was given other options, the trial court could reasonably have found from the evidence that appellant and the college agreed to substitute the NBME score for the final examination, thus, by agreement, overriding the provision in the guidelines and altering the terms of the contract.

Appellant next argues that the college violated its guidelines by allowing him less time than other students for completing both the midterm and final examinations in the remedial course. Specifically, appellant points to Section V(E)(1) of the guidelines, which states, in part:

> "The standards used to evaluate a student's performance when remediating a course shall not differ from the standards applied to evaluate student performance in the class as a whole when the course was offered in the academic year immediately preceding the remediation. * * *"

The trial court considered the fact that other students in the course had four hours to answer one hundred twenty-five questions, while appellant had four hours to answer two hundred questions. The court stated, with regard to this issue:

> "* * * This court might or might not have given plaintiff extra time to complete the midterm exam, but it cannot find that defendant was arbitrary or capricious. While the court was informed that essay questions were included in plaintiff's exams that were held on August 10, 1984, the court has no idea from the evidence that granting plaintiff three hours (and later adding an additional hour) to correctly answer sixty percent of 200 questions was unfair. Further, the standard to be applied is not one of fairness, but rather whether the conduct was arbitrary and capricious."

In determining this issue, we note that appellant's taking of the remedial examinations cannot be viewed as simply another opportunity to earn a grade for the spring semester pharmacology course, since appellant had completed the spring semester course by using his NBME pharmacology subtest score as his final examination grade. He therefore had already failed pharmacology. As a result, appellant's remaining option was to successfully complete the remedial course. Since appellant did not enroll in that class at the beginning of the summer semester, he was not automatically entitled to take the course examination. Nor would it have been appropriate for the college to simply allow him to take the final examination, since appellant had completed and failed the spring semester course, and since other students in the remedial course were required to have taken the midterm examination. The college was not required to give appellant unlimited opportunities to obtain a passing grade in pharmacology, nor would it have been equitable to require appellant to only take the final examination and not the midterm examination as other remedial students were required to do. We therefore agree with the trial court that it was not arbitrary or capricious for the college to require appellant to take both the midterm and final examinations in that course.

Nor do we find that the trial court erred in finding the college had not acted arbitrarily or capriciously in allowing appellant four hours to take both examinations. In this area, the court deferred to the judgment of the college that such was not unreasonable, particularly since the instructor of the remedial course was not required to allow appellant, who had not been a student in the class, to take any examination at all. Despite his personal problems, appellant had had some months to learn pharmacology, not only during the spring semester course but also in preparation for the NBME and in preparation for the remedial examinations. We thus agree with the trial court that appellant failed to produce sufficient evidence of arbitrary or capricious conduct on the part of the college in allowing him four hours to complete the remedial examinations.

. . . .

. . . The trial court properly found that the manifest weight of the evidence supported its conclusion that the academic contract between appellant and the college had not been breached. Appellant's first assignment of error is therefore overruled.

. . . .

Judgment affirmed.

B. ADMISSIONS

1. Race Discrimination and Affirmative Action

SWEATT v. PAINTER

339 U.S. 629 (1950)

MR. CHIEF JUSTICE VINSON delivered the opinion of the Court.

This case and *McLaurin v. Oklahoma State Regents* present different aspects of this general question: To what extent does the Equal Protection Clause of the Fourteenth Amendment limit the power of a state to distinguish between students of different races in professional and graduate education in a state university? . . .

In the instant case, petitioner filed an application for admission to the University of Texas Law School for the February, 1946 term. His application was rejected solely because he is a Negro [with justification pointing to a state statutory law]. Petitioner thereupon brought this suit for mandamus against the appropriate school officials, respondents here, to compel his admission. At that time, there was no law school in Texas which admitted Negroes.

The state trial court recognized that the action of the State in denying petitioner the opportunity to gain a legal education while granting it to others deprived him of the equal protection of the laws guaranteed by the Fourteenth Amendment. The court did not grant the relief requested, however, but continued the case for six months to allow the State to supply substantially equal facilities. At the expiration of the six months, in December, 1946, the court denied the writ on the showing that the authorized university officials had adopted an order calling for the opening of a law school for Negroes the following February. While petitioner's appeal was pending, such a school was made available, but petitioner refused to register therein. The Texas Court of Civil Appeals set aside the trial court's judgment and ordered the cause "remanded generally to the trial court for further proceedings without prejudice to the rights of any party to this suit."

On remand, a hearing was held on the issue of the equality of the educational facilities at the newly established school as compared with the University of Texas Law School. Finding that the new school offered petitioner "privileges, advantages, and opportunities for the study of law substantially equivalent to those offered by the State to white students at the University of Texas," the trial court denied mandamus. The Court of Civil Appeals affirmed. Petitioner's application for a writ of error was denied by the Texas Supreme Court. We granted certiorari. . . .

The University of Texas Law School, from which petitioner was excluded, was staffed by a faculty of sixteen full-time and three part-time professors, some of whom are nationally recognized authorities in their field. Its student body numbered 850. The library contained over 65,000 volumes. Among the other facilities available to the students were a law review, moot court facilities, scholarship funds, and Order of the Coif affiliation. The school's alumni occupy the most distinguished positions in the private practice of the law and in the public life of the State. It may properly be considered one of the nation's ranking law schools.

The law school for Negroes which was to have opened in February, 1947, would have had no independent faculty or library. The teaching was to be carried on by four members of the University of Texas Law School faculty, who were to maintain their offices at the University of Texas while teaching at both institutions. Few of the 10,000 volumes ordered for the library had arrived; nor was there any full-time librarian. The school lacked accreditation.

Since the trial of this case, respondents report the opening of a law school at the Texas State University for Negroes. It is apparently on the road to full accreditation. It has a faculty of five full-time professors; a student body of 23; a library of some 16,500 volumes serviced by a full-time staff; a practice court and legal aid association; and one alumnus who has become a member of the Texas Bar.

Whether the University of Texas Law School is compared with the original or the new law school for Negroes, we cannot find substantial equality in the educational opportunities offered white and Negro law students by the State. In terms of number of the faculty, variety of courses and opportunity for specialization, size of the student body, scope of the library, availability of law review and similar activities, the University of Texas Law School is superior. What is more important, the University of Texas Law School possesses to a far greater degree those qualities which are incapable of objective measurement but which make for greatness in a law school. Such qualities, to name but a few, include reputation of the faculty, experience of the administration, position and influence of the alumni, standing in the community, traditions and prestige. It is difficult to believe that one who had a free choice between these law schools would consider the question close.

Moreover, although the law is a highly learned profession, we are well aware that it is an intensely practical one. The law school, the proving ground for legal learning and practice, cannot be effective in isolation from the individuals and institutions with which the law interacts. Few students and no one who has practiced law would choose to study in an academic vacuum, removed from the interplay of ideas and the exchange of views with which the law is concerned. The law school to which Texas is willing to admit petitioner excludes from its student body members of the racial groups which number 85% of the population of the State and include most of the lawyers, witnesses, jurors, judges and other officials with whom petitioner will inevitably be dealing when he becomes a member of the Texas Bar. With such a substantial and significant segment of society excluded, we cannot conclude that the education offered petitioner is substantially equal to that which he would receive if admitted to the University of Texas Law School.

. . . .

It is fundamental that these cases [*Sweatt* and *McLaurin*] concern rights which are personal and present. . . . These are the only cases in this Court which present the issue of the constitutional validity of race distinctions in state-supported graduate and professional education.

In accordance with [the Supreme Court's equal protection] cases, petitioner may claim his full constitutional right: legal education equivalent to that offered by the State to students of other races. Such education is not available to him in a separate law school as offered by the State. We cannot, therefore, agree with respondents that the doctrine of *Plessy v. Ferguson*, 163 U.S. 537 (1896), requires affirmance of the judgment below. . . .

We hold that the Equal Protection Clause of the Fourteenth Amendment requires that petitioner be admitted to the University of Texas Law School. The judgment is reversed and the cause is remanded for proceedings not inconsistent with this opinion.

Reversed.

NOTES

1. On the same day the Court decided *Sweatt v. Painter*, the court decided *McLaurin v. Oklahoma State Regents for Higher Education*, 339 U.S. 637 (1950). The issue in *McLaurin* was whether a state may, after admitting a student to a graduate program in a state university, treat him differently from other students solely on the basis of his race. Initially, McLaurin was denied admission to the university; but after a trial court hearing and a change in state legislation, he was admitted, albeit with a different experience: he was required to sit apart from his classmates in classrooms (where he was expected to sit in an anteroom), the library (where he was expected to sit on a different floor), and the cafeteria. He filed suit. The Supreme Court ultimately held that the differential conditions under which McLaurin was to receive his education deprived him equal protection of the law. The Court stated:

> Our society grows increasingly complex, and our need for trained leaders increases correspondingly. Appellant's case represents, perhaps, the epitome of that need, for he is attempting to obtain an advanced degree in education, to become, by definition, a leader and trainer of others. Those who will come under his guidance and influence must be directly affected by the education he receives. Their own education and development will necessarily suffer to the extent that his training is unequal to that of his classmates. State-imposed restrictions which produce such inequalities cannot be sustained.

Id. at 641.

2. At the end of the opinion in *Sweatt v. Painter*, the Court made the following statement:

> In accordance with [the Supreme Court's equal protection] cases, petitioner may claim his full constitutional right: legal education equivalent to that offered by the State to students of other races. Such education is not available to him in a separate law school as offered by the State. We cannot, therefore, agree with respondents that the doctrine of *Plessy v. Ferguson*, 163 U.S. 537 (1896), requires affirmance of the judgment below.

No doubt, this statement foreshadows the landmark decision in *Brown v. Board of Education*, 347 U.S. 483 (1954), just four years later. The Court in *Brown v. Board of Education* addressed the question, in four consolidated cases, of whether segregation in public schools based on race violated the Equal Protection clause of the Fourteenth Amendment. The trial courts in three of the cases applied the "separate but equal" doctrine and denied relief. The court in the fourth case acknowledged the doctrine, but held that the segregated schools were not equal and granted relief. The Supreme Court in *Brown* struck down the "separate by equal" doctrine and overruled *Plessy v. Ferguson*, 163 U.S. 537 (1896). Emphasizing both tangible and intangible factors, the Court offered its most cited passage:

> Today, education is perhaps the most important function of state and local governments. Compulsory school attendance laws and the great expenditures for education both demonstrate our recognition of the importance of education to our democratic society. . . . Today it is a principal instrument in awakening the child to cultural values. . . . In these days, it is doubtful that any child may reasonably be expected to succeed in life if he is denied the opportunity of an education. Such an opportunity, where the state has undertaken to provide it, is a right which must be made available to all on equal terms.

Brown, 347 U.S. at 493.

3. Not surprisingly, most racial segregation cases in education originate in K-12 school districts, inspired by the 1954 decision in *Brown v. Board of Education*. There are a few cases, however, that originate in higher education settings. In 1992, the Supreme Court addressed alleged racial segregation in the Mississippi higher education system. In a unanimous opinion, the Court, in *United States v. Fordice*, 505 U.S. 717 (1992), held that the state's practice of requiring all applicants to earn a minimum cut-off score of 15 on the ACT to be admitted to one of the state's three flagship institutions perpetuated vestiges of the state's prior *de jure* segregation. Evidence revealed that the average score for white applicants was 18 and the average score for African-American applicants was only 7. Making matters worse, the regional universities in the state, each with a common mission, had different admissions standards depending on the predominant race at the institution (e.g., predominantly black institutions had lower cut-off scores).

REGENTS OF THE UNIVERSITY OF CALIFORNIA v. BAKKE

438 U.S. 265 (1978)

Mr. Justice Powell announced the judgment of the Court.

[Powell, J., announced the Court's judgment and filed an opinion expressing his views of the case, in Parts I, III-A, and V-C of which White, J., joined; and in Parts I and V-C of which Brennan, Marshall, and Blackmun, JJ., joined.]

This case presents a challenge to the special admissions program of the petitioner, the Medical School of the University of California at Davis, which is designed to assure the admission of a specified number of students from certain minority groups. The Superior Court of California sustained respondent's challenge, holding that petitioner's program violated the California Constitution, Title VI of the Civil Rights Act of 1964, and the Equal Protection Clause of the Fourteenth Amendment. The court enjoined petitioner from considering respondent's race or the race of any other applicant in making admissions decisions. It refused, however, to order respondent's admission to the Medical School, holding that he had not carried his burden of proving that he would have been admitted but for the constitutional and statutory violations. The Supreme Court of California affirmed those portions of the trial court's judgment declaring the special admissions program unlawful and enjoining petitioner from considering the race of any applicant. It modified that portion of the judgment denying respondent's requested injunction and directed the trial court to order his admission.

Affirmed in part and reversed in part.

I

The Medical School of the University of California at Davis . . . devised a special admissions program to increase the representation of "disadvantaged" students in each Medical School class. The special program consisted of a separate admissions system operating in coordination with the regular admissions process.

. . . .

The special admissions program operated with a separate committee, a majority of whom were members of minority groups. On the 1973 application form, candidates were asked to indicate whether they wished to be considered as "economically and/or educationally disadvantaged" applicants; on the 1974 form the question was whether they wished to be considered as members of a "minority group," which the Medical School apparently viewed as "Blacks," "Chicanos," "Asians," and "American Indians." If these questions were answered affirmatively, the application was forwarded to the special admissions committee. No formal definition of "disadvantaged" was ever produced, but the chairman of the special committee screened each application to see whether it reflected economic or educational deprivation. Having passed this initial hurdle, the applications then were rated by the special committee in a fashion similar to that used by the general admissions committee, except that special candidates did not have to meet the 2.5 grade point average cutoff applied to regular applicants. About one-fifth of the total number of special applicants were invited for interviews in 1973 and 1974. Following each interview, the special committee assigned each special applicant a benchmark score. The special committee then presented its top choices to the general admissions committee. The latter did not rate or compare the special candidates against the general applicants, but could reject recommended special candidates for failure to meet course requirements or other specific deficiencies. The special committee continued to recommend special applicants until a number prescribed by faculty vote were admitted. While the overall class size was still 50, the prescribed number was 8; in 1973 and 1974, when the class size had doubled to 100, the prescribed number of special admissions also doubled, to 16.

. . . Although disadvantaged whites applied to the special program in large numbers, none received an offer of admission through that process. Indeed, in 1974, at least, the special committee explicitly considered only "disadvantaged" special applicants who were members of one of the designated minority groups.

Allan Bakke is a white male who applied to the Davis Medical School in both 1973 and 1974. In both years Bakke's application was considered under the general admissions program, and he received an interview. His 1973 interview was with Dr. Theodore C. West, who considered Bakke "a very desirable applicant to [the] medical school." Despite a strong benchmark score of 468 out of 500, Bakke was rejected. His application had come late in the year, and no applicants in the general admissions process with scores below 470 were accepted after Bakke's application was completed. There were four special admissions slots unfilled at that time, however, for which Bakke was not considered. . . .

Bakke's 1974 application was completed early in the year. His student interviewer gave him an overall rating of 94, finding him "friendly, well tempered, conscientious and delightful to speak with." His faculty interviewer . . . gave Bakke the lowest of his six ratings, an 86; his total was 549 out of 600. Again, Bakke's application was rejected. . . . In both years, applicants were admitted under the special program with grade point averages, MCAT scores, and benchmark scores significantly lower than Bakke's.

After the second rejection, Bakke filed the instant suit . . . [alleging] that the Medical School's special admissions program operated to exclude him from the school on the basis of his race[.] . . . The trial court found that the special program operated as a racial quota, . . . [and] the challenged program violative of the Federal Constitution, the State Constitution, and Title VI. The court refused to order Bakke's admission, however, holding that he had failed to carry his burden of proving that he would have been admitted but for the existence of the special program.

Bakke appealed from the portion of the trial court judgment denying him admission[.] . . . The Supreme Court of California . . . accepted the findings of the trial court with respect to the University's program. Because the special admissions program involved a racial classification, the Supreme Court held itself bound to apply strict scrutiny. It then turned to the goals the University presented as justifying the special program. Although the court agreed that the goals of integrating the medical profession and increasing the number of physicians willing to serve members of minority groups were compelling state interests, it concluded that the special admissions program was not the least intrusive means of achieving those goals. . . . [T]he California court held that the Equal Protection Clause of the Fourteenth Amendment required that "no applicant may be rejected because of his race, in favor of another who is less qualified, as measured by standards applied without regard to race."

. . . We granted certiorari to consider the important constitutional issue.

II

. . . .

The language of § 601, 78 Stat. 252 [Title VI of the Civil Rights Act], like that of the Equal Protection Clause, is majestic in its sweep:

> "No person in the United States shall, on the ground of race, color, or national origin, be excluded from participation in, be denied the benefits of, or be subjected to discrimination under any program or activity receiving Federal financial assistance."

. . . .

In view of the clear legislative intent, Title VI must be held to proscribe only those racial classifications that would violate the Equal Protection Clause or the Fifth Amendment.

III

A

. . . The parties . . . disagree as to the level of judicial scrutiny to be applied to the special admissions program. Petitioner argues that the court below erred in applying strict scrutiny. . . . That level of review, petitioner asserts, should be reserved for classifications that disadvantage "discrete and insular minorities." See *United States v. Carolene Products Co.*, 304 U.S. 144, 152 n. 4 (1938). Respondent, on the other hand, contends that the California court correctly rejected the notion that the degree of judicial scrutiny accorded a particular racial or ethnic classification hinges upon membership in a discrete and insular minority and duly recognized that the "rights established [by the Fourteenth Amendment] are personal rights." *Shelley v. Kraemer*, 334 U.S. 1, 22 (1948).

En route to this crucial battle over the scope of judicial review, the parties fight a sharp preliminary action over the proper characterization of the special admissions program. Petitioner prefers to view it as establishing a "goal" of minority representation in the Medical School. Respondent, echoing the courts below, labels it a racial quota.

This semantic distinction is beside the point: The special admissions program is undeniably a classification based on race and ethnic background. To the extent that there existed a pool of at least minimally qualified minority applicants to fill the 16 special admissions seats, white applicants could compete only for 84 seats in the entering class, rather than the 100 open to minority applicants. Whether this limitation is described as a quota or a goal, it is a line drawn on the basis of race and ethnic status.

The guarantees of the Fourteenth Amendment extend to all persons. Its language is explicit: "No State shall . . . deny to any person within its jurisdiction the equal protection of the laws." . . . The guarantee of equal protection cannot mean one thing when applied to one individual and something else when applied to a person of another color. If both are not accorded the same protection, then it is not equal.

Nevertheless, petitioner argues that the court below erred in applying strict scrutiny to the special admissions program because white males, such as respondent, are not a "discrete and insular minority" requiring extraordinary protection from the majoritarian political process. *Carolene Products Co., supra,* at 152-153, n. 4. . . . Racial and ethnic classifications, however, are subject to stringent examination without regard to these additional characteristics. We declared as much in the first cases explicitly to recognize racial distinctions as suspect:

> "Distinctions between citizens solely because of their ancestry are by their very nature odious to a free people whose institutions are founded upon the doctrine of equality." *Hirabayashi* [v. *United States,* 320 U.S. 81, 100 (1943)].
>
> "[All] legal restrictions which curtail the civil rights of a single racial group are immediately suspect. That is not to say that all such restrictions are unconstitutional. It is to say that courts must subject them to the most rigid scrutiny." *Korematsu* [v. *United States,* 323 U.S. 214, 216 (1944)].

. . . Racial and ethnic distinctions of any sort are inherently suspect and thus call for the most exacting judicial examination.

B

. . . .

Petitioner urges us to adopt for the first time a more restrictive view of the Equal Protection Clause and hold that discrimination against members of the white "majority" cannot be suspect if its purpose can be characterized as "benign."[34] The clock of our liberties, however, cannot be turned back to 1868. It is far too late to argue that the guarantee of equal protection to *all* persons permits the recognition

---

[34] In the view of MR. JUSTICE BRENNAN, MR. JUSTICE WHITE, MR. JUSTICE MARSHALL, and MR. JUSTICE BLACKMUN, the pliable notion of "stigma" is the crucial element in analyzing racial classifications. . . . The Equal Protection Clause is not framed in terms of "stigma." Certainly the word has no clearly defined constitutional meaning. It reflects a subjective judgment that is standardless. *All* state-imposed classifications that rearrange burdens and benefits on the basis of race are likely to be viewed with deep resentment by the individuals burdened. . . . One should not lightly dismiss the inherent unfairness of, and the perception of mistreatment that accompanies, a system of allocating benefits and privileges on the basis of skin color and ethnic origin. . . .

of special wards entitled to a degree of protection greater than that accorded others.

Once the artificial line of a "two-class theory" of the Fourteenth Amendment is put aside, the difficulties entailed in varying the level of judicial review according to a perceived "preferred" status of a particular racial or ethnic minority are intractable. The concepts of "majority" and "minority" necessarily reflect temporary arrangements and political judgments. . . . There is no principled basis for deciding which groups would merit "heightened judicial solicitude "and which would not. . . .

. . . .

If it is the individual who is entitled to judicial protection against classifications based upon his racial or ethnic background because such distinctions impinge upon personal rights, rather than the individual only because of his membership in a particular group, then constitutional standards may be applied consistently. . . . When they touch upon an individual's race or ethnic background, he is entitled to a judicial determination that the burden he is asked to bear on that basis is precisely tailored to serve a compelling governmental interest. The Constitution guarantees that right to every person regardless of his background.

. . . .

IV

We have held that in "order to justify the use of a suspect classification, a State must show that its purpose or interest is both constitutionally permissible and substantial, and that its use of the classification is 'necessary . . . to the accomplishment' of its purpose or the safeguarding of its interest." *In re Griffiths*, 413 U.S. 717, 721-722 (1973) (footnotes omitted); *Loving v. Virginia*, 388 U.S., at 11; *McLaughlin v. Florida*, 379 U.S. 184, 196 (1964). The special admissions program purports to serve the purposes of: (i) "reducing the historic deficit of traditionally disfavored minorities in medical schools and in the medical profession;" (ii) countering the effects of societal discrimination; (iii) increasing the number of physicians who will practice in communities currently underserved; and (iv) obtaining the educational benefits that flow from an ethnically diverse student body. It is necessary to decide which, if any, of these purposes is substantial enough to support the use of a suspect classification.

A

If petitioner's purpose is to assure within its student body some specified percentage of a particular group merely because of its race or ethnic origin, such a preferential purpose must be rejected not as insubstantial but as facially invalid. Preferring members of any one group for no reason other than race or ethnic origin is discrimination for its own sake. This the Constitution forbids.

B

The State certainly has a legitimate and substantial interest in ameliorating, or eliminating where feasible, the disabling effects of identified discrimination. The line of school desegregation cases, commencing with *Brown*, attests to the importance of this state goal and the commitment of the judiciary to affirm all lawful means toward its attainment. In the school cases, the States were required by court order to redress the wrongs worked by specific instances of racial discrimination. That goal was far more focused than the remedying of the effects of "societal discrimination," an amorphous concept of injury that may be ageless in its reach into the past.

We have never approved a classification that aids persons perceived as members of relatively victimized groups at the expense of other innocent individuals in the absence of judicial, legislative, or administrative findings of constitutional or statutory violations. . . . Without such findings of constitutional or statutory violations, it cannot be said that the government has any greater interest in helping one individual than in refraining from harming another. Thus, the government has no compelling justification for inflicting such harm.

Petitioner does not purport to have made, and is in no position to make, such findings. Its broad mission is education, not the formulation of any legislative policy or the adjudication of particular claims of illegality. . . .

Hence, the purpose of helping certain groups whom the faculty of the Davis Medical School perceived as victims of "societal discrimination" does not justify a classification that imposes disadvantages upon persons like respondent, who bear no responsibility for whatever harm the beneficiaries of the special admissions program are thought to have suffered. To hold otherwise would be to convert a remedy heretofore reserved for violations of legal rights into a privilege that all institutions throughout the Nation could grant at their pleasure to whatever groups are perceived as victims of societal discrimination. That is a step we have never approved.

C

Petitioner identifies, as another purpose of its program, improving the delivery of health-care services to communities currently underserved. It may be assumed that in some situations a State's interest in facilitating the health care of its citizens is sufficiently compelling to support the use of a suspect classification. But there is virtually no evidence in the record indicating that petitioner's special admissions program is either needed or geared to promote that goal. . . .

Petitioner simply has not carried its burden of demonstrating that it must prefer members of particular ethnic groups over all other individuals in order to promote better health-care delivery to deprived citizens. Indeed, petitioner has not shown that its preferential classification is likely to have any significant effect on the problem.

D

The fourth goal asserted by petitioner is the attainment of a diverse student body. This clearly is a constitutionally permissible goal for an institution of higher education. Academic freedom, though not a specifically enumerated constitutional right, long has been viewed as a special concern of the First Amendment. The freedom of a university to make its own judgments as to education includes the selection of its student body. . . .

. . . The atmosphere of "speculation, experiment and creation" — so essential to the quality of higher education — is widely believed to be promoted by a diverse student body . . . .

Thus, in arguing that its universities must be accorded the right to select those students who will contribute the most to the "robust exchange of ideas," petitioner invokes a countervailing constitutional interest, that of the First Amendment. In this light, petitioner must be viewed as seeking to achieve a goal that is of paramount importance in the fulfillment of its mission.

It may be argued that there is greater force to these views at the undergraduate level than in a medical school where the training is centered primarily on professional competency. But even at the graduate level, our tradition and experience lend support to the view that the contribution of diversity is substantial. . . .

. . . .

Ethnic diversity, however, is only one element in a range of factors a university properly may consider in attaining the goal of a heterogeneous student body. Although a university must have wide discretion in making the sensitive judgments as to who should be admitted, constitutional limitations protecting individual rights may not be disregarded. . . . As the interest of diversity is compelling in the context of a university's admissions program, the question remains whether the program's racial classification is necessary to promote this interest. . . .

V

A

It may be assumed that the reservation of a specified number of seats in each class for individuals from the preferred ethnic groups would contribute to the attainment of considerable ethnic diversity in the student body. But petitioner's argument that this is the only effective means of serving the interest of diversity is seriously flawed. In a most fundamental sense the argument misconceives the nature of the state interest that would justify consideration of race or ethnic background. It is not an interest in simple ethnic diversity, in which a specified percentage of the student body is in effect guaranteed to be members of selected ethnic groups, with the remaining percentage an undifferentiated aggregation of students. The diversity that furthers a compelling state interest encompasses a far broader array of qualifications and characteristics of which racial or ethnic origin is but a single though important element. Petitioner's special admissions program, focused *solely* on ethnic diversity, would hinder rather than further attainment of genuine diversity.

Nor would the state interest in genuine diversity be served by expanding petitioner's two-track system into a multitrack program with a prescribed number of seats set aside for each identifiable category of applicants. Indeed, it is inconceivable that a university would thus pursue the logic of petitioner's two-track program to the illogical end of insulating each category of applicants with certain desired qualifications from competition with all other applicants.

The experience of other university admissions programs, which take race into account in achieving the educational diversity valued by the First Amendment, demonstrates that the assignment of a fixed number of places to a minority group is not a necessary means toward that end. . . .

[Justice Powell described Harvard College's admissions program, in which "race or ethnic background may be deemed a 'plus' " factor in admitting an applicant, that "does not insulate the individual from comparison with all other candidates for the available seats."]

The file of a particular black applicant may be examined for his potential contribution to diversity without the factor of race being decisive when compared, for example, with that of an applicant identified as an Italian-American if the latter is thought to exhibit qualities more likely to promote beneficial educational pluralism. Such qualities could include exceptional personal talents, unique work or service experience, leadership potential, maturity, demonstrated compassion, a history of overcoming disadvantage, ability to communicate with the poor, or other qualifications deemed important. In short, an admissions program operated in this way is flexible enough to consider all pertinent elements of diversity in light of the particular qualifications of each applicant, and to place them on the same footing for consideration, although not necessarily according them the same weight. Indeed, the weight attributed to a particular quality may vary from year to year depending upon the "mix" both of the student body and the applicants for the incoming class.

This kind of program treats each applicant as an individual in the admissions process. The applicant who loses out on the last available seat to another candidate receiving a "plus" on the basis of ethnic background will not have been foreclosed from all consideration for that seat simply because he was not the right color or had the wrong surname. It would mean only that his combined qualifications, which may have included similar nonobjective factors, did not outweigh those of the other applicant. His qualifications would have been weighed fairly and competitively, and he would have no basis to complain of unequal treatment under the Fourteenth Amendment.

It has been suggested that an admissions program which considers race only as one factor is simply a subtle and more sophisticated — but no less effective — means of according racial preference than the Davis program. A facial intent to discriminate, however, is evident in petitioner's preference program and not denied in this case. No such facial infirmity exists in an admissions program where race or ethnic background is simply one element — to be weighed fairly against other elements — in the selection process. "A boundary line," as Mr. Justice Frankfurter remarked in another connection, "is none the worse for being narrow." *McLeod v. Dilworth*, 322 U.S. 327, 329 (1944). And a court would not assume that a university, professing to employ a facially nondiscriminatory admissions policy, would operate it as a cover for the functional equivalent of a quota system. In short, good faith would be presumed in the absence of a showing to the contrary in the manner permitted by our cases.

B

In summary, it is evident that the Davis special admissions program involves the use of an explicit racial classification never before countenanced by this Court. . . .

The fatal flaw in petitioner's preferential program is its disregard of individual rights as guaranteed by the Fourteenth Amendment. . . . Such rights are not absolute. But when a State's distribution of benefits or imposition of burdens hinges on ancestry or the color of a person's skin, that individual is entitled to a demonstration that the challenged classification is necessary to promote a substantial state interest. Petitioner has failed to carry this burden. For this reason, that portion of the California court's judgment holding petitioner's special admissions program invalid under the Fourteenth Amendment must be affirmed.

C

In enjoining petitioner from ever considering the race of any applicant, however, the courts below failed to recognize that the State has a substantial interest that legitimately may be served by a properly devised admissions program involving the competitive consideration of race and ethnic origin. For this reason, so much of the California court's judgment as enjoins petitioner from any consideration of the race of any applicant must be reversed.

. . . .

[Opinions of Justices Brennan, White, Marshall, and Blackmun are omitted.]

NOTES

1. In *Bakke*, what reasons did the University of California assert to justify implementing a quota system for admission? Why did the Court reject those reasons?

2. *Bakke* is one of the most talked-about and most splintered cases in Supreme Court history. The Justices wrote six different opinions. Three of the opinions generate most of the conversation and analysis. Justice Powell's opinion is excerpted above and attracted each of the other Justices, in part, at least in the judgment, if not for similar reasoning. Justice Powell offered essentially two basic judgments. First, he argued that the medical school's program was unlawful and directed Bakke to be admitted. Chief Justice Burger and Justices Stewart, Rehnquist, and Stevens agreed that the policy was flawed and agreed that Bakke should be admitted to the medical school. They wrote separately from Justice Powell, however. Instead of relying on a Fourteenth Amendment equal protection analysis, as Justice Powell did, they relied on Title VI of the Civil Rights Act and did not reach the constitutional issue. Second, Justice Powell argued that race may be used as a "plus factor" in higher education admissions. A second group of four Justices agreed on this point. Justices Brennan, White, Marshall, and Blackmun wrote separately, though, to argue that the policy — subjected to an intermediate level of scrutiny — should be upheld as lawful.

3. Justice Powell's opinion in *Bakke* has generated much conversation and application over the years, with universities continuing to argue that diversity of a student body is, indeed, a compelling governmental interest, and that race and ethnicity may be used as plus factors in admissions decisions. Nonetheless, in those ensuing 25 years, several courts and commentators emphasized the fact that Justice Powell's opinion remained an opinion with only one vote. Consider the following excerpt from *Hopwood v. Texas*, 78 F.3d 932 (5th Cir. 1996). *Hopwood* involved a challenge to the admissions policy at the University of Texas at Austin, where African-American and Mexican-American applicants received preferential treatment by way of lower cut-off scores and a separate committee to review them. The law school offered several justifications for the policy, including diversifying the student body, admitting law school classes that reflect the population in Texas, and remedying past discrimination in Texas public education. The Court of Appeals for the Fifth Circuit struck down the policy, in part, by asserting that diversity is not a compelling governmental interest:

> Justice Powell's argument in *Bakke* garnered only his own vote and has never represented the view of a majority of the Court in *Bakke* or any other case. Moreover, subsequent Supreme Court decisions regarding education state that non-remedial state interests will never justify racial classifications. Finally, the classification of persons on the basis of race for the purpose of diversity frustrates, rather than facilitates, the goals of equal protection.
>
> . . . .
>
> In short, there has been no indication from the Supreme Court, other than Justice Powell's lonely opinion in *Bakke*, that the state's interest in diversity constitutes a compelling justification for governmental race-based discrimination.

Id. at 944–45. For more discussion on the relationship between *Hopwood* and *Bakke*, see Philip T.K. Daniel & Kyle E. Timken, *The Rumors of My Death Have Been Exaggerated: Hopwood's Error in "Discarding" Bakke.* 28 J. L. & Educ. 391 (1999).

GRUTTER v. BOLLINGER
539 U.S. 306 (2003)

Justice O'Connor delivered the opinion of the Court.

. . . .

The [University of Michigan] Law School ranks among the Nation's top law schools. It receives more than 3,500 applications each year for a class of around 350 students. Seeking to "admit a group of students who individually and collectively are among the most capable," the Law School looks for individuals with "substantial promise for success in law school" and "a strong likelihood of succeeding in the practice of law and contributing in diverse ways to the well-being of others." More broadly, the Law School seeks "a mix of students with varying backgrounds and experiences who will respect and learn from each other." . . .

The hallmark of [the admissions] policy is its focus on academic ability coupled with a flexible assessment of applicants' talents, experiences, and potential "to contribute to the learning of those around them." The policy requires admissions officials to evaluate each applicant based on all the information available in the file, including a personal statement, letters of recommendation, and an essay describing the ways in which the applicant will contribute to the life and diversity of the Law School. . . .

The policy . . . requires admissions officials to look beyond grades and test scores to other criteria that are important to the Law School's educational objectives. . . .

The policy aspires to "achieve that diversity which has the potential to enrich everyone's education and thus make a law school class stronger than the sum of its parts." The policy does not restrict the types of diversity contributions eligible for "substantial weight" in the admissions process, but instead recognizes "many possible bases for diversity admissions." The policy does, however, reaffirm the Law School's longstanding commitment to "one particular type of diversity," that is, "racial and ethnic diversity with special reference to the inclusion of students from groups which have been historically discriminated against, like African-Americans, Hispanics and Native Americans, who without this commitment might not be represented in our student body in meaningful numbers." By enrolling a " 'critical mass' of [underrepresented] minority students," the Law School seeks to "ensure their ability to make unique contributions to the character of the Law School."

. . . .

B

Petitioner Barbara Grutter is a white Michigan resident [who filed suit following the rejection of her application, alleging] that respondents discriminated against her on the basis of race in violation of the Fourteenth Amendment; Title VI of the Civil Rights Act of 1964.

Petitioner further alleged that her application was rejected because the Law School uses race as a "predominant" factor, giving applicants who belong to certain minority groups "a significantly greater chance of admission than students with similar credentials from disfavored racial groups." . . . Petitioner requested compensatory and punitive damages, an order requiring the Law School to offer her admission, and an injunction prohibiting the Law School from continuing to discriminate on the basis of race. . . .

. . . .

During the 15-day bench trial, the parties introduced extensive evidence concerning the Law School's use of race in the admissions process. [Several Law School and University administrators testified to their experiences with the policy, including definitions of terms like "critical mass".]

. . . .

. . . [T]he District Court concluded that the Law School's use of race as a factor in admissions decisions was unlawful. Applying strict scrutiny, the District Court determined that the Law School's asserted interest in assembling a diverse student body was not compelling because "the attainment of a racially diverse class . . . was not recognized as such by *Bakke* and is not a remedy for past discrimination." The District Court went on to hold that even if diversity were compelling, the Law School had not narrowly tailored its use of race to further that interest. . . .

Sitting en banc, the Court of Appeals reversed the District Court's judgment and vacated the injunction. The Court of Appeals first held that Justice Powell's opinion in *Bakke* was binding precedent establishing diversity as a compelling state interest. . . . The Court of Appeals also held that the Law School's use of race was narrowly tailored because race was merely a "potential 'plus' factor". . . .

Four dissenting judges would have held the Law School's use of race unconstitutional. . . .

We granted certiorari . . . to resolve the disagreement among the Courts of Appeals on a question of national importance: Whether diversity is a compelling interest that can justify the narrowly tailored use of race in selecting applicants for admission to public universities. . . .

II

A

. . . .

Since this Court's splintered decision in *Bakke*, Justice Powell's opinion announcing the judgment of the Court has served as the touchstone for constitutional analysis of race-conscious admissions policies. Public and private universities across the Nation have modeled their own admissions programs on Justice Powell's views on permissible race-conscious policies. . . .

Justice Powell began by stating that "the guarantee of equal protection cannot mean one thing when applied to one individual and something else when applied to a person of another color. If both are not accorded the same protection, then it is not equal." *Bakke*, 438 U.S., at 289-290. . . .

. . . .

Justice Powell approved the university's use of race to further only one interest: "the attainment of a diverse student body." *Id.*, at 311. . . .

Justice Powell was, however, careful to emphasize that in his view race "is only one element in a range of factors a university properly may consider in attaining the goal of a heterogeneous student body." *Id.*, at 314. For Justice Powell, "it is not an interest in simple ethnic diversity, in which a specified percentage of the student body is in effect guaranteed to be members of selected ethnic groups," that can justify the use of race. *Id.*, at 315. Rather, "the diversity that furthers a compelling state interest encompasses a far broader array of qualifications and characteristics of which racial or ethnic origin is but a single though important element." *Ibid.*

. . . .

B

. . . .

We have held that all racial classifications imposed by government "must be analyzed by a reviewing court under strict scrutiny." [*Adarand Constructors, Inc. v. Pena*, 515 U.S. 200, 215.] This means that such classifications are constitutional only if they are narrowly tailored to further compelling governmental interests. "Absent searching judicial inquiry into the justification for such race-based measures," we have no way to determine what "classifications are 'benign' or 'remedial' and what classifications are in fact motivated by illegitimate notions of racial inferiority or simple racial politics." *Richmond v. J. A. Croson Co.*, 488 U.S. 469, 493 (1989) (plurality opinion). We apply strict scrutiny to all racial classifications to " 'smoke out' illegitimate uses of race by assuring that [government] is pursuing a goal important enough to warrant use of a highly suspect tool." *Ibid.*

. . . .

Context matters when reviewing race-based governmental action under the Equal Protection Clause. . . . Not every decision influenced by race is equally objectionable and strict scrutiny is designed to provide a framework for carefully examining the importance and the sincerity of the reasons advanced by the governmental decisionmaker for the use of race in that particular context.

III

A

With these principles in mind, we turn to the question whether the Law School's use of race is justified by a compelling state interest. Before this Court, as they have throughout this litigation, respondents assert only one justification for their use of race in the admissions process: obtaining "the educational benefits that flow from a diverse student body." In other words, the Law School asks us to recognize, in the context of higher education, a compelling state interest in student body diversity.

We first wish to dispel the notion that the Law School's argument has been foreclosed, either expressly or implicitly, by our affirmative-action cases decided since *Bakke*. It is true that some language in those opinions might be read to suggest that remedying past discrimination is the only permissible justification for race-based governmental action. . . . But we have never held that the only governmental use of race that can survive strict scrutiny is remedying past discrimination. Nor, since *Bakke*, have we directly addressed the use of race in the context of public higher education. Today, we hold that the Law School has a compelling interest in attaining a diverse student body.

The Law School's educational judgment that such diversity is essential to its educational mission is one to which we defer. The Law School's assessment that diversity will, in fact, yield educational benefits is substantiated by respondents and their *amici*. Our scrutiny of the interest asserted by the Law School is no less strict for taking into account complex educational judgments in an area that lies primarily within the expertise of the university. Our holding today is in keeping with our tradition of giving a degree of deference to a university's academic decisions, within constitutionally prescribed limits.

. . . In announcing the principle of student body diversity as a compelling state interest, Justice Powell invoked our cases recognizing a constitutional dimension, grounded in the First Amendment, of educational autonomy: "The freedom of a university to make its own judgments as to education includes the selection of its student body." *Bakke, supra*, at 312. From this premise, Justice Powell reasoned that by claiming "the right to select those students who will contribute the most to the 'robust exchange of ideas,' " a university "seeks to achieve a goal that is of paramount importance in the fulfillment of its mission." 438 US, at 313. . . . Our conclusion that the Law School has a compelling interest in a diverse student body is informed by our view that attaining a diverse student body is at the heart of the Law School's proper institutional mission, and that "good faith" on the part of a university is "presumed" absent "a showing to the contrary." 438 U.S., at 318-319.

As part of its goal of "assembling a class that is both exceptionally academically qualified and broadly diverse," the Law School seeks to "enroll a 'critical mass' of minority students." Brief for Respondents Bollinger et al. 13. The Law School's interest is not simply "to assure within its student body some specified percentage of a particular group merely because of its race or ethnic origin." *Bakke*, 438 U.S., at 307 (opinion of Powell, J.). That would amount to outright racial balancing, which is patently unconstitutional. *Ibid.* Rather, the Law School's concept of critical mass is defined by reference to the educational benefits that diversity is designed to produce.

These benefits are substantial. As the District Court emphasized, the Law School's admissions policy promotes "cross-racial understanding," helps to break down racial stereotypes, and "enables [students] to better understand persons of different races." These benefits are "important and laudable," because "classroom discussion is livelier, more spirited, and simply more enlightening and interesting" when the students have "the greatest possible variety of backgrounds." *Id.*, at 246a, 244a.

The Law School's claim of a compelling interest is further bolstered by its *amici*, who point to the educational benefits that flow from student body diversity. In addition to the expert studies and reports entered into evidence at trial, numerous studies show that student body diversity promotes learning outcomes, and "better prepares students for an increasingly diverse workforce and society, and better prepares them as professionals." . . .

These benefits are not theoretical but real, as major American businesses have made clear that the skills needed in today's increasingly global marketplace can only be developed through exposure to widely diverse people, cultures, ideas, and viewpoints. . . .

. . . This Court has long recognized that "education . . . is the very foundation of good citizenship." *Brown v. Board of Education*, 347 U.S. 483, 493 (1954). For this reason, the diffusion of knowledge and opportunity through public institutions of higher education must be accessible to all individuals regardless of race or ethnicity. . . .

Moreover, universities, and in particular, law schools, represent the training ground for a large number of our Nation's leaders. Individuals with law degrees occupy roughly half the state governorships, more than half the seats in the United States Senate, and more than a third of the seats in the United States House of Representatives. . . .

In order to cultivate a set of leaders with legitimacy in the eyes of the citizenry, it is necessary that the path to leadership be visibly open to talented and qualified individuals of every race and ethnicity. All members of our heterogeneous society must have confidence in the openness and integrity of the educational institutions that provide this training. As we have recognized, law schools "cannot be effective in isolation from the individuals and institutions with which the law interacts." See *Sweatt v. Painter, supra*, at 634. . . .

The Law School does not premise its need for critical mass on "any belief that minority students always (or even consistently) express some characteristic minority viewpoint on any issue." To the contrary, diminishing the force of such stereotypes is both a crucial part of the Law School's mission, and one that it cannot accomplish with only token numbers of minority students. Just as growing up in a particular region or having particular professional experiences is likely to affect an individual's views, so too is one's own, unique experience of being a racial minority in a society, like our own, in which race unfortunately still matters. The Law School has determined, based on its experience and expertise, that a "critical mass" of underrepresented minorities is necessary to further its compelling interest in securing the educational benefits of a diverse student body.

B

Even in the limited circumstance when drawing racial distinctions is permissible to further a compelling state interest, government is still "constrained in how it may pursue that end: [T]he means chosen to accomplish the [government's] asserted purpose must be specifically and narrowly framed to accomplish that purpose." *Shaw v. Hunt*, 517 U.S. 899, 908 (1996). . . . The purpose of the narrow tailoring requirement is to ensure that "the means chosen 'fit' . . . the compelling goal so closely that there is little or no possibility that the motive for the classification was illegitimate racial prejudice or stereotype." *Richmond v. J. A. Croson Co.*, 488 U.S., at 493 (plurality opinion).

. . . .

To be narrowly tailored, a race-conscious admissions program cannot use a quota system — it cannot "insulate each category of applicants with certain desired qualifications from competition with all other applicants." *Bakke, supra*, at 315 (opinion of Powell, J.). Instead, a university may consider race or ethnicity only as a " 'plus' in a particular applicant's file," without "insulating the individual from comparison with all other candidates for the available seats." *Id.*, at 317. In other words, an admissions program must be "flexible enough to consider all pertinent elements of diversity in light of the particular qualifications of each applicant, and to place them on the same footing for consideration, although not necessarily according them the same weight." *Ibid.*

We find that the Law School's admissions program bears the hallmarks of a narrowly tailored plan. As Justice Powell made clear in *Bakke*, truly individualized consideration demands that race be used in a flexible, nonmechanical way. It follows from this mandate that universities cannot establish quotas for members of certain racial groups or put members of those groups on separate admissions tracks. Nor can universities insulate applicants who belong to certain racial or ethnic groups from the competition for admission. *Ibid.* Universities can, however, consider race or ethnicity more flexibly as a "plus" factor in the context of individualized consideration of each and every applicant.

. . . .

The Law School's goal of attaining a critical mass of underrepresented minority students does not transform its program into a quota. As the Harvard plan described by Justice Powell recognized, there is of course "some relationship between numbers and achieving the benefits to be derived from a diverse student body, and between numbers and providing a reasonable environment for those students admitted." *Id.*, at 323. "Some attention to numbers," without more, does not transform a flexible admissions system into a rigid quota. *Ibid.* Nor, as Justice Kennedy [in his dissent] posits, does the Law School's consultation of the "daily reports," which keep track of the racial and ethnic composition of the class (as well as of residency and gender), "suggest[] there was no further attempt at individual review save for race itself" during the final stages of the admissions process. . . . To the contrary, the Law School's admissions officers testified without contradiction that they never gave race any more or less weight based on the information contained in these reports. Moreover, as Justice Kennedy concedes, . . . between 1993 and 2000, the number of African-American, Latino, and Native-American students in each class at the Law School varied from 13.5 to 20.1 percent, a range inconsistent with a quota.

The Chief Justice [in his dissent] believes that the Law School's policy conceals an attempt to achieve racial balancing, and cites admissions data to contend that the Law School discriminates among different groups within the critical mass. But, as the Chief Justice concedes, the number of underrepresented minority students who ultimately enroll in the Law School differs substantially from their representation in the applicant pool and varies considerably for each group from year to year.

That a race-conscious admissions program does not operate as a quota does not, by itself, satisfy the requirement of individualized consideration. When using race as a "plus" factor in university admissions, a university's admissions program must remain flexible enough to ensure that each applicant is evaluated as an individual and not in a way that makes an applicant's race or ethnicity the defining feature of his or her application. The importance of this individualized consideration in the context of a race-conscious admissions program is paramount. . . .

Here, the Law School engages in a highly individualized, holistic review of each applicant's file, giving serious consideration to all the ways an applicant might contribute to a diverse educational environment. The Law School affords this individualized consideration to applicants of all races. There is no policy, either *de jure* or *de facto*, of automatic acceptance or rejection based on any single "soft" variable. . . .

We also find that . . . the Law School's race-conscious admissions program adequately ensures that all factors that may contribute to student body diversity are meaningfully considered alongside race in admissions decisions. With respect to the use of race itself, all underrepresented minority students admitted by the Law School have been deemed qualified. By virtue of our Nation's struggle with racial inequality, such students are both likely to have experiences of particular importance to the Law School's mission, and less likely to be admitted in meaningful numbers on criteria that ignore those experiences.

The Law School does not, however, limit in any way the broad range of qualities and experiences that may be considered valuable contributions to student body diversity. . . . All applicants have the opportunity to highlight their own potential diversity contributions through the submission of a personal statement, letters of recommendation, and an essay describing the ways in which the applicant will contribute to the life and diversity of the Law School.

What is more, the Law School actually gives substantial weight to diversity factors besides race. The Law School frequently accepts nonminority applicants with grades and test scores lower than underrepresented minority applicants (and other nonminority applicants) who are rejected. This shows that the Law School seriously weighs many other diversity factors besides race that can make a real and dispositive difference for nonminority applicants as well. By this flexible approach, the Law School sufficiently takes into account, in practice as well as in theory, a wide variety of characteristics besides race and ethnicity that contribute to a diverse student body. . . .

Petitioner and the United States argue that the Law School's plan is not narrowly tailored because race-neutral means exist to obtain the educational benefits of student body diversity that the Law School seeks. We disagree. Narrow tailoring does not require exhaustion of every conceivable race-neutral alternative. Nor does it require a university to choose between maintaining a reputation for excellence or fulfilling a commitment to provide educational opportunities to members of all racial groups. Narrow tailoring does, however, require serious, good faith consideration of workable race-neutral alternatives that will achieve the diversity the university seeks. . . .

We agree with the Court of Appeals that the Law School sufficiently considered workable race-neutral alternatives. . . . But these alternatives would require a dramatic sacrifice of diversity, the academic quality of all admitted students, or both.

. . . .

We acknowledge that "there are serious problems of justice connected with the idea of preference itself." *Bakke*, 438 U.S., at 298 (opinion of Powell, J.). Narrow tailoring, therefore, requires that a race-conscious admissions program not unduly harm members of any racial group. Even remedial race-based governmental action generally "remains subject to continuing oversight to assure that it will work the least harm possible to other innocent persons competing for the benefit." *Id.*, at 308. To be narrowly tailored, a race-conscious admissions program must not "unduly burden individuals who are not members of the favored racial and ethnic groups." *Metro Broadcasting, Inc. v. FCC*, 497 U.S. 547, 630 (1990) (O'Connor, J., dissenting).

We are satisfied that the Law School's admissions program does not. Because the Law School considers "all pertinent elements of diversity," it can (and does) select nonminority applicants who have greater potential to enhance student body diversity over underrepresented minority applicants. As Justice Powell recognized in *Bakke*, so long as a race-conscious admissions program uses race as a "plus" factor in the context of individualized consideration, a rejected applicant

> "will not have been foreclosed from all consideration for that seat simply because he was not the right color or had the wrong surname . . . . His qualifications would have been weighed fairly and competitively, and he would have no basis to complain of unequal treatment under the Fourteenth Amendment." 438 US, at 318.

We agree that, in the context of its individualized inquiry into the possible diversity contributions of all applicants, the Law School's race-conscious admissions program does not unduly harm nonminority applicants.

We are mindful, however, that "[a] core purpose of the Fourteenth Amendment was to do away with all governmentally imposed discrimination based on race." *Palmore v. Sidoti*, 466 U.S. 429 (1984). Accordingly, race-conscious admissions policies must be limited in time. . . .

In the context of higher education, the durational requirement can be met by sunset provisions in race-conscious admissions policies and periodic reviews to determine whether racial preferences are still necessary to achieve student body diversity. Universities in California, Florida, and Washington State, where racial preferences in admissions are prohibited by state law, are currently engaged in experimenting with a wide variety of alternative approaches. Universities in other States can and should draw on the most promising aspects of these race-neutral alternatives as they develop. . . .

The requirement that all race-conscious admissions programs have a termination point "assures all citizens that the deviation from the norm of equal treatment of all racial and ethnic groups is a temporary matter, a measure taken in the service of the goal of equality itself." *Richmond v. J. A. Croson Co.*, 488 U.S., at 510 (plurality opinion). . . .

We take the Law School at its word that it would "like nothing better than to find a race-neutral admissions formula" and will terminate its race-conscious admissions program as soon as practicable. . . . It has been 25 years since Justice Powell first approved the use of race to further an interest in student body diversity in the context of public higher education. Since that time, the number of minority applicants with high grades and test scores has indeed increased. We expect that 25 years from now, the use of racial preferences will no longer be necessary to further the interest approved today.

IV

. . . The judgment of the Court of Appeals for the Sixth Circuit, accordingly, is affirmed.

It is so ordered.

Chief Justice Rehnquist, with whom Justice Scalia, Justice Kennedy, and Justice Thomas join, dissenting.

I agree with the Court that, "in the limited circumstance when drawing racial distinctions is permissible," the government must ensure that its means are narrowly tailored to achieve a compelling state interest [see majority opinion]. I do not believe, however, that the University of Michigan Law School's (Law School) means are narrowly tailored to the interest it asserts. The Law School claims it must take the steps it does to achieve a " 'critical mass' " of underrepresented minority students. But its actual program bears no relation to this asserted goal. Stripped of its "critical mass" veil, the Law School's program is revealed as a naked effort to achieve racial balancing.

As we have explained many times, "[a]ny preference based on racial or ethnic criteria must necessarily receive a most searching examination." Our cases establish that, in order to withstand this demanding inquiry, respondents must demonstrate that their methods of using race "fit" a compelling state interest "with greater precision than any alternative means."

Before the Court's decision today, we consistently applied the same strict scrutiny analysis regardless of the government's purported reason for using race and regardless of the setting in which race was being used. We rejected calls to use more lenient review in the face of claims that race was being used in "good faith" because "[m]ore than good motives should be required when government seeks to allocate its resources by way of an explicit racial classification system." . . .

Although the Court recites the language of our strict scrutiny analysis, its application of that review is unprecedented in its deference. Respondents' asserted justification for the Law School's use of race in the admissions process is "obtaining 'the educational benefits that flow from a diverse student body.' " They contend that a "critical mass" of underrepresented minorities is necessary to further that interest. Respondents and school administrators explain generally that "critical mass" means a sufficient number of underrepresented minority students to achieve several objectives: To ensure that these minority students do not feel isolated or like spokespersons for their race; to provide adequate opportunities for the type of interaction upon which the educational benefits of diversity depend; and to challenge all students to think critically and reexamine stereotypes. These objectives indicate that "critical mass" relates to the size of the student body. . . . Respondents further claim that the Law School is achieving "critical mass."

In practice, the Law School's program bears little or no relation to its asserted goal of achieving "critical mass." Respondents explain that the Law School seeks to accumulate a "critical mass" of each underrepresented minority group. . . . But the record demonstrates that the Law School's admissions practices with respect to these groups differ dramatically and cannot be defended under any consistent use of the term "critical mass."

From 1995 through 2000, the Law School admitted between 1,130 and 1,310 students. Of those, between 13 and 19 were Native American, between 91 and 108 were African-American, and between 47 and 56 were Hispanic. If the Law School is admitting between 91 and 108 African-Americans in order to achieve "critical mass," thereby preventing African-American students from feeling "isolated or like spokespersons for their race," one would think that a number of the same order of magnitude would be necessary to accomplish the same purpose for Hispanics and Native Americans. Similarly, even if all of the Native American applicants admitted in a given year matriculate, which the record demonstrates is not at all the case, how can this possibly constitute a "critical mass" of Native Americans in a class of over 350 students? In order for this pattern of admission to be consistent with the Law School's explanation of "critical mass," one would have to believe that the objectives of "critical mass" offered by respondents are achieved with only half the number of Hispanics and one-sixth the number of Native Americans as compared to African-Americans. But respondents offer no race-specific reasons for such disparities. Instead, they simply emphasize the importance of achieving "critical mass," without any explanation of why that concept is applied differently among the three underrepresented minority groups.

. . . .

. . . [In] 2000, 12 Hispanics who scored between a 159-160 on the LSAT and earned a GPA of 3.00 or higher applied for admission and only 2 were admitted. Meanwhile, 12 African-Americans in the same range of qualifications applied for admission and all 12 were admitted. Likewise, that same year, 16 Hispanics who scored between a 151-153 on the LSAT and earned a 3.00 or higher applied for admission and only 1 of those applicants was admitted. Twenty-three similarly qualified African-Americans applied for admission and 14 were admitted.

These statistics have a significant bearing on petitioner's case. Respondents have never offered any race-specific arguments explaining why significantly more individuals from one underrepresented minority group are needed in order to achieve "critical mass" or further student body diversity. They certainly have not explained why Hispanics, who they have said are among "the groups most isolated by racial barriers in our country," should have their admission capped out in this manner. True, petitioner is neither Hispanic nor Native American. But the Law School's disparate admissions practices with respect to these minority groups demonstrate that its alleged goal of "critical mass" is simply a sham. . . .

Only when the "critical mass" label is discarded does a likely explanation for these numbers emerge. . . . The Court concludes . . . that the Law School's use of race in admissions, consistent with Justice Powell's opinion in Bakke, only pays "[s]ome attention to numbers."

But the correlation between the percentage of the Law School's pool of applicants who are members of the three minority groups and the percentage of the admitted applicants who are members of these same groups is far too precise to be dismissed as merely the result of the school paying "some attention to [the] numbers." [Chief Justice Rehnquist then presented data from 1995 to 2000 that show that the percentage of admitted applicants who were African American, Hispanic, or Native American closely tracked the percentage of individuals in the school's applicant pool who were from the same groups.]

. . . .

. . . The tight correlation . . . suggests a formula for admission based on the aspirational assumption that all applicants are equally qualified academically, and therefore that the proportion of each group admitted should be the same as the proportion of that group in the applicant pool. . . .

. . . The Law School cannot precisely control which of its admitted applicants decide to attend the university. But it can and, as the numbers demonstrate, clearly does employ racial preferences in extending offers of admission. . . .

I do not believe that the Constitution gives the Law School such free rein in the use of race. The Law School has offered no explanation for its actual admissions practices and, unexplained, we are bound to conclude that the Law School has managed its admissions program, not to achieve a "critical mass," but to extend offers of admission to members of selected minority groups in proportion to their statistical representation in the applicant pool. But this is precisely the type of racial balancing that the Court itself calls "patently unconstitutional."

Finally, I believe that the Law School's program fails strict scrutiny because it is devoid of any reasonably precise time limit on the Law School's use of race in admissions. . . . The Court suggests a possible 25-year limitation on the Law School's current program. Respondents, on the other hand, remain more ambiguous. . . . In truth, they permit the Law School's use of racial preferences on a seemingly permanent basis. Thus, an important component of strict scrutiny-that a program be limited in time-is casually subverted.

. . . .

[Concurring opinion by Justice Ginsburg is omitted. Dissenting opinions by Justices Kennedy, Scalia, and Thomas are omitted.]

GRATZ v. BOLLINGER

539 U.S. 244 (2003)

CHIEF JUSTICE REHNQUIST delivered the opinion of the Court.

We granted certiorari in this case to decide whether "the University of Michigan's use of racial preferences in undergraduate admissions violates the Equal Protection Clause of the Fourteenth Amendment, Title VI of the Civil Rights Act of 1964. . . ." Because we find that the manner in which the University considers the race of applicants in its undergraduate admissions guidelines violates these constitutional and statutory provisions, we reverse that portion of the District Court's decision upholding the guidelines.

I

. . . .

[Petitioners were Caucasian applicants to Michigan University's College of Literature, Science, and the Arts (LSA). Following their rejection, petitioners filed suit, alleging "violations and threatened violations of the rights of the plaintiffs and the class they represent to equal protection of the laws under the Fourteenth Amendment . . . and for racial discrimination in violation of 42 USC §§ 1981, 1983, and 2000d *et seq.*" Michigan's Office of Undergraduate Admissions (OUA), which handles the LSA admissions process, used at the time petitioners' applied a scoring system based on applicants GPA and SAT where a minority applicant with scores identical to petitioners would have been admitted. The OUA later changed its admissions procedure to a 150 point "selection index" where an underrepresented minority applicant received an automatic 20 points.]

. . . .

C

. . . Petitioners asserted that the LSA's use of race as a factor in admissions violates Title VI of the Civil Rights Act of 1964, and the Equal Protection Clause of the Fourteenth Amendment. . . . Respondents contended that the LSA has . . . an interest in the educational benefits that result from having a racially and ethnically diverse student body and that its program is narrowly tailored to serve that interest. . . .

II

. . . .

[The District Court concluded that the LSA's 20 point "bonus" for minorities was narrowly tailored and did not insulate minority candidates from the rest of the applicants. However, the court found the admissions guidelines prior to this to not be narrowly tailored. Both parties appealed these rulings and the Sixth Circuit Court of Appeals heard the case same day as *Grutter v. Bollinger.* The Supreme

Court granted certiorari in both cases prior to the Sixth Circuit's decision in order to address the constitutionality issues therein.]

. . . .

B

Petitioners argue, first and foremost, that the University's use of race in undergraduate admissions violates the Fourteenth Amendment. Specifically, they contend that this Court has only sanctioned the use of racial classifications to remedy identified discrimination, a justification on which respondents have never relied. Petitioners further argue that "diversity as a basis for employing racial preferences is simply too open-ended, ill-defined, and indefinite to constitute a compelling interest capable of supporting narrowly-tailored means." But for the reasons set forth today in *Grutter* v *Bollinger*, the Court has rejected these arguments of petitioners.

Petitioners alternatively argue that even if the University's interest in diversity can constitute a compelling state interest, the District Court erroneously concluded that the University's use of race in its current freshman admissions policy is narrowly tailored to achieve such an interest. . . . Respondents reply that the University's current admissions program *is* narrowly tailored and avoids the problems of the Medical School of the University of California at Davis program (U. C. Davis) rejected by Justice Powell [i.e., Michigan's LSA policy was not a quota]. . . . Specifically, respondents contend that the LSA's policy provides the individualized consideration that "Justice Powell considered a hallmark of a constitutionally appropriate admissions program." For the reasons set out below, we do not agree.

. . . .

. . . [T]he University's policy, which automatically distributes 20 points, or one-fifth of the points needed to guarantee admission, to every single "underrepresented minority" applicant solely because of race, is not narrowly tailored to achieve the interest in educational diversity that respondents claim justifies their program.

In *Bakke*, Justice Powell reiterated that "preferring members of any one group for no reason other than race or ethnic origin is discrimination for its own sake." 438 US at 307. He then explained, however, that in his view it would be permissible for a university to employ an admissions program in which "race or ethnic background may be deemed a 'plus' in a particular applicant's file." *Id.*, at 317. . . .

Justice Powell's opinion in *Bakke* emphasized the importance of considering each particular applicant as an individual, assessing all of the qualities that individual possesses, and in turn, evaluating that individual's ability to contribute to the unique setting of higher education. The admissions program Justice Powell described, however, did not contemplate that any single characteristic automatically ensured a specific and identifiable contribution to a university's diversity. . . . Instead, under the approach Justice Powell described, each characteristic of a particular applicant was to be considered in assessing the applicant's entire application.

The current LSA policy does not provide such individualized consideration. The

LSA's policy automatically distributes 20 points to every single applicant from an "underrepresented minority" group, as defined by the University. . . . [This] has the effect of making "the factor of race . . . decisive" for virtually every minimally qualified underrepresented minority applicant. *Ibid.*

Also instructive in our consideration of the LSA's system is the example provided in the description of the Harvard College Admissions Program, which Justice Powell both discussed in, and attached to, his opinion in *Bakke.* The example was included to "illustrate the kind of significance attached to race" under the Harvard College program. *Id.*, at 324. It provided as follows:

> "The Admissions Committee, with only a few places left to fill, might find itself forced to choose between A, the child of a successful black physician in an academic community with promise of superior academic performance, and B, a black who grew up in an inner-city ghetto of semi-literate parents whose academic achievement was lower but who had demonstrated energy and leadership as well as an apparently abiding interest in black power. If a good number of black students much like A but few like B had already been admitted, the Committee might prefer B; and vice versa. If C, a white student with extraordinary artistic talent, were also seeking one of the remaining places, his unique quality might give him an edge over both A and B. Thus, the critical criteria are often individual qualities or experience *not dependent upon race but sometimes associated with it.*" *Ibid.* (emphasis added).

. . . Clearly, the LSA's system does not offer applicants the individualized selection process described in Harvard's example. Instead of considering how the differing backgrounds, experiences, and characteristics of students A, B, and C might benefit the University, admissions counselors reviewing LSA applications would simply award both A and B 20 points because their applications indicate that they are African-American, and student C would receive up to 5 points for his "extraordinary talent."

Respondents contend that "the volume of applications and the presentation of applicant information make it impractical for [LSA] to use the . . . admissions system" upheld by the Court today in *Grutter.* But the fact that the implementation of a program capable of providing individualized consideration might present administrative challenges does not render constitutional an otherwise problematic system. . . . Nothing in Justice Powell's opinion in *Bakke* signaled that a university may employ whatever means it desires to achieve the stated goal of diversity without regard to the limits imposed by our strict scrutiny analysis.

[The majority reversed and remanded the case for further proceedings].

JUSTICE SOUTER, with whom JUSTICE GINSBURG joins as to Part II, dissenting.

. . . .

II

The cases now contain two pointers toward the line between the valid and the unconstitutional in race-conscious admissions schemes. *Grutter* reaffirms the permissibility of individualized consideration of race to achieve a diversity of students, at least where race is not assigned a preordained value in all cases. On the other hand, Justice Powell's opinion in [*Bakke*] rules out a racial quota or set-aside, in which race is the sole fact of eligibility for certain places in a class. Although the freshman admissions system here is subject to argument on the merits, I think it is closer to what *Grutter* approves than to what *Bakke* condemns, and should not be held unconstitutional on the current record.

The record does not describe a system with a quota like the one struck down in *Bakke*, which "insulate[d]" all nonminority candidates from competition from certain seats. . . . The *Bakke* plan "focused solely on ethnic diversity" and effectively told nonminority applicants that "[n]o matter how strong their qualifications, quantitative and extracurricular, including their own potential for contribution to educational diversity, they are never afforded the chance to compete with applicants from the preferred groups for the [set-aside] special admissions seats."

The plan here, in contrast, lets all applicants compete for all places and values an applicant's offering for any place not only on grounds of race, but on grades, test scores, strength of high school, quality of course of study, residence, alumni relationships, leadership, personal character, socioeconomic disadvantage, athletic ability, and quality of a personal essay. . . .

. . . .

The one qualification to this description of the admissions process is that membership in an underrepresented minority is given a weight of 20 points on the 150-point scale. On the face of things, however, this assignment of specific points does not set race apart from all other weighted considerations. Nonminority students may receive 20 points for athletic ability, socioeconomic disadvantage, attendance at a socioeconomically disadvantaged or predominantly minority high school, or at the Provost's discretion; they may also receive 10 points for being residents of Michigan, 6 for residence in an underrepresented Michigan county, 5 for leadership and service, and so on.

. . . .

The very nature of a college's permissible practice of awarding value to racial diversity means that race must be considered in a way that increases some applicants' chances for admission. Since college admission is not left entirely to inarticulate intuition, it is hard to see what is inappropriate in assigning some stated value to a relevant characteristic, whether it be reasoning ability, writing style, running speed, or minority race. Justice Powell's plus factors necessarily are assigned some values. The college simply does by a numbered scale what the law school accomplishes in its "holistic review," the distinction does not imply that applicants to the undergraduate college are denied individualized consideration or a fair chance to compete on the basis of all the various merits their applications may disclose.

. . . .

[Concurring opinions of Justices O'Connor, Thomas, and Breyer are omitted. Dissenting opinions by Justices Stevens and Ginsburg are omitted.]

NOTES

1. Between *Hopwood* and *Gratz* and *Grutter*, several state legislatures enacted laws designed to attract diverse student bodies, including, for example, laws and policies that guaranteed admission to public universities for any student graduating in the top 10 percent of his or her graduating class. Combating this, however, were several states whose voters passed anti-discrimination ballot initiatives, forbidding the preferential treatment on the basis of race and national origin in public employment and public education. The ballot initiative that perhaps attracted the most public attention was Proposition 209, the California anti-discrimination law passed in 1996. The initiative was upheld against an equal protection clause argument. *See Coalition for Economic Equity v. Wilson*, 122 F.3d 692 (9th Cir. 1997).

2. In *Grutter*, the university argued that diversity of student body is a compelling governmental interest. How? Why? In the law school's policy, the term "diversity" is not specifically defined in terms of race. So how is race used under the policy? How is national origin used? How did the university argue that its policy was narrowly tailored to meet its governmental interest?

3. What is *Grutter*'s contribution to academic freedom philosophy and law?

4. At the end of *Grutter*, the majority stated that it expects, in 25 years, the use of racial preferences will no longer be necessary to further the interest of diversity of student body. Why did the Court make the statement? What force does it hold, legally?

5. Justice Thomas argued in his dissent in *Grutter* that diversity of student body is not a compelling governmental interest: "every time the government places citizens on racial registers and makes race relevant to the provision of burdens or benefits, it demeans us all." 539 U.S. 306 at 353. He further claimed the University of Michigan needed to assert a compelling *state* governmental interest and spent too much of its argument emphasizing its national reputation and selective admissions. Finally, Justice Thomas assailed the majority's reliance on academic freedom, arguing that there is no First Amendment right for a university to do what the Equal Protection Clause would prohibit — governmental racial discrimination. Justice Kennedy argued in his dissent, similar to Chief Justice Rehnquist's dissent presented above, that the stability of application and admission data over time relied on race as a dominant factor "tantamount to quotas."

6. *Gratz*, a 6-3 decision, struck down the admissions policy for the University of Michigan's College of Literature, Science, and the Arts (LSA). What are the differences in the two policies — the law school policy upheld in *Grutter* and the LSA policy struck down in *Gratz*? Why did the undergraduate college's policy in *Gratz* fail the narrow tailoring test?

7. *Gratz* is a case involving an undergraduate college's admissions policy. While it is obvious that the undergraduate college here ought to read *Grutter* and adopt its next policy with the spirit and letter of the *Grutter* decision, what concerns might an undergraduate college or university have when attempting to apply the law school's policy principles in undergraduate admissions?

8. Justice Ginsburg's dissent in *Gratz* discussed long-lasting racial and ethnic disparity in communities and schools and praised the University of Michigan for recognizing and addressing it. She argued that suspect classifications in governmental affairs are subject to strict scrutiny not because such classifications are inevitably impermissible, but because race, historically, had been classified to maintain racial inequality. Justice Ginsburg offered some thoughts on how universities and applicants will proceed post-*Gratz*:

> The stain of generations of racial oppression is still visible in our society . . . and the determination to hasten its removal remains vital. One can reasonably anticipate, therefore, that colleges and universities will seek to maintain their minority enrollment — and the networks and opportunities thereby opened to minority graduates — whether or not they can do so in full candor through adoption of affirmative action plans of the kind here at issue. Without recourse to such plans, institutions of higher education may resort to camouflage. For example, schools may encourage applicants to write of their cultural traditions in the essays they submit, or to indicate whether English is their second language. Seeking to improve their chances for admission, applicants may highlight the minority group associations to which they belong, or the Hispanic surnames of their mothers or grandparents. In turn, teachers' recommendations may emphasize who a student is as much as what he or she has accomplished. . . . If honesty is the best policy, surely Michigan's accurately described, fully disclosed College affirmative action program is preferable to achieving similar numbers through winks, nods, and disguises.

539 U.S. 244, 304–05 (2003) (Ginsburg, J., dissenting).

9. The case of *Fisher v. University of Texas*, 631 F. 3d 213 (2011), *cert. granted*, 132 S. Ct. 1536 (U.S. Feb. 21, 2012) (No. 11-345), has the potential of threatening the decisions in both *Grutter* and *Gratz* and their collective reliance on race-conscious admissions in higher education. The plaintiff in *Fisher* argued that race-neutral plans are equally as capable of achieving a compelling interest in a diverse student body without resorting to race-based classifications. Relying on a Texas state statute supporting the "Top Ten Percent" law, Tex. Educ. Code § 51.803 (1997) (granting admission to any Texas high school student in the top 10% of her class to a public university in the state), Fisher argued that any admissions program that failed to consider available race-neutral alternatives and employ them if efficacious would cause that program to fail strict scrutiny. A concurring appellate opinion went even further in challenging diversity as a compelling governmental interest with the argument that such an approach is nothing more than "invasive social engineering" and that there is no evidence that diversity plans enhance engagement in a democratic society. *Fisher*, 631 F.3d at 254 (Garza, J. concurring). How would such a case be addressed by the Supreme Court in the current affirmative action climate?

Should the Court clarify its holding in *Grutter* and uphold race-conscious diversity? Is it possible to narrow the application of the *Grutter* decision to law schools and graduate level admissions programs? Should the Court overrule the language of *Grutter* by holding that all race-neutral means of achieving diversity must be employed before resorting to race-based classifications?

SMITH v. UNIVERSITY OF WASHINGTON

392 F.3d 367 (9th Cir. 2004)

FISHER, CIRCUIT JUDGE:

Plaintiffs Katuria Smith, Angela Rock and Michael Pyle are white Washington residents who claim that the University of Washington Law School (the "Law School") rejected their applications because of the Law School's unconstitutional consideration of race and ethnicity as factors in its admissions program. They appeal the judgment the district court entered against them following a bench trial.

The question presented is a narrow one due in part to external events that have overtaken this particular litigation. First, the Supreme Court last year ratified our earlier holding in this case that educational diversity constitutes a compelling state interest. . . . [*S*] *ee Grutter v. Bollinger*, 539 U.S. 306, 325 (2003); *Gratz v. Bollinger*, 539 U.S. 244, 268 (2003). In addition, after plaintiffs filed this lawsuit, Washington residents approved a voter initiative in 1998 prohibiting the kind of race-based affirmative action plan at issue here, thereby mooting the plaintiffs' injunctive and declaratory claims, which the district court dismissed. *See Smith*, 233 F.3d at 1192, 1201. Thus, left for us to decide is whether the Law School's admissions program was narrowly tailored to meet the compelling interest of educational diversity during the three years in which the plaintiffs applied — 1994, 1995 and 1996 — in order to determine whether the plaintiffs might be entitled to damages.

In support of their claim that the Law School's admissions program was not narrowly tailored, the plaintiffs cite three specific aspects of the program during the relevant years: (1) a so-called "ethnicity substantiation letter" that the Law School sent only to some minority applicants; (2) that Asian Americans were given a plus; and (3) a large number of white applicants were referred to the Admissions Committee rather than being directly admitted by an administrator. We hold that none of these aspects of the Law School's affirmative action program undermines the district court's finding that the Law School narrowly tailored its consideration of race and ethnicity in order to meet the compelling interest of obtaining the educational benefits of diversity. Accordingly, we affirm the district court judgment in favor of the Law School.

I.

. . . .

During each of the years in question, the Law School received about 2,000 applications for approximately 165 positions. The top 250 to 300 candidates based on an index score (a weighted tabulation of the applicant's undergraduate grade point average ("GPA") and Law School Admission Test ("LSAT") score) were considered "presumptive admits," whereas the remaining applicants were considered "presumptive denies."

All the presumptive admit applications were read by Kathy Swinehart, the Law School's admissions coordinator, who either admitted applicants or referred their applications to the Admissions Committee for further consideration. Sandra Madrid, assistant dean and liaison to the Admissions Committee, reviewed almost all the presumptive deny applications and could admit, deny or refer applicants to the Admissions Committee for further review. Professor Richard Kummert, the Admissions Committee chairman during the relevant times, oversaw Swinehart's and Madrid's decisions. After Kummert, Madrid and Swinehart completed their work, the Admissions Committee ranked the 250 to 300 or so applications that the trio had identified as requiring committee referral, and the committee's top picks were offered admission.

The Law School did not establish any racial quotas, targets or goals for admission or enrollment. Nor is there evidence that the Law School sought to exclude whites from consideration for seats offered to minority applicants or otherwise applied significantly disparate standards to applicants of different races. The Law School did, however, consider racial and ethnic origin, among many other diversity factors, as a "plus" in its admissions decisions. The amount of preference given to a candidate due to his or her race or ethnicity differed depending on his or her race or ethnicity, *e.g.*, Asian American applicants were given a preference lesser in magnitude than that given to African American candidates.

Although race and ethnicity were the most significant factors in the admissions decisions next to the index score, non-racial diversity factors also played a substantial role in admissions decisions. These factors included cultural background, activities or accomplishments, career goals, life experiences (such as growing up in a disadvantaged or unusual environment or with a physical disability) or special talents. No attempt was made to define the weight that could be accorded to any diversity factor; the weight sometimes changed as the pool was reviewed. This consideration of non-racial diversity factors explains in part why the Law School admitted whites scoring at or below every index score level from which minorities were admitted, and why more whites were admitted than any other group in the group of applicants with index scores below the median for the entire applicant pool.

Procedural History

The plaintiffs filed this action on March 5, 1997, alleging that the Law School had discriminated against them on the basis of race in violation of 42 U.S.C. §§ 1981, 1983 and 2000d. In 1998, Washington voters passed Initiative 200, precluding certain state actors from discriminating against, or granting preferential treatment to, any individual or group on the basis of race, sex, color, ethnicity or national origin. *See* Wash. Rev. Code § 49.60.400. The district court on February 10, 1999, dismissed the plaintiffs' requests for declaratory and injunctive relief, as Initiative 200 rendered them moot. We affirmed on appeal, and also held that colleges and universities may consider race or ethnicity in admissions in furtherance of the compelling interest in educational diversity. Accordingly, we remanded the case to the district court for a trial of the individual plaintiffs' claims for liability.

The district court [found] for defendants on all claims. . . . Plaintiffs timely appealed, but we deferred briefing until the Supreme Court decided *Grutter* and *Gratz*. . . .

II.

. . . .

Because the Supreme Court has provided in *Grutter* an example of a narrowly tailored admissions program, we first turn to that opinion as establishing a template of what educational institutions should do and measure the Law School's program against that approved in *Grutter*. . . .

A. *Grutter*

. . . .

As part of its diversity admissions, UMLS [University of Michigan Law School] sought to enroll a "critical mass" of underrepresented minority students — targeting African Americans, Hispanics and Native Americans — to ensure that students of these races had the ability to make unique contributions to the law school. . . .

The Supreme Court held that UMLS had established a compelling interest because "attaining a diverse student body is at the heart of [UMLS]'s proper institutional mission." [539 U.S. 306,] at 329. . . . First, the educational experience itself is greatly enriched by having diverse members. A diverse student body "promotes cross-racial under-standing"; "helps to break down racial stereotypes"; "enables [students] to better understand persons of different races"; results in a "livelier, more spirited, and simply more enlightening" classroom discussion; and "better prepares students for an increasingly diverse workforce and society." *Id.* at 330 (internal quotation marks omitted). Second, the Court recognized that "access to legal education (and thus the legal profession) must be inclusive of talented and qualified individuals of every race and ethnicity, so that all members of our heterogeneous society may participate in the educational institutions that provide the training and education necessary to succeed in America." *Id.* at 332-33. "Effective participation by members of all racial and ethnic groups in the civic life of our Nation is essential if the dream of one Nation, indivisible, is to be realized." *Id.* at 332.

. . . .

Having held that UMLS had a compelling interest in obtaining a critical mass of underrepresented minority students in order to secure the benefits of a diverse student body, the Supreme Court then turned to the question at issue here — whether the means by which UMLS attempted to obtain a diverse student body were constitutional. In approving the UMLS program, the Supreme Court discussed five hallmarks of a narrowly tailored affirmative action plan: (1) the absence of quotas; (2) individualized consideration of applicants; (3) serious, good-faith consideration of race-neutral alternatives to the affirmative action program; (4) that no member of any racial group was unduly harmed; and (5) that the program had a sunset provision or some other end point. *See id.* at 335-43. . . .

. . . .

B. The Law School's Admissions Program

In light of the criteria the Supreme Court has now articulated, we hold that the district court correctly concluded that the Law School's admissions program during 1994-96 "was narrowly tailored to achieve the compelling state interest of educational diversity." . . .

The Law School did not establish quotas, targets or goals for admission or enrollment of minorities. Indeed, the two deans of the Law School during the relevant period testified that they did not direct the admissions staff to admit a certain number of minority applicants. Further, the percentage of minorities varied each year in a manner inconsistent with the existence of a quota.

In addition, the Law School's review of applications demonstrates the sort of "highly individualized, holistic review of each applicant's file, giving serious consideration to all the ways an applicant might contribute to a diverse educational environment" approved of in *Grutter.* 539 U.S. at 337. Applications were divided according to index score. Almost all the top applicants were given offers, unless Swinehart believed the applicant had less academic potential than other presumptive admits, in which case she referred the applicant to the Admissions Committee for further review. The rest of the applicants had to pass the scrutiny of Madrid, the committee or both. These applicants were measured against each other, taking into account all the ways that an applicant might contribute to a diverse educational environment, including that applicant's racial or ethnic minority status. In applying the admissions policy, the reviewers testified that they looked at the whole person for life experiences that most applicants did not possess, trying to imagine that person in the school and what contributions to class diversity they could make.

The Law School also accepted nonminority applicants with grades and test scores lower than underrepresented minority applicants who were rejected, thus showing that the Law School "seriously weigh[ed] many other diversity factors besides race that [could] make a real and dispositive difference." *Grutter*, 539 U.S. at 338. The district court found that nonracial "diversity factors played an important role in the Law School's admissions decisions in all years for all applicants." The consideration of diversity factors other than race and ethnicity further suggests that the admissions program did not unduly harm members of any racial group. *See Grutter*, 539 U.S. at 341. Finally, although the Law School program did not have a sunset provision, the residents of the state of Washington mooted any challenges to this aspect when they passed Initiative 200, prohibiting certain state actors, including the Law School, from considering race or ethnicity in administering state programs.

In sum, the Law School's admissions program comported with the criteria set forth in *Grutter*. . . .

The plaintiffs, however, attempt to differentiate the Law School's program from UMLS's, focusing on three discrete aspects of the admission process. Specifically, they complain that during one or more of the relevant years, the Law School (1) provided an opportunity to some minority applicants to supplement applications through a so-called "ethnicity substantiation letter"; (2) gave a slight "plus" to Asian American applicants; and (3) referred a high number of white applicants to the Admissions Committee. We address each of these practices in turn, but conclude that none of them is inconsistent with the Law School's effort to narrowly tailor its affirmative action program.

1. The Ethnicity Substantiation Letter

Contrary to the plaintiffs' claim, the so-called "ethnicity substantiation letter," as it has been referred to in this lawsuit, supports rather than undermines the constitutionality of the Law School's program. As the district court properly concluded, the Law School used the letter to more narrowly tailor the awarding of a plus for an applicant's race or ethnicity by seeking more information about the role that race or ethnicity played in the applicant's life, rather than simply relying on the applicant's minority status as such. The Law School sent the letter to some applicants who identified themselves as racial or ethnic minorities on the front page of their applications. To help ascertain whether the applicant's race or ethnicity should be considered a plus factor, the letter asked the applicant to provide additional information on "family background (including country of origin), languages spoken, official or government status (for Native Americans), and cultural activities and associations." This was the only letter the school used to seek additional information. Madrid testified that replying to the letter did not guarantee admission; but if the applicant responded, Madrid considered the new information and, as with all applicants, admitted some, referred some to commit-tee and denied others. When applicants did not respond, the file was reviewed as it had been received. In light of this evidence, the district court concluded:

> The Law School further narrowed its use of race by using the ethnicity substantiation letter to better determine which minority students would fulfill the goal of creating a pool of students with diverse back-grounds. The ethnicity substantiation letter allowed the Law School to give preference to those minority students whose race had impacted their views and experiences rather than giving preference to students based on their race alone.
>
> . . .

The plaintiffs argue against this conclusion, first by noting Madrid's testimony that the Law School would examine the application "as is," without any supplementation, if a minority applicant chose not to respond to the Law School's request. They also point to two minority applicants who were sent an ethnicity substantiation letter and who were admitted despite a "perfunctory" response from one applicant and no response from the other. That these two applicants were admitted in the absence of a meaningful response to the ethnicity substantiation letter proves little, however. That their or other non-responsive applicants' chances of admission might have been even better had they responded does not mean that the letter was an inappropriate effort to obtain additional relevant information. Moreover, the history of the two applicants proves nothing about what happened to other minority applicants who either did or did not respond to the letter nor impeaches Madrid's testimony that there was no pattern to the responses to the ethnicity substantiation letter or the letter's effect on who was admitted.

The plaintiffs also complain that white candidates did not receive the same opportunity to supplement their applications. We reject the assumption that the Law School, in adopting a technique to obtain supplemental information about a class of applicants in order to narrowly tailor the category of those who warranted a racial-ethnic diversity plus, had to apply that technique to all applicants. There was no need to seek further substantiation from nonminority applicants who could not receive such a plus. Moreover, this selective inquiry did not unduly harm white applicants. The Law School directed all applicants to write a 700-word essay addressing their potential contributions to diversity. The record also indicates that white applicants could supplement their files on their own initiative.

Assuming the good faith of the Law School in the absence of evidence to the contrary, we agree with the district court that the Law School properly sought to provide meaningful racial or ethnic pluses by seeking more information about minority candidates' backgrounds, thereby helping to narrowly tailor its program. In so doing, the school avoided awarding the type of automatic, decisive bonus that *Gratz* found unconstitutional.

2. The Asian American Plus

The plaintiffs suggest that Asian Americans, who were given a slight plus for racial diversity, should not have been given a plus at all because the Law School could have attracted what the plaintiffs deem a "critical mass" of Asian American students without a preference. With the plus, Asian Americans constituted 18 percent of admitted applicants in 1994 and 14 percent in 1995 and 1996. Asian Americans would have constituted approximately 7 to 9 percent of the class without any racial or ethnic diversity factor.

This argument suffers from several problems. As an initial matter, it assumes that the category "Asian American" is homogenous. In reality, applicants whose families or who themselves originated from the Philippines, Viet Nam, Cambodia, Taiwan and the People's Republic of China — to name a few countries of origin from which the Law School specifically sought applicants — have different cultures, back-grounds and languages, and thus would bring different experiences to the educational environment. The Law School, with its preeminent Asian law program, was particularly interested in achieving such diversity among its Asian American students. This "educational judgment that such diversity is essential to its educational mission is one to which we defer." *Grutter*, 539 U.S. at 328. . . .

In any event, assuming that Asian Americans should be treated as a homogenous group for the purposes of defining a critical mass, the plaintiffs have not provided any support for their theory that a critical mass is achieved whenever a particular group comprises 7 to 9 percent of the student body. *Grutter* did not establish such a cap. . . . Indeed, defining critical mass in terms of specific percentages "would amount to outright racial balancing, which is patently unconstitutional." *Id.* at 330. . . .

. . . .

3. Referral of Some White Applicants to the Admissions Committee

The plaintiffs contend that the Law School created "separate tracks" for white and minority applicants, pointing primarily to the referral in 1994 of white applicants with index scores of 195 and 196 to the Admissions Committee but also to the larger proportion of white applicants referred to the committee rather than directly admitted over all the relevant years. We first address the referral process followed in 1994.

a. The Referral of White Applicants with 195 and 196 Index Scores to the Admissions Committee in 1994

In 1994, the Law School drew the line between "presumptive admits" and "presumptive denies" at 197 and above for the former and 194 and below for the latter, with applicants scoring 195-196 considered a "discretionary" group. Madrid was responsible for initially reviewing the presumptive denies and could admit, deny or refer applicants to the Admission committee for further review.

The entire discretionary group — which consisted of 158 applicants, 136 of whom were white — was supposed to be sent to the Admissions Committee without any review by Madrid, as part of the Law School's efforts to ensure that the committee would have approximately 300 applications to assess. Madrid pulled out the 22 applications from minority applicants, however, in order to make an expedited, albeit not necessarily favorable decision on these strong minority applicants in order "to actively recruit those candidates" who were admitted. She admitted 18, referred three to the Admissions Committee and denied one.

The district court noted that "this separate treatment of the minority applicants with an index score of 195-196" was "troublesome on it face," but found that the Law School provided a reasonable explanation for doing so and that the separate review did not interfere with the Law School's ability to provide appropriate consideration of the white applicants. First, the reason for not including the 22 minority files with the 136 applications reserved for committee review was that the Law School wanted to "make an early decision on minority candidates who were extremely well qualified based solely on their high index scores." . . .

. . . .

Second, the 136 applicants Madrid referred directly to the Admissions Committee received a thorough, individualized consideration by the committee, even though Madrid did not herself provide a first review of those files. Indeed, the percentage of white applicants with 195-196 index scores who were admitted in 1994 as a result of committee review (29%) was approximately the same in all other years when Madrid reviewed the files initially (28%). . . .

We accordingly find no merit in the plaintiffs' argument that separating and accelerating the review of the applications of minorities with relatively high index scores was unconstitutional. The Law School simply sought to achieve the compelling interest of diversity by taking steps to increase the prospects of actually enrolling qualified minority applicants rather than risk losing them to other law schools. Moreover, *Grutter* does not require that a single reviewer evaluate all files, just that all applicants receive an individualized review. . . .

b. The Referral of White Applicants With Index Scores of All Ranges to the Admissions Committee

Plaintiffs finally argue that the admissions program was unconstitutional because in each of the years 1994 through 1996 the Admissions Committee's pool of applicants resulting from Swinehart's and Madrid's referrals (as opposed to direct admissions) was consistently predominantly white. Over the three years, Swinehart — reviewing the presumptive admit category — referred 60 applicants to the committee, 57 of whom were white; she directly admitted 743 applicants, 646 of whom were white. In the same period, Madrid — reviewing the presumptive denies — referred 860 applicants, 782 of whom were white. Of the applicants Madrid admitted directly, 76 of 415 were white. Plaintiffs focus primarily on Madrid's referrals.

To begin with, the large number of white applicants in the Admissions Committee pool must be viewed in context: white applicants ranged from 69 to 74 percent of the total applicant pool from 1994 to 1996. Thus it is not surprising that the committee pool would be predominantly white. In any event, having examined Madrid's review and decision-making process, the district court found that race was never the sole determining factor in Madrid's decision to admit an applicant. The record supports this finding. . . .

Additionally, the Law School put into place a system of checks and balances. Kummert oversaw Madrid's decisions and engaged her in debate when he believed Madrid had recommended admission for less academically promising applicants; any continuing disagreement resulted in the applicant's being referred to the committee. Those applications that were referred to the Admissions Committee received another highly individualistic review, with the benefit of three reviewers and a procedure by which the scores were re-calibrated where the scores were too disparate. No applicants — whether reviewed by Madrid only or by Madrid and the Admissions Committee — were "foreclosed from all consideration for [a] seat simply because [they] were not the right color or had the wrong surname"; instead each applicant's "qualifications would have been weighed fairly and competitively." *Grutter*, 539 U.S. at 341. In short, nonminority applicants were not unduly harmed by this system of review, and the number of white applicants referred to the Admissions Committee does not establish a constitutional violation.

III.

In conclusion, the Law School's narrowly tailored use of race and ethnicity in admissions decisions during 1994-96 furthered its compelling interest in obtaining the educational benefits that flow from a diverse student body. The district court was therefore correct in entering judgment against the plaintiffs' damages claims. . . .

AFFIRMED.

NOTE

In recent years, several states have placed initiatives on the ballot, asking voters to end racial preferencing in university admissions and employment. One such initiative was Michigan's direct response to *Gratz* and *Grutter.* On November 7, 2006, Michigan's Proposal 06-2 (commonly known as "Proposal 2"), passed by a margin of 58% to 42%. Proposal 2 amended the Michigan constitution by adding three provisions to Article I titled "Affirmative Action":

> 1. The University of Michigan, Michigan State University, Wayne State University, and any other public college or university, community college, or school district shall not discriminate against, or grant preferential treatment to, any individual or group on the basis of race, sex, color, ethnicity, or national origin in the operation of public employment, public education or public contracting.
>
> 2. The state shall not discriminate against, or grant preferential treatment to, any individual or group on the basis of race, sex, color, ethnicity, or national origin in the operation of public employment, public education, or public contracting.
>
> 3. For the purposes of this section "state" includes, but is not necessarily limited to, the state itself, any city, county, and public college, university or community college, school district, or other political subdivision or governmental instrumentality of or within the State of Michigan not included in sub-section 1.

Though Proposal 2 removed consideration of "race, sex, color, ethnicity, or national origin" in admissions decisions, other admissions criteria such as grades, athletic ability, or family alumni connections were not affected.

On November 8, 2006, a combination of interest groups and individuals, including the Coalition to Defend Affirmative Action, Integration and Immigration Rights, and Fight for Equality By Any Means Necessary ("Coalition Plaintiffs"), filed suit alleging that the provisions of Proposal 2 affecting colleges and universities violated the Equal Protection Clause of the Fourteenth Amendment. On December 19, 2006, a group of faculty members and prospective and current students at the University of Michigan ("the Cantrell Plaintiffs") filed suit, as well. That same day, the district court issued a preliminary injunction, postponing the application of Proposal 2 to the universities' admissions and financial-aid policies until July 1, 2007. In 2008, the district court granted summary judgment for the Attorney General. The groups appealed to the Sixth Circuit, which reversed. *Coalition to Defend Affirmative Action v. Regents of the Univ. of Mich.*, 652 F.3d 607 (6th Cir. 2011).

The plaintiffs argued that Proposal 2 violated the Equal Protection Clause by unjustifiably restructuring the political process along racial lines, and by impermissibly classifying individuals on the basis of race. Following the *Hunter/Seattle* test (*see Hunter v. Erickson*, 393 U.S. 385 (1969), and *Washington v. Seattle Sch. Dist. No. 1*, 458 U.S. 457 (1982)), the court concluded that Proposal 2 targeted a program that "inures primarily to the benefit of the minority" and alters the political process in Michigan, placing "special burdens" on racial minorities. In prohibiting race as a consideration in admissions decisions, Proposal 2 has a "racial focus." It thus targets a program that operates primarily to the benefit of the minority. Later in 2011, the Sixth Circuit Court of Appeals granted a motion to rehear the case *en banc* and vacated this earlier ruling. 2011 U.S. App. LEXIS 18875 (6th Cir. Sept. 9, 2011).

2. Sex Discrimination and Affirmative Action in Admissions

MISSISSIPPI UNIVERSITY FOR WOMEN v. HOGAN

458 U.S. 718 (1982)

Justice O'Connor delivered the opinion of the Court.

This case presents the narrow issue of whether a state statute that excludes males from enrolling in a state-supported professional nursing school violates the Equal Protection Clause of the Fourteenth Amendment.

I

The facts are not in dispute. In 1884, the Mississippi Legislature created the Mississippi Industrial Institute and College for the Education of White Girls of the State of Mississippi, now the oldest state-supported all-female college in the United States. 1884 Miss. Gen. Laws, Ch. 30, § 6. The school, known today as Mississippi University for Women (MUW), has from its inception limited its enrollment to women.

. . . .

Respondent, Joe Hogan[] . . . applied for admission to the MUW School of Nursing's baccalaureate program. Although he was otherwise qualified, he was denied admission to the School of Nursing solely because of his sex. School officials informed him that he could audit the courses in which he was interested, but could not enroll for credit.

Hogan filed an action in the United States District Court for the Northern District of Mississippi, claiming the single-sex admissions policy of MUW's School of Nursing violated the Equal Protection Clause of the Fourteenth Amendment. Hogan sought injunctive and declaratory relief, as well as compensatory damages.

. . . [T]he District Court denied preliminary injunctive relief. The court concluded that maintenance of MUW as a single-sex school bears a rational relationship to the State's legitimate interest "in providing the greatest practical range of educational opportunities for its female student population." Furthermore, the court stated, the admissions policy is not arbitrary because providing single-sex schools is consistent with a respected, though by no means universally accepted, educational theory that single-sex education affords unique benefits to students. . . .

The Court of Appeals for the Fifth Circuit reversed, holding that, because the admissions policy discriminates on the basis of gender, the District Court improperly used a "rational relationship" test to judge the constitutionality of the policy. Instead, the Court of Appeals stated, the proper test is whether the State has carried the heavier burden of showing that the gender-based classification is substantially related to an important governmental objective. Recognizing that the State has a significant interest in providing educational opportunities for all its citizens, the court then found that the State had failed to show that providing a unique educational opportunity for females, but not for males, bears a substantial relationship to that interest. . . .

. . . .

[On rehearing, the State argued that § 901(a)(5) of Title IX exempted traditional single-sex admissions policies from the gender discrimination prohibition. The Court of Appeals rejected this argument. The Supreme Court granted certiorari and affirmed.]

. . . .

II

We begin our analysis aided by several firmly established principles. Because the challenged policy expressly discriminates among applicants on the basis of gender, it is subject to scrutiny under the Equal Protection Clause of the Fourteenth Amendment. That this statutory policy discriminates against males rather than against females does not exempt it from scrutiny or reduce the standard of review.[8] Our decisions also establish that the party seeking to uphold a statute that classifies individuals on the basis of their gender must carry the burden of showing an "exceedingly persuasive justification" for the classification. The burden is met only by showing at least that the classification serves "important governmental objectives and that the discriminatory means employed" are "substantially related to the achievement of those objectives."

Although the test for determining the validity of a gender-based classification is straightforward, it must be applied free of fixed notions concerning the roles and abilities of males and females. . . . Thus, if the statutory objective is to exclude or "protect" members of one gender because they are presumed to suffer from an inherent handicap or to be innately inferior, the objective itself is illegitimate. . . .

If the State's objective is legitimate and important, we next determine whether the requisite direct, substantial relationship between objective and means is present. The purpose of requiring that close relationship is to assure that the

[8] Without question, MUW's admissions policy worked to Hogan's disadvantage. Although Hogan could have attended classes and received credit in one of Mississippi's state-supported coeducational nursing programs, none of which was located in Columbus, he could attend only by driving a considerable distance from his home. A similarly situated female would not have been required to choose between forgoing credit and bearing that inconvenience. Moreover, since many students enrolled in the School of Nursing hold full-time jobs, . . . Hogan's female colleagues had available an opportunity, not open to Hogan, to obtain credit for additional training. . . .

validity of a classification is determined through reasoned analysis rather than through the mechanical application of traditional, often inaccurate, assumptions about the proper roles of men and women. . . .

. . . .

III

A

The State's primary justification for maintaining the single-sex admissions policy of MUW's School of Nursing is that it compensates for discrimination against women and, therefore, constitutes educational affirmative action.[13] As applied to the School of Nursing, we find the State's argument unpersuasive.

In limited circumstances, a gender-based classification favoring one sex can be justified if it intentionally and directly assists members of the sex that is disproportionately burdened. See *Schlesinger v. Ballard*, 419 U.S. 498 (1975). However, we consistently have emphasized that "the mere recitation of a benign, compensatory purpose is not an automatic shield which protects against any inquiry into the actual purposes underlying a statutory scheme." *Weinberger v. Wiesenfeld*, 420 U.S. 636, 648 (1975). . . .

It is readily apparent that a State can evoke a compensatory purpose to justify an otherwise discriminatory classification only if members of the gender benefited by the classification actually suffer a disadvantage related to the classification. We considered such a situation in *Califano v. Webster*, 430 U.S. 313 (1977), which involved a challenge to a statutory classification that allowed women to eliminate more low-earning years than men for purposes of computing Social Security retirement benefits. Although the effect of the classification was to allow women higher monthly benefits than were available to men with the same earning history, we upheld the statutory scheme, noting that it took into account that women "as such have been unfairly hindered from earning as much as men" and "[worked] directly to remedy" the resulting economic disparity. *Id.*, at 318.

A similar pattern of discrimination against women influenced our decision in *Schlesinger v. Ballard, supra.* There, we considered a federal statute that granted female Naval officers a 13-year tenure of commissioned service before mandatory discharge, but accorded male officers only a 9-year tenure. We recognized that, because women were barred from combat duty, they had had fewer opportunities for promotion than had their male counterparts. By allowing women an additional four years to reach a particular rank before subjecting them to mandatory discharge, the statute directly compensated for other statutory barriers to advancement.

---

[13] In the reply brief, the State understandably retreated from its contention that MUW was founded to provide opportunities for women which were not available to men. . . . Apparently, the impetus for founding MUW came not from a desire to provide women with advantages superior to those offered men, but rather from a desire to provide white women in Mississippi access to state-supported higher learning. . . .

In sharp contrast, Mississippi has made no showing that women lacked opportunities to obtain training in the field of nursing or to attain positions of leadership in that field when the MUW School of Nursing opened its door or that women currently are deprived of such opportunities. . . . [Justice O'Connor presented data indicating that 94 percent of nursing degrees in Mississippi and nearly 99 percent of the nursing degrees nationwide were conferred on women.]. . . .

Rather than compensate for discriminatory barriers faced by women, MUW's policy of excluding males from admission to the School of Nursing tends to perpetuate the stereotyped view of nursing as an exclusively woman's job. . . . Thus, we conclude that, although the State recited a "benign, compensatory purpose," it failed to establish that the alleged objective is the actual purpose underlying the discriminatory classification.

The policy is invalid also because it fails the second part of the equal protection test, for the State has made no showing that the gender-based classification is substantially and directly related to its proposed compensatory objective. To the contrary, MUW's policy of permitting men to attend classes as auditors fatally undermines its claim that women, at least those in the School of Nursing, are adversely affected by the presence of men.

MUW permits men who audit to participate fully in classes. Additionally, both men and women take part in continuing education courses offered by the School of Nursing, in which regular nursing students also can enroll. The uncontroverted record reveals that admitting men to nursing classes does not affect teaching style, that the presence of men in the classroom would not affect the performance of the female nursing students, and that men in coeducational nursing schools do not dominate the classroom. In sum, the record in this case is flatly inconsistent with the claim that excluding men from the School of Nursing is necessary to reach any of MUW's educational goals.

Thus, considering both the asserted interest and the relationship between the interest and the methods used by the State, we conclude that the State has fallen far short of establishing the "exceedingly persuasive justification" needed to sustain the gender-based classification. Accordingly, we hold that MUW's policy of denying males the right to enroll for credit in its School of Nursing violates the Equal Protection Clause of the Fourteenth Amendment.

B

. . . [T]he State contends that MUW is the direct beneficiary "of specific congressional legislation which, on its face, permits the institution to exist as it has in the past." The argument is based upon the language of § 901(a) in Title IX of the Education Amendments of 1972, 20 U. S. C. § 1681(a). . . .

The argument requires little comment. Initially, it is far from clear that Congress intended, through § 901(a)(5), to exempt MUW from any constitutional obligation. Rather, Congress apparently intended, at most, to exempt MUW from the requirements of Title IX.

Even if Congress envisioned a constitutional exemption, the State's argument would fail. Section 5 of the Fourteenth Amendment gives Congress broad power indeed to enforce the command of the Amendment and "to secure to all persons the enjoyment of perfect equality of civil rights and the equal protection of the laws against State denial or invasion . . . ." *Ex parte Virginia*, 100 U.S. 339, 346 (1880). Congress' power under § 5, however, "is limited to adopting measures to enforce the guarantees of the Amendment; § 5 grants Congress no power to restrict, abrogate, or dilute these guarantees." *Katzenbach v. Morgan*, 384 U.S. 641, 651, n. 10 (1966). . . .

. . . .

IV

Because we conclude that the State's policy of excluding males from MUW's School of Nursing violates the Equal Protection Clause of the Fourteenth Amendment, we affirm the judgment of the Court of Appeals.

It is so ordered.

[The dissenting opinions of Chief Justice Burger and Justices Blackmun and Powell are omitted.]

UNITED STATES v. VIRGINIA
518 U.S. 515 (1996)

Justice Ginsburg delivered the opinion of the Court.

. . . .

I

Founded in 1839, VMI [Virginia Military Institute] is today the sole single-sex school among Virginia's 15 public institutions of higher learning. VMI's distinctive mission is to produce "citizen-soldiers," men prepared for leadership in civilian life and in military service. VMI pursues this mission through pervasive training of a kind not available anywhere else in Virginia. Assigning prime place to character development, VMI uses an "adversative method" modeled on English public schools and once characteristic of military instruction. VMI constantly endeavors to instill physical and mental discipline in its cadets and impart to them a strong moral code. The school's graduates leave VMI with heightened comprehension of their capacity to deal with duress and stress, and a large sense of accomplishment for completing the hazardous course.

. . . .

Neither the goal of producing citizen-soldiers nor VMI's implementing methodology is inherently unsuitable to women. And the school's impressive record in producing leaders has made admission desirable to some women. Nevertheless, Virginia has elected to preserve exclusively for men the advantages and opportunities a VMI education affords.

II

A

. . . .

[Justice Ginsburg discussed how VMI's goal is to produce "citizen-soldiers" through an adversative system that includes a lack of privacy, strict behavioral regulations, "a hierarchical 'class system,' " and stringent honor code, ultimately resulting in close bonds amongst cadets].

. . . .

B

[A lawsuit by the United States against Virginia and VMI ultimately resulted in the Fourth Circuit Court of Appeals expressing doubt that VMI's policy of excluding women was a face of the state's goal of "autonomy and diversity" and that VMI's adversative method was not "inherently unsuitable to women." The Fourth Circuit did agree that coeducation would materially affect VMI's program, and therefore gave Virginia the choice of selecting one of three remedial options. "Admit women to VMI; establish parallel institutions or programs; or abandon state support, leaving VMI free to pursue its policies as a private institution."] . . .

C

In response to the Fourth Circuit's ruling, Virginia proposed a parallel program for women: Virginia Women's Institute for Leadership (VWIL). The 4-year, state-sponsored undergraduate program would be located at Mary Baldwin College, a private liberal arts school for women, and would be open, initially, to about 25 to 30 students. Although VWIL would share VMI's mission — to produce "citizen-soldiers" — the VWIL program would differ, as does Mary Baldwin College, from VMI in academic offerings, methods of education, and financial resources. See 852 F. Supp. 471, 476-477 (WD Va. 1994).

The average combined SAT score of entrants at Mary Baldwin is about 100 points lower than the score for VMI freshmen. Mary Baldwin's faculty holds "significantly fewer Ph.D.'s than the faculty at VMI," *id.*, at 502, and receives significantly lower salaries. . . . While VMI offers degrees in liberal arts, the sciences, and engineering, Mary Baldwin, at the time of trial, offered only bachelor of arts degrees. A VWIL student seeking to earn an engineering degree could gain one, without public support, by attending Washington University in St. Louis, Missouri, for two years, paying the required private tuition.

. . . .

. . . In lieu of VMI's adversative method, the VWIL Task Force favored "a cooperative method which reinforces self-esteem." *Id.*, at 476. In addition to the standard bachelor of arts program offered at Mary Baldwin, VWIL students would take courses in leadership, complete an off-campus leadership externship, participate in community service projects, and assist in arranging a speaker series.

. . . .

D

. . . .

[The District Court approved of Virginia's plan, holding that Virginia did not need "to provide a mirror image" of the VMI methodology for women. The Fourth Circuit affirmed, noting that "women could not be accommodated in the VMI plan" without eliminating " 'any sense of decency that still permeates the relationship between the sexes.' "]

. . . .

. . . Exclusion of "men at Mary Baldwin College and women at VMI," the court said, was essential to Virginia's purpose, for without such exclusion, the Commonwealth could not "accomplish [its] objective of providing single-gender education." *Ibid.*

. . . The court . . . added another inquiry, a decisive test it called "substantive comparability." *Ibid.* The key question, the court said, was whether men at VMI and women at VWIL would obtain "substantively comparable benefits at their institution or through other means offered by the State." *Ibid.* Although the appeals court recognized that the VWIL degree "lacks the historical benefit and prestige" of a VMI degree, it nevertheless found the educational opportunities at the two schools "sufficiently comparable." *Id.*, at 1241.

. . . .

The Fourth Circuit denied rehearing en banc. . . .

III

The cross-petitions in this case present two ultimate issues. First, does Virginia's exclusion of women from the educational opportunities provided by VMI — extraordinary opportunities for military training and civilian leadership development — deny to women "capable of all of the individual activities required of VMI cadets," 766 F. Supp., at 1412, the equal protection of the laws guaranteed by the Fourteenth Amendment? Second, if VMI's "unique" situation, *id.*, at 1413 — as Virginia's sole single-sex public institution of higher education — offends the Constitution's equal protection principle, what is the remedial requirement?

IV

. . . .

Today's skeptical scrutiny of official action denying rights or opportunities based on sex responds to volumes of history. As a plurality of this Court acknowledged a generation ago, "our Nation has had a long and unfortunate history of sex discrimination." *Frontiero v. Richardson*, 411 U.S. 677, 684 (1973). . . .

In 1971, for the first time in our Nation's history, this Court ruled in favor of a woman who complained that her State had denied her the equal protection of its laws. *Reed v. Reed*, 404 U.S. 71, 73 (holding unconstitutional Idaho Code prescription that, among " 'several persons claiming and equally entitled to administer [a decedent's estate], males must be preferred to females' "). Since *Reed*, the Court has repeatedly recognized that neither federal nor state government acts compatibly with the equal protection principle when a law or official policy denies to women, simply because they are women, full citizenship stature — equal opportunity to aspire, achieve, participate in and contribute to society based on their individual talents and capacities. . . .

. . . To summarize the Court's current directions for cases of official classification based on gender: Focusing on the differential treatment or denial of opportunity for which relief is sought, the reviewing court must determine whether the proffered justification is "exceedingly persuasive." The burden of justification is demanding and it rests entirely on the State. See *Mississippi Univ. for Women*, 458 U.S. at 724. The State must show "at least that the [challenged] classification serves important governmental objectives and that the discriminatory means employed are substantially related to the achievement of those objectives." *Ibid.* [internal quotation marks omitted]. The justification must be genuine, not hypothesized or invented *post hoc* in response to litigation. And it must not rely on overbroad generalizations about the different talents, capacities, or preferences of males and females. . . . .

The heightened review standard our precedent establishes does not make sex a proscribed classification. Supposed "inherent differences" are no longer accepted as a ground for race or national origin classifications. See *Loving v. Virginia*, 388 U.S. 1 (1967). Physical differences between men and women, however, are enduring: "The two sexes are not fungible; a community made up exclusively of one [sex] is different from a community composed of both." *Ballard v. United States*, 329 U.S. 187, 193 (1946).

"Inherent differences" between men and women, we have come to appreciate, remain cause for celebration, but not for denigration of the members of either sex or for artificial constraints on an individual's opportunity. Sex classifications may be used to compensate women "for particular economic disabilities [they have] suffered," *Califano v. Webster*, 430 U.S. 313, 320 (1977) *(per curiam)*, to "promote equal employment opportunity". . . . But such classifications may not be used, as they once were, see *Goesaert*, 335 U.S. at 467, to create or perpetuate the legal, social, and economic inferiority of women.

Measuring the record in this case against the review standard just described, we conclude that Virginia has shown no "exceedingly persuasive justification" for excluding all women from the citizen-soldier training afforded by VMI. We therefore affirm the Fourth Circuit's initial judgment, which held that Virginia had violated the Fourteenth Amendment's Equal Protection Clause. Because the remedy proffered by Virginia — the Mary Baldwin VWIL program — does not cure the constitutional violation, *i.e.*, it does not provide equal opportunity, we reverse the Fourth Circuit's final judgment in this case.

V

. . . Virginia . . . asserts two justifications in defense of VMI's exclusion of women. First, the Commonwealth contends, "single-sex education provides important educational benefits," and the option of single-sex education contributes to "diversity in educational approaches." Second, the Commonwealth argues, "the unique VMI method of character development and leadership training," the school's adversative approach, would have to be modified were VMI to admit women. We consider these two justifications in turn.

A

. . . Virginia has not shown that VMI was established, or has been maintained, with a view to diversifying, by its categorical exclusion of women, educational opportunities within the Commonwealth. In cases of this genre, our precedent instructs that "benign" justifications proffered in defense of categorical exclusions will not be accepted automatically; a tenable justification must describe actual state purposes, not rationalizations for actions in fact differently grounded. . . .

. . . .

Neither recent nor distant history bears out Virginia's alleged pursuit of diversity through single-sex educational options. In 1839, when the Commonwealth established VMI, a range of educational opportunities for men and women was scarcely contemplated. Higher education at the time was considered dangerous for women; reflecting widely held views about women's proper place, the Nation's first universities and colleges — for example, Harvard in Massachusetts, William and Mary in Virginia — admitted only men. . . . VMI was not at all novel in this respect[]. . . .

Virginia describes the current absence of public single-sex higher education for women as "an historical anomaly." But the historical record indicates action more deliberate than anomalous: First, protection of women against higher education; next, schools for women far from equal in resources and stature to schools for men; finally, conversion of the separate schools to coeducation. The state legislature, prior to the advent of this controversy, had repealed "all Virginia statutes requiring individual institutions to admit only men or women." 766 F. Supp., at 1419. . . .

Our 1982 decision in *Mississippi Univ. for Women* prompted VMI to reexamine its male-only admission policy. Virginia relies on that reexamination as a legitimate basis for maintaining VMI's single-sex character. A Mission Study Committee, appointed by the VMI Board of Visitors, studied the problem from October 1983 until May 1986, and in that month counseled against "change of VMI status as a single-sex college." See 766 F. Supp. at 1429 (internal quotation marks omitted). Whatever internal purpose the Mission Study Committee served — and however well meaning the framers of the report — we can hardly extract from that effort any commonwealth policy evenhandedly to advance diverse educational options. As the District Court observed, the Committee's analysis "primarily focused on anticipated difficulties in attracting females to VMI," and the report, overall, supplied "very little indication of how the conclusion was reached." *Ibid.*

In sum, we find no persuasive evidence in this record that VMI's male-only admission policy "is in furtherance of a state policy of 'diversity.' " See 976 F.2d, at 899. No such policy, the Fourth Circuit observed, can be discerned from the movement of all other public colleges and universities in Virginia away from single-sex education. That court also questioned "how one institution with autonomy, but with no authority over any other state institution, can give effect to a state policy of diversity among institutions." *Ibid.* A purpose genuinely to advance an array of educational options, as the Court of Appeals recognized, is not served by VMI's historic and constant plan — a plan to "afford a unique educational benefit only to males." *Ibid.* However "liberally" this plan serves the Commonwealth's sons, it makes no provision whatever for her daughters. That is not *equal* protection.

B

Virginia next argues that VMI's adversative method of training provides educational benefits that cannot be made available, unmodified, to women. Alterations to accommodate women would necessarily be "radical," so "drastic," Virginia asserts, as to transform, indeed "destroy," VMI's program. Neither sex would be favored by the transformation, Virginia maintains: Men would be deprived of the unique opportunity currently available to them; women would not gain that opportunity because their participation would "eliminate the very aspects of [the] program that distinguish [VMI] from . . . other institutions of higher education in Virginia."

The District Court forecast from expert witness testimony, and the Court of Appeals accepted, that coeducation would materially affect "at least these three aspects of VMI's program — physical training, the absence of privacy, and the adversative approach." 976 F.2d, at 896-897. And it is uncontested that women's admission would require accommodations, primarily in arranging housing assignments and physical training programs for female cadets. It is also undisputed, however, that "the VMI methodology could be used to educate women." 852 F. Supp., at 481. The District Court even allowed that some women may prefer it to the methodology a women's college might pursue. . . . The parties, furthermore, agree that "*some* women can meet the physical standards [VMI] now impose[s] on men." 976 F.2d, at 896. In sum, as the Court of Appeals stated, "neither the goal of producing citizen soldiers," VMI's *raison d'etre*, "nor VMI's implementing methodology is inherently unsuitable to women." *Id.*, at 899.

In support of its initial judgment for Virginia, a judgment rejecting all equal protection objections presented by the United States, the District Court made "findings" on "gender-based developmental differences." 766 F. Supp., at 1434-1435. These "findings" restate the opinions of Virginia's expert witnesses, opinions about typically male or typically female "tendencies." *Id.*, at 1434. For example, "males tend to need an atmosphere of adversativeness," while "females tend to thrive in a cooperative atmosphere." *Ibid.* . . .

The United States does not challenge any expert witness estimation on average capacities or preferences of men and women. Instead, the United States emphasizes that time and again since this Court's turning point decision in *Reed v. Reed*, 404 U.S. 71 (1971), we have cautioned reviewing courts to take a "hard look" at generalizations or "tendencies" of the kind pressed by Virginia, and relied upon by the District Court. . . . State actors controlling gates to opportunity, we have instructed, may not exclude qualified individuals based on "fixed notions concerning the roles and abilities of males and females." *Mississippi Univ. for Women*, 458 U.S. at 725. . . .

. . . Education, to be sure, is not a "one size fits all" business. The issue, however, is not whether "women — or men — should be forced to attend VMI"; rather, the question is whether the Commonwealth can constitutionally deny to women who have the will and capacity, the training and attendant opportunities that VMI uniquely affords.

The notion that admission of women would downgrade VMI's stature, destroy the adversative system and, with it, even the school, is a judgment hardly proved, a prediction hardly different from other "self-fulfilling prophec[ies]," see *Mississippi Univ. for Women*, 458 U.S. at 730, once routinely used to deny rights or opportunities. When women first sought admission to the bar and access to legal education, concerns of the same order were expressed. . . .

. . . .

Virginia and VMI trained their argument on "means" rather than "end," and thus misperceived our precedent. Single-sex education at VMI serves an "important governmental objective," they maintained, and exclusion of women is not only "substantially related," it is essential to that objective. By this notably circular argument, the "straightforward" test *Mississippi Univ. for Women* described, see 458 U.S. at 724-725, was bent and bowed.

. . . Surely that goal [of producing citizen soldiers] is great enough to accommodate women, who today count as citizens in our American democracy equal in stature to men. Just as surely, the Commonwealth's great goal is not substantially advanced by women's categorical exclusion, in total disregard of their individual merit, from the Commonwealth's premier "citizen-soldier" corps. Virginia, in sum, "has fallen far short of establishing the 'exceedingly persuasive justification,' " *Mississippi Univ. for Women*, 458 U.S. at 731, that must be the solid base for any gender-defined classification.

VI

. . . .

A

A remedial decree, this Court has said, must closely fit the constitutional violation; it must be shaped to place persons unconstitutionally denied an opportunity or advantage in "the position they would have occupied in the absence of [discrimination]." See *Milliken v. Bradley*, 433 U.S. 267, 280 (1977). . . . A proper remedy for an unconstitutional exclusion, we have explained, aims to "eliminate [so far as possible] the discriminatory effects of the past" and to "bar like discrimination in the future." *Louisiana v. United States*, 380 U.S. 145, 154 (1965).

Virginia chose not to eliminate, but to leave untouched, VMI's exclusionary policy.

For women only, however, Virginia proposed a separate program, different in kind from VMI and unequal in tangible and intangible facilities. . . .

VWIL affords women no opportunity to experience the rigorous military training for which VMI is famed. . . . Instead, the VWIL program "deemphasize[s]" military education, 44 F.3d, at 1234, and uses a "cooperative method" of education "which reinforces self-esteem," 852 F. Supp., at 476.

VWIL students participate in ROTC and a "largely ceremonial" Virginia Corps of Cadets, see 44 F.3d, at 1234, but Virginia deliberately did not make VWIL a military institute. The VWIL House is not a military-style residence and VWIL students need not live together throughout the 4-year program, eat meals together, or wear uniforms during the school day. VWIL students thus do not experience the "barracks" life "crucial to the VMI experience," the spartan living arrangements designed to foster an "egalitarian ethic." See 766 F. Supp., at 1423-1424. "The most important aspects of the VMI educational experience occur in the barracks," the District Court found, *id.*, at 1423, yet Virginia deemed that core experience nonessential, indeed inappropriate, for training its female citizen-soldiers.

VWIL students receive their "leadership training" in seminars, externships, and speaker series, episodes and encounters lacking the "physical rigor, mental stress, . . . minute regulation of behavior, and indoctrination in desirable values" made hallmarks of VMI's citizen-soldier training, see 766 F. Supp., at 1421. Kept away from the pressures, hazards, and psychological bonding characteristic of VMI's adversative training, VWIL students will not know the "feeling of tremendous accomplishment" commonly experienced by VMI's successful cadets, *id.*, at 1426.

Virginia maintains that these methodological differences are "justified pedagogically," based on "important differences between men and women in learning and developmental needs," "psychological and sociological differences" Virginia describes as "real" and "not stereotypes." The Task Force charged with developing the leadership program for women, drawn from the staff and faculty at Mary Baldwin College, "determined that a military model and, especially VMI's adversative method, would be wholly inappropriate for educating and training *most women.*" 852 F. Supp., at 476 (emphasis added). . . .

As earlier stated, generalizations about "the way women are," estimates of what is appropriate for *most women*, no longer justify denying opportunity to women whose talent and capacity place them outside the average description. Notably, Virginia never asserted that VMI's method of education suits *most men.* It is also revealing that Virginia accounted for its failure to make the VWIL experience "the entirely militaristic experience of VMI" on the ground that VWIL "is planned for women who do not necessarily expect to pursue military careers." 852 F. Supp., at 478. By that reasoning, VMI's "entirely militaristic" program would be inappropriate for men in general or *as a group*, for "only about 15% of VMI cadets enter career military service." See 766 F. Supp., at 1432.

. . . .

B

. . . .

[Justice Gisburg discussed how Mary Baldwin's academic curriculum, faculty, athletic facilities, prestige and endowment all fall far short of VMI's. Additionally the VWIL graduates will not receive equal access to VMI's alumni network]

. . . .

Virginia, in sum, while maintaining VMI for men only, has failed to provide any "comparable single-gender women's institution." Instead, the Commonwealth has created a VWIL program fairly appraised as a "pale shadow" of VMI in terms of the range of curricular choices and faculty stature, funding, prestige, alumni support and influence.

. . . .

VII

. . . .

A prime part of the history of our Constitution, historian Richard Morris recounted, is the story of the extension of constitutional rights and protections to people once ignored or excluded. [See R. Morris, The Forging of the Union, 1781-1789, p. 193 (1987).] VMI's story continued as our comprehension of "We the People" expanded. There is no reason to believe that the admission of women capable of all the activities required of VMI cadets would destroy the Institute rather than enhance its capacity to serve the "more perfect Union."

For the reasons stated, the initial judgment of the Court of Appeals, 976 F.2d 890 (CA4 1992), is affirmed, the final judgment of the Court of Appeals, 44 F.3d 1229 (CA4 1995), is reversed, and the case is remanded for further proceedings consistent with this opinion.

It is so ordered.

Justice Thomas took no part in the consideration or decision of this case.

[Chief Justice Rehnquist's concurring opinion and Justice Scalia's dissenting opinion have been omitted.]

NOTES

1. The discussion and the related claims of the parties in *United States v. Virginia*, in the 1990s, recall the more historical discussions of the "separate but equal" doctrine from the days of *Plessy v. Ferguson* and *Brown v. Board of Education.* Is it clear that single-sex universities continue to exist lawfully? How so, considering the overruling of the "separate but equal" doctrine in *Brown v. Board of Education*?

There are important and applicable exemptions from anti-discrimination laws like Title IX. For instance, under 20 U.S.C. § 1681(a)(5), Title IX does not apply to "any public institution of undergraduate higher education which is an institution that traditionally and continually from its establishment has had a policy of admitting only students of one sex." Also of interest may be the exemption of social fraternities and sororities, which are exempt from taxation under section 501(a) of the Internal Revenue Code. 20 U.S.C. § 1681(a)(6). See also the coverage of *Grove City College v. Bell*, 465 U.S. 555 (1984), in the next section of the chapter.

2. The first time around, the Court of Appeals in the *VMI* case struck down VMI's policy and gave three directives to the university. What were those three options? The second time around, the Court of Appeals approved VMI's implementation of one of those options. Which one did VMI choose? The Supreme Court, however, struck down the chosen option. Why?

3. What is the judicial standard for sex discrimination under the Fourteenth Amendment Equal Protection Clause? Why is it different from the standard applied in cases involving race and national origin?

4. Before the *VMI* case landed at the Supreme Court, another noteworthy case involving sex discrimination at a previously all-male public institution received quite a lot of press. In *Faulkner v. The Citadel*, 51 F.3d 440 (4th Cir. 1995), Shannon Faulkner applied for regular admission to The Citadel not revealing that she was a woman. Initially, the college admitted her, but revoked the admission once Shannon's sex was discovered. The Court of Appeals for the Fourth Circuit found The Citadel's admissions policy violative of the Equal Protection Clause of the Fourteenth Amendment. Faulkner was permitted to enroll immediately. The Court of Appeals then modified and remanded the district court's plan that instructed the college to immediately accept women. Instead, the court held that the university should have been allowed to fashion one of three remedies, identical to those presented to VMI: (1) admit women; (2) create a separate college for women; or (3) forfeit state funds from the college. Following the Supreme Court's decision in *United States v. Virginia*, The Citadel announced that it was admitting women. *Faulkner v. Jones*, 136 F.3d 342 (4th Cir. 1998).

5. What are the laws and policies with respect to disability and college admissions? Under Section 504 of the Rehabilitation Act of 1973, "no otherwise qualified individual with a disability . . . shall, solely by reason of his or her disability, be excluded from the participation in, be denied the benefits of, or be subjected to discrimination under any program or activity receiving Federal financial assistance." 29 U.S.C. § 794(a). Similarly, the Americans with Disabilities Act, 42 U.S.C. § 12101, *et seq.*, prohibits discrimination because of a person's disability as well. With respect to admission and recruitment, the federal regulations for Section 504 prohibit the use of quotas (limitations on the number of people with disabilities admitted), the use of admissions tests that have a disproportionate, adverse effect on people with disabilities (unless such tests are valid and predictive of success), and the inquiry into the disability status of any applicant. *See* 34 C.F.R. § 104.42.

Note, though, that the applicant must be "otherwise qualified," meaning the applicant must be able to perform the essential functions of the program to which he or she is applying in spite of his or her disability. Universities are required to offer reasonable accommodations (e.g., physical and time-based accommodations), but the applicant must still meet the academic and technical standards required for admission. *See Southeastern Cmty. Coll. v. Davis*, 442 U.S. 397 (1979), presented in Chapter XIII. Reasonable accommodations are a part of the "otherwise qualified" analysis. See *Doherty v. Southern College of Optometry*, 862 F.2d 570 (6th Cir. 1988), presented earlier in this chapter.

6. What are your thoughts on in-state versus out-of-state tuition, or other financial aid for students who are illegal immigrants? Under 8 U.S.C. § 1623(a), part of the Illegal Immigration Reform and Immigrant Responsibility Act of 1996,

> an alien who is not lawfully present in the United States shall not be eligible on the basis of residence within a State (or a political subdivision) for any postsecondary education benefit unless a citizen or national of the United States is eligible for such a benefit (in no less an amount, duration, and scope) without regard to whether the citizen or national is such a resident.

Several states have passed laws that provide in-state tuition benefits for illegal immigrants, essentially circumventing the federal law. Most of these state laws condition benefits on the student having completed some or all of high school in that state. What are the pros and cons of such laws?

Litigation under these laws is limited. One noteworthy case is *Day v. Bond*, where the Tenth Circuit dismissed the claims of out-of-state parents and students who argued that in-state tuition benefits granted to illegal immigrants in Kansas violated the Equal Protection Clause of the Fourteenth Amendment. 500 F.3d 1127 (10th Cir.), *reh'g, en banc, denied*, 511 F.3d 1030 (10th Cir. 2007), *cert. denied*, 2008 U.S. LEXIS 5064 (U.S. June 23, 2008). The court held that the plaintiffs had no standing to sue, in that they failed to show that granting in-state tuition to illegal immigrants denied them any benefits under the law. Even if the Kansas law were struck down, the plaintiffs would receive no additional benefits, as they would continue to be ineligible for in-state tuition.

At the federal level, the U.S. Congress, in late 2010, failed to pass the DREAM Act (Development, Relief and Education for Alien Minors Act), which would have provided certain illegal immigrants the opportunity to earn permanent residency if they complete two years of military service or two years of college at a four-year university. To qualify under the DREAM Act, a person must meet several requirements, including the following: (1) must be between the ages of 12 and 29 when the law is enacted, (2) must have arrived in the U.S. before the age of 16, (3) must have resided in the U.S. for at least five consecutive years since the date of arrival, (4) must have graduated from a U.S. high school, or obtained a GED, and (5) must have "good moral character," as determined by the U.S. Department of Homeland Security. The DREAM Act, as considered in the 2010 Congress, did not require states to offer in-state tuition to illegal immigrants. The Act passed in the House, but failed in the Senate.

C. FINANCIAL AID

1. Financial Aid and Contractual Relationships

REVAY v. CLEVELAND STATE UNIVERSITY

Case No. 2002-04003-AD
2003 Ohio Misc. LEXIS 74 (Ohio Ct. Cl. Jan. 7, 2003)

MEMORANDUM DECISION

During the spring semester of 2001, plaintiff, George A. Revay, a student enrolled at defendant, Cleveland State University (CSU), applied for financial aid for the 2001 summer semester. Plaintiff had been attending classes at CSU since 1993 and had completed over 200 hours of class credit[] . . . when he applied for financial aid covering the 2001 summer semester.

On March 26, 2001, defendant university sent plaintiff a letter notifying him that he was being offered a "Part-time Ohio Instructional Grant" of $500.00 for the 2001 summer semester. The letter notifying plaintiff of a financial assistance grant also contained the following: ". . . Cleveland State University reserves the right to adjust any aid offered based on verification of eligibility and enrollment status."

For the 2001 summer semester plaintiff enrolled in one class, Physics-242. . . .

Plaintiff indicated, after the end of the summer semester at some time during August 2001, he received written notice and a voice mail from defendant regarding an eligibility problem with the $500.00 financial aid grant for the 2001 summer semester. Plaintiff stated he was notified by defendant to file a petition to reinstate his financial aid eligibility for the 2001 summer semester. Plaintiff asserted he had previously filed a reinstatement petition, but defendant's financial aid office personnel denied receiving it. Therefore, plaintiff maintained he filed a second reinstatement petition. Plaintiff submitted a letter addressed to him from the university's financial aid office dated August 2, 2001. This letter informed plaintiff his petition for reinstatement of financial aid had been reviewed and reinstatement had been denied. . . .

. . . .

The letter also contained the following written defined guidelines for Satisfactory Academic Progress:

> . . . .
>
> "Total Allowable Attempted Hours (Maximum Time frame). The timely completion of degree requirements. As an undergraduate student you can attempt no more than 192 Credit hours (150% of the required total credit hours to complete a degree program at CSU)."

When plaintiff's petition for reinstatement of financial aid was denied he was charged $500.00 for the Physics-242 class he had taken leaving an unpaid balance on his student account. . . . An outstanding balance of $500.00 remained on plaintiff's student account with an additional late fee charge of $15.00 added on February 13, 2002. . . .

Consequently, plaintiff filed this complaint attempting to appeal the decisions of defendant's administrators in revoking plaintiff's financial aid and denying plaintiff's petition to withdraw from class. Plaintiff has requested this court absolve him of the $515.00 debt he was assessed or alternatively grant his late withdrawal from class with full tuition reimbursement of $853.00. . . .

. . . .

CSU filed an investigation report acknowledging plaintiff was initially granted financial aid for the 2001 summer semester, which was subsequently revoked based on plaintiff's failure to comply with Satisfactory Academic Progress (SAP) requirements. Defendant indicated SAP eligibility requirements are mandated by federal regulations. . . . Specifically, plaintiff became ineligible to receive financial aid by exceeding the maximum time frame [192 hours] for receiving a bachelor's degree. . . . Defendant related plaintiff had successfully petitioned for reinstatement of financial aid eligibility prior to the 2001 summer semester. Defendant's records indicated letters with attached reinstatement petitions were sent to plaintiff on June 20, 2001 and June 21, 2001 notifying him that he had exceeded the maximum time frame and was required to file a reinstatement petition for consideration of financial aid eligibility. Defendant asserted the university Financial Aid Office had not received plaintiff's reinstatement petition as of July 27, 2001. Therefore, defendant's personnel at the Financial Aid Office left a message with plaintiff advising him his reinstatement petition had not been received. Defendant related plaintiff's petition was delivered on July 31, 2001. On August 2, 2001, plaintiff's petition for reinstatement of financial aid eligibility was denied based on SAP standards regarding maximum time frame permitted. Plaintiff was notified of the decision and was billed $500.00, the amount of the financial aid denied.

Defendant insisted the university's SAP standards are clearly specific concerning reinstatement of financial aid eligibility. Defendant asserted proper procedures were followed when plaintiff's petition for reinstatement was denied. Defendant submitted a copy of the SAP Standards for financial aid eligibility requirements [, which outlined in detail the steps a student must take to petition for reinstatement, including forms to be completed, deadlines to be met, requests for statements of mitigating circumstances, offers to meet with advisors, and a requirement that all outstanding balances be paid if the petition is denied]. . . .

Defendant stated all SAP Standards are available in the university's catalogs and on its website. Therefore defendant contended plaintiff had access to all information regarding potential consequences resulting from a revocation of financial aid.

Furthermore, defendant asserted the denial of plaintiff's financial aid reinstatement petition was a determination made in adherence to federal regulations. Defendant apparently believed plaintiff, by needing 47 credits to earn a degree, was not making sufficient academic progress to justify reinstatement of aid in satisfaction of federal guidelines.

. . . .

. . . Plaintiff has asserted he relied on the representations of defendant's staff at the university's Financial Aid Office initially awarding him financial aid for the 2001 summer semester. Plaintiff insisted the revocation of his financial aid was not merited and was unjust.

. . . .

In the instant claim, both plaintiff and defendant were aware of the requirements for financial aid eligibility. Plaintiff had access to information which indicates he either knew or should have known his financial aid award could be revoked. Plaintiff acknowledged he was aware of consequential eligibility problems invoked by exceeding the maximum time frame for obtaining a degree. The fact plaintiff's prior petitions for reinstatement of aid were approved did not constitute a guarantee of approbation of subsequent petitions. Accordingly, the court concludes, plaintiff has failed to prove the decision to deny him financial aid was made improperly or fell outside the bounds of reasonable professional judgment. While the timing of defendant's revocation was unfortunate, the revocation itself did not create an actual event. Defendant had the authority and discretion to grant or deny plaintiff's petition for reinstatement. Under the facts of the instant claim, plaintiff cannot be absolved of a debt arising from defendant's proper act.

Alternatively, plaintiff has evoked some contentions he was defrauded by defendant in regard to the award and revocation of financial aid. Plaintiff has not established fraud. . . . In the present claim, plaintiff has failed to show defendant intended to mislead him about financial aid eligibility. . . . Evidence has shown plaintiff knew of his eligibility obstacle and any reliance professed about a preliminary grant of aid cannot be considered justifiable. Plaintiff has not presented a case of fraud.

In the same vein plaintiff has also failed to produce sufficient proof to invoke promissory estoppel. Promissory estoppel is defined as follows: "A promise which the promisor should reasonably expect to induce action or forbearance on the part of the promisee or a third person and which does induce such action or forbearance is binding if injustice can be avoided only by enforcement of the promise." Restatement of the Law, Contracts 2d (1973), Section 90. The promise of financial aid as characterized by plaintiff in the instant claim contained the following limitation: Cleveland State University reserves the right to adjust any aid offered based on verification of eligibility and enrollment status. The court concludes the initial offer of financial aid should not have been expected to produce action on the part of plaintiff since he knew of his eligibility difficulties. . . .

. . . .

NOTES

1. In *Revay*, the defendant university admitted that Revay's financial aid was revoked because he failed to meet academic progress standards and that he had exceeded the maximum time frame for the degree. But was this not the case before the university initially granted him the aid for the course? Revay had exceeded the maximum number of credits before he enrolled in the physics course. Shouldn't the university have denied the financial request before the course started? Revay argued that, once the university made the offer of financial aid knowing that Revay had exceeded credit hour maximums, it should be bound to that offer under a doctrine of promissory estoppel. The court rejected this argument. Why? Are you convinced by the court's reasoning? Why or why not?

2. Clearly, universities are driven to have strong fundraising and advancement divisions where donations and other gifts are solicited and received to fund, in part, student scholarships. A common question often arises: who has the authority to set scholarship amounts and recipients? Should it be the donors who establish the funds? After all, it is their money. Or is it best to leave such decision making up to the university officials who, presumably, know more about how to measure the merit-based and need-based criteria often found in the scholarship? In *Darcy v. Brown University*, No. KC 94-774, 1997 R.I. Super. LEXIS 34 (R.I. Super. Ct. Feb. 20, 1997), the court gave the university the discretion to make scholarship award decisions. Note, though, that the dispute in *Darcy* was not inspired by the primary donor to the fund. The suit was filed by a student who qualified for a scholarship that supported "needy" and "worthy" students. The student received funding, but felt she deserved more. The scholarship was established via the provisions of a will. The court held that by using imprecise terms like "needy" and "worthy," the will vested discretion in the university to make reasonable judgments regarding qualifications and resource distribution.

2. Financial Aid and the Relationship Between State and Federal Law

GROVE CITY COLLEGE v. BELL
465 U.S. 555 (1984)

Justice White delivered the opinion of the Court.

Section 901(a) of Title IX of the Education Amendments of 1972, . . . 20 U.S.C. § 1681(a), prohibits sex discrimination in "any education program or activity receiving Federal financial assistance," and § 902 directs agencies awarding most types of assistance to promulgate regulations to ensure that recipients adhere to that prohibition. Compliance with departmental regulations may be secured by termination of assistance "to the particular program, or part thereof, in which . . . noncompliance has been . . . found" or by "any other means authorized by law." § 902, 20 U.S.C. § 1682.

. . . We must decide, first, whether Title IX applies at all to Grove City College, which accepts no direct assistance but enrolls students who receive federal grants that must be used for educational purposes. If so, we must identify the "education program or activity" at Grove City that is "receiving Federal financial assistance" and determine whether federal assistance to that program may be terminated solely because the College violates the Department's regulations by refusing to execute an Assurance of Compliance with Title IX. . . .

I

Petitioner Grove City College is a private, coeducational, liberal arts college that has sought to preserve its institutional autonomy by consistently refusing state and federal financial assistance. Grove City's desire to avoid federal oversight has led it to decline to participate, not only in direct institutional aid programs, but also in federal student assistance programs under which the College would be required to assess students' eligibility and to determine the amounts of loans, work-study funds, or grants they should receive. Grove City has, however, enrolled a large number of students who receive Basic Educational Opportunity Grants (BEOG's) . . . under the Department of Education's Alternate Disbursement System (ADS).

The Department concluded that Grove City was a "recipient" of "Federal financial assistance" as those terms are defined in the regulations implementing Title IX, 34 CFR §§ 106.2(g)(1), (h) (1982), and, in July 1977, it requested that the College execute the Assurance of Compliance [with Title IX] required by 34 CFR § 106.4 (1983). . . .

When Grove City persisted in refusing to execute an Assurance, the Department initiated proceedings to declare the College and its students ineligible to receive BEOG's. The Administrative Law Judge held that the federal financial assistance received by Grove City obligated it to execute an Assurance of Compliance and entered an order terminating assistance until Grove City "corrects its noncompliance with Title IX. . . ."

Grove City and four of its students then commenced this action in the District Court for the Western District of Pennsylvania, which concluded that the students' BEOG's constituted "Federal financial assistance" to Grove City but held, on several grounds, that the Department could not terminate the students' aid because of the College's refusal to execute an Assurance of Compliance. . . . The Court of Appeals reversed. . . .

We granted certiorari and we now affirm. . . .

II

. . . Grove City first contends that neither it nor any "education program or activity" of the College receives any federal financial assistance within the meaning of Title IX by virtue of the fact that some of its students receive BEOG's and use them to pay for their education. We disagree.

Grove City provides a well-rounded liberal arts education and a variety of educational programs and student services. The question is whether any of those programs or activities "[receives] Federal financial assistance" within the meaning of Title IX when students finance their education with BEOG's. The structure of the Education Amendments of 1972, in which Congress both created the BEOG program and imposed Title IX's nondiscrimination requirement, strongly suggests an affirmative conclusion. BEOG's were aptly characterized as a "centerpiece of the bill," 118 Cong. Rec. 20297 (1972) (Rep. Pucinski), and Title IX "[related] directly to [its] central purpose." 117 Cong. Rec. 30412 (1971) (Sen. Bayh). In view of this connection and Congress' express recognition of discrimination in the administration of student financial aid programs, it would indeed be anomalous to discover that one of the primary components of Congress' comprehensive "package of federal aid," *id.*, at 2007 (Sen. Pell), was not intended to trigger coverage under Title IX.

. . . The linchpin of Grove City's argument that none of its programs receives any federal assistance is a perceived distinction between direct and indirect aid, a distinction that finds no support in the text of § 901(a). Nothing in § 901(a) suggests that Congress elevated form over substance by making the application of the nondiscrimination principle dependent on the manner in which a program or activity receives federal assistance. . . . As the Court of Appeals observed, "by its all inclusive terminology [§ 901(a)] appears to encompass *all* forms of federal aid to education, direct or indirect." . . .

. . . The economic effect of direct and indirect assistance often is indistinguishable, see *Mueller v. Allen*, 463 U.S. 388, 397, n. 6 (1983); *Committee for Public Education v. Nyquist*, 413 U.S. 756, 783 (1973); *Norwood v. Harrison*, 413 U.S. 455, 463-465 (1973), and the BEOG program was structured to ensure that it effectively supplements the College's own financial aid program. . . . In fact, one of the stated purposes of the student aid provisions was to "[provide] assistance to institutions of higher education." 20 U.S.C. § 1070(a)(5).

. . . Title IX was patterned after Title VI of the Civil Rights Act of 1964, 42 U.S.C. § 2000d *et seq*. . . . The drafters of Title VI envisioned that the receipt of student aid funds would trigger coverage, and, since they approved identical language, we discern no reason to believe that the Congressmen who voted for Title IX intended a different result.

. . . .

. . . There remains the question, however, of identifying the "education program or activity" of the College that can properly be characterized as "receiving" federal assistance through grants to some of the students attending the College.

III

. . . Although the legislative history contains isolated suggestions that entire institutions are subject to the nondiscrimination provision whenever one of their programs receives federal assistance, . . . we cannot accept the Court of Appeals' conclusion that in the circumstances present here Grove City itself is a "program or activity" that may be regulated in its entirety. Nevertheless, we find no merit in Grove City's contention that a decision treating BEOG's as "Federal financial assistance" cannot be reconciled with Title IX's program-specific language since BEOG's are not tied to any specific "education program or activity."

If Grove City participated in the BEOG program through the RDS [Regular Disbursement System, through the Department of Education, that send federal financial aid dollars directly to the institution], we would have no doubt that the "education program or activity receiving Federal financial assistance" would not be the entire College; rather, it would be its student financial aid program. . . .

We see no reason to reach a different conclusion merely because Grove City has elected to participate in the ADS [Alternate Disbursement System, in which BEOG funds are distributed directly to the students]. Although Grove City does not itself disburse students' awards, BEOG's clearly augment the resources that the College itself devotes to financial aid. As is true of the RDS, however, the fact that federal funds eventually reach the College's general operating budget cannot subject Grove City to institution-wide coverage. Grove City's choice of administrative mechanisms, we hold, neither expands nor contracts the breadth of the "program or activity" — the financial aid program — that receives federal assistance and that may be regulated under Title IX.

. . . .

We conclude that the receipt of BEOG's by some of Grove City's students does not trigger institutionwide coverage under Title IX. In purpose and effect, BEOG's represent federal financial assistance to the College's own financial aid program, and it is that program that may properly be regulated under Title IX.

IV

Since Grove City operates an "education program or activity receiving Federal financial assistance," the Department may properly demand that the College execute an Assurance of Compliance with Title IX. . . .

The Assurance of Compliance regulation itself does not, on its face, impose institutionwide obligations. Recipients must provide assurance only that "each education program or activity operated by . . . [them] *and to which this part applies* will be operated in compliance with this part." 34 CFR § 106.4 (1983) (emphasis added). The regulations apply, by their terms, "to every recipient and to *each education program or activity* operated by such recipient *which receives or benefits from Federal financial assistance.*" 34 CFR § 106.11 (1983) (emphasis added). . . . Nor does the Department now claim that its regulations reach beyond the College's student aid program. Furthermore, the Assurance of Compliance currently in use, like the one Grove City refused to execute, does not on its face purport to reach the entire College; it certifies compliance with respect to those "education programs and activities receiving Federal financial assistance." Under this opinion, consistent with the program-specific requirements of Title IX, the covered education program is the College's financial aid program.

A refusal to execute a proper program-specific Assurance of Compliance warrants termination of federal assistance to the student financial aid program. The College's contention that termination must be preceded by a finding of actual discrimination finds no support in the language of § 902, which plainly authorizes that sanction to effect "[compliance] with any requirement adopted pursuant to this section." . . . We conclude, therefore, that the Department may properly condition federal financial assistance on the recipient's assurance that it will conduct the aided program or activity in accordance with Title IX and the applicable regulations.

. . . .

Accordingly, the judgment of the Court of Appeals is

Affirmed.

NOTES

1. The Court of Appeals in *Grove City* held that if the educational institution receives any federal money at all, direct or indirect, it triggers institution-wide coverage of Title IX. The Supreme Court affirmed the Court of Appeals' ruling, but disagreed with the court on this particular point. Why? Do you agree with the Supreme Court's analysis on this issue? What's the impact of such analysis?

2. In comparison to *Grove City* and its interpretation of Title IX, similar arguments can be made with respect to other civil rights laws. The Court in *Grove City* noted that Title IX was patterned after Title VI of the Civil Rights Act and that the drafters of Title VI envisioned that the receipt of funds for student aid would trigger coverage. The Court of Appeals for the Fifth Circuit held similarly for Section 504 of the Rehabilitation Act of 1973. *Bennett-Nelson v. Louisiana Bd. of Regents*, 431 F.3d 448 (5th Cir. 2005) (university is an "intended recipient" of federal financial assistance for purposes of Section 504 when the university distributed federal financial aid to students, who then passed that money back to the university in the form of tuition payments).

3. Congress was not completely supportive of the *Grove City* decision. It subsequently enacted the Civil Rights Restoration Act of 1987 at least partially in response to Part III of the Supreme Court's decision in *Grove City. See Nat'l Collegiate Athletic Ass'n v. Smith*, 525 U.S. 459 (1999). Disagreeing with the conclusion that Title IX, as originally enacted, covered only the specific program receiving federal funding, Congress sought to reiterate the broad coverage of these antidiscrimination provisions in the CRRA. *See also Franklin v. Gwinnett County Public Schools*, 503 U.S. 60, 73 (1992) (noting that Congress endeavored, in the CRRA, "to correct what it considered to be an unacceptable decision on our part in *Grove City*").

3. Non-Discrimination and Affirmative Action in Financial Aid

LOCKE v. DAVEY
540 U.S. 712 (2004)

CHIEF JUSTICE REHNQUIST delivered the opinion of the Court.

. . . .

. . . In 1999, to assist these high-achieving students, the [State of Washington] created the Promise Scholarship Program, which provides a scholarship, renewable for one year, to eligible students for postsecondary education expenses. Students may spend their funds on any education-related expense, including room and board. The scholarships are funded through the State's general fund, and their amount varies each year depending on the annual appropriation, which is evenly prorated among the eligible students. . . .

To be eligible for the scholarship, a student . . . may not pursue a degree in [devotional] theology at that institution while receiving the scholarship. . . . Wash.

Rev. Code § 28B.10.814 (1997) ("No aid shall be awarded to any student who is pursuing a degree in theology"). . . . [T]he statute simply codifies the State's constitutional prohibition on providing funds to students to pursue degrees that are "devotional in nature or designed to induce religious faith." . . .

. . . The institution, rather than the State, determines whether the student's major is devotional. . . .

. . . .

[Respondent Davey was awarded a Promise Scholarship and attended Northwest College, a private Christian college eligible under the program. Respondent chose to pursue a "pastoral ministries degree" and was informed that he could not receive the scholarship as a result].

. . . .

Davey then brought an action under 42 USC § 1983 . . . to enjoin the State from refusing to award the scholarship. . . . He argued the denial of his scholarship based on his decision to pursue a theology degree violated . . . the Free Exercise, Establishment, and Free Speech Clauses of the First Amendment . . . and the Equal Protection Clause of the Fourteenth Amendment. . . . The District Court rejected Davey's constitutional claims and granted summary judgment in favor of the State.

A divided panel of the United States Court of Appeals for the Ninth Circuit reversed. The court concluded that the State had singled out religion for unfavorable treatment and thus under our decision in *Church of Lukumi Babalu Aye, Inc. v. Hialeah*, 508 U.S. 520 (1993), the State's exclusion of theology majors must be narrowly tailored to achieve a compelling state interest. Finding that the State's own antiestablishment concerns were not compelling, the court declared Washington's Promise Scholarship Program unconstitutional. We granted certiorari . . . and now reverse.

The Religion Clauses of the First Amendment provide: "Congress shall make no law respecting an establishment of religion, or prohibiting the free exercise thereof." These two Clauses, the Establishment Clause and the Free Exercise Clause, are frequently in tension. . . . Yet we have long said that "there is room for play in the joints" between them. *Walz v. Tax Comm'n of City of New York*, 397 U.S. 664, 669 (1970). In other words, there are some state actions permitted by the Establishment Clause but not required by the Free Exercise Clause.

. . . The question before us [] is whether Washington, pursuant to its own constitution,[2] which has been authoritatively interpreted as prohibiting even indirectly funding religious instruction that will prepare students for the ministry, . . . can deny them such funding without violating the Free Exercise Clause.

Davey urges us to answer that question in the negative. He contends that under the rule we enunciated in *Church of Lukumi Babalu Aye, Inc. v. Hialeah*, *supra*, the

---

[2] The relevant provision of the Washington Constitution, Art. I, § 11, states: ". . . No public money or property shall be appropriated for or applied to any religious worship, exercise or instruction, or the support of any religious establishment."

program is presumptively unconstitutional because it is not facially neutral with respect to religion. We reject his claim of presumptive unconstitutionality, however; to do otherwise would extend the *Lukumi* line of cases well beyond not only their facts but their reasoning. In *Lukumi*, the city of Hialeah made it a crime to engage in certain kinds of animal slaughter. We found that the law sought to suppress ritualistic animal sacrifices of the Santeria religion. In the present case, the State's disfavor of religion (if it can be called that) is of a far milder kind. It imposes neither criminal nor civil sanctions on any type of religious service or rite. . . . The State has merely chosen not to fund a distinct category of instruction.

Justice Scalia argues, however, that generally available benefits are part of the "baseline against which burdens on religion are measured." (dissenting opinion). . . . But training for religious professions and training for secular professions are not fungible. Training someone to lead a congregation is an essentially religious endeavor. Indeed, majoring in devotional theology is akin to a religious calling as well as an academic pursuit. . . . And the subject of religion is one in which both the United States and state constitutions embody distinct views — in favor of free exercise, but opposed to establishment — that find no counterpart with respect to other callings or professions. That a State would deal differently with religious education for the ministry than with education for other callings is a product of these views, not evidence of hostility toward religion.

. . . .

Far from evincing the hostility toward religion which was manifest in *Lukumi*, we believe that the entirety of the Promise Scholarship Program goes a long way toward including religion in its benefits. The program permits students to attend pervasively religious schools, so long as they are accredited. . . . [U]nder the Promise Scholarship Program's current guidelines, students are still eligible to take devotional theology courses. . . .

In short, we find neither in the history or text of Article I, § 11 of the Washington Constitution, nor in the operation of the Promise Scholarship Program, anything that suggests animus towards religion. . . .

. . . The State's interest in not funding the pursuit of devotional degrees is substantial and the exclusion of such funding places a relatively minor burden on Promise Scholars. If any room exists between the two Religion Clauses, it must be here. . . .

The judgment of the Court of Appeals is therefore reversed.

[The dissenting opinion of Justice Thomas has been omitted.]

Justice Scalia, with whom Justice Thomas joins, dissenting.

. . . .

When the State makes a public benefit generally available, that benefit becomes part of the baseline against which burdens on religion are measured; and when the State withholds that benefit from some individuals solely on the basis of religion, it violates the Free Exercise Clause no less than if it had imposed a special tax.

That is precisely what the State of Washington has done here. It has created a generally available public benefit, whose receipt is conditioned only on academic performance, income, and attendance at an accredited school. It has then carved out a solitary course of study for exclusion: theology. . . . Davey is not asking for a special benefit to which others are not entitled. . . . He seeks only *equal* treatment — the right to direct his scholarship to his chosen course of study, a right every other Promise Scholar enjoys.

. . . .

The Court does not dispute that the Free Exercise Clause places some constraints on public benefits programs, but finds none here, based on a principle of " 'play in the joints.' " . . . If the Religion Clauses demand neutrality, we must enforce them, in hard cases as well as easy ones.

. . . .

NOTES

1. In *Locke v. Davey*, on the dispute over the Promise Scholarship and its non-application to students pursuing degrees in devotional theology, why does the Court ultimately reject the Free Exercise of religion claim by Davey? How does the Court juggle the federal religion clauses with the state's constitutional religion clauses?

2. In the majority opinion, Justice Rehnquist argues that the Promise Scholarship is not hostile to religion and, therefore, not in violation of the religion clauses of the First Amendment. Do you agree with the reasoning? Readers are encouraged to compare this opinion with others written by Justice Rehnquist, who is widely known for his dissenting opinions in Establishment Clause cases, with arguments that school policy and practice are hostile to religion. *See Wallace v. Jaffree*, 472 U.S. 38 (1985) (the Court's majority struck down an Alabama moment of silence law, and Justice Rehnquist, in his dissent, argued that there is no historical foundation for a "wall of separation" between church and state); *Santa Fe Independent School District v. Doe*, 530 U.S. 290 (2000) (the Court struck down a school policy allowing student-initiated, student-led prayer at public school football games, and Rehnquist's dissent argues that the majority opinion bristled with "hostility to all things religious in public life").

3. The majority in *Locke v. Davey* upheld Washington's law prohibiting state-funded Promise Scholarship money from going to students who are pursuing a degree in devotional theology, although the law *did* permit scholarship recipients to attend pervasively religious institutions. What about a law that disallows scholarship recipients from attending "pervasively sectarian" institutions, regardless of their academic major? Colorado Christian University was one of those colleges deemed "pervasively sectarian" and filed suit, alleging that such a restriction in a Colorado law violated the First and Fourteenth Amendments. In *Colorado Christian University v. Weaver*, 534 F.3d 1245 (10th Cir. 2008), the Tenth Circuit held for the university, finding that the law discriminated on the basis of religion and violated both the Free Exercise and Establishment Clauses of the First Amendment. For a complete discussion of the case and its implications, see

Christopher P. Brown, *Colorado Christian University v. Weaver: Implications for the Establishment Clause Following the Death of the "Pervasively Sectarian" Doctrine*, 86 DENV. U.L. REV. 1091 (2009); James A. Davids, *Pounding a Final Stake in the Heart of the Invidiously Discriminatory "Pervasively Sectarian" Test*, 7 AVE MARIA L. REV. 59 (2008).

A similar case decided several years earlier, before *Locke*, also found in favor of the university. In *Columbia Union College v. Oliver*, 254 F.3d 496 (4th Cir. 2001), the Court of Appeals for the Fourth Circuit held that a private college's use of public aid to fund secular educational programs did not violate the Establishment Clause.

PODBERESKY v. KIRWAN
38 F.3d 147 (4th Cir. 1994)

WIDENER, CIRCUIT JUDGE:

The issue in this case is whether the University of Maryland at College Park may maintain a separate merit scholarship program that it voluntarily established for which only African-American students are eligible. Because we find that the district court erred in finding that the University had sufficient evidence of present effects of past discrimination to justify the program and in finding that the program is narrowly tailored to serve its stated objectives, we reverse the district court's grant of summary judgment to the University. We further reverse the district court's denial of Podberesky's motion for summary judgment, and we remand for entry of judgment in favor of Podberesky.

I

The facts and prior proceedings in this case are set forth at length in our earlier opinion, *Podberesky v. Kirwan*, 956 F.2d 52 (4th Cir. 1992) (*Podberesky I*). In sum, Daniel Podberesky challenges the University of Maryland's Banneker scholarship program, which is a merit-based program for which only African-American students are eligible. The University maintains a separate merit-based scholarship program, the Francis Scott Key program, which is not restricted to African-American students. Podberesky is Hispanic; he was therefore ineligible for consideration under the Banneker Program, although he met the academic and all other requirements for consideration. Podberesky was ineligible for consideration under the Key program because his academic credentials fell just shy of its more rigorous standards.

[At the trial court, the] University claimed that four present effects of past discrimination exist at the University: (1) The University has a poor reputation within the African-American community; (2) African-Americans are underrepresented in the student population; (3) African-American students who enroll at the University have low retention and graduation rates; and (4) the atmosphere on campus is perceived as being hostile to African-American students. The district court reasoned that if a strong evidentiary basis existed to support any of the four present effects articulated by the University, the Banneker Program would be justified. The district court then found that there was a strong evidentiary basis to support the existence of each of those four present effects.

The district court also found that the Banneker Program was narrowly tailored to remedy those four present effects of past discrimination which it found at the University. . . . This appeal followed.

II

Because it chose the Banneker Program, which excludes all races from consideration but one, as a remedial measure for its past discrimination against African-Americans, the University stands before us burdened with a presumption that its choice cannot be sustained. . . .

. . . .

We have established a two-step analysis for determining whether a particular race-conscious remedial measure can be sustained under the Constitution: (1) the proponent of the measure must demonstrate a " 'strong basis in evidence for its conclusion that remedial action [is] necessary;' " and (2) the remedial measure must be narrowly tailored to meet the remedial goal. *Maryland Troopers* [*Ass'n v. Evans*], 993 F.2d at 1076. . . .

. . . To have a present effect of past discrimination sufficient to justify the program, the party seeking to implement the program must, at a minimum, prove that the effect it proffers is caused by the past discrimination and that the effect is of sufficient magnitude to justify the program. As to the effect justifying the remedial measure, " 'absent searching judicial inquiry into the justification for such race-based measures, there is simply no way of determining what classifications are "benign" or "remedial" and what classifications are in fact motivated by illegitimate notions of racial inferiority or simple racial politics.' " *Maryland Troopers*, 993 F.2d at 1076 (4th Cir. 1993). Therefore, the district court was incorrect in stating that if the University found strong evidence to support any of its proffered effects, the program would be justified. The effects must themselves be examined to see whether they were caused by the past discrimination and whether they are of a type that justifies the program. Only then could we consider affirming the district court's grant of summary judgment to the University on this issue.

A

Turning to the present effects articulated by the University, we disagree with the district court that the first effect, a poor reputation in the African-American community, and the fourth effect, a climate on campus that is perceived as being racially hostile, are sufficient, standing alone, to justify the single-race Banneker Program. . . . There is no doubt that many Maryland residents, as well as some citizens in other States, know of the University's past segregation, and that fact cannot be denied. However, mere knowledge of historical fact is not the kind of present effect that can justify a race-exclusive remedy. . . .

The hostile-climate effect proffered by the University suffers from another flaw, however. The main support for the University's assertion that the campus climate is hostile to African-American students is contained in a survey of student attitudes and reported results of student focus groups. For an articulated effect to justify the program, however, there must be a connection between the past discrimination and the effect. . . . The district court found that "the very nature of the college experience is that younger students learn from older ones. . . . Since 1970, both black and white students have been handing down racial attitudes that perpetuate a hostile racial climate." . . . The frequency and regularity of the incidents, as well as claimed instances of backlash to remedial measures, do not necessarily implicate past discrimination on the part of the University, as opposed to present societal discrimination, which the district court implicitly held.

. . . .

The district court's analysis cannot be sustained on this point. When we begin by assuming that every predominately white college or university discriminated in the past, whether or not true, we are no longer talking about the kind of discrimination for which a race-conscious remedy may be prescribed. Instead, we are confronting societal discrimination, which cannot be used as a basis for supporting a race-conscious remedy. There is no doubt that racial tensions still exist in American society, including the campuses of our institutions of higher learning. However, these tensions and attitudes are not a sufficient ground for employing a race-conscious remedy at the University of Maryland.

B

We next turn to the two effects that rely on statistical data: underrepresentation of African-American students at the University and low retention and graduation rates for African-American students. . . .

. . . .

. . . As to the low retention and graduation rates, there is a dispute in the evidence about why African American students leave the University of Maryland in greater numbers than other students. Podberesky offered evidence tending to show that the attrition rate revealed by the statistics was the result of economic and other factors and not because of past discrimination. The district court rejected Podberesky's study by reasoning that economic concerns are often more pressing for African-American students because many of those students come from less wealthy backgrounds. The district court then reasoned that the disproportionate number of less wealthy African-American families is the result of past discrimination in society. The district court also found some evidence in some of the University's exhibits that showed that the University's poor reputation and hostile climate have an effect on attrition rates.

As to the underrepresentation, our decisions and those of the Supreme Court have made clear that the selection of the correct reference pool is critical. The district court must first determine as a matter of law whether it is appropriate to apply a pool consisting of the local population or whether another pool made up of people with special qualifications is appropriate. . . .

The district court rejected a pool which consisted of all graduating high school seniors because that pool "does not take into account even flexible minimum admission requirements." Thus, the district court correctly determined the legal issue of whether the appropriate pool was the general population or a smaller qualification specific pool. The district court erred, however, in its attempt to resolve the factual dispute about what are the effective minimum admission criteria. The district court declined to decide the requisite qualification for membership in the reference pool, but mentioned the percentage of students taking the SAT in Maryland, the minimum course curriculum required, and minimum math and verbal SAT scores. It later found that the percentage of African-American incoming freshmen at UMCP (13%) was less than any of them (17.9% for required course curriculum to 22% of students taking the SAT in Maryland who were African-American). It rejected Podberesky's proposed effective minimum criterion for admission, which was based on a combination of SAT scores, high school curriculum requirements, and grade-point averages, because the use of those numbers "ignores the variables in the admissions process and the intergenerational effects of segregated education on the applicant pool." We are of opinion that the goal of the program, remedying any present effects of past discrimination, cannot be used to lower the effective minimum criteria needed to determine the applicant pool. . . .

The factual disputes in this case are not inconsequential and could have been resolved only at trial. A district court may not resolve conflicts in the evidence on summary judgment motions, and the district court erred in so doing here.

III

. . . .

Even if we assumed that the University had demonstrated that African-Americans were underrepresented at the University and that the higher attrition rate was related to past discrimination, we could not uphold the Banneker Program. It is not narrowly tailored to remedy the underrepresentation and attrition problems. . . .

It is difficult to determine whether the Banneker scholarship program is narrowly tailored to remedy the present effects of past discrimination when the proof of present effects is so weak. In determining whether the Banneker Program is narrowly tailored to accomplish its stated objective, we may consider possible race-neutral alternatives and whether the program actually furthers a different objective from the one it is claimed to remedy.

A. *Attraction to Only High-Achieving Black Students*

The district court found that the Banneker Program attracted "high-achieving black students" to the University, which "directly increases the number of African-Americans who are admitted and likely to stay through graduation. . . . The district court further noted that the University's "success in curing the vestiges of its past discrimination depends upon it attracting high-achieving African-Americans to the College Park campus." As we demonstrate below, in conducting its analysis, the district court did not sufficiently connect the problems the University purports to remedy to the Banneker Program: low retention and graduation rates and underrepresentation. If the purpose of the program was to draw only high-achieving African-American students to the University, it could not be sustained. High achievers, whether African-American or not, are not the group against which the University discriminated in the past.

B. *Including Non-Residents of Maryland*

The district court also erred in giving no weight to Podberesky's argument that the Banneker Program is not narrowly tailored because the scholarships are open to non-Maryland residents. The district court stated that the goals of the program would be served "whether Banneker Scholars are Maryland natives or not." It is at once apparent that the Banneker Program considers all African-American students for merit scholarships at the expense of non-African-American Maryland students.

The University, throughout this case, has taken the position that the pool from which the students eligible to enter UMCP is drawn are from "qualified African-American high school students in Maryland," and "the University expects that the racial composition of its student body will reflect the racial composition of qualified college-eligible high school graduates." While all of the prerequisites for membership in the pool were a matter of dispute between the parties, that the University measured its desired number of black students against *Maryland* high school graduates who are qualified to attend the University is not a matter of dispute. That being true, it is obvious that awarding Banneker Scholarships to non-residents of Maryland is not narrowly tailored to correcting the condition that the University argues, that not enough qualified African-American Maryland residents attend at College Park.

C. *Arbitrary Reference Pool*

The district court found the program to be narrowly tailored to increasing representation because an increase in the number of high-achieving African-American students would remedy the underrepresentation problem. The district court so found because it reasoned that the Banneker Scholars would serve as mentors and role models for other African-American students, thereby attracting more African-American students. The Supreme Court has expressly rejected the role-model theory as a basis for implementing a race-conscious remedy, as do we. *Wygant v. Jackson Bd. of Educ.*, 476 U.S. 267, 276 (1986) (plurality opinion).

Furthermore, the district court's analysis of underrepresentation, although it relied on various academic criteria to determine eligibility, relied on each relevant criterion item by item instead of in combination. It is axiomatic that if all of the relevant criteria (270 verbal SAT score, 380 math SAT score, UMCP general course-curriculum requirements, and 2.0 GPA) were applied simultaneously, as indeed UMCP itself claims it most commonly does in determining admissions qualifications, the percentage of eligible Maryland residents who are African-American might well be significantly lower than the percentage satisfying the least burdensome of those criteria relied upon. . . .

. . . [T]he district court failed to account for statistics regarding that percentage of otherwise eligible African-American high school graduates who either (1) chose not to go to any college; (2) chose to apply only to out-of-state colleges; (3) chose to postpone application to a four-year institution for reasons relating to economics or otherwise, such as spending a year or so in a community college to save money; or (4) voluntarily limited their applications to Maryland's predominantly African-American institutions. . . . .

. . . In analyzing underrepresentation, disparity between the composition of the student body and the composition of a reference pool is significant in this case only to the extent that it can be shown to be based on present effects of past discrimination. . . . This the district court simply has not done. The result is no more than a collection of arbitrary figures upon which it held UMCP may rely in its efforts to recruit African-Americans using facially racial classifications.

. . . .

The district court has approved the use of the Banneker Program to affirmatively admit African-American students solely on the basis of race until the composition of African-Americans on the University campus reflects the percentage of African-American Maryland high school graduates who potentially might participate in higher education at UMCP, without an accurate determination of either the extent to which the present disparity exists . . . or the extent to which that disparity flows from past discrimination. . . . The program thus could remain in force indefinitely based on arbitrary statistics unrelated to constitutionally permissible purposes. . . . We are thus of opinion that, as analyzed by the district court, the program more resembles outright racial balancing than a tailored remedy program. As such, it is not narrowly tailored to remedy past discrimination. In fact, it is not tailored at all.

D. *Race-Neutral Alternatives*

The district court also suggested that an increase in the number of high-achieving African-American students would remedy the low retention and graduation rates for African-American students at the University. Podberesky submitted a 1993 study by two University of Maryland professors which indicates that after the freshman year, in which grades are the principal problem, students leave the University for financial and other reasons. Specifically, students who left the University "tended to be more likely to provide their own expenses, live off campus with long commutes, have a job with long hours, spend few free hours on campus, and have few friends on campus." Roger W. McIntire & Sandra Smith, *Work and Life Styles Among Dropouts and Ongoing College Students*, 4 J.A. 1062, 1067 (survey of 455 drop-out and 455 returning University of Maryland students) . . . That study suggests that the best remedy is "campus job opportunities and convenient, attractive, and economically reasonable *campus* housing . . . available to a greater proportion of students." 4 J.A. at 1070-71.

. . . .

The causes of the low retention rates submitted both by Podberesky and the University and found by the district court have little, if anything, to do with the Banneker Program. . . . [T]he University has not made any attempt to show that it has tried, without success, any race-neutral solutions to the retention problem. Thus, the University's choice of a race-exclusive merit scholarship program as a remedy cannot be sustained.

. . . .

NOTES

1. What reasoning does the court use to strike down the race-based scholarship program in *Podberesky*? What arguments did the university make in defense? What arguments would you add? How might you amend the program's policies to help it survive legal scrutiny? Or are such programs not (ever) lawful? It seems that the university did all it could to raise a legitimate defense, yet it lost. For a discussion of the legality of race-based scholarship aid in higher education, see Alexander S. Elson, Note, *Disappearing without a Case — The Constitutionality of Race-Conscious Scholarships in Higher Education*, 86 Wash. U. L. Rev. 975 (2009); Osamudia R. James, *Dog Wags Tail: The Continuing Viability of Minority-Targeted Aid in Higher Education*, 85 Ind. L.J. 851 (2010).

2. What is the impact of *Gratz v. Bollinger* and *Grutter v. Bollinger* — the affirmative action admissions decisions from the University of Michigan — on minority-targeted scholarship programs? Does the recognition of diversity as a compelling governmental interest for admissions justify race-conscious recruitment, outreach, financial aid, and other support programs? After *Grutter*, remedying past discrimination by the educational institution is not the only compelling governmental interest recognized. Would the program in *Podberesky* survive judicial scrutiny under a post-*Grutter* analysis? See the full presentation of *Gratz* and *Grutter* earlier in this Chapter.

3. The federal Office of Civil Rights (OCR) also offers guidance on the legality of minority-targeted aid under Title VI of the Civil Rights Act. In 1994, OCR issued a notice in the Federal Register, entitled *Nondiscrimination in Federally Assisted Programs*, 59 Fed Reg. 8756 (Feb. 23, 1994). The five principles contained in this OCR notice are excerpted below:

> *Principle 1: Financial Aid for Disadvantaged Students*
>
> A college may make awards of financial aid to disadvantaged students, without regard to race or national origin, even if that means that these awards go disproportionately to minority students.
>
> Financial aid may be earmarked for students from low-income families. Financial aid also may be earmarked for students from school districts with high dropout rates, or students from single parent families, or students from families in which few or no members have attended college. None of these or other race-neutral ways of identifying and providing aid to disadvantaged students present Title VI problems. A college may use funds from any source to provide financial aid to disadvantaged students.
>
> *Principle 2: Financial Aid Authorized by Congress*
>
> A college may award financial aid on the basis of race or national origin if the aid is awarded under a Federal statute that authorizes the use of race or national origin.
>
> *Principle 3: Financial Aid To Remedy Past Discrimination*

A college may award financial aid on the basis of race or national origin if the aid is necessary to overcome the effects of past discrimination. A finding of discrimination may be made by a court or by an administrative agency - such as the Department's Office for Civil Rights. Such a finding may also be made by a State or local legislative body, as long as the legislature has a strong basis in evidence identifying discrimination within its jurisdiction for which that remedial action is necessary.

In addition, a college may award financial aid on the basis of race or national origin to remedy its past discrimination without a formal finding of discrimination by a court or by an administrative or legislative body. The college must be prepared to demonstrate to a court or administrative agency that there is a strong basis in evidence for concluding that the college's action was necessary to remedy the effects of its past discrimination. . . .

A State may award financial aid on the basis of race or national origin, under the preceding standards, if the aid is necessary to overcome its own past discrimination or discrimination at colleges in the State.

Principle 4: Financial Aid To Create Diversity

. . . A college should have substantial discretion to weigh many factors — including race and national origin — in its efforts to attract and retain a student population of many different experiences, opinions, backgrounds, and cultures — provided that the use of race or national origin is consistent with the constitutional standards reflected in Title VI, *i.e.*, that it is a narrowly tailored means to achieve the goal of a diverse student body.

. . . .

Among the considerations that affect a determination of whether awarding race-targeted financial aid is narrowly tailored to the goal of diversity are (1) whether race-neutral means of achieving that goal have been or would be ineffective; (2) whether a less extensive or intrusive use of race or national origin in awarding financial aid as a means of achieving that goal has been or would be ineffective; (3) whether the use of race or national origin is of limited extent and duration and is applied in a flexible manner; (4) whether the institution regularly reexamines its use of race or national origin in awarding financial aid to determine whether it is still necessary to achieve its goal; and (5) whether the effect of the use of race or national origin on students who are not beneficiaries of that use is sufficiently small and diffuse so as not to create an undue burden on their opportunity to receive financial aid.

If the use of race or national origin in awarding financial aid is justified under this principle, the college may use funds from any source.

Principle 5: Private Gifts Restricted by Race or National Origin

Title VI does not prohibit an individual or an organization that is not a recipient of Federal financial assistance from directly giving scholarships or other forms of financial aid to students based on their race or national origin. Title VI simply does not apply.

The provisions of Principles 3 and 4 apply to the use of race-targeted privately donated funds by a college and may justify awarding these funds on the basis of race or national origin if the college is remedying its past discrimination pursuant to Principle 3 or attempting to achieve a diverse student body pursuant to Principle 4. In addition, a college may use privately donated funds that are not restricted by their donor on the basis of race or national origin to make awards to disadvantaged students as described in Principle 1.

For a complete copy of the OCR's Notice, see 59 Fed Reg. 8756 (Feb. 23, 1994), *available at* http://www2.ed.gov/about/offices/list/ocr/docs/racefa.html.

D. STUDENT FILES AND RECORDS AND THE FAMILY EDUCATIONAL RIGHTS AND PRIVACY ACT (FERPA)

1. Education Records

OWASSO INDEPENDENT SCHOOL DISTRICT NO. I-011 v. FALVO

534 U.S. 426 (2002)

JUSTICE KENNEDY delivered the opinion of the Court.

. . . .

I

Under FERPA [the Family Educational Rights and Privacy Act, 20 U.S.C. § 1232g], schools and educational agencies receiving federal financial assistance must comply with certain conditions. One condition specified in the Act is that sensitive information about students may not be released without parental consent. The Act states that federal funds are to be withheld from school districts that have "a policy or practice of permitting the release of education records (or personally identifiable information contained therein . . .) of students without the written consent of their parents." § 1232g(b)(1). The phrase "education records" is defined, under the Act, as "records, files, documents, and other materials" containing information directly related to a student, which "are maintained by an educational agency or institution or by a person acting for such agency or institution." § 1232g(a)(4)(A). The definition of education records contains an exception for "records of instructional, supervisory, and administrative personnel . . . which are in the sole possession of the maker thereof and which are not accessible or revealed to any other person except a substitute." § 1232g(a)(4)(B)(i). The precise question for us is whether peer-graded classroom work and assignments are education records.

Three of respondent Kristja J. Falvo's children are enrolled in Owasso Independent School District No. I-011. . . . The children's teachers, like many teachers in this country, use peer grading. In a typical case, the students exchange papers with each other and score them according to the teacher's instructions, then return the work to the student who prepared it. The teacher may ask the students to report their own scores. In this case it appears the student could either call out the score or walk to the teacher's desk and reveal it in confidence, though by that stage, of course, the score was known at least to the one other student who did the grading. Both the grading and the system of calling out the scores are in contention here.

. . . .

We granted certiorari to decide whether peer grading violates FERPA. . . . Finding no violation of the Act, we reverse.

II

. . . .

The parties appear to agree that if an assignment becomes an education record the moment a peer grades it, then the grading, or at least the practice of asking students to call out their grades in class, would be an impermissible release of the records under § 1232g(b)(1). . . . The parties disagree, however, whether peer-graded assignments constitute education records at all. The papers . . . are records under the Act only when and if they "are maintained by an educational agency or institution or by a person acting for such agency or institution." § 1232g(a)(4)(A).

Petitioners . . . contend the definition covers only institutional records — namely, those materials retained in a permanent file as a matter of course. They argue that records "maintained by an educational agency or institution" generally would include final course grades, student grade point averages, standardized test scores, attendance records, counseling records, and records of disciplinary actions — but not student homework or classroom work.

Respondent[] . . . contends student-graded assignments fall within the definition of education records. That definition contains an exception for "records of instructional, supervisory, and administrative personnel . . . which are in the sole possession of the maker thereof and which are not accessible or revealed to any other person except a substitute." § 1232g(a)(4)(B)(i). The Court of Appeals reasoned that if grade books are not education records, then it would have been unnecessary for Congress to enact the exception. Grade books and the grades within, the court concluded, are "maintained" by a teacher and so are covered by FERPA. . . . If Congress forbids teachers to disclose students' grades once written in a grade book, it makes no sense to permit the disclosure immediately beforehand. The court thus held that student graders maintain the grades until they are reported to the teacher.

The Court of Appeals' logic does not withstand scrutiny. Its interpretation, furthermore, would effect a drastic alteration of the existing allocation of responsibilities between States and the National Government in the operation of the Nation's schools. We would hesitate before interpreting the statute to effect such a substantial change in the balance of federalism unless that is the manifest purpose of the legislation. This principle guides our decision.

Two statutory indicators tell us that the Court of Appeals erred in concluding that an assignment satisfies the definition of education records as soon as it is graded by another student. First, the student papers are not, at that stage, "maintained" within the meaning of § 1232g(a)(4)(A). The ordinary meaning of the word "maintain" is "to keep in existence or continuance; preserve; retain." Random House Dictionary of the English Language 1160 (2d ed. 1987). . . . The word "maintain" suggests FERPA records will be kept in a filing cabinet in a records room at the school or on a permanent secure database, perhaps even after the student is no longer enrolled. The student graders only handle assignments for a few moments as the teacher calls out the answers. It is fanciful to say they maintain the papers in the same way the registrar maintains a student's folder in a permanent file.

The Court of Appeals was further mistaken in concluding that each student grader is "a person acting for" an educational institution for purposes of § 1232g(a)(4)(A). The phrase "acting for" connotes agents of the school, such as teachers, administrators, and other school employees. Just as it does not accord with our usual understanding to say students are "acting for" an educational institution when they follow their teacher's direction to take a quiz, it is equally awkward to say students are "acting for" an educational institution when they follow their teacher's direction to score it. Correcting a classmate's work can be as much a part of the assignment as taking the test itself. . . . Even if one were to agree students are acting for the teacher when they correct the assignment, that is different from saying they are acting for the educational institution in maintaining it.

Other sections of the statute support our interpretation. . . . FERPA, for example, requires educational institutions to "maintain a record, kept with the education records of each student." § 1232g(b)(4)(A). This record must list those who have requested access to a student's education records and their reasons for doing so. The record of access "shall be available only to parents, [and] to the school official and his assistants who are responsible for the custody of such records."

Under the Court of Appeals' broad interpretation of education records, every teacher would have an obligation to keep a separate record of access for each student's assignments. Indeed, by that court's logic, even students who grade their own papers would bear the burden of maintaining records of access until they turned in the assignments. We doubt Congress would have imposed such a weighty administrative burden on every teacher, and certainly it would not have extended the mandate to students.

Also FERPA requires "a record" of access for each pupil. This single record must be kept "with the education records." This suggests Congress contemplated that education records would be kept in one place with a single record of access. By describing a "school official" and "his assistants" as the personnel responsible for the custody of the records, FERPA implies that education records are institutional records kept by a single central custodian, such as a registrar, not individual assignments handled by many student graders in their separate classrooms.

FERPA also requires recipients of federal funds to provide parents with a hearing at which they may contest the accuracy of their child's education records. The hearings must be conducted "in accordance with regulations of the Secretary," which in turn require adjudication by a disinterested official and the opportunity for parents to be represented by an attorney. It is doubtful Congress would have provided parents with this elaborate procedural machinery to challenge the accuracy of the grade on every spelling test and art project the child completes.

Respondent's construction of the term "education records" to cover student homework or classroom work would impose substantial burdens on teachers across the country. . . .

We doubt Congress meant to intervene in this drastic fashion with traditional state functions. Under the Court of Appeals' interpretation of FERPA, the federal power would exercise minute control over specific teaching methods and instructional dynamics in classrooms throughout the country. The Congress is not likely to have mandated this result, and we do not interpret the statute to require it.

For these reasons, even assuming a teacher's grade book is an education record, the Court of Appeals erred, for in all events the grades on students' papers would not be covered under FERPA at least until the teacher has collected them and recorded them in his or her grade book. We limit our holding to this narrow point, and do not decide the broader question whether the grades on individual student assignments, once they are turned in to teachers, are protected by the Act.

The judgment of the Court of Appeals is reversed, and the case is remanded for further proceedings consistent with this opinion. . . .

NOTES

1. Justice Kennedy, in writing for the Court, paid close attention to the long-standing nature of the peer-grading exercise and hailed it as important to the learning process. In other words, much of the decision is based on the academic benefit of peer grading and, more generally, deference to the daily decision-making of educators. For practical purposes, then, the ruling in *Owasso* is favorable to school settings. Much of the logic of the Falvos' argument, which the Court says is unable to withstand scrutiny, is played out practically, in demonstrations of what it would be like logistically for teachers and school leaders to comply with record-keeping and hearing requirements. Legally, however, are you convinced by the Falvos' logic? The Court's ultimate legal analysis? Why or why not?

2. In its final paragraph, the majority opinion states:

> For these reasons, even assuming a teacher's grade book is an education record, the Court of Appeals erred, for in all events the grades on students' papers would not be covered under FERPA *at least until the teacher has collected them and recorded them in his or her grade book.* We limit our holding to this narrow point, and do not decide the broader question whether the grades on individual student assignments, *once they are turned in to teachers*, are protected by the Act.

(Emphasis added.) What's the difference between the practice of the teacher transferring a grade to a grade book (with the assumption that the grade book is an education record under FERPA) and the practice of a student announcing that same grade (or revealing the grade) to a teacher, who then transfers it to a grade book (with the same assumption that the grade book is an education record)? The Court declined to answer the "broader question" of whether the grades on individual student assignments are protected by the Act. Is that not the question the Court agreed to hear in the first place? The Falvos' complaint was, indeed, inspired by peer grading: the prospect of individual student assignment grades being revealed to one or more students without parental consent. However, what is the practical and legal difference between the grades obtained through peer grading and any other individual assignment grade that may be revealed to others without consent?

3. Peer grading is not likely common in higher education settings. However, FERPA applies to both K-12 and post-secondary educational institutions. Beyond peer grading, how might *Owasso* apply in higher education?

4. Justice Scalia authored a short concurring opinion, disagreeing with the majority's reliance on a "central custodian theory." In his words, Justice Scalia does not agree that education records include only those records kept in a central repository at school. What do you think? Where should the line be drawn? The Court declined to decide whether a teacher's grade book was an educational record for FERPA purposes. Why did it not decide this question? In other words, why was such a question not necessary for the Court to decide? According to the Court, "[t]he word 'maintain' suggests FERPA records will be kept in a filing cabinet in a records room at the school or on a permanent secure database, perhaps even after the student is no longer enrolled."

What is the impact and application of *Owasso* in an electronic era? In a hard-copy world, perhaps a teacher's grade book cannot be considered "maintained" by the educational agency. But today, we have electronic grade books, often password-protected, that faculty members can update quickly. We also have platforms that allow students to access their own grades during the course of an academic term. These grade books contain grades and scores on individual assignments and are not merely final course grades, grade-point averages, etc. Are electronic grade books, with grades posted in online portals, maintained by the educational agency for FERPA purposes? See the dictionary definition of "maintain" offered by the Court in *Owasso*. Does it make a difference if the electronic grade book is only available online for the duration of a course and for a short time thereafter? What about electronic records that are kept more permanently? For a deeper discussion of FERPA in an electronic age, see Lynn M. Daggett, *FERPA in the Twenty-First Century: Failure to Effectively Regulate Privacy for All Students*, 58 Cath. U.L. Rev. 59 (2008).

5. *Owasso* dealt with the process of grading student work. FERPA has also generated challenges to the *substance* of faculty grading as well. Students have not fared well in such challenges. In *Tarka v. Cunningham*, 917 F.2d 890 (5th Cir. 1990), for example, the court held that there was no cause of action under FERPA for a student's claim based on a disappointing final grade received in a course. While

FERPA does provide an opportunity for a hearing on the accuracy of student records, it does not provide a means for a student to obtain information on how a particular grade was assigned. The battle is, expectedly, even tougher for students who wish to use FERPA to challenge a grade on a particular assignment or exam. In *Lewin v Medical College*, a former medical student used FERPA to challenge his failure of an exam administered to allow students to waive an entire pharmacology course. 931 F. Supp. 443 (E.D. Va. 1996), *aff'd without op.*, 120 F.3d 261, *reported in full*, 1997 U.S. App. LEXIS 20851 (4th Cir. 1997). The court held that there was no cause of action under FERPA, as the exam test score did not appear in the student's permanent school record.

6. Early in the *Owasso* opinion, the Court declined to answer the question whether individuals have a private right of action under FERPA. That question was addressed later that year in *Gonzaga University v. Doe*, 536 U.S. 273 (2002), which follows below.

2. Private Right of Action Under FERPA

GONZAGA UNIVERSITY v. DOE
536 U.S. 273 (2002)

CHIEF JUSTICE REHNQUIST delivered the opinion of the Court.

The question presented is whether a student may sue a private university for damages under . . . 42 U.S.C. § 1983 . . . to enforce provisions of the Family Educational Rights and Privacy Act of 1974 (FERPA or Act), 20 U.S.C. § 1232g, which prohibit the federal funding of educational institutions that have a policy or practice of releasing education records to unauthorized persons. We hold such an action foreclosed because the relevant provisions of FERPA create no personal rights to enforce under 42 U.S.C. § 1983.

. . . .

[Respondent was an undergraduate in the School of Education at Gonzaga University in Washington state. Respondent was denied an "affidavit of good moral character" required by state law at the time in order to teach on the grounds that one of Gonzaga's "teacher certification specialists" overheard rumors of respondent's "act of sexual misconduct" against a female undergraduate. Respondent sued under 42 U.S.C. 1973 and FERPA and a jury awarded him punitive damages. The Washington Court of Appeals reversed on the basis that FERPA did not create "individual rights" and could not be enforced under 1983. The Washington Supreme Court reversed this decision, and the Supreme Court granted certiorari to resolve the conflict.]

. . . .

. . . As relevant here, [FERPA] provides:

> "No funds shall be made available under any applicable program to any educational agency or institution which has a policy or practice of permitting the release of education records (or personally identifiable information

> contained therein . . .) of students without the written consent of their parents to any individual, agency, or organization." 20 U.S.C. § 1232g(b)(1).

. . . .

Respondent contends that this statutory regime confers upon any student enrolled at a covered school or institution a federal right, enforceable in suits for damages under § 1983, not to have "education records" disclosed to unauthorized persons without the student's express written consent. But we have never before held, and decline to do so here, that spending legislation drafted in terms resembling those of FERPA can confer enforceable rights.

. . . [I]n *Pennhurst State School and Hospital v. Halderman*, 451 U.S. 1 (1981), we rejected a claim that the Developmentally Disabled Assistance and Bill of Rights Act of 1975 conferred enforceable rights, saying:

> "In legislation enacted pursuant to the spending power, the typical remedy for state noncompliance with federally imposed conditions is not a private cause of action for noncompliance but rather action by the Federal Government to terminate funds to the State." *Id.*, at 28.

We made clear that unless Congress "speaks with a clear voice," and manifests an "unambiguous" intent to confer individual rights, federal funding provisions provide no basis for private enforcement by § 1983. *Id.*, at 17, 28, and n. 21.

Since *Pennhurst*, only twice have we found spending legislation to give rise to enforceable rights. In *Wright v. Roanoke Redevelopment and Housing Authority*, 479 U.S. 418 (1987), we allowed a § 1983 suit by tenants to recover past overcharges under a rent-ceiling provision of the Public Housing Act, on the ground that the provision unambiguously conferred "a mandatory [benefit] focusing on the individual family and its income." *Id.*, at 430. The key to our inquiry was that Congress spoke in terms that "could not be clearer, "and conferred entitlements "sufficiently specific and definite to qualify as enforceable rights under *Pennhurst*." *Id.*, at 432. Also significant was that the federal agency charged with administering the Public Housing Act "had never provided a procedure by which tenants could complain to it about the alleged failures [of state welfare agencies] to abide by [the Act's rent-ceiling provision]." *Id.*, at 426.

Three years later, in *Wilder v. Virginia Hosp. Ass'n*, 496 U.S. 498 (1990), we allowed a § 1983 suit brought by health care providers to enforce a reimbursement provision of the Medicaid Act, on the ground that the provision, much like the rent-ceiling provision in *Wright*, explicitly conferred specific monetary entitlements upon the plaintiffs. . . .

Our more recent decisions, however, have rejected attempts to infer enforceable rights from Spending Clause statutes. [*Suter v. Artist M.*, 503 U.S. 347 (1992) (the Adoption Assistance and Child Welfare Act of 1980); *Blessing v. Freestone*, 520 U.S. 329 (1997) (Title IV-D of the Social Security Act).]

. . . .

Respondent reads this line of cases to establish a relatively loose standard for finding rights enforceable by § 1983. He claims that a federal statute confers such rights so long as Congress intended that the statute "benefit" putative plaintiffs. He further contends that a more "rigorous" inquiry would conflate the standard for inferring a private right of action under § 1983 with the standard for inferring a private right of action directly from the statute itself, which he admits would not exist under FERPA. . . .

. . . .

We now reject the notion that our cases permit anything short of an unambiguously conferred right to support a cause of action brought under § 1983. Section 1983 provides a remedy only for the deprivation of "rights, privileges, or immunities secured by the Constitution and laws" of the United States. Accordingly, it is *rights*, not the broader or vaguer "benefits" or "interests," that may be enforced under the authority of that section. . . .

. . . For a statute to create such private rights, its text must be "phrased in terms of the persons benefited." *Cannon v. University of Chicago*, 441 U.S. 677, 692, n. 13 (1979). . . . But even where a statute is phrased in such explicit rights-creating terms, a plaintiff suing under an implied right of action still must show that the statute manifests an intent "to create not just a private *right* but also a private *remedy*." *Alexander v. Sandoval*, 532 U.S. 275, 286 (2001) (emphases added).

Plaintiffs suing under § 1983 do not have the burden of showing an intent to create a private remedy because § 1983 generally supplies a remedy for the vindication of rights secured by federal statutes. Once a plaintiff demonstrates that a statute confers an individual right, the right is presumptively enforceable by § 1983. . . .

A court's role in discerning whether personal rights exist in the § 1983 context should therefore not differ from its role in discerning whether personal rights exist in the implied right of action context. . . . Accordingly, where the text and structure of a statute provide no indication that Congress intends to create new individual rights, there is no basis for a private suit, whether under § 1983 or under an implied right of action.

. . . .

With this principle in mind, there is no question that FERPA's nondisclosure provisions fail to confer enforceable rights. To begin with, the provisions entirely lack the sort of "rights-creating" language critical to showing the requisite congressional intent to create new rights. Unlike the individually focused terminology of Titles VI and IX ("no person shall be subjected to discrimination"), FERPA's provisions speak only to the Secretary of Education, directing that "no funds shall be made available" to any "educational agency or institution" which has a prohibited "policy or practice." 20 U.S.C. § 1232g(b)(1). . . .

FERPA's nondisclosure provisions further speak only in terms of institutional policy and practice, not individual instances of disclosure. . . .

Our conclusion that FERPA's nondisclosure provisions fail to confer enforceable rights is buttressed by the mechanism that Congress chose to provide for enforcing those provisions. Congress expressly authorized the Secretary of Education to "*deal with violations*" of the Act, § 1232g(f) (emphasis added), and required the

Secretary to "establish or designate [a] review board" for investigating and adjudicating such violations, § 1232g(g). . . . These administrative procedures squarely distinguish this case from *Wright* and *Wilder*, where an aggrieved individual lacked any federal review mechanism, and further counsel against our finding a congressional intent to create individually enforceable private rights.

Congress finally provided that "except for the conduct of hearings, none of the functions of the Secretary under this section shall be carried out in any of the regional offices" of the Department of Education. 20 U.S.C. § 1232g(g). This centralized review provision was added just four months after FERPA's enactment due to "concern that regionalizing the enforcement of [FERPA] may lead to multiple interpretations of it, and possibly work a hardship on parents, students, and institutions." 120 Cong. Rec. 39863 (1974) (joint statement). . . . It is implausible to presume that the same Congress nonetheless intended private suits to be brought before thousands of federal- and state-court judges, which could only result in the sort of "multiple interpretations" the Act explicitly sought to avoid.

In sum, if Congress wishes to create new rights enforceable under § 1983, it must do so in clear and unambiguous terms — no less and no more than what is required for Congress to create new rights enforceable under an implied private right of action. . . .

. . . .

[Justice Breyer's concurring opinion and Justice Stevens' dissenting opinion omitted]

NOTES

1. Late in its opinion, the majority argued that its finding that FERPA failed to establish a private right of action for monetary damages was buttressed by the administrative review procedures contained in FERPA, for the resolution of claims against an institution. What does FERPA provide in the way of such administrative means, making it unnecessary to allow for a private right of action? What do your college and university policies add? For example, consider the FERPA policies at Bowling Green State University (BGSU): the policy at BGSU contains definitions, FAQs, and specific links for students, faculty, staff, and parents. In its faculty statement, BGSU says the following:

> Faculty members are considered university officials under FERPA regulations when performing specific functions of their position related to the student educational experience. Therefore, in fulfilling your professional responsibilities, you may need to know, use, manage and/or disseminate confidential information about your students. Depending on the specific requirements of your responsibilities, this legitimate educational interest grants you access to all or parts of student educational records.

*Welcome to FERPA at BGSU,** *available at* http://www.bgsu.edu/offices/sa/ferpa/index.html.

The student statement reminds students that the rights and responsibilities under FERPA transfer from parents to students at the college level:

> As a student at BGSU, you have a certain degree of control over who has access to your records depending on your status as a tax dependent, the nature of the information requested, and the reason for accessing or disseminating the information. This means your parents will not have access to your grades without your written authorization.

Rights and Responsibilities for Students, available at http://www.bgsu.edu/offices/sa/ferpa/page51372.html. For administrative purposes, these sites have links to FERPA resources and list the rights that students have under FERPA, including the right to file a complaint of noncompliance against the university. BGSU offers the following statement: "You have the right to file a complaint with the U.S. Department of Education concerning alleged failures by Bowling Green State University to comply with the requirements of FERPA. You do not, however, have the right to sue the University under this federal regulation." The site also contains the contact information for the Family Policy Compliance Office, the federal agency that administers FERPA. The Ohio State University's FERPA site has a tutorial designed for faculty and staff. Interested readers should consult www.ureg.ohio-state.edu/ourweb/more/Content/ferpa_tutorial/main.htm.

Universities are advised to enforce their FERPA policies in order to protect the privacy of their students. *See Ramos v. Tacoma Comm. Coll.*, No. C06-5241 FDB, 2007 U.S. Dist. LEXIS 54691 (W.D. Wash. July 27, 2007) (community college terminated an instructor after the instructor released confidential student information in violation of the college's FERPA policy).

2. The Court in *Gonzaga* held that an individual may not use Section 1983, in a private action, to enforce provisions of FERPA. *P. N. v. Greco*, 282 F. Supp. 2d 221 (D.N.J. 2003), a case decided after *Gonzaga*, held that while FERPA's nondisclosure provisions failed to confer enforceable rights, claims under Section 1983 for violations of confidentiality requirements of the Individuals with Disabilities Education Act were entirely viable.

3. Principles of Nondisclosure

JENNINGS v. UNIVERSITY OF NORTH CAROLINA AT CHAPEL HILL

340 F. Supp. 2d 679 (M.D.N.C. 2004)

TILLEY, CHIEF JUDGE

. . . .

I.

. . . Ms. [Melissa] Jennings was a student soccer player for the University of North Carolina at Chapel Hill ("the University") women's soccer team, coached by

Defendant Anson Dorrance from Aug. '96-May '98. [Jennings brought suit against Dorrance and the University under Title IX and for damages for invasion of privacy and sexual harassment].

In support of their Motion for Summary Judgment, Defendants . . . filed the affidavit of David Lanier, University Registrar, attached to which is Ms. Jennings' final official academic transcript. Defendants at that time also filed a separate motion that those depositions and Mr. Lanier's affidavit be submitted under seal. It is that motion that is addressed here.

. . . .

II.

. . . .

A.

Defendants claim that Ms. Jennings has a privacy interest in her transcript significant enough that Mr. Lanier's affidavit should be sealed. They argue that the existence of the Family Educational Rights and Privacy Act ("FERPA"), 20 U.S.C. § 1232g (2004), elevates her privacy interest to the level of a compelling governmental interest. FERPA prohibits institutions that receive federal funding from releasing a student's educational records without written parental consent. An exception to FERPA arises, however, when a student initiates legal action against the institution. 34 C.F.R. 99.31 (a)(9)(iii)(B) (2004). In that event, the institution may disclose the student's records that are relevant to its defense without obtaining consent. *Id.*

Federal legislation like FERPA may be relevant to a court's determination of whether there is a compelling governmental interest, but alone it is not prima facie evidence of a compelling interest. *In re Washington Post Co.*, 807 F.2d at 393 ("The district court may not simply assume that Congress has struck the correct constitutional balance."). . . .

Even when FERPA is taken into account in this case, Defendants have not shown that there is a compelling governmental interest for sealing Mr. Lanier's affidavit. While FERPA may show that Congress has recognized a student's interest in the privacy of her educational records, the legal action exception contained in the regulations limits that interest. At least part of Ms. Jennings' academic transcript fits that exception. Ms. Jennings' performance from fall 1996 to spring 1998 is relevant to Mr. Dorrance's assertion that he dismissed her from the team in part because of her failure to perform academically, and not in retaliation for any complaints she may have made about him. Thus, that portion of the transcript clearly fits the exception. . . .

FERPA requires written parental consent for the release of academic records. In considering FERPA, however, it must also be considered that (1) Ms. Jennings is an adult capable of making decisions without parental consent and (2) Ms. Jennings had ample opportunity to respond through counsel to Defendants' motion to seal, whether in support of or against it, but chose to take no position. In this context, Ms.

Jennings' failure to take a position amounts to constructive consent to the release of her final transcript. . . .

. . . [D]ue to (1) the potentially integral nature of the document and the corresponding possibility that it is excepted in its entirety from FERPA, (2) Ms. Jennings' constructive consent to its release, and (3) the leeway this Court has in interpreting federal statutes as evidence of compelling governmental interests, it is concluded that there is no compelling governmental interest sufficient to outweigh the First Amendment right to access. Defendants' motion in regard to Mr. Lanier's affidavit will therefore be DENIED.

B.

Defendants also argue that several former students who are not parties to the case have a privacy interest in the alleged comments and conversations recounted in the depositions at issue. In support of this assertion, Defendants argue that an individual has a privacy interest in information about her "body, health, and sexual activities", and that these particular individuals' privacy interests are heightened by FERPA because they were students at a federally funded institution at the time the alleged comments were made. Courts, including this Court, have recognized an individual's interest in avoiding disclosure of certain personal information. However, "as the first step in determining whether the information sought is entitled to privacy protection, courts have looked at whether it is within an individual's reasonable expectations of confidentiality." *Walls v. City of Petersburg*, 895 F.2d 188, 192 (4th Cir. 1990). . . .

Here, the former students could not have had "reasonable expectations of confidentiality" in the information exchanged by and about them in conversations with team members. In many instances, the students themselves were present for and participating in the conversations. Furthermore, the alleged comments made by Mr. Dorrance about the students' bodies do not constitute "personal information" about the students, but are rather the observations of an individual. . . . This is an instance of college students engaged in conversations among themselves, and comments their coach may or may not have made about them. To extend a privacy interest to these conversations and comments would be an impermissible expansion of the interest as defined in past cases.

The existence of FERPA does not heighten the students' privacy interest in these depositions. The information at issue in the depositions is not an "educational record" as defined by FERPA. . . . While some of the information is directly related to students, it was not, and would not have been, part of any documents maintained by the University. . . . Defendants' Motion to Submit Evidence Under Seal . . . will be DENIED.

. . . .

NOTES

1. The court in the *Jennings* case, on a couple of occasions, noted that student education records may not be released without parental consent. This is true, according to 20 U.S.C. § 1232g(b)(1). Note, though, that FERPA transfers the rights to students on the basis of age and/or post-secondary school enrollment:

> . . . For the purposes of this section, whenever a student has attained eighteen years of age, or is attending an institution of postsecondary education, the permission or consent required of and the rights accorded to the parents of the student shall thereafter only be required of and accorded to the student.

See 20 U.S.C. § 1232g(d). You will notice from the above language that FERPA rights transfer to all college students, regardless of whether or not the student is 18 years old. There may be some practicality to this automatic transfer. But what are the implications? Today, the number of school-university partnerships is increasing, and several high school students are taking advantage of post-secondary enrollment options and dual enrollments, allowing them to be both college students and high school students simultaneously. *See, e.g.*, Ohio Rev. Code Ann. § 3313.6013 (dual enrollment program for college credit); §§ 3365.01–3365.15 (post-secondary enrollment options program). How does FERPA apply in such cases? Technically, it would seem that FERPA's transfer-of-rights provision would prevail, regardless of the age of the student. In the dual enrollment program cited here, the students take their courses at high school and earn college credit. In the post-secondary enrollment option program, the students attend classes on the college campuses. Is there a difference for FERPA purposes? It would not seem likely, as there is a university education record for the student in either case.

2. Despite the transfer of FERPA rights from parents to students at age 18 or upon postsecondary enrollment, FERPA does provide ways for educational institutions to share information with parents without the student's consent. For example, a university may disclose education records to parents if the student is an income tax dependent (20 U.S.C. § 1232g(b)(1)(H)), if there is a health and safety emergency involving their child (20 U.S.C. § 1232g(b)(1)(I)), or if the student is involved in a law or policy violation concerning drug or alcohol use or possession (20 U.S.C. § 1232g(i)(1)).

3. One of the common questions faculty members ask about FERPA is whether their personal notes are education records subject to disclosure under one of the FERPA exceptions. Personal observations and knowledge not maintained by the university or shared with others are not considered education records. As an example, a teacher's personal notes about a student with a disability, which she threw out at the end of school year, were not education records. Her act of discarding the notes was not a FERPA violation. *J.P. v. W. Clark Cmty. Schs*, 230 F. Supp. 2d 910 (S.D. Ind. 2002).

4. In 1996, the U.S. Congress passed the Health Insurance Portability and Accountability Act of 1996, or HIPAA (P.L. 104-191, 110 Stat. 1936 (1996)). *See also* 45 C.F.R §§ 160.101 *et seq.* Under HIPAA, individuals are assured of access to their medical records and are provided substantial protection regarding the records' use and disclosure. HIPAA's privacy rule applies to health plans, health care clearinghouses, and health care providers. HIPAA's application to institutions of higher education comes in the form of covered employee health plans and the provision of health care. With respect to students, universities do often serve as health care providers. These universities are required to maintain health records ("protected health information") and their privacy. A health care provider becomes a "covered entity" under HIPAA if it transmits health information in electronic form for the purposes of completing administrative or financial activities. Once a provider becomes a covered entity, all of its protected health information, electronically transmitted or not, becomes subject to HIPAA's privacy rule. Importantly, though, student health information contained in an "education record," as defined by FERPA, is subject to *FERPA*'s nondisclosure provisions and not HIPAA's.

Similar to FERPA, HIPAA has a list of exceptions to nondisclosure. Those who have access to otherwise protected health information include the patient, university staff who must have access to perform health care operations (e.g., nurses, medical assistants, pharmacists, counselors), health insurers, and courts (with a court order or subpoena).

RAGUSA v. MALVERNE UNION FREE SCHOOL DISTRICT

549 F. Supp. 2d 288 (E.D.N.Y. 2008)

A. Kathleen Tomlinson, Magistrate Judge:

I. PRELIMINARY STATEMENT

Plaintiff, a high school mathematics teacher, commenced this action seeking damages based on Defendants' alleged (1) discrimination based upon her disability, age, and national origin, including Defendants' decision to deny Plaintiff tenure, and (2) failure to accommodate Plaintiff's disability, in violation of federal and state law. Before the Court is Plaintiff's motion to compel Defendants to produce . . . "any and all documents, notes or recordings of any kind including but not limited to the grades and/or evaluations given to any and all pupils regarding academic performance and behavior in the Plaintiff's former department of employment by the Defendants, Mathematics Department, from June 2002 to present." . . . For the reasons set forth herein, Plaintiff's motion to compel is GRANTED.

II. PARTIES' ARGUMENTS

Plaintiff argues that the requested records are relevant to this action because they will allow Plaintiff to "show that the reasons Defendants gave for their actions are a mere pretext for discrimination." . . .

Plaintiff asserts that any privacy concerns that may attach to the requested student records may be disposed of, as "[t]his information may be redacted in a manner sufficient to distinguish each student without disclosing complete identifiable personal information."

Defendants argue that the requested documents are not relevant to this action because they will not "go toward meeting [Plaintiff's] burden" to establish that Defendants' articulated legitimate non-discriminatory reasons for denying Plaintiff tenure were merely a pretext for unlawful discrimination. . . .

Defendants further argue that the requested records "are private and are protected by the Family Educational Rights and Privacy Act (FERPA)." . . .

. . . .

IV. DISCUSSION

A. Relevant FERPA Provisions and Framework

The Family Educational Rights and Privacy Act of 1974 ("FERPA") provides in relevant part as follows:

> No funds shall be made available under any applicable program to any educational agency or institution which has a policy or practice of releasing, or providing access to, any personally identifiable information in education records other than directory information, or as is permitted under paragraph (1) of this subsection, unless —
>
> (A) there is written consent from the student's parents specifying records to be released, the reasons for such release, and to whom, and with a copy of the records to be released to the student's parents and the student if desired by the parents, or
>
> (B) except as provided in paragraph (1)(J), such information is furnished in compliance with judicial order, or pursuant to any lawfully issued subpoena, upon condition that parents and the students are notified of all such orders or subpoenas in advance of the compliance therewith by the educational institution or agency.

20 U.S.C. § 1232g(b)(2).

. . . .

Under the provisions of the statute, a school would not be subject to sanctions for disclosure of education records covered by FERPA when such disclosure was made pursuant to a judicial order. The inquiry, however, does not end there because the "privacy violations" that result from any disclosure of FERPA-protected education records are "no less objectionable simply because release of the records is obtained pursuant to judicial approval unless, before approval is given, the party seeking disclosure is required to demonstrate a genuine need for the information that outweighs the privacy interests of the students." *Rios* [*v. Read*, 73 F.R.D. 589, 597 (E.D.N.Y. 1977)].

Accordingly, a party seeking disclosure of education records protected by FERPA bears. . . . "[a] significantly heavier burden" to show that its interests in obtaining the records outweighed the students' privacy interests. . . .

B. Application to Plaintiff's Motion to Compel

Although Defendants' obligations and concerns regarding FERPA are well-grounded, Defendants' arguments in resisting disclosure of the requested information seek to narrow the scope of discovery to a restrictive interpretation of the brief statements contained in the Superintendent's April 20, 2005 letter setting forth three reasons for the denial of tenure. The crux of Plaintiff's Complaint, however, is that these reasons (which Defendants allege are supported by the classroom observation documents) are a pretext for discrimination. Contrary to Defendants' assertions, Plaintiff is not required to prove these allegations (or "disprove" Defendants' articulated reasons for the denial of tenure) at this juncture. Rather, Plaintiff has the right to test Defendants' proffered defenses.

In determining this issue, I have reviewed and considered, among other things, . . . documents and allegations that are relevant to the issue of pretext as well as to Defendants' position that Plaintiff was denied tenure for legitimate, non-discriminatory reasons. . . .

. . . I find that the information sought by Plaintiff's counsel is protected by FERPA. The requested documents . . . are undoubtedly "education records" within the meaning of FERPA . . . contain[ing] personally identifiable information about students. This conclusion, however, does not end the analysis, for two reasons. First, there is nothing in FERPA that would prohibit Defendants from releasing education records that had all "personally identifiable information" redacted. . . .

Second, FERPA permits Defendants to disclose students' education records to comply with a judicial order. In this case, Plaintiff has demonstrated a need for the requested education records — she has shown that these records are relevant at least to some degree in that they may aid her in an attempt to demonstrate that Defendants' articulated reasons for the denial of tenure were a pretext for unlawful discrimination. . . .

. . . .

Accordingly, I find that an order requiring disclosure of the requested education records is appropriate here because the information Plaintiff seeks is arguably relevant to her claims and is in the exclusive control of Defendants. . . . In order to temper the privacy concerns raised under FERPA, all the requested education records sought here must be produced in redacted form and subject to a protective order. . . .

. . . .

SO ORDERED.

NOTES

1. FERPA's nondisclosure rules do contain several important exceptions, including the one applied in *Ragusa,* which allowed a civil plaintiff to access redacted student records to help her make a case for employment discrimination. Other exceptions applicable in higher education, contained in 20 U.S.C. § 1232g(b)(1), include release of education records for the following purposes:

teachers and other school officials who have legitimate educational interests and need to have access to education records to perform professional responsibilities; student transfers to other educational institutions; law enforcement; financial aid applications; research conducted by or on behalf of educational agencies for certain purposes related to testing, student aid, or improving instruction; accreditation; parents (in limited circumstances typically related to a health and safety or law and policy violation); judicial order or subpoena; and national security.

2. There is some sentiment among courts that favoring disclosure of records in cases like *Ragusa* not only aids the particular plaintiff attempting to make a case for a civil rights violation, but is also in furtherance of civil rights law, generally. *See, e.g., United States v. Bertie Cty Bd. of Educ.*, 319 F. Supp. 2d 669 (E.D.N.C. 2004) (federal government's request to obtain student records as evidence of a possible violation of the Civil Rights Act of 1964 was granted, in part, due to the necessity of civil rights laws and the work necessary to enforce compliance of them).

4. Release of Discipline Records

UNITED STATES v. MIAMI UNIVERSITY

294 F.3d 797 (6th Cir. 2002)

Karl S. Forester, District Judge.

Intervening Defendant-Appellant *The Chronicle of Higher Education* ("*The Chronicle*") contests the district court's grant of summary judgment and subsequent permanent injunction in favor of Plaintiff-Appellee the United States. Specifically, the district court concluded that university disciplinary records were "educational records" as that term is defined in the Family Education Rights and Privacy Act ("FERPA"), 20 U.S.C. § 1232g, and that releasing such records and the personally identifiable information contained therein constitutes a violation of the FERPA. The district court permanently enjoined the Defendants-Appellees Miami University and The Ohio State University ("Miami," "Ohio State," or collectively "Universities") from releasing student disciplinary records or any "personally identifiable information" contained therein, except as otherwise expressly permitted under the FERPA. For the reasons that follow, we AFFIRM.

I. FACTUAL AND PROCEDURAL BACKGROUND

This case was born of a dispute between a university newspaper and the university's administration. In the spring of 1995, the editor-in-chief of Miami's student newspaper, *The Miami Student* ("the paper"), sought student disciplinary records from the University Disciplinary Board ("UDB") to track crime trends on campus. *State ex rel. Miami Student v. Miami University*, 680 N.E.2d 956, 957 (Ohio 1997). Miami initially refused to release the requested records, but after the editors made a written request pursuant to the Ohio Public Records Act for all UDB records from 1993-1996, Miami released the records. Pursuant to the FERPA privacy provisions, however, Miami redacted "from these records the identity, sex, and age of the accuseds [sic], as well as the date, time and location of the incidents giving rise to the disciplinary charges." The editors were dissatisfied with Miami's redacted disclosure and subsequently filed an original mandamus action in the Ohio Supreme Court seeking full disclosure of the UDB records, redacting only the "name, social security number, or student I.D. number of any accused or convicted party."

A divided Ohio Supreme Court granted the editors a writ of mandamus. 680 N.E.2d at 958. According to the Court, the Ohio Public Records Act "provides for full access to all public records upon request unless the requested records fall within one of the specific exceptions listed in the Act." *Id.* The relevant exception in the *Miami* case "excludes from the definition of public records those records 'the release of which is prohibited by state or federal law.' " *Id.* . . . [T]he Ohio Supreme Court concluded that university disciplinary records were not "education records" as defined in the FERPA. 680 N.E.2d at 958-59. The Ohio Court reasoned that, because disciplinary records were not protected by the FERPA, they did not fall within the prohibited-by-federal-law exception to the Ohio Public Records Act. . . .

On the heels of the Ohio Supreme Court decision, *The Chronicle*, pursuant to the Ohio Public Records Act, made written requests of Miami and Ohio State for disciplinary records amassed during the calendar years 1995 and 1996. Because the Ohio Supreme Court concluded that student disciplinary records were not educational records covered by the FERPA, *The Chronicle* requested the records with names intact and minimal redaction as required by the Ohio Public Records Act. Upon receipt of the request, and in light of the Ohio Supreme Court decision, Miami contacted the United States Department of Education ("DOE") and explained that it might not be able to comply with the FERPA. The DOE told Miami that it believed the Ohio Supreme Court was incorrect in holding that student disciplinary records are not "education records" under the FERPA. The DOE assured Miami "that the FERPA prohibits the University from releasing personally identifiable information contained in student disciplinary records."

In December of 1997, Miami complied in part with *The Chronicle*'s request by providing the newspaper virtually unredacted disciplinary records from November, 1995, and November, 1996. Miami informed the DOE that it intended to comply with the remainder of *The Chronicle*'s request. In addition, Miami advised the DOE that it "had adopted a policy of releasing disciplinary records to any third-party requestor."

In January of 1998, Ohio State confirmed with the DOE that it too had received *The Chronicle*'s request for all disciplinary records from 1995 and 1996. Ohio State informed the DOE that it already had released unredacted disciplinary records from November, 1995, and November, 1996. Thereafter, Ohio State told the DOE that it intended to comply with the remainder of *The Chronicle*'s request.

Shortly after the DOE learned that Miami and Ohio State intended to release student disciplinary records containing personally identifiable information without the consent of the student, the United States [on its behalf and on behalf of the DOE] filed the underlying complaint against the Universities. In the complaint, the DOE sought declaratory and preliminary and permanent injunctive relief prohibiting the Universities from releasing student disciplinary records that contain personally identifiable information, except as permitted under the FERPA. The

DOE immediately filed a motion to preliminarily enjoin the Universities' release of student disciplinary records. The district court granted the motion. . . .

. . . *The Chronicle* filed an unopposed motion to intervene and the district court granted the motion. *The Chronicle* subsequently filed a motion to dismiss the action and a motion to establish an order of procedure. The motion to dismiss contended that the DOE lacked standing to bring this action and that the DOE's enforcement power was limited to the administrative remedies outlined in the FERPA. The second motion alleged that *The Chronicle* may dispute certain material facts. . . .

The DOE responded to *The Chronicle*'s motions and filed its own motion for summary judgment. The district court denied *The Chronicle*'s motion to dismiss and motion for an order of procedure. Determining that the student disciplinary records were "education records" under the FERPA, the court granted the DOE's motion for summary judgment and permanently enjoined the Universities from releasing student disciplinary records in violation of the FERPA. This timely appeal followed.

II. *THE CHRONICLE'S* APPEAL

. . . .

C. Standing

On appeal, *The Chronicle* contends that the DOE and the United States do not have standing to bring this suit for injunctive relief because Congress has not conferred such authority upon them, and because they are bound by the administrative remedies enumerated in the Act and its corresponding regulations. . . .

The express language of the FERPA provides:

> The Secretary shall take appropriate actions to enforce this section and to deal with violations of this section, in accordance with this chapter, except that action to terminate assistance may be taken only if the Secretary finds there has been a failure to comply with this section, and he has determined that compliance cannot be secured by voluntary means.

20 U.S.C. § 1232g(f). Standing alone, this singular provision, allowing the Secretary to take "appropriate actions" to enforce this section, arguably may not sufficiently empower the DOE to enforce the FERPA through the courts. . . . Congress did not resign the Secretary's enforcement power to this sole, imprecise provision. Instead, 20 U.S.C. § 1234c(a) provides that the Secretary may take the following actions when a recipient of funds fails to comply with the FERPA:

> (1) withhold further payments under that program, as authorized by section 1234d of this title;
>
> (2) issue a complaint to compel compliance through a cease and desist order of the Office, as authorized by section 1234e of this title;
>
> (3) enter into a compliance agreement with a recipient to bring it into compliance, as authorized by section 1234f of this title; or
>
> (4) *take any other action authorized by law with respect to the recipient.*

Id. (emphasis added). We believe that the fourth alternative expressly permits the Secretary to bring suit to enforce the FERPA conditions in lieu of its administrative remedies. . . .

Having reached that conclusion, it follows that the DOE can proceed in equity: a common and "authorized" means to enforce legal obligations. . . .

Even in the absence of statutory authority, the United States has the inherent power to sue to enforce conditions imposed on the recipients of federal grants. "Legislation enacted pursuant to the spending power [, like the FERPA,] is much in the nature of a contract: in return for federal funds, the States agree to comply with federally imposed conditions." *Pennhurst State School and Hospital* [*v. Halderman*], 451 U.S. [1] at 17 [(1981)]. . . .

. . . .

. . . The FERPA unambiguously conditions the grant of federal education funds on the educational institutions' obligation to respect the privacy of students and their parents. . . . Based upon these clear and unambiguous terms, a participant *who accepts federal education funds* is well aware of the conditions imposed by the FERPA and is clearly able to ascertain what is expected of it. . . . [W]e believe that . . . the United States may enforce the Universities' "contractual" obligations through the traditional means available at law. If those remedies are inadequate, then the government may seek contractual relief through a court of equity.

. . . Accordingly, we hold that the DOE had standing to bring the case at bar.

D. The FERPA, *Miami* and the Ohio Public Records Act

The Chronicle finds error in the district court's alleged refusal to respect the Ohio Supreme Court's interpretation of the Ohio Public Records Act. *The Chronicle* contends that, because the Ohio Supreme Court held that disciplinary records are not "education records" as defined by the FERPA, it was unnecessary for the Court to decide whether the FERPA prohibits the disclosure of the requested records within the meaning of [Ohio public records law]. The Ohio Supreme Court noted that "the Ohio Public Records Act is intended to be liberally construed 'to ensure that governmental records be open and made available to the public . . . subject to only a few very limited and narrow exceptions.' " 680 N.E.2d at 958. Among those exceptions is a provision that "excludes from the definition of public records those records 'the release of which is prohibited by state or federal law.' " *Id.* (citing Ohio Rev. Code § 149.43(A)(1)(v)). . . .

. . . [T]he Ohio Supreme Court misinterpreted a *federal* statute — erroneously concluding that student disciplinary records were not "education records" as defined by the FERPA — and prematurely halted its inquiry based upon that erroneous conclusion. . . . Furthermore, whether the release of a particular record is prohibited by federal law necessarily implicates the interpretation of that federal law. The State of Ohio clearly recognized that necessity when it exempted from its definition of public records those records the release of which is prohibited *by federal law.* The prohibition finds its root in the federal law, not the Ohio Public Records Act. Accordingly, to the extent that the district court concluded that the

FERPA prohibited the release of education records, it did so on federal grounds.

. . . .

. . . As noted above, the Ohio Public Records Act does not require disclosure of records the release of which is prohibited by federal law. Based on that exception, the Ohio Public Records Act does not conflict with the FERPA and the state and federal statutes can coexist. . . . Unlike the case at bar, the editors in the *Miami* case permitted Miami to redact significantly the student disciplinary records prior to disclosure. . . .With these court-imposed redactions, the mandamus appears to comport with the FERPA's requirements.

In the case *sub judice, The Chronicle* seeks records fraught with personally identifiable information and virtually untainted by redaction. Given the vast difference in the records sought by *The Chronicle*, it is by no means clear that the *Miami* case would support, without exception, the release of those records.

. . . .

E. Student Disciplinary Records, Education Records and the FERPA

The Chronicle argues that the district court erred in concluding that student disciplinary records are "education records" within the contemplation of FERPA. *The Chronicle* states that there is no evidence that Congress ever intended the FERPA to protect records other than those records relating to individual student academic performance, financial aid or scholastic probation. In addition, *The Chronicle* contends that student disciplinary records involving criminal offenses should be construed as unprotected law enforcement records. Otherwise, the FERPA affords "special" privacy rights to students that the general public does not enjoy.

. . . .

The FERPA broadly defines "education records" as "those records, files, documents, and other materials which (i) contain information directly related to a student; and (ii) are maintained by an educational agency or institution or by a person acting for such agency or institution." 20 U.S.C. § 1232g(a)(4)(A). Under a plain language interpretation of the FERPA, student disciplinary records are education records because they directly relate to a student and are kept by that student's university. Notably, Congress made no content-based judgments with regard to its "education records" definition. . . . [A] detailed study of the statute and its evolution by amendment reveals that Congress intends to include student disciplinary records within the meaning of "education records" as defined by the FERPA. . . .

The FERPA sanctions the release of certain student disciplinary records in several discrete situations through exemption. The Act does not prohibit disclosure "*to an alleged victim* of any crime of violence . . . or a nonforcible sex offense, the final results of any disciplinary proceeding conducted by the institution against the alleged perpetrator . . . ." 20 U.S.C. § 1232g(b)(6)(A) (emphasis added). The *public generally* may be informed of "the final results of any disciplinary proceeding conducted by [an] institution against a student who is an alleged perpetrator of any crime of violence . . . or a nonforcible sex offense, if the institution determines . . . that the student committed a violation of the institution's rules or policies with respect to such crime or offense." *Id.* at § 1232g(b)(6)(B). "The final results of any disciplinary proceeding (i) shall include only the name of the student, the violation committed, and any sanction imposed by the institution on that student; and (ii) may include the name of any other student, such as a victim or witness, only with the written consent of that other student." *Id.* at § 1232g(b)(6)(C).

These two exemptions clearly evolve from a base Congressional assumption that student disciplinary records are "education records" and thereby protected from disclosure. Working from that base, Congress selected two particular situations in which otherwise protected student disciplinary records may be released. And even then, Congress significantly limits the amount of information that an institution may release and the people to whom the institution may release such information. . . . In so doing, Congress acknowledged that student disciplinary records are protected from disclosure but, based on competing public interests, carefully permitted schools to release bits of that information while retaining a protected status for the remainder.

Next, the disciplinary records of a student posing a significant risk to the safety or well-being of that student, other students, or other members of the school community may be disclosed to individuals having a "legitimate educational interest[] in the behavior of the student." *Id.* at § 1232g(h)(2). This provision recognizes that a student has a privacy interest in his or her disciplinary records, even if those records reflect that the student poses a significant safety risk. . . . Obviously this narrow exemption does not contemplate release of the student disciplinary records to the general public.

Finally, if an institution of higher education determines that a student, under the age of twenty-one, "has committed a disciplinary violation with respect to" the use or possession of alcohol or a controlled substance, then the institution may disclose information regarding such violation to a parent or legal guardian of the student. *Id.* at § 1232g(i)(1). Once again, this provision explicitly recognizes that student disciplinary records are education records and therefore are protected from disclosure. In spite of that protection, Congress concluded that a parent, not the general public, had a right to know about such violations.

If Congress believed that student disciplinary records were not education records under the FERPA, then these sections would be superfluous. . . .

In addition to the exemptions discussed above, Congress also provided some exceptions to the "education records" definition. Relevant among those exceptions, the term "education records" does not include "records maintained by a law enforcement unit of the educational agency or institution that were created by that law enforcement unit for the purpose of law enforcement." 20 U.S.C. § 1232g(a)(4)(B)(ii). Because law enforcement records are by definition not education records, the FERPA does not protect law enforcement records or place restriction on their disclosure.

The Chronicle notes, without objection, that student disciplinary proceedings can and sometimes do involve serious criminal conduct. Based upon that fact, it argues that student disciplinary records addressing such conduct are law enforcement records and should be disclosed to the public. Faced with this argument and the fact that this provision is somewhat ambiguous, the district court turned to the DOE's regulations for interpretive assistance. We agree with this approach.

. . . .

The agency draws a clear distinction between student disciplinary records and law enforcement unit records. The former are protected as "education records" under the FERPA without regard to their content while the latter are excluded from the definition of "education records" and receive no protection by the FERPA. In the records request that gave rise to the underlying suit and this appeal, *The Chronicle* asked Miami and Ohio State to please send "copies of records of all disciplinary proceedings handled by the university's internal judicial system for the calendar years 1995 and 1996." Even though some of the disciplinary proceedings may have addressed criminal offenses that also constitute violations of the Universities' rules or policies, the records from those proceedings are still protected "education records" within the meaning of the FERPA.

. . . .

G. Injunctive Relief

. . . .

One explicit purpose of the FERPA is "to protect [students'] rights to privacy by limiting the transferability of their records without their consent." Joint Statement, 120 Cong. Rec. 39858, 39862 (1974). Congress effectuated this purpose by providing that: "No funds shall be made available under any applicable program to any educational agency or institution which has a policy or practice of releasing, or providing access to, any personally identifiable information in education records." 20 U.S.C. § 1232g(b)(2). . . . Once personally identifiable information has been made public, the harm cannot be undone.

. . . It logically follows that if Congress values the privacy interests acknowledged in the Congressional record, and authorizes the DOE to enforce those privacy interests, it must also contemplate that the DOE experiences the irreparable harm suffered by those students whose privacy interests are violated. . . .

Moreover, millions of people in our society have been or will become students at an educational agency or institution, and those people are the object of FERPA's privacy guarantees. Accordingly, systematic violations of the FERPA provision result in appreciable consequences to the public and no doubt are a matter of public interest. . . . In light of the noble and broad objectives of the FERPA and the irreparable harm to the public interest, injunctive relief was appropriate in this case.

. . . .

III. CONCLUSION

Because the district court's grant of summary judgment was consistent with legal precedent and sound statutory interpretation, and because the district court did not abuse its discretion in denying discovery or granting a permanent injunction, we AFFIRM.

NOTES

1. What are the central differences between *Ragusa*, presented earlier, and the *Miami University* case? They are both about a balance of interests — individual privacy and the public's right to access information. In *Ragusa*, the individual privacy interests were balanced against the right of a civil plaintiff to access evidence useful in her discrimination case against her employer. In *Miami University*, the individual interests were weighed against an interest affecting the entire public and not merely one member of it. Was the potential extent of public disclosure a primary difference-maker in the two cases? The *Chronicle of Higher Education* asserted a First Amendment interest in the information it requested. Why did the court reject it? In your opinion, should student discipline records be considered "education records" subject to FERPA? Do you agree with the result in this case? Why or why not?

2. Where a state has a "right to know" provision in its law, the question of access to student disciplinary records may be more easily answered. *See, e.g., Bd. of Trs. v. Cut Bank Pioneer Press*, 160 P.3d 482 (2007) (FERPA does not prevent the public release of redacted student disciplinary records in case where local press brought action under the "right to know" provision of the state's constitution).

3. The *Miami University* case dealt with student disciplinary records. What about student statements made in an employee discipline case? How might FERPA protect students' identities in such cases? Can copies of student statements alleging that a school employee engaged in inappropriate sexual behavior toward them be provided to that employee for his defense with the students' names and addresses redacted? Or do the students' identities have to be disclosed? In other words, do the students' statements become part of their "education records"? *See Wallace v. Cranbrook Educ. Cmty.*, No. 05-73446, 2006 U.S. Dist. LEXIS 71251 (E.D. Mich. Sept. 27, 2006) (magistrate ordered that the students' identities be disclosed). In another example, *Ellis v. Cleveland Mun. Sch. Dist.*, 309 F. Supp. 2d 1019 (N.D. Ohio 2004), the court held that FERPA should not shield allegations of abuse by substitute teachers from discovery in private actions designed to combat such abuse. According to the court, FERPA applies to student records and not educator or employee records. Similar to the discussion in *Ragusa*, however, the court in *Ellis* held that even if the records had been protected by FERPA, discovery would have been permitted to uphold the spirit of the laws designed to combat abuse. In other words, statements from witnesses and victims of alleged abuse ought to be discoverable if we want anti-abuse and anti-harassment laws and policies to be effective.

4. Footnote 15 in *Miami University* explicitly distinguishes the *Miami* decision from *Bauer v. Kincaid*, 759 F. Supp. 575 (W.D. Mo. 1991):

> The holding in *Bauer v. Kincaid*, 759 F. Supp. 575 (W.D. Mo. 1991), does not affect [the] conclusion [that discipline records are education records under FERPA]. Having closely reviewed *Bauer*, we believe that the records sought in that case, criminal investigation and incident records compiled and maintained by the Southwest Missouri State University Safety and Security Department, would likely fall within the *current* law enforcement unit records exception. In fact, the subsequent amendments to the FERPA and its regulations were likely designed to bring the *Bauer* documents clearly within the law enforcement unit records exception. *See* 20 U.S.C. § 1232g(a)(4)(B)(ii); 34 C.F.R. § 99.8(a)(1)(i),(ii). It goes without saying, however, that the records sought in *Bauer*, incident and criminal investigation reports gathered and maintained by a campus safety and security department, are entirely different than the records sought by *The Chronicle* in this case, *to wit*, copies of records of all disciplinary proceedings handled by the university's internal judicial system.

So, according to *Bauer*, a public university student newspaper editor is entitled to receive and publish criminal investigation and incident reports compiled by a campus security department. Do you agree that these records should be legally differentiated from student discipline records? What are the primary differences between the two types of records? And why are these differences sufficient enough to distinguish between the two for FERPA purposes?

5. Both *Bauer* and *Miami University* involved student journalists and their popular First Amendment argument that the public has the right to know. Can a member of the *general* public request such records from university officials? In *Norwood v. Slammons*, 788 F. Supp. 1020 (W.D. Ark. 1991), a prospective law student's action against university officials for failing to release information pursuant to FERPA was dismissed, where the prospective student sought records relating to school disciplinary proceedings against several athletes for a sexual incident in an athletic dorm. According to the court:

> It is a non sequitur to say . . . that merely because the press may have a right to print accurate information, for example, regarding the identities of crime victims and gory details of the crime, does not, by any stretch of the imagination, compel the conclusion that members of the general public have a right to acquire that information from any governmental employee, or body which might possess the same.

788 F. Supp. at 1027. See also the following case.

5. Law Enforcement Exception to Nondisclosure

DEFEO v. MCABOY

260 F. Supp. 2d 790 (E.D. Mo. 2003)

David D. Noce, United States Magistrate Judge.

This matter is before the court upon the motion of defendant for a protective order . . . prohibiting disclosure of documents that plaintiff subpoenaed from

Rockhurst College about defendant. . . .

. . . Plaintiff Ben DeFeo alleges that on March 28, 1999, while he was standing in the front yard of defendant's residence at 5345 Tracy in Kansas City, Missouri, defendant Christopher McAboy while intoxicated negligently drove his motor vehicle into plaintiff injuring him. DeFeo seeks both compensatory and punitive damages.

The record indicates that during March 1999 plaintiff and defendant were post-secondary students at Rockhurst College in Kansas City. The events that occurred at 5345 Tracy on March 27 and 28, 1999, involving plaintiff and defendant were investigated by the Rockhurst College Safety and Security Department and they were the subject matter of college disciplinary proceedings against defendant. Pursuant to an order of this court on September 19, 2002, on September 20 plaintiff issued to Rockhurst a subpoena for the production of "Any and all documents relating to the incident. . . .

Defendant objects to disclosure of these documents to plaintiff, because (1) these documents are privileged from disclosure by the Family Educational Rights and Privacy Act (FERPA), 20 U.S.C. § 1232g; and (2) many of the documents involve incidents unrelated to the alleged driving while intoxicated incident. In response, plaintiff argues (1) he seeks documents that relate only to the incident at 5345 Tracy, and (2) he is entitled to any written statement by defendant about that incident, because such a statement is outside the scope of FERPA.

Subject to certain conditions and exceptions, FERPA generally provides for the confidentiality of colleges' "education records" of students. . . .

FERPA excepts from the confidentiality of "education records" documents and records sought in response to subpoenas issued by a federal grand jury. § 1232g(b)(1)(J)(i). However, the issuing court or agency *must* order the educational institution not to disclose the existence or contents of the subpoena or any information furnished in response to it. Regarding other subpoenas issued for law enforcement purposes, the issuing court or agency *may* issue such a confidentiality order. § 1232g(b)(1)(J)(ii).

Regarding compliance with judicial orders or subpoenas lawfully issued for other purposes than law enforcement, FERPA allows the disclosure of the subject education records, upon condition that "parents and the students are notified of all such orders or subpoenas in advance of the compliance therewith by the educational institution or agency." § 1232g(b)(2).

FERPA allows disclosure of education records to the victims of certain crimes:

> (6)(A) Nothing in this section shall be construed to prohibit an institution of postsecondary education from disclosing, to an alleged victim of any crime of violence . . . , or a nonforcible sex offense, the final results of any disciplinary proceeding conducted by such institution against the alleged perpetrator of such crime or offense with respect to such crime or offense.

20 U.S.C. § 1232g(b)(6)(A).

The Secretary of Education has issued regulations to implement FERPA. Those regulations provide that, without getting the consent of the student, the educational institution may disclose education records if

> (a)(9)(i) [T]he disclosure is to comply with a judicial order or lawfully issued subpoena.
>
> (ii) The educational . . . institution may disclose information under paragraph (a)(9)(i) of this section only if the . . . institution makes a reasonable effort to notify the parent or eligible student of the order or subpoena in advance of compliance, so that the parent or eligible student may seek protective action, unless the disclosure is in compliance with —
>
>> (A) A Federal grand jury subpoena and the court has ordered that the existence or the contents of the subpoena or the information furnished in response to the subpoena not be disclosed; or
>>
>> (B) Any other subpoena issued for a law enforcement purpose and the court or other issuing agency has ordered that the existence or the contents of the subpoena or the information furnished in response to the subpoena not be disclosed.

34 C.F.R. § 99.31(a)(9)(2000).

. . . .

The [forty-two] documents at issue fall into two distinct groups, disciplinary records and law enforcement records. Disciplinary records are within the general definition of protected "education records" in § 1232g(a)(4)(A) (documents containing information about the student and maintained by the educational institution). *See United States v. Miami Univ.*, 294 F.3d 797, 812 (6th Cir. 2002). After reviewing the submitted documents in camera, the court finds that Documents 1, 2, 5 through 29, and 38 are records of the college's disciplinary proceedings against defendant.

The negligent driving while intoxicated, which plaintiff alleges in the instant action, is not alleged to involve a crime of violence or a nonforcible sex offense, as defined by the statute and the regulation; if defendant's actions had involved such a crime, the college may even then disclose only the "final results" of the disciplinary proceedings. Except for the fact that these documents were the subject of a lawful subpoena issued by this court, which is discussed below, the disciplinary record documents enumerated would be protected from disclosure by FERPA.

The campus police department law enforcement records are specifically excluded from the definition of protected education records by § 1232g(b)(4)(F)(ii) (records created and maintained by a law enforcement unit of the educational institution for law enforcement purposes). The court finds that Documents 3, 4, 30 through 37, and 39 through 42 are such documents and are not protected by FERPA.

As mentioned above, Rockhurst College submitted the subject documents to the court under seal for disposition of defendant's motion for a protective order. In doing so it gave defendant, the student involved, notice of the subpoena and an opportunity to seek protective action which defendant did. Thus, although the record is silent on the college's notice to defendant's parents, it substantially complied with 20 U.S.C. § 1232g(b)(2)(B) and 34 C.F.R. § 99.31(a)(9)(i) and (ii). A plain reading of this section of FERPA and the relevant regulation indicates that, the condition of notice having been accomplished, all of the submitted documents are outside the protection of FERPA. . . .

. . . .

NOTES

1. Recall that the courts do not recognize a private right of action for damages under Section 1983 to enforce provisions of FERPA. FERPA, however, does provide for some form of punishment for institutions that ignore its rules. For instance, the statute states that federal funds are to be withheld from educational institutions that have "a policy or practice of permitting the release of education records" without parental consent. 20 U.S.C. § 1232g(b)(1). There are several exceptions to this nondisclosure rule, including disclosure of education records in response to a subpoena or other judicial order. What is the rationale for the judicial order or subpoena exception? And what connection do you think such exceptions have with the overall statement that educational institutions will lose federal funding if they have a "policy or practice" of permitting the release of education records? Is the lack of such a policy or practice a justification for these exceptions?

2. Often, the judicial order of disclosure is based on a ruling of whether the evidence desired is relevant to the case being made, and whether the case is criminal or civil. *See, e.g., State v Birdsall*, 568 P.2d 1094 (Ariz. Ct. App. 1977) (FERPA does not bar disclosure of murder victim's school records in criminal trial of alleged murderer where victim's reputation for belligerence and aggressiveness was at issue); *Fairchild v Liberty Indep. Sch. Dist.*, 466 F. Supp. 2d 817 (E.D. Tex. 2006) (the emergency medical records of special education students were disclosed and admissible in a case where a teacher's aide was allegedly dismissed for complaining about a teacher's dereliction of duty; evidence was admitted to assist the aide's argument that she was dismissed in retaliation for her exercise of the First Amendment).

6. FERPA and Alleged Copyright Infringement

WARNER BROS. RECORDS INC. v. DOES 1-6

527 F. Supp. 2d 1 (D.D.C. 2007)

EMMET G. SULLIVAN, UNITED STATES DISTRICT JUDGE.

Pending before the Court is Plaintiffs' Motion for Leave to Take Expedited Discovery. Upon review of the Motion and the applicable law, the Court GRANTS the motion.

I. BACKGROUND

Plaintiffs are record companies suing a series of John Doe defendants for copyright infringement. Plaintiffs request permission to serve limited, immediate discovery on Georgetown University, a third party internet service provider ("ISP"), in the form of a Rule 45 subpoena. Plaintiffs seek documents and electronically stored information sufficient to identify each defendant's true name, current and permanent addresses and telephone numbers, email address, and Media Access Control ("MAC") address.

Plaintiffs allege that the Doe defendants used an online media distribution system (e.g., a peer-to-peer or "P2P" system) to download plaintiffs' copyrighted works and/or distribute copyrighted works to the public without authorization. Although plaintiffs do not know the true names of the Doe defendants, plaintiffs have identified each defendant by a unique Internet Protocol ("IP") Address assigned to that defendant on the date and at the time of that defendant's allegedly infringing activity. Plaintiffs have identified the ISP that provided Internet access to each defendant by using a publicly available database. Based on that information, plaintiffs have determined that the ISP in this case is Georgetown University. Plaintiffs further represent that when given a defendant's IP address and the time and date of infringing activity, an ISP can quickly and easily identify the name and address of the Doe defendant by referring to the ISP's activity log files. Without this information, plaintiffs aver they will be unable to prosecute their claims or protect their copyrighted works from future infringement.

II. STANDARD OF REVIEW

. . . .

Because Georgetown University is an educational institution, the Family Educational Rights and Privacy Act (FERPA), 20 U.S.C. 1232g, is implicated by this request. Under FERPA, information otherwise protected from disclosure may be released pursuant to a court order. General statutory bans on publication do not bar limited disclosure in judicial proceedings, including court-supervised discovery, so long as the party seeking discovery makes the requisite showing of relevance to the litigation under Federal Rule of Civil Procedure 26. . . .

III. ANALYSIS

The Court finds that plaintiffs have made a showing of good cause for the discovery they seek, as the information is not only relevant but crucial to the prosecution of plaintiffs' claims. This litigation cannot go forward without the true identities of the defendants. Therefore, the Court GRANTS plaintiffs' request for expedited discovery, subject to the following limitations.

Plaintiffs may serve a Rule 45 subpoena upon Georgetown University to obtain the true identity of each Doe defendant. The subpoena must be limited to information sufficient to identify each defendant, including each defendant's true name, current and permanent addresses and telephone numbers, email address, and Media Access Control ("MAC") address. Any information disclosed to plaintiffs in response to the Rule 45 subpoena may be used by plaintiffs solely for the purpose of protecting plaintiffs' rights as set forth in the complaint.

The disclosure of this information is consistent with Georgetown University's obligations under the Family Educational Rights and Privacy Act (FERPA). Though FERPA generally prohibits disclosure of certain records by federally-funded educational institutions, it expressly provides that protected information can be disclosed pursuant to a court order. 20 U.S.C. 1232g(b)(2)(B). If the John Doe defendants are Georgetown University students, FERPA requires that Georgetown University notify the student defendants prior to turning this information over to plaintiffs. *Id.* If and when Georgetown is served with a subpoena, it shall provide written notice to the Doe defendants within five business days. If Georgetown or any defendant wishes to move to quash the subpoena, that party must do so before the return date of the subpoena which shall be 25 days from the date of service. Georgetown University shall preserve any subpoenaed information pending the resolution of any timely filed motion to quash. Plaintiffs shall provide Georgetown University with a copy of this Memorandum Opinion and accompanying Order along with its subpoena.

IV. CONCLUSION

For the foregoing reasons, the plaintiffs' Motion for Leave to Take Expedited Discovery is GRANTED. An appropriate Order accompanies this Opinion.

NOTES

1. As you might guess, *Warner Bros. Records Inc.*, presented above, is one of many, very similar cases filed by copyright holders against college students allegedly illegally downloading copyrighted music. The *Warner Brothers* case is representative of the majority of these cases, in that FERPA's nondisclosure provisions do not prohibit the release of the alleged infringers' name, current and permanent addresses and telephone numbers, email address, and media access control addresses, all released pursuant to a court order. *See also Arista Records, LLC v. John Does 1-19*, 551 F. Supp. 2d 1 (D.D.C. 2008); *Arista Records, LLC v. Does 1-27*, 584 F. Supp. 2d 240 (D. Me. 2008); *Loud Records, LLC v. Minervini*, 621 F. Supp. 2d 672 (W.D. Wis. 2009); *Arista Records LLC v. Does 1-16*, Civ. No. 1:08-CV-765, 2009 U.S. Dist. LEXIS 12159 (N.D.N.Y. 2009), *aff'd*, 2010 U.S. App. LEXIS 8879 (2d Cir. Apr. 29, 2010); *Arista Records LLC v. Does 1-4*, 589 F. Supp.2d 151 (D. Conn. 2008); *Arista Records, LLC v. Does 1-9*, No. 2:07-cv-961, 2008 U.S. Dist. LEXIS 57734 (S.D. Ohio July 29, 2008).

2. Often, these complaints resolve the FERPA issue very quickly and move to more "procedural" matters, like analyzing the actual words in a subpoena. In *Arista Records LLC v. Does 1-14*, No. 7:08cv00205, 2008 U.S. Dist. LEXIS 102974 (W.D. Va. Dec 22, 2008), for example, the plaintiff copyright holders requested information in a two-sentence subpoena. The first sentence requested "[i]nformation, including name, current and permanent addresses, telephone numbers, e-mail addresses, and [MAC] addresses, sufficient to identify the alleged infringers of copyrighted sound recordings, listed by IP address in Attachment A to this Subpoena." Virginia Tech University, the third-party internet service provider in the case, argued that it could not provide the information for some of the defendants because more than one individual lived in the residence hall room associated with the IP addresses provided. There was no single name that the university could provide for that particular address. "Because the four IP addresses in question are associated with a data outlet in a dormitory room, as opposed to an individual, there is no way for Virginia Tech to provide what the subpoena commands, i.e., '[i]nformation . . . sufficient to identify the alleged infringers.' " *Id.* at *23.

The second sentence of the subpoena requested that, if Virginia Tech could not link an IP address to a specific individual, then it had to "provide all documents and electronically-stored information relating to the assignment of the IP address." The university produced network session file logs that indicated the IP addresses that were associated with particular outlets for rooms within the residence halls. The university asserted that this was all it could produce and the court agreed.

3. One of the defenses offered by universities in such cases is a motion to quash the subpoena for imposing an "undue burden of production." Courts are mixed on such motions, and decide them very often on a case-by-case basis. In *Zomba Recording LLC v. Does 1-15*, No. 08-31-HRW, 2008 U.S. Dist. LEXIS 106500 (E.D. Ky. June 2, 2008), for example, the court found that Morehead State University had complied with similar requests in the past and, as a result, did not show an undue burden of production. Its motion to quash was denied. Reaching an opposite result was the court in *Arista Records, LLC v. Does 1-17*, Civ. No. 07-6197-HO, 2008 U.S. Dist. LEXIS 106461 (D. Ore. Sept. 25, 2008). The subpoena required the university to provide "information . . . sufficient to identify the alleged infringers of copyrighted sound recordings," which the court found unduly burdensome. The reason for the burden was that the majority of the defendants accessed the content using IP addresses assigned to single or double occupancy dormitory rooms, or from the university's wireless network. In other words, the university knew the IP addresses, but did not know of the identities of the people who accessed the content at issue in the case.

Chapter VI

STUDENT FREE EXPRESSION

Introduction

In the landmark case of *Tinker v. Des Moines Independent Community School District*, 393 U.S. 503 (1969), the Supreme Court offered one of the most memorable, meaningful statements in education law: "It can hardly be argued that either teachers or students shed their constitutional rights to freedom of speech or expression at the schoolhouse gate." *Id.* at 506. Not only has this statement been applied to support other constitutional rights such as due process and privacy, it also has application and inspiration in higher education settings. In *Tinker*, the Court struck down a policy that prohibited students from wearing black armbands in silent political protest of the Vietnam War, primarily because the wearing of the armbands did not materially or substantially disrupt the work of the school or infringe on the rights of others. Undoubtedly, the school administrators were troubled by the protests they had seen on local college campuses and elsewhere in the community and wished to prevent them on their own campuses. In response, the Court said:

> But, in our system, undifferentiated fear or apprehension of disturbance is not enough to overcome the right to freedom of expression. Any departure from absolute regimentation may cause trouble. Any variation from the majority's opinion may inspire fear. Any word spoken, in class, in the lunchroom, or on the campus, that deviates from the views of another person may start an argument or cause a disturbance. But our Constitution says we must take this risk.

Id. at 508.

The same sentiments are expressed in higher education as well. As it is with most discussions of constitutional rights, the resolution of legal conflict usually leads to a balancing of rights and interests. On one hand, there is the individual right to exercise freedoms so foundational to our nation. On the other hand, there are institutional rights and responsibilities to establish and implement curriculum and policy, and manage the institution's resources, personnel, and facilities. Chapter VI explores this balancing act from the perspectives of both students and their colleges and universities.

This chapter covers students' free speech rights and offers many examples of the classic constitutional balance between individual rights and institutional responsibilities: student protests (*Cox*, *Tinker*, and *Orin*), student organizations and activity fees (*Christian Legal Society*, *Rosenberger*, and *Southworth*), student publications (*Papish* and *Kincaid*), fraternities and sororities (*Pi Lambda Phi*), hate speech codes (*DeJohn*), and student speech in academic settings (*Brown* and *Axson-Flynn*). To be expected, courts are presented with issues of potential disruption and controversial ideas, but they are also presented with a line-drawing affair — between funded and nonfunded activity and between curricular and noncurricular (or cocurricular) activity. In these contexts, the balancing act is sometimes tricky and often variable.

A. STUDENT PROTESTS

COX v. LOUISIANA
379 U.S. 559 (1965)

MR. JUSTICE GOLDBERG delivered the opinion of the Court.

Appellant was convicted of violating a Louisiana statute which provides:

"Whoever, with the intent of interfering with, obstructing, or impeding the administration of justice, or with the intent of influencing any judge, juror, witness, or court officer, in the discharge of his duty pickets or parades in or near a building housing a court of the State of Louisiana . . . shall be fined not more than five thousand dollars or imprisoned not more than one year, or both." La. Rev. Stat. § 14:401 (Cum. Supp. 1962).

. . . Appellant was convicted on this charge also and was sentenced to the maximum penalty under the statute of one year in jail and a $5,000 fine. . . . These convictions were affirmed by the Louisiana Supreme Court. Appellant appealed to this Court contending that the statute was unconstitutional on its face and as applied to him. . . .

I.

We shall first consider appellant's contention that this statute must be declared invalid on its face as an unjustified restriction upon freedoms guaranteed by the First and Fourteenth Amendments to the United States Constitution.

This statute was passed by Louisiana in 1950 and was modeled after a bill pertaining to the federal judiciary, which Congress enacted later in 1950, 64 Stat. 1018, 18 U. S. C. § 1507 (1958 ed.). . . . The federal statute resulted from the picketing of federal courthouses by partisans of the defendants during trials involving leaders of the Communist Party. This picketing prompted an adverse reaction from both the bar and the general public. A number of groups urged legislation to prohibit it. . . . This statute, unlike the two previously considered, is a precise, narrowly drawn regulatory statute which proscribes certain specific behavior. It prohibits a particular type of conduct, namely, picketing and parading, in a few specified locations, in or near courthouses.

There can be no question that a State has a legitimate interest in protecting its judicial system from the pressures which picketing near a courthouse might create. Since we are committed to a government of laws and not of men, it is of the utmost importance that the administration of justice be absolutely fair and orderly. . . . A State may adopt safeguards necessary and appropriate to assure that the administration of justice at all stages is free from outside control and influence. A narrowly drawn statute such as the one under review is obviously a safeguard both necessary and appropriate to vindicate the State's interest in assuring justice under law.

Nor does such a statute infringe upon the constitutionally protected rights of free speech and free assembly. The conduct which is the subject of this statute — picketing and parading — is subject to regulation even though intertwined with expression and association. The examples are many of the application by this Court of the principle that certain forms of conduct mixed with speech may be regulated or prohibited. The most classic of these was pointed out long ago by Mr. Justice Holmes: "The most stringent protection of free speech would not protect a man in falsely shouting fire in a theatre and causing a panic." *Schenck v. United States*, 249 U.S. 47, 52. A man may be punished for encouraging the commission of a crime, *Fox v. Washington*, 236 U.S. 273, or for uttering "fighting words," *Chaplinsky v. New Hampshire*, 315 U.S. 568. This principle has been applied to picketing and parading in labor disputes. See . . . *Giboney v. Empire Storage & Ice Co.*, 336 U.S. 490. . . . These authorities make it clear, as the Court said in *Giboney*, that "it has never been deemed an abridgment of freedom of speech or press to make a course of conduct illegal merely because the conduct was in part initiated, evidenced, or carried out by means of language, either spoken, written, or printed." [*Id.*] at 502.

. . . We are not concerned here with such a pure form of expression as newspaper comment or a telegram by a citizen to a public official. We deal in this case not with free speech alone, but with expression mixed with particular conduct. In *Giboney*, this Court expressly recognized this distinction when it said, "In holding this, we are mindful of the essential importance to our society of a vigilant protection of freedom of speech and press. States cannot consistently with our Constitution abridge those freedoms to obviate slight inconveniences or annoyances. But placards used as an essential and inseparable part of a grave offense against an important public law cannot immunize that unlawful conduct from state control." 336 U.S., at 501-502 [internal citations omitted].

We hold that this statute on its face is a valid law dealing with conduct subject to regulation so as to vindicate important interests of society and that the fact that free speech is intermingled with such conduct does not bring with it constitutional protection.

II.

We now deal with the Louisiana statute as applied to the conduct in this case. The group of 2,000, led by appellant, paraded and demonstrated before the courthouse. Judges and court officers were in attendance to discharge their respective functions. It is undisputed that a major purpose of the demonstration was to protest what the demonstrators considered an "illegal" arrest of 23 students the previous day. While the students had not been arraigned or their trial set for any day certain, they were charged with violation of the law, and the judges responsible for trying them and passing upon the legality of their arrest were then in the building.

It is, of course, true that most judges will be influenced only by what they see and hear in court. However, judges are human; and the legislature has the right to recognize the danger that some judges, jurors, and other court officials, will be consciously or unconsciously influenced by demonstrations in or near their courtrooms both prior to and at the time of the trial. A State may also properly protect the judicial process from being misjudged in the minds of the public. Suppose demonstrators paraded and picketed for weeks with signs asking that indictments be dismissed, and that a judge, completely uninfluenced by these demonstrations, dismissed the indictments. A State may protect against the possibility of a conclusion by the public under these circumstances that the judge's action was in part a product of intimidation and did not flow only from the fair and orderly working of the judicial process.

Appellant invokes the clear and present danger doctrine in support of his argument that the statute cannot constitutionally be applied to the conduct involved here. He says . . . that "no reason exists to apply a different standard to the case of a criminal penalty for a peaceful demonstration in front of a courthouse than the standard of clear and present danger applied in the contempt cases." He defines the standard to be applied to both situations to be whether the expression of opinion presents a clear and present danger to the administration of justice.

. . . Here we deal . . . with a narrowly drafted statute and not with speech in its pristine form but with conduct of a totally different character. Even assuming the applicability of a general clear and present danger test, it is one thing to conclude that the mere publication of a newspaper editorial or a telegram to a Secretary of Labor, however critical of a court, presents no clear and present danger to the administration of justice and quite another thing to conclude that crowds, such as this, demonstrating before a courthouse may not be prohibited by a legislative determination based on experience that such conduct inherently threatens the judicial process. We therefore reject the clear and present danger argument of appellant.

III.

Appellant additionally argues that his conviction violated due process as there was no evidence of intent to obstruct justice or influence any judicial official as required by the statute. *Thompson v. Louisville*, 362 U.S. 199. We cannot agree that there was no evidence within the "due process" rule enunciated in *Thompson v. Louisville*. We have already noted that various witnesses and Cox himself stated that a major purpose of the demonstration was to protest what was considered to be an illegal arrest of 23 students. Thus, the very subject matter of the demonstration was an arrest which is normally the first step in a series of legal proceedings. The demonstration was held in the vicinity of the courthouse where the students' trials would take place. The courthouse contained the judges who in normal course would be called upon to try the students' cases just as they tried appellant. Ronnie Moore, the student leader of the demonstration, a defense witness, stated, as we understand his testimony, that the demonstration was in part to protest injustice; he felt it was a form of "moral persuasion" and hoped it would have its effects. The fact that the students were not then on trial and had not been arraigned is not controlling in the face of this affirmative evidence manifesting the plain intent of the demonstrators to condemn the arrest and ensuing judicial proceedings against the prisoners as unfair and unwarranted. The fact that by their lights appellant and the 2,000 students were seeking justice and not its obstruction is as irrelevant as would be the motives of the mob condemned by Justice Holmes in *Frank v. Mangum*, [237 U.S. 309 (1915) (Holmes, J., dissenting)]. Louisiana, as we have pointed out, has the right to construe its statute to prevent parading and picketing from unduly influencing the administration of justice at any point or time in its process, regardless of whether the motives of the demonstrators are good or bad.

While this case contains direct evidence taking it out of the *Thompson v. Louisville* doctrine, even without this evidence, we would be compelled to reject the contention that there was no proof of intent. Louisiana surely has the right to infer the appropriate intent from circumstantial evidence. At the very least, a group of demonstrators parading and picketing before a courthouse where a criminal charge is pending, in protest against the arrest of those charged, may be presumed to intend to influence judges, jurors, witnesses or court officials.

. . . .

IV.

There are, however, more substantial constitutional objections arising from appellant's conviction on the particular facts of this case. Appellant was convicted for demonstrating not "in," but "near" the courthouse. It is undisputed that the demonstration took place on the west sidewalk, the far side of the street, exactly 101 feet from the courthouse steps and, judging from the pictures in the record, approximately 125 feet from the courthouse itself. The question is raised as to whether the failure of the statute to define the word "near" renders it unconstitutionally vague. . . . It is clear that there is some lack of specificity in a word such as "near." While this lack of specificity may not render the statute unconstitutionally vague, at least as applied to a demonstration within the sight and hearing of those in the courthouse, it is clear that the statute, with respect to the determination of how near the courthouse a particular demonstration can be, foresees a degree of on-the-spot administrative interpretation by officials charged with responsibility for administering and enforcing it. It is apparent that demonstrators, such as those involved here, would justifiably tend to rely on this administrative interpretation of how "near" the courthouse a particular demonstration might take place. Louisiana's statutory policy of preserving order around the courthouse would counsel encouragement of just such reliance. This administrative discretion to construe the term "near" concerns a limited control of the streets and other areas in the immediate vicinity of the courthouse and is the type of narrow discretion which this Court has recognized as the proper role of responsible officials in making determinations concerning the time, place, duration, and manner of demonstrations. . . . It is not the type of unbridled discretion which would allow an official to pick and choose among expressions of view the ones he will permit to use the streets and other public facilities. . . . Nor does this limited administrative regulation of traffic, which the Court has consistently recognized as necessary and permissible, constitute a waiver of law which is beyond the power of the police. . . .

The record here clearly shows that the officials present gave permission for the demonstration to take place across the street from the courthouse. Cox testified that they gave him permission to conduct the demonstration on the far side of the street. This testimony is not only uncontradicted but is corroborated by the State's witnesses who were present. Police Chief White testified that he told Cox "he must confine" the demonstration "to the west side of the street." . . . When Sheriff Clemmons sought to break up the demonstration, he first announced, "now, you have been allowed to demonstrate." The Sheriff testified that he had "no objection" to the students "being assembled on that side of the street." Finally, in its brief before this Court, the State did not contend that permission was not granted. Rather in its statement of the facts and argument it conceded that the officials gave Cox and his group some time to demonstrate across the street from the courthouse. . . .

The record shows that at no time did the police recommend, or even suggest, that the demonstration be held further from the courthouse than it actually was. The police admittedly had prior notice that the demonstration was planned to be held in the vicinity of the courthouse. They were prepared for it at that point and so stationed themselves and their equipment as to keep the demonstrators on the far side of the street. As Cox approached the vicinity of the courthouse, he was met by the Chief of Police and other officials. At this point not only was it not suggested that they hold their assembly elsewhere, or disband, but they were affirmatively told that they could hold the demonstration on the sidewalk of the far side of the street, 101 feet from the courthouse steps. This area was effectively blocked off by the police and traffic rerouted.

Thus, the highest police officials of the city, in the presence of the Sheriff and Mayor, in effect told the demonstrators that they could meet where they did, 101 feet from the courthouse steps, but could not meet closer to the courthouse. In effect, appellant was advised that a demonstration at the place it was held would not be one "near" the courthouse within the terms of the statute.

. . . [U]nder all the circumstances of this case, after the public officials acted as they did, to sustain appellant's later conviction for demonstrating where they told him he could "would be to sanction an indefensible sort of entrapment by the State — convicting a citizen for exercising a privilege which the State had clearly told him was available to him." [*Raley v. Ohio*, 360 U.S. 423,] 426. The Due Process Clause does not permit convictions to be obtained under such circumstances.

This is not to say that had the appellant, entirely on his own, held the demonstration across the street from the courthouse within the sight and hearing of those inside, or *a fortiori*, had he defied an order of the police requiring him to hold this demonstration at some point further away out of the sight and hearing of those inside the courthouse, we would reverse the conviction as in this case. In such cases a state interpretation of the statute to apply to the demonstration as being "near" the courthouse would be subject to quite different considerations.

There remains just one final point: the effect of the Sheriff's order to disperse. The State in effect argues that this order somehow removed the prior grant of permission and reliance on the officials' construction that the demonstration on the far side of the street was not illegal as being "near" the courthouse. This, however, we cannot accept. Appellant was led to believe that his demonstration on the far side of the street violated no statute. He was expressly ordered to leave, not because he was peacefully demonstrating too near the courthouse, nor because a time limit originally set had expired, but because officials erroneously concluded that what he said threatened a breach of the peace. This is apparent from the face of the Sheriff's statement when he ordered the meeting dispersed: "Now, you have been allowed to demonstrate. Up until now your demonstration has been more or less peaceful, but what you are doing now is a direct violation of the law, a disturbance of the peace, and it has got to be broken up immediately." Appellant correctly conceived . . . that this was not a valid reason for the dispersal order. He therefore was still justified in his continued belief that because of the original official grant of permission he had a right to stay where he was for the few additional minutes required to conclude the meeting.

In addition, even if we were to accept the State's version that the sole reason for terminating the demonstration was that appellant exceeded the narrow time limits set by the police, his conviction could not be sustained. Assuming the place of the meeting was appropriate — as appellant justifiably concluded from the official grant of permission — nothing in this courthouse statute, nor in the breach of the peace or obstruction of public passages statutes with their broad sweep and application . . . , authorizes the police to draw the narrow time line, unrelated to any policy of these statutes, that would be approved if we were to sustain appellant's conviction on this ground. . . . In any event, as we have stated, it is our conclusion from the record that the dispersal order had nothing to do with any time or place limitation, and thus, on this ground alone, it is clear that the dispersal order did not remove the protection accorded appellant by the original grant of permission.

Of course this does not mean that the police cannot call a halt to a meeting which though originally peaceful, becomes violent. Nor does it mean that, under properly drafted and administered statutes and ordinances, the authorities cannot set reasonable time limits for assemblies related to the policies of such laws and then order them dispersed when these time limits are exceeded. . . . We merely hold that, under circumstances such as those present in this case, appellant's conviction cannot be sustained on the basis of the dispersal order.

. . . .

Liberty can only be exercised in a system of law which safeguards order. We reaffirm the repeated holdings of this Court that our constitutional command of free speech and assembly is basic and fundamental and encompasses peaceful social protest, so important to the preservation of the freedoms treasured in a democratic society. We also reaffirm the repeated decisions of this Court that there is no place for violence in a democratic society dedicated to liberty under law, and that the right of peaceful protest does not mean that everyone with opinions or beliefs to express may do so at any time and at any place. There is a proper time and place for even the most peaceful protest and a plain duty and responsibility on the part of all citizens to obey all valid laws and regulations. There is an equally plain requirement for laws and regulations to be drawn so as to give citizens fair warning as to what is illegal; for regulation of conduct that involves freedom of speech and assembly not to be so broad in scope as to stifle First Amendment freedoms, which "need breathing space to survive," *NAACP v. Button*, 371 U.S. 415, 433; for appropriate limitations on the discretion of public officials where speech and assembly are intertwined with regulated conduct; and for all such laws and regulations to be applied with an equal hand. We believe that all of these requirements can be met in an ordered society dedicated to liberty. . . .

The application of these principles requires us to reverse the judgment of the Supreme Court of Louisiana.

Reversed.

NOTES

1. On the subject of allegedly vague policy language and the necessary leadership decisions made in implementing the policy, the court in *Cox* made the following statement:

> While this lack of specificity may not render the statute unconstitutionally vague, at least as applied to a demonstration within the sight and hearing of those in the courthouse, it is clear that the statute, with respect to the determination of how near the courthouse a particular demonstration can be, foresees a degree of on-the-spot administrative interpretation by officials charged with responsibility for administering and enforcing it. It is apparent that demonstrators, such as those involved here, would justifiably tend to rely on this administrative interpretation of how "near" the courthouse a particular demonstration might take place.

379 U.S. at 568. Much of the conversation on vagueness in policy and statutory language centers on whether those subject to the laws and policies are well-guided in their conduct. *Cox* makes the important corollary point that those in charge of enforcing the laws and policies must also be well-guided. Is this point the major reason why the convictions in *Cox* were reversed? What lessons does *Cox* teach higher education administrators and policymakers in this regard?

2. *Cox* involved a challenge to the language and the application of a criminal statute. Ultimately, the conviction was overturned on First Amendment speech and assembly grounds. Consider now the hypothetical of a noncriminal university rule on campus protests, in words similar to the ones seen in the Louisiana statute. Consider, as well, a similar challenge on free speech grounds. What defenses should university officials offer? See also the opening section of Chapter VIII on rulemaking authority.

3. The protests involved many students from nearby universities. Would their convictions, if upheld, be relevant in the application of university rules? In other words, can a university use off-campus activity in the application of on-campus codes of conduct? With or without criminal convictions, can a university discipline students for off-campus activities?

4. The Court addressed, albeit quickly, appellant's clear and present danger defense, wherein he argued that the conduct should be judged against the "clear and present danger" doctrine. The Court rejected the argument, distinguishing the criminal statute at issue in *Cox* from the contempt cases more typical of the clear and present danger doctrine. The Supreme Court first enunciated the "clear and present danger" test in *Schenck v. United States*, 249 U.S. 47 (1919), where Justice Oliver Wendell Holmes wrote, "The question in every case is whether the words used are used in such circumstances and are of such a nature as to create a clear and present danger that they will bring about the substantive evils that Congress has a right to prevent." *Id.* at 52. In *Schenck*, the defendants were convicted of violating the Espionage Act, which made it a criminal offense to make false statements with the intent to interfere with the operation of the armed forces (e.g., through the causation of insubordination, disloyalty, or mutiny; or the obstruction of military recruitment and enlistment). The defendants distributed anti-war leaflets opposing the Selective Service Act. Schenck did not deny the intention of his acts, but argued that the actions were protected under the First Amendment.

With the development and application of the clear and present danger doctrine, however, a unanimous Supreme Court upheld the convictions. With some controversy over how "imminent" the violence or disruption must be, the application of the clear and present danger doctrine has held that words alone are not punishable; instead, those words must come with action — clear and present danger must be imminent. *See Gitlow v. New York*, 268 U.S. 652 (1925) (convictions upheld after defendants distributed leaflets advocating the overthrow of the government); *Brandenburg v. Ohio*, 395 U.S. 444 (1969) (criminalization of assembly with others merely to advocate the described type of action, and which failed to distinguish mere advocacy from incitement to imminent lawless action, violates the First and Fourteenth Amendments).

TINKER v. DES MOINES INDEPENDENT COMMUNITY SCHOOL DISTRICT

393 U.S. 503 (1969)

Mr. Justice Fortas delivered the opinion of the Court.

Petitioner John F. Tinker, 15 years old, and petitioner Christopher Eckhardt, 16 years old, attended high schools in Des Moines, Iowa. Petitioner Mary Beth Tinker, John's sister, was a 13-year-old student in junior high school.

In December 1965, a group of adults and students in Des Moines held a meeting at the Eckhardt home. The group determined to publicize their objections to the hostilities in Vietnam and their support for a truce by wearing black armbands during the holiday season and by fasting on December 16 and New Year's Eve. Petitioners and their parents had previously engaged in similar activities, and they decided to participate in the program.

The principals of the Des Moines schools became aware of the plan to wear armbands. On December 14, 1965, they met and adopted a policy that any student wearing an armband to school would be asked to remove it, and if he refused he would be suspended until he returned without the armband. Petitioners were aware of the regulation that the school authorities adopted.

On December 16, Mary Beth and Christopher wore black armbands to their schools. John Tinker wore his armband the next day. They were all sent home and suspended from school until they would come back without their armbands. They did not return to school until after the planned period for wearing armbands had expired — that is, until after New Year's Day.

This complaint was filed in the United States District Court by petitioners, through their fathers, under § 1983 of Title 42 of the United States Code. . . .

On appeal, the Court of Appeals for the Eighth Circuit considered the case *en banc.* The court was equally divided, and the District Court's decision was accordingly affirmed, without opinion. . . . We granted certiorari.

I

. . . .

First Amendment rights, applied in light of the special characteristics of the school environment, are available to teachers and students. It can hardly be argued that either students or teachers shed their constitutional rights to freedom of speech or expression at the schoolhouse gate. This has been the unmistakable holding of this Court for almost 50 years. In *Meyer v. Nebraska*, 262 U.S. 390 (1923), and *Bartels v. Iowa*, 262 U.S. 404 (1923), this Court . . . held that the Due Process Clause of the Fourteenth Amendment prevents States from forbidding the teaching of a foreign language to young students. Statutes to this effect, the Court held, unconstitutionally interfere with the liberty of teacher, student, and parent. . . .

In *West Virginia v. Barnette*, [319 U.S. 624 (1943)], this Court held that under the First Amendment, the student in public school may not be compelled to salute the flag. . . . [T]he Court said:

> The Fourteenth Amendment, as now applied to the States, protects the citizen against the State itself and all of its creatures — Boards of Education not excepted. These have, of course, important, delicate, and highly discretionary functions, but none that they may not perform within the limits of the Bill of Rights. That they are educating the young for citizenship is reason for scrupulous protection of Constitutional freedoms of the individual, if we are not to strangle the free mind at its source and teach youth to discount important principles of our government as mere platitudes. 319 U.S., at 637.

On the other hand, the Court has repeatedly emphasized the need for affirming the comprehensive authority of the States and of school officials, consistent with fundamental constitutional safeguards, to prescribe and control conduct in the schools. *See Epperson v. Arkansas*, [393 U.S. 97 (1969)], at 104; *Meyer v. Nebraska, supra*, at 402. Our problem lies in the area where students in the exercise of First Amendment rights collide with the rules of the school authorities.

II

. . . Our problem involves direct, primary First Amendment rights akin to "pure speech."

The school officials banned and sought to punish petitioners for a silent, passive expression of opinion, unaccompanied by any disorder or disturbance on the part of petitioners. There is here no evidence whatever of petitioners' interference, actual or nascent, with the schools' work or of collision with the rights of other students to be secure and to be let alone. Accordingly, this case does not concern speech or action that intrudes upon the work of the schools or the rights of other students.

Only a few of the 18,000 students in the school system wore the black armbands. Only five students were suspended for wearing them. There is no indication that the work of the schools or any class was disrupted. Outside the classrooms, a few students made hostile remarks to the children wearing armbands, but there were no threats or acts of violence on school premises.

The District Court concluded that the action of the school authorities was reasonable because it was based upon their fear of a disturbance from the wearing of the armbands. But, in our system, undifferentiated fear or apprehension of disturbance is not enough to overcome the right to freedom of expression. Any departure from absolute regimentation may cause trouble. Any variation from the majority's opinion may inspire fear. Any word spoken, in class, in the lunchroom, or on the campus, that deviates from the views of another person may start an argument or cause a disturbance. But our Constitution says we must take this risk, . . . and our history says that it is this sort of hazardous freedom — this kind of openness — that is the basis of our national strength and of the independence and vigor of Americans who grow up and live in this relatively permissive, often disputatious, society.

In order for the State in the person of school officials to justify prohibition of a particular expression of opinion, it must be able to show that its action was caused by something more than a mere desire to avoid the discomfort and unpleasantness that always accompany an unpopular viewpoint. Certainly where there is no finding and no showing that engaging in the forbidden conduct would "materially and substantially interfere with the requirements of appropriate discipline in the operation of the school," the prohibition cannot be sustained.

In the present case, the District Court made no such finding, and our independent examination of the record fails to yield evidence that the school authorities had reason to anticipate that the wearing of the armbands would substantially interfere with the work of the school or impinge upon the rights of other students . . . .

On the contrary, the action of the school authorities appears to have been based upon an urgent wish to avoid the controversy which might result from the expression, even by the silent symbol of armbands, of opposition to this Nation's part in the conflagration in Vietnam . . . .

It is also relevant that the school authorities did not purport to prohibit the wearing of all symbols of political or controversial significance. The record shows that students in some of the schools wore buttons relating to national political campaigns, and some even wore the Iron Cross, traditionally a symbol of Nazism. The order prohibiting the wearing of armbands did not extend to these. Instead, a particular symbol — black armbands worn to exhibit opposition to this Nation's involvement in Vietnam — was singled out for prohibition. Clearly, the prohibition of expression of one particular opinion, at least without evidence that it is necessary to avoid material and substantial interference with schoolwork or discipline, is not constitutionally permissible.

In our system, state-operated schools may not be enclaves of totalitarianism. School officials do not possess absolute authority over their students. Students in school as well as out of school are "persons" under our Constitution. They are possessed of fundamental rights which the State must respect, just as they themselves must respect their obligations to the State. In our system, students may not be regarded as closed-circuit recipients of only that which the State chooses to communicate. They may not be confined to the expression of those sentiments that are officially approved. In the absence of a specific showing of constitutionally valid reasons to regulate their speech, students are entitled to freedom of expression of their views . . . .

In *Meyer v. Nebraska*, Mr. Justice McReynolds expressed this Nation's repudiation of the principle that a State might so conduct its schools as to "foster a homogeneous people" . . .

This principle has been repeated by this Court on numerous occasions during the intervening years. In *Keyishian v. Board of Regents*, 385 U.S. 589, 603, Mr. Justice Brennan, speaking for the Court, said:

> "The vigilant protection of constitutional freedoms is nowhere more vital than in the community of American schools." *Shelton v. Tucker.* The classroom is peculiarly the "marketplace of ideas." The Nation's future depends upon leaders trained through wide exposure to that robust exchange of ideas which discovers truth "out of a multitude of tongues, [rather] than through any kind of authoritative selection."

The principle of these cases is not confined to the supervised and ordained discussion which takes place in the classroom. The principal use to which the schools are dedicated is to accommodate students during prescribed hours for the purpose of certain types of activities. Among those activities is personal intercommunication among the students. This is not only an inevitable part of the process of attending school; it is also an important part of the educational process. A student's rights, therefore, do not embrace merely the classroom hours. When he is in the cafeteria, or on the playing field, or on the campus during the authorized hours, he may express his opinions, even on controversial subjects like the conflict in Vietnam, if he does so "[without] materially and substantially interfer[ing] with . . . appropriate discipline in the operation of the school" and without colliding with the rights of others. *Burnside v. Byars, supra*, at 749. But conduct by the student, in class or out of it, which for any reason — whether it stems from time, place, or type of behavior — materially disrupts classwork or involves substantial disorder or invasion of the rights of others is, of course, not immunized by the constitutional guarantee of freedom of speech.

Under our Constitution, free speech is not a right that is given only to be so circumscribed that it exists in principle but not in fact. Freedom of expression would not truly exist if the right could be exercised only in an area that a benevolent government has provided as a safe haven for crackpots. The Constitution says that Congress (and the States) may not abridge the right to free speech. This provision means what it says. We properly read it to permit reasonable regulation of speech-connected activities in carefully restricted circumstances. But we do not confine the permissible exercise of First Amendment rights to a telephone booth or the four corners of a pamphlet, or to supervised and ordained discussion in a school classroom.

If a regulation were adopted by school officials forbidding discussion of the Vietnam conflict, or the expression by any student of opposition to it anywhere on school property except as part of a prescribed classroom exercise, it would be obvious that the regulation would violate the constitutional rights of students, at least if it could not be justified by a showing that the students' activities would materially and substantially disrupt the work and discipline of the school. . . . In the circumstances of the present case, the prohibition of the silent, passive "witness of the armbands," as one of the children called it, is no less offensive to the Constitution's guarantees.

As we have discussed, the record does not demonstrate any facts which might reasonably have led school authorities to forecast substantial disruption of or material interference with school activities, and no disturbances or disorders on the school premises in fact occurred. These petitioners merely went about their ordained rounds in school. Their deviation consisted only in wearing on their sleeve a band of black cloth, not more than two inches wide. They wore it to exhibit their disapproval of the Vietnam hostilities and their advocacy of a truce, to make their views known, and, by their example, to influence others to adopt them. They neither interrupted school activities nor sought to intrude in the school affairs or the lives of others. They caused discussion outside of the classrooms, but no interference with work and no disorder. In the circumstances, our Constitution does not permit officials of the State to deny their form of expression.

We reverse and remand for further proceedings consistent with this opinion.

NOTES

1. How does *Tinker* apply in higher education settings? Does the substantial disruption standard apply in the same way in colleges and universities as it does in K-12 settings? What are the similarities and differences between the two settings that might dictate how the *Tinker* disruption standard ought to apply? Is the difference in age and maturity of the students a significant factor? What about compulsory attendance statutes that require children of elementary and secondary school age to attend school? Should *Tinker* apply at all to higher education settings? Or should courts rely, instead, on the traditional limits placed on free speech outside of educational arenas: for example, clear and present danger, *Schenck v. United States*, 249 U.S. 47 (1919); imminent lawless action, *Brandenburg v. Ohio*, 395 U.S. 444 (1969); fighting words, *Chaplinsky v. New Hampshire*, 315 U.S. 568 (1942); and obscenity, *Miller v. California*, 413 U.S. 15 (1973)?

2. Under *Tinker*, is there a requirement that actual substantial disruption and material interference occur before speech and conduct can be restricted? If not, then where is the line drawn? Who has the discretion to determine when student speech is substantially and materially disruptive?

3. In *Healy v. James*, 408 U.S. 169 (1972), an eight-member Student Affairs Committee at Central Connecticut State College, by a vote of six to two, approved the application of a proposed chapter of the Students for a Democratic Society (SDS) and recommended to the college president that the chapter be given official recognition on campus. The president rejected the committee's recommendation. The students filed suit, and the District Court and Court of Appeals upheld the president's decision on both due process and free speech grounds. The Supreme Court reversed, holding that the college officials failed to afford the students their First Amendment rights. The Court also recognized that such rights have their limits, particularly with respect to the institutional interest in preventing substantial disruption and material interference with the work of the government and the rights of others.

The majority in *Healy* praised the campus's dedication to welcoming varying viewpoints, but "admonished the organization that immediate suspension would be considered if the group's activities proved incompatible with the school's policies against interference with the privacy of other students or destruction of property." Just as we see in *Healy* and so many free speech cases, the distinction between content and effect of expressive conduct is an important one. For this reason, the drafting of such policies is as important as the proper enforcement of them. The codification of cases like *Tinker* and *Healy* into university policy is welcomed, but the resulting policies must still be clearly written and handled well in their implementation. *See, e.g.*, *Pro-Life Cougars v. Univ. of Houston*, 259 F. Supp. 2d 575 (S.D. Tex. 2003), presented in the next Chapter.

Compare *Tinker* and *Healy*. With an obvious difference in educational setting — *Tinker* at K-12 and *Healy* at university — what are the similarities and differences? Do they both uphold the long-standing tradition that the classroom is the "marketplace of ideas"? Do they both support the notion that speech that substantially disrupts or interferes with the work of the school or university is properly restricted? Is there a particularized legal lesson for student free speech in higher education that *Healy* offers but *Tinker* does not? Perhaps *Healy* more noticeably draws the legal line between advocacy (protected) and action (not protected) than *Tinker* does. But they both recognize the necessity of the "marketplace" and offer classic statements praising the virtues of free speech in educational contexts, with *Tinker*'s "schoolhouse gate" line and the following from *Healy*:

> Though we deplore the tendency of some to abuse the very constitutional privileges they invoke, and although the infringement of rights of others certainly should not be tolerated, we reaffirm this Court's dedication to the principles of the Bill of Rights upon which our vigorous and free society is founded

408 U.S. at 194. *Healy* is presented in full in Chapter IV.

4. In its opinion, the Court in *Tinker* stated that it was "also relevant that the school authorities did not purport to prohibit the wearing of all symbols of political or controversial significance." What do you make of this statement in light of the full opinion in *Tinker*? Much of the discussion and commentary in *Tinker* (and since then) has emphasized the Court's reliance on the lack of evidence of disruption.

What about the argument that the restriction of the armbands was content-related and not based on disruption? Admittedly, the plaintiffs won the case largely on the application of a disruption standard and, very likely, would have been successful with a content discrimination claim, as well. How impactful is the content of the speech in *Tinker*? For an example of the interplay between content and effect of student speech in higher education arenas, see the following case.

ORIN v. BARCLAY

272 F.3d 1207 (9th Cir. 2001)

TALLMAN, CIRCUIT JUDGE:

Plaintiff Benjamin Orin was told by a community college official that he could protest abortion on campus only if he did not create a disturbance, interfere with students' access to school buildings, or couch his protest in overtly religious terms. After four factious hours of demonstration, campus security asked Orin to leave because he was violating these conditions. When he refused, campus security called City of Bremerton police officers who, after asking Orin to leave twice more, arrested him for criminal trespass and failure to disperse.

We must determine whether the conditions imposed on the protest violated Orin's clearly established First Amendment rights such that the school officials, the police officers, or the City of Bremerton may be liable to Orin for damages under 42 U.S.C. §§ 1983 and 1985(3). We must also determine whether the district court properly held that none of Orin's state tort law causes of action can survive summary judgment. We have jurisdiction, and affirm in part and reverse in part.

I

Orin is a member of Positively Pro-Life, an anti-abortion group that demonstrates at high schools, colleges, and medical clinics around the Northwest. On October 30, 1997, Orin and Jim McIntyre appeared unannounced in the office of Richard Barclay, Interim Dean of Students at Olympic Community College ("OCC") [a two-year junior college operated by the state of Washington]. They warned Barclay that they and a third Positively Pro-Life member intended to stage an anti-abortion protest on OCC's main quad. The protest was to include display of two large posters graphically depicting aborted fetuses in various states of dismemberment. They warned Barclay that the signs had elicited strong responses at prior protests, including physical violence.

Barclay informed the protestors that they must apply for and obtain a permit from OCC if they wished to hold an event on the quad. Orin responded, "We have a prior permit. The Bill of Rights says we can be here." Barclay told Orin that he could conduct the demonstration without a permit so long as he did not: (1) breach the peace or cause a disturbance; (2) interfere with campus activities or access to school buildings; or (3) engage in religious worship or instruction. The protestors then left for the main quad. Barclay dispatched two security guards to monitor the demonstration.

The Dean's Office began receiving student complaints about the protestors and their posters soon after the protest began. OCC accommodated the demonstration for approximately four hours. The size and temperament of the crowd attracted by the demonstration waxed and waned. At times there were only five or six students; at other times there were more than one hundred. On two occasions campus security had to interpose themselves between the crowd and the protestors to avert physical violence.

Shortly after 4:00 p.m., OCC security chief Robert "Rocky" Wallace asked the protestors to leave. When they refused, he called to request police assistance. He called again moments later to ask dispatch to expedite the response because the situation was "turning physical." The parties hotly dispute the events that precipitated Wallace's call to the police.

The demonstrators allege that Barclay appeared at the protest and informed them that if they "mentioned God or referred to the Bible [he] would have them arrested and physically removed from campus." Orin allegedly responded that he would continue to decry abortion in religious terms and that Barclay would have to have him arrested. Barclay responded that he would do so, and the police arrived ten to fifteen minutes later. The demonstrators allege that they uttered no incendiary epithets and that they never felt threatened by the crowd.

By contrast, the security officers allege that the demonstration degenerated into an openly hostile incitement of an already angry crowd. Four students submitted declarations in support of the officers, indicating that they felt the demonstrators were "verbally assaulting students" and "attempting to pick a fight." They claim they heard the protestors call students "baby killers" and use incendiary racial and sexist epithets. In the security officers' estimation, physical conflict between the students and the demonstrators was inevitable. The security guards asked the demonstrators to leave because they "could no longer control the situation and the situation was turning physical."

Officer Alan Hornberg of the Bremerton Police Department was dispatched to OCC to respond to "a reported group of protesters that were refusing to leave and a large unruly crowd that was getting out of hand." Wallace met Hornberg at the edge of campus. As they walked to the quad, where the demonstration was being held, Wallace told Hornberg that the protestors had violated the conditions placed on them by Barclay, "the student crowd was agitated to the point of physical violence against the protesters," and "the security staff didn't feel that they had the manpower to protect the anti-abortion protesters from the students." He also informed Hornberg that McIntyre had hit one of the security officers, knocking his hat off his head.

Upon arriving at the quad, Hornberg observed a crowd of forty to fifty students shouting angrily at the demonstrators. Hornberg approached the demonstrators and asked them to leave. Orin told Hornberg that campus officials only wanted him arrested because he was talking about religion. Orin then exclaimed that he was exercising his First Amendment right to free speech and "was not going anywhere." Hornberg again asked Orin to leave. When Orin again refused, Hornberg arrested him for criminal trespass and failure to disperse. Bremerton Police Officer Rick McCluskey arrived after Orin's arrest. Hornberg reported that Orin was under arrest for trespassing and failing to disperse. McCluskey told Hornberg to take Orin to jail for booking.

. . . .

Orin sued Dean Barclay, security officer Wallace, police officers Hornberg and McCluskey, and the City of Bremerton, [claiming, in part, a] violation of his First Amendment rights compensable under 42 U.S.C. § 1983. . . . Defendants moved for summary judgment on all claims.

The district court found that the individual defendants were entitled to qualified immunity against Orin's First Amendment claims. The district court granted all defendants' motions for summary judgment as to Orin's remaining claims. Orin timely appealed.

II

. . . .

A

Section 1983 permits an individual whose federal statutory or constitutional rights have been violated by a public official acting under color of state law to sue the official for damages. Public officials are afforded protection, however, "from undue interference with their duties and from potentially disabling threats of liability." *Harlow v. Fitzgerald*, 457 U.S. 800, 806 (1982). Qualified immunity shields them "from liability for civil damages insofar as their conduct does not violate clearly established statutory or constitutional rights of which a reasonable person would have known." *Id.* at 818. If a public official could reasonably have believed that his actions were legal in light of clearly established law and the information he possessed at the time, then his conduct falls within the protective sanctuary of qualified immunity.

. . . If we determine that Orin has stated a *prima facie* claim that a particular defendant violated his constitutional rights, then we must determine whether the rights allegedly violated were clearly established by federal law. *Id.*

The Supreme Court has explained that a right is clearly established by federal law if:

> The contours of the right [are] sufficiently clear that a reasonable official would understand that what he is doing violates that right. This is not to say that an official action is protected by qualified immunity unless the very action in question has been previously held unlawful, but it is to say that in the light of pre-existing law the unlawfulness must be apparent.

Anderson v. Creighton, 483 U.S. 635, 640 (1987). In other words, Orin's rights were clearly established if reasonable public officials in the defendants' respective positions would have known, "in light of clearly established law *and the information the officers possessed*," that their conduct violated his rights. *Hunter* [*v. Bryant*, 502 U.S. 224], 227 [1991]).

Orin argues that the conditions imposed by Barclay and enforced by Wallace violated his First Amendment rights to free speech and the free exercise of religion. Barclay imposed three conditions on Orin's demonstration. The first two — not to create a public disturbance and not to interfere with campus activities or access to school buildings — are content-neutral regulations. . . . So long as such content-neutral regulations are narrowly tailored to accomplish a legitimate government purpose they are not proscribed by the First Amendment. *Ward v. Rock Against Racism*, 491 U.S. 781, 798 (1989). The first two conditions survive constitutional scrutiny because they do not distinguish among speakers based on the content of their message and they are narrowly tailored to achieve OCC's pedagogical purpose. *See Widmar v. Vincent*, 454 U.S. 263, 268-69 (1981) (holding that a public university may" impose reasonable regulations compatible with [its educational] mission upon the use of its campus and facilities"); *Healy v. James*, 408 U.S. 169, 184 (1972) ("[A] college has a legitimate interest in preventing disruption on the campus.").

The third condition — to refrain from religious worship or instruction — is more problematic. . . . Protection of such expression on public property is not absolute, however. The measure of protection afforded such expression is determined by the status of the public property on which it occurs. Public property may be designated, by law or tradition, as a public forum or may be set aside for some other public purpose.

The record before us does not indicate whether OCC has, in general, designated its quad as a public forum. . . . The parties do not dispute, however, that Dean Barclay told the demonstrators that they could use OCC's quad for expressive purposes so long as they observed three conditions. Having created a forum for the demonstrators' expression, Barclay could not, consistent with the dictates of the First Amendment, limit their expression to secular content. *See Widmar*, 454 U.S. at 267 (holding that once a university creates a forum, it must "justify its discriminations and exclusions under applicable constitutional norms").

The third condition imposed by Barclay constitutes a content-based regulation that we may uphold only if it "is necessary to serve a compelling state interest and . . . is narrowly drawn to achieve that end." *Widmar*, 454 U.S. at 270. Barclay informed Orin that this condition was required by the Establishment Clause in order to maintain the separation of Church and State. The Supreme Court has ruled, however, that the First Amendment does not require public institutions to exclude religious speech from fora held open to secular speakers. In fact, it prohibits them from doing so.

In *Widmar*, a public university defended its regulation excluding religious student organizations from campus facilities on the grounds that it was required by the Establishment Clause to observe a strict separation of Church and State. 454 U.S. at 263. The Court rejected the university's argument, holding that allowing religious organizations the same access to school facilities enjoyed by secular organizations did not violate the Establishment Clause. Since the governmental interest that purported to justify regulation was based on a misunderstanding of the Establishment Clause, the Court struck the regulation down as a content-based regulation of First Amendment rights of assembly, free exercise, and free speech that was not narrowly tailored to serve a compelling government interest. 454 U.S. at 278.

Barclay's "no religion" condition runs squarely afoul of *Widmar*. Having permitted Orin to conduct a demonstration on campus, Barclay could not, consistent with the First Amendment's free speech and free exercise clauses, limit his demonstration to secular content. *Widmar* and its progeny clearly establish this proposition. *See, e.g., Rosenberger v. Rector and Visitors of the Univ. of Va.*, 515 U.S. 819, 842 (1995). *See also Good News Club v. Milford Cent. Sch.*, 533 U.S. 98 (2001). Orin's First Amendment rights, in the context of this case, were clearly established. A reasonable public official should have known that permitting Orin to express his views on abortion only so long as those views were not religious in nature violated his First Amendment rights. We reverse the district court's holding that Barclay has qualified immunity against Orin's First Amendment claim and remand for trial.

We must also reverse the district court's determination that security officer Wallace had qualified immunity against Orin's First Amendment claim. . . . It is unclear on the record before us whether Wallace asked Orin to leave campus because he had violated Barclay's "no religion "condition or because he had violated one of the other two, inoffensive conditions. Construing the facts in the light most favorable to Orin, as we must at this stage, he has properly alleged that Wallace violated his clearly established First Amendment rights. Accordingly, we reverse the district court's determination that Wallace is entitled as a matter of law to qualified immunity against Orin's First Amendment claim.

The district court properly held that police officers Hornberg and McCluskey have qualified immunity. The undisputed evidence indicates that they arrested Orin not because of the religious content of his speech, but rather because they reasonably believed they had probable cause to arrest him for trespass and failure to disperse. Police dispatch informed Hornberg only that a group of protestors was inciting a large, unruly crowd. Security officer Wallace told Hornberg only that the demonstrators had violated the conditions of their revocable license to remain on campus and were creating an unsafe, potentially riotous situation. Hornberg's personal observation of the demonstration confirmed these reports — he witnessed forty to fifty angry people shouting at the demonstrators. The record confirms that Hornberg could reasonably have believed that he was not violating Orin's First Amendment rights because he had probable cause to arrest Orin for violating Washington's laws pertaining to trespass and failure to disperse.

Similarly, Hornberg informed McCluskey that he asked Orin to leave because he was creating a disturbance and blocking entrance to school buildings and that he arrested Orin for trespass and failure to disperse. Based on this information, McCluskey could reasonably have believed that his direction to Hornberg to take Orin to jail for booking did not violate any of Orin's constitutional rights. We affirm the district court's decision that, because police officers Hornberg and McCluskey had probable cause to act against Orin under the Fourth Amendment, they did not violate his First Amendment rights.

Finally, the City of Bremerton is not liable on Orin's First Amendment claim. . . . A § 1983 action against a city fails as a matter of law unless a city employee's conduct violates one of the plaintiff's federal rights. Because the record reveals that neither Officer Hornberg nor Officer McCluskey violated Orin's First Amendment rights, it follows as a matter of course that Orin's action against the City of Bremerton fails. The district court's grant of summary judgment in favor of the City of Bremerton is therefore affirmed.

. . . .

III

. . . The judgment of the district court is

AFFIRMED in part; REVERSED in part; and REMANDED.

NOTES

1. The Court of Appeals in *Orin* affirmed the trial court's findings for the defendant university officials on the grounds that the defendants lawfully enforced content-neutral conditions on the demonstrators' speech. According to the court, there was legitimate reason to ask the demonstrators to disperse, given the conditions imposed not to create public disturbance and not to disrupt or interfere with campus activities and access to buildings. In the opinion of the security officers, "physical conflict between the students and the demonstrators was inevitable." What are the arguments one must make to establish inevitability of disruption in this context?

2. With respect to the district court's findings of qualified immunity for the various government actors in *Orin*, some of those findings were affirmed on appeal, and some were reversed. The police officers retained qualified immunity, as they were acting only on reports of an unsafe, potentially riotous situation on campus. In other words, the arrest of Orin was not motivated by the content of his speech, but rather the reported and later perceived disruptive effect of it. On the other hand, the district court's findings of qualified immunity for Barclay, interim Dean of Students, and Wallace, a campus security officer, were reversed as the facts of the case did not clearly reveal whether Barclay and Wallace asked Orin and his fellow demonstrators to leave campus because of the disruption or the content. While the court found the actions of the defendants permissible with respect to the *effect* of the speech, they found their actions with respect to the *content* more problematic: "A reasonable public official should have known that permitting Orin to express his views on abortion only so long as those views were not religious in nature violated his First Amendment rights." In a civil case like this one, with multiple individual and institutional defendants, it is relatively common for the courts to divide the analysis and concentrate on one government actor at a time.

Is it possible to have a fact pattern that gives rise to such disruptive conduct that a content-based argument in favor of free speech is trumped by the disruption? In other words, is it possible to argue that all of Orin's claims, including the religion-based ones, should be rejected due to the disruptive nature of the demonstration and the necessity to call police? Or will content discrimination claims of speakers, where they can be made successfully, always trump disruption defenses of university officials?

The court in *Orin* stated that, in part, a college's or university's authority to restrict speech on its premises depends on how that premises has been designated for speech purposes. That is, expression rights are higher in public forums than they are in limited public forums or nonpublic forums. In *Orin*, the court found no evidence of a formal designation of the forum, but did find evidence that college officials had granted Orin and his fellow demonstrators the right to speak where they did, subject to the three disputed conditions. In the course of its discussion, the court made the following statement: "Public property may be designated, by law or tradition, as a public forum or may be set aside for some other public purpose." So, how much "tradition" would have to be present in order to designate college or university property a "public forum"? *See Perry Educ. Ass'n v. Perry Local Educators' Ass'n*, 460 U.S. 37 (1983).

In *Perry*, the Supreme Court noted that a traditional public forum is a place "which by long tradition or by government fiat has been devoted to assembly and debate," such as a street or park. *Id.* at 45. In traditional public forums, the government may enforce content-based restrictions only if they are narrowly drawn to serve a compelling interest. Further, the government may enforce content-neutral time, place, and manner regulations only if they are "narrowly tailored to serve a significant government interest, and leave open ample alternative channels of communication." *Id.* See also the discussion of student activity fees and student publications, *infra*.

3. Recall the three conditions that Barclay and Olympic Community College placed on the demonstrations in *Orin*. Two of the conditions, both inspired by the effect of the speech, were permissible. The third one, inspired by the content of the speech, was not. Universities must be careful not to impose unconstitutional "prior restraints" on student speech. Prior restraints are not unconstitutional per se, but they bear a heavy presumption against constitutional validity. In *Burbridge v. Sampson*, 74 F. Supp. 2d 940 (C.D. Cal. 1999), South Orange Community College adopted a speech policy that required non-district individuals and organizations to obtain prior approval to use district property. Non-commercial speech was particularly restricted to three designated areas on campus. The district court held that the policy constituted an overbroad prior restraint. In response to this ruling, the community college adopted a new policy, which was also struck down. *Khedemi v. S. Orange County Comm. Coll. Dist.*, 194 F. Supp. 2d 1011 (C.D. Cal. 2002). The court noted that the policy gave too much discretion to the college president to determine which expressive activities would be permitted and which would not. Seemingly similar to the acceptable conditions in *Orin*, the court found compelling governmental interests in only part of the policy — those designed to prevent criminal activity substantial disruption.

4. In *Widmar v. Vincent*, 454 U.S. 263 (1981), discussed in *Orin*, the Supreme Court held that once a university creates a forum, it must "justify its discriminations and exclusions under applicable constitutional norms." *Id.* at 267. While there was no declaration as to the type of forum created in *Orin*, the university created a forum for demonstrators and subjected the speakers to a content-based condition that did not withstand judicial scrutiny. Judicial scrutiny, however, varies based on the type of forum created. In a nonpublic forum, for example, the government may make reasonable regulations based on subject matter. In *Wilson v. Johnson*, 247

Fed. Appx. 620 (6th Cir. 2007), the Court of Appeals for the Sixth Circuit rejected the First Amendment free speech claims of a university student who posted several, large anti-war banners on university property in contravention of university policy. The university charged him with vandalism and the student filed suit, claiming that the restrictions were unlawful. The court held that the locations where the student posted the banners were nonpublic forums and that the rule forbidding the posting of political messages on university property was a reasonable, content-neutral provision.

B. RECOGNIZED STUDENT ORGANIZATIONS

CHRISTIAN LEGAL SOCIETY v. MARTINEZ
130 S. Ct. 2971 (2010)

Justice Ginsburg delivered the opinion of the Court.

. . . This case concerns a novel question regarding student activities at public universities: May a public law school condition its official recognition of a student group — and the attendant use of school funds and facilities — on the organization's agreement to open eligibility for membership and leadership to all students?

In the view of petitioner Christian Legal Society (CLS), an accept-all-comers policy impairs its First Amendment rights to free speech, expressive association, and free exercise of religion by prompting it, on pain of relinquishing the advantages of recognition, to accept members who do not share the organization's core beliefs about religion and sexual orientation. From the perspective of respondent Hastings College of the Law (Hastings or the Law School), CLS seeks special dispensation from an across-the-board open-access requirement designed to further the reasonable educational purposes underpinning the school's student-organization program.

In accord with the District Court and the Court of Appeals, we reject CLS's First Amendment challenge. Compliance with Hastings' all-comers policy, we conclude, is a reasonable, viewpoint-neutral condition on access to the student-organization forum. In requiring CLS — in common with all other student organizations — to choose between welcoming all students and forgoing the benefits of official recognition, we hold, Hastings did not transgress constitutional limitations. . . .

I

. . . .

Through its "Registered Student Organization" (RSO) program, Hastings extends official recognition to student groups. Several benefits attend this school-approved status. RSOs are eligible to seek financial assistance from the Law School, which subsidizes their events using funds from a mandatory student-activity fee imposed on all students. RSOs may also use Law-School channels to communicate with students: They may place announcements in a weekly Office-of-Student-Services newsletter, advertise events on designated bulletin boards, send e-mails using a Hastings-organization address, and participate in an annual Student Organizations Fair designed to advance recruitment efforts. In addition, RSOs may apply for permission to use the Law School's facilities for meetings and office space. Finally, Hastings allows officially recognized groups to use its name and logo.

In exchange for these benefits, RSOs must abide by certain conditions. . . . Critical here, all RSOs must undertake to comply with Hastings' "Policies and Regulations Applying to College Activities, Organizations and Students."

The Law School's Policy on Nondiscrimination (Nondiscrimination Policy), which binds RSOs, states:

> "[Hastings] is committed to a policy against legally impermissible, arbitrary or unreasonable discriminatory practices. All groups, including administration, faculty, student governments, [Hastings]-owned student residence facilities and programs sponsored by [Hastings], are governed by this policy of nondiscrimination. [Hasting's] policy on nondiscrimination is to comply fully with applicable law.
>
> "[Hastings] shall not discriminate unlawfully on the basis of race, color, religion, national origin, ancestry, disability, age, sex or sexual orientation. This nondiscrimination policy covers admission, access and treatment in Hastings-sponsored programs and activities."

Hastings interprets the Nondiscrimination Policy . . . to mandate acceptance of all comers: School-approved groups must "allow any student to participate, become a member, or seek leadership positions in the organization, regardless of [her] status or beliefs." . . . From Hastings' adoption of its Nondiscrimination Policy in 1990 until the events stirring this litigation, "no student organization at Hastings . . . ever sought an exemption from the Policy."

In 2004, CLS became the first student group to do so. At the beginning of the academic year, the leaders of a predecessor Christian organization — which had been an RSO at Hastings for a decade — formed CLS by affiliating with the national Christian Legal Society (CLS-National). . . . CLS chapters must adopt bylaws that, *inter alia*, require members and officers to sign a "Statement of Faith" and to conduct their lives in accord with prescribed principles. Among those tenets is the belief that sexual activity should not occur outside of marriage between a man and a woman; CLS thus interprets its bylaws to exclude from affiliation anyone who engages in "unrepentant homosexual conduct." CLS also excludes students who hold religious convictions different from those in the Statement of Faith.

On September 17, 2004, CLS submitted to Hastings an application for RSO status. . . . Several days later, the Law School rejected the application; CLS's bylaws, Hastings explained, did not comply with the Nondiscrimination Policy. . . .

CLS formally requested an exemption from the Nondiscrimination Policy but Hastings declined to grant one. . . . If CLS instead chose to operate outside the RSO program, Hastings stated, the school "would be pleased to provide [CLS] the use of Hastings facilities for its meetings and activities." CLS would also have access to chalkboards and generally available campus bulletin boards to announce its events. In other words, Hastings would do nothing to suppress CLS's endeavors, but neither would it lend RSO-level support for them.

Refusing to alter its bylaws, CLS did not obtain RSO status. It did, however, operate independently during the 2004-2005 academic year. . . .

. . . CLS filed suit . . . under 42 U.S.C. § 1983. Its complaint alleged that Hastings' refusal to grant the organization RSO status violated CLS's First and Fourteenth Amendment rights to free speech, expressive association, and free exercise of religion. The suit sought injunctive and declaratory relief.

On cross-motions for summary judgment, the U.S. District Court for the Northern District of California ruled in favor of Hastings. . . .

. . . .

On appeal, the Ninth Circuit affirmed. . . .

We granted certiorari . . . and now affirm. . . .

. . . .

III

A

In support of the argument that Hastings' all-comers policy treads on its First Amendment rights to free speech and expressive association, CLS draws on two lines of decisions. First, . . . this Court has employed forum analysis to determine when a governmental entity, in regulating property in its charge, may place limitations on speech. Recognizing a State's right "to preserve the property under its control for the use to which it is lawfully dedicated," *Cornelius v. NAACP Legal Defense & Ed. Fund, Inc.*, 473 U.S. 788, 800 (1985) (internal quotation marks omitted), the Court has permitted restrictions on access to a limited public forum, like the RSO program here, with this key caveat: Any access barrier must be reasonable and viewpoint neutral, *e.g.*, *Rosenberger* [*v. Rector and Visitors of Univ. of Va.*, 515 U.S. 819 (1995)].[12]

Second, as evidenced by another set of decisions, this Court has rigorously reviewed laws and regulations that constrain associational freedom. In the context of public accommodations, we have subjected restrictions on that freedom to close scrutiny; such restrictions are permitted only if they serve "compelling state interests" that are "unrelated to the suppression of ideas" — interests that cannot be advanced "through . . . significantly less restrictive [means]." *Roberts v. United States Jaycees*, 468 U.S. 609, 623 (1984). . . .

CLS would have us engage each line of cases independently, but its expressive-association and free-speech arguments merge: *Who* speaks on its behalf, CLS reasons, colors *what* concept is conveyed. It therefore makes little sense to treat CLS's speech and association claims as discrete. . . . Instead, three observations lead us to conclude that our limited-public-forum precedents supply the appropriate framework for assessing both CLS's speech and association rights.

---

[12] Our decisions make clear, and the parties agree, that Hastings, through its RSO program, established a limited public forum. . . .

First, the same considerations that have led us to apply a less restrictive level of scrutiny to speech in limited public forums as compared to other environments . . . apply with equal force to expressive association occurring in limited public forums. As just noted, speech and expressive-association rights are closely linked. . . . When these intertwined rights arise in exactly the same context, it would be anomalous for a restriction on speech to survive constitutional review under our limited-public-forum test only to be invalidated as an impermissible infringement of expressive association. . . .

Second, and closely related, the strict scrutiny we have applied in some settings to laws that burden expressive association would, in practical effect, invalidate a defining characteristic of limited public forums — the State may "reserv[e] [them] for certain groups." *Rosenberger*, 515 U.S., at 829. . . .

. . . .

Third, this case fits comfortably within the limited-public-forum category, for CLS, in seeking what is effectively a state subsidy, faces only indirect pressure to modify its membership policies; CLS may exclude any person for any reason if it forgoes the benefits of official recognition. The expressive-association precedents on which CLS relies, in contrast, involved regulations that *compelled* a group to include unwanted members, with no choice to opt out. *See, e.g.*, [*Boy Scouts of America v.*] *Dale*, 530 U.S. [640,] 648 [(2000)] (regulation "forc[ed] [the Boy Scouts] to accept members it [did] not desire" (internal quotation marks omitted)); *Roberts*, 468 U.S., at 623 ("There can be no clearer example of an intrusion into the internal structure or affairs of an association than" forced inclusion of unwelcome participants).

In diverse contexts, our decisions have distinguished between policies that require action and those that withhold benefits. . . . Application of the less-restrictive limited-public-forum analysis better accounts for the fact that Hastings, through its RSO program, is dangling the carrot of subsidy, not wielding the stick of prohibition. . . .

In sum, we are persuaded that our limited-public-forum precedents adequately respect both CLS's speech and expressive-association rights, and fairly balance those rights against Hastings' interests as property owner and educational institution. . . .

B

. . . [W]e have three times before considered clashes between public universities and student groups seeking official recognition or its attendant benefits. First, in *Healy* [*v. James*, 408 U.S. 169 (1972)], a state college denied school affiliation to a student group that wished to form a local chapter of Students for a Democratic Society (SDS). . . . The college, we noted, could require "that a group seeking official recognition affirm in advance its willingness to adhere to reasonable campus law," including "reasonable standards respecting conduct." *Id.*, at 193. But a public educational institution exceeds constitutional bounds, we held, when it "restrict[s] speech or association simply because it finds the views expressed by [a] group to be abhorrent." *Id.*, at 187-188.

We later relied on *Healy* in *Widmar* [*v. Vincent*, 454 U.S. 263 (1981)]. In that case, a public university, in an effort to avoid state support for religion, had closed its facilities to a registered student group that sought to use university space for religious worship and discussion. . . . But because the university singled out religious organizations for disadvantageous treatment, we subjected the university's regulation to strict scrutiny. The school's interest "in maintaining strict separation of church and State," we held, was not "sufficiently compelling to justify . . . [viewpoint] discrimination against . . . religious speech." *Id.*, at 270, 276 (internal quotation marks omitted).

Most recently and comprehensively, in *Rosenberger*, we reiterated that a university generally may not withhold benefits from student groups because of their religious outlook. The officially recognized student group in *Rosenberger* was denied student-activity-fee funding to distribute a newspaper because the publication discussed issues from a Christian perspective. By "select[ing] for disfavored treatment those student journalistic efforts with religious editorial viewpoints," we held, the university had engaged in "viewpoint discrimination, which is presumed impermissible when directed against speech otherwise within the forum's limitations." *Id.*, at 831, 830.

. . . .

C

We first consider whether Hastings' policy is reasonable taking into account the RSO forum's function. . . .

. . . .

2

With appropriate regard for school administrators' judgment, we review the justifications Hastings offers in defense of its all-comers requirement. First, the open-access policy "ensures that the leadership, educational, and social opportunities afforded by [RSOs] are available to all students." . . . [T]he Law School may decide, reasonably in our view, "that the . . . educational experience is best promoted when all participants in the forum must provide equal access to all students." Brief for Hastings 32. RSOs, we count it significant, are eligible for financial assistance drawn from mandatory student-activity fees; the all-comers policy ensures that no Hastings student is forced to fund a group that would reject her as a member.

Second, the all-comers requirement helps Hastings police the written terms of its Nondiscrimination Policy without inquiring into an RSO's motivation for membership restrictions. To bring the RSO program within CLS's view of the Constitution's limits, CLS proposes that Hastings permit exclusion because of *belief* but forbid discrimination due to *status*. But that proposal would impose on Hastings a daunting labor. How should the Law School go about determining whether a student organization cloaked prohibited status exclusion in belief-based garb? . . .

. . . Our decisions have declined to distinguish between status and conduct in this context. *See Lawrence v. Texas*, 539 U.S. 558, 575 (2003). . . .

Third, the Law School reasonably adheres to the view that an all-comers policy, to the extent it brings together individuals with diverse backgrounds and beliefs, "encourages tolerance, cooperation, and learning among students." . . .

Fourth, Hastings' policy, which incorporates — in fact, subsumes — state-law proscriptions on discrimination, conveys the Law School's decision "to decline to subsidize with public monies and benefits conduct of which the people of California disapprove." Brief for Hastings 35. . . . State law, of course, may not *command* that public universities take action impermissible under the First Amendment. But so long as a public university does not contravene constitutional limits, its choice to advance state-law goals through the school's educational endeavors stands on firm footing.

. . . .

3

The Law School's policy is all the more creditworthy in view of the "substantial alternative channels that remain open for [CLS-student] communication to take place." *Perry Ed. Assn.* [*v. Perry Local Educators' Assn.*, 460 U.S. 37, 53 (1983)]. If restrictions on access to a limited public forum are viewpoint discriminatory, the ability of a group to exist outside the forum would not cure the constitutional shortcoming. But when access barriers are viewpoint neutral, our decisions have counted it significant that other available avenues for the group to exercise its First Amendment rights lessen the burden created by those barriers. . . .

In this case, Hastings offered CLS access to school facilities to conduct meetings and the use of chalkboards and generally available bulletin boards to advertise events. Although CLS could not take advantage of RSO-specific methods of communication, the advent of electronic media and social-networking sites reduces the importance of those channels. (CLS maintained a Yahoo! message group to disseminate information to students.) . . .

. . . .

4

CLS nevertheless deems Hastings' all-comers policy "frankly absurd." Brief for Petitioner 49. "There can be no diversity of viewpoints in a forum," it asserts, "if groups are not permitted to form around viewpoints." *Id.*, at 50. . . . This catchphrase confuses CLS's preferred policy with constitutional limitation — the *advisability* of Hastings' policy does not control its *permissibility*. . . . Instead, we have repeatedly stressed that a State's restriction on access to a limited public forum "need not be the most reasonable or the only reasonable limitation." *Cornelius*, 473 U.S., at 808.

CLS also assails the reasonableness of the all-comers policy in light of the RSO forum's function by forecasting that the policy will facilitate hostile takeovers; if organizations must open their arms to all, CLS contends, saboteurs will infiltrate groups to subvert their mission and message. This supposition strikes us as more hypothetical than real. CLS points to no history or prospect of RSO-hijackings at Hastings. . . . Students tend to self-sort and presumably will not endeavor en masse to join — let alone seek leadership positions in — groups pursuing missions wholly at odds with their personal beliefs. And if a rogue student intent on sabotaging an organization's objectives nevertheless attempted a takeover, the members of that group would not likely elect her as an officer.

RSOs, moreover, in harmony with the all-comers policy, may condition eligibility for membership and leadership on attendance, the payment of dues, or other neutral requirements designed to ensure that students join because of their commitment to a group's vitality, not its demise. Several RSOs at Hastings limit their membership rolls and officer slates in just this way.

. . . .

D

We next consider whether Hastings' all-comers policy is viewpoint neutral.

1

. . . It is . . . hard to imagine a more viewpoint-neutral policy than one requiring *all* student groups to accept *all* comers. In contrast to *Healy*, *Widmar*, and *Rosenberger*, in which universities singled out organizations for disfavored treatment because of their points of view, Hastings' all-comers requirement draws no distinction between groups based on their message or perspective. An all-comers condition on access to RSO status, in short, is textbook viewpoint neutral.

2

Conceding that Hastings' all-comers policy is "nominally neutral," CLS attacks the regulation by pointing to its effect: The policy is vulnerable to constitutional assault, CLS contends, because "it systematically and predictably burdens most heavily those groups whose viewpoints are out of favor with the campus mainstream." Brief for Petitioner 51. . . . This argument stumbles from its first step because "[a] regulation that serves purposes unrelated to the content of expression is deemed neutral, even if it has an incidental effect on some speakers or messages but not others." *Ward v. Rock Against Racism*, 491 U.S. 781, 791 (1989). . . .

Even if a regulation has a differential impact on groups wishing to enforce exclusionary membership policies, "[w]here the [State] does not target conduct on the basis of its expressive content, acts are not shielded from regulation merely because they express a discriminatory idea or philosophy." *R.A.V. v. St. Paul*, 505 U.S. 377, 390 (1992). . . .

. . . The Law School's policy aims at the *act* of rejecting would-be group members without reference to the reasons motivating that behavior. . . . CLS's conduct — not its Christian perspective — is, from Hastings' vantage point, what stands between the group and RSO status. . . .

. . . .

IV

. . . .

For the foregoing reasons, we affirm. . . .

JUSTICE ALITO, with whom THE CHIEF JUSTICE, JUSTICE SCALIA, and JUSTICE THOMAS join, dissenting.

. . . .

The Court's treatment of this case is deeply disappointing. The Court does not address the constitutionality of the very different policy that Hastings invoked when it denied CLS's application for registration. Nor does the Court address the constitutionality of the policy that Hastings now purports to follow. And the Court ignores strong evidence that the accept-all-comers policy is not viewpoint neutral because it was announced as a pretext to justify viewpoint discrimination. . . .

I

. . . .

The Court bases all of its analysis on the proposition that the relevant Hastings' policy is the so-called accept-all-comers policy. . . . Overwhelming evidence, however, shows that Hastings denied CLS's application pursuant to the Nondiscrimination Policy and that the accept-all-comers policy was nowhere to be found until it was mentioned by a former dean in a deposition taken well after this case began.

. . . .

When CLS applied for registration, Judy Hansen Chapman, the Director of Hastings' Office of Student Services, sent an e-mail to an officer of the chapter informing him that "CLS's bylaws did not appear to be compliant" with the Hastings Nondiscrimination Policy. . . . As far as the record reflects, Ms. Chapman made no mention of an accept-all-applicants policy.

A few days later, three officers of the chapter met with Ms. Chapman, and she reiterated that the CLS bylaws did not comply with "the religion and sexual orientation provisions of the Nondiscrimination Policy and that they would need to be amended in order for CLS to become a registered student organization." . . .

When CLS refused to change its membership requirements, Hastings denied its request for registration — thus making CLS the only student group whose application for registration has ever been rejected.

. . . .

In May 2005, Hastings filed an answer to CLS's first amended complaint and made an admission that is significant for present purposes. In its complaint, CLS had alleged that the Nondiscrimination Policy discriminates against religious groups because it prohibits those groups "from selecting officers and members dedicated to a particular set of religious ideals or beliefs" but "permits political, social and cultural student organizations to select officers and members dedicated to their organization's ideals and beliefs." In response, Hastings admitted that its Nondiscrimination Policy "permits political, social, and cultural student organizations to select officers and members who are dedicated to a particular set of ideals or beliefs." The Court states that "Hastings interprets the Nondiscrimination Policy, as it relates to the RSO program, to mandate acceptance of all comers." But this admission in Hastings' answer shows that Hastings had not adopted this interpretation when its answer was filed.

. . . In July 2005, Mary Kay Kane, then the dean of the law school, was deposed, and she stated: "It is my view that in order to be a registered student organization you have to allow all of our students to be members and full participants if they want to." In a declaration filed in October 2005, Ms. Chapman provided a more developed explanation, stating: "Hastings interprets the Nondiscrimination Policy as requiring that student organizations wishing to register with Hastings allow any Hastings student to become a member and/or seek a leadership position in the organization."

. . . .

Hastings' effort to portray the accept-all-comers policy as merely an interpretation of the Nondiscrimination Policy runs into obvious difficulties. First, the two policies are simply not the same: The Nondiscrimination Policy proscribes discrimination on a limited number of specified grounds, while the accept-all-comers policy outlaws all selectivity. Second, the Nondiscrimination Policy applies to everything that Hastings does, and the law school does not follow an accept-all-comers policy in activities such as admitting students and hiring faculty.

. . . .

Third, the record is replete with evidence that, at least until Dean Kane unveiled the accept-all-comers policy in July 2005, Hastings routinely registered student groups with bylaws limiting membership and leadership positions to those who agreed with the groups' viewpoints. For example, the bylaws of the Hastings Democratic Caucus provided that "any full-time student at Hastings may become a member of HDC *so long as they do not exhibit a consistent disregard and lack of respect for the objective of the organization* as stated in Article 3, Section 1." The constitution of the Association of Trial Lawyers of America at Hastings provided that every member must "adhere to the objectives of the Student Chapter as well as the mission of ATLA." . . . Since Hastings requires any student group applying for registration to submit a copy of its bylaws, Hastings cannot claim that it was unaware of such provisions. . . .

. . . .

II

To appreciate how far the Court has strayed, it is instructive to compare this case with *Healy v. James*, 408 U.S. 169 (1972), our only First Amendment precedent involving a public college's refusal to recognize a student group. The group in *Healy* was a local chapter of the Students for a Democratic Society (SDS). . . . The president of the college refused to allow the group to be recognized, concluding that the philosophy of the SDS was "antithetical to the school's policies" and that it was doubtful that the local chapter was independent of the national organization, the "'published aims and philosophy'" of which included "'disruption and violence.'" *Id.*, at 174-175.

. . . .

. . . The Court held that the denial of recognition substantially burdened the students' right to freedom of association. After observing that "[t]he primary impediment to free association flowing from nonrecognition is the denial of use of campus facilities for meetings and other appropriate purposes," *id.*, at 181, the Court continued:

> "Petitioners' associational interests also were circumscribed by the denial of the use of campus bulletin boards and the school newspaper. . . . Moreover, the organization's ability to participate in the intellectual give and take of campus debate, and to pursue its stated purposes, is limited by denial of access to the customary media for communicating with the administration, faculty members, and other students. Such impediments cannot be viewed as insubstantial." *Id.*, at 181-182.

It is striking that all of these same burdens are now borne by CLS. . . .

. . . .

In the end, I see only two possible distinctions between *Healy* and the present case. The first is that *Healy* did not involve any funding, but as I have noted, funding plays only a small part in this case. . . .

This leaves just one way of distinguishing *Healy*: the identity of the student group. In *Healy*, the Court warned that the college president's views regarding the philosophy of the SDS could not "justify the denial of First Amendment rights." 408 U.S., at 187. Here, too, disapproval of CLS cannot justify Hastings' actions.

III

. . . While I think that *Healy* is largely controlling, I am content to address the constitutionality of Hastings' actions under our limited public forum cases, which lead to exactly the same conclusion.

. . . .

We have applied this analysis in cases in which student speech was restricted because of the speaker's religious viewpoint, and we have consistently concluded that such restrictions constitute viewpoint discrimination. *E.g.*, *Rosenberger*, *supra*, at 845-846; *Widmar*, *supra*, at 267, n. 5, 269, 277. . . .

IV

. . . As previously noted, when Hastings refused to register CLS, it claimed that the CLS bylaws impermissibly discriminated on the basis of religion and sexual orientation. . . .

. . . [T]he Nondiscrimination Policy "permit[ted] political, social, and cultural student organizations to select officers and members who are dedicated to a particular set of ideals or beliefs." But the policy singled out one category of expressive associations for disfavored treatment: groups formed to express a religious message. Only religious groups were required to admit students who did not share their views. An environmentalist group was not required to admit students who rejected global warming. An animal rights group was not obligated to accept students who supported the use of animals to test cosmetics. But CLS was required to admit avowed atheists. This was patent viewpoint discrimination. . . .

. . . .

. . . The Hastings Nondiscrimination Policy, as interpreted by the law school, also discriminated on the basis of viewpoint regarding sexual morality. CLS has a particular viewpoint on this subject, namely, that sexual conduct outside marriage between a man and a woman is wrongful. Hastings would not allow CLS to express this viewpoint by limiting membership to persons willing to express a sincere agreement with CLS's views. By contrast, nothing in the Nondiscrimination Policy prohibited a group from expressing a contrary viewpoint by limiting membership to persons willing to endorse that group's beliefs. . . . It is hard to see how this can be viewed as anything other than viewpoint discrimination.

. . . .

V

. . . .

The regulations also make it clear that the registration program is not meant to stifle unpopular speech. They proclaim that "[i]t is the responsibility of the Dean to ensure an ongoing opportunity for the expression of a variety of viewpoints." . . . They also emphatically disclaim any endorsement of or responsibility for views that student groups may express.

. . . .

The accept-all-comers policy is antithetical to the design of the RSO forum. . . . As explained above, a group's First Amendment right of expressive association is burdened by the "forced inclusion" of members whose presence would "affec[t] in a significant way the group's ability to advocate public or private viewpoints." *Dale*, 530 U.S., at 648. The Court has therefore held that the government may not compel a group that engages in "expressive association" to admit such a member unless the government has a compelling interest, "'unrelated to the suppression of ideas, that cannot be achieved through means significantly less restrictive of associational freedoms.'" *Ibid.*

There can be no dispute that this standard would not permit a generally applicable law mandating that private religious groups admit members who do not share the groups' beliefs. Religious groups like CLS obviously engage in expressive association, and no legitimate state interest could override the powerful effect that an accept-all-comers law would have on the ability of religious groups to express their views. . . .

While there can be no question that the State of California could not impose such restrictions on all religious groups in the State, the Court now holds that Hastings, a state institution, may impose these very same requirements on students who wish to participate in a forum that is designed to foster the expression of diverse viewpoints. . . .

. . . .

I do not think it is an exaggeration to say that today's decision is a serious setback for freedom of expression in this country. Our First Amendment reflects a "profound national commitment to the principle that debate on public issues should be uninhibited, robust, and wide-open." *New York Times Co. v. Sullivan*, 376 U.S. 254, 270 (1964). . . . Even those who find CLS's views objectionable should be concerned about the way the group has been treated — by Hastings, the Court of Appeals, and now this Court. I can only hope that this decision will turn out to be an aberration.

[Concurring opinions of Justices Stevens and Kennedy are omitted.]

NOTES

1. It is quite clear that Justice Alito's dissenting opinion in *CLS* emphasizes different facts than the majority does (e.g., the presence and application of an "accept all comers" policy, the existence of an amended policy, and the impact of Hastings' offered alternatives to CLS and the legitimate ability of CLS to take advantage of them). With which opinion do you agree? Do you think Hastings interprets its Nondiscrimination Policy as a pretext for discrimination on the basis of religion, in order to exclude CLS from the benefits of registered student organizations? In other words, has Hasting engaged in viewpoint discrimination?

2. Both the majority and dissenting opinions spend a considerable amount of time discussing the reasonableness of Hastings' all-comers policy, with both opinions extolling the virtues of diversity of viewpoint and equality of access. Yet, the Justices disagree sharply on how well the policy's purposes have been met. With which argument do you agree?

3. The dissent in *CLS* compares the present case to *Healy v. James*, 408 U.S. 169 (1972), and argues that the CLS was treated discriminatorily in ways similar to the treatment of the SDS in *Healy*, yet the Court came to opposite conclusions. Do you agree that the circumstances in *Healy* and *CLS* are similar for the two controversial student organizations? If not, why not? If so, then what are the primary reasons why the Court would decide the cases differently?

4. In the years leading up to *CLS v. Martinez*, a few lower courts had addressed similar questions of discrimination and free speech violation, often with varying results. *See, e.g., Christian Legal Society v. Walker*, 453 F.3d 853 (7th Cir. 2006) (CLS' motion for preliminary injunction granted because the CLS was able to show a likelihood that the university violated the free speech rights of the organization);

Christian Legal Society v. Eck, 625 F. Supp. 2d 1026 (D. Mont. 2009) (court ruled that the CLS chapter violated the school's policies regarding open membership and nondiscrimination and were rightfully denied funding from the school's student bar association).

5. Both the majority and dissenting opinions in *CLS* relied, in part, on *Rosenberger v. Rector and Visitors of the University of Virginia*, 515 U.S. 819 (1995), to make their arguments. *Rosenberger* involved a constitutional challenge to the use of student activity fees to fund publications of student organizations, including religious ones. The case is presented below.

C. STUDENT ACTIVITY FEES

ROSENBERGER v. RECTOR AND VISITORS OF THE UNIVERSITY OF VIRGINIA

515 U.S. 819 (1995)

JUSTICE KENNEDY delivered the opinion of the Court.

The University of Virginia, an instrumentality of the Commonwealth for which it is named and thus bound by the First and Fourteenth Amendments, authorizes the payment of outside contractors for the printing costs of a variety of student publications. It withheld any authorization for payments on behalf of petitioners for the sole reason that their student paper "primarily promotes or manifests a particular belief in or about a deity or an ultimate reality." That the paper did promote or manifest views within the defined exclusion seems plain enough. The challenge is to the University's regulation and its denial of authorization, the case raising issues under the Speech and Establishment Clauses of the First Amendment.

I

. . . .

Before a student group is eligible to submit bills from its outside contractors for payment by the fund described below, it must become a "Contracted Independent Organization" (CIO). CIO status is available to any group the majority of whose members are students, whose managing officers are full-time students, and that complies with certain procedural requirements. A CIO must file its constitution with the University; must pledge not to discriminate in its membership; and must include in dealings with third parties and in all written materials a disclaimer, stating that the CIO is independent of the University and that the University is not responsible for the CIO. CIOs enjoy access to University facilities, including meeting rooms and computer terminals. A standard agreement signed between each CIO and the University provides that the benefits and opportunities afforded to CIOs "should not be misinterpreted as meaning that those organizations are part of or controlled by the University, that the University is responsible for the organizations' contracts or other acts or omissions, or that the University approves of the organizations' goals or activities."

All CIOs may exist and operate at the University, but some are also entitled to apply for funds from the Student Activities Fund (SAF). Established and governed by University Guidelines, the purpose of the SAF is to support a broad range of extracurricular student activities that "are related to the educational purpose of the University." The SAF is based on the University's "recognition that the availability of a wide range of opportunities" for its students "tends to enhance the University environment." The Guidelines require that it be administered "in a manner consistent with the educational purpose of the University as well as with state and federal law." The SAF receives its money from a mandatory fee of $14 per semester assessed to each full-time student. The Student Council, elected by the students, has the initial authority to disburse the funds, but its actions are subject to review by a faculty body chaired by a designee of the Vice President for Student Affairs.

Some, but not all, CIOs may submit disbursement requests to the SAF. The Guidelines recognize 11 categories of student groups that may seek payment to third-party contractors because they "are related to the educational purpose of the University of Virginia." One of these is "student news, information, opinion, entertainment, or academic communications media groups." The Guidelines also specify, however, that the costs of certain activities of CIOs that are otherwise eligible for funding will not be reimbursed by the SAF. The student activities that are excluded from SAF support are religious activities, philanthropic contributions and activities, political activities, activities that would jeopardize the University's tax-exempt status, those which involve payment of honoraria or similar fees, or social entertainment or related expenses. . . . A "religious activity" . . . is defined as any activity that "primarily promotes or manifests a particular belief in or about a deity or an ultimate reality."

The Guidelines prescribe these criteria for determining the amounts of third-party disbursements that will be allowed on behalf of each eligible student organization: the size of the group, its financial self-sufficiency, and the University-wide benefit of its activities. If an organization seeks SAF support, it must submit its bills to the Student Council, which pays the organization's creditors upon determining that the expenses are appropriate. No direct payments are made to the student groups. During the 1990-1991 academic year, 343 student groups qualified as CIOs. One hundred thirty-five of them applied for support from the SAF, and 118 received funding. . . .

Petitioners' organization, Wide Awake Productions (WAP), qualified as a CIO. Formed by petitioner Ronald Rosenberger and other undergraduates in 1990, WAP was established "to publish a magazine of philosophical and religious expression," "to facilitate discussion which fosters an atmosphere of sensitivity to and tolerance of Christian viewpoints," and "to provide a unifying focus for Christians of multicultural backgrounds." WAP publishes Wide Awake: A Christian Perspective at the University of Virginia. The paper's Christian viewpoint was evident from the first issue, in which its editors wrote that the journal "offers a Christian perspective on both personal and community issues, especially those relevant to college students at the University of Virginia." The editors committed the paper to a two-fold mission: "to challenge Christians to live, in word and deed, according to the faith they proclaim and to encourage students to consider what a personal relationship with Jesus Christ means." The first issue had articles about racism, crisis pregnancy, stress, prayer, C. S. Lewis' ideas about evil and free will, and reviews of religious music. In the next two issues, Wide Awake featured stories about homosexuality, Christian missionary work, and eating disorders, as well as music reviews and interviews with University professors. Each page of Wide Awake, and the end of each article or review, is marked by a cross. The advertisements carried in Wide Awake also reveal the Christian perspective of the journal. For the most part, the advertisers are churches, centers for Christian study, or Christian bookstores. By June 1992, WAP had distributed about 5,000 copies of Wide Awake to University students, free of charge.

WAP had acquired CIO status soon after it was organized. This is an important consideration in this case, for had it been a "religious organization," WAP would not have been accorded CIO status. As defined by the Guidelines, a "religious organization" is "an organization whose purpose is to practice a devotion to an acknowledged ultimate reality or deity." At no stage in this controversy has the University contended that WAP is such an organization.

A few months after being given CIO status, WAP requested the SAF to pay its printer $5,862 for the costs of printing its newspaper. The Appropriations Committee of the Student Council denied WAP's request on the ground that Wide Awake was a "religious activity" within the meaning of the Guidelines, *i.e.*, that the newspaper "promoted or manifested a particular belief in or about a deity or an ultimate reality." It made its determination after examining the first issue. WAP appealed the denial to the full Student Council, contending that WAP met all the applicable Guidelines and that denial of SAF support on the basis of the magazine's religious perspective violated the Constitution. The appeal was denied without further comment, and WAP appealed to the next level, the Student Activities Committee. In a letter signed by the Dean of Students, the committee sustained the denial of funding.

Having no further recourse within the University structure, WAP, Wide Awake, and three of its editors and members filed suit in the United States District Court for the Western District of Virginia. . . . They alleged that refusal to authorize payment of the printing costs of the publication, solely on the basis of its religious editorial viewpoint, violated their rights to freedom of speech and press, to the free exercise of religion, and to equal protection of the law. . . .

. . . [T]he District Court ruled for the University, holding that denial of SAF support was not an impermissible content or viewpoint discrimination against petitioners' speech, and that the University's Establishment Clause concern over its "religious activities" was a sufficient justification for denying payment to third-party contractors. . . .

The United States Court of Appeals for the Fourth Circuit, in disagreement with the District Court, held that the Guidelines did discriminate on the basis of content. It ruled that, while the State need not underwrite speech, there was a presumptive violation of the Speech Clause when viewpoint discrimination was invoked to deny third-party payment otherwise available to CIOs. The Court of Appeals affirmed the judgment of the District Court nonetheless, concluding that the discrimination by the University was justified by the "compelling interest in maintaining strict separation of church and state." We granted certiorari.

II

It is axiomatic that the government may not regulate speech based on its substantive content or the message it conveys. Other principles follow from this precept. In the realm of private speech or expression, government regulation may not favor one speaker over another. . . . When the government targets not subject matter, but particular views taken by speakers on a subject, the violation of the First Amendment is all the more blatant. Viewpoint discrimination is thus an egregious form of content discrimination. The government must abstain from regulating speech when the specific motivating ideology or the opinion or perspective of the speaker is the rationale for the restriction.

These principles provide the framework forbidding the State from exercising viewpoint discrimination, even when the limited public forum is one of its own creation. In a case involving a school district's provision of school facilities for private uses, we declared that "there is no question that the District, like the private owner of property, may legally preserve the property under its control for the use to which it is dedicated." The necessities of confining a forum to the limited and legitimate purposes for which it was created may justify the State in reserving it for certain groups or for the discussion of certain topics. . . . Once it has opened a limited forum, however, the State must respect the lawful boundaries it has itself set. The State may not exclude speech where its distinction is not "reasonable in light of the purpose served by the forum," . . . nor may it discriminate against speech on the basis of its viewpoint. . . . Thus, in determining whether the State is acting to preserve the limits of the forum it has created so that the exclusion of a class of speech is legitimate, we have observed a distinction between, on the one hand, content discrimination, which may be permissible if it preserves the purposes of that limited forum, and, on the other hand, viewpoint discrimination, which is presumed impermissible when directed against speech otherwise within the forum's limitations.

The SAF is a forum more in a metaphysical than in a spatial or geographic sense, but the same principles are applicable. . . . The most recent and most apposite case is our decision in *Lamb's Chapel, supra.* There, a school district had opened school facilities for use after school hours by community groups for a wide variety of social, civic, and recreational purposes. The district, however, had enacted a formal policy against opening facilities to groups for religious purposes. Invoking its policy, the district rejected a request from a group desiring to show a film series addressing various child-rearing questions from a "Christian perspective." There was no indication in the record in *Lamb's Chapel* that the request to use the school facilities was "denied, for any reason other than the fact that the presentation would have been from a religious perspective." Our conclusion was unanimous: "It discriminates on the basis of viewpoint to permit school property to be used for the presentation of all views about family issues and child rearing except those dealing with the subject matter from a religious standpoint."

The University does acknowledge (as it must in light of our precedents) that "ideologically driven attempts to suppress a particular point of view are presumptively unconstitutional in funding, as in other contexts," but insists that this case does not present that issue because the Guidelines draw lines based on content, not viewpoint. As we have noted, discrimination against one set of views or ideas is but a subset or particular instance of the more general phenomenon of content discrimination. And, it must be acknowledged, the distinction is not a precise one. It is, in a sense, something of an understatement to speak of religious thought and discussion as just a viewpoint, as distinct from a comprehensive body of thought. . . . We conclude, nonetheless, that here, as in *Lamb's Chapel*, viewpoint discrimination is the proper way to interpret the University's objections to Wide Awake. By the very terms of the SAF prohibition, the University does not exclude religion as a subject matter but selects for disfavored treatment those student journalistic efforts with religious editorial viewpoints. Religion may be a vast area of inquiry, but it also provides, as it did here, a specific premise, a perspective, a standpoint from which a variety of subjects may be discussed and considered. The prohibited perspective, not the general subject matter, resulted in the refusal to make third-party payments, for the subjects discussed were otherwise within the approved category of publications.

. . . .

Based on the principles we have discussed, we hold that the regulation invoked to deny SAF support, both in its terms and in its application to these petitioners, is a denial of their right of free speech guaranteed by the First Amendment. It remains to be considered whether the violation following from the University's action is excused by the necessity of complying with the Constitution's prohibition against state establishment of religion. We turn to that question.

III

. . . We granted certiorari on this question: "Whether the Establishment Clause compels a state university to exclude an otherwise eligible student publication from participation in the student activities fund, solely on the basis of its religious viewpoint, where such exclusion would violate the Speech and Press Clauses if the viewpoint of the publication were nonreligious." The University now seems to have abandoned this position, contending that "the fundamental objection to petitioners' argument is not that it implicates the Establishment Clause but that it would defeat the ability of public education at all levels to control the use of public funds." . . . [B]ut as the Court of Appeals rested its judgment on the point and our dissenting colleagues would find it determinative, it must be addressed.

The Court of Appeals ruled that withholding SAF support from Wide Awake contravened the Speech Clause of the First Amendment, but proceeded to hold that the University's action was justified by the necessity of avoiding a violation of the Establishment Clause, an interest it found compelling. . . . [T]he Fourth Circuit . . . declared that the Establishment Clause would not permit the use of public funds to support " 'a specifically religious activity in an otherwise substantially secular setting.' " It reasoned that because Wide Awake is "a journal pervasively devoted to the discussion and advancement of an avowedly Christian theological and personal philosophy," the University's provision of SAF funds for its publication would "send an unmistakably clear signal that the University of Virginia supports Christian values and wishes to promote the wide promulgation of such values."

If there is to be assurance that the Establishment Clause retains its force in guarding against those governmental actions it was intended to prohibit, we must in each case inquire first into the purpose and object of the governmental action in question and then into the practical details of the program's operation. . . .

A central lesson of our decisions is that a significant factor in upholding governmental programs in the face of Establishment Clause attack is their neutrality towards religion. . . . We have held that the guarantee of neutrality is respected, not offended, when the government, following neutral criteria and evenhanded policies, extends benefits to recipients whose ideologies and viewpoints, including religious ones, are broad and diverse. . . . More than once have we rejected the position that the Establishment Clause even justifies, much less requires, a refusal to extend free speech rights to religious speakers who participate in broad-reaching government programs neutral in design.

The governmental program here is neutral toward religion. There is no suggestion that the University created it to advance religion or adopted some ingenious device with the purpose of aiding a religious cause. The object of the SAF is to open a forum for speech and to support various student enterprises, including the publication of newspapers, in recognition of the diversity and creativity of student life. The University's SAF Guidelines have a separate classification for, and do not make third-party payments on behalf of, "religious organizations," which are those "whose purpose is to practice a devotion to an acknowledged ultimate reality or deity." The category of support here is for "student news, information, opinion, entertainment, or academic communications media groups," of which Wide Awake was 1 of 15 in the 1990 school year. WAP did not seek a subsidy because of its Christian editorial viewpoint; it sought funding as a student journal, which it was.

. . . .

It does not violate the Establishment Clause for a public university to grant access to its facilities on a religion-neutral basis to a wide spectrum of student groups, including groups that use meeting rooms for sectarian activities, accompanied by some devotional exercises. This is so even where the upkeep, maintenance, and repair of the facilities attributed to those uses is paid from a student activities fund to which students are required to contribute. The government usually acts by spending money. Even the provision of a meeting room . . . involved governmental expenditure, if only in the form of electricity and heating or cooling costs. The error made by the Court of Appeals, as well as by the dissent, lies in focusing on the money that is undoubtedly expended by the government, rather than on the nature of the benefit received by the recipient. If the expenditure of governmental funds is prohibited whenever those funds pay for a service that is, pursuant to a religion-neutral program, used by a group for sectarian purposes, then *Widmar, Mergens*, and *Lamb's Chapel* would have to be overruled. Given our holdings in these cases, it follows that a public university may maintain its own computer facility and give student groups access to that facility, including the use of the printers, on a religion neutral, say first-come-first-served, basis. If a religious student organization obtained access on that religion-neutral basis and used a computer to compose or a printer or copy machine to print speech with a religious content or viewpoint, the State's action in providing the group with access would no more violate the Establishment Clause than would giving those groups access to an assembly hall. . . . The University provides printing services to a broad spectrum of student newspapers qualified as CIOs by reason of their officers and membership. Any benefit to religion is incidental to the government's provision of secular services for secular purposes on a religion-neutral basis. Printing is a routine, secular, and recurring attribute of student life.

By paying outside printers, the University in fact attains a further degree of separation from the student publication, for it avoids the duties of supervision, escapes the costs of upkeep, repair, and replacement attributable to student use, and has a clear record of costs. As a result, . . . the University can charge the SAF, and not the taxpayers as a whole, for the discrete activity in question. It would be formalistic for us to say that the University must forfeit these advantages and provide the services itself in order to comply with the Establishment Clause. It is, of course, true that if the State pays a church's bills it is subsidizing it, and we must guard against this abuse. That is not a danger here. . . . It is instead a publication involved in a pure forum for the expression of ideas, ideas that would be both incomplete and chilled were the Constitution to be interpreted to require that state officials and courts scan the publication to ferret out views that principally manifest a belief in a divine being.

. . . .

To obey the Establishment Clause, it was not necessary for the University to deny eligibility to student publications because of their viewpoint. . . . That course of action was a denial of the right of free speech and would risk fostering a pervasive bias or hostility to religion, which could undermine the very neutrality the Establishment Clause requires. There is no Establishment Clause violation in the University's honoring its duties under the Free Speech Clause.

The judgment of the Court of Appeals must be, and is, reversed.

It is so ordered.

NOTES

1. *Rosenberger* was a close, 5-4 decision, with the majority authored by Justice Kennedy and joined by Chief Justice Rehnquist and Justices O'Connor, Scalia, and Thomas. Justice O'Connor wrote a concurring opinion to emphasize that the funding program did not unlawfully endorse religion, particularly in light of the possibility that objecting students may have the opportunity to opt out on First Amendment grounds. Justice Thomas wrote a concurring opinion to make the point that the Constitution's framers never intended to keep religious entities from participating in neutral, even-handed governmental programs. The four dissenters — Justice Souter, joined by Justices Stevens, Ginsburg, and Breyer — focused primarily on the Establishment Clause issue and argued that direct funding of the core religious activities at issue is not lawful.

2. How is content discrimination different from viewpoint discrimination? Why is the distinction important for law and policy purposes? If a university official in charge of making such funding and other recognition decisions disagrees with both the content and the viewpoint of a publication like Wide Awake Publications, what advice would you offer in order to remain lawful on content and viewpoint grounds?

3. Recall *Tinker v. Des Moines Independent Community School District*, 393 U.S. 503 (1969). If the expressive activity of the student organization and/or its publication, Wide Awake Publications, were to become substantially disruptive or materially interfering with the work of the university or the rights of others in the university community, would the disruption standards articulated in these cases supersede the viewpoint discrimination standard articulated in *Rosenberger*? How should university policy on student speech and student organizations reflect concerns about content, viewpoint, and effect of student speech effectively enough to withstand legal scrutiny?

4. In the course of its analysis, the Court in *Rosenberger* made the following statement:

> . . . [W]hen the State is the speaker, it may make content-based choices. When the University determines the content of the education it provides, it is the University speaking, and we have permitted the government to regulate the content of what is or is not expressed when it is the speaker or when it enlists private entities to convey its own message. . . . When the government disburses public funds to private entities to convey a governmental message, it may take legitimate and appropriate steps to ensure that its message is neither garbled nor distorted by the grantee.

515 U.S. at 833. The Court then held that the principle stated above did not give the university permission to engage in viewpoint discrimination when, in fact, the university is not the speaker here. Who is the speaker in *Rosenberger*? It appears that the individual grantees of funds would be the speakers. Correct? What about the entire full-time student body as the speakers, considering they are the ones who pay the mandatory fee per semester? How does the Court address this matter? Do the students, in effect, give up some of their individual "speaking" power with this fee, which is designed to help organizations across campus engage in speech? How does this discussion affect the analysis of the Establishment Clause issue? Recall the following statement from *Rosenberger*: "The distinction between the University's own favored message and the private speech of students is evident in the case before us."

5. The student fee of $14 per semester in *Rosenberger* was mandatory. What about students' objections that their money was being used to fund publications whose views were contrary to their own? The Court in *Rosenberger* did not ask or answer the question of whether an objecting student has the First Amendment right to demand a pro rata return to the extent the fee is expended for speech to which he or she does not subscribe. What do you think about such a request? Would a university be required to offer a prorated return? *See Keller v. State Bar of California*, 496 U.S. 1 (1990) (upholding mandatory fees for the state's practicing lawyers to fund activities germane to the state's goals of regulating the legal profession and improving the quality of legal services); *Abood v. Detroit Bd. of Ed.*,

431 U.S. 209 (1977) (holding that fair share fees required for beneficiaries of a collectively bargained teachers' contract are lawful, even if the objecting teachers are not members of the teachers' union). See also the case following these notes, *Board of Regents of the University of Wisconsin v. Southworth*, 529 U.S. 217 (2000).

6. In 2001, following its decisions in *Lamb's Chapel* and *Rosenberger*, the Supreme Court heard a case with similar legal arguments, different factual context, and nearly identical reasoning and result. In *Good New Club v. Milford Central School*, 533 U.S. 98 (2001), the Court held unconstitutional a school district's denial of facilities access to the Good News Club, an after-school Bible study group for children. The Court held that the school's facilities use policy, which allowed outside groups to use school space for instruction in any branch of education, learning, or the arts; social, civic, and recreational meetings and entertainment events; and other uses pertaining to the welfare of the community, permitted the Good News Club to use the facilities, despite the Club's religious viewpoints. Similar to the University of Virginia in *Rosenberger*, Milford Central School asserted that allowing the Club to use the public school would violate the Establishment Clause. The Court disagreed and held, instead, that denying the Club access to the school under the policy would violate the Club's free speech rights and would be discriminatory on viewpoint.

7. Compare "printing services" with "access to website space" for student organizations. The University in *Rosenberger* paid outside printers with funds from the SAF — funds which came first from full-time students. What if the publications were websites, with the websites made available through funds contributed to a fund like the SAF? Does a website bear the "imprimatur" of the university and, therefore, the endorsement of the content?

8. What sorts of challenges may arise with the use of university funds (whether or not filled by student fees) for student government activities, including campaigns and elections? In the area of campaign funding, courts struggle between balancing constitutional protections and the undoubtedly different context of elections at educational institutions. Consider the disconcert within Ninth Circuit precedent over the span of the last decade: In *Welker v. Cicerone*, 174 F. Supp. 2d 1055 (C.D. Cal. 2001), the University of California-Irvine Student Elections Code restricted campaign spending to $100 for students running for seats on the university's Legislative Council. Violations of the code resulted in disqualification. Welker, a senior, spent $233.40. The Elections Commission disqualified Welker and the University Judicial Board affirmed. Welker filed suit for reinstatement to the Legislative Council and expungement of the disciplinary record. The court held for the student, finding that limits on campaign spending directly affect free speech in quantity and in diversity. Generally, universities must show that their funding limits are narrowly tailored to meet a compelling governmental interest. In *Welker*, the defendants offered four such interests, each of which was rejected. First, the court found that the university's stated interest in increasing socio-economic equality was not compelling. Second, the university's interest in encouraging academic pursuits was fine, but not related to student elections. Third, the university's interest in decreasing the influence of private corporate sponsors was compelling, but the elections code already provided for it via limits placed on the amount a candidate could get from any one source. Finally, the university argued that a limit on campaign funding would increase students' creativity. The court found no direct correlation between creativity and spending limits.

However, in 2007, the Ninth Circuit held that First Amendment free speech protections are not fully applicable in the context of state university students' campaigning for student government positions. The court rejected the student's claim that the university could not restrict his campaign spending because it constituted an imposition on his "free speech" rights:

> We may not simply ignore the facts that the campaign expenditure limitations in this case involved election to *student government* and that the expenditures occurred mostly, if not exclusively, on a *university campus.* The educational context of a university, the specific educational purpose of [the university's] student government, and the numerous other limits placed upon student campaigning distinguish the campaign expenditure limitations in this case from those in cases such as *Buckley*, which involved campaigns for national political office.

Flint v. Dennison, 488 F.3d 816, 827 (9th Cir. 2007). The Court further emphasized that due to the educational nature of these "campaigns," "Constitutional protections must be analyzed with due regard to that educational purpose." *Id.* at 827 (quoting *Ala. Student Party v. Student Gov't Ass'n of the Univ. of Ala.*, 867 F.2d 1344, 1346 (11th Cir. 1989)).

Some courts have also held that policies inspired by the maintenance and fair distribution of scarce institutional resources are permissible as well. *See Ala. Student Party v. Student Gov't Ass'n of the Univ. of Ala.*, 867 F.2d 1344 (11th Cir. 1989).

BOARD OF REGENTS OF THE UNIVERSITY OF WISCONSIN v. SOUTHWORTH
529 U.S. 217 (2000)

JUSTICE KENNEDY delivered the opinion of the Court.

. . . Respondents are a group of students at the University of Wisconsin. They brought a First Amendment challenge to a mandatory student activity fee imposed by petitioner Board of Regents of the University of Wisconsin and used in part by the University to support student organizations engaging in political or ideological speech. Respondents object to the speech and expression of some of the student organizations. . . . [B]oth the District Court and the Court of Appeals invalidated the University's student fee program. The University contends that its mandatory student activity fee and the speech which it supports are appropriate to further its educational mission.

We reverse. The First Amendment permits a public university to charge its students an activity fee used to fund a program to facilitate extracurricular student speech if the program is viewpoint neutral. We do not sustain, however, the student referendum mechanism of the University's program, which appears to permit the exaction of fees in violation of the viewpoint neutrality principle. As to that aspect of the program, we remand for further proceedings.

I

. . . .

The responsibility for governing the University of Wisconsin System is vested by law with the board of regents. The same law empowers the students to share in aspects of the University's governance. One of those functions is to administer the student activities fee program. By statute the "students in consultation with the chancellor and subject to the final confirmation of the board [of regents] shall have the responsibility for the disposition of those student fees which constitute substantial support for campus student activities. ". . . The program the University maintains to support the extracurricular activities undertaken by many of its student organizations is the subject of the present controversy.

It seems that since its founding the University has required full-time students enrolled at its Madison campus to pay a nonrefundable activity fee. For the 1995-1996 academic year, when this suit was commenced, the activity fee amounted to $331.50 per year. The fee is segregated from the University's tuition charge. Once collected, the activity fees are deposited by the University into the accounts of the State of Wisconsin. The fees are drawn upon by the University to support various campus services and extracurricular student activities. In the University's view, the activity fees "enhance the educational experience" of its students by "promoting extracurricular activities," "stimulating advocacy and debate on diverse points of view," enabling "participation in political activity," "promoting student participation in campus administrative activity," and providing "opportunities to develop social skills," all consistent with the University's mission.

The board of regents classifies the segregated fee into allocable and nonallocable portions. The nonallocable portion approximates 80% of the total fee and covers expenses such as student health services, intramural sports, debt service, and the upkeep and operations of the student union facilities. Respondents did not challenge the purposes to which the University commits the nonallocable portion of the segregated fee.

The allocable portion of the fee supports extracurricular endeavors pursued by the University's registered student organizations or RSOs. To qualify for RSO status students must organize as a not-for-profit group, limit membership primarily to students, and agree to undertake activities related to student life on campus. During the 1995-1996 school year, 623 groups had RSO status on the Madison campus. To name but a few, RSOs included the Future Financial Gurus of America; the International Socialist Organization; the College Democrats; the College Republicans; and the American Civil Liberties Union Campus Chapter. As one would expect, the expressive activities undertaken by RSOs are diverse in range and content, from displaying posters and circulating newsletters throughout the campus, to hosting campus debates and guest speakers, and to what can best be described as political lobbying.

RSOs may obtain a portion of the allocable fees in one of three ways. Most do so by seeking funding from the Student Government Activity Fund (SGAF), administered by the ASM. SGAF moneys may be issued to support an RSO's operations and events, as well as travel expenses "central to the purpose of the organization." As an alternative, an RSO can apply for funding from the General Student Services Fund (GSSF), administered through the ASM's finance committee. During the 1995-1996 academic year, 15 RSOs received GSSF funding. These RSOs included a campus tutoring center, the student radio station, a student environmental group, a gay and bisexual student center, a community legal office, an AIDS support network, a campus women's center, and the Wisconsin Student Public Interest Research Group (WISPIRG). The University acknowledges that, in addition to providing campus services (*e.g.*, tutoring and counseling), the GSSF-funded RSOs engage in political and ideological expression.

The GSSF, as well as the SGAF, consists of moneys originating in the allocable portion of the mandatory fee. The parties have stipulated that, with respect to SGAF and GSSF funding, "the process for reviewing and approving allocations for funding is administered in a viewpoint-neutral fashion," and that the University does not use the fee program for "advocating a particular point of view."

A student referendum provides a third means for an RSO to obtain funding. While the record is sparse on this feature of the University's program, the parties inform us that the student body can vote either to approve or to disapprove an assessment for a particular RSO. One referendum resulted in an allocation of $45,000 to WISPIRG during the 1995-1996 academic year. At oral argument, counsel for the University acknowledged that a referendum could also operate to defund an RSO or to veto a funding decision of the ASM. In October 1996, for example, the student body voted to terminate funding to a national student organization to which the University belonged. Both parties confirmed at oral argument that their stipulation regarding the program's viewpoint neutrality does not extend to the referendum process.

With respect to GSSF and SGAF funding, the ASM or its finance committee makes initial funding decisions. The ASM does so in an open session, and interested students may attend meetings when RSO funding is discussed. It also appears that the ASM must approve the results of a student referendum. Approval appears *pro forma*, however, as counsel for the University advised us that the student government "voluntarily views the referendum as binding." Once the ASM approves an RSO's funding application, it forwards its decision to the chancellor and to the board of regents for their review and approval. Approximately 30% of the University's RSOs received funding during the 1995-1996 academic year.

RSOs, as a general rule, do not receive lump-sum cash distributions. Rather, RSOs obtain funding support on a reimbursement basis by submitting receipts or invoices to the University. Guidelines identify expenses appropriate for reimbursement. Permitted expenditures include, in the main, costs for printing, postage, office supplies, and use of University facilities and equipment. Materials printed with student fees must contain a disclaimer that the views expressed are not those of the ASM. The University also reimburses RSOs for fees arising from membership in "other related and non-profit organizations."

The University's policy establishes purposes for which fees may not be expended. RSOs may not receive reimbursement for "gifts, donations, and contributions," the costs of legal services, or for "activities which are politically partisan or religious in nature." (The policy does not give examples of the prohibited expenditures.) A separate policy statement on GSSF funding states that an RSO can receive funding if it "does not have a *primarily* political orientation (i.e. is not a registered political group)." The same policy adds that an RSO "shall not use [student fees] for any lobbying purposes." At one point in their brief respondents suggest that the prohibition against expenditures for "politically partisan" purposes renders the program not viewpoint neutral. In view of the fact that both parties entered a stipulation to the contrary at the outset of this litigation, which was again reiterated during oral argument in this Court, we do not consider respondents' challenge to this aspect of the University's program.

The University's Student Organization Handbook has guidelines for regulating the conduct and activities of RSOs. In addition to obligating RSOs to adhere to the fee program's rules and regulations, the guidelines establish procedures authorizing any student to complain to the University that an RSO is in noncompliance. An extensive investigative process is in place to evaluate and remedy violations. The University's policy includes a range of sanctions for noncompliance, including probation, suspension, or termination of RSO status.

One RSO that appears to operate in a manner distinct from others is WISPIRG. For reasons not clear from the record, WISPIRG receives lump-sum cash distributions from the University. University counsel informed us that this distribution reduced the GSSF portion of the fee pool. The full extent of the uses to which WISPIRG puts its funds is unclear. We do know, however, that WISPIRG sponsored on-campus events regarding homelessness and environmental and consumer protection issues. It coordinated community food drives and educational programs and spent a portion of its activity fees for the lobbying efforts of its parent organization and for student internships aimed at influencing legislation.

In March 1996, respondents, each of whom attended or still attend the University's Madison campus, filed suit in the United States District Court for the Western District of Wisconsin against members of the board of regents. Respondents alleged that imposition of the segregated fee violated their rights of free speech, free association, and free exercise under the First Amendment. They contended the University must grant them the choice not to fund those RSOs that engage in political and ideological expression offensive to their personal beliefs. Respondents requested both injunctive and declaratory relief.

. . . .

Other courts addressing First Amendment challenges to similar student fee programs have reached conflicting results. . . . These conflicts, together with the importance of the issue presented, led us to grant certiorari. We reverse the judgment of the Court of Appeals.

II

It is inevitable that government will adopt and pursue programs and policies within its constitutional powers but which nevertheless are contrary to the profound beliefs and sincere convictions of some of its citizens. The government, as a general rule, may support valid programs and policies by taxes or other exactions binding on protesting parties. Within this broader principle it seems inevitable that funds raised by the government will be spent for speech and other expression to advocate and defend its own policies. . . . The case we decide here, however, does not raise the issue of the government's right, or, to be more specific, the state-controlled University's right, to use its own funds to advance a particular message. The University's whole justification for fostering the challenged expression is that it springs from the initiative of the students, who alone give it purpose and content in the course of their extracurricular endeavors.

The University having disclaimed that the speech is its own, we do not reach the question whether traditional political controls to ensure responsible government action would be sufficient to overcome First Amendment objections and to allow the challenged program under the principle that the government can speak for itself. If the challenged speech here were financed by tuition dollars and the University and its officials were responsible for its content, the case might be evaluated on the premise that the government itself is the speaker. That is not the case before us.

The University of Wisconsin exacts the fee at issue for the sole purpose of facilitating the free and open exchange of ideas by, and among, its students. We conclude the objecting students may insist upon certain safeguards with respect to the expressive activities which they are required to support. Our public forum cases are instructive here by close analogy. This is true even though the student activities fund is not a public forum in the traditional sense of the term and despite the circumstance that those cases most often involve a demand for access, not a claim to be exempt from supporting speech. . . . The standard of viewpoint neutrality found in the public forum cases provides the standard we find controlling. We decide that the viewpoint neutrality requirement of the University program is in general sufficient to protect the rights of the objecting students. The student referendum aspect of the program for funding speech and expressive activities, however, appears to be inconsistent with the viewpoint neutrality requirement.

. . . .

The speech the University seeks to encourage in the program before us is distinguished not by discernable limits but by its vast, unexplored bounds. To insist upon asking what speech is germane would be contrary to the very goal the University seeks to pursue. It is not for the Court to say what is or is not germane to the ideas to be pursued in an institution of higher learning.

. . . It is all but inevitable that the fees will result in subsidies to speech which some students find objectionable and offensive to their personal beliefs. If the standard of germane speech is inapplicable, then, it might be argued the remedy is to allow each student to list those causes which he or she will or will not support. If a university decided that its students' First Amendment interests were better protected by some type of optional or refund system it would be free to do so. We decline to impose a system of that sort as a constitutional requirement, however. The restriction could be so disruptive and expensive that the program to support extracurricular speech would be ineffective. The First Amendment does not require the University to put the program at risk.

The University may determine that its mission is well served if students have the means to engage in dynamic discussions of philosophical, religious, scientific, social, and political subjects in their extracurricular campus life outside the lecture hall. If the University reaches this conclusion, it is entitled to impose a mandatory fee to sustain an open dialogue to these ends.

The University must provide some protection to its students' First Amendment interests, however. The proper measure, and the principal standard of protection for objecting students, we conclude, is the requirement of viewpoint neutrality in the allocation of funding support. Viewpoint neutrality was the obligation to which we gave substance in *Rosenberger v. Rector and Visitors of Univ. of Va.*, 515 U.S. 819 (1995). There the University of Virginia feared that any association with a student newspaper advancing religious viewpoints would violate the Establishment Clause. We rejected the argument, holding that the school's adherence to a rule of viewpoint neutrality in administering its student fee program would prevent "any mistaken impression that the student newspapers speak for the University." While *Rosenberger* was concerned with the rights a student has to use an extracurricular speech program already in place, today's case considers the antecedent question, acknowledged but unresolved in *Rosenberger:* whether a public university may require its students to pay a fee which creates the mechanism for the extracurricular speech in the first instance. When a university requires its students to pay fees to support the extracurricular speech of other students, all in the interest of open discussion, it may not prefer some viewpoints to others. There is symmetry then in our holding here and in *Rosenberger:* Viewpoint neutrality is the justification for requiring the student to pay the fee in the first instance and for ensuring the integrity of the program's operation once the funds have been collected. . . .

. . . .

We make no distinction between campus activities and the off-campus expressive activities of objectionable RSOs. Those activities, respondents tell us, often bear no relationship to the University's reason for imposing the segregated fee in the first instance, to foster vibrant campus debate among students. If the University shares those concerns, it is free to enact viewpoint neutral rules restricting off-campus travel or other expenditures by RSOs, for it may create what is tantamount to a limited public forum if the principles of viewpoint neutrality are respected. We find no principled way, however, to impose upon the University, as a constitutional matter, a requirement to adopt geographic or spatial restrictions as a condition for RSOs' entitlement to reimbursement. . . .

Our decision ought not to be taken to imply that in other instances the University, its agents or employees, or — of particular importance — its faculty, are subject to the First Amendment analysis which controls in this case. Where the University speaks, either in its own name through its regents or officers, or in myriad other ways through its diverse faculties, the analysis likely would be altogether different. . . .

. . . In the instant case, the speech is not that of the University or its agents. It is not, furthermore, speech by an instructor or a professor in the academic context, where principles applicable to government speech would have to be considered. . . .

III

It remains to discuss the referendum aspect of the University's program. While the record is not well developed on the point, it appears that by majority vote of the student body a given RSO may be funded or defunded. It is unclear to us what protection, if any, there is for viewpoint neutrality in this part of the process. To the extent the referendum substitutes majority determinations for viewpoint neutrality it would undermine the constitutional protection the program requires. The whole theory of viewpoint neutrality is that minority views are treated with the same respect as are majority views. Access to a public forum, for instance, does not depend upon majoritarian consent. That principle is controlling here. A remand is necessary and appropriate to resolve this point; and the case in all events must be reexamined in light of the principles we have discussed.

It is so ordered.

NOTES

1. In its opinion, the Court made the following important statement: "If the challenged speech here were financed by tuition dollars and the University and its officials were responsible for its content, the case might be evaluated on the premise that the government itself is the speaker. That is not the case before us." So what if the university, perhaps through faculty and staff, is the speaker? How would the analysis and result change here? See the chapters *infra* on faculty personnel speech.

2. No doubt, there are activities and organizations funded through the program in *Southworth* that are contrary to the sincerely held beliefs of many students who are required to pay the fee. But the justification from the university and the conclusion from the Court that the fee is issued to facilitate the free and open exchange of ideas among the students are strong points, indeed. This balance between individual rights and institutional interests, of course, is at the heart of nearly all constitutional analyses. In fact, the Court noted that free and open exchange is better than the alternatives of having university officials decide which speech is "germane" to this purpose or having each student list those activities or organizations that the student wishes not to support for a refund system. What would be the legal and practical impact of such alternative provisions? In *Fry v. Board of Regents of the University of Wisconsin*, No. 96-C-0292-S, 2001 U.S. Dist. LEXIS 3346 (W.D. Wis. Mar. 15, 2001), decided one year after *Southworth*, plaintiff students sought an injunction to prevent the University of Wisconsin from charging the mandatory fee to fund organizations and activities with which they disagreed. The court held for the plaintiffs and invalidated the allocation procedures under the student fee policy. According to the court, the review procedure for the allocation of funds was not viewpoint neutral, as it gave "unbridled discretion" to student government to decide funding allocations.

D. STUDENT PUBLICATIONS

PAPISH v. BOARD OF CURATORS OF THE UNIVERSITY OF MISSOURI
410 U.S. 667 (1973)

PER CURIAM

Petitioner, a graduate student in the University of Missouri School of Journalism, was expelled for distributing on campus a newspaper "containing forms of indecent speech" in violation of a bylaw of the Board of Curators. The newspaper, the Free Press Underground, had been sold on this state university campus for more than four years pursuant to an authorization obtained from the University Business Office. The particular newspaper issue in question was found to be unacceptable for two reasons. First, on the front cover the publishers had reproduced a political cartoon previously printed in another newspaper depicting policemen raping the State of Liberty and the Goddess of Justice. The caption under the cartoon read: ". . . With Liberty and Justice for All." Secondly, the issue contained an article entitled "M — f — Acquitted," which discussed the trial and acquittal on an assault charge of a New York City youth who was a member of an organization known as "Up Against the Wall, M — f —."

Following a hearing, the Student Conduct Committee found that petitioner had violated Par. B of Art. V of the General Standards of Student Conduct which requires students "to observe generally accepted standards of conduct" and specifically prohibits "indecent conduct or speech." Her expulsion, after affirmance first by the Chancellor of the University and then by its Board of Curators, was made effective in the middle of the spring semester. Although she was then permitted to remain on campus until the end of the semester, she was not given credit for the one course in which she made a passing grade.

After exhausting her administrative review alternatives within the University, petitioner brought an action for declaratory and injunctive relief pursuant to 42 U. S. C. § 1983 in the United States District Court for the Western District of Missouri. She claimed that her expulsion was improperly premised on activities protected by the First Amendment. The District Court denied relief and the Court of Appeals affirmed, one judge dissenting. Rehearing *en banc* was denied by an equally divided vote of all the judges in the Eighth Circuit.

The District Court's opinion rests, in part, on the conclusion that the banned issue of the newspaper was obscene. The Court of Appeals found it unnecessary to decide that question. Instead, assuming that the newspaper was not obscene and that its distribution in the community at large would be protected by the First Amendment, the court held that on a university campus "freedom of expression" could properly be "subordinated to other interests such as, for example, the conventions of decency in the use and display of language and pictures." The court concluded that "the Constitution does not compel the University . . . [to allow] such publications as the one in litigation to be publicly sold or distributed on its open campus."

This case was decided [in the Court of Appeals] several days before we handed down *Healy v. James* in which, while recognizing a state university's undoubted prerogative to enforce reasonable rules governing student conduct, we reaffirmed that "state colleges and universities are not enclaves immune from the sweep of the First Amendment." We think *Healy* makes it clear that the mere dissemination of ideas — no matter how offensive to good taste — on a state university campus may not be shut off in the name alone of "conventions of decency." . . . There is language in the opinions below which suggests that the University's action here could be viewed as an exercise of its legitimate authority to enforce reasonable regulations as to the time, place, and manner of speech and its dissemination. While we have repeatedly approved such regulatory authority, . . . the facts set forth in the opinions below show clearly that petitioner was expelled because of the disapproved *content* of the newspaper rather than the time, place, or manner of its distribution.

Since the First Amendment leaves no room for the operation of a dual standard in the academic community with respect to the content of speech, and because the state University's action here cannot be justified as a nondiscriminatory application of reasonable rules governing conduct, the judgments of the courts below must be reversed. . . . [T]he case is remanded to the District Court, and that court is instructed to order the University to restore to petitioner any course credits she earned for the semester in question and, unless she is barred from reinstatement for valid academic reasons, to reinstate her as a student in the graduate program.

Reversed and remanded.

NOTES

1. It is generally understood that courts will afford higher education faculty and administrators great deference in day-to-day decision making in colleges and universities, leaving the application of expertise to those who have it. This is particularly the case in academic decision making. *See, e.g., Bd. of Curators of the Univ. of Mo. v. Horowitz*, 435 U.S. 78 (1978); *Regents of the Univ. of Mich. v. Ewing*, 474 U.S. 214 (1985). How would such an argument be made in *Papish*? Do you think it should be successful? Would it be successful today especially in light of *Rosenberger*?

2. Fifteen years after *Papish* was decided, the Supreme Court heard a landmark case in the context of K-12 education. In *Hazelwood Independent School District v. Kulhmeier*, 484 U.S. 260 (1988), students filed suit against their school district after their principal deleted two pages from the school-sponsored newspaper, produced as part of the school's curriculum. The principal felt that two articles in that issue of the paper were not appropriate for the wide circulation of the paper. The Supreme Court found in favor of the district and held that teachers and administrators may exercise control over the content and style of student speech in school-sponsored activities *if* those controls are reasonably related to legitimate pedagogical concerns. The Court ruled that a school classroom was not a public forum and that student speech in school-sponsored activities bears the imprimatur of the school. Like *Papish*, cases involving student publications in higher education are decided, often, in the spirit of *Tinker v. Des Moines Community School District*, 393 U.S. 503 (1969), and *Healy v. James*, 408 U.S. 169 (1972) (disruption standards applied to student speech). Or, they may be decided in the spirit of *Rosenberger v. University of Virginia*, 515 U.S. 819 (1995) (viewpoint neutrality standards applied). But what about application of *Hazelwood*? See our discussion of *Brown v. Li*, 308 F.3d 939 (9th Cir. 2002), and *Axson-Flynn v. Johnson*, 356 F.3d 1277 (10th Cir. 2004), *infra*, and Chapter IV on faculty rights and responsibilities. Consider also *Kincaid v. Gibson*, 236 F.3d 342 (6th Cir. 2001), following these notes.

3. As much as many readers will be in full favor of student free speech press rights, what argument can be made as to the value assigned to certain expression, particularly in educational institutions? The "legitimate pedagogical concerns" standard, as established in *Hazelwood*, has taken hold in higher education institutions in some jurisdictions. What about other content-based restrictions particular to educational settings? *See, e.g., Bethel Sch. Dist. v. Fraser*, 478 U.S. 675 (1986), where the Supreme Court upheld a short-term suspension of a high school student who delivered a campaign speech, laced with sexual innuendo, to a captive audience of 700 schoolmates. The Court held that lewd and vulgar speech in schools may be restricted by school leaders in ways different from speech restrictions outside of school. Particularly, the Court said that the "First Amendment does not prevent the school officials from determining that to permit a vulgar and lewd speech such as respondent's would undermine the school's basic educational mission." Would such administrative value judgments be permissible in higher education arenas as well, particularly in classroom settings or other learning environments like learning communities or student leadership activities? Surely, professionalism, maturity, and civility in journalism are equally important in higher education as they are in K-12 settings? If not, what content-based standards should apply? Are we, then, left with the traditional restrictions on fighting words, imminent lawless action, clear and present danger, and obscenity?

KINCAID v. GIBSON

236 F.3d 342 (6th Cir. 2001)

R. GUY COLE, JR., CIRCUIT JUDGE.

I. BACKGROUND

A. Factual Background

At the times relevant to this case, both Kincaid and Coffer were registered students at Kentucky State University ("KSU"), a public, state-funded university. Betty Gibson was KSU's Vice President for Student Affairs. KSU funded production and distribution of *The Thorobred*, the student yearbook. KSU students composed and produced *The Thorobred*, with limited advice from the university's student publications advisor. . . .

Coffer served as the editor of the yearbook during the 1993-94 academic year. Although a student-photographer and at least one other student assisted her at one point, Coffer organized and put together the yearbook herself after her staff members lost interest in the project. Coffer endeavored to "do something different" with the yearbook in order to "bring Kentucky State University into the nineties"; she also sought to "present a yearbook to the student population that was what they [had] never seen before." To these ends, Coffer created a purple cover using a material known as "rain shower foil stamp," and, for the first time, gave the yearbook a theme. The theme, "destination unknown," described the atmosphere of "uncertainty" that Coffer believed characterized the time; Coffer found evidence of this uncertainty in students wondering "where are we going in our lives," in high unemployment rates, and in a current controversy regarding whether KSU was going to become a community college. Coffer included pictures in the yearbook depicting events at KSU and in its surrounding community, and political and current events in the nation and world at large. The yearbook covered both the 1992-93 and 1993-94 academic years because the students working on the 1992-93 yearbook had fallen behind schedule. Although the yearbook was originally projected to contain 224 pages, Coffer testified that the final product contained only 128 pages, because she did not have enough pictures to fill 224 pages and because the university administration took no interest in the publication. Coffer completed the yearbook several thousand dollars under budget, and sent the yearbook to the printer in May or June of 1994.

When the yearbook came back from the printer in November 1994, Gibson objected to several aspects of it, finding the publication to be of poor quality and "inappropriate." In particular, Gibson objected to the yearbook's purple cover (KSU's school colors are green and gold), its "destination unknown" theme, the lack of captions under many of the photos, and the inclusion of current events ostensibly unrelated to KSU. After consulting with KSU President Mary Smith and other unnamed university officials, Gibson and Smith decided to confiscate the yearbooks and to withhold them from the KSU community. Gibson contacted Leslie Thomas, KSU's Director of Student Life, and instructed her to secure the yearbooks so that they would not be distributed. Thomas contacted KSU's director for service management, who ensured that the yearbooks were secured. Although Gibson's intention was "perhaps [to] discard [the yearbooks]," Gibson's counsel indicated at oral argument that the yearbooks remain hidden away on KSU's campus.

B. Procedural Background

In November 1995, Kincaid and Coffer sued Gibson, Smith, and individual members of the KSU Board of Regents under 42 U.S.C. § 1983, alleging that the university's confiscation of and failure to distribute the 1992-94 KSU student yearbook violated their rights under the First and Fourteenth Amendments to the United States Constitution. Kincaid and Coffer sought damages and injunctive relief.

. . . .

III. DISCUSSION

The issue before us is whether the university officials violated the First Amendment rights of Kincaid and Coffer by confiscating and failing to distribute the KSU student yearbook. For the reasons that follow, we apply a forum analysis to the question and hold that the KSU yearbook constitutes a limited (or "designated") public forum. Accordingly, we analyze the actions taken by the university officials with respect to the yearbook under strict scrutiny, and conclude that the officials' confiscation of the yearbooks violated Kincaid's and Coffer's First Amendment rights.

A. Application of Public Forum Doctrine

. . . KSU is a state-funded, public university. . . . As such, the actions KSU officials take in their official capacities constitute state actions for purposes of First Amendment analysis. Further, the funds and materials that KSU allocates toward production of *The Thorobred* constitute state property. By confiscating the yearbooks at issue in this case, the KSU officials have restricted access to state property used for expressive purposes. "The Supreme Court has adopted a forum analysis for use in determining whether a state-imposed restriction on access to public property is constitutionally permissible." Accordingly, we find that forum analysis is appropriate in this case.

. . . .

B. Type of Forum

There is no real dispute in this case that the forum in question is *The Thorobred* itself. The parties dispute strenuously, however, the appropriate characterization of *The Thorobred* under forum analysis. Kincaid and Coffer contend that the yearbook is a limited public forum, subject only to reasonable time, place, and manner regulations, and to only those content-based regulations that are narrowly crafted to serve a compelling state interest. The KSU officials respond that the yearbook is a nonpublic forum, subject to all reasonable regulations that preserve the yearbook's purpose.

The Supreme Court has recognized three types of fora. The first type is a traditional public forum. A traditional public forum is a place "which by long tradition or by government fiat has been devoted to assembly and debate," such as a street or park. In traditional public fora, "the rights of the state to limit expressive activity are sharply circumscribed": the government may enforce content-based restrictions only if they are narrowly drawn to serve a compelling interest, and may enforce content-neutral time, place, and manner regulations only if they are "narrowly tailored to serve a significant government interest, and leave open ample alternative channels of communication." The second type of forum has been alternatively described as a "limited public forum," and as a "designated public forum."

The government may open a limited public forum "for use by the public at large for assembly and speech, for use by certain speakers, or for the discussion of certain subjects." Although the government need not retain the open nature of a limited public forum, "as long as it does so it is bound by the same standards as apply in a traditional public forum.". The third and final type of forum is a nonpublic forum. The government may control access to a nonpublic forum "based on subject matter and speaker identity so long as the distinctions drawn are reasonable in light of the purpose served by the forum and are viewpoint neutral."

The parties agree that *The Thorobred* is not a traditional public forum. To determine whether the yearbook is a limited public forum, the touchstone of our analysis is whether the government intended to open the forum at issue. . . . To determine whether the government intended to create a limited public forum, we look to the government's policy and practice with respect to the forum, as well as to the nature of the property at issue and its "compatibility with expressive activity." Further, the context within which the forum is found is relevant to determining whether the government has created a limited public forum. . . . Evaluating these factors — KSU's policy and practice, the nature of *The Thorobred* and its compatibility with expressive activity, and the context in which the yearbook is found — we find clear evidence of KSU's intent to make the yearbook a limited public forum.

1. Policy

KSU's written policy toward *The Thorobred* is found in a section of the student handbook entitled "Student Publications." In addition to stating KSU's policy toward the yearbook, the handbook describes the university's structure for oversight of the publication. The yearbook (along with the student newspaper) is "under the management of the Student Publications Board." The Student Publications Board ("SPB"), in turn, is composed of students, faculty members, and university officials. Both the university's written policy and the structure it created to oversee the yearbook evidence KSU's intention that the yearbook serve as a limited public forum.

First and foremost, the policy places editorial control of the yearbook in the hands of a student editor or editors. Although the policy provides for the establishment of minimum qualifications for student editors, once a student is appointed editor, editorial control of the yearbook's content belongs to her. This is made clear by the policy's description of the Student Publications Advisor, a university employee. The policy directs that the SPB "shall require the use of an experienced advisor," but limits the advisor's role to "assuring that the . . . yearbook is not overwhelmed by ineptitude and inexperience." Indeed, the policy expressly limits the types of changes that the advisor may make to the yearbook:

> In order to meet the responsible standards of journalism, an advisor may require changes in the form of materials submitted by students, *but such changes must deal only with the form or the time and manner of expressions rather than alteration of content.* (emphasis added)

This language is revealing: not only does it direct the university's chosen advisor to refrain from editing the content of the yearbook, it also tracks the Supreme Court's description of the limitations on government regulation of expressive activity in a limited public forum. KSU's intent to limit its own oversight to time, place, and manner aspects of the yearbook is also seen in the policy's treatment of the SPB. The policy declares that one of the duties of the SPB is to "approve the written publications policy of each student publication, including such items as purpose, size, quantity controls, and time, place and manner of distribution." This language reiterates the university's intent to limit its oversight of the yearbook to general and administrative matters, and to cede authority over the yearbook's content to the students who published it. Finally, the publications policy opens with language that indicates that the expressive activity contained in student publications is to be largely unrestrained: "The Board of Regents respects the integrity of student publications and the press, and the rights to exist in an atmosphere of free and responsible discussion and of intellectual exploration." Such self-imposed restraint is strong evidence of KSU's intent to create a limited public forum, rather than to reserve to itself the right to edit or determine *The Thorobred's* content.

The KSU officials argue that the handbook policy shows the university's intent to retain, rather than relinquish, control over the yearbook's content. They point in particular to the fact that the policy requires a disclaimer to be placed on the student newspaper — but not on the yearbook — as evidence of the university's intent to retain control over the content of the yearbook. Such reasoning relies upon a negative inference: in other words, the fact that the policy fails to require a disclaimer to be placed upon the yearbook purportedly implies that the yearbook *is* "an 'official' organ of the University," because the university requires a disclaimer on the newspaper, and the newspaper is *not* such an official organ. This is hardly persuasive. Were we to follow the logic behind this conclusion, we must also conclude that the university has forgone all standards of quality control with relation to the yearbook. After all, the publications policy states minimum standards of quality control for the newspaper, but none for the yearbook. Yet to concede that would require the university officials to concede their entire argument — Gibson argues on appeal that the basis for confiscating the yearbooks is their allegedly "poor quality." Rather than engage in such inferential gymnastics, we read the university's policy in a straightforward manner. . . . KSU's policy leaves room for only one conclusion: that the university intended to open the yearbook as a limited public forum.

2. Practice

. . . The record before us contains substantial evidence from varied sources that the SPB followed its stated "hands off" policy in actual practice. Coffer testified without contradiction that Vice President Gibson — who Coffer described as a "friend[]" with whom she was "on excellent terms" — "never expressed any concern about what the content might be in the yearbook" prior to its publication, but rather limited her concerns to the yearbook's release date. Nor did the SPB exercise oversight of the yearbook's content. Laura Jo Cullen, the university's publications advisor to the yearbook and an ex officio member of the SPB, testified that the SPB limited its oversight of the yearbook to issues such as advertising rates and selection of editors, and that in the time during which she had been associated with the yearbook, the Board had never attempted to control the content of the yearbook. Leslie Thomas, KSU's Director of Student Life and another member of the SPB, testified that the SPB exercised minimal oversight of the yearbook in actual practice: "We just always dealt with the newspaper so I guess that was the major focus." Thomas also testified that it was the student editor rather than the SPB who determined the content of the yearbook. Thus, the record before us is clear that, in actual practice, student editors — not KSU officials, not the student publications advisor, and not the SPB — determined the content of KSU's student yearbook.

3. Nature of the Property and Compatibility with Expressive Activity

. . . The KSU yearbook is a student publication that, by its very nature, exists for the purpose of expressive activity. There can be no serious argument about the fact that, in its most basic form, the yearbook serves as a forum in which student editors present pictures, captions, and other written material, and that these materials constitute expression for purposes of the First Amendment. . . . Nor is *The Thorobred* a closely-monitored classroom activity in which an instructor assigns student editors a grade, or in which a university official edits content. The student handbook itself describes the yearbook as a "student publication" that should "exist in an atmosphere of free and responsible discussion and of intellectual exploration." It is difficult to conceive of a forum whose nature is more compatible with expression.

. . . .

5. KSU Officials' Arguments

The KSU officials dispute this substantial evidence of the university's intent to create a limited public forum in the student yearbook. They argue that a limited public forum cannot exist unless the government has opened the forum at issue for "indiscriminate use by the general public." . . . This reasoning badly distorts a basic tenet of public forum law. It is true that *one of* the ways in which the government may create or designate a public forum is by opening the forum "for indiscriminate use by the general public." But the government may create a limited public forum in other ways as well: "a public forum may be created by government designation of a place or channel of communication for use by the public at large for assembly and speech, for use by certain speakers, *or* for the discussion of certain subjects."

. . . .

In sum, our review of KSU's policy and practice with regard to *The Thorobred*, the nature of the yearbook and its compatibility with expressive activity, and the university context in which the yearbook is created and distributed, all provide strong evidence of the university's intent to designate the yearbook as a limited public forum. Accordingly, we must determine whether the university officials' actions with respect to the yearbook were constitutional.

C. Constitutionality of University Officials' Actions

. . . .

Upon their return from the printer, the 1992-94 yearbooks were delivered to the office of Laura Cullen, the student publications advisor. Before they could be distributed to Kincaid and other KSU students, Gibson ordered Leslie Thomas to have them secured; Thomas complied, and, without any notification or explanation to Cullen, the yearbooks were spirited away. To this day — nearly six years after the yearbooks returned from the printer — the university refuses to distribute them. This is not a reasonable time, place, or manner regulation of expressive activity. . . . . Nor is it a narrowly crafted regulation designed to preserve a compelling state interest. Rather, wholesale confiscation of printed materials which the state feels reflect poorly on its institutions is as broadly sweeping a regulation as the state might muster. Further, the university officials' action leaves open no alternative grounds for similar expressive activity. The record contains no other student forum for recording words and pictures to reflect the experience of KSU students during the 1992 through 1994 school years. . . . Accordingly, the KSU officials' confiscation of the yearbooks violates the First Amendment, and the university has no constitutionally valid reason to withhold distribution of the 1992-94 *Thorobred* from KSU students from that era.

The KSU officials argue that withholding the yearbooks is excusable because they were regulating the style and form of the yearbooks rather than their content. . . . This argument is simply not credible. First, the record makes clear that Gibson sought to regulate the content of the 1992-94 yearbook: in addition to complaining about the yearbook's color, lack of captions, and overall quality, Gibson withheld the yearbooks because she found the yearbook theme of "destination unknown" inappropriate. Gibson also disapproved of the inclusion of pictures of current events, and testified that "there were a lot of pictures in the back of the book that . . . to me, looked like a *Life* magazine." Gibson further stated that the inclusion of pictures of current events "was not exactly what I thought it should have been, and it wasn't what other people who viewed it thought it should have been." And after the yearbooks came back from the printer, Gibson complained to Cullen that "several persons have received the book, and are thoroughly disappointed at the quality and content." Thus, it is quite clear that Gibson attempted to regulate the content of *The Thorobred* once it was printed.

. . . Confiscation ranks with forced government speech as amongst the purest forms of content alteration. There is little if any difference between hiding from public view the words and pictures students use to portray their college experience, and forcing students to publish a state-sponsored script. In either case, the government alters student expression by obliterating it. We will not sanction a reading of the First Amendment that permits government officials to censor expression in a limited public forum in order to coerce speech that pleases the government. The KSU officials present no compelling reason to nullify Coffer's expression or to shield it from Kincaid's view and, accordingly, the officials' actions violate the Constitution. *See Perry*, 460 U.S. at 46.

. . . .

More important, the KSU officials' actions were not reasonable because they were arbitrary and conflicted with the university's own stated policy. The university's publications policy states that "the Thorobred yearbook shall be under the management of the Student Publications Board." Yet Thomas testified that neither Gibson nor any other KSU administrators discussed with the SPB the drastic act of confiscating the yearbooks. Further, the university's policy gave to Cullen the power to "require changes in the form of materials submitted by students [that] . . . deal . . . with the form or the time and manner of expressions." Yet, the KSU officials never even consulted Cullen, the student publications advisor, before they seized the yearbooks. . . . These facts show without doubt that the university's confiscation of the yearbooks was anything but reasonable: rather, it was a rash, arbitrary act, wholly out of proportion to the situation it was allegedly intended to address.

We note that KSU's suppression of the yearbook smacks of viewpoint discrimination as well. The university officials based their confiscation of the yearbook in part upon the particular theme chosen by Coffer, "destination unknown." Coffer characterized that theme, which she described in the yearbook itself, as "my opinion as a student regarding the . . . overall student population." Coffer's choice of theme is a classic illustration of what we mean when we refer to a speaker's "viewpoint." The university officials also based their confiscation of the yearbooks on the fact that the some of its pictures captured particular, well-known individuals whom they deemed to be out of place in a student yearbook. Kincaid summarized the basic premise of First Amendment viewpoint jurisprudence when he testified, "[a] picture that may be relevant to me may be something that would be garbage to you." We might add that in a traditional, limited, or nonpublic forum, state officials may not expunge even "garbage" if it represents a speaker's viewpoint. *See Perry*, 460 U.S. at 46. Finally, the yearbook contained written segments which Coffer described as stating her opinions on various matters. Because the government may not regulate even a nonpublic forum based upon the speaker's viewpoint, *see id.*, and because an editor's choice of theme, selection of particular pictures, and expression of opinions are clear examples of the editor's viewpoint, the KSU officials' actions violated the First Amendment under a nonpublic forum analysis as well as a limited public forum analysis. . . .

IV. CONCLUSION

. . . [W]e *REVERSE* the judgment of the district court and *REMAND* the case with instructions to enter judgment in favor of Kincaid and Coffer, and to determine the relief to which they are entitled.

NOTES

1. What reasons does the court in *Kincaid* offer for declining to apply *Hazelwood*? Is it solely because the levels of education (secondary versus post-secondary) are different? Or were there policy and practice differences that dictated a different forum for First Amendment purposes? Was it the type of speech (yearbook versus newspaper)? For instance, how important is the distinction between classroom teacher/advisor roles played in K-12 schools and higher education institutions with respect to the discretion each one has to make judgment calls on student expression? What practical implications do university faculty and administrators take from *Kincaid*?

2. Is there an "on/off switch" for administrative review of newspapers when we move from K-12 to higher education? *See Hosty v. Carter*, 412 F.3d 731, 734 (7th Cir. 2005), *cert. denied*, 546 U.S. 1169 (2006). What about an on/off switch when we compare classroom curricular activities in higher education and all other speech on those campuses? Plaintiffs in *Hosty*, student writers and editors for the student newspaper at Governors State University, argued that there was such a switch. The Court of Appeals for the Fifth Circuit held otherwise, applying *Hazelwood's* analysis to the review of a university's newspaper, which had begun publishing articles criticizing university administrators directly. On the question of what type of forum had been created, the court declined to draw a line between classroom speech activities and extracurricular student speech, holding that student speech in extracurricular activities is not automatically outside of a nonpublic forum. With that said, however, the court held that the paper was a limited public forum and the writers were not subject to the same level of scrutiny that the high school student writers were in *Hazelwood.* Instead, the paper is subject to a viewpoint discrimination standard. In the end, the court determined that the defendants were entitled to qualified immunity because of a significant split among the circuit courts of appeals on the application of *Hazelwood* in higher education. Ultimately, the applicability of *Hazelwood* in higher education contexts remains variable across the country. For further discussion of the application of *Hazelwood* in higher education, see also *Brown v. Li*, 308 F.3d 939 (9th Cir. 2002), and *Axson-Flynn v. Johnson*, 356 F.3d 1277 (10th Cir. 2004), *infra.*

E. FRATERNITIES AND SORORITIES

PI LAMBDA PHI FRATERNITY v. UNIVERSITY OF PITTSBURGH

229 F.3d 435 (3d Cir. 2000)

BECKER, CHIEF JUDGE.

The University of Pittsburgh chapter of the Pi Lambda Phi fraternity (the Chapter), believing that its members' constitutional rights of freedom of association were violated by disciplinary action taken against it by the University of Pittsburgh (the University), brought suit in the District Court against the University, the City of Pittsburgh, and various individual defendants. The disciplinary action in question occurred when the University stripped the Chapter of its status as a recognized student organization after several of its members were arrested in a drug raid at the Chapter's fraternity house. The Chapter's international parent organization and several current and prospective Chapter members joined the Chapter as plaintiffs.

. . . .

I. Facts

Pi Lambda Phi is an international fraternity with a longstanding local chapter at the University of Pittsburgh. On April 30, 1996, at the beginning of the University's summer recess, the Pittsburgh police raided the house at 225 North Dithridge Street, which is owned by the Chapter and serves as the home of several Chapter members. During the raid, the police found various drugs and drug paraphernalia, including heroin, cocaine, opium, and Rohypnol (the "date rape" drug). Four Chapter members were arrested and charged with possession of controlled substances. One of the arrested Chapter members was the "Risk Manager" for Pi

Lambda Phi, and a second was the president of the University's Interfraternity Council (a student organization composed of representatives from University fraternities). Another of these four was charged with and convicted of possession and distribution of controlled substances, and was expelled from the University.

On May 2, 1996, the University suspended the Chapter pending an investigation into the matter. The University subsequently held a hearing on whether the Chapter should be punished. While the University's investigating panel found that there was "no direct relationship between the drug raid and the Chapter itself," and no evidence that the absent members were involved in, tacitly approved of, or were even aware of the drug activity, the panel did find the Chapter "guilty of a lack of responsibility for its members for the events that occurred at their house on the above date." The panel recommended three years probation.

The Vice Chancellor of student affairs, Dennis Donham (one of the individual defendants in this action), reviewed the panel's decision and concluded that the Chapter was responsible for the drug activity in its house under Section II.1 of the University Compilation of Codes Governing Fraternity and Sorority Activity, which states that "chapters shall be held accountable for actions of individual members and their guests." Donham decided that, instead of probation, the University should revoke the Chapter's status as a "recognized student organization" for one year. Donham also established several restrictions on the Chapter's activities, including a prohibition on participation in University-sponsored Greek activities and a prohibition on recruitment of new members through the University "Rush" process. Donham issued a letter to the Chapter on July 9, 1996, detailing this decision; the letter also stated that the Chapter could reapply to be a recognized student organization on April 30, 1997, although it would have to conform to all the regulations and restrictions placed upon it and subject itself to close scrutiny by the University.

The Chapter appealed Donham's decision to Leon Haley, the Vice Chancellor for Student and Public Affairs. After a hearing, Haley upheld the sanctions. The Chapter then appealed to Haley's successor, Robert Gallagher, the interim Vice Chancellor for Student and Public Affairs, and Gallagher upheld Haley's decision. Both Haley and Gallagher are named as defendants.

In late November 1996, a University Student Affairs hearing panel reviewed the Chapter's status and concluded that it had complied with many of the key requirements set forth in Donham's July 9th letter. The panel recommended to Gallagher that the Chapter be recertified as a recognized student organization on probationary status. Earlier that month, however, the University's Interfraternity Council had voted to recommend to Gallagher that he not grant recognized student group status to the Chapter at that time. Also around this time, Dan Cohen, a member of the Pittsburgh city council, wrote a letter to Gallagher expressing concerns regarding the possible recertification of the Chapter. Cohen stated in his letter that the Chapter had "created a nuisance to the [North Dithridge Street] neighborhood for years with loud parties, vandalism, public urination, and litter, and he urged Gallagher not to recertify the Chapter.

On December 4, 1996, Gallagher decided to continue the Chapter's non-recognized status, as he felt that another term was needed for a full appraisal of the

Chapter. He stated in a deposition that he was influenced by: (1) the seriousness of the drug offense; (2) the fact that the Interfraternity council, a peer group of the Chapter, had voted against recognizing the Chapter; (3) the fact that the Chapter had yet to bring into the house a Graduate Resident Advisor, which Gallagher considered to be a key required condition in Donham's July 9th letter; and (4) concern for other University students and for members of the community who lived near the Chapter house.

On February 27, 1997, the Student Affairs panel held a second hearing on whether the University should restore the Chapter's status as a recognized student organization, and again it recommended that the University should do so as of April 29, 1997. The panel concluded that the Chapter had continued to make progress in addressing its earlier problems by bringing in a Graduate Resident Advisor (who had written the University's Office of Student Affairs with a positive review), by expelling unruly members, and by raising its average GPA up to the highest of any fraternity on campus. On April 18, 1997, before the University ruled on this Student Affairs panel recommendation, the Chapter filed this lawsuit. On May 15, 1997, the University again decided not to recertify the Chapter as a recognized organization. Gallagher based this decision on then recently-disclosed information that the Chapter's Risk Manager had been arrested in the drug raid and that drugs had been purchased in the house several days before the raid, thus supporting the inference that Chapter members had openly possessed and used drugs in the house during the academic year. Gallagher's letter to the Chapter announcing this decision stated that the University would entertain further petitions by the Chapter for recertification beginning May 15, 1998. Even though counsel for the University stated at oral argument (on June 28, 2000) that she knew of nothing that would prevent the University from recertifying the Chapter, the Chapter had not submitted any further petitions or requests for recertification to the University up to that time.

II. Procedural History

This civil action, brought under 42 U.S.C. § 1983, alleged violations of the Chapter members' rights of association under the First Amendment, as well as violations of their Equal Protection and Due Process rights under the Fourteenth Amendment. The University meets the state actor requirement for defendants in § 1983 actions. . . . The Chapter voluntarily dismissed the Due Process claims as well as all claims against the city defendants. After some discovery and testimony at fact-finding hearings, the University defendants' motion for summary judgment was granted by the District Court.

The District Court concluded that the Chapter was primarily engaged in social activities rather than in expressive or intimate association, and that its associational activities were therefore not protected by the First Amendment. The Court held further that even if the Chapter's associational activities were protected by the First Amendment, the government interest underlying the University's action merited whatever associational abridgements did occur. This timely appeal followed. . . .

III. The Chapter's Freedom of Association Claims

The Supreme Court has held that there are two kinds of freedom of association that are constitutionally protected: intimate association and expressive association. The Court summarized these two forms of associational freedom in *Roberts v. United States Jaycees*, 468 U.S. 609 (1984):

> In one line of decisions, the Court has concluded that choices to enter into and maintain certain intimate human relationships must be secured against undue intrusion by the State because of the role of such relationships in safeguarding the individual freedom that is central to our constitutional scheme. In this respect, freedom of association receives protection as a fundamental element of personal liberty. In another set of decisions, the Court has recognized a right to associate for the purpose of engaging in those activities protected by the First Amendment — speech, assembly, petition for the redress of grievances, and the exercise of religion. The Constitution guarantees freedom of association of this kind as an indispensable means of preserving other individual liberties.

The Chapter contends that both kinds of associational rights are implicated in this case. The Supreme Court has held that these two rights may coincide in a particular group's association. We follow the Court's lead in considering each of the associational rights separately.

A. The Right of Intimate Association

The right of intimate association involves an individual's right to enter into and maintain intimate or private relationships free of state intrusion. The types of relationships that give rise to this right may take various forms, but the Supreme Court has held that these relationships must be "distinguished by such attributes as relative smallness, a high degree of selectivity in decisions to begin and maintain the affiliation, and seclusion from others in critical aspects of the relationship." Family relationships are the paradigmatic form of protected intimate associations, as they "by their nature involve deep attachments and commitments to the necessarily few other individuals with whom one shares not only a special community of thoughts, experiences, and beliefs but also distinctively personal aspects of one's life." In determining the nature of a given relationship, relevant factors to consider include a group's "size, purpose, policies, selectivity, congeniality, and other characteristics that in a particular case may be pertinent." . . . [T]he University chapter of Pi Lambda Phi is not a particularly small association. While the number of students in the Chapter was reduced to 22 after certain members had been expelled and the University had prohibited the Chapter from recruiting new members for a year, the chapter had inducted 20 new members during the fall of 1995, before the drug raid. Extrapolating over four years, the Chapter, when recruiting and existing normally, would have approximately 80 members at any one time. At all events, a range of 20 to 80 members would put the Chapter within the same size range as the local Rotary Clubs that the Court held did not engage in intimate association in Duarte.

Furthermore, the Chapter actively recruits new members from the University population at large and it is not particularly selective in whom it admits. The international organization of Pi Lambda Phi strongly encourages its chapters to recruit new members aggressively so as to continue the growth of the organization. The Chapter also invites members of the public into its house for social activities and participates in many public University events. All of these elements — the Chapter's size, lack of selectivity, and lack of seclusion in its activities — support our conclusion that the Chapter lacks the essential characteristics of constitutionally protected intimate association. . . .

B. The Right of Expressive Association

In *Boy Scouts of America v. Dale*, 530 U.S. 640 (2000), the Supreme Court used a three-step process to analyze the Boy Scouts' expressive association claim, which roughly follows the analytical structure that the Court employed in Roberts and Duarte to examine such claims. First, the Court considered whether the group making the claim engaged in expressive association. The Court then analyzed whether the state action at issue significantly affected the group's ability to advocate its viewpoints. Finally, it weighed the state's interest implicated in its action against the burden imposed on the associational expression to determine if the state interest justified the burden.

In the case before us, the District Court ended its analysis at step one, concluding that the Chapter was not a constitutionally protected expressive association because it was essentially a social organization. The analysis required at this step is slightly more complicated, however, as social organizations may receive constitutional associational protection in certain cases. The Supreme Court has recognized a First Amendment "right to associate with others in pursuit of a wide variety of political, social, economic, educational, religious, and cultural ends." Thus, "the First Amendment's protection of expressive association is not reserved for advocacy groups. But to come within its ambit, a group must engage in some form of expression, whether it be public or private." We must therefore engage in a more detailed examination of the Chapter and its expressive characteristics.

1. The Chapter's Allegedly Expressive Character

The Supreme Court has cast a fairly wide net in its definition of what comprises expressive activity. . . . The expansive notions of expressive association . . . demonstrate that there is no requirement that an organization be primarily political (or even primarily expressive) in order to receive constitutional protection for expressive associational activity.

. . . .

The record does not support the Chapter's claim that its level of expression rises to [even]. . . . a de minimis standard required. . . . Nothing in the record indicates that the Chapter ever took a public stance on any issue of public political, social, or cultural importance. The Chapter argues that it engages in expressive activity through its charity work and by promoting the ideals embraced by its parent organization. The specific facts that the Chapter offers in the record to support this claim, however, fall far short of sustaining the assertion that it engages in a level of expressive association that is sufficient for constitutional protection.

While the international organization of Pi Lambda Phi has an admirable history that includes being the country's first non-sectarian fraternity, there is no substantial evidence in the record that the University chapter of Pi Lambda has done anything to actively pursue the ideals underlying this stance. Although members of the Chapter claimed in their deposition testimony that the Chapter still promotes these ideals, they did not give any specific examples of how it does so. Furthermore, while Pi Lambda Phi's international organization runs various programs aimed at individual development, there is no evidence in the record that even a single member of the University chapter participated in any of these programs.

The Chapter also points to a couple of relatively minor acts of charity performed in 1996 as proof of its expressive aspects, but these are underwhelming. The Chapter represents that it once helped run a Halloween haunted house for the Pittsburgh School for the Blind, raised $350 through selling raffle tickets for a charity called the Genesis House, and ran a "Breakfast with Santa" to raise money for Genesis House. The Chapter's counsel admitted at oral argument that this was the extent of the Chapter's charitable activities. A few minor charitable acts do not alone make a group's association expressive, and community service must have more than a merely incidental relationship to the group's character for such service to implicate the constitutional protection of expressive association. The Chapter has not shown in the record that its sporadic acts of community service are related to its basic nature or goals.

In sum, an organization must do more than simply claim to be an expressive association in order to receive the benefits of constitutional protection. The Chapter's contentions along these lines, along with its meager showing of a few minor acts of community service, are insufficient to meet the minimum requirements for an expressive association. Therefore, the Chapter's claim of infringement of its right to expressive association fails. We add that we are not holding that fraternities per se do not engage in constitutionally protected expressive association. . . . We hold only that the University chapter of Pi Lambda Phi has failed to make out such a claim on the record before us.

3. The Chapter's Claim of Infringement of Its Expressive Rights

. . . .

The Chapter argues that its situation is closely analogous to the SDS group in *Healy.* It contends that the practical effect of the University's withdrawal of its recognition of the Chapter is even more severe than CCSC's denial of recognition was for the SDS in *Healy*. . . . As a non-recognized organization, the Chapter submits, its chapter will vanish altogether.

Whether or not it is true that the Chapter is in danger of disappearing — and we are by no means persuaded that the record supports this allegation — *Healy* does not dictate the result suggested by the Chapter. In fact, *Healy* specifically contemplated a situation such as the one before us. . . .

. . . [T]he Court stated in *Healy* that a university has the power to withdraw recognition if an organization breaks university rules. . . . In the case at bar, there is no doubt that the Chapter violated University rules, and *Healy* clearly contemplates the University's power to withdraw recognition from the Chapter without a constitutional violation of associational rights.

. . . .

In the case at bar, the state action had neither a direct nor even an incidental effect on the Chapter's protected associational rights. Unlike in *Dale*, the University's action does not require the Chapter to associate with anyone, nor is the regulation directed on its face at the Chapter's expressive or associational activities. . . . [T]he University's regulation did not sanction conduct that had both speech and nonspeech elements; the regulation was applied simply to the Chapter's drug activity. The Chapter makes no claim that its members engaged in drug activity in order to communicate a political message, nor does it claim that there is any direct connection between its members' drug activity and their First Amendment expression. Therefore, the University's action neither directly nor incidentally affected the Chapter's expressive interests.

. . . [T]he Chapter members' expressive rights were inhibited by a state sanction of activities that themselves had no protected expressive element, and were entirely unrelated to the Chapter members' expressive activities. Therefore, the effect of the state action on the expressive rights was indirect, and there is thus no constitutionally impermissible infringement on the Chapter's right of expressive association.

The judgment of the District Court will be affirmed.

NOTE

From what we learn from *Pi Lambda Phi* and the other cases presented in this part of the chapter, compare the First Amendment protection rights of fraternities and sororities and those of student organizations and publications. Certainly, with student organizations and student publications, whether expressive activity exists is almost entirely without doubt. Yet, for traditional "social" fraternities and sororities, the question does exist. Does the history of social fraternities and sororities largely dictate the answer to the question of whether these organizations are "expressive"? What can these organizations do to be deemed "expressive" and not merely "social" for First Amendment purposes? Is the increased attention, recently, on community service and philanthropy sufficient enough?

F. HATE SPEECH CODES

DeJOHN v. TEMPLE UNIVERSITY

537 F.3d 301 (3d Cir. 2008)

SMITH, CIRCUIT JUDGE.

Christian DeJohn sued Temple University, its former president, David Adamany, and two of his former graduate school professors, Richard H. Immerman and Gregory J.W. Urwin (hereinafter collectively referred to as "Temple" or "the

University") in an eight-count complaint for violations of First Amendment freedom of speech and expression stemming from the University's Policy on Sexual Harassment. . . .

I.

Christian DeJohn served in the Pennsylvania Army National Guard. In January 2002, he enrolled in Temple University to pursue a master's degree in Military and American History. To obtain a master's degree in history at Temple, a student must first successfully complete his course work. The student then has the option of either taking a comprehensive exam or completing a master's thesis. The parties agree that all course work and other requirements must be completed within three years from the date of admission unless a leave of absence has been granted. A graduate student in the history department must form a thesis committee, which includes an advisor selected by the student to serve as the primary reader of the master's thesis and a secondary reader also chosen by the student. The thesis must be acceptable to both readers before the graduate student is allowed to defend it.

DeJohn took four classes in his first semester as a graduate student. Following that semester, DeJohn was called to active military duty and was deployed to Bosnia. He earned graduate level credit while deployed through a correspondence course related to the Vietnam War. By the end of the following fall 2003 semester, DeJohn had completed all of the required course work for his advanced degree. . . . The record indicates that DeJohn is not currently registered as a student at Temple and has not been registered since the 2006 spring semester.

DeJohn filed the instant action on February 22, 2006. Only two of the original counts are at issue in this appeal. These remaining counts embody DeJohn's challenge of Temple University's Student Code of Conduct and related polices, in particular as they address sexual harassment. The Temple policy challenged here reads, in relevant part:

> all forms of sexual harassment are prohibited, including . . . expressive, visual, or physical conduct of a sexual or gender-motivated nature, when . . . (c) such conduct has the purpose or effect of unreasonably interfering with an individual's work, educational performance, or status; or (d) such conduct has the purpose or effect of creating an intimidating, hostile, or offensive environment.

DeJohn claims that this policy is facially overbroad. Specifically, because of the sexual harassment policy, he felt inhibited in expressing his opinions in class concerning women in combat and women in the military. As a history graduate student, DeJohn found himself engaged in conversations and class discussions regarding issues he believed were implicated by the policy. That, in turn, caused him to be concerned that discussing his social, cultural, political, and/or religious views regarding these issues might be sanctionable by the University. Thus, DeJohn contends that the policy had a chilling effect on his ability to exercise his constitutionally protected rights.

. . . .

On January 15, 2007, less than three weeks before the deadline for filing dispositive motions in the case, Temple modified its sexual harassment policy. Temple then filed a motion for a protective order and a motion to quash *duces tecum* — arguing that because there were no longer issues in the case due to the policy modification, DeJohn was not entitled to a . . . deposition on the sexual harassment policy or *duces tecum* discovery of records of past harassment complaints. The District Court denied this motion, concluding in part that there was nothing to prevent Temple from restoring the policy as soon as counts seven and eight of the Complaint were resolved.

After discovery, DeJohn moved for summary judgment on counts seven and eight and Temple moved for summary judgment on all remaining claims. On March 21, 2007, the District Court granted DeJohn's motion, declared the Temple University Policy on Sexual Harassment (as enacted before January 15, 2007) facially unconstitutional and enjoined Temple from reimplementing or enforcing the sexual harassment policy that existed before the changes implemented on January 15, 2007. The District Court granted in part and denied in part Temple's motion for summary judgment on the remaining claims in the case. Temple appealed the partial grant of summary judgment.

After trial, the District Court entered Final Judgment in favor of DeJohn on counts seven and eight, permanently enjoined Temple from reimplementing or enforcing its previous policy, and awarded $1.00 in nominal damages in favor of DeJohn and against Temple University. The Court entered judgment in Temple's favor as to counts one and two.

. . . .

IV.

. . . Here, in order for us to determine the propriety of the injunction, we must review the District Court's determination that Temple University's Policy on Sexual Harassment is facially unconstitutional.

A.

. . . [T]he Supreme Court's resolution of student free speech cases has been, to this point in time, without reference to the overbreadth doctrine. Even so, since the inception of overbreadth jurisprudence, the Supreme Court has recognized its prominent role in preventing a "chilling effect" on protected expression. This laudable goal is no less implicated on public university campuses throughout this country, where free speech is of critical importance because it is the lifeblood of academic freedom. . . . In the context of school anti-discrimination policies, our Court has emphasized that

> "Harassing" or discriminatory speech, although evil and offensive, may be used to communicate ideas or emotions that nevertheless implicate First Amendment protections. As the Supreme Court has emphatically declared, "[i]f there is a bedrock principle underlying the First Amendment, it is that

> the government may not prohibit the expression of an idea simply because society finds the idea offensive or disagreeable."

Saxe v. State Coll. Area Sch. Dist., 240 F.3d 200, 209 (3d Cir. 2001) (quoting *Texas v. Johnson*, 491 U.S. 397, 414 (1989)). Because overbroad harassment policies can suppress or even chill core protected speech, and are susceptible to selective application amounting to content-based or viewpoint discrimination, the overbreadth doctrine may be invoked in student free speech cases.

B.

In reviewing a facial challenge to a racial harassment policy, we have explained:

> A regulation of speech may be struck down on its face if its prohibitions are sufficiently overbroad — that is, if it reaches too much expression that is protected by the Constitution. The harassment policy can be found unconstitutionally overbroad if "there is a 'likelihood that the statute's very existence will inhibit free expression' " to a substantial extent.
>
> . . . .
>
> Furthermore, in response to an overbreadth challenge, a policy can be struck down only if no reasonable limiting construction is available that would render the policy constitutional. "[E]very reasonable construction must be resorted to, in order to save a statute from unconstitutionality." A court, however, "will not rewrite a . . . law to conform it to constitutional requirements." Accordingly, we must determine whether the relatively broad language of the policy can reasonably be viewed narrowly enough to avoid any overbreadth problem.

Sypniewski v. Warren Hills Reg'l Bd. of Educ., 307 F.3d 243, 258-59 (3d Cir. 2002) (internal citations omitted). In addition to the general considerations inherent in reviewing facial challenges to speech regulations, in the present facial challenge we are guided by our decision in *Saxe.* [In *Saxe*, the Court of Appeals for the Third Circuit struck down a K-12 school district's harassment policy as facially overbroad and unconstitutional.]

Saxe, however, involved a public elementary and high school district. Before we employ the overbreadth analysis as used in *Saxe*, we must point out that there is a difference between the extent that a school may regulate student speech in a public university setting as opposed to that of a public elementary or high school.

It is well recognized that "[t]he college classroom with its surrounding environs is peculiarly the 'marketplace of ideas[,]' " *Healy*, 408 U.S. at 180, and "[t]he First Amendment guarantees wide freedom in matters of adult public discourse[,]" *Fraser*, 478 U.S. at 682. Discussion by adult students in a college classroom should not be restricted. Certain speech, however, which *cannot be* prohibited to adults *may* be prohibited to public elementary and high school students. *See Fraser*, 478 U.S. at 682. . . .

In *Sypniewski*, . . . we stressed that, in the context of a public elementary or high school, the "special needs of school discipline" are an important consideration in regulating speech. . . . However, and most important here, we explicitly recognized that, although "[s]peech codes are disfavored under the First Amendment because of their tendency to silence or interfere with protected speech . . . [,] *public secondary and elementary school administrators are granted more leeway* [to restrict speech] *than public colleges and universities* . . . ." *Id.* Accordingly, in determining whether Temple University's policy passes constitutional muster under our reasoning in *Saxe*, we keep in mind that Temple's administrators are granted *less leeway* in regulating student speech than are public elementary or high school administrators.

In *Saxe*, we noted that there is no "harassment exception" to the First Amendment's Free Speech Clause. . . . We explained that while there is no question that non-expressive, physically harassing *conduct* is entirely outside the ambit of the free speech clause, "[w]hen laws against harassment attempt to regulate oral or written expression on such topics, however detestable the views expressed may be, we cannot turn a blind eye to the First Amendment implications. . . ." *Id.* at 206.

Recognizing, then, that some "harassing" speech maybe worthy of First Amendment protection, we look to see whether Temple's Policy on Sexual Harassment reaches too much expression that is constitutionally protected. The relevant portion of Temple's challenged sexual harassment policy reads:

> For all individuals who are part of the Temple community, all forms of sexual harassment are prohibited, including the following: an unwelcome sexual advance, request for sexual favors, *or other expressive, visual or physical conduct of a sexual or gender-motivated nature when . . . (c) such conduct has the purpose or effect of unreasonably interfering with an individual's work, educational performance, or status; or (d) such conduct has the purpose or effect of creating an intimidating, hostile, or offensive environment.*

Temple University Policy on Sexual Harassment, Section II.A.1 (emphasis added). With language mirroring the Policy at issue in *Saxe*, Temple's policy unequivocally prohibits any "expressive, visual or physical conduct" when that conduct "has the purpose or effect of unreasonably interfering with an individual's work, educational performance, or status; or . . . has the purpose or effect of creating an intimidating, hostile, or offensive environment."[15]

. . . Initially, the policy's focus upon the motives of the speaker is rightly criticized. Under the Supreme Court's rule in *Tinker*, a school must show that speech will cause actual, material disruption before prohibiting it. Under the language of Temple's Policy, a student who sets out to interfere with another student's work, educational performance, or status, or to create a hostile environment would be subject to sanctions regardless of whether these motives and actions had their intended effect. As such, the focus on motive is contrary to *Tinker's*

---

[15] We recognize that Temple's sexual harassment policy is not nearly as broad as the anti-harassment policy in *Saxe*. The policy in *Saxe* prohibited conduct based on any "personal characteristic," which included "clothing, physical appearance . . . hobbies or values, etc." *Saxe*, 240 F.3d at 220. Temple's policy, on the other hand, is limited to conduct "of a sexual or gender-motivated nature."

requirement that speech cannot be prohibited in the absence of a tenable threat of disruption.

Further, the policy's use of "hostile," "offensive," and "gender-motivated" is, on its face, sufficiently broad and subjective that they "could conceivably be applied to cover any speech" of a "gender-motivated" nature "the content of which offends someone." This could include "core" political and religious speech, such as gender politics and sexual morality.[18] Absent any requirement akin to a showing of severity or pervasiveness — that is, a requirement that the conduct objectively and subjectively creates a hostile environment or substantially interferes with an individual's work — the policy provides no shelter for core protected speech. . . .

C.

Before declaring whether this or any policy is unconstitutional, we must determine whether it is susceptible to a reasonable limiting construction. Under the Temple Policy the following elements, if present, constitute sexual harassment: (1) expressive, visual or physical conduct (2) of a sexual or gender-motivated nature and which (3) has the purpose or effect of either (3a) unreasonably interfering with an individual's work, educational performance, or status, or (3b) creating an intimidating, hostile, or offensive environment. If we juxtapose this definition of harassment with the limiting construction that this Court placed on the policy at issue in *Saxe*, we find that they are very similar. Importantly, even with the limiting construction, our Court found that the *Saxe* policy still prohibited "a substantial amount of non-vulgar, non-sponsored student speech" and that it still did not satisfy *Tinker*. *Saxe*, 240 F.3d at 216-17. Even more significantly, this case deals with a harassment policy in the university setting, whereas the policy in *Saxe* applied to high-schoolers. Thus, the limitations *Tinker* imposed on a school's ability to promulgate such a policy must *at least* be satisfied. As we indicated before, we must proceed with greater caution before imposing speech restrictions on adult students at a college campus.

First, harassment is defined in the policy as including expressive conduct of a "gender-motivated nature." This phrase gives rise to a number of issues. "Gender-motivated" necessarily requires an inquiry into the motivation of the speaker. Whose gender must serve as the motivation, the speaker's or the listener's? And does it matter? Additionally, we must be aware that "gender," to some people, is a fluid concept. Even if we narrow the term "gender-motivated" to "because of one's sex," we are far from certain that this limitation still does not encompasses expression on a broad range of social issues.

Second, as in *Saxe*, Temple's Policy reaches any speech that interferes or is intended to interfere with educational performance or that creates or is intended to create a hostile environment. Thus, "the Policy punishes not only speech that actually causes disruption, but also speech that merely intends to do so: by its terms, it covers speech 'which has the purpose or effect of' interfering with

---

[18] Indeed, in the instant case, the Plaintiff, a graduate student pursuing a master's degree in Military and American History, argues that he felt inhibited in expressing his opinions in class concerning women in combat and women in the military.

educational performance or creating a hostile environment. This ignores *Tinker's* requirement that a school must reasonably believe that speech will cause actual, material disruption before prohibiting it." [*Saxe*]. at 216-17. Additionally, the Policy prohibits a substantial amount of non-vulgar, non-sponsored student speech. *Id.*

Even if we ignore the "purpose" component, the Policy's prong that deals with conduct that "unreasonably interfere[s] with an individual's work" probably falls short of satisfying the *Tinker* standard. If we were to construe "unreasonable" as encompassing a subjective and objective component, it still does not necessarily follow that speech which effects an unreasonable interference with an individual's work justifies restricting another's First Amendment freedoms. . . .

For similar reasons, some speech that creates a "hostile or offensive environment" may be protected speech under the First Amendment. It is difficult to cabin this phrase, which could encompass any speech that might simply be offensive to a listener, or a group of listeners, believing that they are being subjected to or surrounded by hostility. Certainly speech amounting to "fighting words" would not be protected, but the policy covers much more speech than could be prohibited under *Tinker's* substantial disruption test as well as speech that does not rise to the level of "fighting words."

V.

. . . [W]e will affirm the District Court's March 21 Order granting injunctive relief in favor of DeJohn.

NOTES

1. Consider the following definition of "sexual harassment" from the EEOC:

> Unwelcome sexual advances, requests for sexual favors, and other verbal or physical conduct of a sexual nature constitute sexual harassment when (1) submission to such conduct is made either explicitly or implicitly a term or condition of an individual's employment, (2) submission to or rejection of such conduct by an individual is used as the basis for employment decisions affecting such individual, or (3) such conduct has the purpose or effect of unreasonably interfering with an individual's work performance or creating an intimidating, hostile, or offensive working environment.

29 C.F.R. § 1604.11(a). After *DeJohn,* what is the future of hate speech codes in educational settings? Temple University's policy used language directly from the EEOC guidelines on harassment, particularly the third prong of the EEOC's definition, with reference to "purpose and effect" and an "intimidating, hostile, or offensive" environment. Yet, according to the court, the language as used in the policy remains overbroad and the policy unconstitutional. So what policy guidance does *DeJohn* offer?

2. Hate speech codes have not fared well in the courts over the years, dating back to the late 1980s and early 1990s. In each of three noteworthy cases, the university's attempts at drafting and enforcing hate speech codes were invalidated as infringements on free speech. First, in *Doe v. University of Michigan,* 721 F.

Supp. 852 (E.D. Mich. 1989), a psychology graduate student filed suit challenging the university's hate speech code. The plaintiff argued that, under the policy, classroom discussion of certain controversial theories positing the biological differences between men and women and among races may be perceived as "sexist" or "racist" under the policy. The court struck down the policy as vague and overbroad, finding that it was impossible to determine the scope of the policy as it related to classroom speech, academic discussions, and research. Second, in *UWM Post, Inc. v. Board of Regents of the University of Wisconsin*, 774 F. Supp. 1163 (E.D. Wis. 1991), the court invalidated a similar anti-discrimination policy. Finally, in *Iota Xi Chapter of Sigma Chi Fraternity v. George Mason University*, 993 F.2d 386 (4th Cir. 1993), the Fourth Circuit held in favor of a fraternity that staged an "ugly woman contest" as part of its "Derby Days Events." The court held that such activity, while immature and sophomoric, constituted protected expression.

On the other end of the policymaking spectrum, however, schools, colleges, and universities are required under Title IX of the Education Amendments of 1972 to promulgate policies prohibiting sexual harassment. 20 U.S.C. § 1681(a) (2002). In the late 1990s, the Supreme Court opened the door to institutional liability under Title IX for deliberate indifference to known sexual harassment. *See Gebser v. Lago Vista Indep. Sch. Dist.*, 524 U.S. 274 (1998) (teacher-to-student harassment); *Davis v. Monroe County Bd. of Educ.*, 526 U.S. 629 (1999) (student-to-student harassment). Both *Gebser* and *Davis* are presented in the next Chapter.

3. The case turned from a time-to-degree matter to a facial challenge of a harassment policy without any reported, concrete evidence of chilling effect or damage on the part of *DeJohn*. How important should such evidence be in these cases?

G. STUDENT SPEECH IN ACADEMIC CONTEXTS

BROWN v. LI

308 F.3d 939 (9th Cir. 2002)

Graber, Circuit Judge:

In this appeal, we consider the extent to which the First Amendment and due process guarantees are implicated when a graduate student's thesis committee declines to approve a thesis that meets academic and professional standards in all respects except one: The acknowledgments section does not conform to established academic and professional standards. We conclude that the Amendment does not require university professors to assign a passing grade to such a thesis. . . .

FACTUAL AND PROCEDURAL BACKGROUND

Plaintiff Christopher Brown was a master's degree candidate in the Department of Material Sciences at the University of California at Santa Barbara ("UCSB"), a public university. In order to earn a master's degree, Plaintiff was required to write a thesis under the guidance and subject to the approval of his thesis committee:

Defendants Dr. Galen Stucky (Plaintiff's thesis advisor), Dr. Daniel Morse, and Dr. Fred Lange.

Rules governing the content and structure of master's theses, and the procedures for submitting those theses for approval, are contained in UCSB's Graduate Student's Handbook 1998-99 (Sept. 1998) ("Handbook") and in the UCSB Guide to Filing Theses and Dissertations (Feb. 1998) ("Guide"). The Guide notes that one of the pedagogical purposes of the thesis project is to educate students about how to communicate research results in their chosen disciplines: "The essence of academic research is shared results. Each discipline has a relatively standard method of presenting research results so that other researchers can find and build on past work." With respect to the content of a thesis or dissertation, the Guide states:

> You *and your committee* are responsible for everything between the margins. The organization, presentation, and documentation of your research should meet the standards for publishing journal articles or monographs in your field. . . .

The Guide also provides the general criteria for an optional "Dedication and/or Acknowledgments" section of a student thesis: "You may wish to dedicate this work to someone special to you or to acknowledge particular persons who helped you. Within the usual margin restrictions, any format is acceptable for these pages."

. . . .

The Handbook elaborates further on the supervisory role of the thesis committee with respect to the content of a master's thesis:

> Students, in conjunction with the faculty who supervise the writing of the dissertation, are responsible for the quality of scholarship in theses and dissertations, including presentation in a format that conforms to disciplinary standards. *Faculty should not approve a dissertation that fails to address disciplinary and/or departmental standards.* (emphasis added)

In the spring of 1999, Plaintiff brought his thesis, "The Morphology of Calcium Carbonate: Factors Affecting Crystal Shape," to his committee for final approval. Plaintiff did not include an acknowledgments section of any kind in the document that he delivered to his committee. All three committee members signed an approval page stating, "*This* Thesis of Christopher Brown is approved." (Emphasis added.) In accordance with UCSB rules, that approval page became the second page of the thesis.

After he had obtained the signature page from his committee, Plaintiff inserted an additional, two-page section into his thesis without the knowledge or consent of his committee members. That section, entitled "Disacknowledgements," began: "I would like to offer special *Fuck You's* to the following degenerates for of being an ever-present hindrance during my graduate career. . . ." It then identified the Dean and staff of the UCSB graduate school, the managers of Davidson Library, former California Governor Wilson, the Regents of the University of California, and "Science" as having been particularly obstructive to Plaintiff's progress toward his graduate degree. Plaintiff later explained that he had not revealed the section to the members of his committee because he feared that they would not approve it.

UCSB rules require that graduate students file their approved theses or dissertations in the university's library as a prerequisite to earning a degree. In June of 1999, Plaintiff attempted to file his thesis, including the unapproved "Disacknowledgements" section, with the library. Defendant Charles Li, the Dean of the Graduate Division of UCSB, was alerted to the presence of the "Disacknowledgements." Dean Li, in turn, referred the issue to Plaintiff's thesis committee.

During June and July, Plaintiff met with members of his committee and with Dean Li to discuss the "Disacknowledgements." He also met with the UCSB Ombudsperson and with the Dean of the UCSB School of Engineering. Plaintiff drafted an alternative version of the section, eliminating the profanity.

The committee members agreed that the "Disacknowledgements" section (even in its nonprofane form) did not meet professional standards for publication in the field. They notified Plaintiff of their decision in a memorandum dated August 5, 1999. That memorandum, written by Dr. Stucky, read in part:

> 1) The Dissertation Committee stands by its approval of the thesis (dissertation) as it was presented by you to the Committee for their evaluation, review and approval; and, subsequently signed by the members of the Dissertation Committee.
>
> 2) The disacknowledgement was not submitted to the Dissertation Committee or to the Graduate Division of the University of California, but for deposition in the Library without knowledge of either the Dissertation Committee or the Graduate Division. It is the understanding of the Dissertation Committee members who reviewed your thesis that the signatures of the Dissertation Committee members are a guarantee that the presentation and content of the entire thesis meets the standards and requirements of the Department, College, and the University of California to whom the thesis is submitted for the appropriate advanced degree. The addition or removal of material from a dissertation after the examination, evaluation and signed approval of the original materials that are presented by the candidate to the Committee; and, the subsequent presentation to the scientific community and to the University of such a modified dissertation under the approval signatures of the Committee given only for the original Dissertation presentation to the Committee without the consent of the Committee for the addition or removal of material, is unacceptable to the Committee.

In the August 5 memorandum, the committee also commented that it had consulted with counsel and determined that a thesis or other scientific manuscript is not a "public forum." The committee further said that it would not approve the addition of the "added materials" to the original, approved thesis, nor would it approve a thesis that contained them.

On the same date, Dean Li wrote a letter to Plaintiff, informing him that his degree would be conferred upon the approval of his thesis. The letter further noted that approval would be forthcoming as soon as Plaintiff removed his "Disacknowledgements." It outlined Plaintiff's avenues of appeal, should he opt to challenge the committee's decision not to approve the new version of the thesis.

Plaintiff declined to remove the "Disacknowledgements." Instead, he submitted a written appeal to the Academic Affairs Committee (AAC) of the Department of Material Sciences. The AAC considered Plaintiff's appeal and unanimously rejected it in a written decision. The AAC reasoned that the entire paper, not merely the technical content of the thesis, was subject to the review and approval of the thesis committee - just as the entirety of a scientific paper would be subject to the review and approval of the editorial board of any publication to which it was submitted. . . .

The AAC determined that Plaintiff's "Disacknowledgements" . . . section was otherwise irrelevant to the content of his thesis. The AAC reminded Plaintiff that several other avenues were open to him for disseminating the opinions contained in the "Disacknowledgements". . . . The decision additionally noted the rights of the committee members not to be associated, through their approval, with the content of the "Disacknowledgements" section. Finally, the AAC commented that Plaintiff's conduct was unprofessional in later inserting the material into his thesis without the knowledge or approval of his thesis committee.

Plaintiff appealed the AAC's decision to the Associate Dean of the Graduate Division, Diane Mackie. After reviewing the file, Dean Mackie denied the appeal.

The Graduate Council [also] rejected Plaintiff's appeal in a written decision. It reasoned that, under the university's regulations, the entirety of Plaintiff's thesis was subject to the approval of his thesis committee, and the "committee members [were] within their rights to withdraw their approval, as they do not approve of your added section." The Graduate Council additionally found that Plaintiff had been denied a degree only because he had not completed one of the prerequisites to completing a master's degree: filing a thesis approved by the committee. The Graduate Council suggested two ways in which Plaintiff could complete his degree:

> 1) seek approval of your entire thesis from your current committee, including the content of any acknowledgements/dedication section. All sections of your thesis are subject to their editing and approval.
>
> or.
>
> 2) seek to change the membership of the committee, subject to the approval of your department and the Graduate Division and appropriate university regulations. Submit your complete thesis with the new committee and meet all editing or research requirements imposed by that committee.

Plaintiff chose not to pursue either option proposed by the Graduate Council. Instead, he filed a grievance with the Academic Freedom Committee (AFC). He presented his case orally to the Chair of the AFC and in writing to the full AFC. The AFC rejected his grievance. It reasoned that the rules for filing theses did not impermissibly restrict academic freedom and that Plaintiff had failed to follow those rules.

On May 16, 2000, the Department recommended that Plaintiff receive his degree, based on the draft of the thesis that had received approval, despite Plaintiff's failure to comply with the requirements for earning his degree.

Plaintiff initiated this § 1983 action on June 16, 2000. His complaint alleged three claims: (1) that Defendants (the Dean of the UCSB Graduate Division, the Chancellor of UCSB, the members of Plaintiff's thesis committee, and the Director of the UCSB library) violated his First Amendment rights by "withholding" his degree and by their "conduct"; (2) that Defendants violated his right to procedural due process by withholding his degree without having provided him a formal hearing; and (3) that Defendants' refusal to grant his degree unless he removed the "Disacknowledgements" violated article I, section 2, of the California Constitution. Plaintiff sought damages, declaratory relief, and an injunction to compel Defendants to place Plaintiff's thesis, including the "Disacknowledgements," in the UCSB library.

Defendants moved for summary judgment on the federal claims. They argued that they were entitled to qualified immunity on the damages claims and that Plaintiff was not entitled to injunctive relief. . . .

[The edited portions below examine the First Amendment claim].

. . . .

STANDARD OF REVIEW

We review de novo a grant of summary judgment. Viewing the evidence in the light most favorable to the nonmoving party, we must decide whether there are any genuine issues of material fact and whether the district court correctly applied the substantive law.

DISCUSSION

A. *Qualified Immunity on the First Amendment Claim*

We apply a three-step test to determine whether a defendant is entitled to qualified immunity on a federal constitutional claim. First, we must determine whether the facts alleged, viewed in the light most favorable to the plaintiff, demonstrate that the defendant's conduct violated a constitutional right. Next, if the facts alleged show a constitutional violation, we must decide whether the constitutional right at stake was clearly established at the time of the alleged violation. Finally, if the right was clearly established, we assess whether an objectively reasonable government actor would have known that his or her conduct violated the plaintiff's constitutional right.

Plaintiff primarily contends that the facts, viewed in his favor, demonstrate a violation of his clearly established First Amendment rights. He challenges three acts: (1) the thesis committee's decision not to approve his "Disacknowledgements"; (2) the library's decision not to file his thesis in its archives; and (3) the UCSB's initial decision not to confer his degree.

Plaintiff cannot state separate First Amendment claims with respect to the second and third decisions. Under UCSB's policy, each of those two decisions was nondiscretionary, that is, turned completely on the committee's decision whether to approve the thesis. Had the committee approved the "Disacknowledgements" section, the library would have had to file the thesis containing it. The library had no independent authority to decide whether or not to include the thesis in its collection. Likewise, had Plaintiff filed an approved thesis with the library, UCSB would not have had discretion to decide to withhold or defer the degree.

Because the decisions not to place the thesis in the library and to delay granting Plaintiff's degree were not independent decisions but, rather, were direct consequences of the committee's decision not to approve the "Disacknowledgements," the real question is whether Defendants violated Plaintiff's First Amendment rights when they refused to approve that section. We have found no precedent precisely on point. However, a review of the cases discussing the relationship between students' free speech rights and schools' power to regulate the content of curriculum demonstrates that educators can, consistent with the First Amendment, restrict student speech provided that the limitation is reasonably related to a legitimate pedagogical purpose.

In *Hazelwood School District v. Kuhlmeier*, 484 U.S. 260, 276 (1988), the Supreme Court of the United States held that school officials did not violate students' First Amendment rights when they prohibited the publication in the school newspaper of stories that the officials found objectionable. The Court concluded that the newspaper, which was produced by a high school journalism class, was "fairly . . . characterized as part of the school curriculum" because it was "supervised by faculty members and designed to impart particular knowledge or skills to student participants and audiences." Because of its curricular nature, the newspaper did not qualify as a public forum. The Court then held that, with respect to students' curricular speech, "educators do not offend the First Amendment by exercising editorial control over the style and content of student speech in school sponsored expressive activities so long as their actions are reasonably related to legitimate pedagogical concerns." Both the majority and the dissent in *Hazelwood* agreed that

> "the First Amendment permits educators 'to assure that participants learn whatever lessons the activity is designed to teach' " and that the First Amendment should afford an educator the prerogative not to sponsor the publication of a newspaper article that is "ungrammatical, poorly written, inadequately researched, biased or prejudiced," or that falls short of the "high standards for . . . student speech that is disseminated under [the school's] auspices. . . ." . . . The educator may . . . constitutionally "censor" poor grammar, writing, or research because to reward such expression would "materially disrupt" the newspaper's curricular purpose.

Id. at 283-84 (Brennan, J., dissenting).

Settle v. Dickson County School Board, 53 F.3d 152 (6th Cir. 1995), more strongly resembles the present case. There, the plaintiff argued that her ninth-grade teacher violated her First Amendment rights when she refused to approve the plaintiff's chosen topic for a class research paper and gave the plaintiff a grade of zero on the assignment when the plaintiff refused to comply with requirements related to the assignment. The student had submitted only one topic for the teacher's approval, which the student duly received. Then the student - without the knowledge or approval of the teacher - changed her topic. Relying on *Hazelwood's* recognition of a school's power to regulate classroom speech, the court rejected the plaintiff's First Amendment argument, holding:

> The free speech rights of students in the classroom must be limited because effective education depends not only on controlling boisterous conduct, but also on maintaining the focus of the class on the assignment in question. So long as the teacher violates no positive law or school policy, the teacher has broad authority to base her grades for students on her view of the merits of the students' work. Grades are given as incentives for study, and they are the currency by which school work is measured. . . .

Id. at 155-56 (citations omitted). One judge concurred in the judgment, but concluded that the First Amendment was not implicated at all by the facts presented:

> The bottom line is that when a teacher makes an assignment, even if she does it poorly, the student has no constitutional right to do something other than that assignment and receive credit for it. It is not necessary to try to cram this situation into the framework of constitutional precedent, because there is no constitutional question.

Id. at 158 (Batchelder, J., concurring in the judgment).

Hazelwood and *Settle* lead to the conclusion that an educator can, consistent with the First Amendment, require that a student comply with the terms of an academic assignment. Those cases also make clear that the First Amendment does not require an educator to change the assignment to suit the student's opinion or to approve the work of a student that, in his or her judgment, fails to meet a legitimate academic standard. . . .

Plaintiff argues that the *Hazelwood* standard does not apply in the context of a university-level assignment, as distinct from a primary-school or secondary-school environment. It is true that the Court left open the question "whether the same degree of deference is appropriate with respect to school sponsored expressive activities at the college and university level." *Id.* at 273 n.7. It also is true that courts addressing the extent to which a public college or university, consistent with the First Amendment, can regulate student speech in the context of *extracurricular* activities, such as yearbooks and newspapers, have held that *Hazelwood* deference does not apply.

However, the parties have not identified, nor have we found, any Supreme Court case discussing the appropriate standard for reviewing a university's regulation of students' *curricular* speech. It is thus an open question whether *Hazelwood* articulates the standard for reviewing a university's assessment of a student's academic work. We conclude that it does.

The Supreme Court has suggested that core *curricular* speech - that which is an integral part of the classroom teaching function of an educational institution - differs from students' *extracurricular* speech and that a public educational institution retains discretion to prescribe its curriculum. For example, in *Arkansas Educational Television Commission v. Forbes*, 523 U.S. 666 (1998), the Supreme Court held that a debate sponsored by a state-owned public television station was a nonpublic forum from which the broadcaster could exclude an independent candidate in the exercise of journalistic discretion. In reaching that conclusion, the Court said:

> . . . Much like a university selecting a commencement speaker, a public institution selecting speakers for a lecture series, or *a public school prescribing its curriculum*, a broadcaster by its nature will facilitate the expression of some viewpoints instead of others. Were the judiciary to require, and so to define and approve, preestablished criteria for access, it would risk implicating the courts in judgments that should be left to the exercise of journalistic discretion.

Id. at 673-74 (emphasis added). The Court thus referred to the principle that a public school has discretion to engage in its own expressive activity of prescribing its curriculum. . . .

In summary, under the Supreme Court's precedents, the curriculum of a public educational institution is one means by which the institution itself expresses its policy, a policy with which others do not have a constitutional right to interfere. The Supreme Court's jurisprudence does not hold that an institution's interest in mandating its curriculum and in limiting a student's speech to that which is germane to a particular *academic* assignment diminishes as students age. Indeed, arguably the need for academic discipline and editorial rigor increases as a student's learning progresses.

To the extent that the Supreme Court has addressed the difference between a university's regulation of curricular speech and a primary or secondary school's regulation of curricular speech, it has implied that a university's control may be broader. It has done so in its cases recognizing the doctrine of university professors' academic freedom, a doctrine that encompasses "the idea that universities and schools should have the freedom to make decisions about how and what to teach." *Bd. of Regents of Univ. of Wis. Sys. v. Southworth*, 529 U.S. 217, 237 (2000) (Souter, J., concurring in the judgment). In *Southworth*, Justice Souter summarized the current state of "academic freedom" law:

> In *Regents of Univ. of Mich. v. Ewing*, 474 U.S. 214,(1985), we recognized these related conceptions: "Academic freedom thrives not only on the independent and uninhibited exchange of ideas among teachers and students, but also, and somewhat inconsistently, on autonomous decision-making by the academy itself." Some of the opinions in our books emphasize broad conceptions of academic freedom that if accepted by the Court might seem to clothe the University with an immunity to any challenge to regulations made or obligations imposed in the discharge of its educational mission. . . .

529 U.S. at 237-39 (citations omitted).

We do not know with certainty that the Supreme Court would hold that *Hazelwood* controls the inquiry into whether a university's requirements for and evaluation of a student's curricular speech infringe that student's First Amendment rights. Nevertheless, of all the Supreme Court's cases, *Hazelwood* appears to be the most analogous to the present case.

In view of a university's strong interest in setting the content of its curriculum and teaching that content, *Hazelwood* provides a workable standard for evaluating a university student's First Amendment claim stemming from curricular speech. That standard balances a university's interest in academic freedom and a student's First Amendment rights. It does not immunize the university altogether from First Amendment challenges but, at the same time, appropriately defers to the university's expertise in defining academic standards and teaching students to meet them.

Applying the *Hazelwood* standard to the facts of this case, and viewing those facts in favor of Plaintiff, we conclude that Plaintiff cannot show a violation of his First Amendment rights. In this case . . . , Plaintiff was given an assignment: the writing of a master's thesis. That assignment, like the paper in *Hazelwood*, is "fairly . . . characterized as part of the . . . curriculum," 484 U.S. at 271, because it was designed to teach Plaintiff how to research within an academic specialty and how to present his results to other scholars in his field. Therefore, like the newspaper in *Hazelwood*, Plaintiff's thesis was subject to a reviewing committee's reasonable regulation. Plaintiff was given reasonable standards for that assignment, including a pedagogically appropriate requirement that the thesis comply with professional standards governing his discipline. He was instructed that he should consult a standard style manual, or talk with members of his committee, about those requirements. Like the plaintiff in *Settle*, Plaintiff bypassed the approval process and prepared an assignment that did not comply with the stated criteria. Under *Hazelwood* and *Settle*, Plaintiff's committee members acted well within their discretion, and in conformity with the First Amendment, when they declined to approve the noncompliant section. Their decision was reasonably related to a legitimate pedagogical objective: teaching Plaintiff the proper format for a scientific paper.

Moreover, the committee members had an affirmative First Amendment right not to approve Plaintiff's thesis. . . . That is especially true where, as here, the committee members' names appear in the thesis and where, according to the Guide, they are jointly responsible for its content. The presence of Defendants' affirmative right underscores Plaintiff's lack of a First Amendment right to have his nonconforming thesis approved.

Plaintiff counters, first, that the Guide does not require acknowledgments sections to meet academic and professional standards but, instead, grants students wide discretion to write whatever they want. According to Plaintiff, the use of the word "may" in the part of the Guide defining the "Dedication and/or Acknowledgments" section of a thesis means that a student has complete discretion with respect to the *content* of that section - the student "may" dedicate the thesis to someone special or give thanks to helpful individuals in the section, or the student "may" use the section to communicate some other message. That is not a permissible reading of the Guide. An acknowledgments section has a well-defined form and purpose in academic writing. Moreover, the context is the statement in the Guide that the inclusion of such a section is "optional." Thus, the word "may" simply refers to the fact that a student "may" either include an appropriately drafted section thanking people or "may" omit the section altogether. That is, the discretion to which the term "may" refers is the discretion whether to include the section or not.

Plaintiff also contends that the fact that the Guide permits the section to be in any "format" means that a student has freedom to choose the content of the acknowledgments section. We are not persuaded. "Format" commonly refers to the physical layout of a document, not its substantive content. . . .

In the alternative, whatever the meaning of the Guide, Plaintiff argues that he has a First Amendment right to draft an acknowledgments section from *any* viewpoint. To the contrary, *Hazelwood* and *Settle* establish that - consistent with the First Amendment - a teacher may require a student to write a paper from a particular viewpoint, even if it is a viewpoint with which the student disagrees, so long as the requirement serves a legitimate pedagogical purpose. . . . In this case, the thesis committee was entitled to require that the acknowledgments section (if it were included) recognize those who made a positive contribution to Plaintiff's education. Such requirements are part of the teachers' curricular mission to encourage critical thinking . . . and to conform to professional norms (in this case).

. . . .

Moreover, the summary judgment record does not support an inference that UCSB acted because of the content of Plaintiff's ideas, rather than the format and placement of those ideas. An academic thesis co-signed by a committee of professors is not a public forum, limited or otherwise. As Defendants explained to him, Plaintiff remained free to publish and publicize his ideas in many other ways.

In short, the decision of Plaintiff's committee members not to approve the "Disacknowledgements" section did not violate Plaintiff's First Amendment rights. Because UCSB's decision not to place the thesis in the library and to defer granting Plaintiff's degree cannot be viewed as independent of the approval decision, those actions likewise did not violate Plaintiff's First Amendment rights. Therefore, the district court properly concluded that (a) Defendants are entitled to qualified immunity on Plaintiff's First Amendment claim and (b) Plaintiff cannot compel the library to file the unapproved thesis in the archives.

CONCLUSION

We hold that Plaintiff does not have a First Amendment right to have his nonconforming thesis approved, nor did he have a right to a formal hearing with respect to his committee's academic decision not to approve the thesis. As a result, Defendants are entitled to qualified immunity on Plaintiff's damages claims, and Plaintiff cannot compel Defendants to place the unapproved version of his thesis in the UCSB library.

. . . .

FERGUSON, CIRCUIT JUDGE, concurring in the affirmance of the District Court and the remand on state issues:

. . . .

This case is about an erosion of academic integrity. To put it in the vernacular, the guy cooked the books (his master's thesis), got caught, and now wants to shield his misbehavior under the umbrella of the First Amendment.

. . . University regulations provide that the faculty members who comprise the thesis committee are jointly responsible with the candidate for the content of the thesis. By adding the "Disacknowledgments" section to his thesis for submission to the university library, the plaintiff tried to circumvent the university's requirement of faculty approval and misrepresented to both the university and his academic field that his "Disacknowledgments" had been accepted by the faculty committee for publication.

. . . [It] was the academically dishonest manner in which the plaintiff tried to publish his "Disacknowledgments," rather than his views, that the committee disapproved.

The First Amendment does not protect nor authorize deception. . . . The plaintiff cannot cheat and then seek to evade accountability through the First Amendment.

REINHARDT, CIRCUIT JUDGE, concurring in part and dissenting in part:

First, I emphasize that there is no agreement between my colleagues in the majority as to the legal standard applicable to Brown's First Amendment claims. Thus, there is no majority opinion and no binding precedent with respect to any First Amendment principles. Although Judges Graber and Ferguson reach the same conclusion, they do so for wholly different reasons. . . .

. . . .

Judge Graber would have us adopt a First Amendment standard regarding the authority of public universities to limit the speech of graduate students that I believe to be wholly inappropriate - a standard that would seriously undermine the rights of all college and graduate students attending state institutions of higher learning. Specifically, she would import into the college and graduate academic world the limitations on speech that the Supreme Court has held appropriate for use in the case of emotionally less mature high school students. Because the reasons underlying the deference with respect to the regulation of the speech rights of high school youths do not apply in the adult world of college and graduate students, an arena in which academic freedom and vigorous debate are supposed to flourish, I cannot agree with Judge Graber's conclusion that the First Amendment standard established in *Hazelwood* applies at the university level.

Even were the *Hazelwood* standard applicable to this case, I would vigorously disagree that a university's decision to withhold a graduate student's degree for almost a year, despite the fact that he has successfully completed his masters thesis and complied with all of the department's other academic requirements, is a "reasonable" response to his attachment to his chemistry thesis of a one and a half page prefatory disacknowledgments section in which he caustically expresses his view that university and other public officials obstructed rather than aided his progress toward a graduate degree. Nor, in my opinion, is it a reasonable response to such expressive conduct for the university to exacerbate its retaliatory action by placing the offending graduate student on academic probation for the period during which his degree is being withheld, thus making him ineligible for a teaching or research position or for financial support.

The university's extreme actions in response to Brown's speech - speech that was highly critical of university and other public officials - raises a genuine question of material fact as to whether the university punished him because of the viewpoint he sought to express or whether, as the Judge Graber appears to believe, it simply desired to further a legitimate pedagogical concern. Thus, a genuine issue of fact as to the university's extreme actions exists even if, as I willingly assume for purposes of this dissent, the university had the right to refuse to file Brown's thesis in the library archives as long as he insisted that it not be filed without the hostile disacknowledgments. Summary judgment was therefore wholly inappropriate.

. . . .

I. *Hazelwood's* standard does not apply to college and graduate school student speech.

I vehemently disagree with Judge Graber's conclusion that *Hazelwood* provides the appropriate First Amendment standard for college and graduate student speech. . . .

The Supreme Court has recognized that college and graduate students, unlike high school students, are more mature, independent thinkers who are less likely to be influenced by the school-sponsored publication of controversial ideas. In fact, discussion of controversial ideas on a college campus is essential to the "background and tradition of thought and experiment that is at the center of our intellectual and philosophic tradition" in the university setting. *Rosenberger v. Rector and Visitors of the Univ. of Virginia*, 515 U.S. 819, 835 (1995). . . .

Because college and graduate school students are typically more mature and independent, they have been afforded greater First Amendment rights than their high school counterparts, just as they have been afforded greater legal rights in general. . . .

. . . In *Hazelwood* itself, the Supreme Court recognized that "the same degree of deference" shown to high school officials may not be "appropriate" when analyzing the First Amendment protection available to "school-sponsored expressive activities at the college and university level." 484 U.S. at 273 n.7. When discussing the First Amendment rights of college students generally, the Supreme Court noted that "the precedents of this Court leave no room for the view that, because of the acknowledged need for order, First Amendment protections should apply with less force on college campuses than in the community at large." *Healy v. James*, 408 U.S. 169, 180 (1972). . . .

. . . .

Recognizing that college and graduate student speech should be entitled to greater First Amendment protection than that of high school students, the Sixth Circuit has explicitly declined to apply *Hazelwood's* deferential First Amendment standard in the university setting. In *Kincaid*, a public university attempted to suppress the speech of some of its college students by withholding publication of the school yearbook. The Sixth Circuit, on rehearing en banc, held that the *Hazelwood* standard was inapplicable and instead concluded that the yearbook was a limited public forum in which viewpoint discrimination was impermissible and content-based regulations were permissible only when narrowly drawn to effectuate a compelling state interest.

. . . The yearbook at issue in *Kincaid* was under the management of a "Student Publications Board" consisting of "faculty[] and university officials," as well as students. *Kincaid*, 236 F.3d at 349. Thus, student speech in the yearbook was just as likely to be perceived by members of the public "to bear the imprimatur of the school" as student speech in a curricular context. *Hazelwood*, 484 U.S. at 271. Despite the evident similarity in subject matter in *Hazelwood* and *Kincaid*, the Sixth Circuit refused to apply the *Hazelwood high school* standard to a *university's* decision to withhold publication of a yearbook and instead applied a standard that was more protective of university students' First Amendment rights. When discussing its rationale, the *Kincaid* court emphasized the fact that university students are "less impressionable than younger students" and noted that "the danger of chilling . . . individual thought and expression . . . is especially real in the University setting, where the State acts against a background and tradition of thought and experiment that is at the center of our intellectual and philosophic tradition." *Kincaid*, 236 F.3d at 352. . . .

. . . .

II. There are a number of more speech-protective standards that could be applied to college and graduate student speech.

. . . .

First, there is the limited or designated public forum in which the government opens a forum "for use by the public at large for assembly and speech, for use by certain speakers, or for the discussion of certain subjects." In a limited public forum, the government may impose reasonable time, place, and manner restrictions on speech; viewpoint-based restrictions are impermissible; and all content-based restrictions must be narrowly drawn to effectuate a compelling state interest. This is the standard that the Sixth Circuit applied in *Kincaid* when it held that the university's yearbook constituted a limited or designated public forum in which content-based regulations were subject to strict scrutiny review.

Another possibility is to adopt an intermediate level of scrutiny for regulations of student speech in college and graduate programs. . . . . Under an intermediate level of scrutiny, the university would have the burden of demonstrating that its regulation of college and graduate student speech was substantially related to an important pedagogical purpose. Although intermediate scrutiny is more protective of First Amendment speech rights than the *Hazelwood* standard, it affords more deference to educators' content-based decisions than does the strict scrutiny standard that applies under a limited public forum analysis.

. . . .

III. Even if *Hazelwood* were the applicable standard, the University's decisions to place Brown on academic probation and to withhold his degree for almost a year would raise genuine issues of material fact that preclude summary judgment.

. . . .

In sum, Brown has raised genuine issues of material fact as to whether the university defendants violated his First Amendment rights, even under the most deferential First Amendment standard available - a standard that was clearly established at the time of the events in this case. Moreover, a reasonable school official would have known that, even under *Hazelwood's* "reasonableness" standard, placing a graduate student on academic probation and withholding his degree for almost a year solely because he attempted to include a one and a half page statement highly critical of university and other public officials in his thesis would be unreasonable and would violate the student's First Amendment rights. Accordingly, I respectfully dissent from my colleagues' conclusions (implicit or explicit) on Brown's principal First Amendment claims. I would reverse the district court's grant of summary judgment in favor of the defendants in part, and remand in order to allow Brown to pursue those claims and to seek damages in connection with the principal First Amendment violations he alleges.

AXSON-FLYNN v. JOHNSON

356 F.3d 1277 (10th Cir. 2004)

EBEL, CIRCUIT JUDGE.

. . . .

BACKGROUND

In 1998, Plaintiff-Appellant Christina Axson-Flynn ("Axson-Flynn"), a member of the Church of Jesus Christ of Latter-day Saints ("Mormon church"), applied to the University of Utah's Actor Training Program (ATP). As part of the application process, she attended an audition conducted by ATP instructors Barbara Smith, Sandy Shotwell, Jerry Gardner, and Sarah Shippobotham (hereinafter "Defendants"). During her audition, Sandy Shotwell asked Axson-Flynn if there was anything she would feel uncomfortable doing or saying as an actor. Axson-Flynn replied that she would not remove her clothing, "take the name of God in vain," "take the name of Christ in vain" or "say the four-letter expletive beginning with the letter F." Although the record is unclear as to whether Axson-Flynn explained at the time why she had those objections, the district court summarized her reasons as [related to her religious beliefs.]

At the audition, after challenging Axson-Flynn's refusal to say "fuck" by giving several examples of when it might be appropriate to do so, Defendant Shotwell asked Axson-Flynn, "Well, see, it isn't black and white, is it?" Axson-Flynn responded, "Well I guess not, and I guess it comes down to the individual actor. But as for myself, I will not say the F word, take the Lord's name in vain, or take off my clothes." Defendants then said "Thank you," and the audition ended. At one point during the exchange (the record is unclear as to exactly when), Axson-Flynn said, "I would rather not be admitted to your program than use these words" and "I will not use these words." . . .

Axson-Flynn was admitted to the ATP, and she matriculated in the fall of 1998. As part of a class exercise that fall, she was asked to perform a monologue called "Friday" that included two instances of the word "goddamn" and one instance of the word "shit." Without informing her instructor (Defendant Barbara Smith), Axson-Flynn substituted other words for the two "goddamn"s but otherwise performed the monologue as written. Smith did not notice, and Axson-Flynn received an "A" grade for her performance.

A few weeks later, as part of another class exercise, Smith asked Axson-Flynn to perform a scene from the play "The Quadrangle." Axson-Flynn was to play the part of an unmarried girl who had recently had an abortion. She expressed no concerns about the role itself. She did, however, object to some of the words that she would be required to say, which included "goddamn" and "fucking." Axson-Flynn mentioned her concerns to Smith, who asked why Axson-Flynn was raising these concerns now, when she apparently had no language concerns with respect to the "Friday" monologue. Axson-Flynn replied that she had omitted the offensive words from the "Friday" monologue and that no one had noticed. Smith became angry, told Axson-Flynn her behavior was unacceptable, and said that Axson-Flynn would have to "get over" her language concerns. She told Axson-Flynn that she could "still be a good Mormon and say these words." Axson-Flynn offered to perform a different scene if she were not allowed to change or omit the offensive words, but Smith refused to allow that, saying that Axson-Flynn would either perform the "Quadrangle" scene as written or receive a grade of zero on the exercise. If Axson-Flynn received a zero, the highest grade she would have been able to receive in the class would have been a "C." Axson-Flynn said that she would take a zero on that and any other assignment she could not complete due to her language concerns. Smith suggested that before making such a decision, Axson-Flynn should take the weekend and think about it, which Axson-Flynn agreed to do.

Shortly thereafter (the record is not clear as to when), Smith asked Axson-Flynn if she had changed her mind. Axson-Flynn replied that she had not, and that she would accept a zero. Smith then relented, telling Axson-Flynn that she "admired [her] character" and that she would be allowed "to omit the language that was offensive" to her. Axson-Flynn performed the scene from "The Quadrangle" without the offensive language and received a high grade on her performance. For the rest of the semester, Axson-Flynn was allowed to omit any language she found offensive during class exercises.

At the end of the fall semester, Axson-Flynn attended her semester review, at which Defendants Barbara Smith, Sarah Shippobotham, and Sandy Shotwell were present. Defendants confronted Axson-Flynn about her language concerns and said that her request for an accommodation was "unacceptable behavior." They recommended that she "talk to some other Mormon girls who are good Mormons, who don't have a problem with this." Finally, they told her, "You can choose to continue in the program if you modify your values. If you don't, you can leave. That's your choice." After the review, Axson-Flynn appealed for help to Defendant Xan Johnson, the ATP's coordinator, but Johnson told her that he supported the other Defendants' position on the language issue.

As Axson-Flynn began her second semester in January of 1999, Defendants continued to pressure her frequently to use the language that she found offensive. To clarify the ATP's position on the language issue, Axson-Flynn went to Sandy Shotwell, the director of the ATP. She said to Shotwell, "Sandy, this is what I understand. If I do not — and this is what you said — modify my values by the end of the semester, I'm going to have to find another program. Is that right?" Shotwell replied, "Well, yes. We talked about that, yes." Axson-Flynn told Shotwell that she did not want to leave but that she was not going to change her mind. Shotwell replied, "Neither are we."

Later that month, Axson-Flynn decided to withdraw from the ATP and leave the University of Utah. While she had never been asked to leave, she nonetheless apparently believed that it was only a matter of time before that would happen. After Axson-Flynn left the University of Utah, she enrolled in the acting program at Utah Valley State College. At Utah Valley State, Axson-Flynn was allowed to omit the language she found offensive.

On February 16, 2000, Axson-Flynn filed suit against Defendants pursuant to 42 U.S.C. § 1983 for violating her free speech and free exercise rights under the First Amendment. She sought both monetary damages and declaratory relief in the form of a statement that Defendants had violated her constitutional rights . . . The district court granted Defendants' motion for summary judgment, finding no constitutional violations, and finding that in any event, defendants would be entitled to qualified immunity on both claims. Axson-Flynn timely filed this appeal.

DISCUSSION

. . . .

I. FREEDOM OF SPEECH

Axson-Flynn argues that Defendants' insistence that she speak her lines as written, without omitting the words she found offensive, violated her First Amendment right to refrain from speaking. The district court rejected this argument and granted summary judgment to Defendants, finding that what Axson-Flynn was being asked to do fell outside the bounds of the Supreme Court precedents that prohibit compelled speech.

We review de novo the district court's grant of summary judgment. . . . For the reasons that follow, we reverse the district court's grant of summary judgment and remand for further proceedings.

The Supreme Court has long held that the government may not compel the speech of private actors. *See United States v. United Foods, Inc.*, 533 U.S. 405, 413-15 (2001); *Wooley v. Maynard*, 430 U.S. 705, 714-15 (1977); *W. Va. State Bd. of Educ. v. Barnette*, 319 U.S. 624, 642 (1943). Moreover, it is apodictic that public school students do not "shed their constitutional rights to freedom of speech or expression at the schoolhouse gate." *Tinker v. Des Moines Indep. Cmty. Sch. Dist.*,

393 U.S. 503, 506 (1969). At the same time, however, the Court has emphasized that "the First Amendment rights of students in the public schools are not automatically coextensive with the rights of adults in other settings, and must be applied in light of the special characteristics of the school environment." *Hazelwood Sch. Dist. v. Kuhlmeier*, 484 U.S. 260, 266 (1988). Nowhere is this more true than in the context of a school's right to determine what to teach and how to teach it in its classrooms.

At the outset, we must determine whether the ATP's classroom should be considered a traditional public forum, designated public forum, or nonpublic forum for free speech purposes. As the *Hazelwood* Court stated, "public schools do not possess all of the attributes of streets, parks, and other traditional public forums that time out of mind, have been used for purposes of assembly, communicating thoughts between citizens, and discussing public questions.' " Nothing in the record leads us to conclude that under that standard, the ATP's classroom could reasonably be considered a traditional public forum. Neither could the classroom be considered a designated public forum, as there is no indication in the record that "school authorities have 'by policy or by practice' opened [the classroom] 'for indiscriminate use by the general public,' or by some segment of the public, such as student organizations." We thus find that the ATP's classroom constitutes a nonpublic forum, meaning that school officials could regulate the speech that takes place there "in any reasonable manner."

We next turn to the type of speech at issue in this case. There are three main types of speech that occur within a school setting. First is student speech that "happens to occur on the school premises," such as the black armbands worn by the students in *Tinker*. This type of speech comprises "pure student expression that a school must tolerate unless it can reasonably forecast that the expression will lead to 'substantial disruption of or material interference with school activities.' " The speech at issue in the instant case clearly is not of this type, as it occurred in the classroom setting in the context of a class exercise and did not simply "happen[] to occur on the school premises."

The second type of speech in the school setting is "government speech, such as the principal speaking at a school assembly." Axson-Flynn is a student, not a school official, and recitation of the play is not being advanced as government speech. Therefore, this speech does not fit into this category either.

The third type of speech is "school-sponsored speech," which is "speech that a school 'affirmatively . . . promotes,' as opposed to speech that it 'tolerates.' " " 'Expressive activities that students, parents, and members of the public might reasonably perceive to bear the imprimatur of the school' constitute school-sponsored speech, over which the school may exercise editorial control, 'so long as [its] actions are reasonably related to legitimate pedagogical concerns.' " We conclude that Axson-Flynn's speech in this case constitutes "school-sponsored speech" and is thus governed by *Hazelwood.*

In *Hazelwood*, the Supreme Court upheld against a free speech challenge a school's decision to excise two pages from the school newspaper because of content it deemed inappropriate for publication. The Court determined that the newspaper, which was published as part of a journalism class, constituted "school-sponsored" speech. . . . School-sponsored speech comprises "expressive activities" that "may fairly be characterized as part of the school curriculum, whether or not they occur in a traditional classroom setting, so long as they are supervised by faculty members and designed to impart particular knowledge or skills to student participants and audiences." The Court held that school officials may place restrictions on school-sponsored speech "so long as their actions are reasonably related to legitimate pedagogical concerns."

Here, there is no doubt that the school sponsored the use of plays with the offending language in them as part of its instructional technique. The particular plays containing such language were specifically chosen by the school and incorporated as part of the school's official curriculum. Furthermore, if a school newspaper and a project to paint and post glazed and fired tiles in a school hallway can be considered school-sponsored speech, then surely student speech that takes place inside the classroom, as part of a class assignment, can also be considered school-sponsored speech. . . .

Axson-Flynn argues that forcing her, as part of an acting-class exercise, to say words she finds offensive constitutes compelled speech in violation of the First Amendment. "In order to compel the exercise or suppression of speech, the governmental measure must punish, or threaten to punish, protected speech by governmental action that is regulatory, proscriptive, or compulsory in nature." Compulsion need not take the form of a direct threat or a gun to the head. "The consequence may be an 'indirect discouragement,' rather than a direct punishment. . . ." There is no question that in the instant case, Defendants attempted to compel Axson-Flynn to speak. Although they never suspended her from the ATP or explicitly threatened her with expulsion, Defendants made it abundantly clear that Axson-Flynn would not be able to continue in the program if she refused to say the words with which she was uncomfortable.

. . . Thus, we will uphold the ATP's decision to restrict (or compel) that speech as long as the ATP's decision was reasonably related to legitimate pedagogical concerns. We give substantial deference to educators' stated pedagogical concerns.

That schools must be empowered at times to restrict the speech of their students for pedagogical purposes is not a controversial proposition. By no means is such power limited to the very basic level of a teacher's ability to penalize a student for disruptive classroom behavior. . . . By the same token, schools also routinely require students to express a viewpoint that is not their own in order to teach the students to think critically. . . . Student speech in the classroom context is thus restricted every day in a variety of ways, few of which would be deemed controversial.

In the instant case, Defendants justified their restriction on speech — the requirement that students, including Axson-Flynn, perform the acting exercises as written — as a methodology for preparing students for careers in professional acting. Defendants argue that requiring students to perform offensive scripts advances the school's pedagogical interest in teaching acting in at least three ways: (1) it teaches students how to step outside their own values and character by forcing them to assume a very foreign character and to recite offensive dialogue; (2) it teaches students to preserve the integrity of the author's work; and (3) it measures true acting skills to be able convincingly to portray an offensive part. Requiring an acting student, in the context of a classroom exercise, to speak the words of a script as written is no different than requiring that a law or history student argue a position with which he disagrees. . . . The school's methodology may not be necessary to the achievement of its goals and it may not even be the most effective means of teaching, but it can still be "reasonably related" to pedagogical concerns. A more stringent standard would effectively give each student veto power over curricular requirements, subjecting the curricular decisions of teachers to the whims of what a particular student does or does not feel like learning on a given day. This we decline to do.

Although we do not second-guess the pedagogical wisdom or efficacy of an educator's goal, we would be abdicating our judicial duty if we failed to investigate whether the educational goal or pedagogical concern was pretextual. In *Regents of the Univ. of Mich. v. Ewing*, the Supreme Court directed courts not to override a faculty member's professional judgment "unless it is such a substantial departure from accepted academic norms as to demonstrate that the person or committee responsible did not actually exercise professional judgment." Thus, we may override an educator's judgment where the proffered goal or methodology was a sham pretext for an impermissible ulterior motive.

In her amended complaint, Axson-Flynn posits that Defendants forced her to adhere strictly to the script not because of their educational goals as described above, but rather because of "anti-Mormon sentiment." During her deposition, she queried, "They respect other kids' freedom of religion that aren't [Mormon]. Why won't they respect mine?" Additionally, the program's insistence that Axson-Flynn speak with other "good Mormon girls" and that she could "still be a good Mormon" and say these words certainly raises concern that hostility to her faith rather than a pedagogical interest in her growth as an actress was at stake in Defendants' behavior in this case. Viewing the evidence in a light most favorable to Axson-Flynn, we find that there is a genuine issue of material fact as to whether Defendants' justification for the script adherence requirement was truly pedagogical or whether it was a pretext for religious discrimination. Therefore, summary judgment [on the free speech claim] was improper.

II. FREE EXERCISE

Axson-Flynn also argues that by attempting to force her to say words whose utterance would violate her religious beliefs, Defendants violated the free exercise clause of the First Amendment.

. . . .

Neutral rules of general applicability ordinarily do not raise free exercise concerns even if they incidentally burden a particular religious practice or belief. . . . By contrast, if a law that burdens a religious practice or belief is not neutral or generally applicable, it is subject to strict scrutiny, and the burden on religious conduct violates the Free Exercise Clause unless it is narrowly tailored to advance a compelling government interest.

We first address the threshold requirement . . . of determining whether the strict adherence to offensive script requirement was a "neutral rule of general applicability." A rule that is discriminatorily motivated and applied is not a neutral rule of general applicability. As discussed in the free speech section above, we find a genuine issue of fact in the record as to whether Defendants' requirement of script adherence was pretextual. Therefore, we remand for further proceedings on whether the script adherence requirement was discriminatorily applied to religious conduct (and thus was not generally applicable). Unless Defendants succeed in showing that the script requirement was a neutral rule of general applicability, they will face the daunting task of establishing that the requirement was narrowly tailored to advance a compelling governmental interest.

If Defendants succeed on remand in showing their requirement was not pretextual but rather was a neutral and generally applicable requirement, Axson-Flynn argues that the two exceptions . . . apply, and if she were to be successful in establishing an exemption, Defendants' conduct would not be sheltered by the rational basis test. The first exception . . . has come to be called the "hybrid rights" exception: when a free exercise claim is coupled with some other constitutional claim (such [as] a free speech claim), heightened scrutiny may be appropriate. The second exception, following) is the "individualized exemption" exception: where a state's facially neutral rule contains a system of individualized exemptions, a state "may not refuse to extend that system to cases of 'religious hardship' without compelling reason." The district court held that Axson-Flynn's case fit within neither Smith exception. For the reasons that follow, we disagree and find that Axson-Flynn has raised a genuine issue of material fact as to both exceptions.

A. Hybrid rights

. . . [T]he hybrid-rights theory "at least requires a colorable showing" of infringement of a companion constitutional right left open for later development the definition of "colorable" in this context.

In defining "colorability" for purposes of hybrid-rights claims, the Ninth Circuit has required the companion claim to have a "fair probability or a likelihood, but not a certitude, of success on the merits."

. . . Axson-Flynn urges us to adopt the more generous definition of "colorable" that was utilized by the district court, which only required the companion claim to be "non-frivolous." . . . The adoption of a "non-frivolous" standard would open the floodgates for hybrid-rights claims, as nearly every plaintiff with a free exercise claim would be able to assert an additional non-frivolous constitutional claim. We decline to allow such a result. . . .

On the other hand, it makes no sense to adopt a strict standard that essentially requires a *successful* companion claim because such a test would make the free exercise claim unnecessary. . . .

Therefore, we have chosen the middle ground of requiring the hybrid-rights claimant to show that the companion constitutional claim is "colorable." We define this to mean that the plaintiff must show a fair probability or likelihood, but not a certitude, of success on the merits. This inquiry is very fact-driven and must be used to examine hybrid rights on a case-by-case basis.

Because we are remanding on the free speech issue for fact development, we cannot at this point discern whether Axson-Flynn has a fair probability or likelihood of success on her pretext argument in her free speech claim. However, a remand as to this hybrid-rights issue would be pointless because, as we will explain in the last section of this opinion, although we are remanding Axson-Flynn's free exercise claim, Defendants are entitled to qualified immunity on the hybrid rights theory.

B. The individualized-exemption exception

We turn now to Axson-Flynn's argument that her case is covered by ". . . circumstances in which individualized exemptions from a general requirement are available . . . [whereby] . . . government may not refuse to extend that system to cases of religious hardship without compelling reason."

. . . .

Perhaps the best example of such a system, and indeed the one in which this exception originated, is a system of unemployment benefits which requires claimants to show "good cause" as to why they are unable to find work. In *Sherbert v. Verner*, 374 U.S. 398 (1963), a Seventh Day Adventist was fired by her employer because she refused to work on Saturdays, which her faith did not permit. Sherbert applied for unemployment benefits but was denied for failing to demonstrate "good cause" for her unemployment. The Supreme Court held that the denial of benefits violated the Free Exercise Clause because it "forced [Sherbert] to choose between following the precepts of her religion and forfeiting benefits, on the one hand, and abandoning one of the precepts of her religion in order to accept work, on the other hand."

. . . .

With this understanding of the "individualized exemption" exception, we now address whether Axson-Flynn's case falls within the exception. . . .

The syllabus for First-Year Acting (the ATP class that Axson-Flynn was taking in the fall of 1998) contained a curricular requirement to do improvisational work. However, a Jewish student named Jeremy Rische asked for and received permission to avoid doing an improvisational exercise on Yom Kippur without suffering adverse consequences. Defendant Barbara Smith, who taught First Year Acting, gave him this exemption despite the fact that, in Rische's words, "she said it would be an exercise that couldn't be made up, because it was one of the exercises by — an improv exercise that involved the whole class, and it would be almost impossible to make up." Rische was never penalized, his grades were never lowered, and he was never asked to make up the assignment in any way. Axson-Flynn argues that Defendants' willingness to grant an exemption to Rische demonstrates that the ATP had a system of individualized exemptions in place. That Defendants did not grant her an exemption, Axson-Flynn argues, constitutes "discrimination among members of different religious faiths" that violates the Free Exercise Clause.

When this evidence is coupled with the fact that Defendants sometimes granted Axson-Flynn herself an exemption from their script adherence requirement, we find that the record raises a material fact issue as to whether Defendants maintained a discretionary system of making individualized case-by-case determinations regarding who should receive exemptions from curricular requirements.

The "system of individualized exemptions" need not be a written policy, but rather the plaintiff may show a pattern of ad hoc discretionary decisions amounting to a "system." . . .

Because Axson-Flynn has raised a genuine issue of material fact as to whether Defendants maintained a discretionary system of case-by-case exemptions from curricular requirements, we hold that summary judgment on her free exercise "individualized exemption" claim was improper. Accordingly, we reverse and remand.

. . . .

CONCLUSION

For the foregoing reasons, we REVERSE . . . and REMAND for further proceedings.

NOTES

1. As you have gathered in this section of the chapter, courts are often as uncomfortable discussing precedent from K-12 education as they are comfortable applying it to higher education scenarios. Often, the distinctions made between K-12 and university contexts are made with respect to the age and maturity of the students involved, as well as the comparison between the compulsory nature of elementary and secondary education and the voluntary nature of post-secondary education. More often than not, when courts refrain from applying K-12 precedent to higher education cases, they do so because the students involved in university contexts are adults and generally work and study in more free environments. Judge Graber, however, in his opinion in *Brown v. Li*, makes an interesting statement about the strength of *Hazelwood's* applicability to higher education:

> [T]he curriculum of a public educational institution is one means by which the institution itself expresses its policy, a policy with which others do not have a constitutional right to interfere. The Supreme Court's jurisprudence does not hold that an institution's interest in mandating its curriculum and in limiting a student's speech to that which is germane to a particular *academic* assignment diminishes as students age. Indeed, arguably the need for academic discipline and editorial rigor increases as a student's learning progresses.

Instead of relaxing the application of legal principles based in K-12 education law, Judge Graber argues that the discretion offered to post-secondary academic decision making could, in fact, be higher than it is in K-12 education. Do you agree?

2. In *Axson-Flynn*, the court held that the classroom was a nonpublic forum, permitting the instructors to regulate student speech "in any reasonable manner." While the court upheld the decisions made by the academic leaders at the university here, reasonableness, in most cases, falls on a spectrum and does not dictate a particular response. So, what other reasonable actions could the instructors have made here? If you were the instructor of the course, would you have required Axson-Flynn to swear as part of the completion of her academic work? Would tolerating her refusal to say indecencies be reasonable, as well? Importantly, the court noted that it is common for teachers to require students to make and articulate, in writing or in spoken word, arguments on issues with which they disagree. These requests are generally defended as part of the mission to engage students in critical thinking and reflection. Does *Axson-Flynn* offer one of those examples? Continuing the discussion, what about the obligations educators have to safeguard the best interests of their students and to respect their requests when reasonable to do so? Of course, the court also stated that applying a less stringent free speech standard could give students veto power over the curriculum. Does the fact pattern in *Axson-Flynn* and the safeguarding of the curriculum as a whole present the strongest argument for the application of *Hazelwood* to higher education contexts?

3. So, with *Brown*, *Axson-Flynn*, *Kincaid v. Gibson* and *Hosty v. Carter*, presented in the Chapter on faculty speech, what is the state of affairs in the application of *Hazelwood v. Kuhlmeier* to the work of higher education? The court in *Axson-Flynn* and the lead opinion in *Brown* seemed to apply *Hazelwood* with ease, while the courts in *Brown*, *Kincaid* and *Hosty* engaged a longer, more complicated, and more controversial analyses. What primary factors did the courts in *Axson-Flynn* and *Brown* use to make the case? Where do you stand on the application of *Hazelwood* to student speech in academic contexts? Are university classrooms and other university-sponsored academic activities nonpublic forums?

4. The discussions in *Brown* and *Axson-Flynn* raise questions of the authority faculty members have to grade and assess student work. For more discussion of the legal rights faculty members have with respect to grading policy and faculty relationships with the university, that is, their academic freedom rights in grading, see *Brown v. Armenti*, 247 F.3d 69 (3d Cir. 2001) (upholding a university's suspension and ultimate termination of a faculty member who refused to follow an order to change the grade of a student); *Keen v. Penson*, 970 F.2d 252 (7th Cir. 1992) (upholding a university's decision to demote a faculty member in both salary and rank after he refused to change a student's grade and offer her an apology for the way he treated her in class); *Parate v. Isibor*, 868 F.2d 821 (6th Cir. 1989) (holding that the assignment of a letter grade is speech and is entitled to some measure of First Amendment protection); *Wozniak v. Conry*, 236 F.3d 888 (7th Cir. 2001) (upholding a university dean's decision to cancel the teaching responsibilities of a faculty member who refused to submit grading materials after reasonable requests that he do so). See also Chapter IV on faculty rights and responsibilities.

Chapter VII

STUDENT RIGHTS AND RESPONSIBILITIES

Introduction

The rights and responsibilities of students are mainly protected and created through constitutional and statutory avenues. This is by and large a mid-twentieth century phenomenon, and actions by legal authorities have given rise to a number of concerns in higher education. This chapter is devoted to the sometimes vague nature of college and university rules, academic dismissal, disciplinary dismissal, sexual harassment, and illegal searches and seizures.

Part A explores the rulemaking functions of institutions of higher education and introduces two legal concepts — vagueness and overbreadth — and applies them to both disciplinary and academic contexts. Vagueness and overbreadth are of significant concern to higher education policy makers, as it is critically important to draft and enact policies (e.g., student codes of conduct) that sufficiently define what conduct is expected or prohibited and, at the same time, do not prohibit conduct that would otherwise be lawful. A corollary to this balance is the struggle that college and university officials have when drafting policy specific enough to cover the desired ground, but not so specific that the policy is not useful in the future (e.g., a student code of conduct that is designed to apply to technological media not yet developed). Discussions across the three cases presented in Part A are similar in many regards, but also different in one important area: alleged vagueness of disciplinary rules (as we see with the word "misconduct" in *Soglin* and "potentially disruptive" in *Pro-Life Cougars*) is treated differently by the courts than alleged vagueness in academic policy or curriculum (as we see with "professional dispositions" in *Head*).

Part B continues the discussion of the important distinction the courts have drawn over the years between disciplinary decisions and academic decisions made by higher education professionals. Generally, disciplinary decisions in higher education are subject to a higher level of judicial scrutiny than academic decisions are, due in part to a recognition that academic professionals have a greater level of expertise in their content disciplines. Disciplinary decisions also carry with them measures of punishment more regularly understood by courts. In the discipline and due process divisions of this section, we explore definitions and applications of the traditional due process rights of life, liberty, and property (*Dixon* and *Goss*), and then explore applications of these concepts to student-centered due process systems (*Tigrett*), discipline of off-campus conduct and the technicalities required under the Fourteenth Amendment (*Flaim*), and the obligation a university has to comply with its own policies and procedures, however strict they are (*Denton*).

The academic due process section of the chapter opens with two classic Supreme

Court cases — *Board of Curators of the University of Missouri v. Horowitz* and *University of Michigan v. Ewing* — that further distinguish the due process rights and requirements across discipline and academic contexts. Once again, courts tend to employ a philosophy of judicial deference, allowing education professionals the discretion to make educational decisions, subject to lower levels of scrutiny than we see in disciplinary contexts. As much as courts attempt to differentiate between academics and discipline in due process discussions, readers are encouraged to consult the article excerpts from Fernand Dutile and Lisa Tenerowicz to evaluate whether such distinction is, in the end, persuasive.

Part C addresses gender discrimination against students. Complaints in this area of protection may be consigned under the Equal Protection Clause of the United States Constitution or Title IX of the Education Amendments of 1972. Title IX prohibits educational programs receiving federal funds from treating students unequally on the basis of sex. Two United States Supreme Court decisions, *Gebser v. Lago Vista School District* (staff to student discrimination) and *Davis v. Monroe County Board of Education* (student to student discrimination) are featured under the aegis of Title IX. While both cases target sexual harassment at the K-12 level, the findings of each serve as binding precedent for higher education. Also included in this section is a "Dear Colleague" letter produced by the Office of Civil Rights of the United States Department of Education. The Executive Opinion establishes student violence based on gender as a federal crime. The letter also clarifies the meaning of sexual violence and provides examples of bad acts that constitute a "crime of sexual violence."

Part D, the final section of Chapter VII, explores the application of Fourth Amendment search and seizure law to college campuses, both public and private. The section begins with coverage of two landmark Supreme Court opinions (*Chrisman* and *T.L.O.*). Primary attention, however, is paid to searches conducted in residence halls, with presentation of the time-honored opinion in *Piazzola* to more recent cases (*Limpuangthip* and *Devers*). The chapter concludes with examples of search and seizure in law enforcement contexts, academic settings, cyberspace, and drug testing.

A. RULEMAKING — VAGUENESS AND OVERBREADTH

1. Vagueness and Overbreadth Claims in Disciplinary Contexts

SOGLIN v. KAUFFMAN
418 F.2d 163 (7th Cir. 1969)

CUMMINGS, CIRCUIT JUDGE.

This is an appeal from a declaratory judgment that disciplinary proceedings of the University of Wisconsin instituted on the basis of alleged "misconduct" are unconstitutional.

The named plaintiffs are ten students at the Madison campus of the University of Wisconsin and the Madison chapter of the Students for a Democratic Society. . . . The defendants are various officials of the University of Wisconsin, the State of Wisconsin and the City of Madison allegedly involved in disciplinary actions on the Madison campus. . . .

On October 18, 1967, plaintiffs and others were protesting the presence of recruiting representatives of the Dow Chemical Corporation on the Madison campus. On the following day, the defendant Dean of Student Affairs wrote two of the plaintiffs and other "members of their class" that they were "suspended from the University pending a hearing before the Administrative Division of the Committee on Student Conduct and Appeals." The ground for the suspension was stated to be violation of Chapter 11.02 of the Laws and Regulations of the University of Wisconsin . . . , and the students were informed that a hearing date would be set at a later time. By letter of October 21, 1967, the chairman of the Administrative Division advised them that the hearing would be held on November 2, and that they would be permitted to attend classes and write examinations in the interim.

On November 1, some of the plaintiffs, as well as other individuals, received "Amended Charges" from the chairman of the Administrative Division. These charges specifically described the offensive conduct ascribed to plaintiffs, including the denial of others' rights to job interviews with the Dow Chemical Corporation by physical obstruction of the doorways and corridors of a university building. This behavior was characterized as "misconduct," as well as violative of Chapters 11.02 and 11.15 of the University Policies on the Use of Facilities and Outside Speakers. . . .

The complaint further alleged that some of the defendants had previously expelled two plaintiffs and another member of their class "by application of the doctrine of 'misconduct'," and were threatening to suspend or expel others for "misconduct." This doctrine was alleged to be so vague and overbroad as to violate the rights of plaintiffs under the First and Fourteenth Amendments. The complaint requested a declaratory judgment that the defendants' misconduct doctrine on its face violated the United States Constitution and prayed for an injunction against further application of that doctrine as the basis for disciplinary proceedings.

. . . .

The district court . . . held that the standard of misconduct alone may not serve as the foundation for the expulsion or suspension of students for any significant time. The court concluded that "misconduct", as so used, violates the Due Process Clause of the Fourteenth Amendment by reason of vagueness or, in the alternative, violates the First Amendment (as applied to the states by the Fourteenth Amendment) by reason of vagueness and overbreadth. Injunctive relief, however, was denied so that the University could have a reasonable time to readjust its regulations.

. . . The proper question here is whether defendants were depriving plaintiffs of any constitutional rights regardless of the character of their behavior. . . . This was not an abstract question, for plaintiffs were being charged with "misconduct" and threatened with punishment. . . .

. . . They are entitled to contend that the disciplinary proceedings were invalid deprivations of due process because based upon nonexistent or unconstitutionally vague standards. It is well settled that a statute threatening the exercise of First Amendment freedoms because of overbreadth is subject to attack. . . .

[We cannot agree] with defendants that [an] exception to standing requirements is limited to cases presenting challenges to criminal statutes. . . . Administrative sanctions as harsh as those available to the University in this case, as well as criminal statutes, serve to chill the exercise of free speech. It is accordingly immaterial that this controversy involves a disciplinary rule rather than a criminal statute.

Turning to the merits, defendants contend that the "misconduct" doctrine does not constitute a "standard" of conduct and that it was not employed as such. They argue that "misconduct" represents the inherent power of the University to discipline students and that this power may be exercised without the necessity of relying on a specific rule of conduct. This rationale would justify the *ad hoc* imposition of discipline without reference to any preexisting standards of conduct so long as the objectionable behavior could be called misconduct at some later date. No one disputes the power of the University to protect itself by means of disciplinary action against disruptive students. Power to punish and the rules defining the exercise of that power are not, however, identical. Power alone does not supply the standards needed to determine its application to types of behavior or specific instances of "misconduct." . . . The proposition that government officers, including school administrators, must act in accord with rules in meting out discipline is so fundamental that its validity tends to be assumed by courts engaged in assessing the propriety of specific regulations. The doctrines of vagueness and overbreadth, already applied in academic contexts, presuppose the existence of rules whose coherence and boundaries may be questioned. . . . University administrators are not immune from these requirements of due process in imposing sanctions. Consequently, in the present case, the disciplinary proceedings must fail to the extent that the defendant officials of the University of Wisconsin did not base those proceedings on the students' disregard of university standards of conduct expressed in reasonably clear and narrow rules.

Having specifically charged the students with the offense of "misconduct", the University may not now claim that misconduct was not employed as a standard. When tested as such, however, the term is clearly inadequate in view of constitutional requirements. . . .

The use of "misconduct" as a standard in imposing the penalties threatened here must therefore fall for vagueness. The inadequacy of the rule is apparent on its face. It contains no clues which could assist a student, an administrator or a reviewing judge in determining whether conduct not transgressing statutes is susceptible to punishment by the University as "misconduct." Since the misconduct standard is invalid on its face, it was unnecessary for the district court to make any findings with respect to plaintiffs' activities on October 18, 1967. . . .

It is not an adequate answer to contend, as do defendants, that the particular conduct which is the object of university discipline might have violated an applicable state or local law or otherwise merited punishment. The issue here is not the character of the student behavior but the validity of the administrative sanctions. Criminal laws carry their own definitions and penalties and are not enacted to enable a university to suspend or expel the wrongdoer absent a breach of a university's own rule. Nor is "misconduct" necessarily confined to disruptive actions covered by criminal codes. The ability to punish "misconduct" *per se* affords no safeguard against the imposition of disciplinary proceedings overreaching permissible limits and penalizing activities which are free from any taint of impropriety. Hence we feel compelled to strike down the University's reliance on the doctrine of misconduct in order to ensure that "reasonable regulation of speech-connected activities [of students remains confined to] carefully restricted circumstances." *Tinker v. Des Moines School District*, 393 U.S. 503, 513 [(1969)].

Pursuant to appropriate rule or regulation, the University has the power to maintain order by suspension or expulsion of disruptive students. Requiring that such sanctions be administered in accord with preexisting rules does not place an unwarranted burden upon university administrations. We do not require university codes of conduct to satisfy the same rigorous standards as criminal statutes. We only hold that expulsion and prolonged suspension may not be imposed on students by a university simply on the basis of allegations of "misconduct" without reference to any preexisting rule which supplies an adequate guide. . . .

Affirmed.

NOTES

1. In *Soglin*, the Seventh Circuit, in affirming a finding in favor of the plaintiff students on the grounds that the university rules were unconstitutionally vague, made the following statement: "Requiring that such sanctions be administered in accord with preexisting rules does not place an unwarranted burden upon university administrations." Readers will note that, in cases throughout this chapter and throughout this text, courts have generally deferred to the wisdom and expertise employed by university faculty and administrators. In other words, courts prefer not to intervene in the day-to-day decision making of university officials, unless such decisions sharply and noticeably implicate constitutional interests. What are the pros and cons to this practice of judicial deference?

2. In a case similar to *Soglin*, and decided in the same year, the Eighth Circuit Court of Appeals upheld a campus regulation against a claim of vagueness. In *Esteban v. Central Missouri State College*, 415 F.2d 1077 (8th Cir. 1969), *cert. denied*, 398 U.S. 965 (1970), two students were suspended for two semesters (with the opportunity to apply for readmission) after participating in large-group demonstrations on campus. Each one had been warned that participating would subject them to possible punishment. The plaintiffs argued that words and phrases like "unlawful," "unruly," "spectators," and "which might be considered" were unconstitutionally vague. The court disagreed. In its most blunt statement, the court said the following:

> [W]e do not find the regulation at all difficult to understand and we are positive the college student, who is appropriately expected to possess some minimum intelligence, would not find it difficult. It asks for the adherence to standards of conduct which befit a student and it warns of the danger of mass involvement. We must assume Esteban and Roberds can read and that they possess some power of comprehension. Their difficulty was that they chose not to read or not to comprehend.

Id. See also Sill v. The Penn. State Univ., 462 F.2d 463 (3d Cir. 1972) (finding campus disciplinary rules not void for vagueness or overbreadth).

3. What about a university rule that prohibits "hazing in all forms," but does not define the word "hazing" (and whose state's laws do not define it either)? The court in *Buttny v. Smiley*, 281 F. Supp. 280 (D. Colo. 1968), upheld this rule against a vagueness claim, relying especially on the university's inherent power to make and enforce rules for the safety and well-being of students. The court held that students of common intelligence would not have trouble understanding what conduct is prohibited, despite the lack of a detailed definition. The court, though, was not unsympathetic to the students' claims. However, on balance, it found the university's interests especially viable:

> We are not convinced that because there may be borderline cases the University officials must be denied the goals and protections they seek. Where there is doubt as to the nature of a student's activity we cannot assume that the disciplinary bodies will not accord them full protection. Regulations and rules which are necessary in maintaining order and discipline are always considered reasonable. . . . In fact the recent cases have not denied the validity and reasonableness of some very broad disciplinary regulations. In addition, it cannot be denied that university authorities have an inherent general power to maintain order on campus and to exclude those who are detrimental to its well being.

Id. at 285.

PRO-LIFE COUGARS v. UNIVERSITY OF HOUSTON

259 F. Supp. 2d 575 (S.D. Tex. 2003)

Opinion by: EWING WERLEIN, JR.

. . . .

I. Discussion

This civil rights action was brought under 42 U.S.C. § 1983 by Plaintiffs Pro-Life Cougars and Jeanne S. Tullos against the University of Houston, Dr. William F. Munson, the Assistant Vice President for Student Development and Dean of Students at the University, and Dr. Elwyn C. Lee, Vice President for Student Affairs at the University. Plaintiffs assert that the University has a speech policy in place that discriminates against student expression on campus that is deemed to be potentially disruptive. By this lawsuit, they seek both a declaration that the speech policy is unconstitutional under the First and Fourteenth Amendments to the United States Constitution and preliminary and permanent injunctions preventing Defendants from enforcing the policy against Plaintiffs on the University of Houston campus.

. . . [A]t the time of the events giving rise to this action the University required a student organization that desired to engage in organized expressive activities on the University campus to fill out forms entitled "UH Event Registration" and "University Center Reservation Request" forms. The forms require student organizations requesting permission to access the campus for expressive activities to provide a description of the proposed expressive activity as well as the location and date of the proposed event. For student expression that the University deems "potentially disruptive," the University further requires that student organizations follow the prerequisites listed under the "Disruption of University Operations and Events" policy. . . .

The "Disruption of University Operations and Events" policy in pertinent part provides:

> The right of peaceful expression and/or assembly within the university community must be preserved; however, the University has the right to provide for the safety of individuals, the protection of property, and the continuity of the educational process. The University will not permit any individual or group of individuals to disrupt or attempt to disrupt the operation and functioning of the University by any device, including, but not limited to, the use of pagers, cell phones, and other communication devices.
>
> At least two weeks prior to an event which is potentially disruptive, in addition to making the appropriate facility reservations, the sponsor of the event shall meet with the Dean of Students' designate to determine the time, place and manner of the event. Potentially disruptive events, including events where amplified sound is used outdoors, will be limited to the hours of 11:30 a.m. to 1 p.m. and 4 p.m. to midnight on class days. On non-class days, potentially disruptive events must be over by midnight. . . . Any exception to this policy must be approved by the Dean of Students.
>
> In emergency situations, the president or designated representatives have the responsibility to determine when the conditions cited above prevail and shall have the authority to take such steps as are deemed necessary and reasonable to quell or prevent such disruption.

Expressive activities sponsored by University student organizations that are not deemed to be "potentially disruptive" by Defendants are not required to submit to the same time, location, and content restrictions imposed on expressive activities deemed "potentially disruptive". . . .

On October 2001, in accordance with University policies, Plaintiffs applied for a permit to display their pro-life "Justice For All Exhibit" on Butler Plaza on the University campus. The exhibit was described as an outdoor photographic educational exhibit, presented on panels made of tough vinyl, braced with aluminum pipe, and weighted down with sandbags that require no digging or pegs being driven into the ground. In addition, the exhibit contained eight, two-sided signs, approximately 3 feet by 4 feet in size. The purpose of the exhibit, as described in Plaintiffs' event forms, was to promote "justice and the right to life for the unborn, the disabled, the infirm, the aged, and all vulnerable people; [to] help women and men in crisis pregnancies find support services for themselves and for their unborn children; [to promote] programs designed to assist in abortion recovery needs; [and to promote] discussion of related bio-ethical issues like stem cell research, in vitro-fertilization, RU 486, and 'emergency contraception.' "

Plaintiffs requested to display their exhibit on November 5-8, 2001, at any of three suggested grassy areas on Butler Plaza. Upon reviewing Plaintiffs' event forms, however, Dean Munson determined that the "Justice for All Exhibit" would be "potentially disruptive" and therefore denied Plaintiffs permission to present their exhibit on Butler Plaza. Having deemed Plaintiffs' exhibit "potentially disruptive," Dean Munson determined that the exhibit had to be relegated to one of two more remote sites that he suggested for "potentially disruptive" events. . . . Notably, a few months preceding Plaintiffs' request, the University had granted permission to the Free Speech Coalition, a different student organization, to display the same "Justice for All Exhibit" on Butler Plaza for three consecutive days during March 2001.

Plaintiffs declined to use either of the two alternate "potentially disruptive" event sites proposed by Dean Munson for the stated reasons that one site was too small for the exhibit, and the other site was too far removed from the part of campus where students congregate and was also obscured from view by trees. . . . Following Dean Munson's denial, Plaintiffs filed the present lawsuit seeking a declaration that the First Policy is unconstitutional under the First and Fourteenth Amendments to the United States Constitution and seeking preliminary and permanent injunctions preventing Defendants from enforcing the First Policy against Plaintiffs on the campus.

According to Plaintiffs, the Policy is unconstitutional because it is both a prior restraint and vests Dean Munson with unfettered discretion. . . . In addition, Plaintiffs argue that the Policy is overbroad and vague. Defendants respond that the First Policy is constitutional because it is a content and viewpoint neutral regulation of the time, place, and manner of expressive activities on the University campus.

. . . [T]he Court granted Plaintiffs' Motion for a Preliminary Injunction and ordered Defendants "to cease, desist, and refrain from acting under or invoking the authority of the Policy set forth at page 65 of the Student Handbook 2001-2002, entitled 'Disruption of University Operations and Events,' so as to impose any prior restraint on student expressive activity in Butler Plaza, a designated public forum on the main campus of the University of Houston." . . .

Defendants filed a Motion to Dissolve Preliminary Injunction and a Motion for Stay of Preliminary Injunction Pending Appeal, arguing that the . . . Preliminary Injunction as well as the question regarding the constitutionality of the University Policy became moot the day following the entry of the Order of Preliminary Injunction, because the President of the University . . . signed and formally approved a new speech policy that superseded the First Policy [the policy the plaintiffs challenge]. . . . [T]he Court denied both. . . .

. . . .

III. Discussion

A. Mootness

. . . Defendants maintain that the Court should not consider the constitutionality of the First Policy, because the University, after the Order of Preliminary Injunction issued, adopted a new and revised policy to replace the First Policy. Under the Second Policy, which had been under study and in preparation for some months before it was adopted, all student expressive activity, other than University sponsored events, is banned from Butler Plaza regardless of how quiet, small, or nondisruptive the expressive activity may be. Defendants therefore argue that Plaintiffs' constitutional challenge to the First Policy is moot.

. . . .

On the one hand, Defendants argue that the challenge to the First Policy is moot, but on the other, they continue vigorously to defend the constitutionality of the First Policy. As they have stated in the past and continue to argue in their opposition to Plaintiffs' Motion for Summary Judgment, Defendants "did not, and do not concede the unconstitutionality of the prior Policy." Moreover, following the Court's Order of Preliminary Injunction, Defendants filed an appeal to the Fifth Circuit Court of Appeals challenging the Court's prior rulings and defending the constitutionality of the First Policy Defendants now contend they will not re-adopt. Defendants' persistent defense of the constitutionality of the First Policy, and the power of the University to re-enact it, prevents the Court from finding that the constitutional question is moot. . . .

B. Constitutional Challenge

. . . Defendants assert that Butler Plaza is a limited public forum and that as such they are allowed to impose greater speech restrictions than otherwise allowed for public forums. Plaintiffs on the other hand, argue that the University and in particular Butler Plaza, are traditional public fora. The distinction is significant. . . . [T]he constitutionality of speech restrictions in a limited public forum are judged under the reasonableness standard, while speech restrictions in a traditional or designated public forum are subject to strict scrutiny.

To determine whether a forum is either a limited non-public forum or a designated public forum, a court should consider two factors: (1) the government's intent with respect to the forum; and (2) the nature of the forum and its compatibility with the speech at issue. Moreover, government owned property is considered a traditional public forum when the property has been traditionally used by the public for assembly and debate or when the government intentionally has opened up a non-public forum for public discourse.

The University is a large state university with its main campus within a few miles of downtown Houston. On the campus are many streets, parking facilities, sidewalks and walkways, various stadiums and sports arenas, theaters, bookstores, convenience stores, some 25 restaurants, a Hilton Hotel, and numerous park-like plazas, nearly all of which facilities are open and accessible not only to students and faculty but also to the general public. Approximately 3,000 students live on campus in six resident dormitories. Within the University is Butler Plaza, a plaza that is approximately four acres in size and is centrally located on the University main campus.

Defendants admit that they purposefully opened up Butler Plaza as a forum for student expression. . . . Dean Munson . . . testified at the preliminary injunction hearing . . . that . . . Butler Plaza has been a site used for student expressive activities on campus and that as far back as he can remember, there has been a student expressive event on Butler Plaza on average about once every other month.

This uncontroverted evidence compels the conclusion that both the University, and in particular Butler Plaza, are public fora designated for student speech. . . .

Any restriction imposed by the University on student expressive activity on Butler Plaza must therefore be analyzed under the strict scrutiny standard as opposed to the reasonableness standard suggested by Defendants. Under the strict scrutiny standard, a content-neutral regulation of speech on a public forum "must be narrowly tailored to serve a significant government interest and must leave open ample alternative channels of communication." *Hays* [v. *County Guardian v. Supple*, 969 F.2d 111, 118 (5th Cir. 1992).] "A regulation is 'narrowly tailored' when it does not 'burden substantially more speech than is necessary to further the government's legitimate interests.' " *Id.* . . .

. . . .

Plaintiffs maintain that the University First Policy is unconstitutional because it is a prior restraint and vests Dean Munson with unfettered discretion. The First Policy, as previously observed, provides that a student organization that wishes to use Butler Plaza as a forum for expressive activity must first submit to the University an application for approval. If the University official, in this case, Dean Munson, determines that the proposed expressive activity is "potentially disruptive," the application will not be approved and the student activity will be banned from Butler Plaza. In that respect, the First Policy constitutes a prior restraint. Although prior restraints are not *per se* unconstitutional, the First Policy lacks the procedural safeguards necessary to survive a constitutional challenge.

. . . [T]he First Policy on its face is devoid of any objective guidelines or articulated standards that Dean Munson should consider when determining whether any given student expressive activity should be deemed "potentially disruptive." Under the First Policy, every time a student organization applies for a permit to use Butler Plaza, Dean Munson, *in his sole discretion and without the aid of objective guidelines*, is free to determine whether the proposed student expressive activity is or is not "potentially disruptive." Dean Munson is not required to provide an explanation for his decision. Nor is his decision reviewable. Therefore, under the First Policy, Dean Munson is empowered arbitrarily to deny access to Butler Plaza to students whose expressive activity *he* may deem offensive or undesirable. Such unbridled discretion renders the First Policy unconstitutional. . . .

While Defendants respond that Dean Munson has applied the First Policy in a content-neutral manner and would continue to do so, the Supreme Court has held that "the success of a facial challenge on the grounds that an ordinance delegates overly broad discretion to the decisionmaker rests not on whether the administrator has exercised his discretion in a content-based manner, but whether there is anything in the ordinance preventing him from doing so." *Forsyth County*, 112 S. Ct. at 2403 n.10. . . . In this case, neither the language of the First Policy nor the application of the same support the conclusion that there are narrowly drawn, reasonable, and definite standards guiding the hand of the University official. Moreover, Defendants' argument that Dean Munson considers only content-neutral factors when applying the First Policy presumes that Dean Munson will act in good faith and adhere to standards absent from the ordinance's face. . . .

The First Policy also is not narrowly tailored to serve a significant governmental interest. To be narrowly tailored, a speech regulation must not burden substantially more speech than is necessary to further the stated legitimate governmental interest, which in this case is the preservation of the University's academic mission. . . .

Dean Munson testified that he would regard as "potentially disruptive" even the silent and nondisruptive expression of a single student on Butler Plaza holding a small sign proclaiming "The World is a Beautiful Place." Further, in keeping with his finding that *all* expressive activity on Butler Plaza is "potentially disruptive," Dean Munson testified that during the holiday season, he ordered removed from Butler Plaza a Christmas tree which carried with it some cheerful note of Season's Greetings for University students. The uncontroverted exercise of such sweeping power illustrates the unconstitutionality of the First Policy and Dean Munson's failure to adhere to the constitutional requirement that regulation of speech in a public forum be narrowly tailored and not burden more speech than is necessary to further the stated legitimate governmental interest.

. . . .

For the foregoing reasons, the First Policy fails to pass constitutional muster under the First and Fourteenth Amendments to the United States Constitution. Accordingly, Plaintiffs' Motion for Summary Judgment will be granted.

. . . .

NOTE

The "First Policy," at issue in *Pro-Life Cougars*, gave Dean Munson sole discretion to determine whether the proposed student expressive activity was "potentially disruptive." The court ultimately held that the policy gave too much discretion to one person "without the aid of objective guidelines." Do you agree with this finding? What are the drawbacks of such judicial reasoning? Is there not a significant danger in discounting administrative discretion, even in light of free speech rights? How can university policymakers and administrators inject enough detailed guidelines and process without causing their policies to become formulaic? What discretion does the "First Policy" allow?

2. Vagueness and Overbreadth Claims in Academic Contexts

HEAD v. BOARD OF TRUSTEES OF CALIFORNIA STATE UNIVERSITY

No. H029129, 2007 Cal. App. Unpub. LEXIS 393
(Cal. Ct. App. Jan. 18, 2007)

Opinion by: ELIA

Stephen Head, who was a student in San Jose State University's teaching credential program, filed a "petition for writ of mandate and/or prohibition or other relief" against respondents California State University's Board of Trustees, San Jose State University's Interim President Don W. Kassing, Dean Susan Meyers of the University's School of Education, Associate Professor and Chair of the Department of Secondary Education Cathy Buell, and Associate Professor Helen Kress. Head sought review of the university's denial of a revised October 28, 2004 grievance filed with the university in regard to a course entitled "Social, Philosophical and Multicultural Foundations of Secondary Education" (EDSC 172A), which had been taught by respondent Kress in the fall 2003 semester. The grievance challenged the curriculum, his assigned grade, and the treatment he received during the course. It also challenged, on free speech and due process vagueness grounds, the Secondary Education Department's "professional dispositions," which candidates in the teaching credential program are expected to demonstrate as they progress through the single subject credential program.

Appellant Head's grievance had been rejected by the university's Student Fairness Committee (SFC). One of the responsibilities of the SFC is to hear "complaints of violations of student rights in instructional and curricular matters, including grade appeals. . . ." The SFC denied appellant's grievance petition, finding, among other things, that appellant had not shown his right to free speech had been violated or he was entitled to a change of grade.

Appellant Head's petition sought, among other relief, a judicial order requiring the university to change his grade to an "A" or a "B." . . . [H]e also sought to enjoin (1) the use or enforcement of the "professional dispositions," (2) the infringement of teaching credential students' constitutionally protected speech, and (3) grade discrimination against "White, White-appearing or male" candidates. In his petition, appellant described himself as "a person who holds generally libertarian or conservative beliefs and viewpoints" and "who may appear White." The trial court denied relief on appellant's petition.

Head appeals, claiming that the university's actions deprived him of substantive and procedural due process and the "professional dispositions," which he labeled "student speech codes," are unconstitutionally vague and constituted compelled speech and viewpoint discrimination in violation of the First Amendment right to free speech and Education Code section 66301. . . . We affirm. . . .

A. *Record on Appeal*

In his declaration supporting his petition, appellant Head provided a number of excerpts from instructional materials used in the course. They related to, among other things, culturally sensitive teaching methodology, White preservice teachers' lack of understanding of, and experience with, cultural differences, racism, and discrimination, and the inability of a color blind approach to address these problems. Head also referred to respondent Kress's handout regarding multiculturalism and indicated that respondent Kress had failed to define the meaning of the words "promoting alternative life styles" as used in the handout and expressly disallowed him from citing certain individuals who "contested" multiculturalism in class discussions and class work.

Appellant Head also described a number of other interactions with respondent Kress. He described an incident occurring on October 4, 2003 after the class viewed a videotape regarding discrimination in modern day California. According to Head, he voiced his opinion that immigrants were "generally better off in the United States than in their native countries by way of the greater opportunities afforded by a comparatively better form of government in the United States" and respondent Kress responded by saying, " 'When I hear such opinions coming from someone, it makes me think that that person is unfit to teach.' " Head also reported that on October 18, 2003, he was told by respondent Kress, in regard to an assignment, that it was " 'inadvisable' " for him to focus on a White female student who was prevented from forming a "Caucasian Club" at her high school because "the [W]hite female student was not being discriminated against. . . , and even if she was being discriminated against, it did not matter, since non-Hispanic White Europeans comprised the 'dominant power structure' in the U.S. society and . . . did not qualify for being the focus of the assignment. . . ."

In his declaration, appellant Head stated that he filed a complaint regarding the October 4, 2003 incident with the university's police on October 21, 2003. Head reported receiving an e-mail message from respondent Kress on October 27, 2003 offering to discuss the Secondary Education dispositions to which she had referred in class and informing Head that "[s]o far this semester I have not seen you make progress on displaying these dispositions in our class and I want to know why not and how I can help you with these."

Head also indicated in his declaration that he received an "F" in the course and was placed on academic probation, which prevented him from taking EDSC 184X, the required student teaching course, in Spring 2004. He stated he submitted a "revised complaint, grievance, and appeal" on October 28, 2004, he presented his case to a two-member subcommittee of the University's SFC on November 30, 2004, and he presented his case to the full SFC on December 15, 2004.

The declaration of the University Ombudsman Savander Parker was submitted in opposition to the petition. She received appellant's formal, written grievance from appellant on October 28, 2004. In the grievance, appellant . . . complained that he had suffered a hostile educational environment in the class, violations of his First Amendment rights to free speech, discrimination on the basis of race, and violations of his right as a student to take reasoned exception to the data and views offered in the course. He also asserted, based upon the title of a 2002 conference paper written by professor Kress, that instructor Kress "had a disposition towards discrimination" and she "harbor[ed] hostility towards a concept of multiculturalism and diversity among teachers which is inclusive of 'Whiteness' . . . ."

In his grievance, Head complained that he had been "barred from using conservative and libertarian sources in class discussions and work. . . ." He asserted that the e-mail from respondent Kress indicating that he had not made progress on displaying the professional dispositions could have a chilling effect on students' freedom of speech. He also contended, among other things, that his First Amendment rights were violated by "the existence and threat of enforcement of speech codes in the form of the Secondary Education Department 'Professional Dispositions,' " and those dispositions "require[] that teacher credential students adopt a particular set of beliefs" and are "indistinguishable from 'thought control.' "

The administrative record contains the Secondary Education Department's "professional dispositions." The Department states that candidates for a single subject credential are expected to demonstrate "professional dispositions as they progress through course work and field work experiences." Those "professional dispositions" are reflectiveness, responsibility, commitment to professionalism, and commitment to fairmindedness and equity and are accompanied by "indicators" for assessing student progress. In the category of reflectiveness, some of the specified indicators are "[q]uestions own beliefs and practices," "[p]ractices critical questioning," and is "responsive to opposing views" and "criticism." In the category of commitment to fairmindedness and equity, the indicators are "[t]reats others with equal respect, courtesy, and dignity," "[i]s intolerant of any form of harassment, discrimination, and exploitation," and "[r]ecognizes the need for differences to ensure equal treatment of all."

. . . .

Ombudsman Parker indicated in her declaration that a SFC subcommittee, consisting of faculty member Marty Froomin and a student, investigated appellant's complaints and then submitted a written report summarizing its findings and making a recommendation to the SFC. The report indicated that the subcommittee had met with the parties and had reviewed the student's work and had "noted dates of submission and instructor comments." The report stated that the subcommittee found no evidence to support a claim that marks were assigned based upon criteria other than academic performance and no evidence that grading was based on student Head's personal views. Professor Kress had shown that "student's work does not demonstrate appropriate knowledge of the subject material". . . .

The investigative subcommittee . . . recommended that the grievance be denied.

Ombudsman Parker indicated that appellant's case came before the SFC during a regular meeting of the SFC on December 15, 2004. . . . After a brief discussion, the SFC denied the grievance and confirmed that a grade change should not be granted. Three faculty members in the College of Education and the College of Science abstained.

A letter from the university's ombudsperson informed appellant that the SFC had denied his grievance petition and closed his case. The letter stated that the SFC had not found evidence that appellant's marks had been based on criteria other than academic performance. . . .

. . . .

In opposition to appellant's petition, the university also filed California State University Chancellor's Executive Order 792. That executive order establishes guiding principles governing assignment of grades and grade appeals, including "a presumption that grades assigned are correct" and that "[i]t is the responsibility of anyone appealing an assigned grade to demonstrate otherwise." . . . "[In the] absence of compelling reasons, such as instructor or clerical error, prejudice or capriciousness, the grade assigned by the instructor of record is to be considered final." . . .

Following a hearing, the trial court denied appellant's petition. It stated: "Contrary to the claim of petitioner, the administrative record confirms that his due process rights were assiduously protected and that he was accorded the benefit of appropriate administrative due process. There is no evidence or showing that the decision of the Student Fairness Committee was arbitrary, capricious, or lacking in evidentiary support." . . .

. . . .

C. *Substantive Due Process*

Appellant Head argues that he is entitled to judicial relief because he was denied substantive due process. He contends that he was deprived of due process by the enforcement of an unconstitutionally vague and discriminatory "speech code" and by respondents giving him "failing grades and prevent[ing] him from further pursuing his teaching credential based on his exercise of free speech, his race and/or in retaliation for his filing a faculty complaint" against respondent Kress. We find no basis for overturning the SFC's decision on substantive due process grounds.

. . . .

In *Board of Curators of University of Missouri v. Horowitz* [(1978)] 435 U.S. 78, the U.S. Supreme Court, in finding no showing of arbitrariness or capriciousness had been made in that case, observed that "[c]ourts are particularly ill-equipped to evaluate academic performance." (*Id.* at p. 92.) The high court emphasized the subjective and evaluative nature of academic decision-making and central role of the faculty-student relationship in the educational process and indicated that these factors warned against "judicial intrusion into academic decisionmaking." (*Id.* at pp. 89–92.) The U.S. Supreme Court has also stated: " 'University faculties must have the widest range of discretion in making judgments as to the academic performance of students and their entitlement to promotion or graduation.' *Board of Curators, Univ. of Mo. v. Horowitz*, 435 U.S. 78, 96, n. 6, . . . (Powell, J., concurring). . . .

. . . .

The record does not establish that the SFC acted arbitrarily or capriciously in not finding that the challenged instruction constituted reverse discrimination against Whites. . . . Nothing in the record establishes that the chosen course curriculum did not reflect legitimate sociological theories and philosophies of education recognized within the academic community. In addition, appellant has not pointed to any evidence in the record showing that respondent Kress had an impermissible discriminatory or retaliatory purpose in grading appellant or that the academic reasons given for the failing grade in respondent Kress's class were a pretext.

Appellant Head more specifically attacks the SFC's determination regarding his right to free speech. . . . He suggests that his prohibited speech was relevant to the discussions but disallowed "because . . . the professor's enforcement of the Speech Code prohibited those views from debate." He also states that respondent Kress "refused to grade most, if not all," of his course work because she "disagreed with the views, opinions, analysis or conclusions contained therein," and required him to "conform with the Speech Code and [respondent Kress's] radical political preferences, opinions, and points of view." He asserts that he was given D's and F's because "resubmitted work still did not conform to the Speech Code's vague standards and mandates and [respondent Kress's] worldview. . . ."

Appellant Head also contends that the professional dispositions are unconstitutionally vague, unconstitutionally compel speech, and unconstitutionally discriminate on the basis of viewpoint, and violate Education Code section 66301. Although it is not clear from the record that the "professional dispositions" directly impacted appellant's grade, we consider appellant's free speech claims, keeping in mind that the ultimate question is whether the SFC acted arbitrarily or capriciously.

We begin by noting that "the First Amendment does not guarantee the right to communicate one's views at all times and places or in any manner that may be desired. *Adderley v. Florida*, 385 U.S. 39, 47–48 (1966); *Poulos v. New Hampshire*, 345 U.S. 395, 405 (1953). . . . For one thing, a university classroom where instruction is taking place is not a public forum.

. . . .

An instructor may exercise reasonable control over student expression during class to ensure, among other things, students learn whatever lessons are being taught. . . . Public university instructors are not required by the First Amendment to provide class time for students to voice views that contradict the material being taught or interfere with instruction or the educational mission. Although the First Amendment may require an instructor to allow students to express opposing views and values to some extent where the instructor invites expression of students' personal opinions and ideas, nothing in the First Amendment prevents an instructor from refocusing classroom discussions and limiting students' expression to effectively teach.

A university's "students are inevitably required to support the expression of personally offensive viewpoints in ways that cannot be thought constitutionally objectionable unless one is prepared to deny the University its choice over what to teach." (*Board of Regents of University of Wisconsin System v. Southworth* (2000) 529 U.S. 217, 242–243, opn. of Sutter J. concurring in judgment.) Courts have recognized that a school may compel some speech for legitimate pedagogical purposes by requiring, for example, that a student "write a paper on a particular topic even if the student would prefer to write on a different topic." (*C.N. v. Ridgewood Bd. of Educ.* (3d Cir. 2005) 430 F.3d 159, 178.) Similarly, an instructor at a public school may require student expression, oral or written, to assess whether instructional materials have been adequately mastered.

Furthermore, . . . [a] university is entitled to set its own curriculum and its selection of course materials will express the academic ideas and values that it wishes to inculcate.

In this case, the university's Secondary Education Department had adopted a philosophy of education and established explicit "professional dispositions" that candidates in the Single Subject Credential Program were expected to demonstrate. A university's standards of academic competence are set by a subjective expert evaluation. As previously indicated, judicial deference is generally accorded to academic decision-making. . . .

Although appellant has labeled the university's "professional dispositions" a "speech code," they are not administrative regulations governing students' speech or conduct, the violation of which might subject a student to disciplinary sanction. They are academic standards established by the university's Secondary Education Department. They aim in part in producing credentialed teachers who have particular conceptual understandings and approaches to teaching that the university has impliedly determined will make students more effective educators. Nothing in the First Amendment precludes the university from prescribing the academic standards that must be met to obtain a teaching credential from that institution.

Appellant has not shown that the due process vagueness doctrine invalidates the "professional dispositions." "It is a basic principle of due process that an enactment is void for vagueness if its prohibitions are not clearly defined. Vague laws offend several important values. First, because we assume that [an individual] is free to steer between lawful and unlawful conduct, we insist that laws give the person of ordinary intelligence a reasonable opportunity to know what is prohibited, so that [the person] may act accordingly. Vague laws may trap the innocent by not providing fair warning. Second, if arbitrary and discriminatory enforcement is to be prevented, laws must provide explicit standards for those who apply them. A vague law impermissibly delegates basic policy matters to policemen, judges, and juries for resolution on an ad hoc and subjective basis, with the attendant dangers of arbitrary and discriminatory application. Third, but related, where a vague statute 'abut(s) upon sensitive areas of basic First Amendment freedoms', it 'operates to inhibit the exercise of (those) freedoms.' Uncertain meanings inevitably lead citizens to 'steer far wider of the unlawful zone' . . . than if the boundaries of the forbidden areas were clearly marked." (*Grayned v. City of Rockford* (1972) 408 U.S. 104, 108–109.) As already stated, however, the university's professional dispositions are neither a statute nor an administrative rule, regulation or policy, violation of which could result in punishment or disciplinary action against a student. . . .

Moreover, even if due process vagueness principles apply to academic standards, due process does not demand the clarity required for a criminal statute. . . . A fortiori, assuming due process vagueness doctrine is even applicable to academic standards not carrying the threat of disciplinary sanction, those academic standards are not required to achieve the standard of clarity required of penal statutes or even disciplinary rules. Although the "professional dispositions" reflect abstract ideas, we conclude that they are sufficiently clear, especially as elucidated by the more concrete "indicators," to meet the minimum requirements of due process that might be applicable to academic standards.

Neither has appellant shown that the "professional dispositions" unconstitutionally compel speech even though he argues they do by requiring "credential students to declare and commit to a pre-approved set of beliefs, values and attitudes towards particular subjects, including controversial and unsettled subjects or concepts like 'social justice,' 'equity' and 'multiculturalism' . . . ."

We discern nothing in First Amendment jurisprudence that precludes a public university from adopting, in its exercise of its academic freedom, academic standards that must be satisfied by a student seeking a professional teaching credential even where those standards reflect a certain philosophy of education or academic viewpoints with which a student vehemently disagrees. Obviously, if so-called academic standards were *not* based upon legitimate pedagogical grounds that would be an altogether different matter but the record before us does not demonstrate that is the situation here.

. . . .

In sum, appellant has not established the trial court erred in denying relief. . . . [A]ffirmed.

NOTES

1. The *Head* decision speaks of a general document containing "professional dispositions" for preservice teachers. The plaintiff claims that this document compelled certain speech and violated his First Amendment rights. The court held that the "professional dispositions" and their associated indicators were not unconstitutionally vague. In fact, the court stated that these dispositions were not a part of any administrative rule or regulation that would subject a student to discipline if they were violated; they were merely reasonable academic standards to be accorded a measure of respect. What is the implication of such a case for related claims against a university's mission statements, vision statements, or core values (e.g., respect for one another; creativity and innovation; citizenship, diversity, and leadership in a global society)? Can a similar argument be made that these statements are unenforceable?

2. The plaintiff in *Head* was an undergraduate education major. What about the application of honor codes and professional dispositions in traditional graduate and professional schools? Should the level of education make a difference in the applicability of such provisions? Cases challenging these types of codes are relatively popular with law schools. *See, e.g., Warren v. Drake Univ.*, 886 F.2d 200 (8th Cir. 1989) (law student dismissed after credit card fraud conviction; the provisions of the handbook, honor code, and university catalog created a contract between student and institution, and suspensions, expulsions, and dismissals may be warranted when students violate the contract); *In re Watts*, 557 A.2d 601 (D.C.C. App. 1989) (law student convicted of felony thefts; his case for bar admission was remanded for an independent investigation); *In re Petition of Zbiegnien*, 433

N.W.2d 871 (Minn. Sup. Ct. 1988) (a single incident of plagiarism in a law class did not constitute lack of fitness for bar).

B. DISCIPLINARY AND ACADEMIC GRIEVANCE PROCEDURES

1. Due Process in Discipline

DIXON v. ALABAMA STATE BOARD OF EDUCATION

294 F.2d 150 (5th Cir.), *cert. denied*, 368 U.S. 930 (1961)

Opinion by: Rives

The question presented by the pleadings and evidence, and decisive of this appeal, is whether due process requires notice and some opportunity for hearing before students at a tax-supported college are expelled for misconduct. We answer that question in the affirmative.

The misconduct for which the students were expelled has never been definitely specified. Defendant Trenholm, the President of the College, testified that he did not know why the plaintiffs and three additional students were expelled and twenty other students were placed on probation. The notice of expulsion which Dr. Trenholm mailed to each of the plaintiffs assigned no specific ground for expulsion, but referred in general terms to 'this problem of Alabama State College.'

The acts of the students considered by the State Board of Education before it ordered their expulsion are described in the opinion of the district court reported in 186 F. Supp. 954, 947, from which we quote in the margin.[3]

---

[3] 'On the 25th day of February, 1960, the six plaintiffs in this case were students in good standing at the Alabama State College for Negroes in Montgomery, Alabama. . . . On this date, approximately twenty-nine Negro students, including these six plaintiffs, according to a prearranged plan, entered as a group a publicly owned lunch grill located in the basement of the county courthouse in Montgomery, Alabama, and asked to be served. Service was refused; the lunchroom was closed; the Negroes refused to leave; police authorities were summoned; and the Negroes were ordered outside where they remained in the corridor of the courthouse for approximately one hour. On the same date, John Patterson, as Governor of the State of Alabama and as chairman of the State Board of Education, conferred with Dr. Trenholm, a Negro educator and president of the Alabama State College, concerning this activity on the part of some of the students. Dr. Trenholm was advised by the Governor that the incident should be investigated, and that if he were in the president's position he would consider expulsion and/or other appropriate disciplinary action. On February 26, 1960, several hundred Negro students from the Alabama State College, including several if not all of these plaintiffs, staged a mass attendance at a trial being held in the Montgomery County Courthouse, involving the perjury prosecution of a fellow student. After the trial these students filed two by two from the courthouse and marched through the city approximately two miles back to the college. On February 27, 1960, several hundred Negro students from this school, including several if not all of the plaintiffs in this case, staged mass demonstrations in Montgomery and Tuskegee, Alabama. On this same date, Dr. Trenholm advised all of the student body that these demonstrations and meetings were disrupting the orderly conduct of the business at the college and were affecting the work of other students, as well as work of the participating students. Dr. Trenholm personally warned plaintiffs Bernard Lee, Joseph Peterson and Elroy Embry, to cease these disruptive demonmembers immediately, and advised the members of the student body at the Alabama

As shown by the findings of the district court, just quoted in footnote 3, the only demonstration which the evidence showed that all of the expelled students took part in was that in the lunch grill located in the basement of the Montgomery County Courthouse. The other demonstrations were found to be attended 'by several if not all of the plaintiffs.' We have carefully read and studied the record, and agree with the district court that the evidence does not affirmatively show that all of the plaintiffs were present at any but the one demonstration.

Only one member of the State Board of Education assigned the demonstration attended by all of the plaintiffs as the sole basis for his vote to expel them. Mr. Harry Ayers testified:

'Q. Mr. Ayers, did you vote to expel these negro students because they went to the Court House and asked to be served at the white lunch counter? A. No, I voted because they violated a law of Alabama.

'Q. What law of Alabama had they violated? A. That separating of the races in public places of that kind.

'Q. And the fact that they went up there and requested service, by violating the Alabama law, then you voted to have them expelled? A. Yes.

'Q. And that is your reason why you voted? A. That is the reason.'

The most elaborate grounds for expulsion were assigned in the testimony of Governor Patterson:

'Q. There is an allegation in the complaint, Governor, that . . . the defendants' action of expulsion was taken without regard to any valid rule or regulation concerning student conduct and merely retaliated against, punished, and sought to intimidate plaintiffs for having lawfully sought service in a publicly owned lunch room with service; is that statement true or false?

'A. Well, that is not true; the action taken by the State Board of Education was — was taken to prevent — to prevent incidents happening by students at the College that would bring — bring discredit upon — upon the School and be prejudicial to the School, and the State — as I said before, the State Board of Education took — considered at the time it expelled these students several incidents, one at the Court House at the lunch room demonstration, the one the next day at the trial of this student, the marching on the steps of the State Capitol, and also this rally held at the church, where — where it was reported that — that statements were made against the administration of the School. In addition to that, the — the feeling going around in the community here due to — due to the

State College to behave themselves and return to their classes. . . .

'On or about March 1, 1960, approximately six hundred students of the Alabama State College engaged in hymn singing and speech making on the steps of the State Capitol. Plaintiff Bernard Lee addressed students at this demonstration, and the demonstration was attended by several if not all of the plaintiffs. Plaintiff Bernard Lee at this time called on the students to strike and boycott the college if any students were expelled because of these demonstrations.'

> reports of these incidents of the students, by the students, and due to reports of incidents occurring involving violence in other States, which happened prior to these things starting here in Alabama, all of these things were discussed by the State Board of Education prior to the taking of the action that they did on March 2 and as I was present and acting as Chairman, as a member of the Board, I voted to expel these students and to put these others on probation because I felt that that was what was in the best interest of the College. And the — I felt that the action should be — should be prompt and immediate, because if something — something had not been done, in my opinion, it would have resulted in violence and disorder, and that we wanted to prevent, and we felt that we had a duty to the — to the — to the parents of the students and to the State to require that the students behave themselves while they are attending a State College, and that is (sic) the reasons why we took the action that we did. That is all.'

Superintendent of Education Stewart testified that he voted for expulsion because the students had broken rules and regulations pertaining to all of the State institutions, and, when required to be more specific, testified:

> 'The Court: What rule had been broken is the question, that justified the expulsion insofar as he is concerned?
>
> 'A. I think demonstrations without the consent of the president of an institution.'

The testimony of other members of the Board assigned somewhat varying and differing grounds and reasons for their votes to expel the plaintiffs.

The district court found the general nature of the proceedings before the State Board of Education, the action of the Board, and the official notice of expulsion given to the students as follows:

> 'Investigations into this conduct were made by Dr. Trenholm, as president of the Alabama State College, the Director of Public Safety for the State of Alabama under directions of the Governor, and by the investigative staff of the Attorney General for the State of Alabama.
>
> 'On or about March 2, 1960, the State Board of Education met and received reports from the Governor of the State of Alabama, which reports embodied the investigations that had been made and which reports identified these six plaintiffs, together with several others, as the 'ring leaders' for the group of students that had been participating in the above-recited activities. During this meeting, Dr. Trenholm, in his capacity as president of the college reported to the assembled members of the State Board of Education that the action of these students in demonstrating on the college campus and in certain downtown areas was having a disruptive influence on the work of the other students at the college and upon the orderly operation of the college in general. Dr. Trenholm further reported to the Board that, in his opinion, he as president of the college could not control future disruptions and demonstrations. There were twenty-nine of

> the Negro students identified as the core of the organization that was responsible for these demonstrations. This group of twenty-nine included these six plaintiffs. After hearing these reports and recommendations and upon the recommendation of the Governor as chairman of the Board, the Board voted unanimously, expelling nine students, including these six plaintiffs, and placing twenty students on probation. This action was taken by Dr. Trenholm as president of the college, acting pursuant to the instructions of the State Board of Education. Each of these plaintiffs, together with the other students expelled, was officially notified of his expulsion on March 4th or 5th, 1960. No formal charges were placed against these students and no hearing was granted any of them prior to their expulsion.' *Dixon v. Alabama State Board of Education*, D.C.M.D.Ala.1960, 186 F.Supp. 945, 948, 949.

The evidence clearly shows that the question for decision does not concern the sufficiency of the notice or the adequacy of the hearing, but is whether the students had a right to any notice or hearing whatever before being expelled. . . . After careful study and consideration, we find ourselves unable to agree with the conclusion of the district court that no notice or opportunity for any kind of hearing was required before these students were expelled.

. . . .

Whenever a governmental body acts so as to injure an individual, the Constitution requires that the act be consonant with due process of law. The minimum procedural requirements necessary to satisfy due process depend upon the circumstances and the interests of the parties involved. . . .

. . . .

It is not enough to say, as did the district court in the present case, "The right to attend a public college or university is not in and of itself a constitutional right." That argument was emphatically answered by the Supreme Court in the *Cafeteria and Restaurant Workers Union* case, *supra*, (81 S.Ct. 1748) when it said that the question of whether ". . . summarily denying Rachel Brawner access to the site of her former employment violated the requirements of the Due Process Clause of the Fifth Amendment . . . cannot be answered by easy assertion that, because she had no constitutional right to be there in the first place, she was not deprived of liberty or property by the Superintendent's action. 'One may not have a constitutional right to go to Bagdad, but the Government may not prohibit one from going there unless by means consonant with due process of law.' " As in that case, so here, it is necessary to consider "the nature both of the private interest which has been impaired and the governmental power which has been exercised."

The appellees urge upon us that under a provision of the Board of Education's regulations the appellants waived any right to notice and a hearing before being expelled for misconduct.

> 'Attendance at any college is on the basis of a mutual decision of the student's parents and of the college. Attendance at a particular college is voluntary and is different from attendance at a public school where the pupil may be required to attend a particular school which is located in the

neighborhood or district in which the pupil's family may live. Just as a student may choose to withdraw from a particular college at any time for any personally-determined reason, the college may also at any time decline to continue to accept responsibility for the supervision and service to any student with whom the relationship becomes unpleasant and difficult.'

We do not read this provision to clearly indicate an intent on the part of the student to waive notice and a hearing before expulsion. If, however, we should so assume, it nonetheless remains true that the State cannot condition the granting of even a privilege upon the renunciation of the constitutional right to procedural due process. . . . Only private associations have the right to obtain a waiver of notice and hearing before depriving a member of a valuable right. And even here, the right to notice and a hearing is so fundamental to the conduct of our society that the waiver must be clear and explicit. *Medical and Surgical Society of Montgomery County v. Weatherly*, 75 Ala. 248, 256–259. In the absence of such an explicit waiver, Alabama has required that even private associations must provide notice and a hearing before expulsion. In *Medical and Surgical Society of Montgomery County v. Weatherly, supra*, it was held that a physician could not be expelled from a medical society without notice and a hearing. . . .

The precise nature of the private interest involved in this case is the right to remain at a public institution of higher learning in which the plaintiffs were students in good standing. It requires no argument to demonstrate that education is vital and, indeed, basic to civilized society. Without sufficient education the plaintiffs would not be able to earn an adequate livelihood, to enjoy life to the fullest, or to fulfill as completely as possible the duties and responsibilities of good citizens.

There was no offer to prove that other colleges are open to the plaintiffs. If so, the plaintiffs would nonetheless be injured by the interruption of their course of studies in mid-term. It is most unlikely that a public college would accept a student expelled from another public college of the same state. Indeed, expulsion may well prejudice the student in completing his education at any other institution. Surely no one can question that the right to remain at the college in which the plaintiffs were students in good standing is an interest of extremely great value.

Turning then to the nature of the governmental power to expel the plaintiffs, it must be conceded, as was held by the district court, that that power is not unlimited and cannot be arbitrarily exercised. Admittedly, there must be some reasonable and constitutional ground for expulsion or the courts would have a duty to require reinstatement. The possibility of arbitrary action is not excluded by the existence of reasonable regulations. There may be arbitrary application of the rule to the facts of a particular case. Indeed, that result is well nigh inevitable when the Board hears only one side of the issue. In the disciplining of college students there are no considerations of immediate danger to the public, or of peril to the national security, which should prevent the Board from exercising at least the fundamental principles of fairness by giving the accused students notice of the charges and an opportunity to be heard in their own defense. Indeed, the example set by the Board in failing so to do, if not corrected by the courts, can well break the spirits of the expelled students and of others familiar with the injustice, and do inestimable harm to their education.

The district court, however, felt that it was governed by precedent, and stated that, 'the courts have consistently upheld the validity of regulations that have the effect of reserving to the college the right to dismiss students at any time for any reason without divulging its reason other than its being for the general benefit of the institution.' With deference, we must hold that the district court has simply misinterpreted the precedents.

The language above quoted from the district court is based upon language found in 14 C.J.S. Colleges and Universities § 26, p. 1360, which, in turn, is paraphrased from *Anthony v. Syracuse University*, 224 App.Div. 487, 231 N.Y.S. 435, *reversing* 130 Misc.2d 249, 223 N.Y.S. 796, 797. (14 C.J.S. Colleges and Universities § 26, pp. 1360, 1363 note 70.) This case, however, concerns a private university and follows the well settled rule that the relations between a student and a private university are a matter of contract. The *Anthony* case held that the plaintiffs had specifically waived their rights to notice and hearing. . . . The precedents for public colleges are collected in a recent annotation cited by the district court. 58 A.L.R.2d 903–920. We have read all of the cases cited to the point, and we agree with what the annotator himself says: 'The cases involving suspension or expulsion of a student from a public college or university all involve the question whether the hearing given to the student was adequate. In every instance the sufficiency of the hearing was upheld.' 58 A.L.R.2d at page 909. None held that no hearing whatsoever was required. . . .

The appellees rely also upon *Lucy v. Adams*, D.C.N.D. Ala. 1957, 134 F.Supp. 235, where Autherine Lucy was expelled from the University of Alabama without notice or hearing. That case, however, is not in point. Autherine Lucy did not raise the issue of an absence of notice or hearing.

. . . .

We are confident that precedent as well as a most fundamental constitutional principle support our holding that due process requires notice and some opportunity for hearing before a student at a tax-supported college is expelled for misconduct.

For the guidance of the parties in the event of further proceedings, we state our views on the nature of the notice and hearing required by due process prior to expulsion from a state college or university. They should, we think, comply with the following standards. The notice should contain a statement of the specific charges and grounds which, if proven, would justify expulsion under the regulations of the Board of Education. The nature of the hearing should vary depending upon the circumstances of the particular case. The case before us requires something more than an informal interview with an administrative authority of the college. By its nature, a charge of misconduct, as opposed to a failure to meet the scholastic standards of the college, depends upon a collection of the facts concerning the charged misconduct, easily colored by the point of view of the witnesses. In such circumstances, a hearing which gives the Board or the administrative authorities of the college an opportunity to hear both sides in considerable detail is best suited to protect the rights of all involved. This is not to imply that a full-dress judicial hearing, with the right to cross-examine witnesses, is required. Such a hearing, with the attending publicity and disturbance of college activities, might be detrimental to the college's educational atmosphere and impractical to carry out. Nevertheless, the rudiments of an adversary proceeding may be preserved without encroaching upon the interests of the college. In the instant case, the student should be given the names of the witnesses against him and an oral or written report on the facts to which each witness testifies. He should also be given the opportunity to present to the Board, or at least to an administrative official of the college, his own defense against the charges and to produce either oral testimony or written affidavits of witnesses in his behalf. If the hearing is not before the Board directly, the results and findings of the hearing should be presented in a report open to the student's inspection. If these rudimentary elements of fair play are followed in a case of misconduct of this particular type, we feel that the requirements of due process of law will have been fulfilled.

The judgment of the district court is reversed and the cause is remanded for further proceedings consistent with this opinion.

Reversed and remanded.

NOTE

The court in *Dixon* stated the following: "The precise nature of the private interest involved in this case is the right to remain at a public institution of higher learning in which the plaintiffs were students in good standing." How important to the decision was the fact that these students were students in good standing? The response to this question may be relatively obvious. But what impact does this student status have not only on the existence of due process rights (i.e., liberty and property), but also on the level of due process afforded? In other words, the expulsions here were not motivated by the academic standing of the students, but rather were motivated by alleged infractions of disciplinary rules and state law. For further discussion, see the later cases and materials on due process afforded in purely academic decisions.

GOSS v. LOPEZ

419 U.S. 565 (1975)

Mr. Justice White delivered the opinion of the Court.

This appeal by various administrators of the Columbus, Ohio, Public School System (CPSS) challenges the judgment of a three-judge federal court, declaring that appellees — various high school students in the CPSS — were denied due process of law contrary to the command of the Fourteenth Amendment in that they were temporarily suspended from their high schools without a hearing either prior to suspension or within a reasonable time thereafter, and enjoining the administrators to remove all references to such suspensions from the students' records.

I

Ohio law, Rev. Code Ann. § 3313.64 (1972), provides for free education to all children between the ages of six and 21. Section 3313.66 of the Code empowers the principal of an Ohio public school to suspend a pupil for misconduct for up to 10 days or to expel him. In either case, he must notify the student's parents within 24 hours and state the reasons for his action. A pupil who is expelled, or his parents, may appeal the decision to the Board of Education and in connection therewith shall be permitted to be heard at the board meeting. The Board may reinstate the pupil following the hearing. No similar procedure is provided in § 3313.66 or any other provision of state law for a suspended student. Aside from a regulation tracking the statute, at the time of the imposition of the suspensions in this case the CPSS itself had not issued any written procedure applicable to suspensions.[1] Nor, so far as the record reflects, had any of the individual high schools involved in this case. Each, however, had formally or informally described the conduct for which suspension could be imposed.

The nine named appellees, each of whom alleged that he or she had been suspended from public high school in Columbus for up to 10 days without a hearing pursuant to § 3313.66, filed an action under 42 U. S. C. § 1983 against the Columbus Board of Education and various administrators of the CPSS. The complaint sought a declaration that § 3313.66 was unconstitutional in that it permitted public school administrators to deprive plaintiffs of their rights to an education without a hearing of any kind, in violation of the procedural due process component of the Fourteenth Amendment. It also sought to enjoin the public school officials from issuing future suspensions pursuant to § 3313.66 and to require them to remove references to the past suspensions from the records of the students in question.

The proof below established that the suspensions arose out of a period of widespread student unrest in the CPSS during February and March 1971. [Students were suspended for a number of different infractions, including "disruptive or disobedient conduct committed in the presence of the school administrator," demonstrations, and "a disturbance in the lunchroom which involved some physical damage to school property," Lopez testified that at least 75 other students were suspended from his school on the same day. None of the plaintiffs was provided a hearing.]

On the basis of this evidence, the three-judge court declared that plaintiffs were denied due process of law because they were "suspended without hearing prior to suspension or within a reasonable time thereafter," and that Ohio Rev. Code Ann. § 3313.66 (1972) and regulations issued pursuant thereto were unconstitutional in permitting such suspensions. It was ordered that all references to plaintiffs' suspensions be removed from school files.

. . . .

The defendant school administrators have appealed the three-judge court's decision. . . . We affirm.

---

[1] At the time of the events involved in this case, the only administrative regulation on this subject was § 1010.04 of the Administrative Guide of the Columbus Public Schools which provided: "Pupils may be suspended or expelled from school in accordance with the provisions of Section 3313.66 of the Revised Code." . . .

II

At the outset, appellants contend that because there is no constitutional right to an education at public expense, the Due Process Clause does not protect against expulsions from the public school system. This position misconceives the nature of the issue and is refuted by prior decisions. The Fourteenth Amendment forbids the State to deprive any person of life, liberty, or property without due process of law. Protected interests in property are normally "not created by the Constitution. Rather, they are created and their dimensions are defined" by an independent source such as state statutes or rules entitling the citizen to certain benefits. *Board of Regents v. Roth*, 408 U.S. 564, 577 (1972).

. . . .

Here, on the basis of state law, appellees plainly had legitimate claims of entitlement to a public education. Ohio Rev. Code Ann. §§ 3313.48 and 3313.64 (1972 and Supp. 1973) direct local authorities to provide a free education to all residents between five and 21 years of age, and a compulsory-attendance law requires attendance for a school year of not less than 32 weeks. Ohio Rev. Code Ann. § 3321.04 (1972). It is true that § 3313.66 of the Code permits school principals to suspend students for up to 10 days; but suspensions may not be imposed without any grounds whatsoever. All of the schools had their own rules specifying the grounds for expulsion or suspension. Having chosen to extend the right to an education to people of appellees' class generally, Ohio may not withdraw that right on grounds of misconduct, absent fundamentally fair procedures to determine whether the misconduct has occurred.

Although Ohio may not be constitutionally obligated to establish and maintain a public school system, it has nevertheless done so and has required its children to attend. Those young people do not "shed their constitutional rights" at the schoolhouse door. *Tinker v. Des Moines School Dist.*, 393 U.S. 503, 506 (1969). "The Fourteenth Amendment, as now applied to the States, protects the citizen against the State itself and all of its creatures — Boards of Education not excepted." *West Virginia Board of Education v. Barnette*, 319 U.S. 624, 637 (1943). The authority possessed by the State to prescribe and enforce standards of conduct in its schools although concededly very broad, must be exercised consistently with constitutional safeguards. Among other things, the State is constrained to recognize a student's legitimate entitlement to a public education as a property interest which is protected by the Due Process Clause and which may not be taken away for misconduct without adherence to the minimum procedures required by that Clause.

The Due Process Clause also forbids arbitrary deprivations of liberty. "Where a person's good name, reputation, honor, or integrity is at stake because of what the government is doing to him," the minimal requirements of the Clause must be satisfied. *Wisconsin v. Constantineau*, 400 U.S. 433, 437 (1971); *Board of Regents v. Roth*, *supra*, at 573. School authorities here suspended appellees from school for periods of up to 10 days based on charges of misconduct. If sustained and recorded, those charges could seriously damage the students' standing with their fellow pupils and their teachers as well as interfere with later opportunities for higher education and employment. It is apparent that the claimed right of the State to determine unilaterally and without process whether that misconduct has occurred immediately collides with the requirements of the Constitution.

Appellants proceed to argue that even if there is a right to a public education protected by the Due Process Clause generally, the Clause comes into play only when the State subjects a student to a "severe detriment or grievous loss." The loss of 10 days, it is said, is neither severe nor grievous and the Due Process Clause is therefore of no relevance. Appellants' argument is again refuted by our prior decisions; for in determining "whether due process requirements apply in the first place, we must look not to the 'weight' but to the *nature* of the interest at stake." *Board of Regents v. Roth, supra*, at 570–571. Appellees were excluded from school only temporarily, it is true, but the length and consequent severity of a deprivation, while another factor to weigh in determining the appropriate form of hearing, "is not decisive of the basic right" to a hearing of some kind. *Fuentes v. Shevin*, 407 U.S. 67, 86 (1972). The Court's view has been that as long as a property deprivation is not *de minimis*, its gravity is irrelevant to the question whether account must be taken of the Due Process Clause. *Board of Regents v. Roth, supra*, at 570 n. 8. A 10-day suspension from school is not *de minimis* in our view and may not be imposed in complete disregard of the Due Process Clause.

A short suspension is, of course, a far milder deprivation than expulsion. But, "education is perhaps the most important function of state and local governments," *Brown v. Board of Education*, 347 U.S. 483, 493 (1954), and the total exclusion from the educational process for more than a trivial period, and certainly if the suspension is for 10 days, is a serious event in the life of the suspended child. Neither the property interest in educational benefits temporarily denied nor the liberty interest in reputation, which is also implicated, is so insubstantial that suspensions may constitutionally be imposed by any procedure the school chooses, no matter how arbitrary.

III

"Once it is determined that due process applies, the question remains what process is due." *Morrissey v. Brewer*, 408 U.S., at 481. . . .

. . . .

There are certain bench marks to guide us, however. *Mullane v. Central Hanover Trust Co.*, 339 U.S. 306 (1950), a case often invoked by later opinions, said that "[many] controversies have raged about the cryptic and abstract words of the Due Process Clause but there can be no doubt that at a minimum they require that deprivation of life, liberty or property by adjudication be preceded by notice and opportunity for hearing appropriate to the nature of the case." *Id.*, at 313. "The fundamental requisite of due process of law is the opportunity to be heard," *Grannis v. Ordean*, 234 U.S. 385, 394 (1914), a right that "has little reality or worth unless one is informed that the matter is pending and can choose for himself whether to . . . contest." *Mullane v. Central Hanover Trust Co., supra*, at 314. At the very minimum, therefore, students facing suspension and the consequent interference with a protected property interest must be given *some* kind of notice and afforded *some* kind of hearing. . . .

It also appears from our cases that the timing and content of the notice and the nature of the hearing will depend on appropriate accommodation of the competing interests involved. *Cafeteria Workers v. McElroy, supra*, at 895; *Morrissey v. Brewer, supra*, at 481. The student's interest is to avoid unfair or mistaken exclusion from the educational process, with all of its unfortunate consequences. The Due Process Clause will not shield him from suspensions properly imposed, but it disserves both his interest and the interest of the State if his suspension is in fact unwarranted. The concern would be mostly academic if the disciplinary process were a totally accurate, unerring process, never mistaken and never unfair. Unfortunately, that is not the case, and no one suggests that it is. Disciplinarians, although proceeding in utmost good faith, frequently act on the reports and advice of others; and the controlling facts and the nature of the conduct under challenge are often disputed. The risk of error is not at all trivial, and it should be guarded against if that may be done without prohibitive cost or interference with the educational process.

The difficulty is that our schools are vast and complex. Some modicum of discipline and order is essential if the educational function is to be performed. Events calling for discipline are frequent occurrences and sometimes require immediate, effective action. Suspension is considered not only to be a necessary tool to maintain order but a valuable educational device. The prospect of imposing elaborate hearing requirements in every suspension case is viewed with great concern, and many school authorities may well prefer the untrammeled power to act unilaterally, unhampered by rules about notice and hearing. But it would be a strange disciplinary system in an educational institution if no communication was sought by the disciplinarian with the student in an effort to inform him of his dereliction and to let him tell his side of the story in order to make sure that an injustice is not done. "[Fairness] can rarely be obtained by secret, one-sided determination of facts decisive of rights. . . ." "Secrecy is not congenial to truth-seeking and self-righteousness gives too slender an assurance of rightness. No better instrument has been devised for arriving at truth than to give a person in jeopardy of serious loss notice of the case against him and opportunity to meet it." *Anti-Fascist Committee v. McGrath, supra*, at 170, 171–172 (Frankfurter, J., concurring).

We do not believe that school authorities must be totally free from notice and hearing requirements if their schools are to operate with acceptable efficiency. Students facing temporary suspension have interests qualifying for protection of the Due Process Clause, and due process requires, in connection with a suspension of 10 days or less, that the student be given oral or written notice of the charges against him and, if he denies them, an explanation of the evidence the authorities have and an opportunity to present his side of the story. The Clause requires at least these rudimentary precautions against unfair or mistaken findings of misconduct and arbitrary exclusion from school.

. . . In the great majority of cases the disciplinarian may informally discuss the alleged misconduct with the student minutes after it has occurred. We hold only that, in being given an opportunity to explain his version of the facts at this discussion, the student first be told what he is accused of doing and what the basis of the accusation is. Lower courts which have addressed the question of the *nature* of the procedures required in short suspension cases have reached the same conclusion. . . . Since the hearing may occur almost immediately following the misconduct, it follows that as a general rule notice and hearing should precede removal of the student from school. We agree with the District Court, however, that there are recurring situations in which prior notice and hearing cannot be insisted upon. Students whose presence poses a continuing danger to persons or property or an ongoing threat of disrupting the academic process may be immediately removed from school. In such cases, the necessary notice and rudimentary hearing should follow as soon as practicable, as the District Court indicated.

In holding as we do, we do not believe that we have imposed procedures on school disciplinarians which are inappropriate in a classroom setting. Instead we have imposed requirements which are, if anything, less than a fair-minded school principal would impose upon himself in order to avoid unfair suspensions. Indeed, according to the testimony of the principal of Marion-Franklin High School, that school had an informal procedure, remarkably similar to that which we now require, applicable to suspensions generally but which was not followed in this case. . . .

We stop short of construing the Due Process Clause to require, countrywide, that hearings in connection with short suspensions must afford the student the opportunity to secure counsel, to confront and cross-examine witnesses supporting the charge, or to call his own witnesses to verify his version of the incident. Brief disciplinary suspensions are almost countless. To impose in each such case even truncated trial-type procedures might well overwhelm administrative facilities in many places and, by diverting resources, cost more than it would save in educational effectiveness. Moreover, further formalizing the suspension process and escalating its formality and adversary nature may not only make it too costly as a regular disciplinary tool but also destroy its effectiveness as part of the teaching process.

On the other hand, requiring effective notice and informal hearing permitting the student to give his version of the events will provide a meaningful hedge against erroneous action. At least the disciplinarian will be alerted to the existence of disputes about facts and arguments about cause and effect. He may then determine himself to summon the accuser, permit cross-examination, and allow the student to present his own witnesses. In more difficult cases, he may permit counsel. In any event, his discretion will be more informed and we think the risk of error substantially reduced.

Requiring that there be at least an informal give-and-take between student and disciplinarian, preferably prior to the suspension, will add little to the factfinding function where the disciplinarian himself has witnessed the conduct forming the basis for the charge. But things are not always as they seem to be, and the student will at least have the opportunity to characterize his conduct and put it in what he deems the proper context.

We should also make it clear that we have addressed ourselves solely to the short suspension, not exceeding 10 days. Longer suspensions or expulsions for the remainder of the school term, or permanently, may require more formal procedures. Nor do we put aside the possibility that in unusual situations, although involving only a short suspension, something more than the rudimentary procedures will be required.

IV

The District Court found each of the suspensions involved here to have occurred without a hearing, either before or after the suspension, and that each suspension was therefore invalid and the statute unconstitutional insofar as it permits such suspensions without notice or hearing. Accordingly, the judgment is

Affirmed.

NOTES

1. How do students' property rights and liberty interests manifest themselves in higher education settings? What are the similarities and differences, do you think, between students in public K-12 education settings and students in public colleges and universities with respect to Fourteenth Amendment liberty and property rights? The Court in *Goss* used Ohio's compulsory attendance statute to find the property interest in public education for K-12 students. Where might courts look for property interests of university students who are not compelled to be there under state law? What does the court in *Dixon, supra*, contribute to this discussion?

2. One year following the decision in *Goss*, the Supreme Court decided *Mathews v. Eldridge*, 424 U.S. 319 (1976). In *Mathews*, a recipient of disability benefits under the Social Security Act, filed suit after his benefits were discontinued. A state agency charged with monitoring the medical conditions of recipients distributed a questionnaire to the recipient. Using the recipient's responses and information obtained from the recipient's physician and psychiatric consultant, a state agency determined that the recipient no longer had the disability. The state notified the Social Security Administration (SSA), which in turn notified the recipient. The SSA gave the recipient the opportunity to request a reconsideration of the decision. He declined and, instead, filed suit challenging the administrative procedures. The Supreme Court, in a 6-3 decision, held that in this case, a pre-termination hearing is not required under the Due Process Clause; the procedures outlined and executed by the SSA fully complied with due process. In its decision, the Court presented three factors used to determine what process is due: "first, the private interest that will be affected by the official action; second, the risk of an erroneous deprivation of such interest through the procedures used, and the probable value, if any, of additional or substitute procedural safeguards; and finally, the Government's interest." *Id.* at 335. The first and third factors are rather traditional for constitutional balances — the rights of the individual and the obligations of the institution. The second factor — the risk of erroneous deprivation — is equally important to the determination, though. State actors, like public university administrators, are often called to make tough, adverse decisions against staff and students. The risk of erroneous deprivation of life, liberty, and/or property is, thus, not always low. The best way to avoid such erroneous deprivation is to afford appropriate levels of due process under the circumstances. The three-part analysis from *Mathews v. Eldridge* is seen in the following cases, beginning with *Tigrett v. The Rector and Visitors of the University of Virginia*, 290 F.3d 620 (4th Cir. 2002).

3. In cases like *Dixon* and *Goss*, where there is, at minimum, a deprivation of liberty or property (if not both), some measure of due process is necessary, usually before the deprivation. However, in *Goss*, the Court noted toward the end of its decision that emergency circumstances may dictate the necessity of a disciplinary removal in advance of procedural due process, so long as procedural due process followed shortly thereafter. For example, see *Nguyen v. University of Louisville*, Civ. Action No. 3:04CV-457-H, 2006 U.S. Dist. LEXIS 20082 (W.D. Ky. Apr. 14, 2006), in which a graduate student (Nguyen) was suspended pending a formal hearing on sexual harassment allegations raised by a classmate. Nguyen had been the subject of several earlier reports of harassment, each filed by the same classmate. On each of those prior occasions, university administrators met with Nguyen and, after one of them, placed him on probation. On the final incident at issue, Nguyen was notified by letter that he was suspended pending the formal hearing. In a nice application of *Goss*, with respect to emergency removals in higher education, the court stated the following:

> Here, because of the history of complaints and the evidence discovered in the previous investigations, University officials had legitimate concerns that Nguyen posed a danger to Whitaker. The immediate temporary removal from campus was a reasonable response at the time. Following the suspension, notice and a hearing were provided as soon as practicable. . . . Therefore, the Court concludes that Nguyen's suspension comported with the obligations of due process.

Id. at *13. Note that the university ultimately reinstated Nguyen and he later successfully completed his graduate degree.

4. Following the *Goss* decision, the Ohio legislature took action, seeking to provide students greater due process rights than were afforded the students under the facts of *Goss*. The enacted statute, OHIO REV. CODE ANN. § 3313.66, now requires school officials to "give students written notice of an intention to suspend and an informal hearing before imposing suspension as a disciplinary consequence, in addition to providing for an administrative appeal of suspension decisions." *See Grine v. Sylvania Sch. Bd. of Educ.*, 2004 Ohio 6904, 2004 Ohio App. LEXIS 6393 (Ohio App. 6 Dist. Dec. 17, 2004).

TIGRETT v. THE RECTOR AND VISITORS OF THE UNIVERSITY OF VIRGINIA

290 F.3d 620 (4th Cir. 2002)

KING, CIRCUIT JUDGE:

. . . [Harrison] Tigrett and [Bradley] Kintz, both former students at the University [of Virginia], were punished pursuant to its student disciplinary procedures, and they assert in their lawsuit that they suffered multiple deprivations of their constitutional rights. The district court for the Western District of Virginia denied their claims . . . and this appeal followed. . . . [W]e affirm.

I.

A.

In the early morning hours of November 21, 1997, Tigrett and Kintz (the "Appellants"), along with three of their fraternity brothers, Richard Smith, Wes Kaupinen, and Wes McCluney, travelled to a convenience store in Charlottesville, Virginia. While returning from the store, they encountered Alexander Kory, another University student, walking on the school's main grounds. Kory then engaged in a hostile verbal exchange with at least one of the five men, and the exchange escalated to the point where McCluney stopped his vehicle and Smith, Kaupinen, and the Appellants exited from it. Kaupinen avoided further hostilities by returning to the fraternity house, but the Appellants confronted Kory. In an effort to calm the situation, Smith instructed Kory to leave, and he directed the Appellants to return to the automobile. Kory then called Smith a "fat ass," and in response Smith punched Kory in the face. The Appellants also may have kicked and attacked Kory, and, as a result, Kory suffered extensive injuries to his face, jaw, and teeth. A few days after the incident, Smith turned himself in to the University Police, and he later brought the other four students — the Appellants, plus McCluney and Kaupinen — with him to the police station. All five students then made voluntary statements to the University authorities. On December 3, 1997, pursuant to the procedures of the University Judiciary Committee ("UJC"), Kory initiated a student disciplinary complaint against Smith, McCluney, and the Appellants.

B.

The UJC is a student-operated disciplinary body of the University with responsibility for investigating and hearing complaints involving student misconduct, particularly violations of the University Standards of Conduct ("USOC"). Pursuant to its By-Laws, a UJC trial must be convened within a reasonable time after the filing of a complaint, and an accused must be accorded reasonable notice of any charges and of the time and place for trial. In each case, a UJC member is appointed as Investigator, and he meets with the complainant, the accused, and other witnesses to ascertain the facts underlying the complaint. The Investigator compiles a Report, which is usually presented at a UJC trial. The trial is conducted before a panel of seven members of the UJC. Pursuant to UJC By-Laws, decisions of a trial panel are automatically subject to review by the University's Vice President for Student Affairs. If the Vice President for Student Affairs concludes that the decision of the trial panel is inappropriate, he may remand the matter to the UJC, or he may refer it to an independent body called the Judicial Review Board ("JRB"), which is composed of faculty, administrators, and students. The JRB possesses the authority to remand the case to the UJC for a new trial, or it may reverse or modify the trial panel's decision.

C.

1.

Kory's complaint alleged that Smith, McCluney, and the Appellants violated Section 1 of the USOC, which prohibits physical or sexual assault, and Section 5 of the USOC, by blocking traffic on University property. Because McCluney was scheduled to graduate at the end of the following semester, the Vice President for Student Affairs, William Harmon, determined that he would not be subjected to a UJC trial. Instead, Harmon reprimanded McCluney and required that he attend aggression counseling sessions before he could receive his University diploma. The UJC initially scheduled the trial of Smith and the Appellants (collectively, the "UJC Defendants") for February 19, 1998, but the trial was postponed pending resolution of criminal charges in the state court of Albemarle County, Virginia.

In May 1998, Smith was convicted in state court of assault and battery, on the basis of a nolo contendere plea. The Appellants and McCluney also entered pleas of nolo contendere and were convicted of disorderly conduct. The UJC thereafter rescheduled the trial of the UJC Defendants for November 21, 1998, before a seven-member UJC panel (the "1998 UJC Panel").

Prior to their trial (the "UJC Trial"), the disciplinary charges against the UJC Defendants were amended to include a charge under Section 8 of the USOC, which prohibits disorderly conduct. According to the Investigator, the UJC Defendants were notified of the Section 8 charge when they received his Report, which occurred at least forty-eight hours before the UJC Trial was scheduled.

On November 20, 1998, the day before trial was to begin, the UJC Defendants, along with Smith's father and his student counsel, met with Vice President Harmon to express concerns about the trial. After the Appellants left the meeting, Smith and his father continued their discussions with Harmon. Smith subsequently asserted (as do the Appellants on appeal) that Harmon assured him that the trial would not go forward the next day. At approximately seven o'clock that evening, Smith's student counsel filed a motion requesting that the trial be postponed, which the UJC denied later that night. Smith's student counsel promptly advised the UJC Defendants that their trial would be conducted as scheduled, but they nevertheless decided not to attend. Because Harmon had represented that the trial would not proceed, the UJC Defendants believed that any trial conducted in their absence would be invalid.

Although the UJC Defendants failed to attend, their trial was conducted the next day. Following presentation of the prosecution's evidence, the 1998 UJC Panel found each of the UJC Defendants guilty on all three charges: violating Section 1 (physical assault), Section 5 (blocking traffic), and Section 8 (disorderly conduct), and the Panel recommended their expulsions from the University. By letters of November 21, 1998, the UJC informed the three UJC Defendants of the expulsion sanctions, and it advised them of their right to appeal the decisions to the JRB. These letters failed to reflect that, pursuant to the UJC's By-Laws, the decisions were automatically subject to review by the Vice President for Student Affairs, i.e., Vice President Harmon. On November 23, 1998, the UJC wrote to Harmon, requesting "finalization of its expulsion sanctions." Without a response from or the approval of Harmon, the UJC then wrote the University's Registrar, on November 24, 1998, requesting that she mark "enrollment discontinued" on the transcripts of the UJC Defendants. After consulting with Harmon, however, the Registrar did not mark anything on their transcripts, and she declined to discontinue their enrollments. Instead, the Registrar wrote the words "Not Processed" at the bottom of the UJC's letters.

On November 25, 1998, Vice President Harmon declined to finalize the expulsions. He instead acknowledged "perceived procedural irregularities and misunderstandings," and he referred the case to the JRB. Pursuant to the JRB's Procedures For Appeals, the UJC Defendants each appealed to the JRB. The Chairperson of the JRB then appointed a three-member Appellate Review Panel, consisting of a professor, an administrator, and a student, to handle their appeals. On February 11, 1999, the Review Panel set aside the recommended expulsions and remanded the case to the UJC for a new trial.

2.

Following remand, the UJC convened a new trial panel and scheduled a second trial for April 17, 1999. On April 10, 1999, it again notified the UJC Defendants that they were charged with violations of Sections 1, 5, and 8 of the USOC. Prior to the new trial, however, allegations of bias surfaced concerning the panel Chair, who recused herself. This panel was disbanded, and the UJC then determined that it lacked sufficient membership to form another panel and resolve the charges in a timely manner. By letter of May 4, 1999, the UJC relinquished control of the case, referring the matter to Harmon for disposition.

Vice President Harmon then appointed a five-member factfinding panel, consisting of a law student (a member of the UJC), a professor, and three administrators, to hear the pending charges (the "1999 Panel"). By letters of May 4, 1999, Harmon notified the UJC Defendants that the charges against them would be heard by the 1999 Panel, and they were advised that this panel would not be governed by the rules and practices of the UJC. Harmon further informed them that "the panel will make findings of fact with respect to the pending charges and recommend an appropriate sanction to the President (or his designee) in the event of a finding of guilt." Harmon also specified that President Casteen would be the ultimate decisionmaker, and that the Appellants would have the right to appeal the President's decision to the JRB "on the grounds that the sanction was unduly harsh, clearly excessive or grossly inappropriate to the offense, or for procedural error in violation of due process that had a substantial negative impact on the outcome." The JRB would be the final appeal "except on written permission to the Board of Visitors in the case of expulsion."

The 1999 Panel convened its trial on May 17, 1999 (the "1999 Trial"). At the trial's outset, Smith entered a plea of guilty to Sections 1, 5, and 8 of the USOC; the Appellants, on the other hand, tendered not guilty pleas to all three charges. The 1999 Panel then conducted a thirteen-hour trial at which witnesses were examined and evidence was presented. Shortly thereafter, the Panel completed its "Report of Fact Finding Panel" (the "Report"), and, by letter of May 27, 1999, forwarded it to the University's President, John T. Casteen, III, and copied it to the UJC Defendants. The Report concluded that the Appellants had "engaged in behavior which threatened the health or safety of Mr. Kory," and it found them guilty of violating Section 1 of the USOC. Additionally, the Report unanimously found that they had "engaged in disorderly conduct on University-owned property," and it found them guilty of violating Section 8 of the USOC. However, the 1999 Panel decided that it "could not fairly conclude that the facts constituted an unlawful blocking of normal pedestrian traffic," and it therefore found the Appellants not guilty of violating Section 5 of the USOC. The Report recommended that Smith be suspended for two consecutive semesters (which could include one summer session) and that he be required to perform 100 hours of community service. It also recommended that the Appellants be suspended for one semester (not to include a summer session) and that they each perform seventy-five hours of community service. In response to the Report, the Appellants' lawyers, by letters of May 28, 1999, and June 1, 1999, urged Casteen to reject the recommendations.

After reviewing the Report, the transcript of the 1999 Trial, and the correspondence of the Appellants' lawyers, President Casteen, on June 7, 1999, "affirmed the findings of guilt reached by the panel." He adopted the Report's recommended sanction as to Kintz, imposing academic suspension for one semester plus seventy-five hours of community service. As to Smith and Tigrett, however, Casteen imposed more severe sanctions than had been recommended by the Report. With regard to Smith, he imposed two full years of academic suspension, rather than the one-year suspension recommended by the 1999 Panel, plus 100 hours of community service. Casteen suspended Tigrett for a full academic year, instead of the one semester recommended by the 1999 Panel, and he imposed seventy-five hours of community service. Tigrett promptly appealed Casteen's sanction to the JRB. His appeal was rejected on June 22, 1999, when the JRB determined that his case was "final under University procedure."

3.

Shortly thereafter, on October 27, 1999, Tigrett filed an eleven-count complaint in the Western District of Virginia against the Rector and Visitors of the University, President Casteen, Vice President Harmon, the members of the Board of Visitors (the "Board"), the members of the 1998 UJC Panel, and the members of the 1999 Panel (collectively, the "University Defendants"). Tigrett alleged ten separate due process and First Amendment claims under § 1983, as well as a state law contract claim, all arising from the handling of the student disciplinary charges made against him. . . . [T]he court determined that the Rector and Visitors of the University were immune from suit and it dismissed them. It further concluded that the University Defendants were immune from monetary damages in their official capacities, but that they were subject to suit in their personal capacities and for injunctive relief. With regard to Tigrett's specific claims, the court dismissed his state law contract claim, except to the extent that it sought prospective injunctive relief, and it partially granted the University Defendants' motion for summary judgment.

On April 6, 2000, Kintz filed a separate civil action against the University

Defendants, which contained allegations nearly identical to those made by Tigrett in his . . . complaint. On August 30, 2000, Kintz's lawsuit was consolidated with what remained of Tigrett's claims. On January 30, 2001, the University Defendants sought summary judgment on the claims of the Appellants. The court thereafter [awarded] summary judgment to the University Defendants. . . .

. . . .

III.

In their appeal, the Appellants maintain that the district court erred in three specific respects in its award of summary judgment to the University Defendants. . . . We address each of these contentions in turn.

A.

. . . .

The Appellants first assert that the 1998 UJC Panel in fact expelled them from the University, and that it did so in a manner that violated their Fourteenth Amendment due process rights. Specifically, they maintain that their due process rights were contravened because: (1) they did not receive adequate notice that the UJC Trial was going forward; (2) they had no opportunity to appear and defend themselves; (3) they had no opportunity to cross-examine witnesses; (4) they failed to receive adequate notice of the disorderly conduct charge; and (5) the 1998 UJC Panel violated its internal procedures by, inter alia, allowing the participation of outside attorneys. Each of these claims must fail, however, because the Appellants were not expelled from the University by the 1998 UJC Panel, and hence they could not have been deprived of any constitutionally protected Fourteenth Amendment interest.

. . . .

Assuming the Appellants possessed some constitutionally protected interest in continued enrollment, they were not deprived of such an interest by the actions of the 1998 UJC Panel. Although the Panel recommended the expulsions of the UJC Defendants, that is all the Panel was empowered to do. No expulsions could occur, under University 12 Rules, unless Vice President Harmon ratified the Panel's decision. Pursuant to the UJC's By-Laws, sanctions imposed by the UJC are automatically subject to review by Harmon, and he refused to ratify the recommended expulsions. Instead, citing "procedural irregularities and misunderstandings," he forwarded the case to the JRB, which set the recommended expulsions aside and remanded the matter to the UJC for a new trial. Thus, pursuant to the By-Laws of the UJC, the Appellants were not expelled by the 1998 UJC Panel, nor were they expelled pursuant to its recommendations.

Moreover, the apparent attempts by the UJC to hasten the Appellants' proposed expulsions were rebuffed by the University administration. By letters of November 24, 1998, the UJC requested the Registrar to write "enrollment discontinued" on the Appellants' transcripts. The Registrar, however, consulted with Harmon and was instructed not to comply with this request. Rather than marking the transcripts "enrollment discontinued," she wrote the words "Not Processed" at the bottom of the UJC's letters. The Registrar's refusal to discontinue the Appellants' enrollments confirms the fact that they were not expelled by the 1998 UJC Panel.

. . . .

B.

The Appellants next maintain that their due process rights were violated when President Casteen imposed upon them more severe sanctions than those recommended by the 1999 Panel. Specifically, they assert that Casteen was both the ultimate factfinder and the final decisionmaker, and that they were entitled to appear before him prior to his decisions. This contention is likewise without merit.

As an initial matter, the Appellants are mistaken in their claim that President Casteen was the ultimate factfinder. On the contrary, the 1999 Panel, which afforded them a thirteen-hour trial in which they fully participated, was the factfinder. President Casteen merely reviewed the findings of fact made by the 1999 Panel. While the Appellants correctly maintain that Casteen was the ultimate decisionmaker, and that he meted out their respective one-year and one-semester suspensions, their contention that they possess some due process right to appear before the final decisionmaker is without merit. In *Bates v. Sponberg*, 547 F.2d 325 (6th Cir. 1976), the Sixth Circuit held that a tenured university professor could be dismissed by a Board of Regents without being afforded a hearing before that entity. Bates had appeared and presented evidence before a faculty grievance committee, which recommended his dismissal, but he was denied the opportunity to appear before the Board, which made the ultimate decision to terminate him. . . .

In the absence of a constitutional or statutory deprivation, the federal courts should be loathe to interfere with the organization and operation of an institution of higher education. *See Ewing*, 474 U.S. at 225 n.11 ("University faculties must have the widest range of discretion in making judgments as to the academic performance of students and their entitlement to promotion or graduation."); *Sweezy v. New Hampshire*, 354 U.S. 234, 263 (1957) (Frankfurter, J., concurring in result) (explaining that it is an "essential freedom" of a university to make its own judgments on selection of its student body). . . . There is simply no controlling authority for the proposition that the Appellants possessed a constitutional right to appear before President Casteen prior to his final decisions. Due process . . . mandates only that they be afforded a meaningful hearing. . . .

The thirteen-hour trial accorded the Appellants by the 1999 Panel included the examination of witnesses and a thorough presentation of evidence. They were present throughout, and they were afforded a full opportunity to participate and to testify (which they declined). Their positions were made clear in the record of the 1999 Trial, which was reviewed and analyzed by President Casteen. And those positions and arguments were supplemented by written submissions made to Casteen prior to his decisions in their case. In these circumstances, the Appellants were afforded the meaningful hearing to which they were entitled under *Mathews v. Eldridge*, and their contention to the contrary must be rejected.

C.

Finally, the Appellants contend that President Casteen, Vice President Harmon, and the members of the Board violated their due process rights by failing to properly instruct, train, supervise, and control the 1998 UJC Panel. This claim, made pursuant to a theory of § 1983 liability commonly referred to as "supervisory liability," is without merit as well.

In our recent decision in *Baynard v. Malone*, 268 F.3d 228 (4th Cir. 2001), we had occasion to address the viability of a supervisory liability claim. As Judge Wilkins observed in that case, "it is well settled that supervisory officials may be held liable in certain circumstances for the constitutional injuries inflicted by their subordinates." *Id.* at 235 (citations omitted). . . .

. . . [T]here is no affirmative causal link between the supervisor's inaction and any constitutional injury suffered by the Appellants. As we earlier observed, . . . the Appellants were not expelled by the 1998 UJC Panel, and they were not in any other way deprived of a constitutionally protected interest by that panel. As such, they suffered no constitutional injury in connection with the UJC Trial for which any of the University's supervisory personnel could be liable.

IV.

Pursuant to the foregoing, we affirm the district court's award of summary judgment.

AFFIRMED

NOTES

1. In the *Tigrett* opinion, the court makes passing reference to two landmark decisions of the United State Supreme Court on the issue of constitutionally protected due process rights for university students: *Board of Curators of the Univ. of Missouri v. Horowitz*, 435 U.S. 78 (1978), and *Regents of the Univ. of Michigan v. Ewing*, 474 U.S. 214 (1985), each presented in full later in this chapter. Much of the discussion in both of these cases speaks to the deference courts often show to the internal procedures and decision making of university officials. How heavily does this notion of judicial deference play in the decision in *Tigrett*?

2. Compare the student disciplinary processes in *Tigrett* to the ones you've experienced in your academic and professional experience. According to the facts in *Tigrett*, the University of Virginia has a student-operated disciplinary body called the University Judiciary Committee. What are its powers under University regulations? How did the court use and respect the actions, decisions, and recommendations of the student-based panels in *Tigrett*? The plaintiffs in *Tigrett* argued that the decisions of the UJC deprived them of due process under the Fourteenth Amendment. The court assumed the presence of a constitutional right to continued enrollment and then found that the UJC did actually expel the students. It did not have the power to do so, as there was an automatic administrative review of UJC decisions. So, under the system highlighted in *Tigrett*, is the UJC a "state actor" for constitutional due process purposes?

What are the advantages and disadvantages of a university student-operated disciplinary system for legal and practical purposes? In addition to *Tigrett*, see *Cobb v. The Rector and Visitors of the University of Virginia*, 69 F. Supp. 2d 815 (W.D. Va. 1999) (student who was investigated for cheating and later expelled from the university filed suit alleging due process and equal protection violations under the application of Virginia's student-run disciplinary system).

3. What about a university's authority to discipline off-campus conduct of students? Is a university permitted to apply its student code of conduct against a student for misconduct committed off of university property? After a university wins a major conference or national athletic championship, it is typical to see fans, many of them students, celebrating wildly. In *Rubino v. Saddlemire*, No: 3:05cv1955 (PCD), 2007 U.S. Dist. LEXIS 14893 (D. Conn. Mar. 1, 2007), a student was arrested by campus police at the University of Connecticut after he was caught "jumping on an overturned car, damaging it and inciting the crowd." The incident occurred at a local apartment complex after the university's men's basketball team won the national championship. The student was later charged under the university's student code of conduct and suspended for two years. He filed suit, alleging procedural and substantive due process violations. The district court rejected both parties' motions to dismiss. According to the court, on the procedural due process claim, whether there was substantial evidence to find the student responsible on the student code violations was a question of fact. On the substantive due process claim, it remained a question of fact whether the two-year suspension was arbitrary and capricious and an abuse of the university's authority. Note that the plaintiff returned to the university after his two-year suspension. So a motion for injunctive relief on that matter was denied.

4. Questions of procedural due process violation are relatively common in cases like *Dixon*, *Goss*, and *Tigrett*. Clearly, it is important for universities to follow the general requirements of notice and opportunity to be heard when constitutional due process rights like liberty and property are implicated by disciplinary decisions. Equally important is the requirement that universities comply with substantive due process claims. In *Rubino v. Saddlemire*, *supra*, Note 3, the court denied a motion for summary judgment, holding that there remained a question of fact as to whether a two-year suspension for damage to non-university property was appropriate under the circumstances. Substantive due process claims are difficult to prove, but the necessity remains that university officials impose discipline that is proportional to the infraction committed and that is consistent from case to case. In *Williams v. Wendler*, 530 F.3d 584 (7th Cir. 2008), the Court of Appeals for the Seventh Circuit rejected a substantive due process claim from two African-American students accused of hazing who, in turn, claimed that two white students accused of similar infractions on previous occasions had been disciplined less severely. The court found that the incidents involving the white students were less serious.

FLAIM v. MEDICAL COLLEGE OF OHIO

418 F.3d 629 (6th Cir. 2005)

Boyce F. Martin, Jr., Circuit Judge. We deal here, most regrettably, with a young man who made some unfortunate (and criminal) decisions and the administrators of a medical college who sought to expel him. Sean Michael Flaim was a third-year medical student attending the Medical College of Ohio. He was arrested and convicted of a felony drug crime. Medical College of Ohio subsequently expelled Flaim, who thereupon filed a sixteen-count complaint in federal district court naming Medical College of Ohio and various administrators, in their official and individual capacities, as defendants. The defendants filed a motion to dismiss. . . . [T]he district court granted in full the defendants' motion. . . . Flaim's timely appeal followed, averring error with respect to only his procedural and substantive due process claims against the college administrators in their official capacities. Because Medical College of Ohio's procedural approach was consistent with the bare-minimum requirements of due process, though perhaps less-than-desirable for an institution of higher learning, we affirm.

I.

Flaim was arrested by Toledo police in October 2001 while at his off-campus apartment. At the time, Flaim was a third-year medical student. He was charged with Aggravated Possession of Drugs (Ecstasy), Aggravated Possession of Drugs (D.O.B.), Possession of Cocaine, and Drug Abuse-Possession of L.S.D., all in violation of state law. At the time of his arrest, the police also confiscated a nine millimeter handgun and $9,511 in cash. A grand jury then indicted Flaim on four counts of felony drug possession. He ultimately pleaded guilty to one count of the lesser included offense of Attempted Possession of Drugs, still a felony, and was sentenced to two years of unsupervised probation.

Two days after his arrest, Medical College of Ohio notified Flaim by letter that he was suspended "until external investigations/hearings [were] completed." The letter further informed Flaim of his right to an internal investigation. On the advice of counsel and in an effort to avoid incriminating himself, Flaim declined to schedule a Medical College of Ohio internal investigation until the pending criminal charges were resolved. Medical College of Ohio notified Flaim that he would not be permitted to return to campus until he participated in an internal hearing regarding the "conduct that gave rise to [the] criminal charges."

Flaim's roommate, who had also been arrested in October 2001, but who was only charged with a misdemeanor, was allowed to return to classes later that fall without a hearing. Flaim requested similar treatment, and also requested that Medical College of Ohio certify him to take Step 1 of the United States Medical Licensing Examination. Medical College of Ohio's general counsel informed Flaim that he would not be permitted to return to campus until the completion of an internal hearing on the matter. With the felony charges still pending, Flaim demurred.

In April 2002, Flaim's step-mother, who is an attorney, met with the Dean of Medical College of Ohio, Amira Gohara, with the goal of securing Flaim's return to campus. Dean Gohara informed Flaim's step-mother that Medical College of Ohio was under the impression that Flaim had withdrawn from school upon requesting a tuition refund. Shortly after this meeting, Medical College of Ohio again notified Flaim by letter that he could not return to campus without an internal hearing.

After pleading guilty to one felony drug offense in June 2002, Flaim initiated contact with Medical College of Ohio and requested an internal hearing. On June 21, Flaim received written notice that he was to appear before the college's Student Conduct and Ethics Committee on June 28 to answer the Committee's questions regarding his arrest. The notice informed Flaim that pursuant to Medical College of Ohio policy, only those facing pending criminal charges were entitled to counsel at the hearing and therefore, because the criminal proceedings had concluded, Flaim was not entitled to the presence of counsel. The notice stated, however, that it would make an exception for Flaim and allow his attorney to be present during the internal hearing. On June 26, Flaim contacted Dean Gohara further inquiring about the details of the hearing. Flaim was told that the college had obtained portions of his criminal record and that the arresting officer would testify at the hearing.

At the hearing, the arresting officer testified and Committee members were able to ask the officer questions. Flaim's attorney was not allowed to ask questions or speak with Flaim. Flaim was not permitted to cross-examine the officer. The Committee extensively questioned Flaim to elicit his account of events. At the end of the hearing, the Committee informed Flaim that it would prepare a written recommendation for Dean Gohara for her final consideration. A written recommendation was never prepared, but on July 9, Flaim received a one-page letter from Dean Gohara notifying him that he was expelled from Medical College of Ohio for "violation of institutional standards of conduct." Flaim then requested a meeting with Dean Gohara, at which he was told that the college had a "zero-tolerance policy" regarding drugs, that a more specific reason for the decision would not be provided, that an appeal was not available, and that any further questions would have to be directed to the college's general counsel.

Flaim subsequently requested that Medical College of Ohio produce copies of all of his school records, including the Committee's written recommendation to Dean Gohara and a copy of the so-called zero-tolerance policy. Medical College of Ohio sent all records and documents except for the written recommendation and the zero-tolerance policy. Flaim then requested another hearing under Medical College of Ohio policy to correct his official record and to redress the denial of counsel at the hearing before Committee. Medical College of Ohio responded that because Flaim was no longer a student, he had no existing rights under any Medical College of Ohio policy. The college further stated that it had complied with its due process policy and therefore no further hearings would be held.

On appeal, Flaim argues that the district court erred in dismissing . . . his procedural and substantive due process claims. . . . For the reasons discussed below, we affirm the district court's judgment.

II.

In this Circuit we have held that the Due Process Clause is implicated by higher education disciplinary decisions. *Jaksa v. Regents of Univ. of Mich.*, 597 F. Supp. 1245 (E.D. Mich. 1984), *aff'd*, 787 F.2d 590 (6th Cir. 1986) (finding due process clause implicated in suspension from university for cheating); *see also Goss v. Lopez*, 419 U.S. 565, 575 (1975) (liberty and property interest implicated in high-school suspension). . . . "Once it is determined that due process applies, the question remains what process is due." *Morrissey v. Brewer*, 408 U.S. 471, 481 (1972). The amount of process due will vary according to the facts of each case and is evaluated largely within the framework laid out by the Supreme Court in *Mathews v. Eldridge*, 424 U.S. 319 (1976). . . . Because Flaim's case is a disciplinary expulsion, rather than an academic one, we conduct a more searching inquiry. *See Missouri v. Horowitz*, 435 U.S. 78, 86 (1978) (academic decisions "call[] for far less stringent procedural requirements").

Many times over the Supreme Court has made clear that there are two basic due process requirements: (1) notice, and (2) an opportunity to be heard. *See Goss*, 419 U.S. at 579. . . . The type of notice and hearing will vary and be judged for sufficiency based on the context in which the dispute arose. In this case, Flaim argues that the process he was afforded was less than was required by his circumstances. He points to his very significant interest in his continued medical education and the attendant consequences of expulsion from medical school. Among his assertions of error are: (A) inadequacy of notice; (B) denial of a right to counsel; (C) denial of a right to cross-examine adverse witnesses; (D) denial of a right to receive written findings of facts and recommendation; and (E) denial of a right to appeal the school's decision to expel him.

Our analysis begins with *Goss v. Lopez*. There, a high-school student faced a ten-day suspension. The Court found both a due process property and liberty interest implicated by the potential suspension. Finding that the Due Process Clause applied, the Court held that the student was entitled to "some kind of notice" and "some kind of hearing." *Goss*, 419 U.S. at 579. In *Goss*, oral notice sufficed, and the Court held that due process is satisfied in that context, even if the student denies the charge, so long as the student is provided with an explanation of the evidence supporting the accusation and an opportunity to present an alternative version of the facts. . . . Absent from *Goss*, however, was any requirement for the presentation of evidence against the accused, an opportunity for cross-examination, any representation (legal or otherwise), a transcript of the proceedings, or the opportunity for an appeal.

Two years later, in *Ingraham v. Wright*, 430 U.S. 651 (1977), the Court analyzed corporal punishment in public schools through the framework set out in *Mathews v. Eldridge*. . . . *Ingraham*, applying *Mathews*, instructs that in determining the amount of process due, courts are to look at three factors: (1) the nature of the private interest affected — that is, the seriousness of the charge and potential sanctions, (2) the danger of error and the benefit of additional or alternate procedures, and (3) the public or governmental burden were additional procedures mandated. *Id.* at 676–82. . . .

Notice and an opportunity to be heard remain the most basic requirements of due process. Within this framework — and the generalized, though unhelpful observation that disciplinary hearings against students and faculty are not criminal trials, and therefore need not take on many of those formalities — the additional procedures required will vary based on the circumstances and the three prongs of *Mathews*. Beginning with notice, in *Goss* oral notice sufficed. The stronger the private interest, however, the more likely a formal written notice — informing the accused of the charge, the policies or regulations the accused is charged with violating, and a list of possible penalties — is constitutionally required. . . . In some circumstances where factual issues are disputed, notice might also be required to include the names of witnesses and a list of other evidence the school intends to present. . . .

The hearing, whether formal, informal, live or not, must be meaningful and must provide the accused with the opportunity to "respond, explain, and defend." If the hearing is live, the accused has a right to be present for all significant portions of the hearing. Courts have generally been unanimous, however, in concluding that hearings need not be open to the public . . . , that neither rules of evidence nor rules of civil or criminal procedure need be applied . . . , and witnesses need not be placed under oath. . . .

Ordinarily, colleges and universities need not allow active representation by legal counsel or some other sort of campus advocate. *Jaksa*, 597 F. Supp. at 1252. . . . In *Jaksa*, the court noted, however, that counsel may be required by the Due Process Clause to ensure fundamental fairness when the school proceeds through counsel or the procedures are overly complex. . . . Other courts have concluded that the "weight of authority is against representation by counsel at disciplinary hearings, unless the student is also facing criminal charges stemming from the incident in question." *Gorman* [*v. Univ. of Rhode Island*,] 837 F.2d [7,] 16 [(1st Cir. 1988)]. . . .

An accused individual has the right to respond and defend, which will generally include the opportunity to make a statement and present evidence. It may also include the right to call exculpatory witnesses. . . . Some circumstances may require the opportunity to cross-examine witnesses, though this right might exist only in the most serious of cases. . . .

It is always wise to produce some sort of record of the proceedings, whether it be a transcript or recording, though a record may not always be constitutionally required. *Jaksa*, 597 F. Supp. at 1252 . . . . While due process may not impose upon the university the requirement to produce a record in all cases, fundamental fairness counsels that if the university will not provide some sort of record, it ought to permit the accused to record the proceedings if desired. . . .

An accused individual is generally not entitled to a statement of reasons for a decision against them, at least where the reasons for the decision are obvious. *Hall v. Med. Coll. of Ohio*, 742 F.2d 299, 310 (6th Cir. 1984); *Jaksa*, 597 F. Supp. at 1253–54. Finally, due process generally does not require an appeal from a school's decision that was reached through constitutional procedures. *See e.g., Foo v. Ind. Univ.*, 88 F. Supp. 2d 937, 952 (S.D. Ind. 1999). As discussed further below, most colleges and universities do wisely and justly provide for such appeals to all who are charged in a college or university setting.

The Due Process Clause, however, sets only the floor or lowest level of procedures acceptable. As the Supreme Court noted in *Goss*, however, and as we emphasize here again, the requirements mandated by the Due Process Clause afford, "if anything, less than a fair minded school [administrator] would impose upon himself in order to avoid unfair [decisions]." *Goss*, 419 U.S. at 583. That being said, the procedures used here were far from ideal and certainly could have been better; they were in the end, however, fundamentally fair, and we accordingly affirm the district court's judgment.

III.

At the outset we note that Medical College of Ohio itself is no longer a defendant in this case. Flaim originally sued Medical College of Ohio in his sixteen-count complaint. Ultimately conceding that the Eleventh Amendment precluded a federal lawsuit against Medical College of Ohio, Flaim requested voluntary dismissal of the college as a defendant. . . . Flaim now proceeds only against the college administrators and professors, in their official and individual capacities, and these claims are in no way precluded by the Eleventh Amendment. We turn to them now.

. . . .

. . . In our analysis below, we need not continually reiterate the strength of Flaim's private interest as it remains constant throughout our analysis. We recognize that his private interest is significant. . . . We understand the seriousness and the lifelong impact that expulsion can have on a young person as well as the significant financial costs already incurred. Our review of this matter, however, is circumscribed. We are limited to determining whether the procedures used by Medical College of Ohio were constitutional. . . .

A. Sufficiency of Notice

Flaim argues that Medical College of Ohio failed to provide him with sufficient notice of the charges against him and the procedures that would follow. Notice, of course, is one of the most fundamental aspects of due process when the government seeks to deprive an individual of life, liberty, or property. The more serious the deprivation, the more formal the notice. *Goss*, 419 U.S. at 584. In the context of expulsion from an undergraduate university, "the [written] notice should contain a statement of the specific charges and grounds which, if proven, would justify expulsion under the regulations of the Board of Education." *Dixon*, 294 F.2d at 158. Notice satisfies due process if the student "had sufficient notice of the charges against him and a meaningful opportunity to prepare for the hearing." *See Jaksa*, 597 F. Supp. at 1250, *aff'd* 787 F.2d 590.

As early as October 12, 2001, almost immediately after his arrest, Flaim received written notice from Medical College of Ohio that he was accused of violating two sections of College policies as a result of the state criminal charges. The notice identified the precise College policies that he was charged with violating. The notice also informed Flaim that he was suspended until external investigations/hearings were completed, and informed him that he had the right to an internal investigation in addition to the external investigation. A week later Flaim received additional written notice informing him that he was not permitted back onto campus until an internal hearing could be held regarding the conduct giving rise to the criminal charges. In the following six months, Flaim received two additional letters reminding Flaim that he was required to attend an internal hearing prior to returning to campus.

Flaim, however, chose not to request the internal hearing until his criminal charges were adjudicated. After pleading guilty, Flaim contacted Medical College of Ohio and stated that he wished to schedule his hearing. Medical College of Ohio then provided additional written notice on June 21, 2002, stating that he was required to appear in front of a disciplinary committee on June 28 due to his conviction for attempted possession of a controlled substance. The notice further informed Flaim that he would have the opportunity to present testimony and would be asked to respond to any questions the committee members might have.

Flaim's principal contention regarding notice is that the final notice on June 21 was insufficient because it failed to inform him of the evidence and/or testimony that the college would present and that the college did not produce a written report regarding the specifics of the charges against him. He further asserts that the notice was inadequate because it failed to inform him that the arresting officer would appear and because the notice did not include copies of any documents that Medical College of Ohio intended to produce at the hearing.

The notice provided by Medical College of Ohio, however, was more than adequate. All that is required by the Due Process Clause, which sets a floor or lower limit on what is constitutionally adequate, is "sufficient notice of the charges . . . and a meaningful opportunity to prepare for the hearing." *Jaksa*, 597 F. Supp. at 1250. Flaim certainly received such notice here. Furthermore, considering that it was Flaim himself and not the college that delayed the hearing for six months, it is difficult to see how he was in any way deprived of sufficient opportunity to prepare for the hearing.

. . . .

B. Right to Counsel

Flaim argues that he was denied the right to counsel at his disciplinary hearing in violation of the Due Process Clause. Prior to the hearing, Medical College of Ohio notified Flaim that its policy granted an accused student the right to counsel *only* if the student faced outstanding criminal charges at the time of the hearing. The notice further explained, however, that the college would allow Flaim to have his attorney present. At the hearing, while Flaim's attorney was permitted to remain in the room, Flaim was not permitted to consult with his attorney nor was the attorney permitted to participate in the proceedings. Flaim argues therefore, that Medical College of Ohio unfairly deceived him. We conclude, however, that Flaim was not denied due process based on these procedures.

Assuming Flaim was led to believe that he would be permitted to have active counsel at the hearing, it does not necessarily follow that what occurred violated his constitutional rights. . . .

. . . Here, Medical College of Ohio did not present its case through an attorney. The hearing was not procedurally complex. There were no rules of evidence. Flaim was provided with an opportunity to appear in person before the committee to present his defense. Flaim was permitted to listen to adverse witnesses and to rebut that testimony while addressing the committee with his version of events. Flaim's complaint really boils down to the assertion that he was denied the opportunity to present his case as *effectively* as he would have wished — he could not reasonably claim that he was denied the *opportunity* to present his case at all due to the lack of legal counsel. . . .

Under *Mathews*, Flaim does no better. While the additional safeguard of professional advocacy may lessen the risk of erroneous expulsion by improving the quality of the student's case, the administrative burdens to a university, in the business of education, not judicial administration, are weighty. Full-scale adversarial hearings in school disciplinary proceedings have never been required by the Due Process Clause and conducting these types of hearings with professional counsel would entail significant expense and additional procedural complexity. . . .

C. Cross-Examination

At the hearing, Flaim was not permitted to cross-examine the arresting officer. Flaim alleges that the officer's testimony was unreliable and contradictory. We assume that Flaim is asserting that if he were permitted to cross-examine the officer, he would have been able to expose the testimony's unreliability. In any event, at the hearing and prior to addressing the committee, Flaim was able to listen to and observe the officer's testimony. Flaim then had the opportunity to present his version of events, during which he had the opportunity to point out inconsistencies or contradictions in the officer's testimony.

. . . Flaim was given adequate opportunity to address any discrepancies in the officer's testimony during the hearing, "cross-examination would have been a fruitless exercise," *id.*, and Flaim was not denied due process here.

D. Written Findings

Flaim asserts that he was denied due process because the committee did not produce written findings for his review. He argues that the lack of written findings created a substantial risk that Dean Gohara expelled him erroneously or that she directed the committee to achieve her desired result. Once again, Flaim asserts that this right is based on college policy and/or the verbal or written assurances from the college. He cannot identify, however, any constitutional right to written findings of fact in an academic disciplinary hearing of this ilk and we accordingly reject his claim.

. . . .

E. Right to Appeal

Flaim also takes issue with the finality of Dean Gohara's decision. He argues that he had a right to appeal based on Medical College of Ohio policy, past college practice, and policy requirements from the accrediting body for all United States medical schools. Nonetheless, he fails to tie any of these points to a constitutional right to appeal the decision of an academic institution. Courts have consistently held that there is no right to an appeal from an academic disciplinary hearing that satisfies due process. *See Smith on Behalf of Smith v. Severn*, 129 F.3d 419, 428–29 (7th Cir. 1996) ("Due process does not require review by a school board."); *Winnick*, 460 F.2d at 549 n. 5 ("Winnick had no constitutional right to review or appeal after the disciplinary hearing which satisfied the essential requirements of due process."); *Foo v. Tr., Indiana Univ.*, 88 F. Supp. 2d 937, 952 (S.D. Ind. 1999).

Under *Mathews*, Flaim's claim still fails. Disciplinary hearings, of course, are not flawless. "The risk of error is not at all trivial, and it should be guarded against if that may be done without prohibitive cost or interference with the educational process." *Goss*, 419 U.S. at 580. An appeal's value would be in correcting any such error that might have occurred, even in proceedings satisfying due process. The cost to the college, however, would be substantial, and given the procedural posture of the hearing, we conclude that an appeal was not required in this case.

The costs to the college would include an additional administrative burden on the Dean and other faculty members and administrators involved in the process. The proceedings would be a distraction from the college's primary duty of educating. Additionally, Flaim's internal hearing came after the conclusion of formal state criminal proceedings. We will not speculate as to the outcome were Flaim's internal hearing to have occurred prior to the resolution of the state criminal proceedings, but only note that Flaim came before the committee after having pleaded guilty to state criminal drug charges. While his guilt was not at issue before the committee, there is still the theoretical possibility that Flaim was erroneously expelled because another lesser punishment was more appropriate. This possibility, however, is not sufficient to turn this case in his favor.

. . . .

IV.

Flaim also alleges that Medical College of Ohio violated his substantive due process rights in that the college's actions in expelling him "shock the conscience." *County of Sacramento v. Lewis*, 523 U.S. 833, 846–47 (1998). In *Dixon*, the court stated that "the governmental power to expel [a student] . . . is not unlimited and cannot be arbitrarily exercised. Admittedly, there must be some reasonable and constitutional ground for expulsion or the courts would have a duty to require reinstatement." 294 F.2d at 157. The plaintiffs in *Dixon*, a case argued by Jack Greenberg and Thurgood Marshall, were African-American students and were expelled for seeking to purchase lunch at a publicly owned grill in the basement of the Montgomery, Alabama, county courthouse. That expulsion shocks the conscience. Flaim's expulsion does not and it was supported by substantial evidence. Accordingly, we agree with the district court's conclusion that Flaim failed to state a cognizable substantive due process claim.

. . . .

The district court's judgment is affirmed.

NOTES

1. The court in *Flaim* made the following statement: "Additionally, Flaim's internal hearing came after the conclusion of formal state criminal proceedings. We will not speculate as to the outcome were Flaim's internal hearing to have occurred prior to the resolution of the state criminal proceedings, but only note that Flaim came before the committee after having pleaded guilty to state criminal drug charges." So, Flaim did not pursue an internal hearing until after he pleaded guilty at criminal trial. Would the amount of due process have changed at the university level had he not chosen to wait until after the criminal trial concluded? In other words, would he have gotten the right to active counsel, cross-examination, and appeal had he chosen to accept the internal hearing initially?

In a case in which a university student involved in a disciplinary appeal is also subject to pending criminal charges, how dependent is the university on the outcome or the timeline of the criminal proceedings? Does it have to wait until the criminal proceedings are over? Does it have to abide by the criminal court's result? What if the student argues "double jeopardy" (i.e., one can't be tried for the same crime twice)? For a discussion of the double jeopardy issue, see *Maine v. Sterling*, 685 A.2d 432 (Me. 1996) (holding double jeopardy does not attach in a case where a student is punished under a university code and prosecuted under a criminal code for the same incident).

2. In *Flaim*, the expulsion from the university was based on an already adjudicated felony conviction. As a result, the court, in the due process challenge against the university, found no remaining factual disputes. The lack of factual disputes, it seems, dictated the level of process afforded to the student. Clearly, this may not be the situation in the majority of disciplinary proceedings in higher education. In fact, the court in *Flaim* called its case "rather unique" in this regard. How should university policies and handbooks be drafted to allow for such variation in circumstances? It may not be wise, due to heavy administrative burden and expense, for universities to afford full-blown process protections at the level seen in criminal trials in all discipline cases. In fact, courts, including *Flaim*, note that process at this high level is not necessary under the Fourteenth Amendment Due Process Clause in such cases. But how do university policies make the distinction sufficiently so that administrators are guided properly, offer appropriate process, but are not tied to unnecessary and expensive procedures?

3. The court in *Flaim*, with a citation to *Foo v. Indiana University*, 88 F. Supp. 2d 937, 952 (S.D. Ind. 1999), stated that "due process generally does not require an appeal from a university decision that was reached through constitutional procedures. As discussed further below, most colleges and universities do wisely and justly provide for such appeals to all who are charged in a college or university setting." What, then, are the constitutional minimums for due process in such cases? Why do universities typically offer appeals if the Constitution does not require them?

4. In the past couple decades, there has been much conversation, commentary, and controversy over "zero tolerance policies," particularly in K-12 education settings. *See, e.g.*, Kim Fries & Todd A. DeMitchell, *Zero Tolerance and the Paradox of Fairness: Viewpoints from the Classroom*, 36 J.L. & Educ. 211 (2007); Kevin A.

Gorman & Patrick D. Pauken, *The Ethics of Zero Tolerance*, 41 J. OF EDUC. ADMIN. 24 (2003); Deborah Gordon Klehr, *Addressing the Unintended Consequences of No Child Left Behind and Zero Tolerance: Better Strategies for Safe Schools and Successful Students*, 16 GEO. J. POVERTY LAW & POL'Y 585 (2009); Russell J. Skiba, Suzanne E. Eckes, & Kevin Brown, *African American Disproportionality in School Discipline: The Divide Between Best Evidence and Legal Remedy*, 54 N.Y.L. SCH. L. REV. 1071 (2009/2010). On one hand, as a statement of value, zero tolerance has its benefits, as it articulates to a community that responsibility for actions is necessary for a safe environment conducive to learning. On the other hand, zero tolerance policies also run a risk of reducing policy and practice to mere formula and distorted results. What are the advantages and disadvantages of zero tolerance policies for higher education settings? The specific language of "zero tolerance" in higher education policy is a rarity and will likely remain so. For one example, though, see *Allahverdi v. Regents of the University of New Mexico*, No. CIV 05-277 JB/DJS, 2006 U.S. Dist. LEXIS 27682 (D.N.M. Apr. 25, 2006), where a university's medical school dismissed a medical resident for his failure to comply with a zero tolerance policy on sexual harassment. For another example of "zero tolerance," where strict compliance with procedures haunted the administrators and not the students, see the following case.

SMITH v. DENTON
895 S.W.2d 550 (1995)

ROSALIND M. MOUSER, SPECIAL ASSOCIATE JUSTICE

In this appeal from a decision of the Faulkner County Chancery Court finding the firearms policy of the University of Central Arkansas facially void and violative of substantive due process and setting aside the three-year suspension of appellee Heather A. Denton, a UCA student, the appellants — the University of Central Arkansas and members of its administration and Board of Trustees [hereafter "UCA"] — raise four points for reversal.

. . . These four questions can be grouped more coherently under two broad issues: whether Ms. Denton received (1) procedural due process and (2) substantive due process. Although the chancellor did not address the former topic, we have determined, on *de novo* review, that Ms. Denton was denied procedural due process. . . . It is unnecessary for us to address the substantive due process issue.

. . . .

Facts

In December 1992, after several firearms incidents on its campus, UCA issued a revised firearms policy, which provided that:

> Any student possessing, storing, or using a firearm on University controlled property or at University sponsored or supervised functions, unless authorized by the University, will be suspended from UCA for a period of not less than three years unless a waiver of the suspension is granted by the

President upon the recommendation of the Vice President for Student Affairs.

A copy of the amended firearms policy was delivered to every student organization and residence-hall room and was published on January 11, 1993, in the student newspaper.

On the morning of Saturday, February 13, 1993, Heather A. Denton, a UCA freshman honors student on a full academic scholarship with no disciplinary record, loaned her automobile to a friend, Victor Smith, a non-student. The vehicle was returned to her later in the day.

That evening, Ms. Denton, Eric Patterson, a UCA student, and a mutual friend, Rita Patel, went "cruising" off-campus in Ms. Denton's car, with Mr. Patterson driving. While they were stopped in downtown Conway, a confrontation occurred with unknown occupants of a pickup truck. During the incident, a third vehicle arrived on the scene, and, reportedly, an unidentified person in that car waved a handgun.

Soon after these events, Mr. Patterson drove Ms. Denton's car back to the UCA campus. A Conway police officer, who had received a report about the incident (including the brandished weapon), located and followed Ms. Denton's vehicle to the campus and then stopped and searched it. An unloaded semi-automatic weapon was found in a backpack-style book bag beneath the passenger seat. Ms. Denton, Mr. Patterson, and Ms. Patel denied knowledge of the presence of the gun, though Mr. Patterson stated that it was owned by Victor Smith. Mr. Patterson was arrested and removed from the scene of the stop. No action was taken against either Ms. Denton or Ms. Patel by law enforcement officials.

After becoming aware of the incident, appellant Dr. John Smith, UCA Vice-President for Student Affairs, interviewed Ms. Denton on Monday, February 15, 1993. During the interview, Dr. Smith advised her that she was being charged with a violation of the firearms policy and was being suspended pending a determination by the Student Judicial Board. Dr. Smith ordered Ms. Denton to leave the campus immediately. No written notice of the charge was given to Ms. Denton prior to this meeting, nor did Dr. Smith simultaneously document the interview.

On Wednesday, February 17, 1993, some four days after the incident, the Student Judicial Board conducted a hearing. Various witnesses gave testimony, including Victor Smith, who admitted that he was the owner of the gun and that he had borrowed Ms. Denton's car to go shooting at targets with Mr. Patterson and his brother. He said that after they had finished, he put the gun in the book bag and placed it in the floorboard behind the passenger seat without Ms. Denton's knowledge or permission.

The Board found Ms. Denton not guilty of the charge, declaring its belief that she "did not have knowledge that the weapon was in the car," and recommended that no action be taken against her. Dr. Smith, however, rejected the Student Judicial Board's finding and determined that Ms. Denton should be suspended. Ms. Denton then appealed Dr. Smith's decision to the University Discipline Committee, which found her guilty of a violation of the firearms policy but recommended that the sanction be reduced. Dr. Smith, to whom the recommendation had been referred, withdrew from further consideration of the case.

As a result, Ms. Denton appealed the decision to appellant Dr. Winfred L. Thompson, President of UCA, who upheld the University Discipline Committee's guilt determination but rejected its recommendation of a reduced sanction. Dr. Thompson then imposed the three-year suspension provided for in the UCA firearms policy.

On March 11, 1993, Ms. Denton filed a petition for a temporary restraining order in the Faulkner County Chancery Court, requesting that the court stay or enjoin her suspension from UCA. The following day, the chancellor entered a temporary injunction. Subsequently, on March 31, 1993, Ms. Denton filed an amended petition for a permanent injunction, asserting that UCA's firearms policy failed, on its face, to provide substantive due process and that UCA's actions failed to provide procedural due process. An expedited hearing was held on April 8 and 16, 1993. The chancery court converted the temporary restraining order into a permanent restraining order, finding that:

> the UCA gun policy violates the 5th and 14th Amendments to the Constitution of the United States of America, in that it is violative of substantive due process; that is, the policy is void on its face and violates basic principles of democracy. The policy is hereby struck and any attempts to enforce the said policy against any student subsequent to April 16, 1993, will be sanctioned by the inherent contempt authority of the Court.

Having found that the firearms policy was facially void, the chancery court declared the procedural due process issue moot and declined to issue a ruling on the question. The court also found that the actions of UCA and its agents did not remove their immunity and, therefore, that Ms. Denton was not entitled to damages and attorney's fees. From that order, this appeal and cross-appeal arise.

Standard of review

. . . .

It is undisputed that UCA is a state-supported institution of higher learning which may delegate to its administration disciplinary power over non-academic offenses. A chancery court has no power to interfere in the exercise of a state-supported university's discretion in the promulgation and implementation of disciplinary measures unless it is shown by clear and convincing evidence that the university abused its discretion. . . . We hold that there was clear and convincing evidence, outlined in the discussion below, that UCA's actions constituted an abuse of the university's discretion.

Procedural due process

. . . .

The UCA "Standards of Student Conduct" promulgates disciplinary procedures governing the enforcement of university regulations. The student handbook notes that "the University strives to protect the rights of students involved in the disciplinary process by providing *specific due process procedures*, including appeals, to insure fair and just hearings." (Emphasis added.) The Vice President for Student Affairs is charged with the responsibility of overseeing the disciplinary process and is assisted by several committees and hearing officers who are assigned specialized functions. The Student Judicial Board, comprised of eleven voting student members and the Dean of Students or a designee in an advisory capacity, hears serious, suspendable offenses. Appeals may be made to the University Discipline Committee, UCA's chief appellate body, which consists of three faculty members, three administration representatives, and three students.

The disciplinary process is initiated by the filing of a written report of an alleged incident of non-academic misconduct with the Office of Vice President for Student Affairs. Thereafter, according to the "Standards of Student Conduct":

> *The Dean of Students will receive incident reports and assign discipline cases to the appropriate council and/or hearing officer as needed.* The Student Judicial Board [or other appropriate council or hearing officer] make their recommendations to the Vice President for Student Affairs. Disciplinary action shall be taken only after a hearing is held and the Vice President for Student Affairs has reviewed the action and made a final decision.

(Emphasis added.) The hearings are conducted informally, without strict adherence to the rules of evidence.

A notice provision is set forth in the "Standards":

> The students accused shall be notified, *in writing*, of the alleged charge and of the date, time and place of the hearing. Notice of hearing will be *mailed to the students or delivered to the residence hall room, if the students lives on campus, at least three (3) days prior to the hearing.*

(Emphasis added.) The accused and complainant are afforded the right to be present at the hearing, to present evidence by witness, affidavit, or deposition, to bring an advisor to the hearing, and to question all witnesses.

Appeals are assigned to the University Discipline Committee and must be made in writing to the Vice President for Student Affairs within three days after a disciplinary decision is rendered. One or more of the following reasons may serve as the basis of an appeal:

1. Inadequate opportunity to prepare defense;
2. Inadequate evidence to justify decision; or
3. Sanction not in keeping with gravity of wrong-doing.

The Vice President for Student Affairs is vested with the authority to make the final decision regarding all disciplinary concerns.

In the present case, UCA failed to adhere to its own expressly enunciated standards for ensuring procedural due process. The procedures provided by the university were not structurally flawed; in terms of actual compliance, however, the letter and spirit of procedural due process were violated. To protect due process, the courts, in matters pertaining to a governmental entity's observance and implementation of self-prescribed procedures, must be particularly vigilant and must hold such entities to a strict adherence to both the letter and the spirit of their own rules and regulations. . . .

Here, there was no indication that the Dean of Students reviewed the charge against Ms. Denton before it was referred to Dr. Smith or before the case was assigned to the Student Judicial Board, as required by the UCA "Standards of Student Conduct." Instead, Dr. Smith, Vice President of Student Affairs, interviewed Ms. Denton on Monday, February 15, 1993, and verbally advised her that a disciplinary hearing would be held by the board. Having ordered her to leave the campus immediately, he then caused to be delivered to her vacated residence-hall room a written notice, dated February 15, 1993, of the hearing before the Student Judicial Board to be held "at 7:00 p.m., on Wednesday, February 17, 1993." The notice, which more properly should have been mailed to her permanent address, was sent to the dormitory room two days prior to the hearing rather than three days beforehand, as required by the "Standards."

Thus, UCA, by the terms of its own self-imposed standards, failed to provide Ms. Denton the promised protection of "specific due process procedures." Yet not only was there a failure to comport with the letter of procedural due process, there was also a failure to abide by its spirit. Throughout the proceedings, Dr. Smith acted in a variety of often-conflicting capacities. He was at once investigator, prosecutor, witness, and judge. Although Dr. Smith, as Vice President for Student Affairs, clearly held the ultimate authority in disciplinary matters, he overrode the decision of the Student Judicial Board. No provision was made in the UCA handbook for the Vice President for Student Affairs to step aside from a case, yet Dr. Smith did so following the University Discipline Committee's technical finding of guilt and its recommendation of a reduced sanction.

The matter was submitted for review to UCA President Dr. Winfred Thompson. He retained the three-year suspension because Ms. Denton's appeal was based only on the lack of adequate evidence and not on the appropriateness of the sanction.

While the severity of the sanction is a stated basis for appeal under the UCA "Standards for Student Conduct," the fact remains that "all non-academic discipline hearings are informal," according to the handbook. To deprive a student of her educational property interest on narrowly formal grounds as exemplified in these circumstances is to violate the spirit of procedural due process. We hold that Ms. Denton was denied the "rudimentary elements of fair play" required by the Due Process Clause. . . .

. . . We therefore affirm the decision of the chancery court, albeit for a different reason than that given by the chancellor. . . .

. . . .

DAVID NEWBERN, JUSTICE, concurring. The problem in this case, I think, is that the UCA firearms policy is offended by "possession" of a firearm without knowledge. The Student Judicial Board found Ms. Denton not guilty because she had no knowledge the pistol was in her car. Dr. Smith testified the school policy was violated regardless of knowledge. . . .

. . . .

Substantive due process requires that legislation be rationally related to achieving a legitimate governmental purpose. No doubt UCA had a legitimate governmental purpose for its policy, and the zeal with which the administration sought to implement it is laudable up to a point.

A policy which can be the basis of punishment of one who is the victim of circumstances created by others without her knowledge can also be said to be related to that purpose. It could place even the most innocent student in fear of being punished and thus perhaps serve the purpose. Such a policy is, however, in my view, irrational and unfair to the point that it cannot be said to be rationally related to anything. . . .

Robert L. Brown, Justice, dissenting. . . .

The majority is wrong to equate minor lapses in Student Handbook procedures with a violation of the United States Constitution. . . .

. . . .

Here, if anything, Ms. Denton received more in the way of due process protection than is required. She had two full hearings where she was present and where she testified and other witnesses testified on her behalf: one before the Student Judicial Board, which found her not guilty, and one before the University Discipline Committee, which found her culpable. In addition, her case was reviewed by the University Vice President for Student Affairs, Dr. John Smith, and by the President of the University, Dr. Winfred Thompson. That totals four reviews of her case before she took it to court.

. . . .

The majority cites no case for the principle that failure to adhere strictly to Student Handbook procedures amounts, in itself, to a violation of a constitutional magnitude. That is because there are none. Here, Ms. Denton did not complain of lack of notice of the first hearing because she received notice. She did not complain of surprise witnesses against her because there were none, and she had full opportunity to present her own case. That is all that due process requires.

I am fearful that by requiring such strict adherence to student handbooks and equating those procedures to what the U.S. Constitution requires, we undermine the ability of universities and even primary and secondary schools to enforce their disciplinary policies. In this case, a legitimate school gun policy was violated, and there were no procedural lapses of constitutional significance. Indeed, Ms. Denton was allowed to present her case fully on multiple occasions. I dissent.

NOTES

1. What do you think about the judicial requirement (or expectation) that universities maintain strict compliance with their own procedures? That is, the requirement that the letter of the law trumps the spirit of the law, even when the spirit is, arguably, met? In your opinion, is the majority or the dissent correct in

Denton? See also *Tedeschi v. Wagner College*, 404 N.E.2d 1302 (1980), on the application of these arguments to private university settings, later in the chapter. The letter versus spirit argument is also a matter of contract law. See *Schaer v. Brandeis University*, 735 N.E.2d 373 (2000), in Chapter V.

2. Often, we speak of "notice" in due process cases as notice of the charges against a person cited for alleged misconduct, moving then to an opportunity for a hearing and, perhaps, an opportunity to appeal. In other words, notice of the penalty itself may not be enough to satisfy due process if the penalty is imposed before or at the same time that the student is made aware of the infraction. *See Nickerson v. University of Alaska Anchorage*, 975 P.2d 46 (Alaska 1999) (student denied due process after he was dismissed from a graduate student teaching practicum; he had not been notified of his misconduct or that continued misconduct would result in dismissal until the day he was dismissed).

2. Due Process in Academics

BOARD OF CURATORS OF THE UNIVERSITY OF MISSOURI v. HOROWITZ

435 U.S. 78 (1978)

MR. JUSTICE REHNQUIST delivered the opinion of the Court.

Respondent, a student at the University of Missouri-Kansas City Medical School, was dismissed by petitioner officials of the school during her final year of study for failure to meet academic standards. Respondent sued petitioners under 42 U.S.C. § 1983 in the United States District Court for the Western District of Missouri alleging, among other constitutional violations, that petitioners had not accorded her procedural due process prior to her dismissal. The District Court, after conducting a full trial, concluded that respondent had been afforded all of the rights guaranteed her by the Fourteenth Amendment to the United States Constitution and dismissed her complaint. The Court of Appeals for the Eighth Circuit reversed and a petition for rehearing en banc was denied by a divided court. We granted certiorari to consider what procedures must be accorded to a student at a state educational institution whose dismissal may constitute a deprivation of "liberty" or "property" within the meaning of the Fourteenth Amendment. We reverse the judgment of the Court of Appeals.

I

Respondent was admitted with advanced standing to the Medical School in the fall of 1971. During the final years of a student's education at the school, the student is required to pursue in "rotational units" academic and clinical studies pertaining to various medical disciplines such as obstetrics-gynecology, pediatrics, and surgery. Each student's academic performance at the School is evaluated on a periodic basis by the Council on Evaluation, a body composed of both faculty and students, which can recommend various actions including probation and dismissal. The recommendations of the Council are reviewed by the Coordinating Committee, a body composed solely of faculty members, and must ultimately be approved by the Dean. Students are not typically allowed to appear before either the Council or the Coordinating Committee on the occasion of their review of the student's academic performance.

In the spring of respondent's first year of study, several faculty members expressed dissatisfaction with her clinical performance during a pediatrics rotation. The faculty members noted that respondent's "performance was below that of her peers in all clinical patient-oriented settings," that she was erratic in her attendance at clinical sessions, and that she lacked a critical concern for personal hygiene. Upon the recommendation of the Council on Evaluation, respondent was advanced to her second and final year on a probationary basis.

Faculty dissatisfaction with respondent's clinical performance continued during the following year. For example, respondent's docent, or faculty adviser, rated her clinical skills as "unsatisfactory." In the middle of the year, the Council again reviewed respondent's academic progress and concluded that respondent should not be considered for graduation in June of that year; furthermore, the Council recommended that, absent "radical improvement," respondent be dropped from the school.

Respondent was permitted to take a set of oral and practical examinations as an "appeal" of the decision not to permit her to graduate. Pursuant to this "appeal," respondent spent a substantial portion of time with seven practicing physicians in the area who enjoyed a good reputation among their peers. The physicians were asked to recommend whether respondent should be allowed to graduate on schedule and, if not, whether she should be dropped immediately or allowed to remain on probation. Only two of the doctors recommended that respondent be graduated on schedule. Of the other five, two recommended that she be immediately dropped from the school. The remaining three recommended that she not be allowed to graduate in June and be continued on probation pending further reports on her clinical progress. Upon receipt of these recommendations, the Council on Evaluation reaffirmed its prior position.

The Council met again in mid-May to consider whether respondent should be allowed to remain in school beyond June of that year. Noting that the report on respondent's recent surgery rotation rated her performance as "low-satisfactory," the Council unanimously recommended that "barring receipt of any reports that Miss Horowitz has improved radically, [she] not be allowed to re-enroll in the . . . School of Medicine." The Council delayed making its recommendation official until receiving reports on other rotations; when a report on respondent's emergency rotation also turned out to be negative, the Council unanimously reaffirmed its recommendation that respondent be dropped from the school. The Coordinating Committee and the Dean approved the recommendation and notified respondent, who appealed the decision in writing to the University's Provost for Health Sciences. The Provost sustained the school's actions after reviewing the record compiled during the earlier proceedings.

II

A

To be entitled to the procedural protections of the Fourteenth Amendment, respondent must in a case such as this demonstrate that her dismissal from the school deprived her of either a "liberty" or a "property" interest. Respondent has never alleged that she was deprived of a property interest. Because property interests are creatures of state law, *Perry v. Sindermann*, 408 U.S. 593, 599–603 (1972), respondent would have been required to show at trial that her seat at the Medical School was a "property" interest recognized by Missouri state law. Instead, respondent argued that her dismissal deprived her of "liberty" by substantially impairing her opportunities to continue her medical education or to return to employment in a medically related field.

The Court of Appeals agreed, citing this Court's opinion in *Board of Regents v. Roth*, 408 U.S. 564 (1972). In that case, we held that the State had not deprived a teacher of any liberty or property interest in dismissing the teacher from a nontenured position, but noted:

> "[T]here is no suggestion that the State, in declining to re-employ the respondent, imposed on him a stigma or other disability that foreclosed his freedom to take advantage of other employment opportunities. The State, for example, did not invoke any regulations to bar the respondent from all other public employment in state universities." *Id.* at 573.

We have recently had an opportunity to elaborate upon the circumstances under which an employment termination might infringe a protected liberty interest. In *Bishop v. Wood*, 426 U.S. 341 (1976), we upheld the dismissal of a policeman without a hearing; we rejected the theory that the mere fact of dismissal, absent some publicizing of the reasons for the action, could amount to a stigma infringing one's liberty. . . .

The opinion of the Court of Appeals, decided only five weeks after we issued our opinion in *Bishop*, does not discuss whether a state university infringes a liberty interest when it dismisses a student without publicizing allegations harmful to the student's reputation. Three judges of the Court of Appeals for the Eighth Circuit dissented from the denial of rehearing en banc on the ground that "the reasons for Horowitz's dismissal were not released to the public but were communicated to her directly by school officials." Citing *Bishop*, the judges concluded that "[a]bsent such public disclosure, there is no deprivation of a liberty interest." 542 F. 2d, at 1335. Petitioners urge us to adopt the view of these judges and hold that respondent has not been deprived of a liberty interest.

B

We need not decide, however, whether respondent's dismissal deprived her of a liberty interest in pursuing a medical career. Nor need we decide whether respondent's dismissal infringed any other interest constitutionally protected against deprivation without procedural due process. Assuming the existence of a liberty or property interest, respondent has been awarded at least as much due process as the Fourteenth Amendment requires. The school fully informed respondent of the faculty's dissatisfaction with her clinical progress and the danger that this posed to timely graduation and continued enrollment. The ultimate decision to dismiss respondent was careful and deliberate. These procedures were sufficient under the Due Process Clause of the Fourteenth Amendment. We agree with the District Court that respondent

> "was afforded full procedural due process by the [school]. In fact, the Court is of the opinion, and so finds, that the school went beyond [constitutionally required] procedural due process by affording [respondent] the opportunity to be examined by seven independent physicians in order to be absolutely certain that their grading of the [respondent] in her medical skills was correct."

In *Goss v. Lopez*, 419 U.S. 565 (1975), we held that due process requires, in connection with the suspension of a student from public school for disciplinary reasons, "that the student be given oral or written notice of the charges against him and, if he denies them, an explanation of the evidence the authorities have and an opportunity to present his side of the story." *Id.*, at 581. The Court of Appeals apparently read *Goss* as requiring some type of formal hearing at which respondent could defend her academic ability and performance. All that *Goss* required was an "informal give-and-take" between the student and the administrative body dismissing him that would, at least, give the student "the opportunity to characterize his conduct and put it in what he deems the proper context." *Id.*, at 584. But we have frequently emphasized that "[t]he very nature of due process negates any concept of inflexible procedures universally applicable to every imaginable situation." *Cafeteria Workers v. McElroy*, 367 U.S. 886, 895 (1961). The need for flexibility is well illustrated by the significant difference between the failure of a student to meet academic standards and the violation by a student of valid rules of conduct. This difference calls for far less stringent procedural requirements in the case of an academic dismissal.[3]

Since the issue first arose 50 years ago, state and lower federal courts have recognized that there are distinct differences between decisions to suspend or dismiss a student for disciplinary purposes and similar actions taken for academic reasons which may call for hearings in connection with the former but not the latter. Thus, in *Barnard v. Inhabitants of Shelburne*, 216 Mass. 19, 102 N.E. 1095 (1913), the Supreme Judicial Court of Massachusetts rejected an argument, based on several earlier decisions requiring a hearing in disciplinary context, that school officials must also grant a hearing before excluding a student on academic grounds.

---

[3] We fully recognize that the deprivation to which respondent was subjected — dismissal from a graduate medical school — was more severe than the 10-day suspension to which the high school students were subjected in *Goss*. And a relevant factor in determining the nature of the requisite due process is "the private interest that [was] affected by the official action." *Mathews v. Eldridge*, 424 U.S. 319, 335 (1976). But the severity of the deprivation is only one of several factors that must be weighed in deciding the exact due process owed. *Ibid.* We conclude that considering all relevant factors, including the evaluative nature of the inquiry and the significant and historically supported interest of the school in preserving its present framework for academic evaluations, a hearing is not required by the Due Process Clause of the Fourteenth Amendment.

According to the court, disciplinary cases have

> "no application. . . . Misconduct is a very different matter from failure to attain a standard of excellence in studies. A determination as to the fact involves investigation of a quite different kind. A public hearing may be regarded as helpful to the ascertainment of misconduct and useless or harmful in finding out the truth as to scholarship." *Id.*, at 22–23, 102 N.E., at 1097.

A similar conclusion has been reached by the other state courts to consider the issue. *See, e.g., Mustell v. Rose*, 282 Ala. 358, 367, 211 So. 2d 489, 498, *cert. denied*, 393 U.S. 936 (1968); *cf. Foley v. Benedict*, 122 Tex. 193, 55 S.W. 2d 805 (1932). . . . These prior decisions of state and federal courts, over a period of 60 years, unanimously holding that formal hearings before decisionmaking bodies need not be held in the case of academic dismissals, cannot be rejected lightly. . . .

Reason, furthermore, clearly supports the perception of these decisions. A school is an academic institution, not a courtroom or administrative hearing room. In *Goss*, this Court felt that suspensions of students for disciplinary reasons have a sufficient resemblance to traditional judicial and administrative factfinding to call for a "hearing" before the relevant school authority. . . .

Even in the context of a school disciplinary proceeding, however, the Court stopped short of requiring a *formal* hearing since "further formalizing the suspension process and escalating its formality and adversary nature may not only make it too costly as a regular disciplinary tool but also destroy its effectiveness as a part of the teaching process."

Academic evaluations of a student, in contrast to disciplinary determinations, bear little resemblance to the judicial and administrative factfinding proceedings to which we have traditionally attached a full-hearing requirement. In *Goss*, the school's decision to suspend the students rested on factual conclusions that the individual students had participated in demonstrations that had disrupted classes, attacked a police officer, or caused physical damage to school property. The requirement of a hearing, where the student could present his side of the factual issue, could under such circumstances "provide a meaningful hedge against erroneous action." The decision to dismiss respondent, by comparison, rested on the academic judgment of school officials that she did not have the necessary clinical ability to perform adequately as a medical doctor and was making insufficient progress toward that goal. Such a judgment is by its nature more subjective and evaluative than the typical factual questions presented in the average disciplinary decision. Like the decision of an individual professor as to the proper grade for a student in his course, the determination whether to dismiss a student for academic reasons requires an expert evaluation of cumulative information and is not readily adapted to the procedural tools of judicial or administrative decisionmaking.

Under such circumstances, we decline to ignore the historic judgment of educators and thereby formalize the academic dismissal process by requiring a hearing. The educational process is not by nature adversary; instead it centers around a continuing relationship between faculty and students, "one in which the teacher must occupy many roles — educator, adviser, friend, and, at times, parent-substitute." *Goss v. Lopez*, 419 U.S., at 594 (POWELL, J., dissenting). This is especially true as one advances through the varying regimes of the educational system, and the instruction becomes both more individualized and more specialized. In *Goss*, this Court concluded that the value of some form of hearing in a disciplinary context outweighs any resulting harm to the academic environment. Influencing this conclusion was clearly the belief that disciplinary proceedings, in which the teacher must decide whether to punish a student for disruptive or insubordinate behavior, may automatically bring an adversary flavor to the normal student-teacher relationship. The same conclusion does not follow in the academic context. We decline to further enlarge the judicial presence in the academic community and thereby risk deterioration of many beneficial aspects of the faculty-student relationship. We recognize, as did the Massachusetts Supreme Judicial Court over 60 years ago, that a hearing may be "useless or harmful in finding out the truth as to scholarship." *Barnard v. Inhabitants of Shelburne*, 216 Mass., at 23, 102 N.E., at 1097.

"Judicial interposition in the operation of the public school system of the Nation raises problems requiring care and restraint. . . . By and large, public education in our Nation is committed to the control of state and local authorities." *Epperson v. Arkansas*, 393 U.S. 97, 104 (1968). We see no reason to intrude on that historic control in this case.

III

. . . [A] number of lower courts have implied in dictum that academic dismissals from state institutions can be enjoined if "shown to be clearly arbitrary or capricious." *Mahavongsanan v. Hall*, 529 F. 2d, at 449. . . . Even assuming that the courts can review under such a standard an academic decision of a public educational institution, we agree with the District Court that no showing of arbitrariness or capriciousness has been made in this case. Courts are particularly ill-equipped to evaluate academic performance. The factors discussed in Part II with respect to procedural due process speak a *fortiori* here and warn against any such judicial intrusion into academic decisionmaking.

The judgment of the Court of Appeals is therefore

Reversed.

MR. JUSTICE POWELL, concurring.

I join the Court's opinion because I read it as upholding the District Court's view that respondent was dismissed for academic deficiencies rather than for unsatisfactory personal conduct, and that in these circumstances she was accorded due process.

. . . .

It is well to bear in mind that respondent was attending a medical school where competence in clinical courses is as much of a prerequisite to graduation as satisfactory grades in other courses. Respondent was dismissed because she was as deficient in her clinical work as she was proficient in the "book-learning" portion of the curriculum. Evaluation of her performance in the former area is no less an "academic" judgment because it involves observation of her skills and techniques in actual conditions of practice, rather than assigning a grade to her written answers on an essay question.

Because it is clear from the findings of fact by the District Court that respondent was dismissed solely on academic grounds, and because the standards of procedural due process were abundantly met before dismissal occurred, I join the Court's opinion.

MR. JUSTICE MARSHALL, concurring in part and dissenting in part.

I agree with the Court that, "[a]ssuming the existence of a liberty or property interest, respondent has been awarded at least as much due process as the Fourteenth Amendment requires." I cannot join the Court's opinion, however, because it contains dictum suggesting that respondent was entitled to even less procedural protection than she received. I also differ from the Court in its assumption that characterization of the reasons for a dismissal as "academic" or "disciplinary" is relevant to resolution of the question of what procedures are required by the Due Process Clause. Finally, I disagree with the Court's decision not to remand to the Court of Appeals for consideration of respondent's substantive due process claim.

I

. . . .

These meetings and letters [provided to Horowitz throughout her academic career in the Medical School outlining academic concerns the School had] plainly gave respondent all that *Goss* requires: several notices and explanations, and at least three opportunities "to present [her] side of the story." 419 U.S., at 581. I do not read the Court's opinion to disagree with this conclusion. Hence I do not understand why the Court indicates that even the "informal give-and-take" mandated by *Goss, id.*, at 584, need not have been provided here. This case simply provides no legitimate opportunity to consider whether "far less stringent procedural requirements" than those required in *Goss* are appropriate in other school contexts. While I disagree with the Court's conclusion that "far less" is adequate . . . , it is equally disturbing that the Court decides an issue not presented by the case before us. . . .

II

In view of the Court's dictum to the effect that even the minimum procedures required in *Goss* need not have been provided to respondent, I feel compelled to comment on the extent of procedural protection mandated here. I do so within a framework largely ignored by the Court, a framework derived from our traditional approach to these problems. According to our prior decisions, as summarized in *Mathews v. Eldridge*, 424 U.S. 319 (1976), three factors are of principal relevance in determining what process is due:

"First, the private interest that will be affected by the official action; second, the risk of an erroneous deprivation of such interest through the procedures used, and the probable value, if any, of additional or substitute procedural safeguards; and finally, the Government's interest, including the function involved and the fiscal and administrative burdens that the additional or substitute procedural requirement would entail." *Id.*, at 335.

. . . [A]s the Court of Appeals noted: "The unrefuted evidence here establishes that Horowitz has been stigmatized by her dismissal in such a way that she will be unable to continue her medical education, and her chances of returning to employment in a medically related field are severely damaged." 538 F. 2d 1317, 1321 (CA 8 1976).

. . . .

Neither of the other two factors mentioned in *Mathews* justifies moving from a high level to the lower level of protection involved in *Goss*. There was at least some risk of error inherent in the evidence on which the Dean relied in his meetings with and letters to respondent; faculty evaluations of such matters as personal hygiene and patient and peer rapport are neither as "sharply focused" nor as "easily documented" as was, *e.g.*, the disability determination involved in *Mathews, supra*, at 343. . . .

. . . Under these circumstances — with respondent having much more at stake than did the students in *Goss*, the administration at best having no more at stake, and the meetings between respondent and the Dean leaving some possibility of erroneous dismissal — I believe that respondent was entitled to more procedural protection than is provided by "informal give-and-take" before the school could dismiss her.

The contours of the additional procedural protection to which respondent was entitled need not be defined in terms of the traditional adversary system so familiar to lawyers and judges. . . .

In the instant factual context the "appeal" provided to respondent . . . served the same purposes as, and in some respects may have been better than, a formal hearing. . . . I therefore believe that the appeal procedure utilized by respondent, together with her earlier notices from and meetings with the Dean, provided respondent with as much procedural protection as the Due Process Clause requires.

III

The analysis in Parts I and II of this opinion illustrates that resolution of this case under our traditional approach does not turn on whether the dismissal of respondent is characterized as one for "academic" or "disciplinary" reasons. In my view, the effort to apply such labels does little to advance the due process inquiry, as is indicated by examination of the facts of this case.

. . . .

IV

While I agree with the Court that respondent received adequate procedural due process, I cannot join the Court's judgment because it is based on resolution of an issue never reached by the Court of Appeals. . . .

. . . .

I would reverse the judgment of the Court of Appeals and remand for further proceedings.

NOTES

1. In a practical sense, you may be pleased with the high level of deference the Court has offered to the academic decisions made by school and university officials. But do you agree with the Court's legal argument (i.e., assuming that there's a liberty interest and then holding the level of due process owed in disputes over academic decisions to be less than the level of due process owed in disciplinary disputes)?

2. The due process distinction made between academic and disciplinary decisions appears to be an easy one to make. However, deciding which type of decision has been made in a given case is tough — and it falls to the university employee initially. Once it reaches a court (or even an internal appellate level within the university), the distinction has already been made, or at least asserted, by the university administrator. What factors should be considered in deciding whether a decision is academic or disciplinary?

As an example, consider the case of a graduate medical student who was accepted into a residency program at an American university. Shortly thereafter, but before the residency began, the program's director discovered that the student had been terminated from a previous residency at a Scottish hospital. Based on the lack of truthfulness in his application for the American program, the student was dismissed. Was the decision to dismiss the student an academic one or a disciplinary one? *See Fenje v. Feld*, 398 F.3d 620 (7th Cir. 2005).

3. The Court said on several occasions that the process offered to Horowitz was far more than would have been constitutionally required. What are the procedures like for such academic disputes at your institution? Do you have formal processes spelled out in written policies? Do the required procedures meet or exceed the process that Horowitz received? Are they similar to those offered (and required) by *Goss v. Lopez*, a disciplinary case presented earlier in this chapter?

REGENTS OF THE UNIVERSITY OF MICHIGAN v. EWING
474 U.S. 214 (1985)

Justice Stevens delivered the opinion of the Court.

Respondent Scott Ewing was dismissed from the University of Michigan after failing an important written examination. The question presented is whether the University's action deprived Ewing of property without due process of law because its refusal to allow him to retake the examination was an arbitrary departure from the University's past practice. The Court of Appeals held that his constitutional rights were violated. We disagree.

I

In the fall of 1975 Ewing enrolled in a special 6-year program of study, known as "Inteflex," offered jointly by the undergraduate college and the Medical School. An undergraduate degree and a medical degree are awarded upon successful completion of the program. In order to qualify for the final two years of the Inteflex program, which consist of clinical training at hospitals affiliated with the University, the student must successfully complete four years of study including both premedical courses and courses in the basic medical sciences. The student must also pass the "NBME Part I" — a 2-day written test administered by the National Board of Medical Examiners.

In the spring of 1981, after overcoming certain academic and personal difficulties, Ewing successfully completed the courses prescribed for the first four years of the Inteflex program and thereby qualified to take the NBME Part I. Ewing failed five of the seven subjects on that examination, receiving a total score of 235 when the passing score was 345. (A score of 380 is required for state licensure and the national mean is 500.) Ewing received the lowest score recorded by an Inteflex student in the brief history of that program.

On July 24, 1981, the Promotion and Review Board individually reviewed the status of several students in the Inteflex program. After considering Ewing's record in some detail, the nine members of the Board in attendance voted unanimously to drop him from registration in the program.

In response to a written request from Ewing, the Board reconvened a week later to reconsider its decision. Ewing appeared personally and explained why he believed that his score on the test did not fairly reflect his academic progress or potential. After reconsidering the matter, the nine voting members present unanimously reaffirmed the prior action to drop Ewing from registration in the program.

In August, Ewing appealed the Board's decision to the Executive Committee of the Medical School. After giving Ewing an opportunity to be heard in person, the Executive Committee unanimously approved a motion to deny his appeal for a leave of absence status that would enable him to retake Part I of the NBME examination. In the following year, Ewing reappeared before the Executive Committee on two separate occasions, each time unsuccessfully seeking readmission to the Medical School. On August 19, 1982, he commenced this litigation in the United States District Court for the Eastern District of Michigan.

II

Ewing's complaint against the Regents of the University of Michigan asserted a right to retake the NBME Part I test on three separate theories, two predicated on state law and one based on federal law. As a matter of state law, he alleged that the

University's action constituted a breach of contract and was barred by the doctrine of promissory estoppel. As a matter of federal law, Ewing alleged that he had a property interest in his continued enrollment in the Inteflex program and that his dismissal was arbitrary and capricious, violating his "substantive due process rights" guaranteed by the Fourteenth Amendment and entitling him to relief under 42 U. S. C. § 1983.

The District Court held a 4-day bench trial at which it took evidence on the University's claim that Ewing's dismissal was justified as well as on Ewing's allegation that other University of Michigan medical students who had failed the NBME Part I had routinely been given a second opportunity to take the test. The District Court described Ewing's unfortunate academic history in some detail. Its findings . . . reveal that Ewing "encountered immediate difficulty in handling the work," and that his difficulties — in the form of marginally passing grades and a number of incompletes and makeup examinations, many experienced while Ewing was on a reduced course load — persisted throughout the 6-year period in which he was enrolled in the Inteflex program.

Ewing discounted the importance of his own academic record by offering evidence that other students with even more academic deficiencies were uniformly allowed to retake the NBME Part I. The statistical evidence indicated that of the 32 standard students in the Medical School who failed Part I of the NBME since its inception, all 32 were permitted to retake the test, 10 were allowed to take the test a third time, and 1 a fourth time. Seven students in the Inteflex program were allowed to retake the test, and one student was allowed to retake it twice. Ewing is the only student who, having failed the test, was not permitted to retake it. Dr. Robert Reed, a former Director of the Inteflex program and a member of the Promotion and Review Board, stated that students were "routinely" given a second chance. Ewing argued that a promotional pamphlet released by the Medical School approximately a week before the examination had codified this practice. The pamphlet, entitled "On Becoming a Doctor," stated:

> "According to Dr. Gibson, everything possible is done to keep qualified medical students in the Medical School. This even extends to taking and passing National Board Exams. Should a student fail either part of the National Boards, an opportunity is provided to make up the failure in a second exam." *Id.*, at 113.

The District Court concluded that the evidence did not support either Ewing's contract claim or his promissory estoppel claim under governing Michigan law. There was "no sufficient evidence to conclude that the defendants bound themselves either expressly or by a course of conduct to give Ewing a second chance to take Part I of the NBME examination." With reference to the pamphlet "On Becoming A Doctor," the District Court held that "even if [Ewing] had learned of the pamphlet's contents before he took the examination, and I find that he did not, I would not conclude that this amounted either to an unqualified promise to him or gave him a contract right to retake the examination."

With regard to Ewing's federal claim, the District Court determined that Ewing had a constitutionally protected property interest in his continued enrollment in the Inteflex program and that a state university's academic decisions concerning the qualifications of a medical student are "subject to substantive due process review" in federal court. The District Court, however, found no violation of Ewing's due process rights. The trial record, it emphasized, was devoid of any indication that the University's decision was "based on bad faith, ill will or other impermissible ulterior motives"; to the contrary, the "evidence [demonstrated] that the decision to dismiss plaintiff was reached in a fair and impartial manner, and only after careful and deliberate consideration." To "leave no conjecture" as to his decision, the District Judge expressly found that "the evidence [demonstrated] no arbitrary or capricious action since [the Regents] had good reason to dismiss Ewing from the program."

Without reaching the state-law breach-of-contract and promissory-estoppel claims, the Court of Appeals reversed the dismissal of Ewing's federal constitutional claim. The Court of Appeals agreed with the District Court that Ewing's implied contract right to continued enrollment free from arbitrary interference qualified as a property interest protected by the Due Process Clause, but it concluded that the University had arbitrarily deprived him of that property in violation of the Fourteenth Amendment because (1) "Ewing was a 'qualified' student, as the University defined that term, at the time he sat for NBME Part I"; (2) "it was the consistent practice of the University of Michigan to allow a qualified medical student who initially failed the NBME Part I an opportunity for a retest"; and (3) "Ewing was the only University of Michigan medical student who initially failed the NBME Part I between 1975 and 1982, and was not allowed an opportunity for a retest." *Ewing v. Board of Regents*, 742 F.2d 913, 916 (CA6 1984). The Court of Appeals therefore directed the University to allow Ewing to retake the NBME Part I, and if he should pass, to reinstate him in the Inteflex program.

We granted the University's petition for certiorari to consider whether the Court of Appeals had misapplied the doctrine of "substantive due process." We now reverse.

III

In *Board of Curators, Univ. of Mo. v. Horowitz*, 435 U.S. 78, 91–92 (1978), we assumed, without deciding, that federal courts can review an academic decision of a public educational institution under a substantive due process standard. In this case Ewing contends that such review is appropriate because he had a constitutionally protected property interest in his continued enrollment in the Inteflex program. . . . [W]e again conclude, as we did in *Horowitz*, that the precise facts disclosed by the record afford the most appropriate basis for decision. We therefore accept the University's invitation to "assume the existence of a constitutionally protectible property right in [Ewing's] continued enrollment," and hold that even if Ewing's assumed property interest gave rise to a substantive right under the Due Process Clause to continued enrollment free from arbitrary state action, the facts of record disclose no such action.

As a preliminary matter, it must be noted that any substantive constitutional protection against arbitrary dismissal would not necessarily give Ewing a right to retake the NBME Part I. The constitutionally protected interest alleged by Ewing in his complaint, and found by the courts below, derives from Ewing's implied contract right to continued enrollment free from arbitrary dismissal. The District

Court did not find that Ewing had any separate right to retake the exam and, what is more, explicitly "[rejected] the contract and promissory estoppel claims, finding no sufficient evidence to conclude that the defendants bound themselves either expressly or by a course of conduct to give Ewing a second chance to take Part I of the NBME examination." The Court of Appeals did not overturn the District Court's determination that Ewing lacked a tenable contract or estoppel claim under Michigan law, . . . and we accept its reasonable rendering of state law, particularly when no party has challenged it.

The University's refusal to allow Ewing to retake the NBME Part I is thus not actionable in itself. It is, however, an important element of Ewing's claim that his dismissal was the product of arbitrary state action, for under proper analysis the refusal may constitute evidence of arbitrariness even if it is not the actual legal wrong alleged. The question, then, is whether the record compels the conclusion that the University acted arbitrarily in dropping Ewing from the Inteflex program without permitting a reexamination.

It is important to remember that this is not a case in which the procedures used by the University were unfair in any respect; quite the contrary is true. Nor can the Regents be accused of concealing nonacademic or constitutionally impermissible reasons for expelling Ewing; the District Court found that the Regents acted in good faith.

Ewing's claim, therefore, must be that the University misjudged his fitness to remain a student in the Inteflex program. The record unmistakably demonstrates, however, that the faculty's decision was made conscientiously and with careful deliberation, based on an evaluation of the entirety of Ewing's academic career. When judges are asked to review the substance of a genuinely academic decision, such as this one, they should show great respect for the faculty's professional judgment. Plainly, they may not override it unless it is such a substantial departure from accepted academic norms as to demonstrate that the person or committee responsible did not actually exercise professional judgment. Cf. *Youngberg v. Romeo*, 457 U.S. 307, 323 (1982).

Considerations of profound importance counsel restrained judicial review of the substance of academic decisions. As JUSTICE WHITE has explained:

> "Although the Court regularly proceeds on the assumption that the Due Process Clause has more than a procedural dimension, we must always bear in mind that the substantive content of the Clause is suggested neither by its language nor by preconstitutional history; that content is nothing more than the accumulated product of judicial interpretation of the Fifth and Fourteenth Amendments. This is . . . only to underline Mr. Justice Black's constant reminder to his colleagues that the Court has no license to invalidate legislation which it thinks merely arbitrary or unreasonable." *Moore v. East Cleveland*, 431 U.S. 494, 543–544 (1977) (WHITE, J., dissenting).

. . . Added to our concern for lack of standards is a reluctance to trench on the prerogatives of state and local educational institutions and our responsibility to safeguard their academic freedom, "a special concern of the First Amendment."

Keyishian v. Board of Regents, 385 U.S. 589, 603 (1967). If a "federal court is not the appropriate forum in which to review the multitude of personnel decisions that are made daily by public agencies," *Bishop v. Wood*, 426 U.S. 341, 349 (1976), far less is it suited to evaluate the substance of the multitude of academic decisions that are made daily by faculty members of public educational institutions — decisions that require "an expert evaluation of cumulative information and [are] not readily adapted to the procedural tools of judicial or administrative decisionmaking." *Board of Curators, Univ. of Mo. v. Horowitz*, 435 U.S., at 89–90.

This narrow avenue for judicial review precludes any conclusion that the decision to dismiss Ewing from the Inteflex program was such a substantial departure from accepted academic norms as to demonstrate that the faculty did not exercise professional judgment. . . . The District Court found as a fact that the Regents "had good reason to dismiss Ewing from the program." 559 F.Supp., at 800. Before failing the NBME Part I, Ewing accumulated an unenviable academic record characterized by low grades, seven incompletes, and several terms during which he was on an irregular or reduced course load. Ewing's failure of his medical boards, in the words of one of his professors, "merely [culminated] a series of deficiencies. . . . In many ways, it's the straw that broke the camel's back." Moreover, the fact that Ewing was "qualified" in the sense that he was eligible to take the examination the first time does not weaken this conclusion, for after Ewing took the NBME Part I it was entirely reasonable for the faculty to reexamine his entire record in the light of the unfortunate results of that examination. Admittedly, it may well have been unwise to deny Ewing a second chance. Permission to retake the test might have saved the University the expense of this litigation and conceivably might have demonstrated that the members of the Promotion and Review Board misjudged Ewing's fitness for the medical profession. But it nevertheless remains true that his dismissal from the Inteflex program rested on an academic judgment that is not beyond the pale of reasoned academic decisionmaking when viewed against the background of his entire career at the University of Michigan, including his singularly low score on the NBME Part I examination.

The judgment of the Court of Appeals is reversed, and the case is remanded for proceedings consistent with this opinion.

It is so ordered.

NOTES

1. No doubt, there are countless cases involving academic dismissals of college students and endless requests by those students to get additional opportunities to prove their academic worthiness. For example, when students are placed on academic probation, usually due to the failure to meet GPA minimums or the failure to complete a certain requirement by a certain time, they may be given an opportunity to petition for reinstatement, or they may have a certain number of semesters or credit hours of probation during which they must earn a certain GPA to regain good standing. What a university or program allows in the way of petitions, hearings, and second chances may be based on the particular requirement that must be met (e.g., minimum GPA, passage of an entrance exam, etc.). It also may be based on the level of program (i.e., undergraduate or graduate). Do multiple opportunities to succeed count as due process in academic settings? In other words, if a university gives students second chances (and third chances and beyond) to succeed, does an ultimate decision to dismiss carry sufficiently more weight given these extra opportunities? In *Marx v. The Ohio State University College of Dentistry*, No. 95APE07-872, 1996 Ohio App. LEXIS 798 (Ohio Ct. App. Feb. 27, 1996), a university dentistry program dismissed a student after failing grades and numerous opportunities to improve, including an initial dismissal and reinstatement into a modified program, in which the student also failed. The state court of appeals affirmed the lower court's decision in favor of the university. For an additional example, see *Trotter v. The Regents of the University of New Mexico School of Medicine*, 219 F.3d 1179 (10th Cir. 2000), where the Court of Appeals for the Tenth Circuit upheld a university's decision to dismiss a medical student for poor academic performance after the university had given her three chances to succeed and several subsequent appeals. Even assuming the student had a protected right under the Due Process Clause, the university had afforded the student far more process than the Constitution would require.

The case of *University of Mississippi Medical Center v. Hughes*, 765 So.2d 528 (Miss. 2000), is also illustrative of the point. In *Hughes*, the university had a policy offering students three opportunities to pass the first step of the medical licensing examination. After the third failure, the student was to be dismissed. The court here addressed not only a procedural due process claim, but also a substantive due process claim and held that a judge may not override the faculty's professional judgment in academic matters unless it is such a substantial departure from accepted academic norms as to demonstrate that the person or committee responsible did not actually exercise professional judgment. The court held that the policy was, indeed, rationally related to the university's legitimate function of educating physicians. For a student's successful substantive due process argument, see *Sharick v. Southeastern University of the Health Sciences, Inc.*, 780 So. 2d 136 (Fla. Ct. App. 2000), where the court held that the university's decision to dismiss a fourth-year medical student for failing the final course needed for graduation was arbitrary and capricious. The court remanded for a trial based on damages, but held that tuition reimbursement for successful completion of the degree and loss of future earning potential were reasonable measures of damages, if shown to be appropriate under the circumstances.

2. If a formal hearing is not constitutionally required for student appeals to adverse academic decisions, such as dismissal, then what process should students deserve in such cases? Surely, the damage to a student for an academic dismissal is at least as big as the damage suffered in a disciplinary dismissal. Correct? Do you think the distinction between academic and disciplinary due process is practical? Relevant? Should a single due process system cover both academic and nonacademic disputes?

HABERLE v. UNIVERSITY OF ALABAMA IN BIRMINGHAM

803 F.2d 1536 (11th Cir. 1986)

Hill, Circuit Judge.

FACTS

Appellant Frederick J. Haberle was admitted to graduate school at the University of Alabama at Birmingham in July, 1979, to pursue a Ph.D. in chemistry. The requirements to obtain that degree are set out in a document entitled "Requirements for Degree in Chemistry." Generally it shows that the requirements for a Ph.D. in chemistry are completion of course work, demonstration of competence in two foreign languages, successful completion of the qualifying examination, presentations at two seminars, and the completion of a dissertation. Mr. Haberle was given a copy of this document soon after he entered the program. During his time as a student in the chemistry department, Haberle completed his course work, demonstrated his competency in two foreign languages, and made a presentation at one graduate seminar.

Mr. Haberle completed his course work in the fall of 1981. He registered for his dissertation in research in the winter term of 1980-81 and continued with it through the summer term of 1983-84. In July of 1981, the graduate committee supervising Mr. Haberle's studies met to discuss his curriculum and the qualifying (or "comprehensive") examination requirement. At this meeting the committee listed remaining course requirements, and planned to meet again in order to consider a research proposal and set a date for the qualifying examination. However, the committee did not meet again until January of 1984. At that time the committee noted that Haberle had never taken the qualifying examinations, and suggested he do so promptly. Mr. Haberle objected, stating that he should have taken the exam before beginning his dissertation research three years prior. However, the committee insisted that he take the qualifying exam.

The exam is divided into two portions, a written portion and an oral portion. Mr. Haberle passed the written portion by one point, and failed the oral portion. He was given the choice between accepting a master's degree or retaking the qualifying examination. He chose to take the exam again, and he failed again. He was then dismissed from the Chemistry Ph.D program.

After his dismissal Mr. Haberle complained to Dr. Blaine Brownell, who was then co-dean of the graduate school. He was advised to ask the committee members to reconsider their decision. They refused to do so. Mr. Haberle then addressed a grievance to the two deans of the graduate school, Kenneth J. Roozen and Blaine Brownell, and Peter O'Neal, Dean of the School of Natural Sciences and Mathematics.

O'Neal, along with the dean of the graduate school, decided that O'Neal would appoint an impartial committee to review Mr. Haberle's grievance. O'Neal appointed Professors Joseph Gauthier and Daniel Bearce to review the matter. They had never had any dealings with Mr. Haberle. Haberle was given the opportunity to submit additional information to the committee; he declined the opportunity to do so. The reviewing committee decided that the graduate committee had acted reasonably and that Mr. Haberle had been treated fairly. Their decision was then reviewed by the dean of the graduate school, who concurred.

Soon after, Mr. Haberle filed suit in federal district court, claiming that his dismissal and the procedures used to procure it violated his substantive and procedural due process rights. Haberle objected to the procedure used in disposing of his grievance on the following grounds: (1) the procedures were established on an ad hoc basis, (2) nowhere along the line did any of the administrators review Mr. Haberle's grades, and (3) the procedures did not follow those described in the graduate school bulletin. He also argued that his dismissal was arbitrary and thus a violation of substantive due process.

On summary judgment motion, the district court found that, as a matter of law in the Eleventh Circuit, the right to pursue a degree in the public school system was a constitutionally protectable interest, citing *Debra P. v. Turlington*, 644 F.2d 397 (5th Cir. 1981), *reh'g denied*, 654 F.2d 1079 (5th Cir. 1981). The court then dismissed the procedural due process claims, finding that all the procedures used were constitutionally adequate. After the Supreme Court's decision in *Regents of the University of Michigan v. Ewing*, 474 U.S. 214 (1985), the district court *sua sponte* reconsidered its motion for summary judgment and dismissed the substantive due process claims as well.

I.

With respect to the procedural due process claim, the legal standard governing academic dismissals was enunciated in the Supreme Court's decision *Board of Curators, University of Missouri v. Horowitz*, 435 U.S. 78 (1978). The court emphasized that academic dismissals were not easily adapted to traditional review, and that the standards governing academic dismissals were not as strict as those required in disciplinary actions. Formal hearings are not required in academic dismissals. Rather, the Supreme Court held that the decision-making process need only be "careful and deliberate." *Horowitz*, 435 U.S. at 85–87 (1978).

The district court found that under the *Horowitz* standard, the procedures used in dismissing Mr. Haberle were adequate. The court noted:

> 1. Plaintiff had several discussions with members of the graduate committee during which he expressed objections to taking the preliminary exam.
>
> 2. He was given two opportunities to take the exam.
>
> 3. He had discussions with the co-dean of the graduate school, further consideration by the graduate committee, and further consideration by the Dean of the School of Natural Sciences and Mathematics.
>
> 4. An impartial committee was appointed to review his complaint, and he was given an opportunity to submit further information to the committee.

Obviously Mr. Haberle was given substantial opportunity to complain to all relevant decision-makers. The fact that the procedures used were ad hoc does not violate the *Horowitz* standard; no formal hearing is required. In fact, University officials testified that the procedures afforded Haberle far exceeded the grievance procedure outlined in the University bulletin. There is no reason to reverse the district court's finding that procedural due process requirements were met in this case.

II.

We now turn to the substantive due process issue. In *Ewing*, 474 U.S. 214, the Supreme Court laid out a very narrow standard of substantive review over academic decisions. The Supreme Court stated:

> When judges are asked to review the substance of a genuinely academic decision, such as this one, they should show great respect for the faculty's professional judgment. Plainly, they may not override it unless it is such a *substantial departure from accepted academic norms as to demonstrate that the person or committee responsible did not actually exercise professional judgment.*

Id. at 513. [Emphasis added]

The Court continued:

> . . . Added to our concern for lack of standards is a reluctance to trench on the prerogatives of state and local educational institutions and our responsibility to safeguard their academic freedom, "a special concern of the First Amendment." *Keyishian v. Board of Regents*, 385 U.S. 589, 603 (1967). If a "federal court is not the appropriate forum in which to review the multitude of personnel decisions that are made daily by public agencies," *Bishop v. Wood*, 426 U.S. at 349, far less is it suited to evaluate the substance of the multitude of academic decisions that are made daily by faculty members of public educational institutions — decisions that require "an expert evaluation of cumulative information and [are] not readily adapted to the procedural tools of judicial or administrative decision-making." *Board of Curators, University of Missouri v. Horowitz*, 435 U.S. at 89–90.

Id. at 514. *Ewing* makes it plain that, in the absence of an improper motive, an academic dismissal must be "such a substantial departure from accepted academic norms as to demonstrate that the faculty did not exercise professional judgment," before it will be overturned on substantive due process grounds. *Id.* at 513.

Appellant contends that Mr. Haberle's dismissal was arbitrary because he was required to take the qualifying exam "for no reason." Theoretically the qualifying exam is given to a student before embarking upon dissertation research, to test one's competency and ability to carry out extensive research in one's chosen specialty. Mr. Haberle felt that his three years of dissertation research had already demonstrated his capacity to do extensive research, and that the examination was therefore a totally arbitrary, unnecessary intrusion into his academic career. However, the professors at the Department of Chemistry all felt, as a matter of professional judgment, that such an exam is necessary to test the caliber of one who would enter the company of scholars.

A summary chart submitted to the district court proved that no student had ever been awarded a Ph.D. without having to take the qualifying exam. In fact, the same evidence proved that it was not at all out of the ordinary for a student to take his or her qualifying exam after registering to begin dissertation research. The court found that requiring Mr. Haberle to take it four years after the normal time (i.e. before beginning one's dissertation research) was not such a substantial departure from academic norms as to amount to an arbitrary deprivation of property.

. . . .

Mr. Haberle also argues that the graduate committee "waived" the exam requirement for him by not requiring that he take the exam before beginning his dissertation research. This argument is purely fallacious. While it may have been unfortunate for the committee to allow him to do three year's worth of dissertation research, in fact no one ever told Mr. Haberle that the exam had been waived, and the exam has never been waived for anyone.

Appellant's attempts to distinguish himself from the plaintiff in *Ewing* do not help him. It is true that in *Ewing* the student was dismissed because of a generally poor academic performance. His failure to pass his medical boards was merely the crowning blow. In the instant case, Mr. Haberle's performance in the classroom was very good. However, as appellee points out, the qualifying exam is used to probe one's in-depth knowledge of one's chosen specialty. Only one of the five faculty members who examined Haberle felt that he possessed the overall knowledge of the subject and academic talent necessary for advanced graduate study. Professor Larry K. Krannich, Chairman of the Department of Chemistry, testified in his deposition that, while it is routine to allow a student who fails a qualifying exam a second opportunity to pass, no student has ever been given a third opportunity to take the exam. After two attempts Mr. Haberle was dismissed in accordance with the department's normal procedure.

It may be unfortunate to spend years studying a discipline only to discover that one's capabilities do not pass academic muster. However, the academic community requires a general comprehensive examination to determine whether or not a student is properly qualified for doctoral accomplishments. Had Mr. Haberle learned earlier that he did not have the comprehensive qualifications in chemistry to make him a suitable candidate for a doctoral degree, he might not have pursued the narrow research studies leading towards his dissertation for quite so long. Nevertheless, this is an academic question. The comprehensive exam is a prerequisite to the doctorate. Mr. Haberle failed the exam. There is no dispute about that. Therefore, he is not entitled to continue to pursue the doctorate. There is nothing arbitrary about such a requirement. The courts should not interfere with this academic decision.

Accordingly, the decision of the district court is

AFFIRMED.

NOTES

1. There is continuing debate over the weight a court should place on a university's compliance with its own stated procedures, like those set for grade appeals, academic dismissals, and disciplinary punishments of students. Some will argue that compliance with the letter of the law is required; others will argue that compliance with the spirit of the law is what is necessary. What if a university's procedures are written in a way to afford more due process than is constitutionally required, but then fails to match those procedures in an academic dismissal case where compliance with the letter of those procedures would not have been legally required anyway? In *Schuler v. University of Minnesota*, 788 F.2d 510 (8th Cir. 1986), the Court of Appeals for the Eighth Circuit held in favor of a university that dismissed a doctoral student after she failed a required oral examination twice. The student filed suit, arguing that the university failed to follow its policies on the administration of the exam itself and in the review of student grievances. The court held that the procedures used comported with due process because the student had prior notice of the faculty dissatisfaction with her performance (given the second chance to complete the exam) and the possibility of dismissal after a second failure. The court found that an in-person departmental hearing to review the decision to dismiss was more process than is constitutionally required.

2. If a university adheres to its grade review and appeals procedures in most cases and then deviates from it in one case, courts are likely to find the university's actions constitutionally improper. It is, indeed, rare for courts to jump in and decide academic matters typically reserved for academic decision makers. But when a university diverges from long-standing, appropriate practice in only one noted case, the court may step in. *See Sylvester v. Texas Southern University*, 957 F. Supp. 944 (S.D. Tex. 1997) (granting a law student's motion for summary judgment and ordering the law school to raise the grade in one of the student's final courses from a D to a C and to name her co-valedictorian).

3. With the continuing distinction made between disciplinary and academic decisions, for purposes of constitutional law and judicial deference, would there not be a temptation on the part of university officials to frame disciplinary acts as academic acts in order to avoid more formal due process and future judicial scrutiny? What recourse does an affected student have in a case where the university decision makers are suspected of such a maneuver? Consider also the following article excerpt that explains more fully the arguments and the problems with a legal distinction between academic and disciplinary decisions.

FERNAND N. DUTILE, *DISCIPLINARY VERSUS ACADEMIC SANCTIONS IN HIGHER EDUCATION: A DOOMED DICHOTOMY?*, 29 J. COLL. & UNIV. L. 619 (2003)*

. . . .

III. ACADEMIC VERSUS DISCIPLINARY

A. *A Viable Distinction?*

1. The Problem

The Supreme Court, in denying relief in both *Horowitz* and *Ewing*, made clear that academic situations must be distinguished from disciplinary ones. The Court made no extensive effort, however, to elaborate upon that distinction. The Court seems to have assumed that situations fall easily into one category or the other. But does the distinction survive scrutiny? Or is it, as Justice Marshall said, futile to attempt "a workable distinction between 'academic' and 'disciplinary' dismissals"?

In reality, situations in which higher-education students face adverse institutional decisions occupy a spectrum ranging from the purely academic through the purely disciplinary. On the disciplinary side, the dismissal of a student for stealing the dean's car from a shopping mall parking lot seems virtually all disciplinary, though even that example can be made still less "academic" by substituting for the dean a victim unrelated to the university, an educational factor, the dean, no longer obtains.

On the academic side of the spectrum, the student's dismissal for failing to post the required cumulative grade-point-average seems to approach as nearly as possible the purely academic. But even here, problems with the distinction leap off the page. The matter in dispute might not be the qualitative assessment of the paper but rather whether the instructor (or her research assistant or even a secretary) correctly recorded the grade. In some courses, secretarial staff grade multiple-choice portions of examinations. If a student alleges that the grader mislabeled one answer on a critical examination, reviewing the seemingly academic judgment really implicates no more than the usual factfinding skills involved in purely disciplinary cases. Perhaps the C- in History II that dropped the student below the required average stemmed in part from loss of points under the instructor's attendance policy. . . .

. . . .

Ironically, *Horowitz* provided an apt, though not ideal, vehicle for attacking the very distinction set out there by the Court. Ms. Horowitz had been dismissed in part for erratic attendance and a lack of critical concern for personal hygiene. Both factors present obvious concerns for medical education. Nonetheless, neither conjures up the complex academic judgment demanding virtually total acquiescence to the medical expertise of the faculty. Interestingly, the minutes of an early meeting, reviewing her status, state: "This issue is *not one of academic achievement*, but of performance, relationship to people and ability to communicate."

. . . .

IV. ASSESSING THE DISTINCTION AND THE DEFERENCE

. . . .

At bottom, three rationales seem to underlie the Court's efforts to distance *Horowitz* from *Goss*: 1) the flexibility needed by educational institutions to deal with a panoply of situations; 2) the supposed greater subjectivity involved in "academic" decisions, a subjectivity not given to effective judicial review; and 3) the decreased adversariness typifying the teacher-student relationship in "academic" matters.

Neither the Supreme Court, nor any other court, has provided significant support for the need for more flexibility in academic cases than in disciplinary ones. Indeed, the Court's explanation seems little more than a *non sequitur*: "The need for flexibility is well illustrated by the significant difference between the failure of a student to meet academic standards and the violation by a student of valid rules of conduct." One might say with equal persuasiveness that the significant differences between a Chevrolet and a Ford make the need for different speed limits obvious.

. . . .

Different treatment has also been defended by reference to the supposed greater subjectivity involved in "academic" decisions; unlike the judgments in disciplinary cases, we are told, that subjectivity is not readily adapted to the procedural tools of judicial or administrative decisionmaking. Justice Powell, concurring in *Horowitz*, perhaps put the most nuanced case for the distinction:

> A decision relating to the misconduct of a student requires a factual determination as to whether the conduct took place or not. The accuracy of that determination can be safeguarded by the sorts of procedural protections traditionally imposed under the Due Process Clause. An academic judgment also involves this type of objectively determinable fact, *e.g.*, whether the student gave certain answers on an examination. But the critical decision requires a subjective, expert evaluation as to whether that performance satisfies some predetermined standard of academic competence. That standard, in turn, is set by a similarly expert judgment. These evaluations, which go far beyond questions of mere "conduct," are not susceptible of the same sorts of procedural safeguards that are appropriate to determining facts relating to misconduct.

. . . .

This point might hold true for clinical evaluations in highly specialized fields. Faculty must also be given appropriate rein in deciding, for example, whether an essay responds adequately or well to the question posed or a research paper treats adequately or well the specified topic. The argument, though, carries weight precisely, and only, to the extent that the matter involves a pure assessment of academic performance, *e.g.*, the grade for an examination or research paper or the adequacy of a clinical performance. . . .

. . . .

A third argument for different treatment flows from the claimed decreased adversariness typifying the teacher-student relationship in "academic" matters. . . .

Here again, the Supreme Court has provided little support for its worries about adversariness. It said in *Horowitz*: "Influencing [the] conclusion [in *Goss*] was clearly the belief that disciplinary proceedings . . . may automatically bring an adversary flavor to the normal student-teacher relationship. The same conclusion does not follow in the academic context." Why, pray tell, not? The Court's statement that "[t]he educational process is not by nature adversary" applies to the disciplinary as well as to the academic. That the very situations labeled academic by the courts have, by definition, gone to litigation suggests that students, once threatened with suspension, expulsion, or some other serious sanction, perceive no difference in adversariness between the disciplinary and the academic, even when the situations can be seen as one or the other. Ms. Horowitz and Mr. Ewing, to cite but two examples, took their fight with educational officials all the way to the U.S. Supreme Court; so much for non-adversarial resolution of differences!

. . . .

Yet concerns that more intensive judicial oversight and more extensive internal procedures would promote litigation against colleges and universities and thus perhaps dilute their credibility seem misplaced. First, there has been no shortage of such lawsuits under the current "procedure-lite" approach to academic decisions. Second, one might persuasively counter that the more careful the institutional process, the *less* the judicial involvement. This flows from two different sources. First, the student who feels fairly treated will more likely not sue. Second, courts will more quickly and easily deal with such a case; review may center not on the substance of the decision, but on whether institutional procedures provided a fair method of resolution. Such a fair method of resolution would obviously incorporate academic (and disciplinary) expertise, as relevant, and some method for resolving disputes concerning facts "susceptible of determination by third parties." To some extent, of course, this reflects current judicial practice. Elevating the due process requirements for academic decisionmaking by higher-education institutions can be expected to reduce still further the number of controversies making it to court.

. . . .

V. AN ALTERNATIVE APPROACH

. . . .

. . . The conventional judicial approach holds that a student charged with, say, the use of drugs has the right to a hearing. On the other hand, a student who has failed a three-hour essay examination enjoys no right to a hearing on the matter; the academic aspect of the situation trumps any significant procedural entitlements.

This approach misleads. The second student too has had a hearing: the examination itself. That three-hour exercise allowed the student a full opportunity to persuade the "hearing examiner" — in this case the instructor — that the student has learned the material adequately or even well. This opportunity clearly equals any procedural protection that *Goss* and its progeny provide for disciplinary situations. . . . Especially when one considers that dismissal for academic failure normally results only from several such assessments, it becomes obvious that so-called academic sanctions most often do receive hearings.

In disciplinary cases, the student charged with using drugs now needs a hearing to assess whether the transaction took place as alleged. No official assessment has yet occurred. Even if a university official allegedly witnessed the drug use, the student requires an opportunity to argue that she was misidentified, the object involved was not a proscribed drug, the witness was vindictive, or the like. In cases like *Horowitz* and *Ewing*, the issue should be seen not as whether the student, having been dismissed, *now* should receive a hearing, but whether the assessments that have taken place themselves constituted a hearing. In the test situation, for example, the student by definition has had the opportunity to persuade the instructor of the rightness of her cause. Further assessments are more accurately described as appeals. (Of course, in some cases due process may call for the right to appeal as well, for example if the student claimed bias on the part of the instructor giving the examination or on the part of the hearing examiner in the disciplinary case).

. . . .

Moreover, the deference point as it relates to the academic seems overstated. The fact of the matter is that courts have deferred to educational officials in disciplinary cases as well. School officials in a *Goss* situation enjoy ample deference: Their decisions stand so long as the rudimentary process specified in *Goss* took place. . . . In such cases, then, the courts do not second-guess the substantive decisions of educational officials but rather merely look to whether the prescribed ritual took place — little different from what transpires in the academic cases. . . .

. . . .

One might, of course, extend the disciplinary approach to the academic, thus calling for a hearing in all cases, though recognizing that many forms of academic assessment constitute a hearing. One might attempt to adapt the academic approach to the disciplinary, asking merely whether a "careful and deliberate" assessment has been made. The best approach would merge the two concepts: Students facing a significant loss at the hands of a college or university are entitled to a "careful and deliberate" assessment, including a hearing. The concept of "hearing" would be broadly understood. . . .

Mathews [*v. Eldridge*, 424 U.S. 319 (1976)] seems to require no less. After all, in these cases important interests are at stake; the risk of erroneous deprivation and the probable value of such procedures seem significant; and the burden put on the government by these procedures appears more than manageable. Indeed, this approach will neither add significantly to the current burdens carried by colleges and universities, nor, therefore, change the results of many cases. It will, however, rid the courts of the detritus this untenable distinction has shed, both in separating the academic from the disciplinary, and in setting out the procedures for each. The phrase "careful and deliberate," especially when linked to the notion of a hearing, strikes a nice balance between the substantial interests that both the student and the university bring to academic and disciplinary cases.

. . . .

3. Due Process in Private University Settings

TEDESCHI v. WAGNER COLLEGE

404 N.E.2d 1302 (1980)

Opinion by: MEYER

This appeal concerns the effect of guidelines or rules published by a private educational institution upon its right to suspend a student. We hold that such an institution is bound by its own rules and, therefore, reverse the order of the Appellate Division and remit the matter to the Supreme Court, Richmond County, for entry of a judgment in accordance with this opinion.

Plaintiff Nancy Jean Tedeschi was admitted to Wagner College, a private institution, in September, 1976. She was a part-time student taking courses in mathematics, Latin and psychology. Her performance during the fall semester presented both academic and social problems, however. Dr. Thompson, her Latin professor, testified that she did not participate in class, did not know the required material and only once of the several times called upon was able to answer correctly even a simple question about Latin grammar. Her conduct during class was also disruptive in that three or four times during each period she would pick up her handbag and leave the room, returning after two to five minutes.

On the evening of December 20, 1976 Ms. Tedeschi sat for her Latin examination, but at the end of it dramatically tore up her blue book and did not hand it in. In response to her question, Dr. Thompson advised her that without an examination score her grade for the course would be an F. Beginning at 4 a.m. the next morning and continuing until late in the evening of December 22, Dr. Thompson was subjected to a barrage of telephone calls in which Ms. Tedeschi repeatedly threatened to commit suicide, or to "fix" Dr. Thompson, and at one point appeared in a distraught condition at the front door of his home. Only when the police were summoned and advised plaintiff of the possible criminal consequences did the calls cease.

On January 10, 1977 through his secretary, Dr. Wendel, the academic dean, contacted plaintiff and her mother by telephone to arrange a meeting with them for the purpose of discussing plaintiff's academic situation, in view of her incomplete grades in two courses. Plaintiff, however, refused to meet stating that there was no problem. There followed, nevertheless, another series of harassing calls by plaintiff to Dr. Thompson. Later that evening in a telephone conversation between Dr. Thompson and Nancy's mother, Mrs. Tedeschi refused to discuss the matter with college officials and insisted that any problem should be presented to her in a formal letter from the college. The next day plaintiff was orally advised by Dr. Wendel that she was suspended by the college because of her bad character and the repeated disruption of her Latin class. Thereafter she met with the academic dean, the dean of students and an assistant to the president, who testified that during the interviews plaintiff's conduct was irrational and discussion fruitless. By letter dated January 13, 1977 plaintiff was advised by the dean of students, Dr. Guttu, that after consultation with Dr. Wendel and other members of the faculty and the administration, she was "withdrawn from classes for the 1977 spring semester" but could, if she wished, reapply in the fall. Shortly thereafter plaintiff's tuition for the spring semester was refunded. Plaintiff's mother testified that she called the school several times to arrange a hearing, but without success.

Plaintiff then began this action alleging that she had not been granted a hearing or afforded an opportunity to defend herself and that she had been arbitrarily frustrated in completing her education. She asked for an order reinstating her and for damages. The trial court found that there was no constitutional violation since Wagner College was not State involved, that it could not review the decision to suspend plaintiff on the basis of her academic record, that the disciplinary aspects of her suspension were not arbitrary, that the college was obligated only to act in good faith, that the informal procedure followed was believed to be in plaintiff's best interests and that she had failed to prove any damage. On appeal from the judgment for defendant entered on that decision, the Appellate Division affirmed by a divided court. The majority took note of the college guideline quoted below but held that plaintiff had rebuffed several attempts by the college to arrange a conference; the dissenters reasoned that the relationship between a college and its students is contractual and that the college was bound to follow its own rules relating to suspension. Though we do not arrive at our conclusion on exactly the same reasoning, we agree with the dissenters below that the college has not conformed to the procedure its guidelines prescribed and that plaintiff is entitled to have it do so. We, therefore, reverse.

The guideline referred to is part of a publication distributed by the office of the dean of students entitled 1976-1977 Guidelines of Wagner College. The portion pertinent to this appeal reads:

> "Whenever it shall appear that any student is not making satisfactory progress in his studies, and that his scholastic standing does not meet the requirements specified by the Committee on Academic Standards he shall be discharged from the College. If for any other cause a student is deemed to be an unfit member of the College, the Dean of Students may notify parents or guardians in order that they may have an opportunity to withdraw the student.
>
> "A student may be suspended or expelled from the College by the Dean of Students or the Dean of Academic Affairs. If he is suspended or expelled for any cause other than failure in his academic work, and has not had recourse to a hearing before an established College Court, he shall have the right to be heard by the Student-Faculty Hearing Board which shall present its findings to the President of the College for final determination."

The differentiation between suspension or expulsion for academic unfitness and suspension or expulsion for causes other than academic failure drawn in that guideline reflects the dichotomy in decisional law drawn along similar lines.

As is recognized by our recent decision in *Matter of Olsson v Board of Higher Educ.* (49 NY2d 408) and the cases cited therein, because matters involving academic standards generally rest upon the subjective judgment of professional educators, courts are reluctant to impose the strictures of traditional legal rules. Though such matters are subject to judicial scrutiny, the issue reviewed in such a case is whether the institution has acted in good faith or its action was arbitrary or irrational.

Suspension or expulsion for causes unrelated to academic achievement, however, involve determinations quite closely akin to the day-to-day work of the judiciary. Recognizing the present day importance of higher education to many, if not most, employment opportunities, the courts have, therefore, looked more closely at the actions of educational institutions in such matters.

The legal theory upon which review should be predicated in such cases is, however, not entirely clear. Plaintiff argues, and the dissenters in the Appellate Division agree, that the student-private college relationship is contractual and that it is an implied term of the contract that rules such as the Wagner College Guidelines will be adhered to by the college. There is support for that concept in decisional law . . . and in legal commentary as well. . . .

. . . .

An alternate basis for review of nonacademic disputes between students and private colleges, the application of the principles of the law of associations, is supported by case law in some other States. . . .

The law of associations accords judicial relief to an association member suspended or expelled without adherence to its rules. . . . The courts of this State have consistently recognized the right to such relief (*Browne v Hibbets*, 290 NY 459; *Polin v Kaplan*, 257 NY 277; *Simons v Berry*, 240 NY 463; *People ex rel. Deverell v Musical Mut. Protective Union*, 118 NY 101; *People ex rel. Meads v McDonough*, 8 App Div 591; *Loubat v Le Roy*, 40 Hun 546).

The parallel between associations and universities is, of course, not exact since students do not participate in the governance of a university with the same voice as generally do members in the functioning of an association. . . . The situation is further confused by the facts that at least in part the association law under discussion is stated in terms of contract . . . , and that in several cases the obligation to follow its own rules has been applied to a private university without reference to contract law (*Matter of Kwiatkowski v Ithaca Coll.*, 82 Misc 2d 43, 48; *Matter of Ryan v Hofstra Univ.*, 67 Misc 2d 651, 660–661 . . .).

We do not find it necessary in the present case to resolve such problems as may arise out of the different theoretical predicates. Whether by analogy to the law of associations, on the basis of a supposed contract between university and student, or simply as a matter of essential fairness in the somewhat one-sided relationship between the institution and the individual, we hold that when a university has adopted a rule or guideline establishing the procedure to be followed in relation to suspension or expulsion that procedure must be substantially observed.

We are brought then to a consideration of the guideline in question in relation to the suspension of Nancy Tedeschi. Had her suspension been solely for unsatisfactory progress in her studies, the guideline would have imposed no further obligation on the college and the only judicially reviewable question would have been whether it had acted in good faith (*Matter of Olsson v Board of Higher Educ., supra*). Moreover, there was substantial compliance with so much of the guideline as required that Nancy's parent be notified that Nancy was considered unfit for a cause other than academic, since Dr. Wendel sought to arrange a meeting between Mrs. Tedeschi and college officials to discuss Nancy's problems

The guideline permits either the dean of students or the dean of academic affairs to expel or suspend a student. The withdrawal letter forwarded on January 13, 1977 by the dean of students was, therefore, in conformance with its provisions. But the guideline does not stop there. It requires a further hearing by the Student-Faculty Hearing Board and review of that board's findings by the president of the college in any case in which suspension is for a cause other than academic failure and the student has not had a hearing before an established college court.

Dr. Guttu testified that the college court normally dealt with civil disorders or complaints by one student against another, but that cannot avail the college for it is undisputed that no court or board of any kind ever considered Nancy's case. As to the cause for Nancy's suspension, the Appellate Division found that it was based on her irrational and disruptive conduct. It, thus, apparently tacitly overruled the Trial Judge's reference to academic standing as a cause, but even if it did not, the further proceedings required by the guideline would still be mandated. This is because a suspension for both academic and other causes is necessarily, at least in part, a suspension for a cause other than academic failure. That is not to say that the board would have the right, not given it by the guideline, to review Nancy's scholastic standing as a ground for suspension, but simply to require that she have what the guideline accords her: review of the cause other than academic failure that it involved.

The college argues that Nancy's informal meetings with the two deans and the president's assistant was sufficient compliance with the guideline. Though those meetings may have been sensitive and fair, as the Trial Judge indicated, it constituted no acceptable substitute for a hearing board composed of both students and faculty. The college also suggests that the refusal of Mrs. Tedeschi to meet with its officials constituted a waiver of Nancy's hearing rights, but the guideline itself refutes that, since the purpose of such a meeting is simply to give the parent the possibility of avoiding embarrassment by withdrawing the student. . . . Not only is the guideline phrased in mandatory terms ("shall have the right to be heard") but also it was the obligation of the college in effecting the suspension to call plaintiff's attention to the further procedures provided for by the guidelines. . . .

Under the guideline plaintiff was properly suspended but was entitled to review of her suspension by the hearing board and the president. So much of the complaint as sought money damages and the right to a due process hearing based on claimed "state action" was properly dismissed, but she was entitled to judgment directing review by that body and that official as the guidelines require.

. . . .

Accordingly, the order of the Appellate Division should be reversed, with costs, and the case remitted to Supreme Court, Richmond County, with directions to enter judgment reinstating plaintiff as a student for the September, 1980 term of the college, unless prior to the opening of that term she has been accorded a hearing by the Student-Faculty Hearing Board.

GABRIELLI, J. (dissenting).

More than three and one-half years ago, Nancy Jean Tedeschi, a part-time, nonmatriculated student, was forced to withdraw from classes at Wagner College due to her disruptive and sometimes threatening conduct in and out of the classroom. Today, a majority of this court, after reviewing the extensive evidence that was offered at trial, has nevertheless directed that the college conduct a formal hearing, presumably for the purpose of determining the correctness and wisdom of its original decision. Since I am persuaded that such a hearing could be nothing more than a painful exercise in futility given the peculiar circumstances in this case, I am compelled to dissent.

Preliminarily, it must be noted that the Trial Judge in this case found the testimony of the school officials regarding Ms. Tedeschi's disruptive and irrational behavior to be "extremely credible". Also credited were the statements made by the school authorities concerning their unsuccessful efforts to resolve this delicate matter privately through informal conferences. . . .

The statements of the school authorities, taken together, paint a portrait of a distraught, emotionally disturbed young woman who seemed incapable of controlling her own feelings of aggression and was equally incapable of fulfilling her responsibilities as a student in an institution of higher learning. Ms. Tedeschi habitually disrupted her Latin class throughout her first semester at the college and, indeed, failed to complete two of the three courses in which she was enrolled. The rapid deterioration of her emotional state culminated in a series of harassing telephone calls and suicide threats which, understandably, alarmed the authorities at the school. Under the circumstances, it cannot be said that the college officials reacted in an arbitrary or unfair manner. To the contrary, in attempting to bring Ms. Tedeschi and her mother in for an informal interview to discuss the student's academic and emotional difficulties, the school officials obviously were hoping to reach a solution which would spare this unfortunate young woman further unnecessary embarrassment. That this is so is reflected in the college's final letter to Ms. Tedeschi, which stated that she was being asked to withdraw from classes, but indicated that she was free to apply for readmission if and when she straightened out her emotional difficulties. I cannot imagine a fairer resolution of the immediate problem, particularly in view of Ms. Tedeschi's continued inability to discuss the concerns of the school officials in a calm and rational manner.

Yet, three and one-half years after the fact, a majority of this court concludes that the college is required to afford Ms. Tedeschi a hearing. What possible constructive purpose would be served by such a hearing we are not told. Ordinarily, a hearing serves the salutary purpose of permitting all sides to air their conflicting versions of events and bring forth all of the disputed facts. . . . In the case of Ms. Tedeschi, however, there was never any reason to believe that the student had an alternate version of the facts to present to a neutral hearing body. To the contrary, the evidence accepted by the trial court demonstrates that Ms. Tedeschi and her mother had repeatedly rebuffed efforts by the school authorities to elicit their side of the story. When Ms. Tedeschi finally did come in to speak with the academic dean and the other school officials, she was unable to provide a rational or coherent explanation for her conduct. Significantly, according to the testimony that was credited by the Trial Judge, Ms. Tedeschi never requested an opportunity to have her case heard by a neutral hearing body, although she did speak to school officials personally on at least two occasions. Indeed, everything about the behavior of Ms. Tedeschi and her parent indicated that they had no interest in presenting their case to college officials.

. . . In any event, the special facts presented by Ms. Tedeschi's case cannot be ignored. In view of her continued inability to conduct herself in a rational manner, it cannot be said that a hearing before a student-faculty board would have been an appropriate or effective safeguard of her interests. Inasmuch as the facts concerning her behavior were not seriously disputed, I cannot conclude that the school authorities acted unreasonably or unfairly because they did not think to invite Ms. Tedeschi to present her case to a hearing board.

. . . .

For all these reasons, I respectfully dissent and cast my vote in favor of affirming the decision of the Appellate Division.

NOTES

1. With which opinion do you agree more? On one hand, the majority argues that a university ought to be subject to follow its own rules and, technically, it has not done so. On the other hand, the dissenter makes an argument in spirit of the guideline, rather than letter, stating that the university acted fairly with Tedeschi and gave her opportunities to offer her side of the story. In fact, the ultimate penalty for Tedeschi here is not a permanent exclusion, but rather a dismissal with an opportunity to apply for readmission.

2. What about the possibility, in a case like *Tedeschi*, that university faculty and administrators will simply base their adverse decisions on academic grounds, and not on other grounds, in order to avoid the legal requirement (constitutional and/or contractual) of detailed process? Surely, Wagner College officials could make the argument that Tedeschi failed to perform academically and leave it at that, right? Without reference to non-academic grounds, the university would not have been tied to its own rules and, therefore, its decisions would have been given greater judicial deference. Would such an argument have succeeded in this case? Or do the facts speak to non-academic grounds for dismissal to such an extent that the guideline would have had to have been followed?

3. In private universities, as in public universities, there is a distinction made between dismissal or other penalty for academic issues and dismissal or other penalty for other misconduct. As we saw earlier in this part of the chapter, with cases like *Board of Curators of the University of Missouri v. Horowitz*, and *Regents of the University of Michigan v. Ewing*, the conversation in public university contexts is typically about constitutional law and related university policy and practice. In the private university context, the conversation involves contract law and associated policy and practice. Readers are encouraged to read Chapter V for further discussion of the contractual relationship between both public and private college students and their respective institutions.

4. For a detailed passage on the special context of private universities and judicial deference, consider *Bilut v. Northwestern University*, 645 N.E.2d 536 (1994). Marilyn Bilut, a Ph.D. candidate in speech language pathology worked for several years, and with several faculty members, to secure her dissertation prospectus. On numerous occasions, her committee of faculty members deemed her work unacceptable, in part due to Bilut's choice of a topic that the committee determined was not a strong area for her, and in part due to Bilut's failure to address deficiencies in earlier drafts. After several years of work on her prospectus, Bilut's time-to-degree expired and she requested an extension. The extension was denied. Bilut filed suit, alleging breach of contract and tortious interference with contract (including a claim of sexual harassment against her original committee chair). The trial court denied Bilut's request for an injunction granting her the degree, but did grant an injunction requiring Northwestern University to give her two more years to complete the degree. The university appealed and the Illinois state appellate court reversed in favor of Northwestern. In its opinion, the court stated the following on the nature of judicial deference to academic decision making in private universities:

> The right of a student to attend a private college or university is subject to the condition that the student comply with its academic requirements. The faculty of a private college or university may formulate and enforce reasonable rules and regulations requiring students to adhere to its standards. . . .
>
> . . . .
>
> . . . [W]e agree with defendant's contention that the remedy awarded to plaintiff [by the trial court, an injunction for an extra two years to work on her dissertation] is unworkable. In *Board of Curators of the University of Missouri v. Horowitz* (1978), 435 U.S. 78, 92 the United States Supreme Court stated that "courts are particularly ill equipped to evaluate academic performance." In keeping with the *Horowitz* case, we maintain that our court is ill equipped to run private colleges and universities. Since the Ninth Century, when the first European university was established in Salerno, the university has been a close-knit self-governing community of higher learning which made and applied its own internal rules and disciplines. . . . A private educational institution such as defendant sustains essentially voluntary relationships between itself, its students and its faculty. The foundation of these relationships is the understanding that the students will abide by and adhere to the disciplinary regulations and the academic standards established by the faculty and the university; and that upon the satisfactory completion of their studies, they will be awarded a degree in

> their chosen discipline. . . . Private educational institutions such as defendant have an interest in promoting the academic well being of their students . . . , and in ensuring that the students to whom they award degrees, especially those who will become health care providers, will safely serve the public. . . . To this end, we believe that private colleges and universities must be accorded a generous measure of independence and autonomy with respect to the establishment, maintenance and enforcement of academic standards. . . . For the above reasons, we hold that the trial court erred in awarding plaintiff a mandatory injunction.

Id. at 132–35.

LISA TENEROWICZ, *STUDENT MISCONDUCT AT PRIVATE COLLEGES AND UNIVERSITIES: A ROADMAP FOR "FUNDAMENTAL FAIRNESS" IN DISCIPLINARY PROCEEDINGS*, 42 B.C. L. REV. 653 (2001)*

. . . .

I. BACKGROUND

. . . .

. . . [A]s a general matter, students attending private universities do not possess the same due process rights constitutionally guaranteed to students attending public schools. Accordingly, courts have been more reluctant to review the disciplinary decisions of private schools and have maintained a deferential posture toward private school decisionmaking, particularly in internal disciplinary affairs. In the absence of constitutional protections, courts generally have required that private school disciplinary procedures adhere to a "fundamental" or "basic" fairness standard and not be arbitrary or capricious. More precisely, state and federal courts have often held that a private school's disciplinary decisions are fundamentally fair if they comport with the rules and procedures that the school itself has promulgated.

. . . .

II. ANALYSIS

"The history of liberty," Justice Frankfurter wrote, "has largely been the history of observance of procedural safeguards," for without procedural protection, substantive protections would be virtually useless. . . .

. . . .

. . . Although the Constitution's Due Process Clause affords no protection for a private university student challenging the school's disciplinary procedures or decisions, a number of commentators have argued that the level of procedural protection in disciplinary proceedings should not fall because a student attends a private rather than a public school. This argument is persuasive: procedural due process rights are consistent with the goals of collegiate life, at private as well as public universities. Procedural safeguards benefit the entire school community by serving to legitimize the exercise of disciplinary authority, thereby fostering a sense of justice, fairness and community on campus. These values, in turn, create an effective educational environment. Perhaps more importantly, particularly in emotionally charged cases like those involving student-on-student sexual misconduct, the orderly procedures of requisite due process can mitigate the school's impulse to impose rash penalties and can provide the administrative body with a shield to fend off demands for hasty retaliation. It seems unthinkable that a private school would even consider guaranteeing fewer rights for their students than the minimum rights the Constitution exacts from public schools. Indeed, it would be a "cruel hoax on the integrity of the educational process" for any private school to take refuge in the existing public-private distinction to justify the promulgation of otherwise unsupportable disciplinary procedures. Because colleges and universities perform an essential function in a democratic society and because they have been given a position of esteem, trust and responsibility, they must, in return, treat students fairly, with equal dignity, care and concern.

Changes in disciplinary procedures will come only when initiated by the schools themselves or compelled by the courts as legislative solutions are not to be expected. Consequently, both courts and schools play a vital role in protecting the interests of a student accused of sexual misconduct.

For their part, courts asked to review a private school's disciplinary decision should be more willing to do so. They should employ contract law principles as the doctrinal foundation of their review. The current deferential approach of the courts, finding that a school's disciplinary system is "fundamentally fair" if the school substantially complies with its own established procedures, is inadequate. In effect, it invites private schools to eliminate procedures to avoid violating them. Indeed, potential lawsuits have become a sufficiently potent threat so that counsel advising private schools have cautioned them to protect themselves by avoiding descriptions of highly specific procedural protections (that students might later claim constituted contractual obligations). By employing a heightened standard of scrutiny, however, and recognizing that the contract between the school and the student is essentially adhesionary, courts can better ensure that the administration of discipline in private schools is fundamentally fair. The importance of recognizing the adhesionary nature of the contract cannot be overstated: courts should acknowledge that these contracts are generally executed unilaterally, contain boilerplate language and do not provide opportunity for meaningful negotiation of any of the terms. Moreover, courts should consider, when interpreting the terms of the contract, the extreme inequality in bargaining power and should construe ambiguities and unreasonable terms against the drafting party — the school. Conducting a review of a school's disciplinary procedures would enable the courts to ensure that private schools are administering discipline in a fundamentally fair manner.

Although the role played by the courts is essential to making certain that the discipline systems in private schools are "fundamentally fair," the schools themselves, of course, have the primary responsibility for enacting disciplinary procedures that comport with basic fairness. Student-on-student sexual misconduct cases are hard cases and the procedures a school adopts must consider the competing interests presented. As a result of the evidentiary problems posed by these cases, schools have a heightened duty to weigh the credibility of both parties. Disciplinary procedures designed to uncover the pertinent facts of a contested case will reduce the possibility of an erroneous finding and insulate the school against a potential lawsuit. There are, however, a number of procedural protections a private school can provide to guarantee that the touchstones of fairness and reasonableness govern their disciplinary proceedings.

A. *Right to Written Notice of the Charges and Evidence*

After a complaint of student-on-student sexual misconduct has been filed with school officials, and an initial investigation of the allegations has determined that a disciplinary proceeding is in order, the accused student must be given written notice of the charges. Among the most basic procedural protections, this notice should advise the student of the charges against him as well as the nature of the evidence. The written statement should further include the grounds which, if proven, would justify discipline, and the student should not be subjected to punishment on the basis of some ground other than that stated in the written charge. The formal notice should inform the student of the date, time and place of the disciplinary hearing and afford him or her sufficient time to prepare a defense. Finally, in the interest of fairness reliability, the school should have an ongoing duty to disclose to the student any exculpatory evidence.

B. *Presumption of Innocence and Standard of Proof*

To ensure fundamental fairness in the disciplinary proceedings, the accused student should be entitled to a presumption of innocence. More precisely, the school should bear the burden of production of evidence to sustain the charges against the student. Beyond the burden of proof, the school should have an established standard of production and only discipline a student if there is, at a minimum, substantial evidence to support the charges. The difficulty in student-on-student sexual misconduct cases has caused some schools to go even farther and require that the charges be proved by clear and convincing evidence.

C. *Right to an Impartial Hearing*

As one commentator accurately explained, "if the right to procedural due process means anything, it stands for the principle that the outcome of the hearing is not predetermined." There is little doubt that the disciplinary hearing itself should be conducted with basic fairness, but there is some doubt as to exactly what basic fairness means. First, it is wholly impractical in many schools to guarantee that no one who has had prior contact with the accused student may be involved in the adjudication of the case. It is not unreasonable, however, to require members of the disciplinary board to exercise independent judgment or to recuse themselves if impartiality is impossible. Second, fundamental fairness in cases as sensitive and as emotionally charged as student-on-student sexual misconduct cases requires that the disciplinary decision be based only upon the evidence admitted at the hearing and the charges listed in the notice of hearing letter. To ensure strict adherence to this requirement, training is essential: disciplinary board members should remain neutral and should attempt to identify important factual issues in dispute as evidence is presented. Deliberations should be in good faith and decisions should be based solely on the evidence presented at the hearing. Finally, in the event of an acquittal, the accused student's permanent record should be expunged of any reference to the matter.

D. *Right to a Transcript or Recording of the Proceeding and to an Appeal*

Fundamental fairness in the disciplinary process requires a hearing record that can be used by hearing board members during their deliberations and in the event of an appeal. A verbatim record, either in the form of an audio tape or stenographic transcript enables hearing board members to recall key portions of the testimony without relying on frail human memory and, therefore, ensures that the ultimate decision will be grounded on the evidence presented. A complete record also protects the school on appeal: the accused student must be able to point to error or fundamental unfairness in the record in order to take meaningful advantage of the right to appeal. Finally, knowing that the proceedings are being recorded and may become "public record" if the student appeals the disciplinary decision, hearing board members may have a greater incentive to strictly conform their behavior to established procedures.

E. *Right to Confront, Cross-Examine and Present Witnesses*

Cross-examination is an essential feature of the process by which truthful testimony is distinguished from falsehoods. Although cross-examination reduces the risk of an erroneous expulsion, face-to-face cross-examination of the victim by the accused also maximizes the victim's ordeal. In situations in which the fact of intercourse is not in dispute and consent is the sole contested issue, the importance of cross-examination is magnified. These cases resolve themselves into problems of credibility and the hearing board must choose to believe either the accused student or the alleged victim. A reliable determination of the issues is essential to a fundamentally fair process, but in these highly personal and emotionally grueling cases, a school must consider the toll that the proceeding exacts on the victim.

What can a school do in these situations? One possible solution is to permit indirect cross-examination, in which the victim is shielded from the accused student's view. Another option is to allow the accused student to respond to the testimony of each witness after the witness has testified. Another option is to allow the accused student to offer evidence in defense, to suggest persons who might be interviewed by the hearing board and to suggest questions that might be put to these persons.

F. *Right to Counsel*

Colleges and universities fear that permitting an accused student to be represented by counsel in a school disciplinary hearing will result in an adversarial judicial proceeding. In reality, a case involving student-on-student sexual misconduct is per se adversarial, and there is simply too much at stake to deny an accused student the right to an attorney. Further, in all likelihood the school has sought the advice of counsel in preparation for the disciplinary hearing; thus, fairness dictates that the student should enjoy that same right. One competing consideration is that if lawyers enter the process, the system would advantage only those students able both to find and afford an attorney.

Even if the benefit cannot be shared equally, there are two other reasons that a student accused of sexual misconduct should be entitled to the assistance of counsel in a campus disciplinary hearing. First, because an accused student's statements in a hearing may be relevant to subsequent or concurrent criminal proceedings, accused students should be entitled to representation by an attorney when they face potential criminal charges arising out of the same set of facts that led to the school's disciplinary charges. Otherwise, students in this position face the proverbial Hobson's choice: they can meaning-fully defend themselves in the disciplinary hearings, potentially incriminating themselves and certainly exposing the strengths and weaknesses of the case to the criminal prosecutor, or — wanting most of all to avoid going to prison — they can protect their criminal defense by opting not to contest the school's charges, virtually ensuring expulsion. In the context of sexual misconduct cases, with consent often the key issue and alcohol frequently a factor, piecing together the pertinent details is imperative and the absence of any defense by the accused is likely to lead to sanctions at the school level. Here, the stakes are enormous and basic fairness requires that the accused student be permitted representation by counsel.

Second, faced with serious disciplinary consequences, including expulsion, the accused student undoubtedly experiences an intense emotional response. School disciplinary hearings are intimidating; as a result, the student may not be able to effectively articulate his or her side of the story or version of the facts in a coherent and logical manner. With the potential of an erroneous expulsion, accused students should not be forced to "go at it alone" — an attorney can better articulate the student's position and protect his considerable interests.

CONCLUSION

. . . Although the Fourteenth Amendment's Due Process Clause is not availing to a private school student, concerns for fundamental fairness should not be sacrificed. Indeed, a good student *disciplinary procedure should go beyond the constitutional minimum to avoid arbitrariness and* to promote reasonable decisionmaking and basic fairness.

C. SEXUAL HARASSMENT

1. Employee to Student: Title IX Private Right of Action

GEBSER v. LAGO VISTA INDEPENDENT SCHOOL DISTRICT

524 U.S. 274 (1998)

JUSTICE O'CONNOR delivered the opinion of the Court.

The question in this case is when a school district may be held liable in damages in an implied right of action under Title IX of the Education Amendments of 1972, 86 Stat. 373, as amended, 20 U.S.C. § 1681 *et seq.* (Title IX), for the sexual harassment of a student by one of the district's teachers. We conclude that damages may not be recovered in those circumstances unless an official of the school district who at a minimum has authority to institute corrective measures on the district's behalf has actual notice of, and is deliberately indifferent to, the teacher's misconduct.

I

In the spring of 1991, when petitioner Alida Star Gebser was an eighth-grade student at a middle school in respondent Lago Vista Independent School District (Lago Vista), she joined a high school book discussion group led by Frank Waldrop, a teacher at Lago Vista's high school. Lago Vista received federal funds at all pertinent times. During the book discussion sessions, Waldrop often made sexually suggestive comments to the students. Gebser entered high school in the fall and was assigned to classes taught by Waldrop in both semesters. Waldrop continued to make inappropriate remarks to the students, and he began to direct more of his suggestive comments toward Gebser. . . . He initiated sexual contact with Gebser in the spring, when, while visiting her home ostensibly to give her a book, he kissed and fondled her. The two had sexual intercourse on a number of occasions during the remainder of the school year. Their relationship continued through the summer and into the following school year, and they often had intercourse during class time, although never on school property.

Gebser did not report the relationship to school officials, testifying that while she realized Waldrop's conduct was improper, she was uncertain how to react and she wanted to continue having him as a teacher. In October 1992, the parents of two other students complained to the high school principal about Waldrop's comments in class. The principal arranged a meeting, at which, according to the principal, Waldrop indicated that he did not believe he had made offensive remarks but apologized to the parents and said it would not happen again. The principal also advised Waldrop to be careful about his classroom comments and told the school guidance counselor about the meeting, but he did not report the parents' complaint to Lago Vista's superintendent, who was the district's Title IX coordinator. A couple of months later, in January 1993, a police officer discovered Waldrop and Gebser engaging in sexual intercourse and arrested Waldrop. Lago Vista terminated his employment, and subsequently, the Texas Education Agency revoked his teaching license. During this time, the district had not promulgated or distributed an official grievance procedure for lodging sexual harassment complaints; nor had it issued a formal anti-harassment policy.

Gebser and her mother filed suit against Lago Vista and Waldrop in state court in November 1993, raising claims against the school district under Title IX, Rev. Stat. § 1979, 42 U.S.C. § 1983, and state negligence law, and claims against Waldrop primarily under state law. They sought compensatory and punitive damages from both defendants. After the case was removed, the United States District Court for the Western District of Texas granted summary judgment in favor of Lago Vista on all claims, and remanded the allegations against Waldrop to state court. In rejecting the Title IX claim against the school district, the court reasoned that the statute "was enacted to counter *policies* of discrimination . . . in federally funded education programs," and that "only if school administrators have some type of notice of the gender discrimination and fail to respond in good faith can the discrimination be interpreted as a *policy* of the school district." Here, the court determined, the parents' complaint to the principal concerning Waldrop's comments in class was the only one Lago Vista had received about Waldrop, and that evidence was inadequate to raise a genuine issue on whether the school district had actual or constructive notice that Waldrop was involved in a sexual relationship with a student.

Petitioners appealed only on the Title IX claim. The Court of Appeals for the Fifth Circuit affirmed. . . . The court first declined to impose strict liability on school districts for a teacher's sexual harassment of a student. . . . The court then determined that Lago Vista could not be liable on the basis of constructive notice, finding that there was insufficient evidence to suggest that a school official should have known about Waldrop's relationship with Gebser. Finally, the court refused to invoke the common law principle that holds an employer vicariously liable when an employee is "aided in accomplishing [a] tort by the existence of the agency relation," Restatement (Second) of Agency § 219(2)(d) (1957) (hereinafter Restatement), explaining that application of that principle would result in school district liability in essentially every case of teacher-student harassment.

The court concluded its analysis by reaffirming its holding in *Rosa H.* that, "school districts are not liable in tort for teacher-student sexual harassment under Title IX unless an employee who has been invested by the school board with supervisory power over the offending employee actually knew of the abuse, had the power to end the abuse, and failed to do so," and ruling that petitioners could not satisfy that standard. The Fifth Circuit's analysis represents one of the varying approaches adopted by the Courts of Appeals in assessing a school district's liability under Title IX for a teacher's sexual harassment of a student. We granted certiorari to address the issue and we now affirm.

II

Title IX provides in pertinent part that, "no person . . . shall, on the basis of sex, be excluded from participation in, be denied the benefits of, or be subjected to discrimination under any education program or activity receiving Federal financial assistance." 20 U.S.C. § 1681(a). . . . We subsequently established in *Franklin v.*

Gwinnett County Public Schools, 503 U.S. 60, 112 S. Ct. 1028, 117 L. Ed. 2d 208 (1992), that monetary damages are available in the implied private action.

[The Court described the factual circumstances of *Franklin*. The Court stated] that Title IX supports a private action for damages, at least "in a case such as this, in which intentional discrimination is alleged." *See* 503 U.S. at 74–75. *Franklin* thereby establishes that a school district can be held liable in damages in cases involving a teacher's sexual harassment of a student; the decision, however, does not purport to define the contours of that liability.

We face that issue squarely in this case. . . .

Specifically, [the United States and Petitioners] advance two possible standards under which Lago Vista would be liable for Waldrop's conduct. First, relying on a 1997 "Policy Guidance" issued by the Department of Education, they would hold a school district liable in damages under Title IX where a teacher is " 'aided in carrying out the sexual harassment of students by his or her position of authority with the institution,' " irrespective of whether school district officials had any knowledge of the harassment and irrespective of their response upon becoming aware. That rule is an expression of *respondeat superior* liability, *i.e.*, vicarious or imputed liability, see Restatement § 219(2)(d), under which recovery in damages against a school district would generally follow whenever a teacher's authority over a student facilitates the harassment. Second, petitioners and the United States submit that a school district should at a minimum be liable for damages based on a theory of constructive notice, *i.e.*, where the district knew or "should have known" about harassment but failed to uncover and eliminate it. . . . Both standards would allow a damages recovery in a broader range of situations than the rule adopted by the Court of Appeals, which hinges on actual knowledge by a school official with authority to end the harassment.

. . . .

With respect to Title IX, however, the private right of action is judicially implied, and there is thus no legislative expression of the scope of available remedies, including when it is appropriate to award monetary damages. In addition, although the general presumption that courts can award any appropriate relief in an established cause of action, coupled with Congress' abrogation of the States' Eleventh Amendment immunity under Title IX, *see* 42 U.S.C. § 2000d-7, led us to conclude in *Franklin* that Title IX recognizes a damages remedy, we did so in response to lower court decisions holding that Title IX does not support damages relief at all. We made no effort in *Franklin* to delimit the circumstances in which a damages remedy should lie.

III

Because the private right of action under Title IX is judicially implied, we have a measure of latitude to shape a sensible remedial scheme that best comports with the statute. . . .

. . . [W]e conclude that it would "frustrate the purposes" of Title IX to permit a damages recovery against a school district for a teacher's sexual harassment of a student based on principles of *respondeat superior* or constructive notice, *i.e.*, without actual notice to a school district official. Because Congress did not expressly create a private right of action under Title IX, the statutory text does not shed light on Congress' intent with respect to the scope of available remedies. . . .

As a general matter, it does not appear that Congress contemplated unlimited recovery in damages against a funding recipient where the recipient is unaware of discrimination in its programs. . . .

Congress enacted Title IX in 1972 with two principal objectives in mind: "to avoid the use of federal resources to support discriminatory practices" and "to provide individual citizens effective protection against those practices."

. . . When Congress attaches conditions to the award of federal funds under its spending power, as it has in Title IX and Title VI, we examine closely the propriety of private actions holding the recipient liable in monetary damages for noncompliance with the condition. Our central concern in that regard is with ensuring "that the receiving entity of federal funds [has] notice that it will be liable for a monetary award." . . . If a school district's liability for a teacher's sexual harassment rests on principles of constructive notice or *respondeat superior*, it will [] be the case that the recipient of funds was unaware of the discrimination. It is sensible to assume that Congress did not envision a recipient's liability in damages in that situation. . . .

Most significantly, Title IX contains important clues that Congress did not intend to allow recovery in damages where liability rests solely on principles of vicarious liability or constructive notice. Title IX's express means of enforcement — by administrative agencies — operates on an assumption of actual notice to officials of the funding recipient. The statute entitles agencies who disburse education funding to enforce their rules implementing the non-discrimination mandate through proceedings to suspend or terminate funding or through "other means authorized by law." 20 U.S.C. § 1682. Significantly, however, an agency may not initiate enforcement proceedings until it "has advised the appropriate person or persons of the failure to comply with the requirement and has determined that compliance cannot be secured by voluntary means." The administrative regulations implement that obligation, requiring resolution of compliance issues "by informal means whenever possible," 34 CFR § 100.7(d) (1997), and prohibiting commencement of enforcement proceedings until the agency has determined that voluntary compliance is unobtainable and "the recipient . . . has been notified of its failure to comply and of the action to be taken to effect compliance," § 100.8(d); *see* § 100.8(c).

In the event of a violation, a funding recipient may be required to take "such remedial action as [is] deemed necessary to overcome the effects of [the] discrimination." § 106.3. While agencies have conditioned continued funding on providing equitable relief to the victim, the regulations do not appear to contemplate a condition ordering payment of monetary damages, and there is no indication that payment of damages has been demanded as a condition of finding a recipient to be in compliance with the statute. . . .

. . . .

It would be unsound, we think, for a statute's *express* system of enforcement to require notice to the recipient and an opportunity to come into voluntary compliance while a judicially *implied* system of enforcement permits substantial liability without regard to the recipient's knowledge or its corrective actions upon receiving notice. . . .

IV

Because the express remedial scheme under Title IX is predicated upon notice to an "appropriate person" and an opportunity to rectify any violation, 20 U.S.C. § 1682, we conclude, in the absence of further direction from Congress, that the implied damages remedy should be fashioned along the same lines. An "appropriate person" under § 1682 is, at a minimum, an official of the recipient entity with authority to take corrective action to end the discrimination. Consequently, in cases like this one that do not involve official policy of the recipient entity, we hold that a damages remedy will not lie under Title IX unless an official who at a minimum has authority to address the alleged discrimination and to institute corrective measures on the recipient's behalf has actual knowledge of discrimination in the recipient's programs and fails adequately to respond.

We think, moreover, that the response must amount to deliberate indifference to discrimination. . . . Under a lower standard, there would be a risk that the recipient would be liable in damages not for its own official decision but instead for its employees' independent actions. . . .

Applying the framework to this case is fairly straightforward, as petitioners do not contend they can prevail under an actual notice standard. The only official alleged to have had information about Waldrop's misconduct is the high school principal. That information, however, consisted of a complaint from parents of other students charging only that Waldrop had made inappropriate comments during class, which was plainly insufficient to alert the principal to the possibility that Waldrop was involved in a sexual relationship with a student. Lago Vista, moreover, terminated Waldrop's employment upon learning of his relationship with Gebser. . . .

. . . .

V

The number of reported cases involving sexual harassment of students in schools confirms that harassment unfortunately is an all too common aspect of the educational experience. No one questions that a student suffers extraordinary harm when subjected to sexual harassment and abuse by a teacher, and that the teacher's conduct is reprehensible and undermines the basic purposes of the educational system. The issue in this case, however, is whether the independent misconduct of a teacher is attributable to the school district that employs him under a specific federal statute designed primarily to prevent recipients of federal financial assistance from using the funds in a discriminatory manner. Our decision does not affect any right of recovery that an individual may have against a school district as a matter of state law or against the teacher in his individual capacity under state law or under 42 U.S.C. § 1983. Until Congress speaks directly on the subject, however, we will not hold a school district liable in damages under Title IX for a teacher's sexual harassment of a student absent actual notice and deliberate indifference. We therefore affirm the judgment of the Court of Appeals.

NOTES

1. As described in this case, what are the purposes of Title IX? Does the *Gebser* decision go too far by permitting students to sue colleges and universities that are federal assistance recipients? Does the holding seem to extend the law's reach too far? Why aren't violators subject to a private right of action?

2. In what ways did the Court circumscribe the reach of the private right of action? How did the Court incorporate legislative intent and reasoning into its decision here? Should courts consider mitigating circumstances or the institution's efforts to prevent sexual harassment conduct?

3. *Gebser* was a 5-4 decision. What is the standard articulated by the majority decision regarding liability for teacher's sexual harassment of a student? Is the standard higher, the same, or lower than other forms of institutional liability of an employee's conduct in other settings? What arguments exist for a *respondeat superior* liability, especially when an employee at a college or university may sue under this doctrine for damages when a co-worker's actions arise to employer liability? In Justice Stevens's dissent, which Justices Souter, Ginsburg, and Breyer joined, he raised his concerns stating:

> It is not clear to me why the well-settled rules of law that impose responsibility on the principal for the misconduct of its agents should not apply in this case. As a matter of policy, the Court ranks protection of the school district's purse above the protection of immature high school students that those rules would provide. Because those students are members of the class for whose special benefit Congress enacted Title IX, that policy choice is not faithful to the intent of the policymaking branch of our Government.

Id. at 306.

4. The *Gebser* case dealt with a sexual harassment incident based on a hostile environment. Would the *Gebser* holding apply to a quid pro quo harassment? According to *Liu v. Striuli*, 36 F. Supp. 2d 452 (D.R.I. 1999), "the *Gebser* opinion makes no distinction between the two types of sexual harassment claims in the Title IX context. In fact, neither term is mentioned in the opinion. The Court's broad language, quoted above, applies to both types of harassment in Title IX cases." *Id.* at 465.

5. The Court in *Gebser* suggests that the decision to allow monetary damages to be assessed against federal recipients may apply in other contexts. The majority opinion indicates that "in cases like this one that do not involve official policy of the recipient entity," monetary damages may be limited to certain conditions such as requiring "an official who at a minimum has authority to address the alleged discrimination and to institute corrective measures on the recipient's behalf has actual knowledge of discrimination in the recipient's programs and fails adequately to respond." *Gebser*, 524 U.S. at 290.

2. Student to Student: Title IX Private Right of Action

DAVIS v. MONROE COUNTY BOARD OF EDUCATION
526 U.S. 629 (1999)

JUSTICE O'CONNOR delivered the opinion of the Court.

Petitioner brought suit against the Monroe County Board of Education and other defendants, alleging that her fifth-grade daughter had been the victim of sexual harassment by another student in her class. Among petitioner's claims was a claim for monetary and injunctive relief under Title IX of the Education Amendments of 1972 (Title IX), 86 Stat. 373, as amended, 20 U.S.C. § 1681 et seq. The District Court dismissed petitioner's Title IX claim on the ground that "student-on-student," or peer, harassment provides no ground for a private cause of action under the statute. The Court of Appeals for the Eleventh Circuit, sitting en banc, affirmed. We consider here whether a private damages action may lie against the school board in cases of student-on-student harassment. We conclude that it may, but only where the funding recipient acts with deliberate indifference to known acts of harassment in its programs or activities. Moreover, we conclude that such an action will lie only for harassment that is so severe, pervasive, and objectively offensive that it effectively bars the victim's access to an educational opportunity or benefit.

I

. . . .

A

Petitioner's minor daughter, LaShonda, was allegedly the victim of a prolonged pattern of sexual harassment by one of her fifth-grade classmates at Hubbard Elementary School, a public school in Monroe County, Georgia. According to petitioner's complaint, the harassment began in December 1992, when the classmate, G. F., attempted to touch LaShonda's breasts and genital area and made vulgar statements such as " 'I want to get in bed with you' " and " 'I want to feel your boobs.' " Similar conduct allegedly occurred on or about January 4 and January 20, 1993. LaShonda reported each of these incidents to her mother and to her classroom teacher, Diane Fort. Petitioner, in turn, also contacted Fort, who allegedly assured petitioner that the school principal, Bill Querry, had been informed of the incidents. Petitioner contends that, notwithstanding these reports, no disciplinary action was taken against G. F.

G. F.'s conduct allegedly continued for many months. In early February, G. F. purportedly placed a door stop in his pants and proceeded to act in a sexually suggestive manner toward LaShonda during physical education class. LaShonda reported G. F.'s behavior to her physical education teacher, Whit Maples. Approximately one week later, G. F. again allegedly engaged in harassing behavior, this time while under the supervision of another classroom teacher, Joyce Pippin. Again,

LaShonda allegedly reported the incident to the teacher, and again petitioner contacted the teacher to follow up.

Petitioner alleges that G. F. once more directed sexually harassing conduct toward LaShonda in physical education class in early March, and that LaShonda reported the incident to both Maples and Pippen. In mid-April 1993, G. F. allegedly rubbed his body against LaShonda in the school hallway in what LaShonda considered a sexually suggestive manner, and LaShonda again reported the matter to Fort.

The string of incidents finally ended in mid-May, when G. F. was charged with, and pleaded guilty to, sexual battery for his misconduct. The complaint alleges that LaShonda had suffered during the months of harassment, however; specifically, her previously high grades allegedly dropped as she became unable to concentrate on her studies, and, in April 1993, her father discovered that she had written a suicide note. The complaint further alleges that, at one point, LaShonda told petitioner that she " 'didn't know how much longer she could keep [G. F.] off her.' "

Nor was LaShonda G. F.'s only victim; it is alleged that other girls in the class fell prey to G. F.'s conduct. At one point, in fact, a group composed of LaShonda and other female students tried to speak with Principal Querry about G. F.'s behavior. According to the complaint, however, a teacher denied the students' request with the statement, " 'If [Querry] wants you, he'll call you.' "

Petitioner alleges that no disciplinary action was taken in response to G. F.'s behavior toward LaShonda. In addition to her conversations with Fort and Pippen, petitioner alleges that she spoke with Principal Querry in mid-May 1993. . . . Yet, petitioner alleges, at no point during the many months of his reported misconduct was G. F. disciplined for harassment. . . .

. . . Moreover, petitioner alleges that, at the time of the events in question, the Monroe County Board of Education (Board) had not instructed its personnel on how to respond to peer sexual harassment and had not established a policy on the issue.

B

On May 4, 1994, petitioner filed suit in the United States District Court for the Middle District of Georgia against the Board, Charles Dumas, the school district's superintendent, and Principal Querry. The complaint alleged that the Board is a recipient of federal funding for purposes of Title IX, that "the persistent sexual advances and harassment by the student G. F. upon [LaShonda] interfered with her ability to attend school and perform her studies and activities," and that "the deliberate indifference by Defendants to the unwelcome sexual advances of a student upon LaShonda created an intimidating, hostile, offensive and abusive school environment in violation of Title IX." The complaint sought compensatory and punitive damages, attorney's fees, and injunctive relief.

The defendants (all respondents here) moved to dismiss petitioner's complaint under Federal Rule of Civil Procedure 12(b)(6) for failure to state a claim upon which relief could be granted, and the District Court granted respondents' motion.

With regard to petitioner's claims under Title IX, the court dismissed the claims against individual defendants on the ground that only federally funded educational institutions are subject to liability in private causes of action under Title IX. As for the Board, the court concluded that Title IX provided no basis for liability absent an allegation "that the Board or an employee of the Board had any role in the harassment."

Petitioner appealed the District Court's decision dismissing her Title IX claim against the Board, and a panel of the Court of Appeals for the Eleventh Circuit reversed. Borrowing from Title VII law, a majority of the panel determined that student-on-student harassment stated a cause of action against the Board under Title IX. . . . The Eleventh Circuit panel recognized that petitioner sought to state a claim based on school "officials' failure to take action to stop the offensive acts of those over whom the officials exercised control," and the court concluded that petitioner had alleged facts sufficient to support a claim for hostile environment sexual harassment on this theory.

The Eleventh Circuit granted the Board's motion for rehearing en banc and affirmed the District Court's decision to dismiss petitioner's Title IX claim against the Board. . . .

. . . .

We granted certiorari in order to resolve a conflict in the Circuits over whether, and under what circumstances, a recipient of federal educational funds can be liable in a private damages action arising from student-on-student sexual harassment. . . . We now reverse.

II

Title IX provides, with certain exceptions not at issue here, that

> "no person in the United States shall, on the basis of sex, be excluded from participation in, be denied the benefits of, or be subjected to discrimination under any education program or activity receiving Federal financial assistance." 20 U.S.C. § 1681(a).

. . . .

There is no dispute here that the Board is a recipient of federal education funding for Title IX purposes. Nor do respondents support an argument that student-on-student harassment cannot rise to the level of "discrimination" for purposes of Title IX. Rather, at issue here is the question whether a recipient of federal education funding may be liable for damages under Title IX under any circumstances for discrimination in the form of student-on-student sexual harassment.

A

Petitioner urges that Title IX's plain language compels the conclusion that the statute is intended to bar recipients of federal funding from permitting this form of discrimination in their programs or activities. She emphasizes that the statute prohibits a student from being "subjected to discrimination under any education program or activity receiving Federal financial assistance." 20 U.S.C. § 1681. It is Title IX's "unmistakable focus on the benefited class," *Cannon v. University of Chicago*, 441 U.S. 677, 691, 99 S. Ct. 1946, 60 L. Ed. 2d 560 (1979), rather than the perpetrator, that, in petitioner's view, compels the conclusion that the statute works to protect students from the discriminatory misconduct of their peers.

Here, however, we are asked to do more than define the scope of the behavior that Title IX proscribes. We must determine whether a district's failure to respond to student-on-student harassment in its schools can support a private suit for money damages. . . . This Court has indeed recognized an implied private right of action under Title IX, *see Cannon v. University of Chicago, supra*, and we have held that money damages are available in such suits, *Franklin v. Gwinnett County Public Schools*, 503 U.S. 60, 112 S. Ct. 1028, 117 L. Ed. 2d 208 (1992). Because we have repeatedly treated Title IX as legislation enacted pursuant to Congress' authority under the Spending Clause, however, private damages actions are available only where recipients of federal funding had adequate notice that they could be liable for the conduct at issue. . . .

[R]espondents urge that Title IX provides no notice that recipients of federal educational funds could be liable in damages for harm arising from student-on-student harassment. Respondents contend, specifically, that the statute only proscribes misconduct by grant recipients, not third parties. Respondents argue, moreover, that it would be contrary to the very purpose of Spending Clause legislation to impose liability on a funding recipient for the misconduct of third parties, over whom recipients exercise little control.

We agree with respondents that a recipient of federal funds may be liable in damages under Title IX only for its own misconduct. . . .

We disagree with respondents' assertion, however, that petitioner seeks to hold the Board liable for G. F.'s actions instead of its own. Here, petitioner attempts to hold the Board liable for its own decision to remain idle in the face of known student-on-student harassment in its schools. In *Gebser*, we concluded that a recipient of federal education funds may be liable in damages under Title IX where it is deliberately indifferent to known acts of sexual harassment by a teacher. In that case, a teacher had entered into a sexual relationship with an eighth grade student, and the student sought damages under Title IX for the teacher's misconduct. We recognized that the scope of liability in private damages actions under Title IX is circumscribed by *Pennhurst*'s requirement that funding recipients have notice of their potential liability. 524 U.S. at 287–288. Invoking *Pennhurst*, *Guardians Assn.*, and *Franklin* in *Gebser* we once again required "that 'the receiving entity of federal funds [have] notice that it will be liable for a monetary award' " before subjecting it to damages liability. We also recognized, however, that this limitation on private damages actions is not a bar to liability where a funding recipient intentionally violates the statute. . . .

. . . .

We consider here whether the misconduct identified in Gebser — deliberate indifference to known acts of harassment — amounts to an intentional violation of

Title IX, capable of supporting a private damages action, when the harasser is a student rather than a teacher. We conclude that, in certain limited circumstances, it does. . . .

. . . .

Deliberate indifference makes sense as a theory of direct liability under Title IX only where the funding recipient has some control over the alleged harassment. A recipient cannot be directly liable for its indifference where it lacks the authority to take remedial action.

. . . The statute's plain language confines the scope of prohibited conduct based on the recipient's degree of control over the harasser and the environment in which the harassment occurs. If a funding recipient does not engage in harassment directly, it may not be liable for damages unless its deliberate indifference "subjects" its students to harassment. That is, the deliberate indifference must, at a minimum, "cause [students] to undergo" harassment or "make them liable or vulnerable" to it. . . . Moreover, because the harassment must occur "under" "the operations of" a funding recipient, the harassment must take place in a context subject to the school district's control. . . .

These factors combine to limit a recipient's damages liability to circumstances wherein the recipient exercises substantial control over both the harasser and the context in which the known harassment occurs. Only then can the recipient be said to "expose" its students to harassment or "cause" them to undergo it "under" the recipient's programs. . . .

Where, as here, the misconduct occurs during school hours and on school grounds — the bulk of G. F.'s misconduct, in fact, took place in the classroom — the misconduct is taking place "under" an "operation" of the funding recipient. . . . In these circumstances, the recipient retains substantial control over the context in which the harassment occurs. . . . We thus conclude that recipients of federal funding may be liable for "subjecting" their students to discrimination where the recipient is deliberately indifferent to known acts of student-on-student sexual harassment and the harasser is under the school's disciplinary authority.

. . . .

We stress that our conclusion here — that recipients may be liable for their deliberate indifference to known acts of peer sexual harassment — does not mean that recipients can avoid liability only by purging their schools of actionable peer harassment or that administrators must engage in particular disciplinary action. We thus disagree with respondents' contention that, if Title IX provides a cause of action for student-on-student harassment, "nothing short of expulsion of every student accused of misconduct involving sexual overtones would protect school systems from liability or damages." Likewise, the dissent erroneously imagines that victims of peer harassment now have a Title IX right to make particular remedial demands. In fact, as we have previously noted, courts should refrain from second guessing the disciplinary decisions made by school administrators.

. . . [T]he recipient must merely respond to known peer harassment in a manner that is not clearly unreasonable. . . .

. . . .

While it remains to be seen whether petitioner can show that the Board's response to reports of G. F.'s misconduct was clearly unreasonable in light of the known circumstances, petitioner may be able to show that the Board "subjected" LaShonda to discrimination by failing to respond in any way over a period of five months to complaints of G. F.'s in-school misconduct from LaShonda and other female students.

B

. . . .

[A] plaintiff must establish sexual harassment of students that is so severe, pervasive, and objectively offensive, and that so undermines and detracts from the victims' educational experience, that the victim-students are effectively denied equal access to an institution's resources and opportunities.

. . . .

Courts, moreover, must bear in mind that schools are unlike the adult workplace and that children may regularly interact in a manner that would be unacceptable among adults. . . . Indeed, at least early on, students are still learning how to interact appropriately with their peers. It is thus understandable that, in the school setting, students often engage in insults, banter, teasing, shoving, pushing, and gender-specific conduct that is upsetting to the students subjected to it. Damages are not available for simple acts of teasing and name-calling among school children, however, even where these comments target differences in gender. Rather, in the context of student-on-student harassment, damages are available only where the behavior is so severe, pervasive, and objectively offensive that it denies its victims the equal access to education that Title IX is designed to protect.

. . . .

The fact that it was a teacher who engaged in harassment in *Franklin* and *Gebser* is relevant. The relationship between the harasser and the victim necessarily affects the extent to which the misconduct can be said to breach Title IX's guarantee of equal access to educational benefits and to have a systemic effect on a program or activity. Peer harassment, in particular, is less likely to satisfy these requirements than is teacher-student harassment.

C

Applying this standard to the facts at issue here, we conclude that the Eleventh Circuit erred in dismissing petitioner's complaint. Petitioner alleges that her daughter was the victim of repeated acts of sexual harassment by G. F. over a 5-month period, and there are allegations in support of the conclusion that G. F.'s misconduct was severe, pervasive, and objectively offensive. The harassment was not only verbal; it included numerous acts of objectively offensive touching, and, indeed, G. F. ultimately pleaded guilty to criminal sexual misconduct. Moreover, the complaint alleges that there were multiple victims who were sufficiently disturbed by G. F.'s misconduct to seek an audience with the school principal. Further, petitioner contends that the harassment had a concrete, negative effect on her daughter's ability to receive an education. The complaint also suggests that petitioner may be able to show both actual knowledge and deliberate indifference on the part of the Board, which made no effort whatsoever either to investigate or to put an end to the harassment.

. . . Accordingly, the judgment of the United States Court of Appeals for the Eleventh Circuit is reversed, and the case is remanded for further proceedings consistent with this opinion.

NOTES

1. Should colleges and universities that participate in federal assistance programs be liable for acts of a third party? What other recourse might a student have at a public or private college? A public entity's failure to protect a person against private actions such as physical violence may give rise to a substantive due process claim when a public college or university (1) has a special relationship with that person; (2) created or substantially contributed to the danger (state-created danger theory) then failed to protect *or* limited the person's ability to protect oneself or receive outside protection (i.e., state limitation theory); and (3) behaved in a conscience-shocking manner to address the harm. *Cf. Melendez-Garcia v. Sanchez*, 629 F.3d 25 (1st Cir. 2010).

2. Does the application of Title IX in sexual harassment cases involving a college student extend beyond the powers of authority that Congress intended? In what ways did the Court in *Gebser* and *Davis* attempt to limit the federal recipient's liability? Are the limits too restrictive that colleges and universities might not take appropriate actions to address reported sexual misconduct?

3. Note that Justice O'Connor wrote the majority opinion for both *Gebser* and *Davis*. How is the issue in *Gebser* different from, and yet also similar to, the one in *Davis*? Whose action did the Court focus on in *Gebser* as opposed to in *Davis*? Who was the perpetrator in *Gebser*, and who was the perpetrator in *Davis*?

4. What is the difference between the knowledge standard in *Gebser* with *Davis*?

5. According to the court in *Escue v. Northern Oklahoma College*, 450 F.3d 1146 (10th Cir. 2006), "[l]ower courts differ on whether notice sufficient to trigger liability may consist of prior complaints or must consist of notice regarding current harassment in the recipient's programs." *Id.* at 1153. Generally, the district courts that have examined the issue have required that the school have "actual knowledge of a *substantial risk* of abuse to students based on prior complaints by other students." *Id.* at 1154. While *Escue* is a faculty-to-student sexual harassment case, it highlights differences in what lower courts interpret as actual knowledge.

In an Eleventh Circuit case, *Williams v. Board of Regents of the University System of Georgia*, 477 F.3d. 1282 (11th Cir. 2007), the court applied a "municipal liability" ruling to guide its interpretation of deliberate indifference under Title IX. Under the municipal liability analysis, the court indicated that a "plaintiff can show deliberate indifference by proving that 'the municipality knew of a need to . . . supervise in a particular area and the municipality made a deliberate choice not to take any action.' " *Id.* at 1295 (citing *Gold v. City of Miami*, 151 F.3d 1346, 1350–51 (11th Cir. 1998)). Thus, knowledge of a hostile educational environment based on events prior to the victim's complaint may contribute to the school's actual knowledge.

6. The Eleventh Circuit *Williams* case illustrated other aspects of the *Davis* standard, most notably illustrating deliberate indifference. The facts of *Williams* involved a student "train" rape, in which several football players rotated in and out of the room to rape the victim. While the University of Georgia Police conducted an investigation and filed a report within 48 hours of the event, the university significantly delayed its processes. For instance, the judicial affairs officer did not receive a follow-up police report until three months later. Further, the university waited more than a year after the incident to hold the student conduct hearing. By that time, the perpetrators had left the university.

3. Student to Student: Federal Compliance with Title IX

UNITED STATES DEPARTMENT OF EDUCATION OFFICE FOR CIVIL RIGHTS THE ASSISTANT SECRETARY

April 4, 2011

Dear Colleague:

Education has long been recognized as the great equalizer in America. The U.S. Department of Education and its Office for Civil Rights (OCR) believe that providing all students with an educational environment free from discrimination is extremely important. The sexual harassment of students, including sexual violence, interferes with students' right to receive an education free from discrimination and, in the case of sexual violence, is a crime.

Title IX of the Education Amendments of 1972 (Title IX), 20 U.S.C. §§ 1681 *et seq.*, and its implementing regulations, 34 C.F.R. Part 106, prohibit discrimination on the basis of sex in education programs or activities operated by recipients of Federal financial assistance. Sexual harassment of students, which includes acts of sexual violence, is a form of sex discrimination prohibited by Title IX. In order to assist recipients, which include school districts, colleges, and universities (hereinafter "schools" or "recipients") in meeting these obligations, this letter[1] explains that the requirements of Title IX pertaining to sexual harassment also cover sexual violence, and lays out the specific Title IX requirements applicable to sexual

---

[1] The Department has determined that this Dear Colleague Letter is a "significant guidance document" under the Office of Management and Budget's Final Bulletin for Agency Good Guidance Practices. . . . OCR issues this and other policy guidance to provide recipients with information to assist them in meeting their obligations, and to provide members of the public with information about their rights, under the civil rights laws and implementing regulations that we enforce. OCR's legal authority is based on those laws and regulations. This letter does not add requirements to applicable law, but provides information and examples to inform recipients about how OCR evaluates whether covered entities are complying with their legal obligations. . . .

violence. Sexual violence, as that term is used in this letter, refers to physical sexual acts perpetrated against a person's will or where a person is incapable of giving consent due to the victim's use of drugs or alcohol. An individual also may be unable to give consent due to an intellectual or other disability. A number of different acts fall into the category of sexual violence, including rape, sexual assault, sexual battery, and sexual coercion. All such acts of sexual violence are forms of sexual harassment covered under Title IX.

The statistics on sexual violence are both deeply troubling and a call to action for the nation. A report prepared for the National Institute of Justice found that about 1 in 5 women are victims of completed or attempted sexual assault while in college.3 The report also found that approximately 6.1 percent of males were victims of completed or attempted sexual assault during college.4 According to data collected under the Jeanne Clery Disclosure of Campus Security and Campus Crime Statistics Act (Clery Act), 20 U.S.C. § 1092(f), in 2009, college campuses reported nearly 3,300 forcible sex offenses as defined by the Clery Act. . . . . The Department is deeply concerned about this problem and is committed to ensuring that all students feel safe in their school, so that they have the opportunity to benefit fully from the school's programs and activities.

This letter begins with a discussion of Title IX's requirements related to student-on-student sexual harassment, including sexual violence, and explains schools' responsibility to take immediate and effective steps to end sexual harassment and sexual violence. These requirements are discussed in detail in OCR's *Revised Sexual Harassment Guidance* issued in 2001 (*2001 Guidance*). This letter supplements the *2001 Guidance* by providing additional guidance and practical examples regarding the Title IX requirements as they relate to sexual violence. This letter concludes by discussing the proactive efforts schools can take to prevent sexual harassment and violence, and by providing examples of remedies that schools and OCR may use to end such conduct, prevent its recurrence, and address its effects. Although some examples contained in this letter are applicable only in the postsecondary context, sexual harassment and violence also are concerns for school districts. The Title IX obligations discussed in this letter apply equally to school districts unless otherwise noted.

Title IX Requirements Related to Sexual Harassment and Sexual Violence Schools' Obligations to Respond to Sexual Harassment and Sexual Violence

Sexual harassment is unwelcome conduct of a sexual nature. It includes unwelcome sexual advances, requests for sexual favors, and other verbal, nonverbal, or physical conduct of a sexual nature. Sexual violence is a form of sexual harassment prohibited by Title IX.[9]

---

[9] Title IX also prohibits gender-based harassment, which may include acts of verbal, nonverbal, or physical aggression, intimidation, or hostility based on sex or sex-stereotyping, even if those acts do not involve conduct of a sexual nature. The Title IX obligations discussed in this letter also apply to gender-based harassment. Gender-based harassment is discussed in more detail in the *2001 Guidance*, and in the 2010 Dear Colleague letter on Harassment and Bullying, which is available at http://www2.ed.gov/about/offices/list/ocr/letters/colleague-201010.pdf.

As explained in OCR's *2001 Guidance*, when a student sexually harasses another student, the harassing conduct creates a hostile environment if the conduct is sufficiently serious that it interferes with or limits a student's ability to participate in or benefit from the school's program. The more severe the conduct, the less need there is to show a repetitive series of incidents to prove a hostile environment, particularly if the harassment is physical. Indeed, a single or isolated incident of sexual harassment may create a hostile environment if the incident is sufficiently severe. For instance, a single instance of rape is sufficiently severe to create a hostile environment.

Title IX protects students from sexual harassment in a school's education programs and activities. This means that Title IX protects students in connection with all the academic, educational, extracurricular, athletic, and other programs of the school, whether those programs take place in a school's facilities, on a school bus, at a class or training program sponsored by the school at another location, or elsewhere. For example, Title IX protects a student who is sexually assaulted by a fellow student during a school-sponsored field trip.

If a school knows or reasonably should know about student-on-student harassment that creates a hostile environment, Title IX requires the school to take immediate action to eliminate the harassment, prevent its recurrence, and address its effects. Schools also are required to publish a notice of nondiscrimination and to adopt and publish grievance procedures. Because of these requirements, which are discussed in greater detail in the following section, schools need to ensure that their employees are trained so that they know to report harassment to appropriate school officials, and so that employees with the authority to address harassment know how to respond properly. Training for employees should include practical information about how to identify and report sexual harassment and violence. OCR recommends that this training be provided to any employees likely to witness or receive reports of sexual harassment and violence, including teachers, school law enforcement unit employees, school administrators, school counselors, general counsels, health personnel, and resident advisors.

Schools may have an obligation to respond to student-on-student sexual harassment that initially occurred off school grounds, outside a school's education program or activity. If a student files a complaint with the school, regardless of where the conduct occurred, the school must process the complaint in accordance with its established procedures. Because students often experience the continuing effects of off-campus sexual harassment in the educational setting, schools should consider the effects of the off-campus conduct when evaluating whether there is a hostile environment on campus. For example, if a student alleges that he or she was sexually assaulted by another student off school grounds, and that upon returning to school he or she was taunted and harassed by other students who are the alleged perpetrator's friends, the school should take the earlier sexual assault into account in determining whether there is a sexually hostile environment. The school also should take steps to protect a student who was assaulted off campus from further sexual harassment or retaliation from the perpetrator and his or her associates.

Regardless of whether a harassed student, his or her parent, or a third party files a complaint under the school's grievance procedures or otherwise requests action on the student's behalf, a school that knows, or reasonably should know, about possible harassment must promptly investigate to determine what occurred and then take appropriate steps to resolve the situation. As discussed later in this letter, the school's Title IX investigation is different from any law enforcement investigation, and a law enforcement investigation does not relieve the school of its independent Title IX obligation to investigate the conduct. The specific steps in a school's investigation will vary depending upon the nature of the allegations, the age of the student or students involved (particularly in elementary and secondary schools), the size and administrative structure of the school, and other factors. Yet as discussed in more detail below, the school's inquiry must in all cases be prompt, thorough, and impartial. In cases involving potential criminal conduct, school personnel must determine, consistent with State and local law, whether appropriate law enforcement or other authorities should be notified.

Schools also should inform and obtain consent from the complainant (or the complainant's parents if the complainant is under 18 and does not attend a postsecondary institution) before beginning an investigation. If the complainant requests confidentiality or asks that the complaint not be pursued, the school should take all reasonable steps to investigate and respond to the complaint consistent with the request for confidentiality or request not to pursue an investigation. If a complainant insists that his or her name or other identifiable information not be disclosed to the alleged perpetrator, the school should inform the complainant that its ability to respond may be limited. The school also should tell the complainant that Title IX prohibits retaliation, and that school officials will not only take steps to prevent retaliation but also take strong responsive action if it occurs.

As discussed in the *2001 Guidance*, if the complainant continues to ask that his or her name or other identifiable information not be revealed, the school should evaluate that request in the context of its responsibility to provide a safe and nondiscriminatory environment for all students. Thus, the school may weigh the request for confidentiality against the following factors: the seriousness of the alleged harassment; the complainant's age; whether there have been other harassment complaints about the same individual; and the alleged harasser's rights to receive information about the allegations if the information is maintained by the school as an "education record" under the Family Educational Rights and Privacy Act (FERPA), 20 U.S.C. § 1232g; 34 C.F.R. Part 99. The school should inform the complainant if it cannot ensure confidentiality. Even if the school cannot take disciplinary action against the alleged harasser because the complainant insists on confidentiality, it should pursue other steps to limit the effects of the alleged harassment and prevent its recurrence. Examples of such steps are discussed later in this letter.[15]

Compliance with Title IX, such as publishing a notice of nondiscrimination,

---

[15] For example, the alleged harasser may have a right under FERPA to inspect and review portions of the complaint that directly relate to him or her. In that case, the school must redact the complainant's name and other identifying information before allowing the alleged harasser to inspect and review the sections of the complaint that relate to him or her. In some cases, such as those where the school is required to report the incident to local law enforcement or other officials, the school may not be able to maintain the complainant's confidentiality.

designating an employee to coordinate Title IX compliance, and adopting and publishing grievance procedures, can serve as preventive measures against harassment. Combined with education and training programs, these measures can help ensure that all students and employees recognize the nature of sexual harassment and violence, and understand that the school will not tolerate such conduct. Indeed, these measures may bring potentially problematic conduct to the school's attention before it becomes serious enough to create a hostile environment. Training for administrators, teachers, staff, and students also can help ensure that they understand what types of conduct constitute sexual harassment or violence, can identify warning signals that may need attention, and know how to respond. More detailed information and examples of education and other preventive measures are provided later in this letter.

Procedural Requirements Pertaining to Sexual Harassment and Sexual Violence

Recipients of Federal financial assistance must comply with the procedural requirements outlined in the Title IX implementing regulations. Specifically, a recipient must:

(A) Disseminate a notice of nondiscrimination;

(B) Designate at least one employee to coordinate its efforts to comply with and carry out its responsibilities under Title IX; and

(C) Adopt and publish grievance procedures providing for prompt and equitable resolution of student and employee sex discrimination complaints.

These requirements apply to all forms of sexual harassment, including sexual violence, and are important for preventing and effectively responding to sex discrimination. They are discussed in greater detail below. OCR advises recipients to examine their current policies and procedures on sexual harassment and sexual violence to determine whether those policies comply with the requirements articulated in this letter and the *2001 Guidance*. Recipients should then implement changes as needed.

(A) *Notice of Nondiscrimination*

The Title IX regulations require that each recipient publish a notice of nondiscrimination stating that the recipient does not discriminate on the basis of sex in its education programs and activities, and that Title IX requires it not to discriminate in such a manner. The notice must state that inquiries concerning the application of Title IX may be referred to the recipient's Title IX coordinator or to OCR. It should include the name or title, office address, telephone number, and e-mail address for the recipient's designated Title IX coordinator.

The notice must be widely distributed to all students, parents of elementary and secondary students, employees, applicants for admission and employment, and other relevant persons. OCR recommends that the notice be prominently posted on school Web sites and at various locations throughout the school or campus and published in electronic and printed publications of general distribution that provide information to students and employees about the school's services and policies. The notice should be available and easily accessible on an ongoing basis.

Title IX does not require a recipient to adopt a policy specifically prohibiting sexual harassment or sexual violence. As noted in the *2001 Guidance*, however, a recipient's general policy prohibiting sex discrimination will not be considered effective and would violate Title IX if, because of the lack of a specific policy, students are unaware of what kind of conduct constitutes sexual harassment, including sexual violence, or that such conduct is prohibited sex discrimination. OCR therefore recommends that a recipient's nondiscrimination policy state that prohibited sex discrimination covers sexual harassment, including sexual violence, and that the policy include examples of the types of conduct that it covers.

(B) *Title IX Coordinator*

The Title IX regulations require a recipient to notify all students and employees of the name or title and contact information of the person designated to coordinate the recipient's compliance with Title IX. The coordinator's responsibilities include overseeing all Title IX complaints and identifying and addressing any patterns or systemic problems that arise during the review of such complaints. The Title IX coordinator or designee should be available to meet with students as needed. If a recipient designates more than one Title IX coordinator, the notice should describe each coordinator's responsibilities (*e.g.*, who will handle complaints by students, faculty, and other employees). The recipient should designate one coordinator as having ultimate oversight responsibility, and the other coordinators should have titles clearly showing that they are in a deputy or supporting role to the senior coordinator. The Title IX coordinators should not have other job responsibilities that may create a conflict of interest. For example, serving as the Title IX coordinator and a disciplinary hearing board member or general counsel may create a conflict of interest.

Recipients must ensure that employees designated to serve as Title IX coordinators have adequate training on what constitutes sexual harassment, including sexual violence, and that they understand how the recipient's grievance procedures operate. Because sexual violence complaints often are filed with the school's law enforcement unit, all school law enforcement unit employees should receive training on the school's Title IX grievance procedures and any other procedures used for investigating reports of sexual violence. In addition, these employees should receive copies of the school's Title IX policies. Schools should instruct law enforcement unit employees both to notify complainants of their right to file a Title IX sex discrimination complaint with the school in addition to filing a criminal complaint, and to report incidents of sexual violence to the Title IX coordinator if the complainant consents. The school's Title IX coordinator or designee should be available to provide assistance to school law enforcement unit employees regarding how to respond appropriately to reports of sexual violence. The Title IX coordinator also should be given access to school law enforcement unit investigation notes and findings as necessary for the Title IX investigation, so long as it does not compromise the criminal investigation.

(C) *Grievance Procedures*

The Title IX regulations require all recipients to adopt and publish grievance procedures providing for the prompt and equitable resolution of sex discrimination complaints.21 The grievance procedures must apply to sex discrimination complaints filed by students against school employees, other students, or third parties.

Title IX does not require a recipient to provide separate grievance procedures for sexual harassment and sexual violence complaints. Therefore, a recipient may use student disciplinary procedures or other separate procedures to resolve such complaints. Any procedures used to adjudicate complaints of sexual harassment or sexual violence, including disciplinary procedures, however, must meet the Title IX requirement of affording a complainant a prompt and equitable resolution.[22] These requirements are discussed in greater detail below. If the recipient relies on disciplinary procedures for Title IX compliance, the Title IX coordinator should review the recipient's disciplinary procedures to ensure that the procedures comply with the prompt and equitable requirements of Title IX.

Grievance procedures generally may include voluntary informal mechanisms (*e.g.*, mediation) for resolving some types of sexual harassment complaints. OCR has frequently advised recipients, however, that it is improper for a student who complains of harassment to be required to work out the problem directly with the alleged perpetrator, and certainly not without appropriate involvement by the school (*e.g.*, participation by a trained counselor, a trained mediator, or, if appropriate, a teacher or administrator). In addition, as stated in the *2001 Guidance*, the complainant must be notified of the right to end the informal process at any time and begin the formal stage of the complaint process. Moreover, in cases involving allegations of sexual assault, mediation is not appropriate even on a voluntary basis. OCR recommends that recipients clarify in their grievance procedures that mediation will not be used to resolve sexual assault complaints.

Prompt and Equitable Requirements

As stated in the *2001 Guidance*, OCR has identified a number of elements in evaluating whether a school's grievance procedures provide for prompt and equitable resolution of sexual harassment complaints. These elements also apply to sexual violence complaints because, as explained above, sexual violence is a form of sexual harassment. OCR will review all aspects of a school's grievance procedures, including the following elements that are critical to achieve compliance with Title IX:

- Notice to students, parents of elementary and secondary students, and

[22] These procedures must apply to all students, including athletes. If a complaint of sexual violence involves a student athlete, the school must follow its standard procedures for resolving sexual violence complaints. Such complaints must not be addressed solely by athletics department procedures. Additionally, if an alleged perpetrator is an elementary or secondary student with a disability, schools must follow the procedural safeguards in the Individuals with Disabilities Education Act (at 20 U.S.C. § 1415 and 34 C.F.R. §§ 300.500–300.519, 300.530–300.537) as well as the requirements of Section 504 of the Rehabilitation Act of 1973 (at 34 C.F.R. §§ 104.35–104.36) when conducting the investigation and hearing.

employees of the grievance procedures, including where complaints may be filed;

- Application of the procedures to complaints alleging harassment carried out by employees, other students, or third parties;
- Adequate, reliable, and impartial investigation of complaints, including the opportunity for both parties to present witnesses and other evidence;
- Designated and reasonably prompt time frames for the major stages of the complaint process;
- Notice to parties of the outcome of the complaint; and
- An assurance that the school will take steps to prevent recurrence of any harassment and to correct its discriminatory effects on the complainant and others, if appropriate.

As noted in the *2001 Guidance*, procedures adopted by schools will vary in detail, specificity, and components, reflecting differences in the age of students, school sizes and administrative structures, State or local legal requirements, and past experiences. Although OCR examines whether all applicable elements are addressed when investigating sexual harassment complaints, this letter focuses on those elements where our work indicates that more clarification and explanation are needed, including:

(A) *Notice of the grievance procedures*

The procedures for resolving complaints of sex discrimination, including sexual harassment, should be written in language appropriate to the age of the school's students, easily understood, easily located, and widely distributed. OCR recommends that the grievance procedures be prominently posted on school Web sites; sent electronically to all members of the school community; available at various locations throughout the school or campus; and summarized in or attached to major publications issued by the school, such as handbooks, codes of conduct, and catalogs for students, parents of elementary and secondary students, faculty, and staff.

(B) *Adequate, Reliable, and Impartial Investigation of Complaints*

OCR's work indicates that a number of issues related to an adequate, reliable, and impartial investigation arise in sexual harassment and violence complaints. In some cases, the conduct may constitute both sexual harassment under Title IX and criminal activity. Police investigations may be useful for fact-gathering; but because the standards for criminal investigations are different, police investigations or reports are not determinative of whether sexual harassment or violence violates Title IX. Conduct may constitute unlawful sexual harassment under Title IX even if the police do not have sufficient evidence of a criminal violation. In addition, a criminal investigation into allegations of sexual violence does not relieve the school of its duty under Title IX to resolve complaints promptly and equitably.

A school should notify a complainant of the right to file a criminal complaint, and should not dissuade a victim from doing so either during or after the school's internal Title IX investigation. For instance, if a complainant wants to file a police report, the school should not tell the complainant that it is working toward a solution and instruct, or ask, the complainant to wait to file the report.

Schools should not wait for the conclusion of a criminal investigation or criminal proceeding to begin their own Title IX investigation and, if needed, must take immediate steps to protect the student in the educational setting. For example, a school should not delay conducting its own investigation or taking steps to protect the complainant because it wants to see whether the alleged perpetrator will be found guilty of a crime. Any agreement or Memorandum of Understanding (MOU) with a local police department must allow the school to meet its Title IX obligation to resolve complaints promptly and equitably. Although a school may need to delay temporarily the fact-finding portion of a Title IX investigation while the police are gathering evidence, once notified that the police department has completed its gathering of evidence (not the ultimate outcome of the investigation or the filing of any charges), the school must promptly resume and complete its fact-finding for the Title IX investigation. Moreover, nothing in an MOU or the criminal investigation itself should prevent a school from notifying complainants of their Title IX rights and the school's grievance procedures, or from taking interim steps to ensure the safety and well-being of the complainant and the school community while the law enforcement agency's fact-gathering is in progress. OCR also recommends that a school's MOU include clear policies on when a school will refer a matter to local law enforcement.

As noted above, the Title IX regulation requires schools to provide equitable grievance procedures. As part of these procedures, schools generally conduct investigations and hearings to determine whether sexual harassment or violence occurred. In addressing complaints filed with OCR under Title IX, OCR reviews a school's procedures to determine whether the school is using a preponderance of the evidence standard to evaluate complaints. The Supreme Court has applied a preponderance of the evidence standard in civil litigation involving discrimination under Title VII of the Civil Rights Act of 1964 (Title VII), 42 U.S.C. §§ 2000e *et seq.* Like Title IX, Title VII prohibits discrimination on the basis of sex.

Throughout a school's Title IX investigation, including at any hearing, the parties must have an equal opportunity to present relevant witnesses and other evidence. The complainant and the alleged perpetrator must be afforded similar and timely access to any information that will be used at the hearing.29 For example, a school should not conduct a pre-hearing meeting during which only the alleged perpetrator is present and given an opportunity to present his or her side of the story, unless a similar meeting takes place with the complainant; a hearing officer or disciplinary board should not allow only the alleged perpetrator to present character witnesses at a hearing; and a school should not allow the alleged perpetrator to review the complainant's statement without also allowing the complainant to review the alleged perpetrator's statement.

While OCR does not require schools to permit parties to have lawyers at any stage of the proceedings, if a school chooses to allow the parties to have their lawyers participate in the proceedings, it must do so equally for both parties. Additionally, any school-imposed restrictions on the ability of lawyers to speak or otherwise participate in the proceedings should apply equally. OCR strongly discourages schools from allowing the parties personally to question or cross-examine each other during the hearing. Allowing an alleged perpetrator to question an alleged victim directly may be traumatic or intimidating, thereby possibly escalating or perpetuating a hostile environment. OCR also recommends that schools provide an appeals process. If a school provides for appeal of the findings or remedy, it must do so for both parties. Schools must maintain documentation of all proceedings, which may include written findings of facts, transcripts, or audio recordings.

All persons involved in implementing a recipient's grievance procedures (*e.g.*, Title IX coordinators, investigators, and adjudicators) must have training or experience in handling complaints of sexual harassment and sexual violence, and in the recipient's grievance procedures. The training also should include applicable confidentiality requirements. In sexual violence cases, the fact-finder and decision-maker also should have adequate training or knowledge regarding sexual violence. Additionally, a school's investigation and hearing processes cannot be equitable unless they are impartial. Therefore, any real or perceived conflicts of interest between the fact-finder or decision-maker and the parties should be disclosed.

Public and state-supported schools must provide due process to the alleged perpetrator. However, schools should ensure that steps taken to accord due process rights to the alleged perpetrator do not restrict or unnecessarily delay the Title IX protections for the complainant.

(C) *Designated and Reasonably Prompt Time Frames*

OCR will evaluate whether a school's grievance procedures specify the time frames for all major stages of the procedures, as well as the process for extending timelines. Grievance procedures should specify the time frame within which: (1) the school will conduct a full investigation of the complaint; (2) both parties receive a response regarding the outcome of the complaint; and (3) the parties may file an appeal, if applicable. Both parties should be given periodic status updates. Based on OCR experience, a typical investigation takes approximately 60 calendar days following receipt of the complaint. Whether OCR considers complaint resolutions to be timely, however, will vary depending on the complexity of the investigation and the severity and extent of the harassment. For example, the resolution of a complaint involving multiple incidents with multiple complainants likely would take longer than one involving a single incident that occurred in a classroom during school hours with a single complainant.

(D) *Notice of Outcome*

Both parties must be notified, in writing, about the outcome of both the complaint and any appeal, *i.e.*, whether harassment was found to have occurred. OCR recommends that schools provide the written determination of the final outcome to the complainant and the alleged perpetrator concurrently. Title IX does not require the school to notify the alleged perpetrator of the outcome before it notifies the complainant.

Due to the intersection of Title IX and FERPA requirements, OCR recognizes that there may be confusion regarding what information a school may disclose to the complainant. FERPA generally prohibits the nonconsensual disclosure of personally identifiable information from a student's "education record." However, as stated in the *2001 Guidance*, FERPA permits a school to disclose to the harassed student information about the sanction imposed upon a student who was found to have engaged in harassment when the sanction directly relates to the harassed student. This includes an order that the harasser stay away from the harassed student, or that the harasser is prohibited from attending school for a period of time, or transferred to other classes or another residence hall. Disclosure of other information in the student's "education record," including information about sanctions that do not relate to the harassed student, may result in a violation of FERPA.

Further, when the conduct involves a crime of violence or a non-forcible sex offense,[34] FERPA permits a postsecondary institution to disclose to the alleged victim the final results of a disciplinary proceeding against the alleged perpetrator, regardless of whether the institution concluded that a violation was committed. Additionally, a postsecondary institution may disclose to anyone — not just the alleged victim — the final results of a disciplinary proceeding if it determines that the student is an alleged perpetrator of a crime of violence or a non-forcible sex offense, and, with respect to the allegation made, the student has committed a violation of the institution's rules or policies.

Postsecondary institutions also are subject to additional rules under the Clery Act. This law, which applies to postsecondary institutions that participate in Federal student financial aid programs, requires that "both the accuser and the accused must be informed of the outcome of any institutional disciplinary proceeding brought alleging a sex offense." Compliance with this requirement does not constitute a violation of FERPA. Furthermore, the FERPA limitations on redisclosure of information do not apply to information that postsecondary institutions are required to disclose under the Clery Act. Accordingly, postsecondary institutions may not require a complainant to abide by a nondisclosure agreement, in writing or otherwise, that would prevent the redisclosure of this information.

---

[34] Under the FERPA regulations, crimes of violence include arson; assault offenses (aggravated assault, simple assault, intimidation); burglary; criminal homicide (manslaughter by negligence); criminal homicide (murder and non-negligent manslaughter); destruction, damage or vandalism of property; kidnapping/abduction; robbery; and forcible sex offenses. Forcible sex offenses are defined as any sexual act directed against another person forcibly or against that person's will, or not forcibly or against the person's will where the victim is incapable of giving consent. Forcible sex offenses include rape, sodomy, sexual assault with an object, and forcible fondling. Non-forcible sex offenses are incest and statutory rape. 34 C.F.R. Part 99, App. A.

Steps to Prevent Sexual Harassment and Sexual Violence and Correct its Discriminatory Effects on the Complainant and Others

Education and Prevention

In addition to ensuring full compliance with Title IX, schools should take proactive measures to prevent sexual harassment and violence. OCR recommends that all schools implement preventive education programs and make victim resources, including comprehensive victim services, available. Schools may want to include these education programs in their (1) orientation programs for new students, faculty, staff, and employees; (2) training for students who serve as advisors in residence halls; (3) training for student athletes and coaches; and (4) school assemblies and "back to school nights." These programs should include a discussion of what constitutes sexual harassment and sexual violence, the school's policies and disciplinary procedures, and the consequences of violating these policies.

The education programs also should include information aimed at encouraging students to report incidents of sexual violence to the appropriate school and law enforcement authorities. Schools should be aware that victims or third parties may be deterred from reporting incidents if alcohol, drugs, or other violations of school or campus rules were involved. As a result, schools should consider whether their disciplinary policies have a chilling effect on victims' or other students' reporting of sexual violence offenses. For example, OCR recommends that schools inform students that the schools' primary concern is student safety, that any other rules violations will be addressed separately from the sexual violence allegation, and that use of alcohol or drugs never makes the victim at fault for sexual violence.

OCR also recommends that schools develop specific sexual violence materials that include the schools' policies, rules, and resources for students, faculty, coaches, and administrators. Schools also should include such information in their employee handbook and any handbooks that student athletes and members of student activity groups receive. These materials should include where and to whom students should go if they are victims of sexual violence. These materials also should tell students and school employees what to do if they learn of an incident of sexual violence. Schools also should assess student activities regularly to ensure that the practices and behavior of students do not violate the schools' policies against sexual harassment and sexual violence.

Remedies and Enforcement

As discussed above, if a school determines that sexual harassment that creates a hostile environment has occurred, it must take immediate action to eliminate the hostile environment, prevent its recurrence, and address its effects. In addition to counseling or taking disciplinary action against the harasser, effective corrective action may require remedies for the complainant, as well as changes to the school's overall services or policies. Examples of these actions are discussed in greater detail below.

Title IX requires a school to take steps to protect the complainant as necessary, including taking interim steps before the final outcome of the investigation. The school should undertake these steps promptly once it has notice of a sexual harassment or violence allegation. The school should notify the complainant of his or her options to avoid contact with the alleged perpetrator and allow students to change academic or living situations as appropriate. For instance, the school may prohibit the alleged perpetrator from having any contact with the complainant pending the results of the school's investigation. When taking steps to separate the complainant and alleged perpetrator, a school should minimize the burden on the complainant, and thus should not, as a matter of course, remove complainants from classes or housing while allowing alleged perpetrators to remain. In addition, schools should ensure that complainants are aware of their Title IX rights and any available resources, such as counseling, health, and mental health services, and their right to file a complaint with local law enforcement.

Schools should be aware that complaints of sexual harassment or violence may be followed by retaliation by the alleged perpetrator or his or her associates. For instance, friends of the alleged perpetrator may subject the complainant to name-calling and taunting. As part of their Title IX obligations, schools must have policies and procedures in place to protect against retaliatory harassment. At a minimum, schools must ensure that complainants and their parents, if appropriate, know how to report any subsequent problems, and should follow-up with complainants to determine whether any retaliation or new incidents of harassment have occurred.

When OCR finds that a school has not taken prompt and effective steps to respond to sexual harassment or violence, OCR will seek appropriate remedies for both the complainant and the broader student population. When conducting Title IX enforcement activities, OCR seeks to obtain voluntary compliance from recipients. When a recipient does not come into compliance voluntarily, OCR may initiate proceedings to withdraw federal funding by the Department or refer the case to the U.S. Department of Justice for litigation.

Schools should proactively consider the following remedies when determining how to respond to sexual harassment or violence. These are the same types of remedies that OCR would seek in its cases.

Depending on the specific nature of the problem, remedies for the complainant might include, but are not limited to:

- providing an escort to ensure that the complainant can move safely between classes and activities;
- ensuring that the complainant and alleged perpetrator do not attend the same classes;
- moving the complainant or alleged perpetrator to a different residence hall or, in the case of an elementary or secondary school student, to another school within the district;
- providing counseling services;
- providing medical services;

- providing academic support services, such as tutoring;
- arranging for the complainant to re-take a course or withdraw from a class without penalty, including ensuring that any changes do not adversely affect the complainant's academic record; and
- reviewing any disciplinary actions taken against the complainant to see if there is a causal connection between the harassment and the misconduct that may have resulted in the complainant being disciplined.

Remedies for the broader student population might include, but are not limited to:

Counseling and Training

- offering counseling, health, mental health, or other holistic and comprehensive victim services to all students affected by sexual harassment or sexual violence, and notifying students of campus and community counseling, health, mental health, and other student services;
- designating an individual from the school's counseling center to be "on call" to assist victims of sexual harassment or violence whenever needed;
- training the Title IX coordinator and any other employees who are involved in processing, investigating, or resolving complaints of sexual harassment or sexual violence, including providing training on:
    - o the school's Title IX responsibilities to address allegations of sexual harassment or violence
    - o how to conduct Title IX investigations
    - o information on the link between alcohol and drug abuse and sexual harassment or violence and best practices to address that link;
- training all school law enforcement unit personnel on the school's Title IX responsibilities and handling of sexual harassment or violence complaints;
- training all employees who interact with students regularly on recognizing and appropriately addressing allegations of sexual harassment or violence under Title IX; and
- informing students of their options to notify proper law enforcement authorities, including school and local police, and the option to be assisted by school employees in notifying those authorities.

Development of Materials and Implementation of Policies and Procedures

- developing materials on sexual harassment and violence, which should be distributed to students during orientation and upon receipt of complaints, as well as widely posted throughout school buildings and residence halls, and which should include:
    - o what constitutes sexual harassment or violence
    - o what to do if a student has been the victim of sexual harassment or violence

  - o contact information for counseling and victim services on and off school grounds
  - o how to file a complaint with the school
  - o how to contact the school's Title IX coordinator
  - o what the school will do to respond to allegations of sexual harassment or violence, including the interim measures that can be taken

- requiring the Title IX coordinator to communicate regularly with the school's law enforcement unit investigating cases and to provide information to law enforcement unit personnel regarding Title IX requirements;
- requiring the Title IX coordinator to review all evidence in a sexual harassment or sexual violence case brought before the school's disciplinary committee to determine whether the complainant is entitled to a remedy under Title IX that was not available through the disciplinary committee;
- requiring the school to create a committee of students and school officials to identify strategies for ensuring that students:
  - o know the school's prohibition against sex discrimination, including sexual harassment and violence
  - o recognize sex discrimination, sexual harassment, and sexual violence when they occur
  - o understand how and to whom to report any incidents
  - o know the connection between alcohol and drug abuse and sexual harassment or violence
  - o feel comfortable that school officials will respond promptly and equitably to reports of sexual harassment or violence;
- issuing new policy statements or other steps that clearly communicate that the school does not tolerate sexual harassment and violence and will respond to any incidents and to any student who reports such incidents; and
- revising grievance procedures used to handle sexual harassment and violence complaints to ensure that they are prompt and equitable, as required by Title IX.

School Investigations and Reports to OCR

- conducting periodic assessments of student activities to ensure that the practices and behavior of students do not violate the school's policies against sexual harassment and violence;
- investigating whether any other students also may have been subjected to sexual harassment or violence;
- investigating whether school employees with knowledge of allegations of sexual harassment or violence failed to carry out their duties in responding to those allegations;

- conducting, in conjunction with student leaders, a school or campus "climate check" to assess the effectiveness of efforts to ensure that the school is free from sexual harassment and violence, and using the resulting information to inform future proactive steps that will be taken by the school; and
- submitting to OCR copies of all grievances filed by students alleging sexual harassment or violence, and providing OCR with documentation related to the investigation of each complaint, such as witness interviews, investigator notes, evidence submitted by the parties, investigative reports and summaries, any final disposition letters, disciplinary records, and documentation regarding any appeals.

Conclusion

The Department is committed to ensuring that all students feel safe and have the opportunity to benefit fully from their schools' education programs and activities. As part of this commitment, OCR provides technical assistance to assist recipients in achieving voluntary compliance with Title IX.

. . .

Sincerely,

/s/ Russlynn Ali

Assistant Secretary for Civil Rights

NOTES

1. In light of the *Gebser* and *Davis* decisions, along with the Dear Colleague Letter (DCL), how are the standards for monetary damages versus equitable relief — or monetary damages versus administrative compliance — applied in the higher education context?

2. How did the DCL articulate what qualified as an educational program or activity? In what ways might a student's off-campus or online activities affect another student's participation or ability to benefit from an educational program or activity?

3. What qualifications, training standards, and other expectations are required for individuals participating in the grievance process — particularly in terms of investigators, adjudicators, and Title IX coordinators? What qualifications, training standards, and other expectations are strongly suggested for these individuals? How might these factors change a student grievance policy and the selection of members on the grievance committee hearing?

4. The *Gebser* and *Davis* decisions along with the DCL emphasize protections for the alleged victim. How does the DCL address protections for the alleged victim by considering the inherent power differentials between the alleged victim and alleged perpetrator? What does the DCL indicate as required or recommended actions or protocols to mitigate any further harm onto the alleged victim? How should colleges and universities translate these required and recommended actions or protocols into student grievance and conduct policies?

5. The DCL makes clear that the burden of proof for student conduct proceedings of sexual harassment is a "preponderance of the evidence" standard (i.e., it is more likely than not that sexual harassment or violence occurred). According to the DCL, some schools had used the "clear and convincing" standard (i.e., it is highly probable or reasonably certain that the sexual harassment or violence occurred). The DCL observed that the "clear and convincing" standard is a higher standard of proof, which is inconsistent with Title IX. What are college policy justifications that support a "preponderance of the evidence" standard? What are college policy justifications that support a "clear and convincing" standard? What policy reasons might explain why colleges do not adopt a criminal standard?

6. How does the college's ability to report the adjudicating body's decision, under certain instances, potentially harm a student perpetrator's professional and academic opportunities? Should colleges be able to report publicly any of the adjudicating body's decision? What policy reasons might justify the public disclosure of an adjudicating body's decision that the student perpetrator violated the sexual harassment policy? How is this disclosure process similar or different to an employee perpetrator?

D. SEARCH AND SEIZURE

1. Expectations of Privacy

WASHINGTON v. CHRISMAN

455 U.S. 1 (1982)

Chief Justice Burger delivered the opinion of the Court.

We granted certiorari to consider whether a police officer may, consistent with the Fourth Amendment, accompany an arrested person into his residence and seize contraband discovered there in plain view.

I

On the evening of January 21, 1978, Officer Daugherty of the Washington State University police department observed Carl Overdahl, a student at the University, leave a student dormitory carrying a half-gallon bottle of gin. Because Washington law forbids possession of alcoholic beverages by persons under 21 . . . and Overdahl appeared to be under age, the officer stopped him and asked for identification. Overdahl said that his identification was in his dormitory room and asked if the officer would wait while he went to retrieve it. The officer answered that under the circumstances he would have to accompany Overdahl, to which Overdahl replied "OK."

Overdahl's room was approximately 11 by 17 feet and located on the 11th floor of the dormitory. Respondent Chrisman, Overdahl's roommate, was in the room when the officer and Overdahl entered. The officer remained in the open doorway, leaning against the doorjamb while watching Chrisman and Overdahl. He observed that Chrisman, who was in the process of placing a small box in the room's medicine cabinet, became nervous at the sight of an officer.

Within 30 to 45 seconds after Overdahl entered the room, the officer noticed seeds and a small pipe lying on a desk 8 to 10 feet from where he was standing. From his training and experience, the officer believed the seeds were marijuana and the pipe was of a type used to smoke marijuana. He entered the room and examined the pipe and seeds, confirming that the seeds were marijuana and observing that the pipe smelled of marijuana.

The officer informed Overdahl and Chrisman of their rights . . . ; each acknowledged that he understood his rights and indicated that he was willing to waive them. Officer Daugherty then asked whether the students had any other drugs in the room. The respondent handed Daugherty the box he had been carrying earlier, which contained three small plastic bags filled with marijuana and $112 in cash. At that point, Officer Daugherty called by radio for a second officer; on his arrival, the two students were told that a search of the room would be necessary. The officers explained to Overdahl and Chrisman that they had an absolute right to insist that the officers first obtain a search warrant, but that they could voluntarily consent to the search. Following this explanation, which was given in considerable detail, the two students conferred in whispers for several minutes before announcing their consent; they also signed written forms consenting to the search of the room. The search yielded more marijuana and a quantity of lysergic acid diethylamide (LSD), both controlled substances.

Respondent was charged with one count of possessing more than 40 grams of marijuana and one count of possessing LSD, both felonies. . . . A pretrial motion to suppress the evidence seized in the room was denied; respondent was convicted of both counts. On appeal, the Washington Court of Appeals affirmed the convictions, upholding the validity of the search.

The Supreme Court of Washington reversed. It held that, although Overdahl had been placed under lawful arrest and "there was nothing to prevent Officer Daugherty from accompanying Overdahl to his room," the officer had no right to enter the room and either examine or seize contraband without a warrant. The court reasoned there was no indication that Overdahl might obtain a weapon or destroy evidence, and, with the officer blocking the only exit from the room, his presence inside the room was not necessary to prevent escape. Because the officer's entry into the room and his observations of its interior were not justified by "exigent circumstances," the seizure of the seeds and pipe were held not to fall within the plain-view exception to the Fourth Amendment's warrant requirement. The court went on to hold that because the students' consent to the subsequent search of the room was the fruit of the officer's initial entry, the contraband found during that search should also have been suppressed.

. . . .

We granted certiorari . . . and reverse.

II

A

The "plain view" exception to the Fourth Amendment warrant requirement permits a law enforcement officer to seize what clearly is incriminating evidence or contraband when it is discovered in a place where the officer has a right to be. *Coolidge v. New Hampshire*, 403 U.S. 443 (1971); *Harris v. United States*, 390 U.S. 234 (1968). Here, the officer had placed Overdahl under lawful arrest, and therefore was authorized to accompany him to his room for the purpose of obtaining identification. The officer had a right to remain literally at Overdahl's elbow at all times; nothing in the Fourth Amendment is to the contrary.

The central premise of the opinion of the Supreme Court of Washington is that Officer Daugherty was not entitled to accompany Overdahl from the public corridor of the dormitory into his room, absent a showing that such "intervention" was required by "exigent circumstances." We disagree with this novel reading of the Fourth Amendment. The absence of an affirmative indication that an arrested person might have a weapon available or might attempt to escape does not diminish the arresting officer's authority to maintain custody over the arrested person. Nor is that authority altered by the nature of the offense for which the arrest was made.

Every arrest must be presumed to present a risk of danger to the arresting officer. There is no way for an officer to predict reliably how a particular subject will react to arrest or the degree of the potential danger. Moreover, the possibility that an arrested person will attempt to escape if not properly supervised is obvious. . . .

We hold, therefore, that it is not "unreasonable" under the Fourth Amendment for a police officer, as a matter of routine, to monitor the movements of an arrested person, as his judgment dictates, following the arrest. The officer's need to ensure his own safety — as well as the integrity of the arrest — is compelling. . . .

It follows that Officer Daugherty properly accompanied Overdahl into his room, and that his presence in the room was lawful. With restraint, the officer remained in the doorway momentarily, entering no farther than was necessary to keep the arrested person in his view. It was only by chance that, while in the doorway, the officer observed in plain view what he recognized to be contraband. Had he exercised his undoubted right to remain at Overdahl's side, he might well have observed the contraband sooner.

B

Respondent nevertheless contends that the officer lacked authority to *seize* the contraband, even though in plain view, because he was "outside" the room at the time he made his observations. . . . We agree that on this record such niceties are not relevant. It is of no legal significance whether the officer was in the room, on the threshold, or in the hallway, since he had a right to be in any of these places as an incident of a valid arrest.

Respondent's argument appears to be that, even if the officer could have stationed himself "inside" the room had he done so immediately upon Overdahl's entry, his 30- to 45-second hesitation was fatal; and that having chosen to remain in the doorway, the officer was precluded from proceeding further to seize the contraband. We reject this contention. Respondent's argument, if accepted, would have the perverse effect of penalizing the officer for exercising more restraint than was required under the circumstances. . . .

The "intrusion" in this case occurred when the officer, quite properly, followed Overdahl into a private area to a point from which he had unimpeded view of and access to the area's contents and its occupants. His right to custodial control did not evaporate with his choice to hesitate briefly in the doorway rather than at some other vantage point inside the room. . . .

We therefore conclude that, regardless of where the officer was positioned with respect to the threshold, he did not abandon his right to be in the room whenever he considered it essential. Accordingly, he had the right to act as soon as he observed the seeds and pipe. This is a classic instance of incriminating evidence found in plain view when a police officer, for unrelated but entirely legitimate reasons, obtains lawful access to an individual's area of privacy. The Fourth Amendment does not prohibit seizure of evidence of criminal conduct found in these circumstances.

III

Since the seizure of the marijuana and pipe was lawful, we have no difficulty concluding that this evidence and the contraband subsequently taken from respondent's room were properly admitted at his trial. Respondent voluntarily produced three bags of marijuana after being informed of his rights. . . . He then consented, in writing, to a search of the room, after being advised that his consent must be voluntary and that he had an absolute right to refuse consent and demand procurement of a search warrant. The seizure of the drugs pursuant to respondent's valid consent did not violate the Fourth Amendment.

. . . .

NOTES

1. The Fourth Amendment protects "the right of the people to be secure in their persons, houses, papers, and effects, against unreasonable searches and seizures." In its opinion, the Court acknowledged that one of the historical inspirations behind the Fourth Amendment was a tense relationship between the Crown and the press. What in the language of the Fourth Amendment helps to resolve this conflicted relationship?

2. The Fourth Amendment makes reference not only to the search and seizure of property, but also the seizure of people. Cases touching on the seizure of people in higher education are rare, but the reasonableness standard applies just the same. One example will suffice: In *Desyllas v. Bernstine*, 351 F.3d 934 (9th Cir. 2003), the Court of Appeals for the Ninth Circuit rejected the claim of a university student who argued that he was unlawfully detained and questioned about confidential records he had found outside the newspaper office where he worked. The student realized the documents were confidential and locked them in a cupboard in the newspaper office. Several months later he wrote a letter to the university president informing him that he possessed the records and would be going forward with a press release within two weeks. University officials locked the newspaper office door, located the student, and questioned him. He was never told he was not free to leave their presence and the officials remained with him only until he answered their question about whether he would willingly give them the records that he readily acknowledged belonged to the university. The court concluded that he was not detained within the meaning of the Fourth Amendment. In addition, the court rejected the student's claim that the locking of the door and questioning him amounted to an abridgment of the freedom of the press since the officials did not interfere with the newspaper's publication of news.

3. What do you believe is the more crucial fact in *Chrisman* — the incident giving rise to the lawful arrest; the officer accompanying Overdahl to his room after the arrest; the seeds and pipe in plain view, giving rise to further inquiry and search; or the students' consent to the further search? Why is such dissection of the facts in these cases so important to the Court's ultimate analysis? If Overdahl had not been subject to a lawful arrest, albeit for a scenario unrelated to the use and possession of drugs, what facts would have been necessary to permit the search of the dormitory room?

4. What is the implication of the result in *Chrisman* for the expectation of privacy students have in their residence halls or in their personal belongings? Read the following case, which may help set the scene for the answers to such questions.

NEW JERSEY v. T.L.O.
469 U.S. 325 (1985)

Justice White delivered the opinion of the Court.

. . . .

I

On March 7, 1980, a teacher at Piscataway High School in Middlesex County, N. J., discovered two girls smoking in a lavatory. One of the two girls was the respondent T.L.O., who at that time was a 14-year-old high school freshman. Because smoking in the lavatory was a violation of a school rule, the teacher took the two girls to the Principal's office, where they met with Assistant Vice Principal Theodore Choplick. In response to questioning by Mr. Choplick, T.L.O.'s companion admitted that she had violated the rule. T.L.O., however, denied that she had been smoking in the lavatory and claimed that she did not smoke at all.

Mr. Choplick asked T.L.O. to come into his private office and demanded to see her purse. Opening the purse, he found a pack of cigarettes, which he removed from the purse and held before T.L.O. as he accused her of having lied to him. As he reached into the purse for the cigarettes, Mr. Choplick also noticed a package of cigarette rolling papers. In his experience, possession of rolling papers by high school students was closely associated with the use of marijuana. Suspecting that a closer examination of the purse might yield further evidence of drug use, Mr. Choplick proceeded to search the purse thoroughly. The search revealed a small amount of marijuana, a pipe, a number of empty plastic bags, a substantial quantity of money in one-dollar bills, an index card that appeared to be a list of students who owed T.L.O. money, and two letters that implicated T.L.O. in marijuana dealing.

Mr. Choplick notified T.L.O.'s mother and the police, and turned the evidence of drug dealing over to the police. At the request of the police, T.L.O.'s mother took her daughter to police headquarters, where T.L.O. confessed that she had been selling marijuana at the high school. On the basis of the confession and the evidence seized by Mr. Choplick, the State brought delinquency charges against T.L.O. in the Juvenile and Domestic Relations Court of Middlesex County. Contending that Mr. Choplick's search of her purse violated the Fourth Amendment, T.L.O. moved to suppress the evidence found in her purse as well as her confession, which, she argued, was tainted by the allegedly unlawful search. The Juvenile Court denied the motion to suppress. Although the court concluded that the Fourth Amendment did apply to searches carried out by school officials, it held that

> "a school official may properly conduct a search of a student's person if the official has a reasonable suspicion that a crime has been or is in the process of being committed, *or* reasonable cause to believe that the search is necessary to maintain school discipline or enforce school policies."

. . . .

On appeal from the final judgment of the Juvenile Court, a divided Appellate Division affirmed the trial court's finding that there had been no Fourth Amendment violation, but vacated the adjudication of delinquency and remanded for a determination whether T.L.O. had knowingly and voluntarily waived her Fifth Amendment rights before confessing. T.L.O. appealed the Fourth Amendment ruling, and the Supreme Court of New Jersey reversed the judgment of the Appellate Division and ordered the suppression of the evidence found in T.L.O.'s purse.

The New Jersey Supreme Court agreed with the lower courts that the Fourth Amendment applies to searches conducted by school officials. The court also rejected the State of New Jersey's argument that the exclusionary rule should not be employed to prevent the use in juvenile proceedings of evidence unlawfully seized by school officials. . . .

. . . .

We granted the State of New Jersey's petition for certiorari. . . .

. . . .

II

In determining whether the search at issue in this case violated the Fourth Amendment, we are faced initially with the question whether that Amendment's prohibition on unreasonable searches and seizures applies to searches conducted by public school officials. We hold that it does.

. . . .

These two propositions — that the Fourth Amendment applies to the States through the Fourteenth Amendment, and that the actions of public school officials are subject to the limits placed on state action by the Fourteenth Amendment — might appear sufficient to answer the suggestion that the Fourth Amendment does not proscribe unreasonable searches by school officials. On reargument, however, the State of New Jersey has argued that the history of the Fourth Amendment indicates that the Amendment was intended to regulate only searches and seizures carried out by law enforcement officers; accordingly, although public school officials are concededly state agents for purposes of the Fourteenth Amendment, the Fourth Amendment creates no rights enforceable against them.

. . . But this Court has never limited the Amendment's prohibition on unreasonable searches and seizures to operations conducted by the police. Rather, the Court has long spoken of the Fourth Amendment's strictures as restraints imposed upon "governmental action" — that is, "upon the activities of sovereign authority." *Burdeau v. McDowell*, 256 U.S. 465, 475 (1921). . . .

Notwithstanding the general applicability of the Fourth Amendment to the activities of civil authorities, a few courts have concluded that school officials are exempt from the dictates of the Fourth Amendment by virtue of the special nature of their authority over schoolchildren. Teachers and school administrators, it is said, act *in loco parentis* in their dealings with students: their authority is that of the parent, not the State, and is therefore not subject to the limits of the Fourth Amendment.

Such reasoning is in tension with contemporary reality and the teachings of this Court. We have held school officials subject to the commands of the First Amendment, see *Tinker v. Des Moines Independent Community School District*, 393 U.S. 503 (1969), and the Due Process Clause of the Fourteenth Amendment, see *Goss v. Lopez*, 419 U.S. 565 (1975). If school authorities are state actors for purposes of the constitutional guarantees of freedom of expression and due process, it is difficult to understand why they should be deemed to be exercising parental rather than public authority when conducting searches of their students. More generally, the Court has recognized that "the concept of parental delegation" as a source of school authority is not entirely "consonant with compulsory education laws." *Ingraham v. Wright*, 430 U.S. 651, 662 (1977). Today's public school officials do not merely exercise authority voluntarily conferred on them by individual parents; rather, they act in furtherance of publicly mandated educational and disciplinary policies. . . . In carrying out searches and other disciplinary functions pursuant to such policies, school officials act as representatives of the State, not merely as surrogates for the parents, and they cannot claim the parents' immunity from the strictures of the Fourth Amendment.

III

To hold that the Fourth Amendment applies to searches conducted by school authorities is only to begin the inquiry into the standards governing such searches.

Although the underlying command of the Fourth Amendment is always that searches and seizures be reasonable, what is reasonable depends on the context within which a search takes place. The determination of the standard of reasonableness governing any specific class of searches requires "balancing the need to search against the invasion which the search entails." *Camara v. Municipal Court*, [387 U.S. 523,] 536–537 [(1967)]. On one side of the balance are arrayed the individual's legitimate expectations of privacy and personal security; on the other, the government's need for effective methods to deal with breaches of public order.

. . . .

Although this Court may take notice of the difficulty of maintaining discipline in the public schools today, the situation is not so dire that students in the schools may claim no legitimate expectations of privacy. We have recently recognized that the need to maintain order in a prison is such that prisoners retain no legitimate expectations of privacy in their cells, but it goes almost without saying that "[the] prisoner and the schoolchild stand in wholly different circumstances, separated by the harsh facts of criminal conviction and incarceration." *Ingraham v. Wright*, *supra*, at 669. We are not yet ready to hold that the schools and the prisons need be equated for purposes of the Fourth Amendment.

Nor does the State's suggestion that children have no legitimate need to bring personal property into the schools seem well anchored in reality. Students at a minimum must bring to school not only the supplies needed for their studies, but also keys, money, and the necessaries of personal hygiene and grooming. In addition, students may carry on their persons or in purses or wallets such nondisruptive yet highly personal items as photographs, letters, and diaries. Finally, students may have perfectly legitimate reasons to carry with them articles of property needed in connection with extracurricular or recreational activities. In short, schoolchildren may find it necessary to carry with them a variety of legitimate, noncontraband items, and there is no reason to conclude that they have necessarily waived all rights to privacy in such items merely by bringing them onto school grounds.

Against the child's interest in privacy must be set the substantial interest of teachers and administrators in maintaining discipline in the classroom and on school grounds. Maintaining order in the classroom has never been easy, but in recent years, school disorder has often taken particularly ugly forms: drug use and violent crime in the schools have become major social problems. . . .

How, then, should we strike the balance between the schoolchild's legitimate expectations of privacy and the school's equally legitimate need to maintain an environment in which learning can take place? It is evident that the school setting requires some easing of the restrictions to which searches by public authorities are ordinarily subject. The warrant requirement, in particular, is unsuited to the school environment: requiring a teacher to obtain a warrant before searching a child suspected of an infraction of school rules (or of the criminal law) would unduly interfere with the maintenance of the swift and informal disciplinary procedures needed in the schools. . . . [W]e hold today that school officials need not obtain a warrant before searching a student who is under their authority.

The school setting also requires some modification of the level of suspicion of illicit activity needed to justify a search. Ordinarily, a search — even one that may permissibly be carried out without a warrant — must be based upon "probable cause" to believe that a violation of the law has occurred. . . . However, "probable cause" is not an irreducible requirement of a valid search. The fundamental command of the Fourth Amendment is that searches and seizures be reasonable, and although "both the concept of probable cause and the requirement of a warrant bear on the reasonableness of a search, . . . in certain limited circumstances neither is required." *Almeida-Sanchez v. United States*, [413 U.S. 266, 277 (1973) (Powell, J., concurring)]. . . .

We join the majority of courts that have examined this issue in concluding that the accommodation of the privacy interests of schoolchildren with the substantial need of teachers and administrators for freedom to maintain order in the schools does not require strict adherence to the requirement that searches be based on probable cause to believe that the subject of the search has violated or is violating the law. Rather, the legality of a search of a student should depend simply on the reasonableness, under all the circumstances, of the search. Determining the reasonableness of any search involves a twofold inquiry: first, one must consider "whether the . . . action was justified at its inception," *Terry v. Ohio*, 392 U.S. [1,] 20 [(1969)]; second, one must determine whether the search as actually conducted "was reasonably related in scope to the circumstances which justified the interference in the first place," *ibid.* Under ordinary circumstances, a search of a student by a teacher or other school official will be "justified at its inception" when there are reasonable grounds for suspecting that the search will turn up evidence that the student has violated or is violating either the law or the rules of the school. Such a search will be permissible in its scope when the measures adopted are reasonably related to the objectives of the search and not excessively intrusive in light of the age and sex of the student and the nature of the infraction.

This standard will, we trust, neither unduly burden the efforts of school authorities to maintain order in their schools nor authorize unrestrained intrusions upon the privacy of schoolchildren. By focusing attention on the question of reasonableness, the standard will spare teachers and school administrators the necessity of schooling themselves in the niceties of probable cause and permit them to regulate their conduct according to the dictates of reason and common sense. At the same time, the reasonableness standard should ensure that the interests of students will be invaded no more than is necessary to achieve the legitimate end of preserving order in the schools.

IV

There remains the question of the legality of the search in this case. We recognize that the "reasonable grounds" standard applied by the New Jersey Supreme Court in its consideration of this question is not substantially different from the standard that we have adopted today. Nonetheless, we believe that the New Jersey court's application of that standard to strike down the search of T.L.O.'s purse reflects a somewhat crabbed notion of reasonableness. Our review of the facts surrounding the search leads us to conclude that the search was in no sense unreasonable for Fourth Amendment purposes.

The incident that gave rise to this case actually involved two separate searches, with the first — the search for cigarettes — providing the suspicion that gave rise to the second — the search for marijuana. Although it is the fruits of the second search that are at issue here, the validity of the search for marijuana must depend on the reasonableness of the initial search for cigarettes, as there would have been no reason to suspect that T.L.O. possessed marijuana had the first search not taken place. Accordingly, it is to the search for cigarettes that we first turn our attention.

. . . .

. . . The relevance of T.L.O.'s possession of cigarettes to the question whether she had been smoking and to the credibility of her denial that she smoked supplied the necessary "nexus" between the item searched for and the infraction under investigation. See *Warden v. Hayden*, 387 U.S. 294, 306–307 (1967). Thus, if Mr. Choplick in fact had a reasonable suspicion that T.L.O. had cigarettes in her purse, the search was justified despite the fact that the cigarettes, if found, would constitute "mere evidence" of a violation. *Ibid.*

. . . A teacher had reported that T.L.O. was smoking in the lavatory. Certainly this report gave Mr. Choplick reason to suspect that T.L.O. was carrying cigarettes with her; and if she did have cigarettes, her purse was the obvious place in which to find them. Mr. Choplick's suspicion that there were cigarettes in the purse was not an "inchoate and unparticularized suspicion or 'hunch,' " *Terry v. Ohio*, 392 U.S., at 27; rather, it was the sort of "common-sense [conclusion] about human behavior" upon which "practical people" — including government officials — are entitled to rely. *United States v. Cortez*, 449 U.S. 411, 418 (1981). Of course, even if the teacher's report were true, T.L.O. *might* not have had a pack of cigarettes with her; she might have borrowed a cigarette from someone else or have been sharing a cigarette with another student. But the requirement of reasonable suspicion is not a requirement of absolute certainty: "sufficient probability, not certainty, is the touchstone of reasonableness under the Fourth Amendment. . . ." *Hill v. California*, 401 U.S. 797, 804 (1971). . . .

Our conclusion that Mr. Choplick's decision to open T.L.O.'s purse was reasonable brings us to the question of the further search for marijuana once the pack of cigarettes was located. The suspicion upon which the search for marijuana was founded was provided when Mr. Choplick observed a package of rolling papers in the purse as he removed the pack of cigarettes. Although T.L.O. does not dispute the reasonableness of Mr. Choplick's belief that the rolling papers indicated the presence of marijuana, she does contend that the scope of the search Mr. Choplick conducted exceeded permissible bounds when he seized and read certain letters that implicated T.L.O. in drug dealing. This argument, too, is unpersuasive. The discovery of the rolling papers concededly gave rise to a reasonable suspicion that T.L.O. was carrying marijuana as well as cigarettes in her purse. This suspicion justified further exploration of T.L.O.'s purse, which turned up more evidence of drug-related activities: a pipe, a number of plastic bags of the type commonly used to store marijuana, a small quantity of marijuana, and a fairly substantial amount of money. Under these circumstances, it was not unreasonable to extend the search to a separate zippered compartment of the purse; and when a search of that compartment revealed an index card containing a list of "people who owe me money" as well as two letters, the inference that T.L.O. was involved in marijuana trafficking was substantial enough to justify Mr. Choplick in examining the letters to determine whether they contained any further evidence. In short, we cannot conclude that the search for marijuana was unreasonable in any respect.

Because the search resulting in the discovery of the evidence of marijuana dealing by T.L.O. was reasonable, the New Jersey Supreme Court's decision to exclude that evidence from T.L.O.'s juvenile delinquency proceedings on Fourth Amendment grounds was erroneous. Accordingly, the judgment of the Supreme Court of New Jersey is

Reversed.

NOTES

1. How does the Court in *T.L.O.* define and apply "expectation of privacy" for students? How does this definition translate to students in higher education settings?

2. In an important footnote, the Court in *T.L.O.* stated that it was *not* deciding whether individualized suspicion was a necessary element in the reasonableness standard it was adopting, but recognized that several earlier courts had held that individualized suspicion contributes to the reasonableness of a search; it is not, however, an ironclad requirement. Do you agree with this sentiment? Should individualized suspicion be a legal requirement in searches like the ones that arose in *T.L.O.*?

3. The Court in *T.L.O.* presented a very useful two-part test for the justification of a search in a school setting: (1) was the search justified at its inception?, and (2) was the search reasonable in scope under the circumstances? The searches in *T.L.O.*, of course, took place in a secondary school. What do you think about its application in higher education settings? Are the two central questions written in such a way as to apply to colleges and universities fairly and consistently, so as to strike the proper balance between individual rights and institutional authority? Assuming the Fourth Amendment applies on the campuses of public colleges and universities just as it does on the grounds of public K-12 schools, do you believe the warrant and probable cause requirements of the Fourth Amendment should be relaxed for searches conducted by college and university officials, just as they are for K-12 school administrators? Why? Why not? Does it make a difference who is conducting the searches — administrators, campus police officers? Does it make a difference who obtains the first information leading to the necessity for a search — students, staff, community, campus police, local community police?

2. Fourth Amendment Protection in Residence Halls

PIAZZOLA v. WATKINS
442 F.2d 284 (5th Cir. 1971)

Rives, Circuit Judge:

. . . .

By separate jury trials, each of the appellees [Piazzola and Marinshaw] was convicted of the offense of illegal possession of marijuana in the Circuit Court of Pike County, Alabama, and was sentenced to imprisonment for a period of five years. . . . The State Court of Appeals affirmed both convictions without opinion, and the State Supreme Court granted motions to strike their petitions for certiorari. . . . Their habeas corpus petition to the federal district court was submitted on a stipulation of facts which included . . . a transcript of the testimony taken in the State Circuit Court on their motion to suppress evidence. . . .

The district court condensed the transcript of testimony into the following findings of fact:

> "On the morning of February 28, 1968, the Dean of Men of Troy State University was called to the office of the Chief of Police of Troy, Alabama, to discuss 'the drug problem' at the University. Two State narcotic agents and two student informers from Troy State University were also present. Later on that same day, the Dean of Men was called to the city police station for another meeting; at this time he was informed by the officers that they had sufficient evidence that marijuana was in the dormitory rooms of certain Troy State students and that they desired the cooperation of University officials in searching these rooms. The police officers were advised by the Dean of Men that they would receive the full cooperation of the University officials in searching for the marijuana. The informers, whose identities have not yet been disclosed, provided the police officers with names of students whose rooms were to be searched. Still later on that same day (which was during the week of final examinations at the University and was to be followed by a weeklong holiday) the law enforcement officers, accompanied by some of the University officials, searched six or seven dormitory rooms located in two separate residence halls. The rooms of both Piazzola and Marinshaw were searched without search warrants and without their consent. Present during the search of the room occupied by Marinshaw were two State narcotic agents, the University security officer, and a counselor of the residence hall where Marinshaw's room was located. Piazzola's room was searched twice. Present during the first search were two State narcotic agents and a University official; no evidence was found at this time. The second search of Piazzola's room, which disclosed the incriminating evidence, was conducted solely by the State and City police officials.
>
> "At the time of the seizure the University had in effect the following regulation:

> The college reserves the right to enter rooms for inspection purposes. If the administration deems it necessary, the room may be searched and the occupant required to open his personal baggage and any other personal material which is sealed.

Each of the petitioners was familiar with this regulation. After the search of the petitioners' rooms and the discovery of the marijuana, they were arrested, and the State criminal prosecutions and convictions ensued."

1. *Exhaustion of State Remedies*

. . . .

The district court properly held that the appellees had exhausted the remedies available to them in the courts of the State of Alabama. . . .

2. *Validity of Search and Seizure*

The Fourth Amendment protects "the right of the *people* to be secure in their persons, houses, papers, and effects, against *unreasonable* searches and seizures" (emphasis added). The question is whether in the light of all of the facts and circumstances, including the University regulation, the search which disclosed the marijuana was an unreasonable search. The district judge made reasonableness the touchstone of his opinion as to the validity of the search. We find ourselves in agreement with his view that this search was unreasonable.

In a case where the facts were similar, *People v. Cohen*, 57 Misc.2d 366, 292 N.Y.S.2d 706, aff'd, 61 Misc.2d 858, 306 N.Y.S.2d 788, Judge Burstein said:

> "The police and the Hofstra University officials admitted that they entered the room in order to make an arrest, if an arrest was warranted. This was, in essence, a fishing expedition calculated to discover narcotics. It offends reason and logic to suppose that a student will consent to an entry into his room designed to establish grounds upon which to arrest him. Certainly, there can be no rational claim that a student will self-consciously waive his Constitutional right to a lawful search and seizure. Finally, even if the doctrine of implied consent were imported into this case, the consent is given, not to police officials, but to the University and the latter cannot fragmentize, share or delegate it."

Another case somewhat in point on the facts is *Commonwealth v. McCloskey, Appellant, 1970*, 217 Pa. Super. 432, 272 A.2d 271. There the court reversed a student's marijuana conviction because the policemen who entered his dormitory room to execute a search warrant did not knock or announce their presence and purpose before entering. In part, Judge Cercone speaking for the majority of the court said:

> "It was the Commonwealth's position that the Fourth Amendment protections do not apply to a search of a college dormitory room. The test to be used in determining the applicability of the Fourth Amendment protections is whether or not the particular locale is one '. . . in which there was a

> reasonable expectation of freedom from governmental intrusion'. . . . A dormitory room is analogous to an apartment or a hotel room. . . . The defendant rented the dormitory room for a certain period of time, agreeing to abide by the rules established by his lessor, the University. As in most rental situations, the lessor, Bucknell University, reserved the right to check the room for damages, wear and unauthorized appliances. Such right of the lessor, however, does not mean McCloskey was not entitled to have a 'reasonable expectation of freedom from governmental intrusion' or that he gave consent to the police search, or gave the University authority to consent to such search.

In the case of *Katz v. United States*, 389 U.S. 347 (1967), to which Judge Cercone referred, the Court commented at some length on the concept of "constitutionally protected areas":

> "The petitioner has strenuously argued that the [telephone] booth was a 'constitutionally protected area.' The Government has maintained with equal vigor that it was not. But this effort to decide whether or not a given 'area,' viewed in the abstract, is 'constitutionally protected' deflects attention from the problem presented by this case. For the Fourth Amendment protects people, not places. What a person knowingly exposes to the public, even in his own home or office, is not a subject of Fourth Amendment protection. But what he seeks to preserve as private, even in an area accessible to the public, may be constitutionally protected.

389 U.S. at 351–352.

By a similar process of reasoning, we must conclude that a student who occupies a college dormitory room enjoys the protection of the Fourth Amendment. True the University retains broad supervisory powers which permit it to adopt the regulation heretofore quoted, provided that regulation is reasonably construed and is limited in its application to further the University's function as an educational institution. The regulation cannot be construed or applied so as to give consent to a search for evidence for the primary purpose of a criminal prosecution. Otherwise, the regulation itself would constitute an unconstitutional attempt to require a student to waive his protection from unreasonable searches and seizures as a condition to his occupancy of a college dormitory room. Clearly the University had no authority to consent to or join in a police search for evidence of crime.

The right to privacy is "no less important than any other right carefully and particularly reserved to the people." *Mapp v. Ohio*, 367 U.S. 643, 657 (1961). The results of the search do not prove its reasonableness. This search was an unconstitutional invasion of the privacy both of these appellees and of the students in whose rooms no evidence of marijuana was found. The warrantless search of these students' dormitory rooms cannot be justified. The judgment is therefore

Affirmed.

CLARK, CIRCUIT JUDGE (concurring in part and dissenting in part).

I respectfully dissent from part 2 of the Court's opinion as to the defendant, Marinshaw. The college had a direct interest in keeping its dormitories free of the specific criminal activity here involved — the possession of the drug, marijuana. The regulation was a reasonable means of embodying this interest. Marinshaw was found to be familiar with the regulation. When he chose to place the evidence of this criminal conduct in his dormitory room he knowingly exposed this material to inspections by officials of the University. He cannot now reinstate as private an area he had agreed was thus accessible. A publicly owned dormitory room is not in my mind the equivalent of a private rooming house. I concur in the result as to the defendant, Piazzola, because I do not believe the regulation can be validly construed to authorize the college to consent to an independent police search.

In all other respects I concur in the opinion of the majority.

NOTES

1. Do you agree with the decision in *Piazzola*? Re-read the Troy State regulation: "The college reserves the right to enter rooms for inspection purposes. If the administration deems it necessary, the room may be searched and the occupant required to open his personal baggage and any other personal material which is sealed." The majority held that this rule did not apply to situations giving rise to criminal prosecution. Further, the court implied that if the regulation were to be rewritten to include such authority, then it would be unconstitutional as written *and* as applied. Do you agree? Note that Hofstra University, involved in *People v. Cohen*, 57 Misc. 2d 366 (Dist. Ct. 1968), *aff'd*, 61 Misc. 2d 858, (Sup. Ct. 1969), and cited with persuasive authority in *Piazzola*, had a policy of privacy expectation that recognized that students in dormitory rooms, like all tenants, enjoy the right of privacy and freedom from an unreasonable search or seizure. *See also Limpuangthip v. United States*, 932 A.2d 1137 (D.C. Ct. App. 2007), *infra*.

2. In *Piazzola*, the local police department made initial contact with Troy State University officials in furtherance of its investigation into drug use at the university. The court's majority held that the warrantless search of the dormitory room was unlawful. How important is the sequence of events here, in that the police made the initial contact with the university, as opposed to university officials making initial contact with the police? If the university officials were conducting the investigation, pursuant to Troy State's regulations, and then had contacted the police for assistance, would the search have been lawful? See *People v. The Superior Court of Santa Clara County*, 49 Cal. Rptr. 3d 831 (Cal. Ct. App. 2006), where the Santa Clara County Superior Court in California granted the defendant student's motion to suppress evidence of marijuana possession and trafficking that was obtained as a result of a warrantless search of his dorm room. The court concluded that a campus safety officer did not have actual authority to give valid third-party consent to a police search of defendant's dorm room. Importantly, the court also concluded that defendant's motion to suppress should have been denied on the basis that the seized contraband would have been inevitably discovered: it was unlikely the university would have withheld the contraband from the police to pursue its own internal investigation.

3. What if incriminating evidence had been discovered on a routine inspection and then the police were contacted? Would the search, in that case, have been lawful? In *Commonwealth v. Neilson*, 666 N.E.2d 984 (Mass. 1996), college officials were advised that a cat was living in a dormitory suite, against school regulations. The officials posted notices on the doors alerting residents that a room check would be conducted to ensure the cat was removed. During the check, college officials noticed a light coming from the closet of the one of the bedrooms in one of the four-bedroom suites. They opened it and discovered marijuana plants and cultivation materials. They contacted the campus police, who removed the evidence without seeking or possessing a search warrant. Defendant was charged with illegal possession of marijuana and cultivating and distributing marijuana, but the trial court granted a motion to suppress the evidence. The court affirmed, finding that the warrantless search of the dormitory room by the campus police violated his constitutional rights, and all evidence obtained as a result of the search should be suppressed. Although the college officials' initial search was proper to enforce a reasonable health and safety regulation, the sole purpose of the warrantless entry by the campus police was to confiscate contraband for purposes of a criminal proceeding. A warrant was required as there was no showing of express consent or exigent circumstances. *See also Arizona v. Kappes*, 550 P.2d 121 (Ariz. Ct. App. 1976).

4. How does *New Jersey v. T.L.O.*, 469 U.S. 325 (1985), presented earlier in this chapter and decided 14 years later than *Piazzola*, change this analysis?

5. How do these analyses change when the university is a private institution and not a public one? See the following case.

LIMPUANGTHIP v. UNITED STATES

932 A.2d 1137 (D.C. Ct. App. 2007)

BELSON, SENIOR JUDGE:

Appellant Jason Limpuangthip, a college student, was convicted after a bench trial of possession with intent to distribute marijuana . . . , possession of drug paraphernalia . . . , and possession of psilocylin (mushrooms). . . . Critical evidence supporting the charges was obtained from appellant's dormitory room at George Washington University, a private university, as a result of a warrantless search and seizure by Penny Davis, a community director at the University. Two University police officers from the George Washington University Police Department ("the University Police") and a residential assistant ("R.A.") were present at the time of the search. On appeal, appellant contends that the search that resulted in his arrest violated the Fourth Amendment of the Constitution. We conclude that the search, as it was conducted, did not violate appellant's rights under the Fourth Amendment and, accordingly, affirm the conviction.

I.

Appellant brought a motion to suppress statements and tangible evidence, contending that the evidence supporting the charges against him — i.e., statements, drugs, drug paraphernalia and cash — was illegally obtained by Ms. Davis and the University Police. At a suppression hearing, Ms. Davis testified that she was in charge of supervising three dormitories, including one called the Ivory Tower where appellant lived. As part of her duties, she enforced the University's residential community code of conduct guidelines and conducted administrative searches. She testified that these searches were performed by administrators when there was a concern that activities in a room could endanger the health and welfare of the students. She received training in how to conduct these searches from the University Police. [Her training consisted of four or five hours with university police, ending with a simulation. During the training, it was made clear that the administrators, not the police, should conduct searches. Davis testified that, to her understanding, if police conducted the search, the search could be "thrown out".] The University Police are employees of the University who are appointed as Special Police Officers ("SPOs") by the Mayor of the District of Columbia for the purpose of protecting property on the premises of their employer, and are authorized to exercise arrest powers broader than that of ordinary citizens and security guards.

Ms. Davis testified that she conducted an administrative search in appellant's dorm room, which was initiated when the University Police received an anonymous tip on its website concerning drugs in Room 715 of the Ivory Tower building. The University Police contacted the community director "on call" about the tip, and that person contacted Ms. Davis regarding an administrative search of the room. Ms. Davis then called the University Police to request their presence during the search because she wanted them to provide evidence bags and security. The University Police were in "full uniform," and they were carrying batons and radios, but no firearms.

When Ms. Davis, an R.A. and two SPOs got to room 715, Ms. Davis knocked on the door, and then opened it with a master key which she obtained from one of the SPOs when there was no response. Ms. Davis testified that she "could have obtained the master key in another way." The dorm accommodation was a two-bedroom suite, with a bedroom on either side of a central living area. Ms. Davis testified that once inside, only she and no one else conducted the search. Appellant arrived after a few minutes, and Ms. Davis explained to him that she had information that there were drugs in the apartment and that she was there to perform an administrative search. She requested that he stay in the room until she finished conducting her search. She asked appellant if there was anything he wanted "to present at this time," and he retrieved a wooden case from his desk and a black bag from behind his bed. The case contained a green substance that looked and smelled like marijuana, and the bag contained a bong and two small pipes. Ms. Davis then proceeded to search appellant's bedroom, where she found more drugs and drug paraphernalia. She also found two wallets, which together contained around $5,860. When she asked appellant why he had so much money, he replied that he had received the money as gifts or presents. According to Ms. Davis, appellant acknowledged that the contraband belonged to him.

Ms. Davis placed the contraband in evidence bags provided by the University Police. On cross-examination, she testified that the officers held the bags open for her while she collected the contraband. After the search, one of the University Police officers who was present telephoned the Metropolitan Police Department ("MPD") because he was concerned that the amount of marijuana and money recovered "could be constituted as distribution." When the MPD officers arrived, Ms. Davis showed them the evidence bags and told them what appellant had said.

Ms. Davis testified that the purpose of her search "was to identify any health or safety hazards, to identify any problematic activities that might be occurring in the residence hall," not to "collect evidence for a criminal case." The court admitted into evidence an unsigned "standard residence hall license agreement," which Ms. Davis identified as "the type of agreement" that all students must sign before they can live in a dormitory. The trial court found that appellant had signed the license agreement, and in so doing had agreed to allow authorized representatives of the University to inspect his room at any time for violations of University regulations, including the possession of illegal substances.[3] Thus, there is no contention in this case that the University community director, Ms. Davis, lacked any required reasonable or probable cause for an administrative search.

The trial court concluded that the search did not violate appellant's Fourth Amendment rights; rather, in conducting the search, Ms. Davis had a "legitimate purpose to take cognizance of what goes on in the dormitory rooms and to ensure that there are not illegal substances or . . . any other sort of criminal activities afoot there in addition to maintenance issues, in addition to health and safety issues." The court found that the University Police officers were SPOs "who had the commission that all [SPOs] in D.C. have which basically gives them the . . . limited authority to arrest and search within their jurisdiction." However, the SPOs "never needed to and never exercised any of that authority with respect to the search of appellant's dormitory room." Furthermore, the court found that it was Ms. Davis who made the decision to search room 715, and that she requested the company of the SPOs, questioned appellant, and "did all of the searching." The SPOs "only assisted in terms of providing bags and being able to take away what was recovered. . . ." Based on these factual findings the trial court denied the motion to suppress, concluding that "there was no state action involved in this search" and "the action . . . taken by the [SPOs] did not . . . turn this administrative search into a governmental search." . . . [T]he court found appellant guilty of the charged offenses, noting that Ms. Davis "was a very credible witness" whose testimony the court credited "in its entirety."

---

[3] . . . Paragraph 14 of the license agreement stated the following:

> The University reserves the right for authorized representatives of the University to enter premises at any time for the repair and maintenance of the premises or the inspection thereof pursuant to University rules and regulations. The University further reserves the right to inspect a room at any time and its contents for violations of University or residence hall regulations including but not limited to possessing illegal substances or substances believed by staff to be illegal or conducting activities that could endanger the life, safety, order, or welfare of members of the University community.

II.

. . . .

"[T]he protection of the Fourth Amendment is applicable to intrusions of an individual's privacy interests by governmental officers and, not generally, to those made by private parties." *United States v. Lima*, 424 A.2d 113, 117 (D.C. 1980) (en banc). However, where "[a] private party, 'in light of all the circumstances of the case must be regarded as having acted as an "instrument" or agent of the state,' the Fourth Amendment is called into play." *Id.* (quoting *Coolidge v. New Hampshire*, 403 U.S. 443, 487 (1971)). "What can constitute sufficient government involvement in a search or seizure to trigger application of the Fourth Amendment requires a case by case determination." *Id.*

Preliminarily, we note the government's concession that appellant had a legitimate expectation of privacy in his college dormitory room to contest the search. . . . It is also undisputed that Ms. Davis and the SPOs were employees of George Washington University, a private institution. Appellant argues, however, that the involvement of the SPOs in this case amounted to state action on their part and that their presence and assistance transformed Ms. Davis into an instrumentality of the state. Thus, the issue before us is "whether there was sufficient 'governmental involvement' in the search to bring into play the constraints of the Fourth Amendment." *Alston v. United States*, 518 A.2d 439, 441 (D.C. 1986). We conclude that neither the SPOs nor Ms. Davis acted as agents of the state.

III.

In the District of Columbia, SPOs are appointed by the Mayor upon the "application of any corporation or individual . . . for duty in connection with the property of, or under the charge of, such corporation or individual." D.C. Code § 5-129.02 (2001). SPOs are "commissioned for the special purpose of protecting property on the premises of the employer." *Franklin v. United States*, 271 A.2d 784, 785 (D.C. 1970). This commission "authorizes him or her to exercise arrest powers significantly broader than those of ordinary citizens or licensed security guards." *Woodward & Lothrop v. Hillary*, 598 A.2d 1142, 1144 n.4 (D.C. 1991). In particular, they "have the same powers as a law enforcement officer to arrest without warrant for offenses committed within premises to which his jurisdiction extends. . . ." D.C. Code § 23-582 (a) (2001). This court has said that where security personnel of a private employer have "powers akin to that of a regular police officer and [are] appointed by a governmental official, even though employed by a private company, sufficient trappings of state authority have been found to trigger Fourth Amendment restrictions." *Lima, supra*, 424 A.2d at 118. We clarified, however, that "the commissioning of [SPOs] by the District of Columbia does not make all their actions attributable to the government." *Id.* at 119.

The government argues that the Fourth Amendment is not implicated in this case because the SPOs were not "acting as agents of the state, nor were they significantly involved in the search of appellant's dormitory room." It acknowledges that SPOs act as agents of the state when they exercise their arrest power. . . .

[But] SPOs "are not 'in all their actions' equated with regular police officers. . . ." *Hillary*, 598 A.2d at 1146.

We have not articulated what is required to create a nexus with the state where the SPO has not made an arrest. However, in determining whether state action exists, we have not focused on the fact of an arrest alone. For instance, although an arrest took place in *Lucas v. United States*, 411 A.2d 360, 362 (D.C. 1980), we determined whether SPOs were public officers by focusing broadly on whether they were performing their "police" functions. . . . We further stated that "when they are performing their police functions, they are acting as public officers and assume all the liabilities attaching thereto." *Id.* . . .

. . . .

Thus, an SPO is a state or "public" actor when he or she invokes state authority through manner, word or deed, i.e., he or she acts like a regular police officer. This conclusion is consistent with cases in which the Supreme Court has addressed the constitutional status of SPOs who work for private employers but who are "deputized" with state authority. . . .

. . . .

In this case, the SPOs were "deputized" with special legal powers pursuant to D.C. Code § 23-582(a); however, their actions were directed and controlled by the University whose administrative official, Ms. Davis, made the decision to conduct the search. From the moment Ms. Davis telephoned the SPOs and asked them to accompany her to room 715, Ms. Davis was in control of the situation. She alone spoke to appellant and conducted the search, while the SPOs took little, if any, initiative. They accompanied Ms. Davis to room 715 at her request, produced a master key and evidence bags for her use, and held the evidence bags while she conducted the search. We have held that SPOs are not in all their actions equated with regular police officers. *Woodward & Lothrop v. Hillary, supra*, 598 A.2d at 1146. Rather, the relevant circumstances surrounding the actions in question must be weighed. While the fact that an SPO wore a uniform and carried a baton and a radio, as occurred here, may be a relevant factor, *see Williams, supra*, 341 U.S. at 99 (fact that SPO "went about flashing his badge" relevant to whether he acted under color of law), it does not of itself amount to an assertion of state authority. More is required.

In contrast to the passive behavior of the SPOs in this case, in each of the cases discussed above in which a court found that the SPOs acted as state agents, the SPOs were actively asserting their authority from the state to a significant degree at the time of the challenged act. As they involved questioning, searching, seizing, beating or arresting a suspect, each of the cases is supported by the Supreme Court's holding in *Griffin v. Maryland* [378 U.S. 130 (1964)] that "[i]f an individual is possessed of state authority and purports to act under that authority, his action is state action." 378 U.S. at 135. . . . Here, the SPOs did not employ the arrest power given them pursuant to D.C. Code § 23-582. . . . Here, . . . the trial court found as a matter of fact that "[i]t was Ms. Davis who made the decision to search room 715." . . . Here, the evidence showed that the SPOs' involvement in the search was peripheral and did not indicate that the SPOs were acting in their "public" role or influencing Ms. Davis's actions. Thus, we conclude that under the circumstances of this case, the SPOs were not state actors.

Appellant argues that the "ongoing cooperation" between the University Police and the University administrators, including that members of the University Police passed on the anonymous tip, supplied the key to room 715, and were involved in the search, demonstrates an effort to evade the Fourth Amendment. We cannot agree that the facts of this case indicate a circumvention of the Fourth Amendment. According to Ms. Davis's testimony, which the trial court credited, University administrative searches are to be conducted only by administrators and that the University Police are to "have no role in that" because "the search can actually be thrown out if the University [P]olice contribute to that search." This testimony does not tend to establish that the University policy was designed to circumvent the Fourth Amendment. To the contrary, it is reasonable and appropriate for a university to apply its policies regarding student health and welfare in a manner which, if an administrative search should happen to uncover contraband, does not eliminate any possibility of subsequent prosecution by civil authorities.

. . . .

In sum, the SPOs' conduct in this case does not amount to state action. The trial court found based on record evidence that the University initiated the search and that the purpose of the search was to enforce the University's private policies. . . . The participation of the SPOs was peripheral and secondary to that of the University administrator who carried out the search. Thus, we conclude that the Fourth Amendment was not implicated.

Affirmed

NOTES

1. The court of appeals, in agreeing with the decision by the trial court, found that Ms. Davis, the community director, was the one who made the decision to search the dormitory room and that she was the only person who conducted the search. Factually, this is deemed to be true. However, the search conducted was not a routine administrative search. In fact, initial contact was made by campus police, who also assisted Davis by providing evidence bags to collect the products of the search. Yet the court held that the campus police officers (SPOs) were not public actors for Fourth Amendment purposes. The court stated that "an SPO is a state or 'public' actor when he or she invokes state authority through manner, word or deed, i.e., he or she acts like a regular police officer." When in the fact scenario in *Limpuangthip* did the legal authority move from the SPOs to Davis, a private actor? How is that line important to the ultimate decision in this case? Davis testified that, in her training, she was told that police are not to conduct searches because if they do, the evidence might be thrown out at trial. Does *Limpuangthip*, then, tell us that a different legal standard applies to searches conducted on college and university campuses, including residence halls, when those searches are conducted by university officials and not police officers? Seemingly, this standard is not altered when the police have some connection with the search, including the provision of the initial tip that criminal violations may have occurred on campus.

Compare *Limpuangthip* to *Piazzola* and *T.L.O.*

2. Some non-disciplinary searches occur in buildings other than residence halls. Essentially, though, the same rules of law and policy will apply. In *People v. Lanthier*, 488 P.2d 625 (1971), a university employee, in carrying out his job responsibilities, opened up all the lockers in a locker room to determine the source of an unpleasant odor. Items located in one of the lockers turned out to be marijuana. Defendant student was charged with possession. His motion to suppress on the ground of illegal search and seizure was denied.

3. Routine, non-disciplinary maintenance/safety inspections of residence halls are common. And the policy statements that universities require students to sign are an important piece to the puzzle. In other words, the "right of entry" provisions in housing contracts are very useful to university officials who are called to defend their decisions to not only enter a residence hall room, but also to turn evidence of a criminal violation over to law enforcement for further investigation or, perhaps, additional searches. For example, in *Pearson v. Arkansas*, CACR 04-288, 2005 Ark. App. LEXIS 77 (Ark. Ct. App. Jan. 26, 2005), two resident advisors (RAs) were conducting routine inspections and discovered, in plain view, evidence of drug and alcohol use. Campus police then entered the room and found more evidence. The student argued that the RAs' inspection was lawful, but had only turned up a very small amount of drugs; he argued that the further warrantless search by the police was unlawful. The court held that the searches were legal, in that the right of entry authorized by the student's signature on the housing contract included not only the right to enter to make routine maintenance or safety inspections, but also to enforce the rules and regulations of the university. The court noted that the intrusion was significant, but that the scope of the student's legitimate expectation of privacy was tempered by the right of entry provision in the housing contract. It is clear that the housing agreements are important for the legal defenses of universities in such cases. Note, though, that their mere existence does not shield the university from challenge and the necessity of a solid policy. See the following case.

DEVERS v. SOUTHERN UNIVERSITY

712 So. 2d 199 (La. Ct. App. 1998)

CARTER, J.

. . . .

On March 8, 1995, Devers, a student at Southern University, was arrested following the discovery of twelve bags of marijuana in his dormitory room. The discovery was made pursuant to a dormitory sweep authorized by Southern University's Housing Agreement, which students living in campus housing are required to sign. Devers was issued an administrative expulsion and prohibited from attending classes.

On March 23, 1995, Devers filed a suit for damages and an injunction against Southern University. Devers sought a temporary restraining order from his expulsion. On March 27, 1995, the trial court issued an order vacating Devers' administrative expulsion and ordering Devers to only be suspended from classes until the Judiciary Committee of Southern University determined whether he had violated the Southern University code of conduct manual. The Judiciary Committee was scheduled to hold a hearing on March 30, 1995.

On March 28, 1995, while Devers was on the Southern University campus attempting to gather evidence for his disciplinary hearing before the Judiciary Committee, he was detained, arrested, and forced off the campus. Devers filed a Rule for Contempt on March 30, 1995, alleging Southern University's actions violated the March 27, 1995 court order. After hearing the charges against Devers, the Judiciary Committee found Devers guilty of the following violations of the code of student conduct: 1.13 Manufacturing, Distributing, or Selling Drugs or Narcotics; 1.14 Possession of Drugs, Narcotics or Marijuana.

The Judiciary Committee recommended Devers be expelled from Southern University. In a letter dated March 31, 1995, Gerald Peoples, the Vice Chancellor of Student Affairs, notified Devers that he agreed with the recommendation of expulsion and informed Devers of the appeal procedure. Devers never pursued the appeal procedure. Instead, on April 10, 1995, Devers amended his original suit and asserted an action under 42 U.S.C.A § 1983, arising out of the alleged unconstitutional search of his dormitory room.

On April 17, 1995, Devers filed a second lawsuit. . . . In this suit, Devers named Gerald Peoples, Kevin Jefferson, Joseph Broaden, and Brenda Walton, as defendants in an action seeking damages for their respective roles in having Devers removed from the Southern University campus on March 28, 1995. . . .

. . . .

On May 31, 1995, the trial court rendered a judgment reflecting the settlement of the part of the suit pertaining to the injunction between Devers and Southern University. Pursuant to that judgment, Devers' expulsion was reduced to a suspension for the spring term of 1995, and he would be allowed to enroll at Southern University for the fall term of 1995. . . .

Devers' two suits were consolidated on July 10, 1995. . . . The judgment rendered by the trial court held Southern University's dormitory regulation authorizing warrantless searches of rooms by Southern University officials and police officers, prima facie unconstitutional. . . . .

Southern University assigns the following assignment of error: Did the lower court err in granting plaintiffs motion for summary judgment declaring the dormitory sweep policy of Southern University A&M College unconstitutional on its face?

. . . .

Constitutionality of Dormitory Regulation

The provision of Southern's Rental Agreement at issue provides as follows:

> The University reserves all rights in connection with assignments of rooms, inspection of rooms with police, and the termination of room occupancy. . . .

The trial court ruled this regulation was prima facie unconstitutional in that it violated the Fourth Amendment rights of students living on the campus of Southern University. . . .

The basic purpose of [the Fourth] Amendment is to safeguard the privacy and security of individuals against arbitrary invasion by government officials. *See Camara v. Municipal Court of City and County of San Francisco*, 387 U.S. 523, 526 (1967). To determine the reasonableness of a search, there must be a balancing of the need to search against the invasion in which the search entails. It has been established that students do not shed their constitutional rights at the schoolhouse door. *See Tinker v. Des Moines Independent Community School District*, 393 U.S. 503, 506 (1969). A student who occupies a college dormitory room enjoys the protection of the Fourth Amendment. *Piazzola v. Watkins*, 442 F.2d 284, 289 (5th Cir. 1971). A dormitory room is a student's house for all practical purposes, and a student has the same interest in the privacy of his room as any adult has in the privacy of his home, dwelling, or lodging. *See Smyth v. Lubbers*, 398 F. Supp. 777, 786 (W.D. Mich. 1975). A dormitory room is a student's home away from home, and any student may reasonably expect that once the door is closed to the outside, his or her solitude and secrecy will not be disturbed by a governmental intrusion without at least permission, if not invitation. The Fourth Amendment by its very terms guarantees this.

Southern University argues that the increase in school violence, the increased prevalence of weapons at schools, and the continued involvement of students with drugs form the basis of a substantial state interest in discovering and eliminating weapons and drugs from the educational setting. Southern University asserts that its concern for the safety of its students, faculty, and staff provides the basis for the random dormitory sweeps. Southern argues that its regulation is similar to the Utah State University regulation encountered in *State v. Hunter*, 831 P.2d 1033 (Utah App.), *review denied*, 843 P.2d 1042 (Utah 1992). . . .

In *Hunter*, a warrantless search was made of a student's dormitory room, pursuant to room to room inspections conducted in response to vandalism and other behavior problems. The court held the regulation was a reasonable exercise of the university's authority to maintain an educational environment. It is important to note that the court distinguished this case on the basis of what did not occur, specifically, *Hunter* was not a case in which university officials took action at the behest of or as part of a joint investigation with the police. Nor did the university officials attempt to delegate their right to inspect rooms to the police, which would result in circumvention of traditional restrictions on police activity.

The wording of the Utah State University regulation is quite different from Southern University's housing regulation. The regulation in Hunter specifically stated the purpose of its inspections are for maintenance of university property, the health and safety of students, and maintenance of discipline in an educational atmosphere. Administrative checks of dormitory rooms for health hazards are permissible pursuant to the school's interest in the maintenance of its plant and health of its students, as are searches in emergencies, such as in the case of fire. However, Southern University's regulation does not specify such a purpose, rather it allows entry of dormitory rooms accompanied by police without any stated purpose.

In *Piazzola v. Watkins*, 442 F.2d 284, the United States Fifth Circuit considered the constitutionality of the following provision contained in Troy State University's housing regulations:

> The college reserves the right to enter rooms for inspection purposes. If the administration deems it necessary the room may be searched and the occupant required to open his personal baggage and any other personal material which is sealed.

442 F.2d at 286.

. . . .

Although Troy State University's regulation was upheld as constitutional, the wording of its regulation is clearly different from Southern's regulation. The regulation utilized by Southern University clearly authorizes police involvement in the entry and search of the dormitory rooms. With police routinely assisting in the entry and search of a dormitory room, there are no factors which would characterize such an intrusion as a benign "administrative" search.

In *Smyth v. Lubbers*, [*supra*], Grand Valley State College (Grand Valley) defended the constitutionality of its housing regulation which in part, authorized residence hall staff members to enter and search a dormitory room, if college officials had "reasonable cause" to believe students were continuing to violate federal, state, or local laws, or Grand Valley regulations. Grand Valley defined "reasonable cause" as more than a mere suspicion, but less than probable cause.

Grand Valley asserted its regulation was essential to the maintenance of order and discipline on school property and was constitutionally reasonable, even though such regulation infringed on the outer limits of the students' constitutional rights. Grand Valley contended it could utilize warrantless police searches of student dormitory rooms on less than probable cause, a method which is not available to federal and state law enforcement agencies.

The court found that while Grand Valley had an important interest in enforcing drug laws and regulations, and a duty to do so, it did not have such a special characteristic or such a compelling interest as to justify setting aside the usual rights of privacy enjoyed by adults. The failure of the Grand Valley regulation to require there be "probable cause" to justify a room search rendered the regulation constitutionally invalid.

Likewise Southern asserts that its interest in eliminating weapons and drugs from the educational environment makes its regulation constitutionally permissible. However, we note society as a whole shares this interest with Southern University. Yet, our law enforcement agencies do not have the authority to sweep entire residential areas without a warrant. This is the very essence of the Fourth Amendment protection.

Southern University has many ways to promote the safety interests of students, faculty and staff without the use of warrantless police searches. Where individuals are using or selling marijuana or where weapons have become a threat so as to provoke complaints from the dormitory residents, the alleged offender may be charged and the complaining witnesses may testify against the individual, or Southern may secure a search warrant.

. . . [A] check of a student's dormitory room is unreasonable under the Fourth Amendment unless Southern University can show that the search furthers its functioning as an educational institution. Southern University's housing regulation, as written, clearly authorizes unconstitutional searches. . . .

We reject Southern University's argument that by agreeing to the provisions of the housing contract, students consent to the dormitory sweeps. The state, in operating a public school system of higher education, cannot condition attendance at one of its schools on the student's renunciation of his constitutional rights. *Robinson v. Board of Regents of Eastern Kentucky University*, 475 F.2d 707, 709 (6th Cir. 1973). We find the trial court properly held the regulation prima facie unconstitutional.

. . . .

AFFIRMED.

3. Collaboration with City Police

In the previous subsection, cases were presented that involve searches of residence halls and the discovery of contraband that violates either college policy and/or criminal law. In these circumstances, searches were conducted, by-and-large, as a matter of course by college officials carrying out their own professional responsibilities. There are questions raised, though, that ask whether the decisions made by university officials to conduct such searches are done with the purpose and/or direction of criminal law enforcement. Clearly, the determination of whether the officials conducting the searches are acting as "state actors" or the agents of state actors is an important one. If there is state action, then the Fourth Amendment is implicated and constitutional questions of reasonableness arise, as we saw in *New Jersey v. T.L.O.*, and *Piazzola v. Watkins, supra.* If the Fourth Amendment is not implicated, generally the college or university policy — and the discretion of the official — will prevail. This subsection presents two cases that raise the question of "state action" and "agency." The first case, *Duarte v. Commonwealth of Virginia*, addresses the question of whether private college officials are acting as agents of the state when they conduct searches of residence halls and discover evidence of criminal wrongdoing. The second case in this subsection, *State v. Harber*, is unique in that it asks a question about the extent to which campus police officers may exercise authority to execute a search warrant to search the off-campus residences of their students.

DUARTE v. COMMONWEALTH OF VIRGINIA

407 S.E. 2d 41 (Va. Ct. App. 1991)

William Allen Duarte appeals his conviction of possession of marijuana with intent to distribute. The sole issue Duarte raises is whether the trial court erroneously refused to suppress evidence obtained through the search of his dormitory room by school officials. We find the trial court properly admitted the evidence.

Duarte was a student at Averett College, a private four year liberal arts school in Danville, Virginia. Duarte lived on campus in a dormitory room that he shared with Hugh Thomas Francis, Jr. On February 14, 1990, as part of his investigation into a burglary, Danville detective T.A. Smith telephoned the Averett College Dean of Students, Pat Morgan, to inquire whether Duarte and Francis lived on campus. Smith explained he believed there was a possibility some of the stolen property, namely a microwave oven and a street sign, might be located somewhere on campus. During that conversation, Morgan informed Smith that she would probably search Duarte's room because of some other independently obtained information she had relating to Francis. Smith asked Morgan to refrain from searching Duarte's room at that time due to his concern that her search might interfere with his investigation. The next day, Smith again spoke by telephone with Morgan, who advised him that Francis and Duarte did in fact live in a dormitory room on campus. Smith then told Morgan the police were proceeding with their investigation but never mentioned a search of Duarte's room.

On February 19, 1990, Morgan directed two college officials to conduct an inventory search of Duarte's dormitory room and to confiscate any contraband or stolen items, pursuant to the guidelines for searches and seizures set forth in the Averett College Student Handbook. The handbook is supplied to each student at the beginning of every year. In addition, each dormitory resident is required to sign a residency form that states the resident understands and promises to abide by Averett College's rules and regulations.

Upon searching Duarte's room, the two school officials found several bags of marijuana and drug paraphernalia located in two desk drawers. The officials confiscated the marijuana and paraphernalia and delivered it to Morgan, who notified Smith of the search results. Smith came to Morgan's office and took custody of the contraband. Morgan then spoke with Duarte, who confessed he bought the marijuana intending to sell some of it in order to cover its cost.

Prior to trial, Duarte filed a motion to suppress the evidence obtained through the search of his room. The court denied his motion. Duarte renewed his motion at trial, but it was again denied. The trial court proceeded to convict Duarte of possession of marijuana with intent to distribute. This appeal followed.

On appeal, Duarte contends the search of his room was unreasonable and unlawful, and, therefore, the evidence obtained as a result of the search should have been excluded from his trial. "The rule which excludes evidence obtained by unlawful search because in violation of the Fourth Amendment does not apply where the unlawful search was made by a private individual acting on his own initiative." *Harmon v. Commonwealth*, 209 Va. 574, 577, 166 S.E.2d 232, 234 (1969). Thus, the fourth amendment protections against unreasonable searches and seizures are "wholly inapplicable 'to a search or seizure, even an unreasonable one, effected by a private individual not acting as an agent of the Government or with the participation or knowledge of any governmental official.' " *United States v. Jacobsen*, 466 U.S. 109, 113 (1984). . . . Therefore, in order to exclude evidence based on a fourth amendment violation, a defendant must demonstrate the contested search or seizure was conducted by an officer of the government or someone acting at the government's direction rather than a private individual acting on his own initiative.

> Whether a private party should be deemed an agent or instrument of the Government for Fourth Amendment purposes necessarily turns on the degree of the Government's participation in the private party's activities, a question that can only be resolved "in light of all the circumstances." The fact that the Government has not compelled a private party to perform a search does not, by itself, establish that the search is a private one.

Skinner [*v. Railway Labor Exec. Ass'n*, 489 U.S. 602, 614–15 (1989)] (citations omitted).

. . . .

In the present case, a consideration of all the circumstances leads us to conclude that the fourth amendment is not implicated by the search of Duarte's room at the direction of Morgan. Though Detective Smith informed Morgan that he received Duarte's name while investigating a burglary, he did not compel or even encourage her to conduct a search of Duarte's room. As a part of his investigation into the burglary, Smith telephoned Morgan to inquire whether Duarte and Francis lived on campus. Smith explained he believed there was a possibility stolen property might be located somewhere on campus. Smith told Morgan that he had the names of Francis and Duarte, and that he was trying to determine whether they lived on campus or at another address off campus. Morgan informed Smith that she would probably search Duarte's room because of some other independently obtained information she had relating to Francis. Smith responded by specifically asking her to refrain from searching Duarte's room until after he completed his investigation because he feared he might lose the possibility of talking to Francis and Duarte. The next day, Morgan advised Smith that Francis and Duarte did in fact live in a dormitory room on campus. Smith then told her that the police were proceeding with their investigation, but never withdrew his request that she refrain from searching Duarte's room. Several days after that conversation and without any kind of prompting by the police, Dean Morgan directed officials of Averett College to conduct a search of Duarte's room in accordance with the school's rules and regulations and student handbook.

The record clearly shows that for the purposes of their investigation, the police discouraged rather than encouraged Morgan from searching Duarte's room. . . . Further, the police played no role in the actual search. Though Smith knew Morgan was considering conducting a search based on other information she possessed, he was not notified or consulted about the actual search. Therefore, we find the search was conducted by a private party acting on her own initiative rather than as an agent of the police or with the participation of the police. Thus, we hold the evidence obtained as a result of the search of Duarte's room was properly admitted into evidence at Duarte's trial. Accordingly, we affirm Duarte's conviction.

NOTES

1. Similar to *Duarte*, *Garmon v. Foust*, 741 F.2d 1069 (8th Cir. 1984), presents another story of residence hall employees working with community police in law enforcement. In *Garmon*, a private university student received a package in the mail, delivered to his residence hall. Per typical practice, mail was delivered to the hall's mail room, sorted by residence hall employees, and then placed in the mailboxes of the residents. When a package was too large for the mailbox, a slip of paper was placed in the student's mailbox alerting him or her to come to the front desk to pick it up. The package at issue in *Garmon*, however, took a different path. The employee sorting the mail noticed a strange odor coming from a package addressed to Garmon, the student. She passed it off to a superior who had some training in detection of drugs. He then contacted the local police. Officer Foust came to campus the next day, with a drug-sniffing dog, who detected the marijuana in the package. The package was not opened at that time. Instead, the residence hall employees proceeded with the typical practice, placed a note in Garmon's mailbox, asking him to pick up the package at the front desk. When Garmon did so, the police placed him under arrest and executed a search warrant for his room. The Court of Appeals for the Eighth Circuit reversed the decision of the trial court and held for the police officer. The search was deemed lawful, based on reasonable suspicion, and the police officer was granted immunity.

2. Sometimes the collaboration a university offers a local police department does not involve an investigation with a particular suspect. What if the only information available is the race and gender of an alleged assailant? How can a university help in such a case? In *Brown v. City of Oneonta*, 911 F. Supp. 580 (N.D.N.Y 1996), *reh'g denied and reh'g en banc denied*, 235 F.3d (2d Cir. 2000), *cert. denied*, 534 U.S. 816 (2001), a woman was attacked and reported to the police that the assailant was an African-American male. After initial investigations led the police to the local university, the police asked the university to provide a list of all African-American students. The university complied and the police proceeded to question students (the police also questioned non-students who lived in the area). The plaintiffs, those who were detained and questioned, filed suit against the city claiming race discrimination. The court affirmed the lower court's dismissal of the claims and held that the police were merely acting on a description offered by the alleged victim.

STATE v. HARBER

401 S.E.2d 57 (Ga. Ct. App. 1990)

Appellee was indicted for two counts of violating the Georgia Controlled Substances Act and he filed a pre-trial motion to suppress. The trial court, relying upon *Hill v. State*, 193 Ga. App. 280 (387 S.E.2d 582) (1989), granted appellee's motion and the State appeals from that order.

. . . The issue as presented in *Hill v. State*, supra at 280, was whether "campus police lacked the authority to obtain and execute a search warrant for a residence located more than 500 yards off campus." Relying upon O.C.G.A. § 20-3-72 and Op. Atty. Gen. 70-69, it was held "that the legislature [had not] intended to give to University of Georgia campus police and security personnel carte blanche authority to obtain and execute search warrants directed to residences or businesses located outside the immediate vicinity of university property." *Hill v. State*, supra at 281. It is this holding that must be followed, distinguished or overruled in the instant case.

By its terms, O.C.G.A. § 20-3-72 relates only to the territorial authority of campus police officers to make an *arrest*. In this regard, campus police officers are essentially no different from county and municipal police officers whose authority to make an *arrest* may otherwise be subject to similar territorial restrictions. However, it is *not* the territorial authority of campus police officers to make an arrest that is in question. The issue is the territorial authority of campus police officers to obtain and execute a *search warrant*. Nothing in O.C.G.A. § 20-3-72 purports to address this issue.

Former O.C.G.A. § 17-5-20 is the relevant statute with regard to the authority to *obtain* a search warrant. That statute provided that "[a] search warrant may be issued only upon the application of an *officer of this state* or its political subdivisions charged with the duty of enforcing the criminal laws." (Emphasis supplied.) As employed in this former Code section, an "officer of this state" refers to one who has been authorized by the State to enforce its criminal laws and who has received certification pursuant to the Georgia Peace Officer Standards & Training Act. *Holstein v. State*, 183 Ga. App. 610 (359 S.E.2d 360) (1987). It is clear that such an "officer of this state" *does* have the authority to obtain a search warrant even though it may be directed at locations which lie outside the boundaries of the particular political subdivision that employs him. *Bruce v. State*, 183 Ga. App. 653 (359 S.E.2d 736) (1987). In the instant case, it is undisputed that those campus officers who obtained the search warrant directed at appellee's residence were authorized by the State to enforce its laws *and* that they were also duly certified pursuant to the Georgia Peace Officer Standards & Training Act. Accordingly, pretermitting any territorial limitation on the authority of these duly certified campus police officers to make an *arrest* of appellee . . . , it seems clear that there is no comparable territorial limitation on their authority to obtain a *search warrant* directed at appellee's residence pursuant to former O.C.G.A. § 17-5-20. It would be anomalous to hold that a certified municipal or county police "officer" *is* authorized to obtain an extra-territorial search warrant *notwithstanding* any statutory restriction on his authority to make an extra-territorial arrest, but that a certified campus police "officer" is *not* so authorized *because* of a comparable statutory restriction on his authority to make an extra-territorial arrest.

There is no statutory authority to support a contrary construction of the authority of a duly certified campus police officer to obtain an extra-territorial search warrant. The only authority to the contrary is this court's decision in *Hill v. State*, supra. However, *Hill* relied entirely upon Op. Atty. Gen. 70-69 and that reliance was misplaced. The 1970 opinion of the Attorney General did *not* specifically address the authority to obtain an extra-territorial search warrant of a *duly certified campus police officer*. In this regard, it is important to note that the 1970 opinion of the Attorney General was issued *before* it had been judicially determined that a duly certified county or municipal officer, as an "officer of this state," *does* have the authority to obtain an extra-territorial search warrant notwithstanding his lack of authority to make an extra-territorial arrest. *Fowler v. State*, 128 Ga. App. 501, 503 (c) (197 S.E.2d 502) (1973); *Bruce v. State*, supra.

Likewise, the 1970 opinion of the Attorney General was issued *before* the legislature specifically authorized a campus policeman to obtain certification and thereby become an "officer of this state." See O.C.G.A. § 20-8-1 *et seq*. . . .

Accordingly, *Hill v. State*, supra, erroneously relied upon the 1970 opinion of the Attorney General rather than subsequent judicial and statutory authority and, as the result, O.C.G.A. § 20-3-72 was misconstrued as evincing anything other than a mere expression of the legislative intent that the authority of campus police officers, whether certified or not, to make an *arrest* is to be subject to a territorial limitation comparable to that which is applicable to county and municipal officers. . . . In 1990, the legislature undertook "to *clarify* the authority of peace officers employed by universities . . . to apply for search warrants" and "to *make manifest* the intention of the General Assembly that peace officers who have met the standards established by the Georgia Peace Officer Standards and Training Councils . . . shall be authorized to apply for and obtain search warrants. . . ." (Emphasis supplied.) Ga. L. 1990, p. 1980. The General Assembly apparently found it necessary to enact legislation to *clarify* and make its intent *manifest* because *Hill* had misconstrued the legislative intent of the *then-existing* legislation on the subject. Accordingly, *Hill* is hereby overruled insofar as it holds that certified campus police officers who *obtained* an extra-territorial search warrant directed at locations more than 500 yards from campus property were not authorized to do so under former O.C.G.A. § 17-5-20.

. . . .

In conclusion, *Hill v. State*, supra, is overruled. . . . It follows that the trial court erred in granting appellee's motion to suppress.

. . . .

Judgment reversed.

4. Searches in Academic Contexts

CARBONI v. MELDRUM
949 F. Supp. 427 (W.D. Va. 1996)

MEMORANDUM OPINION

Honorable James C. Turk, United States District Judge

This cause of action stems from the circumstances surrounding Deborah Ann Carboni's dismissal from the veterinary program at the Virginia-Maryland Regional College of Veterinary Medicine at the Virginia Polytechnic Institute (VPI). Plaintiff contends that she was unconstitutionally strip searched in violation of the Fourth and Fourteenth Amendments and that she was denied due process under the Fourteenth Amendment as a result of actions occurring during her university Honor Board proceeding and Faculty Appeal. She also raises various violations of state law including common law battery, negligent and intentional infliction of emotional distress, and tortious interference with contract. Ms. Carboni sues the defendants in both their individual and official capacities, seeking damages and injunctive relief to gain readmission to the program. . . .

. . . The defendants contend that the search of Ms. Carboni's person was reasonable under the circumstances and that she was justifiably dismissed because of her poor academic performance. The court finds that the defendants' actions with respect to the search fall within the scope of qualified immunity, and that the plaintiff received all the process she was due during the Honor Board and Faculty Appeal stages. Summary judgment will be granted for the defendants on the plaintiff's federal claims.

I.

After working on her Master's degree in veterinary neurotoxicology and neuropathology at VPI and securing Virginia residency, Deborah Ann Carboni began her course of study at the Virginia-Maryland Regional College of Veterinary Medicine (VMRCVM). The defendants are all state officials and employees of VPI and VMRCVM. Dr. J. Blair Meldrum is the Associate Dean of Academic Affairs, and also chairs the Faculty Review Board and the Academic Standards Committee. Dr. D. Phillip Sponenberg is a professor at VMRCVM and the faculty advisor to the school's student Honor Board. Dr. Don Waldron is a professor at VMRCVM and Rene Armstrong is the Admissions Coordinator and the administrative assistant to Dean Meldrum.

. . . After beginning her veterinary medicine studies in 1991, Ms. Carboni experienced academic difficulty and fell below the grade point average necessary to continue at VMRCVM. However, the Admissions and Standards Committee allowed her to continue in the program provided that she re-take her first year. The plaintiff also began seeing the university's counselor for help with her alleged "test anxiety." Carboni successfully completed her first year course work in the Spring of 1993 and went on to finish her second year course of study in the Spring of 1994. However, Ms. Carboni again encountered problems with her academic performance during her third year studies (the fourth year she was in the program).

In December, 1994, Carboni received failing grades on two examinations in "core" courses. The veterinary program requires that all students pass every core course, and not doing so can subject a student to dismissal. According to VMRCVM's College Handbook, a student who receives a failing grade in a core course may be allowed to retake the examination at the discretion of the faculty. Ms. Carboni was indeed allowed to retake both examinations and passed.

During the final semester of her third year Ms. Carboni again failed a final examination in a core course, this time in her Urology class. Dr. Waldron agreed to allow her to take a re-test and she was scheduled to do so on April 13, 1995. On that date Ms. Carboni arrived to take the examination and went to pick it up from Ms. Dreama Webb, the secretary for the Department of Small Animal Clinical Sciences. Carboni however, neglected to leave behind all exam preparation material as a note on the door from Dr. Waldron directed. Plaintiff maintains that Ms. Webb was not in her office so she went to the ladies' room to study. Her menstrual period had begun and she was feeling ill. Allegedly, Carboni remained in the bathroom for a while and then went back to Ms. Webb's office to get the exam and inadvertently left some of her notes on the bathroom floor in the process. Ms. Carboni obtained the exam and began it. She maintains that she then left the rest of the notes she had brought with her in a credenza drawer in the exam room.

Sometime after 2:00 p.m. the plaintiff alleges that she felt ill again and proceeded to the ladies' room, leaving a note on the conference room table to that effect. Ms. Carboni was in the bathroom for some time and Dr. Waldron became concerned. He sent Ms. Webb into the ladies' room to find out what was going on and Ms. Webb stated she saw someone in one of the stalls with notes arrayed around her on the floor. Ms. Webb also stated that she heard the sound of "paper rustling" about the waist of Ms. Carboni when she left the bathroom. Webb reported what she saw and heard to Dr. Waldron who confronted the plaintiff and asked her if she had been cheating. Ms. Carboni denied the accusation and said that the only thing she had on her person was something of a "personal nature."

After the confrontation, Dr. Waldron reported the matter to Dean Meldrum and directed Ms. Webb to search the bathroom for notes. None were found at that time. Thinking that Ms. Carboni had hidden the notes on her person, Dean Meldrum and Dr. Waldron directed the plaintiff to go to the restroom with Ms. Webb and Defendant Rene Armstrong and submit to a body search. Carboni was directed to lift her shirt to expose her breast area and back, drop her pants to her knees to expose her waist area and to remove her boots. After she did so and after Ms. Armstrong conducted a "frisk" of Carboni's legs and chest, the plaintiff offered to remove more of her clothing, including her undergarments, but Ms. Armstrong told her that would not be necessary. The search did not turn up the notes or any evidence of cheating. However, when the plaintiff returned to the conference room she was met by Dr. Waldron and Dean Meldrum who had since found the notes which the plaintiff had left there. [Notes found in] the sanitary napkin disposal were also recovered.

Feeling that they had uncovered sufficient evidence of Ms. Carboni's alleged cheating, the plaintiff was not allowed to finish the exam and the entire matter was referred to the student Honor Board for investigation. On April 17, 1995, Ms. Carboni received written notice of the accusations against her and on April 26, 1995, she was told that a hearing would take place and that she was not to discuss the matter with anyone. The hearing before the Honor Board was held on April 30, 1995.

. . . .

Ms. Carboni was found guilty of cheating by the Honor Board and given a two block (six week) academic suspension. Plaintiff immediately advised the Board that she intended to appeal the decision to the Faculty Review Board, as permitted by VMRCVM's Honor Code. . . . During the time between the Honor Board proceeding and the appeal Ms. Carboni alleges that she entered into an agreement with Dean Meldrum that if she agreed to the faculty proposed postponement she would be allowed to take a second re-test of the Urology exam.

The appeal before the faculty board was finally set for May 12, 1995 in order to avoid conflict with the plaintiff's clinical schedule but was later postponed until May

31, 1995. In the meantime Ms. Carboni received a failing grade in Urology, a decision made at Dr. Waldron's discretion and not subject to any determination made by the student Honor Board. Dr. Waldron however, informed Ms. Carboni that the faculty decided, in its discretion, to allow her to take a second re-test if her appeal to the Faculty Review Board was successful.

On May 31, 1995, the appeal went forward. . . .

The faculty panel upheld the Honor Board's six week suspension sentence and as a result, Dr. Waldron did not give Ms. Carboni a second re-test. Solely as a result of the failing grade she received in Urology, Ms. Carboni was dismissed from the veterinary program at VMRCVM and was later denied readmittance based on the totality of her academic performance while in attendance at the veterinary school. On June 6, 1995, the plaintiff timely filed this cause of action with the court.

. . . .

III.

Before looking to the specific facts of this case, the court must determine whether the defendants would be entitled to qualified immunity because that will shape the later inquiry. . . .

[T]his court finds that VPI and VMRCVM are entitled to Eleventh Amendment immunity. . . .

As a result of the foregoing, it is apparent that the defendant employees of VMRCVM enjoy qualified immunity for acts taken in their individual capacities. . . . Under the doctrine, the discretionary decisions of school officials are backed by qualified immunity unless their conduct violates clearly established statutory or constitutional rights of which a reasonable person would have known. *Wood v. Strickland*, 420 U.S. 308, 323 (1975). . . .

IV.

If there is a legitimate question as to whether an official's conduct violated the plaintiff's constitutional rights, the official is entitled to qualified immunity. . . . Thus, qualified immunity protects all but the official who is plainly incompetent, or who knowingly violates the law. *Malley v. Briggs*, 475 U.S. 335, 344–45 (1986). The defendants were reasonable in concluding that their search of the plaintiff's person was justified, either because of the applicable legal standard, or because of the specific facts of this case, and thus, are entitled to summary judgment based on qualified immunity. University officials, no less than the public school administrators in *Wood* must be allowed to exercise their discretion in reliance on the factual information at their disposal at the time. *See Wood*, 420 U.S. at 319.

The specific circumstances of the body search render this issue one of apparent first impression for any federal court. Unlike any prior cases of record, Plaintiff is a graduate student, not a public school pupil. Further, the search was conducted, not to uncover evidence of drugs or a crime, but because Ms. Carboni was suspected of cheating — a violation of school rules, not the penal code. As a result of the foregoing differences between this case and any precedent of which the court is aware, the court is not convinced that a search of a university graduate student undertaken by a faculty member, or at his direction, is *ever* justified if the student objects. However, neither can the court say that the defendants violated the plaintiff's *clearly established* constitutional rights because of the novelty of the issues presented here.

It should be noted that both the plaintiff and defendants cite the case of *New Jersey v. T.L.O.*, 469 U.S. 325 (1985), for the standard they believe this court should utilize. Even in the face of such apparent agreement the court approaches that question with great trepidation. However, regardless of the standard applied, the defendants are entitled to immunity because there is at least a legitimate question as to whether they violated any clearly established constitutional right the plaintiff possessed.

. . . .

. . . Justice White's reasoning in *T.L.O.* partially rested upon the age of public school students and the need for school officials, who are acting *in loco parentis*, to preserve authority over the environment they are charged with controlling. "The preservation of order and a proper educational environment requires close supervision of schoolchildren, as well as the enforcement of rules against conduct that would be perfectly permissible if undertaken by an adult." *T.L.O.*, 469 U.S. at 339. With that in mind it is easy to see that a body search of a graduate student in her late twenties undertaken at the direction of a university professor and Dean is arguably different from the same search performed on a fourteen (14) year old high school freshman by a Vice-Principal. Though higher education administrators must be allowed to make discretionary decisions, *see Wood, supra*, university officials simply do not exercise the same level of disciplinary control over their students as do public school teachers and principals. Thus, there is some question as to whether a state university professor, as opposed to a public school administrator or teacher, could force a student to subject herself to a search performed against her will.

In addition to the distinguishing factor of the plaintiff's age, this case does not involve the sort of general security concern generally at issue in the public school search cases. First, unlike the public school context, it may very well have been improper for Dr. Waldron and Dean Meldrum to order a search of Ms. Carboni's person if she was suspected of drug use or of some other criminal violation which did not immediately affect the safety of others. Such searches should properly be undertaken pursuant to the probable cause standard, and usually with the benefit of a warrant, by either the university's or the locality's police force. In that way, university students have a measurably higher expectation of privacy in their persons, papers, and effects than do similarly situated minors in public schools. Second, violations of school rules by students of any age do not raise the sort of public concern brought about by suspected engagement in criminal acts. This court can find no case which authorizes even public school officials to search their students suspected of cheating and so the court is unwilling to state that such a grave action as a search conducted against a university student's will would be justified by reasonable suspicion [standard, as articulated in *T.L.O.*].

Further, the plaintiff is correct in directing the court's attention to the invasive nature of the search to which she was subjected. . . . However, in the instant case, Dr. Waldron and Dean Meldrum had every justified reason to suspect that Plaintiff was cheating and the court cannot say that the defendants were unreasonable in believing that they could authorize a search of Ms. Carboni's person under the peculiar factual circumstances this case presents.

First, Ms. Carboni was wrong to have classnotes with her in the exam room at all, when the note on the door containing the instructions for the test from Dr. Waldron specifically directed her to discard such items before beginning the examination. Second, the plaintiff admitted to having those notes in the bathroom after spending an inordinately long amount of time there. That admission is corroborated by Ms. Webb who saw the plaintiff in the bathroom with the class notes arrayed around her. Those circumstances alone might justify some sort of questioning and search of Ms. Carboni by the Dean or Dr. Waldron. Add to the foregoing the fact that Ms. Webb heard the sound of paper rustling about Ms. Carboni's waist after she had left the bathroom and that the notes had since apparently disappeared from the bathroom, and it is readily apparent that the defendants were acting reasonably when they thought that a search of Ms. Carboni's person for the classnotes was justified. Ms. Carboni's explanations for all those facts do not serve to negate the likely conclusion that Dean Waldron and Dr. Meldrum drew from them — that the plaintiff was cheating on the exam and that she had hidden the notes seen in the bathroom in the waist of her jeans. The proper yardstick for this court to apply is what VMRCVM's administrators could have reasonably concluded they were entitled to do under the circumstances, not absolute certainty as the plaintiff would apparently have this court believe.

Nor was the scope of the search unreasonable once it was undertaken. The search conducted by Rene Armstrong and Ms. Webb at the direction of Dr. Waldron and Dean Meldrum, instead of by the two men themselves and, in addition, the body search of Ms. Carboni was strictly limited to turning up evidence of the suspected violation. . . .

Even with a recognition that university students may possess a higher degree of privacy than their similarly situated minor counterparts, the court cannot say that such a distinction is clearly established, nor that the defendants should be so schooled in the intricacies of Fourth Amendment jurisprudence that they should be aware of the difference. A State official sued for violating the Fourth Amendment is entitled to qualified immunity if a reasonable person possessing the same information would have believed the conduct engaged in was lawful. There simply has been precious little, if any guidance applicable to the scope of authority possessed by state supported university faculty in this area. As a result of that, this court cannot say that the defendants' belief in their authority to conduct a search of Ms. Carboni's person was unreasonable considering the peculiar facts they were presented with at the time. The defendants are therefore, entitled to summary judgment based on qualified immunity on this point.

V.

The defendants are also entitled to summary judgment on qualified immunity grounds because they were reasonably led to believe that the plaintiff's ready acquiescence to the search indicated her implied consent. Though the question of whether the plaintiff expressly consented to the search is in dispute, the fact that she willingly cooperated with Ms. Armstrong, Dr. Waldron and Dean Meldrum is not. The undisputed fact is that Plaintiff followed Ms. Armstrong and Ms. Webb to the ladies' room without objection and then fully cooperated with the ensuing search. . . .

. . . .

In order to grant summary judgment to a defendant on a qualified immunity basis it is not necessary that the action undertaken be legally justified, just that the official in question reasonably believes he has the justification. A reasonable mistake of consent is no less a factual error than relying on a facially valid warrant, or erroneously searching the wrong premises, and therefore, the proper course of action for this court is granting summary judgment on qualified immunity grounds.

. . . .

VI.

[In Part VI of the opinion, the court held that the defendants did not violate Carboni's procedural due process rights, in that Carboni was given notice of the charges against her and opportunity to tell her side of the story through hearings and appeals.]

VII.

For the reasons set forth above, the defendants' Motion for Summary Judgment is granted on all the federal claims Ms. Carboni's raises pursuant to § 1983 alleging constitutional deprivations of her Fourth and Fourteenth Amendments rights. . . .

NOTES

1. The court in *Carboni* spent quite a bit of its time distinguishing the case from *New Jersey v. T.L.O.* and other cases from K-12 public education. What distinguishing factors did the court offer? Are you convinced that there is and should be a measurable difference between K-12 and higher education settings for search and seizure purposes? What impact does the factual context have in *Carboni*, in that this was a case of suspected violation of an academic, disciplinary code of the university and not a suspected violation of a criminal code? Despite its finding of qualified immunity for defendants, the court generally appeared to disfavor searches like the one conducted here, particularly in light of the age and maturity of the student and noncriminal nature of the alleged infraction. In light of the court's discussion on the legality of the search, what was the ultimate reasoning for the finding of qualified immunity? And why is such immunity important for higher education decision making and the implementation of policy?

2. In 2009, the United States Supreme Court addressed the issue of strip searches in public school settings. In *Safford Unified School District v. Redding*, 557 U.S. 364 (2009), school administrators conducted a strip search of Savana

Redding after receiving a tip from one of Savana's classmates that Savana may have been carrying and distributing prescription-strength pain killers. The search was conducted by a female administrative assistant and a female nurse at the direction of the middle school's assistant principal. No contraband was found. The Court, in a tight 5-4 decision, held that the search was unlawful, but that the school employees involved were entitled to qualified immunity. Applying the reasonable suspicion standard of *T.L.O.*, the Court found the search to be justified at its inception under the circumstances, given the reliable evidence of drug possession and dealing. Regarding the second prong of *T.L.O.*, however, the Court found the search to be unreasonable in scope, in light of the fact that the low number of pills suspected did not present an immediate threat of harm to Savana, others, or the school as a whole. In addition, there was no evidence to suggest that Savana was hiding the pills in her underwear. Finally, relying on the observation that the law of strip searches in public education was not clearly established at the time of the search, the Court then held that the school officials should not be held personally liable for monetary damages, offering them a good faith, qualified immunity defense. In its discussion, the majority in *Safford* found enough differences in the lower courts' opinions on public school strip searches to determine that the law was not so clearly established as to put the school officials in *Safford* on notice that their search of Savana was unconstitutional.

There is no doubt that qualified immunity is a great and useful defense for a government actor in a given case. What about its guidance for future cases, though? In other words, what does it mean to be "clearly established under the law" for purposes of qualified immunity? Surely, the exact fact pattern would not have to be repeated in a future case for the law to be clearly established. The Court in *Safford* offers some guidance here:

> To be established clearly, however, there is no need that "the very action in question [have] previously been held unlawful." *Wilson v. Layne*, 526 U.S. 603, 615, 119 S. Ct. 1692, 143 L. Ed. 2d 818 (1999). The unconstitutionality of outrageous conduct obviously will be unconstitutional, this being the reason, as Judge Posner has said, that "[t]he easiest cases don't even arise." *K. H. v. Morgan*, 914 F.2d 846, 851 (CA7 1990). But even as to action less than an outrage, "officials can still be on notice that their conduct violates established law . . . in novel factual circumstances." *Hope v. Pelzer*, 536 U.S. 730, 741, 122 S. Ct. 2508, 153 L. Ed. 2d 666 (2002).

Safford, 557 U.S. at 377–78.

While the majority in *Safford* noted that conflicting lower courts on the subject of strip searches led, in part, to the finding of qualified immunity, the Court spoke further to reject the notion that "entitlement to qualified immunity is the guaranteed product of disuniform views of the law in the other federal, or state, courts. . . ." *Id.* at 378.

If *Carboni* had been decided after *Safford*, do you think the court would have granted qualified immunity to the defendants? After *Safford*, we may be on notice for strip searches conducted in K-12 settings. Are we also now on notice for such searches in higher education? Or does the language in *Carboni* concerning the differences between K-12 and higher education affect qualified immunity in higher education for strip searches? Recall the following statements from *Carboni*:

> The specific circumstances of the body search render this issue one of apparent first impression for any federal court. Unlike any prior cases of record, Plaintiff is a graduate student, not a public school pupil. . . . As a result of the foregoing differences between this case and any precedent of which the court is aware, the court is not convinced that a search of a university graduate student undertaken by a faculty member, or at his direction, is *ever* justified if the student objects. However, neither can the court say that the defendants violated the plaintiff's *clearly established* constitutional rights because of the novelty of the issues presented here.

Id. at 434. Both parties cited *New Jersey v. T.L.O.* as the applicable search standard here — reasonable suspicion. The court in *Carboni* then followed with, "[h]owever, regardless of the standard applied, the defendants are entitled to immunity because there is at least a legitimate question as to whether they violated any clearly established constitutional right the plaintiff possessed." So should a different legal standard apply to such cases in higher education?

3. Much of the discussion in *Carboni* surrounded the legality of the strip search and the grant of qualified immunity. Note, though, that the case arose from an adverse academic decision made by university officials. For further discussion on such decisions and the associated requirements of due process and policy compliance, see the sections on due process, both academic and disciplinary, *supra.*

5. Privacy and University Computers

UNITED STATES v. BUTLER
151 F. Supp. 2d 82 (D. Me. 2001)

MEMORANDUM DECISION AND ORDER ON DEFENDANT'S MOTIONS TO SUPPRESS, DISMISS AND CONTINUE

The Indictment asserts that the defendant has previously been convicted of a crime relating to sexual abuse and abusive sexual conduct involving a minor or ward. It charges that four times thereafter, he knowingly and illegally received child pornography over the Internet, contrary to 18 U.S.C. § 2252A(a)(2)((A). The defendant's motions to suppress, dismiss and continue are DENIED.

1. Students' Fourth Amendment Rights in University Computers

The Indictment charges that the images in question came over the Internet to computers at the Lewiston-Auburn College of the University of Maine. The defendant moves to suppress the University logs identifying when he used the University computers, as well as the contents of the hard drives from two University computers he used. I accept as true, for purposes of the motion, the assertions in the defendant's motion to suppress.

At the time, the defendant was a student enrolled in the University of Maine system. Because he was an enrolled student, he had access to a computer lab on the

Lewiston-Auburn campus. On one occasion, he left on a University computer screen a frozen image that a University employee considered pedophilia. That incident led to an investigation by University authorities, which revealed more such images on hard drives, and ultimately the police were involved. As a result, the prosecution now has the hard drives of two University computers, as well as session logs showing when the defendant used the computers. The defendant wants all of these suppressed as the product of searches in violation of the Fourth Amendment.

To assert a right under the Fourth Amendment, a defendant must demonstrate both a subjective expectation of privacy and an expectation that society judges as objectively reasonable. *Kyllo v. United States*, 530 U.S. 1305 (2001); *Rakas v. Illinois*, 439 U.S. 128, 143 & n.12 (1978); *Katz v. United States*, 389 U.S. 347 (1967) (Harlan, J., concurring). What that objectively reasonable expectation is for computers, under circumstances of shared usage, presents questions of some difficulty in today's environment of rapidly changing technology and provisions of service. I do not have to confront these difficult issues because the defendant has made not even a minimal showing that he had a reasonable expectation of privacy in either his session logs or the hard drives of these University-owned computers. Session logs are obviously maintained for the benefit of the University and therefore not suppressible on the defendant/student's motion. *See Smith v. Maryland*, 442 U.S. 735, 742–44 (1979) (holding that a telephone customer had no legitimate expectation of privacy in telephone numbers he had dialed because in dialing he voluntarily conveyed the information to the telephone company and thereby assumed the risk that the telephone company would disclose it); *United States v. Miller*, 425 U.S. 435, 442 (1976) (holding that a bank depositor had no legitimate expectation of privacy in bank records that he voluntarily conveyed to the bank and that the bank used in the ordinary course of its business). . . . As for the hard drives, the defendant has pointed to no computer privacy policies in effect at the University, no statements or representations made to him as a user of the computers in this lab, no practices concerning access to and retention of the contents of hard drives, not even password requirements. From all that appears, he, along with other students, was simply using the University computers under circumstances where images on the monitor were visible to others (as occurred here), and no commitments were made as to the privacy of hard drives. *See United States v. Simons*, 206 F.3d 392, 398-99 (4th Cir. 2000) (finding no reasonable expectation of privacy in files downloaded from the Internet to hard drives of employee's office computer where employer had express policy of monitoring Internet activities of employees).

The defendant relies upon "a legitimate and reasonable expectation of privacy recognized by society in any work performed on, or documents and files produced on, computers he used while a student at the University of Maine." Unlike the Supreme Court's treatment of generic payphone booths in 1967 in *Katz*, I conclude that in 2001 there is no generic expectation of privacy for shared usage on computers at large. Conditions of computer use and access still vary tremendously. The burden remains on the defendant to show that his expectations were reasonable under the circumstances of the particular case. Without meeting that burden, he cannot challenge the University's decision to examine the computers he used, nor the warrant the police obtained later to search the hard drives of the University's computers.

. . .

SO ORDERED.

NOTES

1. In *Butler*, the court stated the following: "As for the hard drives, the defendant has pointed to no computer privacy policies in effect at the University, no statements or representations made to him as a user of the computers in this lab, no practices concerning access to and retention of the contents of hard drives, not even password requirements." So does the result in this case change if any of this evidence exists?

2. Recall that the background facts in *Butler* focused on a criminal charge of child pornography. Consider now the following paragraph, edited from the opinion above:

> The First Circuit has already held that the definition of child pornography in 18 U.S.C. § 2256, applicable to 18 U.S.C. § 2252A, is not unconstitutionally overbroad or vague. *United States v. Hilton*, 167 F.3d 61, 71, 76 (1st Cir.), *cert. denied*, 528 U.S. 844 (1999). The fact that the United States Supreme Court has agreed to hear an apparently contrary decision from the Ninth Circuit, *Free Speech Coalition v. Reno*, 198 F.3d 1083, 1095–96 (9th Cir. 1999), *cert. granted sub nom. Ashcroft v. Free Speech Coalition*, 121 S. Ct. 876, 148 L. Ed. 2d 788 (2001), does not change the applicable law in this Circuit or call for any continuance. If the Supreme Court should ultimately rule differently from the First Circuit, that ruling can then be grounds for appeal.

151 F. Supp. 2d at 85.

In its opinion in *Ashcroft v. Free Speech Coalition*, 535 U.S. 234 (2002), the Supreme Court did, in fact, strike down that provision, 18 U.S.C. § 2256(8)(B). The Court held that the definition of "child pornography" was overbroad and an unconstitutional infringement of free speech. The following year, the Congress amended the definition to the following:

> (8) "child pornography" means any visual depiction, including any photograph, film, video, picture, or computer or computer-generated image or picture, whether made or produced by electronic, mechanical, or other means, of sexually explicit conduct, where —
>
> (A) the production of such visual depiction involves the use of a minor engaging in sexually explicit conduct;
>
> (B) such visual depiction is a digital image, computer image, or computer-generated image that is, or is indistinguishable from, that of a minor engaging in sexually explicit conduct; or

(C) such visual depiction has been created, adapted, or modified to appear that an identifiable minor is engaging in sexually explicit conduct.

18 U.S.C. § 2256. For an application of this provision in a search and seizure case, see *United States v. Beatty*, No. 1:08-cr-51-SJM, 2009 U.S. Dist. LEXIS 121473 (W.D. Pa. Dec. 31, 2009) (motion to suppress evidence obtained in a search of defendant's home computer denied).

IN RE PROPERTY OF FORGIONE

908 A.2d 593 (Conn. Super. Ct. 2006)

RUBINOW, J. This memorandum of decision addresses the "Motion for Return of Unlawfully Seized Property and Its Suppression as Evidence" filed by the named petitioner, Perry Forgione, and petitioners Denise Forgione and Meghan Forgione, (Forgiones) under date of July 29, 2005. The Forgiones jointly assert that two search and seizure warrants, issued by separate and independent magistrates, effectively violated the protections guaranteed by the fourth and fourteenth amendments to the United States constitution and §§ 7 and 8 of the Connecticut constitution of Connecticut. They further assert that the searches and seizures enabled by these warrants improperly enabled law enforcement officers to obtain and to hold computers and related materials from the Forgione home, and improperly enabled the officers to ascertain the Internet protocol (IP) address used by the Forgione family members. . . .

It is uncontroverted that the property at issue was identified and seized during the preliminary course of a criminal investigation involving Internet communications with or concerning Meghan Forgione. . . .

. . . [T]he court finds that each of the search warrants at issue presented sufficient basis for the magistrates' determinations of probable cause that a crime had been committed, when viewed in the totality of the circumstances at issue. . . . [The Forgiones'] motion for return and suppression must be denied.

I

FACTUAL AND PROCEDURAL HISTORY

. . . .

On or around October 13, 2004, [Andrew] Hayden, then a freshman at Quinnipiac [University], made a telephone complaint to [Charles] Griffen, who served as the school's information security officer. Hayden complained of computer problems, indicating his belief that someone had been interfering with his Quinnipiac assigned and registered e-mail account. Hayden stated that some of his e-mail messages had been deleted, that his course schedule had been altered and that his Quinnipiac based password had been changed. Hayden assured Griffen that he had never given anyone the password to his e-mail account. Hayden specifically complained of concerns that he was being stalked by an Internet intruder, however, especially since he had recently broken off a relationship with a girlfriend. Although Hayden indicated that his former girlfriend was very angry as the result of their breakup,

Hayden did not provide the identity of this girlfriend when making his fall 2004 complaints.

By June, 2005, Griffen had obtained new computer equipment that would allow him to investigate interferences with student e-mail accounts. Griffen attempted to contact Hayden in order to utilize the new computer equipment to investigate further the student's stated information technology problems. Hayden then explained to Griffen that the previously complained of e-mail interference had continued during the spring, even though Quinnipiac's technology department had "reimaged" his hard drive, with the resultant erasure of digital evidence of the e-mail interference. Using his new equipment, Griffen examined Quinnipiac's network computer e-mail logs and was able to access the times and dates in which Hayden's e-mail account had been entered into by an outside source, ostensibly unrelated to Quinnipiac. Griffen discovered that Hayden's university based e-mail account was accessed by someone from the IP address known as "24.151.1.122." Griffen credibly testified that Quinnipiac's e-mail logs established that someone from the 24.151.1.122 IP address accessed two university e-mail accounts. Quinnipiac had assigned those e-mail accounts to Hayden and to an incoming freshman named Meghan Forgione.

With reasonable technological accuracy, Griffen determined that the IP address 24.151.1.122 originated from Charter Communications (Charter), an Internet service provider. Upon discovering that information, Griffen contacted the Hamden police department and related his suspicion that some person or persons using the IP address 24.151.1.122 from outside the Quinnipiac network had contacted and interfered with two university based e-mail accounts. Hamden police officers procured an affidavit from Griffen relating the aforementioned information and used this affidavit in preparing their own affidavit, which supported an application for a search warrant to access Internet subscriber information at Charter. On the basis of the Hamden police officers' affidavit, on July 13, 2005, the court . . . approved the requested search and seizure warrant after finding probable cause. . . .

In response, on July 14, 2005, Charter identified the 24.151.1.122 IP address as belonging to Perry Forgione of Southbury and so advised the Hamden police. On that same day, but not previously, Hayden told Griffen that Meghan Forgione was his former girlfriend and that he had not been to her residence since March, 2005. Hayden reiterated that he had never given Meghan Forgione any passwords to any of his e-mail accounts.

. . . [T]he Hamden police prepared an affidavit to support their request for a search warrant that would enable them to seize as evidence all computer equipment and devices from the Forgione home in Southbury, the ostensible source of the 24.151.1.122 IP address. . . .

As a result of the subsequent search of the Forgione home, three computers, a wireless router, keyboard, display screen, floppy drive disk and two floppy disks (computer items) were seized. Through their motion, the Forgiones seek return of the seized computer items as well as return of the seized subscriber information. The Forgiones further seek a court order suppressing the use of such evidence in any criminal proceedings that may involve Meghan Forgione or any member of her family. . . .

II

APPLICATION OF LAW TO FACTS

Although the facts of the present case involve late twentieth century features of Internet technology, so-called cybercommunications, computer hardware, software and jargon that developed only late in the twentieth century, the applicable law remains constant insofar as search and seizure issues are concerned. . . . ". . . [The court will] uphold the validity of [a search] warrant . . . [if] the affidavit at issue presented a substantial factual basis for the [issuing judge's] conclusion that probable cause existed. . . . When [an issuing judge] has determined that the warrant affidavit presents sufficient objective indicia of reliability to justify a search and has issued a warrant, a court reviewing that warrant at a subsequent suppression hearing should defer to the reasonable inferences drawn by the [issuing judge]. . . . Probable cause to search exists if: (1) there is probable cause to believe that the particular items sought to be seized are connected with criminal activity or will assist in a particular apprehension or conviction . . . and (2) there is probable cause to believe that the items sought to be seized will be found in the place to be searched. . . ." (Internal quotation marks omitted.) *State v. Eastwood*, 83 Conn.App. 452, 460–61, 850 A.2d 234 (2004).

The Forgiones raise several arguments in support of their claims that the affidavits supporting the search and seizure warrants lack sufficient facts demonstrating probable cause. . . . First, the Forgiones argue that the search warrant affidavits are "infected with double hearsay", information, purporting to represent Griffen's statements about what Hayden told him concerning a romantic relationship and breakup with Meghan Forgione; the Forgiones submit that because this "double hearsay" was never substantiated by independent evidence, it constitutes an unreliable basis for the magistrates' issuance of the search and seizure orders. Second, the Forgiones claim that the IP address found by Griffen does not directly prove that the Forgione computers were used to commit a crime and that Griffen's affidavit does not provide information as to when and where the Internet connection was accessed. Inherently intertwined with the second argument is the Forgiones' further argument that in order to find probable cause, the supporting affidavit would have to include a police interview with Hayden. Had the interview been conducted, they argue, the court would have learned that the Forgiones' residence had a wireless Internet connection that could be accessed by anyone within a 150 foot radius of their home. They claim that anyone, especially Hayden, who has a laptop computer with a wireless Internet adaptor, could access the Internet from inside or outside the Forgione residence and that therefore, there is insufficient evidence to establish probable cause for the searches and seizures at issue. Finally, the Forgiones argue that the search warrant was improperly issued to provide access to their proprietary information held by or at Charter in violation of their privacy interests.

The state counters with several arguments. . . . First, the state responds that the Forgiones have applied the incorrect legal standard in their argument that portions of Griffen's affidavit should not have been considered and contain unreliable double hearsay; the state further argues that the totality of the circumstances promote the finding of sufficiency in the underlying warrant affidavits. Second, the state asserts that the information provided by Griffen, as presented in the warrant affidavits, is sufficient to establish probable cause for search and seizure of the subscriber information linked to the IP address because the Forgiones do not have a fourth amendment privacy interest in this data, thereby rendering it subject to search and seizure. Third, the state argues that the police were not required to interview Hayden prior to obtaining a search warrant because the officers had established probable cause on the basis of the IP address and the information provided by Griffen. . . .

A

"Double Hearsay" Argument

The Forgiones first argue that the evidence should be suppressed and returned because Griffen's affidavit contains an unreliable double hearsay statement from Hayden about his relationship with Meghan Forgione and his access to the Forgione Internet connection. . . .

The Forgiones . . . argue that our Supreme Court . . . established a requirement that whenever law enforcement officers seek a search warrant on the basis of information provided by a third party, that information must meet an "independent basis for reliability test". . . . Although vigorous, this aspect of the movants' argument is derived from miscues and promotes misapplication of *Morrill's* lessons.

Both the text and context of *Morrill* make it clear that its "independent basis for reliability test" is required only in cases in which law enforcement officers attempt to utilize information that is somehow suspect or not subject to a presumption of dependability, such as information from so-called confidential informants, in an effort to invade an individual's constitutionally protected privacy interests. [In *Morrill*, the Connecticut Supreme Court] rejected the defendant's double hearsay argument, finding that "[a] law enforcement officer, *like the general public, is generally presumed to be reliable, and thus no special showing of such reliability . . . is necessary to establish probable cause. . . .* Thus, the fact that [the lieutenant in *Morrill*] received the informant's information from [the detective] does not affect the validity of the affidavit, and this claim is without merit." (Citations omitted; emphasis added; internal quotation marks omitted.) *Id.*, 568–69.

. . . The facts of the present case clearly establish that Griffen here relayed information to the Hamden police department in his capacity as a member of the general public, not as a confidential informant. Accordingly, the information he gave to the law enforcement officers, and which they used in the preparation of the affidavits supporting their search and seizure warrant applications, was not subject to the "independent basis for reliability test" here promoted by the Forgiones. The facts of the present case clearly and convincingly demonstrate that Griffen reviewed the Internet records at issue in the course of his official work capacity at Quinnipiac, not at the request of law enforcement officers, and not in the course of aiding an ongoing criminal investigation. All of the computer accounts which he searched using his new computer equipment, as described in part I, and all of the e-mail transactions and printouts at issue are either the property of Quinnipiac or are accessible through Quinnipiac's proprietary computer services.

Both Quinnipiac and Griffen stand in the position of being citizen-members of the general public. There is, therefore, no reasonable or legal basis for questioning the reliability of Griffen's statements, Quinnipiac's computer data and resources or the link to the Forgione IP address that was exposed by Griffen using Quinnipiac's computer system. Moreover, Griffen was perfectly entitled to view as reliable Hayden's comments to him, and the Hamden police were equally entitled so to view Hayden's comments to Griffen because members of "the general public [are] generally presumed to be reliable, and thus no special showing of such reliability . . . is necessary to establish probable cause. . . . Griffen investigated the Internet activity on the basis of a student complaint of harassment and not directly because of Hayden's relationship with Meghan Forgione. In fact, Griffen testified at the hearing that he was not aware of the name of Hayden's former girlfriend until after he discovered that Hayden's e-mail account had been accessed from the Forgiones' IP address.

. . . .

. . . The evidence clearly and convincingly establishes that only after Griffen had determined the identity of the Forgione IP address did Hayden state to him that he had not been to the Forgione residence or accessed his e-mails from the residence since March, 2005. Hayden inherently possesses the requisite "basis of knowledge" as to when he had been to the Forgione residence and when and where he had accessed his e-mail account. Especially when viewed in the totality of the circumstances of Griffen's Internet identification of the IP address, there is insufficient basis for Griffen to have doubted the reliability of Hayden's statements concerning his contact with the Forgiones or their computer systems. . . .

B

"No Crime Committed" Argument

The Forgiones also claim that the search warrant affidavits used to access the computer materials at their home were further defective in that they lacked the requisite proof that these items seized from their home were the actual items used to commit a crime. They argue that the IP address, found by Griffen, identifies only the computer modem located outside of the house, but that this address cannot be attributed to particular computers located inside the house. As such, the Forgiones protest that the search warrant affidavits at issue do not permit a reasonable determination as to whether one, or indeed any, of the computers or attendant materials in their home had actually been used to access Hayden's e-mail account or otherwise to violate § 53-451. The Forgiones further assert that because of the portability of laptop computers in general, and specifically because of the availability of a "wireless" Internet connection at their home, anyone within a 150 foot radius could have accessed the Internet through their modem, thus rendering the search warrant affidavits at issue fatally flawed. The court finds that the search warrant affidavits at issue sufficiently described the place to be searched and the things to be seized, thus rendering this second argument ineffective in overcoming the presumptive validity of the warrant.

. . . .

. . . The court utilized [a] common sense and practical approach in assessing the information obtained by Griffen concerning the interference with the Quinnipiac computers, and the relationship of Meghan Forgione to the school and to the IP address at issue, as this information was relayed through the warrant affidavits. From this approach, it is apparent that the court found that there was an abundant, reasonable basis for inferring that the computer used to harass Hayden would be found in the Forgione home. Even if the search warrant at issue did not exclude the possibility that another computer, at another location, could have been used to commit the crime, it is a reasonable conclusion to allow a search of the computers located inside the house. . . .

. . . .

C

"Privacy Interest in IP Address" Argument

. . . [T]he Forgiones . . . raised the argument that they had a fourth amendment privacy interest in their subscriber information to their IP address and that this privacy interest was improperly violated through the execution of the warrant permitting Charter to turn over this information to the Hamden police. The state counters that there is no relevant expectation of privacy at issue in the present case because the Forgiones voluntarily provided Charter with this information when they established the IP address. "[The] IP address routing system is essential to the basic functionality of the Internet, in a similar fashion as mailing addresses and telephone numbers are essential to the functionality of the postal service and telecommunications system." *Register. Com, Inc. v. Verio, Inc.*, 356 F.3d 393, 409–10 (2d Cir. 2004). Thus, in the present case, the IP address identified the Forgione street address, like a telephone number would have in a telephone book.

Viewing the evidence as a whole, it is clear that the Forgiones ceded any expectation of privacy in their underlying subscriber information, such as their residential address and other information, when they voluntarily entered into an agreement for Charter to provide them with an Internet account servicing their home in Southbury. . . . [W]hen an individual enters into an agreement for "Internet service, he knowingly revealed all [of the] information connected to the IP address. . . . He cannot now claim to have a Fourth Amendment privacy interest in his subscriber information." *United States v. Kennedy*, 81 F. Supp. 2d 1103, 1110 (D. Kan. 2000). . . .

Wherefore, for the foregoing reasons, the court hereby denies the Forgiones' motion for the return of unlawfully seized property and the suppression of evidence, submitted under date of July 29, 2005.

NOTES

1. Unfortunately, the positive aspects of technology today share much air time with the negative aspects. Among the increasingly common issues facing colleges and universities is the risk of data security breaches, where, for example, the private information (Social Security Numbers, identification numbers, transcripts, etc.) of students, staff, and alumni are made public either by accident or by some criminal activity. In response, institutions of higher education are called to make and enforce new policy and to spend thousands of dollars either compensating those who have been harmed or strengthening their systems to prevent future breaches. The Privacy Rights Clearinghouse regularly updates a list of security breaches nationwide (e.g., stolen laptops, hacked systems, lost files, etc.), including those that occur at colleges and universities. *See Chronology of Data Breaches: Security Breaches 2005 — Present*, PRIVACY RIGHTS CLEARINGHOUSE (Apr. 20, 2005), *available at* http://www.privacyrights.org/data-breach.

2. Much of the legal and policy discussion on bullying and cyberbullying, understandably, focuses on K-12 education. *See, e.g.*, Kathleen Conn, *Cyberbullying and Other Student Misuses of Technology Affecting K-12 Public Schools: Will Public School Administrators Be Held Responsible for the Consequences?*, 244 EDUC. L. REP. 479 (2009); Tiffany Emrick, Comment, *When MySpace Crosses the School Gates: The Implications of Cyberspeech on Student' Free-Speech Rights*, 40 UNIV. TOL. L. REV. 785 (2009); Caitlin May, Comment, *Internet-Savvy Students and Bewildered Educators: Student Internet Speech Is Creating New Legal Issues for the Educational Community*, 58 CATH. UNIV. L. REV. 1105 (2009); Martha McCarthy, *Curtailing Degrading Student Expression: Is a Link to a Disruption Required?*, 38 J.L. & EDUC. 607 (2009); PATRICK D. PAUKEN, *Morse v. Frederick and Cyber-bullying in Schools: The Impact on Freedom of Expression, Disciplinary Authority, and School Leadership in* S. SHARIFF & A. H. CHURCHILL (eds.), TRUTHS AND MYTHS OF CYBER-BULLYING 159 (Peter Lang Pub. 2010); Kevin Turbert, Note, *Faceless Bullies: Legislative and Judicial Responses to Cyberbullying*, 33 SETON HALL LEGIS. J. 651 (2009).

However, higher education settings are not immune from such concerns and accompanying tragedies. For example, on September 22, 2010, Tyler Clementi, a freshman at Rutgers University, committed suicide days after a video, secretly produced by his roommate and a classmate, surfaced on the Internet. The video depicted a sexual act between Tyler and another man in Tyler's dorm room. The tragedy has sparked much law-related conversation nationwide and worldwide, raising questions of civil and criminal liability for the students who produced and posted the video and for the university itself, generating some legislative action. The New Jersey general assembly passed an Anti-Bullying Bill of Rights within two months of the suicide and two federal lawmakers from New Jersey introduced legislation in Congress: the Tyler Clementi Higher Education Anti-Harassment Act of 2010.

3. Another technology-influenced issue facing universities involves the universities as internet service providers and the risks assumed when students and staff use university-provided hardware to engage in illegal downloading of copyrighted materials. For further discussion of this issue as it relates to privacy law, see the section on student records and the Family Educational Rights and Privacy Act (FERPA) in Chapter V.

6. Urinalysis Drug Tests

PIERCE v. SMITH

117 F.3d 866 (5th Cir. 1997)

Garwood, Circuit Judge:

Plaintiff-appellee Dr. Diane Pierce (Dr. Pierce) brought this suit against defendants-appellants Dr. David Smith (Dr. Smith) and Dr. Louis Binder (Dr. Binder), claiming that appellants violated her rights under the Fourth and Fourteenth Amendments when they, as officials of the state medical residency program in which she was enrolled, caused her to undergo a private urinalysis test for drugs and submit the test results to program officials, by informing her that she would be expelled from the program if she was not tested. The jury returned a verdict in favor of Dr. Pierce, awarding her compensatory and punitive damages. Dr. Smith and Dr. Binder appeal. We hold appellants are protected by qualified immunity and accordingly reverse.

Facts and Proceedings below

Dr. Pierce was a medical resident in the emergency medicine residency program at the Texas Tech University Health Science Center (TTUHSC) in El Paso, Texas, from 1988 to 1991. Texas Tech is a state institution. As part of her TTUHSC residency program, Dr. Pierce served a two-month rotation at St. Joseph's Hospital in Phoenix, Arizona, during January and February of 1990, where she trained with the trauma team in emergency medicine.

On February 22, 1990, a patient was admitted to the St. Joseph's emergency room with head injuries sustained after smashing his head through the windshield of his car in an automobile accident. The patient, who was under the influence of alcohol and drugs, was extremely uncooperative and aggressive.

Dr. Dale Stannard, the attending physician on the emergency service that day, ordered that a CAT scan be performed to determine whether the patient had suffered any internal head injury. Hospital orderlies brought the patient to the CAT scan room and placed him on the scan table. As part of the trauma team, Dr. Pierce was called to the CAT scan room to see the patient. When she arrived, she noticed that the orderlies were having difficulty restraining the patient on the table. Dr. Pierce tried to help and as she leaned over the patient to tighten his restraints, he spat in her face. Dr. Pierce, in her words, "hard slapped" the patient at least two times on his face.

Dr. Pierce, the only physician present, left the room to wash off the saliva. When she returned, the nursing supervisor forcefully escorted her out of the room, telling her to stay away from the patient. Dr. Stannard, who was not present in the CAT scan room when the incident occurred, was told by the night supervisor that Dr. Pierce had "karate chopped" the patient. Later on, however, Dr. Stannard learned that Dr. Pierce had actually slapped the patient. He believed that there was no cause to discipline her.

The following day, Dr. Pierce was called in to see Dr. Raymond Shamos, the acting trauma director at St. Joseph's. The administrators at St. Joseph's were upset by the incident and wanted to promptly send Dr. Pierce back to TTUHSC in El Paso. Dr. Shamos, however, felt such steps were unnecessary and instead instructed Dr. Pierce to seek counseling with St. Joseph's employee counseling administrator. She underwent counseling and was allowed to finish the remaining three days of her rotation at St. Joseph's. The counselor recommended that on her return to El Paso Dr. Pierce "contact the University Psychiatric department to continue counseling sessions."

Dr. Smith, the residency director at TTUHSC at the time, learned of the incident through Pat Jones, the emergency medicine department administrator, who told Dr. Smith that Dr. Pierce had "beat up a patient" at St. Joseph's. Dr. Smith began his own investigation of the incident, which included talking with Dr. Brian Nelson, who was chairman of the faculty at TTUHSC, and Dr. Shamos. During Dr. Smith's telephone conversation with Dr. Shamos, Dr. Smith was told that Dr. Pierce had karate chopped the patient in the neck. Later, Dr. Smith met with Dr. Binder, Associate Professor in the Department of Emergency Medicine at TTUHSC and Assistant Dean, to discuss the incident. Due to incorrect information received from St. Joseph's, both Dr. Smith and Dr. Binder thought that Dr. Pierce had karate chopped a patient and had to be physically restrained from the patient. They discussed a number of possible explanations for Dr. Pierce's surprising behavior, including drug use.

Upon Dr. Smith's request, Dr. Pierce met with Dr. Smith in his office on February 28. At that meeting, Dr. Smith handed Dr. Pierce a letter and told her that she was being placed on probation, with pay, pending an investigation into the incident.

This was not the first time Dr. Pierce had been on probation in her TTUHSC residency. During the summer of 1989, she was placed on probation for, among other reasons, excessive tardiness, poor interpersonal relationship problems with the faculty and patients, and failing to carry an acceptable volume of patients. At that time (in 1989), there was some discussion among the faculty members that drug use might be the cause of Dr. Pierce's behavior. When asked during 1989 by Dr. Nelson whether she was using drugs, Dr. Pierce replied that she was not. Dr. Pierce was eventually taken off this probation, and was not on probation when she slapped the patient at St. Joseph's.

Dr. Smith also told Dr. Pierce in the February 28 meeting that she would have to undergo psychiatric evaluations. . . . One evaluation would be performed by a doctor selected by TTUHSC and the other evaluation by a doctor selected by Dr. Pierce.

On that same day, Dr. David Smith contacted Dr. Robert Smith about performing the evaluation on Dr. Pierce on behalf of TTUHSC. Dr. Robert Smith agreed to do so. Dr. David Smith understood that the evaluation would include a urine drug test.

Dr. David Smith met with Dr. Pierce for a third time on March 9. Dr. Pierce handed to Dr. Smith letters written by Dr. Stannard and Dr. Shamos on her behalf, describing their accounts of what had happened at St. Joseph's and, specifically, correcting earlier stories that Dr. Pierce had karate chopped the patient and explaining that Dr. Pierce instead had slapped the patient three times on the face. [T]he letters did not cause the doctors to rule out drug use as a possible explanation for Dr. Pierce's conduct.

Dr. Pierce arrived at Dr. Robert Smith's office on March 14 to undergo her psychiatric evaluation. At that time, she was informed by Dr. Robert Smith that he had scheduled a urinalysis drug test for their next appointment on March 17. Dr. Pierce objected to taking the drug test, and went to speak with Dr. David Smith, informing him of her objection to the urinalysis. . . . Dr. Pierce met with Dr. Robert Smith on March 17, and she told him she would likely refuse to take the urinalysis test. Dr. Pierce next met with Dr. David Smith on March 19. Dr. Pierce testified that on this occasion Dr. David Smith told her "if I didn't take the urinalysis test, I'd be dismissed" and "indicated that he had to be able to prove to Dr. Nelson [TTUHSC faculty chairman] and Dr. Glass [a faculty member] that I wasn't using drugs." Dr. Pierce did not indicate she would submit to urinalysis, but did not definitely say she would not.

Nothing in the record suggests that either Dr. David Smith or Dr. Binder, alone or in combination with each other, had or claimed to have the authority to actually dismiss Dr. Pierce. The only matter in the record speaking to this is the "Personnel Relations & Disciplinary Action" attachment to the TTUHSC Graduate Medical Education Program Agreement between TTUHSC and Dr. Pierce for the period July 1, 1989, to June 30, 1990. This attachment provides that the Program Director has the authority to recommend dismissal to the dean of the Texas Tech medical school, "through" the TTUHSC dean, who in 1990 was Dr. Joseph Brown (to whom Dr. Binder reported), "for review and action." It also provides that a resident has the right to appeal a dismissal, with attendant due process rights, and that compensation and benefits shall continue, and certifying boards and medical associations shall not be notified of the dismissal, during the appeal process.

Although she still would not commit to take Dr. Robert Smith's urinalysis test, on March 23 Dr. Pierce decided to take a urinalysis drug test at an independent laboratory, Pathlab. After receiving the results, which were negative, from the laboratory, Dr. Pierce hand-delivered the report to Dr. David Smith on March 30, which he accepted in place of the urinalysis which had been arranged for by Dr. Robert Smith. The evidence indicates, and there is no evidence to the contrary, that prior to receiving this report neither Dr. David Smith nor Dr. Binder nor anyone else at TTUHSC (nor Dr. Robert Smith) had any indication that Dr. Pierce intended to take (or had taken) a urinalysis drug test, independently or otherwise. On that same day, after reviewing the urinalysis report and the psychiatric evaluations of Dr. Robert Smith and Dr. Ann Salo, Dr. David Smith took Dr. Pierce off her probation.

. . . .

On February 24, 1992, Pierce filed this suit against Dr. David Smith and Dr. Binder, seeking damages and declaratory relief. . . .

All defendants moved for summary judgment. The court granted the defendants' motion on all claims except the Fourth Amendment claim. . . .

. . . .

Over the defendants' objections, the district court submitted a jury instruction stating that, before a government employer may compel an employee to undergo a drug test, the employer must have individualized suspicion that the employee was using drugs. The jury returned a verdict in favor of Dr. Pierce, awarding her $30,000 actual damages against Dr. Smith and Dr. Binder, jointly and severally; $10,000 punitive damages against Dr. Smith; and $10,000 punitive damages against Dr. Binder.

. . . The court also awarded Dr. Pierce $31,153.41 in attorney's fees and expenses and $2,770.82 court costs. Dr. Smith and Dr. Binder bring this appeal.

Discussion

I. Qualified Immunity; Standards and Review

Appellants argue on appeal that, as government officials, they are entitled to qualified immunity.

A state official exercising discretionary authority whose conduct deprives another of a right secured by federal constitutional or statutory law is nonetheless shielded from personal liability for damages under section 1983 by the doctrine of qualified immunity, unless at the time and under the circumstances of the challenged conduct all reasonable officials would have realized that it was proscribed by the federal law on which the suit is founded. *See, e.g., Anderson v. Creighton*, 483 U.S. 635 (1987). . . .

. . . .

Where, as here, a section 1983 defendant pleads qualified immunity and shows he is a governmental official whose position involves the exercise of discretion, the plaintiff then has the burden "to rebut this defense by establishing that the official's allegedly wrongful conduct violated clearly established law." *Salas v. Carpenter*, 980 F.2d 299, 306 (5th Cir. 1992). . . .

. . . .

II. Fourth Amendment

A. Search

. . . .

It is clear that, under certain circumstances, the collection and testing of urine by the government constitutes a search subject to Fourth Amendment constraints. *Chandler v. Miller*, 117 S. Ct. 1295 (1997); *Vernonia School District 47J v. Acton*, 515 U.S. 646 (1995); *Skinner v. Railway Labor Executives' Ass'n*, 489 U.S. 602 (1989); *Treasury Employees v. Von Raab*, 489 U.S. 656 (1989).

B. Non-law enforcement standards generally; Individualized suspicion

. . . "[W]here a Fourth Amendment intrusion serves special governmental needs, beyond the normal need for law enforcement" a more particularized balancing is necessary to determine reasonableness and "neither a warrant nor probable cause, nor, indeed, any measure of individualized suspicion, is an indispensable component of reasonableness in every circumstance." *Von Raab* at 1390. . . .

C. Special needs situations

"Special needs" for these purposes have been found in a variety of circumstances, including "the Government's interest in regulating the conduct of railroad employees to ensure safety . . . its supervision of probationers or regulated industries, . . . [and] its operation of a government office . . . [or] school." *Skinner* at 1415. . . .

. . . .

Plainly, this *is* a "special needs" case. . . . The present setting not only involves the practice of medicine, an endeavor subject to extensive governmental regulation, but also both a student-school and an employee-supervisor relationship. Dr. Pierce was undergoing training in the medical school's emergency medicine residency program, and was in essence both a student and an employee providing professional services to the public. "In the case of searches conducted by a public employer, we must balance the invasion of the employees' legitimate expectations of privacy against the government's need for supervision, control, and the efficient operation of the workplace." *O'Connor* at 1499. What the Court said of the railroad employees in *Skinner* is true "in spades" as to Dr. Pierce, practicing and learning emergency medicine, namely that she "discharged duties fraught with such risks of injury to others that even a momentary lapse of attention can have disastrous consequences." *Id.* at 1419. . . .

D. Privacy expectations; Obtrusiveness

Of course, the fact that "special needs" are present does not alone resolve the matter. The privacy interests of the party searched must also be weighed in the balance. "Whether a particular search meets the reasonableness standard is judged by balancing its intrusion on the individual's Fourth Amendment interests against its promotion of legitimate governmental interests." *Acton* at 2390 (internal quotation marks omitted). . . . Dr. Pierce's status as a student-employee in the emergency medicine residency program diminished her legitimate expectations of privacy vis-a-vis the search at issue. . . . "It is plain that certain forms of public employment may diminish privacy expectations even with respect to . . . personal searches." *Von Raab* at 1394. And, as the Court said of Customs employees required to carry firearms or interdict illegal drugs, so also with those similarly situated to Dr. Pierce, "because successful performance of their duties depends uniquely on their judgment and dexterity, these employees cannot reasonably expect to keep from the Service personal information that bears directly on their fitness." *Id.* . . .

Moreover, the intrusiveness of the search here was entirely minimal. There is no evidence that anyone observed, listened to, or otherwise monitored the excretion of the urine sample. The record suggests that Dr. Pierce excreted the sample alone in a bathroom with the door closed. There is certainly nothing to the contrary, or even to suggest that anyone listened at the door. Moreover, Dr. Pierce took the urinalysis at Pathlab, an independent laboratory that she had hand picked herself, without Dr. Smith (or anyone else) being aware that she was going to undergo (or had undergone) such a test, much less at Pathlab, until she turned over the completely negative results to him. . . . There is no evidence that the urinalysis was used to look for, or that its results reflected, anything other than the presence or absence of drugs, such as whether Dr. Pierce was "epileptic, pregnant, or diabetic." *Acton*, 115 S. Ct. at 2393. The results of the test were negative for drugs, and thus, so far as the evidence shows, nothing else about Dr. Pierce was disclosed thereby. Moreover, had the results been positive, Dr. Pierce could have elected not to disclose them.

Finally, other circumstances of the test also point to nonintrusiveness. . . . [A]s noted, the test was not undertaken for law enforcement purposes, law enforcement personnel were not involved, and there was no threat of force and no potential criminal or civil penalty for refusing. . . . Dr. Pierce was orally threatened by Dr. David Smith with dismissal from the residency program if she did not ultimately undergo a drug test arranged by Dr. Robert Smith. However, only the dean of the medical school had the authority to dismiss her (and any dismissal by the dean was subject to suspensive appeal). . . . Dr. Pierce was *never* tested by anyone acting for any governmental agency or official; and, the wholly noninvasive private test she underwent was not one commanded, requested, or anticipated by any state actor.

. . . .

E. Absence of testing policy; Individualized suspicion

Dr. Pierce does not essentially challenge the foregoing analysis, nor does she contend that appellants were required to obtain a warrant or establish probable cause. Instead, she contends that, as it is undisputed that TTUHSC had no drug testing policy for its physicians or residents, the Fourth Amendment accordingly precluded appellants from telling her she would be dismissed if she did not undergo urinalysis arranged by Dr. Robert Smith, *unless* appellants had reasonable, individualized suspicion that she was using illicit drugs. . . .

However, we conclude that the clearly established law does not now, and did not in March 1990, categorically mandate that sort of reasonable, individualized suspicion for all non-law enforcement, minimally intrusive searches in special needs situations, whenever there was no pre-existing policy authorizing the search.

To begin with, neither the Supreme Court nor this Court has ever articulated such a categorical requirement. To the contrary, the Court has repeatedly stated: "the Fourth Amendment imposes no irreducible requirement of such suspicion," *Acton* at 2391; "neither a warrant nor probable cause, nor, indeed, any measure of reasonable suspicion is an indispensable component of reasonableness in every circumstance," *Von Raab* at 1390; "We have made it clear, however, that a showing of individualized suspicion is not a constitutional floor, below which a search must be presumed unreasonable," *Skinner* at 1417; "the Fourth Amendment imposes no irreducible requirement of reasonable suspicion," *United States v. Martinez-Fuerte*, 428 U.S. 543 (1976). It is true, of course, that in each of these cases there was some sort of policy. However, in none of these cases did the Court condition its quoted statements with any sort of proviso, such as "so long as there was a general policy pursuant to which the search was conducted" or the like. To the contrary, as further elaborated below, these opinions indicate that whether individualized suspicion may be dispensed with depends on the particular context and a weighing of the invasiveness of the search against the "special needs" presented. . . .

. . . What the Supreme Court has expressly left open cannot easily be described as clearly established, particularly as we have never ruled on the matter.

. . . .

Moreover, the presence of a testing policy would not have materially ameliorated the situation from the point of view of one in Dr. Pierce's position. Following *Skinner* and *Martinez-Fuerte*, a presumably permissible policy could have provided that a resident guilty of program misconduct sufficient to justify dismissal — as Dr. Pierce surely was — could, in the discretion of the supervisory program officials as part of their evaluation of whether the underlying misconduct should result in the dismissal of the particular resident, be directed to provide the results of a urine drug test in connection with a psychological evaluation, with the penalty for the underlying misconduct to be dismissal in the event of refusal to furnish the test results. . . .

We conclude that in a situation of this character — a non-law enforcement, employer-school search where there are very special needs and the intrusiveness of the search and the subject's privacy interests are minimal — there is not now, and was not in March 1990, any clearly established Fourth Amendment requirement for either an existing general search policy or individualized suspicion of the type required for a law enforcement *Terry* stop for drug possession. This is not to say that there must not be some legitimate reason for the individual being singled out. The search must be reasonable under all the circumstances, balancing the individual's privacy interests against the interests of the governmental institution.

III. Qualified Immunity Here

We turn now to the final qualified immunity issue: would all reasonable state medical school residency program supervisors, similarly situated to Drs. Smith and Binder and with the information they had, have realized that their conduct was unreasonable under all the circumstances, balancing Dr. Pierce's privacy interests against the interests of TTUHSC, and hence invaded Dr. Pierce's Fourth Amendment rights? On the basis of the undisputed historical facts, we answer this question in the negative.

When Dr. Smith, director of the TTUHSC residency program, learned of the February 22 incident at St. Joseph's in Phoenix, he was objectively faced with what could reasonably be considered as a most serious situation. Dr. Pierce, one of the TTUHSC residents in its emergency medicine residency program, while on brief rotation at St. Joseph's, had slapped an emergency room patient in the face. The patient was about to undergo a CAT scan for a possible internal head injury following an automobile accident in which he had smashed through his car's windshield. He was flat on his back on the CAT scan table, was under restraints, and technicians were holding him down. . . .

. . . .

This was not the first time Dr. Pierce had come to the unfavorable attention of the TTUHSC faculty and administration. During the previous summer, a faculty committee had found that her "performance was not up to the level of acceptable standards" and she had been placed on probation for, among other things, excessive tardiness, failing to carry an acceptable number of patients, and poor interpersonal relationships with faculty and patients. At that time in 1989 some of the faculty discussed drug use as one of the possible explanations for Dr. Pierce's behavior. . . .

. . . .

Objectively, there *was* ample, reasonable basis for singling out Dr. Pierce for special scrutiny and investigation of a kind not applicable to others in the residency program. Dr. Pierce, not long after coming off probation, committed serious professional misconduct in her capacity as a member of the residency program. In light of these occurrences, a decision had to be made as to whether, or under what circumstances, TTUHSC would allow her to remain a part of its emergency medicine residency program. Drug test results — like the psychiatric evaluations — were simply to be one part of that decision-making process, not its ultimate focus or sole determinant. Objectively, something caused Dr. Pierce's behavior in the program to be seriously inappropriate. What things associated with her brought this about? Information in this respect could objectively enhance the reliability of the ultimate decision to be made as to the appropriate future for Dr. Pierce in the residency program.

. . . .

REVERSED

NOTES

1. Unlike so many of the other cases involving drug testing policies (including many cited in the opinion), the drug test in *Pierce* was not administered as part of a random drug testing policy; it was based on suspicion of drug use. Should there, then, have been more conversation and emphasis placed on a "reasonable suspicion" test, instead of the factors most often applied in random urinalysis test cases? How would the two-part analysis from *New Jersey v. T.L.O.*, with its emphasis on "reasonable suspicion," have applied here? Was the search justified at its inception? Was it reasonable in scope, with consideration of the age and maturity of the student and the nature and seriousness of the contraband and the alleged infraction?

2. Random, suspicionless urinalysis drug testing programs are much more common in education settings than suspicion-based programs are. In *Hill v. National Collegiate Athletic Association*, 865 P.2d 633 (Cal. 1994), for example, the California Supreme Court upheld the NCAA's random urinalysis drug testing program against a claim that it violated a right to privacy protected by the state constitution.

The California Supreme Court in *Hill* declined to adopt a standard of analysis that would require the NCAA to assert a "compelling interest" in order to justify its urinalysis drug testing policy against the state constitutional privacy interests claimed by the plaintiffs. Two of the dissenting justices, along with each of the lower courts, argued that the policy should be struck down due to the NCAA's failure to show a compelling interest. The majority, on the other hand, offered and applied the following standard:

> (1) First, the plaintiff alleging an invasion of privacy in violation of the state constitutional right to privacy must establish (a) a legally protected privacy interest; (b) a reasonable expectation of privacy in the circumstances; and (c) conduct by defendant constituting a serious invasion of privacy.
>
> (2) Second, the defendant may prevail in a state constitutional privacy case by negating any of the three elements established by the plaintiff or by pleading and proving, as an affirmative defense, that the invasion of privacy is justified because it substantively furthers one or more countervailing interests.

This test, while fashioned around a state constitutional provision and applied in a state supreme court case, *Hill v. NCAA*, bears some resemblance to two later cases, each involving a K-12 school district's random urinalysis drug testing policy and each decided on Fourth Amendment grounds by the United States Supreme Court. In both cases, *Vernonia School District 47J v. Acton*, 515 U.S. 646 (1995), and *Board of Education of Independent School District No. 92 v. Earls*, 536 U.S. 822 (2002), the court applied a three-factor balancing test and upheld the drug testing policy: (a) the nature of the privacy interest, (b) the character and seriousness of the intrusion, and (c) the nature of the governmental interest. In each case, the Court's majority found that the students' privacy interests were diminished due to the students' acceptance of additional rules and regulations and their representation of the school in athletics (*Vernonia* and *Earls*) and other competitive extracurricular activities (*Earls* only). Similarly, the Courts in *Vernonia* and *Earls* held that the intrusion was negligible, praising the schools for their handling of the students' privacy, sensitivity, sample collection and processing, and record-keeping. Finally, each Court noted the significant interest present in safe and healthy students and in a drug-free school setting. In fact, the Court in *Vernonia* and *Earls* borrowed language from *Treasury Employees v. Von Raab*, 489 U.S. 656 (1989), and found the government's interest in implementing drug testing policies to be "compelling," particularly on the question of whether individualized suspicion is required: "In certain limited circumstances, the Government's need to discover such latent or hidden conditions, or to prevent their development, is sufficiently compelling to justify the intrusion on privacy entailed by conducting such searches without any measure of individualized suspicion." *Earls*, 536 U.S. at 829.

3. Note that the random, urinalysis drug testing policy upheld in *Earls* applied to students in athletics and all other competitive extracurricular activities. What about the application of similar drug testing policies in higher education? Would such policies be advisable under similar institutional interests of health, safety, and student representation of the university? Would they be lawful under a similar three-part analysis? What about any differences that come from the fact that the policy in *Hill v. NCAA* was enacted by the NCAA and its member institutions and the policies in *Vernonia* and *Earls* were enacted by one school system? It would seem that such institutional policies would pass constitutional muster after cases like *Hill*, *Earls*, and *Vernonia*. An earlier state court case, however, held otherwise. In *University of Colorado v. Derdeyn*, 863 P.2d 929 (Colo. 1993), the state appeals court struck down an institutional random, suspicionless drug testing program for student-athletes under both the state and federal constitutions. The court found that the students' expectations of privacy were not diminished by their status as student-athletes and that the policy was significantly intrusive. Furthermore, the court did not find the stated governmental interest to be sufficiently compelling. Finally, against the grain of later cases on the subject, the court found that the required consent to the tests was not voluntary, despite the extracurricular nature of participation in collegiate athletics.

4. How is the NCAA, a private institution, subject to the requirements of state and federal constitutional provisions, like the Fourth Amendment and related state constitutional provisions? More fundamentally, is the NCAA a state actor for the purposes of constitutional analyses? The answer to this second question is seemingly "no" according to the Supreme Court in *NCAA v. Tarkanian*, 488 U.S. 179 (1988), where Jerry Tarkanian, the then-current coach of the men's basketball team at the University of Nevada, Las Vegas, filed suit against the NCAA, claiming due process violations after the NCAA suspended him for a number of rules violations. The Court held in a 5-4 decision that the actions of the NCAA in promulgating and enforcing rules did not amount to state action. For a full discussion of *Tarkanian*, see Chapter VIII.

A precursor to *Tarkanian* was *Barbay v. NCAA*, No. 86-5697, 1987 U.S. Dist. LEXIS 393 (E.D. La. Jan. 20, 1987), which involved a challenge to a suspension of an athlete for testing positive for steroid use. Under NCAA regulations, the athlete was declared ineligible to participate in a college football bowl game. The college athlete filed suit under Section 1983 of the Civil Rights Act of 1871. The court dismissed the suit, holding that the NCAA is not a state actor and, therefore, is not subject to Section 1983. The court held that the regulation of collegiate athletics was not a function reserved to the state.

The question of whether the NCAA is a state actor resurfaces periodically. Several years after *Tarkanian*, in *Brentwood Academy v. Tennessee Secondary School Athletic Association*, 531 U.S. 288 (2001), the Court (in another 5-4 decision) held that the state-level athletics associations that oversee K-12 athletics are, indeed, state actors due in large part to the fact that the member institutions all come from the same state. *See also* James Potter, *The NCAA as State Actor: Tarkanian, Brentwood, and Due Process*, 155 U. Pa. L. Rev. 1269 (2007).

Chapter VIII

INTERCOLLEGIATE ATHLETICS

Introduction

Collegiate athletics have held a central role in the American university system since the first boat race between Yale and Harvard universities in 1852. *See* James L. Shulman & William G. Bowen, The Game of Life: College Sports and Educational Values, 5–6 (2001). By fostering school spirit through competition, providing scholarships to students who would otherwise be unable to attend, and generating both revenue and acclaim for universities, athletics quickly established itself as a major focus of the educational institution. As collegiate athletics have evolved over the years one criticism is that this student-based enterprise has begun to look more like professional sports and less like amateur-level competition. Many collegiate sporting events are now nationally broadcast and viewed by an audience of millions. Further, the revenue produced from events and team merchandising is a substantial source of income for many universities. Competition between student-athletes has spawned the creation of intercollegiate associations, like the National Collegiate Athletic Association (NCAA), charged with the promethean task of regulating and maintaining the amateur nature of college athletics. This gradual shift away from amateurism has created a multitude of complex legal issues facing today's academic institutions, college sports, and intercollegiate associations. This chapter addresses a few of the most controversial and heavily litigated areas of concern.

With the amateur nature of athletics veering into increasingly questionable territory, the university has been forced to strike a balance between athletics and scholastic concerns. Section A of this chapter discusses the issues surrounding the rise of big business and intercollegiate competition. As sporting events, under the direction and authority of organizations like the NCAA, became larger and higher profile, so did the potential to generate exponential profits. These earnings create financial incentives for universities to over-emphasize the role of athletics in the academic institution and possibly massage the rules of athletic associations. *See* Taylor Branch, *The Shame of College Sports*, Atlantic Monthly Magazine, Oct. 2011, *available at* http://www.theatlantic.com/magazine/archive/2011/10/the-shame-of-college-sports/8643/1/. Additionally, controversy surrounds the debate over who should be the recipient of these funds: Should athletes themselves be compensated financially for their talents? Should all the money be distributed to universities? What portion should intercollegiate associations receive? Section B concerns the rights and obligations that accompany athletic scholarships. Generally, the judiciary has analyzed the rights and obligations of student-athletes under the protected interest doctrine of contract law where the terms of the scholarship contract dictate the rights and duties of students and universities. *See Conard v. Univ. of Wash.*, 834

P.2d 17 (Wash. 1992). A case decided by a federal court in Illinois introduces a discussion of the tort "educational malpractice" aimed at compensating student-athletes whose universities, in their rush to craft winning sports teams from students not traditionally equipped for college academics, fail to adequately educate. *Ross v. Creighton Univ.*, 740 F. Supp. 1319 (N.D. Ill. 1990). As a policy matter, what effect might such a tort have on the operation of collegiate sports? Should a university owe any duty to its student-athletes beyond the confines of express contractual language? As collegiate sports teams have grown and expanded, so has the potential for liability. Section C describes the boundaries of university accountability for student-athlete injuries. The duty of care analysis presents potential problems for both the student-athlete plaintiff and the university defendant. *See Kleinknecht v. Gettysburg Coll.*, 989 F.2d 1360 (3d Cir. 1993). Additionally, determining when, and to what extent, injuries are foreseeable can be extremely challenging for universities when student-athletes attend practices and university-sponsored events on a daily basis. Do universities owe any duty to prevent certain injuries to students? If so, what types of preventive measures would satisfy this obligation?

The resurgence in women's rights activism in the 1960s helped usher in a new set of federal legislation, including Title IX of the Education Amendments of 1972. Title IX addresses gender discrimination in education and is applicable to any institution receiving federal financial assistance. Section D discusses some of the issues surrounding Title IX compliance and gender equality in intercollegiate athletics. Deciding whether or not a particular athletic-program framework is discriminatory can be a complex task. Following the passage of Title IX, the Department of Health, Education, and Welfare (and later the Department of Education) released a series of regulations intended to aid educational institutions in monitoring and maintaining compliance. Generally, gender equality in collegiate athletics is measured by interrelated factors including, but not limited to, the proportionality of opportunities to enrollment, the quality and quantity of the resources devoted to the different programs, and the particular history of underrepresentation and response in the institution. *See* 34 C.F.R. § 106; *see also Cohen v. Brown Univ.*, 991 F.2d 888 (1st Cir. 1993). Title IX compliance has forced university officials to change the way they think about intercollegiate athletics and sports related programs such as cheerleading. What sorts of legal challenges and issues might be raised when a university decides to cut well-established male sports teams in order to maintain compliance? Are male-dominated sports entitled to the same protections as women's sports?

Turning towards the heavily regulated (and highly controversial) area of intercollegiate competition, Section E lays out some of the various legal issues regarding athletic associations and conferences. Because athletic associations can regulate and penalize state-run universities and schools, the judiciary has grappled with the question of whether such organizations can properly be considered state actors such that their decisions must comply with constitutional mandates. *See NCAA v. Tarkanian*, 488 U.S. 179 (1988). Also, there is continuing debate about the applicability of the Sherman Act's antitrust regulations to athletic associations. Athletic associations with exclusive control over the operation and lucrative broadcast rights to intercollegiate competitions naturally close out potential competitors in television broadcasting. What are the justifications for these anti-competitive effects in the broadcast market? Further, athletic associations, like the NCAA, attempt to protect amateurism in college sports by promulgating and enforcing an expansive list of rigid regulations affecting both universities and students. This section provides a description of some of the problems created by these rules and the reasons some groups are organizing to decentralize the field of amateur sports. While reading this chapter, it is important to keep in mind the role policy and tradition play in shaping the changes and advances in intercollegiate athletics.

A. AMATEUR ATHLETES, BIG BUSINESS

James L. Shulman & William G. Bowen, The Game of Life: College Sports and Educational Values, 5–6, 9–10 (2001)*

The world of college sports garners a great deal of attention on the pages of the leading newspapers and magazines and in radio and television coverage of sports events. There is no denying that attention given to the NCAA basketball tournament, debates over equal opportunity for women to compete at the intercollegiate level, admissions standards for athletes, an array of highly publicized scandals concerning illegal payments to athletes, and methods of ranking football teams for the purposes of post-season competition. It seems clear that our revealed preference, as a society, is for an extensive commitment to sports within higher education. Anyone who wants to claim that sports has no place in a college or university is quickly going to run headlong into both the insatiable appetite for sports that is evident in our daily lives — and the reality of history.

The first intercollegiate athletic contest took place in 1852 when boats from Harvard and Yale raced on Lake Winnipesaukee in New Hampshire. Though historians record the participants as having thought of the race as "a jolly lark," historian Ronald Smith notes that the first boat race was sponsored by a real estate promoter who was selling land in the area. We should not believe that commercial ties to athletics arose only recently. The race signaled the beginning of an enterprise that would grow rapidly during the second half of the nineteenth century.

In 1859 Williams lost to Amherst in the first intercollegiate baseball game (by a score of 73–32!), and in 1869 Princeton lost to Rutgers in the first football game. But how did such student-organized athletic competitions become embedded in the very core of the leading educational institutions in the country?

. . . .

No other historical development in intercollegiate athletics has been as influential, or as subtle, as the progressive institutionalization of the athletic clubs that students once ran. In institutionalizing these programs, the schools have, in effect, declared, "this is something that we do." This act of assuming ownership of the enterprise has led to a tacit or explicit sanctioning of the goals, values, and norms associated with college sports in a way that has allowed the athletic enterprise to have access to the inner chambers where the educational mission of the school is defined and pursued.

A few attempts were made to resist the institutionalization of college sports. The most notable of these was undertaken by Robert Maynard Hutchins, who declared in 1939 that the University of Chicago (a charter member of the Big Ten) would drop its football program. While Hutchins decried many of the ongoing abuses, his sharpest insight was that how and why colleges play sports tells us a great deal about how they set their overall agendas:

> Several universities have dropped football; but the reason they have stated shows how little they trust the public to understand a good reason for doing so. Almost all universities that have given up the game have said that football lost money. As the public is willing to believe that a university may do anything for money, so it is prepared to agree that it may stop doing it if the money is not forthcoming. If the curriculum were rational and intelligible, the students might not run from it in such large numbers to devote themselves to extracurricular activities.

Hutchins was prescient in seeing the ways that sports were being allowed to influence a school's mission: by inducing schools to follow the money instead of the more abstract academic goals that were central to them and by providing the public with something that was more fun, and more easily digestible, than dry academic debates. But Hutchins's view would not win in the debate over athletics outside Chicago. Standing on principle but losing in the war of public opinion, the University of Chicago's attempt at de-emphasis was based on grounds of institutional control over its own mission and the importance of being able to set its own priorities. Yet the public's continued preference for the clarity of the scoreboard over the confusing goals of the curriculum made Hutchins's decision seem idiosyncratic, out of touch, and, in the minds of some, downright wimpy.

Much later, in the 1970s and 1980s, other college presidents chose to take a stand on the appropriate way to conduct athletics. Paul Hardin's tenure as president of SMU ended abruptly after he brought to light corruption in the athletic department, disciplined the coaches who were involved in it, and made it clear that under his administration all conference and NCAA rules would be followed regardless of the standards set by other schools and whether or not violations known to the school were likely to be discovered externally. . . . In 1990, the Michigan State football coach was also appointed to serve as athletic director, despite President John DiBiaggio's warning to his board that this would be a dangerous arrangement; DiBiaggio subsequently left Michigan State and became president of Tufts. Courage among presidents on questions of athletics rarely portends a long tenure.

TAYLOR BRANCH, *THE SHAME OF COLLEGE SPORTS*, ATLANTIC MONTHLY MAGAZINE, Oct. 2011,* http://www.theatlantic.com/magazine/archive/2011/10/the-shame-of-college-sports/8643/1/

"I'M NOT HIDING," Sonny Vaccaro told a closed hearing at the Willard Hotel in Washington, D.C., in 2001. "We want to put our materials on the bodies of your athletes, and the best way to do that is buy your school. Or buy your coach."

Vaccaro's audience, the members of the Knight Commission on Intercollegiate Athletics, bristled. These were eminent reformers — among them the president of the National Collegiate Athletic Association, two former heads of the U.S. Olympic Committee, and several university presidents and chancellors. The Knight Foundation, a nonprofit that takes an interest in college athletics as part of its concern with civic life, had tasked them with saving college sports from runaway commercialism as embodied by the likes of Vaccaro, who, since signing his pioneering shoe contract with Michael Jordan in 1984, had built sponsorship empires successively at Nike, Adidas, and Reebok. Not all the members could hide their scorn for the "sneaker pimp" of schoolyard hustle, who boasted of writing checks for millions to everybody in higher education.

"Why," asked Bryce Jordan, the president emeritus of Penn State, "should a university be an advertising medium for your industry?"

Vaccaro did not blink. "They shouldn't, sir," he replied. "You sold your souls, and you're going to continue selling them. You can be very moral and righteous in asking me that question, sir," Vaccaro added with irrepressible good cheer, "but there's not one of you in this room that's going to turn down any of our money. You're going to take it. I can only offer it."

. . . .

. . . [W]hat Vaccaro said in 2001 was true then, and it's true now: corporations offer money so they can profit from the glory of college athletes, and the universities grab it. In 2010, despite the faltering economy, a single college athletic league, the football-crazed Southeastern Conference (SEC), became the first to crack the billion-dollar barrier in athletic receipts. The Big Ten pursued closely at $905 million.

. . . .

With so many people paying for tickets and watching on television, college sports has become Very Big Business. According to various reports, the football teams at Texas, Florida, Georgia, Michigan, and Penn State — to name just a few big-revenue football schools — each earn between $40 million and $80 million in profits a year, even after paying coaches multimillion-dollar salaries. When you combine so much money with such high, almost tribal, stakes — football boosters are famously rabid in their zeal to have their alma mater win — corruption [and scandal are] . . . likely to follow.

. . . .

For all the outrage, the real scandal is not that students are getting illegally paid or recruited, it's that two of the noble principles on which the NCAA justifies its existence — "amateurism" and the "student-athlete" — are cynical hoaxes, legalistic confections propagated by the universities so they can exploit the skills and fame of young athletes. The tragedy at the heart of college sports is not that some college athletes are getting paid, but that more of them are not.

. . . .

Fans and educators alike recoil from this proposal as though from original sin. Amateurism is the whole point, they say. Paid athletes would destroy the integrity and appeal of college sports. Many former college athletes object that money would have spoiled the sanctity of the bond they enjoyed with their teammates. I, too, once shuddered instinctively at the notion of paid college athletes.

But after an inquiry that took me into locker rooms and ivory towers across the country, I have come to believe that sentiment blinds us to what's before our eyes. Big-time college sports are fully commercialized. Billions of dollars flow through them each year. The NCAA makes money, and enables universities and corporations to make money, from the unpaid labor of young athletes.

Slavery analogies should be used carefully. College athletes are not slaves. Yet to survey the scene — corporations and universities enriching themselves on the backs of uncompensated young men, whose status as "student-athletes" deprives them of the right to due process guaranteed by the Constitution — is to catch an unmistakable whiff of the plantation. Perhaps a more apt metaphor is colonialism: college sports, as overseen by the NCAA, is a system imposed by well-meaning paternalists and rationalized with hoary sentiments about caring for the well-being of the colonized. But it is, nonetheless, unjust. The NCAA, in its zealous defense of bogus principles, sometimes destroys the dreams of innocent young athletes.

The NCAA today is in many ways a classic cartel. Efforts to reform it — most notably by the three Knight Commissions over the course of 20 years — have, while making changes around the edges, been largely fruitless. The time has come for a major overhaul. And whether the powers that be like it or not, big changes are coming. Threats loom on multiple fronts: in Congress, the courts, breakaway athletic conferences, student rebellion, and public disgust. Swaddled in gauzy clichés, the NCAA presides over a vast, teetering glory.

. . . .

The Myth of the "Student-Athlete"

Today, much of the NCAA's moral authority — indeed much of the justification for its existence — is vested in its claim to protect what it calls the "student-athlete." The term is meant to conjure the nobility of amateurism, and the precedence of scholarship over athletic endeavor. But the origins of the "student-athlete" lie not in a disinterested ideal but in a sophistic formulation designed, as the sports economist Andrew Zimbalist has written, to help the NCAA in its "fight against workmen's compensation insurance claims for injured football players."

"We crafted the term student-athlete," Walter Byers himself wrote, "and soon it was embedded in all NCAA rules and interpretations." The term came into play in the 1950s, when the widow of Ray Dennison, who had died from a head injury received while playing football in Colorado for the Fort Lewis A&M Aggies, filed for workmen's-compensation death benefits. Did his football scholarship make the fatal collision a "work-related" accident? Was he a school employee, like his peers who worked part-time as teaching assistants and bookstore cashiers? Or was he a fluke victim of extracurricular pursuits? Given the hundreds of incapacitating injuries to college athletes each year, the answers to these questions had enormous consequences. The Colorado Supreme Court ultimately agreed with the school's contention that he was not eligible for benefits, since the college was "not in the football business."

The term student-athlete was deliberately ambiguous. College players were not students at play (which might understate their athletic obligations), nor were they just athletes in college (which might imply they were professionals). That they were high-performance athletes meant they could be forgiven for not meeting the academic standards of their peers; that they were students meant they did not have to be compensated, ever, for anything more than the cost of their studies. Student-athlete became the NCAA's signature term, repeated constantly in and out of courtrooms.

. . . .

"They Want to Crush These Kids"

Academic performance has always been difficult for the NCAA to address. Any detailed regulation would intrude upon the free choice of widely varying schools, and any academic standard broad enough to fit both MIT and Ole Miss would have little force. From time to time, a scandal will expose extreme lapses. In 1989, Dexter Manley, by then the famous "Secretary of Defense" for the NFL's Washington Redskins, teared up before the U.S. Senate Subcommittee on Education, Arts, and Humanities, when admitting that he had been functionally illiterate in college.

Within big-time college athletic departments, the financial pressure to disregard obvious academic shortcomings and shortcuts is just too strong. In the 1980s, Jan Kemp, an English instructor at the University of Georgia, publicly alleged that university officials had demoted and then fired her because she refused to inflate grades in her remedial English courses. Documents showed that administrators replaced the grades she'd given athletes with higher ones, providing fake passing grades on one notable occasion to nine Bulldog football players who otherwise would have been ineligible to compete in the 1982 Sugar Bowl. (Georgia lost anyway, 24–20, to a University of Pittsburgh team led by the future Hall of Fame quarterback Dan Marino.) When Kemp filed a lawsuit against the university, she was publicly vilified as a troublemaker, but she persisted bravely in her testimony. Once, Kemp said, a supervisor demanding that she fix a grade had bellowed, "Who do you think is more important to this university, you or Dominique Wilkins?" (Wilkins was a star on the basketball team.) Traumatized, Kemp twice attempted suicide.

In trying to defend themselves, Georgia officials portrayed Kemp as naive about sports. "We have to compete on a level playing field," said Fred Davison, the university president. During the Kemp civil trial, in 1986, Hale Almand, Georgia's defense lawyer, explained the university's patronizing aspirations for its typical less-than-scholarly athlete. "We may not make a university student out of him," Almand told the court, "but if we can teach him to read and write, maybe he can work at the post office rather than as a garbage man when he gets through with his athletic career." This argument backfired with the jurors: finding in favor of Kemp, they rejected her polite request for $100,000, and awarded her $2.6 million in damages instead. (This was later reduced to $1.08 million.) Jan Kemp embodied what is ostensibly the NCAA's reason for being — to enforce standards fairly and put studies above sports — but no one from the organization ever spoke up on her behalf.

. . . .

"The Plantation Mentality"

"Ninety percent of the NCAA revenue is produced by 1 percent of the athletes," Sonny Vaccaro says. "Go to the skill positions" — the stars. "Ninety percent African Americans." The NCAA made its money off those kids, and so did he. They were not all bad people, the NCAA officials, but they were blind, Vaccaro believes. "Their organization is a fraud."

. . . .

Jon King, an antitrust lawyer at Hausfeld LLP in San Francisco, told me that Vaccaro "opened our eyes to massive revenue streams hidden in college sports." King and his colleagues have drawn on Vaccaro's vast knowledge of athletic-department finances, which include off-budget accounts for shoe contracts. Sonny Vaccaro and his wife, Pam, "had a mountain of documents . . ."

. . . .

The college player cannot sell his own feet (the coach does that) nor can he sell his own name (the college will do that). This is the plantation mentality resurrected and blessed by today's campus executives.

. . . .

IN 2010 THE third Knight Commission, complementing a previous commission's recommendation for published reports on academic progress, called for the finances of college sports to be made transparent and public — television contracts, conference budgets, shoe deals, coaches' salaries, stadium bonds, everything. The recommendation was based on the worthy truism that sunlight is a proven disinfectant. But in practice, it has not been applied at all. Conferences, coaches, and other stakeholders resisted disclosure; college players still have no way of determining their value to the university.

. . . .

The most basic reform would treat the students as what they are — adults, with rights and reason of their own — and grant them a meaningful voice in NCAA deliberations. A restoration of full citizenship to "student-athletes" would facilitate open governance, making it possible to enforce pledges of transparency in both academic standards and athletic finances. Without that, the NCAA has no effective checks and balances, no way for the students to provide informed consent regarding the way they are governed. A thousand questions lie willfully silenced because the NCAA is naturally afraid of giving "student-athletes" a true voice. Would college players be content with the augmented scholarship or allowance now requested by the National College Players Association? If a player's worth to the university is greater than the value of his scholarship (as it clearly is in some cases), should he be paid a salary? If so, would teammates in revenue sports want to be paid equally, or in salaries stratified according to talent or value on the field? What would the athletes want in Division III, where athletic budgets keep rising without scholarships or substantial sports revenue? Would athletes seek more or less variance in admissions standards? Should non-athletes also have a voice, especially where involuntary student fees support more and more of college sports? Might some schools choose to specialize, paying players only in elite leagues for football, or lacrosse? In athletic councils, how much would high-revenue athletes value a simple thank you from the tennis or field-hockey players for the newly specified subsidies to their facilities?

. . . .

The greatest threat to the viability of the NCAA may come from its member universities. Many experts believe that the churning instability within college football will drive the next major change. President Obama himself has endorsed the drumbeat cry for a national playoff in college football. This past spring, the Justice Department questioned the BCS about its adherence to antitrust standards. Jim Delany, the commissioner of the Big Ten, has estimated that a national playoff system could produce three or four times as much money as the existing bowl system does. If a significant band of football schools were to demonstrate that they could orchestrate a true national playoff, without the NCAA's assistance, the association would be terrified — and with good reason. Because if the big sports colleges don't need the NCAA to administer a national playoff in football, then they don't need it to do so in basketball. In which case, they could cut out the middleman in March Madness and run the tournament themselves. Which would deprive the NCAA of close to $1 billion a year, more than 95 percent of its revenue. The organization would be reduced to a rule book without money — an organization aspiring to enforce its rules but without the financial authority to enforce anything.

ANDREW ZIMBALIST, UNPAID PROFESSIONALS: COMMERCIALISM AND CONFLICT IN BIG-TIME COLLEGE SPORTS 3–6 (1999)*

On page one of the 1997–98 NCAA Manual the basic purpose of the National Collegiate Athletic Association is written: "to maintain intercollegiate athletics as an integral part of the educational program and the athlete as an integral part of the student body and, by doing so, retain a clear line of demarcation between intercollegiate athletics and professional sports." Some may wonder whom do they think they are kidding.

In December 1996, Notre Dame was playing its final regular season football game against the University of Southern California. The Notre Dame placekicker missed an extra point at the end of the fourth quarter and the game went into overtime where Notre Dame lost, 27–21. The loss quashed Notre Dame's bid to go to an Alliance Bowl game, which would have been worth $8 million to the school. The Fighting Irish turned down an invitation to the $800,000 Independence Bowl. The placekicker blew an $8 million extra point!

Notre Dame has a 7-year, $45 million contract with NBC to televise its regular season games. The major conferences have a $700 million, 7-year contract with ABC to televise the bowl championship series beginning in 1998–99. The NCAA has a $1.725 billion 8–year contract with CBS to broadcast its annual men's basketball tournament.

Like the professional leagues, the NCAA promotes its own line of licensed clothing, as do its leading colleges. Like the National Basketball Association (NBA) and the National Football League (NFL), the NCAA has its own traveling tent show — NCAA Hoop City. It has its own marketing division. Its corporate sponsorships have increased roughly sevenfold in the nineties, with guaranteed income of $75 million between 1997 and 2002. It has its own real estate subsidiary and even its own Learjet. In 1997, the NCAA cut a deal with the city of Indianapolis to build it a new headquarters and provide an estimated $50 million in subsidies, leaving three hundred employees and forty-five years of tradition behind in Kansas City.

The NCAA's total budget, which surpasses $270 million in 1997–98, has grown at an annual rate of 15 percent since 1982. Its Executive Director, Cedric Dempsey, has done even better than this. His salary and benefits package grew 30.2 percent in fiscal 1997 to $647,000, as part of a new five-year deal. Dempsey replaced Dick Schultz in 1993 when the latter ran into ethical problems. As punishment, the Association gave Schultz a golden parachute worth at least $700,000.

Dempsey also gets treated well when he attends the Final Four of the annual basketball tournament. The Kansas City Star reports that "the manual for cities holding Final Fours requires a series of gifts to be delivered every night to the hotel rooms of NCAA officials. These [mementos] cost Indianapolis an estimated $25,000 [in March 1997]. . . . At a minimum, gifts for each official included a Samsonite suit bag, a Final Four ticket embedded in Lucite, a Limoges porcelain basketball and Steuben glass." And to maximize revenue at the Final Four, the NCAA has spurned normal-sized basketball venues and instead chosen cavernous arenas such as the New Orleans Superdome, the San Antonio Alamodome, the St. Louis Trans World Dome, the Indianapolis RCA Dome, and the Georgia Dome, all with seating capacities in excess of forty thousand.

With big bucks dangling before their eyes, many NCAA schools find the temptations of success too alluring to worry about the rules. Schools cheat. They cheat by arranging to help their prospective athletes pass standardized tests. They cheat by providing illegal payments to their recruits. They cheat by setting up special rinky-dink curricula so their athletes can stay qualified. And when one school cheats, others feel compelled to do the same. Then the NCAA passes new rules to curtail the cheating. Sometimes the rules are enforced, sometimes not, but rarely is the penalty harsh enough to be a serious deterrent. The solution, it turns out, is more rules. The NCAA Manual has grown in size from 161 pages in 1970–71 to 579 pages in 1996–97 (and the pages increased in size from 6 x 8 1/2 inches prior to 1989 to 8 1/2 x 11 inches after). In 1998–99, the Manual became so long that the NCAA broke it into three volumes, with 1,268 pages . . . .

So what is the "clear line of demarcation between intercollegiate athletics and professional sports"? It certain is not the presence or absence of commercialism and corporate interests. Rather, two differences stand out. First, unlike their handsomely remunerated coaches and athletic directors (ADs), college athletes don't get paid. Second, the NCAA and its member schools, construed to be amateur organizations promoting an educational mission, do not pay taxes on their millions from TV deals, sponsorships, licensing, or Final Four tickets.

. . . .

In the end, college sports leads a schizophrenic existence, encompassing both amateur and professional elements. The courts, the IRS, and sometimes the universities themselves cannot seem to decide whether to treat intercollegiate athletics as part of the educational process or as a business. The NCAA claims that it manages college sports in a way that promotes both the goals of higher education and the financial condition of the university. Critics say it does neither.

The NCAA wants it both ways. When confronted by the challenges of Title IX and gender equity, the NCAA and its member schools want to be treated as a business. ADs argue that that it is justifiable to put more resources into men's than women's sports, because men's sports generate more revenue. But when the IRS knocks on its door, the NCAA and its member schools want their special tax exemptions as part of the non-profit educational establishment and they claim special amateur status in order to avoid paying their athletes.

Big-time intercollegiate athletics is a unique industry. No other industry in the United States manages not to pay its principal producers a wage or salary. Rather than having many competing firms, big-time college sports is organized as a cartel, like OPEC, through the NCAA

. . . .

Externalities is the word economists use for a phenomenon that arises when a producer or consumer takes an action but does not bear all the costs (negative externality) or receive all the benefits (positive externality) of the action. College sports generates both positive and negative externalities. Among the positive externalities are that they provide a source of entertainment for tens of millions of Americans and of school spirit for college students. Among the negative externalities are that college sports compromise the intellectual standards and educational process at U.S. universities. The challenge is to reform the system in a way that preserves the positives and minimizes the negatives. If the experience with the contradictions and imperfections of college sports over the last hundred years has taught us anything, it is that there are no quick fixes or ideal outcomes. . . .

NOTES

1. Whether to compensate student-athletes for their athletic performance and promotion of the university has long been a source of contention. However, *The Shame of College Athletes*, with its no-nonsense look into the "big business" of student-athletes, has been called "the most important article ever written about college sports." Frank Deford, *The NCAA and the So-Called Student-Athlete*, NPR NEWS, Sept. 14, 2011, *available at* http://www.npr.org/2011/09/14/140433661/the-ncaa-and-the-so-called-student-athlete.

Aside from the general controversial nature of the article, Branch makes use of some provocative analogies: slavery and colonialism. Consider, though, these analogies in light of their barebones definitions, stripped of their usually blinding negative historical connotations.

Merriam Webster defines "slave" as "a person held in servitude as the chattel of another" or "one that is completely subservient to a dominating influence." Based on this definition, is Branch's comparison of collegiate athletics to slavery so inflammatory? Are student-athletes, in essence, completely subservient to the university, the program, and the NCAA? Could athletes' bodies, physicality, and likeness be considered chattel — especially when it comes to the university profiting off of certain jerseys, socks, shoes, or hats that specifically represent one star athlete?

Branch also compares the NCAA and college athletes as having a relationship similar to one of colonialism. Merriam Webster defines "colonialism" as "control by one power over a dependent area or people." Is there any arguing with Branch's classification of the NCAA as an all-powerful colonial power?

2. Professor John C. Weistart has described the state of collegiate basketball and football programs as "The Great American Non Sequitur":

> We have, in this country, embraced the not-wholly-logical notion that if a young man exhibits certain unusual physical skills and wants to secure refinement of his talent, he must also be both motivated and qualified to go to college. Stated more precisely, the notion has even less coherency: a young man who shows promise in the physical skills associated with basketball and football — but not in the areas of baseball, hockey, tennis and golf — must also be academically inclined if he desires to secure further high level pre-professional training. The point, of course, is that college sports effectively provide the only avenue for further training for talented high school football and basketball players.

John C. Weistart, *Legal Accountability and the NCAA*, 10 J.C. & U.L. 167, 174 (1983)*. Assuming the validity of the observation — while acknowledging that the NBA now only allows basketball players to move to the professional level after the first year of college or after sitting one year after high school — are colleges and universities to blame for the prominence of basketball and football programs? Is it inevitable that these programs have evolved the way they have because the NBA and NFL don't have "minor leagues" to develop talent?

3. Professor Stanton Wheeler developed this solution to the "Great American Non Sequitur," suggesting that the NBA, NFL, and NCAA set up a training program for college-aged athletes who do not wish or are not ready for a college education. Stanton Wheeler, *Rethinking Amateurism and the NCAA*, 15 Stan. L. & Pol'y Rev. 213, 234–35 (2004). The NCAA could provide "know-how and experience" with the age group in question and the professional leagues could pay in exchange for the colleges serving essentially as minor league teams. *Id.* at 234. Although colleges would lose some star power, they would make it up in athletes who choose to go to college instead of being forced into it by the system. *Id.* at 235. As Wheeler himself admits, such a collaboration is unlikely to occur. But isn't there some merit in the observation that making aspirant professional athletes attend college against their will is ultimately unfruitful for both the athletes and the schools? Or, given the tiny percentage of college athletes who actually make it to the professional level, would creating some type of alternative along the lines suggested by Wheeler only serve to deprive young athletes of an educational safety net when their professional dreams fail?

4. The creation of the term "student-athlete" has its roots in the NCAA and its member institutions trying to avoid being treated as employers of collegiate athletes. In 1954, the Colorado Supreme Court upheld the ruling of the state industrial commission that a football player at the University of Denver was an "employee," thus making the university liable for his football-related injuries. Worried that other courts and workers' compensation agencies would follow suit, the NCAA coined the term "student-athlete," placed it in its rules and interpretations, and encouraged college presidents to use the term. Robert A. McCormick & Amy Christian McCormick, *The Myth of the Student-Athlete: The College Athlete as Employee*, 81 Wash. L. Rev. 71, 83–84 (2006). This trend only accelerated when, in 1956, postsecondary schools sanctioned full athletic grants to recruit athletes, an arrangement that could be construed as an employer-employee relationship. *Id.* at 84–85.

5. Many argue that paying student-athletes will diminish the "integrity" of college sports, turning collegiate athletics into nothing more than another "minor league" of sorts. If you agree with these sentiments, how do you respond to those who point to the Olympics as a rebuttal? Many of these "diminished integrity" fears were voiced during the debate in the 1970's and 80's over the Olympics required "amateur status." Today, as you are probably well aware, athletes are no longer restricted from receiving money or endorsements. Do you think of the Olympics as any more tainted now than they were in the '70s? Also consider the fact that the NCAA refused to let Michael Phelps swim for his alma mater, the University of Michigan, because of his status as an Olympian and the perks that come along with it. Does this seem fair? Should the NCAA force athletes to give up their collegiate career if they choose, for a year, to train with the Olympic team? Why or why not?

6. The Chronicle of Higher Education conducted a forum in which it asked participants "who should and should not go to college." Richard K. Vedder, director of the Center for College Affordability and Productivity and professor of economics at Ohio University said:

> A large subset of our population should not go to college, or at least not at public expense. The number of new jobs requiring a college degree is now less than the number of young adults graduating from universities, so more and more graduates are filling jobs for which they are academically overqualified.

Are Too Many Students Going to College?, THE CHRON. OF HIGHER EDUC., Nov. 8, 2009,* *available at* http://chronicle.com/article/Are-Too-Many-Students-Going-to/49039/. Bryan Caplan, associate professor of economics at George Mason University added:

> There are two ways to read this question. One is: "Who gets a good financial and/or personal return from college?" My answer: people in the top 25 percent of academic ability who also have the work ethic to actually finish college. The other way to read this is: "For whom is college attendance socially beneficial?" My answer: no more than 5 percent of high-school graduates, because college is mostly what economists call a "signaling game." Most college courses teach few useful job skills; their main function is to signal to employers that students are smart, hard-working, and conformist. The upshot: Going to college is a lot like standing up at a concert to see better. Selfishly speaking, it works, but from a social point of view, we shouldn't encourage it.

Id. However, Sandy Baum, professor emeritus of economics at Skidmore College and senior policy analyst for the College Board responded: "Everyone should have the opportunity to continue his or her education after high school without finances creating an insurmountable barrier. For individuals whose goal is a four-year degree, beginning at a four-year college is generally the most promising option. For others, different types of institutions may be more appropriate." *Id.*

As the debate rages on as to whether or not too many students attend college, does the discussion bolster the idea that athletes should be allowed to participate in minor league sports rather than be forced to go to college? If too many non-athlete students are attending colleges, then should society force athletes to receive an unwanted or unnecessary education? Keep in mind, people who receive a four-year degree still receive a wage premium. Charles Murray, a political scientist and scholar at the American Enterprise Institute, reflected on this issue:

> A large wage premium for having a bachelor's degree still exists. For everything except degrees in engineering and the hard sciences, I submit that most of that premium is associated with the role of the B.A. as a job requirement instead of anything that students with B.A.'s actually learn. The solution to that injustice — and it is one of the most problematic social injustices in contemporary America — is to give students a way to show employers what they know, not where they learned it and how long it took them. In other words, substitute certifications for the bachelor's degree.

Id. Does it change your mind that only one percent of college athletes go on to play professionally? Stacey A. Teicher, *College Athletes Tackle Their Financial Future*, The Christian Sci. Monitor, Oct. 3, 2005, *available at* http://www.csmonitor.com/2005/1003/p13s02-legn.html. Do critics of college athletics focus too much on one percent of student-athletes instead of focusing on the majority that receive educations and go on to other careers? Since student-athletes are undeniably a huge source of income for their institutions shouldn't they at least receive an education in return to promote an opportunity to earn higher wages in the future? Should college athletes be paid with more than a scholarship?

7. Recall the statistic illustrated in the *Shame of College Sports, supra*: 90% of NCAA revenues are attributable to 1% of athletes, 90% of which are African American. Branch further asserts that the major "money making" sports (men's basketball and football) provide a majority of the money the athletic programs use to fund scholarships for other non-mainstream teams such as rowing, tennis, baseball, etc. If a university's basketball and football teams are comprised predominately of African American athletes, and the profits of their work are being diverted to support teams with a traditionally high Caucasian population, is this not a kind of unfair racial subsidization? Is this reverse discrimination with African-American athletes now in the majority in those sports? Or according to Branch (and discussed above in Note 1), slavery or colonialism?

8. Critics of college athletics focus on money and how much revenue men's basketball and football generate for an institution. Would it surprise you that the overwhelming majority of colleges and universities actually lose money? Athletic departments at the I-A level lose $600,000 per year on average. Daniel J. Henderson, *Do Former College Athletes Earn More at Work: A Nonparametric Assessment*, 41 The Journal of Human Resources 558, 559 (2006). Losses at the lower levels are in the millions of dollars per year. *Id.* Only 3.24 percent of NCAA members are profitable, mostly due to football and basketball programs that offset the costs of other sports. *Id.* Even these sports lose money at lower levels because of the lack of national television exposure and post-season rewards. *Id.*

The trend of university subsidization of athletics has not abated. Nor has the loss of revenue. A 2010 article in *USA Today* indicated that subsidies for 99 of the NCAA's 120-team Football Bowl Subdivision — the highest level of play — grew "20% in four years, from $685 million in 2005 to $826 million in 2008," in spite of a funding crisis that has resulted in cut faculty salaries, loss of state-funded financial aid, and tuition and fee hikes. Jack Gillum, Jodi Upton & Steve Berkowitz, *Amid Funding Crisis, College Athletics Soak up Subsidies, Fees*, USA Today, Jan. 13, 2010, *available at* http://www.usatoday.com/sports/college/2010-01-13-ncaa-athletics-funding-analysis_N.htm.

9. Since most institutions actually lose money supporting student athletics, why are colleges and universities so engaged in this enterprise? Proponents of student athletics say that success on the field improves the university's image thereby increasing the number of applications. Since academic reputation is based in part on applications and acceptance rates, it may help increase the university's standing. *Id.* Success in athletics may also help increase donations. Some proponents also say that athletes attain personal skills that they can use later on in the labor market:

they learn "discipline, teamwork skills, a strong drive to succeed, and a better work ethic." *Id.* at 560.

Do these personal skills, allegedly attained by some student-athletes, justify the resources universities use for athletics? Can athletes achieve these skills in other areas of education? Should the institutional support of athletics be better employed in areas of scholarly achievement?

Is it fair that the state, private donors, and other students subsidize athletics when only a minority of students are selected to participate? On the other hand, is it fair that the legislature, donors, and students subsidize students in honors programs, also a small minority, who not only receive scholarship aid but also receive the first pick during course registration and other perquisites?

If universities ceased to support student-athletes who rely on sports scholarships, many could not attend college. Since some percentage of athletic scholarships in the big time sports such as football or basketball go to poor students of color, is this financial aid an instrument to correct social injustice?

10. Despite cuts in state funding and overall declining revenue from their sports' programs, universities continue to pour extravagant amounts of money into athletics. From 2006 to 2010, nearly one-third of Division I-AA schools increased their spending by more than 40 percent, resulting in a median budget deficit of $9 million. Libby Sander & Andrea Fuller, *In Athletics, Ambition Compete with Costs*, THE CHRONICLE OF HIGHER EDUC., June 26, 2011, *available at* http://chronicle.com/article/In-Athletics-Ambitions/128033/. Schools such as Winston-Salem State University, University of Arkansas at Pine Bluff, Southern Illinois University at Carbondale, and Georgia State University, all increased their athletics budget by over *100%* during the five-year period. *Id.* For a list of the top 50 universities with increased athletic-program expenditures, see *Biggest Gainers in Athletic Spending*, THE CHRONICLE OF HIGHER EDUC., June 26, 2011, *available at* http://chronicle.com/article/Sortable-Table-Biggest/127977/.

11. Is it possible for America to develop athletes like England and the rest of Europe? In England, the country is divided into regions where everyone within a community has the opportunity to play football (soccer in America). *See Players*, THEFA.COM, *available at* http://www.thefa.com/GetIntoFootball/Players.aspx. If young players exhibit promise, there is a "player pathway" in place to train and coach more talented players at accelerated levels. *Id.* In fact, this accelerated instruction is performed by the regional professional teams.

> Professional clubs are primarily responsible for talent development in England via their youth academies. There are currently 39 academies in operation in England and Wales, and all Premier League clubs are required to work in concert with the academies. Academies recruit players for coaching and (modified) competitive games from 8 years old, and ultimately offer three-year scholarships for players aged 16–19. At the scholarship level, two teams may be operated (under-17 and under-19), and 'scholars' must receive a minimum of 12 hours football instruction per week. Academy coaches are employed on a full-time basis, but many clubs may employ part-time coaches to assist with younger age group teams. There are

facilities, curricular and coach education requirements established by the EFA that academies must satisfy to maintain their status.

Nicholas L. Holt, *A Comparison of the Soccer Development Systems in England and Canada*, 8 Euro. Physical Educ. Rev. 270, 276 (2002).*

What are the advantages of England's system? Are the players receiving better instruction from professional coaches at a younger age than American athletes? Are they engaged in more heightened competition? Plus, professional teams are shouldering the responsibility of training the nation's premier athletes, not England's universities.

Is a drastic change in developing athletes really possible in America? What would happen to all of the capital schools and states that have invested in university stadiums and arenas? Is there any reasonable way to transition away from the current system?

12. Lower courts generally rule in favor of the NCAA on students-athletes' and universities' many challenges to its regulations and procedures. Students have contested NCAA rules on a number of legal theories, including discrimination against undocumented immigrants, violations of the Americans with Disabilities Act, and violation of the Due Process and Equal Protection clauses of the Fourteenth Amendments. *See Spath v. Nat'l Collegiate Athletic Ass'n*, 728 F.2d 25 (C.A. Mass. 1984) (upholding lower court's denial of student's claim against NCAA for discrimination based on his Canadian nationality); *see also Howard Univ. v. Nat'l Collegiate Athletic Ass'n*, 367 F. Supp. 926 (D.C.D.C. 1973) (where student lost both Equal Protection and Due Process claims against NCAA); *Bowers v. Nat'l Collegiate Athletic Ass'n*, 563 F. Supp. 2d 508 (D.N.J. 2008) (court denied student claim that NCAA regulations on qualifying high school courses violated the Americans with Disabilities Act); *Matthews v. NCAA*, 179 F. Supp. 2d 1209 (E.D. Wash. 2001) (court denied injunction against NCAA for alleged violations of the Americans with Disabilities Act).

Student-athletes and universities have succeeded in a limited number of situations, particularly when the NCAA attempts to apply newly made regulations or interpretations retroactively. *See Tr. of Cal. State Univ. & Colls. v. Nat'l Collegiate Athletic Ass'n*, 82 Cal. App. 3d 461 (Cal. App. 1 Dist. 1978). In *California State University*, the court affirmed an injunction against an NCAA ruling that sanctioned a university for allowing two currently ineligible students to participate in intercollegiate sports. *Id.* at 475. The NCAA released new interpretations of eligibility, but the plaintiff-students had already qualified and begun to participate under the previous rules. *Id.* at 461. Another court granted an injunction precluding the NCAA from enforcing its determination of one student's ineligibility to play college sports based on its findings that his core high school math classes were not sufficient. *Phillip v. Nat'l Collegiate Athletic Ass'n*, 960 F. Supp. 552 (D. Conn. 1997). The court relied on the student's high school principal's testimony and outdated NCAA athletic booklets in deciding that the NCAA's interpretation of the "core classes" at issue was incorrect. *Id.* at 557. The court held that the student would suffer irreparable harm (by losing his scholarship and being financially unable to attend college) if a preliminary injunction were not granted. *Id.* at 558. On review, however, the Second Circuit remanded the case back to the district court as it was unclear from the first opinion whether the lower court had considered Connecticut's good faith and fair dealing requirement in its analysis. *Phillip v. Fairfield Univ.*, 118 F.3d 131 (2d Cir. 1997).

Additionally, one court held that the NCAA must hold some sort of hearing determining a university's knowledge of wrong-doing before imposing any sanctions for knowingly allowing ineligible students to play in intercollegiate events. *Colo. Seminary (Univ. of Denver) v. Nat'l Collegiate Athletic Ass'n*, 417 F. Supp. 885 (D.C. Colo. 1976). At least one court found that students also have the right to some basic form of due process before the NCAA can suspend them from intercollegiate play. *See Behagen v. Intercollegiate Conference of Faculty Representatives*, 346 F. Supp. 602 (D. Minn. 4 Div. 1972). Why do you think the judiciary is generally reluctant to grant injunctions against NCAA rulings? Should the NCAA be considered a public or private entity? Given that adverse NCAA rulings can affect university recruiting and reputation significantly and also take away some students' ability to attend and benefit from higher education, what level of due process should be required?

13. For additional critiques of big-time college sports, see RICK TELANDER, THE HUNDRED YARD LIE: THE CORRUPTION OF COLLEGE FOOTBALL AND WHAT WE CAN DO TO STOP IT (1996); ALLEN L. SACK & ELLEN J. STAUROWSKY, COLLEGE ATHLETES FOR HIRE: THE EVOLUTION AND LEGACY OF THE NCAA'S AMATEUR MYTH (1998); MURRAY SPERBER, COLLEGE SPORTS, INC.: THE ATHLETIC DEPARTMENT VS. THE UNIVERSITY (1990).

B. ATHLETIC SCHOLARSHIPS

CONARD v. UNIVERSITY OF WASHINGTON

834 P.2d 17 (Wash. 1992)

Opinion by DOLLIVER, J.

In February 1983, petitioners Kevin Conard and Vincent Fudzie (plaintiffs) were recruited by the University of Washington (UW) to play football. Both plaintiffs signed national letters of intent and received offers of athletic financial assistance for three consecutive quarters commencing the first day of class of the fall quarter of the 1983 academic year. After signing letters of intent, student-athletes who transfer to another university lose 2 years of athletic eligibility. Each offer of financial assistance covered tuition, compulsory fees, room and board, and course-related books, and each had the following provision regarding renewal:

> This assistance will be considered for renewal during subsequent periods of attendance as long as you are a student in good standing, maintain normal progress toward graduation and are in compliance with all eligibility requirements of this institution, the Pacific-10, and the NCAA.

The offers also stated the assistance "may be gradated or terminated only in accordance with the legislation of the NCAA, principal details of which appear on the attached sheet." The following NCAA rules were attached and signed by Conard, Fudzie, and their guardians:

> 2. Financial aid shall not be revoked or altered during any period for which it has been granted except that the University may revoke aid in whole or in part if the student:
>
> a. is rendered ineligible for intercollegiate competition; or
>
> b. fraudulently misrepresents any information on the application for admission, letter-of-intent or tender; or
>
> c. engages in serious misconduct warranting substantial disciplinary penalty; or
>
> d. voluntarily withdraws from a sport for personal reasons. Any such gradation or cancellation of aid is permissible only if such action is taken for proper cause by the regular disciplinary or scholarship awards authorities of the institution and the student-athlete has had an opportunity for a hearing. Under (d) above, such gradation or cancellation of aid may not occur prior to the conclusion of the academic term.
>
> . . . .
>
> 4. After completion of the above stated period of this award, upon the recommendation of the Head Coach, the Director of Athletics, and the Faculty Representative, the Committee on Financial Aid will consider granting renewal of the assistance, providing you (1) meet the academic requirements of the National Collegiate Athletic Association, the Pacific-10/Nor Pac Conference and the University, and (2) are a student in good standing in every respect as determined by the rules, regulations and administrative decisions of the University, the Pacific-10/Nor Pac Conference and the National Collegiate Athletic Association.

The Department of Intercollegiate Athletics (DIA) makes recommendations regarding the renewal and nonrenewal of athletic scholarships. The DIA policies and procedure manual provides:

> If a coach wishes to withdraw a recommendation for financial aid at anytime, justification within the rules of the Conference and the Associations (AIAW/NCAA) must be fully established. Each student-athlete is entitled to due process and if the student-athlete requests an appeal as well as a hearing, one will be provided.

The opportunity for a hearing is also set forth in section 3-4-(g) of the NCAA constitution:

> In the latter event [a decision of nonrenewal], the institution also shall inform the student-athlete that if he or she believes the grant has not been renewed for questionable reasons, the student-athlete may request, and shall have the opportunity for a hearing before the institutional agency making the financial award. The institution shall have established reasonable procedures for the prompt hearing of such a request.

Both plaintiffs allege they understood their scholarships were for 4 or 5 years depending on whether they were asked not to play or "redshirt" their freshman years. Both stated it is "commonly understood" that such scholarships are to last at least 4 years and neither had heard of an athlete whose scholarship had been "revoked". Each stated his understanding was based upon:

> the offers of aid which I signed, which indicated that as long as I complied with certain criteria as set out in the Offer of Financial Aid and other documentation that my aid would be renewed, and as stated above, the custom of these types of agreements.

Eric S. Godfrey is the Assistant Vice-President for Student Affairs, the Director of Financial Aid, and the Chairman of UW's Athletic Financial Aid Committee which hears appeals from athletes whose awards are not renewed. Godfrey stated that "the commitment on the part of the University, in compliance with the NCAA regulations, is if the student meets these conditions, the aid will be renewed for the next academic period." Both Godfrey and Don James, the head coach of the UW football team, stated that in order for the committee not to renew a student's athletic financial aid there needed to be a finding of serious misconduct.

However, serious misconduct is not defined by any UW, NCAA, or Pac-10 rule or regulation contained in the record. James testified there are no written guidelines as to what constitutes serious misconduct, and it is up to the discretion of the coach and the "financial aid people" on a case-by-case basis to determine whether certain acts constituted serious misconduct. Godfrey stated whether conduct constituted serious misconduct is evaluated generally in light of UW's student conduct code and specifically by the team rules promulgated by James.

The team rules are outlined by James for the players at the beginning of every season and represent broad guidelines governing general conduct, conduct in the dressing room, conduct at practice, and conduct dealing with the press, procedures regarding injuries, and a prohibition on gambling. The rules begin with the following statement:

> The following general rules are for your benefit. Since it is impossible to cover every point or eventuality in a statement of team policy such as this, you are expected to conduct yourself at all times in a manner that will reflect credit upon you, your teammates, the football program, and the University of Washington.

In the fall 1983, plaintiffs matriculated at UW and joined the football team playing on the fifth string. There were a series of incidents involving the plaintiffs, individually and together, between that time and December 1985 when James removed them from the team and told them he would not recommend the renewal of their scholarships. . . .

First, in November 1983, UW police notified James that Conard had been arrested for using a stolen student food credit card. . . .

Next, in 1984 there were several incidents involving plaintiffs. In one incident UW police informed James that Fudzie had punched out some windows in a residence hall. . . . On a separate occasion, it was reported that Fudzie entered a student's room and assaulted a student. In another incident, Fudzie and Conard were reported to have entered a student's room and threatened the student with bodily harm. James alleges he counseled both players as to these incidents and . . . warned them that if such behavior continued, they could lose their scholarships.

Also in 1984, plaintiffs attempted to extort money from a female student by blackmailing her with photographs taken while she was engaged in sexual acts with another student. As a result of the incident, plaintiffs spent a weekend in jail on charges of extortion, but no further action was taken. . . .

In 1985, James counseled Conard for his lack of respect for and unacceptable behavior toward service and equipment personnel. Conard was also counseled for his failure to report an injury to the trainers pursuant to the team rules. Both conversations resulted in a further warning to Conard as to the probability of the nonrenewal of his scholarship.

Finally, in December 1985, the UW football team traveled to Anaheim, California, to participate in the Freedom Bowl. On the morning of December 22, plaintiffs did not report for practice with the rest of the team. Plaintiffs were later found to have spent the night in jail at the Santa Ana Police Department as the result of an altercation at a restaurant the previous evening. . . . The police report states that plaintiffs were asked to leave and then escorted out of the restaurant by police for violating the establishment's dress code; while leaving, they challenged the police officers to a fight; and when the police attempted to arrest plaintiffs after they left the restaurant and were driving away, they resisted arrest. . . . After the incident, James informed plaintiffs they would not play in the Freedom Bowl, they were off the team, and he would not recommend their scholarships be renewed for the next year.

On June 24, 1986, the Athletic Financial Aid Committee convened to review recommendations for renewal and nonrenewal forwarded to them by the DIA. On July 1, 1986, in accordance with the NCAA constitution, Godfrey informed each plaintiff by letter that his athletic financial aid was not being renewed for the 1986-87 academic year. Also in accordance with the NCAA constitution, the letters informed them they could request a hearing before the Athletic Financial Aid Committee to appeal the decision of nonrenewal.

Conard did not request a hearing. As a result of low scholarship, he was dropped from UW and was scholastically ineligible to return to UW after spring quarter 1986. Conard did not petition for reinstatement and transferred to San Diego State University.

By letter dated September 3, 1986, Fudzie requested a hearing which was held on September 22, 1986. . . . [B]ased upon all the evidence, they determined unanimously that the decision of nonrenewal was reasonable and appropriate. Fudzie was notified of the decision and given a copy of the materials submitted by James.

Although Fudzie lost his athletic scholarship, he received financial aid in the amount of $10,118 for the 1986-87 academic year. While Fudzie was not awarded any aid for the following year because his aid application was not received until after the deadline, he remained at UW and received a Bachelor of Arts degree in accounting . . . .

In December 1988, plaintiffs brought suit against UW for breach of contract and against James, his wife, and UW for interference with contractual relations. The trial court granted summary judgment in favor of UW and dismissed the suit in its entirety; the plaintiffs appealed. The Court of Appeals affirmed on the breach of contract and interference of contractual relations claims, but held, sua sponte, that plaintiffs had a constitutionally protected claim of entitlement to the renewal of their scholarships. The Court of Appeals affirmed the dismissal of Conard's complaint because he had not requested a hearing and because he was scholastically ineligible to return for the 1986-87 academic year. The Court of Appeals reversed the dismissal of Fudzie's complaint against UW and remanded the case for an adversarial hearing because it held the informal hearing afforded Fudzie was constitutionally inadequate.

Plaintiffs petitioned for review of the dismissal of their breach of contract claim against UW for not renewing their football scholarships, for finding no violation of Conard's due process rights, and for not providing monetary damages for the violation of Fudzie's due process rights. UW seeks review of the Court of Appeals' decision finding a violation of Fudzie's due process rights and remanding for a new hearing. This court granted review "solely to determine if the University's termination of petitioners' athletic scholarships violated their due process rights and, if so, what remedy is appropriate."

. . . .

The scope of the Fourteenth Amendment's procedural protection of property interests is not coextensive with contract rights. *See Perry v. Sindermann*, 408 U.S. 593, 599-601 (1972); *Board of Regents v. Roth*, 408 U.S. 564, 576-78 (1972). The terms of a contract may be the source of a property interest, *see Roth*, 408 U.S. at 566 n.1, but protected property interests include all benefits to which there is a "legitimate claim of entitlement". *Roth*, 408 U.S. at 577. Such a claim is "more than an abstract need or desire for" and "more than a unilateral expectation of" the benefit. *Roth*, 408 U.S. at 577. Property interests are created by "state law — rules or understandings that secure certain benefits and that support claims of entitlement to those benefits." *Roth*, 408 U.S. at 577.

. . . .

Protected interests also may be created if there are statutes or other rules which contain " 'substantive predicates' " or " 'particularized standards or criteria . . .' " to guide the discretion of decisionmakers and which contain " 'explicitly mandatory language,' i.e., specific directives to the decisionmaker that if the regulations' substantive predicates are present, a particular outcome must follow . . .". *Kentucky Dep't of Corrections v. Thompson*, 490 U.S. 454, 462-63 (1989). . . .

Unless a legitimate claim of entitlement to the renewal of plaintiffs' scholarships was created by the terms of the contract, by a mutually explicit understanding, or by substantive procedural restrictions on the part of the decisionmaker, plaintiffs have no constitutional due process protections.

(1)

Contract

The offers of athletic financial aid to plaintiffs were clear and unambiguous in offering aid for "three consecutive quarters". "If you enroll, you will receive this assistance for three consecutive quarters . . .". . . .

While review of the due process issue raises the question whether the terms of the contract created a protected property interest, the terms of the contract, as found by the Court of Appeals, control this case. Consequently, the duration of the financial aid awards of 1 academic year precludes the contracts from creating a protected property interest for 4 years.

The contract terms also do not create a legitimate claim of entitlement to the renewal of the scholarships. The offers provided only that "[t]his assistance will be considered for renewal during subsequent periods . . ." The NCAA rules, attached to the offers, similarly provided only for consideration of renewal.

. . . .

Thus, the duration of the contracts is for only 1 academic year, and terms are not sufficiently definite to establish a legitimate claim of entitlement to the renewal of plaintiffs' athletic scholarships.

(2)

Mutually Explicit Understandings

The plaintiffs allege they had a claim of entitlement to the renewal of their scholarships as long as they complied with the rules of the UW, the NCAA, and the Pac-10. Plaintiffs assert they relied upon the language of their contracts and the common understanding, based upon the surrounding circumstances and the conduct of the parties, that the aid would be renewed if certain conditions were met. The issue is whether this record supports a "mutually explicit understanding" creating a protected property interest in the renewal of the scholarships.

In *Perry v. Sindermann*, a nontenured college professor, whose contract was not renewed and who was not provided a hearing, alleged a property interest in continued employment based upon the existence of rules and understandings which created a de facto tenure system. . . .

. . . .

In *Roth*, a nontenured college professor alleged a property interest in his continued employment when his 1-year teaching contract was not renewed. However, the plaintiff could point to no "University rule or policy that secured his interest in re-employment or that created any legitimate claim to it." (Footnote omitted.). The plaintiff did assert, similar to the statement of plaintiffs in this case, that most teachers "are, in fact, rehired.". . . .

. . . .

Plaintiffs assert there was a "common understanding" that scholarships were for a minimum of 4 years. Plaintiffs do not cite to any specific persons who made assurances to them regarding a right to renewal. Godfrey did state that "the commitment on the part of the University, in compliance with the NCAA regulations, is if the student meets these conditions, the aid will be renewed for the next academic period." Significantly however . . . nothing in the record indicates Godfrey told this to the plaintiffs, and neither plaintiff asserts he relied upon this or similar statements when accepting the offers.

Both plaintiffs allege they did not know of any student whose aid was not renewed who was in compliance with those conditions. This assertion, like that in *Roth,* however, is insufficient to create a common law of renewal. Like Roth, plaintiffs point to no written UW rule or policy which supports their entitlement. . . .

[T]he language of the offers and the NCAA regulations are not sufficiently certain to support a mutually explicit understanding creating a protected property interest. As in *Roth,* the fact that scholarships are, in fact, normally renewed does not create a "common law" of renewal, absent other consistent and supportive UW policies or rules. . . .

Moreover, plaintiffs have not established they actually met the conditions of the offers. Plaintiffs assert that "a valid finding of misconduct was never made against either Conard or Fudzie." This assertion is made because plaintiffs were apparently exonerated of any misconduct in the restaurant incident at the Freedom Bowl in 1985, and no formal disciplinary proceedings were brought against them as to the alleged prior misconduct.

However, the language of the offers and the NCAA constitution do not require a finding of misconduct in order not to renew the scholarships. Such a finding is required only if the aid is altered or terminated during the period for which it was awarded. . . .

. . . .

Nonetheless, both Godfrey and James testified that in order for the committee not to renew a student's athletic financial aid there needed to be a finding of serious misconduct. Such a finding was made by James and the committee based on plaintiffs' cumulative pattern of misconduct. Even if such a finding were required in making the decision not to renew, however, the record does not establish a mutually explicit understanding that plaintiffs' cumulative pattern of misconduct would not constitute serious misconduct.

. . . .

The broad guidelines set forth in the team rules are not sufficiently specific to create a mutually explicit understanding as to what acts would violate their terms, and plaintiffs have presented no language from the UW student conduct code which would create such an understanding. Therefore, even if there was a mutually explicit understanding that the plaintiffs' scholarships could not be renewed absent a finding of serious misconduct, these broad guidelines are not sufficiently definite to establish a mutually explicit understanding that plaintiffs' cumulative pattern of misconduct would not constitute such serious misconduct.

(3)

Procedural Requirements

Lastly, procedural guaranties may create protected property interests when they contain " 'substantive predicates' " to guide the discretion of decisionmakers and "specific directives to the decisionmaker that if the regulations' substantive predicates are present, a particular outcome must follow . . ." *Kentucky Dep't of Corrections v. Thompson*, 490 U.S. 454, 462-63 (1989).

. . . .

In this case, the NCAA constitution and the DIA policies and procedure manual provide for a hearing and due process respectively. However, there are no articulable standards nor explicitly mandatory language in the contracts, the NCAA constitution, or the DIA manual. The contracts provide that the aid will be considered for renewal if certain conditions are met. . . . [T]he contracts do not state that aid must be renewed if the conditions are met or that aid must not be renewed if they are not met. The NCAA constitution states that there will be an opportunity for a hearing if the student-athlete believes the aid was not renewed for "questionable reasons". This language does not provide an articulable standard and does not mandate a particular outcome. Lastly, the DIA manual states:

> If a coach wishes to withdraw a recommendation for financial aid at anytime, justification within the rules of the Conference and the Associations (AIAW/NCAA) must be fully established.

The record does not indicate and plaintiffs do not point to any other applicable NCAA or AIAW rules other than those already addressed. The discretion of the decisionmakers in this case is not sufficiently limited to create a protected property interest. . . .

We hold, on the record in this case, that plaintiffs do not have a protected property interest in the renewal of their athletic scholarships.

. . . Because plaintiffs do not have a protected interest in the renewal of their scholarships, we need not address whether the hearing provided by UW was constitutionally adequate, or what the appropriate remedy would be if a violation had occurred.

The Court of Appeals' decision holding plaintiffs had a protected property interest in the renewal of their scholarships and remanding Fudzie's case for a rehearing is reversed. The Court of Appeals' decision is affirmed in all other respects.

JACKSON v. DRAKE UNIV.

778 F. Supp. 1490 (S.D. Iowa 1991)

MEMORANDUM OPINION, RULING PARTIALLY GRANTING AND PARTIALLY DENYING DEFENDANT'S MOTION FOR SUMMARY JUDGMENT, AND ORDER

Opinion by VIETOR, J.

Plaintiff Terrell Jackson was recruited to attend, and play basketball at, Drake University. Jackson has several complaints regarding the way he was treated and the manner in which the men's basketball program was run during the period that he was a member of the team. Jackson originally brought suit against defendant Drake University in the Iowa District Court for Polk County. Jackson's complaint states six counts: (I) breach of contract; (II) negligence; (III) negligent misrepresentation; (IV) fraud; (V) negligent hiring; and (VI) violation of civil rights based on 42 U.S.C. § 1981. Drake removed the action to this court on June 4, 1990, based on the section 1981 claim and diversity of citizenship.

Drake moves for summary judgment, and Jackson resists. The motion is submitted.

. . . .

Facts

The following facts are undisputed or represent plaintiff's version. Defendant Drake University is a private educational institution incorporated under the laws of Iowa. In 1988, Drake began looking for a new head coach of the men's basketball team. Drake athletic director Curtis Blake was appointed chairman of the search committee formed to select the new head coach.

In March 1988, Tom Abatemarco was hired as the Drake men's basketball team head coach. Blake made the decision to hire Abatemarco. He based his decision upon, among other things, the search committee's unanimous recommendation. Blake's decision was reported to Michael Ferrari, President of Drake. Ferrari subsequently confirmed Blake's decision. At the time of making his decision, Ferrari did not have all of the information regarding Abatemarco that Blake had. Specifically, Ferrari was not aware of a Sports Illustrated article Blake had read that dealt with, in part, Abatemarco's reputation as a recruiter.

Sometime after assuming the responsibilities of head coach, Abatemarco began recruiting plaintiff Jackson to attend and play basketball at Drake. In recruiting Jackson, Abatemarco emphasized the high quality of education that Jackson would receive at Drake. Abatemarco also told Jackson that the basketball program would be structured around Jackson and he would be the star of the team. Subsequently, Jackson enrolled at Drake in the fall of 1988.

Drake provided Jackson with the assistance of a tutor while playing basketball. Abatemarco and his coaching staff scheduled basketball practices which interfered with Jackson's allotted study time and tutoring schedule. Jackson attended these practices under threats that his scholarship would be taken away if he did not comply. Abatemarco's coaching staff prepared term papers for Jackson which they expected Jackson to turn in for credit as his own work. Jackson refused the offer of term papers provided by the staff. Abatemarco and his staff recommended that Jackson take certain "easy" courses in order to maintain his academic eligibility. Jackson refused to take the recommended easy courses and selected his own courses. Jackson does not question the adequacy of the tutoring and has no complaint with the quality of classroom instruction that he received.

During practices, Abatemarco singled out Jackson and required him to do extra running and exercises in the form of running laps and sprints, and doing situps and pushups. Abatemarco did not, however, physically injure Jackson. Abatemarco yelled at Jackson and called him foul and derogatory names. In January, 1990, Jackson quit the Drake basketball team.

Jackson and Drake executed financial aid agreements on July 12, 1988 and May 11, 1989. The agreements are the only written agreements that exist between the parties, and Drake has fully performed the obligations imposed on it by the agreements.

Count I: Breach of Contract

Jackson complains that Drake breached its contract with him by: failing to provide independent and adequate academic counseling and tutoring; failing to provide adequate study time; requiring Jackson to turn in plagiarized term papers; disregarding Jackson's progress toward an undergraduate degree; and urging Jackson to register for easy classes. Jackson also contends that the financial aid agreements granted him the right to an educational opportunity and the right to play basketball for a Division I school. Drake argues that it is entitled to summary judgment on Count I because it has performed all of the obligations required by the financial aid agreements.

The financial aid agreements entered into by Drake and Jackson constitute valid contracts. Jackson has admitted that Drake has performed all obligations imposed by the financial aid agreements, but argues that implicit in the agreements is the right to play basketball. The financial aid agreements make no mention of such a right. Under Iowa law, where the language of a contract is clear and unambiguous, the language controls. The court concludes that the financial aid agreements do not implicitly contain a right to play basketball. Therefore, and because Drake has met all its obligations under the agreements, Drake's motion for summary judgment on the breach of contract claim will be granted.

Count II: Negligence

Jackson contends that by recruiting him to attend Drake University, Drake "undertook a duty to [Jackson] to provide an atmosphere conducive to academic achievement." According to Jackson, Drake breached this duty by requiring and urging him to enroll in easy courses which would ensure his academic eligibility regardless of the courses' academic worth or his progress toward an undergraduate degree. Jackson also contends that Drake breached its duty by scheduling practices which substantially interfered with his study time and tutoring schedule, and by requiring him to attend these practices under threats that his scholarship would be taken away if he did not comply. Drake argues that Jackson's negligence claim is a claim for "educational malpractice," a claim not recognized under Iowa law.

A prerequisite to establishing a claim of negligence is the existence of a legal duty. Not every claim of negligence creates a civil cause of action, and whether a legal duty arises out of a parties' relationship sufficient to form the basis of a claim of negligence is a matter of law for the court to decide. . . .

Jackson cites several cases in support of his claim, arguing that common law tort principles apply to this case rather than an educational malpractice analysis. Jackson's argument is not persuasive. He argues that the cases cited support the proposition that the court should find Drake had a duty to provide an atmosphere conducive to academic achievement. The cases cited, however, are clearly distinguishable from the instant case. [citations omitted] These cases all involve specific negligent acts or omissions resulting in death or physical injury.

In support of its motion for summary judgment on Jackson's negligence claim, Drake relies on two educational malpractice cases. *See Ross v. Creighton University*, 740 F. Supp. 1319 (N.D. Ill. 1990); *Moore v. Vanderloo*, 386 N.W.2d 108 (Iowa 1986) (in suit by a patient against college of chiropractic for alleged negligent failure to teach one of its former students, the treating chiropractic, the risks associated with certain techniques, the court held there is no recognized cause of action for educational malpractice under Iowa law). While factually distinguishable from the present case, the court finds the policy considerations discussed by the courts in *Moore* and *Ross* in declining to find an educational malpractice claim in those cases to be important considerations in the present case.

. . . .

In *Moore*, the Iowa Supreme Court articulated five reasons for not recognizing a cause of action for educational malpractice. In the context of the case now before this court, several of those reasons provide a strong indication that the Iowa Supreme Court, if called upon to do so, would not recognize a negligence claim in this case. First is a lack of a satisfactory standard of care by which to measure the defendant's conduct. Second, to recognize a negligence claim based on the facts before the court could reasonably be expected to result in an enormous amount of litigation involving college athletic programs. To recognize a negligence claim in this case "would force the courts blatantly to interfere with the internal operations and daily workings of an educational institution." Finally, it has been recognized that academic freedom thrives on the autonomous decision-making of the academy itself. Though Jackson's claim does not specifically challenge the "academic" freedom of Drake, in effect, it does ask the court to pass judgment on the manner in which Drake runs its men's basketball program, a program which does have an academic component. This court judicially estimates that the Iowa Supreme Court would not recognize plaintiff's negligence claim. Drake's motion for summary judgment on Count II, therefore, will be granted.

Count III & Count IV: Negligent Misrepresentation & Fraud

To properly state a claim of negligent misrepresentation, Jackson must allege that the defendant, in the course of its business or profession or employment, supplied false information for the guidance of others in their business transactions, that the information was justifiably relied on by the plaintiff, and the defendant failed to exercise reasonable care or competence in communicating the information.. . . . To state a claim for fraud, Jackson must allege a material misrepresentation, made knowingly, with the intent to induce Jackson to act, upon which he justifiably relied, with damages.

Accepting Jackson's version of the facts, Drake, through Abatemarco, made representations to Jackson that it was committed to academic excellence and that this commitment carried over to the athletic department. Drake promised Jackson a college education and full support services so he could fully utilize his educational opportunity while playing basketball. Jackson relied on Drake's representations, and moved from Chicago to Des Moines to attend Drake. Jackson claims that Drake did not exercise reasonable care in making the representations and had no intention of providing the support services it had promised. Drake argues that these are claims for educational malpractice, a claim not recognized under Iowa law.

The court finds that the policy considerations discussed previously do not weigh as heavily in favor of precluding the claims for negligent misrepresentation and fraud as in the claim for negligence. Furthermore, Jackson has designated specific facts that show there is a genuine issue for trial on these counts. Drake's motion for summary judgment on Counts III & IV will be denied.

Count V: Negligent Hiring

. . . Jackson bases his claim of negligent hiring in large part, if not completely, on the Sports Illustrated article which athletic director Blake read. The court finds no indication, in the article or otherwise, that Abatemarco had a reputation for underhandedness, academic impropriety, or player abuse. Because Jackson has failed to designate specific facts which show there is a genuine issue for trial on his negligent hiring claim, Drake's motion for summary judgment on Count V will be granted.

Count VI: 42 U.S.C. § 1981

Jackson's civil rights claim is based upon Abatemarco's treatment of Jackson while Jackson was a member of the Drake basketball team. Jackson argues that Drake, through Abatemarco, intentionally threatened to revoke his scholarship, physically and mentally abused him, humiliated him and deemphasized his education. Jackson contends that Abatemarco's abusive treatment prevented him from enforcing his contract with Drake. Jackson, who is black, also alleges that as a result of this conduct he has not enjoyed the full and equal protection of the laws or security of his person or property and has been subject to punishment and pains because of his race and disadvantaged background in violation of 42 U.S.C. section 1981.

Section 1981 protects two rights: it prohibits racial discrimination in (1) the making, and (2) enforcement of, employment contracts. Concerning the first of these rights, Jackson does not claim that he was discriminated against in his right to contract; rather, his claims are restricted to post-contract conduct on the part of Abatemarco. The second of these rights, the right to enforce contracts, "prohibits discrimination that infects the legal process in ways that prevent one from enforcing contract rights, by reason of his or her race. . . ." [citation omitted]. Jackson makes no claim that Drake has impaired his ability to enforce his contract through the legal process.

Section 1981 does not apply to conduct which occurs after the formation of a contract and which does not interfere with the right to enforce established contract negotiations. As a matter of law, Jackson is not entitled to recover damages for violation of section 1981 in this case. Accordingly, Drake's motion for summary judgment on Count VI will be granted.

Rulings and Order

The motion for summary judgment by defendant Drake University, filed May 6, 1991, is GRANTED as to Counts I, II, V, and VI of plaintiff Terrell Jackson's complaint, but is DENIED as to Counts III and IV.

IT IS ORDERED that Counts I, II, V, and VI be DISMISSED.

ROSS v. CREIGHTON UNIVERSITY

957 F.2d 410 (7th Cir. 1992)

RIPPLE, CIRCUIT JUDGE. Kevin Ross filed suit against Creighton University (Creighton or the University) for negligence and breach of contract arising from Creighton's alleged failure to educate him. The district court dismissed Mr. Ross' complaint for failure to state a claim. For the following reasons we affirm in part and reverse in part the judgment of the district court.

I

BACKGROUND

A. *Facts*

. . . Mr. Ross' complaint reveals the following story.

In the spring of 1978, Mr. Ross was a promising senior basketball player at Wyandotte High School in Kansas City, Kansas. Sometime during his senior year in high school, he accepted an athletic scholarship to attend Creighton and to play on its varsity basketball team.

Creighton is an academically superior university. Mr. Ross comes from an academically disadvantaged background. At the time of his enrollment at Creighton, Mr. Ross was at an academic level far below that of the average Creighton student. For example, he scored in the bottom fifth percentile of college-bound seniors taking the American College Test, while the average freshman admitted to Creighton with him scored in the upper twenty-seven percent. According to the complaint, Creighton realized Mr. Ross' academic limitations when it admitted him, and, to induce him to attend and play basketball, Creighton assured Mr. Ross that he would receive sufficient tutoring so that he "would receive a meaningful education while at CREIGHTON."

Mr. Ross attended Creighton from 1978 until 1982. During that time he maintained a D average and acquired 96 of the 128 credits needed to graduate. However, many of these credits were in courses such as Marksmanship and Theory of Basketball, and did not count towards a university degree. Mr. Ross alleges that he took these courses on the advice of Creighton's Athletic Department, and that the department also employed a secretary to read his assignments and prepare and type his papers. Mr. Ross also asserts that Creighton failed to provide him with sufficient and competent tutoring that it had promised.

When he left Creighton, Mr. Ross had the overall language skills of a fourth grader and the reading skills of a seventh, grader. Consequently, Mr. Ross enrolled, at Creighton s expense, for a year of remedial education at the Westside Preparatory School in Chicago. At Westside, Mr. Ross attended classes with grade school children. He later entered Roosevelt University in Chicago, but was forced to withdraw because of a lack of funds. In July 1987, Mr. Ross suffered what he terms a "major depressive episode," during which he barricaded himself in a Chicago motel room and threw furniture out the window. To Mr. Ross, this furniture "symbolized" Creighton employees who had wronged him. *Id.*

B. *District Court Proceedings*

. . . .

Mr. Ross' complaint advances three separate theories of how Creighton was negligent towards him. First, he contends that Creighton committed "educational malpractice" by not providing him with a meaningful education and preparing him for employment after college. Second, Mr. Ross claims that Creighton negligently inflicted emotional distress upon him by enrolling him in a stressful university environment for which he was not prepared, and then by failing to provide remedial programs that would have helped him survive there. Third, Mr. Ross urges the court to adopt a new cause of action for the tort of "negligent admission," which would allow recovery when an institution admits, and then does not adequately assist, a woefully unprepared student. The complaint also sets forth a contract claim, alleging that Creighton contracted to provide Mr. Ross "an opportunity . . . to obtain a meaningful college education and degree, and to do what was reasonably necessary . . . to enable [Mr. Ross] to obtain a meaningful college education and degree." It goes on to assert that Creighton breached this contract by failing to provide Mr. Ross adequate tutoring; by not requiring Mr. Ross to attend tutoring sessions; by not allowing him to "red-shirt," that is, to forego a year of basketball, in order to work on academics; and by failing to afford Mr. Ross a reasonable opportunity to take advantage of tutoring services. Mr. Ross also alleges that Creighton breached a promise it had made to him to pay for a college education.

Creighton moved to dismiss the complaint under Federal Rule of Civil Procedure 12(b)(6), and the district court granted this motion. . . .

. . . .

II

ANALYSIS

A. *Guiding Principles*

As an appellate court, we review de novo a Rule 12(b)(6) dismissal for failure to state a claim. . . . .In this diversity case, because neither party raises an issue as to what state's law to apply, we apply the substantive law of Illinois, the forum state. Our task, therefore, is to analyze Mr. Ross' complaint against the backdrop of Illinois law to determine if it states a claim. . . .

B. *The Negligence Claims*

Mr. Ross advances three separate theories of how Creighton was negligent towards him: educational malpractice for not educating him, a new tort of "negligent admission" to an educational institution, and negligent infliction of emotional distress. We believe that, on the facts of this case, Illinois law would deny Mr. Ross recovery on all three theories.

1. Educational malpractice

Illinois courts have never ruled on whether a tort cause of action exists against an institution for educational malpractice. However, the overwhelming majority of states that have considered this type of claim have rejected it. Only Montana allows these claims to go forward, and its decision was based on state statutes that place a duty of care on educators, a circumstance not present here.

Courts have identified several policy concerns that counsel against allowing claims for educational malpractice. First, there is the lack of a satisfactory standard of care by which to evaluate an educator. Theories of education are not uniform, and "different but acceptable scientific methods of academic training [make] it unfeasible to formulate a standard by which to judge the conduct of those delivering the services." *Swidryk v. St. Michael's Medical Center*, 201 N.J. Super. 601, 493 A.2d 641, 643 (N.J. Super. Ct. Law Div. 1985). "Factors such as the student's attitude, motivation, temperament, past experience and home environment may all play an essential and immeasurable role in learning." *Donohue v. Copiague Union Free School Dist.*, 47 N.Y.2d 440, 418 N.Y.S.2d 375, 391 N.E.2d 1352, 1355 (N.Y. 1979) (Wachtler, J., concurring). Consequently, it may be a "practical impossibility [to] prove that the alleged malpractice of the teacher proximately caused the learning deficiency of the plaintiff student." *Id.* A third reason for denying this cause of action is the potential it presents for a flood of litigation against schools. As the district court noted, "education is a service rendered on an immensely greater scale than other professional services." *Ross v. Creighton Univ.*, 740 F. Supp. 1319, 1329 (N.D. Ill. 1990). The sheer number of claims that could arise if this cause of action were allowed might overburden schools. *Id.* This consideration also suggests that a common-law tort remedy may not be the best way to deal with the problem of inadequate education. *Id.* A final reason courts have cited for denying this cause of action is that it threatens to embroil the courts into overseeing the day-to-day operations of schools. *Donohue*, 391 N.E.2d at 1354; *Hoffman v. Board of Educ.*, 49 N.Y.2d 121, 424 N.Y.S.2d 376, 400 N.E.2d 317, 320 (N.Y. 1979). . . . This oversight might be particularly troubling in the university setting where it necessarily implicates considerations of academic freedom and autonomy. *Moore*, 386 N.W.2d at 115.

We believe that the Illinois Supreme Court would find the experience of other jurisdictions persuasive and, consequently, that these policy considerations are compelling. Consequently, the Illinois Supreme Court would refuse to recognize the tort of educational malpractice. We therefore affirm the district court's dismissal of Mr. Ross' claim based on that theory.

2. "Negligent admission"

In his complaint, Mr. Ross alleges that Creighton owed him a duty "to recruit and enroll only those students reasonably qualified and able to academically perform at CREIGHTON." He then contends that Creighton breached this duty by admitting him, not informing him of how unprepared he was for studies there, and then not providing tutoring services or otherwise enabling him to receive a meaningful education. As a result, Mr. Ross underwent undue stress, which brought about, among other things, the incident at the motel.

We believe that Illinois would reject this claim for "negligent admission" for many of the same policy reasons that counsel against recognizing a claim for educational malpractice. First, this cause of action would present difficult, if not insuperable, problems to a court attempting to define a workable duty of care. Mr. Ross suggests that the University has a duty to admit only students who are "reasonably qualified" and able to perform academically. However, determining who is a "reasonably qualified student" necessarily requires subjective assessments of such things as the nature and quality of the defendant institution and the intelligence and educability of the plaintiff. Such decisions are not open to ready determination in the judicial process. Second, such a cause of action might unduly interfere with a university's admissions decisions, to the detriment of students and society as a whole. As the district court noted, if universities and colleges faced tort liability for admitting an unprepared student, schools would be encouraged to admit only those students who were certain to succeed in the institution. The opportunities of marginal students to receive an education therefore would likely be lessened. *Id.* Also, the academic practice of promoting diversity by admitting students from disadvantaged backgrounds might also be jeopardized.

3. Negligent infliction of emotional distress

Finally, Mr. Ross argues that his allegations that Creighton wrongfully admitted him, and then caused him emotional harm, present a claim under the traditional tort theory of negligent infliction of emotional distress. In *Corgan v. Muehling*, 574 N.E.2d 602, 606, (Ill. 1991), the Illinois Supreme Court made clear that the "essential question" when evaluating whether a complaint states a claim for negligent infliction of emotional distress "is whether the plaintiff properly alleged negligence on the part of the defendant." We have already held that policy reasons would compel Illinois not to recognize Mr. Ross' claims for educational malpractice and negligent admission. We believe that these same concerns would cause it to refuse to recognize in this situation a claim for negligent infliction of emotional distress.

C. *The Contract Claims*

In counts two and three of his complaint, Mr. Ross alleges that Creighton breached an oral or a written contract that it had with him. When read as a totality, these allegations fairly allege that Creighton agreed, in exchange for Mr. Ross' promise to play on its basketball team, to allow him an opportunity to participate, in a meaningful way, in the academic program of the University despite his deficient academic background. The complaint further alleges, when read as a totality, that Creighton breached this contract and denied Mr. Ross any real opportunity to participate in and benefit from the University's academic program when it failed to perform five commitments made to Ross: (1) "to provide adequate and competent tutoring services," (2) "to require [Mr. Ross] to attend tutoring sessions," (3) to afford Mr. Ross "a reasonable opportunity to take full advantage of tutoring services," (4) to allow Mr. Ross to red-shirt, and (5) to provide funds to allow Mr. Ross to complete his college education.

It is held generally in the United States that the "basic legal relation between a student and a private university or college is contractual in nature. The catalogues, bulletins, circulars, and regulations of the institution made available to the matriculant become a part of the contract." *Zumbrun v. University of Southern California*, 101 Cal. Rptr. 499, 504 (Ct. App. 1972) (collecting cases from numerous states). Indeed, there seems to be "no dissent" from this proposition. As the district court correctly noted, Illinois recognizes that the relationship between a student and an educational institution is, in some of its aspects, contractual. It is quite clear, however, that Illinois would not recognize all aspects of a university-student relationship as subject to remedy through a contract action. *DeMarco* makes the point quite clearly. "A contract between a private institution and a student confers duties upon both parties which cannot be arbitrarily disregarded and may be judicially enforced." *DeMarco*, 352 N.E.2d at 361-62. However, "a decision of the school authorities relating to the academic qualification of the students will not be reviewed. . . . [C]ourts are not qualified to pass an opinion as to the attainments of a student . . . and . . . courts will not review a decision of the school authorities relating to academic qualifications of the students." *Id.*

There is no question, we believe, that Illinois would adhere to the great weight of authority and bar any attempt to repackage an educational malpractice claim as a contract claim. As several courts have noted, the policy concerns that preclude a cause of action for educational malpractice apply with equal force to bar a breach of contract claim attacking the general quality of an education. "Where the essence of the complaint is that the school breached its agreement by failing to provide an effective education, the court is again asked to evaluate the course of instruction . . . [and] is similarly called upon to review the soundness of the method of teaching that has been adopted by an educational institution." *Paladino v. Adelphi Univ.*, 89 A.D.2d 85, 454 N.Y.S.2d 868, 872 (App. Div. 1982).

To state a claim for breach of contract, the plaintiff must do more than simply allege that the education was not good enough. Instead, he must point to an identifiable contractual promise that the defendant failed to honor. Thus, as was suggested in *Paladino*, if the defendant took tuition money and then provided no education, or alternately, promised a set number of hours of instruction and then failed to deliver, a breach of contract action may be available. *Paladino*, 454 N.Y.S.2d at 873; *see also Zumbrun*, 25 Cal. App. 3d 1, 101 Cal. Rptr. 499 (breach of contract action allowed against university when professor declined to give lectures and final exam, and all students received a grade of "B"). Similarly, a breach of contract action might exist if a student enrolled in a course explicitly promising instruction that would qualify him as a journeyman, but in which the fundamentals necessary to attain that skill were not even presented. *See Wickstrom*, 725 P.2d at 156-58. In these cases, the essence of the plaintiff's complaint would not be that the institution failed to perform adequately a promised educational service, but rather that it failed to perform that service at all. Ruling on this issue would not require an inquiry into the nuances of educational processes and theories, but rather an objective assessment of whether the institution made a good faith effort to perform on its promise.

We read Mr. Ross' complaint to allege more than a failure of the University to provide him with an education of a certain quality. Rather, he alleges that the University knew that he was not qualified academically to participate in its curriculum. Nevertheless, it made a specific promise that he would be able to participate in a meaningful way in that program because it would provide certain specific services to him. Finally, he alleges that the University breached its promise by reneging on its commitment to provide those services and, consequently, effectively cutting him off from any participation in and benefit from the University's academic program. To adjudicate such a claim, the court would not be required to determine whether Creighton had breached its contract with Mr. Ross by providing deficient academic services. Rather, its inquiry would be limited to whether the University had provided any real access to its academic curriculum at all.

Accordingly, we must disagree respectfully with our colleague in the district court as to whether the contract counts of the complaint can be dismissed at the pleadings stage. In our view, the allegations of the complaint are sufficient to warrant further proceedings. We emphasize, however, the narrow ground of our disagreement. We agree — indeed we emphasize — that courts should not "take on the job of supervising the relationship between colleges and student-athletes or creating in effect a new relationship between them." *Ross*, 740 F. Supp. at 1332. We also recognize a formal university-student contract is rarely employed and, consequently, "the general nature and terms of the agreement are usually implied, with specific terms to be found in the university bulletin and other publications; custom and usages can also become specific terms by implication." *Wickstrom*, 725 P.2d at 157 (quoting *Peretti*, 464 F. Supp. at 786). Nevertheless, we believe that the district court can adjudicate Mr. Ross' specific and narrow claim that he was barred from *any* participation in and benefit from the University's academic program without second-guessing the professional judgment of the University faculty on academic matters.

Conclusion

Accordingly, the judgment of the district court is affirmed in part and reversed and remanded in part for proceedings consistent with this opinion.

AFFIRMED in part, REVERSED in part and REMANDED

NOTES

1. The court in *Jackson* refused to recognize the student-athlete's educational malpractice and contract claims. But the court did allow the case to move forward on Jackson's negligent misrepresentation and fraud claims. If the court concluded that there was enough evidence for trial that the coach recruiting Jackson fraudulently induced him to attend Drake by promising full educational opportunities and support services, and then failed to follow through on those promises, how is that distinguishable from an educational malpractice claim? If the coach had been upfront about writing term papers for Jackson, encouraging him to take easy classes, and denying him the promised support services, would that have freed the athletic department from all legal liability?

2. Like the *Jackson* decision the federal district court in *Ross v. Creighton University*, 740 F. Supp. 1319 (N.D. Ill. 1990) refused to recognize a student's educational malpractice claims. While the federal appeals court affirmed the decision as to the malpractice claim, it held that Ross plead sufficient facts to show the university made specific promises to provide access to education. The court further found that addressing the narrow question of whether the university breached its express promises did not require the lower court to evaluate the deficiency or quality of the education. *Id.* at 417. The appeals court emphasized that a contract claim is not a "Trojan Horse" for educational malpractice claims and that contract actions must concern specific promises, not implicit agreements respecting the quality of instruction. With the acceptance of the breach of contract claim, the *Ross* decision has now become a landmark case for higher education law. *See also* Chapter II. Is there a way to distinguish a student-athlete's educational malpractice claim and contract claims? Wouldn't it be possible to hold that a postsecondary school *does* have a special contractual relationship with student-athletes without recognizing an educational malpractice claim that would affect the entire student body? As the *Conard* case indicates, there are certain pledges expected of student-athletes in return for their athletic scholarships. Does a college or university owe anything else to compliant student-athletes aside from their scholarships?

3. At least one court has found that there may be some constitutionally protected interest in participation in college athletics. In *Richard v. Perkins*, the court stated, in dicta, that a student-athlete might have some limited form of a constitutionally protected interest in his track scholarship and participation on the college track team. *Richard v. Perkins*, 373 F. Supp. 2d 1211 (D. Kan. 2005). Though the student's claims were ultimately rejected on other grounds, the court hinted that a constitutional right to college-athletic participation stemming from the state constitution or common law might exist in certain situations. *Id.* at 1219. What situations might create such a right? What role should coaches' oral promises and recruitment efforts play in interpreting the rights arising from an athletic scholarship?

4. Should colleges and universities expect less academically of student-athletes participating in the big-time programs of basketball and football? Is collective bargaining for student-athletes a viable avenue to win such concessions? Consider this:

> It seems anomalous for the NCAA to be enforcing strict academic eligibility requirements for its college athletes, when the main reason such athletes are recruited is that they are outstanding athletes. . . . [T]he NCAA's eligibility requirements may supply a certain amount of satisfaction, but they distract from the reality of big-time college sports as a huge money-making enterprise that has little to do with the mission of the university.
>
> A student does not attain the level of play necessary for Division I football and basketball without spending many long, hard hours on the playing field during his or her high school years. Those who have dedicated themselves to excellence in sports have often neglected their studies in order to do so. Young people in disadvantaged urban communities, furthermore, are apt to see sports as their way to a prosperous adulthood.
>
> . . . The disparate impact of athletic eligibility requirements on African-American students should not be confronted in the courtroom but should be attacked on several fronts as stemming from many societal phenomena as the glorification and commercialization of big-time college sports and the concomitant neglect of the mission of the university; the NCAA's failure to acknowledge that Division I basketball and football teams constitute a quasi-professional league that develops a rich pool of outstanding athletes from which the National Football League and the National Basketball Association will skim the very best for professional play; the role of athletic scholarships in developing that quasi-professional league rather than in promoting scholarly achievement, and the accompanying treatment of athletes that many see as exploitation; the economic and educational disadvantages suffered by young African-Americans; the widespread misimpression that sports are the only way for middle and low-income students to obtain a college education; and the illusions entertained by high school basketball and football players that they will play professionally.
>
> Maybe Division I student-athletes don't need civil-rights lawyers after all. Maybe what they need is what any other workers could use to protect

> themselves — a union. Recently Division I NCAA football and basketball players have enlisted the aid of the United Steelworkers of America in developing the Collegiate Athletes' Coalition (CAC), which seeks to negotiate better conditions for Division I athletes. The players complain of poverty and exploitation in a business to which they contribute to the generation of billions of dollars of revenue. One way of changing the dynamics of the athletic scholarships in big-time sports would be to "pay" the athletes for their hard work with scholarships — which could be taken advantage of whenever the athlete chose, perhaps after the athlete is injured, after retirement, or after he fails to make the pros. Of course, the students are, formally and legally speaking, not workers, and such a change would lead to the professionalization of college sports. But that may be exactly what college sports need. If so, the United Steelworkers might be just what is needed to pierce the NCAA's steel-plated armor.

Lesley Chenoweth Estevao, *Student-Athletes Must Find New Ways to Pierce the NCAA's Legal Armor*, 12 SETON HALL. J. SPORT L. 243, 278–80 (2002).* Is there a way to establish some kind of collective-bargaining system without reclassifying student-athletes as employees, which the NCAA has successfully resisted for a half century?

For additional commentary on empowering student-athletes participating in big-time college sports, see Nathan McCoy & Kerry Knox, *Flexing Union Muscle: Is It the Right Game Plan for Revenue Generating Student-Athletes in Their Contest for Benefits Reform with the NCAA?*, 69 TENN. L. REV. 1051 (2002); Marc Jenkins, *The United Student-Athletes of America: Should College Athletes Organize in Order to Protect Their Rights and Address the Ills of Intercollegiate Athletics?*, 5 VAND. J. ENT. L. & PRAC. 39 (2003); Jonathan L. H. Nygren, *Forcing the NCAA to Listen: Using Labor Law to Force the NCAA to Bargain Collectively with Student-Athletes*, 2 VA. SPORTS & ENT. L.J. 359 (2003).

5. The Collegiate Athletes' Coalition mentioned in the above excerpt subsequently renamed itself the National College Players Association. Its web site contains a section titled, *The 'Free Ride' — Should We Complain?*:

> There is no question about it — college athletes are fortunate. We have been given an opportunity to get an education while playing sports that we enjoy.
>
> However . . .
>
> Just because we are fortunate does not mean that we should not try to minimize risks and secure basic protections.
>
> The NCAA tries to convince us that we have little, if anything, to complain about because we are getting a "free ride" through college. This is not true. Our scholarships are not free — we WORK for them.

> The following explains how college athletes EARN an opportunity to get a college education:
>
> Year-round strength and conditioning workouts.
>
> Countless hours per week of mandatory participation in a sport (hours per week greatly increase because "voluntary" activities are performed).
>
> Injuries and surgeries that are endured throughout an athlete's career.
>
> Risk of permanent physical disability and death.
>
> Generating billions of dollars from TV contracts, ticket sales, etc.
>
> Giving national exposure to our schools.
>
> College athletes do not get a "free ride." Our education definitely has a price. Hard work and high risks are the trade-off for our scholarships. We should not have to keep quiet while being subjected to unethical conditions.

The "Free Ride" — Should We Complain?, NAT'L COLL. PLAYERS ASS'N (Mar. 13, 2009),* *available at* http://ncpanow.articulatedman.com/news_articles?id=0005. Do you agree?

6. In many colleges and universities black athletes have a higher graduation rate than black students. *The Academic Performance of Black Student Athletes at Highly Ranked Universities*, J. OF BLACKS IN HIGHER EDUC., Autumn 2003, at 30.* The biggest factor explaining this phenomenon is that black athletes do not face the financial pressures their black non-athlete peers do: the number one reason black students drop out is financial pressure. *Id.* However, the graduation rate of black athletes at highly ranked universities is far lower than other black students at the same institutions:

> [R]esearch shows that black athletes at almost all highly selective universities with major college sports programs graduate at rates lower than black students generally at the same institutions. At some of these universities, blacks graduate at a rate that is 20 percentage points or more below the rate of other black students.

Id. Why might this happen? Black athletes are given tremendous preference in their admissions process. They are accepted with lower grades and test scores — resulting in athletes isolating themselves from the rest of the university and suffering in the classroom. *Id.* William G. Bowen, the former president of Princeton University, and other advocates for reform recommend that universities "decrease their emphasis on athletics and recruit more well-rounded students who would be more engaged with the rest of the campus community." *Id.* at 31.

Are higher education institutions setting students up for failure by luring them to a university with high academic standards that they are ill prepared to meet?

Would it be better for these athletes to attend less prestigious schools, prep schools, or junior colleges in order to better prepare them for the rigors of university academics?

Do some black athletes have lower graduation rates at prestigious schools because those institutions refuse to have an "athlete curriculum"?

7. Do college coaches, recruiters, and even universities themselves have an incentive to make promises and even misrepresentations to athletes in order to ensure they choose their respective institutions? The University of Texas football coach, Mack Brown, makes $5.1 million a year. Steve Berkowitz, *Texas Mack Brown Becomes Highest-Paid Football Coach*, USA TODAY, Dec. 10, 2009, *available at* http://www.usatoday.com/sports/college/football/big12/2009-12-09-mack-brown-salary_N.htm. The Big Ten and Southeastern athletic conferences each received $22.2 million, to be divided up amongst the schools, following their BCS football appearances. *Non-BCS conferences get $24 million; Big Ten receives $22.2 million*, ASSOCIATED PRESS, Jan. 25, 2010, *available at* http://www.annarbor.com/sports/um-football/non-bcs-conferences-get-24-million-big-ten-receives-222-million/. Coaches receive better jobs and higher salaries when they win, and they cannot win without better athletes than the competition. If a university attracts the best athletes, it has a better chance to market a winning team nationally and receive revenue from merchandising, television contracts, and championship appearances. Are there any real checks and balances against personal and institutional ambition? Can student-athletes become victims to a system that uses them to further private agendas as opposed to educating them in the best way for their future?

8. Athletic programs use a variety of recruiting techniques to attract "blue-chip" athletes. Unfortunately, for some institutions, recruiting does not necessarily center on academics. The case of *Simpson v. University of Colorado Boulder* demonstrates an unfortunate but not uncommon method of recruiting. Here, high-school athletes visited the university and the resulting activity ended in sexual-harassment charges:

> Plaintiffs were sexually assaulted in Ms. Simpson's apartment by CU football players and high-school students on a recruiting visit. The CU football team recruited talented high-school players each fall by bringing them to campus. Part of the sales effort was to show recruits "a good time." To this end, recruits were paired with female "Ambassadors," who showed them around campus, and player-hosts, who were responsible for the recruits' entertainment. At least some of the recruits who came to Ms. Simpson's apartment had been promised an opportunity to have sex.
>
> By the time of the alleged assaults of Plaintiffs, there were a variety of sources of information suggesting the risks that sexual assault would occur if recruiting was inadequately supervised. These included reports not specific to CU regarding the serious risk of sexual assaults by student-athletes. There was also information specific to CU. In 1997 a high-school girl was assaulted by CU recruits at a party hosted by a CU football player. The local district attorney initiated a meeting with top CU officials, telling them that CU needed to develop policies for supervising recruits and implement sexual-assault-prevention training for football players. Yet CU

> did little to change its policies or training following that meeting. In particular, player-hosts were not instructed on the limits of appropriate entertainment.
>
> Moreover, events within the football program did not suggest that training relating to recruiting visits was unnecessary. Not only was the coaching staff informed of sexual harassment and assault by players, but it responded in ways that were more likely to encourage than eliminate such misconduct.

Simpson v. Univ. of Colo. Boulder, 500 F.3d 1170, 1173–74 (2007).

Do these recruiting techniques simply illustrate how far coaches and administrators are willing to go to get top-tier athletes? *See, e.g.*, Andy Staples, *Photo Reveals Vols Recruit had Contact with Hostesses at Game*, SPORTS ILLUSTRATED, Dec. 11, 2009, *available at* http://sportsillustrated.cnn.com/2009/writers/andy_staples/12/11/tennessee-recruiting/index.html (calling into question the University of Tennessee's recruiting practices when the university's hostesses attend high-school prospects' game three and a half hours away from university).

9. Some commentators think that coaches have a fiduciary duty to their players. A fiduciary is someone "who owes to another the duties of good faith, trust, confidence, and candor . . ." BLACK'S LAW DICTIONARY, 506 (7th ed. 2000). This way, student-athletes would have a private cause of action against coaches which is strong incentive for coaches to tell the truth; otherwise, they could be sued by their players and the players' families.

> While case law on the fiduciary duty of coaches in the college and university context is limited, there are potential legal obligations arising from the relationship. Scholars and commentators support finding fiduciary duties in intercollegiate athletics. The relationship between student-athletes and coaches (and the college or university) is more intimate than for many students. Student-athletes have a great deal riding on their success at their college or university, particularly athletes with potential at the professional level. Consequently, these student-athletes are highly regulated by the college or university and by the NCAA. Additionally, student-athletes rely heavily on academic advisors and coaches for their achievement.
>
> The relationship between a coach and a student-athlete is different from the relationship between the average teacher and student. Unlike a classroom teacher, who works to guide students through discussion and debate, the "[e]xecution of the coach's will is paramount" and what he/she says is seldom up for debate. "Coaches possess vast control over the lives of athletes on the field, in class, and away from school." This relationship lends itself to abuse by a coach and requires that the student-athlete have some sort of protection from a coach. Additionally, as one commentator notes, "Coaches and student-athletes do not necessarily have the same goals. Coaches . . . retain job security by winning, not by guiding student-athletes to graduation."

> This relationship between student-athlete and coach is more similar to that between a graduate student and faculty advisor, than to that between a non-athlete student and teacher.

Sarah Young, *Does A Coach Owe Players A Fiduciary Duty? Examining the Relationship Between Coach And Team*, 35 J.C. & U.L. 475, 488–89 (2009).*

10. How much control can a university exercise over academic decisions made by student-athletes? At least one lower court found, as a matter of law, that a student-athlete violated his scholarship agreement by failing to attend sports practices in favor of academic tutoring. *Taylor v. Wake Forest Univ.*, 16 N.C. App. 117 (N.C. App. 1972). The scholarship agreement required attendance at all practices and the student was making "reasonable academic progress" in his current course work. *Id.* at 121. Accordingly, the court determined that failure to attend practices without evidence of clear academic problems constituted a breach of the scholarship contract. *Id.* at 121. Should athletic administrators or the students themselves be the judge of "reasonable academic progress"?

In another case, a lower court found that a university had no duty of care when counseling student-athletes in academic compliance with intercollegiate association rules. *Hendricks v. Clemson Univ.*, 353 S.C. 449 (S.C. 2003). The court held that the scholarship contract created no fiduciary duty to accurately counsel students in NCAA academic requirements. *Id.* at 460. The student-athlete subsequently became ineligible to play and lost his scholarship. *Id.* at 454. Could this outcome have been avoided by more careful wording in the scholarship agreement? When does the scholarship agreement imply academic duties or rights? Who should be in charge of monitoring academic progress and eligibility?

11. Outside of misconduct, what kinds of acts can justify non-renewal of an athletic scholarship? In *Marcum v. Dahl*, the court found that several student-athletes' comments to the press regarding a university basketball coach were valid grounds for non-renewal of their scholarships. *Marcum v. Dahl*, 658 F.2d 731, 734–35 (10th Cir. 1981). Further, the court found that a player's comments to the press did not touch on "[a matter] of public concern" and were not subject to free speech protection. *Id.* at 734. The court determined that public comments about the students' coach and their scholarship renewals were not constitutionally protected by free speech rights or the Due Process clause of the Fourteenth Amendment. *Id.* at 735. Should off-campus speech ever affect scholarship status? The court noted that the speech in question caused division and disruption among the players of the university basketball team and that the decision not to renew scholarship contracts was entirely justified by this disruptive effect of the off-campus speech. *Id.* at 734.

C. LIABILITY FOR STUDENT-ATHLETE INJURIES

HANSON v. KYNAST

494 N.E.2d 1091 (Ohio 1986)

PRIOR HISTORY: APPEAL from the Court of Appeals for Ashland County.

On May 1, 1982, appellee, Brian K. Hanson, sustained a paralyzing injury while playing in a lacrosse game between Ohio State University ("OSU") and Ashland University, Inc. ("Ashland") at the Ashland lacrosse field. During the game Roger Allen, an OSU player, intercepted an Ashland player's pass and scored a goal. As Allen was scoring the goal, he was body-checked from behind by Ashland defender William D. Kynast. Allen fell and Kynast allegedly stood over Allen taunting him. Brian Hanson saw the contact and Kynast's subsequent behavior. Concerned for Allen's welfare, Hanson grabbed Kynast from the side or back and held him in a bear hug. Kynast immediately twisted and threw Hanson off his back. Hanson's head struck the ground and he sustained serious injuries.

The trainers for both teams came onto the field to attend Hanson. After discovering the seriousness of his injury . . . an assistant trainer for Ashland was sent to telephone the fire department for an ambulance.

Upon arriving on the scene, the ambulance driver discovered that the main entrance to the playing field was blocked by an illegally parked automobile. As a result, the ambulance driver had to find another entrance.

After immobilizing Hanson, the attendants transported him to Ashland Samaritan Hospital where he remained for almost an hour. He was then transferred to Mansfield General Hospital for surgery. . . . The surgery successfully relieved vascular compression thus preventing possible brain damage. Hanson, however, had sustained a serious spinal cord injury on impact. . . . Hanson is now an incomplete quadriplegic.

On December 13, 1983, Brian Hanson filed an amended complaint in the Court of Common Pleas of Ashland County against William Kynast and Ashland University, Inc. Hanson maintained, in relevant part, that because Kynast was acting as the agent of Ashland, the university was therefore liable for Kynast's alleged wrongful acts under the doctrine of respondeat superior. Hanson also alleged that Ashland was directly liable for negligently failing to have an ambulance or emergency vehicle present at the site of the game, and in permitting a motor vehicle to be parked in such a manner that the main entrance to the playing field was blocked. Ashland filed a timely answer denying the material allegations of the complaint.

On April 11, 1984, Ashland filed a motion for summary judgment. . . . The trial court granted Ashland's motion on November 16, 1984. The court held that no agency relationship existed between Kynast and Ashland, and that Ashland did not have a legal duty to have an ambulance at the game. In a split decision, the court of appeals reversed the trial court's judgment, holding that genuine issues of fact existed on the question of agency and upon Ashland's duty to provide medical personnel at the game.

The cause is now before this court pursuant to the allowance of a motion to certify the record.

Opinion by: PARRINO, J.

The first issue to be decided is whether the relationship of principal and agent existed between Kynast and Ashland. Because of the absence of proof as to the existence of a principal-agent relationship, the trial court essentially found as a matter of law that Ashland was not bound by Kynast's conduct under the doctrine of respondeat superior. We agree.

This court has held that the relationship of principal and agent or master and servant exists only when one party exercises the right of control over the actions of another, and those actions are directed toward the attainment of an objective which the former seeks. [citations omitted]. Therefore, a principal-agent relationship can be found in the instant case only if Kynast was under the control of Ashland, and if he took some action directed toward the attainment of Ashland's objective.

In order to make this determination we must examine the relevant documentary evidence produced before the trial court. A review of the evidence reveals that William Kynast expressed an interest in Ashland when he was in high school. He requested and received written information from the university and he spoke with Ashland lacrosse coach Dick Fahrney. In his deposition Kynast testified that he chose Ashland because it had a good business school, he could live away from home, and he would be able to play lacrosse. He also testified that no promises were made to him by any Ashland official to induce him to attend the university.

Kynast attended Ashland for three semesters, starting in August 1981. He financed his education through bank loans and with the assistance of his parents. While at Ashland, Kynast decided to play lacrosse; however, he was never obligated to play lacrosse for the university. In addition, Kynast did not receive a scholarship, he used his own equipment while playing, and he was not compensated for his participation.

. . . Ashland provides a coach and the players are each given a game shirt which displays the university's name. The players also received free transportation to games at other schools, and on one occasion while Kynast played for Ashland, they received overnight lodging on a road trip. No admission fee is charged at the home games.

This court is of the opinion that this relationship between Kynast and Ashland is a relationship common to many students attending universities. A university offers a diversified educational experience which includes classroom instruction in a great variety of subjects as well as optional participation in events such as school clubs, and intramural and intercollegiate sports. . . . Students evaluate and determine which university best meets their needs, and then pay a fee to attend that university. The relationship formed under these conditions has previously been characterized as contractual. *Zumbrun v. U.C.L.A.* (1972), 25 Cal. App. 3d 1, 10. The student pays a fee and agrees to abide by the university rules. In exchange, the university provides the student with a worthwhile education.

This relationship does not constitute a principal-agent relationship. The student is a buyer of education rather than an agent. Restatement of the Law 2d, Agency (1958) 73, Section 14 J, states that a buyer retains goods primarily for his own benefit, while an agent is one who retains goods primarily for the benefit of the one who delivers those goods. In the instant case, the "goods" to be delivered is an education and the university delivers that education to the student for a fee. It is clear that a student retains the benefit of that education for himself rather than for the university.

. . . .

In summary, the relationship discussed above constitutes a contractual one between the student and his university. The university is selling and the student is buying an education, and the formation of a principal-agent relationship was not intended, nor was one established, between the parties.

The appellee, however, maintains that Kynast's participation in lacrosse converted his status from the usual university-student relationship to that of principal-agent due to the control exercised by the lacrosse coach over Kynast, and because his participation in lacrosse resulted in beneficial publicity for Ashland. We disagree. In applying the law of agency to the facts of this case, we must conclude that Kynast was not controlled by Ashland, and that he was not playing the game for the school's benefit.

The degree of control necessary to establish agency has not been clearly defined. Instead, courts have generally examined various factors in determining whether the requisite amount of control exists. One such factor is whether the individual is performing in the course of the principal's business rather than in some ancillary capacity. In the case at bar, Kynast was not performing in the course of the principal's business, i.e., he was not educating students. On the contrary, he was participating in one of the educationally related opportunities offered by the university. Another factor to be considered is whether the individual was receiving any compensation from the principal. It is undisputed that Kynast was never compensated for playing on the Ashland lacrosse team. A third factor is whether the principal supplied the tools and the place of work in the normal course of the relationship. Kynast supplied his own equipment in order to play lacrosse. The university did, however, provide the playing field.

A review of these factors clearly shows that Kynast was not controlled by Ashland for the purpose of establishing an agency relationship. The control exerted over Kynast by the university, i.e., the Ashland coach running the lacrosse team, was merely incidental to the educational opportunity in which Kynast voluntarily participated. . . .

Further, the documentary evidence considered in determining appellee's motion for summary judgment clearly establishes that Kynast's activity was not directed toward the attainment of an objective by Ashland. Lacrosse at Ashland is not an income-producing sport. In fact, as previously noted, an admission fee is not charged to attend the games. . . .

The appellee's claim that Ashland derived a benefit through the publicity the team generated is not persuasive. In *Toms v. Delta Savings & Loan Assn.* (1955),

162 Ohio St. 513 . . . this court specifically held that an agency relationship is not established between a savings and loan company and a softball player, even though the savings and loan company sponsored the softball team for publicity and provided the team with uniforms bearing the company's name. In the instant case, there is no evidence that Ashland derived a benefit from publicity; nor is there evidence that Kynast participated in lacrosse so that Ashland could benefit from publicity. . . . Under such a circumstance no agency relationship is created.

To summarize, we conclude that a student who attends a university of his choice, receives no scholarship or compensation, voluntarily becomes a member of the university lacrosse team that engages in intercollegiate contests with other universities for which games no attendance fee is charged, who purchases his own equipment and who receives instructions from a coach while preparing for and playing such games, but is not otherwise controlled by the coach, and who participates in the game as a part of his total educational experience while attending school, is not the agent of the university at the time he is playing the game of lacrosse. Thus, appellee's claim that Ashland was liable for Kynast's wrongful acts through the doctrine of respondeat superior was properly rejected and the trial court properly entered summary judgment for appellant on this issue.

The second and final issue to be resolved is whether the trial court properly entered summary judgment for Ashland upon Hanson's claims that Ashland was negligent for failing to have an ambulance and medical personnel at the game, and for permitting an illegally parked car to block the playing field's entrance. The appellee maintains that such negligence resulted in the delay of his treatment.

In order to successfully establish negligence, the appellee must prove the existence of the following elements: (1) a duty owed by Ashland to Hanson, (2) a breach of this duty by Ashland, and (3) that Hanson's injuries were a proximate result of Ashland's conduct. It is unnecessary at this time to consider whether genuine issues of fact existed as to the first two elements of negligence for the reason that the uncontradicted evidence submitted by Ashland established that no damages proximately resulted from Ashland's alleged wrongdoing.

Submitted in support of Ashland's motion for summary judgment was an affidavit from Dr. Thomas L. Strachan stating that Hanson's injury was sustained at the moment that his head hit the ground. Dr. Strachan further stated that there was no evidence of neurological deterioration subsequent to impact; in other words, Hanson did not suffer additional injury as a proximate result of any delay in treatment. . . .

One of the elements necessary to establish negligence was not present; therefore, as a matter of law, the trial court properly granted Ashland's motion for summary judgment on Hanson's claim of negligence.

Accordingly, the judgment of the court of appeals is reversed.

KLEINKNECHT v. GETTYSBURG COLLEGE

989 F.2d 1360 (3d Cir. 1993)

OPINION OF THE COURT

HUTCHINSON, CIRCUIT JUDGE.

Suzanne W. Kleinknecht and Richard P. Kleinknecht (collectively "the Kleinknechts") appeal an order of the United States District Court for the Middle District of Pennsylvania granting summary judgment to appellee Gettysburg College ("the College"). . . . We will reverse the district court's order granting summary judgment to the College for the following reasons.

I. Procedural History

Drew Kleinknecht died of cardiac arrest on September 16, 1988, while a student at the College and during a practice session of its intercollegiate lacrosse team. His parents filed this wrongful death and survival action against the College on August 15, 1990. The College filed an answer on September 11, 1990, and a motion for summary judgment on August 31, 1991. The district court initially denied the motion on November 1, 1991, but then granted the College's motion for reconsideration on January 9, 1992.

Following oral argument on January 30, 1992, the district court reversed its earlier decision and entered summary judgment in favor of the College on March 12, 1992. In its opinion, the court first held that the College had no duty to anticipate and guard against the chance of a fatal arrhythmia in a young and healthy athlete. The court also held that the actions taken by school employees following Drew's collapse were reasonable, and thus the College did not negligently breach any duty that might exist.

. . . .

The Kleinknechts filed a timely appeal . . . .

II. Factual History

In September 1988, Drew Kleinknecht was a twenty-year old sophomore student at the College, which had recruited him for its Division III intercollegiate lacrosse team. The College is a private, four-year liberal arts school. . . .

Lacrosse is a contact sport. . . . Lacrosse players can typically suffer a variety of injuries, including unconsciousness, wooziness, concussions, being knocked to the ground, and having the wind knocked out of them. Before Drew died, however, no athlete at the College had experienced cardiac arrest while playing lacrosse or any other sport.

In September 1988, the College employed two full-time athletic trainers, Joseph Donolli and Gareth Biser. Both men were certified by the National Athletic Trainers Association, which requires, inter alia, current certification in both cardiopulmonary resuscitation ("CPR") and standard first aid. In addition, twelve student trainers participated in the College's sports program. The trainers were stationed in the College's two training room facilities at Musselman Stadium and Plank Gymnasium.

Because lacrosse is a spring sport, daily practices were held during the spring semester in order to prepare for competition. . . . Fall practice was held only for the players to learn "skills and drills" . . . . No student trainers were assigned to the fall practices.

Drew participated in a fall lacrosse practice on the afternoon of September 16, 1988. Coaches Janczyk and Anderson attended and supervised this practice. . . . No trainers or student trainers were present. Neither coach had certification in CPR. Neither coach had a radio on the practice field. The nearest telephone was inside the training room at Musselman Stadium, roughly 200-250 yards away. The shortest route to this telephone required scaling an eight-foot high cyclone fence surrounding the stadium. According to Coach Janczyk, he and Coach Anderson had never discussed how they would handle an emergency during fall lacrosse practice.

The September 16, 1988 practice began at about 3:15 p.m. with jogging and stretching, some drills, and finally a "six on six" drill in which the team split into two groups at opposite ends of the field. Drew was a defenseman and was participating in one of the drills when he suffered a cardiac arrest. . . .

. . . .

According to the College, Coach Janczyk acted in accordance with the school's emergency plan by first assessing Drew's condition, then dispatching players to get a trainer and call for an ambulance. Coach Janczyk himself then began to run toward Musselman Stadium to summon help.

The Kleinknechts dispute the College's version of the facts. They note that although Coach Janczyk claims to have told two players to run to Apple Hall, a nearby dormitory, for help, Coach Anderson did not recall Coach Janczyk's sending anyone for help. Even if Coach Janczyk did send the two players to Apple Hall, the Kleinknechts maintain, his action was inappropriate because Apple Hall was not the location of the nearest telephone. It is undisputed that two other team members ran for help, but the Kleinknechts contend that the team members did this on their own accord, without instruction from either coach.

The parties do not dispute that Polizzotti, the team captain, ran toward the stadium, where he knew a training room was located and a student trainer could be found. In doing so, Polizzotti scaled a chain link fence that surrounded the stadium and ran across the field, encountering student trainer Traci Moore outside the door to the training room. He told her that a lacrosse player was down and needed help. . . . Polizzotti continued into the training room where he told the student trainers there what had happened. One of them phoned Plank Gymnasium and told Head Trainer Donolli about the emergency.

Contemporaneously with Polizzotti's dash to the stadium, Dave Kerney, another team member, ran toward the stadium for assistance. Upon seeing that Polizzotti was going to beat him there, Kerney concluded that it was pointless for both of them to arrive at the same destination and changed his course toward the College Union Building. He told the student at the front desk of the emergency on the practice field. The student called his supervisor on duty in the building, and she immediately telephoned for an ambulance.

Student trainer Moore was first to reach Drew. . . . Because Drew was breathing, she did not attempt CPR or any other first aid technique . . . .

By this time, Coach Janczyk had entered the stadium training room and learned that Donolli had been notified and an ambulance called. Coach Janczyk returned to the practice field at the same time Donolli arrived in a golf cart. Donolli saw that Drew was not breathing, and turned him on his back to begin CPR . . . . [D]espite repeated resuscitation efforts, Drew could not be revived. He was pronounced dead at 4:58 p.m.

As the district court observed, the parties vigorously dispute the amount of time that elapsed in connection with the events following Drew's collapse. . . . The College estimates that an ambulance was present within eight to ten minutes after Drew's collapse.

The Kleinknechts, on the other hand . . . contend that evidence exists from which a jury could infer that as long as twelve minutes elapsed before CPR was administered. They also estimate that roughly ten more minutes passed before the first ambulance arrived on the scene.

Prior to his collapse on September 16, 1988, Drew had no medical history of heart problems. . . .

Medical evidence indicated Drew died of cardiac arrest after a fatal attack of cardiac arrhythmia. Post-mortem examination could not detect the cause of Drew's fatal cardiac arrhythmia. . . .

III. Issues on Appeal

The Kleinknechts . . . . first argue that the district court erred in determining that the College had no legal duty to implement preventive measures assuring prompt assistance and treatment in the event one of its student-athletes suffered cardiac arrest while engaged in school-supervised intercollegiate athletic activity. Second, the Kleinknechts maintain that the district court erred in determining that the actions of school employees following Drew's collapse were reasonable and that the College therefore did not breach any duty of care. . . .

. . . .

IV. Analysis

1. The Duty of Care Issue

Whether a defendant owes a duty of care to a plaintiff is a question of law. In order to prevail on a cause of action in negligence under Pennsylvania law, a plaintiff must establish: (1) a duty or obligation recognized by the law, requiring the actor to conform to a certain standard of conduct; (2) a failure to conform to the standard required; (3) a causal connection between the conduct and the resulting injury; and (4) actual loss or damage resulting to the interests of another.

The . . . theories upon which [the Kleinknechts] predicate the College's duty to establish preventive measures capable of providing treatment to student-athletes in the event of a medical emergency [include]: (1) existence of a special relationship between the College and its student-athletes; [and] (2) foreseeability that a student-athlete may suffer cardiac arrest while engaged in athletic activity . . . .

a. Special Relationship

The Kleinknechts argue that the College had a duty of care to Drew by virtue of his status as a member of an intercollegiate athletic team. . . . The Kleinknechts argue that although the Supreme Court has not addressed this precise issue, it would conclude that a college or university owes a duty to its intercollegiate athletes to provide preventive measures in the event of a medical emergency.

In support of their argument, the Kleinknechts cite the case of *Hanson v. Kynast*, No. CA-828 (Ohio Ct. App. June 3, 1985), *rev'd on other grounds*, 494 N.E.2d. 1091 (Ohio 1986). In *Hanson*, an intercollegiate, recruited lacrosse player was seriously injured while playing in a lacrosse game against another college. The plaintiff alleged that his university breached its legal duty to have an ambulance present during the lacrosse game. The trial court granted the defendant's motion for summary judgment based on its holding, inter alia, that

> There is no duty as a matter of law for the Defendant College or other sponsor of athletic events to have ambulances, emergency vehicles, trained help or doctors present during the playing of a lacrosse game or other athletic events, and the failure to do so does not constitute negligence as a matter of law.

Id. at 10. The court of appeals reversed, concluding, "It is a question of fact for the jury to determine whether or not appellee University acted reasonably in failing to have an ambulance present at the field or to provide quick access to the field in the event of an emergency." By directing the trial court to submit the case to a jury, the court of appeals implicitly held that the university owed a duty of care to the plaintiff.

Although the *Hanson* court did not specify the theory on which it predicated this duty, we think it reached the correct result, and we predict that the Supreme Court of Pennsylvania would conclude that a similar duty exists on the facts of this case. Like the lacrosse student in *Hanson*, Drew chose to attend Gettysburg College because he was persuaded it had a good lacrosse program, a sport in which he wanted to participate at the intercollegiate level. Head Trainer Donolli actively recruited Drew to play lacrosse at the College. At the time he was stricken, Drew was not engaged in his own private affairs as a student at Gettysburg College. Instead, he was participating in a scheduled athletic practice for an intercollegiate team sponsored by the College under the supervision of College employees. On these facts we believe that the Supreme Court of Pennsylvania would hold that a special relationship existed between the College and Drew that was sufficient to impose a duty of reasonable care on the College. . . .

The Supreme Court of Pennsylvania has not specifically addressed the issue whether schools owe its athletes a duty based on that special relationship. The Supreme Court has, however, held that a university cannot be held liable for property damage incurred in a fire started by an intoxicated minor student of the university. In *Alumni Association v. Sullivan*, 572 A.2d 1209, 1211 (Pa. 1990), the plaintiff alleged that the university knew or should have known that alcohol was being provided to minors in a dormitory and a fraternity house. Finding no evidence that either the fraternity or the university was involved in serving, supplying or purchasing the liquor, the Court declined to impose a duty based on a custodial relationship between the university and its students. *Id.* at 1213.

In so holding, the *Sullivan* Court quoted from this Court's decision in *Bradshaw v. Rawlings*, on which the College relies in support of its position that it has no duty of care to its students. *Bradshaw* is clearly distinguishable, for the same reasons. There the plaintiff had attended a sophomore class picnic sponsored by his college. He left the picnic with another visibly intoxicated student who, while driving, was involved in an automobile accident that left the plaintiff with severe injuries. We held that the college owed no duty to the plaintiff in this situation based on a recognition that "the modern American college is not an insurer of the safety of its students." 612 F.2d at 138. . . .

Here, unlike *Sullivan* and *Bradshaw*, Drew was not acting in his capacity as a private student when he collapsed. Indeed, the Kleinknechts concede that if he had been, they would have no recourse against the College. . . . [T]he fact that Drew's cardiac arrest occurred during an athletic event involving an intercollegiate team of which he was a member does impose a duty of due care on a college that actively sought his participation in that sport. We cannot help but think that the College recruited Drew for its own benefit, probably thinking that his skill at lacrosse would bring favorable attention and so aid the College in attracting other students.

. . . .

In conclusion, we predict that the Supreme Court of Pennsylvania would hold that the College owed Drew a duty of care in his capacity as an intercollegiate athlete engaged in school-sponsored intercollegiate athletic activity for which he had been recruited.

b. Foreseeability

This does not end our inquiry, however. The determination that the College owes a duty of care to its intercollegiate athletes could merely define the class of persons to whom the duty extends, without determining the nature of the duty or demands it makes on the College. Because it is foreseeable that student-athletes may sustain severe and even life-threatening injuries while engaged in athletic activity, the Kleinknechts argue that the College's duty of care required it to be ready to respond swiftly and adequately to a medical emergency.

Foreseeability is a legal requirement before recovery can be had.

The type of foreseeability that determines a duty of care, as opposed to proximate cause, is not dependent on the foreseeability of a specific event. Instead, in the context of duty, "the concept of foreseeability means the likelihood of the occurrence of a general type of risk rather than the likelihood of the occurrence of the precise chain of events leading to the injury." Only when even the general likelihood of some broadly definable class of events, of which the particular event that caused the plaintiff's injury is a subclass, is unforeseeable can a court hold as a matter of law that the defendant did not have a duty to the plaintiff to guard against that broad general class of risks within which the particular harm the plaintiff suffered befell.

Even this determination that the harm suffered was foreseeable fails to end our analysis. If a duty is to be imposed, the foreseeable risk of harm must be unreasonable. The classic risk-utility analysis used to determine whether a risk is unreasonable "balances the risk, in light of the social value of the interest threatened, and the probability and extent of the harm, against the value of the interest which the actor is seeking to protect, and the expedience of the course pursued."

. . . .

Although the district court correctly determined that the Kleinknechts had presented evidence establishing that the occurrence of severe and life-threatening injuries is not out of the ordinary during contact sports, it held that the College had no duty because the cardiac arrest suffered by Drew, a twenty-year old athlete with no history of any severe medical problems, was not reasonably foreseeable. Its definition of foreseeability is too narrow. Although it is true that a defendant is not required to guard against every possible risk, he must take reasonable steps to guard against hazards which are generally foreseeable. *Kimble v. Mackintosh Hemphill Co.*, 359 Pa. 461, 59 A.2d 68, 71 (Pa. 1948). Though the specific risk that a person like Drew would suffer a cardiac arrest may be unforeseeable, the Kleinknechts produced ample evidence that a life-threatening injury occurring during participation in an athletic event like lacrosse was reasonably foreseeable. . . . Therefore, the College did owe Drew a duty to take reasonable precautions against the risk of death while Drew was taking part in the College's intercollegiate lacrosse program.

Having determined that it is foreseeable that a member of the College's interscholastic lacrosse team could suffer a serious injury during an athletic event, it becomes evident that the College's failure to protect against such a risk is not reasonable. The magnitude of the foreseeable harm — irreparable injury or death to one of its student-athletes as a result of inadequate preventive emergency measures — is indisputable. With regard to the offsetting cost of protecting against such risk, the College prophesied that if this Court accepts that the College owed the asserted duty, then it will be required "to have a CPR certified trainer on site at each and every athletic practice whether in-season or off-season, formal or informal, strenuous or light," and to provide similar cardiac protection to "intramural, club sports and gym class." This "slippery slope" prediction reflects an unwarranted extension of the holding in this case. First, the recognition of a duty here is limited to intercollegiate athletes. . . . Second, the determination whether the College has breached this duty at all is a question of fact for the jury. This Court recognizes only that under the facts of this case, the College owed a duty to Drew to have measures in place at the lacrosse team's practice . . . in order to provide prompt treatment in the event that he or any other member of the lacrosse team suffered a life-threatening injury.

We also must reject the College's vigorous and lengthy argument that Drew's cardiac arrest could not have been foreseeable because his parents' encouragement to engage in athletic activity shows that Drew's death as a result of cardiac arrest while participating in athletics was not foreseeable even to them . . . . This argument is unavailing because it addresses foreseeability as relating to causation, not duty. It is not pertinent to the issue of the College's duty of care to Drew.

. . . .

. . . In reversing the district court's grant of summary judgment to the College, we predict that the Supreme Court of Pennsylvania would hold that a college also has a duty to be reasonably prepared for handling medical emergencies that foreseeably arise during a student's participation in an intercollegiate contact sport for which a college recruited him. It is clearly foreseeable that a person participating in such an activity will sustain serious injury requiring immediate medical attention.

. . . .

Whether the College breached that duty is a question of fact. If the factfinder concludes that such a breach occurred, we think that the question whether that breach was the proximate or legal cause of Drew's death would likewise be a question of fact.

. . . .

2. The Reasonableness of the College's Actions

On the duty question, it remains only for us to address the district court's second holding that the conduct of the College's agents in providing Drew with medical assistance and treatment following his cardiac arrest was reasonable. The court based this determination in part, if not in whole, on its conclusion that the College had no duty to consider what emergency assistance measures would be necessary were one of its student-athletes to suffer a cardiac arrest during athletic activity . . . . The question of breach must be reconsidered on remand in light of this Court's holding that the College did owe Drew a duty of care to provide prompt and adequate emergency medical assistance to Drew while participating as one of its intercollegiate athletes in a school-sponsored athletic activity.

. . . .

V. Conclusion

The district court's holding that the College's duty of care to Drew as an intercollegiate athlete did not include, prior to his collapse, a duty to provide prompt emergency medical service while he was engaged in school-sponsored athletic activity will be reversed. The district court's holding that the College acted reasonably and therefore did not breach any duty owed to Drew following his collapse will likewise be reversed. We will remand this matter to the district court for further proceedings consistent with this opinion. . . .

NOTES

1. Even if you agree with the conclusion of the *Hanson* court on the negligence claim (because Hanson's injuries were instantaneous, thus rendering it immaterial whether Ashland had medical personnel at the game to tend to his injuries), do you think the court's agency analysis would have held up if Kynast — the one who caused Hanson's injuries — had been a scholarship athlete? Recall that Kynast received no financial assistance from Ashland for his participation on the lacrosse team. This prompted the court to conclude that Kynast's relationship with Ashland could not be that of principal and agent because Kynast was a "buyer of education rather than an agent," keeping the "goods" for his own benefit rather than that of the university. *Hanson v. Kynast*, 494 N.E.2d 1091, 1094 (Ohio 1986).

2. The question of what duties, if any, a college or university owes to its student-athletes remains unsettled. Consider this:

> In recent years, courts and commentators have taken differing views as to what duties schools have to the scholarship athletes that they have recruited. Some are of the view that the unequal bargaining power in the recruitment process, the degree of influence that a school and its coaches have over a student-athlete's daily life, the pressures placed on student-athletes to win at all costs (which may cause some students to risk their own health and safety), and the enormous sums of money schools now reap from their successful teams, are such that schools should be deemed to have a "special relationship" with their own scholarship athletes and a corresponding duty to protect those athletes from injury. Others have rejected that theory on the ground that there is nothing different about a student-athlete's relationship with a university which would justify the conclusion that a student-athlete is a custodial ward of the university while the non-athlete student is an emancipated adult.

Kavanagh v. Trs. of Boston Univ., 795 N.E.2d 1170, 1176–77 (Mass. 2003).

3. What role should the assumption-of-risk negligence doctrine have in this discussion? *See* Donald T. Meier, Note, *Primary Assumption of Risk and Duty in Football Indirect Injury Cases: A Legal Workout from the Tragedies on the Training Ground for American Values*, 2 VA. SPORTS & ENT. L.J. 80, 125–26 (2002) (arguing that assumption of risk should have precluded financial recovery by the family of a Northwestern University football player who died during a preseason conditioning workout); *but see* Lura Hess, Note, *Sports and the Assumption of Risk Doctrine in New York*, 76 ST. JOHN'S L. REV. 457, 476 (2002) (arguing that assumption of risk should not be used for student-athletes in comparative fault jurisdictions because it is "illogical, cumbersome, and unnecessarily harsh.").

4. While it remains an open question as to what duties postsecondary schools owe to their own student-athletes, it appears settled that a college or university owes extremely limited duties to student-athletes from other schools. *See, e.g., Fox* *v. Bd. of Supervisors of LSU*, 576 So. 2d 978 (La. 1991) (holding that the only duty LSU owed to a visiting rugby player who had been severely injured when he missed a tackle was to keep the playing field safe); *Kavanagh v. Trs. of Boston Univ.*, 795 N.E.2d 1170 (Mass. 2003) (holding that unless Boston University officials had reason to foresee that one of its basketball players was likely to punch an opposing player, they owed no duty to the injured player).

5. Should a lower standard of liability apply to athletic activities that naturally imply higher risks of injury to student-athletes, like cheerleading? Lower courts typically differ widely on the answer. In *Fisher v. Northwestern State University*, the court found that a university had no duty to provide even minimal adult supervision or coaching to university cheerleaders. *Fisher v. Northwestern State Univ.*, 624 So. 2d 1308 (La. App. 3 Cir. 1993). The court relied heavily on evidence that collegiate cheerleaders are generally aware of the high risk of injury inherent in cheerleading at that level. *Id.* at 1309. Additionally, the court determined that supervision of athletics should be proportionate to the experience and age of the students and that no supervision was necessary for experienced and well-trained collegiate cheerleaders. *Id.* at 1311. Conversely, the Washington Supreme Court affirmed an award of $350,000 to a university cheerleader who was permanently injured during a practice. *Kirk v. Wash. State Univ.*, 109 Wash. 2d 448 (Wash. 1987). The court found that a university could be negligent for failing to adequately supervise cheerleaders, train students in safety, and for failing to provide safe equipment for practice. *Id.* at 449. Unlike *Fischer*, the court determined that assumption of the risk was not a complete bar to recovery of damages. *Id.* at 457. The university had a duty to provide safe practice conditions, training, and adequate supervision to university-sponsored cheerleaders, though Kirk herself was found partially negligent and her award was reduced accordingly. *Id.* at 451.

Should universities be required to monitor all athletic practices that might cause injury? Should college students, as trained adult athletes, be required to supervise themselves? Should a higher standard of supervision and liability apply in cheerleading and other injury-prone sports?

6. Can a university be liable for failure to investigate and provide support services to a student-athlete rape victim? One court found that a university was not at fault for failure to investigate a sexual assault, take action against the alleged students/rapists, or provide support services to a student-athlete who claimed she had been raped by two other students. *Ruegsegger v. Western NM Univ. Bd. of Regents*, 141 N.M. 306 (N.M. App. 2006). Ruegsegger argued that her scholarship agreement with the university created a contractual obligation on the part of the university to follow university handbook procedures on sexual assault support and investigation. *Id.* at 308. The court found that the scholarship agreement wasn't specific enough on the university's obligation to provide non-academic services, and hence, there was no breach for failure to provide support services and take action on behalf of Ruegsegger. *Id.* at 311. Should sexual assault services be explicitly stated in athletic scholarship agreements? Should a student-athlete reasonably expect her university to investigate incidents of sexual assault and provide support services where needed? Notably, the alleged rapists in question were both student-athletes and members of the university football team. *Id.* at 308. Does a university have a duty to monitor student-athletes it specifically recruits into the student population? Should universities ever be responsible for the emotional and psychological well-being of athletes?

7. Should colleges and universities be liable for the crimes committed by its student-athletes? *See* Ann Scales, *Student Gladiators and Sexual Assault: A New Analysis of Liability for Injuries Inflicted by College Athletes*, 15 MICH. J. GENDER & L. 205 (2009).

D. GENDER EQUALITY IN INTERCOLLEGIATE ATHLETICS

COHEN v. BROWN UNIVERSITY

991 F.2d 888 (1st Cir. 1993)

OPINION

SELYA, CIRCUIT JUDGE. In this watershed case, defendants-appellants Brown University, Vartan Gregorian, and David Roach appeal from the district court's issuance of a preliminary injunction ordering Brown to reinstate its women's gymnastics and volleyball programs to full intercollegiate varsity status pending the resolution of a Title IX claim. After mapping Title IX's rugged legal terrain and cutting a passable swath through the factual thicket that overspreads the parties' arguments, we affirm.

I. BROWN ATHLETICS: AN OVERVIEW

College athletics, particularly in the realm of football and basketball, has traditionally occupied a prominent role in American sports and American society. For college students, athletics offers an opportunity to exacuate leadership skills, learn teamwork, build self-confidence, and perfect self-discipline. In addition, for many student-athletes, physical skills are a passport to college admissions and scholarships, allowing them to attend otherwise inaccessible schools. These opportunities, and the lessons learned on the playing fields, are invaluable in attaining career and life successes in and out of professional sports.

The highway of opportunity runs in both directions. Not only student-athletes, but universities, too, benefit from the magic of intercollegiate sports. Successful teams generate television revenues and gate receipts which often fund significant percentages of a university's overall athletic program, offering students the opportunity to partake of sports that are not financially self-sustaining. Even those institutions whose teams do not fill the grandstands of cavernous stadiums or attract national television exposure benefit from increased student and alumni cohesion and the support it engenders. . . .

In these terms, Brown will never be confused with Notre Dame or the more muscular members of the Big Ten. . . . Brown's athletic program has only occasionally achieved national prominence or, for that matter, enjoyed sustained success. Moreover, at Brown, as at most schools, women are a relatively inconspicuous part of the storied athletic past. Historically, colleges limited athletics to the male sphere, leaving those few women's teams that sprouted to scrounge for resources.

. . . .

II. THE PLAINTIFF CLASS

In the spring of 1991, Brown announced that it, like many other schools, was in a financial bind, and that, as a belt-tightening measure, it planned to drop four sports from its intercollegiate varsity athletic roster: women's volleyball and gymnastics, men's golf and water polo. The University permitted the teams to continue playing as "intercollegiate clubs," a status that allowed them to compete against varsity teams from other colleges, but cut off financial subsidies and support services routinely available to varsity teams (e.g., salaried coaches, access to prime facilities, preferred practice time, medical trainers, clerical assistance, office support, admission preferences, and the like). Brown estimated that eliminating these four varsity teams would save $77,813 per annum, broken down as follows: women's volleyball, $37,127; women's gymnastics, $24,901; men's water polo, $9,250; men's golf, $6,545.

Before the cuts, Brown athletics offered an aggregate of 328 varsity slots for female athletes and 566 varsity slots for male athletes. Thus, women had 36.7% of the athletic opportunities and men 63.3%. Abolishing the four varsity teams . . . did not materially affect the athletic opportunity ratios; women retained 36.6% of the opportunities and men 63.4%. At that time . . . Brown's student body comprised approximately 52% men and 48% women.

Following Brown's announcement of the cutbacks, disappointed members of the women's volleyball and gymnastics teams brought suit. They proceeded on an implied cause of action under Title IX, 20 U.S.C. §§ 1681-1688 (1988). See *Franklin v. Gwinnett* County Pub. Sch.,112 S. Ct. 1028, 1032 (1992) (recognizing implied private right of action under Title IX). The plaintiffs charged that Brown's athletic arrangements violated Title IX's ban on gender-based discrimination, a violation that was allegedly exacerbated by Brown's decision to devalue the two women's programs without first making sufficient reductions in men's activities or, in the alternative, adding other women's teams to compensate for the loss.

. . . [T]he district court certified a class of "all present and future Brown University women students and potential students who participate, seek to participate, and/or are deterred from participating in intercollegiate athletics funded by Brown." . . . [T]he judge granted a preliminary injunction requiring Brown to reinstate the two women's teams pending the outcome of a full trial on the merits. We stayed execution of the order and expedited Brown's appeal.

III. TITLE IX AND COLLEGIATE ATHLETICS

Title IX prohibits gender-based discrimination by educational institutions receiving federal financial support — in practice, the vast majority of all accredited colleges and universities. The statute sketches wide policy lines, leaving the details to regulating agencies. . . .

A. Scope of Title IX.

At its inception, the broad proscriptive language of Title IX caused considerable consternation in the academic world. The academy's anxiety chiefly centered around identifying which individual programs, particularly in terms of athletics, might come within the scope of the discrimination provision, and, relatedly, how the government would determine compliance. The gridiron fueled these concerns: for many schools, the men's football budget far exceeded that of any other sport, and men's athletics as a whole received the lion's share of dedicated resources — a share that, typically, was vastly disproportionate to the percentage of men in the student body.

. . . .

In 1984, the Supreme Court . . . held that Title IX was "program-specific," so that its tenets applied only to the program(s) which actually received federal funds and not to the rest of the university. *Grove City College v. Bell*, 465 U.S. 555, 574 (1984). Because few athletic departments are direct recipients of federal funds — most federal money for universities is channeled through financial aid offices or invested directly in research grants — Grove City cabined Title IX and placed virtually all collegiate athletic programs beyond its reach.

In response to *Grove City*, Congress scrapped the program-specific approach and reinstated an institution-wide application of Title IX by passing the Civil Rights Restoration Act of 1987, 20 U.S.C. § 1687 (1988). The Restoration Act required that if any arm of an educational institution received federal funds, the institution as a whole must comply with Title IX's provisions. Although the Restoration Act does not specifically mention sports, the record of the floor debate leaves little doubt that the enactment was aimed, in part, at creating a more level playing field for female athletes.

The appellants do not challenge the district court's finding that, under existing law, Brown's athletic department is subject to Title IX. . . .

B. Statutory Framework.

Title IX, like the Restoration Act, does not explicitly treat college athletics. Rather, the statute's heart is a broad prohibition of gender-based discrimination in all programmatic aspects of educational institutions:

> No person in the United States shall, on the basis of sex, be excluded from participation in, be denied the benefits of, or be subjected to discrimination under any education program or activity receiving Federal financial assistance . . . .

20 U.S.C. § 1681(a) (1988). After listing a number of exempt organizations, section 1681 makes clear that, while Title IX prohibits discrimination, it does not mandate strict numerical equality between the gender balance of a college's athletic program and the gender balance of its student body. . . . Put another way, a court assessing Title IX compliance may not find a violation solely because there is a disparity between the gender composition of an educational institution's student constituency, on the one hand, and its athletic programs, on the other hand.

That is not to say, however, that evidence of such a disparity is irrelevant. . . .

C. Regulatory Framework.

. . . .

1. *The Regulations.* [The Department of Education's] regulations begin by detailing Title IX's application to college athletics.[insert footnote] The regulations also recognize, however, that an athletic program may consist of gender-segregated teams as long as one of two conditions is met: either the sport in which the team competes is a contact sport or the institution offers comparable teams in the sport to both genders. See 34 C.F.R. § 106.41(b).

Finally, whether teams are segregated by sex or not, the school must provide gender-blind equality of opportunity to its student body. The regulations offer a non-exclusive compendium of ten factors which OCR will consider in assessing compliance with this mandate:

> (1) Whether the selection of sports and levels of competition effectively accommodate the interests and abilities of members of both sexes;
>
> (2) The provision of equipment and supplies;
>
> (3) Scheduling of games and practice time;
>
> (4) Travel and per diem allowance;
>
> (5) Opportunity to receive coaching and academic tutoring;
>
> (6) Assignment and compensation of coaches and tutors;
>
> (7) Provision of locker rooms, practice and competitive facilities;
>
> (8) Provision of medical and training facilities and services;
>
> (9) Provision of housing and dining facilities and services;
>
> (10) Publicity.

34 C.F.R. § 106.41(c) (1992). The district court rested its preliminary injunction on the first of these ten areas of inquiry: Brown's failure effectively to accommodate the interests and abilities of female students in the selection and level of sports. . . .

2. *The Policy Interpretation.* In the three years next following the initial issuance of the regulations, [the Department of Health, Education, and Welfare] received over one hundred discrimination complaints involving more than fifty schools. In order to encourage self-policing and thereby winnow complaints, HEW [adopted a Policy Interpretation in 1979,] a matter of months before the effective date of the statute through which Congress, emulating King Solomon, split HEW. The parties are in agreement that, at DED's birth, it clutched the Policy Interpretation, and, as a practical matter, that appears to be the case. . . . Although we can find no record that DED formally adopted the Policy Interpretation, we see no point to splitting the hair, particularly where the parties have not asked us to do so. Because this document is a considered interpretation of the regulation, we cede it substantial deference.

. . . .

Equal opportunity to participate lies at the core of Title IX's purpose. Because the third compliance area delineates this heartland, we . . . hold that, with regard to the effective accommodation of students' interests and abilities, an institution can violate Title IX even if it meets the "financial assistance" and "athletic equivalence" standards. In other words, an institution that offers women a smaller number of athletic opportunities than the statute requires may not rectify that violation simply by lavishing more resources on those women or achieving equivalence in other respects.

3. *Measuring Effective Accommodation.* The parties agree that the third compliance area is the field on which this appeal must be fought. In surveying the dimensions of this battleground, that is, whether an athletic program effectively accommodates students' interests and abilities, the Policy Interpretation maps a trinitarian model under which the university must meet at least one of three benchmarks:

> (1) Whether intercollegiate level participation opportunities for male and female students are provided in numbers substantially proportionate to their respective enrollments; or
>
> (2) Where the members of one sex have been and are underrepresented among intercollegiate athletes, whether the institution can show a history and continuing practice of program expansion which is demonstrably responsive to the developing interest and abilities of the members of that sex; or
>
> (3) Where the members of one sex are underrepresented among intercollegiate athletes, and the institution cannot show a continuing practice of program expansion such as that cited above, whether it can be demonstrated that the interests and abilities of the members of that sex have been fully and effectively accommodated by the present program.

44 Fed. Reg. at 71,418. The first benchmark furnishes a safe harbor for those institutions that have distributed athletic opportunities in numbers "substantially proportionate" to the gender composition of their student bodies. Thus, a university which does not wish to engage in extensive compliance analysis may stay on the sunny side of Title IX simply by maintaining gender parity between its student body and its athletic lineup.

The second and third parts of the accommodation test recognize that there are circumstances under which, as a practical matter, something short of this proportionality is a satisfactory proxy for gender balance. For example, so long as a university is continually expanding athletic opportunities in an ongoing effort to meet the needs of the underrepresented gender, and persists in this approach as interest and ability levels in its student body and secondary feeder schools rise, benchmark two is satisfied and Title IX does not require that the university leap to complete gender parity in a single bound. Or, if a school has a student body in which one sex is demonstrably less interested in athletics, Title IX does not require that the school create teams for, or rain money upon, otherwise disinterested students; rather, the third benchmark is satisfied if the underrepresented sex's discernible interests are fully and effectively accommodated.

It seems unlikely, even in this day and age, that the athletic establishments of many coeducational universities reflect the gender balance of their student bodies. Similarly, the recent boom in Title IX suits suggests that, in an era of fiscal austerity, few universities are prone to expand athletic opportunities. It is not surprising, then, that schools more often than not attempt to manage the rigors of Title IX by satisfying the interests and abilities of the underrepresented gender, that is, by meeting the third benchmark of the accommodation test. Yet, this benchmark sets a high standard: it demands not merely some accommodation, but full and effective accommodation. If there is sufficient interest and ability among members of the statistically underrepresented gender, not slaked by existing programs, an institution necessarily fails this prong of the test.

Although the full-and-effective-accommodation standard is high, it is not absolute. Even when male athletic opportunities outnumber female athletic opportunities, and the university has not met the first benchmark . . . or the second benchmark . . . the mere fact that there are some female students interested in a sport does not ipso facto require the school to provide a varsity team in order to comply with the third benchmark. Rather, the institution can satisfy the third benchmark by ensuring participatory opportunities at the intercollegiate level when, and to the extent that, there is "sufficient interest and ability among the members of the excluded sex to sustain a viable team and a reasonable expectation of intercollegiate competition for that team . . . ." 44 Fed. Reg. at 71,418. . . .

Brown argues that DED's Policy Interpretation, construed as we have just outlined, goes so far afield that it countervails the enabling legislation. Brown suggests that, to the extent students' interests in athletics are disproportionate by gender, colleges should be allowed to meet those interests incompletely as long as the school's response is in direct proportion to the comparative levels of interest. Put bluntly, Brown reads the "full" out of the duty to accommodate "fully and effectively." . . . .

. . . .

We think that Brown's perception of the Title IX universe is myopic. The fact that the overrepresented gender is less than fully accommodated will not, in and of itself, excuse a shortfall in the provision of opportunities for the underrepresented gender. Rather, the law requires that, in the absence of continuing program expansion (benchmark two), schools either meet benchmark one by providing athletic opportunities in proportion to the gender composition of the student body . . . or meet benchmark three by fully accommodating interested athletes among the underrepresented sex . . . .

In the final analysis, Brown's view is wrong on two scores. It is wrong as a matter of law, for DED's Policy Interpretation, which requires full accommodation of the underrepresented gender, draws its essence from the statute. Whether Brown's concept might be thought more attractive, or whether we, if writing on a pristine page, would craft the regulation in a manner different than the agency, are not very important considerations. Because the agency's rendition stands upon a plausible, if not inevitable, reading of Title IX, we are obligated to enforce the regulation according to its tenor. *See Chevron*, 467 U.S. at 843 n.11.

Brown's reading of Title IX is legally flawed for yet another reason. It proceeds from the premise that the agency's third benchmark countervails Title IX. But, this particular imprecation of the third benchmark overlooks the accommodation test's general purpose: to determine whether a student has been "excluded from participation in, [or] denied the benefits of" an athletic program "on the basis of sex . . . ." 20 U.S.C. § 1681(a). While any single element of this tripartite test, in isolation, might not achieve the goal set by the statute, the test as a whole is reasonably constructed to implement the statute. No more is exigible. *See Chemical Mfrs. Ass'n v. Natural Resources Defense Council, Inc.*, 470 U.S. 116, 125(1985).

. . . Brown's approach cannot withstand scrutiny on either legal or policy grounds. We conclude that DED's Policy Interpretation means exactly what it says. This plain meaning is a proper, permissible rendition of the statute.

IV. THE CONSTITUTIONAL CHALLENGE

We turn now to a series of case-specific issues, starting with Brown's constitutional challenge to the statutory scheme.

A. Equal Protection.

Brown asseverates that if the third part of the accommodation test is read as OCR wrote it — to require full and effective accommodation of the underrepresented gender — the test violates the Fifth Amendment's Equal Protection Clause. We think not.

Brown assumes that full and effective accommodation disadvantages male athletes. While it might well be that more men than women at Brown are currently interested in sports, Brown points to no evidence in the record that men are any more likely to engage in athletics than women, absent socialization and disparate opportunities. In the absence of any proof supporting Brown's claim, and in view of congressional and administrative urging that women, given the opportunity, will naturally participate in athletics in numbers equal to men, we do not find that the regulation, when read in the common-sense manner that its language suggests . . . offends the Fifth Amendment.

What is more, even if we were to assume, for argument's sake, that the regulation creates a gender classification slanted somewhat in favor of women, we would find no constitutional infirmity. It is clear that Congress has broad powers under the Fifth Amendment to remedy past discrimination. . . .

B. Affirmative Action.

Brown rehashes its equal protection argument and serves it up as a nominally different dish, arguing that the district court's preliminary injunction constitutes "affirmative action" and violates the Equal Protection Clause because the court lacked a necessary factual predicate to warrant such a step. It is, however, established beyond peradventure that, where no contrary legislative directive appears, the federal judiciary possesses the power to grant any appropriate relief on a cause of action appropriately brought pursuant to a federal statute. Hence, this initiative, too, is bootless.

V. BURDEN OF PROOF

. . . [A] Title IX plaintiff makes out an athletic discrimination case by proving numerical disparity, coupled with unmet interest, each by a fair preponderance of the credible evidence, so long as the defendant does not rebut the plaintiff's showing by adducing preponderant history-and-practice evidence.

VI. THE PRELIMINARY INJUNCTION

We come at long last to the cynosure of the appeal. This is familiar territory. A district court, faced with a motion for preliminary injunction, must assess the request in four particular ways, evaluating (1) the movant's probability of victory on the merits; (2) the potential for irreparable harm if the injunction is refused; (3) the balance of interests as between the parties, i.e., whether the harm to the movant if the injunction is withheld outweighs the harm to the nonmovant if the injunction is granted; and (4) the public interest. . . .

If, in conducting this tamisage, the district court has made no clear error of law or fact, we will overturn its calibration of the four factors only for a manifest abuse of discretion.

Here, the district court found that the quadrat of factors favored plaintiffs' position. Brown disagrees with these findings up and down the line, but offers developed argumentation only as to three of the four components. Because Brown does not explain its challenge to the district court's finding that the public interest would be disserved by leaving the two women's teams on the sidelines until the suit is finally resolved, we ignore its pro forma protest in that respect. . . .

A. Likelihood of Success.

. . . In this case, the district court paid meticulous attention to the parties' prospects for success over the long haul. The court plainly visualized both the factual intricacies and legal complexities that characterize Title IX litigation. It held a lengthy adversary hearing and reviewed voluminous written submissions. And at journey's end, it correctly focused on the three-part accommodation test.

The court faultlessly dispatched the first two elements of the test. With respect to the comparison between Brown's athletic agenda and student body, we adopt the lower court's record-rooted finding that the University did not meet — or even closely approach — the "substantial proportionality" threshold because it offered too few varsity opportunities for women. Cognizant, perhaps, that the raw numbers tell an unambiguous tale, Brown does not challenge the inviolability of this finding.

As to the test's second part, the court below found that, although Brown could point to "impressive growth" in its women's athletic program in the 1970s, the school had not continued filling the gap during the next two decades. *Id.* On this basis, the court concluded that Brown had not met the benchmark. Brown asserts that the district court erred by not crediting it sufficiently for its dramatic expansion of women's sports in the 1970s, and we are not entirely unsympathetic to this plea. In the last analysis, however, this was a judgment call and the trial court's judgment was not unreasonable. . . .

The third benchmark presents a more problematic scenario. The district court incorrectly held that Brown bore the burden of showing that it had fully and effectively accommodated the interests and abilities of its women athletes. Section 1681(b) requires that the plaintiffs, rather than the University, prove a shortfall in the full and effective accommodation of interested female athletes by showing, initially, both numerical disparity and unmet interest. Nonetheless, we do not think that the court's bevue is fatal. Even when a trial court has misconstrued the law, an appellate tribunal may avoid remanding if the record is sufficiently developed and the facts necessary to shape the proper legal matrix are sufficiently clear.

. . . .

In this instance, the district court's subsidiary findings of fact render it beyond cavil that the plaintiffs carried their burden of proof. The court found, for example, that there was "great interest and talent" amongst Brown's female undergraduates which, following the cuts, would go unserved. . . . [T]he court also found the interest and talent on campus ample to support women's varsity volleyball and gymnastics teams, a finding that is hardly surprising in view of the teams' robust health before the budget-cutters arrived on the scene. . . .

The potency of this evidence is an effective antidote to the district court's partial misapplication of the burden of proof. Because the record contains nothing that would allow a trier to find that Brown's athletic agenda reflects the makeup of its student body or that the plaintiff class is so poorly populated as to warrant a reduction in women's sports, the court's error was harmless.

B. Irreparable Injury.

The next area of inquiry is irreparable harm. The district court heard from a variety of athletic administration experts. The court concluded that, absent judicial intervention, the plaintiffs would suffer irremediable injury in at least three respects: competitive posture, recruitment, and loss of coaching. As club teams, the district court thought women's volleyball and gymnastics would increasingly become less competitive, have fewer players, be unable to schedule varsity teams from other schools, become unattractive to potential stars making college choices, and suffer stagnation in the growth of individual talent due to the absence of coaching. . . . Although the types of harms the court catalogued might not all rise to the same level of seriousness, the overall record supports, even though it does not compel, the court's assessment of their cumulative severity . . . [W]e will not second-guess the district court's finding of irreparable injury.

C. The Balance of Harms.

Finally, the district court found that the competing equities weighed in favor of granting the injunction. After hearing testimony from Brown's Financial Vice-President and its Associate Athletic Director, the district court concluded that the cost of the interim injunction would be relatively slight; and that, in view of discretionary funds already contained in the Athletic Department budget and a presidential "contingency fund," Brown possessed the wherewithal to defray the costs without undue hardship. By contrast, the court noted the volleyball and gymnastics programs' continuing deterioration in the aftermath of the demotion. On balance, the court determined that the financial burden on Brown was tolerable, and, in any event, was overbalanced by the potential harm to the plaintiff class if the court took no action.

Brown contests the results of this balancing on the premise that the district court wrongly discounted the testimony of one of its witnesses and did not adequately consider the possibility that false hopes might be raised by a preliminary injunction. It is, however, axiomatic that a district court, sitting without a jury, may selectively discount testimony as it weighs conflicting viewpoints and adjudicates the facts. . . .

It is similarly fundamental that a preliminary injunction, by its very nature, is sometimes ephemeral. Hence, the risk that some observers might read into a temporary restrainer more than it eventually proves to mean is endemic to the equitable device and cannot tip the scales against its use in any particular circumstance. . . .

In fine, the district court did not overspill its discretion either in taking Brown's self-interested description of its financial plight with a grain of salt or in limiting the role that raising false hopes might play in the equitable calculus.

D. Summing Up.

We summarize succinctly, beginning with the probability of plaintiffs' success. In an era where the practices of higher education must adjust to stunted revenues, careening costs, and changing demographics, colleges might well be obliged to curb spending on programs, like athletics, that do not lie at the epicenter of their institutional mission. Title IX does not purport to override financial necessity. Yet, the pruning of athletic budgets cannot take place solely in comptrollers' offices, isolated from the legislative and regulatory imperatives that Title IX imposes.

This case aptly illustrates the point. Brown earnestly professes that it has done no more than slash women's and men's athletics by approximately the same degree, and, indeed, the raw numbers lend partial credence to that characterization. But, Brown's claim overlooks the shortcomings that plagued its program before it took blade in hand. If a school, like Brown, eschews the first two benchmarks of the accommodation test, electing to stray from substantial proportionality and failing to march uninterruptedly in the direction of equal athletic opportunity, it must comply with the third benchmark. To do so, the school must fully and effectively accommodate the underrepresented gender's interests and abilities, even if that requires it to give the underrepresented gender . . . what amounts to a larger slice of a shrinking athletic-opportunity pie.

The record reveals that the court below paid heed to these realities. It properly recognized that even balanced use of the budget-paring knife runs afoul of Title IX where, as here, the fruits of a university's athletic program remain ill-distributed after the trimming takes place. Because the district court understood this principle, and because its findings of fact as to the case's probable outcome are based on substantial evidence, the court's determination that plaintiffs are likely to succeed on the merits is inexpugnable.

The district court displayed similar dexterity in touching the other three bases en route to a grant of injunctive relief: irreparability of injury, the relative weight of potential harms, and impact on the public interest. . . .

VII. REMEDIATION

After applying the preliminary injunction standard, the district court ordered relief pendente lite, temporarily reinstating the women's volleyball and gymnastics teams. Brown argues that such specific relief is inappropriate because it intrudes on Brown's discretion. The point has some cogency. We are a society that cherishes academic freedom and recognizes that universities deserve great leeway in their operations. In addition, Title IX does not require institutions to fund any particular number or type of athletic opportunities — only that they provide those opportunities in a nondiscriminatory fashion if they wish to receive federal funds.

Nonetheless, the district court has broad discretionary power to take provisional steps restoring the status quo pending the conclusion of a trial. Considering the district court's proper estimation and deft application of the preliminary injunction standard . . . we think that requiring Brown to maintain the women's volleyball and gymnastics teams in varsity status for the time being is a remedial choice within the district court's discretion. That is not to say, however, that the same remedy will be suitable at trial's end if the Title IX charges prove out against Brown. . . .

VIII. CONCLUSION

. . . .

This appeal exemplifies many of the difficulties inherent in Title IX litigation. We do not presume to say that the district court's interim solution is perfect, but it is fair and it is lawful. On the record compiled to date, the preliminary injunction requiring Brown to reinstate its women's volleyball and gymnastics teams for the time being came well within the encincture of judicial discretion. We will not meddle.

The preliminary injunction is affirmed, the temporary stay is dissolved, and the cause is remanded to the district court for further proceedings. Costs to appellees.

NEAL v. CALIFORNIA STATE UNIVERSITY

198 F.3d 763 (9th Cir. 1999)

OPINION

HALL, CIRCUIT JUDGE:

The instant case requires us to consider whether Title IX prevents a university in which male students occupy a disproportionately high percentage of athletic roster spots from making gender-conscious decisions to reduce the proportion of roster spots assigned to men. We hold that Title IX does not bar such remedial actions.

The Board of Trustees of the California State Universities and other defendants appeal from the district court's order granting the motion of Neal and other plaintiffs for a preliminary injunction. Neal's suit alleged that the decision of California State University, Bakersfield ("CSUB") to reduce the number of spots on its men's wrestling team, undertaken as part of a university-wide program to achieve "substantial proportionality" between each gender's participation in varsity sports and its composition in the campus's student body, violated Title IX and the Equal Protection Clause of the United States Constitution. The district court determined that regulations promulgated pursuant to Title IX, and CSUB's program, which was modeled after those regulations, violated Title IX. . . . We reverse, and vacate the injunction.

I.

Defendant/Appellant CSUB is a large public university where female students outnumbered male students by roughly 64% to 36% in 1996. The composition of CSUB's varsity athletic rosters, however, was quite different. In the 1992-93 academic year, male students took 61% of the university's spots on athletic rosters and received 68% of CSUB's available athletic scholarship money.

This imbalance helped prompt a lawsuit by the California chapter of the National Organization for Women, alleging that the California State University system was violating a state law that is similar to the federal government's Title IX. That lawsuit eventually settled, resulting in a consent decree mandating, inter alia, that each Cal State campus have a proportion of female athletes that was within five percentage points of the proportion of female undergraduate students at that school. This portion of the consent decree was patterned after the first part of the three-part Title IX compliance test promulgated by the Department of Education's Office for Civil Rights ("OCR").

When the university agreed to the consent decree, California was slowly emerging from a recession, and state funding for higher education was declining. . . . CSUB administrators were seriously constrained in what they could spend on athletic programs. The university chose to adopt squad size targets, which would encourage the expansion of the women's teams while limiting the size of the men's teams. . . . CSUB opted for smaller men's teams across the board, rejecting the alternative of eliminating some men's teams entirely. CSUB's plan was designed to bring it into compliance . . . by the 1997-98 academic year, meaning that female students would fill at least 55% of the spaces on the school's athletic teams.

As part of this across-the-board reduction in the number of slots available to men's athletic teams, the size of the men's wrestling team was capped at 27. Although the reduction was protested vigorously by wrestling coach Terry Kerr, and team captain Stephen Neal expressed concerns that a smaller squad would prove less competitive, the smaller CSUB team performed exceptionally well, winning the Pac-10 Conference title and finishing third in the nation in 1996. In 1996-97, the men's wrestling roster was capped at 25, and four of these spots went unused. Nevertheless, in response to the rumored elimination of the men's wrestling team, on January 10, 1997, the team filed the instant lawsuit, alleging that the university's policy capping the size of the men's team constituted discrimination on the basis of gender in violation of Title IX and the Equal Protection Clause of the Federal Constitution.

The team sought declaratory and injunctive relief to prevent the squad size reductions. CSUB responded by filing a motion to dismiss. The district court initially granted a temporary restraining order preventing the reductions, then granted a preliminary injunction to prevent CSUB from reducing the size of the wrestling team. The district court concluded as a matter of fact that CSUB's primary motivation for capping the size of the men's teams was to meet the gender proportionality requirements in the consent decree. The district court concluded as a matter of law that capping the male teams in order to comply with the consent decree violated Title IX. Although the district court refused to rule on Plaintiffs' equal protection challenge to the CSUB policy, the court did reject a reading of Title IX that created a "safe harbor" for any school that achieved substantial proportionality between the percentage of athletes of one gender and the percentage of students of that same gender. . . .

II.

On appeal, this Court reviews the district court's grant of a preliminary injunction for abuse of discretion, and "that discretion is abused where the district court based its ruling on an erroneous view of the law or on a clearly erroneous assessment of the evidence."

III.

This case has its origins in Congress's passage of Title IX in 1972. Title IX was Congress's response to significant concerns about discrimination against women in education. . . .

The regulations promulgated pursuant to Title IX require schools receiving federal funding to "provide equal athletic opportunity for members of both sexes". 34 C.F.R. § 106.41(c). In evaluating schools' compliance with that provision, one factor that will be considered is "whether the selection of sports and levels of competition effectively accommodate the interests and abilities of members of both sexes". *Id.* at § 106.41(c)(1). . . . The drafters of these regulations recognized a situation that Congress well understood: Male athletes had been given an enormous head start in the race against their female counterparts for athletic resources, and Title IX would prompt universities to level the proverbial playing field.

Appellees recognize that, given this backdrop, it would be imprudent to argue that Title IX prohibits the use of all gender-conscious remedies. Appellees therefore suggest that gender-conscious remedies are appropriate only when necessary to ensure that schools provide opportunities to males and females in proportion to their relative levels of interest in sports participation. By contrast, Appellants contend that schools may make gender-conscious decisions about sports-funding levels to correct for an imbalance between the composition of the undergraduate student body and the composition of the undergraduate student athletic participants pool. This disagreement has real significance: Men's expressed interest in participating in varsity sports is apparently higher than women's at the present time — although the "interest gap" continues to narrow — so permitting gender-conscious remedies until the proportions of students and athletes are roughly proportional gives universities more remedial freedom than permitting remedies only until expressed interest and varsity roster spots correspond.

Appellees' argument that equal opportunity is achieved when each gender's athletic participation roughly matches its interest in participating is hardly novel. Several courts of appeals have considered and rejected Appellees' approach as fundamentally inconsistent with the purpose of Title IX.

Cohen v. Brown University, 991 F.2d 888 (1st Cir. 1993) ("*Cohen I*"), was the first case to rule on the issues raised in the instant appeal. . . .

The *Cohen I* court interpreted Title IX's requirements in light of the three-part test set forth in the Policy Interpretation promulgated by the Department of Health, Education, and Welfare in 1979. That test is used to assess whether a school's athletic program is in compliance with Title IX. Appellees attack only the first part of this test, which declares a university Title IX-compliant if participation levels for each gender are "substantially proportionate" to their representation in the student body.

The *Cohen I* court explicitly rejected Brown's argument that, because male athletes were more interested in athletics, the school could bring itself into Title IX compliance by providing females with fewer athletic roster spots "as long as the school's response is in direct proportion to the comparative levels of interest." *Cohen I*, 991 F.2d at 899. In *Cohen II*, the rejection of Brown's argument was even more emphatic: "Brown's relative interests approach cannot withstand scrutiny on either legal or policy grounds, because it disadvantages women and undermines the remedial purposes of Title IX by limiting required program expansion for the underrepresented sex to the status quo level of relative interests." *Cohen v. Brown Univ.*, 101 F.3d 155, 174 (1st Cir. 1996) ("*Cohen II*") (citations and internal quotations marks omitted).

. . . .

Appellees and the district court relied heavily on a lone district court opinion, *Pederson v. Louisiana State Univ.*, 912 F. Supp. 892 (M.D. La. 1996), which criticized the Policy Interpretation test's first part. However, this criticism is entirely dicta: The court still found Louisiana State University ("LSU") to be in violation of Title IX and ordered it to bring itself into Title IX compliance immediately, hinting that it should do so by funding women's soccer and softball teams. *See id.* at 922. The court never addressed the issue of whether LSU could bring itself into Title IX compliance by cutting the opportunities available to male athletes because the parties there never suggested such an approach. . . .

Title IX is a dynamic statute, not a static one. It envisions continuing progress toward the goal of equal opportunity for all athletes and recognizes that, where society has conditioned women to expect less than their fair share of the athletic opportunities, women's interest in participating in sports will not rise to a par with men's overnight. The percentage of college athletes who are women rose from 15% in 1972 to 37% in 1998, and Title IX is at least partially responsible for this trend of increased participation by women. Title IX has altered women's preferences, making them more interested in sports, and more likely to become student-athletes. Adopting Appellees' interest-based test for Title IX compliance would hinder, and quite possibly reverse, the steady increases in women's participation and interest in sports that have followed Title IX's enactment.

A number of courts of appeals have addressed another potentially dispositive issue in this appeal - namely, whether Title IX permits a university to diminish athletic opportunities available to men so as to bring them into line with the lower athletic opportunities available to women. Every court, in construing the Policy Interpretation and the text of Title IX, has held that a university may bring itself into Title IX compliance by increasing athletic opportunities for the underrepresented gender (women in this case) or by decreasing athletic opportunities for the overrepresented gender (men in this case). *See Horner*, 43 F.3d at 275; *Kelley v. Board of Trustees*, 35 F.3d 265, 269 (7th Cir. 1994); *Roberts v. Colorado State Bd. of Agric.*, 998 F.2d 824, 830 (10th Cir. 1993); *Cohen I*, 991 F.2d at 898 n.15. . . .

There is a second reason why a reversal of the district court's order granting injunctive relief on the Title IX claim is warranted. The district court failed to defer properly to the interpretation of Title IX put forward by the administrative agency that is explicitly authorized to enforce its provisions. It is well-established that the federal courts are to defer substantially to an agency's interpretation of its own regulations. *See Martin v. Occupational Safety & Health Review Comm'n*, 499 U.S. 144, 150 (1991). The Department of Education, "acting through its OCR [is] the administrative agency charged with administering Title IX." *Cohen I*, 991 F.2d 888 at 895. In this instance, Congress explicitly delegated to the agency the task of prescribing standards for athletic programs under Title IX. . . .

. . . .

Finally, the district court below rejected the interpretation of Title IX advocated by the OCR and Appellants on the ground that such a reading of the statute might violate the Constitution. In the court's words, OCR's interpretation would "effectively transform Title IX from an anti-discrimination statute to a statute enacted to remedy past discrimination, thus subjecting it to heightened scrutiny." Without speculating whether Title IX would survive such searching constitutional scrutiny, the court notes that it remains unsatisfied with the *Cohen* majority's treatment of these important questions. The court is satisfied that avoiding serious constitutional questions such as an equal protection challenge to a very important Congressional statute is itself ample reason for rejecting the safe harbor idea as part of Title IX.

The district court thus strained to interpret Title IX in a way that ostensibly would avoid these concerns. . . .

The First and Seventh Circuits both have considered at length the constitutionality of the first prong of the OCR's test. In *Cohen I*, 991 F.2d at 899-901; *Cohen II*, 101 F.3d at 181-84; and *Kelley*, 35 F.3d at 272-73, the courts emphatically rejected the claim that the Policy Interpretation was unconstitutional under the Fourteenth Amendment. The separate reasoning in the two *Cohen* opinions is particularly well-developed. It applied intermediate scrutiny, which we would also do were we addressing the constitutional merits. *Cohen II* noted that the Policy Interpretation furthered the "clearly important" objectives of "avoiding the use of federal resources to support discriminatory practices, and providing individual citizens effective protection against those practices." 101 F.3d at 184 (citation and internal quotations omitted). Moreover, it found that "judicial enforcement of federal anti-discrimination statutes is at least an important governmental objective." *Id.* And *Cohen II* held that the district court's relief, which was essentially identical to what the OCR Policy Interpretation calls for, was "clearly substantially related" to these objectives. *Id.* Along the same lines, the Seventh Circuit has held that "the remedial scheme established by Title IX and the applicable regulation and policy interpretation are clearly substantially related to" the objective of prohibiting "educational institutions from discriminating on the basis of sex." *Kelley*, 35 F.3d at 272. We adopt the reasoning of *Cohen I, Cohen II*, and *Kelley*, and hold that the constitutional analysis contained therein persuasively disposes of any serious constitutional concerns that might be raised in relation to the OCR Policy Interpretation. The district court's final basis for rejecting the OCR's interpretation of Title IX was therefore erroneous.

IV.

This past summer, 90,185 enthusiastic fans crowded into Pasadena's historic Rose Bowl for the finals of the Women's World Cup soccer match. An estimated 40 million television viewers also tuned in to watch a thrilling battle between the American and Chinese teams. The match ended when American defender Brandi Chastain fired the ball past Chinese goalkeeper Gao Hong, breaking a 4-4 shootout tie. The victory sparked a national celebration and a realization by many that women's sports could be just as exciting, competitive, and lucrative as men's sports. And the victorious athletes understood as well as anyone the connection between a 27-year-old statute and tangible progress in women's athletics. Title IX has enhanced, and will continue to enhance, women's opportunities to enjoy the thrill of victory, the agony of defeat, and the many tangible benefits that flow from just being given a chance to participate in intercollegiate athletics. Today we join our sister circuits in holding that Title IX does not bar universities from taking steps to ensure that women are approximately as well represented in sports programs as they are in student bodies. We REVERSE, and VACATE the preliminary injunction.

NOTES

1. After years of additional litigation — during which Brown University had its compliance plans rejected by the district court — the court approved a final settlement agreement in 1998. Based on the provisions, Brown: (1) agreed to ensure that its women's athletics participation rate was within 3.5 percentage points of the women's undergraduate enrollment rate; (2) agreed to move women's water polo from club to donor-funded varsity status; and (3) guaranteed funding to the four women's teams the district court had found to be the original source of the discrimination, namely, gymnastics, fencing, skiing, and water polo. *Brown Title IX Case Settled*, NAT'L COLLEGIATE ATHLETIC ASS'N, July 6, 1997, *available at* http://web1.ncaa.org/web_files/NCAANewsArchive/1998/19980706/briefly.html#1. The full text of the settlement agreement is available at the Public Justice Foundation website: http://www.publicjustice.net/content/cohen-v-brown-university.

For a similar case in which the disproportionality between male and female athletic participation was even more severe, see *Pederson v. Louisiana State University*, 213 F.3d 858 (5th Cir. 2000). In holding that LSU violated Title IX, the court observed that while the overall student population was 51% male and 49% female, the population participating in athletics was 71% male and 29% female. *Id.* at 878. Remember, also, that the *Pederson* case made an appearance in *Neal* because of the *Pederson* court's criticism of the first prong of the Department of Health, Education, and Welfare's Policy Interpretation.

2. The plaintiffs in *Neal v. California State University*, presented above, challenged the university's decision to reduce the numbers of positions available on the men's wrestling team. The court ultimately upheld the university's decision, holding that such decisions did not violate the law. Other universities, in their efforts to comply with Title IX and to provide equitable opportunities for women athletes, have gone farther and have eliminated some men's sports entirely. For example, in *Miami University Wrestling Club v. Miami University* [Ohio], 302 F.3d 608 (6th Cir. 2002), the university eliminated men's wrestling, tennis, soccer, and golf programs. The golf program, however, was restored because participants and alumni were able to raise enough money to keep the team operating without university assistance. The plaintiffs — the Soccer Club, Tennis Club, Wrestling Club, and several individual athletes — filed suit against Miami University, individual members of the Board of Trustees, the University President, and the university athletic director under Title IX and the equal protection clause of the Fourteenth Amendment. They alleged discrimination in that the university excluded them from participation in educational and athletic programs on the basis of sex. Miami had conducted a self-study in 1993 and determined that elimination of men's sports became necessary to make the percentages of participation more representative of the study body. By 1999–2000, women represented 55% of the student body and 53% of the athletes. Furthermore, the university had increased financial aid to women students by $400,000.

Applying the 1979 Policy Interpretation Letter, the Court of Appeals for the Sixth Circuit held that Miami's decision did not violate Title IX. Despite the obvious classification based on gender, the university's focus on the underrepresented gender is permissible and is in line with the spirit of the law. Although the court held against the plaintiffs, the holding was not without sympathy for them. It just came with similar sympathy for the position of the university:

> The Policy Interpretation implicitly recognizes that universities and other recipients of federal funds do not have infinite money supplies. If a university cannot afford to add sports teams in order to provide equal athletic opportunity for men and women, it may be forced to subtract in order to equalize. It is anomalous in an allegedly free society to accomplish equality of opportunity by decreasing rather than increasing opportunities, but in the real world of finite resources, this approach may be the only way for an educational institution to comply with Title IX while still maintaining the other niceties of its mission, such as its academic offerings.

Id. at 613. For similar claims at other universities, with identical legal results upholding the decisions to eliminate men's sports, see also *Kelley v. Bd. of Trustees*, 35 F.3d 265 (7th Cir. 1994) (University of Illinois eliminated men's swimming); *Chalenor v. Univ. of N. Dakota*, 291 F.3d 1042 (8th Cir. 2002) (University of North Dakota eliminated men's wrestling). An important decision to address the issue of eliminating men's sports is *Equity in Athletics, Inc., v. Dep't of Educ.*, 639 F.3d 91 (4th Cir. 2011) where a nonprofit organization consisting of representatives of male-dominated teams challenged James Madison University's decision to eliminate seven men's sports and three women's sports. The case challenged the efficacy of the Title IX regulations involving athletics particularly that portion of the "Effective Accommodation Test" requiring an examination of "[w]hether the selection of sports and levels of competition effectively accommodate the interests and abilities of both sexes." 34 C.F.R. § 106.41(c)(1) (2011). The Court of Appeals for the Fourth Circuit found no violation adding that the plaintiffs brought no position that had not been heard by previous courts. The United States Supreme Court denied certiorari. 132 S. Ct. 1004 (2012).

3. As seen in *Neal* and in the cases cited in the above note, one of the primary criticisms of Title IX's proportionality requirement is that it violates equal protection by increasing female athletic opportunities at the expense of male athletes. This criticism became more pointed in some respects after the Supreme Court decided *United States v. Virginia*, 518 U.S. 515 (1996). In that case, the Court sided with the United States by holding that it was a violation of the Fourteenth Amendment's Equal Protection Clause for the Virginia Military Institute, a state-supported college, to deny admission to women. The Court's decision in *Virginia* came down several months before so-called *Cohen IV*, 101 F.3d 155 (1st Cir. 1996), in which the appeals court once again affirmed the district court's determination that Brown's athletics program discriminated against women. Critics of the *Cohen* line of cases, however, argue that *Virginia* fundamentally changed gender-based discrimination cases and should have forced the *Cohen* court to reach a different conclusion. Consider this:

> Prior to *United States v. Virginia*, classifications based on gender were considered "quasi-suspect." Gender classifications would be upheld if the classification: (1) served important governmental objectives; and (2) was substantially related to the achievement of those objectives. In applying this pre-*Virginia* standard, the Supreme Court generally upheld statutes

which seem to be a reasonable means of compensating one gender for past societal discrimination. However, the Court would invalidate statutes which drew unreasonable distinctions between the sexes. Under this standard, it is quite likely that *Cohen IV*'s interpretation of Title IX would be upheld. . . .

United States v. Virginia refined the standard for gender classifications with an additional requirement. The Court . . . held that gender classifications will be sustained only if: (1) an exceedingly persuasive justification for the gender classification exists; (2) the classification served important governmental objectives; and (3) the classification is substantially related to the achievement of those objectives. This is true regardless of the gender which is favored by the classification. Thus, after *Virginia*, it is not sufficient that the gender classification be substantially related to an important government objective. There is an additional requirement of articulating an exceedingly persuasive justification.

The additional requirement of an exceedingly persuasive justification represents a fundamental change in the interpretation of the Equal Protection Clause. *Virginia* effectively transformed gender classifications from "quasi-suspect" classifications to "de facto suspect" classifications. Since "suspect" classifications, such as those based on race, "are by their very nature odious to a free people whose institutions are founded upon the doctrine of equality," they are permitted only if they are narrowly tailored to promote a compelling state interest. Thus, if something is a compelling state interest for purposes of a racial classification, it also would be regarded as an exceedingly persuasive justification for purposes of a gender classification. Conversely, if something were not a compelling state interest for purposes of a racial classification, it generally would not be regarded as an exceedingly persuasive justification for purposes of a gender classification. The only significant difference between the two terms is that "exceedingly persuasive justification" would allow for accommodation of physical differences and privacy interests. Thus, although the government would never be allowed to have separate but equal locker room facilities for different races, the government would be allowed to have separate but equal locker room facilities for different genders. In all other instances, "exceedingly persuasive justification" would be synonymous with the compelling state interest.

Since *Virginia* elevated gender classification to "de facto suspect" status and since "exceedingly persuasive justification" is almost synonymous with "compelling state interest," then, under current case law, it logically follows that the only exceedingly persuasive justification would be the elimination of prior discrimination by the government. In the context of suspect classifications, the only interest which has been found to be compelling is the need to remedy the present day effects of specific incidents of prior discrimination by the government. Indeed, in determining what is a compelling state interest, the Supreme Court has rejected the desire to have greater representation from specific groups, the elimination of societal discrimination, the need for diverse role models, and compliance with the demands of the federal government. Presumably, such interests would not be regarded as exceedingly persuasive justifications in the gender context.

Consequently, the reasoning of *Cohen IV* will not pass constitutional muster except in those rare instances where there is a specific finding of present day effects of previous intentional discrimination on the basis of gender in the context of intercollegiate athletics. Moreover, the findings of present day effects of past discrimination to be remedied must be highly specific. Although the findings of legislative bodies are generally entitled to great deference, a "suspect or de facto suspect" classification cannot rest on some generalized assertion that discrimination exists in society or on a particular campus. Furthermore, the mere fact that a particular racial or gender group is underrepresented at a particular institution is not, by itself, sufficient to establish intentional discrimination in violation of the Constitution. Indeed, the entire notion of underrepresentation "rests on the completely unrealistic assumption" that minorities will choose a particular trade in lockstep proportion to their representation in the local population." Therefore, most institutions will have difficulty finding sufficient evidence to justify a finding of present day effects of prior intentional discrimination.

Even if an institution could articulate an exceedingly persuasive justification for the differing treatment mandated by *Cohen IV*, the institution would still have to demonstrate that (1) the classification served important governmental objectives; and (2) the classification is substantially related to the achievement of those objectives. As noted above, prior to *Virginia*, these two requirements were the standard. . . .

[O]ne could argue that by imposing the exceedingly persuasive justification requirement, *Virginia* transformed these two additional requirements into something that is synonymous with the "narrow tailoring" requirement in the context of "suspect classifications." If this occurred, then the burden on an institution is almost impossible to meet. In the context of "suspect classifications," narrow tailoring involves four factors. First, the efficacy of using remedies which do not involve suspect classifications must be fully explored. Suspect classifications will be only where they are "necessary to break down patterns of deliberate exclusion." Second, the classification must be flexible and temporary. Third, there must be a realistic numerical relationship between the classification and the relevant population. Fourth, the racial remedy generally may not favor one group over another.

The differing treatment mandated by *Cohen IV* does not meet this test. First, there is no suggestion that alternative remedies were even considered. Second, since the differing treatment apparently continues indefinitely, it cannot be regarded as flexible and temporary. Third, *Cohen IV* implicitly assumes that both genders have equal interest in participating in intercollegiate athletics. Such an assumption might not be realistic. Fourth, as explained above, the classification clearly favors one gender over the other. In sum, if the addition of the exceedingly persuasive justification

> requirement has transformed the other requirements into something synonymous with "narrow tailoring," then the differing treatment of *Cohen IV* will not pass constitutional review. This is true even if there is an exceedingly persuasive justification.

William E. Thro & Brian A. Snow, *The Conflict Between the Equal Protection Clause and Cohen v. Brown University*, 123 EDUC. L. REP. 1013, 1030–35 (1998).*

Are Thro and Snow overreaching in their analysis? If the Court wanted to apply narrow tailoring in gender-based cases, would it not have said so? Regardless of the label applied to the *Virginia* test, is there an argument that the solution in the *Cohen* line of cases easily satisfies it? For other critical commentary regarding *Cohen* and the ill effects of Title IX on men's collegiate athletic programs, see Suzanne Sangree, *The Secretary's Commission on Opportunity in Athletics Squandered Its Opportunity to Understand Commercial Collegiate Sports: Why They Eliminate Minor Men's Sports and Prevent Title IX from Achieving Full Gender Equality*, 3 MARGINS 257 (2003); Sarah E. Gohl, Note, *A Lesson in English and Gender: Title IX and the Male Student Athlete*, 50 DUKE L.J. 1123 (2001); Brian A. Snow & William E. Thro, *Still on the Sidelines: Developing the Non-Discrimination Paradigm Under Title IX*, 3 DUKE J. GENDER L. & POL'Y 1(1996); Earl C. Dudley, Jr. & George Rutherglen, *Ironies, Inconsistencies, and Intercollegiate Athletics: Title IX, Title VII, and Statistical Evidence of Discrimination*, 1 VA. J. SPORTS & L. 177 (1999); Donald C. Mahoney, Comment, *Taking a Shot at the Title: A Critical Review of Judicial and Administrative Interpretations of Title IX as Applied to Intercollegiate Athletic Programs*, 27 CONN. L. REV. 943 (1995); George A. Davidson & Carla A. Kerr, *Title IX: What Is Gender Equity?*, 2 VILL. SPORTS & ENT. L.J. 25 (1995).

4. One concern of Title IX's proportionality requirement is the idea that it contravenes the "careers-open-to-talents model envisioned by Title VII," under which "individuals compete for jobs that are awarded based on relevant talents and abilities." Kimberly A. Yuracko, *One for You and One for Me: Is Title IX's Sex-Based Proportionality Requirement for College Varsity Athletic Positions Defensible?*, 97 NW. U. L. REV. 731, 731–32 (2003).* To critics, "the proportionality requirement does not fit this model because it guarantees female students proportional varsity athletic spots even if they have lower levels of athletic interest and ability than do male students." *Id.* at 732. This line of reasoning, however, does not comport with the fact that most critics do not really "favor[] a meritocratic distribution of college varsity athletic spots along the careers-open-to-talents model." *Id.* at 799.

In fact, critics do not "recommend an abandonment of sex-segregated athletic teams":

> Instead, they argue for a distribution of sex-segregated varsity athletic positions between female and male students based on their relative levels of athletic interest and ability. These proposals are, however, thoroughly incompatible with a straight careers-open-to-talents meritocracy-based

> distribution. First, interest is necessary, but not sufficient, to justify the distribution of rewards under a straight meritocracy model. Second, there is in fact no way to do real merit comparisons across groups when the measure of merit is distinctly group specific. Therefore, while the dominant denunciation of proportionality as being non-meritocratic are correct, the criticisms themselves reveal that even those who do not like proportionality do not really favor distributing varsity athletic spots along a true careers-open-to-talents meritocracy model. The proportionality requirement must be justified on grounds other than a straight careers-open-to-talents meritocracy model.

Id. at 799. Professor Yuracko argues that the proportionality requirement "cannot be justified by a standard liberal civil rights model in which resources and rewards are distributed based on neutral principles of merit, utility, or capacity to benefit." *Id.* But she concludes that proportionality can be defended on other grounds:

> Social policy often does and should reflect widely shared social ideals about the skills, traits, and attributes that are necessary for human flourishing. Such widely shared perfectionist ideals in fact provide the strongest justification for the proportionality requirement. Proportionality is probably best justified as a perfectionist resocialization measure aimed at providing girls with a set of alternative viable conceptions of themselves either through the role-modeling effects of having visible college varsity female athletes or, more indirectly, through helping to change the social meanings attached to athleticism, specifically, and physical agency, more generally. Proportionality is thus best justified on the grounds that it encourages girls to develop a set of traits, skills, and possible self-conceptions that are considered important for their future success and also important, more generally, for a good human life. Although a complete social transformation of what it means to be female or what it means to be an athlete has assuredly not taken place, just as assuredly, Title IX has been tremendously successful as a resocialization measure. Title IX's proportionality requirement may be best understood by recognizing this social transformation as both its goal and justification.

Id. Do you agree with this conclusion? Is this the statutory intent of the drafters of Title IX and its regulations? Or were they being driven by the types of distribution justifications that Yuracko dismisses? Moreover, notice that Yuracko conflates Title IX, a federal education statute, with Title VII, which is federal employment legislation, as the foundation of her thesis. Does this position begin with a desired end (a change in the interpretation of Title IX) with unsupportable means (Title VII)?

5. Are other factors at play in the decline of so-called "nonrevenue sports" — that is, wrestling, water polo, rowing, etc. — in men's collegiate athletic programs? An empirical study in 2003 concluded that the unbridled growth in men's football and basketball budgets at major universities might be the real culprit. Daniel R. Marburger & Nancy Hogshead-Makar, *Is Title IX Really to Blame for the Decline* *in Intercollegiate Men's Nonrevenue Sports?*, 14 MARQ. SPORTS L. REV. 65 (2003).* According to Professors Marburger and Hosgshead-Makar, it would be logical to assume that Title IX would harm nonrevenue men's sports at the Division II and III levels the most; while at the Division I level, the often immensely profitable men's basketball and football programs could "effectively cross-subsidize the men's nonrevenue sports, sparing [them] from the 'deleterious' effects of Title IX." *Id.* at 91. They conclude, however, that "the reverse is true": between 1978 and 1996, the number of men's sports offered at the Division II and III levels rose by 58 percent and 131 percent, respectively. *Id.* The only decreases occurred at the Division I and Division I-AA levels, with the largest decrease occurring in Division I men's nonrevenue sports. Although these statistics may seem counterintuitive, Marburger and Hogshead-Makar explained the trends in light of the economic model of budget allocation:

> Because the "marginal benefit" of a dollar spent on football and men's basketball at the Division I (especially I-A) level exceeds the marginal benefit of the same sports at Divisions II and III, Division I athletic directors have an economic incentive to dedicate a greater proportion of the budget to these sports. The evidence clearly supports this contention. In fact, the largest allocation of resources in favor of football and men's basketball occurs at the Division I-A level, where significant profits in these sports serve as the norm.
>
> If Division I athletic directors behave as profit-maximizers (or as "budget-maximizers," whose budget increases and/or salaries are tied to the success of the football and/or men's basketball teams), then any expenditure on a nonrevenue sport will reduce the athletic department's profit. In time, expenditures on nonrevenue sports would be reduced until the last dollar spent on a nonrevenue sport serviced the investment/consumption interests of the university as much as the last dollar spent on football and men's basketball (as investment/consumption and profit-generating programs). If the athletic director has significant autonomy in decision-making and does not stand to benefit materially from the investment/consumption interests of the university, the incentive is to phase out nonrevenue sports entirely.
>
> In practice, the profit-maximizing athletic director cannot eliminate all nonrevenue sports because of NCAA requirements. Division I-A, for example, will require a minimum of sixteen sponsored intercollegiate sports beginning in 2004. Most of these, of course, will be nonrevenue sports. Given the economic incentives of the profit-maximizing athletic director, one would expect "surplus" nonrevenue sports to be cut or their budgets reduced in favor of the income-generating sports.
>
> In this regard, Title IX serves to insulate women's nonrevenue sports from the budgetary axe. This is exhibited in the "expenditures per participant" data. At the Division I level, the expenditures per football/men's basketball player dwarf those of the other sports. To allow for

> unbridled growth in their budgets (driven primarily by the prisoner's dilemma), athletic directors resort to exempting football and men's basketball from budgetary considerations and cut men's nonrevenue sports as a means to comply with Title IX.

Id. at 92.

6. What happens when intercollegiate athletic association regulations bump heads with Title IX compliance? A federal district court in Alaska found that the NCAA could not enforce rules which in effect discriminated against female students and interfered with the university's responsibility to comply with federal law. *Pavey v. Univ. of Alaska*, 490 F. Supp. 1011, 1014 (D.C. Alaska 1980). Even though an athletic association's regulations appear facially neutral on gender, they can still be invalidated on grounds that they in effect create inequality and conflict with the university's Title IX obligations. *Id.* at 1015. What different kinds of regulations might interfere with Title IX compliance? Procedurally, the University of Alaska had to bring in the NCAA as a third party defendant to argue against the offending regulations. *Id.* at 1011. How could a university challenge athletic association regulations directly? Would any university be willing to challenge gender discriminating regulations without the pressure of student-initiated litigation?

7. Can a university consider factors other than gender equality in deciding how to structure athletic programs to be in compliance with Title IX? At least one court found that a university can consider financial interests when cutting teams in order to maintain gender equality. *Lichten v. State Univ. of N.Y. at Albany*, 223 A.D.2d 302, 306 (N.Y. A.D. 3 Dept.1996). Students argued that financial issues were improperly considered when their university-sponsored sports team was cut in order to comply with Title IX. *Id.* at 302. The court said that gender equality was only one of many important factors that may be considered when a university decides how to comply with Title IX. *Id.* at 306. What impact might this rule have on low-revenue sports? What other factors might affect compliance decisions in one direction or another?

8. Is it possible to achieve a satisfactory balance between men's and women's collegiate athletic programs without pursuing broader reforms of collegiate athletics in general? Are the issues associated with Title IX just a symptom of a larger problem? *See* Ellen J. Staurowsky, *Title IX and College Sport: The Long Painful Path to Compliance and Reform*, 14 Marq. Sports L. Rev. 95 (2003).

E. ATHLETIC ASSOCIATIONS AND CONFERENCES

1. Constitutional Concerns

NCAA v. TARKANIAN
488 U.S. 179 (1988)

JUSTICE STEVENS delivered the opinion of the Court.

When he became head basketball coach at the University of Nevada, Las Vegas (UNLV), in 1973, Jerry Tarkanian inherited a team with a mediocre 14-14 record. Four years later the team won 29 out of 32 games and placed third in the championship tournament sponsored by the National Collegiate Athletic Association (NCAA), to which UNLV belongs.

Yet in September 1977 UNLV informed Tarkanian that it was going to suspend him. No dissatisfaction with Tarkanian, once described as "the 'winningest' active basketball coach," motivated his suspension. Rather, the impetus was a report by the NCAA detailing 38 violations of NCAA rules by UNLV personnel, including 10 involving Tarkanian. The NCAA had placed the university's basketball team on probation for two years and ordered UNLV to show cause why the NCAA should not impose further penalties unless UNLV severed all ties during the probation between its intercollegiate athletic program and Tarkanian.

Facing demotion and a drastic cut in pay, Tarkanian brought suit in Nevada state court, alleging that he had been deprived of his Fourteenth Amendment due process rights in violation of 42 U. S. C. § 1983. Ultimately Tarkanian obtained injunctive relief and an award of attorney's fees against both UNLV and the NCAA. NCAA's liability may be upheld only if its participation in the events that led to Tarkanian's suspension constituted "state action" prohibited by the Fourteenth Amendment and was performed "under color of" state law within the meaning of § 1983. We granted certiorari to review the Nevada Supreme Court's holding that the NCAA engaged in state action when it conducted its investigation and recommended that Tarkanian be disciplined. We now reverse.

I

In order to understand the four separate proceedings that gave rise to the question we must decide, it is useful to begin with a description of the relationship among the three parties — Tarkanian, UNLV, and the NCAA.

Tarkanian initially was employed on a year-to-year basis but became a tenured professor in 1977. He receives an annual salary with valuable fringe benefits, and his status as a highly successful coach enables him to earn substantial additional income from sports-related activities such as broadcasting and the sponsorship of products.

UNLV is a branch of the University of Nevada, a state-funded institution. The university is organized and operated pursuant to provisions of Nevada's State

Constitution, statutes, and regulations. In performing their official functions, the executives of UNLV unquestionably act under color of state law.

The NCAA is an unincorporated association of approximately 960 members, including virtually all public and private universities and 4-year colleges conducting major athletic programs in the United States. Basic policies of the NCAA are determined by the members at annual conventions. Between conventions, the Association is governed by its Council, which appoints various committees to implement specific programs.

One of the NCAA's fundamental policies "is to maintain intercollegiate athletics as an integral part of the educational program and the athlete as an integral part of the student body, and by so doing, retain a clear line of demarcation between college athletics and professional sports." It has therefore adopted rules, which it calls "legislation," governing the conduct of the intercollegiate athletic programs of its members. This NCAA legislation applies to a variety of issues, such as academic standards for eligibility, admissions, financial aid, and the recruiting of student-athletes. By joining the NCAA, each member agrees to abide by and to enforce such rules.

The NCAA's bylaws provide that its enforcement program shall be administered by a Committee on Infractions. The Committee supervises an investigative staff, makes factual determinations concerning alleged rule violations, and is expressly authorized to "impose appropriate penalties on a member found to be in violation, or recommend to the Council suspension or termination of membership." . . . .

During its investigation of UNLV, the Committee on Infractions included three law professors, a mathematics professor, and the dean of a graduate school. Four of them were on the faculties of state institutions; one represented a private university.

The NCAA Investigation of UNLV

On November 28, 1972, the Committee on Infractions notified UNLV's president that it was initiating a preliminary inquiry into alleged violations of NCAA requirements by UNLV. As a result of that preliminary inquiry, some three years later the Committee decided that an "Official Inquiry" was warranted and so advised the UNLV president on February 25, 1976. That advice included a series of detailed allegations concerning the recruitment of student-athletes during the period between 1971 and 1975. Many of the allegations implicated Tarkanian. It requested UNLV to investigate and provide detailed information concerning each alleged incident.

With the assistance of the Attorney General of Nevada and private counsel, UNLV conducted a thorough investigation of the charges. On October 27, 1976, it filed a comprehensive response containing voluminous exhibits and sworn affidavits. The response denied all of the allegations and specifically concluded that Tarkanian was completely innocent of wrongdoing. . . . Ultimately the Committee decided that many of the charges could not be supported, but it did find 38 violations of NCAA rules, including 10 committed by Tarkanian. Most serious was the finding that Tarkanian had violated the University's obligation to provide full cooperation with the NCAA investigation. . . .

UNLV's Discipline of Tarkanian

Promptly after receiving the NCAA report, the president of UNLV directed the University's vice president to schedule a hearing to determine whether the Committee's recommended sanctions should be applied. Tarkanian and UNLV were represented at that hearing; the NCAA was not. Although the vice president expressed doubt concerning the sufficiency of the evidence supporting the Committee's findings, he concluded that "given the terms of our adherence to the NCAA we cannot substitute — biased as we must be — our own judgment on the credibility of witnesses for that of the infractions committee and the Council." . . . [T]he president [ultimately] notified Tarkanian that he was to "be completely severed of any and all relations, formal or informal, with the University's Intercollegiate athletic program during the period of the University's NCAA probation."

Tarkanian's Lawsuit Against UNLV

The day before his suspension was to become effective, Tarkanian filed an action in Nevada state court for declaratory and injunctive relief against UNLV and a number of its officers. He alleged that these defendants had . . . deprived him of property and liberty without the due process of law guaranteed by the Fourteenth Amendment to the United States Constitution. Based on a stipulation of facts and the testimony offered by Tarkanian, the trial court enjoined UNLV from suspending Tarkanian on the ground that he had been denied procedural and substantive due process of law. UNLV appealed.

The NCAA, which had not been joined as a party, filed an amicus curiae brief arguing that there was no actual controversy between Tarkanian and UNLV; thus, the suit should be dismissed. Alternatively, the NCAA contended that the trial court had exceeded its jurisdiction by effectively invalidating the enforcement proceedings of the NCAA, even though the Association was not a party to the suit. Should a controversy exist, the NCAA argued, it was a necessary party to litigate the scope of any relief. Finally, it contested the trial court's conclusion that Tarkanian had been denied due process. The Nevada Supreme Court concluded that there was an actual controversy but agreed that the NCAA was a necessary party and therefore reversed and remanded to permit joinder of the NCAA.

The Lawsuit Against NCAA

Tarkanian consequently filed a second amended complaint adding the NCAA. . . . The court concluded that NCAA's conduct constituted state action for jurisdictional and constitutional purposes, and that its decision was arbitrary and capricious. It reaffirmed its earlier injunction barring UNLV from disciplining Tarkanian or otherwise enforcing the Confidential Report. Additionally, it enjoined the NCAA from conducting "any further proceedings against the University," from enforcing its show-cause order, and from taking any other action against the University that had been recommended in the Confidential Report.

[The NCAA again sought removal to Federal District Court. But the court again ordered the litigation remanded.]

The Nevada Supreme Court agreed that Tarkanian had been deprived of both property and liberty protected by the Constitution and that he was not afforded due process before suspension. It thus affirmed the trial court's injunction insofar as it pertained to Tarkanian, but narrowed its scope "only to prohibit enforcement of the penalties imposed upon Tarkanian in Confidential Report No. 123(47) and UNLV's adoption of those penalties." 741 P. 2d, at 1353. . . .

As a predicate for its disposition, the State Supreme Court held that the NCAA had engaged in state action. Several strands of argument supported this holding. First, the court assumed that it was reviewing "UNLV's and the NCAA's imposition of penalties against Tarkanian," rather than the NCAA's proposed sanctions against UNLV if it failed to discipline Tarkanian appropriately. Second, it regarded the NCAA's regulatory activities as state action because "many NCAA member institutions were either public or government supported." Third, it stated that the right to discipline a public employee "is traditionally the exclusive prerogative of the state" and that UNLV could not escape its responsibility for such disciplinary action by delegating that duty to a private entity. The court next pointed to our opinion in *Lugar v. Edmondson Oil Co.*, 457 U.S. 922, 937 (1982), in which we held that the deprivation of a federal right may be attributed to the State if it resulted from a state-created rule and the party charged with the deprivation can fairly be said to be a state actor. . . .

II

Embedded in our Fourteenth Amendment jurisprudence is a dichotomy between state action, which is subject to scrutiny under the Amendment's Due Process Clause, and private conduct, against which the Amendment affords no shield, no matter how unfair that conduct may be. . . .

. . . When Congress enacted § 1983 as the statutory remedy for violations of the Constitution, it specified that the conduct at issue must have occurred "under color of" state law; thus, liability attaches only to those wrongdoers "who carry a badge of authority of a State and represent it in some capacity, whether they act in accordance with their authority or misuse it." *Monroe v. Pape*, 365 U.S. 167, 172 (1961). . . .

In this case Tarkanian argues that the NCAA was a state actor because it misused power that it possessed by virtue of state law. He claims specifically that UNLV delegated its own functions to the NCAA, clothing the Association with authority both to adopt rules governing UNLV's athletic programs and to enforce those rules on behalf of UNLV. Similarly, the Nevada Supreme Court held that UNLV had delegated its authority over personnel decisions to the NCAA. Therefore, the court reasoned, the two entities acted jointly to deprive Tarkanian of liberty and property interests, making the NCAA as well as UNLV a state actor.

These contentions fundamentally misconstrue the facts of this case. In the typical case raising a state-action issue, a private party has taken the decisive step that caused the harm to the plaintiff, and the question is whether the State was sufficiently involved to treat that decisive conduct as state action. This may occur if the State creates the legal framework governing the conduct, *e. g.*, *North Georgia*

Finishing, Inc. v. Di-Chem, Inc., 419 U.S. 601 (1975); if it delegates its authority to the private actor, *e. g., West v. Atkins*, 487 U.S. 42 (1988); or sometimes if it knowingly accepts the benefits derived from unconstitutional behavior, *e. g., Burton v. Wilmington Parking Authority*, 365 U.S. 715 (1961). Thus, in the usual case we ask whether the State provided a mantle of authority that enhanced the power of the harm-causing individual actor.

This case uniquely mirrors the traditional state-action case. Here the final act challenged by Tarkanian — his suspension — was committed by UNLV. A state university without question is a state actor. When it decides to impose a serious disciplinary sanction upon one of its tenured employees, it must comply with the terms of the Due Process Clause of the Fourteenth Amendment to the Federal Constitution. Thus when UNLV notified Tarkanian that he was being separated from all relations with the university's basketball program, it acted under color of state law within the meaning of 42 U. S. C. § 1983.

The mirror image presented in this case requires us to step through an analytical looking glass to resolve the case. Clearly UNLV's conduct was influenced by the rules and recommendations of the NCAA, the private party. But it was UNLV, the state entity, that actually suspended Tarkanian. Thus the question is not whether UNLV participated to a critical extent in the NCAA's activities, but whether UNLV's actions in compliance with the NCAA rules and recommendations turned the NCAA's conduct into state action.

We examine first the relationship between UNLV and the NCAA regarding the NCAA's rulemaking. UNLV is among the NCAA's members and participated in promulgating the Association's rules; it must be assumed, therefore, that Nevada had some impact on the NCAA's policy determinations. Yet the NCAA's several hundred other public and private member institutions each similarly affected those policies. Those institutions, the vast majority of which were located in States other than Nevada, did not act under color of Nevada law. It necessarily follows that the source of the legislation adopted by the NCAA is not Nevada but the collective membership, speaking through an organization that is independent of any particular State.

State action nonetheless might lie if UNLV, by embracing the NCAA's rules, transformed them into state rules and the NCAA into a state actor. *See Lugar*, 457 U.S., at 937. UNLV engaged in state action when it adopted the NCAA's rules to govern its own behavior, but that would be true even if UNLV had taken no part in the promulgation of those rules. . . . [Yet,] UNLV retained the authority to withdraw from the NCAA and establish its own standards. The university alternatively could have stayed in the Association and worked through the Association's legislative process to amend rules or standards it deemed harsh, unfair, or unwieldy. Neither UNLV's decision to adopt the NCAA's standards nor its minor role in their formulation is a sufficient reason for concluding that the NCAA was acting under color of Nevada law when it promulgated standards governing athlete recruitment, eligibility, and academic performance.

Tarkanian further asserts that the NCAA's investigation, enforcement proceedings, and consequent recommendations constituted state action because they resulted from a delegation of power by UNLV. UNLV, as an NCAA member, subscribed to the statement in the Association's bylaws that NCAA "enforcement procedures are an essential part of the intercollegiate athletic program of each member institution." It is, of course, true that a State may delegate authority to a private party and thereby make that party a state actor. . . . But UNLV delegated no power to the NCAA to take specific action against any university employee. The commitment by UNLV to adhere to NCAA enforcement procedures was enforceable only by sanctions that the NCAA might impose on UNLV itself.

Indeed, the notion that UNLV's promise to cooperate in the NCAA enforcement proceedings was tantamount to a partnership agreement or the transfer of certain university powers to the NCAA is belied by the history of this case. It is quite obvious that UNLV used its best efforts to retain its winning coach — a goal diametrically opposed to the NCAA's interest in ascertaining the truth of its investigators' reports. During the several years that the NCAA investigated the alleged violations, the NCAA and UNLV acted much more like adversaries than like partners engaged in a dispassionate search for the truth. . . .

The NCAA enjoyed no governmental powers to facilitate its investigation. It had no power to subpoena witnesses, to impose contempt sanctions, or to assert sovereign authority over any individual. Its greatest authority was to threaten sanctions against UNLV, with the ultimate sanction being expulsion of the university from membership. Contrary to the premise of the Nevada Supreme Court's opinion, the NCAA did not — indeed, could not — directly discipline Tarkanian or any other state university employee. The express terms of the Confidential Report did not demand the suspension unconditionally; rather, it requested "the University . . . to show cause" why the NCAA should not impose additional penalties if UNLV declines to suspend Tarkanian. . . .

Finally, Tarkanian argues that the power of the NCAA is so great that the UNLV had no practical alternative to compliance with its demands. We are not at all sure this is true, but even if we assume that a private monopolist can impose its will on a state agency by a threatened refusal to deal with it, it does not follow that such a private party is therefore acting under color of state law.

In final analysis the question is whether "the conduct allegedly causing the deprivation of a federal right [can] be fairly attributable to the State." *Lugar*, 457 U.S., at 937. It would be ironic indeed to conclude that the NCAA's imposition of sanctions against UNLV — sanctions that UNLV and its counsel, including the Attorney General of Nevada, steadfastly opposed during protracted adversary proceedings — is fairly attributable to the State of Nevada. It would be more appropriate to conclude that UNLV has conducted its athletic program under color of the policies adopted by the NCAA, rather than that those policies were developed and enforced under color of Nevada law.

The judgment of the Nevada Supreme Court is reversed, and the case is remanded to that court for further proceedings not inconsistent with this opinion.

NOTES

1. Footnote 5 of the *Tarkanian* decision predicted the outcome in one of the Court's more recent pronouncements on state action: *Brentwood Acad. v. Tenn. Secondary Sch. Athletic Ass'n*, 531 U.S. 288 (2001). In *Brentwood*, the Tennessee Secondary School Athletic Association, a nonprofit organization that regulates athletics at the state's public and private high schools, sanctioned Brentwood Academy for violating the Association's recruiting rule. The Court held that the Association's sanction was state action because of the "pervasive entwinement of public institutions and public officials in [the Association's] composition and workings . . . ." *Id.* at 298. Describing the "entwinement" analysis as a "necessarily fact-bound inquiry," Justice Souter, writing for the majority, noted that 84 percent of the Association's member institutions were public schools. *Id.* "[D]ictum in *Tarkanian*," Souter wrote, "pointed to a contrary result on facts like ours . . . ." *Id.* at 298.

2. Justice Thomas, writing for the four dissenters, concluded that the majority's new "entwinement" test "extends state action doctrine beyond its permissible limits [and] also encroaches upon the realm of individual freedom that the doctrine was meant to protect." *Id.* at 305 (Thomas, J., dissenting). Prior to *Brentwood*, the Court had used three different tests to determine whether an action was state action: (1) the symbiotic relationship test, examining whether a public and private entity had developed an interdependent relationship that turned the private entity's actions into actions of the state; (2) the public function test, analyzing whether a private entity was performing a traditionally public function; and (3) the state compulsion test, a look at whether a state coerced or encouraged a private entity to take a particular action. Megan M. Cooper, *Dusting Off the Old Play Book: How the Supreme Court Disregarded the Blum Trilogy, Returned to Theories of the Past, and Found State Action Through Entwinement in Brentwood Academy v. Tennessee Secondary School Athletic Ass'n*, 35 Creighton L. Rev. 913, 913–14 (2002).

Justice Thomas worried that the entwinement test was too vague:

> Because the majority never defines "entwinement," the scope of its holding is unclear. If we are fortunate, the majority's fact-specific analysis will have little bearing beyond this case. But if the majority's new entwinement test develops in future years, it could affect many organizations that foster activities, enforce rules, and sponsor extracurricular competition among high schools — not just in athletics, but in such diverse areas as agriculture, mathematics, music, marching bands, forensics, and cheerleading. Indeed, this entwinement test may extend to other organizations that are composed of, or controlled by, public officials or public entities, such as firefighters, policemen, teachers, cities, or counties. I am not prepared to say that any private organization that permits public entities and public officials to participate acts as the State in anything or everything it does, and our state-action jurisprudence has never reached that far. The state-action doctrine was developed to reach only those actions that are truly attributable to the State, not to subject private citizens to the control of federal courts hearing § 1983 actions.

Brentwood, 531 U.S. at 314–15 (Thomas, J., dissenting).

3. Is there a real difference between the symbiotic relationship and entwinement tests? For additional analysis of the holding in *Brentwood*, see Michael A. Culpeper, *Casenote: A Matter of Normative Judgment: Brentwood and the Emergence of the "Pervasive Entwinement" Test*, 35 U. Rich. L. Rev. 1163 (2002); Lisa Mastrogiovanni, *Casenote: Fourteenth Amendment: Deeds of Private Organizations Constitute State Action Under the Fourteenth Amendment Where There Is Pervasive Entwinement Between the Private Organization and a Governmental Entity*, 12 Seton Hall. Const. L. J. 711 (2002). In light of Justice Thomas' concern about the symbiotic relationship and entwinement tests, see also Chapter IV for state action issues.

2. Antitrust Concerns

NCAA v. BOARD OF REGENTS OF THE UNIVERSITY OF OKLAHOMA

468 U.S. 85 (1984)

Justice Stevens delivered the opinion of the Court.

The University of Oklahoma and the University of Georgia contend that the National Collegiate Athletic Association has unreasonably restrained trade in the televising of college football games. . . . [T]he District Court found that the NCAA had violated § 1 of the Sherman Act and granted injunctive relief. The Court of Appeals agreed that the statute had been violated but modified the remedy in some respects. We granted certiorari and now affirm.

I

The NCAA

Since its inception in 1905, the NCAA has played an important role in the regulation of amateur collegiate sports. It has adopted and promulgated playing rules, standards of amateurism, standards for academic eligibility, regulations concerning recruitment of athletes, and rules governing the size of athletic squads and coaching staffs. In some sports, such as baseball, swimming, basketball, wrestling, and track, it has sponsored and conducted national tournaments. It has not done so in the sport of football, however. With the exception of football, the NCAA has not undertaken any regulation of the televising of athletic events.

The NCAA has approximately 850 voting members. The regular members are classified into separate divisions to reflect differences in size and scope of their athletic programs. Division I includes 276 colleges with major athletic programs; in this group only 187 play intercollegiate football. Divisions II and III include approximately 500 colleges with less extensive athletic programs. Division I has been subdivided into Divisions I-A and I-AA for football.

Some years ago, five major conferences together with major football-playing independent institutions organized the College Football Association (CFA). The original purpose of the CFA was to promote the interests of major football-playing schools within the NCAA structure. The Universities of Oklahoma and Georgia, respondents in this Court, are members of the CFA.

History of the NCAA Television Plan

In 1938, the University of Pennsylvania televised one of its home games. From 1940 through the 1950 season all of Pennsylvania's home games were televised. That was the beginning of the relationship between television and college football.

On January 11, 1951, a three-person "Television Committee," appointed during the preceding year, delivered a report to the NCAA's annual convention in Dallas. Based on preliminary surveys, the committee had concluded that "television does have an adverse effect on college football attendance and unless brought under some control threatens to seriously harm the nation's overall athletic and physical system." . . . As a result, the NCAA decided to retain the National Opinion Research Center (NORC) to study the impact of television on live attendance . . . . A television committee was appointed to implement the decision and to develop an NCAA television plan for 1951.

The committee's 1951 plan provided that only one game a week could be telecast in each area, with a total blackout on 3 of the 10 Saturdays during the season. A team could appear on television only twice during a season. . . . The plan received the virtually unanimous support of the NCAA membership . . . .

During each of the succeeding five seasons, studies were made which tended to indicate that television had an adverse effect on attendance at college football games. During those years the NCAA continued to exercise complete control over the number of games that could be televised.

From 1952 through 1977 the NCAA television committee followed essentially the same procedure for developing its television plans. It would first circulate a questionnaire to the membership and then use the responses as a basis for formulating a plan for the ensuing season. The plan was then submitted to a vote by means of a mail referendum. Once approved, the plan formed the basis for NCAA's negotiations with the networks. Throughout this period the plans retained the essential purposes of the original plan. Until 1977 the contracts were all for either 1- or 2-year terms. In 1977 the NCAA adopted "principles of negotiation" for the future and discontinued the practice of submitting each plan for membership approval. Then the NCAA also entered into its first 4-year contract granting exclusive rights to the American Broadcasting Cos. (ABC) for the 1978-1981 seasons. . . .

The Current Plan

The plan adopted in 1981 for the 1982-1985 seasons is at issue in this case. This plan, like each of its predecessors, recites that it is intended to reduce, insofar as possible, the adverse effects of live television upon football game attendance. It provides that "all forms of television of the football games of NCAA member institutions during the Plan control periods shall be in accordance with this Plan."

The plan recites that the television committee has awarded rights to negotiate and contract for the telecasting of college football games of members of the NCAA to two "carrying networks." . . .

In separate agreements with each of the carrying networks, ABC and the Columbia Broadcasting System (CBS), the NCAA granted each the right to telecast the 14 live "exposures" described in the plan . . . . Each of the networks agreed to pay a specified "minimum aggregate compensation to the participating NCAA member institutions" during the 4-year period in an amount that totaled $131,750,000. In essence the agreement authorized each network to negotiate directly with member schools for the right to televise their games. The agreement itself does not describe the method of computing the compensation for each game, but the practice that has developed over the years and that the District Court found would be followed under the current agreement involved the setting of a recommended fee by a representative of the NCAA for different types of telecasts, with national telecasts being the most valuable . . . . The aggregate of all these payments presumably equals the total minimum aggregate compensation set forth in the basic agreement. Except for differences in payment between national and regional telecasts, and with respect to Division II and Division III games, the amount that any team receives does not change with the size of the viewing audience, the number of markets in which the game is telecast, or the particular characteristic of the game or the participating teams. Instead, the "ground rules" provide that the carrying networks make alternate selections of those games they wish to televise, and thereby obtain the exclusive right to submit a bid at an essentially fixed price to the institutions involved.

The plan also contains "appearance requirements" and "appearance limitations" which pertain to each of the 2-year periods that the plan is in effect. . . . Under the appearance limitations no member institution is eligible to appear on television more than a total of six times and more than four times nationally, with the appearances to be divided equally between the two carrying networks. The number of exposures specified in the contracts also sets an absolute maximum on the number of games that can be broadcast.

Thus, although the current plan is more elaborate than any of its predecessors, it retains the essential features of each of them. It limits the total amount of televised intercollegiate football and the number of games that any one team may televise. No member is permitted to make any sale of television rights except in accordance with the basic plan.

Background of this Controversy

Beginning in 1979 CFA members began to advocate that colleges with major football programs should have a greater voice in the formulation of football television policy than they had in the NCAA. CFA therefore investigated the possibility of negotiating a television agreement of its own, developed an independent plan, and obtained a contract offer from the National Broadcasting Co. (NBC). This contract, which it signed in August 1981, would have allowed a more liberal number of appearances for each institution, and would have increased the overall revenues realized by CFA members.

In response the NCAA publicly announced that it would take disciplinary action against any CFA member that complied with the CFA-NBC contract. . . . On September 8, 1981, respondents commenced this action in the United States District Court for the Western District of Oklahoma and obtained a preliminary injunction preventing the NCAA from initiating disciplinary proceedings or otherwise interfering with CFA's efforts to perform its agreement with NBC. Notwithstanding the entry of the injunction, most CFA members were unwilling to commit themselves to the new contractual arrangement with NBC in the face of the threatened sanctions and therefore the agreement was never consummated.

Decision of the District Court

After a full trial, the District Court held that the controls exercised by the NCAA over the televising of college football games violated the Sherman Act. The District Court defined the relevant market as "live college football television" because it found that alternative programming has a significantly different and lesser audience appeal. . . .

The District Court found that competition in the relevant market had been restrained in three ways: (1) NCAA fixed the price for particular telecasts; (2) its exclusive network contracts were tantamount to a group boycott of all other potential broadcasters and its threat of sanctions against its own members constituted a threatened boycott of potential competitors; and (3) its plan placed an artificial limit on the production of televised college football.

. . . .

Decision of the Court of Appeals

The Court of Appeals held that the NCAA television plan constituted illegal per se price fixing, 707 F.2d, at 1152. It rejected each of the three arguments advanced by NCAA to establish the procompetitive character of its plan. First, the court rejected the argument that the television plan promoted live attendance, noting that since the plan involved a concomitant reduction in viewership the plan did not result in a net increase in output and hence was not procompetitive. Second, the Court of Appeals rejected as illegitimate the NCAA's purpose of promoting athletically balanced competition. It held that such a consideration amounted to an argument that "competition will destroy the market" — a position inconsistent with the policy of the Sherman Act. . . . Third, the Court of Appeals refused to view the NCAA plan as competitively justified by the need to compete effectively with other types of television programming, since it entirely eliminated competition between producers of football and hence was illegal *per se.*

Finally, the Court of Appeals concluded that even if the television plan were not per se illegal, its anticompetitive limitation on price and output was not offset by any procompetitive justification sufficient to save the plan even when the totality of the circumstances was examined. The case was remanded to the District Court for an appropriate modification in its injunctive decree.

II

There can be no doubt that the challenged practices of the NCAA constitute a "restraint of trade" in the sense that they limit members' freedom to negotiate and enter into their own television contracts. In that sense, however, every contract is a restraint of trade, and as we have repeatedly recognized, the Sherman Act was intended to prohibit only unreasonable restraints of trade.

It is also undeniable that these practices share characteristics of restraints we have previously held unreasonable. The NCAA is an association of schools which compete against each other to attract television revenues, not to mention fans and athletes. As the District Court found, the policies of the NCAA with respect to television rights are ultimately controlled by the vote of member institutions. By participating in an association which prevents member institutions from competing against each other on the basis of price or kind of television rights that can be offered to broadcasters, the NCAA member institutions have created a horizontal restraint — an agreement among competitors on the way in which they will compete with one another. A restraint of this type has often been held to be unreasonable as a matter of law. Because it places a ceiling on the number of games member institutions may televise, the horizontal agreement places an artificial limit on the quantity of televised football that is available to broadcasters and consumers. By restraining the quantity of television rights available for sale, the challenged practices create a limitation on output; our cases have held that such limitations are unreasonable restraints of trade. Moreover, the District Court found that the minimum aggregate price in fact operates to preclude any price negotiation between broadcasters and institutions, thereby constituting horizontal price fixing, perhaps the paradigm of an unreasonable restraint of trade.

Horizontal price fixing and output limitation are ordinarily condemned as a matter of law under an "illegal per se" approach because the probability that these practices are anticompetitive is so high; a per se rule is applied when "the practice facially appears to be one that would always or almost always tend to restrict competition and decrease output." *Broadcast Music, Inc. v. Columbia Broadcasting System, Inc.*, 441 U.S. 1, 19-20 (1979). . . . . Nevertheless, we have decided that it would be inappropriate to apply a *per se* rule to this case. . . . [W]hat is critical is that this case involves an industry in which horizontal restraints on competition are essential if the product is to be available at all.

As Judge Bork has noted: "[Some] activities can only be carried out jointly. Perhaps the leading example is league sports. When a league of professional lacrosse teams is formed, it would be pointless to declare their cooperation illegal on the ground that there are no other professional lacrosse teams." R. Bork, The Antitrust Paradox 278 (1978). What the NCAA and its member institutions market in this case is competition itself — contests between competing institutions. Of course, this would be completely ineffective if there were no rules on which the competitors agreed to create and define the competition to be marketed. A myriad of rules affecting such matters as the size of the field, the number of players on a team, and the extent to which physical violence is to be encouraged or proscribed, all must be agreed upon, and all restrain the manner in which institutions compete. Moreover, the NCAA seeks to market a particular brand of football — college football. The identification of this "product" with an academic tradition differentiates college football from and makes it more popular than professional sports to which it might otherwise be comparable, such as, for example, minor league baseball. In order to preserve the character and quality of the "product," athletes must not be paid, must be required to attend class, and the like. And the integrity of the "product" cannot be preserved except by mutual agreement . . . . Thus, the NCAA plays a vital role in enabling college football to preserve its character, and as a result enables a product to be marketed which might otherwise be unavailable. In performing this role, its actions widen consumer choice — not only the choices available to sports fans but also those available to athletes — and hence can be viewed as procompetitive.

Broadcast Music squarely holds that a joint selling arrangement may be so efficient that it will increase sellers' aggregate output and thus be procompetitive. *See* 441 U.S., at 18-23. Similarly, as we indicated in *Continental T. V., Inc. v. GTE Sylvania Inc.*, 433 U.S. 36, 51-57 (1977), a restraint in a limited aspect of a market may actually enhance marketwide competition. . . . Thus, despite the fact that this case involves restraints on the ability of member institutions to compete in terms of price and output, a fair evaluation of their competitive character requires consideration of the NCAA's justifications for the restraints.

Our analysis of this case under the Rule of Reason, of course, does not change the ultimate focus of our inquiry. Both *per se* rules and the Rule of Reason are employed "to form a judgment about the competitive significance of the restraint." *National Society of Professional Engineers v. United States*, 435 U.S. 679, 692 (1978). A conclusion that a restraint of trade is unreasonable may be

> based either (1) on the nature or character of the contracts, or (2) on surrounding circumstances giving rise to the inference or presumption that they were intended to restrain trade and enhance prices. Under either branch of the test, the inquiry is confined to a consideration of impact on competitive conditions.

Id. at 690 (footnotes omitted).

. . . .

III

. . . .

The anticompetitive consequences of this arrangement are apparent. Individual competitors lose their freedom to compete. Price is higher and output lower than they would otherwise be, and both are unresponsive to consumer preference. . . . A restraint that has the effect of reducing the importance of consumer preference in setting price and output is not consistent with this fundamental goal of anti-trust law. Restrictions on price and output are the paradigmatic examples of restraints of trade that the Sherman Act was intended to prohibit. At the same time, the television plan eliminates competitors from the market, since only those broadcasters able to bid on television rights covering the entire NCAA can compete. Thus, as the District Court found, many telecasts that would occur in a competitive market are foreclosed by the NCAA's plan.

Petitioner argues, however, that its television plan can have no significant anticompetitive effect since the record indicates that it has no market power — no ability to alter the interaction of supply and demand in the market. We must reject this argument for two reasons, one legal, one factual.

As a matter of law, the absence of proof of market power does not justify a naked restriction on price or output. To the contrary, when there is an agreement not to compete in terms of price or output, "no elaborate industry analysis is required to demonstrate the anticompetitive character of such an agreement." *Professional Engineers*, 435 U.S., at 692. Petitioner does not quarrel with the District Court's finding that price and output are not responsive to demand. Thus the plan is inconsistent with the Sherman Act's command that price and supply be responsive to consumer preference. We have never required proof of market power in such a case. This naked restraint on price and output requires some competitive justification even in the absence of a detailed market analysis.

As a factual matter, it is evident that petitioner does possess market power. The District Court employed the correct test for determining whether college football broadcasts constitute a separate market — whether there are other products that are reasonably substitutable for televised NCAA football games. Petitioner's argument that it cannot obtain supracompetitive prices from broadcasters since advertisers, and hence broadcasters, can switch from college football to other types of programming simply ignores the findings of the District Court. It found that intercollegiate football telecasts generate an audience uniquely attractive to advertisers and that competitors are unable to offer programming that can attract a similar audience. These findings amply support its conclusion that the NCAA possesses market power. . . . Thus, respondents have demonstrated that there is a separate market for telecasts of college football which "[rests] on generic qualities differentiating" viewers. *Times-Picayune Publishing Co. v. United States*, 345 U.S. 594, 613 (1953). It inexorably follows that if college football broadcasts be defined as a separate market — and we are convinced they are — then the NCAA's complete control over those broadcasts provides a solid basis for the District Court's conclusion that the NCAA possesses market power with respect to those broadcasts. . . .

Thus, the NCAA television plan on its face constitutes a restraint upon the operation of a free market, and the findings of the District Court establish that it has operated to raise prices and reduce output. Under the Rule of Reason, these hallmarks of anticompetitive behavior place upon petitioner a heavy burden of establishing an affirmative defense which competitively justifies this apparent deviation from the operations of a free market. We turn now to the NCAA's proffered justifications.

IV

Relying on *Broadcast Music*, petitioner argues that its television plan constitutes a cooperative "joint venture" which assists in the marketing of broadcast rights and hence is procompetitive. . . . [A] joint selling arrangement may "[make] possible a new product by reaping otherwise unattainable efficiencies." *Arizona v. Maricopa County Medical Society*, 457 U.S. 332, 365 (1982) (Powell, J., dissenting). The essential contribution made by the NCAA's arrangement is to define the number of games that may be televised, to establish the price for each exposure, and to define the basic terms of each contract between the network and a home team. The NCAA does not, however, act as a selling agent for any school or for any conference of schools. The selection of individual games, and the negotiation of particular agreements, are matters left to the networks and the individual schools. . . .

The District Court did not find that the NCAA's television plan produced any procompetitive efficiencies which enhanced the competitiveness of college football television rights; to the contrary it concluded that NCAA football could be marketed just as effectively without the television plan. There is therefore no predicate in the findings for petitioner's efficiency justification. Indeed, petitioner's argument is refuted by the District Court's finding concerning price and output. . . .

Neither is the NCAA's television plan necessary to enable the NCAA to penetrate the market through an attractive package sale. Since broadcasting rights to college football constitute a unique product for which there is no ready substitute, there is no need for collective action in order to enable the product to compete against its nonexistent competitors. This is borne out by the District Court's finding that the NCAA's television plan reduces the volume of television rights sold.

V

Throughout the history of its regulation of intercollegiate football telecasts, the NCAA has indicated its concern with protecting live attendance. . . . [T]he concern is that fan interest in a televised game may adversely affect ticket sales for games that will not appear on television.

Although the NORC studies in the 1950's provided some support for the thesis that live attendance would suffer if unlimited television were permitted, the District Court found that there was no evidence to support that theory in today's market. Moreover, as the District Court found, the television plan has evolved in a manner inconsistent with its original design to protect gate attendance. Under the current plan, games are shown on television during all hours that college football games are played. The plan simply does not protect live attendance by ensuring that games will not be shown on television at the same time as live events.

There is, however, a more fundamental reason for rejecting this defense. The NCAA's argument that its television plan is necessary to protect live attendance is not based on a desire to maintain the integrity of college football as a distinct and attractive product, but rather on a fear that the product will not prove sufficiently attractive to draw live attendance when faced with competition from televised games. At bottom the NCAA's position is that ticket sales for most college games are unable to compete in a free market. The television plan protects ticket sales by limiting output — just as any monopolist increases revenues by reducing output. . . .

VI

Petitioner argues that the interest in maintaining a competitive balance among amateur athletic teams is legitimate and important and that it justifies the regulations challenged in this case. We agree with the first part of the argument but not the second.

Our decision not to apply a per se rule to this case rests in large part on our recognition that a certain degree of cooperation is necessary if the type of competition that petitioner and its member institutions seek to market is to be preserved. It is reasonable to assume that most of the regulatory controls of the NCAA are justifiable means of fostering competition among amateur athletic teams and therefore procompetitive because they enhance public interest in intercollegiate athletics. The specific restraints on football telecasts that are challenged in this case do not, however, fit into the same mold as do rules defining the conditions of the contest, the eligibility of participants, or the manner in which members of a joint enterprise shall share the responsibilities and the benefits of the total venture.

The NCAA does not claim that its television plan has equalized or is intended to equalize competition within any one league. The plan is nationwide in scope and there is no single league or tournament in which all college football teams compete. There is no evidence of any intent to equalize the strength of teams in Division I-A with those in Division II or Division III, and not even a colorable basis for giving colleges that have no football program at all a voice in the management of the revenues generated by the football programs at other schools. The interest in maintaining a competitive balance that is asserted by the NCAA as a justification for regulating all television of intercollegiate football is not related to any neutral standard or to any readily identifiable group of competitors.

. . . .

Perhaps the most important reason for rejecting the argument that the interest in competitive balance is served by the television plan is the District Court's unambiguous and well-supported finding that many more games would be televised in a free market than under the NCAA plan. . . . The finding that consumption will materially increase if the controls are removed is a compelling demonstration that they do not in fact serve any such legitimate purpose.

VII

The NCAA plays a critical role in the maintenance of a revered tradition of amateurism in college sports. There can be no question but that it needs ample latitude to play that role, or that the preservation of the student-athlete in higher education adds richness and diversity to intercollegiate athletics and is entirely consistent with the goals of the Sherman Act. But consistent with the Sherman Act, the role of the NCAA must be to preserve a tradition that might otherwise die; rules that restrict output are hardly consistent with this role. Today we hold only that the record supports the District Court's conclusion that by curtailing output and blunting the ability of member institutions to respond to consumer preference, the NCAA has restricted rather than enhanced the place of intercollegiate athletics in the Nation's life. Accordingly, the judgment of the Court of Appeals is

Affirmed.

NOTES

1. Justice Stevens, writing for the majority, noted that "[t]he NCAA plays a critical role in the maintenance of a revered tradition of amateurism in college sports." *NCAA v. Bd. of Regents of the Univ. of Okla.*, 468 U.S. 85, 120 (1984). This argument — that the NCAA is the guardian of amateurism — has been one of the Association's primary defenses in antitrust cases. Kristin R. Muenzen, *Weakening Its Own Defense? The NCAA's Version of Amateurism*, 13 Marq. Sports L. Rev. 257, 258 (2003). Should that argument hold, however, given the recent trend of liberalization of the restrictions placed on college athletes and the ever-increasing profits generated by collegiate athletics, particularly at the Division I level?

In 2002, Division III schools loosened its rules for student-athletes by allowing pre-enrolled students to accept prize money in open athletic events, sign contracts for participation in professional athletics, enter professional drafts and be drafted, and compete in professional athletics. In return, for each year in which a pre-enrolled student engages in one of the specified activities, that student loses a year of athletic eligibility at the collegiate level. *Id.* at 279. Division II schools passed a similar deregulation package in 2001. *Id.* at 277. At the Division I level — the level "most susceptible to blurring the lines between amateurs and professionals" — schools passed a more modest deregulation package in 2002. *Id.* at 282. Under the Division I plan, prospects can enter a draft and be drafted, receive prize money, not to exceed expenses, in athletic competitions, and receive funds to attend a high school or prep school as long as the funds do not come from an agent, athletics representative, or professional sports team. *Id.* Prospects who participate in the specified activities for no more than one year after high school lose one year of eligibility and must spend a year of academic residence at whatever college they enroll in. *Id.* Division I prospects, however, are not allowed to sign professional contracts or compete at the professional level. *Id.*

How has the definition of amateurism changed from the early days of the NCAA in the first part of the twentieth century to today? As these rules continue to loosen, how long can the NCAA continue to position itself as the guardian of amateurism in collegiate athletics? Is there a point of no return, where amateurism and professionalism become indistinguishable?

2. One of the more interesting current questions involving antitrust laws at the collegiate level is whether the Bowl Championship Series ("BCS") — in which football powers from the major Division I athletic conferences, such as the Big Ten, Pac-10, and SEC, compete in the marquee bowl games, including a national championship game — violates antitrust law. Senate and House committees considered the question in 2003 and 2005. C. Paul Rogers III, *The Quest for Number One in College Football: The Revised Bowl Championship Series, Antitrust, and the Winner Take All Syndrome*, 18 Marq. Sports L. Rev. 285 (2008). Consider that in the 2006–07 season, more than $122 million went to the 64 BCS schools from the four BCS bowls, while the remaining conferences divided only $20.5 million. Further, only $75 million was divided among all schools from the 27 non-BCS bowl games. *Id.* at 290. Additionally, the BCS had a $320 million contract with the Fox Network through 2010 to televise all of the BCS bowl games except for the Rose Bowl. *Id.* at 289. Does the BCS act as a pro-competitive force in college football? If you represented a non-BCS school, how would you attack the current BCS system? Can a sport truly be considered nonprofessional if it generates television contracts worth hundreds of millions of dollars?

3. Former UCLA basketball star Ed O'Bannon is heading a class-action, antitrust law suit against the NCAA "claiming that former athletes should be compensated for the use of their images and likenesses in television advertisements, video games, and on apparel." Pete Thamel, *N.C.A.A. Fails to Stop Licensing Lawsuit*, N.Y. TIMES, Feb. 8, 2010, at B14; *see also* Diamond Leung, *Ed. O'Bannon's NCAA Antitrust Lawsuit Lives*, ESPN College Basketball Nation Blog (May 6, 2011, 8:09 p.m.), *available at* http://espn.go.com/blog/collegebasketballnation/post/_/id/30717/ed-obannons-ncaa. The NCAA's motion for summary judgment was denied and now, NCAA business records are subject to discovery for possibly the first time. Many commentators suspect that this is an opportunity for someone to pull the curtain back and reveal the business of college athletics with possible consequences on the NCAA's future with respect to amateurism. *Id.*

4. As *NCAA v. Board of Regents of the University of Oklahoma* makes clear, the NCAA is afforded protection from the Sherman Act because the horizontal restrictions are necessary to make college athletics possible and protect amateurism, which the Court declared a social good. However, as amateurism in college athletics deteriorates and college athletics becomes more and more commercial, some commentators suspect that the protection universities once received from the Sherman Act will no longer exists:

> The myth of amateurism is likewise at the heart of the NCAA's insulation from the antitrust laws, and any antitrust challenge to NCAA rules governing players will encounter the Association's amateurism defense. This defense has been variously formulated, but essentially provides that the NCAA produces a singular product, one that is by its nature amateur, and that the NCAA must be accorded broad latitude to administer and regulate college sports for the preservation of that product.
>
> The United States Supreme Court embraced this reasoning in *NCAA v. Board of Regents*, when it wrote, "the preservation of the student-athlete in higher education adds richness and diversity to intercollegiate athletics and is entirely consistent with the goals of the Sherman Act." There, the Court distinguished between the NCAA's commercial business activities, like the television marketing plan under examination, and its so-called noncommercial activities, which the Court characterized as necessary to protect amateurism and to preserve the college football product, rendering those noncommercial activities outside the reach of the Sherman Act. The Court wrote, "[i]t is reasonable to assume that most of the regulatory controls of the NCAA are justifiable means of fostering competition among amateur athletic teams and therefore procompetitive because they enhance public interest in intercollegiate athletics." Indeed, a primary reason NCAA rules forbidding athlete compensation beyond a certain level — an act of naked price fixing among commercial competitors — have not been condemned "is

the belief that the restrictions somehow preserve an amateur tradition."

The foundation for the NCAA's immunity from antitrust law rests upon the false premise that its activities promote and preserve an amateur, noncommercial product. If the NCAA's activities were viewed as commercial, they would not merit exemption through the amateurism defense to the antitrust laws.

Amy Christian, *The Emperor's New Clothes: Lifting the NCAA's Veil of Amateurism*, 45 SAN DIEGO L. REV. 495, 500–01 (2008).*

According to Merriam-Webster's Dictionary, an amateur "engages in a pursuit, study, science, or sport as a pastime rather than a profession." According to the definition, are student-athletes actually amateurs? Does it change your mind to know that college athletes are paid with tuition, books, housing, food money, clothing stipends, and traveling stipends? Are athletes essentially receiving a heavily regulated salary for their labor? Despite all this, would it surprise you to know that while "the NCAA and its members reap billions of dollars in revenues, the average 'student-athlete' earns less than the federal minimum wage"? In fact, many such athletes live below the poverty line. *Id.* at 507.

5. Despite the holding in *NCAA v. Board of Regents of the University of Oklahoma*, the NCAA's cartel-like activities continue to garner their fair share of accusations of antitrust violations. In one recent case, walk-on players challenged NCAA regulations limiting scholarships under an antitrust law theory. *In re NCAA I-A Walk-On Football Players Litigation*, 398 F. Supp. 2d 1144 (W.D. Wash. 2005). The court found that setting regulations for athletic scholarships was activity that affected trade and commerce and that, accordingly, the NCAA could be sued for such regulations as a violation of Section 1 and 2 of the Sherman Act. *Id.* at 1152. Should the NCAA have the authority to fix scholarship amounts for universities? Are there policy justifications for limiting the scholarship amounts offered to walk-on student-athletes (those who try out for a university team after already being admitted)? At what point does intercollegiate sports regulatory activity cross into the territory of illegal cartel activity?

3. Policy — Calls for Reform

THE KNIGHT FOUNDATION COMMISSION ON INTERCOLLEGIATE ATHLETICS, A CALL TO ACTION: RECONNECTING COLLEGE SPORTS AND HIGHER EDUCATION, 12–14 (2001)*

http://www.knightcommission.org/images/pdfs/2001_knight_report.pdf

It is tempting to turn away from bad news. To the cynic, corruption has been endemic in big-time sports as long as they have existed. To the rationalizer, reform is already under way and things are not nearly as bad as the critics make them out to be. More time is all that is needed. But to the realist, the bad news is hard to miss. The truth is manifested regularly in a cascade of scandalous acts that, against a backdrop of institutional complicity and capitulation, threaten the health of American higher education. The good name of the nation's academic enterprise is even more threatened today than it was when the Knight Commission published its first report a decade ago. Despite progress in some areas, new problems have arisen, and the condition of big-time college sports has deteriorated.

Consider as an example some simple statistics: As noted in the foreword, 57 out of 106 Division I-A institutions (54 percent) had to be censured, sanctioned or put on probation for major violations of NCAA rules in the 1980s. In the 1990s, 58 out of 114 Division I-A colleges and universities (52 percent) were similarly penalized. In other words, more than half the institutions competing at the top levels continue to break the rules. Wrongdoing as a way of life seems to represent the status quo.

The fact that such behavior has worked its way into the fiber of intercollegiate sports without provoking powerful and sustained countermeasures from the many institutions so besmirched speaks for itself. It appears that more energy goes into looking the other way than to finding a way to integrate big-time sports into the fabric of higher education.

At the heart of these problems is a profound change in the American culture of sports itself. At one time, that culture was defined by colleges, high schools, summer leagues, and countless community recreational programs. Amateurism was a cherished ideal. In such a context, it made sense to regard athletics as an educational undertaking. Young people were taught values ranging from fitness, cooperation, teamwork and perseverance to sportsmanship as moral endeavor.

All of that seems somehow archaic and quaint today. Under the influence of television and the mass media, the ethos of athletics is now professional. The apex of sporting endeavor is defined by professional sports. This fundamental shift now permeates many campuses. Big-time college basketball and football have a professional look and feel — in their arenas and stadiums, their luxury boxes and financing, their uniforms and coaching staffs, and their marketing and administrative structures. In fact, big-time programs have become minor leagues in their own right, increasingly taken into account as part of the professional athletics system.

In this new circumstance, what is the relationship between sport and the university as a place of learning?

At the time the Knight Commission was formed in 1989, the answers to that question were already sounding alarm bells. For example, the late A. Bartlett Giamatti, a former president of Yale who went on to become commissioner of major league baseball, said that "failures of nerve, principle and purpose" were threatening to "engulf higher education in ways unfair and dangerous." He argued that what had been "allowed to become a circus — college sports — threatens to become the means whereby the public believes the whole enterprise is a sideshow."

Now, in this new millennium, informed critics are equally scathing in their evaluations. James Duderstadt, president emeritus of the University of Michigan, put it this way before the Knight Commission in late 2000: Major college sports "do far more damage to the university, to its students and faculty, its leadership, its reputation and credibility than most realize — or at least are willing to admit." The ugly disciplinary incidents, outrageous academic fraud, dismal graduation rates, and uncontrolled expenditures surrounding college sports reflect what Duderstadt and others have rightly characterized as "an entertainment industry" that is not only the antithesis of academic values but is "corrosive and corruptive to the academic enterprise."

Ten years ago, the Commission's efforts focused largely on big-time football and basketball programs. The most glaring problems seemed concentrated in these two sports. While that is just as true today, the Commission notes the influence-by-emulation of big-time programs on sports other than football and basketball. William Bowen and James Shulman of The Andrew W. Mellon Foundation detail the full impact of this "contagion" in their book, *The Game of Life*, which concludes that the skewed priorities of top programs have infected men's and women's sports at all levels, including, perhaps most remarkably, the Ivy League and elite private liberal arts colleges. It all leads, they write, to a single conclusion:

> Intercollegiate programs in these academically selective institutions are moving steadily in the direction of increased tension with core educational values, and more substantial calls on the tangible and intangible resources of their host institutions. We cannot think of a single set of data that contradicts this proposition . . . We are unable to identify any forces inside the system that — without considerable help — can be expected to alter these directions.

Nevertheless, what the Knight Commission has concentrated on again in this review of intercollegiate athletics is the impact and control of football and basketball at the most competitive level. At the core of the problem is a prevailing money madness. These sports programs have created a universe parallel to — but outside the effective control of - the institutions that house them. They answer not to the traditional standards of higher education but to the whims and pressures of the marketplace.

There is no question about who is winning this open, ever-escalating war between the academic and athletic cultures. In too many places, the tail already wags the dog. The continuation and possible acceleration of this development is a prospect that demands the engagement of presidents, trustees, faculties, and higher education associations.

Coalition on Intercollegiate Athletics, Framing The Future: Reforming Intercollegiate Athletics 7–12 (2007)*

http://coia.comm.psu.edu/FTF/FTFtext&appendix.pdf

1. Academic Integrity and Quality Reforms

. . . .

1.1 Institutional Admission and Recruiting Policies

1.1.1 Student-athletes should be admitted based on their potential for academic success and not primarily on their athletic contribution to the institution. General admissions policies should be the same for all students, student-athletes and non-student-athletes. Campus administrators and campus faculty governance bodies should work together to develop admission policies consistent with the educational mission of the institution.

1.1.2 The academic profiles of freshmen or transfer student-athletes as a group and by sport should be similar to those of the entering freshman class or the non-athlete transfer cohort, as applicable. Data on the academic profiles of entering student-athletes and non-student-athletes should be reviewed at least annually by the Campus Athletics Board or the campus faculty governance body.

1.1.3 Special admissions of freshman and transfer student-athletes should reflect the same philosophy as special admissions of non-student-athletes. Data on the academic performance of student-athlete special admits should be reviewed at least annually by the Campus Athletic Board or the campus faculty governance body.

1.1.4 Faculty should be involved in developing and overseeing campus policies regarding recruiting of student-athletes.

1.2 The Primacy of Academics

1.2.1 No academic programs or majors should be designed specifically for student-athletes or created for the purpose of allowing student-athletes to maintain their eligibility. Qualified student-athletes should be allowed and in fact encouraged to pursue the major of their choice and to have the same access to academic classes and programs as other students without explicit or implicit athletic consequences. Data on student-athletes' choice of major should be gathered and evaluated by the campus faculty governance body or the Campus Athletic Board and should also be provided to all prospective recruits.

1.2.2 To preserve academic integrity, the campus faculty governance body or the Campus Athletic Board should monitor student-athlete enrollment by course.

1.2.3 Academic Progress Rate (APR), Graduation Success Rate (GSR) and other available graduation rate data should be reviewed annually by the campus faculty governance body to sustain processes that will improve the academic success and graduation rates of student-athletes.

1.2.4 The NCAA should continue to enforce rigorously contemporaneous and historical penalties for teams and institutions that fail to meet NCAA APR and GSR standards.

1.2.5 To ensure that student-athletes are acquiring the educational foundation leading to a degree, athletic eligibility shall be dependent on the maintenance of a minimum cumulative GPA of 2.0 on a 4.0 scale.

2. Student-Athlete Welfare Reforms

. . . .

2.1 Athletics Scholarships

2.1.1 Athletics scholarships should be awarded on a year-by-year basis with the presumption that they should be renewed up to four times for a total award of five years, or until graduation, whichever comes first, for students who are in good academic standing, conform to campus codes for student behavior, conform to the athletics department's standards of conduct, and adhere to team rules. Institutions should establish criteria and a mechanism for revoking a scholarship. The final authority for revoking a scholarship should rest with the campus' chief financial aid officer or with the chief academic officer. A student awarded an athletics scholarship who is no longer participating in athletics should be counted against the NCAA maximum number of awards for that sport, unless the scholarship is revoked or unless the student has exhausted athletic eligibility.

2.2 Competition and Practice Scheduling

2.2.1 Individual athletic competitions, as distinct from conference, regional and national tournaments and championships, shall not be scheduled during final exam periods unless an exception is granted by the Campus Athletics Board or equivalent. [COIA 2005 Academic Integrity in Intercollegiate Athletics section 4.3.6; local, conferences, and national (NCAA legislation)]

2.2.2 Individual athletic competitions and associated travel should be scheduled to minimize lost class time. Institutional policies designed to minimize lost class time should be described.

2.2.3 Athletically-related activities (e.g., formal and informal practices, team meetings, and any activities at which the attendance of student-athletes is required) should be scheduled outside the prime times for academic classes. Each institution should explain how it achieves this scheduling goal.

2.3 Integration into Campus Life

2.3.1 Life skills and personal development programs for student-athletes should have as a goal the integration of the student-athlete into the rest of the student population. These programs should help student-athletes develop an appropriate balance between their athletic time requirements and their paramount need for academic and social integration. Administrators, faculty and athletic departments should mitigate the time demand on student-athletes to allow them to pursue the full range of educational experiences open to other students.

2.4 Campus Integration of Academic Advising for Student-Athletes

2.4.1 Academic advising and academic support for student-athletes should be structured to give student-athletes as valuable and meaningful an educational experience as possible and not just to maintain their athletic eligibility.

2.4.2 The academic advising facility for student-athletes should be integrated into and report through the existing academic advising structure and not through the Athletics Department.

2.4.3 The campus academic advising structure or the office of the chief academic officer should have oversight of and regularly review the academic advising of student-athletes.

2.4.4 Athletic academic advisors should be appointed by and work for the campus academic advising structure and not solely for the Athletics Department.

3. Campus Governance of Intercollegiate Athletics Reforms

. . . .

3. Campus Governance of Intercollegiate Athletics

3.1 Each NCAA member institution should establish a Campus Athletic Board. The charge of this Board should be to monitor and oversee campus intercollegiate athletics. A majority of Board members should be tenured faculty who should be appointed or elected through rules established by the campus faculty governance body. The Faculty Athletic Representative should be an ex officio voting or non-voting member of the Board. The chair of the Board should be a senior (tenured) faculty member. An Athletic Director should not be chair.

3.2 Major athletic department decisions (e.g., hiring of the athletic director and key athletic department personnel, changes in the total number of intercollegiate sports, initiation of major capital projects, etc.) should be made in consultation with the Campus Athletic Board and leaders of the campus faculty governance body and appropriate faculty committee(s).

3.3 The Faculty Athletic Representative (FAR) should be appointed by the University President based on recommendation by the campus faculty governance body. The FAR appointment should be made for a specific term and a review of the performance of the FAR should take place prior to reappointment. Such a review should include meaningful participation by the campus faculty governance body, or the Campus Athletic Board.

3.4 The Athletic Director, Faculty Athletic Representative and the Campus Athletic Board chair should report orally and in writing at least once a year to the campus faculty governance body. Their reports should include a focus on academic benchmarks including the APR, GSR, graduation rates and the percentage and progress of student-athlete special admits.

3.5 Leaders of campus faculty governance body should report annually to the University President (1) that the faculty has been able to fulfill its responsibilities in regard to athletic governance, or (2) that it has not, in which case the report should specify the obstacles that have prevented it from doing so. These reports should be made available to the NCAA during re-certification

4. Fiscal Responsibility

4.1 The Athletic Department's budgets, revenues and expenditures should be transparent and aligned with the mission, goals and values of the institution. The University President should take the lead to ensure that fiscal reports, including dash board indicators as listed in the 2006 NCAA Presidential Task Force report, are issued annually and made available to the campus faculty governance body. The President should work closely with faculty leaders, existing faculty committees, and athletic department personnel to achieve these goals.

4.2 The overall annual growth rate in the Athletic Department's operating expenditures should be no greater than the overall annual growth rate in the university's operating expenditures.

4.3 The athletic department budget should be integrated into the university general budget process where feasible. The proposed athletic department budget should be evaluated by the same process as the budget for academic units.

4.4 The University President should take the appropriate steps to fuse athletic fundraising efforts into those of the rest of the university, including eliminating separate, athletic-only 501(c)(3) entities and establishing faculty representation on the board of the institutional fund-raising entity

4.5 Commercialization policies in athletics should be comparable to other commercialization policies conducted throughout the University and should include meaningful faculty participation in their oversight.

NOTES

1. The John S. and James L. Knight Foundation's Commission on Intercollegiate Athletics has a membership composed of a broad cross-section of respected college and university officials, attorneys, and journalists. The Coalition on Intercollegiate Athletics is an alliance of 55 Division I-A faculty senates. After reading the above excerpts, is it possible to maintain collegiate athletics as we know them now if a serious reform effort taking into account their observations and recommendations, gains momentum? What is the likelihood of meaningful reform? Is reform even necessary? What are the benefits, if any, of the current system?

2. Students themselves are also attempting to take on reform. The National College Players Association, mentioned earlier, is a non-profit organization founded by former UCLA football player Ramogi Huma. The NCPA focuses on organizing former and current student-athletes for major reform in the NCAA. Among their many campaigns, the NCPA hopes to raise scholarship amounts for student-athletes, increase graduation rates, and hold universities accountable for students' medical injuries. For more information on this organization, see www.ncpanow.org. The NCPA has succeeded on a number of issues, including establishing a fund to help former student-athletes complete their undergraduate degrees or attend graduate school.

Further, with the encouragement of the NCAA, several universities sponsor a Student Athlete Advisory Council. The Council is comprised of student-representatives from each of the universities' athletic teams and meets on a periodic basis to "serve as a conduit of communication among student-athletes, coaches and athletics administrators on issues to improve the student-athlete experience and promote growth and education through sports participation." *Campus SAACS*, NAT'L COLLEGIATE ATHLETIC ASS'N, 2011, *available at* http://www.ncaa.org/wps/portal/ncaahome?WCM_GLOBAL_CONTEXT=/ncaa/ncaa/academics+and+athlathl/saac/campus+conference+division+saacs. In essence, these student-centered groups serve as liaisons between athletes and university administration. To promote greater student-athlete influence at the decision-making level, there are Conference and Division Student Athlete Advisory Boards. For example, the Division I SAAC "reports directly to the Division I Management Council, and two SAAC members participate in each meeting of the Management Council as nonvoting members." *Id.*

3. For additional commentary on potential reforms, see JAMES L. SHULMAN & WILLIAM G. BOWEN, THE GAME OF LIFE: COLLEGE SPORTS AND EDUCATIONAL VALUES

(2001); Ellen J. Staurowsky & B. David Ridpath, *The Case for a Minimum 2.0 Standard for NCAA Division I Athletes*, 15 J. Legal Aspects of Sport 113 (2005); Rodney K. Smith, *Increasing Presidential Accountability in Big-Time Intercollegiate Athletics*, 10 Vill. Sports & Ent. L.J. 297 (2003); Matthew R. Salzwedel & Jon Ericson, *Cleaning Up Buckley: How the Family Educational Rights and Privacy Act Shields Academic Corruption in College Athletics*, 2003 Wis. L. Rev. 1053 (2003).

Chapter IX

FEDERAL FUNDING AND REGULATION

Introduction

Over time, the government has played an increasing role in the funding and regulating of postsecondary institutions. By tying statutory rules to large sources of funding or the rights to conduct certain types of scientific research, the federal government has effectively imposed some form of regulation on nearly every educational institution in America. Despite the multitude of complex regulatory schemes that apply to institutions of higher education, there is no single federal agency that oversees postsecondary education regulation generally. Many federal agencies, including the U.S. Department of Education, the Food and Drug Administration (FDA), and the Internal Revenue Service (IRS), participate in interpreting and enforcing federal regulations.

The first section of this chapter will examine the various agencies involved in the funding of higher education. By making large federal funds contingent upon compliance with statutory requirements, the federal government can shape and manipulate the policies of higher educational institutions in numerous ways. In *Rumsfeld v. Forum for Academic and Institutional Rights* (*FAIR*), an association of educators challenged as unconstitutional an Act that conditioned federal funds on a military recruiter's equal access to campus employment events. 547 U.S. 47 (2006). While reading this section it is important to keep in mind several issues: What different kinds of activities or programs can the federal government regulate through funding conditions? Are there any constitutional limits placed on the restrictions and regulations tied to federal educational funds?

The second section focuses on federal regulation involving human and animal participants in university research. Each university is required to establish an Institutional Review Board (IRB) to approve planned university research on humans or animals based on regulations promulgated by the FDA and the Department of Health and Human Services. Following the discovery of several infamous experiments that abused human participants, including the Tuskegee Syphilis Experiment, the federal government created a new regulatory scheme to monitor and approve postsecondary research through the use of IRBs. Since their implementation, IRBs have come under fire by some, questioning their ability to review accurately scientific experiments and their overall level of involvement in postsecondary research. Some central questions have repeatedly been asked: How much can IRBs regulate university research without implying any academic freedom concerns? How do IRBs review highly specialized scientific experiments?

Finally, the third section examines the effect of tax benefits and exemptions on postsecondary institutions. By reading a public policy element into the definition of "charitable" under the charitable tax exemption statute in *Bob Jones University v. United States*, the Supreme Court was able to uphold the revocation of the university's tax exempt status due to a racially discriminatory admissions policy. 461 U.S. 574 (1983). What legal theories justify allowing tax exemption status for private or for-profit universities? How much influence does tax regulation have on the policies and regulation of educational institutions? More broadly, are there certain areas of postsecondary operation that the federal government shouldn't be allowed to regulate? What authority do universities and educators have to challenge these regulations?

A. FEDERAL AID TO POSTSECONDARY INSTITUTIONS

Federal aid for postsecondary education is disbursed by a number of federal agencies. Several important players include the U.S. Department of Education, the U.S. Department of Health and Human Services, the National Foundation for the Arts and Humanities, and the National Science Foundation. Each agency follows a specific statutory and regulatory framework for its own aid program. The General Education Provisions Act, 20 U.S.C. § 1221 *et seq.*, applies specifically to the Department of Education, but is illustrative, generally, of most of the statutory and regulatory provisions. Below are a few key provisions.

20 U.S.C. § 1221-1. National policy with respect to equal educational opportunity

Recognizing that the Nation's economic, political, and social security require a well-educated citizenry, the Congress (1) reaffirms, as a matter of high priority, the Nation's goal of equal educational opportunity, and (2) declares it to be the policy of the United States of America that every citizen is entitled to an education to meet his or her full potential without financial barriers.

20 U.S.C. § 1228a. Equity for students, teachers, and other program beneficiaries

(a) Purpose. The purpose of this section is to assist the Department in implementing the Department's mission to ensure equal access to education and to promote educational excellence throughout the Nation, by —

(1) ensuring equal opportunities to participate for all eligible students, teachers, and other program beneficiaries in any project or activity carried out under an applicable program; and

(2) promoting the ability of such students, teachers, and beneficiaries to meet high standards.

(b) Requirement to develop steps to insure equity. The Secretary shall require each applicant for assistance under an applicable program (other than an individual) to develop and describe in such applicant's application the steps such applicant proposes to take to ensure equitable access to, and equitable participation in, the project or activity to be conducted with such assistance, by addressing the special needs of students, teachers, and other program beneficiaries in order to overcome barriers to equitable participation, including barriers based on gender, race, color, national origin, disability, and age.

. . . .

20 U.S.C. § 1232a. Prohibition against Federal control of education

No provision of any applicable program shall be construed to authorize any department, agency, officer, or employee of the United States to exercise any direction, supervision, or control over the curriculum, program of instruction, administration, or personnel of any educational institution, school, or school system, or over the selection of library resources, textbooks, or other printed or published instructional materials by any educational institution or school system, or to require the assignment or transportation of students or teachers in order to overcome racial imbalance.

The Department of Education has promulgated an extensive set of regulations that govern the implementation of the General Education Provisions Act. These regulations covering higher education institutions are located at 34 C.F.R. Parts 74 and 81. Some key provisions include:

34 C.F.R. § 74.14 Special award conditions.

(a) The Secretary may impose special award conditions, if an applicant or recipient —

(1) Has a history of poor performance;

(2) Is not financially stable;

(3) Has a management system that does not meet the standards prescribed in this part;

(4) Has not conformed to the terms and conditions of a previous award; or

(5) Is not otherwise responsible.

. . . .

34 C.F.R. § 74.51 Monitoring and reporting program performance.

(a) Recipients are responsible for managing and monitoring each project, program, subaward, function, or activity supported by the award. Recipients shall monitor subawards to ensure subrecipients have met the audit requirements . . . .

(b) The Secretary prescribes the frequency with which the performance reports shall be submitted. . . . [P]erformance reports are not required more frequently than quarterly or, less frequently than annually. Annual reports are due 90 calendar days after the grant year; quarterly or semi-annual reports are due 30 days after the reporting period. The Secretary may require annual reports before the anniversary dates of multiple year awards in lieu of these requirements. The final performance reports are due 90 calendar days after the expiration or termination of the award.

. . . .

(d) When required, performance reports must generally contain, for each award, brief information on each of the following:

(1) A comparison of actual accomplishments with the goals and objectives established for the period, the findings of the investigator, or both. Whenever appropriate and the output of programs or projects can be readily quantified, this quantitative data should be related to cost data for computation of unit costs.

(2) Reasons why established goals were not met, if appropriate.

(3) Other pertinent information including, when appropriate, analysis, and explanation of cost overruns or high unit costs.

. . . .

(f) Recipients shall immediately notify the Secretary of developments that have a significant impact on the award-supported activities. Also, notification must be given in the case of problems, delays, or adverse conditions which materially impair the ability to meet the objectives of the award. This notification must include a statement of the action taken or contemplated, and any assistance needed to resolve the situation.

(g) The Secretary may make site visits, as needed.

. . . .

34 C.F.R. § 74.61 Termination.

(a) Awards may be terminated in whole or in part only —

(1) By the Secretary, if a recipient materially fails to comply with the terms and conditions of an award . . . .

34 C.F.R. § 74.62 Enforcement.

(a) Remedies for noncompliance. If a recipient materially fails to comply with the terms and conditions of an award, whether stated in a Federal statute, regulation, assurance, application, or notice of award, the Secretary may, in addition to imposing any of the special conditions outlined in § 74.14, take one or more of the following actions, as appropriate in the circumstances:

(1) Temporarily withhold cash payments pending correction of the deficiency by the recipient or more severe enforcement action by the Secretary.

(2) Disallow (that is, deny both use of funds and any applicable matching credit for) all or part of the cost of the activity or action not in compliance.

(3) Wholly or partly suspend or terminate the current award.

(4) Withhold further awards for the project or program.

(5) Take other remedies that may be legally available.

In addition to creating conditions tied to specific aid programs, Congress has also created conditions that apply generally to all aid programs, stemming from a variety of federal agencies. An example is the so-called Solomon Amendment, which is actually a group of restrictions that cuts off the federal funding support of a number of federal agencies — including the Departments of Education and Health and Human Services — if an institution of higher learning hinders on-campus ROTC operations.

An association of law schools and law faculties challenged the restrictions, and the case reached the U.S. Supreme Court. The Court ruled 8–0 that the restrictions do not violate the First Amendment.

RUMSFELD v. FORUM FOR ACADEMIC AND INSTITUTIONAL RIGHTS, INC.

547 U.S. 47 (2006)

Chief Justice Roberts delivered the opinion of the Court.

. . . .

I

Respondent Forum for Academic and Institutional Rights, Inc. (FAIR), is an association of law schools and law faculties. Its declared mission is "to promote academic freedom, support educational institutions in opposing discrimination and vindicate the rights of institutions of higher education." FAIR members have adopted policies expressing their opposition to discrimination based on, among other factors, sexual orientation. They would like to restrict military recruiting on their campuses because they object to the policy Congress has adopted with respect to homosexuals in the military. *See* 10 U.S.C. § 654. The Solomon Amendment, however, forces institutions to choose between enforcing their nondiscrimination policy against military recruiters in this way and continuing to receive specified federal funding.

In 2003, FAIR sought a preliminary injunction against enforcement of the Solomon Amendment, which at that time — it has since been amended — prevented the Department of Defense (DOD) from providing specified federal funds to any institution of higher education "that either prohibits, or in effect prevents" military recruiters "from gaining entry to campuses." [10 U.S.C.] § 983(b). FAIR considered the DOD's interpretation of this provision particularly objectionable. Although the statute required only "entry to campuses," the Government — after the terrorist attacks on September 11, 2001 — adopted an informal policy of " 'requir[ing] universities to provide military recruiters access to students equal in quality and scope to that provided to other recruiters.' " [citation omitted]. Prior to the adoption of this policy, some law schools sought to promote their nondiscrimination policies while still complying with the Solomon Amendment by having military recruiters interview on the undergraduate campus. But under the equal access policy, military recruiters had to be permitted to interview at the law schools, if other recruiters did so. FAIR argued that this forced inclusion and equal treatment of military recruiters violated the law schools' First Amendment freedoms of speech and association. According to FAIR, the Solomon Amendment was unconstitutional because it forced law schools to choose between exercising their First Amendment right to decide whether to disseminate or accommodate a military recruiter's message, and ensuring the availability of federal funding for their universities.

The District Court denied the preliminary injunction on the ground that FAIR had failed to establish a likelihood of success on the merits of its First Amendment claims. The District Court held that inclusion "of an unwanted periodic visitor" did not "significantly affect the law schools' ability to express their particular message or viewpoint." [citation omitted]. The District Court based its decision in large part on the determination that recruiting is conduct and not speech, concluding that any expressive aspect of recruiting "is entirely ancillary to its dominant economic purpose." The District Court held that Congress could regulate this expressive aspect of the conduct under the test set forth in *United States v. O'Brien*, 391 U.S. 367 (1968).

In rejecting FAIR's constitutional claims, the District Court disagreed with "the DOD's proposed interpretation that the statute requires law schools to 'provide military recruiters access to students that is at least equal in quality and scope to the access provided other potential employers.' " In response to the District Court's concerns, Congress codified the DOD's informal policy. The Solomon Amendment now prevents an institution from receiving certain federal funding if it prohibits military recruiters "from gaining access to campuses, or access to students . . . on campuses, for purposes of military recruiting in a manner that is at least equal in quality and scope to the access to campuses and to students that is provided to any other employer." 10 U.S.C. § 983(b).

FAIR appealed the District Court's judgment, arguing that the recently amended Solomon Amendment was unconstitutional for the same reasons as the earlier version. A divided panel of the Court of Appeals for the Third Circuit agreed. According to the Third Circuit, the Solomon Amendment violated the unconstitutional conditions doctrine because it forced a law school to choose between surrendering First Amendment rights and losing federal funding for its university. Unlike the District Court, the Court of Appeals did not think that the *O'Brien* analysis applied because the Solomon Amendment, in its view, regulated speech and not simply expressive conduct. The Third Circuit nonetheless determined that if the regulated activities were properly treated as expressive conduct rather than speech, the Solomon Amendment was also unconstitutional under *O'Brien*. As a result, the Court of Appeals reversed and remanded for the District Court to enter a preliminary injunction against enforcement of the Solomon Amendment.

We granted certiorari.

II

. . . The Government and FAIR agree on what [the Solomon Amendment] requires: In order for a law school and its university to receive federal funding, the law school must offer military recruiters the same access to its campus and students that it provides to the nonmilitary recruiter receiving the most favorable access.

Certain law professors participating as amici, however, argue that the Government and FAIR misinterpret the statute. According to these amici, the Solomon Amendment's equal access requirement is satisfied when an institution applies to military recruiters the same policy it applies to all other recruiters. On this reading, a school excluding military recruiters would comply with the Solomon Amendment so long as it also excluded any other employer that violates its nondiscrimination policy.

. . . .

We conclude that they cannot and that the Government and FAIR correctly interpret the Solomon Amendment. The statute requires the Secretary of Defense to compare the military's "access to campuses" and "access to students" to "the access to campuses and to students that is provided to any other employer." (Emphasis added.) The statute does not call for an inquiry into why or how the "other employer" secured its access. Under amici's reading, a military recruiter has the same "access" to campuses and students as, say, a law firm when the law firm is permitted on campus to interview students and the military is not. We do not think that the military recruiter has received equal "access" in this situation — regardless of whether the disparate treatment is attributable to the military's failure to comply with the school's nondiscrimination policy.

The Solomon Amendment does not focus on the content of a school's recruiting policy, as the amici would have it. Instead, it looks to the result achieved by the policy and compares the "access . . . provided" military recruiters to that provided other recruiters. Applying the same policy to all recruiters is therefore insufficient to comply with the statute if it results in a greater level of access for other recruiters than for the military. Law schools must ensure that their recruiting policy operates in such a way that military recruiters are given access to students at least equal to that "provided to any other employer."

Not only does the text support this view, but this interpretation is necessary to give effect to the Solomon Amendment's recent revision. Under the prior version, the statute required "entry" without specifying how military recruiters should be treated once on campus. The District Court thought that the DOD policy, which required equal access to students once recruiters were on campus, was unwarranted based on the text of the statute. Congress responded directly to this decision by codifying the DOD policy. Under amici's interpretation, this legislative change had no effect — law schools could still restrict military access, so long as they do so under a generally applicable nondiscrimination policy. Worse yet, the legislative change made it easier for schools to keep military recruiters out altogether: Under the prior version, simple access could not be denied, but under the amended version, access could be denied altogether, so long as a nonmilitary recruiter would also be denied access. That is rather clearly not what Congress had in mind in codifying the DOD policy. We refuse to interpret the Solomon Amendment in a way that negates its recent revision, and indeed would render it a largely meaningless exercise.

We therefore read the Solomon Amendment the way both the Government and FAIR interpret it. It is insufficient for a law school to treat the military as it treats all other employers who violate its nondiscrimination policy. Under the statute, military recruiters must be given the same access as recruiters who comply with the policy.

III

The Constitution grants Congress the power to "provide for the common Defence," "[t]o raise and support Armies," and "[t]o provide and maintain a Navy." Art. I, § 8, cls. 1, 12-13. Congress' power in this area "is broad and sweeping," *O'Brien*, 391 U.S. at 377, and there is no dispute in this case that it includes the authority to require campus access for military recruiters. That is, of course, unless Congress exceeds constitutional limitations on its power in enacting such legislation. *See Rostker v. Goldberg*, 453 U.S. 57, 67 (1981). . . .

Although Congress has broad authority to legislate on matters of military recruiting, it nonetheless chose to secure campus access for military recruiters indirectly, through its Spending Clause power. The Solomon Amendment gives universities a choice: Either allow military recruiters the same access to students afforded any other recruiter or forgo certain federal funds. Congress' decision to proceed indirectly does not reduce the deference given to Congress in the area of military affairs. Congress' choice to promote its goal by creating a funding condition deserves at least as deferential treatment as if Congress had imposed a mandate on universities.

Congress' power to regulate military recruiting under the Solomon Amendment is arguably greater because universities are free to decline the federal funds. In *Grove City College v. Bell*, 465 U.S. 555, 575-576 (1984), we rejected a private college's claim that conditioning federal funds on its compliance with *Title IX of the Education Amendments of 1972* violated the First Amendment. We thought this argument "warrant[ed] only brief consideration" because "Congress is free to attach reasonable and unambiguous conditions to federal financial assistance that educational institutions are not obligated to accept." *Id.*, at 575. We concluded that no First Amendment violation had occurred — without reviewing the substance of the First Amendment claims — because *Grove City* could decline the Government's funds. *Id.*, at 575-76.

Other decisions, however, recognize a limit on Congress' ability to place conditions on the receipt of funds. We recently held that " 'the government may not deny a benefit to a person on a basis that infringes his constitutionally protected . . . freedom of speech even if he has no entitlement to that benefit.' " *United States v. Am. Library Ass'n*, 539 U.S. 194, 210 (2003). Under this principle, known as the unconstitutional conditions doctrine, the Solomon Amendment would be unconstitutional if Congress could not directly require universities to provide military recruiters equal access to their students.

This case does not require us to determine when a condition placed on university funding goes beyond the "reasonable" choice offered in *Grove City* and becomes an unconstitutional condition. . . . Because the First Amendment would not prevent Congress from directly imposing the Solomon Amendment's access requirement, the statute does not place an unconstitutional condition on the receipt of federal funds.

A

The Solomon Amendment neither limits what law schools may say nor requires them to say anything. Law schools remain free under the statute to express whatever views they may have on the military's congressionally mandated employment policy, all the while retaining eligibility for federal funds. . . .

Nevertheless, the Third Circuit concluded that the Solomon Amendment violates law schools' freedom of speech in a number of ways. First, in assisting military recruiters, law schools provide some services, such as sending e-mails and distributing flyers, that clearly involve speech. The Court of Appeals held that in supplying these services law schools are unconstitutionally compelled to speak the Government's message. Second, military recruiters are, to some extent, speaking while they are on campus. The Court of Appeals held that, by forcing law schools to permit the military on campus to express its message, the Solomon Amendment unconstitutionally requires law schools to host or accommodate the military's speech. Third, although the Court of Appeals thought that the Solomon Amendment regulated speech, it held in the alternative that, if the statute regulates conduct, this conduct is expressive and regulating it unconstitutionally infringes law schools' right to engage in expressive conduct. We consider each issue in turn.

1

Some of this Court's leading First Amendment precedents have established the principle that freedom of speech prohibits the government from telling people what they must say. In *West Virginia Bd. of Ed. v. Barnette*, 319 U.S. 624, 642 (1943), we held unconstitutional a state law requiring schoolchildren to recite the Pledge of Allegiance and to salute the flag. And in *Wooley v. Maynard*, 430 U.S. 705, 717 (1977), we held unconstitutional another that required New Hampshire motorists to display the state motto — "Live Free or Die" — on their license plates.

The Solomon Amendment does not require any similar expression by law schools. Nonetheless, recruiting assistance provided by the schools often includes elements of speech. For example, schools may send e-mails or post notices on bulletin boards on an employer's behalf. Law schools offering such services to other recruiters must also send e-mails and post notices on behalf of the military to comply with the Solomon Amendment. As FAIR points out, these compelled statements . . . are subject to First Amendment scrutiny.

This sort of recruiting assistance, however, is a far cry from the compelled speech in *Barnette* and *Wooley*. The Solomon Amendment, unlike the laws at issue in those cases, does not dictate the content of the speech at all, which is only "compelled" if, and to the extent, the school provides such speech for other recruiters. There is nothing in this case approaching a Government-mandated pledge or motto that the school must endorse.

The compelled speech to which the law schools point is plainly incidental to the

Solomon Amendment's regulation of conduct, and "it has never been deemed an abridgment of freedom of speech or press to make a course of conduct illegal merely because the conduct was in part initiated, evidenced, or carried out by means of language, either spoken, written, or printed." *Giboney v. Empire Storage & Ice Co.*, 336 U.S. 490, 502 (1949). Congress, for example, can prohibit employers from discriminating in hiring on the basis of race. The fact that this will require an employer to take down a sign reading "White Applicants Only" hardly means that the law should be analyzed as one regulating the employer's speech rather than conduct. . . .

2

Our compelled-speech cases are not limited to the situation in which an individual must personally speak the government's message. We have also in a number of instances limited the government's ability to force one speaker to host or accommodate another speaker's message. *See Hurley v. Irish-American Gay, Lesbian and Bisexual Group of Boston, Inc.*, 515 U.S. 557, 566 (1995) (state law cannot require a parade to include a group whose message the parade's organizer does not wish to send); *Pacific Gas & Elec. Co. v. Public Util. Comm'n of Cal.*, 475 U.S. 1, 25 (1986) (Marshall, J., concurring in judgment) (state agency cannot require a utility company to include a third-party newsletter in its billing envelope); *Miami Herald Publishing Co. v. Tornillo*, 418 U.S. 241, 258 (1974) (right-of-reply statute violates editors' right to determine the content of their newspapers). Relying on these precedents, the Third Circuit concluded that the Solomon Amendment unconstitutionally compels law schools to accommodate the military's message "[b]y requiring schools to include military recruiters in the interviews and recruiting receptions the schools arrange."

The compelled-speech violation in each of our prior cases, however, resulted from the fact that the complaining speaker's own message was affected by the speech it was forced to accommodate. . . .

In this case, accommodating the military's message does not affect the law schools' speech, because the schools are not speaking when they host interviews and recruiting receptions. Unlike a parade organizer's choice of parade contingents, a law school's decision to allow recruiters on campus is not inherently expressive. Law schools facilitate recruiting to assist their students in obtaining jobs. A law school's recruiting services lack the expressive quality of a parade, a newsletter, or the editorial page of a newspaper; its accommodation of a military recruiter's message is not compelled speech because the accommodation does not sufficiently interfere with any message of the school.

The schools respond that if they treat military and nonmilitary recruiters alike in order to comply with the Solomon Amendment, they could be viewed as sending the message that they see nothing wrong with the military's policies, when they do. We rejected a similar argument in *PruneYard Shopping Center v. Robins*, 447 U.S. 74 (1980). In that case, we upheld a state law requiring a shopping center owner to allow certain expressive activities by others on its property. We explained that there was little likelihood that the views of those engaging in the expressive activities would be identified with the owner, who remained free to disassociate himself from those views and who was "not . . . being compelled to affirm [a] belief in any governmentally prescribed position or view." *Id.*, at 88.

The same is true here. Nothing about recruiting suggests that law schools agree with any speech by recruiters, and nothing in the Solomon Amendment restricts what the law schools may say about the military's policies. . . .

Having rejected the view that the Solomon Amendment impermissibly regulates speech, we must still consider whether the expressive nature of the conduct regulated by the statute brings that conduct within the First Amendment's protection. In *O'Brien*, we recognized that some forms of " 'symbolic speech' " were deserving of First Amendment protection. 391 U.S. at 376. But we rejected the view that "conduct can be labeled 'speech' whenever the person engaging in the conduct intends thereby to express an idea." *Ibid.* Instead, we have extended First Amendment protection only to conduct that is inherently expressive. In *Texas v. Johnson*, 491 U.S. 397, 406 (1989), for example, we applied *O'Brien* and held that burning the American flag was sufficiently expressive to warrant First Amendment protection.

Unlike flag burning, the conduct regulated by the Solomon Amendment is not inherently expressive. Prior to the adoption of the Solomon Amendment's equal access requirement, law schools "expressed" their disagreement with the military by treating military recruiters differently from other recruiters. But these actions were expressive only because the law schools accompanied their conduct with speech explaining it. For example, the point of requiring military interviews to be conducted on the undergraduate campus is not "overwhelmingly apparent." *Johnson, supra*, at 406. An observer who sees military recruiters interviewing away from the law school has no way of knowing whether the law school is expressing its disapproval of the military, all the law school's interview rooms are full, or the military recruiters decided for reasons of their own that they would rather interview someplace else.

The expressive component of a law school's actions is not created by the conduct itself but by the speech that accompanies it. The fact that such explanatory speech is necessary is strong evidence that the conduct at issue here is not so inherently expressive that it warrants protection under *O'Brien*. If combining speech and conduct were enough to create expressive conduct, a regulated party could always transform conduct into "speech" simply by talking about it. . . . Neither *O'Brien* nor its progeny supports such a result.

Although the Third Circuit also concluded that *O'Brien* does not apply, it held in the alternative that the Solomon Amendment does not pass muster under *O'Brien* because the Government failed to produce evidence establishing that the Solomon Amendment was necessary and effective. The Court of Appeals surmised that "the military has ample resources to recruit through alternative means," suggesting "loan repayment programs" and "television and radio advertisements." As a result, the Government . . . failed to establish that the statute's burden on speech is no greater than essential to furthering its interest in military recruiting.

We disagree with the Court of Appeals' reasoning and result. We have held that "an incidental burden on speech is no greater than is essential, and therefore is permissible under *O'Brien*, so long as the neutral regulation promotes a substantial government interest that would be achieved less effectively absent the regulation." *United States v. Albertini*, 472 U.S. 675, 689 (1985). The Solomon Amendment clearly satisfies this requirement. Military recruiting promotes the substantial Government interest in raising and supporting the Armed Forces — an objective that would be achieved less effectively if the military were forced to recruit on less favorable terms than other employers. . . .

B

The Solomon Amendment does not violate law schools' freedom of speech, but the First Amendment's protection extends beyond the right to speak. We have recognized a First Amendment right to associate for the purpose of speaking, which we have termed a "right of expressive association." *See, e.g., BSA v. Dale*, 530 U.S. 640, 644 (2000). The reason we have extended First Amendment protection in this way is clear: The right to speak is often exercised most effectively by combining one's voice with the voices of others. If the government were free to restrict individuals' ability to join together and speak, it could essentially silence views that the First Amendment is intended to protect.

FAIR argues that the Solomon Amendment violates law schools' freedom of expressive association. According to FAIR, law schools' ability to express their message that discrimination on the basis of sexual orientation is wrong is significantly affected by the presence of military recruiters on campus and the schools' obligation to assist them. Relying heavily on our decision in *Dale*, the Court of Appeals agreed.

In *Dale*, we held that the Boy Scouts' freedom of expressive association was violated by New Jersey's public accommodations law, which required the organization to accept a homosexual as a scoutmaster. After determining that the Boy Scouts was an expressive association, that "the forced inclusion of *Dale* would significantly affect its expression," and that the State's interests did not justify this intrusion, we concluded that the Boy Scouts' First Amendment rights were violated.

The Solomon Amendment, however, does not similarly affect a law school's associational rights. To comply with the statute, law schools must allow military recruiters on campus and assist them in whatever way the school chooses to assist other employers. Law schools therefore "associate" with military recruiters in the sense that they interact with them. But recruiters are not part of the law school. Recruiters are, by definition, outsiders who come onto campus for the limited purpose of trying to hire students — not to become members of the school's expressive association. This distinction is critical. Unlike the public accommodations law in *Dale*, the Solomon Amendment does not force a law school " 'to accept members it does not desire.' " The law schools say that allowing military recruiters equal access impairs their own expression by requiring them to associate with the recruiters, but just as saying conduct is undertaken for expressive purposes cannot make it symbolic speech, so too a speaker cannot "erect a shield" against laws requiring access "simply by asserting" that mere association "would impair its message." 530 U.S. at 653.

FAIR correctly notes that the freedom of expressive association protects more than just a group's membership decisions. For example, we have held laws unconstitutional that require disclosure of membership lists for groups seeking anonymity, *Brown v. Socialist Workers '74 Campaign Comm.*, 459 U.S. 87, 101-102 (1982), or impose penalties or withhold benefits based on membership in a disfavored group, *Healy v. James*, 408 U.S. 169, 180-184 (1972). Although these laws did not directly interfere with an organization's composition, they made group membership less attractive, raising the same First Amendment concerns about affecting the group's ability to express its message.

The Solomon Amendment has no similar effect on a law school's associational rights. Students and faculty are free to associate to voice their disapproval of the military's message; nothing about the statute affects the composition of the group by making group membership less desirable. The Solomon Amendment therefore does not violate a law school's First Amendment rights. . . .

In this case, FAIR has attempted to stretch a number of First Amendment doctrines well beyond the sort of activities these doctrines protect. . . .

Because Congress could require law schools to provide equal access to military recruiters without violating the schools' freedoms of speech or association, the Court of Appeals erred in holding that the Solomon Amendment likely violates the First Amendment. We therefore reverse the judgment of the Third Circuit and remand the case for further proceedings consistent with this opinion.

NOTES

1. Despite the unanimous opinion in *FAIR* (Justice Alito did not participate in the case), the case was subject to criticism from civil rights advocates. Consider this:

> The nation is currently engaged in rethinking both the acceptability of sexual orientation discrimination and our personal and institutional responsibilities upon encountering entrenched discrimination. Not long ago, most institutions had a nondiscrimination policy that only spoke to discrimination by the institution itself and only against classes of people named in civil rights laws. As political movements effected social progress, those policies developed to include discrimination based on sexual orientation. The policies also articulated a belief that not only should the institution refuse to discriminate directly, but it also should not associate itself with anyone who does discriminate.
>
> The *FAIR* decision allows the heavy hand of government to block social progress on this issue. Due to the holding in this case, universities are prevented from doing precisely what institutions traditionally do when understandings of principles of equality evolve — reflect those new understandings by modifying and adhering to nondiscrimination policies. *FAIR* allows the government to interfere with the critical and vulnerable process of public discourse that seriously engages meaning of "equality." The First Amendment protects this dialogue and activist speech.

Additionally, *FAIR* violates freedom of association principles. Members of the law school community have determined that they do not want discriminatory employers soliciting applications in the school's publications and setting up tables in their facilities. But now, students will receive communications from their school administrators advertising an interviewing opportunity for an employer that only welcomes straight students. Universities will facilitate scheduling and even arrange for space for interested students, but gay students need not apply. It is patently offensive to require students, professors, and other members of the law school community to tolerate such messages from their own institutions.

Chief Justice Roberts claims no message is conveyed when the university supports an employer that openly and systematically discriminates against particular students. He finds that nondiscrimination policies are not deserving of First Amendment protection. We need Justices willing to identify and support equality. We need Justices who understand the opposition to discrimination that the university community is striving to advance and institutionalize. Such a Justice would have recoiled at the premise of the Chief Justice's opinion.

Zachary Wolfe, *The Right to Say No to Discrimination: A Commentary on Rumsfeld v. Fair*, 2 Am. U. Modern Am. 30, 31 (2006).*

As a reply to this type of argument, legal scholars and practitioners who advocate for judicial restraint reasoned that the case could not have come out any other way. Judge Richard A. Posner of the Seventh Circuit Court of Appeals, who falls squarely into this camp, chided the so-called "elite" law schools participating in the case for allowing normative judgments to trump sound legal reasoning:

> The Supreme Court's 8-0 decision . . . in *Rumsfeld v. Forum for Academic & Institutional Rights, Inc.* (*FAIR*) was neither momentous nor unexpected (a decision the other way would have been both). Its chief interest lies in the participation of the legal professoriat in the litigation. The suit was in effect an academic project, from which we can learn some things about the faculties of today's law schools, especially elite law schools like Harvard and Yale.
>
> . . . .
>
> The Harvard professors (who did their stretching on the principles of statutory interpretation) were right that invalidating the Solomon Amendment would foster discrimination by educational institutions by curtailing the government's authority to use its spending power to prevent discrimination. It would even empower conservative law schools — and there are some (Ave Maria, for example) — to refuse to assist employers who will not promise not to hire homosexuals. But the Harvard professors' solution — an untenable interpretation of the amendment — raises a question of academic integrity. FAIR's constitutional arguments were weak, but the Harvard professors' statutory argument bordered on the frivolous. A

lawyer whom you hire to represent you can in perfect good faith make any argument on your behalf that is not downright frivolous. But the professors were not parties to *Rumsfeld v. FAIR* and so a reader of their amicus curiae brief might expect the views expressed in it to represent their best professional judgment on the meaning of the Solomon Amendment. The brief identifies them as full-time faculty members of the Harvard Law School rather than as concerned citizens, and one expects law professors when speaking ex cathedra as it were to be expressing their true belief rather than making any old argument that they think might have a 5 percent chance of persuading a court. They could have said "we happen to be law professors but we're also citizens and it is in the latter capacity that we have decided to participate as amici curiae." But they did not. I cannot imagine that all the professors who subscribed to the Harvard brief thought that interpreting the Solomon Amendment as a nullity was the best interpretation. I doubt also that they are interpretive nihilists, who believe that the meaning of a text is entirely in the eye of the beholder.

I do not make the same criticism of the law schools themselves, or of their association (the Association of American Law Schools, another amicus curiae), or of FAIR itself insofar as it is composed of law schools (but it also has law professors as members). Of course a law school (and its university) would prefer to have federal money given to it without strings attached, especially strings that will get it in trouble with students and faculty members who are strongly hostile to the military's policy on homosexuals. The law school merely wants to have its cake and eat it — and who doesn't? It is not an edifying desire — it is embarrassing for a law school to have to tell its irate homosexual students that it loves them but loves federal money even more — but the reality is that universities nowadays are giant corporations and behave accordingly, whatever their pretensions. It is hyperbole for the AALS to argue that the price of a law school's retaining its federal funding is to "abandon its commitment to fight discrimination" or that the issue in the case is the right of a university to decide what may be taught, but one understands that this is merely lawyer rhetoric in the service of a conventional client interest.

. . . .

What is especially curious about the law professor amicus curiae briefs is how conventional they are. In all but one instance the professors did not write the briefs themselves but instead hired a practicing lawyer to do so. No doubt they approved what he wrote, and I am told that at least in the case of the Yale professors' brief the intellectual input by the professors was substantial. I would be more comfortable had it been insubstantial. For there is nothing in any of these briefs that distinguishes them from the ordinary product of practicing lawyers.

The way in which a law professor could be a true friend of the court would be by offering an academic perspective on a case. Long gone are the days when elite law schools were dominated by law professors who identified with the practicing legal profession rather than with a distinctive legal academic culture. That culture might have a contribution to make to the judicial consideration of a case like *Rumsfeld v. FAIR*. Yet absent from the briefs is any discussion of why our armed forces want to continue a ban on homosexuals that has been abandoned by most of the countries that we consider to be our peers and what effect invalidating the Solomon Amendment would have. Maybe the military has reason to believe that lifting the ban would undermine military morale, complicate recruitment, and further strain our already overstretched military. If so, this belief would have to be weighed against the harm to homosexuals (indeed, the harm to the military itself) from the ban. For what it is worth, I have long considered that harm significant. But the military perforce recruits heavily from a segment of the American male population that might be deeply upset if it thought that homosexuals were entitled to serve with them; and that anxiety — that prejudice — is something that a conscientious administration would have to weigh, especially when the nation is at war. (And I am referring not to the "war on terrorism," a locution imprecise and misleading, but rather to our military combat in Iraq and Afghanistan.)

. . . .

The practical causes and real-world consequences of the ban on homosexuals in the military, of the "don't ask, don't tell" policy, and of the Solomon Amendment are the kind of sociopolitical facts that academics are in a better position to investigate than practicing lawyers are. Inquiring into those facts and presenting the results to the courts would be a more useful employment of law professors' time than hiring practitioners to flog precedents. There is a sheeplike character to all these professors signing on to a practitioner's brief (the sheep being led by the goat). One might have thought that some of these professors would speak in their own voice — express an individual view. Can't a law professor at Harvard or Yale write a brief? Well, maybe not any more; but he or she could do the research that only academics can do well, and let the practitioner convey the results in the brief. Do these professors perhaps not care about the issue strongly enough to actually work on it? Do they want more than to show that their heart is in the right place, or at least in the same place as their students' hearts?

But [Joshua] Rosenkranz[, the organizer of the FAIR organization] is on to something, though not to what he thinks he's on to, when he says that "law schools are more than just vocational schools that teach students to draft briefs and close deals. Law schools are, and define themselves as, normative institutions. They aspire to shape future lawyers who 'can profoundly change our society, its mores and values,' and who will urge their visions of justice on society at large. Law schools admonish their students that 'issues of justice are at the core of [their] missions,' and urge students 'to accept the challenge of more clearly defining a just system.' " Soaring rhetoric, but inaccurate. American law schools are professional schools, not secular madrasahs, and they spend a lot more time teaching their students how to defend society's "mores and values" than how to challenge them. The vast majority of the students at the elite law schools become corporate lawyers and defend the mores and values of giant corporations. Revolutionaries they are not. Rosenkranz's brief invokes a selected subset of American mores and values in defense of his constitutional claim.

What is particularly revealing about the passage I've just quoted is the uncritical assumption that legal education has a liberal agenda, specifically a liberal agenda in which homosexual rights occupy a high place. The Solomon Amendment must go because law schools are normative institutions. Rosenkranz invokes "visions of justice" (plural) but does not acknowledge the possibility that there is a military vision of justice that challenges justice as homosexual rights. So comfortable are Rosenkranz and the legal professoriat with that agenda that it does not occur to him or to it to inquire into the practical dimensions of JAG recruiting at elite law schools, including the possibility that by discouraging military recruiters the schools are helping to perpetuate a conservative military culture; JAG recruiters are surely welcome at Ave Maria.

The left-liberal domination of elite law school faculties has had the debilitating effect on the intellect that John Stuart Mill in *On Liberty* assigned to the groupthink of his day. When you inhabit a cozy burrow of like thinkers, your ideas are not challenged and they grow flabby. They become unexamined habits of mind — articles of faith that when finally challenged provoke anger rather than reasoned response because the ability to reason about them has atrophied. Missing from the professors' briefs is an awareness that there are two sides to the issue of the right of homosexuals to full equality in the armed forces and that law professors could contribute more to a sound resolution by dispassionate study than by signing their names to conventional briefs written by practicing lawyers. Even a sense of irony withers in an atmosphere of intellectual conformity. Law professors should be "reluctant to promiscuously hurl accusations of discrimination at the military, especially since many of the law professors had only a few years ago argued for, and won from the Supreme Court in *Grutter v Bollinger* (2003), a special exemption to classify at their law schools on the basis of race because of their presumed special expertise concerning the need in legal education for diverse student bodies." The military has its needs as well, and perhaps even some expertise.

Judges sense a growing chasm between the professoriat and the judiciary. In *Rumsfeld v. FAIR* we glimpse its breadth.

Richard A. Posner, *A Note on Rumsfeld v. FAIR and the Legal Academy*, 2006 Sup. Ct. Rev. 47, 47, 51–53, 54–55, 55–57 (2006).* For a similarly blistering take on "elite" law schools by a Judge Advocate with the U.S. Air Force, see Matthew D. van Dalen, *Rumsfeld v. FAIR, A Free Speech Setback or a Strategic Military Victory?*, 31 J. Legal Prof. 75 (2007).

What role should normative judgments have in these types of cases? How could *FAIR* propose an interpretation of the Solomon Amendment when that interpretation would nullify the clear purpose of the law? As Judge Posner correctly notes in his article, "Nullification is not an accepted method of statutory interpretation." Posner, *supra*, at 50. Do you agree with Posner's contention that there is a growing divide between the judiciary and the academy? Or is the judiciary moving away from a normative judicial philosophy that was closely aligned with the academy? What role should the judiciary play in today's civil rights litigation? Should the deference it owes to Congress's spending power vary depending on the type of case that is brought?

2. Apart from the debate over "liberal" and "conservative" judicial philosophies, the *FAIR* case raises other questions.

> Many rules and exceptions come out of the [*FAIR*] opinion: (1) Congress may place reasonable conditions on its provision of aid so long as these conditions do not infringe on freedom of speech, but one must keep in mind that maximum deference is due to Congress when they are operating under their authority to build an army; (2) government compelled speech violates the First Amendment, but only if the government is mandating the content of speech or if that speech is affecting a message the complaining speaker is trying to convey - not if the required speech is merely incidental to the government policy; (3) the First Amendment does protect conduct, but that conduct must be "inherently expressive" and "overwhelmingly apparent"; and (4) the First Amendment protects freedom of association, but freedom of association only protects individuals from being forced to admit someone into their "expressive association."
>
> On a broader note, *Rumsfeld* cites precedents to fit the Solomon Amendment somewhere along the spectrum of free speech cases. What stands out in opinions like Rumsfeld is how vulnerable to manipulation precedent is. Couldn't a military recruiter who visits a law school multiple times a year, spending days at a time with the school's students and staff, be considered within the law school's "expressive association?" Is the speech compelled by the Solomon Amendment truly incidental to the law? Is even more deference owed to Congress when they are operating under their authority to build and support armies when our country is at war? With so many potential factors at play and no decipherable rule to guide us, predictions are very difficult to make. . . .

Crandall Close, *Note: Speech and Subsidies: How Government Uses Financial Threats and Incentives to Dampen First Amendment Protections*, 6 First Amendment L. Rev. 285, 303–04 (2008).* Another important question left after the decision is whether both public and private law schools are considered "expressive associations."

> Note that in all of these passages the Court is not assuming for the sake of argument that the law schools in *FAIR* are expressive associations; it is saying the law schools are expressive associations and doing so with a glaring absence of any analysis.

Why might the Court have made this assumption? This is necessarily speculation, but since the government did not contest the point that the law schools qualified as expressive associations, the Court apparently did not think this issue worthy of any mention. It also might be that the Court did not want to distinguish between the public and private law school members of FAIR because it would have required an additional, and potentially difficult, analysis that was not necessary to decide the case.

So, what's the big deal? After all, FAIR lost the case. No harm, no foul. The issue lurking is that the Court strongly gestures in the direction that public law schools, as members of FAIR, have expressive association rights. In fact, of the known FAIR members, four are public law school faculties: the faculty of the City University of New York (CUNY) School of Law, the faculty of the District of Columbia David A. Clarke School of Law, the faculty of the University of Minnesota Law School, and the faculty of the University of Puerto Rico Law School. The Court did not distinguish between institutional membership and faculty membership in the FAIR organization, suggesting that recognition of FAIR law school faculties as expressive associations is tantamount to recognizing public law schools as expressive associations for purposes of First Amendment analysis.

Although the Court found in *FAIR* that the Solomon Amendment did not significantly burden the law schools' expressive association rights, it is possible that public law schools and other public employers could argue in future cases that their expressive association rights permit them to not accept employee members they do not desire. Indeed, the *FAIR* Court's expressive association analysis hinged to a large degree on the critical point that military recruiters were not seeking to become "members of the schools' expressive association."

Paul M. Secunda, *The Solomon Amendment, Expressive Associations, and Public Employment*, 54 UCLA L. Rev. 1767, 1779–80 (2007).* For an argument that all postsecondary institutions, including public schools, should be considered "expressive associations," see Paul Horwitz, *Universities as First Amendment Institutions: Some Easy Answers and Hard Questions*, 54 UCLA L. Rev. 1497 (2007).

3. The legal attacks on the military's policy of prohibiting homosexuals from serving predate the "Don't Ask, Don't Tell" policy enacted during President Clinton's first term. The first case challenging the military's policy was *Steffan v. Perry*, 41 F.3d 677 (D.C. Cir. 1994), in which the Court of Appeals affirmed the district court's grant of summary judgment to the government based on its argument that discharging a midshipman at the U.S. Naval Academy because he stated he was gay was constitutional. For an interesting description of the development of *Steffan* by the plaintiff himself, Joseph Steffan, see *Conference Remark: Harvard Law School Lambda Second Annual Gay and Lesbian Advocacy Conference: "Don't Ask, Don't Tell,"* 14 Duke J. Gender L. & Pol'y 1173 (2007). The "Don't Ask, Don't Tell" policy was mandated and codified in 10 U.S.C. § 654. After contentious debate in the United States Congress, President Barack Obama signed the repeal of the policy in December 2010. After formal certification in July 2011, the policy became effective in September 2011.

4. *Rumsfeld v. FAIR* is not a Spending Clause case because the Court held that the federal government could impose the Solomon Amendment on states *directly* without violating the First Amendment. The Spending Clause kicks into effect only when Congress must impose a spending restriction *indirectly* on states because a direct imposition would be unconstitutional. Nevertheless, the type of analysis the Court engages in with either type of case is similar and squarely tackles a troublesome question of federalism: specifically, the balance of power between the federal government and the states.

The seminal Spending Clause decision is *South Dakota v. Dole*, 483 U.S. 203 (1987). In *Dole*, South Dakota (where the legal drinking age was 19), challenged a federal law that directed the Secretary of Transportation to withhold a certain percentage of federal highway funds from states that had a legal drinking age of less than 21. The Court ruled against South Dakota, holding that the law did not violate the Constitution. In reaching its conclusion, the Court delineated four restrictions on Congress's spending power: (1) the power must be exercised in pursuit of the general welfare; (2) Congress must describe the conditions on funding "unambiguously"; (3) the conditions must be related "to the federal interest in particular national projects or programs"; and (4) there must not be an "independent constitutional bar" to the conditions. *Id.* at 207, 209.

In remarks on the 20th anniversary of the *Dole* decision, Craig Eichstadt, counsel to the state of South Dakota in the case, noted that Chief Justice Roberts, as a young associate, wrote an amicus brief on behalf of the alcoholic beverages industry and in favor of South Dakota's case. Craig Eichstadt, *Twenty-Year Legacy of South Dakota v. Dole*, 52 S.D. L. Rev. 458 (2007). South Dakota argued in *Dole* that the statute at issue violated the 21st Amendment — which repealed Prohibition — because it essentially mandated that states adopt a legal drinking age of 21. And that issue, the state argued, was strictly within the purview of state authority. Eichstadt described the philosophy behind South Dakota's argument as seeking to prevent federal government from becoming overly powerful and subsequently "dictatorial." *Id.* at 464. State governments serve as "laboratories for testing new ideas" because they are closer to their electorates, but this can be stifled by the federal government. *Id.* Ultimately, according to Eichstadt, this is a matter of "fighting the good fight" and that as a result the Supreme Court has limited federal authority on the states in the exercise of the Commerce Clause, if not the Spending Clause. *Id.* at 465.

If the Court, as it has moved rightward in its judicial philosophy during the past two decades, has generally moved to limit the federal government's power vis-a-vis the states, why has it not done so in Spending Clause cases? How would Chief Justice Roberts square his amicus brief in *Dole* to his opinion in *FAIR*? Consider this:

> [T]here is little reason to believe that the conservative Justices have any desire to impose significant direct limitations on the conditional spending power. When the Rehnquist Court imposed direct limitations on the Commerce power in [*United States v.*] *Lopez*[, 514 U.S. 549 (1995)] and

> [*United States v.*] *Morrison*[, 529 598 (2000)] it was responding in part to the concern that the failure to do so would abandon all pretense of limitations on federal power — a concern underlined by the solicitor general's oral argument in *Lopez*, in which he was unable to come up with a single hypothetical statute that would be beyond Congress's commerce authority under his theory. Opponents of the *Dole* regime often speak of the conditional spending power as effectively unlimited, but that is not quite right. Even in the absence of judicially imposed limits, the conditional spending power contains an intrinsic limit that does not constrain other federal powers: Congress cannot impose Spending Clause regulations on unwilling states; those regulations depend on the consent states are willing to give (and Congress's willingness to find the revenue to purchase that consent). Even a conservative Court has reason to be relatively unconcerned with a broad congressional power to try to persuade states to agree to spending conditions.
>
> And there are substantial reasons why a conservative Court would hesitate before imposing meaningful direct limitations on the spending power. One involves the fear of Lochnerism. Strengthening the direct limitations on the conditional spending power will require courts to engage in the kind of second-guessing of Congress's means-ends judgments that conservative jurists foreswore in the wake of *Lochner*.
>
> Even aside from their interest in avoiding the appearance of judicial activism, conservative judges have strong reasons to defend a broad conditional spending power. . . . [C]onditional spending legislation can just as readily be used to achieve conservative ends as it can liberal ones. . . .

Samuel R. Bagenstos, *Spending Clause Litigation in the Roberts Court*, 58 Duke L.J. 345, 381–82 (2008).*

5. Recall the case of *Rust v. Sullivan*, 500 U.S. 173 (1991), in which the Supreme Court upheld federal regulations that excluded funding for family planning services that included abortion as an option. The Court reasoned that the federal government was free to implement policies in favor of non-abortion related methods of family planning and thus restrict the activities, even the speech activities, of clinics and researchers who receive federal funds. How is the Court's reasoning in *Rust* related, if at all, to its reasoning in *FAIR*? Is there a rule to be taken from both cases? Can the government enforce generally applicable laws, regardless of their incidental infringement of constitutional rights, while postsecondary schools cannot enforce generally applicable regulations if they conflict with Congress's spending power — even if that spending power, as employed, incidentally infringes on the schools' constitutional rights? Note that *Rust*, while still good law, has been criticized or distinguished by a number of other decisions, particularly subsequent to the Court's decision in *Planned Parenthood v. Casey*, 505 U.S. 833 (1992). At least one federal court's opinion suggested that *Casey* abrogated *Rust*, and a Ninth

Circuit decision to strike down a state abortion law similar to the one in *Rust*, on the basis of *Casey*, suggests that courts may doubt the validity of *Rust. See Richmond Med. Ctr. for Women v. Gilmore*, 55 F. Supp. 2d 441 (E.D. Va. 1999); *Planned Parenthood of S. Ariz. v. Lawall*, 180 F.3d 1022 (9th Cir. 1999).

Also consider the case of *National Endowment for the Arts v. Finley*, 524 U.S. 569 (1998):

> Using the holding in *Rust*, the United States Supreme Court analogized federally funded pregnancy counseling to the funding of art. Specifically, if one kind of counseling can be funded over another, one point of view about art can be valued over another. Hence, artists who create consistent with societal values can be funded while those who create "indecent" art can be refused. This activity began with the controversy surrounding the funding by the National Endowment for the Arts of the photography exhibits of Robert Mapplethorpe (the sexual demeanor of gay men as seen through several very suggestive poses) and Andres Serrano (the image of a crucifix immersed in a cup of urine). Objecting to the funding by a federal organization of art images that were judged to be obscene, anti-religious, and anti-family, the United States Congress amended the legislation to include the following:
>
> No payment shall be made under this section except upon application therefor which is submitted to the National Endowment for the Arts in accordance with regulations issued and procedures . . . In establishing such regulations and procedures, [the NEA] shall ensure that-
>
> > (1) artistic excellence and artistic merit are the criteria by which applications are judged, taking into consideration general standards of decency and respect for the . . . values of the American public.
>
> Four artists, who were refused funding, filed suit claiming that the "decency" and "respect" clauses of the statute were unconstitutional and a violation of their first amendment rights to free expression. In *NEA v. Finley*, the . . . Court took up the issue whether government may control the content of art produced by artists in its role as patron and whether funds can be distributed to art programs based on the messages expressed.
>
> The majority opinion reviewed the legislation, both original and as amended, and determined that there was nothing unconstitutional about making awards based on considerations of generally accepted standards of decency and respect for common American values. The Court interpreted the provisions to be mere guidelines for funders to use, worthy of some consideration, but nonetheless necessary with every proposal. There is a strong message here and this should not be lost on those in academe. The Court found the "decency" and "respect" prongs of the legislation to be permissible factors when assessing educational suitability. . . . [T]he majority opinion stated that "[s]urely it is a highly appropriate function of public school education to prohibit the use of vulgar and offensive terms in public discourse." As such, the NEA could decide to fund particular projects for a wide variety of reasons including, "anticipated public interest

> in the work, . . . educational value, . . . [and its] suitability to [certain] audiences . . ." More importantly, the dissent in the case interpreted this to mean that any possible activity that competed for public funds could be declared ineligible if it offended the sensibilities of a portion of the public. Examples might include not only the works of artists like Mapplethorpe and Serrano, but also teachers who decorated their offices with African or other non-European art, teachers who wore non-mainstream clothing, or student or faculty art projects with an anti-American theme.
>
> . . . .
>
> The message from both *Rust* and *Finley* is that government may allocate the public's resources on the basis of viewpoint. The majority decisions in both cases essentially postulate that one is free to express, but not necessarily with the support of public funds. The result of such a position is that government funding can be used as a weapon to limit controversial issues or ones that certain persons simply disagree with. Indeed, the decisions leave artistic expression in a compromising position inasmuch as funding in any given year may be dependent upon who is in power at the time. . . .

Philip T.K. Daniel & Vesta A.H. Daniel, *A Legal Portrait of the Artist and Art Educator in Free Expression and Cyberspace*, 140 Educ. L. Rep. 431, 456–58 (2000).* After *Finley*, are there any limits to Congress's ability to silence speech that it finds distasteful through funding cuts? In one case, a federally funded non-profit organization that provided legal services for indigent clients brought an action claiming that congressional regulations restricting the kinds of cases the corporation could hear were unconstitutional. *Velazquez v. Legal Svcs. Corp.*, 164 F.3d 757 (2d Cir. 1999), *aff'd*, 531 U.S. 533 (2001). The Second Circuit said that "different types of speech enjoy different degrees of protection" and that one provision in particular, preventing LSC from representing a client for welfare relief, where such a suit "involve[s] an effort to amend or otherwise challenge existing law" was speech criticizing government policy. This speech is guaranteed the "strongest protection" and according to the court this statute was not viewpoint neutral. *Id.* at 771.

> In our view, a lawyer's argument to a court that a statute, rule, or governmental practice standing in the way of a client's claim is unconstitutional or otherwise illegal falls far closer to the First Amendment's most protected categories of speech than abortion counseling or indecent art. The fact that Congress can make grants that favor family planning over abortion, or that favor decency over indecency, in no way suggests that Congress may also make grants to fund the legal representation of welfare applicants under terms that bar the attorney from arguing the unconstitutionality or illegality of whatever rule blocks the client's success. Among the only directly effective ways to oppose a statute, regulation or policy adopted by government is to argue to a court having jurisdiction of the matter that the rule is either unconstitutional or unauthorized by law. . . .

> The Supreme Court's discussion in *Finley* . . . seemed to imply that an absolute prohibition, of the sort "calculated to drive 'certain ideas or viewpoints from the marketplace,' " would have required a different result. The limitation on the suit-for-benefits exception is just such an absolute prohibition: It muzzles grant recipients from expressing any and all forbidden arguments.

Id. at 771–72. But note that the court held as constitutional "program integrity requirements" that restricted LSC's use of funds on the grounds that they did not leave the organization's grantees "adequate alternative avenues for expression" even though there was some restriction on the grantees' First Amendment rights. *Id.* at 766.

Another case distinguishing *Finley* is *Gentala v. City of Tucson.* In that case the City Council of Tucson rejected the Gentalas' application for funds to support a local observation of the National Day of Prayer. The court held this to be unconstitutional on grounds that the rejection was not viewpoint neutral as it denied the application "due to the religious character of the event." 213 F.3d 1055, 1063 (9th Cir. 2000). Although this case involves a local decision, not a congressional one, it is likely that similar restrictions passed by Congress would not pass muster under *Finley.*

Is there something to be said about legislators aligning the distribution of tax funds with their constituents' standards of decency and morality? Essentially, does this practice embody representative democracy, the government employed in America? Or, does it frustrate you that the majority can oppress the abilities and rights of the minority just because they do not agree with them?

> The essence of representative democracy is to provide a layer of protection between the majority will and legislative enactments. This separation permits the reasoned, educated, and experienced minds of elected officials to temper passions and compromise in order to legislate in the public interest, which serves the common good, rather than specific interests and constituencies. However, the founders recognized that even elected legislators may not always be appropriately responsive to the will of the people electing them.
>
> Out of a concern that on certain issues the elected representatives may be unresponsive to the popular will, the founders argued that an aspect of direct democracy should be included in the federal constitution. Madison recognized the democratic ideal that people also operate as a check on the government. Where the government departments are not adequately representing the interests of the populace or of society, the people retain the right to address those inadequacies. The right does not exist solely to expand or contract government, as was arguably the rationale for the Constitution replacing the Articles of Confederation, but also to correct failures in the system.

Chris Goodman, *(M)ad Men: Using Persuasion Factors in Media Advertisements to Prevent a "Tyranny of the Majority" on Ballot Propositions*, 32 HASTINGS COMM.

& Ent. L.J. 247, 253 (2009)* (footnote omitted).

Politicians have incentives to pass laws and distribute tax funds according to their constituents; otherwise, they could be voted out of office or impeached for not representing the people that elected them. This is the crux of the gay marriage debate right now. The judiciary and legislation in some states want to legalize gay marriage, but then the state's residents vote against it.

6. In 2010, the United States Supreme Court agreed to hear an appeal from a Christian student group — The Christian Legal Society — that was denied recognition by the Hastings College of Law in San Francisco for excluding homosexuals and nonbelievers. *Christian Legal Society Chapter of the Univ. of Calif. v. Martinez*, 130 S. Ct. 2971 (2010). The Court ruled in favor of Hastings, holding that the law school's policy of recognizing only those student groups that did not discriminate on various grounds, including religion and sexual orientation, did not violate the Constitution. The Court reasoned that Hastings' policy applied to all groups and was thus "viewpoint neutral and reasonable." Though it is not a Spending Clause case, it involves a similar balancing of constitutional interests as that seen in *FAIR*.

7. There are still unresolved issues for schools and administrators in light of *Martinez*. In particular, the Court's decision did not squarely address the constitutionality of a school's right to refuse funding to an organization that violates a school's written nondiscrimination policy. It has been suggested that the Court should find this right to refusal as constitutionally permissible in order to "prevent public sponsorship" of discriminatory beliefs held by these organizations. *See* Jennifer Hennessy, Note, *University-Funded Discrimination: Unresolved Issues After the Supreme Court's "Resolution" of the Circuit Split on University Funding for Discriminatory Organizations*. 96 Iowa L. Rev. 1767, 1777–78, 1789. (2011).

8. As a matter of policy, is there anything that postsecondary schools can do to maintain their commitment to anti-discrimination rules while still complying with federal regulations? Should they make more of an effort, in the context of the *FAIR* case, to express explicitly their dissatisfaction with the military's homosexual policy? Would more "speech" be an effective counterbalance to the policy?

9. This section has explored the ways Congress can condition the funds it provides to postsecondary schools. Can Congress condition funds that schools provide students in the form of financial aid? Does the federal government have an interest in regulating that? After the federal government launched an antitrust investigation into the financial aid practices of the so-called "Ivy Overlap Group" (the Ivy League schools and Massachusetts Institute of Technology), in which the schools collectively calculated the financial aid packages of its applicants, Congress placed a statutory note after Section 1 of the Sherman Antitrust Act that provides an exemption for postsecondary schools. The Overlap investigation and subsequent court cases examined whether schools "engaged in commercial activity" when they collected tuition and provided financial aid. The statutory note, set to expire in 2015 (although there is little reason to believe that it will not be reauthorized after a string of reauthorizations dating to 1997), allows postsecondary schools to collaborate on financial aid decisions as long as students are admitted on a need-blind basis. The note, according to two commentators, revives the meaning of educational opportunity and diverts judicial analysis from the commercial aspects of tuition and financial aid.

> That is, the statutory note offers protection so that schools can again focus on the collegiate goals of scholarship, service, and student development. In the absence of such legislation, many colleges and universities would be unable to provide adequate financial aid packages for some of the brightest young men and women. Without the provision of adequate financing, the basic goals of education, the passing of traditions and values from one generation to the next, would not be met.

Jeffrey C. Sun & Philip T.K. Daniel, *The Sherman Antitrust Act Provisions and Collegiate Action: Should There Be a Continued Exception for the Business of a University?*, 25 J.C. & U.L. 451, 492 (1999). Federal oversight and conditions on student aid are elaborated on in Chapter XI of the book.

10. Thus far, postsecondary schools have avoided the type of student achievement requirements that K-12 schools must meet under the No Child Left Behind Act. The 2008 reauthorization of the Higher Education Act — originally enacted in 1965 to provide more funding to postsecondary schools and students — "forbids [the U.S. Department of Education] from establishing criteria that specify, define or prescribe the standards accreditors use in assessing an institution's success with respect to student achievement." AM. COUNCIL ON EDUC., ACE ANALYSIS OF HIGHER EDUCATION ACT REAUTHORIZATION 2–3 (2008), *available at* http://www.acenet.edu/AM/Template.cfm?Section=Search§ion=Government_Relations&template=/CM/ContentDisplay.cfm&ContentFileID=5713. The development of achievement standards is left to the institutions themselves and accrediting organizations.

11. Has the Solomon Amendment Controversy been settled? Not long after this decision, a non-profit organization attempted to compel the federal government to revoke funds from a university for discriminating against military recruiters as prohibited by the Solomon Amendment. *Young America's Found. v. Gates*, 573 F.3d 797 (C.A.D.C. 2009). The Young America's Foundation argued that student and faculty protesters at University of California- Santa Cruz (UCSC) had disrupted military recruiters on campus. *Id.* at 798. Ultimately, the court determined that the organization (unlike FAIR) lacked any standing to pursue the issue. *Id.* at 800. The concurrence alone explicitly said the Administrative Procedure Act prohibits the judiciary from compelling the Secretary of Defense to enforce or not enforce the Solomon Amendment. *Id.* at 801. Should postsecondary federal funding decisions be entirely discretionary, without judicial redress? Would this outcome have been the same if something other than the Solomon Amendment had been at issue?

12. On December 22, 2010, President Obama signed the Don't Ask Don't Tell Repeal Act of 2010 into law. H.R. 2965, S. 4023, amending 10 U.S.C. § 654. Though the Act doesn't specify what the new military policy on gay and lesbian service members should be, it does repeal the portion discriminating against LGBT individuals' ability to serve openly. *Id.* Though it remains to be seen what direction military policy will take, much of the concern felt by the educators in FAIR about LGBT discrimination has been essentially eliminated. Does the Solomon Amendment still serve some purpose? Are there other reasons a postsecondary institution might not want military recruiters on campus?

B. FEDERAL REGULATION OF RESEARCH

The Food and Drug Administration and Department of Health and Human Services require institutions of higher education conducting tests on humans to establish Institutional Review Boards to oversee such research and ensure that colleges comply with federal regulations.

The regulations are substantially similar and provide:

45 C.F.R. § 46.111 and 21 C.F.R. § 56.111. Criteria for IRB approval of research.

(a) In order to approve research covered by this policy the IRB shall determine that all of the following requirements are satisfied:

(1) Risks to subjects are minimized: (i) By using procedures which are consistent with sound research design and which do not unnecessarily expose subjects to risk, and (ii) whenever appropriate, by using procedures already being performed on the subjects for diagnostic or treatment purposes.

(2) Risks to subjects are reasonable in relation to anticipated benefits, if any, to subjects, and the importance of the knowledge that may reasonably be expected to result. In evaluating risks and benefits, the IRB should consider only those risks and benefits that may result from the research (as distinguished from risks and benefits of therapies subjects would receive even if not participating in the research). The IRB should not consider possible long-range effects of applying knowledge gained in the research (for example, the possible effects of the research on public policy) as among those research risks that fall within the purview of its responsibility.

(3) Selection of subjects is equitable. In making this assessment the IRB should take into account the purposes of the research and the setting in which the research will be conducted and should be particularly cognizant of the special problems of research involving vulnerable populations, such as children, prisoners, pregnant women, mentally disabled persons, or economically or educationally disadvantaged persons.

(4) Informed consent will be sought from each prospective subject or the subject's legally authorized representative, in accordance with, and to the extent required by § 46.116.

. . . .

(6) When appropriate, the research plan makes adequate provision for monitoring the data collected to ensure the safety of subjects.

(7) When appropriate, there are adequate provisions to protect the privacy of subjects and to maintain the confidentiality of data.

(b) When some or all of the subjects are likely to be vulnerable to coercion or undue influence, such as children, prisoners, pregnant women, mentally disabled persons, or economically or educationally disadvantaged persons, additional safeguards have been included in the study to protect the rights and welfare of these subjects.

45 C.F.R. § 46.116 and 21 C.F.R. § 50.20
General requirements for informed consent.

Except as provided elsewhere in this policy, no investigator may involve a human being as a subject in research covered by this policy unless the investigator has obtained the legally effective informed consent of the subject or the subject's legally authorized representative. An investigator shall seek such consent only under circumstances that provide the prospective subject or the representative sufficient opportunity to consider whether or not to participate and that minimize the possibility of coercion or undue influence. The information that is given to the subject or the representative shall be in language understandable to the subject or the representative. No informed consent, whether oral or written, may include any exculpatory language through which the subject or the representative is made to waive or appear to waive any of the subject's legal rights, or releases or appears to release the investigator, the sponsor, the institution or its agents from liability for negligence.

The federal government also regulates research involving animals. The Animal Welfare Act, 7 U.S.C. § 2131 *et seq.*, is administered by the Animal and Plant Health Inspection Service of the U.S. Department of Agriculture. The regulations supplementing the Act require that institutions performing research on animals establish an Institutional Animal Care and Use Committee. Those committees are similar to the Institutional Review Boards required for research involving humans, operating as the entity responsible for ensuring the college or university comply with federal law in this area.

Barbara A. Noah, *Bioethical Malpractice: Risk and Responsibility in Human Research*, 7 J. Health Care L. & Pol'y 175 (2004)*

I. INTRODUCTION

In the past decade, the pace of medical research involving human subjects has accelerated substantially, promising the development of new treatments that extend life, improve its quality, and prevent disease. Estimates suggest that about seven million people participate in clinical trials funded by the National Institutes of Health (NIH) and another twelve million subjects participate in private trials annually. Looking ahead into the new millennium, the rapidly evolving sciences of genetics and proteomics, along with the continued development of traditional therapies, offer the hope of treatment or cure for currently untreatable illnesses, and ultimately may transform the practice of medicine.

Clinical research provides the necessary bridge from scientific theory to practical medical application, but research involving human subjects sometimes exacts a high price from those who participate. Patients who enroll in therapeutic research protocols take risks, sometimes unwittingly, that they might not ordinarily tolerate in the clinical setting. Healthy volunteers, motivated by altruism or a desire to make money, also encounter risks when they agree to participate in non-therapeutic research designed to advance scientific understanding. The medical community often assumes, perhaps over-optimistically, that clinical research enhances scientific knowledge in ways that ultimately will benefit many patients. Sometimes, experimental protocols actually benefit research subjects directly. Other times, however, as with the recent deaths of several research participants, hindsight suggests that no amount of improved scientific understanding or medical benefit appears to justify the risks of a particular research plan.

Recent events have drawn public attention to flaws in the regulatory system that is designed to protect human research subjects and have prompted demands for reform. Although calculating the number of research-related deaths and injuries has proven difficult, one expert suggests that as many as 5,000 people die annually in federally-funded research protocols, while tens of thousands more suffer injuries. Injuries in privately-funded research remain even more difficult to estimate due to the lack of any unified tracking system.

Institutional review boards (IRBs), the entities charged with the task of protecting human research subjects from coercion and unreasonable risk, suffer from significant limitations that impede their mission. The United States General Accounting Office (GAO) and the Department of Health and Human Services (HHS) have sounded the alarm, issuing highly critical reports about the ineffectiveness of IRBs. Federal regulatory agencies and state health policy bodies also have increased their scrutiny of research activities. HHS's Office for Human Research Protections (OHRP) temporarily suspended research under the supervision of IRBs at more than a dozen research institutions because of non-compliance with regulatory requirements, and it continues to criticize the conduct of specified trials. In several of these cases, the suspension followed the death or serious injury of a patient or healthy volunteer.

In 1999, eighteen-year-old Jesse Gelsinger, a young man with a fairly mild form of an inherited liver disease, volunteered for a gene therapy protocol at the University of Pennsylvania, hoping to improve his condition and to provide scientific information that might be useful in treating infants born with a more severe form of the disease. After receiving a massive dose of a viral vector designed to deliver healthy genes to his liver cells, Mr. Gelsinger developed multiple-organ failure and died. Subsequent investigation revealed that the Recombinant DNA Advisory

Committee (RAC), an NIH committee charged with the oversight of all federally-funded gene therapy research, had approved the study notwithstanding some reservations about performing the risky procedure on patients who were coping relatively well with the disorder. Worse still, it later became apparent that the consent form given to Mr. Gelsinger failed to reveal that similar studies had caused deaths in monkeys, or that two other people who had received the viral vector treatment experienced serious side effects. In addition to these gaps in the information conveyed to subjects, the principal investigator (PI) in the study neglected to disclose the fact that he was the founder of the company with rights to all treatments developed by his research laboratory, a potential conflict of interest that very well may have affected the family's decision to participate in the study.

The Gelsinger family eventually sued the University of Pennsylvania, the director of the university's bioethics program, and the PI, among others, claiming that the information provided in the informed consent documents was incomplete and that the research team deliberately misled the family about the safety of the protocol by withholding information about previous adverse events associated with the gene therapy procedure. The lawsuit also alleged that the IRB should never have approved the protocol and claimed that the University and the PI inappropriately held equity stakes in a company with a financial interest in the investigational therapy. The suit settled for an undisclosed amount.

In 2001, Ellen Roche, a 24-year old healthy volunteer, died while participating in an NIH-funded study at the Johns Hopkins University School of Medicine designed to understand the physiologic mechanisms of asthma. The non-therapeutic research protocol required volunteers to inhale an unapproved drug called hexamethonium into their lungs to irritate the bronchial linings. After the PI's search of a medical literature database failed to turn up any serious risks associated with the chemical, the university's IRB approved the research. It later became apparent that the investigator's research efforts had missed older published research reporting serious side effects associated with inhalation of the compound.

In addition, although at least one previous study volunteer developed a persistent cough and shortness of breath, the investigator had failed to report the adverse event and continued the research. OHRP suspended all federally-funded research at the Johns Hopkins University, citing numerous deficiencies in the institution's IRB processes in general, and particular problems with the IRB's approval and oversight of the asthma study. Although research subsequently resumed at Hopkins, critics continue to find fault with the University's protection of human subjects.

In still another recent incident, patients in a clinical trial of a melanoma vaccine at the University of Oklahoma sued the principal investigator, the manufacturer of the experimental vaccine, and the members of the IRB that approved the study, alleging that the researchers had failed to inform the participants of relevant risks and had misrepresented information in order to obtain government permission to conduct the trial. The nurse coordinator for the study became concerned when she realized that the PI continually enrolled subjects who did not meet the medical inclusion criteria for the approved protocol and that the chair of the IRB routinely approved major deviations from the study procedures retroactively, in clear violation of federal regulations. When the University conducted an audit of the research, it discovered serious safety problems with the manufacture and testing of the vaccine and it shut down the research.

This accumulation of events has real consequences for the future of biomedical research. Already, researchers are encountering growing suspicion from prospective trial participants, and are experiencing increased difficulty in recruiting subjects. Moreover, as these examples illustrate, inappropriate research conduct and flaws in oversight pose risks to human subjects that may form the basis for liability actions against IRBs and the institutions that house them. Institutional and investigator failures to comply with basic research regulations certainly contributed to some of the recent injuries, but other less easily remedied flaws in the system of human subjects protection pose even greater challenges. Conscientious compliance with the minimal standards in the federal rules satisfies only a portion of the legal and ethical obligations in clinical research. Because the regulations only provide basic parameters for acceptable research, IRBs and investigators must work harder to interpret and implement the rules appropriately for the myriad individual research plans that they consider.

The changing climate of medical research — particularly pressures arising from increased research volume, the lack of effective training mechanisms, lack of expertise on IRBs in highly specialized fields of medicine, and complex relationships between academic researchers and private funding sources — increases the likelihood that these boards will fail in their mission to protect human subjects. In addition to failures to comply with explicit human subjects protection regulations, IRBs may underestimate risks, miss ethical or scientific deficiencies in the design of research protocols, or make other similar errors of judgment, thereby subjecting unwitting research participants to inappropriate and avoidable jeopardy. IRBs increasingly may face tort liability for what I will call "bioethical malpractice" — a failure to exercise reasonable judgment within the confines of the regulatory scheme governing human subjects research. Although tort claims brought by injured research subjects remain rare, recent events suggest that this type of litigation will increase in frequency. Several lawsuits against IRBs are pending and more will surely follow.

. . . .

II. IRB OPERATIONS

Existing federal regulations delegate to IRBs the responsibility to safeguard research subjects who participate in clinical trials of experimental treatments and in non-therapeutic trials designed to gain generalizable scientific knowledge. In order to protect human research subjects effectively, IRBs must use their combined expertise to assess the scientific, ethical, and legal validity of every proposed research protocol and must continue vigilant monitoring of approved protocols. . . .

A. The Regulatory Framework

The existing system of human research regulation evolved over time in reaction to a series of publicized incidents of research abuse. The Nuremburg Code, which emerged out of the trials of Nazi physicians after the Second World War, sets out essential principles for permissible medical experiments. In 1964, the World Medical Association adopted the Declaration of Helsinki, which provides additional commentary on the Nuremburg Code. In 1979, in response to several notorious research abuses in the United States, such as the Tuskegee syphilis study, the National Commission for the Protection of Human Subjects issued the Belmont Report. Finally, the American Medical Association (AMA) has published a variety of opinions dealing with ethical issues in clinical research.

These ethical codes and guidelines provided the underpinnings for today's federal oversight regime. In 1974, the Department of Health, Education, and Welfare (HEW, the predecessor of HHS) promulgated the first formal regulations governing human research. Seven years later, the Food and Drug Administration (FDA) issued its own regulations. Both the OHRP and the FDA have the authority to inspect records and suspend research activities at institutions that receive federal funding. IRBs represent a central feature of this system, and they have become widespread, with an estimated 3,000 to 5,000 such boards now operating in academic medical centers, hospitals, and at government agencies like NIH. . . .

The federal rules apply to most, though not all, clinical research conducted in the United States. The FDA regulations apply to all human subjects research involving articles such as drugs, medical devices, and biological products that eventually will support a licensing application to the agency, while the HHS regulations cover all research conducted or supported by the federal government. All institutions receiving HHS funding must provide the Department with assurances that every project conducted at the institution, regardless of the source of funding, will abide by the human subjects protection regulations.

These two overlapping sets of federal research regulations provide a wealth of detail about standards for approval and supervision of human research. Nevertheless, the regulations leave some of the most difficult scientific issues unresolved, and they leave important ethical questions to the discretion of IRBs, which may vary substantially in their interpretation and application of the regulatory requirements. In effect, the federal government has deputized these boards, delegating to private groups composed of relevant experts primary responsibility for applying the rules. Thus, variations in IRB workload, institutional support and resources, and attitudes towards the informed consent process can lead to significant differences in the implementation of the federal regulations among boards, thereby potentially compromising this core mission.

1. Review of New Research Protocols

With few exceptions, all new research protocols involving human subjects require full board review. The regulations which set out criteria for approval require the IRB to assess a variety of scientific and ethical factors. First, the study design must minimize the risks to the subjects by using sound research procedures and, in the case of therapeutic research, by preferring procedures that typically would comprise standard diagnostic tests or treatment. In addition to ensuring that risks to subjects are minimized, the IRB must evaluate whether those risks, whatever their magnitude, are reasonable in relation to the probable benefits to the subjects and the importance of the anticipated scientific knowledge. Thus, the IRB must weigh potential risks and benefits to subjects who participate in the research.

This inquiry is necessarily complex and fact-intensive. In the case of therapeutic research, where the subjects suffer from the condition under investigation, there are both potential risks and direct benefits to participation. In non-therapeutic research, however, there is no prospect of direct benefit to the participants and concerns about coercion loom large. In such cases, the IRB evaluates whether the possible benefit to society in the form of improved scientific understanding justifies the risks to individual research participants. . . .

IRBs also must assess the broader scientific merit of each research proposal, a task that includes risk-benefit analysis but also considers the place of a particular research plan in the broader field of scientific inquiry. Research that lacks scientific merit is per se unethical and must not receive IRB approval. The assessment of scientific merit may prove difficult, however, even for a board of scientists and physicians. . . .

The informed consent process is designed to reduce the knowledge gap between physician and patient by mandating the communication of sufficient information to allow the patient to make meaningful decisions about health care. It serves much the same purpose for potential subjects in their dealings with investigators. Informed consent represents a necessary, though insufficient, requirement for ethically appropriate research. . . .

Once the IRB approves the protocol and the consent form, the process of obtaining consent is left to the principal investigator or, more often, to his or her staff. Unfortunately, the actual process of obtaining consent in research often emphasizes form over substance and thus falls short of promoting the ethical ideal of patient autonomy in making medical decisions. . . .

Research designed primarily to advance medical knowledge, with only a speculative possibility of some secondary benefit to the research subjects, heightens these concerns and makes meaningful informed consent essential. Even when the IRB and the principal investigator manage to draft an easy-to-read informed consent document and provide the potential research participant with an oral explanation of the research and an opportunity to ask questions, research subjects sometimes fail to understand the distinction between the standard therapy that they would ordinarily receive for their condition and the experimental therapy. . . .

In addition, even in protocols that offer some real possibility of prospective benefit, informed consent seldom includes information about the likelihood that such benefit will occur for any one research subject. Moreover, consent forms rarely discuss the possibility that the experimental intervention under study may not work as well as standard therapy for a given condition, or remind research subjects of their option not to participate based on concerns that experimental therapy entails additional and often unpredictable risks compared with standard medical interventions. . . .

In addition to requiring meaningful informed consent, the regulations prohibit research that employs "coercive" tactics, but IRBs sometimes struggle to determine what sorts of recruitment techniques would constitute coercion. For many years, recruitment of research subjects has involved payment for participation, although most IRBs agree that this practice poses difficult ethical problems. Depending on how they are structured, such incentives clearly can pose a risk of coercion, particularly because low-income or uninsured individuals are more likely to enroll in a research study in order to obtain otherwise unavailable treatment and are more likely to underestimate the risks. . . .

2. Ongoing Supervision of Approved Protocols

IRBs must revisit approved protocols at least annually, and more frequently if the degree of risk demands it, in a process called "continuing review." In such a review, the board examines adverse events (with particular attention to serious, unexpected events) and should ensure that the investigator has complied with informed consent requirements by obtaining consent from each subject, documenting that consent, and providing the subject with a copy of the consent document and information about whom to contact in case of problems. The IRB also must inquire whether there have been any deviations from the approved protocol, such as enrolling more than the approved number of subjects or changing study procedures. If an IRB discovers that clinical investigators are not complying with the board's requirements, or have deviated from an approved protocol, it has the authority to suspend or terminate approval of the project. Unfortunately, continuing review remains a "paper-based" activity at most IRBs, which generally lack the resources to visit study sites or to interview principal investigators or research subjects. Instead, IRBs usually rely on self-reporting from researchers as the basis for continuing review.

. . . .

The recent increase in the pace of clinical research has left IRBs inundated with adverse event reports. OHRP has noted a tripling of research-related injury reports between 1997 and 2000, which it attributes in part to an increased awareness of federal reporting regulations among researchers. Not surprisingly, boards find it difficult to devote serious attention to reviewing and addressing these reports. . . .

. . . .

B. Changes in the Climate of Biomedical Research

A variety of recent developments in clinical research may contribute to the likelihood of regulatory violations or errors in supervisory judgments by IRBs. Although research administrators have acknowledged problems in the clinical research environment, not all of the problematic aspects of academic medical research receive the same degree of attention. As the pace of medical research increases, many IRBs are staggering under the weight of their oversight responsibilities. One recent survey found that requests for initial protocol reviews increased 42% between 1993 and 1998 and that some IRBs supervise up to 2,000 ongoing research plans. The burgeoning load of protocols requiring initial review and continuing supervision, combined with lack of adequate institutional support for IRBs, can create a situation where an overworked IRB may be forced to do only the bare minimum required by the regulations. Despite governmental recommendations that institutions supply their IRBs with adequate staff, funding, space, and equipment, many boards continue to muddle along with insufficient support.

Frequently, IRB members also lack the necessary training and expertise in the regulatory requirements, ethics, and relevant scientific principles to perform their duties optimally. One recent study of IRB practices concluded that a quarter of the boards provide no training to their new members, while the remaining boards require only minimal training — an average of four hours for each new member, along with "a stack of material to read." Moreover, as medical research becomes more complex and specialized, even larger IRBs at major medical centers may lack expertise in particular scientific specialties such as gene therapy. Despite recommendations from government reports calling for significant improvements in funding and training, none of the relevant federal agencies has imposed educational requirements for investigators or IRB members.

. . . .

Most IRBs are comprised primarily of physicians and other health professionals employed at the research institution. IRBs have an obligation to subject every protocol to the same level of scrutiny, whether the principal investigator is a stranger or a close colleague, but complete evenhandedness is probably unrealistic. Although board members must recuse themselves from voting on protocols in which they are listed as investigators, IRB members frequently review their colleagues' protocols and, understandably, may find it difficult to avoid bias in favor of approval. . . .

The federal regulations forbid institutional reversals of IRB decisions to reject a protocol, but they do little to prevent lobbying of board members. Junior faculty at academic institutions who serve on the IRB may fear reprisals in the form of delayed promotion or tenure, or subtler forms of "shunning," if they fail to support their senior colleagues' research. . . .

Financial conflicts of interest are disturbingly prevalent in biomedical research. Every year, more dollars flow into the clinical trials business. The pharmaceutical industry spends approximately $9 billion annually on research, while the NIH and other government programs provide $5 billion yearly in research funding. Financial arrangements between medical technology companies and academic researchers, community physicians, and private contract research organizations (CROs) have captured the attention of regulatory agencies and the academic and medical communities. These increasingly common collaborative research agreements between private corporations and universities, which can include stock options, profitable research subject enrollment bonuses, and generous consulting fees, have the potential to generate immense profits for both types of entities. At the same time, however, such arrangements complicate the process of IRB review and supervision because they increase the potential for inappropriate research conduct.

IRBs can serve as a bulwark against the potentially negative consequences of academic-industry partnerships. By overseeing research protocols designed to test the safety and effectiveness of investigational drugs, medical devices, and biotechnology products, IRBs enable sponsors to collect the data necessary for FDA review of potentially profitable products. Despite the fact that most clinical research receives extramural funding support, the IRB must resist a pattern of presumptive cooperation with investigators who rely on board approval to facilitate the receipt of research grants for the institution.

Unfortunately, financial connections between researchers and sponsors may cause deliberate or unintentional distortion of the risks and benefits of research in ways that IRBs may find difficult to detect and correct. When investigators receive substantial grant money from study sponsors in the form of consulting fees, subject enrollment fees, corporate equity interests, or honoraria, these payments can increase the risk of subjecting the research participants to avoidable harm. The IRB ordinarily relies on the promise of generating sound scientific data as part of the justification for placing human subjects at risk in research. Financial connections between industry and clinical investigators can make a mockery of these assumptions or at least can add complexity to the risk-benefit calculus. Even if the conflict of interest does not cause direct harm to research subjects, the very fact that individuals are enrolled in a clinical trial (with its additional attendant risks compared to standard treatment) may be ethically objectionable if the study design lacks scientific merit.

. . . .

These concerns about biases and conflicts are not merely speculative. Recent studies have documented a relationship between industry sponsorship and favorable outcomes. . . .

The federal regulations do little to insulate the integrity of the initial IRB review from internal or external pressures. Although the FDA and HHS regulations do contain provisions that address financial conflicts of interest, these rules focus primarily on disclosure of conflicts to government agencies rather than to IRBs and research subjects. The HHS regulations require investigators receiving funding under the Public Health Service Act (such as NIH grants) to disclose "significant financial conflicts of interest." FDA regulations require that sponsors disclose to the agency their investigators' financial interests in products that are the subject of research protocols. These rules do not require IRBs to address conflicts of interest or require their disclosure to research subjects in consent documents. . . .

In addition to institutional and industry pressures on IRB performance, changing expectations among research subjects and a rapidly developing consumerist attitude towards medical services (including experimental therapies) add to the complexities of IRB review. In 1997, Congress required that NIH establish a publicly-accessible database of all clinical trials for drugs designed to treat serious or life-threatening conditions, and private websites with names like "Hopelink.com" and "Emergingmed.com" continue to proliferate. Increased advertising of research protocols in print media and on television and radio improves clinical trial enrollment but may contribute to unrealistic expectations about prospective benefit. With easy access to information about clinical trials, many patients now question their physicians about experimental therapies or pursue such opportunities independently.

. . . .

Finally, IRBs and clinical researchers are no longer viewed as above reproach. The recent surge in media coverage of injuries and deaths at prominent research institutions and the concurrent decision by regulatory entities to reexamine existing research protections suggest that significant changes lay ahead. Ethicists and health care providers have begun to express concern about individual and institutional preoccupation with the financial and professional rewards of scientific discovery, conflicts of interest, problems with disclosure of risks to research subjects, and coercive recruiting tactics. Recent evaluations have identified a disturbing pattern of researcher noncompliance with important human subjects protections and a concomitant failure by IRBs to detect and correct deficiencies. In the past two years, the FDA and OHRP have temporarily shut down research programs in at least seven institutions while they remediated a host of compliance problems. In response to these and other apparent deficiencies in research oversight, the FDA and OHRP have begun to scrutinize more closely research institutions with a spotty history of regulatory compliance, while the media has brought these issues to the public's attention.

III. CONSTRUCTING A LIABILITY CLAIM AGAINST AN IRB

The failure of IRBs to exercise reasonable care in the review and supervision of clinical research sometimes results in injury to human subjects. In addition to satisfying the minimal standards set forth in the research regulations described in Part II, IRBs must exercise substantial judgment about complex ethical and scientific issues and opportunities for negligence abound. Some research injury lawsuits are still framed as traditional malpractice claims against physicians using experimental procedures. Although lawsuits naming IRBs as defendants remain relatively rare, the inclusion of boards as parties has begun to increase. . . .

A. Finding a Duty of Care and Defining Its Scope

Under general tort principles, a court first must conclude that the defendant owes a duty of care to the plaintiff before inquiring into the question of the defendant's negligence. The existence of a duty of care usually depends on some kind of direct relationship between plaintiff and defendant. Thus, absent some relationship with a patient, courts will not impose a duty of care on hospital employees.

. . . .

Holding IRBs, and the institutions that house them, responsible in tort for injuries to research subjects would stretch the boundaries of conventional tort doctrine . . . . As with other traditional negligence actions, courts first would have to determine, as a matter of law, whether IRBs and the institutions in which they operate owe a duty of care to research participants that might support a finding of liability. In cases where courts conclude that such a duty exists, they must then define its scope and consider whether the IRB breached this duty of care.

How might a court justify a conclusion that an IRB-a relatively distant entity with no direct relationship to research subjects — owes a duty of care to these individuals? Courts typically consider a variety of factors in deciding whether a duty of care exists in a particular context. Although no contractual relationship exists between an IRB and subjects of research conducted by an unrelated investigator, the subjects are intended third-party beneficiaries of the agreements between the institution, the board, and the researcher. In the research setting, a court might reason that the IRB voluntarily has undertaken the task of protecting research subjects (even if they do not know this) and in fact exists solely for that purpose; that it has undertaken to protect an identifiable and limited class of individuals (future enrollees in the study); and that the protected group reasonably relies on that IRB to provide responsible research oversight.

In addition, public policy arguments support the imposition of a duty of care on IRBs. Although institutions typically furnish necessary medical care to treat research subject injuries free of charge, the current regulatory system permits institutions to refuse to provide financial compensation for injuries incurred during research procedures. That fact, combined with the reality that some researchers are likely to be judgment-proof, while their institutions have significant resources and derive financial rewards from the research, supports an argument that IRBs and/or the institutions that house them should provide appropriate compensation. . . .

Assuming that IRBs have a tort-based duty to protect research subjects, how far does it extend? Courts must calibrate the scope of the duty appropriately in order to address competing concerns about the effects of imposing such a duty on IRBs. The paucity of litigation against IRBs to this point leaves the question of the appropriate standard of care unresolved. Theoretically, courts simply could apply a general standard of negligence — namely, an obligation to act reasonably under the circumstances. Because such an open-ended duty might impose unacceptable constraints on the progress of research, however, courts should attempt to place some more precise limitations on the scope of the duty.

. . . .

Ideally . . . [b]ecause actual customary practice remains inadequate, courts . . . should describe the scope of the duty in terms of the aspirational standards set out in ethical guidelines such as the Nuremberg Code and the Declaration of Helsinki, layered onto the basic regulatory requirements. The international research community created these guidelines through a thoughtful, collaborative approach, using the collective experience of scientists and ethicists, and they command significant respect among experts on clinical research ethics. Such an approach would create a higher standard of care than a simple regulatory compliance approach, while at the same time avoiding the adverse consequences of an open-ended general negligence standard.

. . . .

IV. CONCLUSION

. . . .

A variety of changes in the human research "machine," including overwork, lack of expertise and training, and greater conflicts of interest, pose formidable challenges to the protection of human subjects and likely will serve as a basis for a proliferation of negligence claims against IRBs and the institutions that house them. This litigation trend is not necessarily cause for hand-wringing. Although IRBs strive to protect human research subjects from harm and are largely successful in their efforts, these boards labor under less than ideal circumstances that contribute to a tendency towards shortcuts and misjudgments. The regulations serve as a starting point for resolving difficult ethical and scientific problems in proposed research, but truly effective human subjects protection requires IRBs to exceed the minimal regulatory requirements for the protection of research subjects.

This endeavor will require more financial and institutional support, better training, and more specialized expertise. Institutions also must work to foster a cooperative mindset between clinical researchers and the supervising IRB, helping researchers to view the board as a partner in clinical investigations — an entity that can help to assure the highest ethical standards and thereby protect the value and validity of the scientific results — rather than as an obstacle to successful research. Increased regulatory surveillance and guidance also may help to enhance IRB performance. Courts certainly ought to be attentive to concerns about broad expansion of IRB duties of care. Realistically, however, holding IRBs accountable in negligence for the injuries that result from their shortcomings will serve as an efficient catalyst for meaningful improvement to the system of human subjects protections.

NOTES

1. Professor Noah argues that the Nuremberg Code — developed in the wake of Nazi atrocities involving human research subjects — and the Declaration of Helsinki — developed by the World Medical Association using the Nuremberg Code as a template — should themselves serve as a template for the standard of care that should be applied to Institutional Review Boards. The Nuremberg Code provides:

> a. The voluntary consent of the human subject is absolutely essential. This means that the person involved should have legal capacity to give consent; should be so situated as to be able to exercise free power of choice, without the intervention of any element of force, fraud, deceit, duress, over-reaching, or other ulterior form of constraint or coercion; and should have sufficient knowledge and comprehension of the elements of the subject matter involved as to enable him to make an understanding and enlightened decision. This latter element requires that before the acceptance of an affirmative decision by the experimental subject there should be made known to him the nature, duration, and purpose of the experiment; the method and means by which it is to be conducted; all inconveniences and hazards reasonable to be expected; and the effects upon his health or person which may possibly come from his participation in the experiment.
>
> The duty and responsibility for ascertaining the quality of the consent rests upon each individual who initiates, directs or engages in the experiment. It is a personal duty and responsibility which may not be delegated to another with impunity.

b. The experiment should be such as to yield fruitful results for the good of society, unprocurable by other methods or means of study, and not random and unnecessary in nature.

c. The experiment should be so designed and based on the results of animal experimentation and knowledge of the natural history of the disease or other problem under study that the anticipated results will justify the performance of the experiment.

d. The experiment should be so conducted as to avoid all unnecessary physical and mental suffering and injury.

e. No experiment should be conducted where there is an a priori reason to believe that death or disabling injury will occur; except, perhaps, in those experiments where the experimental physicians also serve as subjects.

f. The degree of risk to be taken should never exceed that determined by the humanitarian importance of the problem to be solved by the experiment.

g. Proper preparations should be made and adequate facilities provided to protect the experimental subject against even remote possibilities of injury, disability, or death.

h. The experiment should be conducted only by scientifically qualified persons. The highest degree of skill and care should be required through all stages of the experiment of those who conduct or engage in the experiment.

i. During the course of the experiment the human subject should be at liberty to bring the experiment to an end if he has reached the physical or mental state where continuation of the experiment seems to him to be impossible.

j. During the course of the experiment the scientist in charge must be prepared to terminate the experiment at any stage, if he has probable cause to believe, in the exercise of the good faith, superior skill and careful judgment required of him that a continuation of the experiment is likely to result in injury, disability, or death to the experimental subject.

Office of Human Subjects Research, Nat'l Inst. of Health, Regulations and Ethical Guidelines: Nuremberg Code (1949), *available at* http://history.nih.gov/research/downloads/nuremberg.pdf. For a copy of the Declaration of Helsinki, see World Med. Ass'n, Declaration of Helsinki: Ethical Principles for Medical Research Involving Human Subjects (2008), *available at* http://www.wma.net/en/30publications/10policies/b3/index.html.

For an argument that a lenient standard of care should be applied to IRBs, similar to the business judgment rule that is applied to corporate decision making, see Carla M. Stalcup, Note, *Reviewing the Review Boards: Why Institutional Review Board Liability Does Not Make Good Business Sense*, 82 Wash. U. L. Q. 1593 (2004).

As a matter of policy, if you were a member of a university advisory board that was trying to develop new regulations to minimize the liability of the school's research operations, and if the state of the law involving IRBs remained in question, would the Nuremberg Code provide enough guidance in the crafting of those regulations? Is the Nuremberg Code any different from the aspirational goals of existing federal regulations and IRB policies? *See, e.g.*, General Research Policies, Ohio State Univ. Office of Research Compliance (2009), *available at* http://orc.osu.edu/resources/.

Consider this: what if you were a judge trying to develop a standard of care for IRBs? Should the standard of care be based on research best practices, or should it be based on more of a medical or legal malpractice standard, that is, a researcher in good standing in the community?

2. Should research colleges and universities reform their Institutional Review Boards in the spirit of recent reforms applicable to corporate boards? The Sarbanes-Oxley Act of 2002, 116 Stat. 745, for example, requires increased director independence and monitoring oversight. But can the corporate regulations cross over to the IRB context?

> IRBs and corporate boards suffer from remarkably similar drawbacks regarding their structure, composition, procedures, and operations. All of these factors combine to make these entities imperfect monitoring agents to represent the interests of their purported principals-research subjects and shareholders. For example, individuals serving on IRBs and corporate boards face enormous conformity pressures and possible social sanctions for aggressive oversight. They can become entangled in and compromised by complex, personal relationships with each other and the very actors they are supposed to monitor. Additionally, IRBs and corporate boards are comprised of a mix of "inside" and "outside" interests. Corporate boards ordinarily include "inside" directors who are directly employed by the firm and "outside" directors, non-employees who are nominally more independent. Similarly, IRBs include "inside" members, typically researchers and other personnel who work within the institution, as well as "outside" members, usually non-scientists drawn from the larger community who have no affiliation with the institution. This inside/outside mix is fraught with complications in terms of how it affects a board's or IRB's overall monitoring effectiveness.
>
> More generally, IRBs and corporate boards share a significant degree of insularity. They operate largely free from the controlling influence of individual research subjects and shareholders. Additionally, IRB members and corporate directors suffer from similar informational and time constraints in performing their duties. While IRB members and corporate directors are expected to exert monitoring effort, there exist disappointingly few clear external incentives for them to do so. As so much depends upon the goodwill and commitment of dedicated individuals serving on the boards, the effective performance of IRBs and corporate boards becomes quite difficult to ensure. Goodwill and commitment can be in short supply and, in any event, cannot compensate for all the inherent problems with corporate board and IRB review. IRBs and corporate boards raise the same critical challenge for health law and corporate law: who is monitoring

the monitors? Moreover, why should these oversight bodies be trusted and even expected to do a good job?

. . . .

The IRB-corporate board comparison does much more than simply highlight a monitoring trade-off dilemma [wherein researchers lose their trust of and willingness to work with IRBs that step up their monitoring function]. The experience of corporate boards can help in predicting how particular changes in structure, mandate, and procedures will likely affect an IRB's overall performance. This Part preliminarily explores such implications of the corporate governance perspective by considering two significant IRB reform proposals currently attracting much support: (1) attempts to increase the number of outside, community members serving on IRBs; and (2) calls for IRBs to take on a more direct role in reviewing financial conflicts of interest.

. . . .

In theory, increasing the outside presence on IRBs offers several important advantages for improving IRB oversight. A greater number of outside members could have more practical success, through the force of sheer numbers, in getting the IRB to consider layperson and noninstitutional viewpoints. Additional outside members could help establish stronger links between the IRB and the greater community, enhancing perceptions of the IRB's legitimacy. They also could serve as a sounding board for researcher and inside IRB members seeking insight about layperson and other professionals' perspectives. Moreover, the very prospect of having their protocols reviewed and discussed by a sizable number of outside members can encourage researchers to take more care in designing protocols. Presumably, they would be concerned about wider exposure of potentially questionable research activities, as well as anticipate receiving a qualitatively different level of scrutiny from outside members, as compared to insiders.

But the corporate governance perspective cautions that merely adding more outside members offers no simple, quick-fix remedy. Indeed, there are limits to how much numerical changes in the insider/outsider mix, without more, can realistically affect board operations. The corporate board experience teaches that pursuit of shareholder interests and active monitoring do not go hand in hand with outside status. With regard to corporate boards, the traditional label of outside director may not entirely reflect that director's capacity for independence. True independence turns on the director's state of mind and willingness to act, including readiness to buck management. An outside director, although not employed by the firm, may still have significant business and financial relationships with the company that affect his willingness to challenge management. Indeed, for this reason the new NYSE and NASDAQ listing requirements have tried to define "independent" directors for public corporations more narrowly, accounting for such financial ties.

Even if an outside director avoids significant business relationships with the firm, however, the outside status still does not mean that director will vigorously represent shareholders as a truly independent director. In other words, "[g]ood character and financial independence from management may be necessary conditions for effective monitoring, but they are hardly sufficient." A number of additional factors can affect an outside director's monitoring ability. First, and critically important, many outside directors have on-going personal relationships or socially identify with the firm's senior executives. Such outside directors can face considerable social pressures. Indeed, in the recent *In re Oracle Corp. Derivative Litigation* proceeding, the Delaware Court of Chancery recognized the degree to which social ties and other affiliations between directors and management can compromise an outside director's capacity for independence. The court questioned whether two outside directors, both Stanford University professors, could maintain sufficient independence in evaluating insider trading allegations against a fellow colleague at their university in light of other personal relationships between the outside directors and the interested parties.

. . . .

Plus, as previously discussed, any director, whether inside or outside, has few clear incentives to consider shareholder views when making board decisions. A nominally independent director may have joined the board primarily to increase his social reputation and because of perceived perks of director service, and thus care very little about the monitoring role and seeking shareholder input.

. . . .

Financial conflicts of interest "have come center-stage" as one of the most pressing challenges confronting human subjects research today. The private sector finances a greater percentage of medical research today than in the past. The general increase in private sector funding, as well as more commercialization opportunities for researchers and medical centers emanating from publicly funded studies, have spawned a plethora of funding arrangements and related financial conflicts of interest. The powerful economic incentives provide rewards for enrolling subjects and completing a greater volume of clinical trials speedily and with favorable results. Consequently, the objectivity of the research and the welfare of the participating subjects can be significantly compromised.

The push to do something more about financial conflicts of interest has extended to IRBs. For most of their history, IRBs have occupied an uncertain, ill-defined, and relatively passive role in policing financial ties in clinical research. For example, neither the general IRB regulations, nor the existing financial conflict of interest requirements imposed by the FDA regulations, the Public Health Service (PHS) regulations, and the funding policies of the National Science Foundation (NSF) clearly require an IRB to evaluate financial conflicts in deciding whether to approve or disapprove a research protocol. The research regulations and federal agency funding policies also have not clearly required disclosure of financial conflicts to potential research subjects. Accordingly, IRBs traditionally did not investigate financial conflicts when performing protocol review. Nor have IRBs ordinarily scrutinized consent forms for full disclosure of any financial ties. The Office of Inspector General found that seventy-five percent of IRBs do not review any financial arrangements between sponsors and investigators. Although such practices may be changing in light of increased concern regarding financial conflicts, for many decades IRBs rarely took an active role in such matters.

Now, however, many urge IRBs to do much more. The National Bioethics Advisory Commission has recommended that IRBs investigate financial arrangements as part of the risk/benefit analysis done for overall protocol review and determine what information needs to be disclosed to research subjects. Academic commentators have similarly advocated for more direct involvement by IRBs in monitoring financial conflicts. In a significant new regulatory development, the Department of Health and Human Services (HHS) has promulgated guidance that envisions considerable expansion of IRB activities in this area. HHS recommends that IRBs consider whether methods "used for management of financial interests of parties involved in the research adequately protect the rights and welfare of human subjects." The HHS guidance also cautions IRBs to consider, before approving a protocol, whether additional corrective actions are required to minimize the risks subjects face in light of any conflicting financial interests.

. . . .

Unfortunately, the corporate governance perspective cautions that an increased role for IRBs in reviewing financial conflicts of interest may be misguided and prove disappointing. Corporate boards, unlike IRBs, have a well-developed track record in reviewing financial conflicts of interest. Indeed, corporate statutes encourage the firm to obtain the approval of disinterested, independent directors on the board for a transaction raising conflict of interest problems. Whether independent directors have performed well in this assigned role is another story. For example, in the Enron fiasco, a board comprised overwhelmingly of outside directors nonetheless performed dismally in monitoring financial conflicts of interest for key senior executives. Similarly, empirical studies of corporate board action in setting CEO compensation do not necessarily support the view that the participation of nominally independent, outside directors has a clearly measurable impact in controlling potential financial conflicts of interest for the firm's top executive. Boards with greater participation by outside directors in the compensation process do not determine executive compensation in a manner markedly different from boards with less participation by outsiders.

. . . .

This evidence does not bode well for IRBs. Currently, IRBs have very few outside members. Meanwhile, financial ties to industry already compromise the potential objectivity of many inside IRB members. A recent study indicates that almost half of all faculty IRB members have served as consultants to pharmaceutical or medical device companies, calling into question whether such inside IRB members can sufficiently distance themselves from industry and neutrally evaluate potential financial conflicts faced by fellow investigators and their respective institutions. Expecting that the typical board's one to two outside members will do all the heavy work of financial conflicts review seems unrealistic. Moreover, hoping the outside members can stand up to powerful institutional and investigator constituencies and take the uncomfortable position of regularly challenging investigator and institutional financial conflicts — especially when the other faculty IRB members already have so many ties to industry — may simply be too much to ask.

This difficulty points to a related expertise and capacity problem for IRB review of financial conflicts. IRBs may be even less suited to do this type of review than corporate boards. The typical outside director on a corporate board is better trained and equipped to address financial conflict situations than the typical outside member on an IRB. Outside directors include a sizable number of CEOs and senior executives of other companies. They can call upon their business acumen and financial expertise in evaluating numerous economic conflict of interest scenarios, such as considering whether a CEO's proposed compensation package truly aligns the CEO's interests with the firm's performance. Many IRB members reviewing financial conflict of interest situations have no equivalent financial and business background upon which to draw. The complex economic arrangements involved in funding clinical trials can include the award of stock contingent on certain occurrences, licensing rights, "put" options, seed money for commercial start-ups, limited partnership and other joint venture opportunities, royalty-based payments, and specialized grant funding to individual investigators and to institutions. These arrangements raise complicated, arcane financial issues far beyond what the ordinary IRB member is used to seeing.

. . . .

Richard S. Saver, *Medical Research Oversight from the Corporate Governance Perspective: Comparing Institutional Review Boards and Corporate Boards*, 46 Wm. & Mary L. Rev. 619, 630–31, 699, 700–02, 710–12, 713–14, 715–16 (2004).* Are Professor Saver's observations about outside directors really applicable to IRB members? There is certainly something to the contention that many outside corporate directors join corporate boards for the prestige and the compensation (through direct payments and stock options), and thus have little incentive to closely monitor the corporation. But can outside IRB board members count on that same level of prestige and compensation? If current IRB members are ill-equipped to monitor conflicts of interest and other financial issues, would it not make good sense to have an outside member or two who could handle those matters? On a more fundamental level, given the deep interconnections between industry and research institutions, is trying to eliminate conflicts of interest akin to tilting at windmills?

3. Are the extensive federal consent requirements for IRBs really a form of prior restraint that restrict researchers' freedom of speech? Consider this:

> The danger of the IRB laws is evident from their practical implications for teachers and students who do human subjects research. Such persons need permission to begin their research; they need permission to continue the research; they need permission to observe, ask questions, talk, or take notes; indeed, they need permission to use data received from other scholars, to analyze much already published data, and to share, disclose, or otherwise publish significant elements of what they learn. Sometimes they are denied permission altogether. More typically, they are partly denied permission in a process by which IRBs withhold consent unless researchers modify their plans. Although an IRB can thereby require a researcher not to engage in some types of physical contact, it more typically interferes with the researcher's words — for example, by refusing permission unless he agrees not to ask, say, look at, write down, keep records of, disclose, or otherwise publish what the IRB does not want him to ask, say, etc. In such ways, IRBs censor the entire range of observation, inquiry, recording, talking, writing, and publishing protected by the First Amendment, and far from making a single outrageous assault on this Amendment, IRBs modify or censor well over 100,000 research proposals every year in the United States and stifle countless others that get abandoned or never get started. As a result, IRBs bar important avenues of research — even in fields involving techniques no more dangerous than observation, reading, asking questions, and printing.

Philip Hamburger, *Getting Permission*, 101 Nw. U.L. Rev. 405, 406–07 (2007).* For an opposing argument, see James Weinstein, *Institutional Review Boards and the Constitution*, 101 Nw. U.L. Rev. 493 (2007).

4. Do universities unnecessarily bind themselves to IRB oversight and regulation which results in limited academic freedom?

> Notice the unsettling irony in the current IRB regulatory situation at most U.S. universities and colleges. There is no legal requirement to universalize the IRB process beyond federally funded projects. Consequently, OHRP, DHHS, and other federal agencies have structured the FWA form in such a way that academic administrators are offered the opportunity to decide for themselves whether to over regulate their own faculties, which they typically do; at the same time, preoccupied members of faculty ruling bodies, unaware of the legal alternatives, allow this to be done. Those who value academic freedom (university faculty and university administrators) just give it away, readily, passively, and unnecessarily.
>
> . . . .

> Given the options now explicitly offered by the DHHS and OHRP on the FWA form, we (members of the academy: administrators, faculty, and students) can no longer blame the federal government for our own internal ethical-oversight policies with regard to research that is not federally funded. It is not DHHS or OHRP (or NSF) that requires everyone who does research with human beings (regardless of funding source) to fully formulate and declare what they are doing before they do it. It is not DHHS or OHRP (or NSF) that stipulates that privately funded, personally funded, and unfunded researchers (faculty and students) must annually seek and receive permission from an appointed board of local academics and a member of the nonacademic public (an IRB is composed of both) to do research at all. We have only ourselves to blame, which is not necessarily a bad thing, because it means we have the option to reform the system.

Richard A. Shweder, *Protecting Human Subjects and Preserving Academic Freedom*, 33 AM. ETHNOLOGIST 507, 509–10 (2006).*

5. Professor Noah concludes that IRBs require "more financial and institutional support, better training, and more specialized expertise" in order to better regulate human testing. Who should bear those costs? If the corporation bears the costs, they will have to pay universities more for research and clinical testing, resulting in higher overall costs passed on to consumers. Socially, is there a cost-benefit equilibrium we are comfortable with? In other words, how much IRB oversight does society require in order to protect human testing participants while still producing medicine and procedures that potentially improve thousands of peoples' quality of life? Would you be comfortable with spending $5,000,000 on IRB oversight if it produced a 70% chance of curing cancer but posed a 15% chance of death to human participants? Would you change your response if spending $50,000,000 on IRB oversight if it produced a 30% chance of curing cancer but posed only a 3% chance of death to human participants?

6. Informed-consent suits, one of the most common suits that result from human testing, are private actions that patients can bring against their doctors for treatments and procedures that result in injury if the doctor failed to reasonably inform the patient concerning the risks involved. It is typically brought as a cause of action under state law, and varies from state to state, but it generally is comprised of the same elements. One Massachusetts court succinctly enunciated the principles underlying the claim:

> Under Massachusetts law, to recover under a theory of informed consent, a plaintiff must show (1) that his doctor had a duty to disclose the information in question, and (2) that the doctor's breach of that duty caused the plaintiff's injury. The "duty" prong of this analysis comprises four elements. A plaintiff must prove (a) a sufficiently close doctor-patient relationship; (b) that the doctor knew or should have known of the information allegedly not disclosed; (c) that the doctor should reasonably

> have recognized that this information would be material to the patient; and (d) that the doctor failed to disclose this information. The "causation" prong of this analysis then requires a plaintiff to show that the unrevealed risk materialized, and that, had the proper information been provided, neither he nor a reasonable person in similar circumstances would have undergone the procedure.

Harrison v. United States, 233 F. Supp. 2d 128, 132 (D. Mass. 2002) (citations omitted).

7. Human research constitutes only one area of university research. For example, engineering and technology departments generate a significant revenue stream for many universities, especially since legislation in the 1980s that encouraged corporate-university research and development.

> Beginning in the 1980s, a series of legislative and policy changes were enacted in the United States to promote university-industry partnerships. Notable among these were the Bayh-Dole Act of 1980, which permitted universities to retain the property rights of innovations arising out of federally-funded projects and the Stevenson-Wydler Technology Innovation Act of 1980, which directed agencies with research budgets to allocate 5 percent of R&D funds to technology transfer. The Economic Recovery Tax Act of 1981 provided a tax credit for incremental increases in research and development (R&D). These acts were intended to aid economic development, boost US economic competitiveness, and augment university R&D budgets.
>
> The new legislation was enacted against the backdrop of important economic and political change. By the late 1970s, American business had lost the global advantage it gained in the aftermath of World War II, and the country faced both recession and inflation. The Reagan and Bush administrations were oriented toward privatization and deregulation as a stimulus to economic growth. Eliminating the "bottleneck" between university research and commercial application was identified by Republican policy makers as a potential source of renewed advantage in the marketplace, at the same time that industry funding of research was seen as an alternative to federal funding.
>
> Universities had their own reasons for interest in new partnerships with industry. They faced shrinking R&D budgets as funds from federal sources declined. By establishing or expanding ties with industry, universities saw the opportunity to increase their resources for research and to enhance their reputations. Changes in organized science further encouraged university interests in expanding technology transfer. Time from discovery to application had been shrinking, while the scale of research in the sciences and applied sciences continued to grow. Thus, the interest of leaders in government, industry, and universities converged just enough for the establishment of a more attractive environment for university-industry partnerships.

Of course, some universities had long been involved with industry. From the time of their founding, the land grant universities were expected to contribute to the economic vitality of their states, and some private universities with strong engineering programs also encouraged collaborative relations with industry from the beginning (MIT and Stanford are noteworthy examples). Citing these historical examples, some researchers have argued that the new industry partnerships of the 1980s and 1990s did not substantially alter the priorities of research universities.

Most researchers, however, have argued that the scale and nature of university-industry partnerships during the 1980s and 1990s set them apart from earlier, more limited collaborations. The increase in the number of ties, and especially in the magnitude of investments, has been sizeable, whether one measures patenting, licensing, or industry expenditures on university R&D. Perhaps equally important, the conditions under which grants are made have also changed dramatically. Unrestricted funding, which allowed universities to define how funds would be used, comprised a larger share of R&D funding from industry before the 1980s. Over the last quarter century, relationships have been increasingly based on restricted funds targeting specific research. This can have a significant impact on the way individuals and even units conduct research, skewing effort toward commercially attractive projects.

Lori Turk-Bicakci & Steven Brint, *University-Industry Collaboration: Patterns of Growth for Low- and Middle-Level Performers*, 49 Higher Educ. 61, 63–64 (2005) (citations omitted).*

Is industrial R&D on university campuses commercialization of the education process, or is it a source of revenue for universities and a practicum for students to acquire skills that translate to the workplace? Just how much has university R&D benefited the economy? Consider this:

University research creates more than 29 billion dollars in economic activity and more than 246,000 jobs. This data are based on reports delivered by 175 institutions which include 132 universities, research centers and companies that exploit the patents.

All these institutions produced in year 1997 11,303 new discoveries as a consequence of their research activities and 2,465 patents. A total of 333 startup companies were reported in the survey. The University of Washington had 25 startups, MIT had 17, Stanford had 15 and Berkeley 13. Eighty-three percent of all start-ups were located in the same state as the research university or other patent generator. Since 1980 (till 1997), 2,214 new entrepreneurial ventures have been created to commercialize university technologies. Of these, nearly half (1,045) were formed in the period 1993-1997.

In 1997, academic institution signed 3,328 new licenses and options with industrial companies and received $611 million in royalties and fees. The

> top earners included the University of Berkeley ($61.3 million), Columbia (46.1), Stanford (34), Florida (29.9), MIT (19.8), Michigan (18.3), Wisconsin (11.2), Harvard (13.4) and Yale (13). Universities reinvest the major portion of their licensing revenues into teaching and research activities. In patents (1997): Berkeley (206), MIT (134), Wisconsin (69), Minnesota (66), Stanford (65), Cornell (62). In licenses (1997): Berkeley (528), Stanford (272), MIT (255), Harvard (232), Columbia (201). With these licenses, most of them exclusive, companies have their rights granted in exchange of their commitment to develop inventions and yield them to products.

Gregorio Martin Quetglas, *Aspects of University Research and Transfer to Private Industry*, 39 J. BUS. ETHICS 51, 53 (2002).*

8. Who owns the rights to genetic material obtained in the course of university research? University research often involves the collection of genetic material from participants. When a research participant provides genetic material as part of an experiment, do they lose all rights to that material? The answer to this question generally is yes: donors receive no rights to their DNA, receive no financial benefit from either donating their genetic material or any revenue derived from the usage of their DNA, and have no say in what researchers do with their DNA once it is collected. *See* Gary Marchant, *Property Rights and Benefit-Sharing for DNA Donors?*, 45 JURIMETRICS J. 153, 155 (2005).

The leading case in this area is *Moore v. Regents of California*, 793 P.2d 479 (Cal. 1990). In that case researchers used a donor's spleen to patent an apparently lucrative cell line. The donor alleged that the researchers did not properly inform him of their intent to use his tissue in for-profit work and that he had a property interest in his cells that the researchers had improperly converted. *Id.* The California Supreme Court rejected the donor's argument on the basis that, because cell lines are frequently copied, creating such a property interest would impose a duty on every researcher to ensure that they had not acquired the cells from a non-consenting party. *Id.* at 161–63. This strict liability would economically disincentivize crucial medical research. *Id.*

Further, who would own the rights to that genetic material: the researcher or the university? In one case, a university challenged a former researcher's rights to use genetic material obtained while conducting research at the university. *Wash. Univ. v. Catalona*, 490 F.3d 667 (8th Cir. 2007). The court determined that the genetic material was a gift donated by the participants, based on the wording of the informed consent agreement required by the experiment. *Id.* at 676. Additionally, the court found that the university, not the researcher, was the recipient of this inter vivos gift and had the sole rights to use the genetic material. *Id.*. Why would the university want the rights to genetic material used in experiments on campus? How could an informed consent agreement be worded to avoid this outcome?

9. University researchers can face serious career consequences if denied approval or investigated by an Institution Review Board. One researcher brought suit against a university after the IRB publicly investigated the ethical elements of his medical experiment on human subjects — after he had received approval and voluntarily ended the experiment. *Halikas v. Univ. of Minn.*, 856 F. Supp. 1331 (D. Minn. 1994). The IRB publicly suspended the researcher's ability to perform or participate in any experiments involving human subjects, including those projects unrelated to the experiment at issue. *Id.* at 1334. The university-tenured professor alleged that the IRB's review process and investigations failed to meet the standards of due process as required by the Fourteenth Amendment. Among other things, the researcher alleged that the IRB's actions would create "irreparable harm to his reputation and career" without judicial intervention. *Id.* at 1334. Ultimately, the court found that the university's interests in protecting human subjects and maintaining safe and ethical research standards outweighed the researcher's interests in his reputation and career. *Id.* at 1336. Should IRB procedures and decisions be public? Why would due process rights attach or not attach to the IRB procedures? Should university researchers have any rights in the IRB process?

C. FEDERAL TAXATION OF POSTSECONDARY INSTITUTIONS

BOB JONES UNIVERSITY v. UNITED STATES

461 U.S. 574 (1983)

Chief Justice Burger delivered the opinion of the Court.

We granted certiorari to decide whether petitioners, nonprofit private schools that prescribe and enforce racially discriminatory admissions standards on the basis of religious doctrine, qualify as tax-exempt organizations under § 501(c)(3) of the Internal Revenue Code of 1954.

I

A

Until 1970, the Internal Revenue Service granted tax-exempt status to private schools, without regard to their racial admissions policies, under § 501(c)(3) of the Internal Revenue Code, 26 U.S.C. § 501(c)(3),[1] and granted charitable deductions

---

[1] Section 501(c)(3) lists the following organizations, which, pursuant to § 501(a), are exempt from taxation unless denied tax exemptions under other specified sections of the Code:

> "Corporations, and any community chest, fund, or foundation, *organized and operated exclusively for religious, charitable*, scientific, testing for public safety, literary, *or educational purposes*, or to foster national or international amateur sports competition (but only if no part of its activities involve the provision of athletic facilities or equipment), or for the prevention of cruelty to children or animals, no part of the net earnings of which inures to the benefit of any private shareholder or individual, no substantial part of the activities of which is carrying on propaganda, or otherwise attempting, to influence legislation . . ., and which does not participate in, or intervene in (including the publishing or distributing of statements), any political campaign on behalf of any candidate for public office." (Emphasis added.)

for contributions to such schools under § 170 of the Code, 26 U.S.C. § 170.[2]

On January 12, 1970, a three-judge District Court for the District of Columbia issued a preliminary injunction prohibiting the IRS from according tax-exempt status to private schools in Mississippi that discriminated as to admissions on the basis of race. *Green v. Kennedy*, 309 F. Supp. 1127, *appeal dism'd sub nom. Cannon v. Green*, 398 U.S. 956 (1970). Thereafter, in July 1970, the IRS concluded that it could "no longer legally justify allowing tax-exempt status [under § 501(c)(3)] to private schools which practice racial discrimination." At the same time, the IRS announced that it could not "treat gifts to such schools as charitable deductions for income tax purposes [under § 170]." By letter dated November 30, 1970, the IRS formally notified private schools, including those involved in this litigation, of this change in policy, "applicable to all private schools in the United States at all levels of education."

On June 30, 1971, the three-judge District Court issued its opinion on the merits of the Mississippi challenge. *Green v. Connally*, 330 F. Supp. 1150, *summarily aff'd sub nom. Coit v. Green*, 404 U.S. 997 (1971). That court approved the IRS's amended construction of the Tax Code. The court also held that racially discriminatory private schools were not entitled to exemption under § 501(c)(3) and that donors were not entitled to deductions for contributions to such schools under § 170. The court permanently enjoined the Commissioner of Internal Revenue from approving tax-exempt status for any school in Mississippi that did not publicly maintain a policy of nondiscrimination.

The revised policy on discrimination was formalized in Revenue Ruling 71-447, 1971-2 Cum. Bull. 230:

> "Both the courts and the Internal Revenue Service have long recognized that the statutory requirement of being 'organized and operated exclusively for religious, charitable, . . . or educational purposes' was intended to express the basic common law concept [of 'charity']. . . . All charitable trusts, educational or otherwise, are subject to the requirement that the purpose of the trust may not be illegal or contrary to public policy."

Based on the "national policy to discourage racial discrimination in education," the IRS ruled that "a [private] school not having a racially nondiscriminatory policy as to students is not 'charitable' within the common law concepts reflected in sections 170 and 501(c)(3) of the Code." *Id.*, at 231.

The application of the IRS construction of these provisions to petitioners, two private schools with racially discriminatory admissions policies, is now before us.

---

[2] Section 170(a) allows deductions for certain "charitable contributions." Section 170(c)(2)(B) includes within the definition of "charitable contribution" a contribution or gift to or for the use of a corporation "organized and operated exclusively for religious, charitable, scientific, literary, or educational purposes. . . ."

B

No. 81-3, Bob Jones University v. United States

Bob Jones University is a nonprofit corporation located in Greenville, S. C. Its purpose is "to conduct an institution of learning . . . , giving special emphasis to the Christian religion and the ethics revealed in the Holy Scriptures." The corporation operates a school with an enrollment of approximately 5,000 students, from kindergarten through college and graduate school. Bob Jones University is not affiliated with any religious denomination, but is dedicated to the teaching and propagation of its fundamentalist Christian religious beliefs. It is both a religious and educational institution. Its teachers are required to be devout Christians, and all courses at the University are taught according to the Bible. Entering students are screened as to their religious beliefs, and their public and private conduct is strictly regulated by standards promulgated by University authorities.

The sponsors of the University genuinely believe that the Bible forbids interracial dating and marriage. To effectuate these views, Negroes were completely excluded until 1971. From 1971 to May 1975, the University accepted no applications from unmarried Negroes, but did accept applications from Negroes married within their race.

Following the decision of the United States Court of Appeals for the Fourth Circuit in *McCrary v. Runyon*, 515 F.2d 1082 (1975), *aff'd*, 427 U.S. 160 (1976), prohibiting racial exclusion from private schools, the University revised its policy. Since May 29, 1975, the University has permitted unmarried Negroes to enroll; but a disciplinary rule prohibits interracial dating and marriage. . . .

. . . .

The University continues to deny admission to applicants engaged in an interracial marriage or known to advocate interracial marriage or dating.

Until 1970, the IRS extended tax-exempt status to Bob Jones University under § 501(c)(3). By the letter of November 30, 1970, that followed the injunction issued in *Green v. Kennedy*, 309 F. Supp. 1127 (DC 1970), the IRS formally notified the University of the change in IRS policy, and announced its intention to challenge the tax-exempt status of private schools practicing racial discrimination in their admissions policies.

[The University subsequently tried and failed to enjoin the IRS from revoking the school's tax-exempt status.]

Thereafter, on April 16, 1975, the IRS notified the University of the proposed revocation of its tax-exempt status. On January 19, 1976, the IRS officially revoked the University's tax-exempt status, effective as of December 1, 1970, the day after the University was formally notified of the change in IRS policy. The University subsequently filed returns under the Federal Unemployment Tax Act for the period from December 1, 1970, to December 31, 1975, and paid a tax totaling $21 on one employee for the calendar year of 1975. After its request for a refund was denied, the University instituted the present action, seeking to recover the $21 it had paid to the IRS. The Government counterclaimed for unpaid federal unemployment taxes for the taxable years 1971 through 1975, in the amount of $489,675.59, plus interest.

The United States District Court for the District of South Carolina held that revocation of the University's tax-exempt status exceeded the delegated powers of the IRS, was improper under the IRS rulings and procedures, and violated the University's rights under the Religion Clauses of the First Amendment. The court accordingly ordered the IRS to pay the University the $21 refund it claimed and rejected the IRS's counterclaim.

The Court of Appeals for the Fourth Circuit, in a divided opinion, reversed. . . . [T]he Court of Appeals concluded that § 501(c)(3) must be read against the background of charitable trust law. To be eligible for an exemption under that section, an institution must be "charitable" in the common-law sense, and therefore must not be contrary to public policy. In the court's view, Bob Jones University did not meet this requirement, since its "racial policies violated the clearly defined public policy, rooted in our Constitution, condemning racial discrimination and, more specifically, the government policy against subsidizing racial discrimination in education, public or private." The court held that the IRS acted within its statutory authority in revoking the University's tax-exempt status. Finally, the Court of Appeals rejected petitioner's arguments that the revocation of the tax exemption violated the Free Exercise and Establishment Clauses of the First Amendment. The case was remanded to the District Court with instructions to dismiss the University's claim for a refund and to reinstate the IRS's counterclaim.

C

No. 81-1, Goldsboro Christian Schools, Inc. v. United States

[The IRS also revoked the tax-exempt status of a Christian school in North Carolina. The school, which offered classes from kindergarten through high school, maintained a racially discriminatory admissions policy, primarily accepting Caucasians only. The school filed suit, and the revocation of its tax-exempt status was eventually upheld by the Fourth Circuit.]

We granted certiorari in both cases, 454 U.S. 892 (1981), and we affirm in each.

II

A

In Revenue Ruling 71-447, the IRS formalized the policy, first announced in 1970, that § 170 and § 501(c)(3) embrace the common-law "charity" concept. Under that view, to qualify for a tax exemption pursuant to § 501(c)(3), an institution must show, first, that it falls within one of the . . . categories expressly set forth in that section, and second, that its activity is not contrary to settled public policy.

Section 501(c)(3) provides that "[corporations] . . . organized and operated exclusively for religious, charitable . . . or educational purposes" are entitled to tax exemption. Petitioners argue that the plain language of the statute guarantees them tax-exempt status. They emphasize the absence of any language in the statute expressly requiring all exempt organizations to be "charitable" in the common-law sense, and they contend that the disjunctive "or" separating the categories in § 501(c)(3) precludes such a reading. Instead, they argue that if an institution falls within one or more of the specified categories it is automatically entitled to exemption, without regard to whether it also qualifies as "charitable." . . .

It is a well-established canon of statutory construction that a court should go beyond the literal language of a statute if reliance on that language would defeat the plain purpose of the statute . . . .

. . . .

Section 501(c)(3) therefore must be analyzed and construed within the framework of the Internal Revenue Code and against the background of the congressional purposes. Such an examination reveals unmistakable evidence that, underlying all relevant parts of the Code, is the intent that entitlement to tax exemption depends on meeting certain common-law standards of charity — namely, that an institution seeking tax-exempt status must serve a public purpose and not be contrary to established public policy.

This "charitable" concept appears explicitly in § 170 of the Code. That section contains a list of organizations virtually identical to that contained in § 501(c)(3). It is apparent that Congress intended that list to have the same meaning in both sections. In § 170, Congress used the list of organizations in defining the term "charitable contributions." On its face, therefore, § 170 reveals that Congress' intention was to provide tax benefits to organizations serving charitable purposes. The form of § 170 simply makes plain what common sense and history tell us: in enacting both § 170 and § 501(c)(3), Congress sought to provide tax benefits to charitable organizations, to encourage the development of private institutions that serve a useful public purpose or supplement or take the place of public institutions of the same kind.

Tax exemptions for certain institutions thought beneficial to the social order of the country as a whole, or to a particular community, are deeply rooted in our history, as in that of England. The origins of such exemptions lie in the special privileges that have long been extended to charitable trusts.

More than a century ago, this Court announced the caveat that is critical in this case:

> "[It] has now become an established principle of American law, that courts of chancery will sustain and protect . . . a gift . . . to public charitable uses, provided the same is consistent with local laws and public policy. . . ." *Perin v. Carey*, 24 How. 465, 501 (1861) (emphasis added).

Soon after that, in 1877, the Court commented:

> "A charitable use, where neither law nor public policy forbids, may be applied to almost any thing that tends to promote the well-doing and well-being of social man." *Ould v. Washington Hospital for Foundlings*, 95 U.S. 303, 311 (emphasis added).

. . . .

These statements clearly reveal the legal background against which Congress enacted the first charitable exemption statute in 1894: charities were to be given preferential treatment because they provide a benefit to society.

What little floor debate occurred on the charitable exemption provision of the 1894 Act and similar sections of later statutes leaves no doubt that Congress deemed the specified organizations entitled to tax benefits because they served desirable public purposes. . . .

. . . .

A corollary to the public benefit principle is the requirement, long recognized in the law of trusts, that the purpose of a charitable trust may not be illegal or violate established public policy. In 1861, this Court stated that a public charitable use must be "consistent with local laws and public policy," *Perin v. Carey*, 24 How., at 501. Modern commentators and courts have echoed that view. *See, e. g.*, RESTATEMENT (SECOND) OF TRUSTS § 377, Comment c (1959); 4 Scott § 377, and cases cited therein; Bogert § 378, at 191-192.

When the Government grants exemptions or allows deductions all taxpayers are affected; the very fact of the exemption or deduction for the donor means that other taxpayers can be said to be indirect and vicarious "donors." Charitable exemptions are justified on the basis that the exempt entity confers a public benefit — a benefit which the society or the community may not itself choose or be able to provide, or which supplements and advances the work of public institutions already supported by tax revenues. History buttresses logic to make clear that, to warrant exemption under § 501(c)(3), an institution must fall within a category specified in that section and must demonstrably serve and be in harmony with the public interest. The institution's purpose must not be so at odds with the common community conscience as to undermine any public benefit that might otherwise be conferred.

B

We are bound to approach these questions with full awareness that determinations of public benefit and public policy are sensitive matters with serious implications for the institutions affected; a declaration that a given institution is not "charitable" should be made only where there can be no doubt that the activity involved is contrary to a fundamental public policy. But there can no longer be any doubt that racial discrimination in education violates deeply and widely accepted views of elementary justice. Prior to 1954, public education in many places still was conducted under the pall of *Plessy v. Ferguson*, 163 U.S. 537 (1896); racial segregation in primary and secondary education prevailed in many parts of the country. This Court's decision in *Brown v. Board of Education*, 347 U.S. 483 (1954), signaled [sic] an end to that era. Over the past quarter of a century, every pronouncement of this Court and myriad Acts of Congress and Executive Orders attest a firm national policy to prohibit racial segregation and discrimination in public education.

An unbroken line of cases following *Brown v. Board of Education* establishes beyond doubt this Court's view that racial discrimination in education violates a most fundamental national public policy, as well as rights of individuals.

. . . .

Congress, in Titles IV and VI of the Civil Rights Act of 1964, Pub. L. 88-352, 78 Stat. 241, 42 U.S.C. §§ 2000c, 2000c-6, 2000d, clearly expressed its agreement that racial discrimination in education violates a fundamental public policy. Other sections of that Act, and numerous enactments since then, testify to the public policy against racial discrimination.

The Executive Branch has consistently placed its support behind eradication of racial discrimination. Several years before this Court's decision in *Brown v. Board of Education, supra*, President Truman issued Executive Orders prohibiting racial discrimination in federal employment decisions, and in classifications for the Selective Service. In 1957, President Eisenhower employed military forces to ensure compliance with federal standards in school desegregation programs. And in 1962, President Kennedy announced:

> "[The] granting of Federal assistance for . . . housing and related facilities from which Americans are excluded because of their race, color, creed, or national origin is unfair, unjust, and inconsistent with the public policy of the United States as manifested in its Constitution and laws."

These are but a few of numerous Executive Orders over the past three decades demonstrating the commitment of the Executive Branch to the fundamental policy of eliminating racial discrimination.

Few social or political issues in our history have been more vigorously debated and more extensively ventilated than the issue of racial discrimination, particularly in education. Given the stress and anguish of the history of efforts to escape from the shackles of the "separate but equal" doctrine of *Plessy v. Ferguson*, it cannot be said that educational institutions that, for whatever reasons, practice racial discrimination, are institutions exercising "beneficial and stabilizing influences in community life," *Walz v. Tax Comm'n*, 397 U.S. 664, 673 (1970), or should be encouraged by having all taxpayers share in their support by way of special tax status.

There can thus be no question that the interpretation of § 170 and § 501(c)(3) announced by the IRS in 1970 was correct. That it may be seen as belated does not undermine its soundness. It would be wholly incompatible with the concepts underlying tax exemption to grant the benefit of tax-exempt status to racially discriminatory educational entities, which "[exert] a pervasive influence on the entire educational process." *Norwood v. Harrison*, [413 U.S. 455] at 469. Whatever may be the rationale for such private schools' policies, and however sincere the rationale may be, racial discrimination in education is contrary to public policy. Racially discriminatory educational institutions cannot be viewed as conferring a public benefit within the "charitable" concept discussed earlier, or within the congressional intent underlying § 170 and § 501(c)(3).

C

Petitioners contend that, regardless of whether the IRS properly concluded that racially discriminatory private schools violate public policy, only Congress can alter the scope of § 170 and § 501(c)(3). Petitioners accordingly argue that the IRS overstepped its lawful bounds in issuing its 1970 and 1971 rulings.

Yet ever since the inception of the Tax Code, Congress has seen fit to vest in those administering the tax laws very broad authority to interpret those laws. In an area as complex as the tax system, the agency Congress vests with administrative responsibility must be able to exercise its authority to meet changing conditions and new problems. Indeed as early as 1918, Congress expressly authorized the Commissioner "to make all needful rules and regulations for the enforcement" of the tax laws. Revenue Act of 1918, ch. 18, § 1309, 40 Stat. 1143. The same provision, so essential to efficient and fair administration of the tax laws, has appeared in Tax Codes ever since, see 26 U.S.C. § 7805(a); and this Court has long recognized the primary authority of the IRS and its predecessors in construing the Internal Revenue Code, *see, e.g., Commissioner v. Portland Cement Co. of Utah*, 450 U.S. 156, 169 (1981); *United States v. Correll*, 389 U.S. 299, 306-307 (1967); *Boske v. Comingore*, 177 U.S. 459, 469-470 (1900).

Congress, the source of IRS authority, can modify IRS rulings it considers improper; and courts exercise review over IRS actions. In the first instance, however, the responsibility for construing the Code falls to the IRS. . . .

In § 170 and § 501(c)(3), Congress has identified categories of traditionally exempt institutions and has specified certain additional requirements for tax exemption. Yet the need for continuing interpretation of those statutes is unavoidable. For more than 60 years, the IRS and its predecessors have constantly been called upon to interpret these and comparable provisions, and in doing so have referred consistently to principles of charitable trust law. In Treas. Regs. 45, Art. 517(1) (1921), for example, the IRS's predecessor denied charitable exemptions on the basis of proscribed political activity before the Congress itself added such conduct as a disqualifying element. In other instances, the IRS has denied charitable exemptions to otherwise qualified entities because they served too limited a class of people and thus did not provide a truly "public" benefit under the common-law test. Some years before the issuance of the rulings challenged in these cases, the IRS also ruled that contributions to community recreational facilities would not be deductible and that the facilities themselves would not be entitled to tax-exempt status, unless those facilities were open to all on a racially nondiscriminatory basis. . . .

Guided, of course, by the Code, the IRS has the responsibility, in the first instance, to determine whether a particular entity is "charitable" for purposes of § 170 and § 501(c)(3). This in turn may necessitate later determinations of whether given activities so violate public policy that the entities involved cannot be deemed to provide a public benefit worthy of "charitable" status. We emphasize, however, that these sensitive determinations should be made only where there is no doubt that the organization's activities violate fundamental public policy.

On the record before us, there can be no doubt as to the national policy. In 1970, when the IRS first issued the ruling challenged here, the position of all three branches of the Federal Government was unmistakably clear. The correctness of the Commissioner's conclusion that a racially discriminatory private school "is not 'charitable' within the common law concepts reflected in . . . the Code," is wholly consistent with what Congress, the Executive, and the courts had repeatedly declared before 1970. . . . Clearly an educational institution engaging in practices affirmatively at odds with this declared position of the whole Government cannot be seen as exercising a "beneficial and stabilizing [influence] in community life," *Walz v. Tax Comm'n*, 397 U.S., at 673, and is not "charitable," within the meaning of § 170 and § 501(c)(3). We therefore hold that the IRS did not exceed its authority when it announced its interpretation of § 170 and § 501(c)(3) in 1970 and 1971.

D

The actions of Congress since 1970 leave no doubt that the IRS reached the correct conclusion in exercising its authority. It is, of course, not unknown for independent agencies or the Executive Branch to misconstrue the intent of a statute; Congress can and often does correct such misconceptions, if the courts have not done so. Yet for a dozen years Congress has been made aware — acutely aware — of the IRS rulings of 1970 and 1971. As we noted earlier, few issues have been the subject of more vigorous and widespread debate and discussion in and out of Congress than those related to racial segregation in education. Sincere adherents advocating contrary views have ventilated the subject for well over three decades. Failure of Congress to modify the IRS rulings of 1970 and 1971, of which Congress was, by its own studies and by public discourse, constantly reminded, and Congress' awareness of the denial of tax-exempt status for racially discriminatory schools when enacting other and related legislation make out an unusually strong case of legislative acquiescence in and ratification by implication of the 1970 and 1971 rulings.

. . . .

Nonaction by Congress is not often a useful guide, but the nonaction here is significant. During the past 12 years there have been no fewer than 13 bills introduced to overturn the IRS interpretation of § 501(c)(3). Not one of these bills has emerged from any committee, although Congress has enacted numerous other amendments to § 501 during this same period, including an amendment to § 501(c)(3) itself. Tax Reform Act of 1976, Pub. L. 94-455, § 1313(a), 90 Stat. 1730. It is hardly conceivable that Congress — and in this setting, any Member of Congress — was not abundantly aware of what was going on. In view of its prolonged and acute awareness of so important an issue, Congress' failure to act on the bills proposed on this subject provides added support for concluding that Congress acquiesced in the IRS rulings of 1970 and 1971.

The evidence of congressional approval of the policy embodied in Revenue Ruling 71-447 goes well beyond the failure of Congress to act on legislative proposals. Congress affirmatively manifested its acquiescence in the IRS policy when it enacted the present § 501(i) of the Code, Act of Oct. 20, 1976, 90 Stat. 2697. That provision denies tax-exempt status to social clubs whose charters or policy statements provide for "discrimination against any person on the basis of race, color, or religion." Both the House and Senate Committee Reports on that bill articulated the national policy against granting tax exemptions to racially discriminatory private clubs.

Even more significant is the fact that both Reports focus on this Court's affirmance of *Green v. Connally*, 330 F. Supp. 1150 (D.D.C. 1971), as having established that "discrimination on account of race is inconsistent with an educational institution's tax-exempt status." (emphasis added). These references in congressional Committee Reports on an enactment denying tax exemptions to racially discriminatory private social clubs cannot be read other than as indicating approval of the standards applied to racially discriminatory private schools by the IRS subsequent to 1970, and specifically of Revenue Ruling 71-447.

III

Petitioners contend that, even if the Commissioner's policy is valid as to nonreligious private schools, that policy cannot constitutionally be applied to schools that engage in racial discrimination on the basis of sincerely held religious beliefs. As to such schools, it is argued that the IRS construction of § 170 and § 501(c)(3) violates their free exercise rights under the Religion Clauses of the First Amendment. This contention presents claims not heretofore considered by this Court in precisely this context.

This Court has long held the Free Exercise Clause of the First Amendment to be an absolute prohibition against governmental regulation of religious beliefs. As interpreted by this Court, moreover, the Free Exercise Clause provides substantial protection for lawful conduct grounded in religious belief. However, "[not] all burdens on religion are unconstitutional. . . . The state may justify a limitation on religious liberty by showing that it is essential to accomplish an overriding governmental interest." *United States v. Lee*, 455 U.S. 252, 257-258 (1982).

. . . .

The governmental interest at stake here is compelling. As discussed in Part II-B, *supra*, the Government has a fundamental, overriding interest in eradicating racial discrimination in education — discrimination that prevailed, with official approval, for the first 165 years of this Nation's constitutional history. That governmental interest substantially outweighs whatever burden denial of tax benefits places on petitioners' exercise of their religious beliefs. The interests asserted by petitioners cannot be accommodated with that compelling governmental interest; and no "less restrictive means," are available to achieve the governmental interest.

IV

The remaining issue is whether the IRS properly applied its policy to these petitioners. Petitioner Goldsboro Christian Schools admits that it "[maintains] racially discriminatory policies," but seeks to justify those policies on grounds we have fully discussed. The IRS properly denied tax-exempt status to Goldsboro Christian Schools.

Petitioner Bob Jones University, however, contends that it is not racially discriminatory. It emphasizes that it now allows all races to enroll, subject only to its restrictions on the conduct of all students, including its prohibitions of association between men and women of different races, and of interracial marriage. Although a ban on intermarriage or interracial dating applies to all races, decisions of this Court firmly establish that discrimination on the basis of racial affiliation and association is a form of racial discrimination, *see, e. g., Loving v. Virginia*, 388 U.S. 1 (1967); *McLaughlin v. Florida*, 379 U.S. 184 (1964); *Tillman v. Wheaton-Haven Recreation Assn.*, 410 U.S. 431 (1973). We therefore find that the IRS properly applied Revenue Ruling 71-447 to Bob Jones University.

The judgments of the Court of Appeals are, accordingly,

Affirmed.

John D. Colombo, *Why Is Harvard Tax-Exempt? (And Other Mysteries of Tax Exemption for Private Educational Institutions)*, 35 Ariz. L. Rev. 841 (1993)*

I. INTRODUCTION

Why is Harvard tax-exempt? Better yet, why do entities offering continuing legal education for lawyers and seminar training for bankers (who probably are not anyone's first choice as groups in need of charity) qualify as tax-exempt educational organizations? The issue of tax exemption for private educational institutions is certainly a curious one. Many private educational institutions, after all, "sell" education much the same way Microsoft sells software, and their "customers" (students) certainly pay for the product. In fact, recent data indicates that more than 60% of the annual gross revenues of private universities came from student tuition and sales. Yet while no one would suggest that we give Microsoft an exemption from federal and state income, property and other taxes, tax exemption for private educational institutions has been virtually unquestioned since colonial times and remains so. . . .

. . . .

II. BACKGROUND: THE HISTORY OF TAX EXEMPTION FOR PRIVATE EDUCATIONAL INSTITUTIONS

Tax exemption for private educational institutions extends to the beginning of colonial America. Indeed, the seeds of tax exemption for private schools can be traced to Fourteenth Century England, where William Langland wrote in the poem Piers the Plowman that in order to save their souls, wealthy merchants should devote their fortunes to "repair hospitals[,] help sick people[,] mend bad roads[,] build up bridges that had been broken down[,] help maidens to marry or to make them nuns[,] find food for prisoners and poor people[,] put scholars to school or to some other crafts[,] help religious orders, and ameliorate rents or taxes." . . .

In colonial America, religious and educational institutions were exempted from local taxes from the beginning. In fact, several colonies even extended local tax exemption to the professors who taught in colleges or universities as well as their students. The educational exemption appears to have been connected to the historic exemption for churches and religious institutions, since virtually all educational institutions of the time had the training of ministers as a primary objective. Moreover, many of these institutions began life as quasi-public schools. Harvard, for example, was chartered with a grant of public funds, as were Yale, Brown, Dartmouth and William & Mary. These exemptions survived the formation of the United States, and today virtually every state has either a constitutional or statutory provision exempting educational institutions from state and local property and income taxes.

At the federal level, tax exemption for schools or other charities was simply not an issue until the passage of the first income tax act in 1894. Prior to this, federal revenues came mostly from import duties and excise taxes, which did not affect the charitable organizations of that time. The first federal income tax law adopted in 1894, however, contained a broad exemption for "corporations, companies or associations organized and conducted solely for charitable, religious or educational purposes." . . .

III. CURRENT LEGAL STANDARDS FOR EXEMPTING PRIVATE EDUCATIONAL INSTITUTIONS

A. Federal Standards For Exemption

1. Education as a Charitable Purpose

All charitable organizations must meet certain general standards for exemption under Internal Revenue Code ("Code") § 501(c)(3). These general standards include organizing documents that limit the entity's purpose and operations to a charitable purpose, such as education; actual pursuit of such charitable purpose in the entity's operations; an absence of "private inurement"; and compliance with limits on political lobbying and campaign activity.

The major issue that has faced both the Internal Revenue Service (IRS) and the courts in interpreting the scope of federal tax exemption for educational institutions has been defining what constitutes "education." Unfortunately, the statutory language has never attempted to define "education" for purposes of the exemption. The Treasury Department, moreover, never has confined the exemption to traditional schools. Even as early as the 1920's, the IRS concluded that the educational exemption applied to activities as diverse as studying ruffled grouse, maintaining wild bird sanctuaries and forest land, and disseminating geographic knowledge. This approach apparently derived from the general law of charitable trusts, which recognizes a broad range of activities as educational.

The current Treasury regulations include in the definition of education "instruction or training of the individual for the purpose of improving or developing his capabilities" as well as "instruction of the public on subjects useful to the individual and beneficial to the community." Within this definition fall "schools" as one might colloquially think of them: institutions with a regularly scheduled curriculum, a regular faculty and a regularly enrolled body of students, including primary and secondary schools, colleges, professional schools and trade schools. The definition, however, also extends to a number of entities that one would not immediately classify as educational institutions, such as entities presenting public discussion groups, forums, panels or lectures, entities providing correspondence courses through radio or television, and "museums, zoos, planetariums, symphony orchestras, and other similar organizations." The educational exemption also has been applied to organizations that provided continuing legal education and other professional skills training, university bookstores, a jazz festival, various counseling services, research organizations, and a number of organizations whose stated purpose was to disseminate information to the public. Even the IRS, however, has its limits: a dog obedience school was held not exempt since it neither trains individuals nor educates the public.

2. Limitations on the Definition

The breadth of the federal tax definition of an "educational institution" has resulted in numerous problems for both the IRS and the courts in drawing the line between exempt and non-exempt institutions. . . .

a. The Commerciality Doctrine

Perhaps the most unsuccessful attempt at limiting the scope of the educational definition has been the "business activity" or "commerciality" doctrine. This doctrine arises from the regulations' interpretation of the exemption requirement that an organization pursue exclusively a charitable purpose. According to the regulations, an organization may be exempt under § 501(c)(3) even if it operates a trade or business, as long as such trade or business is either "insubstantial" or, if substantial, is "in furtherance of the organization's exempt purpose." The IRS has invoked this "primary purpose" test to deny exemption to organizations that it believes operate largely like for-profit businesses. In the educational area, for example, the doctrine has been invoked in a number of "publication" cases in which the IRS claimed that the entity seeking exemption was nothing more than a commercial publisher.

. . . .

The major problem with the commerciality doctrine as applied by the IRS and the courts is that no clear guidance exists for when an activity crosses the line from exempt to "commercial." While courts tend to focus on whether the activity results in net receipts and is otherwise conducted in a "commercial manner," this focus is simply wrong-headed. Nothing in the statute or regulations requires charitable entities to operate at a loss or inefficiently to achieve exemption. Moreover, the case-by-case analysis employed by the courts to date invites inexplicable variations in result. . . .

Another example of inconsistency lies in the fact that a number of activities in the educational area clearly are capable of being run as stand-alone businesses, such as university-associated bookstores or restaurants. If the focus of the commerciality doctrine is that goods and services provided by for-profit businesses are not appropriate subjects for tax-exemption, then any activity in an area populated by for-profit enterprise ought to lose exemption. This, however, clearly is not the existing law. Accordingly, the commerciality limitation, at least as applied by the IRS and courts to the current exemption standard, appears to lack any consistent theoretical base and hence is incapable of producing anything close to uniform results.

b. Private Benefit/Inurement

A second theory used by the IRS to police the educational exemption (and the exemption area in general) is the private benefit/inurement doctrine. This doctrine arises from the statutory provision that no entity will be exempt unless "no part of [its] net earnings inures to the benefit of any private shareholder or individual. . . ." The IRS actually breaks this doctrine into two parts: the private inurement limitation that is actually part of the statutory language, and a limitation on private benefit that is derived from the statutory language and separately stated in the regulations ("[an entity must not be] operated for the benefit of private interests such as designated individuals").

The private inurement concept is easy to define and well-developed in the tax exemption case law. It simply refers to a situation in which the entity's economic benefits are diverted from the charitable class the entity is supposed to serve into the hands of "insiders" such as officers, directors, employees and the like. . . . Since most private inurement situations are not subtle and involve a clear abuse of the economic benefits of exemption, this limitation is both appropriate and relatively straightforward.

The related private benefit concept, however, is another story. One recent IRS pronouncement equates private benefit to the situation in which an entity's benefits appear to flow primarily to a narrow group, rather than to the general community. . . .

The private benefit limitation as applied to the educational exemption suffers the same problem as the commerciality doctrine: no obvious line exists for deciding when the benefits conferred by an organization otherwise clearly engaged in "training the individual" are "too private." . . .

c. Education vs. "Propaganda"

Since the early days of the educational exemption, the IRS has taken the position that certain "advocacy groups" do not qualify for exemption. The regulations state that an organization can qualify as educational even if it advocates a particular viewpoint, as long as it presents "a sufficiently full and fair exposition of the pertinent facts to permit an individual or the public to form an independent opinion or conclusion." If, however, an organization's purpose is merely the "presentation of unsupported opinion," it will not qualify. Nor will an organization qualify if its presentation of viewpoint crosses the line into an impermissible amount of legislative lobbying.

The D.C. Circuit, however, held the "full and fair exposition" test unconstitutionally vague . . . .

In response . . . the IRS adopted a four-part "methodology test" that purports to decide educational status based upon the methodology used by the organization in promoting its viewpoint, rather than on the viewpoint itself. The four factors identified by the IRS in this test are (1) whether the presentation of viewpoints or positions unsupported by facts is a significant portion of the organization's communications; (2) whether the facts that purport to support the viewpoints or positions are distorted; (3) whether the organization's presentations make substantial use of inflammatory and disparaging terms, expressing conclusions based more on strong emotional feelings than on objective evaluations; and (4) whether or not the approach used in the organization's presentations is aimed at developing an understanding on the part of the intended audience or readership by considering their background or training in the subject matter. . . .

. . . .

d. The Public Policy Limitation

Perhaps no aspect of tax exemption for educational institutions (or, for that matter, exemption in general) has received more commentary than the IRS's decision to withhold exemption from racially discriminatory schools, a decision upheld by the United States Supreme Court in *Bob Jones University v. United States*. . . .

. . . .

By far the most common complaint . . . is that the "fundamental public policy" standard is "open-ended and beclouded," leaving far too much discretion in the hands of the IRS. Because the requirement appears to have been taken from the common law of charitable trusts, it has no theoretical grounding in the tax laws and no development other than in a body of law primarily concerned with whether a donor can place money in trust for a specific cause in perpetuity. As a concurring Justice worried, if not adequately restrained, the Court's decision could reach organizations with unpopular ideas that contribute to diversity of viewpoint essential to a pluralistic society; in any event, the IRS should not be making such substantive decisions. . . . Thus the public policy constraint appears to suffer from the same lack of theoretical grounding and definitional consistency observed for the other limiting principles.

B. State Exemption Standards

While generalizations about state exemption standards are somewhat hazardous, state tax exemption tends to follow the federal pattern. . . .

C. Summary

Both the federal and most state tax definitions of education for exemption purposes are extremely broad, grounded in common-law definitions of charity taken from charitable trust law that have little in common with tax administration. At the federal level, this breadth has required the IRS to turn to various other doctrines to limit the scope of the exemption, and states appear to follow this federal lead. With the exception of the private inurement (as opposed to private benefit) doctrine, however, all these limiting doctrines suffer to a greater or lesser degree from their own lack of definition, leaving the IRS and its state counterparts with virtually unlimited discretion in their application and little in the way of guidance for applying that discretion. One is tempted to call the situation a mess.

IV. THEORIES OF EXEMPTION AND PRIVATE EDUCATIONAL INSTITUTIONS

. . . .

A. The Nature of Exemption: Bittker's Income Measurement Theory

While several theories of exemption exist, these theories break into two general groups: tax-base theories and subsidy theories. In general, the subsidy theories view the tax exemption as an implicit subsidy to the exempt organization equal to the amount of taxes foregone as a result of exemption. The tax-base theories, on the other hand, justify exemption as a natural outgrowth of the inability to accurately measure the income of nonprofit organizations or to assess the incidence of tax that would occur if exemption were not available. Whether one views exemption as the equivalent of a government subsidy or simply as a natural outgrowth of a taxing system aimed at measuring income (or property value) impacts one's view of the proper scope of exemption: if the tax-base theories are correct, for example, then questions regarding whether society might be better off taxing that entity and applying the revenues elsewhere simply do not arise, because those entities cannot be brought into the taxing system in the first place.

. . . .

Perhaps the biggest problem with the [tax-based] theory . . . is that it simply is wrong with respect to a number of exempt organizations. As Henry Hansmann has observed, many "charitable" organizations in fact derive all or nearly all their income from sales of goods or services they produce, and measuring income for such "commercial" nonprofits is no more difficult than for any other business. Hospitals are one notable example, deriving virtually all their income from service fees. Another commentator has noted that more charities are operating in a "business-like" fashion, generating surplus receipts, hiring professional managers, creating reserves for operations and so on. Thus whatever historic problems regarding income measurement may have existed are rapidly disappearing today. . . .

More importantly . . . many private schools and other educational institutions fall into the "businesslike" category, deriving the great majority of their receipts from tuition and sales. Whatever the difficulties of measuring income under the I.R.C. § 61 definition may be for other entities, tuition (fees for educational services rendered) and sales revenues fall squarely within the definition of § 61. In addition, aside from the profit motive issue, the expenses of most educational institutions (teacher salaries, maintenance and the like) are classic examples of deductible business expenses under I.R.C. § 162. One has the sneaking suspicion that Harvard, for example, could come up with a taxable income number if pressed to do so. Finally . . . most private school students come from high income classes that otherwise would be subject to income tax, thus making the rate-setting problem less of a concern. . . .

The "no income" theory, therefore, ultimately is an unsatisfying explanation for both the exemption of charitable entities in general and the exemption of educational institutions in particular. . . .

B. The Subsidy Theories

Once one eliminates as a reason for exemption the impossibility of bringing exempt entities into the tax base, then the question regarding exemption simply becomes one of normative standards to justify the benefit conferred by exemption. Under this view, which I broadly characterize as the subsidy view, certain evaluative criteria become obvious. The first is that such a benefit should be conferred on an entity only when it is deserved. This criterion breaks into two subcomponents: worth and need. The worth component requires an entity to prove that the function it performs is one that society should support. Proving worth alone, however, is insufficient. The entity must also show need for the benefit. An entity might well continue its worthy function without government intervention. This is most obvious in the case of functioning private markets. We may view the software produced by Microsoft as a worthy social benefit, but because the private market supports Microsoft's continued production of software, no government intervention is necessary to ensure this continued production. A functioning private market, however, is not the only aspect of need. Even if the private market does not function with respect to a particular good or service, the need component is not necessarily satisfied; instead, need also requires showing that the undersupplied good or service cannot (or would not) be replaced as efficiently by the government providing such goods or services directly.

The second major evaluative criterion is proportionality. Once an entity demonstrates that a benefit is deserved, the amount of the benefit should relate in some way to the level of production of the worthy good or service. In a sense, proportionality overlaps need: there is no reason to give an entity a larger benefit than is necessary to ensure optimum production of the worthy good or service. In this criteria list, however, I view "need" as the threshold showing that a benefit is necessary to avoid irreparable diminution in the worthy good or service, and "proportionality" as the answer to the question "how much benefit is necessary?"

In addition to these two major criteria, two lesser, but still important considerations exist. These I have referred to as universality, which is the hope that a particular theory of exemption can serve to explain both the income and property tax, and historical consistency, which refers to whether the theory adequately accounts for the general historical scope of exemption.

1. The Quid-Pro-Quo Theory

Perhaps the oldest justification for exemption of charitable institutions is that the exemption is a rough "quid-pro-quo" to charities for the cost of performing services that otherwise would have to be borne by the government. This theory posits that the benefit of exemption is deserved because in the absence of the exemption, government would be required to pay the cost of the service or product provided by the exempt entity. While this theory establishes that exemption is deserved (as the quid-pro-quo for providing the desired services), the theory suffers from at least three serious deficiencies when applied to the educational area.

First is the question of need. If the justification for exemption is that the economic benefits conferred are a rough quid-pro-quo for the costs that would otherwise be borne by the government in providing the exempt service, then exemption should be available to all providers of that service, whether or not they operate for profit. For-profit educational institutions certainly exist. . . . [T]he obvious problem here is that for-profit institutions clearly cannot demonstrate a need for government assistance, since the private market appears to be working in this area. Thus the quid-pro-quo theory fails to adequately delimit the need factor of the deservedness criterion.

Second, the theory has serious proportionality problems. To begin with, it is difficult to trace the burden being relieved by private schools to the governmental units granting exemption. As noted above, tax exemption for charitable institutions is a unified system: the "educational" label invokes not only federal income tax exemption, but also state income, sales and local property tax exemptions. Thus even if one finds indisputable the proposition that government in general should provide all levels of education to its populace, tax exemption is a peculiar way to allocate the costs involved. This is best illustrated by the local property tax exemption for private research universities, such as Harvard. Surely the city of Cambridge or the state of Massachusetts would not find it necessary to supply college and post-graduate education at their expense to the out-of-state (or out-of-city) students who attend Harvard. . . .

. . . .

Finally, the theory fails on the historical consistency criterion because it does not even come close to explaining the traditional scope of the educational exemption. While one might view traditional schools as a necessary government function and argue that traditional private schools relieve the government from the burden of educating those students attending private schools, the quid-pro-quo theory fails to address the myriad of nontraditional educational activities that historically have been exempt but are not government responsibilities. Organizations that disseminate information, for example, historically have fallen into the educational ambit . . . . While some of these organizations in fact may not deserve exemption under any theory, limiting exemption to true quid-pro-quo situations would both unduly restrict the exemption in terms of activities exempted and, if followed to logical conclusion, unduly expand the exemption to for-profit providers of activities within the ambit of the quid-pro-quo rationale.

2. The Community Benefit Theory

While the quid-pro-quo theory at one time was the most cited reason for exemption, that theory largely has been displaced in popularity today by the community benefit theory. This theory claims that exemption is warranted not as a direct quid-pro-quo for goods or services that the government otherwise would have to provide, but rather as government support for institutions that provide socially worthy goods or services with a special quality or ethic. Often this theory is expressed in terms of the way nonprofit organizations contribute to pluralism by providing the public goods and services that either are undersupplied by the private market or by the government or else not provided in the same socially desirable manner. . . .

While the community benefit theory has had its most explicit delineation in the context of exemption for nonprofit hospitals and health care providers, the same points made in the hospital context concerning the special role of private nonprofit entities have also been made, albeit in different contexts, with respect to educational institutions (at least, private nonprofit schools). Thus private schools have been defended on the grounds that they promote parental choice in education, promote diversity in schooling and in society as a whole, provide wider opportunities for the socially disadvantaged, and provide better quality education than their public counterparts.

As an exemption theory, however, the community benefit doctrine suffers many of the same problems as the quid-pro-quo theory, as well as some new ones. Perhaps the most serious of these is the inherent inability to quantify the particular ethic or quality that results in exemption, and thus to properly identify when exemption is deserved. . . .

In the educational area, for example, the special qualities cited in support of private nonprofit schools would seem to be equally applicable to for-profit counterparts: the existence of for-profit private schools also would increase parental choice, educational opportunity and promote diversity. Similarly, in higher education at least, some government institutions might supply many or all of these same qualities: surely whatever "special ethic" Harvard and other premier private institutions bring to higher education can be found as well in the premier public institutions such as Berkeley, Illinois, Michigan, Texas, Virginia and the like. Education researchers, in fact, are skeptical that private schools in general provide much, if any, quality improvement over government counterparts, despite common perceptions to the contrary.

The vagueness of the community benefit standard is especially troubling because it takes the substantive policy decisions regarding what activities are so socially desirable as to deserve exemption out of the hands of Congress, state legislatures, or other government agencies charged with substantive policy decisions and puts such decisions in the hands of the IRS or state taxing authorities, all primarily charged with the task of tax collection. . . .

The community benefit standard suffers from other problems, as well. Like the quid-pro-quo standard, it fails the proportionality criterion because it is no better at matching the level of "special ethic" of the exempt entity to the value of the exemption. Indeed, no specific reason exists to believe that whatever special qualities nonprofit enterprise brings to the educational sector would not exist absent exemption. Put positively, the argument is as follows. If consumers prefer the special ethic in education provided by Harvard, why would they not continue to prefer Harvard even absent exemption? Would Harvard really go out of business if it were not tax exempt? . . . .

5. The Donative Theory

The subsidy theories of exemption examined so far all suffer from serious defects in either deservedness, proportionality or both. . . . Faced with this situation, Professor Mark Hall and I revisited the theoretical grounds for exemption and noted, curiously, that virtually all commentators agreed that "donative entities" (whatever they were) were clearly deserving of exemption; the commentators then devoted most of their energy to developing a rationale for exempting other kinds of nonprofits. . . . [I]nstead of trying to justify expanding exemption beyond the donative standard, we embarked on justifying limiting the exemption to only donative entities. Our theory thus posits that exemption should be available only when a given percentage of an entity's revenues come from donations.

a. The Economic Basis for the Donative Theory

The donative theory begins with Professor Hansmann's observation that nonprofits tend to exist in markets characterized by contract failure — that is, a failure of the private market to function properly. This observation, however, fails to explain why nonprofits in these markets deserve the benefit of tax exemption. . . . In order to satisfy the deservedness criterion, a theory of exemption must explain why exemption, rather than direct government intervention, is an appropriate response. The donative theory does just that, because it posits that exemption is warranted not in all cases of private market failure, but only in those cases in which private market failure is accompanied by government failure, i.e., a failure of the government to intervene directly to provide the optimal level of production.

Government failure occurs as a result of the vagaries of the democratic system, which requires a majority vote of the legislature to enact government programs. Economist Burton Weisbrod observed that because of this phenomenon, minority blocs of voters will lack the voting strength to force the government to meet their demand for certain goods and services. In effect, the government will provide any good or service at approximately the demand of the median voter, since any attempt to provide more than this will be voted down by the majority. The result, of course, is that high-demanding minority blocs will be chronically underserved.

It is this "twin failure" scenario (private market failure coupled with government failure) that justifies exemption, because it answers the question why direct government intervention is not a more appropriate response to private market failure. When twin failure occurs, there cannot be any direct government intervention because the majority of the electorate will not vote for it. Why, then, would the majority permit exemption, which constitutes an indirect government subsidy?

The answer here is that although a majority of voters may resist paying the full cost of government directly providing certain goods and services, a majority may be willing for government to "contribute" to such production because, while they do not value the particular good or service enough to pay for all of it, they recognize that they would receive some marginal benefit from increased production and hence would be willing to pay for a portion of that increased production, especially if such agreement would permit a partial cross-subsidy of their own special interest. . . .

b. The Role of Donations in General

The next issue, of course, is identifying when this twin failure occurs. The donative theory hypothesizes that the best evidence of twin failure is donations by more than a de minimis number of individuals to a given entity. Where neither the private markets nor the government supplies a good or service at an optimum level of production, high-demanders have no choice but to donate to the supplying entity to encourage more production. These donations, however, are virtually certain not to provide the entire needed production because of the free-riding problem: some high-demanders will not pay their "fair share" of the cost of increased production but rather free-ride on the donations of others. Higher education is a good example. Some have theorized that alumni donations to higher education are a form of delayed payment for one's education. Private colleges and universities keep tuition artificially low to expand the number of students who can afford to attend, and then impress upon their alumni the "moral obligation" to make donations post-graduation in order to make up the difference between the true value of the education received and the amount actually charged as tuition. Because this is only a moral obligation, however . . . many graduates fail to donate or fail to donate at an appropriate level, free-riding on the donations of other alumni. In these situations exemption comes to the rescue: by forgiving the tax liability otherwise due on income or property, the exemption becomes a form of "shadow subsidy" equal to the tax rate, permitting an entity to produce more based on its income and capital base than would be possible if the government took its tax cut.

This, then, is the case for restricting exemption to donative entities. Exemption is warranted only when both the private market and direct government subsidies fail to produce goods and services desired by segments of the population at their optimum level — the "twin failure" phenomenon. Donations signal both the desire of a particular population segment to have increased production of a given good or service and that both private markets and direct government intervention are failing to produce the desired good or service at its optimum level.

c. Defining a Donation and The Donative Threshold

. . . .

The major issue . . . concerns what level of donative support is necessary to invoke exemption. We previously have proposed based upon both historical evidence and current provisions of the Internal Revenue Code defining public charities that exemption be available only when one-third of an entity's gross receipts come from donations from a minimum number . . . of donors. Nevertheless, we also recognized that what the threshold should be is essentially a political judgment concerning when donations are high enough as a percentage of the entity's revenues to signify sufficient twin failure that granting the "shadow subsidy" of exemption is an appropriate response. Specifically, we noted that the donative percentage might well be reduced for those institutions that suffered greater free-riding behavior than average . . .

In fact, educational institutions, particularly colleges and universities, are one example where free-riding is rampant. . . . During the period 1986-1988, only approximately 28.3% of the alumni of four-year private colleges and universities made contributions. Thus over 70% of alumni of these institutions chose to free-ride on the donations of others. A lower donative percentage also guards against the possibility that entities receive exemption solely because they have rich alumni with money to throw around.

In the educational area, therefore, one could argue for a donative threshold much lower than the one-third previously suggested on the basis of general historical evidence. . . .

. . . .

V. CONCLUSION

This Article began with a question, why is Harvard tax-exempt? I believe that the donative theory provides the best answer to that question: To the extent Harvard can justify exemption, it is because of its reliance on private donations, which in turn indicate that Harvard produces some product or service valued by a significant portion of society but undersupplied by the private market and undersupported by government. . . .

Whatever donative threshold is chosen, however, the donative theory provides an administrable, objective standard for exemption sorely lacking either in the law as applied today by the IRS and state tax agencies, or in other theories of exemption. With it, we can supplant litigation over "commerciality," "private benefit," "propaganda," and "community benefit" with a standard dependent on the objective conduct of the parties most interested in where tax dollars go, the taxpaying public. Without it, we will be condemned to an ever-expanding definition of what constitutes a charitable institution, reined in only by the subjective notions of "goodness" of the Internal Revenue Service and courts. Surely taxpayers, and tax policy, deserve better.

NOTES

1. In *Bob Jones University*, did the Court stretch the bounds of statutory interpretation in reaching its conclusion? Is § 501(c)(3) not abundantly clear on its face? Why resort to another section of the Internal Revenue Code that mentions charitable contributions, but never defines "charity"? At the start of the chapter, the Court appeared to shun normative arguments in *FAIR*. Did a normative argument trump a strong statutory interpretation argument in *Bob Jones University*?

What if the Court's public-policy driven approach in *Bob Jones University* was applied to the facts of *FAIR*, creating the legal question of whether postsecondary schools lose their tax exemption for denying full access to military recruiters? How would the Court weigh the different policy questions involved, that is, the military's national security justification for having full access to law schools versus the law professors' civil rights justification? One commentator has gone so far as to write an article containing four opinions in a hypothetical case exploring a *Bob Jones*-type analysis to the *FAIR* facts, including one opinion (by a Justice Wisdom) that exposes the flaws in that approach:

> Justice Wisdom's opinion thoroughly explains why the doctrinal framework of *Bob Jones* is unworkable, dangerous, and based on a contestable rationale for the charity income tax exemption. Although *Bob Jones* reached the proper result, to strive to apply the public policy doctrine in the language of *Bob Jones* is to embrace and perpetuate its flawed doctrinal framework. Consequently, attempting to demonstrate the "correct" application of the public policy doctrine of *Bob Jones* is not simply futile; it is misguided and counter-productive.

Johnny Rex Buckles, *Do Law Schools Forfeit Federal Income Tax Exemption When They Deny Military Recruiters Full Access to Career Services Programs?: The Hypothetical Case of* Yale University v. Commissioner, 41 ARIZ. ST. L.J. 1 (2009).*

2. Are all tax exempt charitable organizations in "harmony with the public interest," as the Court suggests they should be? *Bob Jones Univ.*, 461 U.S. 574, 592 (1983). In his concurrence, Powell says that it is "impossible to believe" that all non-profit organizations actually conform to generally accepted public policy or to "common community consciousness." *Id.* at 609. According to Powell, it is important that a diverse, pluralistic society support "sharply conflicting viewpoints and activities." *Id.* at 609. Does the majority's standard for tax exemption status go too far?

The Court emphasizes that all three branches of the federal government were in explicit agreement that racial discrimination in education was against public policy. *Id.* at 598–99. Ask yourself what if the branches had been in disagreement on the exact boundaries of public policy? Would the case have come out the same way? How does the Court determine what constitutes "accepted" public policy? Is this definition flexible to changes in public thought over time?

Are there flaws in the public policy approach? Consider this:

> Critics have disparaged the Court for concluding that a charitable overlay to section 501(c)(3) exists and imposing a public-policy limitation on the statute. They have likewise rebuked the Court for "abdicat[ing] its supervisory powers to the IRS" and "supplant[ing] the role of Congress as lawmaker by making broad tax policy pronouncements," rather than exercising the oversight necessary to ensure that the IRS properly enforces the tax laws.
>
> Professor David A. Brennen has criticized the doctrine as lacking legal or statutory authority and a "clearly defined scope of applicability." Since

the IRS's adoption of its racial nondiscrimination policy in 1970, Congress has neither enacted any law that codifies the public-policy doctrine nor provided the IRS with the "legal authority to act solely on public policy grounds." As a consequence, Brennen questioned whether the IRS is the appropriate federal agency to determine if a charitable organization violates an established public policy.

. . . .

Ultimately, the absence of a clearly defined public policy forces the IRS to balance its unfettered discretion in exercising public-policy power with the heavy burden of proving that an "established" policy exists. This difficult balancing act may explain why the IRS has used the public-policy doctrine as the basis for revocation only in instances involving racial discrimination, civil disobedience, or illegal activity. Furthermore, the lack of a defined public policy also leaves charitable organizations in the precarious position of monitoring the current political climate to ensure that their activities do not violate a contemporary public policy. Reliance on the public-policy doctrine to combat discrimination on the basis of marital status, sexual orientation, or even religion has been futile because such bases are not "established" public policy. Only Congress's enactment of a well-defined nondiscrimination requirement in section 501(c)(3) will effectively end discrimination by charitable organizations.

Nichola Mirkey, *Is it "Charitable" to Discriminate? The Necessary Transformation of Section 501(c)(3) into the Gold Standard for Charities*, 2007 Wis. L. Rev. 45, 65–68 (2007).*

3. Could the Court have reached the same result without stretching the rules of statutory construction? In Footnote 24, the court declines to address the issues of whether Bob Jones University should be denied tax exempt status on Equal Protection grounds. *Id.* at 599. What does the Equal Protection Clause of the Fourteenth Amendment require? Would this have been an easier argument to make? Why does the Court decline to address it?

4. After losing its tax exempt status, Bob Jones University (BJU) continued its racially discriminatory policies for another 17 years. In 2000, Bob Jones III, acting as the university president, publicly lifted BJU's policy against interracial dating. *See Statement about Race at BJU*, Bob Jones Univ., http://www.bju.edu/communities/ministries-schools/position-statements/race-statement.php (last visited Sept. 1, 2012). The university has also created two scholarship programs specifically for minority students. *Id.* In their online public statement on racial diversity, BJU says that it is "profoundly sorry" for its prior institutional policies and is currently dedicated to creating a diverse learning environment. *Id.*

5. Will the various rationales for the educational institution tax exemption retain their analytical force as colleges and universities increasingly look like for-profit corporate enterprises — with profitable research partnerships, lucrative athletic programs, and large land holdings that are not dedicated exclusively to educational purposes? *See, e.g.*, DEREK BOK, UNIVERSITIES IN THE MARKETPLACE: THE COMMERCIALIZATION OF HIGHER EDUCATION (2003); Peter D. Blumberg, *From "Publish or Perish" to "Profit or Perish": Revenues from University Technology Transfer and the 501(c)(3) Tax Exemption*, 145 U. PA. L. REV. 89 (1996); *see also* Barbara K. Bucholtz, *Reflections on the Role of Nonprofit Associations in a Representative Democracy*, 7 CORNELL J.L. & PUB. POL'Y 555 (1998); John M. Bello, Note, *Economics 101: A Study of the Tax-Exempt Status of Colleges and Universities*, 34 SUFFOLK U. L. REV. 615 (2001).

6. As a matter of policy, is there anything colleges and universities can do to counteract the increasing corporatization of higher education to ensure that they maintain their tax exemptions? What about expanding unprofitable or less-profitable endeavors, stepping up pure charitable activities, or investing more heavily in, say, core humanities departments that do not spin off the type of money that athletic programs and research activities do?

7. Organizations that qualify for an income tax exemption under § 501(c)(3) are not exempt from taxes on income derived from activities that do not relate to the organizations' charitable purpose. The technical term for this income is "unrelated business taxable income," or UBIT.

> Internal Revenue Code § 512(a)(1) provides the definition of unrelated business taxable income: '[T]he term unrelated business taxable income means the gross income derived by any organization from any unrelated trade or business . . . regularly carried on by it . . . .' Section 513(a) then proceeds to define the term 'unrelated trade or business' as 'any trade or business the conduct of which is not substantially related . . . to the exercise or performance by such organization of its charitable, educational, or other purpose or function constituting the basis for its exemption under section 501.' Therefore, the determination whether a[n] . . . endeavor is substantially related to the exempt purpose of the university lies at the heart of the inquiry as to whether subsequent income generated by the project should be taxable.

Blumberg, *supra* note 5, at 110–11 (citations omitted). In fact, courts, using UBIT, have already recognized that some university activities are unrelated to their charitable, educational mission to the public and should be taxed.

One of the most well-known applications of UBIT in the university setting occurred in *Iowa State University of Science and Technology v. United States*, 205 Ct. Cl. 339 (Court of Claims 1974). In that case, Iowa State University operated a revenue-generating television station affiliated with the American Broadcasting Corporation. Only 14% of the station's programming was "educational"; the balance consisted of network and syndicated programming. The Court of Claims noted that "[t]he presence of an income tax exemption for the University, however, does not automatically exempt all activities in which it may participate." While the court recognized that the station may have provided some educational benefit, it ultimately concluded that "the commercial aspects and the emphasis on revenue maximization were the overwhelming goals of the operation of the station; and, thus, the business was not substantially related to the educational purposes of the University." The court held the station to be an unrelated trade or business of the university and its income taxable under UBIT.

> Higher education's attempt to find collateral sources of income by engaging in activities that are arguably unrelated to its educational or scientific purpose has generated considerable media attention. No single source of income has been more hotly debated than the revenues — still largely tax-exempt — derived from participation in major college athletics. The Service has recently ruled on other, less high-profile revenue sources. Income from the rental of university facilities to outside parties has been declared taxable, as has income from university operation of hotels and motels. Income from university-operated parking lots and travel tours, on the other hand, has been declared exempt. Some of these dispositions, however, were "easy cases" in the sense that the activity had only the most attenuated relationship to an educational or other charitable purpose. Furthermore, the amount of money generated by these activities is not so great that the institution sustains a tremendous loss from being subject to taxation. Making a determination on research income, however, does not present an easy resolution, because an obvious relationship exists between the activity and the university's exempt purposes, and the amount of money at issue is considerable for both the institution and the Service.

Id. at 109–10. Is UBIT an adequate solution to the commercialization of universities and colleges in America? Should academic activities remain exempt while commercial research and profitable sports become taxable? If you were counsel for a university, what arguments would you develop to show that sports and corporate research are related to the educational purpose of a university and the income derived from them should be tax exempt? What arguments can you develop for the IRS? Do your arguments hold up against the IRS's definition of what constitutes "educational activities"?

> The term educational, as used in section 501(c)(3), relates to:
>
> (a) The instruction or training of the individual for the purpose of improving or developing his capabilities; or
>
> (b) The instruction of the public on subjects useful to the individual and beneficial to the community.

26 C.F.R. § 1.501(d)(3)(i) (2009). Do your arguments hold up against how the IRS defines "scientific research" as a tax exempt activity under § 501(c)(3)?

> (5) Scientific defined. (i) Since an organization may meet the requirements of section 501(c)(3) only if it serves a public rather than a private interest, a scientific organization must be organized and operated in the public interest (see subparagraph (1)(ii) of this paragraph). Therefore, the term scientific, as used in section 501(c)(3), includes the carrying on of scientific research in the public interest. . . .
>
> . . . .
>
> (iii) Scientific research will be regarded as carried on in the public interest:

(a) If the results of such research (including any patents, copyrights, processes, or formulae resulting from such research) are made available to the public on a nondiscriminatory basis;

(b) If such research is performed for the United States, or any of its agencies or instrumentalities, or for a State or political subdivision thereof; or

(c) If such research is directed toward benefiting the public. The following are examples of scientific research which will be considered as directed toward benefiting the public, and, therefore, which will be regarded as carried on in the public interest: (1) Scientific research carried on for the purpose of aiding in the scientific education of college or university students; (2) scientific research carried on for the purpose of obtaining scientific information, which is published in a treatise, thesis, trade publication, or in any other form that is available to the interested public; (3) scientific research carried on for the purpose of discovering a cure for a disease; or (4) scientific research carried on for the purpose of aiding a community or geographical area by attracting new industry to the community or area or by encouraging the development of, or retention of, an industry in the community or area. . . .

(iv) An organization will not be regarded as organized and operated for the purpose of carrying on scientific research in the public interest and, consequently, will not qualify under section 501(c)(3) as a scientific organization, if:

(a) Such organization will perform research only for persons which are (directly or indirectly) its creators and which are not described in section 501(c)(3), or

(b) Such organization retains (directly or indirectly) the ownership or control of more than an insubstantial portion of the patents, copyrights, processes, or formulae resulting from its research and does not make such patents, copyrights, processes, or formulae available to the public. . . .

(v) The fact that any organization (including a college, university, or hospital) carries on research which is not in furtherance of an exempt purpose described section 501(c)(3) will not preclude such organization from meeting the requirements of section 501(c)(3) so long as the organization meets the organizational test and is not operated for the primary purpose of carrying on such research . . .

26 C.F.R. § 1.501(d)(5) (2009). Are college sports and industrial research close enough to universities' primary, educational purpose to justify a tax exempt status? Do you think they adequately benefit the public, even if research, licenses, and patents are not available to the public, and only a minority of students get to play sports, with only a handful of athletic programs actually creating revenue for the school? Could the revenue generated by these activities justify their tax exempt status because they can potentially finance other university activities that are more academic?

If universities were taxed for these activities how do you think they would respond? Would they cut sports programs, starting with the least popular sports, or simply charge more tuition or divert funds away from other campus activities?

Chapter X

STATE & LOCAL GOVERNMENTS

Introduction

The Tenth Amendment of the U.S. Constitution states that "[t]he powers not delegated to the United States by the Constitution, nor prohibited by it to the States, are reserved to the States respectively, or to the people." U.S. CONST. AMEND. X. Since the federal government has no articulate powers over education, states maintain primary responsibility for education. The role of the state in higher education has changed significantly since the establishment of the higher education system. As Dr. Aims McGuinness of the National Center for Higher Education Management Systems describes:

> Higher education in the nineteenth century was primarily private. With only a few exceptions-such as the establishment of the University of Georgia in 1785, Ohio University in 1804, and the University of Virginia in 1819-states played a limited role in higher education until the establishment of land-grant universities in the 1860s and the 1870s. Another important development was the establishment of state normal schools to prepare teachers, schools that evolved into state colleges and universities by the mid-twentieth century. Historically, states have always provided the legal framework within which both public and private institutions operated. Following the principles established by the U.S. Supreme Court's ruling in the Dartmouth College case (*Dartmouth College v. Woodward*, 17 U.S. 518 (1819)) . . . , states accorded both public and private institutions significant autonomy, especially on "substantive" decisions on whom to admit, what should be taught, and who should teach. It was not until the massive expansion of higher education in the 1950s and 1960s that the states began to undertake more deliberate efforts to promote the coordinated development of public higher education to establish more systematic approaches to the allocation of state funding.
>
> From the 1950s to the end of the 1980s, the share of total enrollments in public institutions (including many community colleges partially funded by local revenue) increased from about 60 to 76 percent. The private sector continued to grow, but this was outstripped by enrollment increases of one and a half times in public four-year institutions and five times in public two-year ones. The proportions of the institutions in the private sector dropped from 65 to 59 percent.
>
> State and local governments now provide approximately 35 percent of the current revenue for higher education, both public and private, excluding sales and services (for example, hospitals, dormitories, and restaurants).

> This compares with 16 percent from the federal government, 38 percent from student tuition and fees, and 11 percent from other sources (including endowments, private gifts, and grants).

Aims C. McGuinness, Jr., *The States and Higher Education, in* AMERICAN HIGHER EDUCATION IN THE TWENTY-FIRST CENTURY: SOCIAL, POLITICAL, AND ECONOMIC CHALLENGES 140–41 (3d ed. 2011).* While state support in terms of funding has declined, the state's oversight function had not changed as dramatically.

Section A of this chapter presents cases and materials regarding state regulation of public colleges and universities. First, it examines regulations of institutions created by the respective state's constitution. Then, the chapter discusses a different level of institutional autonomy by exploring the legal authority of public institutions established by state statute.

Having established the regulatory parameters for public institutions, Section B explores state authority over private colleges and universities in its respective jurisdiction. It provides an overview of the basic implementation of state rules regarding chartering and licensing an institution in the state. It also raises the nuance of regulating religiously affiliated, private colleges and universities. Section C continues the emphasis on state authority; however, it presents laws that support transparency of public institutions. Specifically, it explores sunshine laws for public meetings and records. Section D, then, discusses the effect a poor economic climate has on higher education, addressing the fiscal strategies institutions have attempted to counter declining state funds while staying faithful to the university's mission.

In Section E, this chapter shifts its focus to local government. At the heart of many of the cases presented are the conflicts that often arise between state and local government. While the general rule is that states may regulate local government and communities (also known as Dillon's Rule from the 1868 case of *Iowa City of Clinton v. Cedar Rapids and Missouri River Railroad Company*, 24 Iowa 455 (1868)), as the sections below explore, states have granted certain rights and privileges to local government — ones that state colleges and universities have argued do not apply to them. Further, at times, local government may raise concerns about the actions of public and private colleges and universities operating within their jurisdiction. In particular, this chapter addresses local laws, from a resources and planning framework, in terms of land use and taxation rights. "Land use" refers to the legal enjoyment and benefit of real property. "Land use planning" includes the development process and considerations, which include land use rights (e.g., quiet enjoyment), regulations (e.g., zoning ordinance), restrictions (e.g., covenants), and transference (e.g., takings).

Typically, the land use cases involving higher education address questions about zoning. Zoning laws articulate how a lawful owner or possessor of real property may use the property and land. These zoning restrictions limit landowners by categorizing the land according to a particular "zone," for example, permitted use only for residential, commercial, agricultural, or industrial purposes. In addition, the zoning restrictions may place related building code requirements on the property such as height of the building, square footage, and physical building to lot ratios. Often, zoning changes take place in the form of variances, special use permits rezoning initiatives, or through an enabling act that sets out a comprehensive plan to change an area. The approval process typically involves a city or town council; in larger organized locales, municipalities or the local entities may have established a Board of Zoning Authority (BZA) to approve changes. Zoning laws are presumed to be legal, but issues often arise regarding substantive due process, matters of fairness (such as questions of illegitimate motives), equal protection challenges under the Fourteenth Amendment, and "takings" issues, that change the relationship between the local government and the landowner and/or possessor of the real property. The latter issue is raised in Section F.

Finally, in Section F, this chapter explores legal challenges that affect a local government's efforts to collect taxes from private and public colleges and universities. Private institutions claim tax exemptions as charitable organizations; however, one case questions whether an auxiliary service (i.e., housing), which generates significant income, qualifies under the tax exempt status. Further, the cases examine the extent that special organizational groups affiliated with the university such as a fraternity should be captured under the exemption. To close, this chapter addresses the tension between state institutions and local admission taxes for ticketed events that do not reflect the academic core.

Put simply, the overall theme of this chapter captures the conflicts arising from governmental authority over colleges and universities — often in terms of one public interest in conflict with another.

A. STATE REGULATION OF PUBLIC POSTSECONDARY SCHOOLS

1. Institutions Established by State Constitution

SAN FRANCISCO LABOR COUNCIL v. REGENTS OF THE UNIVERSITY OF CALIFORNIA

608 P.2d 277 (Cal. 1980)

Opinion by: Clark, J.

Plaintiffs petitioned the superior court for writ of mandate to compel the Regents of the University of California to fix minimum salary rates for certain employees at or above the prevailing wage rates in various localities in accordance with Education Code section 92611. The trial court sustained defendants' demurrer without leave to amend on ground the statute conflicts with article IX, section 9 of the California Constitution. Plaintiffs appeal from judgment of dismissal. The judgment must be affirmed.

Education Code section 92611 provides: "The minimum and maximum salary limits for laborers, workmen, and mechanics employed on an hourly or per diem basis need not be uniform throughout the state, but the regents shall ascertain, as to each such position, the general prevailing rate of such wages in the various localities of the state.

"In fixing such minimum and maximum salary limits within the various localities of the state, the regents shall take into account the prevailing rates of wages in the localities in which the employee is to work and other relevant factors, and shall not fix the minimum salary limits below the general prevailing rate so ascertained for the various localities."

Article IX, section 9 of the California Constitution provides: "(a) The University of California shall constitute a public trust, to be administered by the existing corporation known as 'The Regents of the University of California,' *with full powers of organization and government, subject only to such legislative control* as may be necessary to insure the security of its funds and compliance with the terms of the endowments of the university and such competitive bidding procedures as may be made applicable to the university by statute for the letting of construction contracts, sales of real property, and purchasing of materials, goods, and services . . . ."

Article IX, section 9, grants the regents broad powers to organize and govern the university and limits the Legislature's power to regulate either the university or the regents. This contrasts with the comprehensive power of regulation the Legislature possesses over other state agencies.

The courts have also recognized the broad powers conferred upon the regents as well as the university's general immunity from legislative regulation. " 'The Regents have the general rule-making power in regard to the University . . . and are . . . fully empowered with respect to the organization and government of the University . . . .' [citations omitted]. '[The] power of the Regents to operate, control, and administer the University is virtually exclusive.' "

We recently pointed out "the University is intended to operate as independently of the state as possible. . . . [W]e concluded the university is so autonomous that, unlike other state agencies, it is subject to the usury laws then applicable to private persons and private universities.

It is true the university is not completely free from legislative regulation. In addition to the specific provisions set forth in article IX, section 9, there are three areas of legislative regulation. First, the Legislature is vested with the power of appropriation, preventing the regents from compelling appropriations for salaries.

Second, it is well settled that general police power regulations governing private persons and corporations may be applied to the university. For example, workers' compensation laws applicable to the private sector may be made applicable to the university.

Third, legislation regulating public agency activity not generally applicable to the public may be made applicable to the university when the legislation regulates matters of statewide concern not involving internal university affairs.

Education Code section 92611 cannot be brought within any of the three categories. A provision requiring an employer to pay prevailing wages in the community does not constitute an appropriation bill. Moreover, the Legislature remains free to refuse to appropriate the money necessary to pay prevailing wages.

Nor may section 92611 be construed as a general regulation pursuant to the police power applicable to private individuals and corporations. Prevailing wage regulations are substantially different from minimum wage statutes. A prevailing wage is in the nature of an average wage, and private persons and corporations will pay both above and below the average. Although, as petitioners point out, the Legislature and some local agencies have adopted statutes and ordinances requiring payment of prevailing wages by some governmental agencies and some of their contractors, a number of governmental agencies are not required to pay the prevailing wage. There is no showing that prevailing wage requirements have been made generally applicable to private persons and corporations.

Finally, our recent decision in *Sonoma County Organization of Public Employees v. County of Sonoma* (1979) 23 Cal.3d 296, leads us to conclude a prevailing wage requirement is not a matter of statewide concern. In that case we held "the determination of wages paid to employees of charter cities as well as charter counties is a matter of local rather than statewide concern." Sonoma invalidated statutory provisions cutting off state appropriations to cities and counties giving wage raises to employees. We pointed out that the fact the Legislature had declared the matter to be one of statewide concern is not controlling. Even before the 1970 constitutional amendment giving charter cities "plenary" authority over employee compensation, it was "held that the salaries of local employees of a charter city constitute municipal affairs and are not subject to general laws."

A statute requiring payment of prevailing wages or more is effectively a salary setting statute. Public agencies' use of taxpayers' funds to pay in excess of a prevailing wage is unwarranted, and while the statute purports to establish a minimum wage, it in effect determines the wage. Like the statute in *Sonoma* which did not set actual wages but relied upon an extrinsic fact — prior wages — the statute now before us also relies upon an extrinsic fact — prevailing wages — to fix compensation. . . .

Plaintiffs seek to distinguish *Sonoma* by noting that unlike cities and counties, the university possesses neither tax power nor delegated police power. However, the Sonoma decision was based not on existence of tax or delegated police power but on constitutional power in local authority, to the exclusion of legislative interference. As we have seen, article IX, section 9, establishing the independence of the university also curtails legislative power. Salary determination is as important to the autonomy of the university as it is to the independence of chartered cities and counties.

. . . .

The judgment of dismissal is affirmed.

NOTES

1. *Regents of the University of Michigan v. State*, 419 N.W.2d 773 (Mich. Ct. App. 1988), is also illustrative of courts' deference to constitution-based postsecondary schools. The Michigan legislature passed a law that forbade public schools from investing in, or maintaining investments in, organizations operating in Apartheid South Africa. Although it had, at the time of the lawsuit, divested itself of most of its South African investments, the University of Michigan challenged the law. The state appellate court, in reversing an order entering summary judgment for the state, held:

> The [Michigan] Constitution confers on [the] plaintiff, as it does on the controlling boards of the other institutions of higher education established by Michigan law and authorized to grant baccalaureate degrees, the general supervision of its institution and the control and direction of all expenditures from the institution's funds. Mich. Const. art 8, §§ 5 and 6 (1963).
>
> . . . .
>
> . . . [W]ithin the confines of the operation and the allocation of funds of the university, the university is supreme.

Id. at 774, 780 (internal quotation marks and citations omitted).

More recently, in *Federated Publications v. Board of Trustees of Michigan State University*, 460 Mich. 75 (1999), a newspaper publisher sued the university claiming that the procedure used for selecting a university president violated Michigan's Open Meeting Act. The Michigan Supreme Court held that "[g]iven the constitutional authority to supervise the institution generally, application of the OMA to the governing boards of our public universities is likewise beyond the realm of legislative authority." *Id.* at 89. Basically, the court held that the constitutional power endowing the university's board with authority was superior to latter legislation that encroached on its ability to operate the university. *Id.* at 88–90; *see also Regents of the Univ. of Cal. v. Aubry*, 42 Cal. App. 4th 579 (Cal. Ct. App. 1996) (constitutional power endowed to university allowed it to avoid paying prevailing wages while building married housing in furtherance of its educational mission).

But consider *Star Tribune Co. v. University of Minnesota Board of Regents*, 683 N.W.2d 274 (Minn. 2004). In that case the newspaper brought an action to compel the University of Minnesota to disclose information in regards to the University's presidential search process pursuant to Minnesota's Open Meeting Law and Government Data Practices Act. *Id.* at 278. The Regents attempted to argue based on the holding in *Federated Publications* that they had the same constitutional authority to supervise presidential searches *without* oversight from an open information law. *Id.* at 288. Not only did the Minnesota Supreme Court expressly reject the Michigan Court's logic as contradictory, they also pointed out that the constitutional provision that court relied on requires only "[f]ormal sessions of the governing board" to be open to the public, and that Minnesota lacked a similar provision on which the University could rely. *Id.*

2. While it is generally true that courts are more deferential to constitution-based schools than statute-based schools, there is one significant exception: courts normally apply statutes of general applicability regulating the employment relationship between public employers and their employees to constitution-based institutions. *See, e.g., Colo. Civil Rights Comm'n v. Regents of the Univ. of Colo.*, 759 P.2d 726 (Colo. 1988); *Regents of the Univ. of Mich. v. Mich. Emp't Relations Comm'n*, 204 N.W.2d 218 (Mich. 1973).

2. Institutions Established by State Statute

SOUTH TEXAS COLLEGE OF LAW v. TEXAS HIGHER EDUCATION COORDINATING BOARD

40 S.W.3d 130 (Tex. Ct. App. 2000)

Opinion by: MARILYN ABOUSSIE, C.J.

Appellants South Texas College of Law ("South Texas") and Texas A&M University ("A&M") appeal from a summary judgment declaring their Affiliation Agreement void and enjoining them from acting, or purporting to act, under the Agreement. We will affirm the trial court's judgment.

BACKGROUND

On January 23, 1998, appellants entered into an "Agreement for Exclusive Affiliation between South Texas College of Law and Texas A&M University" ("Affiliation Agreement" or "Agreement"). The Agreement's preamble states that A&M is a public institution of higher education "offering courses of study and degrees in a broad range of undergraduate academic pursuits, but with no specialized curriculum for the teaching of law and granting of degrees in that field." South Texas is a free-standing, private institution offering only law degrees. According to the Agreement, A&M "believes that an exclusive affiliation with South Texas would further A&M's goals and missions by broadening its coverage of the academic disciplines and by providing a means for interdisciplinary study programs." Finally, the Agreement notes that the Education Code "provides that the Texas Higher Education Coordinating Board shall consider, enlist and encourage cooperation and cooperative undertakings between public and private institutions of higher education" and recites A&M and South Texas's belief that the affiliation will promote the best interests of each institution and "will promote the best interests of higher education in the State of Texas through the strategic utilization of public sector assets, talents and goals."

. . . .

After appellee Texas Higher Education Coordinating Board ("Coordinating Board" or "the Board") expressed concern that the Agreement could not be implemented unless and until the Board approved the addition of law to A&M's role and mission, South Texas filed suit against the Board in April 1998 seeking, *inter alia*, declarations that the Agreement did not exceed A&M's power and that the Board did not have authority to review and approve the Agreement. The Board filed a counterclaim, and A&M intervened as plaintiff. Each party filed a motion for summary judgment regarding the validity of the Agreement. In the motion on its counterclaim, the Board contended that the Agreement violated the Education Code, the Texas Constitution, and the state's public policy.

In its final judgment and order of severance, the district court found "the Affiliation Agreement to be void because it exceeds the authority granted Texas A&M University in the Texas Education Code, and because its essential purpose violates public policy as expressed in the Texas Education Code." The court expressly did not reach the question of whether the Agreement violated the Texas Constitution. The court awarded the Board permanent injunctive relief and prohibited A&M and South Texas from acting or purporting to act pursuant to the Agreement. South Texas and A&M then brought appeal to this Court.

DISCUSSION

. . . .

Public Policy

In its summary judgment motion, the Coordinating Board asserted that the Affiliation Agreement violated the public policy of the State of Texas as expressed in the Education Code. A court can declare a contract void as against public policy and refuse to enforce it. The State's public policy is expressed through its statutes. Our primary goal in interpreting statutes is to discern legislative intent, and we do so by looking first to the plain and unambiguous meaning of the words used. We thus look to the plain language of the Education Code to determine the public policy contained therein.

Entitled "Purpose," section 61.002 of the Education Code unequivocally states:

> The purpose of this chapter is to establish in the field of public higher education in the State of Texas an agency to provide leadership and coordination for the Texas higher education system, institutions, and governing boards, to the end that the State of Texas may achieve excellence for college education of its youth through the efficient and effective utilization and concentration of all available resources and the elimination of costly duplication in program offerings, faculties, and physical plants.

Tex. Educ. Code § 61.002(a) (1996). The Code further states that the Coordinating Board represents "*the* highest authority in the state in matters of public higher education." *Id.* § 61.051(a) (emphasis added). Moreover, the Board is charged with the duty to take an active part in promoting quality education in the various regions of the state. As part of that duty, the Coordinating Board is under a responsibility to develop, after consultation with the governing board of the institution, the role and mission for each public institution of higher education in Texas. A public institution of higher education cannot change its role or mission without the authorization of the Board; instead, the Board hears applications from the institutions for changes in role and mission and *itself* makes changes necessary to update the role and mission statements of each institution. The Coordinating Board also has direct control over the initiation or consolidation of degree or certificate programs. If a program is disapproved by the Coordinating Board, no funds appropriated to any institution of higher education may be expended for the disapproved program unless the program is subsequently specifically approved by the legislature.

The present issue is before us because the Affiliation Agreement implicates the Board's authority as illustrated in the above provisions. The Agreement's terms, which purport to enhance and expand A&M's existing programs, coupled with the fact that the Board has approved neither a law school nor a program in law for Texas A&M, directly infringe upon the Board's statutory authority in determining whether degree programs are in the best interest of the state's public institutions and in determining how public resources should be allocated in order to best serve the educational needs of the state. Absent specific legislative action, the Board alone has the role of ensuring the efficient and effective utilization and concentration of public assets available for higher education and eliminating unnecessary duplication. By entering into an agreement that purports to "promote the best interests of higher education in the State of Texas through the strategic utilization of public sector and private sector assets, talents and goals," appellants usurp the Coordinating Board's singular purpose and frustrate clear legislative intent. If each individual public institution of higher education had the power to determine how public-sector education assets under its control could be "strategically utilized," there would be dozens of decision-makers — an unnecessary duplication — and no single leader. Construing the statutes to result in such a situation would render those sections creating the Coordinating Board and designating it as *the* body to provide leadership and coordination for the Texas higher education system nugatory. Permitting the Agreement to stand absent the Coordinating Board's approval would not only deprive the Board of its statutorily prescribed role, but would also undermine the Board's ability to perform its designated functions of coordinating public resources and eliminating duplication.

South Texas's argument that the Affiliation Agreement is merely a compact with a private institution, and therefore does not come under the auspices of the Board's authority, fails. Section 61.051 of the Education Code requires the Board to develop a five-year master plan for higher education in the state; such plan must specifically take into account the resources of *private* institutions of higher education in the state. Even if the Agreement only implicated the resources of a private institution, the Board's role in developing the State's master plan for higher education would nevertheless be affected. However, the instant case presents a situation beyond the mere expenditure of private resources. As previously stated, the Education Code mandates that no funds appropriated to any institution of higher education be expended for any program which has been disapproved by the Board. Because the Agreement is an exclusive affiliation, Texas A&M necessarily assumes responsibility for deciding where some of its resources shall be placed. The Agreement also dictates that A&M "make available to [South Texas] appropriate office space and related support personnel for use by a Law School representative . . . ." Because the use of public property can constitute a use of public funds, and because the Agreement effectively allows A&M to expend resources without Board approval or consideration, the Agreement necessarily implicates authority reserved for the Board.

Because courts generally construe statutes so as to give effect to the whole and avoid rendering any portion surplusage, we cannot ignore those portions of the Education Code confirming the Coordinating Board's role as the highest authority in matters of public education. We accordingly overrule appellants' issues to the extent they contend that the Affiliation Agreement does not violate public policy.

Limitation on University's Authority under the Education Code

In its motion for summary judgment, the Coordinating Board argued that by entering into the Agreement, Texas A&M not only infringed on the authority of the Coordinating Board, but also exceeded the University's own authority. A&M's governing board possesses broad power to govern and manage the University. *See* Tex. Educ. Code §§ 85.21, 86.02 (1991). However, the Education Code limits A&M's powers to performing acts that are related to the University's approved role as an institution of higher education. *See id.* § 61.002(b) (1996) (charging Coordinating Board with aiding institutions of higher education to realize their full potential "within their prescribed role and scope").

The Education Code requires that each institution of higher education have a role and mission statement. *See* Tex. Educ. Code § 61.0511 (1996). The legislature has charged the Coordinating Board with adopting criteria to be used in reviewing the role and mission statements and has required that institutions apply to the Board for approval in order to make changes. The Coordinating Board's rules provide that an institution's mission statement consists of its (1) table of programs, (2) mission description, (3) historical statement, and (4) additional background information.

Neither A&M's mission description nor its table of programs state that instruction in law is within A&M's role and mission. An institution's table of programs includes all degree and certificate programs currently authorized for that institution; A&M's table of programs is blank next to "Law & Legal Studies." Under agency rules, a blank means that a degree program has not been approved for the institution and that such a program does not fall within the institution's approved mission. According to the legend on A&M's table of programs, the blank also means that "the institution has no degree programs and *no planning authority* in the category." The Agreement expressly states that the affiliation would "broaden A&M's coverage of the academic disciplines." In attempting to "broaden its coverage of the academic disciplines," A&M is attempting to expand its role and mission without prior Board approval in violation of section 61.051.

Appellants contend that the Affiliation Agreement does not envision A&M offering, or planning to offer, a law degree; thus, they argue, the Agreement is beyond the concern of the Board. Again, we disagree. In the Agreement, the parties promise to "take such action as may be necessary or appropriate from time to time to foster the effective *assimilation* of South Texas graduates, students, administration and faculty into *all aspects* of A&M's culture and affairs." (Emphasis added.) The Agreement expressly provides that an operating committee of South Texas and A&M representatives will meet at least twice a year to discuss joint degrees, combined degrees, and certification programs, and that an affiliation committee of representatives from both institutions will meet as needed to discuss "development and joint and combined degree plans." The Agreement also allows Texas A&M to plan for ultimately issuing a law degree by implicating A&M in the hiring and administration at South Texas; the Agreement allows A&M to have input regarding candidates for tenure and faculty appointments at South Texas, allows A&M to have representatives present on the Board of Directors, Executive Committee of the Board of Directors, each other standing committee of the Board of Directors,

Operating Committee, and Admissions Committee, and allows A&M's President to submit to South Texas's Board of Directors an evaluation of the law school's President and Dean and make recommendations for a replacement for South Texas's President and Dean should the position become vacant. In addition, the record contains evidence of A&M's own president stating, "It has been our ambition for many years to have a law college." Clearly the Affiliation Agreement contemplates more than merely "enhancing" A&M's existing programs; it represents a conspicuous step in planning for the addition of legal studies and for a law degree to be issued by A&M, an action for which A&M now lacks authority. Before A&M can even "plan" to expand its role and mission, it must gain approval of the Board.

As noted in the Coordinating Board's summary judgment motion, a public institution may not add any "new department, school, degree program, or certificate program . . . except with specific prior approval of the Coordinating Board." "New" is a relative term. . . . Even if, as appellants contend, the Affiliation Agreement merely allows A&M to offer existing, approved programs in different ways, changing the way in which A&M offers the existing programs would create "new" programs requiring Coordinating Board approval.

We are likewise unpersuaded by appellants' argument that the Affiliation Agreement fulfills the legislative directive that the Coordinating Board encourage cooperation between public and private institutions of higher education. Section 61.064 provides that the Coordinating Board shall "(2) encourage cooperation between public and private institutions of higher education wherever possible and may enter into cooperative undertakings with those institutions on a shared-cost basis as permitted by law; . . . and (4) cooperate with these private institutions, within statutory and constitutional limitations, to achieve the purposes of this chapter." As the Coordinating Board noted in its motion for summary judgment, however, this section only addresses *the Board's* authority to enter into these cooperative undertakings. The Education Code does direct *the Board* to encourage cooperative programs and agreements among institutions of higher education, including agreements relating to degree offerings and library sharing. Even assuming this section relates to agreements between public and private institutions, it clearly suggests *Board* involvement. The Coordinating Board decided that this Affiliation Agreement violated both statutory and constitutional provisions. We overrule appellants' complaints that the trial court erred by finding that the Agreement exceeds A&M's authority and infringes upon the Coordinating Board's authority. Because we have held that general provisions of the Agreement violate both the law and public policy, we need not address appellants' contention that the Coordinating Board is attempting, without authority, to regulate A&M's use of its name. Without regard to whether A&M's name is used in connection with the affiliation, A&M has exceeded its authority by implicating itself in the governance of a law school, thereby expanding its role and mission; this it cannot do without Board approval.

. . . .

CONCLUSION

Having determined that the district court did not err (1) in granting summary judgment on the basis that appellants' Affiliation Agreement violated the laws and public policy of this state and is therefore void and (2) in ordering appellants to cease operating pursuant to the void Agreement, we affirm the district court judgment.

NOTES

1. The above case was later distinguished by *Texas A&M University-Kingsville v. Lawson*, 127 S.W.3d 866 (Tex. App. 2004). The University in *Lawson* tried to get out of a settlement agreement with a wrongfully dismissed professor by arguing that the original contract was void. *Id.* at 873. The language in the contract described the professor as an "assistant professor" when his actual position was that of "instructor"; on this basis the University argued the settlement agreement would force them to lie about the nature of Lawson's employment and that such an act was both illegal and against public policy. *Id.* The court rejected that logic, holding that for an agreement to be against public policy, there must be an injury to the public good. *Id.* at 874. Simply referring to an employee as a different position was not, in this case, injurious to the public. Does this holding modify the holding in *South Texas* in any way?

2. Being a statute-based institution can have its positives and negatives. On the positive side, as exemplified in *Board of Trustees of Howard Community College v. John K. Ruff, Inc.*, 366 A.2d 360 (Md. 1976), the court held that the board of Howard Community College was a state agency allowing the board to argue that sovereign immunity barred a lawsuit against it for breach of contract.

On the negative side, in *Moore v. Board of Regents of the University of the State of New York*, 390 N.Y.S.2d 582 (N.Y. Sup. Ct. 1977), a New York trial court held that the state commissioner of education, acting for the constitutionally created state board of regents, had the authority to deregister the history and English doctoral programs at the State University of New York at Albany, an institution created by statute. The decision was ultimately affirmed by the New York Court of Appeals, although the state's highest court noted that the Regents' power "is not unbridled and is not an all-encompassing power permitting the Regents' intervention in the day-to-day operations of the institutions of higher education in New York." 407 N.Y.S.2d 452, 457 (N.Y. 1978).

For another example of a university's statutory incorporation limiting its board's administrative freedom, see *Board of Governors of University of North Carolina v. U.S. Department of Labor*, 917 F.2d 812 (4th Cir. 1990), in which the court held that the North Carolina statute delegating power to the Board of Governors limited the Board's ability to divest power away from itself to other campuses.

3. What is the modern rationale for treating constitution-based postsecondary schools and statute-based postsecondary schools differently? Is it enough that, as an accident of state constitutional history, some schools enjoy exponentially more discretion than others? Did the drafters of state constitutions intend for schools written into constitutional law to enjoy preferential treatment over other schools?

As the Florida Supreme Court succinctly put it: "The Constitution is the supreme law of the land," and all subsequent legislation is created by the power of the constitution and subject to it. *Coleman v. State*, 118 Fla. 201, 205 (1935); *see also Am. Bush v. City of S. Salt Lake*, 140 P.3d 1235, 1243 (Utah 2006) (Utah's constitution is "a superior, paramount law that fixes the boundaries of power granted to the branches of state government, including this court.") (internal quotation marks and citations omitted). If you were charged with organizing public, postsecondary education for a new state, would you constitutionally or statutorily delegate authority to the institutions? Since statutes are more easily modified than constitutions, are statutes a better way for states and citizenry to flexibly regulate their universities and adapt over time?

B. STATE REGULATION OF PRIVATE POSTSECONDARY SCHOOLS

1. Chartering and Licensure

SHELTON COLLEGE v. STATE BOARD OF EDUCATION

226 A.2d 612 (N.J. 1967)

Opinion by: WEINTRAUB, C.J.

Shelton College (herein Shelton) attacks the constitutionality of our statute relating to the granting of baccalaureate degrees. The vehicle for this attack is an appeal to the Appellate Division from so much of a resolution of the State Board of Education "as purports to limit the duration of the authority of Appellant to confer the degree of Bachelor of Arts to September 15, 1966," which date was extended by further resolution to June 30, 1967. We certified the appeal before argument in the Appellate Division.

. . . .

Before turning to the specific challenges, we will summarize the statute and its history.

Prior to 1889 the power to confer degrees had been granted expressly in special acts of incorporation. In that year a statute . . . was adopted empowering any college founded under a general act of our Legislature to confer degrees other than a degree authorizing the practice of medicine, dentistry, or law.

In 1912 the Legislature adopted [another statute that] prohibited the conferring of a degree "until the terms and conditions of such degree * * * shall first be submitted to and approved of by the State Board of Education," with the proviso that the statute shall not apply to a school "established and conducted within this State for a period of twenty-five years prior to the passage of this act." This 25-year exemption excluded from the statute's ambit colleges formed prior to the adoption of the 1889 act already referred to, and thus excluded . . . those institutions which had received the power to confer degrees under special acts of incorporation.

In 1916 the Legislature adopted [another statute that] superseded the 1912 act just referred to . . . . Section 2 of the 1916 statute rephrased the substance of the 1912 statute, including the 25-year exemption. In addition to thus continuing the 1912 requirement for "approval" of the basis for the conferring of degrees, the 1916 statute innovated in section one the further requirement of a "license" for all institutions which confer degrees, without any exemption. We note also, for later reference, the fact that section 8 of the 1916 statute expressly stated that "If any provision of this act shall be held to be unconstitutional or invalid, such unconstitutional or invalid provision shall be considered severable from the remainder of this act, and shall be exscinded therefrom.

. . . .

In sum, then, Shelton challenges the constitutionality of a statute (1) which requires all degree-conferring colleges to obtain a license and (2) which requires approval of the basis and conditions for conferring a degree except as to institutions within the 25-year exemption.

I

First Shelton says it is beyond the power of government to regulate in any way the award of the bachelor degree, and this because of the right of free speech guaranteed in *Art.* I, para. VI of the State Constitution and the First Amendment to the United States Constitution.

It should be noted that the resolution in question does not limit in any way what Shelton may teach. Rather the resolution concerns the power to confer the bachelor degree. Hence Shelton's thesis, logically extended, must be that everyone has the absolute power to bestow degrees evidencing higher educational achievement, no matter how remote the course of instruction may be from the values the educational degree is commonly thought to hold. It contends that society may protect itself from the obvious evils of that proposition only by relying upon private evaluations of colleges, such as those made by the regional accreditation associations which now pass upon the standing of colleges on a voluntary basis.

Shelton points to no authority to support its position. The history of the subject runs strongly the other way. The public interest in higher education has been evident since medieval times. Today in most countries ministries of education control educational standards. The story in the United States has been uniquely different, for here, overall, government has played a modest role. The result has been a chaotic scene with which private interests have had to contend on a wholly cooperative basis. There emerged a system of regional associations which continue to set standards and accredit institutions. . . .

Whatever the reason for the modest governmental activity in this area, it was not for doubt as to the power of the States to act. In *Trustees of Dartmouth College v. Woodward*, 4 *L. Ed.* 629, 658 (1819), in which the charter of incorporation was held to be a contract the State could not undo, Chief Justice Marshall said, in axiomatic style:

"That education is an object of national concern, and a proper object of legislation, all admit."

And it is the degree, evidential as it is of academic attainment, which especially is an appropriate object of regulation. . . .

. . . .

In our State, the power to confer degrees has traditionally been deemed to depend upon legislative grant. . . .

That the Legislature may provide for licensure of medical colleges and condition the license upon suitable standards was held in *State Board of Medical Examiners of New Jersey v. The College of Mecca of Chiropractic, Inc.*, 6 N.J. Misc. 677 (Sup. Ct. 1928), and in further litigation between those parties. Shelton accepts those decisions but would avoid them because they involved the practice of a profession rather than the academic bachelor degree with which we are concerned. The point pressed is that as to professional matters there is danger from incompetence and fraud, and hence there is an evil to which the police power may be addressed, whereas with respect to academic education there is no necessity for governmental intervention. But the claim that the public needs no protection with respect to a nonprofessional degree rests upon nothing more than argumentative assertion.

We have no difficulty in assuming the Legislature found a public interest in the bachelor degree, for it is commonplace that government and private segments of our society look to the degree for evidence of achievement and capacity. Hence the opportunity for imposition upon the student and those who will deal with him is quite as evident as in the case of a professional degree. Indeed, today some or all of the study required for the bachelor degree is prerequisite for most professional degrees, and licensing authorities, as for example our own Court, must depend upon the quality of the instruction given by the colleges, academic as well as professional.

It was an undisputed need for standardization with respect to degrees, both academic and professional, which sparked the development of private accreditation. But useful as private accreditation has been, it cannot deal directly with the non-accredited school. It cannot stop the substandard school or close the out-and-out degree mill. Hence bogus degrees have been vended, and no doubt still are, not only to citizens here but as well to residents of foreign countries . . . .

The statute of 1912, which sought for the first time in our State to protect the academic degree by requiring the "approval" of the State Board of Education, was a direct response to the widespread concern over the abuse of the public. . . .

. . . .

In 1897 the National Education Association resolved "that the States should exercise supervision over degree-conferring institutions through some properly constituted tribunal having the power to fix a minimum standard of requirements for admission to or graduation from such institutions, and with the right to deprive of the degree-granting power such institutions not conforming to the standards so prescribed." In 1907 Woodrow Wilson, then president of Princeton University, proclaimed that "We are on the eve of a period when we are going to set up standards," and five years later, as Governor of this State, he signed the 1912 enactment to that end.

As of 1959 apparently less than half the States required governmental approval of a school as prerequisite for the conferring of a degree. The problem being thus but partly resolved, the Council of State Governments in 1961 prepared a model statute which would require such approval. . . .

. . . .

The public stake in education has never been more evident, for today higher education is essential for the survival of man himself. The academic degree is the more meaningful on that account. The State may protect it unless the police power is restrained by some constitutional guaranty. Shelton would find that restraint in the guaranty of free speech, arguing that the power to regulate the conferring of a degree could be used to harry an institution whose teachings may be unpopular. Shelton describes its own tenets in some such vein, but has not charged or attempted to prove that the State Board has subjected it to harassment. Rather Shelton relies upon the abstract possibility that a power to regulate could be used illicitly to destroy by indirection a value secured from destruction by the Constitution, and from that premise contends that the power to regulate may not be allowed at all.

Of course the power to regulate does not depend upon a power to destroy. If government were denied the power to regulate unless it could also prohibit, there could hardly be law and order. Our statutes abound with needful restrictions upon rights of the person and of property notwithstanding the Constitution would protect those rights from destruction. Rather the Constitution condemns such exercises of the police power as are arbitrary, and leaves it to its constituted officers to say when the boundaries of that power have been breached.

Here there is no proof whatever that the State Board is bearing down upon Shelton because of Shelton's convictions upon any topic. Indeed, as we said at the outset, there is no record at all relating to the propriety of the standards adopted by the Board or their application to Shelton. The attack rests wholly upon the untenable proposition that the Constitution guarantees to everyone an absolute right to bestow the degree of bachelor of arts upon any basis or upon none at all.

II

Next, Shelton says the statute fails to set forth a sufficient standard for the exercise of the legislative power delegated to the State Board and therefore violates our State Constitution, *Art.* IV, § I, para. 1, and *Art.* III, para. 1.

The statute does not tell the State Board what standards should be met by a college worthy of the power to confer a degree, nor does the statute specify areas within which the school's capabilities should be tested. Instead the whole subject is committed to the judgment of the State Board with a statement of the goal rather than of the path to be followed to reach it. Thus *N.J.S.A.* 18:2-4 empowers the State Board in subsection "*l*" to "Advance the education of people of all ages," and to that end equips the Board with sundry powers of which the following may be mentioned here from the catalogue in the section just cited:

> b. Prescribe and enforce rules and regulations necessary to carry into effect the school laws of this State;
>
> . . . .
>
> m. Establish standards of higher education;
>
> n. License institutions of higher education as authorized by sections 18:20-5, 18:20-6, and 18:20-7 of this Title;
>
> o. Approve the basis or conditions for conferring degrees as authorized by sections 18:20-8, 18:20-9, and 18:20-10 of this Title;
>
> . . . .
>
> u. The State Board shall have all other powers requisite to the performance of its duties.

Shelton's complaint is quite like the one rejected in *Douglas v. Noble*, 261 U.S. 165 (1923). That case involved a state statute concerning the practice of dentistry. The attack made under the Fourteenth Amendment was based upon the claim that the discretion given the board of examiners with respect to licensure was so standardless as to furnish no guard against arbitrariness. Specifically the complaint was the legislature did not itself fix the scope or the character of the qualifying examination but rather left it to the board to decide what would demonstrate fitness to practice dentistry. The highest court of the State had held the statute was not intended to authorize arbitrary action, and of course the United States Supreme Court accepted that judicially found restriction. The Supreme Court unanimously upheld the statute, saying that, although the legislature could itself specify (1) what knowledge and skill will fit one to practice dentistry and leave it to the board to decide (2) whether the individual applicant had the specified knowledge and skill, the legislature was free to commit both matters to the agency, adding that "it is not to be presumed that powers conferred upon the administrative boards will be exercised arbitrarily."

And so in the case at hand, the Legislature, to protect the sundry interests in the integrity and value of the bachelor degree, could itself have written the qualifying specifications for the school and then left it to the Board to decide in each case whether the specifications were met. But the Legislature could decide, as it did, that the wiser course was to leave it to the Board to make the specifications, thus to profit from the expertise of the Board and to permit those specifications to develop with a changing educational scene. Whether that approach to the problem will better serve the public interest is itself a matter which the Constitution commits to the judgment of the Legislature. The judiciary of course may not intervene unless the legislative decision is palpably arbitrary. There is nothing before us to suggest the Legislature exceeded its constitutional authority in deciding to delegate the subject in such fullness to the State Board. Nor is there any reason to suppose the Legislature intended that the power thus delegated may be used by the Board capriciously. On the contrary, it is elementary in our State that delegated power must be exercised reasonably in its substantive aspects and that the procedural demands of due process must be honored whenever they apply. The statutory provision for rules and regulations plainly imports that the Legislature had these fundamental values in mind.

As we have said, the attack in *Douglas v. Noble*, supra, was under the Fourteenth Amendment. Here Shelton invokes provisions of our State Constitution. We therefore add that our Constitution is no more restrictive. We have recognized the power of the Legislature to leave with an administrative agent the task of achieving a goal, expressed or implied, if the Legislature could reasonably believe it was better to have the agency prepare the blueprint. . . .

. . . .

III

Shelton further charges the statute creates an unconstitutional classification in that it exempts colleges which had the power to confer the degree 25 years before the enactment of the statute. . . .

The question then is whether the exemption from this regulatory measure of degree-conferring colleges which had received the degree-conferring power by special acts of incorporation 25 or more years before the statute was enacted created a constitutionally impermissible class.

. . . .

The power to classify is pervasive, and a court may not declare the legislative judgment to be invalid unless . . . the classification is "invidious." The burden of so proving is a heavy one, and the burden is not obviated merely because the classification depends upon a date. It remains to be shown that the date is not relevant to the legislative aim and that there is no reasonable basis upon which the Legislature could find the exemption is fair or prudent. And where the evaluation depends upon the factual milieu, as we apprehend is here the case, the burden is upon the complainant to make the record, which . . . Shelton made no effort to do.

Here the Legislature apparently used a date as a way to identify colleges which had received the degree-conferring power under a special act of incorporation. Perhaps the Legislature concluded that where a prior Legislature had thus made an individual determination that the recipients of the degree-conferring power were equipped to discharge the responsibility involved, the college ought not to be called upon to seek initial approval again. Perhaps the Legislature entertained doubt as to whether the degree-conferring power could be taken away from any, or some, of the colleges which held it by special acts of incorporation, and rather than risk a challenge to the new statute on that account, chose to improve the total scene by such limited activity as was beyond contest, perhaps with the hope that the executive branch could question by litigation the right of such a college to exercise the degree-conferring power if it were no longer equal to the responsibility implied in the grant of the power. Perhaps the Legislature concluded that it could secure the maintenance by the exempted colleges of proper standards under the *licensing* provisions of *N.J.S.A.* 18:20-5, which apply to all degree-conferring colleges without exception. . . .

It seems evident that the constitutional issue cannot be resolved intelligently in the absence of a full factual picture. If it were necessary to decide the issue in order to conclude this case, it might be appropriate to permit Shelton to make a record even now. But that course seems unwarranted, for we are satisfied that if the exemption clause were invalid, the statute would nonetheless survive. There is no reason to suppose the Legislature would be so opposed to overseeing the exempted schools that it would prefer to have the degree-conferring power go unregulated in this important respect. As we noted earlier, the 1916 statute contained an express severability clause, and we find support in that provision for our evaluation of the legislative intent. We are therefore satisfied that if Shelton could demonstrate factually that the classification is bad, Shelton nonetheless could not escape the statute's provisions. This being so, we need go no further, especially since the institutions which would be affected if the exemption fell are not parties to this litigation.

IV

Finally, Shelton contends that, assuming the statute is valid, nonetheless the State Board had no power to condition the "approval" upon terms to be met and thus to subject the "approval" to annual decisions as to whether it should be withdrawn for failure to attain the standards.

We see no reason to deny the State Board the power to give a conditional "approval." The alternative would be to require all standards to be met at once. New colleges would find it difficult to get under way if total compliance were prerequisite. The State Board's approach is in the public interest and is amply authorized by *N.J.S.A.* 18:2-4(u) which grants the Board "all other powers requisite to the performance of its duties."

The resolution under appeal is therefore affirmed.

NOTES

1. In *Ramos v. California Committee of Bar Examiners*, 857 F. Supp. 702 (N.D. Cal. 1994), a federal district court also recognized the broad authority that states have over private postsecondary schools. In *Ramos*, the plaintiff operated a correspondence law school from Hawaii and was seeking to register the school with the California Committee of Bar Examiners. The Committee provided the plaintiff with a hearing and later declined the registration. The court held that the Eleventh Amendment barred the plaintiff from bringing suit against the Committee, a state agency, in federal court. The court also dismissed the plaintiff's claims of procedural due process violations against two members of the Committee. The court ruled that the plaintiff did not have the constitutionally required "legitimate claim of entitlement" to the benefit in question: here, the benefit of being registered with the state.

> In considering whether there is a legitimate claim to an entitlement here, the Court looks to the statutory and regulatory provisions pertaining to the availability of registration. There can be no doubt that the Committee may exercise discretion in determining whether to remove a correspondence law school from registration. Further, the Committee is specifically empowered to inquire into the scholastic and financial resources of a school so as to

> determine its appropriateness for students preparing to take the California bar exam. In addition, the generally broad mandate given the Committee to carry out its function indicates that the exact fashion in which registration and other goals need be carried out is left broadly to the Committee, and its governing state supervisors. The record before this Court does not indicate that registration is intended to be a right or entitlement, granted automatically like a permit.

Id. at 706.

Not only do private institutions have to register with states to become legitimate, they also have to meet and maintain accreditation requirements from private accreditation associations. In *Hiwassee College v. The Southern Ass'n of Colleges and Schools*, 531 F.3d 1333 (11th Cir. 2008), Hiwassee claimed that the Southern Association of Colleges and Schools, a private accrediting agency responsible for accreditation in the southeastern United States, violated its due process rights when the Association revoked its accreditation. The court held that the Association was not a government actor and was not bound by the Fifth Amendment's due process clause; rather, it owed Hiwassee a common law duty of due process which it had met. *Id.* at 1335. A majority of courts have made similar decisions. *See McKeesport Hosp. v. Accreditation Council for Graduate Med. Educ.*, 24 F.3d 519, 524–25 (3d Cir. 1994); *Chicago Sch. of Automatic Transmissions, Inc. v. Accreditation Alliance of Career Schs. & Colls.*, 44 F.3d 447, 449 n.1 (7th Cir. 1994); *see also Thomas M. Cooley Law Sch. v. Am. Bar Ass'n.*, 376 F. Supp. 2d 758, 766 (W.D. Mich. 2005) (declining to extend *Automatic Transmission* to find a private right of action under federal statute and holding that the common law duty of due process is the only means of challenging an agency's denial of accreditation).

Does it seem fair that an agency who, on its face, serves a public function by accrediting private and public universities and colleges does not owe the institutions it monitors a constitutional protection of due process? If states rely on these associations to accredit their public and private institutions to ensure quality academia, should the associations be held out as agents of the state?

2. Even though private universities must register with states and work closely with them to maintain their status, they remain private institutions, and in most instances, do not owe students and staff constitutional protections associated with public universities and colleges. For example, in *Grossner v. Trustees of Columbia University in City of New York*, 287 F. Supp. 535 (S.D.N.Y. 1968), a group of students sued Columbia University for violating their constitutional rights. The students occupied university buildings and performed "sit ins" to protest the university's contracts with the Department of Defense and Columbia's decision to construct a gymnasium on public land used for recreation. Columbia used police to dispel the students, and the students sued claiming that Columbia had violated their First and Fifth Amendment rights, incorporated and applicable to the states via the Fourteenth Amendment. The court held however, that in order for the Fourteenth Amendment to apply, the actions taken by Columbia had to be deemed a "state action." *Id.* at 546. Plaintiffs asserted that Columbia's mission to educate the public, large receipt of government funds, and contracts to perform research for the government qualified its actions as state actions; in response, the court stated:

> A more fundamental point against plaintiffs is that receipt of money from the State is not, without a good deal more, enough to make the recipient an agency or instrumentality of the Government. Otherwise, all kinds of contractors and enterprises, increasingly dependent upon government business for much larger proportions of income than those here in question, would find themselves charged with state action in the performance of all kinds of functions we still consider and treat as essentially private for all presently relevant purposes.
>
> . . . .
>
> Plaintiffs' remaining thought — that Columbia performs a public function in education persons which may be likened to a company town or a party primary system — is, briefly, without any basis. It is not sounder for Columbia than it would be for Notre Dame or Yeshiva. Of course, plaintiffs are correct in a trivial way when they say education is impressed with a public interest. Many things are. And it may even be that action in some context or other by such a University as Columbia would be subject to limitations like those confining the State. . . . Even the plaintiffs have not yet suggested that the University must allow all comers to demonstrate within its buildings. . . . No case anywhere, and no acceptable extension of any pertinent principle, indicates that a University like Columbia is engaged in state action when it takes such measures and conducts such procedures as those here in question.

Id. at 547–49. This finding is consistent with other circuits' decisions that have encountered similar claims against private universities. Courts almost uniformly reject the notion that private institutions are state actors. *See Furumoto v. Lyman*, 362 F. Supp. 1267 (N.D. Cal. 1973); *Blackburn v. Fisk Univ.*, 443 F.2d 121 (6th Cir. 1971); *but see Guillory v. Admins. of Tulane Univ.*, 203 F. Supp. 855 (E.D. La. 1962) (suggesting that private university may not discriminate in admissions on the basis of race because the involvement of the state is sufficient to make it a state action); *Isaacs v. Bd. of Temple Univ. of Com. Sys. of Higher Educ.*, 385 F. Supp. 473 (holding that University was a state actor because of its "statutory incorporation into the Commonwealth system of higher education, the substantial, though not controlling, representation of the Commonwealth on the University's board of trustees, and the massive financial subsidies bestowed on the University [by the Commonwealth] in order that it might provide relatively inexpensive higher education to residents of The Commonwealth").

3. A minority of courts more narrowly interpret states' authority over private colleges and universities. *See, e.g.*, Matthew Bender & Company, 1–3 Education Law § 3.02 (2009); *State v. Williams*, 117 S.E.2d 444 (N.C. 1960). In *Williams*, the state of North Carolina prosecuted the operator of a Virginia-based correspondence school that was not licensed in North Carolina, as required by state law (a law very similar to the one at issue in *Shelton, supra*). The Supreme Court of North Carolina reversed the operator's conviction, noting that while the state had broad authority over public schools, its authority over private schools was much more limited. The court wrote: "[T]he regulation of private schools under the police power of the state must be reasonable and in response to a manifest present public need or emergency." *Id.* at 448. The court ultimately held that the statute in question was an unconstitutional grant of legislative authority because it set no standards for the state Board of Education to use when evaluating license applications. *Id.* at 451.

4. The saga of Shelton College did not end with the above-mentioned decision. The school, as seen in the material that follows, again challenged New Jersey's licensing system for colleges and universities — this time on First Amendment grounds.

2. State Regulation of Religious Postsecondary Schools

NEW JERSEY BOARD OF HIGHER EDUCATION v. SHELTON COLLEGE

448 A.2d 988 (N.J. 1982)

Opinion by: O'HERN, J.

Two provisions of New Jersey's education law, *N.J.S.A.* 18A:68-3 and *N.J.S.A.* 18A:68-6, prohibit the conferring of baccalaureate degrees by any institution that has not secured a license from the State Board of Higher Education. We hold that application of these statutes to a sectarian college whose religious doctrine precludes state licensure does not violate the First Amendment.

I.

Shelton College is an institution of higher education operated by the Bible Presbyterian Church as part of the church's religious mission. Members of this fundamentalist Christian church believe that every aspect of their lives, including education, must be governed by their faith. Shelton's teachers and students believe that their presence at the college is for the purpose of preparing themselves and others to undertake missions that their Lord calls upon them to perform. Religion pervades Shelton College. Every academic subject is taught from a Christian fundamentalist perspective and students must conform their behavior to religiously derived codes of conduct. Shelton College is a school of approximately 30 students, but those who attend it cherish its mission.

The procedural pilgrimage of Shelton College to this point of decision began after the school opened operations in New Jersey in the 1950's under a temporary license issued by the State. In 1965, the State Board of Education passed a resolution proposing to terminate Shelton's power to confer baccalaureate degrees because the college had failed to comply with certain minimum requirements. Shelton appealed the Board's action, challenging the constitutionality of *N.J.S.A.* 18A:68-3 and *N.J.S.A.* 18A:68-6, the statutes that regulate the award of baccalaureate degrees. *Shelton College v. State Bd. of Ed.*, 48 *N.J.* 501 (1967) (*Shelton I*). . . .

The Court upheld the statutes against Shelton's constitutional attacks and affirmed the action of the State Board of Education. . . .

Thus, *Shelton I* held that the State has a substantial interest in regulating the bachelor's degree and that it may constitutionally prohibit the granting of such degrees by unlicensed institutions.

In 1971, after *Shelton I* and the conclusion of related litigation, the State Board of Higher Education revoked Shelton's temporary license to award degrees in New Jersey. Shelton College moved its operations to Florida where it obtained a license to confer bachelor's degrees in that state. It has continued to operate there up to the present time and, as late as May 1981, applied to Florida officials for renewal of its license.

In February of 1979, Shelton College submitted a new application to the New Jersey State Board of Higher Education, seeking authorization to award baccalaureate degrees in Biblical Literature, Christian Education, Elementary Education, Secondary Education, English, History, Business Management, Music Education and Natural Science. Before it secured such authorization, however, Shelton began to offer credit-bearing courses in New Jersey that it represented would lead to a bachelor's degree. On November 15, 1979, the State Board of Higher Education brought suit in the Superior Court, Chancery Division, alleging that Shelton's New Jersey operations violated *N.J.S.A.* 18A:68-3 and *N.J.S.A.* 18A:68-6 which prohibit the conferring of degrees or the furnishing of instruction for the purpose of conferring degrees, except by licensed institutions. The State Board sought an injunction restraining Shelton from engaging in any form of educational instruction, offering any credits, or granting any degrees until it obtained a license authorizing it to do so. The Chancery Court granted a preliminary injunction to that effect.

On November 19, 1979, Shelton College and various students and faculty members instituted an action under 42 U.S.C. § 1983 in the United States District Court for the District of New Jersey. The federal plaintiffs alleged that application of the New Jersey licensing statutes to Shelton College violated rights guaranteed them by the First, Ninth and Fourteenth Amendments to the United States Constitution. . . .

The District Court issued a preliminary injunction, enjoining the State from taking any action to prevent Shelton College from engaging in religious teaching or educational activities, or from publicizing or advertising these activities. Although the court granted partial injunctive relief to the federal plaintiffs, it abstained from deciding whether the New Jersey licensing statutes apply to religious institutions, such as Shelton College. The District Court stayed the federal action to permit the state courts to resolve this issue.

In February 1980, the State Board appealed the District Court's order to the United States Court of Appeals for the Third Circuit, and the federal plaintiffs cross-appealed. While the federal appeal was pending, the state court action proceeded to trial in June 1980. . . . The Superior Court upheld the constitutionality of the licensing statutes as applied to Shelton College and on December 10, 1980 entered a permanent injunction which, among other things, restrained the college from awarding course credits or degrees in New Jersey without a license from the State Board of Higher Education. . . .

On April 14, 1981, a divided Third Circuit upheld the Federal District Court's order granting injunctive relief, and approved the court's decision to stay further federal proceedings pending completion of the state court action. On May 18, 1981, the District Court entered a revised preliminary injunction that prohibited the State Board of Higher Education from enforcing or implementing the Superior Court's order of December 10, 1980, "until such time as the Supreme Court of New Jersey definitively construes the New Jersey statutes and regulations which are the subject of this action." We directly certified the matter on petition of the parties.

II.

Before addressing the constitutional issues raised by this appeal, we first consider whether *N.J.S.A.* 18A:68-3 and *N.J.S.A.* 18A:68-6 apply to religious institutions such as Shelton College. Read literally, these statutes clearly encompass Shelton College. They require that *all* institutions — regardless of religious character or affiliation — obtain a license before offering degree programs or conferring degrees. Nonetheless, defendants urge us to adopt a narrowing construction of these statutes — excluding Shelton from their ambit — so as to avoid the constitutional issues that otherwise would emerge. . . .

. . . .

Under New Jersey law, a challenged statute will be construed to avoid constitutional defects if the statute is "reasonably susceptible" of such construction. . . .

The Legislature's intent with regard to these statutes is clear and unambiguous. *N.J.S.A.* 18A:68-3 and *N.J.S.A.* 18A:68-6 speak in absolute terms. They prohibit the granting of baccalaureate degrees by *any* institution that has not secured a license from the State Board of Higher Education. The sole exception to this regulatory scheme appears in *N.J.S.A.* 18A:68-6. There the Legislature expressly exempted institutions that were operating on April 1, 1887 by virtue of special legislative grant. No such exemption was created for sectarian colleges. Nor does the legislative history even hint at intent to exclude religious schools from the scope of these statutes. To the contrary, the history of the higher education licensing provisions demonstrates a legislative intent to regulate the conferring of baccalaureate degrees by religious as well as secular institutions.

The first higher education "approval" statute, entitled "An Act to prescribe the terms and conditions under which degrees may be conferred by any school or institution of learning within this State," was adopted in 1912. This legislation did not, however, mark the State's first involvement with the bachelor's degree. Prior to 1912 the Legislature passed several special acts of incorporation that authorized a number of secular and sectarian institutions to confer baccalaureate degrees. Passage of these acts evidenced the Legislature's belief that even a sectarian college's power to confer degrees could be conditioned on state authorization. There is no reason to infer that the Legislature's view in this regard changed before passage of [the 1912 act]. We must assume therefore that when the Legislature adopted [the 1912 Act], it was aware of the existence of religiously oriented colleges. We must also assume that the Legislature understood that such institutions would come within the literal terms of the statute. Yet, although the act included an express exemption clause, it contained no exemption for religious colleges.

Related provisions of New Jersey education law supply further evidence of legislative intent. Thus *N.J.S.A.* 18A:68-2 provides that seminaries and schools of theology may grant bachelor's degrees "*subject to the provisions of this chapter.*" (Emphasis added.) This statute appears in Chapter 68 of the education laws, together with the licensing statutes.

The current statutory scheme also confirms that the Legislature affirmatively intended to regulate the conferring of degrees by religious institutions. In 1966, the Legislature created a Department of Higher Education, the office of Chancellor of Higher Education, and a Board of Higher Education. The Board has been given broad authority over the system of higher education in this State. Pursuant to *N.J.S.A.* 18A:3-13, it is the duty of the Board "to advance long-range planning for the system of higher education *as a whole* in the State." (Emphasis added.) Religious oriented colleges and universities comprise a significant proportion of the institutions of higher learning in this State. If such institutions were permitted to reject even minimal state regulation, the legislative intent manifested by these education laws would be defeated.

Finally, the practice relative to *N.J.S.A.* 18A:68-3 and *N.J.S.A.* 18A:68-6 has been to apply the licensing requirements to all degree-granting institutions, regardless of religious affiliation. The Legislature has acquiesced in this long-standing practice. This is strong evidence that the current application of these statutes conforms to legislative intent.

In summary, we see no basis to infer that the Legislature intended to exempt Shelton College and like institutions from the requirements of *N.J.S.A.* 18A:68-3 and *N.J.S.A.* 18A:68-6. We construe statutes in accord with the Legislature's intent, even if to do so will give rise to substantial constitutional questions. We hold that *N.J.S.A.* 18A:68-3 and *N.J.S.A.* 18A:68-6 apply to Shelton College.

III.

We turn now to defendants' claim that application of *N.J.S.A.* 18A:68-3 and *N.J.S.A.* 18A:68-6 to Shelton College unconstitutionally infringes upon the free exercise of their religion. Decisions in cases such as this regrettably involve courts in an examination of religious practices and inevitably call for "a delicate balancing of important but conflicting interests." *Wisconsin v. Yoder*, 406 U.S. 205, 237 (1972) (White, J., concurring). In this case we must decide whether the State's interest in regulating academic degrees constitutionally justifies the burden that such regulation may impose on defendants' freedom to hold and practice their religious beliefs.

We begin by determining whether application of the statutory licensing requirements to Shelton College interferes with the free exercise of defendants' religion. Defendants profess as a principle of their faith that the Bible commands the separation of church and state. Recently, the Bible Presbyterian Church interpreted this religious precept as prohibiting Shelton College from submitting to licensure by the New Jersey Board of Higher Education. . . .

Although the First Amendment wisely prohibits courts from questioning the validity of religious beliefs, it does not preclude judicial inquiry into the sincerity of those who claim exemption on religious grounds from a law of general application.

Despite defendants' apparently inconsistent adherence to the asserted religious tenet, however, we decline to inquire into their sincerity on the record before us. Rather, we shall assume, for purposes of this appeal, that licensure of Shelton College would conflict with a principle of defendants' religion.

Accepting this assumption, the Board of Higher Education nonetheless maintains that application of *N.J.S.A.* 18A:68-3 and *N.J.S.A.* 18A:68-6 to Shelton College does not abridge defendants' Free Exercise rights. The Board points out that even if enforcement of those statutes against Shelton causes the college to close, no direct interference with religious practice occurs because defendants' religion does not require attendance at Shelton College.

This argument undervalues the constitutional right to exercise one's religion freely. The First Amendment guarantee of religious freedom protects against more than direct state proscription of religious practices. Any state action that unduly burdens the free exercise of religion violates the First Amendment. Even facially neutral legislation may give rise to a burden on religion if, as applied to a particular religious sect, it forces individuals to choose between abandoning their religious beliefs or sacrificing an important government benefit.

. . . .

. . . *N.J.S.A.* 18A:68-3 and *N.J.S.A.* 18A:68-6 require defendants to choose between a tenet of their religion and the privilege of conferring baccalaureate degrees. . . . [W]e must conclude that the New Jersey licensing statutes, as applied to Shelton College, impose some burden on the exercise of religion.

This conclusion does not, however, terminate the inquiry. Not all burdens on religion are unconstitutional. Legislation that impedes the exercise of religion may be constitutional if there exists no less restrictive means of achieving some overriding state interest. . . .

Assuming that the revocation of [tax exempt] status does impinge upon the university's practice to some extent the question remains one of balancing — giving due consideration to the weight of the interests asserted by the government and the extent and nature of the burden on the religious practice and the religion as a whole.

The legislation at issue here advances the State's interest in ensuring educational standards and maintaining the integrity of the baccalaureate degree. Chief Justice Weintraub amply described the depth and importance of this interest from medieval times to the present in *Shelton I, supra.* We need not reconstruct that discussion here. . . .

. . . .

Shelton's education expert testified that the bachelor's degree has been severely devalued by recent trends in education and that therefore the State currently has no significant interest in regulating the award of such degrees. Other educators have earnestly urged the contrary. In their *amicus* brief to this Court, the Association of Independent Colleges and Universities of New Jersey maintained that "there is a general expectation that institutions permitted to award degrees in this State will at least meet basic standards of educational integrity." . . .

In addition, the legislation supports the State's purpose of protecting students, as potential consumers of higher education, from substandard education. It allows them to assume by virtue of a school's ability to grant degrees that it meets certain minimum standards.

That maintenance of minimum educational standards in all schools constitutes a substantial state interest is now beyond question. Nothing in this record persuades us to the contrary. The Legislature has attached great importance to the fulfillment of these goals. We have no doubt of that legislative appraisal and conclude that the New Jersey licensing statutes are supported by a strong state interest in maintaining minimum academic standards and preserving the basic integrity of the baccalaureate degree.

Having reached this conclusion, we must now decide whether granting defendants a religious exemption from the licensing statutes would significantly hinder attainment of the state interest. If so, the statutes present the least restrictive means of fulfilling an overriding governmental interest and, as such, do not abridge defendants' rights of religious freedom.

In New Jersey, the conferring of a baccalaureate degree connotes that certain minimum standards have been met by the issuing institution, and that the degree recipient has attained at least a basic level of academic proficiency. To this extent the value of academic degrees from New Jersey institutions traces directly to state regulation. Thus, by claiming a complete exemption from all state regulation defendants in effect ask that they be given a benefit without having to accept the correlative burden. In this sense, if the First Amendment requires that Shelton be permitted to confer degrees without a license, it must also require that unemployment compensation be disbursed to individuals who for religious reasons refuse to accept any employment whatsoever. . . . [T]he First Amendment compels no such result.

. . . Here, accommodation of defendants' religious beliefs would entail a complete exemption from state regulation. As noted above, such accommodation would cut to the heart of the legislation and severely impede the achievement of important state goals. Furthermore, if an exemption were created here, Shelton College would receive an advantage at the expense of those educational institutions that have submitted to state regulation. Such a development would undermine the integrity of the baccalaureate degree, erode respect for the state higher education scheme, and encourage others to seek exemptions. Thus, the uniform application of these licensing requirements is essential to the achievement of the State's interests.

In sum, although defendants' freedom of religion may suffer some indirect burden from this legislation, the constitutional balance nonetheless favors the state interest in uniform application of these higher education laws. . . .

We conclude that *N.J.S.A.* 18A:68-3 and *N.J.S.A.* 18A:68-6 as applied to Shelton College do not abridge rights guaranteed by the Free Exercise Clause of the First Amendment.

IV.

The Establishment Clause requires that a law reflect a secular legislative purpose, have a primary effect that neither advances nor inhibits religion, and avoid excessive entanglement with religion. The secular purpose of the State's program for higher education is unassailable. Defendants assert, however, that this regulatory scheme creates an excessive state entanglement with religion.

The United States Supreme Court has never questioned a state's interest in insuring, through licensure or accreditation, minimal academic standards in church-operated institutions. . . .

The Establishment Clause permits minor, unobtrusive state supervision of religiously oriented schools. *Roemer v. Maryland Public Works Bd.*, 426 U.S. 736 (1976). Only excessive entanglement is proscribed. None of the education statutes or regulations here in question mandates "active involvement of the sovereign in religious activity." *Walz v. Tax Commissioner*, 397 U.S. 664, 668 (1970). None authorizes state regulation of the *content* of an educational program. Nor does the regulatory scheme on its face require "comprehensive, discriminating and continuing state surveillance." *Lemon v. Kurtzman*, 403 U.S. [602, 619 (1971)]. Although the regulations in this area, *N.J.A.C.* 9:1-1 to -2.14, appear to be burdensome, especially as applied to a college of approximately 30 students, they explicitly call for flexibility in their administration so as to accommodate various institutions with diverse educational goals. Because Shelton College declined even to complete the licensing process, the allegation of excessive entanglement rests on speculation about the manner in which these statutes and regulations might be applied. Although one could imagine an unconstitutional application of this regulatory scheme, we are confident that the Board of Higher Education will pursue the least restrictive means to achieve the State's overriding concerns. Of course, should the Board exercise its discretion in a manner that unnecessarily intrudes into Shelton's religious affairs, the college would then be free to challenge the constitutionality of such action. At this juncture, however, we need not invalidate these statutes merely because they may be amenable to an unconstitutional application.

. . . .

V.

In sum, we find that the State's program for licensing institutions of higher education is applicable to sectarian institutions and that facially it does not unduly interfere with the free exercise of religion nor create an excessive state entanglement with religion. At the same time, we recognize the good faith with which the students of Shelton College have pursued their educational and religious goals. To accommodate the free exercise interests of the individual students without unduly interfering with the state regulatory program, and in consideration of the difficulty involved in transferring to a different college at the end of three years, we modify the judgment below to allow the awarding of earned credits and degrees to all eligible students through the end of the 1982–83 academic year and to the class of 1984 through the end of the 1983–84 academic year. No other credits or degrees shall be awarded without licensure.

As modified, the judgment of the Chancery Division is affirmed.

NOTE

The analysis used by the Supreme Court of New Jersey in *Shelton II* is somewhat dated now because of a U.S. Supreme Court case decided in 1990, *Employment Division v. Smith*, 494 U.S. 872 (1990). *See also Church of the Lukumi Babalu v. City of Hialeah*, 508 U.S. 520 (1993). In *Smith*, the Court held that a lower standard of review under the federal free exercise clause is permissible when the licensing scheme is "generally applicable" and religiously "neutral." Such a standard of review — rather than the type of strict scrutiny applied in *Shelton II* — makes it much easier for states to regulate religious postsecondary schools. However, following the *Smith* decision, Congress enacted the Religious Land Use and Institutionalized Person Act in 2000, commonly known as RLUIPA and codified as 42 U.S.C. § 2000cc, *et seq.* The Act, in pertinent part states:

> No government shall impose or implement a land use regulation in a manner that imposes a substantial burden on the religious exercise of a person, including a religious assembly or institution, unless the government can demonstrate that imposition of the burden on that person, assembly or institution
>
> a. is in furtherance of a compelling governmental interest; and
>
> b. is the least restrictive means of furthering that compelling governmental interest.

42 U.S.C. § 2000cc(a). Is this statutory standard more aligned with the analysis in *Shelton II* or *Smith*?

The following case incorporates more recent developments in case law that many courts currently rely on in reaching their decisions.

HEB MINISTRIES, INC. v. TEXAS HIGHER EDUCATION COORDINATING BOARD

235 S.W.3d 627 (Texas 2007)

Opinion by: Nathan L. Hecht, J.

The State of Texas requires a private post-secondary school to meet prescribed standards before it may call itself a "seminary" or use words like "degree", "associate", "bachelor", "master", and "doctor" — or their equivalents — to recognize attainment in religious education and training. We must decide whether this requirement impermissibly intrudes upon religious freedom protected by the United States and Texas Constitutions. We hold it does and therefore reverse the judgment of the court of appeals and remand the case to the trial court for further proceedings.

I

A

The State of Texas goes to great lengths to ban "diploma mills" . . . . The Higher Education Coordinating Act of 1965, codified as chapter 61 of the Texas Education Code, states that "the policy and purpose of the State of Texas [are] to prevent deception of the public resulting from the conferring and use of fraudulent or substandard college and university degrees [and] to regulate the use of academic terminology in naming or otherwise designating educational institutions, the advertising, solicitation or representation by educational institutions or their agents, and the maintenance and preservation of essential academic records."

To achieve this purpose, subchapter G of the Act denies a "private post-secondary educational institution" use of certain terminology common to graduate education unless it has a certificate of authority from the Texas Higher Education Coordinating Board. Section 61.313 restricts what an institution can call itself. . . . and . . . states in part

> (a) Unless the institution has been issued a certificate of authority under this subchapter, a person may not:
>
> (1) use the term "college," "university," "seminary," "school of medicine," "medical school," "health science center," "school of law," "law school," or "law center" in the official name or title of a nonexempt private postsecondary educational institution; or
>
> (2) describe an institution using a term listed in Subdivision (1) or a term having a similar meaning.

Section 61.304 restricts the designations of educational attainment an institution may use. In 1998, when the events in this case occurred, section 61.304 stated:

> A person may not grant or award a degree on behalf of a private postsecondary educational institution unless the institution has been issued a certificate of authority to grant the degree by the board in accordance with the provisions of this subchapter. A person may not represent that credits earned or granted by that person or institution are applicable for credit toward a degree to be granted by some other person or institution except under conditions and in a manner specified and approved by the board. The board is empowered to specify and regulate the manner, condition, and language used by an institution or person or agents thereof in making known that the person or institution holds a certificate of authority and the interpretation of the significance of such certificate.

Current section 61.302(1) defines "degree" expansively:

> "Degree" means any title or designation, mark, abbreviation, appellation, or series of letters or words, including associate, bachelor's, master's, doctor's, and their equivalents, which signifies, purports to, or is generally taken to signify satisfactory completion of the requirements of all or part of

a program of study leading to an associate, bachelor's, master's, or doctor's degree or its equivalent.

. . . .

To obtain a certificate of authority, an institution must satisfy the Coordinating Board that it meets standards the Board has adopted. There are 21 at present. . . . According to the Board, its standards "represent generally accepted administrative and academic practices and principles of accredited institutions of higher education in Texas" and "are generally set forth by regional and specialized accrediting bodies". The standards are lengthy, detailed, rigorous, and comprehensive, covering every aspect of an institution's operation. Some are quite explicit, [including provisions on teacher qualifications and required curricula in associate and baccalaureate degree programs].

Other standards leave much to the Coordinating Board's discretion to determine compliance[, including general provisions on faculty members and administrators maintaining good character, and schools maintaining adequate financial resources].

An institution is exempt from subchapter G if it is fully accredited by a "recognized accrediting agency" designated by the Coordinating Board. In 1998, the Board had designated only three accrediting agencies, two of which were specifically oriented toward religious institutions. Since then, four others have been added, none with a religious focus. Although no recognized accrediting agency's standards are included in the record, for Board recognition, an accrediting agency's standards "must be at least as comprehensive and rigorous as [the Board's standards for a certificate of authority] and be as rigorously applied." An exempt institution may, and according to the Board *should*, obtain a certificate of authorization, which is not to be confused with a certificate of authority.

In sum, with a few exceptions, none material to this case, subchapter G of the Act requires that a private post-secondary institution either have Board-approved accreditation or satisfy Board-adopted standards before it can describe itself and its students' attainments with words commonly used for those purposes by such institutions. A violation is a Class A misdemeanor, may be investigated and enjoined by the Attorney General, is punishable by a civil penalty of $1,000 per day and an administrative penalty of $1,000–5,000 per offense imposed by the Commissioner of Higher Education, the Board's executive officer, and is a false, misleading, or deceptive act or practice actionable under the Texas Deceptive Trade Practices-Consumer Protection Act.

B

The parties have stipulated to all the facts.

Petitioner HEB Ministries, Inc., a church in Fort Worth, operates a school, Tyndale Theological Seminary and Bible Institute, which was founded in the early 1990s to offer a biblical education in preparation for ministry in churches and missions. By 1999, its campus consisted of a library, four or five classrooms, administrative offices, a small bookstore, and a computer department, and its enrollment was 300–350 students, with over three-fourths in correspondence courses. Tyndale is a "private postsecondary educational institution" as defined by subchapter G.

Tyndale's 1997–1998 course catalog . . . . contained a lengthy "Doctrinal Statement" setting out Tyndale's positions on issues of faith. The catalog listed 172 courses, 162 of which were in religious subjects. Of the other ten, three were in general education — "Basic English Grammar & Composition", "Read, Research & Study Basics", and "Ancient World History" — and seven were in typing, word processing, and use of the Internet, offered by the "Department of Theological and Biblical Research". The catalog offered 20 "diplomas", all in religious subjects.

Tyndale's catalog offered no "diploma" in any secular subject and no "degree" of any kind, but it characterized programs of study required for a diploma as equivalent to programs of study required for a degree at the same level. For example, the catalog referred to its "Diploma Of Theological Studies" program as a "bachelor equivalent program" and "bachelor equivalent course of studies", and the "Master of Arts Level Diploma" in "Counseling" as a "Masters Level Program".

The course catalog did not state that Tyndale's diplomas were the equivalent of college degrees, but neither did it state that they were not; it was silent on the subject. . . .

In 1998, Tyndale had never been accredited by an agency recognized by the Coordinating Board and had never obtained a certificate of authority from the Board. Tyndale never sought accreditation or a certificate of authority for what it describes as "doctrinal reasons". . . .

. . . .

At commencement exercises on June 26, 1998, Tyndale recognized graduates with 34 awards, listed in the program with titles [such as Bachelor Level Diploma in Biblical Studies, Master of Theology, and Doctor of Theology].

. . . .

In conferring these awards, Tyndale did not use the word "degree". Nevertheless, the Commissioner of Higher Education sent Tyndale a letter dated July 22, 1998, which stated [that because it had violated the Texas Education Code by granting degrees without authority and using the protected term "seminary" in its name, the school was being assessed an administrative penalty of $173,000].

. . . .

C

. . . HEB Ministries sued the Coordinating Board, the Commissioner, and the Attorney General for a declaratory judgment that sections 61.304 and 61.313(a), as applied to a school like Tyndale, violate the Establishment Clause and Free Exercise Clause of the First Amendment to the United States Constitution as well as article I, section 6 of the Texas Constitution. . . . The Coordinating Board and the Commissioner counterclaimed for collection of the previously assessed $173,000 administrative penalty, an injunction prohibiting HEB Ministries from engaging in the conduct for which it had been sanctioned, and attorney fees.

. . . .

Both sides moved for summary judgment. In their motion, the plaintiffs . . . argued, in addition to the allegations in HEB Ministries' petition, that sections 61.304 and 61.313 also violate the First Amendment's Free Speech Clause and article I, section 8 of the Texas Constitution. . . . The trial court held that section 61.313's regulation of the word "seminary" violates the First Amendment and article I, sections 6 and 8 of the Texas Constitution. In all other respects, the trial court granted summary judgment for the defendants. It ordered HEB Ministries to pay the State $170,000, the penalty assessed for granting 34 degrees . . . . The court also enjoined HEB Ministries from awarding degrees, as defined in Subchapter G, or representing that Tyndale's educational credits would be applied toward a degree at another institution, until it obtained a certificate of authority from the Coordinating Board.

The court of appeals held that neither 61.304 nor 61.313 violates the First Amendment or article I, sections 6 and 8 of the Texas Constitution. Thus, it reinstated the $3,000 administrative penalty against HEB Ministries for Tyndale's use of "seminary", and upheld the $170,000 administrative penalty for granting degrees. The court remanded the case for entry of a permanent injunction consistent with its opinion.

We granted the plaintiffs' petition for review. Petitioners, to whom we shall refer collectively as "HEB Ministries", contend that the Establishment and Free Exercise Clauses of the First Amendment and corresponding state constitutional provisions preclude the State from requiring a post-secondary school with a religious mission to meet specified standards for its operation and curriculum before it can call itself a "seminary" or use words like "associate", "bachelor's", "master's", and "doctor's" to mark student attainment in religious education and training. HEB Ministries does not challenge the State's authority to impose such standards on secular institutions and on religious institutions offering a secular education. Nor does HEB Ministries contend that the State cannot regulate use of the word "degree". It contends only that the State cannot deny the use of such higher education terminology to religious schools that do not meet its standards. Respondents, the Coordinating Board and the Commissioner (collectively "the Coordinating Board"), insist that sections 61.304 and 61.313(a) are constitutionally sound because they are part of a neutral law that is secular in purpose and generally applicable to all institutions of higher education, and that only incidentally impacts institutions offering religious instruction. The Coordinating Board argues that use of the statutorily restricted words is unimportant to the religious mission of a school like Tyndale when there are other words it can use to describe itself and its students' attainment.

. . . .

II

The Establishment Clause prohibits any "law respecting an establishment of religion". Correspondingly, article I, section 6 of the Texas Constitution states that "no preference shall ever be given by law to any religious society". We have referred to this provision and article I, section 7 as "Texas' equivalent of the Establishment Clause." The parties do not argue that there is any difference in the application of these federal and state constitutional provisions to this case, and we will assume for present purposes that they are coextensive.

Fundamentally, "[t]he 'establishment of religion' clause of the First Amendment means at least this: Neither a state nor the Federal Government can set up a church. Neither can pass laws which aid one religion, aid all religions, or prefer one religion over another." [*Everson v. Bd. of Educ.*, 330 U.S. 1, 15 (1947).] Since the government cannot determine what a church should be, it cannot determine the qualifications a cleric should have or whether a particular person has them. [*See Gonzalez v. Roman Catholic Archbishop*, 280 U.S. 1, 16 (1929).] Likewise, the government cannot set standards for religious education or training. [*See Lemon v. Kurtzman*, 403 U.S. 602, 625 (1971).] As the United States Supreme Court said long ago in *Watson v. Jones*:

> The law knows no heresy, and is committed to the support of no dogma, the establishment of no sect. The right to organize voluntary religious associations to assist in the expression and dissemination of any religious doctrine . . . is unquestioned

[80 U.S. (13 Wall.) 679, 728–729 (1872).] That said, the Supreme Court has also written:

> A system of government that makes itself felt as pervasively as ours could hardly be expected never to cross paths with the church. In fact, our State and Federal Governments impose certain burdens upon, and impart certain benefits to, virtually all our activities, and religious activity is not an exception. The Court has enforced a scrupulous neutrality by the State, as among religions, and also as between religious and other activities, but a hermetic separation of the two is an impossibility it has never required. . . .
>
> Neutrality is what is required. The State must confine itself to secular objectives, and neither advance nor impede religious activity.

[*Roemer v. Bd. of Pub. Works*, 426 U.S. 736, 745–747 (1976) (plurality opinion) (footnote omitted).]

The Coordinating Board asserts that subchapter G meets this requirement of neutrality. Though the statute regulates religious education, it does so, the Board argues, only incidentally in pursuit of its secular objective of regulating all post-secondary educational institutions generally, irrespective of whether their programs are secular or religious. In the sense that subchapter G applies to institutions across the board, we agree that it is neutral; that is, it does not single out religious programs for special treatment. But the fact that subchapter G burdens all private post-secondary institutions does not lessen its significant, peculiar impact on religious institutions offering religious courses of study. Subchapter G requires a clear, public, instantly identifiable differentiation between a religious education that meets the Coordinating Board's standards and one that does not: only an institution that meets those standards may call itself a seminary and its graduate associates, bachelors, masters, doctors, and the like. But setting standards for a religious education is a religious exercise for which the State lacks not only authority but competence, and those deficits are not erased simply because the State concurrently undertakes to do what it *is* able to do — set standards for secular educational programs. The State cannot avoid the constitutional impediments to setting substantive standards for religious education by making the standards applicable to all educational institutions, secular and religious.

Subchapter G expresses a preference for one manner of religious education over another. The religious school that chooses to educate in the manner of secular schools may use education terminology with the State's approval. Other religious schools cannot. The Coordinating Board's standards we have set out above, adopted as authorized by subchapter G, require "academic freedom" and faculty "independence" inconsistent with a doctrinal statement like Tyndale's that is at the core of its mission. Those standards set minimum faculty qualifications and require that one-fourth of the hours required for graduation from a baccalaureate program be in *each* of three groups: the humanities and fine arts, the social and behavioral sciences, and the natural sciences and mathematics. The standards also give the Board wide discretion to determine the adequacy of an institution's operations and curriculum. An accrediting agency's standards must be at least as comprehensive and rigorous for the agency to receive recognition by the Board. Such standards, prescribing as they do a detailed model for any institution offering post-secondary education, can hardly be said to impact religious institutions offering religious instruction incidentally. Subchapter G does not target religious institutions, but it directly and substantively impacts them by impeding their ability to describe themselves or their students' religious educational attainment.

HEB Ministries does not argue that the Coordinating Board's standards offend constitutional protections when applied to secular educational programs, even if provided by religious institutions, and we need not consider that issue. HEB Ministries argues only that it is constitutionally impermissible for the State to require an indication of its preference for one manner of religious education over another. HEB Ministries' course offerings are almost exclusively in religious subjects . . . . HEB Ministries offers no secular program of study. . . . It is one thing for the State to require that English majors in a baccalaureate program take science or math courses, that they be taught by professors with master's degrees from accredited institutions, and that professors have the freedom to teach that the works sometimes attributed to Shakespeare were really written by Edward de Vere, Christopher Marlowe, Francis Bacon, or Queen Elizabeth I. It is quite another for the State to require that a religious institution's baccalaureate-level education in religion include psychology courses, or that preaching or evangelism or missions be taught only by professors with master's degrees instead of practitioners from the field, or that a school's faculty have the freedom to teach that the Bible was not divinely inspired, contrary to the school's tenets of faith. As the United States Supreme Court has observed,

> training for religious professions and training for secular professions are not fungible. Training someone to lead a congregation is an essentially religious endeavor. Indeed, majoring in devotional theology is akin to a religious calling as well as an academic pursuit.

[*Locke v. Davey*, 540 U.S. 712, 721 (2004).]

The Coordinating Board acknowledges that the State cannot control religious education and training and insists that subchapter G does not do so. Compliance is voluntary. Any institution is free to choose to operate without a certificate of authority from the Coordinating Board or accreditation from a recognized agency as long as it does not use restricted terminology. But subchapter G cannot avoid the Establishment Clause merely because it allows institutions a degree of choice. The issue is whether it operates to prefer one kind of religious instruction over another. By restricting the terminology a religious institution can use, the State signals its approval or disapproval of the institution's operation and curriculum as vividly as if it hung the state seal on the institution's front door. . . .

As Tyndale explained in its course catalog, views vary on how post-secondary religious instruction should be provided. For some, the secular education model is preferred, with programs structured like those of any liberal arts school, and accreditation, though expensive, is affordable. For others, religious instruction is more insular, steeped in the doctrine and experience of a specific faith, and limited resources practically preclude obtaining accreditation. The Coordinating Board admits that subchapter G takes sides in this debate, but insists that subchapter G does so only incidentally as part of its overall regulation of private post-secondary education. We disagree that the State's expression of a preference for how religion should be taught can fairly be characterized as incidental. . . . By limiting the educational terminology a religious institution may use without the approval of the Coordinating Board, subchapter G prefers one course of religious instruction over another.

The Coordinating Board argues that subchapter G's standards are no different than sanitation standards a state might set for churches butchering meat to religious specifications. A state in such circumstances need not interfere with religious beliefs and practices to ensure that food is minimally safe for human consumption, and it cannot interfere in religious requirements when health is no longer an issue. Thus, government standards for determining that food is not only safe but kosher — a religious requirement only partly concerned with health — would involve an impermissible state preference among religious views. . . . Subchapter G helps prevent harm to students by requiring that educational institutions be financially responsible and candid about their operations. But the State's legitimate concern for student safety does not authorize it to take sides in the religious debate over how religion should be taught by setting substantive standards for religious educational curriculum and process. We have upheld regulations protecting the health, safety, and well-being of students in daycare facilities. Subchapter G is much different.

We think sections 61.304 and 61.313(a) clearly effectuate a state preference for one model of religious education over others, a preference that the Establishment Clause simply does not permit. We are mindful, however, that

> [t]he Supreme Court has rejected any absolute approach in applying the Establishment Clause. At times it has relied on the principles enunciated in *Lemon v. Kurtzman* . . . to guide it through this "extraordinarily sensitive area of constitutional law." Under *Lemon*, a government practice is constitutional if: (1) it has a secular purpose; (2) its principal or primary

effect neither advances nor inhibits religion; and (3) it does not excessively entangle the government with religion.

[*Williams v. Lara*, 52 S.W.3d 171, 189 (Tex. 2001) (footnote and citations omitted)]. In our view, the statutory provisions at issue do not pass this test.

There is nothing to suggest that either the Legislature in enacting subchapter G or the Coordinating Board in enforcing it intended any purpose other than the secular one of maintaining high standards for post-secondary education to protect legitimate institutions and their graduates and prevent public deception by "diploma mills", even though the distinct impact on religious instruction is apparent. Nor can we say that *the* principal or primary effect of subchapter G is to advance or inhibit religion, although as we have explained at length, a substantial effect of the statute is to indicate the State's preference for post-secondary religious instruction that meets the Board's standards. But it is fair to say that *a* principal or primary effect is to advance religious education the State approves and inhibit what it does not. We think it beyond serious dispute that the statute clearly and excessively entangles the government in matters of religious instruction. . . .

. . . .

Several Justices of the Supreme Court have criticized the *Lemon* test, and while we are not at liberty to take criticism for rejection, from our vantage point, the Court seems over time to have become "particularly attuned to whether the challenged government practice purposefully or effectively 'endorses' religion, an inquiry courts generally consider a component of the *Lemon* test's first and second parts." [footnote omitted] As we have explained, subchapter G clearly expresses the State's endorsement of particular religious education by allowing institutions that meet its standards to use restricted terminology. . . .

We are aware of only one other court that has considered whether state regulation of post-secondary religious education conflicts with the Establishment Clause. In *New Jersey State Board of Higher Education v. Shelton College*, the New Jersey Supreme Court upheld that state's regulation against an Establishment Clause challenge. But the school in that case, Shelton College, offered secular as well as religious programs, including elementary education, secondary education, English, history, business management, music education, and natural science. And the court's reasoning[, in which it described the regulations at issue as "minor" and "unobtrusive,"] illustrates the significant differences between the level of regulation involved in that case and this one . . . .

Subchapter G's certification process is certainly not minor or unobtrusive; it is, the Coordinating Board insists, "comprehensive and rigorous". The statute prohibits an institution from using common terminology if the sovereign is not actively involved in the institution's religious education. State examination extends to content and presentation. There is no special provision for religious instruction, and not only is the Board given no discretion to treat such education differently than secular education, it has given no indication that it would be willing to do so if it could. . . .

. . . It is hard to imagine a more active involvement in religious training than by determining whether it meets the comprehensive standards set by the Coordinating

Board, and equally hard to imagine a more direct state sponsorship of religious education than by indicating in every institution's name and on every academic award whether the State approves the programs of study. We therefore hold that sections 61.304 and 61.313(a) violate the Establishment Clause and article I, section 6 of the Texas Constitution as applied to a religious institution's programs of religious instruction.

III

A

The First Amendment also forbids any "law . . . prohibiting the free exercise" of religion. [Article I, section 6 of the Texas Constitution contains a similar prohibition.]

We have treated the state and federal Free Exercise guarantees as coextensive absent parties' argument to the contrary, and we do so again here. . . .

HEB Ministries contends . . . that subchapter G violates its Free Exercise rights by requiring that it either comply with state standards, and thereby compromise its religious training mission, or forego the use of restricted terms, including "seminary" and common program-level designations for its diplomas. The Coordinating Board asserts that subchapter G does not violate the Free Exercise Clause because it is a neutral law of general applicability, or if not, then because the State has a compelling interest in regulating post-secondary schools. The Board stresses that compliance with subchapter G is voluntary and that other terms are available to schools that do not comply.

This dispute centers on whether and how to apply the United States Supreme Court's decision in *Employment Division v. Smith*, 494 U.S. 872 (1990). In *Smith*, two Native American Church members who used peyote for sacramental purposes were fired and then denied unemployment benefits because their conduct violated state drug laws. They complained that the criminal law thus infringed on their Free Exercise rights. The Supreme Court disagreed, noting that it had "consistently held that the right of free exercise does not relieve an individual of the obligation to comply with a valid and neutral law of general applicability on the ground that the law proscribes (or prescribes) conduct that his religion prescribes (or proscribes)." The only exceptions, it stated, had

> involved not the Free Exercise Clause alone, but the Free Exercise Clause in conjunction with other constitutional protections, such as freedom of speech . . . . And it is easy to envision a case in which a challenge on freedom of association grounds would likewise be reinforced by Free Exercise Clause concerns. . . .
>
> The present case does not present such a hybrid situation, but a free exercise claim unconnected with any communicative activity . . . . Respondents urge us to hold, quite simply, that when otherwise prohibitable conduct is accompanied by religious convictions, not only the convictions but the conduct itself must be free from governmental regulation. We have

> never held that, and decline to do so now. There being no contention that Oregon's drug law represents an attempt to regulate religious beliefs [or] the communication of religious beliefs, . . . the rule to which we have adhered . . . plainly controls.

The Court specifically noted that the case did not involve "the communication of religious beliefs" or "any communicative activity". The fact that the use of peyote was prohibited by a general criminal law was "critical". In that situation, the state could not be held to showing a compelling interest to justify the law:

> The government's ability to enforce generally applicable prohibitions of socially harmful conduct, like its ability to carry out other aspects of public policy, cannot depend on measuring the effects of a governmental action on a religious objector's spiritual development.

Three years later, the Supreme Court expounded on *Smith*'s neutrality and general applicability requirements in *Church of the Lukumi Babalu Aye, Inc. v. City of Hialeah*[, 508 U.S. 520 (1993).] There, a church of the Santeria religion challenged city ordinances passed to prohibit it from sacrificing animals as part of its religious ritual. The requirement that a law be neutral toward religion, the Court said, is basic: "At a minimum, the protections of the Free Exercise Clause pertain if the law at issue discriminates against some or all religious beliefs or regulates or prohibits conduct because it is undertaken for religious reasons." Non-neutrality, the Court said, was indicated but not established by the ordinances' use of the words "sacrifice" and "ritual" because the words, though religious in origin, also have secular meanings. But even if a law is neutral on its face, if its object "is to infringe upon or restrict practices because of their religious motivation, the law is not neutral". The Court readily found that "suppression of the central element of the Santeria worship service was the object of the ordinances." The requirement of general applicability, the Court explained, was based on "[t]he principle that government, in pursuit of legitimate interests, cannot in a selective manner impose burdens only on conduct motivated by religious belief." The Court deemed that principle "essential to the protection of the rights guaranteed by the Free Exercise Clause." Clearly, the Court found, the ordinances "pursue[d] the city's governmental interests only against conduct motivated by religious belief." Having determined that the ordinances were neither neutral nor generally applicable, the Court concluded:

> A law burdening religious practice that is not neutral or not of general application must undergo the most rigorous of scrutiny. To satisfy the commands of the First Amendment, a law restrictive of religious practice must advance interests of the highest order and must be narrowly tailored in pursuit of those interests. The compelling interest standard that we apply once a law fails to meet the *Smith* requirements is not watered down but really means what it says. A law that targets religious conduct for distinctive treatment or advances legitimate governmental interests only against conduct with a religious motivation will survive strict scrutiny only in rare cases. It follows from what we have already said that these ordinances cannot withstand this scrutiny.
>
> . . . .

Lukumi was an easy case — the Court was unanimous on the result — because the clear genesis and purpose of the ordinances was to restrict the church's sacramental animal sacrifices. . . . Though *Smith* also involved a law restricting a church's sacramental practice, its purpose was to prevent drug abuse generally and its enactment was completely unrelated to the church's practice. . . .

HEB Ministries and amici curiae argue the [Smith] rule does not apply in this case because subchapter G directly interferes with a religious group's education and training of its ministers, activities that are specifically protected by the First Amendment. In support of this argument, amici cite a Supreme Court decision prior to *Smith* that prohibited a court from deciding whether a bishop deposed by his church should be reinstated and state and federal decisions prohibiting suits against churches for employment discrimination. [footnotes omitted] But these cases address government interference in selection of the clergy, not in education and training. Subchapter G only obliquely affects religious groups' selection of their clergy. It may influence students' choices in seeking a religious course of study, but it does not prohibit a group from calling a minister who does not hold a "degree" from a "seminary" or otherwise limit a group's freedom to select whomever it chooses. While subchapter G's impact on religious education is direct and undeniable, the authorities cited shed little light on whether it infringes on Free Exercise rights. . . . Thus, we decline the invitation to analyze the Free Exercise issues here apart from *Smith* . . . .

Accordingly, we turn to the matter of how Smith applies, first to section 61.313's limitation on the use of "seminary", and then to section 61.304's limitation on terms reflecting program-level educational attainment.

B

Undoubtedly, a statute regulating the use of words like "church", "mosque", and "synagogue" by groups that do not meet state standards would not be a neutral law of general applicability permissible under Smith because the words' meanings are exclusively religious, and a law regulating their use would thus target religion. The Supreme Court said as much in *Lukumi* when it concluded that regulation of "sacrifice" and "ritual" was consistent with but not conclusive of facial discrimination because those words did not refer exclusively to religious practices, implying that if they had, it would have reached the opposite conclusion.

The meaning of "seminary" is also not exclusively religious. Its origin is secular and only metaphorically related to education. Derived from the Latin *semen*, meaning "seed", "seminary" once meant a seedbed but later a school, where, figuratively speaking, seeds of knowledge are planted. . . .

Primarily, however, "seminary" is used to refer to a religious school. The Coordinating Board has not pointed us to a single secular seminary in Texas, or even in the United States, for that matter, either at present or in 1997 when the Legislature amended section 61.313 to include "seminary" with "college", "university", and other institutional names as restricted words. That is not to say there are none at all, but the fact that they are rare describes the context in which the 1997 amendment was proposed and adopted.

. . . .

No legislative history explains the Legislature's intent in amending section 61.313 to add "seminary" to names institutions are restricted in using, but it must have recognized that the amendment would ensure regulation of the kind of religious study and clerical training for which seminaries primarily are known. . . . Although the amendment may not have been aimed at religious practices quite as squarely as the ordinances in *Lukumi*, its target was certainly smaller than the general public health protected by the statute in *Smith*.

The Coordinating Board argues that the amendment did not alter the fact that section 61.313 is neutral in its purposes of setting high standards for post-secondary education and prohibiting "diploma mills". Even if all seminaries were religiously affiliated, the Board contends, a seminary education is respected in the secular world and should meet the standards the public expects for graduate education. Furthermore, the Board notes, religious subjects can be taught in secular programs. Sacred texts may be studied as literature, religious history without belief in divine direction, even creeds without a profession of faith, and the same standards should apply as for other programs. But these arguments exaggerate HEB Ministries' contention in this case. HEB Ministries does not contend that secular education, whether provided by seminaries or other institutions, even in religious subjects, is beyond state regulation; it contends only that the State cannot regulate the religious education and training of students as part of a religious mission.

The Coordinating Board insists that section 61.313 does not violate HEB Ministries' Free Exercise rights by restricting its use of a single word, "seminary", when others are available, like "Biblical Institute", "Academy", "Center", "School", "School of Religion", or "School of Theology". It is not clear that the Board's reading of the statute is correct. Section 61.313 restricts not only the use of a listed term but also "a term having a similar meaning". If the meanings of "seminary", "school", and "school of religion" are not similar, then the meaning of "similar" is itself unclear. . . . [T]he statute, in its application to schools offering only religious instruction, targets religious practices, discriminating between those that comply with state standards from those that do not, and is not merely a neutral regulation of post-secondary education.

"[A] law restrictive of religious practice must advance interests of the highest order and must be narrowly tailored in pursuit of those interests[," *Lukumi*, 508 U.S. at 546.] . . . The Coordinating Board tells us: "The State has a strong interest in ensuring that 'seminaries' are in fact genuine places of study and academic learning." With respect to religious courses of study, we think the State has no such interest at all and is in fact incapable of determining what is "genuine" religious study and learning and what is not. The Board argues that to exclude seminaries from the State's regulation of post-secondary education would seriously undermine its effectiveness, but HEB Ministries does not argue for so broad an exclusion. It contends only that a school's religious programs need not meet state standards before it can call itself a seminary. None of the instances of diploma mills' fraud on the public cited by the Board involves such programs. In sum, the Board has failed to show that the State has any interest in restricting use of the word "seminary" by schools offering religious instruction, let alone an interest of the highest order.

Accordingly, we conclude that section 61.313's restriction on the use of the name "seminary" by schools offering only religious programs of study violates the Free Exercise guarantees of the First Amendment and the Texas Constitution.

C

HEB Ministries does not challenge the State's authority to require that a private post-secondary educational institution meet prescribed standards before it can grant degrees, which is what section 61.304 does, but contends that section 61.302(1) defines "degree" so broadly that a noncompliant school is effectively left with no words to describe educational attainment. For religious study programs, HEB Ministries asserts, this pressure to comply with subchapter G's standards governing a school's operation and curriculum content violates the Free Exercise Clause.

The first premise of HEB Ministries' constitutional complaint is correct. Section 61.302(1) casts a wide net, defining "degree" to include not only the designations "associate", "bachelor's", "master's", and doctor's", but "their equivalents", as well as "any title or designation, mark, abbreviation, appellation, or series of letters or words . . . which signifies, purports to [signify], or is generally taken to signify satisfactory completion of the requirements of all or part of a program of study leading to [a] . . . degree *or its equivalent*." The last clause forms a linguistic Mobius strip: a degree is not only anything that could possibly signify a degree, but also the equivalent of anything that could possibly signify a degree, which includes the equivalent of . . . , and so on. The Coordinating Board suggests in its brief that the definition excludes four terms, "certificate", "advanced certificate", "diploma", and "higher diploma", but those exceptions are nowhere to be found in subchapter G or in the Board's regulations. The Board offers no explanation why they alone do not signify, do not purport to signify, and are not generally taken to signify a degree or its equivalents, and no explanation is apparent, especially in the context of this case. HEB Ministries was fined $30,000 for awarding two "certificates" and four "diplomas" in "Biblical Studies" because the Commissioner concluded that Tyndale alleged that completed courses could be applied toward a degree. HEB Ministries was fined another $10,000 for awarding two "diplomas" in "Christian Studies" because the Commissioner found that Tyndale would accept them for admission to more advanced study in what it called "master's" programs. Not one of these eight awards was called a "degree" or designated "associate", "bachelors", "master's", or "doctor's" or otherwise seems to have signified a degree.

We realize we must construe statutes to avoid constitutional problems when we can, but we cannot create exceptions where none appears to exist. It is hardly surprising, of course, that "degree" is defined broadly; the purpose of subchapter G is to ensure compliance, not to provide a safe haven for noncompliant schools. Even if the definition of "degree" admits exceptions, the use of any words remotely resembling ordinary educational terminology is risky. A violation of section 61.304 carries criminal, civil, and administrative liability. If Subchapter G does not actually restrict all terminology ordinarily used to mark educational attainment, it effectively does so.

The second premise of HEB Ministries' complaint is also correct: section 61.304's prohibition against granting degrees, defined to include all useful terminology, strongly encourages, to the point of coercion, compliance with standards set by the Coordinating Board. Again, this is hardly surprising. Subchapter G is designed to ensure that private post-secondary schools operating in Texas meet prescribed standards. If it were easier for a school not to comply, the statute's effectiveness would be impaired. The Board insists that compliance is voluntary, by which it means that it is possible for a school to refuse, but the consequences of refusal are severe.

We come, then, to the issue of whether this state regulation of the terminology used in recognizing student attainment, as applied to religious educational programs, violates the Free Exercise Clause. The Coordinating Board argues that because the regulation does not target religious programs, but applies to secular and religious programs alike, it is a neutral law of general applicability that, according to the rule in *Smith*, does not impact Free Exercise rights. This argument, we think, focuses too narrowly on the concepts of neutrality and general applicability, separate from the First Amendment's concerns they are meant to help analyze, and reduces them to a rule that a regulation is permitted as long as it is universal. . . . A law is not neutral or generally applicable for purposes of applying the Free Exercise Clause merely because it affects everyone; it is important how religion is affected differently because it is religion. This concern is critical when the law affects communication, as the Supreme Court plainly implied in *Smith* by reemphasizing that the law there had no such effect.

Standards for the content of educational instruction are not neutral with regard to religious studies merely because they also apply to secular studies, as the standards under subchapter G plainly show. Academic freedom, for example, which the Coordinating Board's standards require, has no more than a limited role, and perhaps no place at all, in a school whose mission is to advance the doctrinal tenets of a specific faith. Study in general subjects outside a student's major, a desirable requirement for a liberal arts education, may be considered a distraction or worse by someone preparing for the ministry or other religious service. . . . The Board argues that section 61.304 regulates only the granting of degrees, something that is well within the State's authority, not how religious subjects are taught. But the statute's prohibition on granting degrees is so pervasive that its effect is necessarily coercive, as indeed it is intended to be.

In the sense that section 61.304 is directed to a problem, diploma abuse, that did not originate in or have any distinct association with any religious practice, the statute more closely resembles the drug law upheld in *Smith* than the animal sacrifice ordinances struck down in *Lukumi*. But section 61.304 strongly encourages compliance with state educational standards, which in turn affect the content and operation of religious educational programs, and in that sense, the statute not only differs from the laws in both cases, it affects "the communication of religious beliefs" against which *Smith* pointedly warned. We therefore conclude[, applying *Lukumi*,] that the Free Exercise Clause requires that it "must advance interests of the highest order and must be narrowly tailored in pursuit of those interests."

. . . The Legislature has identified the State's interests as "prevent[ing] deception of the public resulting from the conferring and use of fraudulent or substandard college and university degrees", "regulation by law of the evidences of college and university educational attainment", and "protection of legitimate institutions and of those holding degrees from them". . . .

We do not doubt the importance of the State's interests, but we nevertheless conclude that section 61.304 is not narrowly tailored to pursue those interests and avoid unnecessary interference with religious studies. The Board has not identified any instance of diploma fraud involving religious programs, or any complaint that an award of a diploma in religious studies did not represent the expected academic achievement. Thus, it is not clear that the purpose of subchapter G would be impaired in any way if religious programs were exempted altogether. At the very least, section 61.304's restrictions on all terminology relating to degrees need not be so pervasive for religious programs. The Board worries that any exception for religious schools might violate the Establishment Clause, but HEB Ministries does not argue that religious institutions offering secular education programs should be exempt from state standards. Amici argue that the State's interest would be fully served by requiring noncompliant institutions to disclose their lack of accreditation, even on academic award certificates. The Board does not argue that this, too, would raise First Amendment concerns but asserts only that it would be ineffective. It has not, however, provided support for its assertion.

. . . .

Accordingly, we conclude that section 61.304's restriction on the words that a religious institution may use to refer to completion of religious programs of study is so broad that it violates the Free Exercise guarantees of the First Amendment and the Texas Constitution. The State may not deny a religious program of study clearly denominated as such the use of all words capable of describing educational achievement. . . .

. . . .

The judgment of the court of appeals is reversed and the case is remanded to the trial court to vacate its injunction and award of penalties . . . and for further proceedings in accordance with this opinion.

NOTES

1. The court in *HEB Ministries* wrote that "[b]y restricting the terminology a religious institution can use, the State signals its approval or disapproval of the institution's operation and curriculum as vividly as if it hung the state seal on the institution's front door." Could it not also be said that by allowing a purely religious school to use state-sanctioned terminology applied to secular schools the court is hanging a state seal of approval on HEB Ministries?

2. What happens when an ostensibly religious institution offers a secular degree with a religious slant? In another decision from Texas, the court upheld the Texas Higher Education Coordinating Board's rejection of a certificate of authority to an institution attempting to "offer a Master of Science Degree with a major in science education from a Biblical scientific creationist viewpoint[.]" *Inst. for Creation for Research Graduate Sch. v. Tex. Higher Educ. Coordinating Bd.*, 2010 U.S. Dist. LEXIS 60699 (W.D. Tex. June 18, 2010) (internal quotation marks omitted). The Board argued that such a degree failed to meet the Board's standard for a science curriculum because the program ignored a significant amount of research and data and thus "did not adequately prepare students in the field of science education." *Id.* at *1. The court found that Subchapter G is facially neutral, that the Board's decision met the rational basis test because it had a legitimate state interest and did not specifically draft its standards to target schools that offer "science-related degrees with creationist viewpoints." Thus, the free speech and free exercise rights of the Institute for Creation for Research Graduate School (ICRGS) were not restricted because it could still offer the program as long as it did not offer it as a degree. *Id.* at *5–10, *12–13. Does this decision fit with the holding in *HEB Ministries*? Note that the court here, when holding Subchapter G is facially neutral, cited *HEB Ministries*, but cited the partial dissent without apparently recognizing it as such. *See id.* at *7. Does it matter that ICRGS specifically described its program as a degree? It is perhaps also worth noting that the court in this case had difficulty understanding plaintiff's complaint, describing it as "overly verbose, disjointed, incoherent, maundering, and full of irrelevant information." *Id.* at *6.

3. The court acknowledges that the statute at issue in *HEB Ministries* was similar in form to the statute at issue in *Employment Division v. Smith*, 494 U.S. 872 (1990): a neutral law of general applicability that forbade the use of a particular drug. But the court distinguished the Texas statute this way: "[The statute] strongly encourages compliance with state educational standards, which in turn affect the content and operation of religious educational programs, and in that sense, the statute not only differs from the laws in both cases, it affects 'the communication of religious beliefs' against which *Smith* pointedly warned." How did regulating the use of such words as "diploma" and "master's" affect HEB Ministries' communication of its religious beliefs? Does the use of other words to describe its degrees somehow interfere with HEB Ministries' ability to describe to others the core tenets of its particular type of Christianity?

4. The second prong of the oft-cited *Lemon v. Kurtzman* test asks whether a law's "principal or primary effect" advances or inhibits religion. Applying this prong, the court in *HEB Ministries* acknowledged that neither *the* principal nor primary effect of the Texas statute was to inhibit or advance religion. But the court nonetheless found the statute suspicious because "it is fair to say that *a* principal or primary effect is to advance religious education the State approves and inhibit what it does not." Aside from questionably applying the *Lemon* test, did the court not stretch the meaning of "principal or primary effect"? What did the court rely on to show that a principal or primary effect of the statute was to advance particular religious programs over secular ones, rather than, say, improving the overall quality of postsecondary education in the state by requiring schools applying and reapplying for licenses to comply with certain standards?

5. The court noted that HEB Ministries was not arguing that the Texas regulations should not apply to secular schools or religious schools with secular educational programs. But as to the latter group, what kind of line-drawing problems would there be for a court trying to determine the secularity or non-secularity of a religious school's educational program? How would a court

balance the secular and non-secular aspects of a particular curriculum without walking into thorny questions of faith?

6. The *Lemon* test has attracted controversy almost from the moment it was decided. While it is still officially good law, the court in *HEB Ministries* correctly noted that several Justices have been critical of the test, and that, over time, the Court has shifted to an analysis that looks most closely at whether a particular government practice "endorses" a religion. Developed by Justice O'Connor in *Lynch v. Donnelly*, 465 U.S. 668 (1984), the endorsement test requires a court to examine "both the subjective and the objective components of the message communicated by a government action . . . to determine whether the action carries a forbidden meaning."

Justice Scalia has been the most vocal critic of the *Lemon* test. He once had this to say about it:

> Like some ghoul in a late-night horror movie that repeatedly sits up in its grave and shuffles abroad, after being repeatedly killed and buried, *Lemon* stalks our Establishment Clause jurisprudence . . . . Over the years . . . no fewer than five of the currently sitting Justices have, in their own opinions, personally driven pencils through the creature's heart . . . and a sixth has joined an opinion doing so.
>
> . . .
>
> The secret of the *Lemon* test's survival, I think, is that it is so easy to kill. It is there to scare us (and our audience) when we wish it to do so, but we can command it to return to the tomb at will. When we wish to strike down a practice it forbids, we invoke it; when we wish to uphold a practice it forbids, we ignore it entirely. Sometimes, we take a middle course, calling its three prongs "no more than helpful signposts." [Citation omitted.] Such a docile and useful monster is worth keeping around, at least in a somnolent state; one never knows when one might need him.

Lamb's Chapel v. Ctr. Moriches Union Free Sch., 508 U.S. 384, 398–99 (1993) (Scalia, J., concurring).

7. Justice Scalia's criticism of the *Lemon* test is part of a broader disagreement he has with the judicial philosophy that stresses the importance of maintaining a strict wall of separation between church and state. His dissent in *McCreary County v. ACLU*, 545 U.S. 844 (2005), illustrates this point of view. In that case, the Court affirmed the decision of a federal district court ordering the removal of copies of the Ten Commandments from two Kentucky courthouses. The Court held that the displays had presented a predominantly religious purpose. Justice Scalia dissented, arguing that the mixing of the secular with the religious in civic life is as old as the nation itself.

> Those who wrote the Constitution believed that morality was essential to the well-being of society and that encouragement of religion was the best way to foster morality. The "fact that the Founding Fathers believed devotedly that there was a God and that the unalienable rights of man were rooted in Him is clearly evidenced in their writings, from the Mayflower

> Compact to the Constitution itself." *School Dist. of Abington Township v. Schempp*, 374 U.S. 203, 213 (1963). President Washington opened his Presidency with a prayer, and reminded his fellow citizens at the conclusion of it that "reason and experience both forbid us to expect that National morality can prevail in exclusion of religious principle." President John Adams wrote to the Massachusetts Militia, "we have no government armed with power capable of contending with human passions unbridled by morality and religion. . . . Our Constitution was made only for a moral and religious people. It is wholly inadequate to the government of any other."

Id. at 887–88.

Despite Justice Scalia's criticism of the Court's jurisprudence in this area, it seems that the gradual morphing of the *Lemon* test into an endorsement or nonendorsement test has gradually eroded the type of strict wall between church and state that Scalia derides. Consider this:

> The nonendorsement principle replaces the bright line of separationism with an uncertain screen, through which many symbols and practices of an obvious religious character will pass. The nonendorsement principle thus tolerates substantial governmental use of religious symbols; separationism as a coherent philosophy did not.
>
> More fundamentally, the nonendorsement principle rests on a foundation profoundly different from that of separationism. The nonendorsement principle is concerned with the individual alienation, or feelings of exclusion, that an observer of a government-sponsored religious symbol might experience; separationism focuses upon the social, rather than individual, harms that a church-state merger may create. Similarly, the attention paid in nonendorsement writing to insiders and outsiders rings with equal protection considerations. Though separationism achieves minority-protecting functions, it reflects the broader social purpose of secularizing the public arena and discouraging sectarian rivalries. These rivalries are more likely to occur as separationism wanes and the new regime emerges.

Ira C. Lupu, *The Lingering Death of Separationism*, 62 Geo. Wash. L. Rev. 230, 240–41 (1994).*

Must states exempt *all* religious postsecondary schools from substantive regulation, as *HEB Ministries* suggests? Would a state that enacted such an exemption be erecting an unduly strict wall between church and state? What would Justice Scalia have to say about it?

C. THE IMPACT OF OTHER STATE LAWS AND REGULATIONS ON POSTSECONDARY SCHOOLS

1. Open Meetings Laws

ASSOCIATED PRESS v. CROFTS
89 P.3d 971 (Mont. 2004)

JUSTICE JOHN WARNER delivered the Opinion of the Court.

The Respondents, members of the print and television media, filed a complaint against Appellant Richard A. Crofts in the First Judicial District Court, Lewis and Clark County. The complaint alleged that meetings between Crofts and other employees of Montana's University System were subject to Montana's open meeting laws. Crofts and the Respondents filed cross-motions for summary judgment. The District Court granted the Respondents' summary judgment motion, and awarded the Respondents their attorneys' fees and costs. Crofts appeals. We affirm in part and reverse in part the judgment of the District Court.

We restate the issues on appeal as follows:

1. Did the District Court err when it concluded that meetings between senior employees of the University System were subject to Article II, Section 9, of the Montana Constitution and Montana's open meeting laws?

2. Did the District Court correctly award the Respondents their attorneys' fees?

FACTUAL AND PROCEDURAL BACKGROUND

Montana's University System is a public education system supervised and controlled by the Board of Regents of Higher Education (the Board of Regents). Art. X, Sec. 9, Mont. Const.; § 20-25-301, MCA (2001). One of the responsibilities of the Board of Regents is to hire the Commissioner of Higher Education, who serves as the chief executive officer of the University System. The Board of Regents also prescribes the Commissioner's official duties. Art. X, Sec. 9(2)(c), Mont. Const. One of the Commissioner's official duties is to act as the person through whom all matters are presented to the Board of Regents, including reports, recommendations and suggestions from the different units of the University System.

At all times relevant to the instant case, Crofts was Montana's Commissioner of Higher Education. During the period between June 30, 1999, and December 7, 2001, Crofts held fourteen meetings with a group of upper-level employees of the University System, such as University presidents and chancellors. For its first twelve meetings, this group referred to itself in its agendas as the Policy Committee. Then, the Committee's name was changed to the Senior Management Group. The meetings were called by Crofts to discuss issues directly related to the operation of the University System. Crofts also used the meetings to seek input from Committee members on proposed actions within the realm of his authority. The various members of the Policy Committee attended the meetings in their official capacity as upper-level University employees and were compensated for their attendance with public funds.

The fifteenth meeting between Crofts and the Policy Committee was scheduled for February 1, 2002. However, before such meeting could commence, a reporter for the Associated Press entered the meeting room and requested to observe, and report on, the meeting. Crofts declined this request. The reporter refused to leave. Crofts then canceled the meeting.

On February 8, 2002, the Respondents filed a complaint against Crofts, in his official capacity as Montana's Commissioner of Higher Education. The complaint sought a declaration that the meetings between Crofts and the Policy Committee were subject to Montana's open meeting laws. The complaint also sought an order enjoining Crofts from excluding the public from such meetings.

Crofts moved for summary judgment on the Respondents' complaint on August 9, 2002. The Respondents filed a cross-motion for summary judgment that same day. . . . On January 3, 2003, the District Court issued its order, granting the Respondents' summary judgment motion, and denying Crofts' summary judgment motion.

On January 9, 2003, the Respondents filed a motion requesting that they be awarded attorneys' fees. . . . Crofts filed a notice of appeal on March 11, 2003. On April 3, 2003, the District Court granted the Respondents their attorneys' fees and costs. Crofts then filed an amended notice of appeal on April 7, 2003.

. . . .

DISCUSSION

ISSUE 1

Did the District Court err when it concluded that meetings between senior employees of the University System were subject to Article II, Section 9, of the Montana Constitution and Montana's open meeting laws?

Crofts maintains that the District Court erred when it concluded that the Policy Committee's meetings were subject to Montana's open meeting laws. The Respondents counter that the District Court's decision was proper, as Article II, Section 9, of the Montana Constitution and the open meeting laws apply to the type of meetings at issue in this case.

Article II, Section 9, of the Montana Constitution provides:

> No person shall be deprived of the right to examine documents or to observe the deliberations of all public bodies or agencies of state government and its subdivisions, except in cases in which the demand of individual privacy clearly exceeds the merits of public disclosure.

The above provision, commonly referred to as the "Right to Know" provision of the Montana Constitution, has been implemented primarily through Montana's open meeting laws, located at §§ 2-3-201 through -221, MCA (2001). The legislature created the open meeting laws with the intent that the deliberations of the public agencies of this State be conducted openly. To that end, the provisions of the open meeting laws are to be liberally construed.

Section 2-3-203(1), MCA (2001), which addresses the types of meetings subject to the open meeting laws, provides:

All meetings of public or governmental bodies, boards, bureaus, commissions, agencies of the state, or any political subdivision of the state or organizations or agencies supported in whole or in part by public funds or expending public funds must be open to the public[.]

We have previously determined that, in the context of § 2-3-203(1), MCA (2001), the phrase "public or governmental bodies" means a group of individuals organized for a governmental or public purpose. Therefore, pursuant to § 2-3-203(1), MCA (2001), any group of individuals organized for a governmental or public purpose must allow their meetings to be open to the public.

In past cases, this Court has concluded that various types of committees created by government entities to perform some type of function were public or governmental bodies required to open their meetings to the public.

In this case, while the Policy Committee was not formally created by a government entity to accomplish a specific function, we agree with the District Court that the committee in question, whether it was called the Policy Committee or the Senior Management Group, was organized to serve a public purpose. The Policy Committee met fourteen times over two and a half years to discuss matters directly related to the governance of the University System. The Committee deliberated on issues relating to, *inter alia*: (1) policy changes; (2) tuition and fee changes; (3) budgeting issues; (4) contractual issues; (5) employee salaries; and (6) legislative initiatives. The Policy Committee also advised Crofts on matters related to his duties as the Commissioner of Higher Education. How the University System conducts its business, both academically and administratively, and the job-related actions of the Commissioner of Higher Education, are public matters. Thus, the Policy Committee's meetings brought together public officials for an undeniably public purpose.

Crofts admits that the meetings in question are occasions where public officials gather for a public purpose. However, he argues that because the Policy Committee has no definite membership, no specific charter or goal to accomplish, is not created by a specific order of either the Board of Regents or Crofts, and neither votes on propositions nor takes any direct action, it is not a public body as contemplated by Article II, Section 9, of the Montana Constitution and the open meeting laws.

The determination of whether advisory committees are public bodies subject to the open meeting laws has been recognized as presenting special problems for courts. Moreover, the legislation enacted by the different states on this issue is so varied that decisions from other jurisdictions are of little help in resolving the instant question. Many factors have been considered in deciding if a particular committee's meetings were required to be open to the public. Additionally, each situation must be examined in the context of the applicable constitutional and statutory provisions.

Consideration of Montana's particular constitutional and statutory schemes leads us to the conclusion that Crofts' interpretation of what constitutes a public body is too narrow. We conclude that under Montana's constitution and statutes, which must be liberally interpreted in favor of openness, factors to consider when determining if a particular committee's meetings are required to be open to the public include: (1) whether the committee's members are public employees acting in their official capacity; (2) whether the meetings are paid for with public funds; (3) the frequency of the meetings; (4) whether the committee deliberates rather than simply gathers facts and reports; (5) whether the deliberations concern matters of policy rather than merely ministerial or administrative functions; (6) whether the committee's members have executive authority and experience; and (7) the result of the meetings. This list of factors is not exhaustive, and each factor will not necessarily be present in every instance of a meeting that must be open to the public. A proper consideration of these factors does not mandate that every internal department meeting meet the requirements of the open meeting laws. Meetings where staff report the result of fact gathering efforts would not necessarily be public. Deliberation upon those facts that have been gathered and reported, and the process of reaching decisions would be open to public scrutiny. The guiding principles are those contained in the constitution; that is "no person shall be deprived of the right to examine documents or to observe the deliberations of all public bodies or agencies of state government and its subdivisions," and "all meetings of public or governmental bodies . . . supported in whole or in part by public funds . . . must be open to the public." Art. II, Sec. 9, Mont. Const.; § 2-3-203(1), MCA (2001).

The Policy Committee is not merely a fact finding body, nor is it an *ad hoc* group which came together to consider a specific matter or to gather facts concerning a particular issue. It is a committee that was created and continued by Crofts . . . . the head of a department of the State of Montana[,] to tender advice and make recommendations.

The Policy Committee came together at times that were noticed, and agendas were prepared. Moreover, while the record does not contain minutes of the Policy Committee's meetings, the agendas make it clear that the matters deliberated were somehow memorialized, as such matters were remembered, and re-discussed at successive meetings. The Policy Committee's meetings required substantial time, inconvenience and travel by the attendees, all of whom were expected to attend. Further, the various costs of conducting the meetings were paid with public funds.

A review of the record reveals that the District Court was correct that the meetings of the Policy Committee were more than simply staff meetings. The meetings in question were held for much more than mere fact gathering and reporting. Crofts used these meetings to seek input, opinions, and guidance from the Committee regarding the policy decisions he was required to make as Montana's Commissioner of Higher Education.

As we noted above, the Policy Committee was made up of upper-level employees of Montana's University System. These upper-level employees did not convene for the purpose of delivering the results of factual investigations to Crofts. Rather, the agendas indicate that the Policy Committee deliberated, discussed, and debated a wide variety of issues. The Committee then applied their considerable knowledge to the issues, and advised Crofts on how he should proceed. The District Court found that these meetings: "included tuition and fees, student financial planning, course fees, distance education fees, athletic funding, salaries, Indian education planning, diversity, writing proficiency, credit cap, students called to active duty, and reciprocal campus services." It then went on to conclude: "All of these matters are important to the public and in particular to prospective students and employees of the University System."

In addition, the record reveals that the Committee deliberated on legislative strategy; the extent to which the Board of Regents should be involved in campus planning; guidelines for determining what percentage of the cost of a college education should be covered by tuition; budget planning, including consideration of salary increases; tuition and fees; development of information technology policies; the fiscal and political implications of a retired school district administrator teaching at a unit of the University while drawing retirement pay; whether to use interest income arising out of non-resident tuition for scholarships for non-resident students; dental hygiene pre-admission course requirements and how to attract students to the program; the implementation of writing proficiency standards; the policy concerning continuous enrollment of transfer students; and policies concerning the transfer of class credits. The facts had been gathered when the members arrived at the meeting and once there they deliberated positions and solutions. The function performed by the committee, as revealed by the record, was to make decisions on how to proceed.

Clearly, the Policy Committee met to deliberate on matters of substance. Accordingly, we hold that the Policy Committee is a public body within the meaning of Article II, Section 9, of the Montana Constitution and Montana's open meeting laws.

Crofts argues that even if the Policy Committee is deemed to be a public body, it does not hold "meetings," as contemplated in the open meeting laws, because the Committee's membership is not fixed, no number of members were required to attend to constitute a quorum, and neither direct action nor votes were taken at its meetings.

Section 2-3-202, MCA (2001), defines the term "meeting" as:

> The convening of a quorum of the constituent membership of a public agency or association described in 2-3-203, whether corporal or by means of electronic equipment, to hear, discuss, or act upon a matter over which the agency has supervision, control, jurisdiction, or advisory power.

Nothing in the plain language of § 2-3-202, MCA (2001), requires that a meeting produce some particular result or action, or that a vote on something be taken. All that is required is that a quorum of the membership convene to conduct its public business.

In this case, the parties stipulated that each person who attended a meeting of the Policy Committee was invited because he or she was an employee of the University System that held a responsible position. It was also agreed that there were no established rules of procedure and no quorum requirements. Thus, a quorum of the Policy Committee consisted of the members who were in attendance at any particular meeting. The common law rule is that a quorum of any body of an indefinite number consists of those who assemble at any meeting thereof. There being no statute, rule, or precedent to the contrary, this rule of common law applies in this instance to our interpretation of § 2-3-202, MCA (2001). Moreover, our constitution mandates that the deliberations of public bodies be open, which is more than a simple requirement that only the final voting be done in public. Devices such as not fixing a specific membership of a body, not adopting formal rules, not keeping minutes in violation of § 2-3-212, MCA, and not requiring formal votes, must not be allowed to defeat the constitutional and statutory provisions which require that the public's business be openly conducted. Therefore, we hold that the meetings of the Policy Committee were meetings within the meaning of § 2-3-202, MCA (2001).

Article II, Section 9, of the Montana Constitution provides that no person shall be deprived of the right to observe the deliberations of public bodies. Government operates most effectively, most reliably, and is most accountable when it is subject to public scrutiny. The Policy Committee is a public body which deliberates on substantive issues that are the public's business. Accordingly, we hold that the meetings of the Policy Committee are subject to the requirements of Montana's open meeting laws and Article II, Section 9, of the Montana Constitution.

ISSUE 2

[The court proceeded to reverse the lower court on the issue of awarding Respondents' attorney fees because the lower court failed to rule on Respondents' motion for attorney fees within sixty days, as required by Montana Rules of Civil Procedure.]

. . . .

For the foregoing reasons, the judgment of the District Court requiring the meetings of the Policy Committee to be open to the public is affirmed, and its award of attorneys' fees to the Respondents is reversed.

NOTES

1. Writing in dissent, another Justice of the Supreme Court of Montana criticized the majority for casting the open meetings net so broadly that it encompassed governmental bodies that were not clearly "deliberative":

> Although the Court here pays lip service to a distinction between deliberative decision-making and fact-finding, its conclusion that the Senior Management Group is a "deliberative" body does not withstand scrutiny. The Senior Management Group was not created by law, rule or regulation and thus has no legally imposed charge or mandate to decide anything. It has no definite membership and does not vote on propositions or take any direct action. Rather it is a group of upper-level university employees formed at the behest of the Commissioner of Higher Education with no specific charge to perform any function other than confer with the Commissioner. The Commissioner in turn makes recommendations to the

> Board of Regents, which, in open meetings, deliberates and makes final decisions. The management group is too far removed from the decision-making process to trigger the need for public access. Given that the Commissioner is free to disband the management group and dispense with any further meetings, it seems anomalous to hold that a group which has no collective authority, no constituent membership, and no legal obligation to meet in the first instance, must, if it does meet, give notice of its meeting, vote and maintain minutes . . . .
>
> Clearly, the Constitution guarantees the public access to the "deliberative" process whereby public agencies with governmental authority make decisions. The Court, however, needs to meaningfully define "deliberative" in such a manner that the open meeting requirements (quorums, minutes, voting and advance notice) are not counterproductively imposed on administrative or fact-finding meetings of public agencies. In deeming this ill-defined, amorphous Senior Management Group a "deliberative" decision-making body subject to open meeting requirements, the Court is creating more, not less, confusion.

Id. at 980–81 (Mont. 2004) (Leaphart, J., dissenting).

The Commissioner, in effect, was making an executive privilege-type of argument. If he could not get candid opinions from high-level employees of the University System — because of their privacy concerns — how could he hope to formulate informed policy that would then face public scrutiny through meetings of the Board of Regents? Clearly, the Policy Committee "deliberated" in one sense of the word; but did it really "deliberate" in the way envisioned by the drafters of Montana's open meeting laws? Is the court's interpretation of the laws overly formalistic?

2. As a practical matter, how could the Commissioner hold the same kinds of meetings without coming within the sweep of Montana's open meeting laws?

3. For other examples of courts construing open meeting laws against educational bodies, see *Sandoval v. Bd. of Regents of the Univ. and Cmty. Coll. System of Nev.*, 67 P.3d 902 (Nev. 2003) (rejecting claims by the state board of regents that forbidding them to stray from the published agenda violated their First Amendment rights); *Ark. Gazette Co. v. Pickens*, 522 S.W.2d 350 (Ark. 1975) (holding that committees of the board of trustees, and not just the entire board itself, were subject to the state's open meeting laws).

2. Open Records Laws

STATE EX REL. JAMES v. OHIO STATE UNIVERSITY
637 N.E.2d 911 (Ohio 1994)

Opinion by WRIGHT, J.

[William Calvin James, an assistant professor in the department of geological sciences at Ohio State University, sought access to and copies of records contained in tenure and promotion files maintained by the university in various college and departmental offices. James Garland, dean of the college of math and physical sciences, offered James access to a redacted version of James's own promotion and tenure file, but refused James access to any other employee's promotion and tenure file. As to James's promotion and tenure file, Garland refused to provide James access to the chairperson's evaluation letter and any information which might reveal the identity of persons evaluating James's work. James brought this original action in mandamus to compel the university to provide access to the disputed records.]

At issue in this case is whether documents contained in promotion and tenure files maintained by the university are public records subject to disclosure under R.C. 149.43(B), or whether the records meet any of the exceptions contained in R.C. 149.43(A)(1) so as to prevent disclosure.

The university does not dispute that it is a state agency and public office under R.C. 149.011. Rather, it argues that the records are excepted from disclosure under R.C. 149.43(A)(1). In considering the university's arguments, we are mindful that exceptions to disclosure are to be construed strictly against the custodian of public records and doubt should be resolved in favor of disclosure. Further, the burden to establish an exception is on the custodian of the public records.

The university makes two claims that the records are not subject to disclosure: that R.C. 149.43(A)(2)(a) and (b) justify redaction of the evaluators' names, and that disclosure would substantially infringe the university's constitutionally protected right to academic freedom. We reject both arguments.

The university contends that an evaluator is the equivalent of "an information source or witness to whom confidentiality has been reasonably promised" under R.C. 149.43(A)(2)(a) and (b). However, in making this argument the university ignores R.C. 149.43(A)(2), which limits the applicability of R.C. 149.43(A)(2)(a) and (b) to "[c]onfidential law enforcement investigatory record[s]." Under no stretch of the imagination can the personnel records in question be deemed confidential law enforcement investigatory records. Therefore, the university's reliance on R.C. 149.43(A)(2)(a) and (b) is at best misplaced and, at worst, disingenuous.

This is particularly true in light of the university's statement in its own "GUIDELINES FOR PROMOTION AND TENURE PROCEDURES AT THE DEPARTMENT, COLLEGE, AND UNIVERSITY LEVELS," that "[i]t is the policy of the Ohio State University to maintain confidentiality, within the limits of law, regarding access to all letters of evaluation, including those from the inside and outside evaluators, promotion and tenure committees, the chairperson, and the dean. *However, these materials are not exempted from the Ohio Public Records Act at this time.* Prospective external evaluators should be informed of both these facts." (Emphasis added.)

The university's other contention is that disclosure of the records at issue would substantially infringe its constitutionally protected right to academic freedom. Without specifically so stating, it would appear that the university is arguing that the records are not public records under R.C. 149.43(A)(1) because their release "is prohibited by state or federal law."

Basically the university's argument is as follows. Academic freedom implicates core First Amendment values. The tenure process is at the heart of academic freedom; therefore, the tenure process also implicates these values. Since the integrity of the tenure process depends on the confidentiality of evaluators of candidates, the disclosure of evaluators' names violates the university's constitutionally protected right to academic freedom.

The university's argument is based on unfounded premises and we reject its conclusion for the same reasons the United States Supreme Court rejected a similar argument when it considered whether promotion and tenure peer review documents are discoverable by the Equal Employment Opportunity Commission in a Title VII investigation. In *Univ. of Pennsylvania v. E.E.O.C.*, 493 U.S. 182 (1990), the University of Pennsylvania, a private institution, argued that its constitutional right of academic freedom would be infringed by disclosure of peer review documents to the E.E.O.C. The court rejected this argument because disclosure of the documents did not relate to the right of the university to make tenure decisions on academic grounds. Similarly, in the present case, the issue is not whether the university is permitted to decide on academic grounds who receives promotion and tenure, but whether the *records* of those decisions are public records. The university's only explanation as to how disclosure of the records will infringe on its decisions to award promotion and tenure on academic grounds is that it will not receive candid information necessary to make those decisions. As the United States Supreme Court found, the claimed injury to academic freedom purportedly caused by disclosure of the records is "remote and attenuated." In addition, it is ironic that the university here argues that academic freedom is challenged by the disclosure of the documents. It seems the antithesis of academic freedom to maintain secret files upon which promotion and tenure decisions are made, unavailable even to the person who is the subject of the evaluation.

Further, we are not convinced the integrity of the promotion and tenure system will be diminished if disclosure occurs. Academic scholars routinely critique each other's work in public forums such as conferences, journal articles, and book reviews. The existence of a tradition of confidentiality in the promotion and tenure setting does not mean that scholars will refuse to provide candid evaluations in the future simply because the records could be made available to the public. As Justice Blackmun said in *Univ. of Pennsylvania v. E.E.O.C.*, "[f]inally, we are not so ready as petitioner seems to be to assume the worst about those in the academic community. Although it is possible that some evaluators may become less candid as the possibility of disclosure increases, others may simply ground their evaluations in specific examples and illustrations in order to deflect potential claims of bias or unfairness. Not all academics will hesitate to stand up and be counted when they evaluate their peers."

Even if we were convinced that the integrity of the promotion and tenure process could be diminished by the disclosure of the documents at issue, this is a public policy consideration which it is not our place to evaluate. As we have previously recognized . . . in enumerating very narrow, specific exceptions to the public records statute, the General Assembly has already weighed and balanced the competing public policy considerations between the public's right to know how its state agencies make decisions and the potential harm, inconvenience or burden imposed on the agency by disclosure.

Therefore, we hold that promotion and tenure records maintained by a state-supported institution of higher education are "public records" pursuant to R.C. 149.43(A)(1), are not subject to any exception, and are, therefore, subject to the public records disclosure requirements of R.C. 149.43(B). Accordingly, the writ is granted.

NOTES

1. Open records cases more often involve members of the public trying to obtain information from a public college, university, or affiliated body, rather than the situation in *James*, where a university employee was trying to obtain information from the university. *See, e.g., State ex rel. Toledo Blade Co. v. Univ. of Toledo Found.*, 602 N.E.2d 1159 (Ohio 1992) (holding that a foundation affiliated with the University of Toledo was a "public office," and that the foundation had to turn over the names of its donors to a newspaper); *Western v. Carolina Research and Dev. Found.*, 401 S.E.2d 161 (S.C. 1991) (holding that South Carolina's open records laws applied to a foundation that developed land for the University of South Carolina, and that it had to make its records public).

2. In a case similar to *James* a professor was denied tenure due to his apparent lack of collegiality. *Kirsch v. Bowling Green State University*, 1996 Ohio App. LEXIS 2247 (Ohio Ct. App. 1996). Plaintiff sought to overturn a protection order under open records laws in order to gain access to the individual votes of tenure and the tenure review board's private notes recorded during the review process. *Id.* at *10. The court denied plaintiff's motion *in limine* to overturn the protection order, holding that the evidence he sought represented the private communications and mental processes of the review board and were thus not public records. *Id.* at *11. How exactly are private notes and communications different from the promotion and tenure files in *James*? Isn't it likely that those notes had an important impact on the information in such files? Why should or shouldn't a plaintiff have access to the individual votes and evaluations of a review board if that information was part of the promotion and tenure file?

3. Courts often liberally construe open records laws, placing the burden on a state college or university to either come forward with a specific statutory exception or a strong public policy argument to defeat application of the laws to the school. This applies even if the information sought will be used for commercial purposes. *See, e.g., Lieber v. Bd. of Trustees of S. Ill. Univ.*, 680 N.E.2d 374 (Ill. 1997) (holding that a university had violated Illinois' open records laws by not providing the names and addresses of admitted students to the operator of for-profit student housing); *but see Stern v. Wheaton-Warrenville Cmty. Unit Sch. Dist. 200*, 233 Ill. 2d 396 (Ill. 2009). In *Stern*, the Illinois Supreme Court held that an *in camera* inspection of the employment contract of a superintendant (that plaintiff was trying to have disclosed) was necessary to determine if there was personal information, such as a social security number, that would result in an invasion of privacy. *Id.* at 414. That information would not be subject to disclosure and would not place a burden of a specific statutory exemption on a public school. *Id.* Does this case suggest that a university could rely on a right to personal privacy to avoid disclosing information it would otherwise have to?

4. The court in *James* noted that it was not its place to consider the university's public policy argument because the state legislature had "already weighed and balanced the competing public policy considerations between the public's right to know how its state agencies make decisions and the potential harm, inconvenience or burden imposed on the agency by disclosure." Should it ever be presumed that a legislature has "weighed and balanced" all "competing public policy considerations" that might ever arise under a particular law? Is the court unduly diminishing the judiciary's role in cases such as these?

5. As a matter of policy, how can a college or university guard itself against open records claims? Is developing a formal open records policy enough? Should all state schools have an open records committee to consider such requests?

6. There are numerous state laws and regulations that vary from state to state and materially affect institutions in numerous ways. For example, a former professor at Georgia Tech sued administrators for tortious interference. *Edmonds v. Bd. of Regents of the Univ. Sys. of Ga.*, 689 S.E.2d 352 (Ga. Ct. App. 2009). Edmonds claimed that when university administrators locked him out of his lab, they interfered with his contractual obligations to third parties. *Id.* However, Edmonds' claims were dismissed because the Georgia Tort Claims Act granted "immunity to state employees for liability arising from the performance or nonperformance of their official duties or functions." *Id.* at 358. Since the administrators acted in their official state capacity when they denied Edmonds access to his lab, they were protected from personal liability. *Id.* These immunity statutes are common; *see also* CONN. GEN. STAT. § 4-165 (2007); 745 ILL. COMP. STAT. 10/2-201 (2010).

In Missouri, a baseball coach at the University of Missouri-St. Louis sued the university for age discrimination and retaliation under the Missouri Human Rights Act after the university reduced his hours to part time and withdrew his retirement and medical benefits while hiring young coaches and paying them salaries considerably higher than his. *Brady v. Curators of the Univ. of Mo.*, 213 S.W.3d 101, 104–06 (Mo. Ct. App. 2006). The coach, uninsured and suffering from colon cancer, won and received over one million dollars in damages. *Id.* at 106, 115.

These cases demonstrate the range of state laws and regulations that affect postsecondary institutions. They are not exhaustive, and reflect the need for university and college administrators to familiarize themselves with their respective state laws to protect themselves and the university from litigation.

D. THE IMPACT OF DECLINING STATE FUNDS

DENNIS JONES & JANE WELLMAN, RETHINKING CONVENTIONAL WISDOM ABOUT HIGHER ED FINANCE (2009)

America faces a growing crisis in public postsecondary education, as an unprecedented fiscal meltdown plays out at a time of growing consensus about the urgent need to nearly double levels of degree attainment. Instead of taking steps to develop an investment strategy to reduce access and achievement gaps, we are moving in the opposite direction: reductions in state finances, increases in tuition, cutbacks in enrollments, and reductions in courses and programs students need to succeed.

One might wish that this crisis is short-lived and that once it blows over, we can return to business as usual. But this storm has been brewing for the better part of the last decade, with no serious or sustained attention to what it will take to dig out of it. Part of the problem is that policy makers on all sides of the table keep looking to revenue solutions to the problem, when the evidence tells us that there isn't going to be enough new money to return us to the funding levels of the past. That means that institutional and state policy makers need to look to better ways of using the money they have — to cut unnecessary costs, increase productivity, and find better ways to target subsidies to the areas that are the most urgent public priorities.

Clearly, changing postsecondary finance without a lot of new money to grease the skids will be difficult. The status quo is always easier than change, particularly change that will be objectionable to those who benefitted most in the previous system. But political objections aren't the only barrier to changing funding in higher education; a much bigger impediment emerges in the form of conventional wisdoms about college finance, truisms about costs that aren't based in fact. The power of these myths is that they are held uncritically by people inside and outside of the academy, from presidents and trustees to governors and legislators. In an effort to advance the conversation about improving performance in higher education, we've identified our 'top ten' list of conventional wisdoms about higher education finance.

Conventional Wisdom #1: Spending increases in higher education are inevitable, because there is no way to improve the productivity of teaching and learning without sacrificing quality.

This myth equates institutional productivity with faculty labor productivity, as if all costs in higher education are driven by faculty workload and compensation. It's not true: spending on faculty is a minority of total spending in most institutions, a proportion that has been declining in all sectors for the last two decades. The belief in the inevitability of rising costs may be the most damaging truism of all, as it affects how institutions and states budget and plan, beginning with the assumption of automatic annual increases in the "base" budget. These adjustments — for things like employee benefits, and utilities, and pay increases — are typically not counted as 'real' increases in the base budget, but because they are first in line for funding increases, they end up being higher priorities than funding for programs, or new student enrollments, or student aid.

Conventional Wisdom #2: More money means more quality, and quality means higher performance.

Another enduring myth of higher education finance is that money buys quality, which is presumed to equate with performance. This logic holds if quality is synonymous with academic reputation, but neither money nor reputation equate to getting students to a degree with acceptable learning outcomes. Research in K-12 and postsecondary education shows no consistent relationship between spending and student results, but instead shows that the absolute level of resources is less important than the way resources are used within the institution. This means that leadership and intentionality matter more to educational performance than money alone.

Conventional Wisdom #3: Institutions can make up for lost public subsidies by increasing research revenue.

While there are many reasons for institutions to pursue federal research funds, supplementing unrestricted revenues isn't one of them. Research grants almost never pay for their full costs, instead requiring institutions to bear part of the cost, either overtly or covertly. The cost of faculty time goes up significantly, through reduced teaching loads. Institutions, as well as states and students, pay for this, so costs per student increase even as the amount of faculty time available for teaching goes down. Institutional leaders and policy makers share responsibility for supporting this 'mission creep,' as does the federal government, which has limited reimbursements for the indirect costs of research administration for years.

Conventional Wisdom #4: Because state governments are now minority shareholders in higher education, public policy goals should take a backseat to market rules in steering institutions.

This rationale is most commonly used to justify deregulation of tuition-setting. True, state funds have declined as a proportion of revenues among public institutions in recent years. However, the taxpayer is still the single largest funder of instruction, student services, and academic support at most public colleges and universities. State government can drive a major change agenda focusing on goals and performance with as little as 20 percent or 30 percent of total unrestricted revenues. The private sector provides an example of this, as shareholders can leverage major changes in a company's management performance with as little as three percent of the voting stock. There's plenty of room for deregulation of finance for higher education at the state level, beginning with deregulation of benefit costs that now represent at least 30 percent of payroll in most states. But no state should entirely absent itself from decisions about tuition levels or other major policy questions simply because it is not the majority shareholder.

Conventional Wisdom #5: Colleges and universities cannot be expected to invest in change or to pursue state priorities without new money. Any reductions in funds must be replaced before funds can be considered as "new."

In this budget climate, the standard of efficiency has to be met by looking at spending against performance in light of current priorities. A new financing agenda for the future has to begin by pressing the "reset" button on the usual rules for constructing the base budget, focusing on how to spend the resources that are available, rather than on how much might have been available if the past ten years had gone differently.

Conventional Wisdom #6: Instructional costs rise by the level of the student taught . . . upper-division students are more expensive than lower-division students, graduate students are more expensive than undergraduates, and doctoral candidates are the most expensive of all.

Higher spending levels don't necessarily mean higher "costs." Upper division and graduate coursework are more expensive because we've always spent more money on them. Granted, the specialized nature of coursework and smaller class sizes in upper-division and graduate coursework are partially responsible for higher costs. But institutional spending preferences, including subsidized faculty time for departmental research, are the primary reason for increased spending at higher levels. Spending patterns also reflect historic funding advantages for institutions with research and graduate education functions, since departmental research is counted as a cost of instruction. Finally, upper-division costs are higher in part because institutions lose so many first and second year students to attrition. The marginal costs of adding more upper-division students to courses that are under enrolled are very low. Increasing retention will drive down the unit cost of upper-division instruction simply because class sizes will be larger.

Conventional Wisdom #7: An expansive undergraduate curriculum is a symbol of quality, and necessary to attract students.

Many institutions equate a wide selection of undergraduate courses with quality, and a necessary asset for student recruitment. The reality for most institutions is that more than half of the lower-division credit hours are generated in 25 or fewer courses, resulting in a few high-enrollment courses and a lot of low-enrollment courses. Moreover, there is mounting evidence that a more prescribed path through a narrower and more coherent range of curricular options leads to better retention, since advising is more straightforward, scheduling is easier to predict, and students are less likely to get lost in the process. So an educationally effective undergraduate curriculum is also the most cost-effective curriculum.

Conventional Wisdom #8: States can improve postsecondary productivity if they direct more students to community colleges.

If states want to make cost-effective investment decisions, they need to pay attention to what it costs to get students to a degree, and not just entry-level costs per student. Moving more students to community colleges is a case where cutting costs may actually hurt productivity if the goal is to increase bachelor's degree attainment. Costs per *student* are lower in community colleges than in four-year and research universities, but costs per *degree* are highest in community colleges, not because they have more money, but because they award so few degrees or other credentials relative to student enrollment. This does not mean that states should increase enrollments in public research universities, but it does mean that states should be investing in institutions that put teaching and student success at the front of their missions: community colleges that are effective in translating access to a credential or to transfer, or to public four-year teaching institutions.

Conventional Wisdom #9: The state financing mechanism for higher education is broken, and we should turn to the federal government to generate the resources needed for the future.

This is a relatively new "myth," probably more of a displacement fantasy than a myth, but it's being voiced more often as states and institutions rush to get in line for new spending proposed by the Obama administration. There's little question that the state funding model for higher education is badly frayed, if not broken. But the primary problem is not a failure of postsecondary finance policy, but a function of state budgets, where growing spending on health care and public safety are crowding out other priorities. The federal policy agenda is already very crowded, and cannot realistically be looked to as a sustaining source of operating revenues for public higher education. That doesn't mean that there is no federal responsibility for the higher education funding crisis; in fact, the most significant actions the federal government could take to stabilize resources for higher education would be to reduce the growth in health care spending and pick up the full cost of the Medicaid program.

Conventional Wisdom #10: American higher education is grossly overfunded, and the investments needed to increase attainment can be achieved entirely by reallocating resources within existing institutions.

International comparisons consistently show that, on average, the U.S. funds higher education more generously than any other nation — approximately $21,000 per student per year, compared with $8,100 per student per year for OECD member nations. True enough, but these statistics include private institutions, which are on average funded much more generously than public institutions, and include tuition revenues as well as public funds. Public investment in higher education in the U.S. actually falls below the OECD average. Moreover, the majority of our students are enrolled in public community colleges and comprehensive masters' institutions, which spend between $9,000 and $11,000 per student per year — much closer to the OECD average, and well behind other American universities. These are the institutions that will do the lion's share of the work to increase access and attainment in the future.

We can no longer afford to allow false or unexamined "truths" to dominate conversations about higher education finance and performance. Costs can be contained without sacrificing either quality or access. This will require better management of resources, including using data to make decisions, paying attention to spending, and looking at the relationship between spending and results. Even so, better management of spending is a necessary but insufficient step toward doubling current levels of degree attainment. To meet that goal, we need to be reinvesting public resources in higher education, beginning with state appropriations. In this political environment, that won't happen without stronger accountability for the resources we have. We need to change our thinking about higher education finance, beginning with institutions and extending to government. Getting rid of conventional wisdoms that stand in the way of new approaches is a good place to start.

Dennis Jones is president of the National Center for Higher Education Management Systems (NCHEMS); Jane Wellman is executive director of the Delta

Project on Postsecondary Education Costs, Productivity, and Accountability. This essay is based on an earlier version that ran in Inside Higher Education.

CENTER FOR COLLEGE AFFORDABILITY AND PRODUCTIVITY, 25 WAYS TO REDUCE THE COST OF COLLEGE, #5: OUTSOURCE MORE SERVICES (2010)*

Abstract

Colleges and universities are ostensibly in the business of producing and distributing knowledge. Yet huge portions of universities are given over to doing other things: running food and lodging operations, hospitals, recreational centers, building repair and maintenance, high school education (remedial education), entertainment operations (especially intercollegiate sports), information technology services, etc. Many of these operations could be more efficiently provided by specialists in those activities. Many colleges have made some progress in this area, especially in food services, but vastly more can be done.

Colleges should explore contracting out or selling their food and lodging businesses, but also much more, such as IT operations, building maintenance, student health centers, remedial education, and even campus recreational centers. Universities with large hospitals should consider separating the hospital operations from the core university businesses. In some cases, the sale or long-term lease of capital assets is appropriate, particularly dormitories and dining halls. Resources from assets sales can finance capital projects in core academic areas. Done adroitly, colleges can rid themselves of some money-losing auxiliary operations and actually earn revenues from the leasing of campus facilities to private entrepreneurs to operate businesses (e.g., fast food restaurants in student union buildings). Some schools are even outsourcing some instructional services to for-profit companies, partnering with such companies in, for example, offering on-line or remedial education.

Although more controversial radical, the complete separation of highly commercial intercollegiate athletic activities from the university would seem to be appropriate. This is particularly true of schools with big time sports programs that often have budgets approaching and even exceeding $100 million annually. . . .

Center for College Affordability and Productivity

The Center for College Affordability and Productivity (CCAP) is an independent, nonprofit research center based in Washington, DC that is dedicated to researching public policy and economic issues relating to postsecondary education.

. . . .

---

25 Ways to Reduce the Cost of College — #5: Outsource More Services

With recent financial difficulties, it is more important than ever for colleges to make the best use of their limited resources. Responsible fiscal management necessitates that colleges decide whether their many functions should be performed internally or outsourced to an external service provider. Private enterprises increasingly outsource a wide variety of functions, but colleges have remained averse to the prospect of outsourcing. Matt Johner described the state of outsourcing as:

"[B]y no means a mainstay in higher education. It is quite the opposite . . . All other vertical markets have been employing this tool for years."

Instead, many colleges continue to perform the majority of their functions in-house, passing the cost of unnecessary inefficiencies on to students in the form of higher tuition. A 2001 AACRAO survey indicated that only a third of colleges outsourced a service that was once fulfilled in-house. Another national survey, conducted by the Mackinac Center for Public Policy, indicated that colleges were outsourcing fewer services in 2001 than they were two years prior, with only 36 percent of institutions responding that they planned to increase their use of outsourcing in the future. This trend is partly due to a common attitude among some in higher education that was expressed by a labor union official who stated bluntly, "We have a visceral dislike of outsourcing."

Rather than expend vast sums from limited resources in an effort to perform functions in-house for which they do not have any particular expertise, colleges should focus on improving the value of their core functions, for which they do possess a comparative advantage. For higher education, this is most often instructional education and research. Institutions should therefore focus on performing these functions in the most efficient manner possible, and consider outsourcing non-core, but often necessary, functions to an external vendor who specializes in providing them. When determining which functions to outsource, colleges must make a decision about whether to produce the service or procure it from elsewhere. That decision should include consideration for a number of local issues and utilize a cost-benefit analysis. There are a great number of functions that colleges should consider outsourcing that fit into three general categories: student services, business functions, and educational functions.

The Produce vs. Procure Decision

Colleges are complex institutions that perform a variety of functions and offer a number of services that require resources to provide. This section will not question whether colleges should perform certain functions or provide certain services, but instead will discuss how they should go about doing so. After an institution has decided that it wants or needs a particular function or service, there are two options for how to provide it: in-house or external (outsourced). In other words, an institution must decide whether to provide the service with its own staff and resources, or to procure it from an external vendor who specializes in providing a particular function or service. We will describe both the benefits and the potential costs and limitations of outsourcing, which must be considered when making an outsourcing decision. Cost-benefit analysis should be performed after all pertinent information is addressed.

Benefits of Outsourcing

Outsourcing has become an important aspect of the contemporary business world that is not limited to large corporations. Increasingly, small and medium-sized firms are outsourcing at least some of their functions, primarily in an effort to reduce costs. Aside from reducing costs, outsourcing has the potential to confer a number of other benefits, such as improving efficiency and enhancing organizational flexibility. These are attractive propositions for colleges that have growing bureaucratic workforces and sprawling campuses filled with a plethora of buildings for administrative, classroom, office and recreational use, all of which entail operational and maintenance costs.

Cost Reduction — Labor costs are often one of an organization's largest expenses, and include not only wages, benefits, and payroll taxes, but also the costs related to hiring, managing, and training employees. By outsourcing some functions, organizations are able to transfer these responsibilities to a firm that is able to provide such services at a lower cost, due to its expertise in providing a particular service and the fact that it likely already has access to a highly trained professional workforce. Organizations are also able to control their capital costs by outsourcing, as it permits them to convert fixed costs into variable ones and free up capital for alternative uses. This allows organizations to limit their need for plant, property, and equipment, which also reduces the expenses associated with maintenance and upgrades of such capital assets.

Improve Efficiency — A lack of in-house skills and the desire to improve operating efficiencies were cited as the two most common reasons that colleges outsource in a 2002 survey. Outsourcing allows organizations to operate more efficiently by removing tasks that would absorb valuable resources. It also provides them with access to technology and expertise that they might not otherwise have. In other words, outsourcing often permits greater efficiencies than managing functions in-house, as firms specializing in a particular function often have a *comparative advantage* in producing it. Specialization allows firms to develop an expertise in a particular function that permits them to operate more efficiently through greater economies of scale and process innovation.

Specialization often also results in enhanced production speed and quality. This creates a greater value proposition by allowing organizations to focus resources on improving the value of their core products and services, rather than spending limited resources on functions that they do not have a comparative advantage in performing. For higher education, "Cost efficiencies may be achieved by focusing on non-academic functions and employing outsourcing," without having to "threaten academic quality or institutional independence."

Enhance Organizational Flexibility — As noted above, outsourcing permits organizations to free up resources for alternative uses. This provides them with a greater degree of flexibility to adapt to a changing environment more quickly and to meet the demands of their consumers. This permits new initiatives such as programs or polices that relate to an organization's core functions to be streamlined and implemented at a more rapid pace, rather than being queued at the back of the line because scarce resources are tied up. Outsourcing also gives organizations the flexibility to alter their workforce in response to economic or other environmental changes.

Potential Costs and Limitations

The U.S. has a diverse set of institutions of higher education that serve various missions. As such, there are a number of potential costs and limitations that a college should consider when deciding whether to outsource a particular function or service or to produce it in-house. A 2005 study by the Institute of Higher Education Policy identified six general areas of concern that an institution should consider when making an outsourcing decision. The areas are listed below, along with some related concerns and questions that should be assessed when making an outsourcing decision.

Human Resources — How will the change affect faculty and staff, especially when labor unions and other contract employees are involved?

Financial Implications — How do the costs of producing internally compare to that of outsourcing? Both immediate costs and potential long-run savings should be considered, and some assumptions must be made.

Service Quality — Will outsourcing reduce the quality of service provided to the student, and if so, will this reduction in quality result in lower enrollment?

Legal and Ethical Considerations — What are the potential legal, tax, and ethical ramifications? Are there privacy issues that need to be addressed, such as FERPA?

Institutional Mission — Is the service being considered for outsourcing essential to fulfilling an institution's educational mission, and would outsourcing it detract from that mission?

Management Control — To be efficient, colleges must be able to adapt to a changing environment. Would outsourcing a service hinder an institution's ability to make critical decisions in the face of a changing environment?

Areas that Can Likely Be Outsourced

There are three general areas in which colleges will find the most opportunities for outsourcing: student services, professional services and educational services.

Student Services

Colleges provide a plethora of student services, such as dining, recreation, housing, and health care, among others. Most often, these services are provided in-house by the institutions themselves. Colleges do not have any particular advantage over the private sector in providing such services, so they should consider outsourcing many of these services.

Food Services — Residential colleges have historically provided students with meals at the infamous campus dining halls and, more recently, in food courts and other dining facilities. Colleges have also historically provided these food services internally. More recently, however, many institutions have begun outsourcing some aspects of food services. In fact, around 61 percent of colleges reported outsourcing some aspect of food service in a 2002 survey. Central Michigan University, for example, consistently lost money on its retail food services prior to contracting with a private provider in 1994. In the following five years, CMU reported savings of approximately $890,000, along with an improvement in service.

University of Southern Mississippi CFO Gregg Lassen said that he ascribed to legendary management guru Peter Drucker's business philosophy of focusing on core strengths when deciding to outsource his institution's dining services. Lassan said that, "In a higher ed setting, those strengths would be research, instruction, and services . . . cooking is not on the list." By outsourcing, USM has realized cost savings, an upgrade to its dining facilities, and a professionally trained service staff. In addition, USM is now in a position to hold its contractor accountable for the quality and service that it provides through the use of a legally enforceable contract and the option to solicit bids for competition.

Recreation — High-quality recreation facilities have become increasingly common on campus, as the current generation of students has come to expect state-of-the art recreation facilities that contain modern exercise equipment, climbing walls, Olympic-sized pools, golf courses, and more. Such facilities are expensive to build and maintain, and the costs of doing so are often passed on to students in the form of mandatory fees, regardless of whether they make use of the facilities.

There are several approaches that colleges could take to outsource recreation, depending on each institution's particular circumstances. If a college already has a recreation center, then it could outsource its management to an outside firm. One such firm that has found a niche in this market is Centers, which provides recreational management services to small institutions that have high-tech recreation facilities but don't have adequate resources or expertise to staff and operate them. Centers has a policy of not advertising its name or logo on campus facilities or equipment, in order to allow colleges to maintain their brand and to avoid the stigma of being an outsider. Centers has thus far landed contracts with Cleveland State University, Depaul University, and Jackson State University.

Some colleges may not have a recreation center, but would like to provide students with access to one. For such institutions, building and managing an exercise center is likely not the optimal strategy. Rather, it might be more cost effective to contract with area fitness centers to provide students with memberships at a group rate. This would be not only save the college money, but could also benefit the students who gain access to fitness centers at a lower cost. The College of Charleston (CofC) took this approach in partnering with a local athletic club, East Shore Athletic Club (ESAC), instead of building its own facility.

Housing — Many colleges have traditionally provided students with housing in dormitories and other institutionally-owned facilities, at least for the first year or two of college. Colleges house approximately 28 percent of students nationwide in institutionally-owned housing. As the cost of operating such facilities and demand for college have grown, some colleges have begun to outsource portions of their housing needs to the private market. Around 10 percent of universities outsourced some of their housing to private firms in 2006.

The University of Texas system began outsourcing some of its campus housing needs in 1989, when [University of Texas at] Dallas [(UTD)] contracted with a private firm to construct and manage Waterview Park Apartments, which contains around 1,000 units and houses about 3,000 students. One senior UTD official estimated that the arrangement saved the institution at least $500,000 a year, and the model was emulated at other UT campuses. According to this official, the school has two types of management agreements with its privatized housing system. Under the first, the "university receives a commission based on gross revenues from those units built, owned, and operated on campus by a private developer." Under the second type, "the university receives from the units it owns all income minus a flat percentage fee, which is paid to the private developer that manages the units and pays the operating expenses." The two main advantages conferred to the institution are to ability to offer off-campus student housing without making a capital investment, and the opportunity to avoid the operational expenses associated with managing a housing operation.

Healthcare Services — Most residential colleges provide students with healthcare services, often with a campus facility dedicated to providing counseling, examinations, vaccinations, and other medical treatments. As the American public is well aware, the costs of providing healthcare continue to rise. Although students require access to healthcare facilities and colleges must often comply with public health requirements, it is questionable whether colleges should be in the business of managing such facilities and performing medical services, with the possible exception being universities that run a hospital or other medical training facilities. For most colleges, however, it would be much more cost effective, and likely create higher quality care, to outsource healthcare services to a private organization with expertise in the field.

In an effort to reduce the costs and improve the accuracy of compliance with a meningitis vaccination law in New York, Columbia University hired FairChoice Systems to move its paper-based management compliance system online. Columbia not only reported higher compliance rates with the electronic system, but also realized a 25 to 30 percent reduction in staff time devoted to compliance with the law. The Polytechnic Institute of NYU also hired FairChoice to automate its vaccination compliance efforts, and was able to reduce its processing cost from $26 to $1 per vaccination. It also saw a significant reduction in the delay time and resources required for processing.

Professional Services

Colleges are often complex institutions that require professional services such as accounting and financial management, information technology, and maintenance in order to operate. Albino Barrera of Providence College suggested that many professional "services that used to be non-tradable (back-office operations, call centers, data management, and accounting sectors) have now been made fully tradable because of advances in communications and computational technologies.

Location is increasingly insignificant in the provision of these services." With a growing number of private firms dedicated to providing expert services for hire, colleges stand to benefit by outsourcing professional services.

Information Technology — Colleges have become increasingly information-based and electronically organized, and, therefore, IT has become an important function. In the past some universities were capable of developing and maintaining an IT-based infrastructure, but as technology has evolved at a rapid pace and become increasingly integrated into the higher education landscape, universities are no longer able to provide IT-related services at a level of quality and efficiency comparable to private specialized IT firms. Information technology is an area that is commonly outsourced in the private sector because it is more cost-effective and efficient to hire specialists when needed rather than keep them on staff permanently. Yet there remains a certain amount of resistance in higher education to outsourcing IT services to private firms. EDUCAUSE estimated that outsourcing comprised about 6 percent of total higher education IT spending in 2002, a proportion that was about two thirds of that in the commercial market and one third of that of the U.S. federal government.

The private sector has realized the biggest gains in outsourcing help desk, desktop support, data center operations, and website functions. Most of these functions can be described as transaction processes, for which Bill Bradfield suggested that colleges outsource, stating that "accountability structures in higher education don't motivate them to do transaction processing services very well. . . . functions that require 'productivity driven operations' are best left to folks who specialize in them." Other IT functions that higher education institutions have started to outsource include asset management, disaster recovery, security, and vulnerability detection.

Financial Services — Colleges are large institutions that require accounting and financial services such as accounts payable and receivable, audit and compliance support, endowment auditing, financial management, and payroll and tax reporting, among others. Although the outsourcing of similar financial services is common practice in the private sector, especially among small to medium-sized firms, higher education has been more reluctant to transfer responsibility for many back-office functions from campus employees to specialized private firms. For instance, a 2001 survey indicated that only 10.8 percent of colleges outsourced payroll processing.

The private market now offers financial aid processing and customer support for outsourcing. In 2008, Matt Johner estimated that only about 100 colleges and universities have thus far made use of financial aid outsourcing services. The University of Mississippi, for instance, outsourced its financial aid customer service to an inbound call center in 2004, reducing its financial aid office call volume by 90 percent, and freeing up staff to focus on more strategic work and on-site counseling.

Custodial and Maintenance Services — Most colleges are brick-and-mortar operations, consisting of a (sometimes) large number of facilities that require custodial and maintenance work. Because most colleges own rather than lease their facilities, this places the burden of cleaning and maintaining the facilities on these colleges. This does not, however, necessitate that colleges themselves employ persons to perform these tasks in-house, yet colleges have historically done just that. This policy often leads to costs much greater than could have been delivered in the private sector. Table 5.1 shows the percentage of colleges that outsourced various custodial and maintenance services in 2001, according to a national survey by the Mackinac Center for Public Policy.

With the exception of custodial food services, the great majority of colleges performed basic cleaning and maintenance services in-house rather than hiring a private contractor to do so. Colleges do not have any particular strength in performing such services, yet they do so in-house, in many cases employing unionized labor that costs significantly more than work performed by similarly skilled, non-union workers. The fact that many custodial and maintenance workers are unionized makes it difficult to outsource such services.

Recently, the unionized custodians and groundskeepers at Boston College were generating significant overtime pay at wages up to $40 per hour, creating a financial burden for the institution. Rather than engage in a heated battle with the union by trying to outsource the work completely, BC sought somewhat of a compromise by trying to outsource only its overtime work to a third party whose employees also belong to a union. This would have enabled the school to reduce its expenses and become more flexible, while at the same time not have to lay off any current employees. At the time of this writing, it is not known whether BC was successful in persuading the union to agree to the new terms or not.

Table 5.1: Percentage of Colleges Using Privatized Services, 2001

Type of Service	Percentage
Food Service - Custodial	74.6%
Academic Buildings - Custodial	26.3%
Academic Buildings - Maintenance	9.2%
Facility Management	9.2%
Grounds Maintenance	18.1%
HVAC Maintenance	18.1%
Instructional-Equipment Upkeep	2.5%
Laundry	20.6%
Office-Equipment Upkeep	9.8%
Printing	19.4%
Residential Buildings - Custodial	18.7%
Residential Buildings - Maintenance	8.3%

JOE AGRON, KEEPING IT CLOSE TO HOME: A SURVEY OF EDUCATION-RELATED OUTSOURCING, MICH. PRIVATIZATION REP. (Spring 2002).*

E. Gordon Gee, *Colleges Must Find Innovative Ways to Finance Their Missions,* CHRON. OF HIGHER EDUC. (2011),* http://chronicle.com/article/Colleges-Must-Find-Innovative/129568/

At this moment, American public higher education faces a reality check of the highest order. Distilled to its essence, the concern takes us back to first principles: Who are we as a community of learners, and how do we reconfigure ourselves for a financially sustainable future? Even in Ohio, where state government is supportive and understands our public universities' critical role, we must face facts squarely. The pie — our resources from both the state and the federal government — is unlikely to get any larger than it is today.

This nation and our world are not merely in a recession; we are also experiencing a resetting of the global economy. All signs point to a new normal in which those of us engaged in higher education must accept that no amount of pleading or whining or denying will alter what now seems an inexorable reality. We will earn what support we get by virtue of our excellence — and our hustle, our ingenuity, and our creativity.

Indeed, my own role as a university president is shifting. No longer is it sufficient for me to argue Ohio State's case for financial support with legislators and alumni and friends. Those constituents are fully supportive, and they are stepping forward in the most generous ways possible. Still, to ensure that my institution is able to pursue its mission with unbridled passion and purpose, I must do more. I must look further for the resources required to fuel the work of our faculty, staff, and students.

Each and every day, I grapple with the central question of how to finance a great public research university in a future of radically changed financing.

Earlier this month, I delivered my annual fall address to the faculty, and that was the major theme I explored. My aim was to set off what will be a cascade of conversations in department meetings, faculty senate meetings, town halls, small lunches, and other settings throughout the year. We must ask ourselves a series of questions that are critical to our existence. We must ask how we sustain ourselves, how we fund excellence, how we invest in new ideas and new partnerships, and how we extend our reach even further to those in need.

I do not know all of the answers, but my firm belief is that we must seek fundamentally new ways to fund our core purposes, and we must reshape and simplify ourselves both to make it easier to do what we need to do and to save time and resources in the process. Reconceptualizing how we finance our core mission is not recession thinking, it is future thinking.

As a starting point, this means the following: finding innovative ways to leverage the market, assessing university-owned assets and considering shedding those that do not contribute to our central mission, commercializing technological innovations, and simplifying processes.

Last week Ohio State University issued a Century Bond, the first public university in this country to do so. Demand was so great that we raised the amount of the offering to $500 million. The interest rate was the lowest ever on this type of bond, which allows the university to pay out only the interest for a hundred years and then make a full payment of all the principal. Good economic timing helps: Investors are seeking safe and durable investments and, I am proud to say, they judged the university to be a wise investment for the long haul.

This is clearly a creative way to get an infusion of capital, which will be used for building projects over the coming decades, and it comes at an all-time low cost. Because of the long life of the loan, we will set aside a small portion of our general receipts (less than $20-million) and invest it. Assuming a very modest interest rate, we will earn back the loan amount over the course of the payback period.

I will say that my recent faculty address was perhaps better attended than usual because one topic I was assumed to be commenting on was the potential leasing of the management of campus parking operations. We are studying this issue and asking what the market might bring, and, if the offer is sufficient, what parameters we would put around the management and pricing structure.

Now, a faculty discussion about parking might seem less than strategic. And yet we must consider all options that can ennoble our institution for generations to come by providing funds directly to our core purposes. No one is learning art history or chemistry in a 9-by-18-foot parking space in one of our garages, but what if we could turn that parking space into a teaching position? Or a research grant?

Along those same lines, this past spring and summer we began using a new approach to commercializing our technology innovations. Ohio State's tech-commercialization effort is just beginning, but we believe it holds great promise — for bringing innovations by faculty members to market, for rewarding them for their work, and for helping to sustain the university in the process. Doing so is not turning the university into a business, it is enabling us to support our core academic values despite volatility in the world around us.

While we are gaining new money on one side of the balance sheet, we are also reducing expenditures on the other side. Ohio State is a large and complex university, and we are making strides in simplifying what we do. For example, through efforts to streamline procurement, financial, travel, and other processes in the nonacademic units, the university saved $5-million last year, we are projected to save $20-million this year, and we are likely to save $50-million annually thereafter. That money will be funneled directly back to support the work of our faculty and our students.

The gains come through seemingly simple things: reducing the number of people who process transactions; making routine products centrally available for purchase online; thinking twice before sending a courier instead of using UPS. These are institutionally driven changes that do not impinge upon individual freedom. They do not change the quality of services we provide. They do not impact the quality of teaching or research. But the savings are enormous — and now that they have proved successful, they will be expanded upon in the coming year.

Taken together, these approaches to our financing streams are new and vast, some might even say radical. Yet a sea change is precisely what is required to ensure that my own institution, with its noble land-grant mission — to improve lives and enrich communities — not only endures but also thrives. We teach, we learn, we think, we discover, we write and create in service of our students, our community, our times, and our future. That will never change.

NOTES

1. What was Jones and Wellman's primary message about higher education finance? Should states participate in assisting public institutions in making the decisions of where and what to cut?

Jones and Wellman challenge public colleges and universities to reassess their positions and find ways to cut funding. If cutting costs represents one of the more viable options, what would happen if colleges and universities opted to cut more expensive programs such as the lab sciences as its solution? How might that decision significantly hinder national science policies?

Should institutions also use more adjuncts to reduce salaries and benefits? What effect might these decisions have on students' progress? *See, e.g.*, Audrey J. Jaeger & Derik Hinz, *The Effects of Part-Time Faculty on First Semester Retention: A Predictive Model Using Logistic Regression*, 10 J. of Coll. Student Retention: Research Theory & Practice 265–86 (2008–2009) (finding a decreased likelihood of college student retention as their instruction by part-time faculty increased); Paul D. Umbach, *How Effective Are They? Exploring the Impact of Contingent Faculty on Undergraduate Education*, 30 Rev. of Higher Educ. 91–123 (2007) (concluding that part-time faculty are less likely to engage with undergraduate students than their full-time peers). As Umbach points out, "it should surprise few that contingent faculty display a lack of commitment and perform less effectively than their tenured and tenure-track peers" because their work environment consists of low wages, little support for professional development, and few opportunities to participate fully in the institution. *Id.* at 110.

2. Jones and Wellman suggest that financial reductions do not necessarily mean compromising quality. If that is the case, is higher education too well funded? Are Jones and Wellman more likely to advocate for re-examining public investment of higher education? If the latter argument is consistent with the Jones and Wellman piece, what claims do they assert in support of this idea of rethinking public reinvestment of higher education?

3. How might streamlining services and offerings impact students and faculty? For instance, Jones and Wellman recommend fewer choices for undergraduate classes to increase class sizes (*see* Conventional Wisdom #7, *supra*). How might that change the notion of college students exploring or limiting their options to specialize in an academic area?

4. The excerpt from the Center for College Affordability and Productivity (CCAP) suggests outsourcing more services for efficiency purposes. Do you agree? How might an outside vendor provide better services at lower costs and achieve economies of scale? How are outsourced vendors more experienced and specialized? What might be reasons against outsourcing services?

5. What services should public colleges and universities outsource and why? *See* Ben Gose, *The Companies that Colleges Keep*, CHRON. OF HIGHER EDUC. at B1 (Jan. 28, 2005) (reporting on numerous successful outsourcing experiences for college and university administrators; however, he also discusses some unsuccessful arrangements); Martin Van Der Werf, *U. of Pennsylvania Ends Landmark Outsourcing Agreement*, CHRON. OF HIGHER EDUC. at B1 (Sept. 4, 2002); Martin Van Der Werf, *How the U. of Pennsylvania Learned That Outsourcing Is No Panacea: Trammell Crow's Academic Clients*, CHRON. OF HIGHER EDUC. at A38 (Apr. 7, 2000).

6. The CCAP excerpt argues that campus housing may be outsourced to housing agents with more experience and specialization in maintaining the facilities; however, the student affairs literature suggests that college residence halls are more than just a place to sleep and "hang out." Instead, the literature indicates that through campus housing programming events and peer effects, colleges can have a positive impact on students' development such as experiencing levels of independence, reducing odds of binge drinking, and engaging more in campus activities. *See* Sandra Y. Vasquez & Bradley A. Rohrer, *Students Living in Residence Halls, in* UNDERSTANDING COLLEGE STUDENT SUBPOPULATIONS: A GUIDE FOR STUDENT AFFAIRS PROFESSIONALS 215–38 (Lyle A. Gohn & Ginger Albin, eds., 2006). Further, colleges have used the residence halls in a much more intentional manner as a way to construct organized learning. This idea is probably most evident through living-learning communities such as engineering students taking classes and living in a designated area of a residence hall or an ally group such as students who seek a social justice component of their educational experience. Karen Kurotsuchi Inkelas et al., *Measuring Outcomes of Living-Learning Programs: Examining College Environments and Student Learning and Development*, 55 J. GEN. EDUC. 40–76 (where researchers found that students who lived in a living-learning community reported greater likelihood than other students living in residence halls of engaging in discussions about academic/career and sociocultural issues with their peers).

7. What should the business officers and general counsel of public colleges and universities consider when deciding whether to outsource? Richard Bartem & Sherry Manning, *Outsourcing in Higher Education: A Business Officer and Business Partner Discuss a Controversial Management Strategy*, 33 CHANGE MAGAZINE 42–47 (2001) (stating that "leaders need to know that they cannot abrogate management responsibility"). Bartem and Manning recommend that "[e]very Monday morning, [administrators] need to ask questions like: 'What do I expect from this contract?' 'What did I ask for?' 'What did they commit to?' 'Am I getting it?' " Kimberly VanHorn-Grassmeyer and Kenneth Stoner also illustrated how universities and outsourcing vendors partnered to reach successful and collaborative relationships. Kimberly VanHorn-Grassmeyer & Kenneth Stoner, *Adventures in Outsourcing*, 96 NEW DIRECTIONS FOR STUDENT SVCS. 13–29 (2002); RONALD PHIPPS & JAMIE MERISOTIS, INST. FOR HIGHER EDUC. POL'Y, IS OUTSOURCING PART OF THE SOLUTION TO THE HIGHER EDUCATION COST DILEMMA? A PRELIMINARY EXAMINATION (2005).

8. The three treatises in this section highlight the need for public colleges and universities to reduce reliance on state support and suggest more innovative ways to manage this increasingly normalized environment of reduced state financial support. Which of these recommendations seem most viable and why? The

underlying message among the three positions centers on the college or university's core mission. They generally pose questions that ask what it is and how we further that mission (in the present and future). Do the recommendations provided appear as long-term, sustainable solutions? What legislative or other political mechanisms within the state might colleges and universities seek to aid in this environment of financial constraint? How would public colleges and universities and policymakers assess their effectiveness?

E. LOCAL LAW GOVERNING LAND USE

1. Application of Zoning Ordinance to State Institution

RUTGERS v. PILUSO

286 A.2d 697 (N.J. 1972)

Opinion by: HALL, J.

The question presented by this litigation is whether Rutgers, The State University, ("Rutgers") is subject to the zoning ordinance provisions of a municipality in which one of its campuses is located-here Piscataway Township, Middlesex County. Although the provision precisely involved is a limitation on the permissible number of housing facilities for student families, the broader issue necessarily present encompasses the matter of intergovernmental land use regulation in general as well as the particular status of Rutgers. The Law Division, granting Rutgers' motion for summary judgment, held that it is an instrumentality of the state and immune from local zoning enactments. We certified the township's appeal while it was pending in the Appellate Division.

This legal problem arises in the following panoramic context. It is well known that New Jersey has long lagged in providing public higher education facilities. To commence to meet that unquestioned need, Rutgers has expanded tremendously during the past few years in undergraduate and graduate enrollment and necessary teaching buildings, student housing and other physical facilities required for a larger university for the benefit of the people of the whole state. Further expansion in all these aspects will undoubtedly continue for many years to come. As far as the New Brunswick center of operations is concerned (two other centers are situated in Newark and Camden), the original College Avenue campus within the city is fully occupied. A second campus, which includes Douglass College and the College of Agriculture and Environmental Science, located in the southern end of the city and running over into North Brunswick Township, offers some room for expansion. But it is apparent that the greater part of the necessary future physical growth will have to take place on the Piscataway campus, where a substantial number of new buildings and other facilities have already been erected.

That campus, across the Raritan River from the College Avenue campus, comprises many hundreds of acres and occupies almost all of the southwesterly corner of the township. It is quite set apart, physically, from other land uses and is roughly composed of two segments-University Heights and the Kilmer section-separated only by a county road. (A small portion of the Kilmer section extends into Edison Township and the Borough of Highland Park.) The University Heights area has been owned by Rutgers for many years; the Kilmer section is a recent acquisition from the federal government. It is a portion of former Camp Kilmer, a military installation during World War II.

University Heights is already rather substantially occupied by collegiate buildings and facilities. These comprise classroom and research buildings, mostly new and principally used for science and engineering studies, the College of Pharmacy, and the Medical School (now administered by a separate governing body). Also located there are the stadium, golf course and playing fields, as well as apartments and small dwellings for the housing of married students. The Kilmer section is the site of recently opened Livingston College, an undergraduate unit of the university; the rest of its very sizeable area is largely vacant land where most future expansion will have to take place.

The township as a whole is a large, sprawling area-until fairly recently mostly unimproved land with few centers of population, but now, typical of so many such municipalities in the northeastern New Jersey suburban ring, in the throes of extensive development of all kinds. Many housing developments, a few garden apartments, and a very considerable number of industrial establishments adjacent to new Interstate Highway Route 287 have come in, and there is room for a lot more of each. This growth has necessitated great extensions of municipal services and facilities, including schools, which must be principally financed, under New Jersey's present tax system, out of local property taxes. The result has been financial and other growing pains.

The township's present zoning ordinance, enacted in 1964, along with amendments thereto, reflects the usual means employed by this type of municipality in attempting to meet local financial problems by land use regulation, i.e., so-called "fiscal zoning." The legally dubious stratagems of zoning wide expanses of vacant land for industrial use only, requiring large lots for undeveloped residential land, and rigidly regulating multi-family dwellings are all utilized to restrict private growth to land uses which will produce few school children and show a "tax profit."

Also included in the ordinance are detailed regulations of all of Rutgers' lands. They are placed in and comprise most of the area of an education and research zone (E-R). Permitted uses are "educational and research activities and related service activities" conducted by non-profit public and private educational institutions and by 'scientific or research laboratories of private corporations, institutions, or other agencies' together with accessory uses, as well as uses allowed in the highest residential zone. Accessory uses are spelled out in considerable detail, as are minimum lot size, setback, first floor building area and percentage of lot coverage requirements. It may be observed in passing that while these detailed regulations are pertinent with respect to a private research enterprise, they are not physically suited to a vast university complex comprising dozens of buildings and allied collegiate uses on huge tracts of land having their own private interior roads. . . .

The ordinance provision here precisely involved is found among the permitted accessory uses in the E-R zone and reads as follows:

> Dormitories for matriculated students; dormitories and other housing facilities for use by matriculated students and their families, provided, however, that such facilities do not exceed 500 units.

In other words, the township purported to allow unlimited housing facilities for unmarried students, but to arbitrarily restrict the number of those which could be used by married students and their families.

In 1969 Rutgers had reached the maximum of 500 student family housing units in Piscataway. It sought to build 374 more garden apartments in the middle of the Kilmer section (together with an additional number in adjacent Edison Township). Building permits were refused because of the ordinance restriction. The university then sought a variance, which the Board of Adjustment denied.

Rutgers thereupon started the instant suit. Originally it asserted three claims for relief: one, to compel grant of the variance; two, to declare the ordinance restriction invalid; and three, to declare Rutgers, as an instrumentality of the state, not subject to a local zoning ordinance. The variance aspect was remanded for further evidence before the township agency. When that was completed, Rutgers abandoned the first two claims and successfully moved in the trial court for summary judgment on the third, thereby producing the ruling now on review. The trial judge had before him on that motion the evidence developed before the Board of Adjustment, as do we.

Rutgers' proofs demonstrated the public need for the proposed housing beyond question, although in the view we take of the case that matter is of little relevance. These proofs showed that, as of the time of the agency hearing, there were almost 10,000 full- and part-time students enrolled on the New Brunswick campuses, and that the enrollment there is expected to increase to something over 19,000 by 1980. The present number of full-time graduate students is 1,788, of whom about half are married, and the projected number in 1980 is about 5,900, of whom again approximately half will be married. Graduate students, for whom the planned garden apartments are primarily designed, play an indispensable role in assisting in undergraduate instruction and will not come to this institution absent available accommodations for themselves and their families. There is already such a shortage of facilities for this purpose that all the proposed units will be immediately used. It is estimated that a minimum of 1,500 apartments will be required for such purposes by 1980.

The local interest which may be said to constitute the reason for the detailed zoning regulation of Rutgers' lands is in one respect somewhat difficult to fathom and in another, quite obvious. The campus is physically well insulated and substantially self-sufficient from the municipal service point of view. Reference has already been made to the interior roads constructed and maintained by the university. It has its own police force for routine purposes. At oral argument, counsel for the township agreed that the only municipal services it had to furnish were fire protection and access roads. The presence of the campus in the township nonetheless does have a local impact. For one thing, municipal traffic policing is undoubtedly required outside the tracts by reason of the thousands of students and staff using the campus as well as by attendance of the public at events held on the grounds. This and other peripheral consequences may well be the reason for the municipality to attempt to regulate even non-residential growth on the campus by zoning regulations. Perhaps the greatest impact is the exemption from property taxation of hundreds of acres of prime land which would otherwise produce local tax revenues. But zoning regulation obviously cannot cure that consequence. We fully recognize the fiscal problem that exists, so long as our present municipal property tax structure remains, in municipalities having large governmental or other exempt installations and land ownerships. However, relief on this score can only be financial and has to come from the Legislature.

As to university residential growth, the reason for the 500 unit limitation on student family housing is made exceedingly plain by the township's evidence and the discussions at the Board of Adjustment hearings. That reason is 'fiscal zoning' in its most baneful aspect. The township fears that if the 500 unit limitation does not stand and the university ultimately builds the number of student apartments it now estimates will be needed within the next few years, the township will be required to build a new elementary school to accommodate the increased number of children of married students who will live in them. And such construction will, of course, under the present fiscal scheme, have to be at the expense of Piscataway taxpayers. While this result may be burdensome to property owners, as it is in the case of providing education for children from private housing, residential limitations imposed for such a reason may well be beyond the bounds of legitimate land use regulation.

From what has been said so far, it is apparent that municipal zoning regulation of state university property can, and in the case before us certainly would, very materially interfere with the development and growth of the institution, for the benefit of all the people of the state, as planned and felt necessary by the educational authorities. As the trial court commented: "The absence of immunity would result in local municipalities controlling virtually every decision concerning physical development of the University." In this connection, the township's brief projects the astonishing point of view that in its opinion public collegiate education in this state needs more classrooms rather than additional student housing facilities.

The question of what governmental units or instrumentalities are immune from municipal land use regulations, and to what extent, is not one properly susceptible of absolute or ritualistic answer. Courts have, however, frequently resolved such conflicts in perhaps too simplistic terms and by the use of labels rather than through reasoned adjudication of the critical question of which governmental interest should prevail in the particular relationship or factual situation.

Thus, speaking generally, black letter law frequently says: "Absent a waiver expressed by, or necessarily inferred from, the language of a state statute, a state is not amenable to the zoning regulations of its political subdivisions" and "(a) public corporation or authority created by the state to carry out a function of the state is not bound by local zoning regulations," thereby turning the matter on the scope of the political authority of the governmental unit seeking exemption. Often the decision is reached on the basis of whether the function, use or activity as to which exemption is claimed is "governmental" or "proprietary." Whether the claimant has been granted the right of eminent domain has been found to be conclusive in some cases.

Our own prior cases in the field, while referring to some of these considerations, cannot be said to have adopted any absolute criteria as decisive. Brief mention may be made of our leading decisions. In *Hill v. Borough of Collingswood*, a county park commission was held not to be subject to the provisions of a municipal zoning ordinance permitting only residential uses in the area covered by the park, on the thesis that dual land use control "is at variance with the evident sense of the legislative expression" and "would militate against the fulfillment of the basic statutory policy" in authorizing a county park for the use of all the county's residents. In *Town of Bloomfield v. New Jersey Highway Authority*, a state agency empowered to construct and operate a toll parkway running the full north-south length of the state was held immune from the zoning enactments of a municipality through which it passed and entitled to erect an adjacent food and motor vehicle service area in a residential zone. The court found the parkway to be an essential governmental function and a facility for the use of the people of the whole state which the Legislature could not have intended to be restricted by the enactments of the municipalities along its route.

In *Aviation Services v. Board of Adjustment of Hanover Township*, the Town of Morristown had established a municipal airport in Hanover Township pursuant to legislation authorizing such a municipal enterprise within or without the boundaries of the municipality creating and operating it. The township's effort to prevent expansion of the airport by zoning the land against such a use was held ineffective because it would thwart the legislation's design and purpose. *Washington Township v. Village of Ridgewood* also involved a conflict between two municipalities. Ridgewood sought to erect a water storage tank on residential lands in Ho-Ho-Kus under legislation authorizing the location of municipal water facilities outside the boundaries of the municipality operating the system. Chief Justice Weintraub rejected the governmental-proprietary distinction . . . and held Ridgewood was not bound by the use restrictions of the zoning ordinance of Ho-Ho-Kus. He found, however, . . . that Ridgewood had been arbitrary and unreasonable, from the standpoint of impact upon legitimate local interests in Ho-Ho-Kus, in the selection of the proposed site and in the type of storage facility constructed, and its demolition was ordered.

The rationale which runs through our cases and which we are convinced should furnish the true test of immunity in the first instance, albeit a somewhat nebulous one, is the legislative intent in this regard with respect to the particular agency or function involved. That intent, rarely specifically expressed, is to be divined from a consideration of many factors, with a value judgment reached on an overall evaluation. All possible factors cannot be abstractly catalogued. The most obvious and common ones include the nature and scope of the instrumentality seeking immunity, the kind of function or land use involved, the extent of the public interest to be served thereby, the effect local land use regulation would have upon the enterprise concerned and the impact upon legitimate local interests. In some instances one factor will be more influential than another or may be so significant as to completely overshadow all others. No one, such as the granting or withholding of the power of eminent domain, is to be thought of as ritualistically required or controlling. And there will undoubtedly be cases, as there have been in the past, where the broader public interest is so important that immunity must be granted even though the local interests may be great. The point is that there is no precise formula or set of criteria which will determine every case mechanically and automatically.

With regard to a state university (passing for the moment the matter of any peculiar status of Rutgers), there can be little doubt that, as an instrumentality of the state performing an essential governmental function for the benefit of all the people of the state, the Legislature would not intend that its growth and development should be subject to restriction or control by local land use regulation. Indeed, such will generally be true in the case of all state functions and agencies.

It is, however, most important to stress that such immunity in any situation is not completely unbridled. Even where it is found to exist, it must not . . . be exercised in an unreasonable fashion so as to arbitrarily override all important legitimate local interests. This rule must apply to the state and its instrumentalities as well as to lesser governmental entities entitled to immunity. For example, it would be arbitrary, if the state proposed to erect an office building in the crowded business district of a city where provision for off-street parking was required, for the state not to make some reasonable provision in that respect. And, at the very least, even if the proposed action of the immune governmental instrumentality does not reach the unreasonable stage for any sufficient reason, the instrumentality ought to consult with the local authorities and sympathetically listen and give every consideration to local objections, problems and suggestions in order to minimize the conflict as much as possible. As far as Rutgers' proposal here, to erect the student family housing on the Kilmer tract, is concerned, we fail to see the slightest vestige of unreasonableness as far as Piscataway's local interests are concerned or in any other respect. (The university did present the proposal to the local authorities by its variance application.) The possible additional local cost of educating children living in the housing is clearly not a legitimate local interest from any proper land use impact point of view.

This brings us to the final point in the case, upon which the township principally relies. It urges in effect that under the "Rutgers, the state university law," the entity thereby created is not such an instrumentality of the state as to qualify it for immunity from local land use regulation on that basis. The contention appears to be that only a contract relationship was thereby established between the state and the Board of Trustees of the prior institution and that the Legislature did not intend to confer immunity. The point confuses the Method of creation of Rutgers, as the state university, which was by legislative contract, with the Nature of the entity that resulted, from the standpoint of the problem before us.

A brief bit of history is first in order. . . . Rutgers remained a private institution managed and operated by the Board of Trustees of Rutgers College in New Jersey until 1956. . . . [Prior to that time], it had had substantial governmental financial connections since it became the state's land grant college in 1864. This included not only federal aid as a land grant institution, but also, commencing in the early part of this century, substantial state appropriations for both operating and capital expenditures designated for particular purpose or segments of the university, which need not be recounted in detail. This conglomeration of private and public funds and facilities first resulted in [a law], which designated the whole "as the State University of New Jersey to be utilized as an instrumentality of the State for providing public higher education and thereby to increase the efficiency of the public school system of the State." That statute, in effect, provided for a purely contractual arrangement between the Trustees and the state whereby the state bought collegiate educational services from the Trustees in return for annual appropriations to the institution by the Legislature in an amount to be agreed upon each year, with the Trustees given full operational responsibility, as well as custody and control of state property in the university complex, under visitorial general powers of supervision of the State Board of Education. Whether the form of institution and arrangement thereby created, i.e., still a private institution under private management and control, was immune from local land use regulations need not be considered.

The 1956 act provided for the creation, by contract between the Trustees and the state, of an entirely different kind of entity and arrangement. At the time of the adoption of the statute the institution represented an even greater and more complex conglomeration of public and private assets, physical and financial, than existed when the 1945 statute was enacted. The large investment of state monies both previously and in the eleven year interim dictated the need for public rather than private control. At the same time the private properties and funds held by the Trustees were so intermixed, in the operation of the entire institution, with those derived from state appropriations that the university could not be conducted without the use of both the public and private assets. Separation was practically impossible. And there was a general demand for a true state university, with financial and other potentialities sufficient to meet present and future needs of the state. Also the Trustees could not, consistent with their general and special trust obligations with respect to the private assets, simply turn them over to the state.

The solution provided by the statute, which became a consummated contract by the acquiescence of the Trustees following the decision of the Chancery Division heretofore mentioned, was a unique one. A Board of Governors was created, with the majority of its members state appointed, and was given full authority and control over all aspects of the conduct and operation of the university, subject to collaboration in budget aspects with and to the general visitorial powers of the State Board of [Higher] Education. The old Board of Trustees remained, augmented by the state appointed Governors as additional members, but with practically no powers as far as the running of the institution is concerned. . . . [T]heir principal function is to retain title to and to control, pursuant to general or special trust obligations, properties, funds and trusts vested in them at the effective date of the new institution . . . or subsequently vested in them by specific designation.. . . . The Trustees' absolute obligation in this regard is limited only by the reservation of their right to withhold or withdraw the use of these private properties and funds, but only with court approval, if certain underlying commitments, relating generally to the proper continuance of the university in accordance with the provisions of the statute, fail to be maintained. Parenthetically, it may be observed that this right of withdrawal is more theoretical than realistic, since it would seemingly be an impossible task to unscramble the conglomeration, and any court to which the matter was presented would quite likely require the state to specifically perform these commitments rather than direct a separation.

The overall result of the legislative contract therefore is an autonomous public university-not merely a contractual relationship or an institution both public and private at the same time. This conclusion is further buttressed by several additional expressions in the act. The institution is specifically designated as "the instrumentality of the state for the purpose of operating the state university," The public policy of the state is expressly declared to be, indicative of an intent to create a full-fledged state agency, that:

> a. the corporation and the university shall be and continue to be given a high degree of self-government and that the government and conduct of the corporation and the university shall be free of partisanship; and
>
> b. resources be and continue to be provided and funds be and continue to be appropriated by the state adequate for the conduct of a state university with high educational standards and to meet the cost of increasing enrollment and the need for proper facilities.

Most significantly for present purposes, these governmentally autonomous powers are directed to be exercised "without recourse or reference to any department or agency of the state, except as otherwise Expressly provided by this chapter or other applicable statutes." And finally, it is provided that the act,

> . . . being deemed and hereby declared necessary for the welfare of the state and the people of New Jersey to provide for the development of public higher education in the state and thereby to increase the efficiency of the public school system of the state, shall be liberally construed to effectuate the purposes and intent thereof.

The whole picture demonstrates to us beyond any doubt that the Legislature must be said to have intended that the growth and development of Rutgers, as a public university for the benefit of all the people of the state, was not to be thwarted or restricted by local land use regulations and that it is immune therefrom. In this respect it is a statewide facility entitled to the same protection from local enactments as the turnpike and the parkway, so long as it does not act unreasonably or arbitrarily. The township urges that the failure to grant the university the power of eminent domain and the omission from the statute of a provision that all other inconsistent laws should be deemed inapplicable compel a contrary conclusion. As previously indicated, the absence of the right of eminent domain is not decisive. The quoted provision from that the powers granted by the act may be exercised without recourse or reference to any department or agency of the state (which we take it includes municipal corporations), except as otherwise expressly provided, amounts to the same thing as an inconsistent law provision if, indeed, it is not even stronger.

A procedural item deserves passing mention. The claim for relief here sought a declaratory judgment. The matter was disposed of by the granting of Rutgers' motion for summary judgment. The judgment entered states only that 'Plaintiff's Motion for Summary Judgment . . . be and the same is hereby granted.' A judgment in a declaratory judgment action, no matter by what mechanics the case is decided or whether plaintiff or defendant is the winner, should spell out in detail the affirmative or negative declaration which the court is making. Although failure to do so is not error if the details of the adjudication can be clearly ascertained from the court's findings in the record (here by the trial judge's opinion), good practice dictates that such a judgment should so specify.

The judgment of the Law Division is affirmed.

2. Application of Zoning Ordinance to State Related Institution

TOWNSHIP OF DERRY v. PENNSYLVANIA DEPARTMENT OF LABOR & INDUSTRY

940 A.2d 1265 (Pa. Commw. Ct. 2008)

Opinion by: JUDGE MCGINLEY:

Presently before this Court is the Pennsylvania Department of Labor and Industry's (L & I), The Milton S. Hershey Medical Center's (Medical Center), and Pennsylvania State University's (PSU) (collectively, the Respondents) preliminary objection in the nature of a demurrer to the Township of Derry's (Derry) Petition for Review brought in this Court's original jurisdiction.

This dispute arose as a result of construction on the Medical Center campus initiated by the Medical Center under the Pennsylvania Construction Code Act (PCCA). The campus is located in Derry Township and owned in part by the Medical Center and by PSU. In *Derry I*, the facts were summarized as follows:

> In 1999, the General Assembly enacted the PCCA. Except for certain limited exceptions, the PCCA applies to the construction, alteration, repair, and occupancy of all buildings in the Commonwealth. One of the provisions contained in the PCCA provides, "[t]he department shall maintain plan and specification review and inspection authority over all State-owned buildings. State-owned buildings shall be subject to the regulations promulgated under this act. The department shall notify municipalities of all inspections of State-owned buildings and give municipalities the opportunity to observe the department inspections of such buildings."
>
> The PCCA also provided for the adoption of a Uniform Construction Code (UCC) and directed the Department to promulgate regulations adopting the 1999 Building Officials and Code Administrators International, Inc. (BOCA) code as the UCC. In 2004, the Department adopted the UCC, which includes a regulation that defines "State-owned building" as "a building owned by or to be constructed for Commonwealth entities consisting of the General Assembly, the Unified Judicial System, the Pennsylvania Higher Education Assistance Agency, an executive agency, independent agency, and a State affiliated entity or State related institution as defined in [the Pennsylvania Consolidated Statutes]. . . . "State-related institutions" are "The Pennsylvania State University, the University of Pittsburgh, Lincoln University or Temple University."
>
> The Township's zoning ordinance provides for the issuance of building permits and certificates of occupancy for buildings within the Township. Under the zoning ordinance, the Township zoning officer examines all

applications for building permits and land use. The officer determines whether the proposed activity conforms to the zoning ordinance before issuing building permits and/or certificates of occupancy. The Township zoning ordinance also states that no building permit shall be issued until the associated fees are paid to the Township.

The Medical Center operates a significant portion of its health care system on a campus located in Township, which is owned by the Medical Center and PSU. The Medical Center is a subsidiary or affiliate of PSU. The Medical Center campus is a substantial facility on large tracts of real estate. The campus includes multiple improvements, such as an acute care hospital, parking areas, and buildings housing various physician practices and other functions. PSU's College of Medicine conducts certain operations on the Medical Center's campus, but Petitioner (Derry) does not believe that PSU operates the health care system, which includes the acute care hospital.

The Township has a zoning ordinance that provides for the issuance of building permits and certificates of occupancy for buildings within the Township. Under the zoning ordinance, the Township zoning officer examines all applications for building permits and land use, determines whether the proposed activity conforms to the zoning ordinance, and after inspecting the use or structure, issues building permits and/or certificates of occupancy. The zoning ordinance also provides that no building permit shall be issued until the associated fees are paid to the Township.

During the last several decades, the Medical Center has undertaken various construction and renovation projects, which were subject to the Township's review, permitting, and approval process. Prior to the PCCA's enactment, both PSU and the Medical Center submitted applications for building permits to the Township. Since 2004, neither the Medical Center nor PSU has sought the Township's approval for the construction of any buildings or issuance of any permits.

On March 23, 2004, the Medical Center submitted an Application for Plan Examination and Building Permit to the Township in connection with the proposed renovation and upgrading of the pharmacology lab located in the Medical Center Science & Education Building. Although the Township reviewed the plans and prepared a building permit, the Medical Center did not pay the Township the permit fee or pick up the building permit. The Medical Center proceeded with the pharmacology lab renovation without obtaining or paying for a building permit from the Township. The Township asserts, "[u]pon information and belief, the Department approved the plans, issued the building permit, and conducted inspections for the pharmacology lab renovations project based upon the provision of PCCA, which provides the Department shall have plan review and inspection authority over 'state-owned buildings,' and based upon the Department's own over inclusive definition of 'state-owned building.' " The Township also asserts that the Department did not provide the Township with notice of the construction inspections. . . .

On February 7, 2006, the Medical Center filed a Revised Preliminary/ Final Land Development and Lot Consolidation Plan with the Township, which indicated that the Medical Center planned to build a facility called "The Cancer Institute" in the Township. The Township approved the plan, but the Medical Center has not sought the Township's approval of construction plans or the issuance of a building permit. The Township asserts, "[u]pon information and belief, Hershey Medical Center has sought the Department's approval of the construction plans for the Cancer Institute or for one or more proposed construction projects on the basis of the Department's over inclusive definition of 'state-owned building.' "

In the present action, *Derry II*, Derry contends that the demurrer should be denied because Derry has asserted a legally sufficient cause of action.

When reviewing preliminary objections, this Court must treat as true all well-pleaded material and relevant facts together with all reasonable inferences that may be drawn therefrom. Preliminary objections that assert a pleading is legally insufficient may only be sustained where "it appears with certainty that the law permits no recovery under the allegations pleaded." When any doubt exists whether a demurrer should be sustained, the preliminary objection should be denied.

Derry first argues that L & I is overreaching the bounds of its statutorily granted authority. The General Assembly vested certain authority to L & I pursuant to Section 105 of the PCCA, which provides that:

> [t]he department shall maintain plan and specification review and inspection authority over all *State-owned buildings*. State-owned buildings shall be subject to regulations promulgated under this act. The department shall notify municipalities of all inspections of State-owned buildings and give municipalities the opportunity to observe the department inspection of such buildings.

Pursuant to the PCCA, L & I promulgated a regulation defining a "State-owned building" as "[a] building owned by or to be constructed for Commonwealth entities consisting of the General Assembly, the Unified Judicial System, the Pennsylvania Higher Education Assistance Agency, an executive agency, and a *State-affiliated entity or State-related institution* as defined in 62 Pa.C.S. § 103 (relating to definitions)."[3] The Commonwealth Procurement Code, (Procurement Code), . . . provides that PSU is a state-related institution.

---

[3] 62 Pa.C.S. § 103 provides:

"State-affiliated entity." A Commonwealth authority or a Commonwealth entity. The term includes the Pennsylvania Turnpike Commission, the Pennsylvania Housing Finance Agency, the Pennsylvania Municipal Retirement System, the Pennsylvania Infrastructure Investment Authority, the State Public School Building Authority, the Pennsylvania Higher Educational Facilities Authority and the State System of Higher Education. The term does not include any court or other officer or agency of the unified judicial system, the General Assembly and its officers and agencies, any State-related institution, political subdivision or any local, regional or metropolitan transportation authority.

"State-related institution." *The Pennsylvania State University*, the University of Pittsburgh, Lincoln University or Temple University. (emphasis added).

The crux of the issue before this Court is whether Derry might succeed in its argument that the regulation exceeds the scope of L & I's authority. The General Assembly authorized L & I to develop regulations pursuant to its plan and specification review and inspection authority over state-owned buildings. Whether L & I's definition of "state-owned buildings" improperly expands its authority to buildings owned not by the state, but to buildings owned by state-related institutions, or potentially even private corporations, is one of law for this Court to decide. "[W]hen convinced that the interpretive regulation adopted by the agency is unwise or violative of legislative intent, courts are free to disregard the regulation."

Courts traditionally accord some deference to the interpretation of a statute by an agency charged with its administration. Further, an agency's interpretation of a statute is entitled to substantial deference where the regulation tracks the meaning of the statute and does not violate the legislative intent.

When an agency adopts a regulation pursuant to its legislative rule-making power, "it is valid and binding upon courts so long as it is *(a) adopted within the agency's granted power*, (b) issued pursuant to proper procedure, and (c) reasonable." The statutory grant of authority by which the General Assembly vested authority in the L & I extends to buildings *owned by the Commonwealth.*

PSU is a state-related institution. According to the pleadings, the Medical Center is a not-for-profit corporation, a separate legal entity, that is a subsidiary or affiliate of PSU. The question of ownership hinges on whether the "real property is so thoroughly under the control of the Commonwealth, that, effectively, the institution's property functions as Commonwealth property. *PSU's property does not meet this test.*"

Accordingly, it appears to this Court that the application of the regulation to the Medical Center property, as the property is not owned by the Commonwealth, is erroneous. The regulation, as applied, is potentially overbroad, and preempts Derry's ability to grant permits and receive fees for construction and occupancy of buildings within its confines. Simply stated, state-owned and state-related are clearly distinguishable. For example, "while PSU is only a 'state-related' university, [the State Employees' Retirement System] is a Commonwealth agency and therefore an extension of the Commonwealth."

Because the buildings in question are owned by PSU and the Medical Center, and not by the Commonwealth, application of the L & I regulation to the construction and renovation of the pharmacology lab and the Cancer Institute demonstrates the overbroad nature of the regulation, and calls into question whether L & I has exceeded the scope of its statutorily granted authority. The standard for a demurrer has not been met by Respondents.

Accordingly, Respondents' demurrer is overruled, and Respondents ordered to file an answer to Derry's pleadings.

ORDER

AND NOW, this 23rd day of January, 2008, the preliminary objections of the Respondents Pennsylvania Department of Labor and Industry, The Milton S.

Hershey Medical Center, and Pennsylvania State University are overruled, and Respondents are ordered to file an answer within thirty (30) days from the date of this order to the Township of Derry's Petition for Review.

NOTES

1. Both the *Piluso* and *Township of Derry* cases balanced the interests between state and local governments. The general rule is that a state may regulate local government and communities (also known as Dillon's Rule derived from the historic case of *Iowa, City of Clinton v. Cedar Rapids & Missouri River Railroad Company*, 24 Iowa 455 (1868)).

2. What were the various tests that *Piluso* and *Township of Derry* entertained? How was the formation and state support for Rutgers and Pennsylvania State University different? What difference did this formation and support make to the analysis of the cases? (See Chapter II for a discussion on state governance.) What alternative arguments might the local governments have asserted if the institutions had differing state relationships?

3. As the Supremacy Clause in the U.S. Constitution grants the federal government preemption rights over state laws and policies, state constitutions declare similar language and effect over local laws and policies. Therefore, when a local law or policy, such as a city ordinance, conflicts with state law, state law prevails. State preemption prevails particularly in instances where express language grants state authority over local laws and policies, implied terms present irreconcilable language, local laws permit what the state forbids, and the local government forbids what the state expressly permits.

3. Application of Zoning Ordinance to Private Institution

GEORGE WASHINGTON UNIVERSITY v. DISTRICT OF COLUMBIA

318 F.3d 203 (D.C. Cir. 2003)

Opinion by Senior Circuit Judge Stephen F. Williams:

This case is the most recent stage of a long-running land-use dispute between George Washington University ("GW" or "the university") and the District of Columbia's Board of Zoning Adjustment (the "Board" or the "BZA"). GW's campus is bounded on the west and north by the District's Foggy Bottom and West End neighborhoods (here referred to collectively as "Foggy Bottom"), and the BZA has been concerned about protecting their residential character and "stability." In an order approving the university's long-term campus improvement plan (the "BZA Order" or the "Order") the BZA imposed conditions aimed at limiting, and even rolling back, encroachment into Foggy Bottom by the university-or, more precisely, its students. The district court upheld some of the conditions, but also found some to be unconstitutional denials of substantive due process. Both sides appealed; we find no constitutional violation.

. . . .

The District's zoning scheme for universities, promulgated by the Zoning Commission pursuant to the authority granted by D.C.Code § 6-641 and codified at 11 District of Columbia Municipal Regulations ("DCMR") §§ 210, 302.2 & 507, permits university use as a matter of right in areas zoned for high-density commercial use. For land zoned residential or "special purpose," it permits university use as a special exception. GW's land evidently includes high-density commercial, special purpose, and residential portions. In the areas where university use is by special exception, the owner must secure permission for specific university projects in a two-stage application process. In the first stage, the university submits a "campus plan" that describes its general intentions for new land use over a substantial period (GW's preceding plan was for 15 years). On approval by the Board-an approval that can be subject to a set of conditions designed to minimize the impact of the proposed development-the campus plan "establish[es] distinct limitations within which all future construction must occur." In the second stage, the BZA reviews individual projects that the university proposes to undertake, evaluating them both for consistency with the campus plan and the zoning regulations.

In both stages, the BZA has substantial, but not unbounded, discretion to reject or approve the university's application. It is instructed to make sure that any university use is located so that it is "not likely to become objectionable to neighboring property because of noise, traffic, number of students or other objectionable conditions." When reviewing a special exception application for a university, the BZA is also to consider the policies of the so-called "District Elements of the [Comprehensive] Plan," a planning document setting out development policies for the District. If the application meets these criteria-that is to say, the proposed use is consistent with the Comprehensive Plan and is not likely to become objectionable to users of neighboring property-the Board "ordinarily must grant [the] application."

In late 1999 the university submitted a campus plan for the years 2000–10, reflecting its intentions to expand. Although BZA's concern over the university's effects on Foggy Bottom had been expressed in review of its 1985 plan, the sharp expansion of its enrollment in the 1990s made the issue more acute. Relying in part on submissions of the District's Office of Planning, the BZA found that the university's past acquisition of buildings in Foggy Bottom (and their subsequent conversion into dormitories or student apartments), as well as undergraduates' informal off-campus housing, threatened the "livability and residential character" of the Foggy Bottom neighborhood. As a result, it conditioned its approval of the 2000 Campus Plan on a series of measures designed to limit the presence of undergraduates; these measures included provisions requiring the university to house its freshmen and sophomores on campus and to provide on-campus housing for at least 70% of its students, and imposing an enrollment cap tied to the university's supply of on-campus housing.

The university challenged the BZA action in federal district court in 2001, and won a preliminary injunction against enforcement of parts of the BZA order. But the court conditioned enforcement of the injunction on GW's pursuit of the same relief before the District of Columbia Court of Appeals, which in turn remanded the order to the BZA for revision. The BZA then eliminated the enrollment cap but required the university to provide housing on campus or outside of Foggy Bottom for 70% of its approximately 8000 undergraduates, plus one on-campus or non-Foggy Bottom bed for every fulltime undergraduate student over 8000. The new Order issued on January 23, 2002, and GW promptly renewed its court challenge. The district court found that several conditions of the BZA Order, including the new housing requirements, violated the university's right to substantive due process, but rejected its claims that the zoning regulations were facially unconstitutional and that the District's actions infringed on its First Amendment rights. *George Washington University v. District of Columbia*, Civil Action No. 01-0895 (D.D.C. Apr. 12, 2002). Both sides appealed. We reverse in part, finding no constitutional infirmities.

. . . .

The university's primary challenges sound in substantive due process. Although that doctrine normally imposes only very slight burdens on the government to justify its actions, it imposes none at all in the absence of a liberty or property interest.

In the land-use context courts have taken (at least) two different approaches for determining the existence of a property interest for substantive due process purposes. In *DeBlasio v. Zoning Bd. of Adjustment*, the Third Circuit held that an ownership interest in the land qualifies. Other circuits, including the Second, Fourth, Eighth, Tenth and Eleventh Circuits, have focused on the structure of the land-use regulatory process, pursuing a "new property" inquiry and looking to the degree of discretion to be exercised by state officials in granting or withholding the relevant permission. GW urges us to adopt the Third Circuit's approach but also contends that it has a "new property." Because we agree on the latter point, we need not decide whether the Third Circuit's approach is sound or exactly how it would apply.

The majority approach may seem at odds with ordinary language, in which we would say, for example, that a particular piece of land in Washington is "the property" of GW. But an all-encompassing land use regulatory system may have either replaced that "property" with a "new property" (or with several, one for each authorized class of use), or conceivably have replaced it with less than a new property (thereby, one would suppose, effecting a taking).

Within the majority there is considerable variety in the courts' formulae for how severely official discretion must be constrained to establish a new property. The Second Circuit apparently will not find one if the authority has any discretion to deny approval of the proposed land use. The Eighth Circuit, in contrast, inquires whether the "statute or regulation places substantial limits on the government's exercise of its licensing discretion," finding a property interest if the agency is so constrained. In our view, the Eighth Circuit's analysis is more in line with analogous Supreme Court precedent and the precedent of this circuit.

In practice, the fact patterns of new property cases in the land use arena seem to divide into two sets, one set involving virtually unlimited discretion, the other rather absolute entitlement. In *Bituminous Materials*, for instance, the regulation in question specified that the agency "may" grant the permit, without setting out any substantive standards to follow. . . . [By contrast], *Walz v. Town of Smithtown*, handily found a property interest when the highway superintendent was to issue a permit for street excavation to a public utility so long as its application stated "the nature, location, extent and purpose" of the excavation, and gave adequate undertakings that it would restore the street to its original condition.

The university's expectations for a "special exception" fall between these poles, but we think closer to establishing, as *Bituminous Materials* said, "substantial limits on the government's exercise of its licensing discretion." Here, for a residential or special purpose parcel, university use "shall be permitted as a special exception" if the criteria for the exception are met. Moreover, the District of Columbia courts have interpreted this provision to mean what it says-namely, that special exceptions must be issued as a matter of right if the qualifying criteria are met. "The Board's discretion . . . is limited to a determination whether the exception sought meets the requirements of the regulation. . . . [If so,] the Board ordinarily must grant [the] application."

Of course, some of these qualifying criteria are by no means self-defining. In particular, 11 DCMR § 210.2 says that university use shall be located so that it is "not likely to become objectionable to neighboring property." But combining this provision with 11 DCMR § 210.1 . . . , it seems inescapable that the BZA can deny the university a special exception only by an explicit finding that the proposed use is likely to become "objectionable"-a term that we think clearly places "substantive limitations on official discretion." Although 11 DCMR § 210.2 speaks of uses "objectionable to neighboring property because of noise, traffic, number of students or other objectionable conditions," plainly the final wrap-up clause does not invite the BZA members to apply their own personal tastes; they must rest the "objection [s]" either on the criteria specified in § 210.2or otherwise made relevant by the Code, regulations, the Comprehensive Plan or other pertinent legal provisions.

In addition, the BZA's conduct and procedures indicate that it interprets the regulations as imposing substantive limits on its discretion. For instance, its Order of March 29, 2001 started with a series of detailed "findings of fact" establishing for the record the objective conditions created by the university's property use. It states that it is "authorized to grant a special exception where, in the judgment of the Board *based on a showing of substantial evidence*, the special exception . . . will not tend to affect adversely the use of neighboring property." Although of course a local law mandate of minimum procedures cannot generate an entitlement, the District's provision of fairly formal procedures supports our reading of the regulations as imposing "substantial limits on the [Board's] exercise of its licensing discretion."

Once a property interest is found, however, the doctrine of substantive due process constrains only egregious government misconduct. We have described the doctrine as preventing only "grave unfairness," and identified two ways in which such unfairness might be shown: "Only [1] a substantial infringement of state law prompted by personal or group animus, or [2] a deliberate flouting of the law that trammels significant personal or property rights, qualifies for relief under § 1983."

In attacking the conditions, the university makes a stab at the "group animus" angle suggested in *Silverman*, saying that the BZA Order reflects the hostility of the Foggy Bottom residents to students. As Foggy Bottom is a residential area, and apartments occupied by students are indisputably a residential use, it seems inescapable that the District is drawing a distinction based on student status. But just what sort of "group animus" the *Silverman* court had in mind is unclear. An equal protection violation would of course be independently unlawful, and the university does not make a serious analytical case for the proposition that students should be viewed as a "suspect class" for equal protection purposes. On the other hand, creation of a sort of shadow equal protection doctrine in the name of "substantive due process" seems just the sort of error against which we and others have cautioned.

In any event, even assuming the legitimacy of any such shadow doctrine, the university offers us neither a "Brandeis brief" nor any other basis for even doubting the implicit basis for the Board's distinction of students from others-namely, that on average they pose a risk of behavior different from that generally preferred by non-student residents and legally relevant. Instead GW invokes District law to show the impropriety of such a distinction, pointing to provisions such as D.C.Code § 2-1402.21, which bars discrimination "based on . . . matriculation" for certain types of real estate transactions, and *id.* § 2-1401.01, saying that it "is the intent of the Council of the District of Columbia . . . to secure an end in the District of Columbia to discrimination . . . by reason of . . . matriculation." It also notes the District of Columbia Court of Appeals' observation that "a university - even a law school - is not to be presumed, for the purposes of the Zoning Regulations, to be the land use equivalent of the bubonic plague." But even if GW reads District law correctly, a breach of local law does not of itself violate substantive due process. Accordingly, we think the university falls short in its effort to show a deprivation of substantive due process by reference to "group animus."

Perhaps implicitly pointing to a "deliberate flouting of the law that trammels significant . . . property rights," GW also complains of what the District now calls the "transitional housing plan," Conditions 9(a)-(c) of the Order, which the district court found unconstitutional. These require the university to provide its undergraduates, no later than August 31, 2002, with a total of approximately 5600 beds (corresponding to 70% of the approximately 8000 undergraduates) located either on campus or off campus but outside the Foggy Bottom area. After August 31, 2006, the 5600 beds must be located entirely on campus. The parties agree that this requirement will force the university to acquire temporary accommodations for about 1400 students in off-campus, nonFoggy Bottom locations-accommodations that might be not only expensive (though the university has offered no data on just how large an expense) but less desirable for students than the university housing already available to students off-campus in Foggy Bottom.

GW spins these conditions as generating a completely irrational expense. It says that they in effect render "duplicative" the university's current off-campus student housing in Foggy Bottom, which is (concededly) in full conformity to the residential zoning there. But in reality nothing in the transitional housing plan forces the university to give up its off-campus Foggy Bottom dorms or prevents it from continuing to house students there. If it chooses, it can continue supplying that housing *in addition* to the 5600 beds required by Conditions 9(a)-(c). If it chose that option, it would be providing housing to approximately 85% of its undergraduate students, a percentage that is hardly extraordinary for modern urban American universities; Harvard University, for instance, houses 98% of its undergraduates on campus, and Columbia University about 90%. Of course, the university might choose instead to sell its off-campus Foggy Bottom properties or convert them to another use. But the fact that it might do so doesn't render the District's regulation an improper encroachment on its by-right use of those properties.

Nor is there any irrationality in the District's policy. Given the District's concern that an excess of students in the Foggy Bottom area is negatively affecting the character of the neighborhood, it cannot be irrational for the District to adopt rules likely to limit or reduce the number of students in the area. That seems to be the effect of the BZA Order: it guarantees that, of the approximately 8000 undergraduates, at least 5600 (70%) of them will be provided housing on-campus or outside of Foggy Bottom; and since about 1250 students are commuters, married, disabled or for some other reason are not considered by GW to be "well suited for dormitory life", this leaves only about 1150 traditional undergraduates living off-campus in Foggy Bottom, whether their residence was in university properties or in private apartments. Obviously the university's alternative proposal-to count the off-campus Foggy Bottom properties towards the 70% requirement-would not as effectively limit the student presence in Foggy Bottom.

The district court also found a violation in certain provisions that the District characterizes as enforcement and severability mechanisms. Condition 9(e) prohibits the issuance of any new "permit to construct or occupy buildings for nonresidential use on campus" whenever "a semiannual report reveals that [GW] is not in compliance" with the conditions of the Order. The university claims that this condition is purely punitive, as it lacks any relationship to the District's goal of protecting the neighborhood. After all, it says, prohibiting the construction of non-residential buildings will not cause the new dormitories currently under construction to be completed more rapidly. But Condition 9(e) clearly serves two functions that advance the District's goals. First, it strengthens the university's incentive to comply with the housing provisions. Second, even though the new non-housing construction that Condition 9(e) holds hostage may not relate directly to new housing demands (e.g., new labs replacing old ones do not necessarily meet needs generated by *increased* students), the condition as a general matter keeps housing and non-housing growth proceeding in parallel.

The district court also found a constitutional flaw in Condition 10, which requires freshmen and sophomores to live on campus "to the extent such housing is available." But as the District notes, it was the university that originally proposed this measure as an element of its campus plan. Normally, a party cannot attack its own proposed agency action, although presumably that concept would not apply where the proposal was closely tied to some other proposed action that the agency rejected. Here, there is no evidence of such close ties to any other specific condition not granted to the university. And, even apart from the university's self-contradiction, the condition seems readily to meet the latitudinarian standards of substantive due process. A city might reasonably consider the youngest college students to be the ones most likely to disturb residents in the surrounding communities, as well as most likely to need whatever shreds of parietal rules may subsist on campus.

Finally, the district court rejected Condition 9(f), which provides that the other provisions of Condition 9 are "integral, non-severable aspect[s] of the Board's approval of this application. If any [provision] . . . is declared void for any reason . . . no application for a special exception will be processed and no permit to construct or occupy buildings . . . may be issued." The university characterizes this provision as an unconstitutional incursion into the province of the judiciary, because it punishes the university for exercising its legal right to challenge invalid provisions. Under our conclusion here that no other provisions of the Order are void, however, we see no need to address a condition that would take effect only on the opposite contingency.

On its cross-appeal the university claims that the BZA Order infringed its First Amendment rights to academic freedom. It did this, in the university's view, by constraining its determinations of where to build dormitories, how much campus space to devote to dormitories and how many students to admit. In support it points to Justice Frankfurter's concurrence in *Sweezy v. New Hampshire*, saying that a university has the right to "determine for itself on academic grounds who may teach, what may be taught, how it shall be taught and who may be admitted to study." But the university cites no case giving universities any special status vis-à-vis neutral, generally applicable zoning and land-use regulations of the standard externality-constraining type. Thus our case is wholly different from, for example, *Keyishian v. Bd. of Regents*, which found unconstitutional vagueness in a statute requiring removal of state university faculty members for "treasonous or seditious" utterances or acts, noting the university's place in the "marketplace of ideas." By contrast, the BZA Order merely requires the university to house its students in a way that is compatible with the preservation of surrounding neighborhoods.

The university also argues that the District's zoning regulations are facially unconstitutional under the equal protection element of Fifth Amendment due process because their requirement of two stages of approval imposes burdens on university landowners not imposed on similarly situated non-university actors. But GW acknowledges that universities do not constitute a protected class and so the legislation need only "classify the persons it affects in a manner rationally related to legitimate governmental objectives." As universities are larger, make more intensive use of their land, and have greater spillover effects on neighboring communities than most other landowners, however, the District's legislative classifications meet this criterion.

Accordingly, the decision of the district court is reversed in so far as it found constitutional violations in the BZA Order and is otherwise affirmed.

So ordered.

Karen LeCraft Henderson, Circuit Judge, concurring:

Although I concur in the judgment in this case, I believe the majority erroneously recognizes a constitutionally protected property interest where there is none. In doing so, the majority chooses not to embrace firmly, as I would, the substantial authority that employs the claim to entitlement approach. . . .

The majority instead simply recognizes that two (at least) approaches exist to answer the question, concluding that under either GW has the requisite property interest. But under the "majority" approach of the Second, Fourth, Eighth, Tenth and Eleventh Circuits, a landowner has a protected property interest in a favorable land-use decision only if a "statute or regulation places substantial limits on the government's exercise of its [land-use] discretion," Those courts follow the U.S. Supreme Court's guidance found in *Bd. of Regents v. Roth* ("To have a property interest in a benefit, a person clearly must have more than an abstract need or desire for it. He must have more than a unilateral expectation of it. He must, instead, have a legitimate claim of entitlement to it."). At the same time, their approach uses a standard that properly "balances the need for local autonomy in a matter of paramount local concern with recognition of constitutional protection at the very outer margins of municipal behavior."

Using this approach, I would not recognize a constitutionally protected property interest in GW's expectation of a "special exception." Indeed, I find it impossible to conclude the zoning regulations under which the BZA "ordinarily must," approve a special exception for a campus plan only if it determines that the proposed plan is "not likely to become *objectionable* to neighboring property" substantially limit the exercise of its discretion.

The majority finds sufficient constraint on the BZA's authority in the regulation's command that university use " 'shall be permitted as a special exception' if the criteria for the exception are met." But the crucial criterion upon which the BZA's decision depends is whether the proposed use is "objectionable," . . . a criterion that requires the BZA to use its judgment in considering numerous factors. D.C. MUN. REGS. tit. 11, § 210.2 ("Use as a college or university shall be located so that it is not likely to become objectionable to neighboring property because of noise, traffic, number of students, or other objectionable conditions."). Heeding advice to hesitate before intervening in local land disputes, I find only a minimal limitation on the Board's discretion that is far from a case where "the discretion of the issuing agency is so narrowly circumscribed that approval of a proper application is virtually assured." In fact, the zoning authority has been given "wide discretion" in making its decisions; hence, no constitutionally protected property interest in the special exception exists. [See] *Jacobs, Visconsi & Jacobs Co. v. City of Lawrence* (where zoning authority's decision must be "reasonable" and reasonable decision under state law should consider factors such as "zoning and uses of properties nearby," "suitability of the subject property for the uses to which it has been restricted" and "extent to which removal of the restrictions will detrimentally affect nearby property," authority had sufficient discretion to checkmate property interest). It is because GW does not possess a constitutionally protected property interest that I would reverse the district court to the extent it found otherwise.

For the foregoing reasons, I concur in the judgment reversing the district court and I otherwise fully concur in the majority opinion.

GEORGE WASHINGTON UNIVERSITY v. DISTRICT OF COLUMBIA
391 F. Supp. 2d 109 (D.D.C. 2005)

Opinion By: OBERDORFER, DISTRICT JUDGE.

This case involves constitutional challenges to various conditions imposed by the District of Columbia's Board of Zoning Adjustment ("the Board") on the development of George Washington University's campus in the District's Foggy Bottom and West End neighborhoods ("Foggy Bottom"). Currently pending is defendants' motion for summary judgment on four of the University' claims: unconstitutional taking/unconstitutional conditions (Claims I and II); denial of equal protection (Claim VI); and violation of the University students' right to equal protection and due process (Claim VIII). As explained below, the D.C. Circuit's opinion requires that defendants' motion should be granted on all four counts.

I. Procedural History

Pursuant to D.C. zoning laws, in 1999 the University submitted to the Board for its review and approval a "campus plan" for the years 2000–2010. The Board approved the plan, but issued an Order ("Initial Order") imposing several conditions, including particularly Condition 9. This condition imposed a cap on student enrollment to the number admitted as of February 13, 2001, and it imposed this cap after the University had already admitted a substantial number of its students for the immediately forthcoming semester. The Initial Order also imposed a sanction on the University if it failed to meet its requirement to house 70% of its students on-campus, by barring the University from building any non-residential buildings on campus while out of compliance. The University filed suit, seeking to enjoin enforcement of the Initial Order.

On June 15, 2001, I granted the University's motion for a preliminary injunction, finding that the University was substantially likely to succeed in demonstrating that Condition 9 of the Initial Order was so arbitrary and capricious as to violate the University's right to substantive due process.

On January 23, 2002, the Board issued its corrected Final Order, which differed in some respects from the Initial Order. Whereas the Initial Order required the University to house 70% of its undergraduates and capped student enrollment to the number enrolled as of February 13, 2001, the Final Order imposed a "soft cap" of housing 5,600 (or 70%) of its 8,000 undergraduates, and additionally required the University to house every undergraduate above the 8,000 threshold either on campus or outside Foggy Bottom.[3] The Final Order also provided a six-month grace period for the University to comply. In addition, it allowed the University to house the students either on-campus or outside of Foggy Bottom until August 2006. Thereafter, it was required to use only on-campus housing.

---

[3] For example, if the University enrolled 8,100 students, then it would be required to house 5,600 + (8,100-8,000) = 5,700 students.

After the Board issued its Final Order, the University amended and supplemented its complaint. The parties then cross-moved for summary judgment on all claims, including particularly Claims III (substantive due process) and XII (substantive due process and separation of powers). An April 12, 2002 Order granted summary judgment in favor of the University on Claims III and XII-concluding that the Board Order violated the University's due process rights on the theory that, while the government's purpose was legitimate, the government's regulations were not rationally related to its legitimate purpose. Both parties appealed.

II. The D.C. Circuit's Opinion

The court of appeals affirmed in part and reversed in part, and held that the Final Order was not unconstitutional in all respects. Although the court's decision did not directly address the remaining claims specified above (Claims I, II, VI, and VIII) . . . , the clear implication of the court's ruling is that the University's remaining claims cannot succeed.

In its ruling, the court noted that the Final Order found that the property purchased by the University in the Foggy Bottom neighborhood for undergraduate housing, and undergraduates' "informal" off-campus housing, "threatened the 'livability and residential character' of the Foggy Bottom neighborhood." The court concluded that "on average [students] pose a risk of behavior different from that generally preferred by non-student residents and legally relevant."

The University argued that the on-campus or outside Foggy Bottom housing requirements rendered the University's off-campus student housing *in* Foggy Bottom "duplicative," which was plainly irrational. The court disagreed, concluding that "nothing in the transitional housing plan forces the University to give up its off-campus Foggy Bottom dorms or prevents it from continuing to house students there. If it chooses, it can continue supplying that housing *in addition* to the 5600 beds required by Conditions 9(a)-(c)."

The court then turned to Condition 9(e) of the Final Order, which prohibited "the issuance of any new 'permit to construct or occupy buildings for nonresidential use on campus' whenever 'a semiannual report reveals that [the University] is not in compliance' with the conditions of [the Final] Order." The court held-without extensive discussion-that this condition "clearly serves two important functions that advance the District's goals." This condition "strengthens the University's incentive to comply with the housing provisions" and it generally "keeps housing and non-housing growth proceeding in parallel."

The court also held that Condition 10-which required freshmen and sophomores to live on campus "to the extent such housing is available"-was not problematic, in part because the University proposed it as part of its own plan (although it was tied to another proposal that the Board rejected). Moreover, "the condition seems readily to meet the latitudinarian standards of substantive due process. A city might reasonably consider the youngest college students to be the ones most likely to disturb residents in the surrounding communities, as well as most likely to need whatever shreds of parietal rules may subsist on campus."

Finally, the court affirmed that the District's zoning regulations were not unconstitutional as violative of the equal protection element of Fifth Amendment due process rights. Because universities are not a protected class, the legislation need only "classify the persons it affects in a manner rationally related to legitimate governmental objectives." The court found that the regulations meet this standard: "As universities are larger, make more intensive use of their land, and have greater spillover effects on neighboring communities than most other landowners . . . , the District's legislative classifications meet this criterion."

III. The University's Takings Claims (Claims I and II)

In its amended complaint, the University alleged that the Board's Final Order effects an unconstitutional taking of (1) its properties that cannot be used for non-residential purposes (assuming the University is not in compliance with the Final Order); (2) its off-campus housing, which cannot be counted in determining whether the University is complying with the Final Order; (3) its financial resources, which will be expended to build on-campus housing; and (4) tuition revenue, which will be limited by the *de facto* cap on undergraduate enrollment. The University's takings claims were not reached in this court or on appeal, because the case was disposed of on due process grounds. None of these claims has merit, however; in fact, they appear to be largely a restatement of the University's due process and equal protection claims.

Takings claims in the D.C. Circuit are governed by *District Intown Prop. Ltd. P'ship, et al. v. District of Columbia.* There are two types of takings claims-a *per se* taking, and a taking based on a three-part balancing test. Under either test, the relevant inquiry is an economic assessment of the entire property, and not just the parcels of land that a party claims have lost value.

A. *Per Se Taking*

A *per se* taking occurs either if governmental regulations result in " 'permanent physical occupation of property,' " or alternatively leads to a loss of "*all* economically beneficial or productive use of property." The Board's Final Order does not result in a physical occupation of property, nor does it lead to a loss of "*all* economically beneficial or productive use of property." At worst, the Final Order requires the University to use its property for a certain purpose, but these requirements do not deprive the University of all economic benefit of the property.

B. *Penn Central Taking*

In determining if there is a taking under the balancing test [established in the U.S. Supreme Court's decision of *Penn Central Transp. Co. v. City of New York*], there are "three primary factors weighing in the balance: the regulation's economic impact on the claimant, the regulation's interference with the claimant's reasonable investment-backed expectations, and the character of the government action." The parties disagree about whether a claimant must meet all three *Penn Central* elements, or if these are simply three factors to balance. Under either approach, however, the claims of the University fail.

1. Economic Impact

Claimants " 'must put forth striking evidence of economic effects to prevail even under the [balancing] inquiry.' " The University, however, makes no showing that the Final Order diminishes the property's value. Instead, the University alleges that the District has restricted the use of the University's property-without tying these restrictions to an actual economic loss of property value.

At most, the University alleges that it will cost money to comply. This is not, however, a substantial loss of property value. For example, the University argues that the Final Order "deprives the University of the existing use of its off-campus properties in Foggy Bottom that were developed by right for student housing." As the D.C. Circuit noted, however, the University can still use the off-campus housing; it simply cannot count this housing towards its 70% requirement.

2. Investment-Backed Expectations

There is no interference with the University's investment-backed expectations here, because it was on notice that its property was subject to governmental regulation. Moreover, the Board expressed concern in 1985 about the University's growth, and-following its decision to undergo a "sharp expansion" in enrollment in the late 1990s-the University should have anticipated that further regulation might be imminent.

3. Character of the Government's Action

To assess the character of the government's action, the central question is whether the regulation advances a "common good" or "public purpose." The D.C. Circuit has already concluded here that the regulations were rationally related to a legitimate government objective, in light of a university's potential impact on the surrounding neighborhood. This ruling that the regulations and Order are rationally related to a legitimate government objective suffices to establish that they are in furtherance of a common good or public purpose.

IV. Equal Protection (Claim VI)

Claim VI alleges that the Final Order imposes greater restrictions on the University's ability to use its property than imposed on others similarly situated, thereby denying equal protection as guaranteed by the Fifth Amendment. The D.C. Circuit has already indicated, however, that the Final Order is rationally related to a legitimate government objective. Although this finding was in the context of analyzing the due process claim (and not equal protection), in practice these tests are almost indistinguishable.

V. Due Process and Equal Protection Rights of the University Students (Claim VIII)

Finally, the University claims that the Final Order violates the University students' due process and equal protection rights by forcing them to live on campus and not in the University's off-campus dorms in Foggy Bottom.

A. *Standing*

Defendants first challenge this claim on the ground that the University lacks standing to represent the students. Resolution of the standing issue is a close call, but, because the underlying claims fail, there is no need to reach this issue.

B. *Constitutional Claims*

The University's arguments on behalf of its students are largely duplicative of its constitutional arguments on its own behalf. The University alleges that the Final Order discriminates against its students by dictating where they can live. On this theory, the University alleges both due process and equal protection violations.

As previously discussed, for both the equal protection and substantive due process claims, the Court of Appeals has already held that the Final Order was rationally related to a legitimate government objective. The court found that the University provided no grounds "for even doubting the implicit basis for the Board's distinction of students from others-namely, that on average they pose a risk of behavior different from that generally preferred by non-student residents and legally relevant." Moreover, it has decided that the means employed by the University are rationally related to its ends. For the substantive due process claim, it similarly rejected any claim that the Final Order was motivated by group animus towards the University's students. In sum, it has already considered and upheld the Board's Final Order in full. The University makes no showing as to why claims on behalf of the students compel a different conclusion.

. . . .

Accordingly, the Court of Appeals leaves no alternative but to dismiss the University's complaint, and leaves it with no further recourse beyond seeking relief by further appeal, or by legislation. . . .

ORDER

On this 16th day of September, 2005, for reasons stated in an accompanying memorandum, it is hereby ORDERED: that Defendants' Motion for Summary Judgment on Plaintiff's Remaining Claims . . . is GRANTED.

NOTES

1. How do the arguments in the George Washington University cases differ from the cases involving public universities? While the zoning ordinances in *Piluso* and *Township of Derry* involved a conflict between state and local laws, the two George Washington University cases raised concerns about a private entity's right to property, and even initiated a question of government takings.

2. Colleges and universities contribute to the economic development of an area. How could George Washington University fashion an argument based on the public good that the institution brings to an area?

3. While many local zoning ordinances grant exceptions to "educational institutions," the application of that exception has been rather inconsistent on whether parking lots fulfill the ordinance language of advancing the interests of the public generally and more specifically, the educational institution.

4. Whether a college campus may be located in a residential or commercial area also presents inconsistencies. For example, the court in *Duke v. American University*, 675 A.2d 26 (D.C. 1996), notes that the D.C. ordinance does not permit educational institutions, as a matter of right, to operate within residential neighborhood. By contrast, in D.C., universities are permitted to operate in commercially zoned areas.

4. Zoning Board — Conflicts of Interest

HUGHES v. MONMOUTH UNIVERSITY

925 A.2d 741 (N.J. Super. Ct. App. Div. 2007)

Per Curiam.

Monmouth University applied for site plan approval and several variances to the Borough of West Long Branch Board of Adjustment to construct a 48,800 square foot, three-story 196-bed student dormitory with parking for 126 vehicles, six tennis courts and associated parking lot, public restroom, and storm water detention basin. Plaintiffs Joseph and Pamela Hughes, neighboring residential property owners, objected to the application as a non-residential use of property zoned for low-density residential uses. After hearing extensive testimony from both sides, the Board voted five to one to approve the application, granting thirteen distinct use and bulk variances. Thereafter, plaintiffs filed a complaint in lieu of prerogative writs with the Law Division, claiming that several Board members should have been disqualified because of financial or personal involvement with the University. Plaintiffs also claimed the Board's grant of the variances was improper and a usurpation of the Borough's zoning power. Judge Lehrer affirmed the Board's decisions, and plaintiffs appealed to this court. We affirm substantially for the reasons expressed by Judge Lehrer in his decision [from the lower court].

The Municipal Land Use Law (MLUL) provides in pertinent part that "no member of the board of adjustment shall be permitted to act on any matter in which he has, either directly or indirectly, any *personal or financial interest.*" This conflict-of-interest provision codified the existing common law and has been interpreted as precluding action by board members in four situations:

> (1) "Direct pecuniary interests," when an official votes on a matter benefiting the official's own property or affording a direct financial gain; (2) "Indirect pecuniary interests," when an official votes on a matter that financially benefits one closely tied to the official, such as an employer, or family member; (3) "Direct personal interest," when an official votes on a matter that benefits a blood relative or close friend in a non-financial way, but a matter of great importance, as in the case of a councilman's mother

being in the nursing home subject to the zoning issue; and (4) "Indirect Personal Interest," when an official votes on a matter in which an individual's judgment may be affected because of membership in some organization and a desire to help that organization further its policies.

In 1996, the Local Government Ethics Law was enacted, barring a public official, such as a member of a board of adjustment from acting in any matter in which he or she "has a direct or indirect *financial or personal involvement* that might reasonably be expected to impair his[/her] objectivity or independence of judgment." The Ethics Law also extends the prohibition to immediate family members or business associates.

As we indicated in *Shapiro v. Mertz*, "[t]he Ethics Law expanded the definition of a conflict of interest which had been established through common law and codified by the MLUL." Indeed, one of the leading land-use scholars believes that "the Ethics Law broadens the areas of disqualification at least by its extension of reach to the indirect involvements of family members and business associates." According to Cox, "it is unclear whether the use of the word 'involvement' instead of 'interest' bears significance," but "intangible relations such as a friendship or being an alumnus of the same school as the applicant could be held to be grounds for disqualification depending upon the circumstances." Nevertheless, whether considering the MLUL's definition or the broader Ethics Law, we still agree with Judge Lehrer's determination that none of the involvements and interests highlighted by plaintiff, under the circumstances presented herein, constituted disqualifying conflicts.

It is clear that an alumnus of a University applicant has an "involvement" with the school. But here, where the board members obtained their degrees many years ago, were not active alumni members, and did not substantially contribute to the University or otherwise evidence any special attachment to the school, no reasonable person could conclude that such involvement would have tempted them "to depart from [their] sworn public duty."

We also note that none of the board members or their family members is a current student at the University.

It is true that one of the board member's children, who had attended the University in the past, received a $4,500 tuition credit from the school. However, the credit was awarded because of the student's academic record and was available to all similarly situated students. Consequently, this credit would not have interfered with the members' impartial performance of his duties. Similarly, the fact that a board member's child may in the future consider attending the University or that a member's company won a public bid and performed some work for the school over ten years ago, are both much too remote to constitute conflicts.

Furthermore, the fact that board members participated in various University events, such as concerts, wine tastings, and athletic events, would similarly not be disqualifying. None of these involvements, which were open to the public generally, could "reasonably be expected to impair [the board member's] objectivity or independence of judgment."

Plaintiffs further argue that board member Juliano was disqualified from voting and improperly participated in one of the final hearings, thereby rendering the result void in its entirety. The final hearings plaintiffs reference, however, dealt with the site plan and occurred well after the variances had been approved. Plaintiffs also complain of Juliano "questioning objector Hughes, especially as related to the tennis court aspect of the plan. In addition, she also questioned the objector's Professional Planner" regarding the placement of the tennis courts.

However, Juliano's relatively minimal participation was not fatal because she was not disqualified "for cause." Instead, she disqualified herself from voting because she had missed several meetings due to her ill son. Had she read the transcripts from the missed meetings, she could have voted. Under these circumstances, she was not precluded from commenting on those issues for which she was properly prepared.

Finally, plaintiffs claim that when the entire 19.277 acre proposal is considered, and not just the 4.38 acres relating to the tennis courts, the project was clearly an usurpation of the Borough's zoning authority. However, the entire proposal constituted only three percent of the R-22 zone and was hardly a substantial modification of the zone. Moreover, unlike *Twp. of N. Brunswick v. Zoning Bd. of Adjustment of Twp. of N. Brunswick*, there was no indication in the record that the Borough clearly disapproved of the proposed use within the zone. In fact, the surrounding area includes numerous other resident dorms and other University structures that are similar in style and size to the proposed plan. Consequently, the variances did not significantly alter the township's zoning plan, and Judge Lehrer correctly found that the variance approvals were not usurpations of the Borough's zoning authority.

Affirmed.

F. TAKINGS

WAMPLER v. TRUSTEES OF INDIANA UNIVERSITY
172 N.E.2d 67 (Ind. 1961)

Opinion by: BOBBITT, CHIEF JUSTICE.

Appellee brought this action to condemn and appropriate the absolute fee simple title to certain real estate owned by appellants, and to be used by Indiana University as a parking lot in connection with a student dormitory located across the street from such real estate.

Appellants filed objections to appellee's complaint thereby raising, *inter alia*, the following questions:

(1) Did appellee have the power to condemn appellant's land for the intended purpose?

(2) Is there a necessity for the taking?

(3) Was there a 'good faith' effort to purchase?

From an order overruling appellants' objections this appeal is prosecuted.

We shall consider the questions here presented in the order of their discussion in appellants' brief.

First: Does appellee have the authority and power to condemn appellants' property for the intended purpose?

Acts 1911, ch. 189, § 1, p. 468, being § 22-503, Burns' 1950 Replacement, provides in pertinent part as follows:

> Whenever the board of trustees, * * * of any * * * educational * * * institution belonging to the state of Indiana shall deem it necessary or desirable for the welfare or convenience of such institution, to acquire real estate for its use, said institution, by its board of trustees, * * * is hereby authorized and empowered to condemn such real estate, and, for that purpose, shall possess the right and powers secured by an act of the general assembly concerning proceedings in the exercise of eminent domain, approved February 27, 1905, shall be subject to the duties imposed thereby, and shall conduct such condemnation proceedings in conformity therewith. . . .

The resolution adopted by the Board of Trustees of Indiana University and which is made a part of the complaint and marked Exhibit 'A' states, *inter alia,* that:

> Whereas, the Board of Trustees of Indiana University, for the furtherance of its public educational purposes deem it necessary and proper to acquire absolute fee simple title to that certain real estate described as Lot Number 8 in Ray Rogers Addition to the City of Bloomington, Monroe County, Indiana, as shown by the recorded plat thereof an file in the office of the Recorder of Monroe County, Indiana.

The necessity and expediency of taking for public use is a legislative question, and where the intended use is public, this question may be determined by such agency and in such manner as the Legislature may designate.

It is not contended that the property which appellee here seeks to appropriate will not be devoted to a public use.

The statute vests discretion in appellee to condemn and appropriate property which it deems necessary and desirable for the 'welfare or convenience' of the University, and its judgment cannot be questioned or superseded by the courts except for fraud, capriciousness or illegality.

While we recognize that reasonable standards must be imposed where the Legislature delegates discretionary duties to administrative officers and bodies, we are also aware that the specific nature of the purposes to be accomplished by the Act may be considered in determining whether the standards therein provided are as specific, definite and certain as the necessities of the case permit.

Clearly, the purpose to be accomplished in the present case is to prepare adequately to meet the expansion problems inherent in this era of college and university growth and development. The members of the Board of Trustees are the best qualified to determine whether or not it is necessary or desirable for the welfare or convenience of the University to condemn and appropriate the property here in question for the intended purpose. Measured by these qualifications it must be concluded that the standards provided by § 22-503, *supra*, are reasonable and adequate for the purpose to be accomplished by the Act, and appellee acted within its statutory power and authority in proceeding to condemn and appropriate appellants' property for the intended use.

Second: Appellants assert that it was not necessary to appropriate their land, and that appellee seeks to condemn more land than the University needs because sufficient parking space could be provided to serve the "Tower Dormitory area of the University Campus" by using available land in the area already owned by the University.

The question of the necessity or expediency of a taking in eminent domain lies within the discretion of the Legislature and is not a proper subject for judicial review. Consequently appellants here cannot show in defense of the present proceedings that a quantity of land less than that described in the complaint would suffice, or that the University owned other land which might have been converted to parking space instead of appropriating appellants' land for such use.

Third: Appellants further assert that appellee did not make a "good faith" effort to purchase the land pursuant to [the statutory language of the Eminent Domain Act] before instituting condemnation proceedings.

An effort to purchase the property sought to be acquired is a condition precedent to the right to maintain an action to condemn property pursuant to the Eminent Domain Act, and the burden is on the appellee here to show a good faith effort to purchase and an inability to agree.

Appellants contend that the effort to purchase their land was not made in good faith because they were not offered what they considered to be the market price of the property. They rely upon *In re Rogers*, which states, "A bona fide effort to purchase involves a willingness to pay the market value of the land wanted, and this means the amount for which the property would actually sell at the time."

In the *Rogers* case an agent of the State Highway Commission attempted to make a settlement with the property owners on the basis of an offer of $300 per acre in one location and $500 per acre in another, which offer had been made two years before the attempted settlement. The lowest value placed upon the land at the hearing was $2,500 per acre. The court held that the offer of $300 per acre "constituted no real effort to purchase; was perfunctory only, for it negatived any purpose to negotiate.". . . . [T]he court further stated that:

> The highway department need not pay the price asked by a property owner, if not reasonable; neither is the property owner required to accept an inadequate price offered by the department or, in case of refusal, be subjected to the expense and trouble of condemnation proceedings. The law intends a purchase based upon a fair and reasonable price reached in a good faith effort to purchase.

The evidence at the hearing in the present case discloses that appellants' property here involved is Lot Number 8 in Ray Rogers Addition to the City of

Bloomington, Indiana; that Lot Number 7 in such addition was purchased by the University for $18,000; Lot Number 9 for $21,000; and that the highest price paid for any single lot acquired in the addition was $25,000. Under these circumstances it cannot be said that an offer of $30,000 for appellant's property "constituted no real effort to purchase." The University was not required to pay the price asked by appellants if it was not reasonable.

The facts and circumstances in the *Rogers* case vary so widely from those in the present case that it cannot be controlling or persuasive here.

Prior decisions of this court have not followed the "market value of the land" theory and appellants here have advanced no persuasive reason to depart from the general rule, which has been applied in Indiana to determine whether or not an effort to purchase has been made which satisfies the requirements of our statutes on Eminent Domain, and to adopt in lieu thereof the 'market value of the land' theory.

What constitutes a "good faith" or "bona fide" offer to purchase? Each case must be determined in light of its own particular circumstances. However, the authorities generally indicate that where there is disagreement regarding the value of property, if a reasonable offer is made honestly and in good faith and a reasonable effort has been made to induce the owner to accept it, the requirements of the statute for an offer to purchase have been met.

In our judgment the statute here . . . does not contemplate an impossibility to purchase at any price, however large, but merely an unwillingness on the part of the owner to sell only at a price which in the petitioner's judgment is excessive. In such an event the attempt to agree need not be pursued further than to develop the fact that an agreement to purchase is not possible at any price which the condemnor is willing to pay.

The record here discloses that appellee first contacted appellants in the spring of 1955 concerning the acquisition of their property. Appellants' answer to appellee's first contact was that they did not want to sell. Appellants were contacted on three or four subsequent occasions and such oral negotiations resulted in an offer by appellee first of $25,000, and subsequently of $30,000. On July 17, 1957, appellee, by registered mail, made its final offer of $30,000, and served therewith notice of intent to condemn. On July 30, 1957, appellants requested appellee to withdraw its notice of intention to condemn. On August 3, 1957, appellee demanded acceptance of its offer of $30,000 by August 8, 1957. On July 14, 1958, appellants again indicated their desire not to sell but offered to take $50,000 for the property. This offer was rejected on July 17, 1958, by appellee. Appellee's complaint to condemn and appropriate was filed on August 15, 1958. At the hearing on appellants' objections the director of the real estate division of Indiana University testified that no further negotiations were entered into with appellants because they had, through their attorneys, stated that they would accept nothing less than $50,000 for the property.

In our judgment the record here clearly discloses not only an offer honestly made in good faith, but also a reasonable effort to induce the owners to accept it, and an unwillingness on the part of the owners, appellants, to sell only at a price which appellee deemed excessive. This meets fully the requirements of the statute pertaining to an offer to purchase prior to the filing of condemnation proceedings.

The appellee here possessed the power and authority to condemn and appropriate the subject land for the use intended. It is not alleged that appellee acted fraudulently or capriciously. Its actions herein were not illegal.

The judgment of the trial court overruling appellants' objections to the condemnation and appropriation of their land described in appellee's complaint and appointing appraisers to assess the damages, if any, must be affirmed.

Judgment affirmed.

NOTES

1. Local board members may have connections with university officials in college towns. How, then, might college administrations and the institutions' boards create arms-length transactions?

2. *Mt. San Jacinto Community College District v. Superior Court*, 54 Cal. Rptr. 3d 752 (Cal. 2007), was a taking clause case involving two institutions of higher education, Azusa Pacific University as the original landowner and Mt. San Jacinto Community College as the land recipient. The pertinent facts of the case are as follows:

> In October 2000, Mt. San Jacinto Community College District (the District) commenced an eminent domain action against Azusa Pacific University (the University), seeking to condemn approximately 30 acres of vacant land in Riverside County. On December 15, 2000, the District deposited $1.789 million into court as probable compensation for the property. In October 2001, the District applied for a prejudgment order for possession. The trial court granted the application effective upon the University's completion of improvements to the property. The District took possession of the property in January 2002. The University did not move to stay the order for possession on hardship grounds or pending the trial court's adjudication of the District's right to take the property. In addition, the University did not withdraw any portion of the deposited funds.
>
> In February 2002, the University petitioned the court to increase the deposit of probable compensation from $1.789 million to $4.2 million. The University argued that the property was worth $4.2 million when the deposit was made in December 2000. The trial court determined that the amount of probable compensation on December 15, 2000 was $1.789 million, and denied the University's petition.

Id. at 756. The issue that the California Supreme Court eventually addressed was whether the District's valuation of the property at the date of the deposit provided just compensation to the property owner. Azusa Pacific argued that the valuation should take place at the commencement of trial after the property value had increased instead of at the date of deposit. The state high court disagreed with Azusa's argument and ruled that when the government entity deposited funds as the probable compensation for a taking, that value was the appropriate determination for just compensation.

G. LOCAL TAXES

1. Property Taxes — Student Housing

LOCK HAVEN UNIVERSITY FOUNDATION v. CLINTON COUNTY BOARD OF ASSESSMENT APPEALS AND REVISION OF TAXES

920 A.2d 207 (Pa. Commw. Ct. 2007)

Opinion by: JUDGE LEADBETTER

Lock Haven University Foundation appeals from an order of the Clinton County Court of Common Pleas that affirmed the decision of the Office of the Board of Assessment Appeals & Revision of Taxes denying the Foundation's appeal from the assessment of its Evergreen Commons property as "no longer exempt improvements."

According to its bylaws, the purpose of the Foundation, which was formerly known as the "Friends of Lock Haven State College," is as set forth in its Articles of Incorporation, including "serving as the authoritative body to approve and coordinate all fundraising activities carried out on behalf of Lock Haven University[.]" Plaintiff's Exhibit 3, Lock Haven University Foundation Bylaws, as amended July 2003 at 1. The Articles of Incorporation provide that the corporation was formed to "further the program and purposes of Lock Haven State College" and

> [t]o receive and administer a fund or funds of real or personal property, or both, and, subject to the restrictions and limitations hereinafter set forth, to use and apply the whole or any part of the income therefrom and the principal thereof exclusively for charitable, scientific, literary or educational purposes either directly or by contributions to organizations that qualify as exempt organizations under Section 501(c)(3) of the Internal Revenue Code and its regulations. . . .
>
> No part of the Foundation's net earnings inure to the benefit of its shareholders or other individuals, and no shareholder or other individual is entitled to share in distribution of the Foundation's assets if the corporation is dissolved.

In April 2005, the Chief Assessor for Clinton County issued the Foundation a notice of new or corrected assessed valuation with respect to its Evergreen Commons property, a student housing complex adjacent to the Lock Haven University campus. The assessment was changed from $107,840 to $2,278,240. The notice explained: "REASON FOR CHANGE: NO LONGER EXEMPT IMPROVEMENTS." Thereafter, the Foundation filed a "Statement of Intention to Appeal/Reclassification of Property." After a hearing, the Board denied the Foundation's appeal. The Foundation then appealed to common pleas, asserting that it is a charitable, tax-exempt institution under applicable law, including the Pennsylvania Constitution and the Institutions of Purely Public Charity Act

(Charity Act), and that the uses of Evergreen Commons qualify the property for exemption under applicable law, including the "Assessment Statute."

After a hearing, Common Pleas denied the Foundation's appeal, concluding that "Evergreen Commons is not entitled to a real estate tax exemption." Common Pleas also stated that, because "Evergreen Commons is not a purely public charity," the court need "not address whether it is tax exempt under the Fourth to Eighth Class County Assessment Law." Before us, the Foundation essentially queries whether common pleas misconstrued applicable law in denying its assessment appeal and determining that Evergreen Commons is not tax exempt.

Our Supreme Court stated in *Community Options, Inc. v. Board of Property Assessment, Appeals and Review*:

> An entity seeking a statutory exemption for taxation must first establish that it is a "purely public charity" under Article VIII, Section 2 of the Pennsylvania Constitution before the question of whether that entity meets the qualifications of a statutory exemption can be reached. In *Hospital Utilization Project [HUP]*, this Court set forth a five-part test for determining whether an entity qualifies as a "purely public charity" under the Pennsylvania Constitution:
>
> [A]n entity qualifies as a purely public charity if it possesses the following characteristics.
>
> (a) Advances a charitable purpose;
>
> (b) Donates or renders gratuitously a substantial portion of its services;
>
> (c) Benefits a substantial and indefinite class of persons who are legitimate subjects of charity;
>
> (d) Relieves the government of some of its burden; and
>
> (e) Operates entirely free from private profit motive.
>
> The question of whether an entity is a "purely public charity" is a mixed question of law and fact on which the trial court's decision is binding absent an abuse of discretion or lack of supporting evidence.

Once an institution qualifies as a "purely public charity" under Article VIII, Section 2 of the Pennsylvania Constitution, the next relevant question is whether it qualifies for tax exemption status under the Charity Act. In this regard, our Supreme Court stated:

> Section 372 of the Charity Act states that the intent of the Act is to provide "standards to be applied uniformly throughout this Commonwealth for determining eligibility for exemption from State and local taxation which are consistent with traditional legislative and judicial applications of the constitutional term 'institution of purely public charity.' " Section 375(a) of the Charity Act, titled "Criteria for institutions of purely public charity", states that an institution of purely public charity is an institution that meets

the criteria set forth. . . .[8] Each of the five subsections to which Section 375(a) refers has an opening sentence that tracks the language of one of the *Hospital Utilization Project* test prongs.

In this instance, however, common pleas did not engage in a step-by-step analysis of whether the Foundation proved that it is a "purely public charity" under Article VIII, § 2 of the Pennsylvania Constitution, nor did it thoroughly discuss whether the Foundation is an institution of purely public charity under the standards of the Charity Act. Instead, it assumed that the Foundation meets the constitutional test for a purely public charity. Nevertheless, it denied the Foundation an exemption for its property known as Evergreen Commons on the ground that Evergreen Commons is not itself a purely public charity pursuant to the relevant statutory criteria. We do not believe that this analysis is supported by the law.

Section 3 of the Charity Act defines "institution" as "[a] domestic or foreign nonprofit corporation, association or trust or other similar entity." Relying on this definition, we explained in *Chartiers Valley School District v. Board of Property Assessment, Appeals, Review and Registry of Allegheny County* that, for purposes of considering whether an institution is one of purely public charity under the Charity Act, "[o]ur evaluation focuses on a corporation, not on multiple corporations and not on parts of a corporation." In so stating, we acknowledged as accurate common pleas' determination that, because the South Hills Branch of the Jewish Community Center of Pittsburgh "was not incorporated separately, it could not be evaluated as a separate institution" from the Center itself. Further, we determined that common pleas rightly decided that the Center "actually and regularly use [d] the Branch for the advancement of its charitable purposes." Last, we concluded that, due to our decision, we did not need to discuss whether the Branch independently met the requirements of Section 5(d) and (e) of the Charity Act. We therefore affirmed common pleas' decision that the Center, including its South Hills Branch, was an institution of purely public charity.

. . . .

Therefore, to reiterate, the proper legal analysis is, first, whether the Foundation, as a whole, meets the constitutional criteria for an institution of purely public charity, and, second, whether the Foundation, as a whole, meets the specific statutory criteria under Section 5(b)-(f) for an institution of purely public charity. Because the board's responsive arguments challenged only Evergreen Commons' failure to fulfill these statutory criteria, there appears to be no real question that the Foundation is an institution of purely public charity under both the constitutional and statutory standards. That being said, Evergreen Commons, as part and parcel of the Foundation, will not qualify for tax exempt status unless it, too, meets certain constitutional and statutory standards, as hereafter set forth.

---

[8] [Relevant sections of the] Charity Act specifically provide[]: "General rule. An institution of purely public charity is an institution which meets the criteria set forth . . . "the institution must advance a charitable purpose"; . . . it "must operate entirely free from private profit motive"; . . . it "must donate or render gratuitously a substantial portion of its services"; . . . it "must benefit a substantial and indefinite class of persons who are legitimate subjects of charity"; and . . . it "must relieve the government of some of its burden." These criteria, in turn, have specific sub-elements that must be met before the criteria can be satisfied.

Article VIII, § 2 of the Constitution provides in relevant part: "(a) The General Assembly may by law exempt from taxation: . . . (v) Institutions of purely public charity, *but in the case of any real property tax exemptions only that portion of real property of such institution which is actually and regularly used for the purposes of the institution.*" (Emphasis added).

Moreover, Section 5(h) of the Charity Act, . . . specifically provides:

> (1) Nothing in this act shall affect, impair or hinder the responsibilities or prerogatives of the political subdivision responsible for maintaining real property assessment rolls to make a determination *whether a parcel of property or a portion of a parcel of property is being used to advance the charitable purpose of an institution of purely public charity* or to assess the parcel or part of the parcel of property as taxable based on the use of the parcel or part of the parcel for purposes other than the charitable purpose of that institution. (Emphasis added).
>
> (2) Nothing in this act shall prohibit a political subdivision from filing challenges or making determinations as to whether a particular parcel of property is being used to advance the charitable purpose of an institution of purely public charity.

This Section grants authority for the Board of Assessment Appeals to tax Evergreen Commons independently from the Foundation itself.

Last, Section 202 of the Fourth to Eighth Class County Assessment Law, 72 P.S. § 5453.202(a)(3), provides in relevant part:

> (a) The following property shall be exempt from all county, borough, town, township, road, poor, county institution district and school (except in cities) tax, to wit:
>
> . . . .
>
> (3) All hospitals, universities, colleges, seminaries, academies, associations and institutions of learning, benevolence or charity, including fire and rescue stations, with the grounds thereto annexed and necessary for the occupancy and enjoyment of the same, *founded, endowed and maintained by public or private charity:* Provided, That the entire revenue derived by the same be applied to the support and to increase the efficiency and facilities thereof, the repair and the necessary increase of grounds and buildings thereof, and for no other purpose: Provided further, *That the property of associations and institutions of benevolence or charity be necessary to and actually used for the principal purposes of the institution and shall not be used in such a manner as to compete with commercial enterprise.* (Emphasis added).

We explained in *Mars Area School District v. United Presbyterian Women's Association of North America*, that

> [i]n order to be entitled to a real estate exemption under Section 202, an entity must affirmatively show that: (1) the entire institution is a "purely public charity"; (2) it was founded by a public or private charity; and (3) it

> is maintained by a public or private charity. In addition, the institution must establish that its property is necessary to and actually used for its charitable purpose and not used in such a manner as to compete with commercial enterprise.

Because, here, there seems to be no real question that the Foundation is an institution of purely public charity, which, pursuant to Section 5(a) of the Charity Act, would then be "founded, endowed and maintained by public or private charity," we are left with the determination of whether Evergreen Commons is a property that (1) is necessary to and actually used for the Foundation's principal purposes; and (2) is not used in a manner that competes with private enterprise. The law is clear that, in establishing whether the property is necessary to the charity's use, proof of absolute necessity is not required.

Again, the purpose of Lock Haven University Foundation is "[t]o receive and administer a fund or funds of real or personal property, or both, and, subject to the restrictions and limitations hereinafter set forth, to use and apply the whole or any part of the income therefrom and the principal thereof exclusively for charitable, scientific, literary or educational purposes. . . ." Moreover, the articles provide that, as a means of accomplishing its purposes, the Corporation shall have the following powers:

> 1. To accept, acquire, receive, take and hold by bequest, devise, grant, gift, purchase, exchange, lease, transfer, judicial order or decree, or otherwise, for any of its objects and purposes, any property, both real and personal, of whatever kind, nature or description and wherever situated.
>
> 2. To sell, exchange, convey, mortgage, lease, transfer, or otherwise dispose of, any such property, both real and personal, as the objects and purposes of the Corporation may require, subject to such limitations as may be prescribed by law.
>
> 3. To borrow money and, from time to time, to make, accept, endorse, execute and issue bonds, debentures, promissory notes, bills of exchange and other obligations of the Corporation, for monies borrowed or in payment of property acquired or for any of the other purposes of the Corporation, and to secure the payment of any such obligations by mortgage, pledge, deed, indenture, agreement or other instrument of trust, or by other lien upon, assignment of, or agreement in regard to all or any part of the property, rights or privileges of the Corporation wherever situated, whether now owned or hereafter to be acquired.

Although common pleas never discussed whether Evergreen Commons was exempt from tax under the Fourth to Eighth Class County Assessment Law, it did conclude that the Foundation provides student housing; it sets the rents so that, in combination, they will be enough to repay the bond and the expenses of the facility; there is presently no profit; and when the bond is paid back, any income the Foundation receives would benefit the programs and purposes of the University. We believe that these findings are enough to satisfy the Foundation's burden of proving that Evergreen Commons is necessary to and actually used for the Foundation's principal purposes and is not used in a manner that competes with private enterprise.

Further, to be exempt from taxation, Section 202(b) of the Assessment Law requires that the revenue derived from the subject property come from the recipients of the bounty of the institution or charity, 72 P.S. § 5453.202(b), and Section 202(c) requires the institution to prove that it has legal or equitable title in the property at issue. There is no question that the revenue derived from Evergreen Commons comes from the Lock Haven University students who reside there and that the Foundation is the owner of Evergreen Commons.

For all of the above reasons, the order of the Court of Common Pleas of Clinton County is reversed.

NOTES

1. The language that exempts nonprofit private colleges typically describes the qualifying institution as a "nonprofit, educational institution," a "purely public charity," or a nonprofit "college or university." What was different about *Lock Haven* from traditional nonprofit educational institutions?

2. What test did the court articulate? Describe each of the elements. What type of housing arrangements might have changed the *Lock Haven* case outcome?

3. Many jurisdictions permit exemptions for property used exclusively for educational functions. For instance, in *Bexar Appraisal Dist. v. Incarnate Word College*, 824 S.W.2d 295 (Tex. App. 1992), the court iterated the standard as property "used exclusively for educational functions and that the property is reasonably necessary for the operation of the school." Accordingly, the tax exemption did not apply to the private university's college president's house.

4. Historically, while state colleges and universities were developing in the mid to late 1800s, municipal colleges and universities also emerged — though to a lesser degree. Publically owned, municipal colleges reported to and relied much in part on the local government. CHRISTOPHER J. LUCAS, AMERICAN HIGHER EDUCATION 153–54 (1996). Examples of established publically owned, municipal colleges include the College of Charleston, City College of New York (formerly known as the Free Academy of New York City), University of Louisville, University of Toledo, University of Akron, and Washburn University. Today, many of these institutions rely largely on state support and operate under state control. That is, the institutions merely retain historical roots as a municipal college without the same level of local governance.

Similarly, in many states, community colleges emerged with the similar historical formation as municipal colleges. Local school districts initially established community colleges. ARTHUR M. COHEN & FLORENCE B. BRAWER, THE AMERICAN COMMUNITY COLLEGE 117–23 (4th ed. 2008). Funding and governance sources differ widely today, but as a whole, the states are significantly more involved with community colleges than at the time of their establishment. *See id.* at 158–60; EDUC. COMM'N OF THE STATES, STATE FUNDING FOR COMMUNITY COLLEGES: A 50-STATE SURVEY (2000), *available at* http://www.ecs.org/clearinghouse/22/86/2286.pdf (identifying the revenue sources for community colleges).

2. Property Taxes — Greek Life

ZACH, INC. v. FULTON COUNTY
520 S.E.2d 899 (Ga. 1999)

Opinion by: Carley, Justice.

Zach, Inc. is a non-profit corporation created by a national fraternity for the sole purpose of owning real property, which is surrounded by the campus of the Georgia Institute of Technology (Georgia Tech) and which is used to house fraternity members. Zach filed a property tax challenge, relying on the exemption from ad valorem property taxes for "[a]ll buildings erected for and used as a college, incorporated academy, or other seminary of learning. . . ." In prior appeals related to the issue of taxability vel non, the Court of Appeals . . . held that the exemption at issue does not apply to the property because it is not owned by Georgia Tech and Zach is not an "arm or extension" thereof. However, the Court of Appeals did not address Zach's contention that denial of the application of the exemption to its property violated its right to equal protection, because the trial court did not distinctly pass or rule on that issue. Thereafter, Zach filed a "renewed" motion for summary judgment. The trial court rejected the equal protection challenge and directed the entry of final judgment. . . . The Court of Appeals affirmed. We granted certiorari to consider whether the holding that Zach's property is not tax-exempt is consistent with this Court's decisions in *Johnson v. Southern Greek Housing Corp., supra*, and *Alford v. Emory University, supra.* Because we hold that the educational use exemption from ad valorem property taxes found in OCGA § 48-5-41(a)(6) applies only to residential property owned by an educational institution or an "arm or extension" thereof, we affirm the judgment of the Court of Appeals.

With few exceptions the courts have held that college fraternities and sororities are not exempt from taxation, because they exist primarily for the convenience of their members, and are mainly concerned with providing them with board, lodging, and recreation, while any educational, charitable, and benevolent purposes are of secondary importance.

In this state, it is clear that property used for purely residential purposes does not come within the educational use exemption, even if college students or teachers happen to live there. The owner, not the residents, constitutes the determinative factor for eligibility for the tax exemption. A residential building may come within the exemption only if there is a sufficient nexus between the property and a legitimate educational institution. "Thus, it is clear, at least *where the university owns the property*, that residential buildings may be 'used as a college' and qualify for ad valorem tax exemption under OCGA § 48-5-41(a)(6). . . ." "In the absence of a provision to the contrary, it is ordinarily essential to exemption that the property should be owned by the educational institution." The title to the residential property in *Johnson* was not formally in the college's name, but the nonprofit corporate owner was an arm and extension of the college and performed an educational function in conjunction with and under the auspices of the college. Therefore, the *Johnson* decision reaches the outer limit of the application of the educational use exemption to residential buildings. If a property has a residential use, but no direct educational use, then it can only meet the statutory requirement of use "as a college" if the college itself, or at least an arm or extension thereof, owns the property as part of that institution's overall nonprofit educational endeavor. Indeed, OCGA § 48-5-41(b) refers to the exemption as "apply[ing] to . . . colleges. . . ." See also OCGA § 48-5-41(d) (which provides that the various exemptions, including subsection (a)(6), "shall not apply to real estate or buildings which are not used for the *operation* of religious, *educational*, and charitable *institutions*." (Emphasis supplied.))

If ownership by an educational institution or arm thereof were not the decisive factor in eligibility for the educational use exemption, then any entrepreneur could claim the exemption, so long as he provided some service or had another connection, however attenuated, to a few students or teachers. Furthermore, the exemption would effectively become in personam, and the owner could repeatedly lose and regain it based upon the actions of the educational institution. For example, Zach's entitlement to the educational use exemption would anomalously depend upon whether Georgia Tech continues or withdraws its official recognition of the fraternity. Such consequences are inconsistent with the statutory scheme of the property tax exemption, which applies unconditionally to property that is "used as a college," rather than to property only so long as it continues to be used by a fraternity in good standing with a nearby educational institution.

Zach exists solely to own and operate a fraternity house in proximity to the Georgia Tech campus. Its articles of incorporation do not mention education, but list recreation and pleasure as its purposes. Zach does not contend that it is an arm or extension of Georgia Tech. Zach is an arm or extension of the national fraternity which created it, and that fraternity, in turn, is not an arm or extension of Georgia Tech. Accordingly, the ad valorem property tax exemption set forth in OCGA § 48-5-41(a)(6) does not apply to the property owned by Zach and used for private residential and recreational purposes.

Judgment affirmed.

All the Justices concur, except HINES, J., not participating.

3. Admission Taxes

CITY OF BOULDER v. REGENTS OF UNIVERSITY OF COLORADO

501 P.2d 123 (Colo. 1972) (en banc)
rehearing denied Oct. 10, 1972

Opinion by: GROVES, JUSTICE.

This action against the Regents involves an ordinance of the City of Boulder which provides for an admissions tax upon charges made to attend public events. Boulder sought a declaratory judgment and asked for judgment for past taxes. The trial court held the ordinance to be valid but, as applied to events held under the auspices of the University of Colorado, the defendant Regents of the University could not be compelled to collect the tax. We affirm in part and reverse in part as to the validity of the ordinance, and affirm the ruling that the Regents cannot be compelled to collect the tax. This disposition of the matter renders moot the issues of whether the Board of Regents is liable for taxes which it did not collect in the past and whether they are liable for interest thereon and penalties as specified in the ordinance.

The ordinance (No. 3661) provides that every person who pays to gain admission to any place or event in the City that is open to the public shall pay an excise tax of 5% of the admission price. It places a duty upon the "owner or operator," who charges the admission fee, to collect and remit the tax. By way of illustration, the ordinance lists the following as being included within the events giving rise to the imposition of the tax:

> (1) Any performance of a motion picture, stage show, play, concert or other manifestation of the performing arts.
>
> (2) Any sporting or athletic contest, exhibition or event whether amateur or professional.
>
> (3) Any lecture, rally, speech of (sic) dissertation.
>
> (4) Any showing, display or exhibition of any type, such as an art exhibition. . . .

Under an administrative regulation the "owner or operator" may retain 1 1/2% of the tax as a collection and remittal fee.

The parties stipulated as follows:

> Certain portions of the curricula offered at the University of Colorado require students to attend events held on campus for which an admission is charged. Such event would be taxable by the Boulder Ordinance. For example, students taking certain English Drama and English Literature courses are sometimes required by the their professors to attend various "MANIFESTATIONS OF THE PERFORMING ARTS" held at the university theatre. Students in the Social Science Departments are some-

> times required to attend "lectures, dissertations and speeches" held out of class at Macky Auditorium. Those in the Fine Arts Department are sometimes required to attend various "art exhibitions" which come to the Boulder campus. Those in the Music Department are required to attend various concerts while many of the dramatic performances and plays are made compulsory for those in the Performing Arts Department. Many of these lectures, dissertations, art exhibitions, concerts and dramatic performances are brought in directly by the University, through its various academic departments, or by the faculty or various student groups.

I

We consider first the question of whether the Regents can be compelled to collect the tax, assuming for the moment that the tax is valid. It is the position of the City that, since it has not been shown that collection of the tax created an undue burden upon or interference with the operation of the University, the Regents can be compelled to make collection. The City relies upon *Bedford v. Colorado National Bank.*

Colo. Const. art. VIII, § 5 provides that the University is an institution of the State of Colorado. Colo. Const. art. IX, § 14 states: "The board of regents shall have the general supervision of the university, and the exclusive control and direction of all funds of, and appropriations to, the university."

Colo. Const. art. IX, § 12 provides that the Regents constitute a body corporate.

We quote with approval the following portion of the ruling by the trial court:

> [I]n the instant case the City is attempting to impose duties on the Board of Regents which would necessarily interfere with the Regents' control of the University. The Constitution establishes a state-wide University and vests control in the Board of Regents. The Board of Regents has Exclusive control and direction of all funds of, and appropriations to, the University. . . . Thus, the City of Boulder cannot force the Regents to apply any funds toward the collection of the tax in question. Even if the City claims that sufficient funds would be generated by the tax to compensate the Regents for collection expense and, arguably, such funds could be paid to the Regents by the City, the Regents are still vested with the 'general supervision' of the University. The University would necessarily be required to expend both money and manpower for the collection, identification and payment of such funds to the City. This interferes with the financial conduct of the University and the allocation of its manpower for its state-wide educational duties. Argument then might be raised that when the framers of the Constitution utilized the word 'general' rather than 'exclusive' in describing the supervisory power of the Regents that some area might be open for a city to impose duties without conflicting with the Regents' authority. However, this argument is incompatible with Article VIII, Section 5 of the Constitution of Colorado which, in establishing the state institutions provides the management thereof to be subject, ". . . to the control of the state, under the provisions of the Constitution, and such

laws and regulations as the General Assembly may provide . . ."

Thus, since the Constitution has established a state-wide University at Boulder and vested general supervisory control in a state-wide Board of Regents and management in control of the state, a city, even though a home rule city, has no power to interfere with the management or supervision of the activities of the University of Colorado. If the City of Boulder was allowed to impose duties on the University, such duties would necessarily interfere with the functions of the state institution. There is no authority to permit the City of Boulder to force a state institution to collect such a local tax. Consequently, the City of Boulder cannot require the Board of Regents of the University of Colorado to become involuntary collectors of the City of Boulder's Admission Tax.

Involved in *Bedford v. Colorado National Bank* was the imposition by the State of a 2% Tax on the service of furnishing safe deposit boxes. The tax was to be paid by the person who rented the box, and was to be collected and remitted by those furnishing the boxes. The issue was whether the State could compel a national bank-an instrumentality of the federal government-to collect and remit the tax. It was ruled that the bank was required to collect the tax. The reasoning there was that (1) the incidence of the tax was on the customer, not the bank; and (2) the duty of collecting the tax did not constitute an undue burden on the bank because (a) furnishing safe deposit boxes was not an essential function of the bank, and (b) the bank was permitted to keep 3% of the sum collected to reimburse it for the cost of collection.

Bedford was a 4 to 2 decision. We need not comment upon the correctness of this opinion because we find it distinguishable from the instant matter. There the State was the taxing authority and here a city is the taxing agency. So far as the questions involved here are concerned, the Regents are the State. Even with all the powers granted home rule cities under COLO. CONST. art. XX, § 6, a home rule city is still a subdivision of the State. We hold that no municipality, absent statutory authority, can compel the State or its officials to collect municipal taxes.

In *Hamilton v. City and County of Denver, Colo.*, we held the application of Denver's occupational privilege tax against state employees to be valid. We did not say that the State could be compelled to collect it. We take judicial notice of the fact that the State now is voluntarily deducting that tax from the compensation paid to those State employees who request the State to do so, and is remitting the amount collected to Denver. The State has not been compelled to do this.

II

We now consider the validity of the tax as applied to University functions, and we emphasize that we do not rule on any other application of the tax. When academic departments of the University, or others acting under the auspices of the University, sponsor lectures, dissertations, art exhibitions, concerts and dramatic performances, whether or not an admission fee is charged, these functions become a part of the educational process. This educational process is not merely for the enrolled students of the University, but it is a part of the educational process for those members of the public attending the events. In our view the home rule authority of a city does not permit it to tax a person's acquisition of education furnished by the State. We hold that the tax is invalid when applied to University lectures, dissertations, art exhibitions, concerts, and dramatic performances.

. . .

We now consider the tax as applied to University football games held on the campus. It is alleged in the complaint that the anticipated annual tax realized from University of Colorado football admissions would be approximately $41,000 (and that $9,000 tax would be raised annually from all other University events). It is obvious that the primary interest of the City is to obtain the tax from paid admissions to football games. *Allen v. Regents*, [a U.S. Supreme Court case,] has been cited to us and there is a statement in the brief by the City, "It is debatable whether an intercollegiate football game or a folk rock musical is an essential part of a liberal education." Rather anomalously, except for that citation and that statement, the record and the briefs are devoid of any facts or arguments disclosing a connection or lack of connection between football and the educational process. In *Allen*, the Court assumed that the holding of athletic contests is an integral part of the program of public education. It nevertheless upheld a federal 10% Admissions tax as applied to the University of Georgia and the Georgia Tech football games. We do not find *Allen* persuasive, one way or another.

Absent a showing that football is so related to the educational process that its devotees may not be taxed by a home rule city, we should not make a finding of fact or conclusion of law that it is so related. The alternative is to affirm, and, therefore, we affirm on the validity of the tax as applied to football. We surmise that, under our ruling in the first portion of this opinion combined with the rights of the Regents to control the operation of football games on the campus, any ruling on the validity of the tax as applied to University football games is probably academic.

The judgment of the trial court is reversed in part on the question of the validity of the tax as we have expounded, and otherwise is affirmed.

CITY OF MORGANTOWN v. WEST VIRGINIA BOARD OF REGENTS

354 S.E.2d 616 (W.Va. 1987)

Opinion by: Brotherton, Justice:

The City of Morgantown filed a declaratory judgment action in the Circuit Court of Kanawha County in July, 1985, asking whether the Board of Regents was required to collect the City's two-percent amusement tax on the sale of tickets to entertainment events such as carnivals, basketball and football games, and big time entertainers, which are open to the general public. Judge Canady of the Circuit Court of Kanawha County granted summary judgment to the Board of Regents, from which the City now appeals. We agree with the circuit court that the events sought to be taxed are not conducted for private profit, and therefore affirm.

The legislature granted cities the power to levy amusement taxes in W.Va. Code

§ 8-13-6 (1984). It reads, in pertinent part:

> Every municipality shall have plenary power and authority to levy and collect an admission or amusement tax upon any public amusement or entertainment conducted within the corporate limits thereof *for private profit or gain.* The tax shall be levied upon the purchaser and added to and collected by the seller with the price of admission, or other charge for the amusement or entertainment. The tax shall not exceed two percent of the admission price or charge, but a tax of one cent may be levied and collected in any case. (emphasis added).

In order to uphold the summary judgment, we must find that there is no genuine issue of material fact as to whether sports and entertainment events sponsored by West Virginia University are conducted "for private profit or gain."

The City of Morgantown relies to a large extent on depositions taken of various University employees that indicate that the West Virginia University Department of Intercollegiate Athletics is a separate, self-supporting unit and that money generated by sports activities does not go directly to the support of the academic function of the University. The City also points out that these receipts do not go into the general revenue fund, but are sequestered in special revenue accounts, and that the State collects consumers sales tax on them. The Board of Regents counters that there is no "private" party that stands to gain from profits generated by West Virginia University's athletic or entertainment events; that the legislature and this Court have recognized that West Virginia University exercises a governmental (as opposed to private) function when it sponsors athletic contests, and that special revenue funds are nonetheless State funds. Further, the Board of Regents asserts that imposition of the sales tax on certain state activities is expressly authorized by W.Va. Code § 11-15-2(7), and that such authorization does not convert a public function to private status.

The appellant cites two cases that have sustained taxes on football ticket receipts. The first is *Allen v. Regents of Univ. Sys. of Ga.*, in which the United States Supreme Court sustained a federal ten percent admissions tax on tickets to University of Georgia and Georgia Tech football games. That case focused on whether the federal exaction would unconstitutionally burden a governmental activity of the state. The Court assumed that public education was a governmental function, and that athletic contests were an integral part of the program of public education conducted by the State of Georgia. It concluded that the State of Georgia was conducting a business "having the incidents of similar enterprises usually prosecuted for private gain," and that even if education was an essential governmental function, funds generated by conducting a business enterprise were nonetheless subject to federal taxation. This case supports the City of Morgantown's argument to the extent that it finds that two universities were conducting a business enterprise "for gain" in the form of their athletic programs. It also compares such programs to "enterprises usually prosecuted for private gain." It does not, however, hold that the football games sponsored by Georgia universities were *conducted* "for private profit or gain." It does not, therefore, compel us to accept the City of Morgantown's position.

The second case is *City of Boulder v. Regents of the Univ. of Colorado.* There the

City of Boulder sought a declaratory judgment regarding the validity of its admissions tax on charges made to attend public events sponsored by the University of Colorado. The Supreme Court of Colorado held that the City's ordinance was valid as applied to university football games, but invalid as applied to university lectures, dissertations, art exhibitions, concerts, and dramatic performances. The statute in the Colorado case, however, imposed a tax on "admission to any place or event in the city that is open to the public," and made no reference to "private profit or gain." Thus the Colorado case, like the *Allen* case, did not address the issue before us.

Proceeds from athletic and entertainment events sponsored by West Virginia University are state funds held in special revenue accounts under W.Va.Code § 12-2-2 (1985). Special revenue accounts are state accounts kept separate from the general revenue due to a legislative determination that money generated by a particular activity should be allocated to a specific purpose. Such accounting does not remove the funds from the state treasury or destroy the public accountability of those who spend them.

This Court has held that admission fees collected by state educational institutions at athletic events are "public moneys." Similarly, we have observed that athletic programs are a proper and integral part of the education provided by state universities. We believe that the same is true of entertainment events such as concerts, lectures, exhibits, dramatic performances, and similar functions, the profits from which accrue to the benefit of a public university.

The City of Morgantown asks us to hold that such public moneys are collected for private profit or gain. The word "private" means "intended for or restricted to the use of a particular person or group or class of persons: not freely available to the public . . . belonging to or concerning an individual person, company, or interest." *Webster's Third New International Dictionary* 1804–05 (1966). There is no individual person, company, or interest that stands to profit from university-sponsored events, and the profits therefrom are not "private."

In a case construing the term "private gain," Washington, D.C., had a statute providing that property used for educational purposes that was not used for private gain was exempt from taxation, and all other property used for educational purposes was to be taxed as any other property. The court in *District of Columbia v. Mt. Vernon Seminary*, held that the seminary was not taxable under the statute even though operation of the school resulted in a profit. The court held:

> The term "private gain," as used in the statute, has reference only to gain realized by any individual or stockholder who has a pecuniary interest in the corporation and not . . . to profits realized by the institution but turned back into the treasury or expended for permanent improvements. . . .
>
> If it had been intended to tax institutions earning a profit, i.e., having income in excess of expenditures, Congress would have used the word *profit* or the word *gain* instead of *private gain*.

The same is true in this case.

For the reasons discussed, we conclude that sports and entertainment events sponsored by West Virginia University are not conducted for private profit or gain, and are not subject to the amusement tax levied by the City of Morgantown. We find no genuine issue of material fact in this regard, and no error in the circuit court's application of the law. We therefore affirm the grant of summary judgment.

Affirmed.

NOTES

1. Often, private nonprofit, as well as public, colleges and universities are exempt from paying local property taxes. The basis for this exemption is that the public institution falls within the state sovereignty, and the home rule does not permit the collection of taxes from the state. The basis for private colleges and universities somewhat vary, but generally speaking, its role as a nonprofit educational institution exempts it from the local property tax collection.

2. Legal construction and standards to collect property taxes are based on three principles:

(i) Narrow review of statutory language;

(ii) Construing tax exemptions strongly against those who claim the exemption;

(iii) Differences in "purpose": the purpose of the parcel of land versus the purpose of the institutional type and its use of the land.

3. Off-campus sites of public universities may also qualify for tax exemptions. For instance in *Trustees of Indiana University v. Town of Rhine*, 488 N.W.2d 128 (Wis. Ct. App. 1992), the state appellate court held that a summer camp which served as an off-campus site for a university to conduct a mandatory portion of its physical education curriculum constituted "grounds" of the university for purposes of the property tax exemption statute. The university's leasing of the camp to its alumni association for use as family campground and vacation site did not destroy its tax exempt status. *Id.* at 132.

4. These cases collectively support two points: (1) the plain statement of the legislation plays a role in determining application of special tax and (2) the educational versus non-educational function analysis likely is factored.

Chapter XI

INSTITUTIONAL AND ACADEMIC PROGRAM INTEGRITY

Introduction

In the United States, most institutions of higher education engage in multiple institutional and academic program integrity processes. Historically referred to as the program integrity triad, colleges and universities that receive federal financial aid adhere to standards established by the federal government, respective state governments, and U.S. Department of Education approved accreditors (which, for the most part, are regional accreditation agencies). This chapter presents the case law involving institutional and academic program integrity standards and discusses the policy considerations associated with the roles that each entity plays in the institutional and academic program integrity check process [hereinafter integrity check]. Given this U.S. process for integrity checks, the authors pay special attention to cases and policy matters that involve standards established by the federal government, state licensing offices, and accreditation bodies, as these three entities tend to generate most of the litigation within this area and largely shape the form and manner of these integrity checks.

At the federal level, the integrity checks provide institutional certification, so an institution may qualify as a recipient of Title IV federal funding (e.g., Pell Grants, student loan programs, and work study). That is, the certification permits the institution to award federal financial aid. The awarding of these federal funds is quite significant for students to pay for their college education, and consequently, these awards are critical to institutions of higher education. For the 2009–2010 school year, eligible colleges and universities awarded approximately $146.5 billion in federal student aid. *See* Nat'l Ass'n of Student Financial Aid Admins., Federal Student Financial Aid: 2011 National Profile of Programs in Title IV of the Higher Education Act 2 (2011), *available at* http://www.nasfaa.org/EntrancePDF.aspx?id=5328. With 19.5 million college students qualifying for federal aid in 2010–2011 and projections of increasing obligations to more students in the future, the federal contribution is expected to remain quite significant. As part of the process, in 2011, over 4300 colleges and universities — both private and public — participated in continued integrity program checks, in order to be eligible to make these awards of federal aid. As Section A of this chapter illustrates, institutional challenges of federal policies center around meeting program integrity standards, so they may qualify for Title IV funding.

Similarly, at the state level, these institutional and academic program integrity checks are incorporated into the laws and policies that certify educational institutions to operate in that respective jurisdiction. As presented in Chapter II and illustrated in Section B of this chapter, state law governs these checks through state licensure requirements for educational institutions. For instance, in *State v. Clarksville School of Theology*, 636 S.W.2d 706 (Tenn. 1982), the Supreme Court of Tennessee ruled that the state Postsecondary Education Authorization Act required approved colleges and universities in the state to adhere to minimum standards in order to qualify as an educational institution that issues degrees or diplomas. Although Clarksville argued that the approval requirements burdened its free exercise of religion, the state high court determined that the state authorization process did not violate the rights of the operators of the school.

States also have policies for schools that maintain a physical presence or issue degrees to citizens of its state, and these policies tend to generate challenges regarding the reach of the state's authority. Further, the state is involved when questions of professional qualification or recognition of a degree arise for the purpose of meeting state board standards. These challenges often raise concerns about the tension between the educational institution and the entity representing the professional certification.

In Section C of this chapter, several significant legal challenges and policy debates surrounding accreditation are presented. Although accreditation represents a mechanism for the profession to maintain self-regulation, the cases question the fairness of the gatekeepers' actions and the extent to which these gatekeepers should have authority over the operations and decision making of a college or university's operations. Given the high stakes of accreditors' decisions, numerous cases have emerged to contest them.

Throughout this chapter, the reader will discover several cross-cutting themes. One theme is the participation of For-Profit Colleges and Universities (FPCUs) as a major player within higher education. FPCU enrollments have grown significantly in the last decade. *For Profit Colleges: Hearing Before the Sen. Comm. on Health, Education, Labor & Pensions*, 111th Cong. 1 (Aug. 4, 2010) (statement of Gregory D. Kutz, Managing Director Forensics Audits and Special Investigations at the U.S. Government Accountability Office) (Enrollment at FPCUs "has grown from about 365,000 students to almost 1.8 million in the last several years."). Because their enrollment growth has been quite substantial, these students account for larger shares of student aid, especially, federal grant programs. *See* NAT'L ASS'N OF STUDENT FINANCIAL AID ADMINS., *supra*, at 2. As a growing provider of higher education, FPCUs also serve as an access point for students, who might not have chosen to enroll (or re-enroll) in higher education *but for* the offerings of a FPCU. In short, FPCUs present new challenges and opportunities for higher education, especially in terms of regulation. *See* GUILBERT C. HENTSCHKE, ET AL., FOR-PROFIT COLLEGES AND UNIVERSITIES: THEIR MARKETS, REGULATION, PERFORMANCE, AND PLACE IN HIGHER EDUCATION 1–22 (2010).

Another theme highlighted in this chapter is maintaining educational quality in an environment that presents competing interests. For instance, in some cases, business ventures established so-called "educational providers" to issue degrees based on no or questionably substandard educational experiences. One of the cases presented in this chapter is a Federal Trade Commission opinion from 1958. While the case appears outdated, current reports and investigations indicate otherwise.

See Diploma Mills: Hearing Before the H. Subcomm. on 21st Century Competitiveness, Committee on Education & the Workforce, 108th Cong. (Sept. 23, 2004) (statement of Robert J. Cramer, Managing Director of the Office of Special Investigations at the U.S. Government Accountability Office). Similarly, these cases also arise from decisions by state professional licensing boards and accrediting agencies.

A third theme discusses the benefits and drawbacks of the heterogeneous system of U.S. higher education. Each state has authority to decide how to certify and oversee colleges and universities engaged with its state. This authority grants states discretion to establish the standards and processes for approval, but it also creates a very confusing and complex system for educational providers that wish to have a presence in more than one state. As Sir John Daniel of the British Open University remarked: "I thought that when I brought the Open University to the U.S. I would be dealing with one country. I was mistaken." MICHAEL B. GOLDSTEIN. REGULATION OF E-LEARNING: REGULATING THE MEDIUM AND THE MESSENGER (2001). Sir John Daniel observed 50 different standards implemented by the states, along with different standards from D.C. and U.S. territories. In addition, while the United States maintains great diversity within higher education among its more than 4600 colleges and universities, this chapter draws attention to the variability in determining student learning outcomes. In other words, state standards are different and institutional variation might dictate further differences. Accordingly, this lack of uniformity calls into question whether higher education accreditation, state authorization policies, and degree outcomes should be standardized across the nation. *See* CLIFFORD ADELMAN., LEARNING ACCOUNTABILITY FROM BOLOGNA: A HIGHER EDUCATION POLICY PRIMER (2008), *available at* http://www.ihep.org/assets/files/publications/g-l/Learning_Accountability_from_Bologna.pdf.

A. FEDERAL REGULATIONS

ASSOCIATION OF PRIVATE SECTOR COLLEGES AND UNIVERSITIES v. DUNCAN

681 F.3d 427 (D.C. Cir. 2012)

EDWARDS , SENIOR CIRCUIT JUDGE

Every year, Congress provides billions of dollars through loan and grant programs to help students pay tuition for their postsecondary education. The Department of Education ("the Department" or "the agency") administers these programs, which were established under Title IV of the Higher Education Act of 1965 ("the HEA" or "the Act") . . . . Students must repay their federal loans; the costs of unpaid loans are borne by taxpayers.

To participate in Title IV programs — i.e., to be able to accept federal funds — a postsecondary institution ("a school" or "an institution") must satisfy several statutory requirements. These requirements are intended to ensure that participating schools actually prepare their students for employment, such that those students can repay their loans. Three requirements are at issue here. First, a school must qualify as an "institution of higher education," 20 U.S.C. § 1094(a) (2006) — meaning, *inter alia*, that the school is "legally authorized" to provide education in the state in which it is located, *id.* § 1001(a)(2). Second, a school must "enter into a program participation agreement with the Secretary" of Education ("the Secretary"), pursuant to which the school agrees, *inter alia*, not to "provide any commission, bonus, or other incentive payment based directly or indirectly on success in securing enrollments or financial aid to any" recruiters or admissions employees. *Id.* § 1094(a)(20). Third, a school must not engage in "substantial misrepresentation of the nature of its educational program, its financial charges, or the employability of its graduates." *Id.* § 1094(c)(3)(A).

In 2009, based on experiences that it had faced in administering the Title IV programs, the Department concluded that the existing regulations covering the state authorization, compensation, misrepresentation, and other statutory requirements created opportunities for abuse by schools, because the regulations were too lax. The Department thus initiated a rulemaking process to strengthen the regulations so as to protect the integrity of these programs. On October 29, 2010, following notice and comment, the agency issued final regulations.

The new regulations included several new provisions that are the focus of the dispute in this case. First, the Department adopted for the first time substantive regulations addressing the HEA's state authorization requirement. *See* 34 C.F.R. § 600.9 (2011) ("the State Authorization Regulations"). Under the applicable regulations, a school is now legally authorized by a state, only if the state has a process to review and act on complaints concerning institutions, and if the state has authorized that specific school by name. *See id.* § 600.9(a)(1)(i)(A) ("the school authorization regulation"). In addition, in order to be "legally authorized," a school offering distance or correspondence education, including online courses, must obtain authorization from all states in which its students reside that require such authorization. *See id.* § 600.9(c) ("the distance education regulation"). Second, the regulations covering compensation practices were amended to eliminate regulatory "safe harbors" pursuant to which schools had adopted compensation practices that effectively circumvented the HEA's proscription against certain incentive payments. *See id.* § 668.14(b)(22) ("the Compensation Regulations"). Finally, the Department amended the regulations covering the HEA's misrepresentation requirement, *see id.* §§ 668.71-.75 ("the Misrepresentation Regulations"), by, *inter alia*, specifying that a "misleading statement includes any statement that has the likelihood or tendency to deceive or confuse," *id.* § 668.71(c), and restyling the Secretary's menu of enforcement options, *see id.* § 668.71(a).

The Association of Private Sector Colleges and Universities ("Appellant" or "the Association") filed suit in the District Court challenging the State Authorization, Compensation, and Misrepresentation Regulations (collectively, "the challenged regulations") under the Administrative Procedure Act ("the APA"), *see* 5 U.S.C. § 706 (2006), and the Constitution. Both parties moved for summary judgment. The District Court granted summary judgment to the Department on Appellant's challenges to the Compensation and Misrepresentation Regulations; found that Appellant lacked standing to challenge the school authorization regulation; and granted summary judgment to Appellant on its challenge to the distance education regulation. *See Career Coll. Ass'n v. Duncan*, 796 F. Supp. 2d 108 (D.D.C. 2011).

We affirm in part, reverse in part, and remand for further proceedings consistent with this opinion. First, we affirm the judgment of the District Court holding that the Compensation Regulations do not exceed the HEA's limits. And we mostly reject Appellant's claim that these regulations are not based on reasoned decision-making. We remand two aspects of the Compensation Regulations, however, that are lacking for want of adequate explanations. Second, we hold that the Misrepresentation Regulations exceed the HEA's limits in three respects: by allowing the Secretary to take enforcement actions against schools sans procedural protections; by proscribing misrepresentations with respect to subjects that are not covered by the HEA; and by proscribing statements that are merely confusing. We reject Appellant's other challenges to the Misrepresentation Regulations. Finally, with respect to the State Authorization Regulations, we conclude that Appellant has standing to challenge the school authorization regulation, but hold that the regulation is valid. However, we uphold Appellant's challenge to the distance education regulation, because that regulation is not a logical outgrowth of the Department's proposed rules.

I. BACKGROUND

A. The Higher Education Act

Congress created the Title IV programs to foster access to higher education. "Every year [these] programs provide more than $150 billion in new federal aid to approximately fourteen million post-secondary students and their families." *Career Coll. Ass'n*, 796 F. Supp. 2d at 113-14. Students receiving this aid attend private for-profit institutions, public institutions, and private nonprofit institutions. *See id.* at 114. These students are expected to repay their federal loans; their failure to do so shifts their tuition costs onto taxpayers. But schools receive the benefit of accepting tuition payments from students receiving federal financial aid, regardless of whether those students are ultimately able to repay their loans. Therefore, Congress codified statutory requirements in the HEA to ensure against abuse by schools. Three are at issue in this dispute.

First, the HEA stipulates that "[i]n order to be an eligible institution for the purposes of any [Title IV] program[,] . . . an institution must be an institution of higher education." 20 U.S.C. § 1094(a). Federal law defines an "institution of higher education" as an institution in any state that *inter alia* "is legally authorized within such State to provide a program of education beyond secondary education." *Id.* § 1001(a)(2); *see also id.* § 1002(a)(1), (b)-(c). The HEA does not define "legally authorized." This lack of a statutory definition has meant that, for virtually all of the HEA's history, each state has determined for itself the method of authorizing schools within its borders.

Second, as noted above, each school must enter into a program participation agreement with the Secretary. Pursuant to this statutory requirement, a school must agree not to "provide any commission, bonus, or other incentive payment based directly or indirectly on success in securing enrollments or financial aid to any persons or entities engaged in any student recruiting or admission activities or in making decisions regarding the award of student financial assistance." *Id.* §

1094(a)(20). Congress adopted this provision in 1992 based on its concern that schools were creating incentives for recruiters to enroll students who could not graduate or could not find employment after graduating. *See* H.R. Rep. No. 102-447, at 10 (1992), *reprinted in* 1992 U.S.C.C.A.N. at 343; *see also United States ex rel. Lee v. Corinthian Colls.*, 655 F.3d 984, 989 (9th Cir. 2011) ("This requirement is meant to curb the risk that recruiters will sign up poorly qualified students who will derive little benefit from the subsidy and may be unable or unwilling to repay federally guaranteed loans." (citations omitted) (internal quotation marks omitted)). The Department may initiate an enforcement action against a school that violates this prohibition to seek the imposition of a civil fine or the limitation, suspension, or termination of the institution's eligibility to participate in Title IV programs.

Third, the HEA prohibits schools from engaging in "substantial misrepresentation" regarding "the nature of its educational program, its financial charges, or the employability of its graduates." Congress adopted this provision to protect students from "false advertising" and other forms of manipulative "sharp practice." If the agency determines "after reasonable notice and opportunity for a hearing" that an institution has engaged in proscribed substantial misrepresentation, it may "suspend or terminate" the institution's eligibility to participate in Title IV programs. 20 U.S.C. § 1094(c)(3)(A). The agency may alternatively seek the imposition of a civil fine.

B. Regulatory History

Congress has delegated to the Secretary the authority to promulgate regulations governing the Department's administration of Title IV and other federal programs. The grant of authority provides that "[t]he Secretary, in order to carry out functions otherwise vested in the Secretary by law or by delegation of authority pursuant to law, . . . is authorized to make, promulgate, issue, rescind, and amend rules and regulations governing the manner of operation of, and governing the applicable programs administered by, the Department." *Id.* § 1221e-3; *see also id.* § 1098a(a)(1) (directing the Secretary to obtain public involvement in the development of regulations through negotiated rulemaking). In 2009, the Secretary established a negotiated rulemaking committee to develop new rules related to its administration of Title IV programs.

The reason for the Department's new regulations is clear. The agency had determined that the existing regulations were too lax, allowing schools to circumvent the proscriptions of the HEA and threaten the integrity of Title IV programs. For example, following an investigation, agency officials found that the University of Phoenix had "systematically engage[d] in actions designed to mislead the [Department] and to evade detection of its improper incentive compensation system for those involved in recruiting activities." Letter from Donna M. Wittman, Institutional Review Specialist, to Todd S. Nelson, President, Apollo Grp., Inc. (Feb. 5, 2004) ("Phoenix Report"), reprinted in J.A. 145. The Department ultimately chose to settle with the university's parent company rather than to pursue a formal sanction, but allegations of impropriety continued. . . .

Nor did the Department have any reason to believe that the University of Phoenix's alleged misconduct was aberrational. In 2007, admissions and financial aid employees filed a *qui tam* false claims action against Alta Colleges, alleging that the organization had, in contravention of the HEA, both misrepresented the nature of its degrees to prospective students and provided salary increases and bonuses to recruiters based solely on the number of students they recruited. . . . A former recruiter filed a similar action against DeVry in 2009. . . . There were also media reports during this period indicating that other schools had engaged in compensation and marketing practices proscribed by the HEA. . . .

The Secretary's negotiated rulemaking committee failed to reach consensus. The Department moved forward, however, and submitted proposed regulations for public comment. . . . "Approximately 1,180 parties submitted comments" during the comment period. The Department issued its final regulations on October 29, 2010.

C. The Challenged Regulations

1. The State Authorization Regulations

The Department's 2002 regulations did not impose any substantive rules covering state authorization. Before the promulgation of the new regulations, states determined for themselves the methods of authorizing schools. But the new regulations eliminate the old regime and require states to follow specified standards in order to satisfy the HEA's state authorization requirement. Two are at issue here.

First, the school authorization regulation applies to all institutions participating in Title IV programs. It establishes that:

> [a]n institution . . . is legally authorized by a State if the State has a process to review and appropriately act on complaints concerning the institution including enforcing applicable State laws, and the institution . . . is established by name as an educational institution by a State through a charter, statute, constitutional provision, or other action issued by an appropriate State agency or State entity and is authorized to operate educational programs beyond secondary education.

34 C.F.R. § 600.9(a)(1)(i)(A) (2011).

Second, the new regulations include a provision covering providers of distance education. It sets forth that:

> [i]f an institution is offering postsecondary education through distance or correspondence education to students in a State in which it is not physically located or in which it is otherwise subject to State jurisdiction as determined by the State, the institution must meet any State requirements for it to be legally offering postsecondary distance or correspondence education in that State.

Id. § 600.9(c).

2. The Compensation Regulations

The Department's 2002 regulations allowed schools to engage in specific compensation practices under a series of safe harbors. As the Department explained in its 2002 rulemaking, the safe harbors were created to "clarify the current law for most institutions by setting forth specific payment arrangements that an institution may carry out that have been determined not to violate the incentive compensation prohibition in" the HEA. In 2010, the Department eliminated the codified safe harbors and expressly interpreted the HEA to prohibit some of the practices that had previously been deemed safe. Of the compensation arrangements that were previously permitted and are now prohibited, three are at issue.

First, the 2002 regulations allowed schools to provide salary adjustments — e.g., raises — to persons engaged in recruiting and admission activities, so long as those adjustments were not made "more than twice during any twelve month period" and were not "based *solely* on the number of students recruited, admitted, enrolled, or awarded financial aid." 34 C.F.R. § 668.14(b)(22)(ii)(A) (2010) (emphasis added). In contrast, the current Compensation Regulations prohibit institutions from offering any "sum of money or something of value, other than a fixed salary or wages," 34 C.F.R. § 668.14(b)(22)(iii)(A) (2011), "based *in any part, directly or indirectly*, upon success in securing enrollments or the award of financial aid," *id.* § 668.14(b)(22)(i) (emphasis added). In other words, under the Compensation Regulations, an institution may a make merit-based salary adjustment to a recruiter's salary, but only if the adjustment is not based in any part, directly or indirectly, on the recruiter's success in securing either enrollments or the award of financial aid. *See id.* § 668.14(b)(22)(ii)(A).

Second, the 2002 regulations allowed schools to provide incentive based compensation to employees "based upon students successfully completing their educational programs, or one academic year of their educational programs, whichever is shorter." The Department eliminated this safe harbor.

Third, the 2002 regulations allowed schools to provide incentive based compensation "to managerial or supervisory employees who do not directly manage or supervise employees who are directly involved in recruiting or admission activities, or the awarding of title IV, HEA program funds." The Department eliminated this safe harbor. Moreover, it interpreted the HEA's prohibition — which applies to "persons . . . engaged in any student recruiting or admission activities or in making decisions regarding the award of student financial assistance" — to reach "any higher level employee with responsibility for recruitment or admission of students, or making decisions about awarding title IV, HEA program funds" . . . .

3. The Misrepresentation Regulations

The current Misrepresentation Regulations differ in several respects from the 2002 regulations. First, the 2002 regulations defined "*misrepresentation*" to mean "[a]ny false, erroneous or misleading statement an eligible institution makes to a student enrolled at the institution, to any prospective student, to the family of an enrolled or prospective student, or to the Secretary." The 2002 regulations further defined "*substantial misrepresentation*" as "[a]ny misrepresentation on which the person to whom it was made could reasonably be expected to rely, or has reasonably relied, to that person's detriment."

Under the new regulations, "misrepresentation" is defined as:

> [a]ny false, erroneous or misleading statement an eligible institution, . . . *organization, or person with whom the eligible institution has an agreement to provide educational programs, or to provide marketing, advertising, recruiting or admissions services* makes *directly or indirectly to* a student, prospective student or *any member of the public, or to an accrediting agency, to a State agency*, or to the Secretary. *A misleading statement includes any statement that has the likelihood or tendency to deceive or confuse. A statement is any communication made in writing, visually, orally, or through other means.*

34 C.F.R. § 668.71(c) (2011) (emphases added). The Misrepresentation Regulations do not, however, establish a new definition of "*substantial misrepresentation*."

Second, the 2002 regulations set forth that the Secretary could initiate a proceeding against a participating institution for making any substantial misrepresentation "regarding the nature of its educational program, its financial charges or the employability of its graduates." The 2002 regulations then clarified what kinds of statements would fall within those three subject areas. In contrast, the current Misrepresentation Regulations describe that the agency may initiate a proceeding against an institution for engaging in misrepresentation "regarding *the eligible institution, including about* the nature of its educational program, its financial charges, or the employability of its graduates." 34 C.F.R. § 668.71(b) (2011) (emphasis added). The regulations then clarify what statements fall within those subject areas and identify an additional covered subject area — an institution's relationship with the Department. . . .

Third, the 2002 regulations and the current Misrepresentation Regulations differ in their respective descriptions of the steps that the Secretary must or may follow after receiving notice of an alleged misrepresentation. The 2002 regulations established that "[i]f the misrepresentation is minor and can be readily corrected, the designated department official informs the institution and endeavors to obtain an informal, voluntary correction." The regulations provided in the alternative that "[i]f the designated department official finds that the complaint or allegation is a substantial misrepresentation," then he or she initiates a formal action against the institution, pursuant to the procedural requirements set forth in subpart G of the Department's regulations.

In promulgating the current Misrepresentation Regulations, the Department restyled the agency's menu of enforcement options. The relevant provision reads:

> If the Secretary determines that an eligible institution has engaged in substantial misrepresentation, the Secretary may —
>
> (1) Revoke the eligible institution's program participation agreement;
>
> (2) Impose limitations on the institution's participation in the title IV, HEA programs;

(3) Deny participation applications made on behalf of the institution; or

(4) Initiate a proceeding against the eligible institution under subpart G of this part.

34 C.F.R. § 668.71(a) (2011). There is no provision in the regulations specifically addressing how the Secretary should proceed in the event of a minor misrepresentation. . . .

Like the 2002 regulations, the Department's final regulations lay out in subpart G the procedures that the Secretary must follow to initiate a formal proceeding against an institution for violating any of the HEA's requirements. . . .

D. Procedural History

Appellant is "an association of for-profit schools in the private sector education industry, representing more than 1,500 such schools. Every year, [its] members educate more than one and a half million students." *Career Coll. Ass'n*, 796 F. Supp. 2d at 114. Shortly after the Department issued its final regulations, Appellant filed this suit in the District Court, challenging the regulations under both the Constitution and the APA. Appellant claimed that the Compensation Regulations include provisions that exceed the authority of the Secretary under the HEA and are otherwise arbitrary and capricious. Appellant claimed that the Misrepresentation Regulations: (1) exceed the HEA's scope in several respects; (2) are otherwise arbitrary and capricious; and (3) violate the First Amendment by imposing content-based and speaker-based prohibitions on both core noncommercial and protected commercial speech. Appellant additionally claimed that the school authorization regulation exceeds the Department's statutory authority, because it impermissibly alters the allocation of power between the federal government and the states in a traditional area of state concern. Appellant also claimed that the school authorization regulation is otherwise arbitrary and capricious. Finally, Appellant claimed that the distance education regulation is arbitrary and capricious. Both parties moved for summary judgment.

During the proceedings in the District Court, the Department issued a Dear Colleague Letter to address questions that regulated parties had raised regarding the challenged regulations. . . . The letter purported to "provide[] additional guidance" without "mak[ing] any changes to the regulations." . . . The letter specifically addressed the arguments that Appellant had raised in its complaint.

The District Court granted the Department's motion for summary judgment in almost all respects. The court upheld the Compensation and Misrepresentation regulations entirely, and it held that Appellant lacked standing to challenge the school authorization regulation. However, the court granted Appellant's motion for summary judgment with respect to the distance education regulation. It found that the regulation violated the APA, because the Department had failed to provide adequate notice that it was contemplating the new rule. Both parties appealed.

II. Analysis

A. Standard of Review

We review the District Court's grant of summary judgment de novo. . . . Furthermore, "[i]n a case like the instant one, in which the District Court reviewed an agency action under the APA, we review the administrative action directly, according no particular deference to the judgment of the District Court."

Appellant's claims that various provisions of the challenged regulations are "in excess of statutory jurisdiction, authority, or limitations, or short of statutory right," 5 U.S.C. § 706(2)(C), are reviewed under the well-known *Chevron* framework. *See Chevron U.S.A. Inc. v. Natural Res. Def. Council, Inc.*, 467 U.S. 837 (1984).

> Pursuant to *Chevron* Step One, if the intent of Congress is clear, the reviewing court must give effect to that unambiguously expressed intent. If Congress has not directly addressed the precise question at issue, the reviewing court proceeds to *Chevron* Step Two. Under Step Two, "[i]f Congress has explicitly left a gap for the agency to fill, there is an express delegation of authority to the agency to elucidate a specific provision of the statute by regulation. Such legislative regulations are given controlling weight unless they are . . . manifestly contrary to the statute." *Chevron*, 467 U.S. at 843-44.

HARRY T. EDWARDS & LINDA A. ELLIOTT, FEDERAL STANDARDS OF REVIEW — REVIEW OF DISTRICT COURT DECISIONS AND AGENCY ACTIONS 141 (2007) (alterations in original).

The fact that some of the challenged regulations are inconsistent with the Department's past practice "is not a basis for declining to analyze the agency's interpretation[s] under the *Chevron* framework." *Nat'l Cable & Telecomms. Ass'n v. Brand X Internet Servs.*, 545 U.S. 967 (2005). As the Supreme Court has stated, "if the agency adequately explains the reasons for a reversal of policy, 'change is not invalidating, since the whole point of *Chevron* is to leave the discretion provided by the ambiguities of a statute with the implementing agency.'" *Id.* (citations omitted). An agency's departure from past practice can, however, if unexplained, render regulations arbitrary and capricious. *See id.*; *Rust v. Sullivan*, 500 U.S. 173, 186-87 (1991).

Appellant's claims that the challenged regulations are "arbitrary, capricious, an abuse of discretion, or otherwise not in accordance with law," 5 U.S.C. § 706(2)(A), require us to determine whether the regulations are the product of reasoned decisionmaking. As the Supreme Court has explained:

> Normally, an agency rule would be arbitrary and capricious if the agency has relied on factors which Congress has not intended it to consider, entirely failed to consider an important aspect of the problem, offered an explanation for its decision that runs counter to the evidence before the agency, or is so implausible that it could not be ascribed to a difference in view or the product of agency expertise.

Motor Vehicle Mfrs. Ass'n of the U.S., Inc. v. State Farm Mut. Auto. Ins. Co., 463 U.S. 29, 43 (1983). In evaluating an agency's decisionmaking, our review is "fundamentally deferential." EDWARDS & ELLIOTT 172. But we are limited to assessing the record that was actually before the agency. . . .

A regulation will be deemed arbitrary and capricious, if the issuing agency failed to address significant comments raised during the rulemaking. . . . An agency's obligation to respond, however, is not "particularly demanding." A regulation also violates the APA, if it is not a "logical outgrowth" of the agency's proposed regulations. . . . This rule ensures that regulated parties have an opportunity to comment on new regulations. . . .

Two additional points merit mention before turning to Appellant's claims. First, Appellant is pursuing a facial challenge to the regulations. "To prevail in such a facial challenge, [Appellant] 'must establish that no set of circumstances exists under which the [regulations] would be valid.' That is true as to both the constitutional challenges and the statutory challenge[s]." *Reno v. Flores*, 507 U.S. 292, 301 (1993) (citations omitted); *see also Sherley v. Sebelius*, 644 F.3d 388, 397 (D.C. Cir. 2011). "[I]t is not enough for [Appellant] to show the [challenged regulations] could be applied unlawfully." *Sherley*, 644 F.3d at 397 (citations omitted); *see also Rust*, 500 U.S. at 183. As we explain below, this limited exception to the rule for an overbreadth challenge to a regulation of speech has no application in this case. Where we conclude that a challenged regulatory provision does not exceed the HEA's limits and otherwise satisfies the requirements of the APA, we will uphold the provision and preserve the right of complainants to bring as-applied challenges against any alleged unlawful applications.

Second, the Department offered interpretations of the challenged regulations in its Dear Colleague Letter and also in its briefs to the District Court and this court. An agency's permissible interpretation of its own regulation normally "must be given controlling weight unless it is plainly erroneous or inconsistent with the regulation," *Thomas Jefferson Univ. v. Shalala*, 512 U.S. 504, 512 (1994) (citations omitted) (internal quotation marks omitted), even when the interpretation is first articulated in the course of litigation, *see Auer v. Robbins*, 519 U.S. 452 (1997). The Supreme Court has specified additional constraints on the deference owed to an agency's interpretation of its own regulation in *Thomas Jefferson*, *Auer*, and other decisions. *See, e.g., Chase Bank USA, N.A. v. McCoy*, 131 S. Ct. 871, 178 L. Ed. 2d 716 (2011); *Christensen v. Harris Cnty.*, 529 U.S. 576 (2000). Pursuant to this line of authority, Appellant argues that the Department's interpretations are not entitled to any deference. As we make clear, however, it is unnecessary to resolve this contention.

B. The Compensation Regulations

1. The Regulations Do Not Exceed the HEA's Limits

Appellant offers two arguments in support of its claim that the Compensation Regulations exceed the HEA's prohibition on incentive based compensation. Neither is persuasive.

• *Salary Adjustments*

The HEA prohibits institutions from providing "any commission, bonus, or other incentive payment based directly or indirectly on success in securing enrollments or financial aid." In the Compensation Regulations, the Department interpreted the phrase "commission, bonus, or other incentive payment" to mean "a sum of money or something of value, other than a fixed salary or wages." 34 C.F.R. § 668.14(b)(22)(iii)(A) (2011). The Compensation Regulations thus allow a school to provide a salary adjustment to a recruiter, only if the adjustment is not "based in any part, directly or indirectly, upon success in securing enrollments or the award of financial aid." At *Chevron* step one, Appellant must demonstrate that the HEA "unambiguously forecloses" that interpretation. *Vill. of Barrington, Ill. v. Surface Transp. Bd.*, 636 F.3d 650, 661 (D.C. Cir. 2011) (citation omitted). Appellant has not satisfied that "heavy burden."

Starting with the HEA's text, we have no trouble concluding that the phrase "any commission, bonus, or other incentive payment" is broad enough to encompass salary adjustments. We need look no further than to the phrase "other incentive payment." Since that term is not defined, we must give it its ordinary meaning. *See FCC v. AT & T Inc.*, 131 S. Ct. 1177, 1182, 179 L. Ed. 2d 132 (2011) (citation omitted). When used as an adjective, incentive means "[i]nciting" or "motivating," American Heritage Dictionary 650 (2d Coll. ed. 1982), and a payment is "[t]hat which is paid," Webster's International Dictionary 1797 (2d ed. 1957). A salary adjustment fits within the plain meaning of the statutory term, because it is something paid by a school to recruiters to motivate improved performance.

Appellant's theory that a standard salary adjustment is not a prohibited form of compensation is perplexing. After all, Appellant defends the 2002 regulations, . . . which established that at least some salary adjustments — *i.e.*, those made more than twice a year as well as those based solely on recruitment numbers — are prohibited commissions, bonuses, or other incentive payments. Appellant has not meaningfully explained how the HEA could authorize the agency to prohibit some salary adjustments but not others. But quite apart from this incongruity, we find Appellant's arguments to be unpersuasive.

Appellant argues that the Department's interpretation is foreclosed by basic rules of statutory interpretation. Invoking the related canons *expressio unius est exclusio alterius and ejusdem generis*, Appellant claims that the phrase "other incentive payment" cannot be a "catch-all that dramatically changes the scope of the statute." . . . *see also Hall St. Assocs., L.L.C. v. Mattel, Inc.*, 552 U.S. 576 (2008) ("[W]hen a statute sets out a series of specific items ending with a general term, that general term is confined to covering subjects comparable to the specifics it follows."). And invoking the canon against surplusage, Appellant argues that to construe "other incentive payment" broadly would impermissibly render the prohibition on bonuses and commissions superfluous. Appellant thus urges that we limit "other incentive payment" to mean payments such as "rewards or prizes." . . .

This court's decisions discussing the application of these canons at *Chevron* step one are not entirely consistent. *Compare Indep. Ins. Agents of Am., Inc. v. Hawke*, 211 F.3d 638, 644-45 (D.C. Cir. 2000) (rejecting agency's interpretation at step one based on the tandem canons "of avoiding surplusage and *expressio unius*"), *with*

Mobile Commc'ns Corp. of Am. v. FCC, 77 F.3d 1399, 1405 (D.C. Cir. 1996) ("*Expressio unius* 'is simply too thin a reed to support the conclusion that Congress has clearly resolved [an] issue.'" (alteration in original) (citations omitted)), *and Tex. Rural Legal Aid, Inc. v. Legal Servs. Corp.*, 940 F.2d 685, 694 (D.C. Cir. 1991) ("[A] congressional prohibition of particular conduct may actually support the view that the administrative entity can exercise its authority to eliminate a similar danger." (citation omitted)). But it is clear that a court need not follow these canons, when they do "not hold up in the statutory context." *Hawke*, 211 F.3d at 644 (citations omitted). Here, Congress phrased the relevant provision broadly — employing words and phrases like "any" and "directly or indirectly." 20 U.S.C. § 1094(a)(20); *see also United States v. Gonzales*, 520 U.S. 1, 5 (1997) (noting that "'any' has an expansive meaning"); *Roma v. United States*, 344 F.3d 352, 360 (3d Cir. 2003) (describing "directly or indirectly" as "extremely broad language"). Thus, Congress intended the phrase "other incentive payment" to broadly cover abuses that Congress had not enumerated. Appellant's objection that "[s]alary adjustments are not an obscure form of payment beyond Congress's foresight," misses the point. While Congress was undoubtedly aware that many schools provide salary-based compensation to recruiters, it may not have anticipated that schools would circumvent the HEA's prohibition on incentive based compensation through the strategic use of salary adjustments.

Nor do we find any other indication that Congress unambiguously intended to exclude salary adjustments from the prohibition on incentive based compensation. Appellant directs us to the Conference Report for the 1992 amendments to the HEA. But that report demonstrates merely that Congress was concerned with schools' "use of commissioned sales representatives." It certainly does not show or even suggest that Congress was affirmatively unconcerned with the use of "salaried recruiters." . . .

Finally, the fact that courts have interpreted the HEA not to prohibit certain compensation practices does not compel a different outcome here. In *Corinthian Colleges*, the Ninth Circuit stated that "the HEA does not prohibit *any and all* employment-related decisions on the basis of recruitment numbers; it prohibits only a particular type of incentive compensation." 655 F.3d at 992. But the court held only that "adverse employment actions, including termination, on the basis of recruitment numbers remain permissible" under the HEA. It did not address salary adjustments at all. More importantly, neither that decision nor the Ninth Circuit's unpublished decision in *United States ex rel. Bott v. Silicon Valley Colleges*, 262 Fed. Appx. 810 (9th Cir. 2008), is binding law in this circuit. And neither decision stated that its holding was unambiguously compelled by the HEA; hence, neither can trump the Department's interpretation. . . .

We therefore proceed to *Chevron* step two. Appellant initially argues that the Department forfeited its right to invoke step-two deference. In the final rule, the Department responded to comments that its test for identifying prohibited compensation was unclear, stating that it "believe[d] that the prohibition identified in section 487(a)(20) of the HEA is clear and that institutions should not have difficulty maintaining compliance with the new regulatory language." An agency cannot claim deference, when it adopts a regulation based on its judgment that a particular "interpretation is compelled by Congress." *Peter Pan Bus Lines, Inc. v.*

Fed. Motor Carrier Safety Admin., 471 F.3d 1350, 1354 (D.C. Cir. 2006) (citations omitted) (internal quotation marks omitted). However, it would be a stretch, to say the least, to hold that the Department's use of the word "clear" demonstrates that the agency meant to suggest that its regulatory interpretation was "compelled by Congress." *Id.* In *Peter Pan*, the agency had declared that a private party's interpretation of a statutory term was "*not consistent with the plain language of the statute and the legislative history*," and the agency had further stated what the statutory phrase "*clearly meant.*" *Id.* at 1353 (citation omitted) (internal quotation marks omitted). But the regulations at issue here reflect more than mere "parsing of the statutory language." *Id.* at 1354 (citation omitted) (internal quotation marks omitted). The agency adopted the regulations based on its "experience and expertise," *id.* (citation omitted) (internal quotation marks omitted), after administering the safe harbors for almost a decade.

At step two, we easily conclude that the Compensation Regulations are entitled to deference, because they are not manifestly contrary to the HEA. The agency promulgated the regulations based on known abuses. As the Department explained, "unscrupulous" institutions used the safe harbor for salary adjustments to "circumvent the intent" of the HEA and to avoid detection and sanction for engaging in unlawful compensation practices. . . . The safe harbor enabled a school to tell the Department that it was basing compensation on both recruitment numbers and other qualitative factors, when in fact, "these other qualitative factors [were] not really considered when compensation decisions [were] made." . . . As we have already discussed, the agency's assessment of the safe harbor finds support in the record — specifically, in the Department's investigation into the practices of one school, several *qui tam* actions against other schools, and media reports, as well as from comments the agency received during the rulemaking. . . .

Appellant's reliance on GAO Report Number 10-370R to refute the Department's assessment of the safe harbor is misplaced. Appellant summarizes that report as finding that "substantiated violations of the HEA's compensation restriction have not significantly increased in frequency or severity since the adoption of the 2002 regulations." . . . But that report expressly "d[id] not . . . assess the overall impact of the safe harbor regulations on Education's efforts to enforce the incentive compensation ban." U.S. Gov't Accountability Office, GAO-10-370R, Higher Education 2 (2010), J.A. 268. Indeed, the Department justified the regulations partially on its conclusion that the safe harbors had made it more difficult to substantiate violations of the HEA in the first place. Moreover, the Compensation Regulations address this problem. They allow the Department to use any evidence that an institution based compensation on recruitment numbers to substantiate a violation; thus, the Department no longer needs to see through an institution's "smoke and mirrors." Phoenix Report at 10.

Appellant also argues that the Department's interpretation is arbitrary and capricious, because it deprives institutions of the ability to provide any merit-based salary adjustments to recruiters. After all, Appellant insists, a recruiter's job is to recruit. But the Department adequately addressed this claim. A recruiter's job goes beyond maximizing recruitment numbers; a recruiter also offers students "a form of counseling" about whether they are a good fit for a particular institution. . . . Therefore, a school may still provide merit-based salary adjustments based on a recruiter's ability effectively to match students with that school. Moreover, the Department has identified a number of other factors on which permissible salary adjustments may be based — *e.g.*, professionalism, expertise, student evaluations, and seniority.

Indeed, even under the 2002 regulations, schools were not allowed to offer salary adjustments "based solely" on recruitment numbers. Schools have thus been required to take into account job-performance factors unrelated to recruitment numbers for nearly a decade. We think it implausible that schools are now at a loss for such factors. Appellant objects that its members cannot rely on the factors that they identified under the 2002 regulations, because the Department has sought to punish schools for using those factors. . . . This argument is farcical. The Department means to sanction institutions for using these factors *to hide their true compensation practices*. The Department has never adopted Appellant's straw-person position that factors such as professionalism or experience are inherently related to recruitment numbers. And because of the facial nature of Appellant's challenge, we need not address the concern that the Department could adopt that position under the regulations in the future. In the event that the Department does so, a school may seek relief through an as-applied challenge.

• Managers and Supervisors

The Compensation Regulations apply the HEA's incentive based compensation prohibition to higher level employees. To achieve this effect, the Department interpreted the phrase "any persons . . . engaged in any student recruiting or admission activities or in making decisions regarding the award of student financial assistance," . . . to include "higher level employee[s] with responsibility for recruitment or admission of students, or making decisions about awarding title IV, HEA program funds," 34 C.F.R. § 668.14(b)(22)(iii)(C)(2) (2011). This interpretation easily passes muster under *Chevron*.

At step one, the statutory phrase is broad, using the word "any" to modify "persons," "recruiting," and "admission activities." Appellant argues that the phrase "engaged in" must be construed narrowly. But the term is undefined, and Appellant offers no authority suggesting that the term has a limited, specific meaning. The Department, by contrast, argues persuasively that "engaged in" should be read broadly based on both the plain meaning of "engage" — "[t]o involve oneself," American Heritage Dictionary 454 — and case law . . . . The phrase "admission activities" is also broad and can connote supervision as well as participation. *See* American Heritage Dictionary 77 (defining "activity" to include "[a] specified form of supervised action or field of action"). Therefore, there was a statutory basis for the Department to conclude that persons "with responsibility for" recruitment or admission activities can be "engaged in" recruitment or admission activities.

At step two, the Department's interpretation that the HEA's prohibition on incentive based compensation can apply to higher level employees is permissible, because it is not manifestly contrary to the statute. Here too, the Department was responding to known abuses. As the Department explained in its proposed rulemaking, "senior management may drive the organizational and operational culture at an institution, creating pressures for top, and even middle, management to secure increasing numbers of enrollments from their recruiters." This conclusion finds support in the administrative record — particularly, the Department's investigation into the practices of the managers overseeing recruitment at the University of Phoenix.

Appellant's argument that the Department's application of the HEA to higher level employees is counter to the Act's legislative history — whether intended as a *Chevron* step-one or step-two argument — is unpersuasive. The House Report on which Appellant relies demonstrates merely that Congress was concerned with "salespeople," . . . not that Congress manifestly did not intend to regulate managers and supervisors. Appellant's claim that the Department forfeited its right to invoke *Chevron* is also unavailing for the reasons discussed above.

Finally, the Department has committed to evaluating whether a specific employee or manager is subject to the incentive based compensation prohibition on a case-by-case basis. . . . If the agency overreaches by pursuing actions against institutions that provide incentive based compensation to employees or managers who are not responsible for driving organizational culture toward a focus exclusively on recruitment numbers, those institutions may seek appropriate as-applied relief.

2. Two Aspects of the Regulations Are Arbitrary and Capricious for Want of Reasoned Decisionmaking

Appellant argues that the Compensation Regulations fail for want of reasoned decisionmaking. For the most part, we find Appellant's arguments to be specious and unworthy of serious discussion. The Compensation Regulations "have sufficient content and definitiveness as to be a meaningful exercise in agency lawmaking," . . . with or without reference to the Department's Dear Colleague Letter. The Department provided an adequate and more-than-conclusory explanation for why it adopted the regulations, primarily based on its experience administering the 2002 safe harbors. The Department's budgetary analysis does not call into question the benefits of the regulations — it reflects that the benefits were difficult to quantify. And the Department was entitled to replace bright-line rules with contextual rules.

Business Roundtable v. SEC, 647 F.3d 1144 (D.C. Cir. 2011), on which Appellant places much emphasis, is easily distinguishable, even apart from our conclusion that the Department has satisfactorily justified its adoption of the Compensation Regulations. In *Business Roundtable*, we found a regulation to be arbitrary and capricious, because, in promulgating it, the SEC had failed to satisfy its "unique [statutory] obligation to consider the effect of a new rule upon 'efficiency, competition, and capital formation.'" *Id.* at 1148 (citation omitted). Appellant points to no such "unique" statutory obligation here. Moreover, in *Business Roundtable*, this court criticized the SEC for failing to consider empirical studies and quantitative data. *See id.* at 1150-51. The Appellant points to no data or study the Department ignored and thus *Business Roundtable* is of no help to its argument.

There are two aspects of the regulations, however, that are lacking for want of adequate explanations. First, the elimination of the safe harbor for compensation "based upon students successfully completing their educational programs, or one academic year of their educational programs," is arbitrary and capricious without some better explanation from the Department. Congress created the Title IV programs to enable more students to attend and graduate from postsecondary institutions. This specific safe harbor seems perfectly in keeping with that goal. Indeed, the elimination of this safe harbor could even discourage recruiters from focusing on the most qualified students.

The Department offered a brief explanation for its elimination of this safe harbor.But its fleeting reference to "short-term, accelerated programs" and its isolated examples of students who graduated from schools but could not find commensurate work . . . are insufficient. Furthermore, the Department points to nothing in the record supporting these assertions. It may well be that the Department actually eliminated this safe harbor based on the agency's belief that institutions have used graduation rates as a proxy for recruitment numbers. But the Department never offered that explanation. We thus remand to the District Court with instructions to remand to the Department to allow it to explain its decision to eliminate this specific safe harbor.

Second, the Department failed to address the concern, identified by at least two commenters, that the Compensation Regulations could have an adverse effect on minority enrollment. During the comment period, the Career Education Corporation posed the following question to the Department:

> How will the new regulations apply to employees who are not involved in general student recruiting, but who are involved in recruiting certain types of students? Examples would include college coaches who recruit student athletes, and employees in college diversity offices who recruit minority students.

Letter from Career Educ. Corp. to Jessica Finkel, U.S. Dep't of Educ. 40 (Aug. 1, 2010), J.A. 357. DeVry, Inc. asked similar questions:

> Can schools increase compensation to personnel involved in diversity outreach programs for successfully assembling a diverse student body? Does the Department intend to foreclose schools' ability to compensate their staffs for successfully managing outreach programs for students from disadvantaged backgrounds . . . ?

Letter from DeVry, Inc. to Jessica Finkel (Aug. 1, 2010), J.A. 359.

As noted, an agency's obligation to address specific comments is not demanding. Here, the Department fell just short. In the rulemaking, the Department appears to have grouped together related comments. In one such bundle, the Department summarized that "[s]ome commenters . . . asked whether the proposed regulations would permit a president to receive a bonus or other payment if one factor in attaining the bonus or other payment was meeting an institutional management plan or goal that included increasing minority enrollment."

In the discussion that followed, the Department stated that the Compensation Regulations "apply to all employees at an institution who are engaged in any student recruitment or admission activity or in making decisions regarding the award of title IV, HEA program funds." However, the Department never really answered the questions posed by Career Education Corporation and DeVry, Inc., because it failed to address the commenters' concerns. It may be that the Department misinterpreted the concerns raised by the comments to be limited to minority recruitment by higher-level employees. Nevertheless, the agency's "failure to address these comments, or at best its attempt to address them in a conclusory manner, is fatal to its defense." *Int'l Union, United Mine Workers*, 626 F.3d at 94 (citation omitted). We therefore remand to the District Court with instructions to remand to the Department to allow it to address these concerns. It will be a simple matter for the Department to address these matters on remand.

In short, because the Department has not adequately explained its reasoning with respect to two aspects of the Compensation Regulations, we reverse, in part, the judgment of the District Court. The case is remanded with instructions to remand to the Department for further consideration. On remand, the Department must better explain its decision to eliminate the safe harbor based on graduation rates, and it must offer a reasoned response to the comments suggesting that the new regulations might adversely affect diversity outreach.

C. The Misrepresentation Regulations

1. The Regulations Exceed the HEA's Limits in Three Respects

Appellant claims that the Misrepresentation Regulations exceed the HEA's limitations in several respects: by allowing the Secretary to sanction an institution without providing it with statutorily required procedural protections; by allowing the Secretary to sanction an institution for making misrepresentations regarding subjects that are not covered by the HEA; and by allowing the Secretary to take action against an institution for making statements that are not substantial misrepresentations.

- *Procedural Protections*

The HEA provides that the Secretary may — following reasonable notice and opportunity for a hearing — limit, suspend, or terminate a school's eligibility to participate in Title IV programs for making certain misrepresentations. Section 668.71(a) of the Misrepresentation Regulations states that, upon determining that an institution has engaged in substantial misrepresentation, the agency may: "(1) Revoke the eligible institution's program participation agreement; (2) Impose limitations on the institution's participation in the title IV, HEA programs; (3) Deny participation applications made on behalf of the institution; or (4) Initiate a proceeding against the eligible institution under subpart G of this part." 34 C.F.R. § 668.71(a) (2011). Subpart G of the Department's regulations sets forth the procedures that the agency must follow to initiate a formal proceeding against a school.

According to Appellant, because section 668.71(a) lists the agency's options using "or," and because only the fourth option requires the agency to follow subpart G's procedures, the effect of the provision is to allow the agency to take the first three actions without following those procedures. Appellant does not challenge section 668.71(a)(3), which deals only with applicants, as opposed to participating schools.

But Appellant argues that sections 668.71(a)(1) and (a)(2) exceed the HEA's limits by allowing the agency — without affording any procedural protections — to revoke certified schools' program participation agreements and to impose limitations on certified schools' participation. We agree.

The Department does not contest that if sections 668.71(a)(1) and (a)(2) have the described effect, they are impermissible. Instead, it attempts to salvage section 668.71(a) as a whole by interpreting sections 668.71(a)(1) and (a)(2) not to affect the procedural rights of certified schools. We acknowledge that the Department has consistently maintained the same position with respect to these sections throughout the rulemaking. *See, e.g.*, Dear Colleague Letter at 14, J.A. 143 ("There is nothing in revised section 668.71(a) that reduces the procedural protection given by the HEA and applicable regulations to an institution to contest the specific action the Department may take to address substantial misrepresentation by the institution."); Final Regulations, 75 Fed. Reg. at 66,915 ("[N]othing in the proposed regulations diminishes the procedural rights that an institution otherwise possesses to respond to [an adverse] action."). The Department's explanations are unconvincing. They merely purport to explain why the disputed regulatory provisions were never erroneous in the first place by reinterpreting the regulation in a way the text does not support.

With respect to section 668.71(a)(1), the Department contends that the word "revoke" is a term of art that refers specifically and only to the act of ending an agreement with a provisionally certified institution. *See* 20 U.S.C. § 1099c(h) (allowing for provisional certification of schools). The Department apparently uses the word "terminate" to describe the process of ending an agreement with a fully certified school. *See* 34 C.F.R. § 668.86(a) (2011). Under this interpretation, section 668.71(a)(1) would be valid, because the Department may "revoke" provisional certification without following the procedures required to "terminate" an agreement with a fully certified school. But section 668.71(a)(1) simply cannot bear the Department's interpretation. The section authorizes the agency to revoke the agreement of an "eligible institution," not of any provisionally certified institution. We thus cannot defer to the Department's interpretation, because it is inconsistent with the terms of the regulation.

The Department's interpretation of section 668.71(a)(2) fares no better. The agency interprets that section to require the Secretary to follow the procedures for imposing limitations on the eligibility of institutions that are found in subpart G of the Department's regulations. . . . But section 668.71(a)(4) independently authorizes the Secretary to initiate proceedings under subpart G. In other words, under the Department's interpretation, section 668.71(a)(2) is wholly included within section 668.71(a)(4). The interpretation is thus plainly inconsistent with section 668.71(a) as a whole, which lists the Secretary's options using the disjunctive. Under principles of statutory construction, "terms connected by a disjunctive [should] be given separate meanings, unless the context dictates otherwise; here it does not." *Reiter v. Sonotone Corp.*, 442 U.S. 330, 339 (1979) (citation omitted); *see also In re ESPY*, 80 F.3d 501, 505 (D.C. Cir. 1996) (per curiam) ("[A] statute written in the disjunctive is generally construed as 'setting out separate and distinct alternatives.'" (citation omitted)).

In sum, section 668.71(a) exceeds the Act's limits by allowing the Secretary — without affording procedural protections — to revoke a program participation agreement with a fully certified school and to impose limitations on the eligibility of a fully certified school. The judgment of the District Court is reversed on this point, and we remand to the trial court with instructions to remand to the Department, so that it can revise this provision.

• *Misrepresentations Regarding Nonproscribed Subjects*

The HEA authorizes the agency to sanction an institution for engaging in "substantial misrepresentation of the nature of its educational program, its financial charges, or the employability of its graduates." 20 U.S.C. § 1094(c)(3)(A). In notable contrast, the Misrepresentation Regulations provide that the agency may sanction an institution for engaging in "substantial misrepresentation *regarding the eligible institution, including* about the nature of its educational program, its financial charges, or the employability of its graduates." 34 C.F.R. § 668.71(b) (2011) (emphasis added). The regulations then clarify *four* categories of proscribed misrepresentations — *i.e.*, about the nature of an eligible institution's educational program, about the nature of an institution's financial charges, about the employability of an institution's graduates, and *about an institution's relationship with the Department.*

Appellant claims that the regulations allow the agency to sanction schools for making misrepresentations regarding subjects that are not covered by the HEA. We agree. Section 668.71(b) prohibits institutions from engaging in "misrepresentation regarding the eligible institution." That phrase obviously covers the three subjects listed in the HEA, but it also plainly encompasses more. Because it is followed by the word "including," the phrase encompasses both the enumerated subjects listed in 20 U.S.C. § 1094(c)(3)(A) and anything falling within the ordinary meaning of "misrepresentation regarding the eligible institution." And an institution can clearly make misrepresentations "regarding the institution" that do not fall within the HEA's three listed subject areas. We find immediate support for that proposition in section 668.75, which prohibits an institution from misrepresenting its relationship with the Department — a subject that is not proscribed by the HEA.

Here too, the Department essentially concedes the point. It explained in the Dear Colleague Letter, and it argues here, that the Misrepresentation Regulations should not be read to authorize the agency to sanction misrepresentations regarding nonproscribed topics. We cannot defer to this belated interpretation, however, because it is plainly inconsistent with the terms of the regulation. *Thomas Jefferson Univ.*, 512 U.S. at 512; *see also Appalachian Power Co. v. EPA*, 249 F.3d 1032, 1048 (D.C. Cir. 2001) (per curiam) ("[W]e should not defer to an agency's interpretation imputing a limiting provision to a rule that is silent on the subject, lest we 'permit the agency, under the guise of interpreting a regulation, to create de facto a new regulation.'" (citation omitted)). We therefore reverse on this point and remand to the District Court with instructions to remand to the Department, so that it can revise sections 668.71(b) and 668.75 to match its description of how the regulations should function.

• *"Substantial Misrepresentation"*

The HEA prohibits institutions from engaging in "substantial misrepresentation," a phrase which is not defined in the statute. In the Misrepresentation Regulations, the Department adopted a new regulatory definition of misrepresentation but kept the existing definition of substantial misrepresentation. Appellant argues that the regulations as modified exceed the HEA's limits in several respects; we find only one claim persuasive.

The agency has long defined "*misrepresentation*" as used in the HEA to mean "[a]ny false, erroneous or misleading statement." The new Misrepresentation Regulations start with that same definition, but further define "[a] misleading statement" to "include[] any statement that has the likelihood or tendency to deceive or confuse." Appellant's primary argument is that the provision exceeds the HEA's limits, insofar as it reaches statements that merely have the likelihood or tendency to confuse. We review this claim under *Chevron,* and we reject the Department's interpretation at step one.

"Misrepresentation" means "[t]he act of making a false or misleading statement about something, usually. with the intent to deceive." BLACK'S LAW DICTIONARY 1016 (7th ed. 1999). Appellant argues that the statute unambiguously proscribes only statements that are "false" or "misleading" — *i.e.*, "[t]ending to [lead in the wrong direction]" or "deceptive." AMERICAN HERITAGE DICTIONARY 803. A statement that is merely confusing falls outside of that scope. The Department counters that a "misrepresentation" can be a statement that is true, *see* BLACK'S LAW DICTIONARY 1016 ("[A]n assertion need not be fraudulent to be a misrepresentation." (alteration in original) (quoting RESTATEMENT (SECOND) OF CONTRACTS § 159 cmt. a. (1981)), as well as a statement that is not made with the intent to deceive, *see id.* ("Thus a statement intended to be truthful may be a misrepresentation because of ignorance or carelessness, as when the word 'not' is inadvertently omitted or when inaccurate language is used." (quoting RESTATEMENT (SECOND) OF CONTRACTS § 159 cmt. a. (1981)).

If there is any merit to the Department's claim that a *misrepresentation* may include a statement that is both truthful and nondeceitful, this view can hold no water in the context of the HEA, which prohibits institutions from engaging in *substantial* misrepresentation. *See* American Heritage Dictionary 1213 (defining "substantial" as "[c]onsiderable in importance, value, degree, amount, or extent"). Furthermore, to allow the Department to proscribe statements that are merely confusing would raise serious First Amendment concerns — even with respect to commercial speech. We therefore hold that, under the HEA, "substantial misrepresentation" unambiguously means something more than a statement that is merely confusing. We accordingly vacate section 668.71(c), insofar as it defines misrepresentation to include true and nondeceitful statements that have only the tendency or likelihood to confuse.

We do not take Appellant to be challenging the Department's interpretation that the HEA reaches "misleading statement[s]," insofar as that term encompasses "any statement," truthful or otherwise, "that has the likelihood or tendency to deceive." 34 C.F.R. § 668.71(c) (2011). Nor do we see how Appellant could challenge that aspect of the Misrepresentation Regulations. At *Chevron* step one, as we have already noted, a misrepresentation can be a true statement that is deceitful. And at step two, the Department justified the regulations based on known abuses . . . that are borne out by the record, *see, e.g.*, U.S. GOV'T ACCOUNTABILITY OFFICE, GAO-10-948T, FOR-PROFIT COLLEGES (2010) . . . . Moreover, the fact that one of the studies the Department cited in the rulemaking was subject to methodological criticisms and revision after the Department promulgated the regulations . . . does not call into question the Department's reasoning.

Appellant separately argues that the Misrepresentation Regulations exceed the HEA's limitations by defining "substantial misrepresentation" without an intent requirement. The scope of Appellant's argument is unclear. On the one hand, Appellant could be challenging only the Department's regulatory definition that "misleading statement[s]" include nondeceitful, confusing statements. If that is the extent of Appellant's position, then we have already addressed it.

On the other hand, Appellant could be objecting to the Department's longstanding interpretation that the HEA prohibits "false" and "erroneous" statements, regardless of the speaker's intent. If Appellant sought to advance that broader argument, it needed to do so more much clearly. But the position is untenable in any event. At *Chevron* step one, we have already explained that "misrepresentation" does not unambiguously exclude inadvertent and negligent, factually untrue statements. Nor does the legislative history to which Appellant directs us demonstrate that Congress unambiguously intended to prohibit only intentionally false statements. And at step two, we think that allowing the Secretary to sanction schools for making substantial, negligent or inadvertent, false statements is consistent with the HEA's goals.

Finally, Appellant argues that the Department has read "substantial" out of the statute. Here too, the breadth of Appellant's position is unclear. In its narrowest form, Appellant's argument is that the Department impermissibly "eliminat[ed] a regulation that expressly stated that the Department would address 'minor' misrepresentations that could be 'readily corrected' on 'an informal' and 'voluntary' basis." We find no merit in this argument. The fact that "substantial" appears in the HEA does not mean that the Department must have a specific regulation stating how it will respond to minor misrepresentations; it means that the Department may not seek to sanction schools for engaging in minor misrepresentations. The Department claims that its decision to delete that provision was administrative house keeping . . . and that it will pursue enforcement taking into account aggravating and mitigating factors. We have no reason — beyond Appellant's speculation — to think otherwise, and such speculation cannot be the basis for declaring the regulations facially invalid.

Appellant might instead be making the broader argument that the regulatory definition of "substantial misrepresentation" exceeds the HEA's limits by omitting a "materiality or objective reliance requirement." The Misrepresentation Regulations use the same definition of "substantial misrepresentation" that the Department has used for over thirty years: "Any misrepresentation on which the person to whom it was made could reasonably be expected to rely, or has reasonably relied, to that person's detriment." *Compare* 34 C.F.R. § 668.71(c) (2011), *with* 34 C.F.R. § 668.62 (1981). Appellant claims that the definition should instead be: any misrepresentation on which "a reasonably prudent person would rely." This argument is unpersuasive. It lacks entirely the hallmarks of *Chevron* analysis — recourse to the plain meaning of text, legislative history, context, etc. — and rests instead on speculation. To prevail on its facial challenge, Appellant must demonstrate that there is no set of circumstances under which the Department's interpretation of "substantial misrepresentation" can be applied lawfully. Appellant cannot possibly satisfy this standard.

2. The Regulations Are Not Unconstitutional

Appellant argues that the Misrepresentation Regulations impermissibly prohibit both core political speech and protected commercial speech. We disagree.

• *Noncommercial Speech*

The Misrepresentation Regulations set forth that the Department may sanction an institution for making a misrepresentation "directly or indirectly to a student, prospective student or any member of the public, or to an accrediting agency, to a State agency, or to the Secretary." 34 C.F.R. § 668.71(c) (2011). Appellant claims that the regulations suppress core First Amendment speech, specifically by authorizing the Department to sanction a statement made "'directly or *indirectly* to . . . any member of the public' . . . even if made with the best intentions and completely outside of any advertising context." To illustrate the breadth of the regulations, Appellant offers the example that the Department could invoke section 668.71(c) to sanction an institution for statements made by its president during a public debate about education policy.

If Appellant were correct that the regulations apply to all of an institution's communications to "the public," then we would have some misgivings about the regulations' constitutionality. But we think that Appellant's interpretation cannot be squared with the regulations, when read as a whole and in context. Furthermore, a law "must be construed, if fairly possible, so as to avoid not only the conclusion that it is unconstitutional but also grave doubts upon that score." *Weaver v. U.S. Info. Agency*, 87 F.3d 1429, 1436 (D.C. Cir. 1996) (citation omitted) (internal quotation marks omitted). We therefore interpret the regulations facially to reach only "commercial speech" — at least insofar as statements to "the public" are concerned. And because Appellant's position is linked exclusively to the potential application of the regulations to statements to the public, we have no occasion to address the scope of the regulations, insofar as statements to other entities, such as state accrediting agencies or the Secretary, are concerned.

The Supreme Court has defined "commercial speech" to be "expression related solely to the economic interests of the speaker and its audience," as well as "speech proposing a commercial transaction." *Cent. Hudson Gas & Electric Corp. v. Pub. Serv. Comm'n of N.Y.*, 447 U.S. 557, 561, 562 (1980). This court has added that "material representations about the efficacy, safety, and quality of the advertiser's product, and other information asserted for the purpose of persuading the public to purchase the product" also can qualify as commercial speech. *United States v. Philip Morris USA Inc.*, 566 F.3d 1095, 1143 (D.C. Cir. 2009) (per curiam) (citations omitted). We construe the regulations facially to apply to nothing more.

As a threshold matter, a number of contextual clues make it clear that — at least with respect to communications to the public — the regulations encompass only advertisements, direct solicitations, and other promotional and marketing materials and statements. For example, the only parties prohibited from engaging in misrepresentation under the regulations are "the institution itself, one of its representatives, or any ineligible institution, organization, or person with whom the eligible institution has an agreement to provide educational programs, *marketing, advertising*, recruiting or admissions services." 34 C.F.R. § 668.71(b) (2011) (emphasis added). Additionally, in describing the forms of proscribed misrepresentations, the regulations specifically list only those "made in any *advertising, promotional materials, or in the marketing or sale* of courses or programs of instruction offered by the institution." *Id.* (emphasis added). And finally, the Department's explanation for adopting the regulations supports our reading. *See* Final Regulations, 75 Fed. Reg. at 66,913-14 (documenting that the regulations are a response to "overly aggressive advertising and marketing tactics" and summarizing a study of "fraudulent, deceptive, or otherwise questionable marketing practices").

We understand that "[t]he mere fact that [statements] are conceded to be advertisements clearly does not compel the conclusion that they are commercial speech." *Bolger v. Youngs Drug Prods. Corp.*, 463 U.S. 60, 66 (1983) (citation omitted). However, when statements reference particular services or products, and when they are offered to advance the economic interests of the institution, they "constitute commercial speech notwithstanding the fact that they contain discussions of important public issues." *Id.* at 67-68. "[A]dvertising which links a product to a current public debate is not thereby entitled to the constitutional protection afforded noncommercial speech. [An institution] has the full panoply of protections available to its direct comments on public issues, so there is no reason for providing similar constitutional protection when such statements are made in the context of" promoting a service or product. *Id.* at 68 (footnote omitted) (citations omitted) (internal quotation marks omitted). "Advertisers should not be permitted to immunize false or misleading product information from government regulation simply by including references to public issues." *Id.* (citation omitted).

As Appellant points out, commercial speech does not "retain[] its commercial character when it is inextricably intertwined with otherwise fully protected speech." *Riley v. Nat'l Fed'n of the Blind of N.C., Inc.*, 487 U.S. 781, 796 (1988). Thus, when the government seeks to restrict *inextricably intertwined* commercial and noncommercial speech, courts must subject the restriction to the test "for fully protected expression." *Id.* But even if the regulations create the possibility that the Department could sanction an institution's misrepresentations made in the context of mixed commercial and noncommercial speech — or contained in a purely informational pamphlet that does not qualify as commercial speech at all — that possibility, without more, does not require facial invalidation of the regulations. *See, e.g., Reno*, 507 U.S. at 301; *Sherley*, 644 F.3d at 397. If the Department ever overreaches, schools will be able to challenge particular applications as unconstitutional.

Lorillard Tobacco Co. v. Reilly, 533 U.S. 525 (2001), is not to the contrary. There, on a facial challenge, the Supreme Court invalidated state regulations of speech without expressly following *Reno*'s no-set-of-circumstances test. But because the regulations at issue were conceded facially to encompass purely *protected* speech, *see id.* at 555, the state bore the burden of demonstrating that the regulations were tailored to achieve the state's purpose, *see id.* at 561. The regulations were not so tailored, hence their facial invalidation. *See id.* at 561-66. Here, however, we face the inverse situation. The regulations reach only commercial speech; and we have vacated the regulations insofar as they reach anything other than false, erroneous, or deceitful commercial speech. Therefore, Appellant's argument that the regulations could be applied unlawfully is precisely the kind of argument that is disfavored in the posture of a facial challenge.

Nor does the "overbreadth" doctrine save Appellant's challenge. At the outset, it is not clear that Appellant is entitled to invoke the overbreadth doctrine here. That doctrine is intended to prevent the chilling of speech by allowing a plaintiff to challenge a restriction, even if the restriction could be lawfully applied to that plaintiff. But the Supreme Court has recognized that chilling is unlikely where, as here, the speech is "the offspring of economic self-interest," because such speech "is a hardy breed of expression that is not 'particularly susceptible to being crushed by overbroad regulation.'" *Cent. Hudson*, 447 U.S. at 564 n.6 (citation omitted).

But even were we to consider Appellant's overbreadth challenge, we would reject it. In bringing an overbreadth attack, a plaintiff bears the burden of demonstrating that the challenged law reaches a "'substantial' amount of protected free speech, 'judged in relation to the [regulations'] plainly legitimate sweep.'" *Virginia v. Hicks*, 539 U.S. 113, 118-19 (2003). The Court established this high threshold because

> there comes a point at which the chilling effect of an overbroad law, significant though it may be, cannot justify prohibiting all enforcement of that law — particularly a law that reflects "legitimate state interests in maintaining comprehensive controls over harmful, constitutionally unprotected conduct." For there are substantial costs *created* by the overbreadth doctrine when it blocks application of a law to constitutionally unprotected speech, or especially to constitutionally unprotected conduct. To ensure that these costs do not swallow the social benefits of declaring a law "overbroad," we have insisted that a law's application to protected speech be "substantial," not only in an absolute sense, but also relative to the scope of the law's plainly legitimate applications, before applying the "strong medicine" of overbreadth invalidation.

Id. at 119-20 (citations omitted).

Appellant has failed to satisfy this standard. The Misrepresentation Regulations clearly serve a legitimate state interest: ensuring that schools receiving federal funds do not deceive prospective students into accepting loans that they cannot repay. And we have no basis to think that the regulations' potential application to noncommercial speech will be substantial in either the absolute sense or relative to their application to unprotected commercial speech.

• *Commercial Speech*

"[C]ommercial speech enjoys First Amendment protection only if it . . . is not misleading." *Whitaker v. Thompson*, 353 F.3d 947, 952 (D.C. Cir. 2004). Furthermore, misleading commercial speech is not only subject to restraint; "[it] may be prohibited entirely." *In re R.M.J.*, 455 U.S. 191, 203 (1982); *see also Cent. Hudson*, 447 U.S. at 563 ("[T]here can be no constitutional objection to the suppression of commercial messages that do not accurately inform the public about lawful activity. The government may ban forms of communication more likely to deceive the public than to inform it . . . ." (citations omitted)). Appellant argues that even if the Misrepresentation Regulations reach only commercial speech, they are still impermissible. But its position is predicated entirely on the fact that section 668.71(c) interprets the HEA to reach statements that have the "tendency or likelihood . . . to confuse." We have already vacated that provision, insofar as it reaches merely confusing statements. And since the regulations now facially reach only false statements, erroneous statements, or statements that have the likelihood or tendency to *deceive*, there can be no doubt that the regulations are constitutional: They regulate speech that is not entitled to protection in the first place.

D. The State Authorization Regulations

1. The School Authorization Regulation Is Valid

The school authorization regulation sets forth that an institution is legally authorized within a state only if "the state has a process to review and appropriately act on complaints concerning the institution" and if "[t]he institution is established by name as an educational institution by a State through" one of several specifically designated actions. 34 C.F.R. § 600.9(a)(1)(i)(A) (2011). The District Court held that Appellant lacks standing to challenge these requirements. *See Career Coll. Ass'n*, 796 F. Supp. 2d at 133 n.16. We reverse on that point.

To have standing to seek injunctive relief,

> [Appellant] must show that [it] is under threat of suffering "injury in fact" that is concrete and particularized; the threat must be actual and imminent, not conjectural or hypothetical; it must be fairly traceable to the challenged action of [Appellee]; and it must be likely that a favorable judicial decision will prevent or redress the injury.

Summers v. Earth Island Inst., 555 U.S. 488 (2009) (citation omitted). Where, as here, the challenged regulations "neither require nor forbid any action on the part of [the challenging party]," — *i.e.*, where that party is not "the object of the government action or inaction" — "standing is not precluded, but it is ordinarily substantially more difficult to establish." *Id.* (citation omitted) (internal quotation marks omitted). In such situations, the challenging party must demonstrate that "application of the regulations by the Government will affect [it]" in an adverse manner. *Id.*

Appellant satisfies this standard. "If States bend to the Department's will, [Appellant's] members are harmed because they will face even greater compliance costs." Appellant's Br. at 55. That injury is not speculative or conclusory; indeed, even the Department implicitly recognized it. *See* Final Regulations, 75 Fed. Reg. at 66,859 ("Since the final regulations only establish minimal standards for institutions to qualify as legally authorized by a State, we believe that, in most instances, they do not impose *significant* burden or costs." (emphasis added)). Alternatively, "[i]f the States ignore the regulations, [Appellant's] members will be barred from Title IV programs through no fault of their own. Whatever States do in response to the regulations, [Appellant]'s members will suffer cognizable injury." Appellant's Br. at 55 (citation omitted).

• *Statutory Authority*

Appellant's primary argument is that the Department lacked authority to promulgate the school authorization regulation. Appellant argues that

> [t]he Department can point to nothing in the HEA that empowers it to dictate to States how to "authorize" institutions of higher education. Oversight of education has long been a state prerogative, and it is well established that agencies may not alter the allocation of power between federal and state governments in a traditional area of state concern unless Congress has clearly authorized them to do so.

Appellant's Br. at 56 (citing *Gregory v. Ashcroft*, 501 U.S. 452, 461 (1991)).

We find this argument unpersuasive for two reasons. *First*, the school authorization regulation does not impose any mandatory requirements on states. In *Gregory*, the Court confronted whether the Federal Age Discrimination in Employment Act ("the ADEA") covered state judges, such that they could challenge a state constitutional provision requiring their retirement. The Court explained that to interpret the law in such manner would interfere with a "decision of the most fundamental sort for a sovereign entity." Here, by contrast, the regulations merely establish criteria for schools that choose to participate in federal programs. *See* Final Regulations, 75 Fed. Reg. at 66,858 ("The proposed regulations do not seek to regulate what a State must do, but instead considers [sic] whether a State authorization is sufficient for an institution that participates, or seeks to participate, in Federal programs.").

This difference is constitutionally significant, because in *Gregory* the Court was concerned with congressional overreach in an area of state concern pursuant to Congress's powers under the Commerce Clause. Congress unquestionably enacted the ADEA pursuant to its commerce powers . . . and the Court in *Gregory* justified adopting a plain statement rule on the basis that "[a]s against [*those*] powers . . ., the authority of the people of the States to determine the qualifications of their government officials may be inviolate." *Id.* (emphasis added) (citation omitted). In contrast, Congress enacted the HEA pursuant to its spending power. "Incident to [that] power, Congress may attach conditions on the receipt of federal funds, and has repeatedly employed the power 'to further broad policy objectives by conditioning receipt of federal moneys upon compliance by the recipient with federal statutory and *administrative directives*.'" *South Dakota v. Dole*, 483 U.S. 203, 206 (1987) (emphasis added) (citations omitted).

We are not aware of any case in which a court has applied *Gregory* to an exercise of Congress's spending power. This absence of authority is hardly surprising: The Supreme Court has consistently maintained that more permissive limitations apply when Congress acts pursuant to its spending powers than when it acts pursuant to its commerce power. *See id.* at 209 ("[T]he constitutional limitations on Congress when exercising its spending power are less exacting than those on its authority to regulate directly.").

We understand that the Supreme Court's spending power case law is not directly apposite, because states are not the recipients of federal funds under the HEA; schools are. But the school authorization regulation's requirements are more analogous to conditions on federal grants to states than they are to direct requirements on states, if for no other reason than that the decision of whether to comply actually rests with the states. And we have no basis to think that the Department's presenting states a noncoercive choice somehow "upset[s] the usual constitutional balance of federal and state powers," *Gregory*, 501 U.S. at 460.

Second, the *Gregory* rule is not inviolate, and we see no reason to apply it here. This court has suggested that the rule might apply in instances in which an agency regulates in an area of state oversight — for example, the practice of law — without plain authorization from Congress. *See Am. Bar Ass'n v. FTC*, 430 F.3d 457, 471-72 (D.C. Cir. 2005). But the Supreme Court has also upheld federal regulation of activity in those same areas of state concern. *See, e.g., Milavetz, Gallop & Milavetz, P.A. v. United States*, 130 S. Ct. 1324, 1331-33, 176 L. Ed. 2d 79 (2010) (holding that Bankruptcy Abuse Prevention and Consumer Protect Action of 2005 plainly covers lawyers as "debt relief agencies"). Moreover, Appellant's claim that "[o]versight of education has long been a state prerogative" is a non sequitur in the context of a federal program in which the Department has clear oversight responsibility. *Cf. Sistema Universitario Ana G. Mendez v. Riley*, 234 F.3d 772, 778 (1st Cir. 2000) ("This is a federal program, federal dollars are at stake, and the most sensible reading of the statute is that the Secretary has discretion to determine what is 'legal authorization' in order to protect federal interests.").

• *Reasoned Decisionmaking*

Appellant also argues that the school authorization regulation is arbitrary and capricious — because it is "not a solution to any problem" in the record, and because it "penalize[s] *schools and their students* for the failure of *States* to adopt compliant authorization regimes even though schools and their students obviously cannot control States' compliance." As noted, our review of agency regulations is deferential, especially where the administrative action "involve[s] legislative-type policy judgments." Edwards & Elliott 172 (citation omitted). During the rulemaking, the Department identified three problems that the regulation addresses. We can find no basis, and Appellant offers none, to set aside the agency's policy judgment.

First, the agency was concerned that the historical lack of state oversight had prompted "movement of substandard institutions and diploma mills from State to State in response to changing requirements." The Department reiterated and amplified this concern in the final rulemaking, describing that it had "anecdotally observed institutions shopping for States with little or no oversight." This court has said that while we "accord deference to a determination by [an agency] that a problem exists within its regulatory domain, [that] deference is not a blank check." *ALLTEL Corp. v. FCC*, 838 F.2d 551, 561 (D.C. Cir. 1988). Furthermore, we have warned that even plausible claims of "abuse" can fall short where an agency offers no demonstration that "such abuse exists" or that a challenged rule "targets [entities] engaged in such abuse." *Id.* at 560. But we think that, in this case, the Department has offered more than a conclusory assertion of abuse. Furthermore, the record certainly bears out that institutions have engaged in other deceptive practices, and the Department was entitled to adopt this regulation as a prophylactic response to burgeoning forms of abuse.

Second, the Department was apparently concerned that the absence of specific authorization requirements had "contributed to the recent lapse in the existence of California's Bureau for Private Postsecondary and Vocational Education." Commenters asked whether this "lapse" had produced any actual harm to California's students, and the Department's answer certainly leaves something to be desired. The agency responded that it had been informed of at least one instance of a school's shutting down during the lapse, and it asserted that "the absence of a regulation created uncertainty." It further suggested that other problems might have occurred. But the Department also provided some explanation for why it believed that such lapses could present risks to students in the future, and why the regulation would likely prevent states from allowing similar lapses, lest their institutions lose Title IV eligibility. Those explanations are sufficient.

Third, the agency was concerned that states were "deferring all, or nearly all, of their oversight responsibilities to accrediting agencies," thereby "[compromising] the checks and balances provided by the separate processes of accreditation and State legal authorization." The Department offered a similar explanation in the final rulemaking. Here too, we understand the Department to be justifying the regulation — and the dual authorization-accreditation requirements — as a prophylactic component to a larger regulatory regime. We are unwilling to second-guess the Department's policy judgment in that regard.

The Department also offered two justifications for its decision to revoke schools' eligibility for states' failure to adopt compliant authorization procedures. First, the agency claimed that the HEA compels that outcome by requiring schools to be legally authorized. It noted that the HEA separately requires schools to be "accredited," even though institutions lack control over accrediting agencies. The Department therefore claimed that an institution in a state which has not complied with the school authorization regulation is not "any different than an institution failing to comply with an accreditation requirement that results in the institution's loss of accredited status."

Second, the Department explained why it is likely that states will comply with the school authorization regulation's requirements, such that most schools will not lose their eligibility. . . . But the agency also concluded that "[u]nless a State provides at least this minimal level of review, we do not believe it should be considered as authorizing an institution to offer an education program beyond secondary education." This conclusion is precisely the type of policy judgment that an agency is entitled to make.

2. The Distance Education Regulation Violates the APA

The distance education regulation establishes specific requirements for schools that offer distance education. It sets forth that a school offering education "to students in a State in which it is not physically located . . . must meet any State requirements for it to be legally offering postsecondary distance or correspondence education in that State." 34 C.F.R. § 600.9(c) (2011). The District Court held that the regulation violated the APA, because the Department had failed to provide adequate notice of the rule to regulated parties. *See Career Coll. Ass'n*, 796 F. Supp. 2d at 133-35; *see also* 5 U.S.C. § 553(b)(3) (requiring agencies to provide notice of proposed rulemaking that includes "either the terms or substance of the proposed rule or a description of the subjects and issues involved"). We agree.

This court succinctly summarized the governing standard for the APA's notice requirement in *CSX Transportation, Inc. v. Surface Transportation Board*, 584 F.3d 1076 (D.C. Cir. 2009):

> [T]he NPRM and the final rule need not be identical: "[a]n agency's final rule need only be a 'logical outgrowth' of its notice." A final rule qualifies as a logical outgrowth "if interested parties 'should have anticipated' that the change was possible, and thus reasonably should have filed their comments on the subject during the notice-and-comment period." By contrast, a final rule fails the logical outgrowth test and thus violates the APA's notice requirement where "interested parties would have had to 'divine [the agency's] unspoken thoughts,' because the final rule was surprisingly distant from the proposed rule."

Id. at 1079–80.

The Department does not point to anything in its Notice of Proposed Rulemaking that specifically addressed distance education. Nor did the Department solicit comments about the adoption of such a rule. These failures cut against the Department's claim that the distance education regulation is a logical outgrowth of the proposed rules. *See id.* at 1081. More importantly, we find the Department's claims that parties should have anticipated the regulation wanting.

First, the Department emphasizes that whereas the previous regulations required authorization "in the State in which the institution is physically located," 34 C.F.R §§ 600.4(a)(3), 600.5(a)(4), 600.6(a)(3) (2010), the proposed regulations stated that the HEA requires authorization "from the States where [institutions] operate to provide postsecondary educational programs." But, as Appellant points out, the word "operate" is not a term of art that clearly refers only to distance education providers; "[m]any brick-and-mortar programs 'operate' in several physical locations." Appellant's members thus had no way of knowing that the Department was contemplating specific requirements for distance education providers. The agency counters that "if the proposed regulation gave fair notice that the Department was considering changing its 'physically located' rule . . ., and such a change has obvious relevance to distance education programs . . ., then it is irrelevant that the proposed change might *also* have relevance for brick-and-mortar schools as well." But the critical point is that "operate" is, at best, an oblique — and hence, insufficient — indication that the Department was considering the distance education regulation.

Second, the Department claims that its repeated references to "reciprocal agreements between appropriate State agencies," in the proposed regulations, and during the negotiated rulemaking proceedings provided notice that the Department was contemplating regulation of distance and correspondence education. But this argument suffers from the same shortcomings as the Department's first argument. The reason the reference to reciprocal agreements did not put parties on notice of the eventual regulation is that such agreements would be equally applicable to brick-and-mortar institutions with locations in multiple states.

Third, the Department claims that "various commenters took the proposed regulation . . . as contemplating a requirement for state authorization beyond where a school is physically located." This court has made clear that "[t]he fact that some commenters actually submitted comments" addressing the final rule "is of little significance. . . . [T]he [agency] must *itself* provide notice of a regulatory proposal." *Fertilizer Inst. v. EPA*, 935 F.2d 1303, 1312 (D.C. Cir. 1991) (citations omitted) (internal quotation marks omitted). The Department seeks to avoid this instruction by expressly not arguing that interested parties received notice from other parties' comments; instead, it claims that the fact that parties commented demonstrates that the Department provided adequate notice. But at least some of the commenters that the Department cites merely requested clarification as to the Department's new language without offering evaluations of the final rule. Therefore, we cannot conclude that the "purposes of notice and comment have been adequately served. *Fertilizer Inst.*, 935 F.2d at 1311 (citation omitted).

Finally, the Department argues that in the proposed regulations, it made clear its intent to impose, for the first time, substantive requirements related to the legal authorization of institutions by states. The Department urges that institutions were therefore put on notice that authorization requirements for distance education programs were possible. We agree that the "final rule did not amount to a complete turnaround from the NPRM." *CSX Transp., Inc.*, 584 F.3d at 1081-82. But the APA simply requires more.

The Department does not challenge that its failure to provide notice was prejudicial to Appellant, which never had the chance to explain why, in its view, the rule exceeded the HEA's limits or was arbitrary and capricious. We are thus constrained to affirm that section 600.9(c) violates the APA and must be vacated.

III. CONCLUSION

For the foregoing reasons, the judgment is affirmed in part and reversed in part. The case is remanded to the District Court with instructions to remand the challenged regulations to the Department for reconsideration consistent with this opinion.

So ordered.

NOTES

1. The 2010 U.S. Department of Education regulations addressing the Higher Education Act potentially involve high stakes for a college or university found in violation. As mentioned in the case, Title IV financial aid programs provide more than $150 billion annually to 14 million college students. These programs include federally subsidized loans, federal work study, and many federal grants issued to college students. Without these programs, for a significant number of college students, higher education would not be financially accessible. *See, e.g.*, Laura W. Perna, Toward a More Complete Understanding of the Role of Financial Aid in Promoting College Enrollment: The Importance of Context 129–179 (John C. Smart ed., 2010); Neil S. Seftor & Sarah E. Turner, *Back to School: Federal Student Aid Policy and Adult College Enrollment*, 37 J. Hum. Resources 336 (2002). Further, according to a study by Professor Cellini, if a for-profit college increases a student's federal Pell Grant aid, it is more likely the student will enroll into that for-profit college. Stephanie Riegg Cellini, *Financial Aid and For-Profit Colleges: Does Aid Encourage Entry?*, 29 J. Pol'y Analysis & Mgmt. 526 (2010). Put simply, a college or university's receipt of Title IV federal funding plays a critical role in student enrollment, and actions that jeopardize an institution's eligibility could in some cases be quite devastating to its enrollment. Do any of these points change your interpretation of this case? If so, explain.

2. In *APSCU*, the Association contested the rulemaking process. Based on your review of this case, to what extent, if any, does consensus or majority non-agency opinions have on the rulemaking process? Should it influence or dictate the agency's decision? If not, why is the process in place?

Was there any evidence of bad faith in the rulemaking process for the regulations at issue in this case? What standards did the court need to follow to determine the acceptability of these regulations?

3. In light of this case, how might university legal counsel and administrators understand conceptual principles governing when a Dear Colleague Letter qualifies as sufficient clarity of a regulation and when it does not? Should the fact that a subsequent U.S. Secretary of Education may re-clarify or change a regulation factor into the weight afforded "Dear Colleague" letters? As the court even noted, "A new Secretary is not limited by the regulatory choices of his predecessor if he adequately states the reasons for any changes." *See Sistema Universitario Ana G. Mendez v. Riley*, 234 F.3d 772, 780 (1st Cir. 2000) (holding that the U.S. Secretary of Education has discretion to determine the standards of institutional eligibility to participate in student financial assistance programs).

Following the announcement of the *APSCU* decision, the Department of Education issued a Dear Colleague Letter (DCL). Letter from David A. Bergeron, Acting Assistant Secretary of Postsecondary Education, Dear Colleague Letter Regarding *Guidance on Program Integrity Regulations to Legal Authorization by a State* (Jul. 27, 2012). Because the federal appellate court ruled that the Department failed to comply with administrative procedures in promulgating its distant education regulations, the DCL noted that the Department would not enforce the rule, but it reminded colleges and universities that they may be subject to a state's authorization policies. Several states have moved forward with policies and procedures to address authorization of distant education programs. *See, e.g.*, Eric Kelderman, *Despite Halt in Federal Enforcement, States Move Ahead with Regulations for Online Programs*, CHRON. OF HIGHER EDUC. (Aug. 8, 2012) (citing Minnesota's cease and desist letters for noncompliance, Maryland's passage of a registration fee, and several states' attempts to create cooperative agreements). What arguments exist for the Department to stay out of this matter and simply leave the authorization to states? What other options may the Department or states have? What are the pros and cons of a reciprocity agreement or a centralized licensing board? As you read ahead to the discussion about accreditation, ask yourself — why can't accrediting bodies satisfy requirements for the state?

4. With respect to the state authorization regulations for distance and online programs, the court in *Duncan* determined that the Department failed to comply with the notice requirement under the Administrative Procedure Act (APA). If you were advising the Department, what would you discuss with the Secretary about possible next steps? What reasons would you raise? How might state agencies that oversee higher education respond to this decision and your possible avenues presented to the Secretary? If you were advising APSCU, what would you state to the APSCU as the possible next steps and what reasons would you raise? Would your statements change if you were aware of the recommendations presented to the states and U.S. Secretary of Education? If so, explain.

5. Should the U.S. Department of Education ("Department") regulate bonuses and merit pay of admissions' officers? *See, e.g., United States ex rel. Main v. Oakland City Univ.*, 426 F.3d 914, 916 (7th Cir. 2005) ("The concern is that recruiters paid by the head are tempted to sign up poorly qualified students who will derive little benefit from the subsidy and may be unable or unwilling to repay federally guaranteed loans."); *United States ex rel. Hendow v. Univ. of Phoenix*, 461 F.3d 1166, 1169 (9th Cir. 2006) ("The [incentive payment] ban was enacted based on evidence of serious program abuses."). In your opinion, would the Department's and district court's recommendation regarding other ways to determine admissions' officer pay incentives sufficiently motivate the staff? Why or why not?

6. The compensation regulations, specifically in terms of providing bonuses to recruiters and others engaged in the admission and financial aid processes, do not apply to recruiters of foreign students. Often, these recruiters are commission-based agents. What arguments likely justify this distinction, at least in the context of regulations pertaining to the Higher Education Act? There have been numerous debates about this issue, which largely revolve around professional ethics. Generate a list of the arguments for and against a regulation that forbids payment to commission-based agents, who recruit students internationally to attend U.S. colleges and universities. *See* NATIONAL ASSOCIATION FOR COLLEGE ADMISSION COUNSELING, INTERNATIONAL INTEREST IN U.S. HIGHER EDUCATION AND INSTITUTIONAL RECRUITING PRACTICE 1 (Sept. 2010), *available at* http://www.nacacnet.org/studentinfo/InternationalStudentResources/Documents/InternationalRecruiting.pdf.

For some colleges and universities, international students represent new sources of revenue generation. In July 2011, an *Inside Higher Ed* survey of chief financial officers at 606 colleges and universities indicated that a significant percentage of them (51.1% at doctoral institutions, 49.1% at master's institutions, and 40% at baccalaureate institutions) reported that they plan to recruit more international students as a critical strategy to increase revenues. KENNETH C. GREEN ET AL., THE 2011 INSIDE HIGHER ED SURVEY OF COLLEGE & UNIVERSITY BUSINESS OFFICERS (2011), *available at*

> http://www.insidehighered.com/download?file=insidehigheredcfosurveyfinal7-5-11.pdf

According to an article in *Inside Higher Ed*, the State University of New York has a typical "international recruitment agent" contract, and it pays the agents 10% of the student's net first-year tuition. Elizabeth Redden, *SUNY Bets Big on Agents*, INSIDE HIGHER ED (July 26, 2011)

> http://www.insidehighered.com/news/2011/07/26/suny_plans_broad_use_of_commission_based_agents_to_boost_international_enrollment

7. At the beginning of the opinion, the federal appellate court notes that the statutory requirements under the federal financial aid program "are intended to ensure that participating schools actually prepare their students for employment, such that those students can repay their loans." To what extent should colleges be responsible for their students getting a job? What measures should be used to evaluate whether the college adequately prepared students to obtain a job and should colleges that have high placement rates be rewarded by federal or state funds? What impact might such a policy have in terms of admission criteria, major offerings, and financial aid package awards? In Section I.A of the opinion, the court attaches statutory purpose behind the federal financial aid provisions within the Higher Education Act of dealing with schools benefiting from tuition dollars collected, which might have come from federal aid, yet not bearing sufficient responsibility in terms of "whether those students are ultimately able to repay their loans."

8. What freedoms or latitude may an academic institution that receives federal funds have in terms of what it states about its program offerings and the student experience? How much leeway, if any, should be given to colleges and universities to make statements that members of the institution believe to be true yet raise questions of accuracy? What constitutes "substantial misrepresentation"? What constitutes a minor misrepresentation? Consider the battle of college and program rankings. How much of a role do market effects play in creating higher education as a business transaction infused with customers, competition, and revenue generating concerns? In this case, how does the Department attempt to salvage its Misrepresentation Rules? What arguments does it assert? Why is the appellate court unconvinced? How could the Department reconstruct its Misrepresentation Regulations to conform with this decision? What other factors might arise to challenge any subsequent proposed regulations? Assuming the Misrepresentation Regulations are permissible under federal law (e.g., Constitution and Administrative Procedures Act), what might the Department have done to address "minor misrepresentation"?

9. In 2012, a system audit disclosed that Dickinson State University had not complied with its International Articulation Agreement that it established with various foreign colleges and universities. According to the report, numerous students in the program had failed to demonstrate that the students met graduation requirements, yet the institution still issued the students a degree. *See* NORTH DAKOTA UNIVERSITY SYSTEM. INTERNATIONAL TRANSFER AGREEMENT REVIEW (2012) *available at* http://www.ndus.edu/uploads/reports/96/dsu-internal-review-ddj-final-draft1-020912.pdf.

B. STATE LICENSURE OF ACADEMIC INSTITUTIONS

State licensure represents one form of approval for institutional and academic program integrity. In Chapter II, *supra*, cases such as *Shelton College v. State Board of Education*, 226 A.2d 612 (N.J. 1967) and *New Jersey Board of Higher Education v. Shelton College*, 448 A.2d 988 (N.J. 1982) illustrate the state-level review process known as the state licensure process (to recognize an institution of higher education and the state-level oversight that follows). Here, in this context, state licensure refers to the process by which states issue a license to an educational institution, allowing the institution to operate in the state under the respective license regulations. The term "state licensure" also refers to a state issuing a license to an individual who meets regulatory guidelines to practice a learned profession in the jurisdiction. This would include, for example, those seeking licensure to teach or practice law.

While the standards and procedures for licensure vary widely among the states, most state licensing offices maintain some degree of oversight over the institutions and their academic programs. (For a historical review and more detailed discussion about academic program integrity checks for program approvals and reviews, see Robert J. Barak, STATE HIGHER EDUC. EXEC. OFFICERS, THIRTY YEARS OF ACADEMIC REVIEW AND APPROVAL BY STATE POSTSECONDARY COORDINATING AND GOVERNING BOARDS (2007), *available at* http://www.sheeo.org/academic/Barak%20final.pdf.) This section of the chapter reveals conflicts that arise between the state licensing office and an institution of higher education or an organization that claims to offer diplomas without proper state recognition as a degree-conferring college or university.

1. General Oversight Provisions

NOVA UNIVERSITY v. BOARD OF GOVERNORS OF UNIVERSITY OF NORTH CAROLINA

287 S.E.2d 872 (N.C. 1982)

Opinion by: EXUM, JUSTICE.

The question dispositive of this litigation is whether General Statute 116-15 authorizes the Board of Governors of the University of North Carolina (herein "Board") to regulate through a licensing procedure teaching in North Carolina by Nova University (herein "Nova") when the teaching leads to Nova's conferral of academic degrees in Florida and pursuant to Florida law. The Court of Appeals concluded that the statute contains no such authorization. We agree and affirm.

Defendant Board, acting under G.S. 116-15 and various regulations adopted by it pursuant to the statute, denied plaintiff Nova, a Florida nonprofit corporation, a license to teach in North Carolina curricula designed by Nova to lead to its conferral in Florida of certain academic degrees. Nova has challenged this ruling by filing in superior court what it denominates a "Petition and Complaint." Its petition is filed pursuant to G.S. 150A-45, the section of our Administrative Procedure Act (herein "APA") which provides that "judicial review of a final agency decision" may be obtained through "a petition" filed in Wake Superior Court. By its complaint, or civil action, Nova seeks both a declaratory judgment that the Board has no authority to license its teaching in North Carolina or its conferral of degrees in Florida under Florida law and injunctive relief against the Board's attempt at this kind of regulation. In superior court Nova filed both a motion for summary judgment and a motion for extension of time to conduct discovery. Both motions appear to be related to Nova's civil action, rather than its APA petition for review; but the Board resisted only Nova's motion to extend time for discovery on the ground that Nova's relief, if any, from the Board's decision was via its APA petition for review. The Board argued that the superior court could not entertain a separate civil action and Nova had no right to discovery in a proceeding to review an administrative decision.

Judge Hobgood, after a hearing, denied Nova's motion for summary judgment "without prejudice" to Nova's having its "appeal from an adverse ruling of an administrative agency heard pursuant to [the APA]." Concluding, however, that Nova had a right to conduct discovery, Judge Hobgood allowed Nova's motion to extend time for discovery.

The Court of Appeals allowed both Nova's and the Board's petitions for certiorari, each party having sought review of the ruling adverse to it. The Court of Appeals, after concluding that under G.S. 116-15 the Board "does not have the power to license or regulate Nova University in its teaching program in this state so long as Nova does not confer degrees in this state," reversed Judge Hobgood's denial of Nova's summary judgment motion and remanded for entry of a judgment consistent with its opinion. The Court of Appeals did not, therefore, reach the discovery question raised by the Board's petition for certiorari.

Before us the Board has not sought to sustain the denial of Nova's summary judgment motion on the ground that the superior court had no jurisdiction to entertain it. It continues to argue that Nova's exclusive judicial remedy is under the APA only as a challenge to the superior court's ruling on Nova's discovery motion. Both parties have before us treated the case as if Nova's motion for summary judgment was procedurally a proper way to raise the question of the Board's authority to act. Both have vigorously and ably argued this question here and in the Court of Appeals on the basis that a conclusion that the Board lacked such authority would effectively terminate the litigation in Nova's favor whether the matter is considered as a petition under the APA or civil action against the Board, or both. We approach this aspect of the case as have the parties.

We now proceed to the question at hand.

General Statute 116-15 provides:

> Licensing of nonpublic educational institutions; regulation of degrees.-

(a) *No nonpublic educational institution created or established in this State after December 31, 1960 by any person, firm, organization, or corporation shall have power or authority to confer degrees upon any person except as provided in this section.* For the purposes of this section, the term "created or established in this State" or "established in this State" shall mean, in the case of an institution whose principal office is located outside of North Carolina, the act of issuance by the Secretary of State of North Carolina of a certificate of authority to do business in North Carolina. The Board of Governors shall call to the attention of the Attorney General, for such action as he may deem appropriate any institution failing to comply with the requirements of this section.

(b) *The Board of Governors, under such standards as it shall establish, may issue its license to confer degrees in such form as it may prescribe to a nonpublic educational institution established in this State after December 31, 1960,* by any person, firm, organization, or corporation; but no nonpublic educational institution established in the State subsequent to that date shall be empowered to confer degrees unless it has income sufficient to maintain an adequate faculty and equipment sufficient to provide adequate means of instruction in the arts and sciences, or in any other recognized field or fields of learning or knowledge.

(c) All nonpublic educational institutions licensed under this section shall file such information with the President as the Board of Governors may direct, and the said Board may evaluate any nonpublic educational institution shall fail to maintain the required standards, the Board shall *revoke its license to confer degrees,* subject to a right of review of this decision in the manner provided in Chapter 150A of the General Statutes.

Acting pursuant to subsection (b) of the statute, the Board adopted "Rules and Standards for Licensing Non-Public Educational Institutions To Confer Degrees." (Herein "Standards"). These Standards provide for a number of "minimum standards" with which "a non-public degree-granting educational institution operating wholly or in part in North Carolina" must comply. They relate, in part, to "the quality and content of each course or program of instruction;" the adequacy of "space, equipment, instructional materials, and personnel;" the qualifications of administrators and instructors; financial soundness; and absence of discriminatory practices. "Accreditation by the appropriate accrediting agency . . . may be accepted by the Board . . . as evidence of compliance with [the] minimum standards." The Standards then provide for a procedure whereby an institution may apply for a license. After application, an "examination visit" to the applicant institution's campus by a "team of examiners" is conducted. The Team then files its report and recommendations with the President of the University of North Carolina. After opportunity is given to the applicant to discuss and make additions to the report of the examining team, the matter is submitted to the Board for its "decision and final disposition of the institution's request for licensing." The Rules provide for judicial review of the Board's decision pursuant to article 4 of G.S. 150A.

In addition to its Standards, the Board on 13 February 1976 adopted revised "Guidelines for Interpretation and Implementation" of its Standards (herein

"Guidelines"). The Guidelines are expressly designed to "interpret the rules and minimum standards under which the Board . . . issues licenses to non-public educational institutions to confer degrees in North Carolina." (Emphasis supplied). The Guidelines, after stating the Board's conception of the "broad purpose of higher education", outline in detail requirements for an acceptable "educational program" for each of several types of academic degrees. After stating the Board's conception of the capacities of "[a] generally educated person" and how these capacities are generally developed, the Guidelines provide:

> *Extension work Offered by Out-of-State Institutions.* Any institution legally operating in another state that wishes to offer in North Carolina courses leading to a degree is to apply in the same manner *for a license to grant degrees*, and is to be judged by the same standards as institutions applying for initial licensure in North Carolina.

The Guidelines close with a section on how an educational institution should be organized and administered. It is against this legislative and regulatory backdrop that the dispute before us arose.

It is undisputed that Nova is a nonprofit corporation organized and existing under the laws of Florida with its principal place of business in Fort Lauderdale, Florida. In addition to undergraduate, graduate and professional curricula taught at its 200 acre campus in Fort Lauderdale, Nova, beginning in 1972 and thereafter, instituted various "non-resident" curricula designed to lead to the conferral by Nova in Florida of various degrees for professional persons [Note: The degrees of concern here are (1) the Doctor of Education Degree for "educational leaders"; (2) the Doctor of Education Degree for "community college faculty"; (3) master's and doctor's degrees in public administration; (4) a master's degree in "criminal justice."] Candidates for these degrees are not required to fulfill traditional residence requirements at the Nova campus in Fort Lauderdale. Instead, they form "clusters" of 25 to 30 persons who meet regularly at a site in the state where they live. They are taught by professors, most of whom also teach at universities with traditional residency requirements and who are flown in for weekend sessions with the candidates. The candidates listen to lectures, take notes, have class discussions and undergo examinations. In addition, candidates are required to attend summer institutes at Nova's home campus. Courses and research projects required for the degrees usually require three or more years to complete. Successful candidates receive their degrees in Florida by virtue of Nova's charter under the laws of that state. Nova is and has been since 1971 fully accredited by the Southern Association of Colleges and Schools, the officially recognized accrediting association of the southeastern United States. Nova's accreditation was most recently affirmed for a ten-year period after a review in 1974–75 of its educational programs including its extension courses such as those here at issue. Nova offered its first nonresident curriculum leading to the Doctor of Education Degree for community college faculty in North Carolina in the fall of 1973.

According to Nova's complaint, it did not believe that it was subject to the jurisdiction of the Board; but with confidence in the quality of its curriculum and desire to cooperate with North Carolina authorities, it applied to the Board on 19 November 1976 for licensure.

This application was processed according to the Board's Standards and Guidelines. After reviewing documentary material, contacting persons familiar with Nova's curriculum and making site visits both to the North Carolina "clusters" and to the Fort Lauderdale campus, a team of examiners appointed by the Board recommended on 31 October 1977 denial of Nova's license applications. This recommendation was seconded by staff personnel of the University of North Carolina; and on 7 December 1978 the Board's Committee on Educational Planning, Policies and Programs recommended that the Board deny Nova's license applications. The Board by resolution on 8 December 1978 denied the application. According to the Board's resolution it found that the curriculum leading to the degrees in question lacked "sufficient depth and extensiveness in terms of time and effort required of students," lacked "an adequate faculty in terms of faculty members' contact with and accessibility to their students" and lacked "equipment in terms of libraries and instructional facilities sufficient to provide adequate means of instruction in any of the fields of learning in which" Nova proposed to confer degrees. The Board apparently had no dispute with the qualifications of the faculty generally.

In due time Nova brought this proceeding in Wake Superior Court challenging the Board's action on a multitude of grounds.[1] Nova's most compelling argument, and the one with which we agree, is that G.S. 116-15 expressly authorizes the Board to license only the conferral of degrees. The statute, therefore, should not be interpreted beyond its terms to authorize the Board to license teaching even though the teaching is designed to lead to a degree conferral.

The Board argues to the contrary. It agrees that the statute by its terms speaks only of the Board's authority to license degree conferrals. The Board argues, however, that because the statute authorizes the Board to license degree conferrals, the power to license teaching designed to lead to degree conferrals is necessarily implied.

The Court of Appeals answered the Board's argument by stating "[t]he difficulty we have with the Board's position is that the statute does not specifically grant the power it seeks. What they ask is the power to regulate and license Nova's right to teach which is a restriction on freedom of speech. As Nova points out, other constitutional questions would also arise if we interpreted the statute as contended by the Board. We do not believe we should find a power in the statute by implication which could lead to such constitutional problems. If the General Assembly wants to give the Board the power to so restrict teaching in this state, it may do so specifically and the constitutional questions may then be raised. The statute is not clear in giving the Board the power it seeks. We do not believe we should find this power by implication."

We agree essentially with these conclusions. Insofar as the statute is susceptible

---

[1] Grounds other than the one discussed in the text are the contentions that if G.S. 116-15 is construed to permit the Board to regulate Nova's teaching in North Carolina, then the statute violates the Interstate Commerce and Free Speech Clauses of the United States Constitution and the Free Speech, Law of the Land, Anti-monopoly and Equal Protection Clauses of the North Carolina Constitution. Nova also argues that G.S. 116-15 is an unconstitutional delegation of authority to the Board because it fails to provide any legislative standards for the Board's exercise of its administrative discretion.

to two reasonable interpretations, the one proffered by the Board and the other by Nova, the Board is met head-on by the canon of statutory construction that "[w]here one of two reasonable constructions will raise a serious constitutional question, the construction which avoids this question shall be adopted." *In re Arthur*, 231 S.E.2d 614, 616 (1977).

All that Nova does in North Carolina is teach. Teaching and academic freedom are "special concern[s]" of the First Amendment to the United States Constitution, *Keyishian v. Board of Regents of New York*, 385 U.S. 589, 603 (1967); and the freedom to engage in teaching by individuals and private institutions comes within those liberties protected by the Fourteenth Amendment to the United States Constitution.

State v. Williams, 117 S.E.2d 444 (N.C. 1960), dealt with G.S. 115-253 . . . , which provided generally for the regulation of business, trade and correspondence schools, i.e., certain private schools. The statute in question required persons soliciting students in North Carolina for schools "located within or without the State" to secure a license from the State Board of Education. A representative of a Virginia school solicited a North Carolina high school teacher to take a course of instruction by correspondence from the Virginia school. The representative was prosecuted for the misdemeanor of soliciting the student "without first having secured a license from the State Board of Education" in violation of the statute making such act a crime. She defended on the ground that the statute was unconstitutional. This Court sustained her defense. In a thorough opinion, canvassing the law from both the United States Supreme Court and our sister jurisdictions, this Court held that the state had "a limited right, under the police power, to regulate private schools and their agents and solicitors, provided: (1) there is a manifest present need which affects the health, morals, or safety of the public generally, (2) the regulations are not arbitrary, discriminatory, oppressive or otherwise unreasonable, and (3) adequate legislative standards are established." 117 S.E.2d at 450. Noting that the need in the case before it for regulation was "meager at best", the Court also pointed out:

> "But it should be remembered that, though the schools involved are not of equal dignity with many old and revered private institutions of learning in our State, the same law applies to all. The principles the Legislature may follow in regulating one, it may apply to all. Standardization and regimentation in the field of learning is contrary to the American concept of individual liberty. It would be difficult to over-estimate the contribution of private institutions of learning to the initiative, progress and individualism of our people. Regulation should never be resorted to unless the need is compellingly apparent." (Emphasis supplied).

The Court ultimately concluded that G.S. 115-253 was clearly "an unwarranted delegation of legislative power . . . violat[ing] the 'law of the land' section of the Constitution of North Carolina." *Id.* at 451. The Court closed its opinion by saying, "it might be well to point out that it appears settled that statutes such as G.S. 115-253, insofar as they attempt to regulate solicitors for nonresident schools, burden interstate commerce and are unconstitutional (citations omitted)." *Id.* at 452.

In *Keyishian v. Board of Regents of New York, supra*, the Supreme Court struck down a New York regulatory scheme designed to prevent the hiring and retention in state employment of "subversive" personnel. Those challenging the regulations in the case were faculty members of the State University of New York. Insofar as the regulations applied to these teachers the Supreme Court had occasion to note, 385 U.S. at 603:

> Our Nation is deeply committed to safeguarding academic freedom, which is of transcendent value to all of us and not merely to the teachers concerned. That freedom is therefore a special concern of the First Amendment, which does not tolerate laws that cast a pall of orthodoxy over the classroom. "The vigilant protection of constitutional freedoms is nowhere more vital than in *Shelton v. Tucker*, [364 U.S. 479] at 487the community of American schools." *Shelton v. Tucker*, [364 U.S. 479] at 487. The classroom is peculiarly the "marketplace of ideas." The Nation's future depends upon leaders trained through wide exposure to that robust exchange of ideas which discovers truth "out of a multitude of tongues, [rather] than through any kind of authoritative selection." *United States v. Associated Press*, 52 F.Supp. 362, 372. *In Sweezy v. New Hampshire*, 354 U.S. 234, 250, we said:
>
> > The essentiality of freedom in the community of American universities is almost self-evident. No one should underestimate the vital role in a democracy that is played by those who guide and train our youth. To impose any strait jacket upon the intellectual leaders in our colleges and universities would imperil the future of our Nation. No field of education is so thoroughly comprehended by man that new discoveries cannot yet be made. Particularly is that true in the social sciences, where few, if any, principles are acquired as absolutes. Scholarship cannot flourish in an atmosphere of suspicion and distrust. Teachers and students must always remain free to inquire, to study and to evaluate, to gain new maturity and understanding; otherwise our civilization will stagnate and die.

Were we, therefore, to interpret G.S. 116-15 as the Board suggests, serious constitutional questions arising under the First Amendment and the Interstate Commerce and Fourteenth Amendment Due Process Clauses of the United States Constitution and the Law of the Land clause of the North Carolina Constitution would arise.

Further, we do not think the Board's proffered interpretation of G.S. 116-15 is a reasonable one. The Board argues as follows: The legislature has made clear in other provisions of Chapter 116, dealing with higher education in North Carolina, that the Board is to preside over the planning and development of a coordinated system of higher education in this state.[2] In order to accomplish this broad

---

[2] The Board notes particularly, the following provisions of Chapter 116:

> § 116-1. *Purpose. — In order to foster the development of a well-planned and coordinated system of higher education*, to improve the quality of education, to extend its benefits and to encourage an economical use of the State's resources the University of North Carolina is hereby redefined in accordance with the provisions of this Article.

legislative purpose the Board argues that it must have the power not only to license degree conferrals, but also the teaching of curricula which lead to such conferrals. Thus, argues the Board, the meaning of this statute is to be found in what it necessarily implies as much as in what it specifically expresses. The Board reminds us that "[w]e are not at liberty to give a statute a construction at variance with [the legislature's] intent, even though such construction appears to us to make the statute more desirable and free it from constitutional difficulties." *State v. Fulcher*, 243 S.E.2d 338, 350 (1978).

It is true that portions of Chapter 116 do purport to give the Board broad powers in the planning and coordination of a system of higher education in North Carolina. These powers of planning and coordination are granted to the Board in a number of subsections of G.S. 116-11, each of which deals with a specific power. These grants of power, however, are expressly relative to the Board's governance of the constituent institutions of the University of North Carolina.[3] Only G.S. 116-15, dealing specifically with the licensing of degree conferrals, purports to give the Board authority over private educational institutions, and even this authority is severely limited by the grandfather clause exempting all institutions established before 31 December 1960.

Neither does the Board need, by implication or otherwise, the power to license teaching leading to degree conferrals apart from and in addition to its power to license those conferrals made by North Carolina colleges and universities in order to accomplish the purpose of the legislation. Although a private North Carolina educational institution may remain free to teach what it will without the Board's sanction, it cannot, under the statute, grant a degree based on such instruction unless the Board approves. Inherent in the power to license degrees is the power to establish minimum criteria which a North Carolina institution must meet in order to be licensed to grant degrees. This is sufficient power for the Board to ensure that degrees conferred by North Carolina institutions are backed by curricula meeting

---

§ 116-11. *Powers and duties generally.* — The powers and duties of the Board of Governors shall include the following:

The Board of Governors shall plan and develop a coordinated system of higher education in North Carolina. To this end it *shall govern the 16 constituent institutions* [as defined in another portion of the statute], subject to the powers and responsibilities given in this Article to the boards of trustees of the institutions, *and* to this end it *shall maintain close liaison with* the State Board of Education, the Department of Community Colleges and the *private colleges and universities of the State. The Board, in consultation with representatives of the State Board of Education and of the private colleges and universities, shall prepare and from time to time revise a long-range plan for a coordinated system of higher education,* supplying copies thereof to the Governor, the members of the General Assembly, the Advisory Budget Commission and the institutions.

[3] In addition to subsection (1), quoted [in the earlier footnote], some of the other subsections provide in pertinent part as follows:

(2) The Board of Governors shall be responsible for the general determination, control, supervision, management and governance of all affairs of *the constituent institutions.*

(3) The Board shall determine the functions, educational activities and academic programs of *the constituent institutions.*

(6) The Board shall approve the establishment of any new *publicly supported institution* above the community college level.

(8) The Board shall set enrollment levels of *the constituent institutions.*

the minimum standards of quality prescribed by the Board's regulations. We believe it is all the power the legislature intended to confer.[4]

The difficulty, of course, is that the Board cannot regulate Nova's degree conferrals made in Florida under the auspices of Florida law. The Board concedes that it does not have this extraterritorial jurisdiction. Therefore, the Board argues, the power to license teaching conducted by Nova in North Carolina leading to a degree from the Florida institution must necessarily be implied if the Board is properly to guard against the possibility that this state's citizens will be awarded degrees which are not, in the Board's view, supported by adequate academic preparation.

The Board, however, may not exercise more licensing power over Nova than it has over North Carolina institutions. Thus, the Board cannot be given authority to license Nova's teaching in North Carolina when it has no authority to license teaching by a North Carolina institution. Since the statute gives the Board no such authority, either expressly or by necessary implication, to license teaching by North Carolina private institutions, even when such teaching may lead to a degree conferral, it likewise gives the Board no authority to license this kind of teaching on the part of Nova.[5]

Indeed the Board in its Brief concedes, "Nova is free to teach what it . . . wishes to teach, and its students are entitled to learn the same. This remains true even though Nova was denied a license to offer degree programs and confer degrees in this state." If this is true, and we agree that it is, then Nova must prevail. For, by whatever name it is called, all that Nova does in North Carolina is teach. To say that it is conducting a "degree program" which is somehow different from or more than mere teaching, as the Board would have it, is nothing more than the Board's euphemization. Teaching is teaching and learning is learning notwithstanding what

---

[4] We are satisfied that the legislature had in mind only North Carolina institutions when it enacted in 1971 those provisions of G.S. 116-15 now under consideration. In the Act of October 30, 1971, ch. 1244, § 1, 1971 N.C.Sess.Laws (1st Sess.), the legislature spoke of "non-public educational institution[s] created or established in this State" without assigning any meaning to "created or established" other than their ordinary connotation. It was not until 1977, four years after Nova offered its first external program in North Carolina and seven months after it applied for a license, that the legislature amended G.S. 116-15(a) to define the phrase "created or established." It was then that the legislature first mentioned out-of-state institutions in connection with "[l]licensing of nonpublic educational institutions" and "regulation of degrees." The amendment stated: "For the purposes of this section, the term 'created or established in this State' or 'established in this State' shall mean, in the case of an institution whose principal office is located outside of North Carolina, the act of issuance by the Secretary of State of North Carolina of a certificate of authority to do business in North Carolina." Act of June 14, 1977, ch. 563, supra, § 3. Thus, it is apparent that the legislature did not even contemplate out-of-state schools like Nova when the licensing provisions of the statute were designed. Even after the 1977 amendment purporting to bring out-of-state institutions within the statute's ambit, the legislature did not broaden the reach of the licensing scheme itself. The Board's power remained limited to the licensing of "degree conferrals." Whether a statute could be constitutionally designed to regulate in-state teaching or even in-state degree conferrals by out-of-state schools operating under the laws of other states is a question not now before us and one which we do not now decide.

[5] To say, as we do, that the Board has no power under the statute to license teaching, whether by an out-of-state or an in-state institution, is not to say, as the dissenters contend, that the Board has no power to regulate degree conferrals by in-state institutions operating under North Carolina law if they occur outside the state. This again is a question not now before us and one which we do not now decide.

reward might follow either process. The Board's argument that the power to license teaching is necessarily implied from the power to license degree conferrals simply fails to appreciate the large difference, in terms of the state's power to regulate, between the two kinds of activities. The Board accuses Nova of trying to accomplish an "end run" around the statute. In truth, the Board, if we adopted its position, would be guilty of an "end run" around the statutory limits on its licensing authority.

Finally, the Board's proffered canons of statutory construction, including the canon that "[t]he construction of statutes adopted by those who execute and administer them is evidence of what they mean," *Commissioner of Insurance v. Automobile Rate Office*, 241 S.E.2d 324, 329 (1978), are designed to help courts construe statutes where the statute is susceptible to construction. When the language of the statute is unambiguous and the meaning clear, there is no room for judicial construction. "[T]he province of construction lies wholly within the domain of ambiguity, and . . . if the language used is clear and admits but one meaning, the Legislature should be taken to mean what it has plainly expressed." *Asbury v. Town of Albemarle*, 78 S.E. 146, 148 (1913).

Here the legislature has clearly authorized the Board to license only degree conferrals, not teaching. Because of the statute's clear language limiting the Board's authority to license only degree conferrals and not separately to license the teaching which may lead to the conferral, the statute is simply not reasonably susceptible to a construction which would give the Board the power to license such teaching.

Since this determination effectively ends this litigation, we, like the Court of Appeals, need not reach the question of whether Judge Hobgood erred in granting Nova an extension of time to conduct discovery.

The decision of the Court of Appeals is, for the reasons stated, AFFIRMED.

CARLTON, JUSTICE, dissenting.

I respectfully dissent from the majority opinion. Its interpretation of G.S. 116-15 as applying only to the physical conferral in this state of academic degrees emasculates that statute and seriously erodes the power of the Board of Governors in carrying out its statutory mandate to plan and develop a coordinated system of higher education in this state. The law created by the majority would allow any private organization which teaches in this state to avoid regulation and minimum standards of quality by simply stepping a few feet across the state line on graduation day and handing out diplomas to its North Carolina students. Such a result could not possibly have been the intent of our Legislature. In order to accomplish its statutorily expressed purposes, the Board must have the power to license all degree conferral programs offered within this state, regardless of where the graduation ceremony is held. I believe it does have that power.

I cannot argue with the majority's statement that G.S. 116-15 expressly mentions only the regulation of degree conferrals; our disagreement lies in whether this statute implicitly authorizes the licensing or regulation of the programs which lead to degree conferrals. In my opinion, the power to regulate or license degree conferral programs is essential to the power to regulate degree conferral itself and is necessarily implied by the statute. My conclusion is based on two grounds: (1) the language of G.S. 116-15 itself and (2) the purpose and function of the Board of Governors.

(1) In pertinent part, G.S. 116-15 provides:

> § 116-15. Licensing of nonpublic educational institutions; regulation of degrees.-(a) No nonpublic educational institution created or established in this State after December 31, 1960, by any person, firm, organization, or corporation shall have *power or authority to confer degrees* upon any person except as provided in this section.
>
> (b) The Board of Governors, under such standards as it shall establish, may issue its license to confer degrees in such form as it may prescribe to a nonpublic educational institution established in this State after December 31, 1960, by any person, firm, organization, or corporation; but *no nonpublic educational institution established in the State subsequent to that date shall be empowered to confer degrees unless it has income sufficient to maintain an adequate faculty and equipment sufficient to provide adequate means of instruction in the arts and sciences, or in any other recognized field or fields of learning or knowledge.*
>
> (c) All nonpublic educational institutions licensed under this section shall file such information with the President as the Board of Governors may direct, and the said Board may evaluate any nonpublic educational institution applying for a license to confer degrees under this section. If any such nonpublic educational institution shall fail to maintain the required standards, the Board shall revoke its license to confer degrees, subject to a right of review of this decision in the manner provided in Chapter 150A of the General Statutes.

(Emphases added).

From the emphasized portions of this statute it is obvious that the Legislature intended that licensure to confer degrees depend upon "income sufficient to maintain an adequate faculty and equipment sufficient to provide adequate means of instruction" in the fields of knowledge in which a degree is sought. This language clearly evinces a legislative concern over the quality of a program leading to the conferral of a degree. Hence, inherent in the authority to license private entities to confer degrees is the power to license the programs leading to those degrees. To separate the physical act of bestowing a diploma from the program which leads to the degree is to exalt form above substance. The concern of the Legislature that degree programs be sufficiently funded and equipped to provide adequate means of instruction shows that it considered the degree conferral program to be an inherent and inseparable part of the ability and authority to confer degrees.

(2) The purpose of the Board of Governors is to plan and develop a coordinated system of higher education in North Carolina. To this end it is authorized to license private institutions to confer degrees. If the licensing requirement can be met by side-stepping the statute, literally, then the Board of Governors has few means available to accomplish its purposes.

If this loophole exists in G.S. 116-15, all institutions now subject to the licensing requirement and the minimum standards and regulations attendant to it may escape the coverage of the statute by holding their graduation ceremonies just across the state line. It will not matter that their students are North Carolina citizens who are solicited and taught in this state and that their graduates will remain in North Carolina to use their degrees. In truth, these students will have acquired their knowledge through programs conducted in this state, and those programs, good or bad, will be part of the system of higher education in this state. Under the majority's decision, these institutions will be immune from any licensing requirement and cannot be part of the plan for a coordinated system of higher education. Such an exception, grounded on the geographical location of the graduation ceremony, cannot have been within the legislative intent. Both the language of the licensing statute indicating a concern with adequate funding and facilities and the statutorily stated purpose of the Board of Governors evince a clear legislative intent that the "power or authority to confer degrees" implicitly includes the power or authority to offer degree conferral curricula within this state. Because the former is expressly required to be licensed, then the latter must also be licensed.

Although the majority makes much of the canon of statutory construction that " '[w]here one of two reasonable constructions will raise a serious constitutional question, the construction which avoids this question shall be adopted,' " (quoting *In re Arthur*, 231 S.E.2d 614, 616 (1977)), I find it unpersuasive. The intent of the Legislature is the polar star which guides the courts in determining the meaning of a statutory provision. In ascertaining the legislative intent a court should consider the language of the statute, the spirit of the act and what the act seeks to accomplish. As stated above, the language, purpose and spirit of the statutory scheme in question, in my opinion, clearly indicate a legislative intent to require that programs leading to degree conferral, and not just the handing out of a diploma, be licensed by the Board of Governors. That this construction of the statute raises numerous constitutional questions is of no consequence: if such is found to be the legislative intent, this Court "[is] not at liberty to give to a statute a construction at variance with [the legislative] intent, even though such construction appears . . . to make the statute more desirable and to free it from constitutional difficulties." *State v. Fulcher*, 243 S.E.2d 338, 350 (1978).

The majority's adoption of a literal construction of G.S. 116-15 is premised on the assumption that the interpretations proffered by Nova and by the Board of Governors are both reasonable. I submit that the interpretation adopted by the majority is not reasonable and renders the statutory scheme devoid of rhyme or reason.

The majority makes much of the distinction between teaching and the conferral of degrees. According to the majority, Nova merely teaches within North Carolina. Because teaching is a right protected by the first amendment, it cannot be regulated. G.S. 116-15 does not purport to regulate mere teaching. Thus, the majority concludes, because Nova's activities in this state are confined to teaching, those activities cannot be regulated:

> [B]y whatever name it is called, all that Nova does in North Carolina is teach. To say that it is conducting a "degree program" which is somehow different from or more than mere teaching, as the Board would have it, is nothing more than the Board's euphemization. Teaching is teaching and learning is learning notwithstanding what reward might follow either process. The Board's argument that the power to license teaching is necessarily implied from the power to license degree conferrals simply fails to appreciate the large difference, in terms of the state's power to regulate, between the two kinds of activities.

I must confess that I also fail to appreciate the "large difference, in terms of the state's power to regulate, between [teaching and degree conferral]." Assuming, as does the majority, that the Board constitutionally may license degree conferral by private institutions within this state, I am at a loss to understand how the licensing of degree conferrals differs, in practical terms, from the licensing of the program. In considering whether to grant a private institution a license to confer degrees, the Board considers such factors as years in operation, safety and health standards, maintenance of records, financial soundness, reputation of officers and staff, admissions policies, adequacy of facilities for classes and study, adequacy of faculty, and academic quality of the programs offered. Most of these factors deal with adequacy of educational resources and the degree to which the school's environment is conducive to learning, *not with what is taught or how it is taught.*[1] To the degree that these factors concern the teaching or learning in the case of an institution which confers degrees in North Carolina, they regulate, *to the same extent and no more*, the teaching of degree conferral programs designed to lead to conferral of degrees outside the state. In asserting that Nova is subject to the licensing requirement contained in G.S. 116-15, the Board is attempting to assert *exactly the same* authority it does over institutions operating wholly within this state.

That the Board attempts to evaluate only the ability to teach or opportunity for and sufficiency of learning and not what is taught is reflected in its evaluation of Nova. Nova was found to have satisfied the following criteria:

> (1) It was properly chartered and had been in operation for at least two years;
>
> (2) Its safety and health standards were adequate;
>
> (3) Its record-keeping system was adequate;
>
> (4) It was financially sound;
>
> (5) Its officers and staff had good reputation and character;
>
> (6) Its admissions policies were nondiscriminatory.

Deficiencies were found, however, in the requirements of adequate facilities and adequate faculty. Nova was found to have no formal arrangements for facilities in which to hold classes or for access for its students to library facilities. One cluster

---

[1] In its evaluation of Nova, the investigative team did find inadequacies in the amount of material covered. This, however, does not regulate what is taught, but sets minimum standards of coverage for degree recognition.

group was holding its meetings in a motel. The lack of specific arrangements for meeting and library space did not ensure continuity of the program nor did it provide an academic setting conducive to the in-depth study and research required for graduate degrees. Deficiencies were also noted in specific degree programs. These deficiencies concerned mainly the inadequacy of testing, little opportunity for in-depth study, insufficient amount of material, and little opportunity to interact with faculty.

I wish to make it clear that I agree that Nova is free to teach anything it wants to teach without a license from the Board of Governors. However, the factor which makes Nova subject to the licensing requirement is that it does not merely teach; the programs it offers in this state are advertised and do indeed lead to conferral of a degree. It is not the fact of teaching that makes Nova subject to licensure, it is the offering of a degree program, the promise of a degree.

I freely admit that the construction urged by the Board and which I find persuasive is not free from constitutional difficulties. Those presented to us are infringement on freedom of speech, violation of the commerce clause, equal protection and invalid delegation of legislative authority. I do not purport by this dissent to deal with those issues. My purpose in writing this dissent is to state what I believe to be the clear legislative intent and to emphasize that this Court should not shirk its responsibility to interpret statutes according to the legislative intent even when complex constitutional issues loom on the horizon. I leave for another day and another majority, one in which I will gladly participate, the task of determining whether the mandatory licensing of degree conferral programs by a legislatively created administrative agency is constitutionally permissible. For now, it is enough to say that I believe our statutory scheme passes constitutional muster.

I also leave untouched the question of whether Nova's exclusive remedy is under the APA or whether it may initiate a separate action under the Declaratory Judgment Act and, thus, obtain discovery. I do, however, wish to make this observation: questions of law or assignments of error which, because of their nature, can be adequately handled by a reviewing court on the basis of the record of the proceedings before the administrative agency ought to be reviewable solely under the APA; claims which, by their nature, cannot be substantiated or challenged on the basis of the "cold record" ought not to be ignored merely because the APA does not provide for discovery. These latter claims, I believe, fall outside the intended coverage of the APA and may be brought under the Declaratory Judgment Act.

In conclusion, I cannot accept the majority's construction of the application of G.S. 116-15 to be dependent upon the location of the graduation ceremony and not on the location of the teaching which forms the basis for the degree. Such a construction places form above substance, contravenes the clear legislative intent, and creates a gaping loophole in the statutory scheme for a coordinated system of higher education in this state.

COPELAND, J., joins in this dissent.

NOTES

1. The differing opinions rested on statutory interpretation, but both opinions considered several legal parameters such as the Commerce Clause, First Amendment, and Fourteenth Amendment. What statutory language would have properly permitted the Board to regulate Nova's academic programs?

2. Nova also challenged another jurisdiction's licensure policy; however, in that case, the licensing office prevailed. In *Nova University v. Educational Institution Licensure Commission*, 483 A.2d 1172 (D.C. 1984), *cert. denied*, 470 U.S. 1054 (1985), the court concluded, among its findings, that the District of Columbia's statutory provisions pertaining to licensing of educational institutions contained nondiscriminatory language. That is, the statute treated educational institutions the same, regardless of where the degree was conferred (i.e., in state or out of state), and the language focused on establishing criteria for minimal academic standards, not restricting speech. An excerpt of the relevant portion of the statute is restated below.

§ 29-815. License to confer degrees — Issuance by Educational Institution Licensure Commission required.

No institution . . . incorporated under the provisions of this chapter shall have the power to confer any degree in the District of Columbia or elsewhere, nor shall any institution incorporated outside of the District of Columbia . . . , undertaking to confer any degree, operate in the District of Columbia, unless . . . , by virtue of a license from the Educational Institution Licensure Commission, which before granting any such license may require satisfactory evidence:

(1) That in the case of . . . an incorporated institution, a majority of the trustees, directors, or managers of said institution are persons of good repute and qualified to conduct an institution of learning;

(2) That any such degree shall be awarded only after such quantity and quality of work shall have been completed as are usually required by reputable institutions awarding the same degree . . . [.]

Here is a brief synopsis of the case:

In 1929, Congress passed a law to regulate degree-conferring institutions in the District of Columbia. Congress enacted the law to combat the problem of "diploma mills" in D.C. At the time of this case, the District established regulations that governed licensure for degree-granting institutions. Among the regulations, the statute outlines provisions regarding minimum criteria for degree programs such as number of faculty, availability of library resources, and dedicated, physical space. When Nova University, a private, nonprofit institution of higher education based in Florida, underwent its review, it failed to seek approval. A review committee concluded that Nova failed to meet several criteria — particularly, the number of faculty, availability of library resources, and dedicated, physical space. In reaction, the University sued the District agency asserting several claims: Nova's primary argument was that the statute was inapplicable to private educational institutions that only planned to offer select courses in D.C. (when, in the end, the degrees would be issued from another jurisdiction (i.e., Florida)). Additionally, Nova claimed that the statute violated the First Amendment in two ways: According to Nova, (1) the statute regulated speech on the basis of its quality because of the licensing controls, and (2) the law's language was impermissibly vague.

The federal district court disagreed with all of Nova's claims. First, the court found that the statute applied to degree-conferring institutions that operate in the District of Columbia. Thus, the statute applied to Nova University's purpose of seeking permission to operate in D.C. Second, the court concluded that the statute did not regulate pure speech. The court rationalized that the statute did not bar Nova's right to speak or teach "so long as no degree credits or degrees" were issued. *Id.* at 1180. Further, the court emphasized that "[e]ducational institutions have no inherent or constitutional right to confer degrees; rather, degree conferral is business conduct, a corporate privilege conferred by the state of incorporation." *Id.* at 1181. The court continued its analysis, finding that the law achieved its purpose of responding to the government's interest of setting standards for educational institutions within its jurisdiction. Third, in reviewing the statute's language, the court concluded that the criteria as a business regulation — which is not subject to the strict vagueness test as other statutory language — was sufficiently clear for the purposes of determining minimum standards for an educational institution to operate.

What are the differences between the North Carolina and Washington, D.C. policies and how did the legal analyses change?

3. What arguments might have been made in the North Carolina case if the state oversight pertained to courses for professional practice in accountancy, law, medicine, or nursing? *See Excelsior Coll. v. California Bd. of Registered Nursing*, 39 Cal. Rptr. 3d 618 (Cal. App. Ct. 2006).

4. These cases focus on physical resources such as classroom space and library collections. Many state regulations that examine physical resources have been modified to accommodate new educational delivery methods, particularly online, distance education. With these modified regulations, distance education programs and enrollments have increased substantially. For example, in the 1997–1998 academic year, approximately 34% of colleges and universities reported some form of distance education. LAURIE LEWIS ET AL., NAT'L CENTER FOR EDUC. STATS., DISTANCE EDUCATION AT POSTSECONDARY EDUCATION INSTITUTIONS: 1997–98 (1999), *available at* http://nces.ed.gov/pubs2000/2000013.pdf. In that same year, distance education courses yielded 710,000 enrollees. By the 2006–2007 academic year, those figures increased substantially: during that time frame, approximately two-thirds of colleges and universities indicated that they offered some form of distance education, which for many of these institutions included complete degree programs. BASMAT PARSAD & LAURIE LEWIS, NAT'L CENTER FOR EDUC. STATS., DISTANCE EDUCATION AT DEGREE-GRANTING POSTSECONDARY INSTITUTIONS: 2006–07 (2008), *available at*

http://nces.ed.gov/pubs2009/2009044.pdf. In addition, from 2006–2007, distance education courses reached an estimated 12,200,000 enrollees. For a more detailed discussion regarding state regulations and distance education, particularly in terms of oversight of interstate educational delivery, see MICHAEL B. GOLDSTEIN ET AL., DOW LOHNES PLLC, THE STATE OF STATE REGULATION OF CROSS-BORDER POSTSECONDARY EDUCATION: A SURVEY AND REPORT ON THE BASES FOR THE ASSERTION OF STATE AUTHORITY TO REGULATE DISTANCE LEARNING (2006), *available at* http://www.dowlohnes.com/files/upload/survey.pdf. Nevertheless, as forms of educational media advance even further and the supply and demand for online education increase (particularly as this form of educational delivery gains academic and employer legitimacy), questions of institutional and academic integrity will continue to surface. State regulations have the challenge of balancing new legitimate educational delivery approaches with proper oversight of questionable educational programs, particularly diploma mills, discussed *infra*.

2. Provisions Addressing Diploma Mills

State licensing offices also establish regulations to prevent and eliminate so-called "diploma mills." Under the Higher Education Opportunity Act, Congress defines a diploma mill as an organization that "offers, for a fee, degrees, diplomas, or certificates, that may be used to represent to the general public that the individual possessing such a degree, diploma, or certificate has completed a program of postsecondary education or training; and requires such individual to complete little or no education or coursework to obtain such degree, diploma, or certificate." 20 U.S.C. § 1003(5) (2011). In addition, that organization is not accredited by a recognized accrediting agency. As discussed in greater detail below, the U.S. Department of Education, other federal agencies, state government, and specially identified accreditation associations identify certain accrediting agencies that they "recognize." These "recognized" agencies conform with the accreditation requirement under the law. Put simply, as a special investigation unit within the Government Accountability Office refers to them, diploma mills are organizations that sell "bogus academic degrees." Letter from Robert J. Cramer, Office of Special Investigations, Government Accountability Office, to Senator Susan M. Collins (Nov. 21, 2002), *available at* http://www.gao.gov/new.items/d03269r.pdf.

IN THE MATTER OF JOSEPH JAYKO TRADING

55 F.T.C. 242 (1958)

FTC CHAIRMAN GWYNNE

. . . .

I.

Appeal From the Initial Decision and Order

The complaint charges respondent with violation of the Federal Trade Commission Act by the making of false representations in connection with the sale of printed material, consisting of tests designed to determine the knowledge and ability of persons regarding certain specific subjects. The passing of such tests was made the basis for issuance of "equivalency diplomas" and degrees as hereinafter described.

The false statements charged against respondent in the complaint and which are the basis of the initial order are as follows:

> 1. That respondent has authority to award degrees and diplomas.
>
> 2. That the educational qualifications of persons awarded degrees and diplomas by respondent is equivalent to those acquired by attendance at accredited institutions of learning.
>
> 3. That the certification or diploma issued by respondent is recognized by industry, commerce and by Federal and State organizations.
>
> 4. That thousands of persons have purchased respondent's material and have been awarded diplomas.
>
> 5. That the degrees and diplomas awarded by respondent will guarantee better paid positions and jobs.
>
> 6. Through the use of the word "Institute" as a part of the trade names "Cramwell Institute" and "Cramwell Research Institute" and references to the use of the words "Institute" and "Institution" in his advertising, that respondent is conducting an institution of higher learning with a staff of competent, experienced and qualified educators offering instruction in the arts, sciences and subjects of higher learning.

In his answer, respondent admits the allegations contained in paragraph 2, subparagraphs 3 and 6, but denies, in whole or in part, the remaining allegations. He also denies in toto that such allegations were false, misleading and deceptive.

The initial decision reviews the evidence as to each matter in controversy. Only a brief summary thereof will be given here.

From about 1944 to 1950 or 1951, respondent engaged in business as "Air Institute." This business consisted of compiling and selling courses in air navigation. In about 1951, respondent broadened his program to include testing procedures and abandoned the name "Air Institute" and adopted the names "Cramwell Institute" or "Cramwell Research Institute." Respondent also claims to have operated a publishing business with various trade names, such as "Cramwell Books," "Cramwell Publishing Company," etc.

At the time of the hearing, respondent operated his testing service in an office consisting of two rooms and a foyer, located in Adams, Mass[achusetts]. He had a reference library of 300 to 500 volumes. He had no laboratory and no class rooms. The staff consisted of his wife as secretary, and four consultants on a part-time basis, two of whom were employed full time commercially as electrical engineers, and the other two as full time teachers. The amount of time and money spent by respondent on these consultants appears to have been relatively small.

Upon receipt of applications, respondent prepares written tests which are mailed to applicants and the questions thereon answered in writing, usually before a designated impartial person. Respondent then grades the papers and in some cases, issues his equivalency diplomas. He has tested 302 persons and issued 200 diplomas.

Respondent offers "college equivalency diplomas" in the following, among other, areas: business administration, business law, personnel management, advertising, English language, aeronautical science and engineering, and general science.

The type of document issued is indicated in the following in evidence as an exhibit.

CRAMWELL INSTITUTE

Educational Testing System
To all before whom these letters may come, greeting
Be It Known That
JOHN ZELEM
having satisfactorily completed the requirements
comparable
in accredited college curricula in
GENERAL SCIENCE
Degree of Bachelor of Science
prescribed for certification by this Institution, is awarded
this College Equivalency
DIPLOMA
as an honorable testimonial of attainment. Given at
Adams, Massachusetts, this 4th day of Nov. 1954
(s) Joseph Jayko
Director of Education.

In the educational field, the words "diploma" and "degree" have come to have a well-established meaning. A diploma is a document issued by an educational institution witnessing the fact that the grantee has met certain requirements of the institution. These are often the passing of examinations, together with attendance at classes and compliance generally with the established discipline. It is a matter which is handled by the respective states, either through general law or by agencies to whom the power has been delegated. The respondent does not claim that he has authority to issue diplomas within the above meaning of the term. He claims that through his method of testing, he is able to determine whether an individual's level of intelligence is equivalent to that of a person who has completed the requirements for a standard diploma and that his "diplomas" are issued on that basis. However, his representations go beyond that, and either expressly or impliedly assert that his equivalency diplomas are comparable to those issued by educational institutions and are equally acceptable to interested parties.

For example, in connection with his operations, respondent disseminated in commerce advertising brochures, letters, etc. in which he made statements, of which the following are typical:

> Would you like a raise in salary? Would you like a better job? Are you interested in a promotion? Are you always left behind when promotions are made in your department? Do you feel secure in your present job? Are you in constant fear of being laid off to make room for someone else? Do you want more social prestige? * * * You know the answers. But regardless of how you answer these questions, your employment status can be improved by improving your educational status. Have you ever taken the trouble to provide your employer with evidence showing your educational growth since leaving school or coming to work for him?
>
> * * *
>
> You may possess the equivalent of a college education in your field of endeavor. The Cramwell College Equivalency Diploma will provide the evidence you need to prove you have superior ability and help put you in line for real promotion.
>
> * * *
>
> Remember: This system of self-advancement is guaranteed. * * * It helps you toward promotions and better pay or your money is refunded in full. This guarantee is backed by the U. S. Government Postal Laws.
>
> * * *
>
> DOUBLE YOUR CHANCES for promotion with a College Equivalency Diploma — Awarded through certification of your on-the-job educational development. Business Administration, Liberal Arts, etc. Wonderful opportunities. Qualify by comprehensive examination at home. No courses. Free details. Cramwell Institute, A.B.-7, Adams, Massachusetts.
>
> * * *
>
> Cramwell Institute has devised an educational testing system that has helped thousands of students and mature adults to obtain educational level and specialized knowledge by taking a monitored test * * *.

We agree with the finding of the hearing examiner that the false and deceptive character of the statements alleged in paragraph 2 of the complaint have been established by the evidence.

II.

Respondent's Motion

The motion to set aside the order and remand the case was based in part on the claim that the findings in the initial decision are not made in accordance with the Administrative Procedure Act. We think that the findings cover the ultimate facts and are adequate.

Respondent also objects to the general tone of the initial decision, objects to certain statements and "innuendoes" contained therein and refers to it as "decision by assumption, conclusion and innuendo." We have examined the record with care, and conclude that respondent had a fair hearing, that the examiner gave him adequate opportunity to present his case and to cross-examine witnesses testifying for the complaint. We conclude that the ultimate findings are well supported by the record. We do not, however, approve of some of the language contained in the initial decision.

Respondent's motion to reopen the case for the receiving of newly discovered evidence is based on three documents.

> (1) Copies of portions of the Federal income tax returns of respondent showing that Cramwell Institute operated at a loss.
>
> (2) "Meaning and Use of the Term Institute" prepared by Donald O. Bolander, M.A., Director of Education, Career Institute.
>
> (3) Copies of certificate from the Secretary of Massachusetts showing that, as of July 19, 1957, respondent Joseph Jayko and six others incorporated as Cramwell Research Institute for the following purpose:
>
> To conduct research in the fields of education industry and commerce. To promote the development of better methods for the identification, evaluation and classification of human aptitudes and achievements related to commercial, industrial, and national defense needs. To develop more efficient methods for the utilization of the educational resources in the United States through human resources engineering.

The Federal income tax returns were obviously known to respondent at all times, or at least the information contained therein could have been discovered by the exercise of reasonable diligence. In any event, the proposed evidence would not be material. The evidence in the record shows that respondent's representations had the tendency and capacity to deceive and that an action to prevent them is in the public interest. Whether respondent made or lost money in carrying on his business would have no bearing on any of the issues in the case.

The document above referred to prepared by Donald O. Bolander was received as an exhibit in Docket 6515, Chicago School of Nursing, Division of Career Institute. It contains a list of 629 organizations using the term "institute" as part of their trade name. Included in the list are a large number listed as "Technical, Trade, Vocational and Miscellaneous Private Schools." Included are some correspondence schools. Other organizations are grouped under the heading, "Trade Associations, Research and Product Promotion Groups, Etc."

The word "institute" both as a verb and as a noun has a wide variety of meanings. It is often used by organizations in the strictly educational field. However, it is also used by other organizations as an examination of the telephone directory of any large city will demonstrate.

When used in the educational field, the word seems to connote a group of people organized for the purpose of education and carrying out that purpose as schools ordinarily do. For example, in *Branch v. Federal Trade Commission*, 141 F. 2d 31, in which respondent was charged with misrepresentation by the use of the term in connection with its courses, the Court said: "Petitioner's school is neither a university nor an institute. It has no entrance requirements, no resident teachers, no library, no laboratory, and no faculty."

The word "institute" by itself does not necessarily connote an educational institution, although it is often used by organizations in the educational field. The inquiry in the instant case is limited by the issues presented by the pleadings. The complaint charged that by the use of the word "institute," respondent represented that he "is conducting an institution of higher learning with a staff of competent, experienced and qualified educators offering instructions in the arts, sciences and subjects of higher learning." In his answer, respondent admitted that through the use of "institute," he had made the representations as alleged.

As to the truth or falsity of the representations, there is no substantial dispute. Respondent admitted that he did not provide any courses of instruction in connection with his examination procedure other than recommending titles of books available to applicants through public libraries, etc. His services are limited exclusively to the evaluation of an individual's educational background and intellectual potentialities.

Subsequent to the closing of the case and taking of testimony, respondent joined with others in organizing under Massachusetts law, "Cramwell Research Institute," a corporation not for profit.

The right to issue educational diplomas and degrees in Massachusetts is regulated by the laws of that State which lay down a program and procedure in regard thereto. Unfair methods of competition in commerce, and unfair or deceptive acts or practices in commerce are by Federal law made matters over which the Federal Trade Commission has jurisdiction. This is true of the acts of respondent in regard to his equivalency diplomas and degrees which are the subject matter of the present complaint. A photostatic copy of the incorporation of Cramwell Research Institute which respondent now asks to present as newly discovered evidence would have no bearing on the issues in the present case. Nor would any of the documents referred to in his motion have any bearing.

Respondent's motion and appeal are denied. The findings and order of the hearing examiner are adopted as the findings and order of the Commission. It is directed that an order issued in accordance with this opinion.

FINAL ORDER

This matter having been heard by the Commission upon respondent's appeal from the hearing examiner's initial decision as well as respondent's motion to set aside the initial decision and remand or to reopen for the receipt of newly discovered evidence, and upon briefs and oral argument in support thereof and in opposition thereto; and the Commission having rendered its decision denying the appeal and the motion and adopting the initial decision as the decision of the Commission:

It is ordered, That the respondent, Joseph Jayko, shall, within sixty (60) days after service upon him of this order, file with the Commission a report, in writing, setting forth in detail the manner and form in which he has complied with the order to cease and desist contained in the initial decision.

NOTES

1. State and federal governments tend to use consumer protection laws to cease operations of diploma mills. *See, e.g., Kensington Univ. v. Council for Private Postsecondary Educ.*, 62 Cal. Rptr. 2d 582 (Cal. App. Ct. 1997) (where the state asserted claims related to state deceptive trade acts and practices for Kensington's false advertising); *Federal Trade Comm'n v. Mountain View Sys., Ltd.*, Case No. 03-CV-00021-RMC (2003), *available at* http://www.ftc.gov/os/caselist/mountainview/031125mountainviewstip.pdf (where Mountain View entered into a settlement agreement with the Federal Trade Commission to cease operations); *State v. Colorado State Christian Coll. of Church of Inner Power, Inc.*, 346 N.Y.S.2d 482 (N.Y. Sup. Ct. 1973) (granting the state's request for injunctive relief, so defendant-organization would stop offering to sell, as well as actually sell, honorary Ph.D. degrees in New York even though its operations originated in another jurisdiction).

2. Allen Ezell and John Bear trace the history and development of diploma mills, discuss the reasons sellers and buyers are attracted to engage in such transactions, and discuss governmental efforts to curb these transactions. *See* Allen Ezell & John Bear, Degree Mills: The Billion-Dollar Industry That Has Sold Over A Million Fake Diplomas (2005).

In 2005, Ezell and Bear referred to the selling of diplomas as a $1 billion industry. *Id.* Nevertheless, state oversight of diploma mills is not consistent. Ezell and Bear refer to legislation in North Dakota and Oregon as containing strong language prohibiting diploma mills (as well as penalties), along with other provisions to protect consumers from these fraudulent degrees. *See also* Valerie Strauss, *Hundreds Linked to Diploma Mill: Government, Military Probed For Violators*, Washington Post (July 31, 2008), http://www.washingtonpost.com/wp-dyn/content/article/2008/07/30/AR2008073002300_pf.html.

There are many states at the opposite end of the spectrum, however. Oregon, which is noted as a state with relatively high standards for degree authorization, states on its website:

> Idaho, Hawaii, Montana, Alabama, Wyoming, Mississippi and California have either no meaningful standards, excessive loopholes or poor enforcement owing to local policy or insufficient staff. Degrees issued by unaccredited private colleges in Alabama, Idaho, Mississippi or Wyoming should be evaluated with great caution. In particular, Mississippi has no oversight standards.

Oregon Office of Degree Authorization, *Diploma Mills*, http://www.osac.state.or.us/oda/diploma_mill.html.

3. Grolleau, Lakhal, and Mzoughi argue that the social costs associated with diploma mills — such as deceit, losses to legitimate educational institutions, and the individual's lack of knowledge and skill acquisition — far exceed any social benefits derived from this greater access to educational degrees through reduced societal costs. Gilles Grolleau, Tarik Lakhal, & Naoufel Mzoughi, *An Introduction to the Economics of Fake Degrees*, 42 J. ECON. ISSUES 673 (2008).

4. The literature on diploma mills cites several sources of the problem: the proliferation of distance education through online media, the incentives and structure of for-profit educational institutions, and the lack of control and oversight over foreign organizations. Creola Johnson, *Degrees of Deception: Are Consumers and Employers Being Duped By Online Universities and Diploma Mills?*, 32 J. COLL. & UNIV. L. 411 (2006). Johnson attributes the growing problem of diploma mills and their deceptive practices as an outgrowth of online education. She brings attention to the deceptive practices used to lure potential students into enrolling in unaccredited degree programs, with emphasis on the online diploma mills. Johnson disagrees with legislation that summarily permits civil and criminal actions against employees with substandard degrees; instead, she suggests a media campaign to educate the public matched with a more robust scale of penalties for the employees including demotions, salary reductions, and terminations after evaluation based on an employer's multi-part review.

Amanda Harmon Cooley and Aaron Cooley raise concerns regarding the consumer accessibility to diploma mills, particularly those emerging as for-profit educational enterprises. Amanda Harmon Cooley & Aaron Cooley, *From Diploma Mills to For-Profit Colleges and Universities: Business Opportunities, Regulatory Challenges, and Consumer Responsibility in Higher Education*, 18 S. CAL. INTERDISC. L.J. 505 (2009).

In *Corruption in Education: A Global Legal Challenge*, Vincent Johnson looks outside the United States and outlines typical illustrations of educational corruption associated with degree or course completion throughout the world. These foreign-based organizations use, or participate in, practices that violate educational standards such as bribery, plagiarism, and issuing fake degrees. Vincent R. Johnson, *Corruption in Education: A Global Legal Challenge*, 48 SANTA CLARA L. REV. 1 (2008).

C. STATE PROFESSIONAL BOARD

TOWNSHEND v. GRAY
19 A. 635 (Vt. 1890)

POWERS, J.

This is a petition by the complainant, claiming to be a graduate of the Vermont Medical College, and holding a diploma of that college conferring upon her the degree of M.D., against the defendants, who are the censors of the Vermont State Eclectic Medical Society, praying that a writ of mandamus be issued commanding the defendants, as such censors, to issue to the complainant a certificate authorizing her to practice medicine in this state.

Our [state] statute provides that every medical society chartered by the legislature "shall issue certificates to physicians and surgeons who furnish evidence by diploma from a medical college or university, or by certificate of examination by an authorized board, which satisfies said censors that the person presenting such credentials has been, after due examination, deemed qualified to practice the branches mentioned in such diploma or certificate." The case shows that the complainant presented to the defendants, as such censors, her diploma aforesaid, and the defendants refused to issue the certificate above referred to on the ground that the Vermont Medical College had no legal power to issue a diploma conferring the degree of M.D., and so the complainant had not shown credentials entitling her to a license to practice medicine.

The main question in issue is whether said medical college has the power to issue diplomas which entitle the holder to the license provided for in the statute. Without going into the question at length, touching the power conferred by the statute upon the censors, which has been discussed in argument, it is plain that this board has the power to decide in the first instance whether a diploma presented to it as evidence of the holder's right to a license is a genuine or spurious document. So far, at least, the board may sit in judgment upon a diploma; and in this case the board adjudged that this diploma did not have such legal efficacy, as evidence, as would warrant the issue of a license.

The Vermont Medical College was organized under the provisions of the tenth subdivision of section 3664, R. L. That section provides that "persons may associate together and have the powers of a corporation for either of the following purposes: * * * (10) To establish and maintain literary and scientific institutions." Later sections in the same chapter enumerate the powers which such associations may have, namely: May have a corporate name, a corporate seal; may adopt by-laws; may sue and be sued; purchase and hold real estate; may raise money, and divide their capital stock into shares. Under this subdivision, it is argued that a medical college may be organized with the power to confer the degree of M.D. It is fundamental that a corporation has such power only as is conferred by its charter, with such incidental powers as are necessary to enable it to exercise its chartered power. No express power to confer degrees can be found in the statute under which this medical college was organized, and hence the power to confer degrees must be classed as incidental to the general powers of a corporation formed for the purpose of maintaining a literary or scientific institution, if it exists all. It would hardly do to say that literary or scientific institutions have such power upon any theory that without it they cannot answer the ends of their creation. The degree of M.D. is something more than a mere honorary title. It is a certificate attesting the fact that the person upon whom it has been conferred has successfully mastered the curriculum of study prescribed by the authorities of an institution created by law, and by law authorized to issue such certificate. It thus has a legal sanction and authority. But it has more. In practical affairs, it introduces its possessor to the confidence and patronage of the general public. Its legal character gives it a moral and material credit in the estimation of the world, and makes it thereby a valuable property right of great pecuniary value.

The scope of subdivision 10 of the statute in question may be discovered by looking at the other subdivisions of the same section. These provide for the organization of library associations; bands of music; associations for breeding fish, for bringing to justice thieves and burglars, building meetinghouses, securing burial grounds, etc. The articles of association are to be filed in the town clerk's office, in the town where the association is organized. All this points to association of limited and local scope. The filing of the articles of association, which constitute the charter under which the association proceeds with its work, in the town clerk's office, indicates that the legislature did not regard such associations as having powers, the exercise of which concerned the general public. The power to confer degrees, not being conferred explicitly by the statute, and not being necessary to enable a literary or scientific institution to carry forward studies of a literary or scientific character, clearly does not exist at all. It is no more appropriate to say that a literary or scientific institution, without special statutory power, can confer the degree of M.D., than to say that it may confer the degree of LL.D. or D.D. or A.B.; for it is plain that law schools, theological schools, universities, and colleges can be organized under this subdivision equally well with medical schools. Every state in the Union has chartered these institutions, and it is believed that none of them has ever supposed that, with all the widely enumerated powers delegated to them, it had the power to confer degrees of any kind unless such power was expressly conferred in its charter. In the case of the Castleton Medical School, chartered many years ago, the charter as first granted contained no delegation of power to confer degrees, but at the next session of the legislature it was amended by an act giving such power. Such has, manifestly, been the legislative idea respecting the necessity of special authority from the law-making power of the government touching the right to confer degrees; and, construing this general statute, providing for the organization, by voluntary association, of persons for local and comparatively unimportant purposes, in the light of the common usages and common understanding of people respecting the rights, privileges, and emoluments universally accorded to persons upon whom degrees have been conferred, we are clearly of the opinion that the Vermont Medical College has no power, under its articles of association, to confer degrees of any kind. To hold that the legislature, by a general law, intended that any three men in any town in the state, however illiterate or irresponsible, might organize and flood the state with doctors of medicine, doctors of law, doctors of divinity, masters of arts, civil engineers, and all the other various titles that everywhere in the civilized world have signified high attainments and special equipment for professional work, is to liken it to the witty French minister who threatened to create so many dukes that it would be no honor to be one, and a burning disgrace not to be one.

The complainant, therefore, in submitting her diploma to the board of censors, did not furnish that board any sufficient evidence of qualification that entitled her to the license asked for. The petition is dismissed, with costs.

NOTES

1. Creola Johnson contends that employers participate in the credentialing system when they reimburse employees for diploma mill programs and encourage or require a college degree as a requisite to job placement or advancement. Johnson argues that when hiring practices disproportionately impact a protected class from qualifying for a low-to-moderate skill position because the employer requires a specified educational level that does not support job performance, this may present a valid claim of employment discrimination under the disparate impact theory; the educational requirement potentially presents a seemingly neutral employment policy with a discriminatory impact on a protected class. Pursuant to the case of *Griggs v. Duke Power Co.*, 401 U.S. 424 (1971), involving discrimination on the basis of the disparate impact theory, such a policy likely presents an employment discrimination case. Creola Johnson, *Credentialism and the Proliferation of Fake Degrees: The Employer Pretends to Need a Degree; the Employee Pretends to Have One*, 23 HOFSTRA LAB. & EMP. L.J. 269 (2006).

2. State professional standards, such as nursing practice laws, govern qualifications in terms of what degrees are accepted and/or how an individual qualifies as a candidate to sit for the state board examination. *See, e.g., Excelsior Coll. v. California Bd. of Registered Nursing*, 39 Cal. Rptr. 3d 618 (Cal. App. Ct. 2006). In some instances, whether an individual qualifies as a candidate for a state license to practice a profession may be associated with whether the individual received the proper professional education, according to the profession's accreditation process. For example, in *Dep't of Prof. Reg., Bd. of Dentistry v. Florida Dental Hygienist Ass'n, Inc.*, 612 So. 2d 646 (Fla. Ct. App. 1993), the state board of dentistry changed its standards to recognize individuals from neighboring states with reported lower standards and academic preparation. The appellate court in Florida upheld the regulation indicating that "those hygienists who are already qualified, licensed and practicing in Florida have a sufficient interest in maintaining the levels of education and competence required for licensing to afford them standing to challenge an unauthorized encroachment upon their practice." *Id.* at 651. *See also Thomas M. Cooley Law Sch. v. Am. Bar Ass'n*, 459 F.3d 705 (6th Cir. 2006).

D. ACCREDITATION

Besides (and sometimes in lieu of) state level reviews, accreditation serves as a check for institutional or academic program integrity. Accreditation is a peer review process to maintain oversight of institutions of higher education and programs in terms of "quality assurance and quality improvement." JUDITH S. EATON, ACCREDITATION, IN HIGHER EDUCATION IN THE UNITED STATES: AN ENCYCLOPEDIA 29 (J. J. F. Forest & K. Kinser eds., 2002). It is generally designed as a self-regulatory system for accredited institutions or programs.

An "accrediting agency" administers the review process. An accreditation agency is a private, nongovernmental body that sets the quality standards and coordinates the program and/or institutional reviews. Often viewed as an academic gatekeeper, the accrediting agency ultimately decides whether a program or institution satisfactorily complies with the standards of the accreditation agency.

In *Auburn University v. Southern Association of Colleges and Schools, Inc.*, 489 F. Supp. 2d 1362 (N.D. Ga. 2002), the court provides a brief historical overview of accreditation and its significance to the federal government as the single most important entity to provide financial assistance to higher education:

> In the late nineteenth century, a number of voluntary associations were created in an attempt to formalize the country's system of higher education. These organizations were not part of the federal government because of the traditional conception that education was not a federal concern, but rather

was an issue left to local governments. The standards used by the regional associations varied during the course of the twentieth century, but eventually evolved into the notion that an institution should be evaluated in relation to the educational mission it established for itself.

The federal government became involved in the accreditation process when the government required institutes of higher education to be accredited in order for the school and its students to qualify for federal financial aid. The predecessor to the Department of Education was first given statutory authority to "recognize" accrediting agencies in the G.I. Bill passed during the Korean War. Congress wanted to assure that federal money was not being spent on "fly by night" educational programs. To that end, the Commissioner of Education was authorized to "publish a list of nationally recognized accrediting agencies and associations which he determines to be reliable authority as to the quality of training offered by an educational institution." The cooperative efforts of the federal and state governments working with the accrediting agencies became known as the "triad." The continued reliance on a "private" system to regulate the accreditation of institutions again appears to have its origins in congressional desire to maintain local control over education and to avoid the development of federal standards for educational policy. ("The establishment of the Department of Education shall not increase the authority of the Federal Government over education or diminish the responsibility for education which is reserved to the States and the local school systems and other instrumentalities of the States.").

Federal financial aid, however, increased in importance when Congress passed the Higher Education Act of 1965 (HEA), which established federal financial aid programs beyond students who were veterans of the armed services. As the federal government became more involved in the accrediting process, accrediting associations became concerned that their educational independence would be threatened by such cooperation. The executive director of an association of accrediting agencies testified in 1974 that accrediting organizations have been enticed to become reluctant extensions of the U.S. Office of Education in order that the accredited schools, programs, and colleges might share in the largesse writ large. Many now would like to break off the relationship, and some have indicated they intend to do so, in order to return to the prerogative which historically and professionally has belonged to them-that of promoting and insuring quality programs of education. All are capable of doing just that and are perfectly willing to abide the scrutiny of the federal benefactor in so doing. They are not willing much longer to abide the prod which inevitably has followed the scrutiny.

In 1992, following investigations related to the high rate of default in the student loan program, Congress again amended the terms of the Higher Education Act to include a subsection on "Program Integrity" to assure reliability in the distribution of federal aid to educational institutions. Under the amendments, Congress continues to delegate to the Secretary of Education the responsibility of determining whether an accrediting agency should be recognized as "a reliable authority as to the quality of education or training offered." The Secretary may promulgate regulations setting forth the criteria for recognition. If an accrediting agency fails to meet these criteria, the Secretary has the option of terminating his recognition of the agency. The amendments set forth several requirements placed on the accrediting agencies, including: that they be "separate and independent" from trade associations; have public participation on the agencies' governing boards; have operating procedures that include provisions for arbitration and due process, specifically "adequate specification of requirements and deficiencies," "notice of an opportunity for a hearing," a "right to appeal any adverse action," and a "right to representation by counsel"; that they perform site visits; and inform the Secretary of Education of any adverse decisions in the accrediting process within thirty days. For the first time, the amendments also provide for statutory requirements related to the substance of accreditation. Specifically, accrediting agencies must review student achievement, faculty, curricula, admissions practices, completion rates, default rates in student loan programs, and facilities; although the agency may go beyond these categories in its review of educational institutions.

In developing the regulations to implement the 1992 amendments, the Secretary of Education described the HEA as providing "the framework for a shared responsibility among accrediting agencies, States, and the Federal government to ensure that the 'gate' to Title IV, HEA [financial aid] programs is opened only to those institutions that provide students with quality education or training worth the time, energy, and money they invest in it." The Secretary also noted that the 1992 amendments "significantly increased the gatekeeping responsibilities of each member of the triad" by enacting "requirements that accrediting bodies must meet if they are to be recognized by the Secretary as 'gatekeepers' for Title IV or other Federal purposes." He indicated that the Department of Education would "take steps to ensure that the various responsibilities of the triad members are carried out in a manner that, in fact, results in the identification of institutions that should not be eligible to participate in the Title IV, HEA programs, on the basis of either the quality of education they offer or their inability to handle program funds" because "the Secretary is committed to effective management of the gatekeeping function."

JUDITH S. EATON, COUNCIL FOR HIGHER EDUCATION ACCREDITATION, AN OVERVIEW OF U.S. ACCREDITATION 2–3 (2009),* *available at* http://www.chea.org/pdf/2009.06_Overview_of_US_Accreditation.pdf.

The accreditation process generally serves the following functions:

- ***Assuring quality.*** Accreditation is the primary means by which colleges, universities, and programs assure quality to students and the public. Accredited status is a signal to students and the public that an institution or program meets at least threshold standards for its faculty, curriculum, student services, libraries, etc. Accredited status is conveyed only if institutions and programs provide evidence of fiscal stability.

- ***Access to federal and state funds.*** Accreditation is required for access to federal funds such as student aid and other federal programs. Federal student aid funds are available to students only if the institution or program they are attending is accredited by a recognized accrediting organization. The federal government awarded $86 billion in student grants and loans in 2006–2007 alone. State funds to institutions and students are contingent on accredited status.

- ***Engendering private sector confidence.*** Accreditation status of an institution or program is important to employers when evaluating credentials of job applicants and when deciding whether to provide tuition support for current employees seeking additional education. Private individuals and foundations look for evidence of accreditation when making decisions about private giving.

- ***Easing transfer.*** Accreditation is important to students for smooth transfer of courses and programs among colleges and universities. Receiving institutions take note of whether or not the credits a student wishes to transfer have been earned at an accredited institution. Although accreditation is but one among several factors taken into account by receiving institutions, it is viewed carefully and is considered an important indicator of quality.

Today, the U.S. Department of Education generally recognizes three types of accreditation agencies: institutional, programmatic/disciplinary, and hybrid agencies. In the United States, the most common form of institutional accreditation is performed by regional accreditation agencies. Although that may seem counter-intuitive, unlike other countries that centralize educational standards, the United States has historically operated with a decentralized educational system — one initially driven by the states. The six[1] regional accreditation agencies are Middle States Association of Colleges and Schools ("Middle States"), New England Association of Schools and Colleges (NEASC), North Central Association of Colleges and Schools (NCA), Northwest Commission on Colleges and Universities (NWCCU), Southern Association of Colleges and Schools (SACS), and Western Association of Schools and Colleges (WASC). In addition, programmatic or disciplinary accreditation agencies examine specific areas such as the American Medical Association, the American Bar Association, and the Council on Education for Public Health. These accreditation agencies only examine their specific programmatic areas. Finally, the U.S. Department of Education also recognizes hybrid accreditation bodies. There are four faith-based accrediting organizations and seven national career-related accreditors that fall under this category. They have focused programmatic areas but they also review the entire institution. These accreditation agencies include the Commission on Massage Therapy Accreditation, the Council on Chiropractic Education, and the National Association of Schools of Theatre's Commission on Accreditation.

---

[1] There are six regional accreditation agencies, but two of them maintain separate divisions or commissions. Thus, in reality, there are eight commissions.

1. Accrediting Agency's Qualifications

MARJORIE WEBSTER JUNIOR COLLEGE, INC. v. MIDDLE STATES ASSOCIATION OF COLLEGES AND SECONDARY SCHOOLS, INC.

432 F.2d 650 (D.C. Cir. 1970), *cert. denied*, 400 U.S. 965 (1970)

BAZELON, CHIEF JUDGE:

Middle States Association of Colleges and Secondary Schools, Inc., is a voluntary nonprofit educational corporation, the successor to an unincorporated association of the same name established in 1887. Its general purposes are to aid and encourage the development of quality in secondary schools and institutions of higher education located within its geographical domain (New York, New Jersey, Pennsylvania, Delaware, Maryland, and the District of Columbia) or outside of the continental United States. Chief among its activities is that of accrediting member institutions and applicants for membership. Marjorie Webster Junior College, Inc., is a proprietary junior college for women located in the District of Columbia. In 1966, it applied to Middle States for accreditation. Relying upon a policy statement of the Federation of Regional Accrediting Commissions of Higher Education, and upon its own past practice, Middle States refused to consider Marjorie Webster for accreditation because the latter was not "a nonprofit organization with a governing board representing the public interest." Following this refusal, Marjorie Webster brought suit to compel its consideration for accreditation without regard to its proprietary character. The District Court found Middle States' refusal to consider proprietary institutions of higher education for accreditation a violation of § 3 of the Sherman Act and of the developing common law regarding exclusion from membership in private associations; in addition, it found that Middle States' activities in the field of accreditation were sufficiently under the aegis of the Federal Government as to make applicable the limitations of the Due Process Clause; and that to deny accreditation to all proprietary institutions solely by reason of their proprietary character was arbitrary and unreasonable, in violation of the Fifth Amendment. Concluding, finally, that continued denial of consideration for accreditation would result in irreparable injury to Marjorie Webster, the District Court enjoined Middle States from denying Marjorie Webster accreditation solely because of its proprietary character, and ordered it to accredit Marjorie Webster if it should otherwise qualify for accreditation under Middle States' standard. On the application of Middle States, we stayed the District Court's order pending our determination of this appeal. For the reasons hereafter set forth, we conclude that the Sherman Act is not applicable to Middle States' conduct as indicated by the present record; that the circumstances are not such as to warrant judicial interference with the accreditation and membership policies of Middle States; and that, assuming the Due Process Clause to be applicable, Marjorie Webster has not sustained its burden of showing the irrationality of the policy in question as applied to bar consideration of Marjorie Webster for accreditation. Accordingly, we reverse the judgment of the District Court.

I.

Appellee strongly urges, and the court below concluded, that once it be determined that appellee is engaging in "trade," restraint of that "trade" by appellant's conduct is subject to the limitations of the Sherman Act. If this were the ordinary case of a trade association alleged to have transgressed the bounds of reasonable regulation designed to mitigate the evils afflicting a particular industry, this reasoning might be conclusive. But in our view, the character of the defendant association, and the nature of the activities that it regulates, require a finer analysis.

Despite the broad wording of the Sherman Act, it has long been settled that not every form of combination or conspiracy that restrains trade falls within its ambit. For the language of the Act, although broad, is also vague; and in consequence of that vagueness, "perhaps not uncalculated, the courts have been left to give content to the statute, and in the performance of that function it is appropriate that courts should interpret its word in light of its legislative history and of the particular evils at which the legislation was aimed." The Act was a product of the era of "trusts" and of "combinations" of businesses and of capital organized and directed to control of the market by suppression of competition in the marketing of goods and services, the monopolistic tendency of which had become a matter of public concern.

. . . .

That appellant's objectives, both in its formation and in the development and application of the restriction here at issue, are not commercial is not in dispute. Of course, when a given activity falls within the scope of the Sherman Act, a lack of predatory intent is not conclusive on the question of its legality. But the proscriptions of the Sherman Act were "tailored * * * for the business world," not for the noncommercial aspects of the liberal arts and the learned professions. In these contexts, an incidental restraint of trade, absent an intent or purpose to affect the commercial aspects of the profession, is not sufficient to warrant application of the antitrust laws.

We are fortified in this conclusion by the historic reluctance of Congress to exercise control in educational matters.[1] We need not suggest that this reluctance is of such depth as to immunize any conceivable activity of appellant from regulation under the antitrust laws. It is possible to conceive of restrictions on eligibility for accreditation that could have little other than a commercial motive; and as such, antitrust policy would presumably be applicable. Absent such motives, however, the process of accreditation is an activity distinct from the sphere of commerce; it goes rather to the heart of the concept of education itself. We do not believe that Congress intended this concept to be molded by the policies underlying the Sherman Act.

---

[1] E.g., 20 U.S.C. § 401 (1964): "The Congress reaffirms the principle and declares that the States and local communities have and must retain control over and primary responsibility for public education." § 402: "Nothing contained in this Act shall be construed to authorize any department, agency, officer, or employee of the United States to exercise any direction, supervision, or control over the curriculum, program of instruction, administration, or personnel of any educational institution or school system."

II.

The increasing importance of private associations in the affairs of individuals and organizations has led to substantial expansion of judicial control over "The Internal Affairs of Associations not for Profit." Where membership in, or certification by, such an association is a virtual prerequisite to the practice of a given profession, courts have scrutinized the standards and procedures employed by the association notwithstanding their recognition of the fact that professional societies possess a specialized competence in evaluating the qualifications of an individual to engage in professional activities. The standards set must be reasonable, applied with an even hand, and not in conflict with the public policy of the jurisdiction. Even where less than complete exclusion from practice is involved, deprivation of substantial economic or professional advantages will often be sufficient to warrant judicial action.

The extent of judicial power to regulate the standards set by private professional associations, however, must be related to the necessity for intervention. Particularly when, as here, judicial action is predicated not upon a legislative text but upon the developing doctrines of the common law, general propositions must not be allowed to obscure the specific relevant facts of each individual case. In particular, the extent to which deference is due to the professional judgment of the association will vary both with the subject matter at issue[2] and with the degree of harm resulting from the association's action.

With these factors in mind, we turn to consider the harm appellee will suffer by virtue of the challenged exclusion. We note in this regard that denial of accreditation by Middle States is not tantamount to exclusion of appellee from operating successfully as a junior college. It has been, and without regard to accreditation by appellant will remain, accredited by the District of Columbia Board of Education, and licensed to award the Associate in Arts degree. The record indicates that appellee's listing in the major publications available for use by high school guidance counsellors (and often, by students and their families) does not depend upon its accreditation by appellant. Appellee's lack of accreditation does not appear to render it, or its students, ineligible to receive federal aid.[3] Appellee's students seeking to transfer to four-year colleges at the completion of their programs are not necessarily barred from obtaining credit for their studies because of the unaccredited status of the institution.[4] We recognize, as the trial court found, that lack of

---

[2] Less deference may be due professional judgment when the question is not one of substantive standards, but rather one concerning the fairness of the procedures by which the challenged determination was reached. In the present case, however, no such issue is raised.

[3] Eligibility for a number of federal funding programs that provide grants to institutions or their students does turn upon the institution's being accredited by a "nationally recognized accrediting agency" listed by the Commissioner of Education. However, as an alternative to such accreditation, an institution or its students will become eligible upon showing that its credits "are accepted on transfer by not less than three institutions which are so accredited, for credit on the same basis as if transferred from an institution so accredited." This is known as "three-letter certification," and appellee has such certification at the Office of Education. It appears that appellee is ineligible for federal funds, if at all, because the applicable statutes preclude grants and loans to proprietary liberal arts institutions or their students.

[4] It appears that some 34 educational institutions throughout the United States re-fused to give full

accreditation may be a not insignificant handicap to appellee both in the effect that such lack may have on students considering application for admission, and in the loss of the substantial benefits that the accreditation process itself has upon the institution under study. But appellee has operated successfully as a junior college since 1947. Although it suffered a decline in applications for admission in the years immediately preceding the instant suit, this decline was shared by the other women's institutions in the District of Columbia. In the last year for which figures were introduced, it received over 100 more applications than Mount Vernon Junior College, the institution receiving the second highest number. We do not believe, therefore, that the record supports the conclusion that appellee will be unable to operate successfully as a junior college unless it is considered for accreditation by appellant.

Accordingly, we believe that judicial review of appellant's standards should accord substantial deference to appellant's judgment regarding the ends that it serves and the means most appropriate to those ends. Accreditation, as carried out by appellant, is as involved with educational philosophy as with yardsticks to measure the "quality" of education provided. As found by the trial court,

> [Appellant] seeks to determine in broad qualitative terms whether an institution has clearly defined appropriate objectives, whether it has established conditions under which it can reasonably be expected to obtain them, and whether it appears to be obtaining them. Under this criteria [sic], Middle States, in its publication, The Nature of a Middle States Evaluation, notes that "Organization, administration, facilities, and resources are not important in themselves." Accreditation means that the institution has achieved quality within the context of its own aims and program- not that such institution is more qualified than any other accredited or unaccredited institution.

Appellee does not challenge this view of the accreditation process as improper. And given this view, we cannot say that appellant's refusal to consider proprietary institutions is an unreasonable means of seeking to reach the ends sought. Of course no institution, no matter how well endowed, can afford to entirely ignore the balance sheet. But when the institution itself is responsible in large part for setting the measure by which it is to be judged, we do not think it has been shown to be unreasonable for appellant to conclude that the desire for personal profit might influence educational goals in subtle ways difficult to detect but destructive, in the long run, of that atmosphere of academic inquiry which, perhaps even more than any quantitative measure of educational quality, appellant's standards for accreditation seek to foster. Likewise, we may recognize that, even in nonprofit institutions, the battle for academic freedom and control of educational policy is still sporadically waged; but this factor would seem to strengthen, rather than weaken, the reasonableness of appellant's judgment that motives of personal profit should not be allowed to influence the outcome. Finally, we need not say that appellant's views of the proper measure for accreditation of an educational institution are the only, the best, or even particularly well chosen ones. The core of appellant's argument is not

---

credit to appellee's transfer students in the period 1962–1969. Appellee was able to show only 11 such institutions which did so because of its lack of accreditation by appellant.

that proprietary institutions are unworthy of accreditation, but rather that they, like many trade and professional schools, should properly be measured by standards different from those used by appellant, and which appellant is possessed of no special competence or experience in using. In this regard appellee is unlike the individual denied membership in or certification by a professional society. Rarely, if ever, could it be said that such an individual could realistically be expected to combine with others excluded on the same grounds to form his own association. Appellee, however, is free to join with other proprietary institutions in setting up an association for the accreditation of institutions of such character; and such an association, if recognized, could obtain for its members all the benefits of accreditation by appellant save, perhaps, prestige. Appellee has made no attempt to show that any such course has ever been attempted. In these circumstances, we do not think that appellant's refusal to consider appellee for accreditation as a proprietary institution lacks sufficient basis in reason to warrant judicial intervention.

In reaching this conclusion, we need neither disregard not disbelieve the extensive testimony introduced by appellee below regarding the values and benefits, both for the educational process and for the country as a whole, that flow from proprietary educational institutions. We do not conclude, not does appellant even suggest, that competition from proprietary institutions is anything but wholesome for the nonprofit educational establishment. We merely find that, so far as can be discerned from the present record, appellant does not wield such monopoly power over the operation of educational institutions that its standards for accreditation may be subject to plenary judicial review; and that in light of the substantial latitude that must accordingly be allowed appellant in setting its criteria for accreditation, appellee's exclusion solely on the basis of its proprietary character is not beyond the bounds of appellant's allowable discretion.

III.

What has been said above should also dispose of so much of appellee's argument as is based upon the Due Process Clause. We may assume, without deciding, that either the nature of appellant's activities or the federal recognition which they are awarded renders them state action subject to the limitations of the Fifth Amendment. If so, however, the burden remains with appellee to show the unreasonableness of the restriction, not simply in the abstract but as applied specifically to it. We need not decide here the precise limits of those circumstances under which governmental action may restrict or injure the activities of proprietary educational institutions. For the reasons already discussed, we conclude that appellee has failed to show that the present restriction was without reasonable basis. Accordingly, it must be upheld.

Reversed.

NOTES

1. Middle States Association of Colleges and Secondary Schools, Inc. ("Middle States") denied Marjorie Webster accreditation because it had concerns with its institutional control as a proprietary organization. While that decision is a substantive one, an area where the court very reluctantly treads, accreditation agencies today approve many for-profit colleges and universities. In fact, since the 1970s, the number of for-profit, higher education institutions has grown approximately 10-fold — from 96 schools in the 1978–1979 academic year to 1,043 in the 2007–2008 academic year.

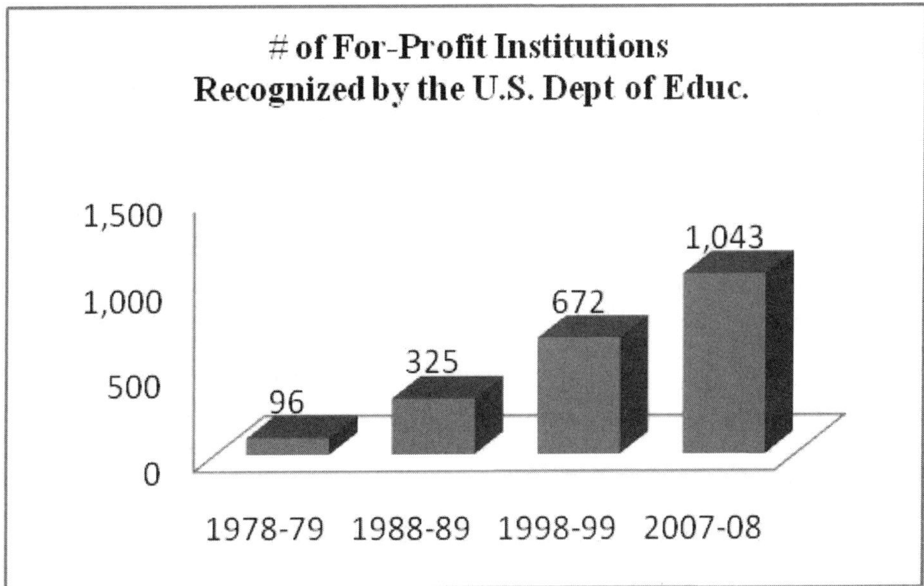

Source: Authors' presentation based off IPEDS data

2. What impact does a regional accreditation group such as Middle States have on student financial aid? How might that change a college's financial position?

FOUNDATION FOR INTERIOR DESIGN EDUCATIONAL RESEARCH v. SAVANNAH COLLEGE OF ART & DESIGN

244 F.3d 521 (6th Cir. 2001)

Merritt, Circuit Judge

I. Facts

Savannah College of Art & Design, a private, non-profit institution located in Savannah, Georgia, offers a variety of educational programs in the fields of art and design, including interior design. The College is accredited by the Commission on Colleges of the Southern Association of Colleges and Schools. The Foundation for Interior Design Education Research, also a non-profit organization, is the sole accrediting body for interior design education programs in the United States. The Foundation is organized under the laws of New York. It is located in Grand Rapids, Michigan.

In January 1995, the College applied to the Foundation for accreditation of the College's interior design program. In April 1995, the Foundation sent a group of three interior design practitioners/educators to the College to conduct an evaluation of the College's interior design program. The visiting team prepared a report that generally praised the College's program, but that recommended a denial of accreditation. The team based its recommendation on deficiencies it found in ten areas of "student achievement" at the College. The Foundation's accreditation committee reviewed both the team's report and comments from the College in response to the report. Three members of that committee responded to the report. One member agreed with the visiting team's recommendation; two others disagreed with the recommendation. One of the committee members who disagreed with the visiting team found that "the report is written in such a manner that it sets the program up for denial."

The Foundation's board of trustees, the organ responsible for making accreditation decisions, reviewed the team report, the College's comments, and the comments of members of the accreditation committee. The board decided to deny the College's application for accreditation on August 22, 1995. The College appealed this decision to the Foundation's internal board of appeals. The Foundation's board of appeals determined that the visiting team's findings concerning the College's student achievement deficiencies were not sufficiently substantiated in the team report, and it decided that the board of trustees should reconsider the College's application. Upon reconsideration, the Foundation's board of trustees recommended that the Foundation conduct a second on-site evaluation of the College's interior design program.

The Foundation conducted a second on-site evaluation of the College in December 1996. The second team of visitors to the College did not include any members of the first visiting team, and it did not read the first team's report before visiting the College. The second team identified deficiencies in twenty areas of "student achievement" at the College, and it recommended that the Foundation reject the College's application for accreditation of its interior design program. The accreditation committee then reviewed a combination of the reports prepared by both visiting teams. Five members of the accreditation committee responded to the combined report; each agreed that the Foundation should deny the College's application. The Foundation's board of trustees denied the College's application once again, and it informed the College of this decision on August 25, 1997.

The College appealed the Foundation's second decision to deny accreditation to the Foundation's appeal panel, the successor organ to the board of appeals. At this time, the College also demanded that the Foundation provide the College with its accreditation re-ports dating from 1994 forward to enable the College to prove that it had been disparately treated. The Foundation refused this demand. The College then submitted to the appeal panel eleven of the Foundation's accreditation reports that it had obtained from other sources. On April 22, 1998, the appeal panel notified the College that, based on its finding that the board's decision was supported by substantial evidence, it had affirmed the board's decision to deny the College's application for accreditation. The appeal panel also found that the board's decision was not inconsistent with its previous accreditation decisions cited by the College because the other successful schools had not been as deficient as the College.

On at least three occasions during the pendency of its application for accreditation, the College suggested to the Foundation that it was considering taking legal action against the Foundation. In a letter to the Foundation concerning the Foundation's second on-site evaluation, sent on July 31, 1996, the College's attorney wrote: "While we prefer to resolve this matter privately and confidentially, should [the Foundation] decline to award earned accreditation, the College will consider all of its options, including the filing of a lawsuit. . . ." In another letter sent to the Foundation on September 16, 1996, in the midst of discussions about the second on-site visit, the College's attorney suggested that, if discussions broke off, "the College [would] explore the numerous options available." Finally, on February 9, 1998, less than two months before the College's second appeal of the Foundation's decision to deny it accreditation, the College's attorney informed the Foundation that, if the Foundation did not grant accreditation upon appeal, "the College will have no choice but to pursue its claims against [the Foundation], and expose its disparate practices to a public whose trust in [the Foundation's] ability to objectively evaluate applicant programs is clearly misplaced."

Anticipating legal action by the College, the Foundation filed a complaint on April 22, 1998, seeking a declaratory judgment that its decision to deny the College's accreditation application was lawful. This complaint was filed ten minutes after the Foundation transmitted to the College its decision to affirm its second denial of the College's application for accreditation. The College subsequently filed counterclaims against the Foundation alleging breach of contract, violation of common law due process, breach of fiduciary duty, antitrust violations, and fraud. On December 21, 1998, the district court granted the Foundation's motion for summary judgment on its declaratory judgment claim. On September 3, 1999, the district court granted the Foundation's motion to dismiss each of the College's counterclaims for failure to state a claim.

. . . .

III. The Foundation's accreditation decision

The College appeals the district court's decision granting the Foundation's motion for summary judgment on its claim for declaratory judgment. Michigan law controls the Foundation's claim. Unfortunately, there are no Michigan cases directly on point. There is, however, a body of jurisprudence concerning academic accreditation in decisions from other jurisdictions.

This jurisprudence derives from early common law relating to private, voluntary organizations. Despite the traditional reluctance of courts to review such membership decisions, the Seventh Circuit indicated as early as 1938 that it would interfere with an accrediting association's decision to rescind a school's accreditation if the decision was "arrived at arbitrarily and without sufficient evidence to support [it]." Falcone and Blende, two influential state court cases on physician licensing from the 1960's, articulated a similar rule for professional associations. These cases reasoned that, because the medical societies in question exercised a monopolistic power in areas of public concern, they were required to base their decisions on substantial evidence and were not allowed to act arbitrarily or unreasonably.

In a landmark case, the Court of Appeals for the District of Columbia refined and generalized the rule from Falcone and Blende, finding that, where membership in an organization is a significant requirement to practice in a given profession, courts will scrutinize the standards and procedures used by the organization to select its membership. Reviewing a decision by the Middle States Association of Colleges and Secondary Schools to deny accreditation to Marjorie Webster Junior College, however, the D.C. Circuit found that the denial did not greatly hinder the school's ability to continue to operate successfully and that it did not warrant heightened scrutiny. The court found that "judicial review of [Middle States]'s standards should accord substantial deference to [Middle State]'s judgment regarding the ends that it serves and the means most appropriate to those ends." In subsequent cases reviewing school accreditation decisions, courts have held that such decisions are accorded "great deference" and have "consistently limited their review . . . to whether the decisions were 'arbitrary and unreasonable' and whether they were supported by 'substantial evidence.' " *Wilfred Acad. of Hair & Beauty Culture*, 957 F.2d at 214 (citing *Medical Inst. of Minnesota*, 817 F.2d at 1314; *Marjorie Webster Junior Coll., Inc.*, 432 F.2d at 657; *Rockland Inst.*, 412 F.Supp. at 1016; *Parsons Coll.*, 271 F.Supp. at 73). Courts have refused to conduct de novo accreditation reviews, and they have refused to consider claims of disparate treatment of accreditation applicant.

In 1992, Congress provided that federal courts have exclusive jurisdiction over suits brought by schools challenging accreditation decisions made by certain organizations approved by the Secretary of Education. *This statute does not apply in this case because the Foundation was not at any relevant time approved by the Secretary of Education* [emphasis added by eds.]. In Chicago School, a case decided under this statute, the Seventh Circuit determined that the common law standard for reviewing accreditation decisions is essentially the same as the standard used to review decisions by administrative agencies — i.e., "whether the . . . decision was 'arbitrary, capricious, an abuse of discretion, . . .' or reached 'without observance of procedure required by law.' " *Chicago Sch. of Automatic Transmissions, Inc.*, 44 F.3d at 449–50 (quoting 5 U.S.C. § 706(2)(A), (D)).

The parties and the district court have taken notice of two cases, *Maitland v. Wayne State Univ. Med. Sch.* and *Dietz v. American Dental Ass'n*, that strongly suggest that Michigan courts would adopt the common law standard of review for school accreditation decisions discussed above. *Maitland* involved a suit by a medical student seeking to be reinstated in good standing at his school. The Michigan court reviewed the defendant's actions for arbitrariness, capriciousness, and denial of procedural due process-a standard very similar to the school accreditation cases. *Dietz* involved a challenge by an individual denied membership in a medical association. There, citing *Marjorie Webster*, the court found that it should not afford great deference to membership decisions by professional organizations that exercise monopoly power in their professions. The court found that, in such cases, "the association has a fiduciary duty to be substantively rational and procedurally fair." The *Dietz* court applied this standard and found that there were disputed issues of fact requiring discovery — e.g., whether or not the plaintiff had been given the standard amount of time to take an exam and whether or not the reviewing members of the association had made comments about the plaintiff's appearance. The court specifically found, however, that it would not review the plaintiff's qualifications for membership. *Id.* ("This court may only determine whether the procedure was fair and whether arbitrary factors were used to determine the result. If the result was not based on arbitrary factors, but on substantive factors within the [defendant's] competence, this court cannot substitute its judgment for theirs.").

The district court therefore applied the correct standard in reviewing the Foundation's accreditation decision. The College argues that, even under the deferential standard of review adopted by the district court, it is entitled to prevail because the Foundation's decision was arbitrary and/or discriminatory. In making this claim, the College relies on the comments made by members of the Foundation accreditation committee who disagreed with the first visiting team's report. Such comments, however, are reasonably understood as part of a procedurally fair deliberative process. The College also contends that the Foundation's decision to conduct a second on-site evaluation represents a significant deviation from the Foundation's own procedural rules and that it provides evidence of arbitrariness or discrimination. If the second visit was a deviation, however, it was one that provided the College additional procedural safeguards; it made the Foundation's accreditation decision-making process more fair, not less.

Finally, the College claims that the Foundation has awarded accreditation to a number of schools with qualifications similar to those of the College. According to the College, this is evidence that the Foundation treated the College disparately and/or that it discriminated against the College. Because the record does not provide any credible indication that the Foundation had acted in an arbitrary or unreasonable manner in denying the College's accreditation application, and because the record indicates that the Foundation's accreditation decision was based on substantial evidence, the district court was correct in deciding not to give consideration to the relative qualifications of other schools accredited by the Foundation. We find that the court did not err in granting the Foundation's motion for summary judgment on its declaratory judgment claim.

IV. The College's antitrust claims

The College also appeals the district court's dismissal of its federal and state antitrust claims. The district court found that the College did not properly allege that the Foundation has substantial market power in the relevant market. It also found that the College did not allege that the Foundation injured competition through its accreditation activities. The court determined that, even with the opportunity for additional discovery, the College would not be able to state a claim for antitrust violations. We review the district court's dismissal *de novo.*

The Sherman Act provides: "Every contract, combination in the form of trust or otherwise, or conspiracy, in restraint of trade or commerce among the several states . . . is hereby declared to be illegal." 15 U.S.C. § 1.[1] Despite the broad language of the statute, it has been held to prohibit only unreasonable restraints of commerce

[1] The same analysis applies to the College's federal and state antitrust claims.

or trade. "[A]greements or practices which because of their pernicious effect on competition and lack of any redeeming virtue are conclusively presumed to be unreasonable and therefore illegal without elaborate inquiry as to the precise harm they have caused or the business excuse for their use." Here, although the College alleged a group boycott by the Foundation and its members, the action giving rise to the College's complaint does not constitute a per se violation. As the district court noted, accreditation serves an important public purpose and can enhance competition. Because the Foundation's activity is not a per se antitrust violation, we analyze it according to a rule of reason, which requires the College to allege and to prove that the Foundation's action "may suppress or even destroy competition." The College must prove more than its own damages because the antitrust laws are designed for "the protection of competition, not competitors." "Plaintiffs must prove antitrust injury, which is to say injury of the type the antitrust laws were intended to prevent and that flows from that which makes defendants' acts unlawful."

The essential elements of a private antitrust claim must be alleged in more than vague and conclusory terms to prevent dismissal of the complaint on a defendant's 12(b)(6) motion. While the pleading standard under the federal rules is very liberal, "the price of entry, even to discovery, is for the plaintiff to allege a factual predicate concrete enough to warrant further proceedings, which may be costly and burdensome."

A. Trade or commerce

As a threshold question, the district court considered whether or not the Foundation's activities represent "trade or commerce," for the purpose of antitrust analysis. It noted that, in *Marjorie Webster*, discussed *supra*, the D.C. Circuit held that, unless an accreditation decision was based on commercial motives, "accreditation is an activity distinct from the sphere of commerce." After the Supreme Court's decision in *Goldfarb v. Virginia State Bar*, however, the status of this holding in *Marjorie Webster* is questionable. In *Goldfarb*, the Court dismissed the argument that there was an antitrust exception for the "learned professions." The Court read the scope of Section 1 of the Sherman Act very broadly and found that there is no public-service exemption from the antitrust laws. *Id.* The Foundation's accreditation decision may fall within the scope of commerce described in *Goldfarb*. In this case, however, the district court did not discuss *Goldfarb*, finding instead that the College successfully alleged that the Foundation had a commercial motive in reaching its accreditation decision. The parties do not challenge the court's determination, so we do not reach the question of whether or not the Foundation's accreditation decision is trade or commerce pursuant to the Sherman Act.

B. Market power

The College appeals the district court's decision that it did not sufficiently allege that the Foundation enjoys market power in the relevant market. Generally, a plaintiff must show that his defendant has market power in the relevant market to prove an antitrust injury. Furthermore, "[t]o establish a claim under section 1, the plaintiff must establish that [a] . . . combination or conspiracy produced adverse, anti-competitive effects within relevant product and geographic markets. . . ." The relevant market for this purpose "is composed of products that have reasonable interchangeability for the purposes for which they are produced. . . ."

The College alleged in its counterclaim complaint that the Foundation abused its market power in the "market for accredited interior design programs" by restricting output and suppressing competition. The district court rejected the College's market definition, finding that non-accredited programs for the study of interior design are interchangeable with accredited programs, and that the proper market definition includes all interior design programs. The district court then found that the College did not allege that the Foundation enjoyed substantial market power in the market of all interior design programs.

Market definition is a highly fact-based analysis that generally requires discovery. Here, however, definition of the relevant market requires relatively little factual analysis. Based on a review of the record, we find that the College competes with schools that have non-accredited interior design programs and with schools that have accredited programs. Thus, the relevant market in this case includes all interior design programs. We find that the College did not provide a sufficient factual predicate to support its allegations that the Foundation enjoys market power in the market of all interior design programs.

C. Injury

Alternatively, the College also appeals the district court's decision that, as a matter of law, the College did not suffer an antitrust injury. Professional associations are generally capable of violating antitrust laws and causing antitrust injuries. We have not found a case, however, in which a denial of school accreditation gave rise to a successful allegation of antitrust injury. At most, courts in other jurisdictions have found that a denial of school accreditation results in a loss of reputation or a drop in school enrollment, neither of which constitute antitrust injuries. [Three earlier cases illustrate this point.] *Massachusetts School of Law*, *Zavaletta*, and *Brandt* involved allegations of antitrust violations stemming from the denial of law school accreditation. The plaintiff in *Massachusetts School of Law*, for example, argued that the American Bar Association based its accreditation decisions on anticompetitive standards, including target faculty salaries and limitations on the transfer of credits from nonaccredited law schools. *Massachusetts School of Law* experienced a 40% drop in enrollment after being denied accreditation. The School claimed that the Association's anticompetitive conduct caused the school to suffer an antitrust injury because 1) its students were not allowed to sit for state bar exams; 2) the school suffered stigma due to the denial of accreditation; 3) the Association's standards increased the cost of faculty salaries, directly or indirectly, through marketplace inflation; and 4) the limitation on transferring credits constituted a boycott. Affirming a grant of summary judgment against the school, the *Massachusetts School of Law* court found 1) that stigma — i.e., loss of prestige-is not an antitrust injury; 2) that the decision of states bar associations not to admit students from nonaccredited schools was protected government action; 3) that the effect of accreditation standards on price was either nonexistent or indirect; and 4) that the school had not provided any evidence that it had been injured by the limitations on transfer credits. Here, the College has not alleged that the Foundation has conducted any activities more potentially damaging to competition than the activities of the defendants in *Massachusetts School of Law*, *Zavaletta*, and *Brandt*. Similarly, the College has not alleged that it suffered any greater, or any different, injury than the injuries suffered by the plaintiffs in those cases.

As a final matter, the College argues that an allegation of unlawful purpose can independently sustain a claim under Section 1 of the Sherman Act. The College relies on [three Sixth Circuit cases involving anti-trust claims]. These cases refer in passing to "the general rule that a civil violation can be established by proof of either an unlawful purpose or an anticompetitive effect." None of these cases, however, stand for the proposition that an antitrust plaintiff in a rule of reason case does not need to plead and to prove antitrust injury. Even if an allegation of unlawful purpose could sustain an antitrust claim, however, the College has made only speculative and conclusory allegations that the Foundation acted with an unlawful purpose. Because the College did not allege that the Foundation has market power in the relevant market, and because the College did not allege that it has suffered an antitrust injury, we find that the district court was correct to dismiss the College's antitrust claims.

V. The College's common law claims

Finally, the College argues that the district court erred in dismissing its common law claims for breach of contract, breach of fiduciary duty, violation of common law procedural and substantive due process, and fraud. We agree with the district court that these claims arise from the Foundation's decision to deny the College's accreditation application. We therefore review the Foundation's decision as an accreditation decision, not as a contract, fiduciary duty, fraud or other common law claim. As discussed *supra*, our review of the Foundation's accreditation decision is limited to alleged procedural violations; it does not extend to the substance of the accreditation decision. We have found *supra* that the Foundation did not act in an arbitrary or unreasonable manner in denying the College's accreditation application and that its decision was based on substantial evidence. The College cannot prevail on its common law claims as a matter of law. We find that the district court did not err in dismissing these claims.

VI. Conclusion

For the foregoing reasons, we affirm the district court's decision granting the Foundation's motion for summary judgment on its claim for declaratory judgment, and the court's decision granting the Foundation's motion to dismiss the College's counterclaims.

NOTES

1. Compare and contrast the causes of action asserted between *Marjorie Webster* and *Foundation for Interior Design Education Research.* What might account for the differences? How and why did the legal analyses, particularly in terms of due process claims, differ between the two cases? What are the general principles uncovered in the due process claims?

2. Colleges and universities that seek recourse from an adverse accreditation decision have attempted to assert a private right of action under the Higher Education Act (HEA). The courts uniformly concluded that the HEA does not create a private right of action because the construction of the statute does not benefit the college or university (but rather students) and works contrary to the legislative scheme. *See, e.g., Thomas M. Cooley Law Sch. v. Am. Bar Ass'n*, 459 F.3d 705 (6th Cir. 2006); *Hiwassee Coll., Inc. v. Southern Ass'n of Colls. and Schs.*, 531 F.3d 1333 (11th Cir. 2008).

When a federal statute does not expressly indicate whether a private right of action exists, the court attempts to decipher whether the statute contains implicit references to a private right of action. Most frequently, the courts refer to a four-part test, established in the U.S. Supreme Court decision of *Cort v. Ash*, 422 U.S. 66 (1975). The test asks: (1) Is the plaintiff part of the class who is intended to benefit from the statute's enactment? (2) Is there any indication of legislative intent, explicit or implicit, either to create such a remedy or to deny one? (3) Is it consistent with the underlying purposes of the legislative scheme to imply such a remedy for the plaintiff? (4) Is the cause of action one traditionally relegated to state law, in an area basically the concern of the States, so that it would be inappropriate to infer a cause of action based solely on federal law? *Id.* at 78. Subsequent Supreme Court decisions have brought the viability of this four-part standard into question and have even mentioned that stronger indicators, not just any indicators, of Congress's intent is needed to recognize a private right of action. *See, e.g., Karahalios v. Nat'l Federation of Fed. Employees*, 489 U.S. 527 (1989). Despite the volatility of the test, the appellate courts that have addressed whether the HEA intended a private right of action refer to the *Cort* four-part test and have concluded that Congress did not intend a private right of action.

3. The courts consistently declare that accreditation entities are not state actors. *See, e.g., McKeesport Hosp. v. Accreditation Council for Graduate Med. Educ.*, 24 F.3d 519, 524 (3d Cir. 1994) (accreditation body was not a state actor; state board did not delegate powers to accreditation group, as it retained authority over approving medical training facilities); *Chicago Sch. of Automatic Transmissions, Inc. v. Accreditation Alliance of Career Schls. and Colls.*, 44 F.3d 447 (7th Cir. 1994); *Peoria Sch. of Business, Inc. v. Accrediting Council for Continuing Educ. & Training*, 805 F. Supp. 579, 582 (N.D. Ill. 1992). As courts indicate, "[a] governmental body may rely on the decisions of a private association without turning that association into 'the government' itself." *Chicago Sch. of Automatic Transmissions, Inc.*, 44 F.3d at 449. Since accrediting agencies are not state actors, constitutional claims, particularly assertions that the accrediting body violated a school's constitutional due process rights, fail. *See Hiwassee Coll., Inc. v. Southern Ass'n of Colls. and Schs.*, 531 F.3d 1333, 1335 (11th Cir. 2008). While accreditation bodies are private, nonprofit organizations, several courts refer to these agencies as "quasi-governmental" entities because they often serve as the certifying entity, which determines a college or university's eligibility for federal financial assistance and state licensure of an educational institution. *See, e.g., Thomas M. Cooley Law Sch. v. Am. Bar Ass'n*, 459 F.3d 705 (6th Cir. 2006); *Marlboro Corp. v. Ass'n of Indep. Colls. & Schs.*, 556 F.2d 78, 79–80 (1st Cir. 1977).

4. The U.S. Department of Education provides limited regulatory oversight of the accreditation agencies that they recognize. In addition, accreditation agencies may seek associational membership with the Council for Higher Education Accreditation, a voluntary organization that represents the interests of accreditation agencies.

5. The purpose of this section is to address accreditation of academic units (e.g., academic programs and entire institutions) as a way to ensure institutional and academic program integrity; however, at times, the term "accreditation" also applies to accrediting operational units within an institution of higher education such as libraries and healthcare sites. For example, college medical health facilities may be accredited by one of the agencies for medical care such as the American Association for Ambulatory Health Care or the Joint Commission on the Accreditation of Healthcare Organizations. In addition, the college medical health unit might also be a member of the Association of Academic Health Centers.

6. In 2008, President George W. Bush signed into law the Higher Education Opportunity Act of 2008. It reauthorized and amended the Higher Education Act of 1965, which built upon prior amended language from earlier reauthorizations of the Act.[2] Today, the Higher Education Act, codified as 20 U.S.C. § 1099b(6), outlines in greater detail an accreditation agency's due process guidelines. For example, the language in 20 U.S.C. § 1099b(6)(C) indicates that an appeal process shall not consist of the original body that concluded the adverse decision (e.g., accreditation denial, withdrawal, suspension or termination) and the composition of the group is subject to a conflict of interest policy. Furthermore, the law provides additional avenues for institutions to appeal or gather more information after receiving an adverse accreditation decision based on the school's finances. 20 U.S.C. § 1099b(6)(E)–(G) (2009).

2. Scope of Accrediting Agency's Authority

The cases discussed above clearly articulate that the accreditation agency must follow its own policies. Based on this foundational principle, the court in *Auburn University v. Southern Association of Colleges and Schools, Inc.*, 489 F. Supp. 2d 1362, 1369 (N.D. Ga. 2002), observed that one accreditation agency, Southern Association of Colleges and Schools, exceeded its review to areas outside of the accreditation criteria. The focus of the dispute concerned conflict between the university administration and the Board of Trustees, and particularly one member of the Board. The court described the conflict as follows:

> This case arises amidst a tumultuous time in the life of this institution. Historical events that may have fueled some of the clamor included the dismissal of the University's President and athletic coaches, and the denial of tenure to a faculty member whose views were controversial. It proceeds in part upon charges that one of the Board of Trustees seeks to operate the school as his personal fiefdom and that other trustees have conflicts of interest in that their enterprises do business with the University.

---

[2] Note: The Higher Education Act of 1965 was reauthorized and amended in 1968, 1972, 1976, 1980, 1986, 1992, and 1998. The Higher Education Act expires in 2013. — Eds.

Id. at 1365.

While issues of institutional governance may arise in an accreditation review or a special accreditation investigation, the court in *Auburn* concluded that several areas of the SACS review, such as the Board's new policy on minimum standards for admission, retention, and graduation, fell in the purview of the Board's rights to institute university policies. *See id.* at 1378–79.

The *Auburn* case along with several other disputes between boards of colleges and universities and their respective accrediting agencies led to several public criticisms about the accreditation process. A report, A TEST OF LEADERSHIP: CHARTING THE FUTURE OF U.S. HIGHER EDUCATION (2006), which the then-U.S. Secretary of Education Margaret Spellings commissioned, recommended a re-examination of the accreditation process. It questioned the effectiveness of accreditation as a means to determine educational quality at the postsecondary level. That report was the final product of a bigger program entitled A NATIONAL DIALOGUE: THE SECRETARY OF EDUCATION'S COMMISSION ON THE FUTURE OF HIGHER EDUCATION, which also included criticisms on the role and process of accreditation.

ANNE D. NEAL, WHY ACCREDITATION DOESN'T WORK AND WHAT POLICYMAKERS CAN DO ABOUT IT: A POLICY PAPER FROM THE AMERICAN COUNCIL OF TRUSTEES AND ALUMNI (2007)*

Accreditation does nothing to ensure educational quality.

In passing the Higher Education Act, Congress linked accreditation and federal student aid to prevent students from squandering money on diploma mills. According to the Act, recognized accreditors serve as a "reliable authority" on the "quality of education or training offered." Accreditation was thought to be a good proxy for quality. But this assumption was wrong. Today, virtually all colleges and universities in the United States are accredited (sometimes by more than one accrediting body); yet, there are widespread concerns that college quality has been on a steady decline. According to the September 2006 report of the Secretary of Education's Commission on the Future of Higher Education: "Unacceptable numbers of college graduates enter the workforce without the skills employers say they need in an economy in which . . . knowledge matters more than ever." . . . .

Accreditation examines inputs and ignores the output that matters to parents and students: educational quality.

Parents, students, and citizens may assume that accreditation ensures good educational quality, but quality is not what the process measures. Accreditation only shows that the school is following what the accreditors think is the *proper formula* for a successful educational institution, not whether an institution is in fact successful at teaching students.

. . . Nothing in the accreditation process concretely measures student learning, instructional quality, or academic standards. Nothing measures whether students have made intellectual progress since high school or have attained a level of basic knowledge and competence that would be expected of college graduates. If the accrediting process were applied to automobile inspection, cars would "pass" as long as they had tires, doors, and an engine — without anyone ever turning the key to see if the car actually operated.. . . .

Accreditation undermines traditional strengths of American higher education: institutional autonomy and diversity.

. . . Accreditors' recipe for educational inputs oft en includes the idea that colleges should employ individuals who hold "appropriate degrees." The Southern Association, for example, states that "when determining acceptable qualifications of its faculty, an institution gives primary consideration to the highest earned degree in the discipline." The assumption is that a Ph.D. trumps all other qualifications. The difficulty with such a one-size-fits-all standard is that it rules out the employment of individuals who may be very knowledgeable in a field and perfectly capable of teaching, but who don't possess the preferred credential.

People can and do gain knowledge outside of graduate schools. Some best-selling historians would be wonderful history instructors but do not have advanced degrees. Many writers are good at teaching literature, regardless of their academic credentials. There are exemplary economists who never earned a Ph.D. in economics. Following accreditors' imperatives, schools are encouraged to rank the possession of certain credentials above other aspects of individual ability and achievement. Restricting hiring to individuals with these credentials may not lead to better teaching, but is virtually guaranteed to drive up costs.. . . .

Accreditation contributes to ever-mounting education costs.

. . . [A]ccreditation itself helps to inflate the cost of higher education. The regional accreditors charge schools for conducting campus visits and reviews of the self-study documents, and schools can incur expensive direct and in-kind expenditures. But that's not the only cost.

Abiding by accreditors' one-size-fits-all formulae also drives up costs. Having to meet a particular standard for library size, for example, may do nothing to help students learn, but diverts resources from other institutional needs that the school may regard as more pressing.. . . .

Accreditation creates an unaccountable, federally-mandated monopoly.

. . . Accreditors do not sell their services in competition with other firms. Instead, they operate as regional monopolies. As such, they have nearly unchecked power — often making the accreditation process a high-wire act for schools. Indeed, accreditors are "private" in name only since their power derives solely from their role as gatekeepers for the federal student loan program.

Accreditors also present colleges and universities with a labyrinth of standards. A school that needs or seeks multiple accreditor approvals may be faced with a medley of inconsistent and uncoordinated standards. The direct result — intended or not — is to make it more difficult and more costly for institutions to enter the higher education marketplace.. . . .

Accreditation is largely a secret process.

From the vantage point of parents, students and even policymakers, accreditation is largely a secret process. Accreditation associations do not publish their evaluations of colleges and universities. The associations do publish lists of their members and any sanctions that they have imposed on schools. But this is scant information.

Although for many prospective students, knowledge about the quality of an academic department could be very useful, accreditation offers no such guarantee. Accrediting associations do not publish any rankings of institutions, nor do they evaluate individual programs and departments. The New England Association asserts that, "Meeting the standards does not guarantee the quality of individual programs, courses, or graduates. . . ." That admission is extremely important.. . . .

Accreditation is a conflicted, closed, and clubby system

Federal accreditation creates serious conflicts of interest. When colleges and universities seek accreditation, they are being evaluated by an association of which they themselves are members. They pay annual dues and an accreditation fee to this association. The fact that accreditation is rarely denied or revoked may be explained, at least in part, by the reluctance of accreditors to cast off paying members.

The accreditation review process is also a closed, clubby system. The accreditation teams that visit and evaluate schools are generally composed of college and university personnel from other schools in the region, people whose own schools will be evaluated by a team that might include someone from the school under evaluation. It is not surprising that this system produces little valuable information because accreditation agencies do not see themselves in an adversarial relationship with their members.

NOTES

1. The American Council of Trustees and Alumni published its policy paper to outline reasons to either eliminate or modify the accreditation system. What are their interests and how might they differ from accreditation agencies?

2. How might the tension between an accreditation body and religious institution change the legal arguments of cases such as *Auburn* or *The Foundation for Interior Design Education Research*?

Barbara Brittingham, *An Uneasy Partnership Accreditation and the Federal Government*, CHANGE, Sept.–Oct. 2008, at 32*

Soon we will have an election, a new President, and a new Secretary of Education, and while we can hope for a more informed and nuanced understanding of higher education from a new administration than we have received from the current one, we also expect a continuation of the calls for accreditors to require increased attention to student achievement and success and greater transparency about results.

At the 35,000-foot level, these expectations are reasonable. However, things are more problematic on the ground. For the past two years, accreditation has been the focus of attention by the current Secretary of Education, Margaret Spellings, and others who believe that accreditors, in the words of Spellings' Commission on the Future of Higher Education, should "make performance outcomes, including completion rates and student learning, the core of their assessment," develop frameworks that allow "comparisons among institutions regarding learning outcomes and other performance measures," and make "the findings of final reviews easily accessible to the public." Those proposals and the attempt to enforce them through new regulations have been widely viewed as unacceptable by the higher education community.

Anticipating the new administration, now is the time to step back, take a deep breath, review some basic principles, and make recommendations for the future.

The basic argument here is as follows: Regional accreditation is fundamentally sound and should not be harmed by abrupt regulatory changes. At the same time, understanding why accreditation hasn't met this Secretary's expectations can be helpful, because accreditation must address increased expectations for transparency, including information about student learning. Further, the federal system of "recognizing" accreditors, while imperfect, serves the public purpose of assuring satisfactory educational quality for purposes of making federal financial aid available to students.

FIRST, DO NO HARM

Accreditation — imperfect as it is — serves a valuable function for both institutions and the public. Any change imposed through law or regulation should be weighed against the consequences of harming a fundamentally sound system.

Accreditation serves two functions: institutional quality improvement among its members (the "private" function) and quality assurance (the "public" function). While the quality-improvement role can be traced to accreditation's beginnings, the quality-assurance role has been explicit only since the 1950s, when the federal government began its system of recognizing accreditors as "reliable authorities concerning the quality of education or training offered by the institutions of higher education . . . they accredit" (http://www.ed.gov/admins/finaid/accred/index.html).

The role of accreditors as gatekeepers for federal funds has brought increasing expectations that accreditation serve the public interest by focusing more directly and with greater consequence on educational effectiveness as indicated by student learning and success. It is the quality-assurance function that is under question. But change should not come at the cost of harm to the quality-improvement function.

Moreover, the strength of American higher education is in the diversity of its institutions: large and small; public and private; comprehensive and single-purpose; local, national, and international; religious and secular; non-profit and for-profit; urban and rural; single-sex and coed; military and civilian; [Historically Black Colleges & Universities (HBCUs)], Hispanic-serving, and tribal colleges; selective and open-access; all online and all on the ground. American higher education is porous and forgiving, allowing for many second and third acts in American lives. It is market-sensitive, robust, and sufficiently differentiated to encompass world-class research universities and teaching-only institutions. The system supports both institutional competition and cooperation.

While accreditation is not responsible for this diversity, its peer-review system of self-regulation has provided the conditions under which it has flourished and allowed our country's collection of the best institutions in the world to soar. And while self-regulation is sensitive to differences among members, regulation seeks — and may demand — a consistency which threatens both the diversity and excellence of those institutions and the quality-improvement function of accreditation.

And as a quality-assurance system, accreditation is highly cost effective. Though not designed to hold down costs, by its nature as a system of self-regulation, accreditation relies on small staffs and large pools of active volunteers. In 2005, regional commissions accredited 3,000 institutions using 3,500 volunteers in a system overseen by 105 full-time staff. Quality-assurance systems in most other countries are more regulatory than in the United States and therefore more expensive. It is not unusual for a government-based quality-assurance system to have, on average, one employee for every two or three institutions overseen. The Quality Assurance Authority in the United Kingdom has 130 employees to oversee the quality of 165 institutions. Increasing the regulatory burden placed on accreditation may threaten the peer-review system, which will in turn drive up costs.

WHY HASN'T ACCREDITATION PRODUCED BETTER INFORMATION ON STUDENT LEARNING?

Nevertheless, the critique of accreditation persists and must be taken seriously. Since accreditors have been engaged with assessment of student learning for approximately two decades, why have they not produced "solid evidence, comparable across institutions, of how much students learn in colleges or whether they learn more at one college than another"?

We have had different goals for assessment. The expectation that accreditors should provide the public with information "comparable across institutions" on what students are learning is new. Accreditors' approach to assessment has hitherto been to support the quality-improvement function; by understanding student learning in light of program and institutional goals, the institution can judge its own effectiveness and have information useful for improvement. Regional accreditors are far more likely to use the word 'inquiry' than 'testing' when speaking of assessment. Inquiry engages the curiosity and scholarly skills of faculty and helps assessment be appropriate to the field of study and useful for improvement. The paths taken by inquiry diverge and don't necessarily lead to results that are comparable.

While "accountability" is mentioned by some regional accreditors in the context of assessment — knowing what one's students are learning, and judging their success, is a form of accountability — assessment for purposes of comparison has not been on the radar screen. For the goal of improvement, accreditation has had considerable success; for the goal of accountability, there has been measurably less. Commenting on the impressive number of sessions on assessment at the annual meeting of the Higher Learning Commission (of the North Central Association of Colleges and Schools), the commission's president, Steve Crow, noted that the glow of the "1,000 twinkling lights . . . does not add up to national accountability." Nor has that been the goal of assessment for accreditors.

Standardization threatens institutional diversity. Much of the Spellings' Commission's accountability agenda — for instance, measures of student achievement with comparable results, or the annotated student unit record system — are applicable to large state public systems of higher education (think of Texas, home of both Spellings and the chair of the Commission on the Future of Higher Education, Charles Miller).

However, accreditation serves independent institutions as well. And while three quarters of undergraduate students attend public institutions, half of regionally accredited institutions are independent institutions. Expanding the goals and methods of a state accountability system for public institutions to a national collection of independent and public institutions represents a serious misapplication of a solution to a problem.

The Secretary and her surrogates are quick to say they are not arguing that "one size fits all" for purposes of comparing student outcomes, though it does sometimes seem as though they believe that perhaps three sizes do. But as anyone involved in accreditation well knows, the position that institutions can handily be grouped by type to compare outcomes may be possible to take in a large state system but is impossible to sustain nationally, given the rich variety of American higher education.

Consider for example the New England Conservatory, MIT, the Rhode Island School of Design, Amherst College, Berklee College of Music, and the Maine Maritime Academy. Students choose these institutions with very different goals in mind. At the very highest level of abstraction, among undergraduate institutions there may be common learning goals, but students come to these institutions because of their distinctiveness, not their commonality or comparability. Students choosing the New England Conservatory do not have learning goals comparable to those of students at the Maine Maritime Academy or vice versa, nor should they.

Moreover, while nearly all of the discussion relevant here has been on undergraduate education, higher education is more complex than this focus implies. New England has 17 accredited and candidate institutions offering only graduate degrees, ranging from seminaries, law schools, and a medical school to institutions focused on the fine arts, psychology, psychoanalysis, music, intercultural service, oceanography, and landscape design — not to mention the U.S. Naval War College. Some but not all of these institutions could find peers whose learning outcomes could help them judge the success of their students' achievement. But for many the student bodies are so different and the set of peer institutions so small that comparisons made for purposes of public accountability would be meaningless or misleading — and potentially harmful. Should these institutions compare their student achievement with that of peer institutions? Yes. Are the comparisons robust enough to be used for public comparisons and accountability? No.

And many institutions are more complex than either these specialized ones. Could Boston University or the University of Connecticut pick a set of peer institutions against which to compare the performance of their students? Likely not a single set — more likely a dozen or more, depending on the programs picked for comparison. Identifying these comparison sets is more an art than a science, with enough complexity to warrant its own discussion.

Could a regional accrediting commission pick peer institutions for any of the above, as was suggested by the Secretary? Please, no. As H. L. Mencken said, "For every difficult problem, there is a solution that is simple, neat, and wrong."

Assessment is still in its (relatively) early days. The development of useful assessment in colleges and universities has, on the one hand, been impressive for an industry not known for swift change and, on the other, predictably uneven and not fully mature. There are beacons of good practice and institutions in which the assessment culture has taken firm root. And much has been learned about assessment's usefulness — for example, the powerful effect of faculty members' collectively considering the work of their students. But assessment robust enough to make comparative judgments about important learning outcomes across a diverse array of institutions? Not ready for prime time.

There is much interest among policy makers and higher-education leaders in the Collegiate Learning Assessment (CLA), which presents students with engaging tasks that measure higher-order thinking and offers institutions the ability to compare how much their students have learned with the gains of students at other similar institutions. We all stand to benefit from what institutions learn by using the CLA. While much effort has been put into this measure by its developers, we are now at the institutional R&D phase, as colleges and universities determine whether using it is practical (how *do* you get those seniors to take the exam seriously?), affordable (particularly for small institutions), and useful (is the feedback to institutions sufficient to tell where their students are particularly successful and where they struggle? Can the results be used for improvement?) There is promising work underway, notably the by the members of the Collegiate Learning Assessment (CLA) Consortium . . . for a discussion of this project, which is . . . described at http://www.cic.edu/projects_services/coops/cla.asp]. But the jury is still out.

Meanwhile, a host of local assessment methods are being developed and used, including electronic portfolios. Institutions have demonstrated the usefulness of such methods for their own purposes; whether or how the information they generate can serve the expectations for public accountability remains to be seen.

Big change takes time. We are in the midst of a sea change in how we think about undergraduate education, and assessment is part of this larger movement. The move from a primary focus on teaching, with responsibility for learning placed almost entirely on the student, to the assumption — right or wrong — that colleges should make public institutionally comparable information on how much their students have learned is a shift of tectonic proportions.

Regional accreditation has been deeply involved with assessment since the early 1990's. Accreditors have designed new and alternative accreditation processes that highlight the effectiveness of institutions in educating students: for example, the Quality Enhancement Plan by the Southern Association of Colleges and Schools (SACS), the Academic Quality Improvement Program (AQIP) process by North Central's Higher Learning Commission, and the capacity and effectiveness reviews by the Western Association of Schools and Colleges (WASC).

These processes differ to some degree, reflecting the higher education landscape in each region. The two-stage process developed by WASC . . . is responsive to the needs of large institutions, predominantly in the public sector — 68 percent of students in the WASC region attend institutions of 10.000 or more students (the comparable number in New England is 29 percent). In New England, where half of all undergraduates and 75 percent of all graduate students attend independent institutions, the word "mission" is used 100 times in the *Standards for Accreditation* (in the WASC standards, the comparable number is 41 times), and the focus of review is explicitly mission centered. Nevertheless, all regions have an intensified focus on student learning.

To support this increased emphasis on learning, institutions have added teaching and learning centers, enlarged and refocused institutional research offices, and supported a host of faculty-development activities. Accreditors have written and applied standards, trained volunteers, and made judgments. Foundations have funded a host of developmental projects. And associations have held conferences and workshops and published a rich array of resources.

On campus, the basic ideas of assessment have gained increasing acceptance and become the norm among most professional schools, supported and expected by specialized accreditors. In some instances, faculty have had sufficient experience with assessment for the "culture of evidence" to take hold and for the results to be used for improvement. At most institutions, for unaccredited programs and especially the humanities, the struggle is still apparent.

So there is progress, overall and at nearly every institution. But these are early days. No institution has yet been through these redesigned processes or refocused standards a second time. Accreditors do know that forcing a system that values public accountability *über alles*, and imposing it in ways not sensitive to differences in institutional mission using instruments that are not fit for the purpose, will result in unnecessary harm to many institutions, and may lead to perceived but not actual understanding of student achievement.

WHAT CHALLENGES DOES ACCREDITATION FACE FOR THE FUTURE?

Accreditation is a mature enterprise, still changing. Given the challenges ahead, the rate of change will need to accelerate. What are those challenges?

Maintaining a self-regulatory system in an era of increasing regulation. The principal challenge accreditation faces is being overtaken by federal regulation. The threat was previewed in the attempted re-writing of the regulations for recognition in 2007. The Department of Education's appetite for regulating how accreditors judge student success was ultimately unsatisfied, but the discussions revealed the scope of the intent, including requiring accreditors to set minimal levels for student achievement or ensure that levels set by institutions were satisfactory.

While that bullet was dodged, there is every reason to believe the push for increased regulation will continue over the next several years. The newly re-authorized HEA, or Higher Education Act, has approximately 100 *new* reporting and record-keeping requirements for colleges and universities. The collapse of Enron and the turmoil in the financial sector have created conditions for increased regulation. And as social scientist Dan Yankelovich has pointed out, in an era of mistrust, when many Americans feel their ability to assure a better future for their children is threatened, increased regulation of higher education is predictable. Judith Eaton, president of the Council for Higher Education Accreditation, has suggested that increased regulation could allow the federal government to make its own quality judgments if "higher education's otherwise compelling and forceful responses [do] not match the urgency of the accountability demands," and accreditors and higher education do not argue effectively for self-regulation.

The best defense against excessive regulation is a trustworthy system of self-regulation. Self-regulation works well with the involvement of creative, committed, and accomplished members of the academy. Accreditors must work with institutions, professional associations, and others in higher education to ensure the vitality of accreditation and communicate the value and effectiveness of accreditation.

Accreditors must also respond to the concerns of the public and policy makers. An assumption commonly made is that accreditors haven't stepped up to the accountability plate because they are membership organizations. There's some truth to this charge, but every federally recognized accreditor has public members — at least one of every seven commissioners — who reliably bring a public perspective to bear on accreditation decisions. Accreditation is stronger for their participation.

Building public trust by strengthening accreditation. To avoid having federal regulation turn accreditors into government contractors, the self-regulation system must address priorities related to the public interest: increasing transparency and providing more information about student achievement and success.

Transparency. Discussions of increased transparency on the part of accreditation predictably begin with calls for making team reports public. But while such reports are sometimes made public by state-supported and a few confident independent institutions, requiring that institutions do so would violate the safe space required for them to be candid in their own self-evaluation, a cornerstone of regional accreditation.

Indeed, what the public wants to know is not what's found in an eight-year-old team report. The New England Association of Schools and Colleges standard on public disclosure (http://cihe.neasc.org/standards_policies/standards/standard_ten/) was designed to specify the information prospective students and other stakeholders would find most useful so they could "make informed decisions about the institution." Last year's initiatives by the national associations for independent and public institutions — the National Association of Independent Colleges and Universities' (NAICU's) University and College Accountability Network (U-CAN) and the American Association of State Colleges and Universities (AASCU) and the National Association of State Universities and Land-Grant Colleges' (NASULGC's) Voluntary System of Accountability — focused on making much of the same information available to the public in common formats. [. . . see http://www.ucan-network.org/ and http://www.voluntarysystem.org/index.cfm.] These are useful beginnings, a foundation that can support expansion.

Going forward, accreditors can help the public understand the dimensions of educational quality and how to find the best match between their own priorities and suitable institutions.

Student Achievement and Success. While all of the regional accreditors have substantially increased their focus on assessment and student learning during the last decade, it has become clear that we need to do more. Last year, the New England Association's Commission on Institutions of Higher Education (CIHE) developed an initiative to make student achievement and success more explicit in the accreditation process. In part a response to the calls from the Spellings Commission to increase accreditation's emphasis on learning, the initiative was also the accreditor's way of signaling its expectation that institutions be more forthcoming about the way assessment results are reviewed internally and used for improvement.

Through this initiative the CIHE is also challenging institutions to identify and develop quantitative measures of student success keyed to the institution's mission. We know, for example, that the IPEDS retention and graduation rates are not satisfactory measures of success for many community colleges. The CIHE has challenged those institutions to specify which measures of retention and graduation are meaningful, given their student bodies: semester-to-semester retention rates for all students? Four- or five-year graduation rates? Rates of transfer to four-year institutions? For baccalaureate institutions, the measures of success may be the percent of graduates who get jobs in their field within six months, or the number who make their living in the arts, or the number who join the Peace Corps or Teach for America or who are accepted into medical schools or a designated list of graduate programs each year. Graduate institutions may track time-to-degree, placements in post-docs, fellowships, starting salaries, or the proportion of graduates entering public service. The challenge is to identify, define, measure, record, and evaluate student success based on measures important to the institution's mission.

Much remains to be done. In the coming years, look for accreditors to:

* encourage institutions to improve their assessment programs — and push them when necessary;
* provide a safe space for experimentation;
* devise ways for institutions to learn from each other;
* help policy-makers and the public understand that assessment at its current state of development is not the only way — and arguably not yet the most powerful way — to judge academic quality;
* make appropriate judgments and apply sanctions when institutions do not meet expectations that they have systematic and effective methods to understand what their students are learning; and
* develop the means to ensure that the public gets useful and appropriate information about student learning and student success.

Maintaining a system that relies on volunteers as the work gets harder. As institutions become more complex and quality-assurance expectations increase, the expectations on volunteers increase as well. Visiting teams must now deal with learning outcomes, distance education, and off-campus and overseas locations, as well as increased expectations for institutional effectiveness generally. Certainly academics typically find demanding work interesting, so there is reason for optimism, but increased demands also sharpen the importance of accreditors' selecting, training, and evaluating members of visiting teams.

While most of the discussion about assessment concerns the need for institutions to do more and better assessment, it is also necessary for accreditors to make judgments about that assessment. The challenge is not so much in offering observations for improvement as it is in drawing the line between what is and what is not satisfactory. When are the assessment methods not sufficiently robust? When are assessment results used insufficiently? And most difficult: When, given an institution's mission and student population, is student learning (or student success) too low to warrant accreditation's stamp of approval?

Accreditors will rightly resist bright-line indicators, given the vastly different missions and student populations of member institutions. But they must develop the capacity to make sharper, valid judgments on assessment. Happily, while this is a difficult problem, it is not a large one. If three to five percent of institutions at any given time are in serious financial difficulties, the likelihood is that a comparable or smaller percent of institutions would be found to have student achievement problems serious enough to warrant probation or termination. But we must face the challenges of identifying such instances and having the ability and the will to respond.

Increasing capacity without becoming bureaucratic. Regional accreditation is under-resourced, given the increased expectations, and the work outlined above will take increased capacity. Accreditors must ensure that the increases provide value to institutions and that in increasing capacity, accrediting organizations do not become bureaucratic.

FEDERAL RECOGNITION: A MIXED BLESSING FOR ALL

Accreditation and the federal government are joined through the Secretary's process of recognizing accreditors to serve as gatekeepers for federal financial aid. The use of accreditors for this purpose is not a perfect system. Indeed, the Association of College Trustees and Alumni (ACTA) has suggested that the link between accreditors and the federal government be severed, limiting government oversight of institutional eligibility for federal financial aid to the financial certification system now in place.

But while the system is a mixed blessing to institutions, accreditors, and the federal government, there are several advantages to this arrangement when it works well. First, the system achieves its intended purpose: Accreditation provides an oversight of educational quality sufficient for purposes of access to federal financial aid. Through a complex system developed over decades, accreditation articulates and applies standards of quality for institutions deserving the public trust. It is not a perfect system, but it is a very good one for this purpose.

Also, federal recognition imposes a reasonable consistency among accreditors that serves institutions and the public. Standards must address specified areas (e.g., curriculum, faculty, fiscal capacity), and certain processes are required (e.g., accreditors must review "substantive changes," such as the addition of branch campuses). Further, the recognition system serves as a buffer, keeping government at arm's length from colleges and universities.

The system of government recognition, focused on quality assurance, balanced against the natural tendency of accreditors as membership organizations to focus on quality improvement, has created a constructive ambiguity. Accreditation's special genius is that these two functions operate in balance; its challenge is that they also operate in tension.

Finally, properly done, recognition is a nudge for timely change. For nearly two decades, the recognition system has pushed accreditors in the area of student achievement, student outcomes, and student success. Done steadily but judiciously, this push is a plus.

However, the recognition system has disadvantages as well — for the government, accreditors, and institutions. The principal disadvantage for the government is that recognition of accreditation is the strongest federal link to the academic programs of colleges and universities. Thus, when the government wants higher-education institutions to be more accountable for student learning, regulating what accreditors are required to do is the available lever, though not always a satisfactory one.

Peter Ewell has identified a major cause of the tension between federal regulators and accreditors as the "the principal-agent problem." In this case the principal is the federal government and the agent is the accreditor, authorized to carry out a quality-assurance function on behalf of the principal. But because the agent — the accreditor — is close to the institutions whose quality it oversees, it is "captured" and imperfectly fulfills the expectations of the principal. And in fact, accreditors do not think of their primarily role as federal agents. Thus, the agendas of the principal and the actors are not entirely congruent, resulting in a heightened desire for control — regulation — on the part of the government-as-agent.

For *accreditors*, the principal disadvantage is that recognition overlays a regulatory system on top of a self-regulatory system. Regulation seeks consistency: self-regulation is sensitive to differences. Further, the regulations haven't changed since 1998, and the application of the same regulations two or three times has resulted in a drilling down to ever finer details of accreditation. The benefit of this heightened scrutiny on the minutiae of accreditation is not clear. More fundamentally, the recognition process, addressing as it does the quality-assurance function of accreditation, is blind to the improvement function, arguably accreditation's greatest strength. A more robust recognition function driven by federal interests has the potential of throwing accreditation out of balance.

Further, recognition as a regulatory system is not friendly to experimentation by accreditors with new ways of doing business; any change an accreditor considers potentially threatens its federal recognition. Ironically, [Accreditation Board for Engineering and Technology (ABET)], the engineering accreditor, voluntarily withdrew from the recognition system because it wanted to focus more directly on student learning outcomes and concluded it could not follow that path the way it wanted to while maintaining federal recognition.

For *institutions*, the recognition system is a mixed blessing as well. On the plus side, of course, is that through it their students have access to federal financial aid. But accreditation imposes elements of government regulation: new branch campuses must be overseen and the addition of higher degrees reviewed. Institutions will always argue for more autonomy, but the linked system of accreditation and federal recognition sometimes complicates the audience for that argument, as happened in the ultimately unsuccessful attempt of the Secretary to renegotiate the regulations for recognition last year.

Given all of the difficulties described above, should the link be severed? No. During 2005–2006, federal financial aid to college and university students exceeded $88 billion. The public deserves a system to ensure that students receiving this aid are attending institutions of satisfactory academic quality that have sufficient financial resources and administrative capacity to administer that aid. Currently, accreditation is that system. The major problem with breaking the federal link is that there is no reasonable proposal for an alternate system for assuring educational quality.

And so we are left with an imperfect accreditation system overseen by an imperfect federal recognition system, both seeking to increase transparency and provide the public with more information about student learning and success. What to do? We are reminded of Winston Churchill famous line: "No one pretends that democracy is perfect or all-wise. Indeed, it has been said that democracy is the worst form of government except all those other forms that have been tried from time to time," The same may be said of accreditation. And as with democracy, we must keep trying to perfect it.

NOTES

1. Although this article refers to the regulatory goals of a policymaker who is now a former U.S. Secretary of Education, the debate regarding assessment measures, comparing institutions, and public access still continues today.

2. Do you agree with Barbara Brittingham's arguments about the value of the accreditation system as it currently operates? The U.S. accreditation system largely relies on regional accreditors. Should the United States move to a national system of accreditation? Since the argument is about diversity among institution types, which are at least arguably differentiated by their mission statements, why is the accreditation based on region rather than institution type and their respective mission statements?

3. Given the role of accreditation and its process, should the federal government use accreditation to qualify an institution for purposes of eligibility to receive federal dollars such as federal financial aid? What other system might work? What advantages does the current U.S. system of accreditation offer that your identified alternatives do not?

4. Tom Loveless, a Senior Fellow at a non-profit public policy organization, The Brookings Institution, described the wide variation in educational expectations at the primary and secondary levels, stating:

> Unlike most countries, the United States does not have national education standards, no single set of expectations for what all American teachers should teach and all American students should learn. It never has. A question that the rest of the world considers foundational to its national school systems — deciding the content of the curriculum — sits in the hands of local authorities. That is because the United States has 50 state school systems. Heterogeneity extends to the deepest levels of schooling. Even students transferring from one teacher to another within the same school may, as a consequence, learn a different curriculum than their former classmates.

TOM LOVELESS, THE 2010 BROWN CENTER REPORT ON AMERICAN EDUCATION: HOW WELL ARE AMERICAN STUDENTS LEARNING? 20 (2011),* *available at* http://www.brookings.edu/~/media/Files/rc/reports/2011/0207_education_loveless/0207_education_loveless.pdf.

5. At the primary and secondary levels of education, educational leaders and policymakers have been in discussion to adopt common core standards by grade level and completion of schooling before postsecondary education. At present, the National Governors Association and the Council of Chief State School Officers are working together to roll out the "common core" standards. Should colleges and universities have a standard conception of what is a bachelor's, master's, and doctoral degree? Are these differences factors of wide gaps in expectations and instructional quality?

Clifford Adelman, Institution for Higher Education Policy, Learning Accountability from Bologna: A Higher Education Policy Primer 1–3, 6, 10–11, 14 (2008)*

. . . .

It's about accountability in the enterprise of higher education, a big abstraction that we think we know as well as we know the lifelines on the palms of our hands. It's simple, isn't it? Our colleges, community colleges, and universities are "accountable" to those who subsidize them or pay their tuition and fees if they make public their graduation rates, demographic mix, and job placement rates, and throw in a test or two to show that a random sample of their students know how to write or solve a problem. Everybody goes home assured that this is what higher education is about.

This document challenges that assumption, demonstrates what we can learn if we lift our eyes beyond our own borders, and, based on that learning, offers a very different set of prescriptions on accountability. It contends that none of the major pronouncements on accountability in U.S. higher education that we have heard in the recent past — from Secretary of Education Margaret Spellings' Commission on the Future of Higher Education to platitude pronouncements and wish lists for student learning from the higher education community — even begin to understand what accountability means. Even the "voluntary system of accountability" adopted by a large segment of higher education — which tells the public how many pieces of paper colleges and universities handed out (to whom and when), how much students liked different aspects of their experience at an institution, and how much scores on tests of something called "critical thinking" improved for a sample of students between entrance and senior year — is more show than substance.

All these pronouncements and efforts were genuine. All of them sought improvement — in something. But that "something" is not really accountability. At best, it's "accountability light." None of it says what credentials represent or what students must do to earn those credentials. There are no public reference points, and no public performance criteria. And students neither played a role in fashioning these efforts nor will be affected by them at all.

But imagine a system of higher education with 4,000 institutions and 16 million students that is changing all its rules, procedures, and standards so that —

- Everyone is singing in the same key, though not necessarily the same tune.
- Every degree is publicly defined so that everyone knows what it means in terms of the demonstration of knowledge; the application of knowledge; fluency in the use of information; breadth, depth, and effectiveness of communication; and degree of autonomy gained for subsequent learning.
- Students whose performance does not meet the public definition do not receive the degree.

- Everyone can recite the difference in performance standards for an associate's degree, a bachelor's degree, and a master's degree, and the public language of these standards clearly ratchets up the scope and performance bar at each level.
- Faculty in each discipline agree and publicly state the reference points of knowledge, skills, and competence that define the qualifications for a degree in their field at each level.
- Credits are based on a common standard of student workload, not faculty contact hours, and each course is assigned a level of challenge so that the combination of workload and level guarantees transfer of credits.
- Distinctive routes to degrees integrating associate's and bachelor's degrees, part-time status, and recognition of prior learning are set out in public maps to create alternative paths to participation and, thus, increased access rates.
- Every student who earns a degree receives, as a supplement to the diploma (and in addition to a transcript), an official documented summary of the setting, nature, purpose, and requirements of the degree and the major program — and a shorthand warrantee of what that student did to earn the degree.

That's *not* a description of the U.S. system of higher education, though the size of the system — 4,000 institutions and 16 million students — is comparable.

It *is* the description of the core features of the system of higher education under development for the past decade in 46 European countries, across 23 major languages; one that is standing 800-year-old traditions on their heads. It is producing the European Higher Education Area, and some of the core features have already been imitated in Latin America, Africa, and Australia. While it is still a work in progress and has some bugs to fix, it has sufficient momentum to become the dominant global model of higher education within two decades.

It is called the Bologna Process, and is the most far-reaching and ambitious reform of higher education ever undertaken, one in which student unions have actively participated.

This policy brief brings to its readers in the United States highlights of what European higher education authorities, academic leaders, faculty, and students have accomplished and learned in the course of their efforts, particularly in the challenging matters of student learning outcomes (set in what are called "qualification frameworks"); the relationship of these frameworks to credits and curriculum reform; and the reflection of all this in the documentation of student attainment called "diploma supplements." These highlights have been selected because they are extraordinarily relevant to accountability challenges that face U.S. higher education, and this document urges us to learn something from beyond our own borders that just might help us rethink our higher education enterprise. These highlights clearly indicate that accountability in higher education begins with the establishment of public definitions of degrees and criterion referenced statements of academic performance so that when an institution awards a credential it can assert, with confidence: 'This is what this degree represents, this is what the student did to earn the degree, and a warrantee has been issued on behalf of both institution and student.'

On the basis of what we can learn from the experience of our European colleagues, this policy brief makes some very concrete — and bold — reconstructive suggestions for change across the U.S. higher education system, all of them following a student-centered story line of accountability, including:

- Developing detailed and public degree qualification frameworks for state higher education systems and for all institutions in students' major fields;
- Revising the reference points and terms of our credit system; and
- Developing a distinctive version of a diploma supplement that summarizes individual student achievement.

These suggestions, derived from studying what the Bologna Process has wrought — for better or for less — are intended as "constructive irritants" to U.S. higher education. They clearly say that there is no free lunch, no easy way out. A college, community college, or university does not demonstrate its accountability by issuing more public statistics about how many of its entering students come back for a second year, or by giving a test on critical thinking to 100 student volunteers, or by refreshing its mission and goal statements. That is all easy avoidance behavior with no penetration of the organization. Students — our constituents — will not sense that anything has changed. If we want things to work better, then we have to work, and work hard. Most of the national higher education systems participating in the Bologna Process have been at it for a decade — with another decade to come. We think we solved it all in the two years since the Spellings Commission put the first draft of its report up. . . .

. . . .

What does each level of degree we award (associate's, bachelor's, master's, doctoral) mean?

What does it represent in terms of student learning? What does a degree in a particular field at each of those levels mean, and what does it represent in terms of student learning? These sound like common sense questions that have obvious and public answers. But obvious and public answers are not easily available, and that's what some of our recent arguments about accountability in the United States have been about. Furthermore, the U.S. arguments tend to stagnate on process issues, whereas, under Bologna, these questions are about content. The

Bologna Process has been very clear about the conceptual elements with which degrees should be described: learning outcomes, level of challenge, "competences," and student workload. Our first guidance for answering these questions can best be found in "qualification frameworks."

WHAT IS A QUALIFICATIONS FRAMEWORK?

A qualifications framework is a statement of learning outcomes and competencies a student must demonstrate in order for a degree at a specific level to be awarded. It is not a statement of objectives or goals: it is a warrantee. When an institution of higher education is governed by a qualifications framework, it must "demonstrate" that its *students* have "demonstrated." While a qualifications framework does not dictate *how* that demonstration takes place (the nature and form of assessments employed), it does provide learning outcome constructs within which the demonstration is conducted. This is a *form* of accountability worth our serious consideration.

A second key characteristic of a qualifications framework is that the description of learning outcomes for a degree clearly indicates how that degree differs from the degree level below it and the degree level above it. The language of the frameworks accomplishes this end by a *ratcheting up* of benchmarks. This "ratchet principle" pervades all of the content challenge and performance statements of Bologna — and penetrates the credit system as well. This principle is an *engine* of accountability worth our serious consideration.

Three levels and types of qualifications frameworks have been developed or are in the process of being developed under the Bologna Process: Transnational, National, and Disciplinary/Field.

"Tuning" is a methodology, including a consultation phase with recent graduates and employers, that produces reference points for faculty members who are writing criterion referenced statements of learning outcomes and competencies in the disciplines. It provides a common language for academic-subject-specific knowledge and for generic competencies or shared attributes. Tuning Educational Structures in Europe is a university-level project that was brought into the Bologna portfolio. As it relates to qualifications frameworks, it seeks to help institutions and faculty describe "degree programs at the level of subject areas."

Does that mean standardization of content, sequence, and delivery modes? Does it mean that the business program at the Warsaw School of Business will be a carbon copy of the business program at the University of Coimbra in Portugal? Hardly. Tuning goes to great lengths to balance academic autonomy with the tools of transparency and comparability. It's a delicate balancing act, but the participation evidence says they've done it, though more successfully in some disciplines than others. The official Tuning documents stress that criterion-referenced competency statements are not straightjackets. They provide a common language for expressing what a curriculum at a specific institution aims to do but do not prescribe the means of doing it. Thus, the Tuning notion is like convergence. Everybody winds up with the same music staffs, range of time signatures, tempo commands, and system of notation. All programs in the same discipline sing in the same key — engineering in A-minor, history in G, business in B-flat — but they don't necessarily sing the same tune.

For example, the Tuning group in business first engaged in a consultative survey involving previous graduates of business programs, business faculty, and employer representatives with considerable knowledge and experience in the various facets of business programs (finance, accounting, marketing, organizational behavior, etc.) The objectives of such a survey (carried out in each field involved in Tuning) include gleaning current perspectives on the diversity of practice and commonality of knowledge across borders and traditions, and seeking a simple and accessible language to create scaffolding on which the various degree programs can work in comfort and trust.

On the basis of this consultation, the Tuning group in business developed guidelines for statements of learning outcomes in core knowledge (e.g., operations management, marketing, accounting), in supporting knowledge (economics, statistics, law, and information technology [IT]), and in communication skills (language, presentation, and teamwork). The Tuning group in business did not specify outcomes statements (that is the responsibility of institutional faculty) but did recommend their distribution for the bachelor's degree: 50 percent in core knowledge, 10 percent in economics, and 5 percent each in quantitative methods, law, and IT. For the remaining 15 percent, the group recommended a choice (made locally) among a bachelor's thesis, an internship, or "activities documenting ability to solve problems across different business subject areas."

. . .

. . . Faculty obviously agree that it is possible to arrive at consensus for the *nature* and *form* of learning objectives in a field at different degree levels and at every institution that offers degrees in that field, without dictating the way to deliver a curriculum to match those objectives.

. . .

When U.S. colleges, community colleges, and universities describe what students must do to earn a degree in a specific field, they list courses (required and suggested), credits, and minimum grade point average, not learning outcomes. Sometimes, departments issue a statement of the purpose of the degree in terms of the careers to which it traditionally leads or careers in which its subject may be useful. Sometimes one finds flowery mission statements extolling the vision or heritage or human benefits of the field. But rarely is there an attempt to provide a statement of the summative knowledge, skills, and capacities expected of graduates — let alone criterion-referenced performance criteria. Students themselves thus have little idea of the meaning of either their learning or the credential they receive.

In the emerging Bologna-inspired world higher education order, other countries would be taking a great leap of faith by recognizing U.S. undergraduate degrees without operational outcomes statements in the disciplines. If other countries have to make that leap of faith, our own employers and governance authorities are attempting to leap tall buildings in a single bound. We can do a lot better in the service of accountability.

. . . .

NOTES

1. Under the "Bologna Process," the system also calculates college credits differently. The system "uses the *student* as the primary reference point — it asks how many hours the average student must spend to accomplish the various tasks in a course module and converts the total to credits." *Id.* at 16. By contrast, in the United States, colleges and universities base credit assignments "on faculty contact hours, with the assumption that for each faculty contact hour, the student engages in additional learning activities." *Id.*

2. As higher education enters into a more global environment, the international policy community becomes more keenly aware of postsecondary educational systems abroad. The Bologna Process is an accountability system adopted in over 40 countries around the world (though principally in Europe). *See id.* The Bologna Process establishes a more uniform set of qualifications for college degrees. Under Bologna, countries or educational systems define a qualifications framework, which outlines the overarching learning outcomes and competencies that a graduate must demonstrate for each respective degree level. This process is followed by a tuning approach for specific disciplines and fields of study.

While states and accrediting bodies push for more student assessment measures, under Bologna, the explicit degree construction around student achievement of outcomes and competencies is more evident in the degree requirements and course expectations. How would the Bologna Process roll out in the United States, where, under the Tenth Amendment, education is primarily under the control of the states? That is, how does a nationally decentralized educational system create policies that, in relative terms, standardize qualifications for college degrees? While a uniform set of measures offer a form of data comparisons among colleges and universities, which might serve well for accountability purposes, how might these mandated levels of uniformity alter the face of American higher education? What legal arguments might arise from the implementation of a national system such as the Bologna Process? What significance might the Bologna Process have as colleges and universities blur the lines on state and national borders?

3. Recall a question posed following the last article: should the United States adopt a uniform or national system to identify what is a bachelor's, master's, or doctoral degree? How would you respond now?

4. What are the pros and cons of the Bologna Process for educators, students, administrators, accreditation teams, and regulators? In other words, what are the logistical and criteria-based advantages and drawbacks to assessing student learning, evaluating instructor performance, and comparing institutional educational practices? Would this process help accreditation teams and regulators in terms of determining the adequacy of student learning? Under the Bologna Process, how can institutions still incorporate their respective mission and values, and yet, still maintain the standardization of the degree outcomes.

5. At present, state assessments of student learning vary widely, yet policymakers and policy research teams have offered few options to resolve this disparate outcome *unless* as a matter of policy heterogeneous outcomes are intended. *See* STACEY ZIS, MARIANNE BOEKE, & PETER EWELL. STATE POLICIES ON THE ASSESSMENT OF STUDENT LEARNING OUTCOMES: RESULTS OF A FIFTY-STATE INVENTORY (2010), *available at* http://www.nchems.org/pubs/detail.php?id=132. If so, what implications might there be as our society adopts a more global infrastructure, where the labor market is defined more at the international level rather than the national level?

Chapter XII

INTELLECTUAL PROPERTY AND COMMERCIALIZATION

Introduction

Consider the following excerpt:

> "Intellectual property" is a product of the human intellect — literary or artistic works, inventions, business methods, or industrial processes — distinct from personal property and real property. Intellectual property law is covered in the law of copyrights, patents, and trademarks. From the words of this definition alone, it can be argued quite easily that nearly every activity engaged by students, staff, and faculty at colleges and universities is in furtherance of the production or protection of "intellectual property."

Philip T.K. Daniel & Patrick Pauken, *Intellectual Property and Higher Education, in* CONTEMPORARY ISSUES IN HIGHER EDUCATION 495 (Richard Fossey, Kerry Melear & Joseph Beckham, eds., 2011).

As is evidenced by the above statement, intellectual property (IP) concerns are major issues at the college and university levels. Based on this broad definition of "intellectual property," can you think of any activity of students, staff, or faculty that has ties to intellectual property protection or production? A few common examples in the higher education setting include copyright protection for teaching aids, texts, and methods, patent ownership and allocation of profit for researchers and their respective universities and departments, and trademark licensing and protection of names, logos, symbols, and pictures associated with colleges, universities, students and faculty. *Id.* The following cases and remainder of this chapter provide further examples and a general understanding of these IP concerns and the complex litigation that often arises from them.

A. INTELLECTUAL PROPERTY ISSUES

1. Copyright Law

BASIC BOOKS v. KINKO'S GRAPHICS CORP.
758 F. Supp. 1522 (S.D.N.Y. 1991)

CONSTANCE BAKER MOTLEY, UNITED STATES DISTRICT JUDGE

Plaintiffs, all major publishing houses in New York City, brought this suit against Kinko's alleging copyright infringement pursuant to the Copyright Act of 1976. 17 U.S.C. § 101, *et seq.* More specifically, plaintiffs allege that Kinko's infringed their copyrights when Kinko's copied excerpts from books, whose rights are held by the plaintiffs, without permission and without payment of required fees and sold the copies for a profit. Plaintiffs request relief in the form of statutory damages, injunction, declaratory judgment and attorney's fees and costs.

Kinko's admits that it copied the excerpts in suit without permission, compiled them into course "packets," and sold them to college students. It defends on four grounds. First, Kinko's claims their use of the excerpts was a "fair use," specifically provided for in § 107 of the Copyright Act. Second, Kinko's alleges that plaintiffs misused their copyrights by trying to create an industry standard beyond that established by congressional mandate and which impermissibly precludes all use of plaintiffs' works without permission and royalty. Third, Kinko's claims that plaintiffs are estopped from complaining of the copying because they have known for a long time about Kinko's 20-year practice of selling course packets and did nothing about it and Kinko's detrimentally relied upon their silence. Fourth, Kinko's argues that, with respect to two of the alleged infringements, plaintiffs failed to record their copyrights before filing this complaint and, therefore, this court lacks jurisdiction with respect to those two excerpts.

This court finds and concludes that defendant did violate the Copyright Act, that plaintiffs did not misuse their copyrights nor are they estopped from asserting their rights under the copyrights. With regard to the copyrights that were not recorded before filing the complaint, this court finds them to be validly asserted. Finally, Kinko's has not convincingly shown that the excerpts it appropriated without seeking permission were a fair use of the works in question. This court hereby awards plaintiffs injunctive relief, as well as statutory damages in the amount of $510,000, attorney's fees and costs.

FINDINGS OF FACT

There are 12 instances of copyright infringement alleged in this case. The 12 excerpts, which vary in length from 14 to 110 pages, were copied from books previously published by the plaintiffs, compiled in five numbered packets ("anthologies") with excerpts from other books and distributed by Kinko's. Kinko's neither sought nor obtained permission to copy any of these works. There are two stores from which Kinko's sold the excerpts included in this suit: one at 24 E. 12th

Street (which services, among others, students at New York University and the New School for Social Research) and a second at 2872 Broadway (which services Columbia University students). Below is a list of the 5 packets, by number and title, and a list of the titles of the works copied. Next to the latter title is the total number of pages copied, the approximate percentage of the entire book that was copied and whether the work was in- or out- of print.

PACKET #1: "WORK AND COMMUNITY"

This packet included 388 pages of copied work taken from 25 books. This course was taught at the New School for Social Research by Professor Hoffman; 3 students were enrolled. This packet was sold for $24.00 . . . .

1. *Understanding Capitalism* 22 pp. [5%], in-print, by Samuel Bowles & Richard Edwards.

. . . .

2. *Community: A Critical Response* 23pp. [18–21%], out-of-print, by Joseph Gusfield.

. . . .

3. *Work and Community in the West* 34pp. [22–24%], out-of-print. An anthology with contributions from six authors, edited by Edward Shorter.

. . . .

4. *The Deindustrialization of America* 53pp. [16–20%], in-print, by Barry Bluestone & Bennett Harrison.

. . . .

5. *All Our Kin: Strategies for Survival in a Black Community* 14pp. [8–11%], in-print, by Carol Stack.

. . . .

6. *A Lesser Life* 37pp. [8–9%], in-print, by Sylvia Ann Hewlett.

. . . .

PACKET #7: "ART THERAPY WITH GROUPS"

This packet included 383 pages taken from 43 sources. The course was taught at New York University by Professor Haeseler; 10 students were enrolled. This packet sold for $20.07.

7. *Group Dynamics: The Psychology of Small Group Behavior* 40pp. [7–8%], in-print, by Marvin Shaw.

. . . .

8. *Art Psychotherapy* 20pp. [6%], in-print, by Harriet Wadeson.

. . . .

PACKET #34: untitled

This packet includes 324 pages taken from 23 sources. This course was taught at Columbia University by Professor Ichniowski. Thirty-three students were enrolled. This packet was sold for $21.50 . . . .

9. *Business Ethics* 22pp. [14%], in-print, by Norman Bowie.

. . . .

PACKET #36: "INTERNATIONAL AFFAIRS"

This packet included 292 pages taken from 22 sources. This course was taught at Columbia University by Professor Lissakers; 48 students were enrolled. The packet sold for $17.75 . . . .

10. *The Money Market* 100pp. [13–14%], in-print, by Marcia Stigum.

. . . .

11. *The Money Bazaars* 65pp. [17–18%], out-of-print, by Marvin Mayer.

. . . .

PACKET # 70: "U.S. SINCE 1945"

This packet included copies of 212 pages of materials taken from 7 sources. This course was taught by Professor Freeman at Columbia University. It enrolled 132 students. This packet was sold for $11.00 . . . .

12. *Lyndon Johnson and the American Dream* 110pp. [25–28%], in-print, out-of-stock, by Doris Kearns.

. . . .

Each packet has a cover page, printed with the Kinko's logo, "Kinko's Copies: Professor Publishing," the name of the course and professor, the designated packet number, and a price listing. There is a space on the price listing to designate the royalty charges included. Only one packet lists a charge for royalty fees. On the inside cover of three of the five packets is a sheet entitled "Education and Fair Use: The Federal Copyright Law." It lists the § 107 fair use factors and displays the Professor Publishing logo and course information. None of the excerpts carries a copyright creditline as required by copyright law.

It is undisputed that Kinko's markets and provides its copying services directly to university professors and students. At trial, Kinko's presented marketing brochures produced by the company which are distributed by their marketing representatives to university professors and used as the subject of follow-up visits. These brochures openly solicit from the professors lists of readings they plan to use in their courses. Kinko's then copies excerpts, some quite large, and sells them in bound form with excerpts copied from other books as well. Unaudited financial statements of Kinko's Graphics Corporation for the years 1988 and 1989 show revenue of $42 million and $54 million, respectively, and net profit of $200,000 and $3 million, respectively. Its assets totalled $12 million in 1988 and $15 million in

1989. Appropriately, plaintiffs refer to this bound packet as an "anthology." Plaintiffs derive a significant part of their income from textbook sales and permissions fees. Kinko's has conducted its Professor Publishing business at least since the mid-1980's.

DISCUSSION

I. FAIR USE.

Coined as an "equitable rule of reason," the fair use doctrine has existed for as long as the copyright law. It was codified in § 107 of the Copyright Act of 1976, Article 17 of the United States Code. The Section reads in its entirety:

> Notwithstanding the provisions of section 106, the fair use of a copyrighted work, including such use by reproduction in copies or phonorecords or by any other means specified by that section, *for purposes such as criticism, comment, news reporting, teaching (including multiple copies for classroom use), scholarship, or research*, is not an infringement of copyright. In determining whether the use made of a work in any particular case is a fair use the factors to be considered shall include:
>
> (1) the purpose and character of the use, including whether such use is of a commercial nature or is for *nonprofit* educational purposes;
>
> (2) the nature of the copyrighted work;
>
> (3) the amount and substantiality of the portion used in relation to the copyrighted work as a whole; and
>
> (4) the effect of the use upon the potential market for or value of the copyrighted work.

17 U.S.C. § 107 (1976) (emphasis added).

. . . .

Courts and commentators disagree on the interpretation and application of the four factors . . . . The search for a coherent, predictable interpretation applicable to all cases remains elusive. This is so particularly because any common law interpretation proceeds on a case-by-case basis. . . .

This case is distinctive in many respects from those which have come before it. It involves multiple copying. The copying was conducted by a commercial enterprise which claims an educational purpose for the materials. The copying was just that — copying — and did not "transform" the works in suit, that is, interpret them or add any value to the material copied, as would a biographer's or critic's use of a copyrighted quotation or excerpt. Because plaintiffs specifically allege violation of both, this court has the task of evaluating the copying under fair use doctrine and the "Agreement on Guidelines for Classroom Copying in Not-For-Profit Educational Institutions" ("Classroom Guidelines").

A. The 4 Factors of Fair Use.

1. Purpose and Character of the Use.

Section 107 specifically provides that under this factor we consider "whether [the] use is of a commercial nature or is for nonprofit educational purposes." The Supreme Court has held that "commercial use of copyrighted material is presumptively an unfair exploitation of the monopoly privilege that belongs to the owner of the copyright." *Sony Corp.* [*v. Universal City Studios, Inc.*, 464 U.S. 417, 451 (1984)]. Additionally, the Supreme Court has found that "the distinction between 'productive' and 'unproductive' uses may be helpful in calibrating the balance [of interests]." *Id.* at 455 n. 40. While both are significant considerations, neither of these is determinative.

Transformative use.

It has been argued that the essence of "character and purpose" is the transformative value, that is, productive use, of the secondary work compared to the original. District Court Judge Leval has noted that, "the use . . . must employ the quoted matter in a different manner or for a different purpose from the original. A quotation of copyrighted material that merely repackages or republishes the original is unlikely to pass the test." Leval, *Toward a Fair Use Standard*, 103 Harv. L. Rev. 1105, 1111 (1990).

Most contested instances of copyright infringement are those in which the infringer has copied small portions, quotations or excerpts of works and represents them in another form, for example, a biography, criticism, news article or other commentary. In this case, there was absolutely no literary effort made by Kinko's to expand upon or contextualize the materials copied. The excerpts in suit were merely copied, bound into a new form, and sold. The plaintiffs refer to this process as "anthologizing." The copying in suit had productive value only to the extent that it put an entire semester's resources in one bound volume for students. It required the judgment of the professors to compile it, though none of Kinko's.

Commercial use.

The use of the Kinko's packets, in the hands of the students, was no doubt educational. However, the use in the hands of Kinko's employees is commercial. Kinko's claims that its copying was educational and, therefore, qualifies as a fair use. Kinko's fails to persuade us of this distinction.

Kinko's has not disputed that it receives a profit component from the revenue it collects for its anthologies. The amount of that profit is unclear; however, we need only find that Kinko's had the intention of making profits. Its Professor Publishing promotional materials clearly indicate that Kinko's recognized and sought a segment of a profitable market, admitting that "tremendous sales and profit potential arise from this program."

. . . .

Kinko's offers a 10% discount if professors get in their orders early, emphasizes student savings, convenience, and service — all "at no cost to your department." Kinko's shows that it is keenly aware of students' and professors' preoccupation with educational costs and provides additional services to get their business: offering campus pick-up and delivery and free copyright permission assistance. The extent of its insistence that theirs are educational concerns and not profitmaking ones boggles the mind.

Kinko's has periodically asserted that it acted at the instruction of the educational institution, that is, as the agent of the colleges and is without responsibility. Yet, Kinko's promotional materials belie this contention particularly because Kinko's takes responsibility for obtaining copyright permission while touting the expertise of its copyright permissions staff . . . .

Kinko's is paid directly by students who come into its stores to purchase the packets. Professors do not pay a fee; in fact, Kinko's provides incentives to professors for choosing their copy center over others. . . .

. . . .

"The crux of the profit/nonprofit distinction is not whether the sole motive of the use is monetary gain but whether the user stands to profit from exploitation of the copyrighted material without paying the customary price." *Harper & Row [v. Nation Enterprises*, 471 U.S. 539, 562 (1985)]. This is precisely the concern here and why this factor weighs so strongly in favor of plaintiffs.

Courts' consideration of the profit factor usually arises because the alleged infringing work competes in the same market as the copyrighted work, thus making the "commerciality" more harmful to the copyright holder. In cases in which a defendant is claiming fair use for a criticism, commentary or other scholarly research, the courts are more likely to find fair use under this factor. In *New Era Publications v. Carol Publishing*, [904 F.2d 152, 156 (2d Cir. 1990)], the Second Circuit found fair use under the character and use factor since the publication in suit was not an economic exploitation of the original work but a legitimate critical biography. In that case, a critic and biographer of L. Ron Hubbard and the Church of Scientology defended his use of quotes from 48 of Hubbard's works.

A potentially widespread use which was notably non-commercial has been held to be a fair use. In *Sony Corp., supra*, television viewers taped plaintiffs' television programs on home video recorders, doing nothing to enhance the program — simply copying them in order to view them later. The Court decided this "time-shifting" was fair use and placed emphasis on the fact that the viewers were not selling their copies of these programs for profit.

2. The Nature of the Copyrighted Work.

The second factor concerns the nature of the copyrighted work. Courts generally hold that "the scope of fair use is greater with respect to factual than non-factual works." [citation omitted]. Factual works, such as biographies, reviews, criticism and commentary, are believed to have a greater public value and, therefore, uses of them may be better tolerated by the copyright law. Works containing information in the public interest may require less protection. Fictional works, on the other hand, are often based closely on the author's subjective impressions and, therefore, require more protection. These are general rules of thumb. The books infringed in suit were factual in nature. This factor weighs in favor of defendant.

3. The Amount and Substantiality of the Portion Used.

. . . This third factor considers not only the percentage of the original used but also the "substantiality" of that portion to the whole of the work; that is, courts must evaluate the qualitative aspects as well as the quantity of material copied. A short piece which is "the heart of" a work may not be fair use and a longer piece which is pedestrian in nature may be fair use. The balancing of the four factors must be complete, relying solely upon no one factor. The purpose of the use may be balanced against the amount and substantiality of the use. For example, "even substantial quotations might qualify as fair use in a review of a published work." *See Harper & Row*, 471 U.S. at 564–65.

Courts have found relatively small quantitative uses to be fair use. See, e.g., New Era Publications, 904 F.2d at 158 (court found as fair that defendant used a "minuscule" amount of 25 works: 5–6% of 12 works, 8% or more of 11 works "each of the 11 being only a few pages in length."); *Iowa State Univ. Research Found., Inc. v. Am. Broadcasting Cos., Inc.*, [621 F.2d 57, 61–62 (2d Cir. 1980)] (court found unfair copying of 8% of videotape never before broadcast); *Maxtone-Graham [v. Burtchaell*, 803 F.2d 1253, 1263 (2d Cir. 1986)] (inclusion of 4.3% of work was fair); *Salinger [v. Random House, Inc.*, 811 F.2d 90, 98–99 (2d Cir. 1987)] (finding this factor weighed "heavily" in favor of Salinger, the court found no fair use of quotation and paraphrasing totalling one-third of 17 letters, and 10% of 42 letters); *Harper & Row*, 471 U.S. at 564–65 (the 300 copyrighted words appropriated to the Times article were an insubstantial portion of the work but " 'essentially the heart of the book.' ").

Additionally, "reference to a work's availability is appropriate." [citation omitted]. Therefore, longer portions copied from an out-of-print book may be fair use because the book is no longer available. (This has been thought to be true because, presumably, there is little market effect produced by the copying. However, plaintiffs in this case convincingly argue that damage to out-of-print works may in fact be greater since permissions fees may be the only income for authors and copyright owners.).

This court finds and concludes that the portions copied were critical parts of the books copied, since that is the likely reason the college professors used them in their classes. While it may be impossible to determine . . . that the quoted material was "essentially the heart of" the copyrighted material, it may be inferred that they were important parts.

This factor, amount and substantiality of the portions appropriated, weighs against defendant. In this case, the passages copied ranged from 14 to 110 pages, representing 5.2% to 25.1% of the works. In one case Kinko's copied 110 pages of someone's work and sold it to 132 students. Even for an out-of-print book, this amount is grossly out of line with accepted fair use principles.

In almost every case, defendant copied at least an entire chapter of a plaintiff's book. This is substantial because they are obviously meant to stand alone, that is, as a complete representation of the concept explored in the chapter. This indicates that these excerpts are not material supplemental to the assigned course material but the assignment. Therefore, the excerpts, in addition to being quantitatively substantial, are qualitatively significant.

4. The Effect of the Use on Potential Markets for or Value of the Copyrighted Work.

The fourth factor, market effect, also fails the defendant. This factor has been held to be "undoubtedly the single most important element of fair use." *Harper & Row*, 471 U.S. at 566. "To negate fair use one need only show that if the challenged use 'should become widespread, it would adversely affect the *potential* market for the copyrighted work.' " *Id.* at 568 (quoting *Sony Corp.*, 464 U.S. at 451, emphasis added).

Kinko's confirms that it has 200 stores nationwide, servicing hundreds of colleges and universities which enroll thousands of students. The potential for widespread copyright infringement by defendant and other commercial copiers is great. In this case, Kinko's has admitted that its market for these anthologies or packets is college students. The packets were compiled as a result of orders placed by professors at Columbia University, New York University and the New School for Social Research as to what readings they needed to supply their courses. In this case, the competition for "student dollars" is easily won by Kinko's which produced 300 to 400-page packets including substantial portions of copyrighted books at a cost of $24 to the student. . . . While it is possible that reading the packets whets the appetite of students for more information from the authors, it is more likely that purchase of the packets obviates purchase of the full texts. This court has found that plaintiffs derive a significant part of their income from textbook sales and permissions. This court further finds that Kinko's copying unfavorably impacts upon plaintiffs' sales of their books and collections of permissions fees. This impact is more powerfully felt by authors and copyright owners of the out-of-print books, for whom permissions fees constitute a significant source of income. This factor weighs heavily against defendant.

5. Other Factors.

In this case an important additional factor is the fact that defendant has effectively created a new nationwide business allied to the publishing industry by usurping plaintiffs' copyrights and profits. This cannot be sustained by this court as its result is complete frustration of the intent of the copyright law which has been the protection of intellectual property and, more importantly, the encouragement of creative expression. Because of the vastness and transitory nature of its business (Kinko's has 200 stores nationwide which are typically located near colleges), it has become difficult for plaintiffs to challenge defendant.

Additionally, the Classroom Guidelines express a specific prohibition of anthologies. The fact that these excerpts were compiled and sold in anthologies weighs against defendant.

Kinko's claims that "the evidence shows that course packets are of tremendous importance to teaching and learning, and are the subject of widespread and extensive use in schools throughout the country" and that "an injunction against the educational photocopying at issue would pose a serious threat to teaching and the welfare of education." This appears to be a "fair use by reason of necessity" argument. Kinko's has failed to prove this central contention which is that enjoining them from pirating plaintiffs' copyrights would halt the educational process.

Kinko's did not produce any professor to testify that he or she uses course packets and would be disabled from teaching effectively if Kinko's could not copy without paying permissions fees. Defendant did produce a witness, Dr. Bruce Johnson, who testified to the results of a survey he conducted which showed the widespread use of course packets by college professors and the reasons for this use. Notwithstanding professors' complaints of costly original materials, rapid change in course subject matter, and inadequate current offerings — which are all good reasons for desiring anthologies — defendant's witnesses did not produce evidence which would explain why they could not seek and pay for permission to create these anthologies. Dr. Johnson's survey fails to do so. This argument also fails.

B. The Classroom Guidelines.

The Classroom Guidelines, entitled the "Agreement on Guidelines for Classroom Copying in Not-For-Profit Educational Institutions," are a part of the legislative history of the Copyright Act of 1976. These Guidelines were the result of negotiation and agreement among the Ad Hoc Committee of Educational Institutions and Organizations on Copyright Law Revision, the Authors League of America, Inc., and the Association of American Publishers. . . . The legislative history acknowledges "the long controversy over the related problems of fair use and the reproduction (mostly by photocopying) of copyrighted material for educational and scholarly purposes." This indicates that Congress saw the maelstrom beginning to churn and sought to clarify, through broad mandate, its intentions.

For a proper analysis, there must be initial consideration given to the issue of what comprises educational copying and whether Kinko's status as a for-profit corporation, and its profitmaking intent, renders it outside of a Guidelines review. We believe that it does.

Kinko's contends that it serves an important function in the educational process — providing prompt, cost-effective service to educational institutions. If they did not provide this service to colleges and universities, they claim, these institutions and their students would suffer educationally and financially. However, Kinko's is *in the business* of providing copying services for whomever is willing to pay for them and, as evidenced in this case, students of colleges and universities are willing to pay for them.

. . . .

This court finds and concludes that even if Kinko's copying warranted review under the Classroom Guidelines, it is excessive and in violation of the Guidelines requirements.

. . . .

II. COPYRIGHT MISUSE AND UNCLEAN HANDS.

Kinko's alleges that the plaintiff publishers have collectively attempted to "impede and prohibit educational copying for classroom use as carried out by Kinko's on behalf of professors" and have "combined with each other to promulgate as a purported 'industry standard' with respect to photocopying a version of 'fair use' that is inimical to Section 107 of the Copyright Act as enacted by Congress." The defense of copyright misuse through violation of the antitrust laws has generally been held not to exist.

. . . .

Kinko's asserts that plaintiffs have misused their copyrights by impermissibly "broaden[ing] or extend[ing] the monopoly of [their] copyright in an effort to restrain competition." However, the facts of this case do not support a legal finding of copyright abuse. They show no agreement among plaintiffs to advocate any industry standard in excess of fair use. Plaintiffs' efforts to restrain competition by Kinko's is simultaneously an effort to stop Kinko's from infringing their copyrights. Plaintiffs have acted reasonably in so doing, not collusively for some illegal, monopolistic purpose. Consequently, Kinko's contentions fail.

Defendant posits other arguments in favor of copyright misuse. They contend that plaintiffs "arbitrarily and capriciously refused to grant permission to Kinko's" while granting it to others, plaintiffs understaffed their permissions departments in order to delay processing and, in some cases, failed to process them at all.

Kinko's first contention is barred since it failed to *request* permission for any of the excerpts in suit.

Kinko's fails to establish its second contention in two respects. Plaintiffs convincingly assert that they are in this business to make money and want to collect permissions fees. Therefore, it is unlikely that plaintiffs, in an attempt to spite Kinko's, are intentionally delaying their permissions process. Further, this court is unconvinced that a slow or backlogged permissions department constitutes a misuse of copyright. Kinko's alleges that, not only the timing, but the cost of obtaining these permissions presents obstacles for the copiers and universities. Kinko's failed to prove this as well.

Similarly, Kinko's fails in its unclean hands defense. Defendant unconvincingly reasserts its "anticompetitive scheme" argument to support this defense.

III. ESTOPPEL AND ACQUIESCENCE.

[To establish the estoppel defense] [p]laintiff must know of the defendant's infringing conduct; plaintiff must intend that his conduct be acted on or must act in a way that the party asserting the estoppel had a right to believe it was so intended;

defendant must be ignorant of the true facts; and defendant must rely on plaintiff's conduct to his detriment.

. . . .

Defendant cites the testimony of one of plaintiff's witnesses in which he admits to continuous knowledge of Kinko's anthologizing since 1984 and his "general" perception that Kinko's copying constituted infringement. Kinko's argues that "the continued and open expansion of Kinko's educational photocopying without protest by plaintiffs created Kinko's detrimental reliance." Kinko's convincingly asserts that it has expended much time and energy in its Professor Publishing business and "has continued to expand its educational photocopying . . . over the years in line with its [own] policies and procedures. . . ." However, this does not reach the level of detrimental reliance.

Plaintiffs argue they had no knowledge Kinko's was infringing, only that they were copying. Once they realized Kinko's was copying without permission, they complained and demanded fees. Plaintiffs urge that only through discovery did they realize the extent of Kinko's copying without permission. Defendant has not supplied any proof to the contrary. Additionally, Kinko's has not shown that plaintiffs *intended* their inaction to be interpreted as a "license" to infringe its works nor that any action of plaintiffs' gave Kinko's the *right* to believe it had such a license. Plaintiffs have denied any such intent.

Lastly, the extent of the harm experienced by Kinko's works no substantial prejudice against it. Its detriment is that it will have to request permission the next time it wishes to copy and publish its Professor Publishing anthologies.

. . . .

CONCLUSION

This court finds the excerpts copied by defendant Kinko's are not a fair use of plaintiffs' copyrights and, therefore, constitute infringement. Further, Kinko's defenses of copyright misuse, unclean hands, and estoppel fail. Plaintiff is granted statutory damages [of $510,000], injunctive relief and attorneys' fees and costs. . . .

PRINCETON UNIVERSITY PRESS v. MICHIGAN DOCUMENT SERVICES, INC.

99 F.3d 1381 (6th Cir. 1996)

DAVID A. NELSON, CIRCUIT JUDGE.

This is a copyright infringement case. The corporate defendant, Michigan Document Services, Inc., is a commercial copyshop that reproduced substantial segments of copyrighted works of scholarship, bound the copies into "coursepacks," and sold the coursepacks to students for use in fulfilling reading assignments given by professors at the University of Michigan. The copyshop acted without permission from the copyright holders, and the main question presented is whether the "fair use" doctrine codified at 17 U.S.C. § 107 obviated the need to obtain such permission.

Answering this question "no," and finding the infringement willful, the district court entered a summary judgment order in which the copyright holders were granted equitable relief and were awarded damages that may have been enhanced for willfulness. A three-judge panel of this court reversed the judgment on appeal, but a majority of the active judges of the court subsequently voted to rehear the case *en banc*. The appeal has now been argued before the full court.

We agree with the district court that the defendants' commercial exploitation of the copyrighted materials did not constitute fair use, and we shall affirm that branch of the district court's judgment. We believe that the district court erred in its finding of willfulness, however, and we shall vacate the damages award because of its possible linkage to that finding.

I

Thanks to relatively recent advances in technology, the coursepack — an artifact largely unknown to college students when the author of this opinion was an undergraduate — has become almost as ubiquitous at American colleges and universities as the conventional textbook. From the standpoint of the professor responsible for developing and teaching a particular course, the availability of coursepacks has an obvious advantage; by selecting readings from a variety of sources, the professor can create what amounts to an anthology perfectly tailored to the course the professor wants to present.

The physical production of coursepacks is typically handled by a commercial copyshop. The professor gives the copyshop the materials of which the coursepack is to be made up, and the copyshop does the rest. Adding a cover page and a table of contents, perhaps, the copyshop runs off as many sets as are needed, does the necessary binding, and sells the finished product to the professor's students.

Ann Arbor, the home of the University of Michigan, is also home to several copyshops. Among them is defendant Michigan Document Services (MDS), a corporation owned by defendant James Smith. We are told that MDS differs from most, if not all, of its competitors in at least one important way: it does not request permission from, nor does it pay agreed royalties to, copyright owners.

Mr. Smith has been something of a crusader against the system under which his competitors have been paying agreed royalties, or "permission fees" as they are known in the trade. The story begins in March of 1991, when Judge Constance Baker Motley, of the United States District Court for the Southern District of New York, decided the first reported case involving the copyright implications of educational coursepacks. See *Basic Books, Inc. v. Kinko's Graphics Corp.*, 758 F. Supp. 1522 (S.D.N.Y. 1991), holding that a Kinko's copyshop had violated the copyright statute by creating and selling coursepacks without permission from the publishing houses that held the copyrights. After *Kinko's*, we are told, many copyshops that had not previously requested permission from copyright holders began to obtain such permission. Mr. Smith chose not to do so. He consulted an attorney, and the attorney apparently advised him that while it was "risky" not to obtain permission, there were flaws in the *Kinko's* decision. Mr. Smith also undertook his own study of the fair use doctrine, reading what he could find on this subject in a law library. He ultimately concluded that the *Kinko's* case had been wrongly decided, and he publicized this conclusion through speeches, writings, and advertisements. His advertisements stressed that professors whose students purchased his coursepacks would not have to worry about delays attendant upon obtaining permission from publishers.

Not surprisingly, Mr. Smith attracted the attention of the publishing industry. Three publishers — Princeton University Press, MacMillan, Inc., and St. Martin's Press, Inc. — eventually brought the present suit against Mr. Smith and his corporation.

Each of the plaintiff publishers maintains a department that processes requests for permission to reproduce portions of copyrighted works. . . . MacMillan and St. Martin's, both of which are for-profit companies, claim that they generally respond within two weeks to requests for permission to make copies for classroom use. Princeton, a non-profit organization, claims to respond within two to four weeks. Mr. Smith has not put these claims to the test, and he has not paid permission fees.

The plaintiffs allege infringement of the copyrights on six different works that were excerpted without permission. The works in question, and the statistics on the magnitude of the excerpts, are as follows: Nancy J. Weiss, *Farewell to the Party of Lincoln: Black Politics in the Age of FDR* (95 pages copied, representing 30 percent of the entire book); Walter Lippmann, *Public Opinion* (45 pages copied, representing 18 percent of the whole); Robert E. Layne, *Political Ideology: Why the American Common Man Believes What He Does* (78 pages, 16 percent); Roger Brown, *Social Psychology* (52 pages, 8 percent); Milton Rokeach, *The Nature of Human Values* (77 pages, 18 percent); James S. Olson and Randy Roberts, *Where the Domino Fell, America and Vietnam*, 1945–1950 (17 pages, 5 percent). The extent of the copying is undisputed, and the questions presented by the case appear to be purely legal in nature.

II

The fair use doctrine, which creates an exception to the copyright monopoly, "permits [and requires] courts to avoid rigid application of the copyright statute when, on occasion, it would stifle the very creativity which that law is designed to foster." *Campbell v. Acuff-Rose Music, Inc.*, 510 U.S. 569 (1994), quoting *Stewart v. Abend*, 495 U.S. 207, 236 (1990). Initially developed by the courts, the doctrine was codified at 17 U.S.C. § 107 in 1976. Congress used the following formulation in Section 107:

> "The fair use of a copyrighted work . . . is not an infringement of copyright. In determining whether the use made of a work in any particular case is a fair use the factors to be considered shall include —
>
> (1) the purpose and character of the use, including whether such use is of a commercial nature or is for nonprofit educational purposes;
>
> (2) the nature of the copyrighted work;

(3) the amount and substantiality of the portion used in relation to the copyrighted work as a whole; and

(4) the effect of the use upon the potential market for or value of the copyrighted work. . . ."

. . . .

The four statutory factors may not have been created equal. In determining whether a use is "fair," the Supreme Court has said that the most important factor is the fourth, the one contained in 17 U.S.C. § 107(4). See *Harper & Row Publishers, Inc. v. Nation Enters.*, 471 U.S. 539, 566(1985), citing 3 M. Nimmer, *Copyright* § 13.05[A], at 13–76 (1984). . . . We take it that this factor, "the effect of the use upon the potential market for or value of the copyrighted work," is at least *primus inter pares*, figuratively speaking, and we shall turn to it first.

The burden of proof as to market effect rests with the copyright holder if the challenged use is of a "noncommercial" nature. The alleged infringer has the burden, on the other hand, if the challenged use is "commercial" in nature. *Sony Corp. v. Universal City Studios, Inc.*, 464 U.S. 417, 451 (1984). In the case at bar the defendants argue that the burden of proof rests with the publishers because the use being challenged is "noncommercial." We disagree.

It is true that the use to which the materials are put by the students who purchase the coursepacks is noncommercial in nature. But the use of the materials by the students is not the use that the publishers are challenging. What the publishers are challenging is the duplication of copyrighted materials for sale by a for-profit corporation that has decided to maximize its profits — and give itself a competitive edge over other copyshops — by declining to pay the royalties requested by the holders of the copyrights.

The defendants' use of excerpts from the books at issue here was no less commercial in character than was *The Nation* magazine's use of copyrighted material in *Harper & Row*, where publication of a short article containing excerpts from the still unpublished manuscript of a book by President Ford was held to be an unfair use. Like the students who purchased unauthorized coursepacks, the purchasers of *The Nation* did not put the contents of the magazine to commercial use — but that did not stop the Supreme Court from characterizing the defendant's use of the excerpts as "a publication [that] was commercial as opposed to nonprofit. . . ." And like the use that is being challenged in the case now before us, the use challenged in *Harper & Row* was "presumptively an unfair exploitation of the monopoly privilege that belongs to the owner of the copyright."

The strength of the *Sony* presumption may vary according to the context in which it arises, and the presumption disappears entirely where the challenged use is one that transforms the original work into a new artistic creation. Perhaps the presumption is weaker in the present case than it would be in other contexts. There *is* a presumption of unfairness here, nonetheless, and we are not persuaded that the defendants have rebutted it.

If we are wrong about the existence of the presumption — if the challenged use is not commercial, in other words, and if the plaintiff publishers have the burden of proving an adverse effect upon either the potential market for the copyrighted work or the potential value of the work — we believe that the publishers have carried the burden of proving a diminution in potential market value.

One test for determining market harm — a test endorsed by the Supreme Court in *Sony, Harper & Row*, and *Campbell* — is evocative of Kant's categorical imperative. "To negate fair use," the Supreme Court has said, "one need only show that *if the challenged use 'should become widespread, it would adversely affect the potential market* for the copyrighted work.' " *Harper & Row*, 471 U.S. at 568, quoting *Sony*, 464 U.S. at 451 (emphasis supplied in part). Under this test, we believe, it is reasonably clear that the plaintiff publishers have succeeded in negating fair use.

As noted above, most of the copyshops that compete with MDS in the sale of coursepacks pay permission fees for the privilege of duplicating and selling excerpts from copyrighted works. The three plaintiffs together have been collecting permission fees at a rate approaching $500,000 a year. If copyshops across the nation were to start doing what the defendants have been doing here, this revenue stream would shrivel and the potential value of the copyrighted works of scholarship published by the plaintiffs would be diminished accordingly.

The defendants contend that it is circular to assume that a copyright holder is entitled to permission fees and then to measure market loss by reference to the lost fees. They argue that market harm can only be measured by lost sales of books, not permission fees. But the circularity argument proves too much. Imagine that the defendants set up a printing press and made exact reproductions — asserting that such reproductions constituted "fair use" — of a book to which they did not hold the copyright. Under the defendants' logic it would be circular for the copyright holder to argue market harm because of lost copyright revenues, since this would assume that the copyright holder had a right to such revenues.

A "circularity" argument indistinguishable from that made by the defendants here was rejected by the Second Circuit in *American Geophysical*, 60 F.3d at 929–31 (Jon O. Newman, C.J.), where the photocopying of scientific articles for use by Texaco researchers was held to be an unfair use. It is true, the Second Circuit acknowledged, that "a copyright holder can *always* assert some degree of adverse effect on its potential licensing revenues as a consequence of [the defendant's use] . . . simply because the copyright holder has not been paid a fee to permit that particular use." But such an assertion will not carry much weight if the defendant has "filled a market niche that the [copyright owner] simply had no interest in occupying." Where, on the other hand, the copyright holder clearly does have an interest in exploiting a licensing market — and especially where the copyright holder has actually succeeded in doing so — "it is appropriate that potential licensing revenues for photocopying be considered in a fair use analysis." Only "traditional, reasonable, or likely to be developed markets" are to be considered in this connection, and even the availability of an existing system for collecting licensing fees will not be conclusive. But Congress has implicitly suggested that licensing fees should be recognized in appropriate cases as part of the potential market for or value of the copyrighted work, and it was primarily because of lost licensing revenue that the Second Circuit agreed with the finding of the district court in *American Geophysical* that "the publishers have demonstrated a substantial harm to the value of their copyrights through [Texaco's] copying." *Id.* at 931 (quoting the district court opinion (Pierre N. Leval, J.) reported at 802 F. Supp. 1, 21 (S.D.N.Y. 1992)).

The approach followed by Judges Newman and Leval in the *American Geophysical* litigation is fully consistent with the Supreme Court case law. In *Harper & Row*, where there is no indication in the opinion that the challenged use caused any diminution in sales of President Ford's memoirs, the Court found harm to the market for the licensing of excerpts. The Court's reasoning — which was obviously premised on the assumption that the copyright holder was entitled to licensing fees for use of its copyrighted materials — is no more circular than that employed here. And in *Campbell*, where the Court was unwilling to conclude that the plaintiff had lost licensing revenues under the fourth statutory factor, the Court reasoned that a market for critical parody was not one "that creators of original works would in general develop or license others to develop."

The potential uses of the copyrighted works at issue in the case before us clearly include the selling of permission to reproduce portions of the works for inclusion in coursepacks — and the likelihood that publishers actually will license such reproduction is a demonstrated fact. A licensing market already exists here . . . . Thus there is no circularity in saying, as we do say, that the potential for destruction of this market by widespread circumvention of the plaintiffs' permission fee system is enough, under the *Harper & Row test*, "to negate fair use."

Our final point with regard to the fourth statutory factor concerns the affidavits of the three professors who assigned one or more of the copyrighted works to be read by their students. The defendants make much of the proposition that these professors only assigned excerpts when they would not have required their students to purchase the entire work. But what seems significant to us is that none of these affidavits shows that the professor executing the affidavit would have refrained from assigning the copyrighted work if the position taken by the copyright holder had been sustained beforehand.

It is true that Professor Victor Lieberman, who assigned the excerpt from the Olson and Roberts book on America and Vietnam, raises questions about the workability of the permission systems of "many publishers." In 1991, Professor Lieberman avers, a Kinko's copyshop to which he had given materials for inclusion in a coursepack experienced serious delays in obtaining permissions from unnamed publishers. Professor Lieberman does not say that timely permission could not have been obtained from the publisher of the Olson and Roberts book, however, and he does not say that he would have refrained from assigning the work if the copyshop had been required to pay a permission fee for it.

It is also true that the publisher of one of the copyrighted works in question here (*Public Opinion*, by Walter Lippmann) would have turned down a request for permission to copy the 45-page excerpt included in a coursepack prepared to the specifications of Professor Donald Kinder. The excerpt was so large that the publisher would have preferred that students buy the book itself, and the work was available in an inexpensive paperback edition. But Professor Kinder does not say that he would have refrained from assigning the excerpt from the Lippmann book if it could not have been included in the coursepack. Neither does he say that he would have refrained from assigning any of the other works mentioned in his affidavit had he known that the defendants would be required to pay permission fees for them.

The third professor, Michael Dawson, assigned a 95-page excerpt from the book on black politics by Nancy Weiss. Professor Dawson does not say that a license was not available from the publisher of the Weiss book, and he does not say that the license fee would have deterred him from assigning the book.

III

In the context of nontransformative uses, at least, and except insofar as they touch on the fourth factor, the other statutory factors seem considerably less important. We shall deal with them relatively briefly.

A

As to "the purpose and character of the use, including whether such use is of a commercial nature or is for nonprofit educational purposes," 17 U.S.C. § 107(1), we have already explained our reasons for concluding that the challenged use is of a commercial nature.

. . . .

B

The second statutory factor, "the nature of the copyrighted work," is not in dispute here. The defendants acknowledge that the excerpts copied for the coursepacks contained creative material, or "expression;" it was certainly not telephone book listings that the defendants were reproducing. This factor too cuts against a finding of fair use.

C

The third statutory factor requires us to assess "the amount and substantiality of the portion used in relation to the copyrighted work as a whole." . . .

The amounts used in the case at bar — 8,000 words in the shortest excerpt — far exceed the 1,000-word safe harbor that we shall discuss in the next part of this opinion. The defendants were using as much as 30 percent of one copyrighted work, and in no case did they use less than 5 percent of the copyrighted work as a whole. These percentages are not insubstantial. And to the extent that the third factor requires some type of assessment of the "value" of the excerpted material in relation to the entire work, the fact that the professors thought the excerpts sufficiently important to make them required reading strikes us as fairly convincing "evidence of the qualitative value of the copied material." *Harper & Row*, 471 U.S. at 565. We have no reason to suppose that in choosing the excerpts to be copied, the professors passed over material that was more representative of the major ideas of the work as a whole in preference to material that was less representative.

The third factor may have more significance for the 95-page excerpt from the black politics book than for the 17-page excerpt from the Vietnam book. In each instance, however, the defendants have failed to carry their burden of proof with respect to "amount and substantiality."

IV

We turn now to the pertinent legislative history. The general revision of the copyright law enacted in 1976 was developed through a somewhat unusual process. Congress and the Register of Copyrights initiated and supervised negotiations among interested groups — groups that included authors, publishers, and educators — over specific legislative language. Most of the language that emerged was enacted into law or was made a part of the committee reports. The statutory fair use provisions are a direct result of this process. So too is the "Agreement on Guidelines for Classroom Copying in Not-for-Profit Educational Institutions With Respect to Books and Periodicals" — commonly called the "Classroom Guidelines" — set out in H.R. Rep. No. 1476 at 68–71, 94th Cong., 2d Sess. (1976). The House and Senate conferees explicitly accepted the Classroom Guidelines "as part of their understanding of fair use" . . . .

There are strong reasons to consider this legislative history. The statutory factors are not models of clarity, and the fair use issue has long been a particularly troublesome one. Not surprisingly, courts have often turned to the legislative history when considering fair use questions. . . .

Although the Classroom Guidelines purport to "state the minimum and not the maximum standards of educational fair use," they do evoke a general idea, at least, of the type of educational copying Congress had in mind. The guidelines allow multiple copies for classroom use provided that (1) the copying meets the test of brevity (1,000 words, in the present context); (2) the copying meets the test of spontaneity, under which "the inspiration and decision to use the work and the moment of its use for maximum teaching effectiveness [must be] so close in time that it would be unreasonable to expect a timely reply to a request for permission;" (3) no more than nine instances of multiple copying take place during a term, and only a limited number of copies are made from the works of any one author or from any one collective work; (4) each copy contains a notice of copyright; (5) the copying does not substitute for the purchase of "books, publishers' reprints or periodicals;" and (6) the student is not charged any more than the actual cost of copying. The Classroom Guidelines also make clear that unauthorized copying to create "anthologies, compilations or collective works" is prohibited.

In its systematic and premeditated character, its magnitude, its anthological content, and its commercial motivation, the copying done by MDS goes well beyond anything envisioned by the Congress that chose to incorporate the guidelines in the legislative history. Although the guidelines do not purport to be a complete and definitive statement of fair use law for educational copying, and although they do not have the force of law, they do provide us general guidance. The fact that the MDS copying is light years away from the safe harbor of the guidelines weighs against a finding of fair use.

Although the Congress that passed the Copyright Act in 1976 would pretty clearly have thought it unfair for a commercial copyshop to appropriate as much as 30 percent of a copyrighted work without paying the license fee demanded by the copyright holder, the changes in technology and teaching practices that have occurred over the last two decades might conceivably make Congress more sympathetic to the defendants' position today. If the law on this point is to be changed, however, we think the change should be made by Congress and not by the courts.

V

We take as our text for the concluding part of this discussion of fair use Justice Stewart's well-known exposition of the correct approach to "ambiguities" (see *Sony*, 464 U.S. at 431–32) in the copyright law:

> "The immediate effect of our copyright law is to secure a fair return for an 'author's' creative labor. But the ultimate aim is, by this incentive, to stimulate artistic creativity for the general public good. 'The sole interest of the United States and the primary object in conferring the monopoly,' this Court has said, 'lie in the general benefits derived by the public from the labors of authors.' . . . When technological change has rendered its literal terms ambiguous, the Copyright Act must be construed in light of this basic purpose." *Twentieth Century Music Corp. v. Aiken*, 422 U.S. 151, 156 (1975) (footnotes and citations omitted).

The defendants attach considerable weight to the assertions of numerous academic authors that they do not write primarily for money and that they want their published writings to be freely copyable. The defendants suggest that unlicensed copying will "stimulate artistic creativity for the general public good."

This suggestion would be more persuasive if the record did not demonstrate that licensing income is significant to the publishers. It is the publishers who hold the copyrights, of course — and the publishers obviously need economic incentives to publish scholarly works, even if the scholars do not need direct economic incentives to write such works.

The writings of most academic authors, it seems fair to say, lack the general appeal of works by a Walter Lippmann, for example. . . . One suspects that the profitability of at least some of the other books at issue here is marginal. If publishers cannot look forward to receiving permission fees, why should they continue publishing marginally profitable books at all? And how will artistic creativity be stimulated if the diminution of economic incentives for publishers to publish academic works means that fewer academic works will be published?

The fact that a liberal photocopying policy may be favored by many academics who are not themselves in the publishing business has little relevance in this connection. As Judge Leval observed in *American Geophysical*,

> "It is not surprising that authors favor liberal photocopying; generally such authors have a far greater interest in the wide dissemination of their work than in royalties — all the more so when they have assigned their royalties

> to the publisher. But the authors have not risked their capital to achieve dissemination. The publishers have. Once an author has assigned her copyright, her approval or disapproval of photocopying is of no further relevance." 802 F. Supp. at 27.

In the case at bar the district court was not persuaded that the creation of new works of scholarship would be stimulated by depriving publishers of the revenue stream derived from the sale of permissions. Neither are we. On the contrary, it seems to us, the destruction of this revenue stream can only have a deleterious effect upon the incentive to publish academic writings.

VI

The district court's conclusion that the infringement was willful is somewhat more problematic, in our view. The Copyright Act allows the collection of statutory damages of between $500 and $20,000 for each work infringed. Where the copyright holder establishes that the infringement is willful, the court may increase the award to not more than $100,000. If the court finds that the infringement was innocent, on the other hand, the court may reduce the damages to not less than $200. Here the district court awarded $5,000 per work infringed, characterizing the amount of the award as "a strong admonition from this court."

. . . .

The plaintiffs do not contest the good faith of Mr. Smith's belief that his conduct constituted fair use; only the reasonableness of that belief is challenged. "Reasonableness," in the present context, is essentially a question of law. The facts of the instant case are not in dispute, and the issue is whether the copyright law supported the plaintiffs' position so clearly that the defendants must be deemed as a matter of law to have exhibited a reckless disregard of the plaintiffs' property rights. . . .

Fair use is one of the most unsettled areas of the law. . . . The potential for reasonable disagreement here is illustrated by the forcefully argued dissents and the now-vacated panel opinion. In the circumstances of this case, we cannot say that the defendants' belief that their copying constituted fair use was so unreasonable as to bespeak willfulness. Accordingly, we shall remand the case for reconsideration of the statutory damages to be awarded.

VIII

The grant of summary judgment on the fair use issue is AFFIRMED. The award of damages is VACATED, and the case is REMANDED for reconsideration of damages and for entry of a separate judgment not inconsistent with this opinion.

NOTES

1. Usually, "original works" are not copyrightable until they are reduced to a "fixed" medium. In other words, the work has to be embodied in some tangible form. For example, if a student is in the process of typing up his term paper, that paper is not technically "protected" until it is saved as a file on his computer. Similarly, a professor's lectures are usually not "protected" if he is just speaking to his students in a classroom. Do you foresee any issues with these requirements in the emerging field of "distance learning" and online courses? Can you think of any way one could argue that a professor's lecture that is broadcast to long-distance students is protected even though it is just the professor's words?

2. The original basis for copyright protection can be found in Article I, § 8 of the U.S. Consitution: "The Congress shall have Power . . . To promote the Progress of Science and useful Arts, by securing for limited Times to Authors and Inventors the exclusive Right to their respective Writings and Discoveries." As with many other constitutional rules, however, Congress has supplemented this general protection with detailed legislation. One such example is the Copyright Act, passed in 1976. The Copyright Act lists eight categories of "protected" works:

Literary works.

Musical works, including any accompanying words.

Dramatic works, including any accompanying music.

Pantomimes and choreographic works.

Pictorial, graphic, and sculptural works.

Motion pictures and other audiovisual works.

Sound recordings.

Architectural works.

17 U.S.C. § 102. Can you think of an example of each of these categories that occurs on a university or college campus on a daily basis?

3. The legislature provided for a few exceptions to the strict protections given copyrighted works that are germane to the education context. For example, 17 U.S.C. § 107 states, "the fair use of a copyrighted work, including such use by reproduction in copies . . . for purposes such as criticism, comment, news reporting, teaching (including multiple copies for classroom use), scholarship, or research, is not an infringement of copyright." The statute continues to describe factors used in determining whether a use is "fair." One factor is whether the purpose and character of the use is of a "commercial nature" or is for "nonprofit educational purposes." 17 U.S.C. § 107(1).

Another equally important exception is found in 17 U.S.C. § 110(1), which permits the performance or display of a copyrighted work by instructors or students "in the course of face-to-face teaching activities" of a nonprofit educational institution, in a classroom or similar place devoted to instruction. Related to this exception is the TEACH Act, 17 U.S.C. § 110(2) — the Technology, Education, and Copyright Harmonization Act — which broadens the definition of the classroom to include educational activities in distance or online settings. The TEACH Act permits, essentially, the same activities in distance/online settings as would be permitted in traditional face-to-face settings. There are several institutional requirements, though. First, the activities must be directly supervised by an instructor. Second, activities must be a part of a regular class session and must be related to the content taught. Third, the activities must be accessible only to those students enrolled in the course. Finally, the institution must implement policies and programming regarding copyright. Do these limitations on traditional copyright protection demonstrate a practical consideration on behalf of the legislature? Without this exception isn't it arguable that schools or their faculty would have to pay copyright fees for every handout or educational video shown to students?

4. The court in *Princeton University Press v. Michigan Document Services* makes reference to the "*Sony* presumption" of unfairness. What is this presumption and how does it dictate the burden of proof for the parties in a copyright infringement case?

2. Trademark Law

BOARD OF GOVERNORS OF THE UNIVERSITY OF NORTH CAROLINA v. HELPINGSTINE

714 F. Supp. 167 (M.D.N.C. 1989)

MEMORANDUM OPINION

FRANK W. BULLOCK, JR., UNITED STATES DISTRICT JUDGE

Plaintiffs instituted this action against Defendants under the Lanham Act, specifically 15 U.S.C. §§ 1114 and 1125, and N.C. Gen. Stat. § 75-1.1, alleging trademark infringement, false designation of source or origin, and unfair and deceptive trade practices. Defendants denied such practices and brought counterclaims under the Sherman Act, 15 U.S.C. § 1, and N.C. Gen. Stat. §§ 66-58 and 75-1.1, asserting restraint of trade, unlawful competition with state citizens in the sale of goods, and unfair and deceptive trade practices. Defendants also claimed that their activities were protected by the First Amendment to the United States Constitution.

Defendants have moved for summary judgment on their claims under N.C. Gen. Stat. § 66-58 and Plaintiffs' claims under the Lanham Act. Plaintiffs have countered with their own motion for summary judgment on their trademark infringement claim as well as all of the Defendants' counterclaims. For the reasons stated below, summary judgment will be denied on both parties' motions regarding the alleged Lanham Act violations; summary judgment will also be denied on Defendants' motion on their claim under N.C. Gen. Stat. § 66-58. However, summary judgment will be granted for Plaintiffs on all of the Defendants' counterclaims.

STATEMENT OF FACTS

The record reveals the following facts to be undisputed:

The University of North Carolina is comprised of sixteen institutions including its main campus at Chapel Hill (hereinafter "UNC-CH"). UNC-CH opened its doors to students in 1795 and has developed a tradition of excellence with regard to both its academic and athletic programs.

As the University's reputation expanded, a market emerged for items bearing the University's name, symbols, and insignia. Prior to 1982, the University made no efforts to license the manufacture and retail sale of such items. By the University's own admission, at least 107 suppliers and 79 manufacturers were users of the symbols in 1982.

However, in late 1982, the University, prompted in large measure by the proliferation of collegiate products, decided to develop and implement a trademark licensing program. As part of this program UNC-CH registered four trademarks with the United States Patent and Trademark Office: (1) the University seal; (2) the letters "UNC"; (3) the words "University of North Carolina"; and (4) the Tarheel foot. Also, effective October 1, 1982, UNC-CH granted to Golden Eagle Enterprises (now Collegiate Concepts, Inc.) the "right to use and the exclusive right to grant sub-licenses" to use its registered trademarks "on merchandise sold in the United States" in the manner set forth in the agreement. This agreement is currently in full force and effect, and today approximately 225 manufacturers have been licensed under the agreement.

Licensing is not automatic, though; instead, applications are reviewed by UNC-CH officers who approve or disapprove of the applications according to criteria developed in 1982. These criteria include whether the merchandise is offensive, whether the use of the merchandise might result in injury, whether the use of the merchandise would suggest University sponsorship, and whether the price of the merchandise is commensurate with its quality. Products which have been rejected under these criteria include items promoting alcoholic beverage consumption, play football helmets, and blankets and other merchandise with a high degree of flammability.

In August 1983 the Defendants Helpingstine opened Johnny T-Shirt, a retail shop in Chapel Hill, North Carolina. The business was incorporated in January of 1987 and currently employs between twenty and forty persons in various capacities. Its gross sales revenue for 1986, the most recent figure before this court, was $621,681.05.

Johnny T-Shirt sells collegiate merchandise, fraternity and sorority merchandise, and other types of apparel and merchandise to the public. It also imprints plain merchandise with various names, symbols, and other designs through various processes. Although UNC-CH and its licensing agent have offered on many occasions to grant Johnny T-Shirt a license to utilize the University's marks on apparel and other merchandise, Johnny T-Shirt has always refused to accept such license. Thus, since 1983 Johnny T-Shirt has never been nor is it now licensed to sell merchandise bearing UNC-CH's registered trademarks. However, it is undisputed that a large portion of the merchandise sold by Johnny T-Shirt bears UNC-CH's registered marks.

Defendant JTS Promotions is a companion business to Johnny T-Shirt, incorporated in October of 1986. JTS's primary business is the sale of advertising specialties. JTS has also sold items bearing UNC-CH's registered trademarks despite the fact that it also is not licensed to sell such merchandise.

Defendants admit that they have sold goods bearing UNC's marks knowing that the University has a trademark program and that it has claimed trademark rights in the marks. Defendants have also added that they were aware of the trademark licensing program even before they opened Johnny T-Shirt in 1983. However, Defendants maintain that even with this knowledge and use they have not infringed UNC-CH's trademarks because the trademarks were abandoned through extensive non-licensed used prior to 1982, and also that even if such marks are valid UNC-CH has not established the requisite likelihood of confusion that is the hallmark of copyright infringement. These contentions are discussed below.

DISCUSSION

A. Plaintiffs' Claim of Infringement of Trademark

In determining the outcome of a trademark dispute, two questions must be addressed: first, does the plaintiff have a protectable property right in the name or mark it seeks to defend; and second, is defendant's use of a similar mark likely to cause confusion, mistake or deception in the market as to the source, origin, or sponsorship of the products on which the marks are used. If both of these questions are answered in the affirmative, then trademark infringement has been established. However, simply because the plaintiff has a valid trademark does not mean that another's use of a similar or even the same mark will always meet the likelihood-of-confusion test necessary to establish infringement.

Plaintiffs contend that as its marks are validly registered and there is no dispute that Johnny T-Shirt is using the exact marks registered by Plaintiffs, both elements of the test are met as a matter of law and thus UNC is entitled to summary judgment on its claims. Defendants contend, however, that as Plaintiffs abandoned their trademark rights by allowing widespread uncontrolled use of the marks prior to 1982, they cannot now assert valid trademark rights in these marks. Alternatively, Defendants contend that their use does not create likelihood of confusion. Each prong of the test will be discussed below.

1. Plaintiffs' property right in marks

Under Section 7(b) of the Lanham Act, 15 U.S.C. § 1057(b), registration of a mark with the United States Patent and Trademark Office constitutes *prima facie* evidence that the registrant owns the mark and has the exclusive right to use the mark as well as that the registration itself is valid. As it is undisputed that UNC-CH has registered the four marks in question with the Patent and Trademark Office, it is entitled to the presumptions of Section 7(b). . . .

Defendants do not dispute that UNC-CH's registration of the marks in question constitutes *prima facie* evidence of their validity, but they point out that the presumptions of Section 7(b) are rebuttable. Defendants maintain that they have rebutted the presumptions in this case through evidence that the University abandoned its rights in the marks at issue. Defendants assert that this abandonment occurred in two interrelated ways — first, by UNC-CH's failure to prosecute those individuals who used its marks prior to 1982; and, second, by UNC-CH's allowance of substantial uncontrolled use of the marks prior to 1982.

Defendants are correct that abandonment is one means by which an individual or entity can relinquish rights to a mark in which it once had a property interest. *See* 15 U.S.C. § 1064(c). However, to establish abandonment it is imperative that the Defendants show both an intent to abandon as well as the loss of all indication as to the source of the mark's origin. *See Sweetheart Plastics, Inc. v. Detroit Forming, Inc.*, 743 F.2d 1039 (4th Cir. 1984). Evaluating Defendants' assertions and proof in light of this standard, the court finds that abandonment has not been established.

The court recognizes that many manufacturers used UNC-CH's marks prior to the licensing program's institution and is also dubious of UNC-CH's contention that it had no actual knowledge of any alleged unauthorized third-party use of its marks. However, as *Sweetheart* points out,

> 'It appears that the only relevancy of failure to prosecute others is as to the possible impact such failure may have on the strength of the plaintiff's mark. It is possible that plaintiff's mark has been "weakened" by widespread use in the market and that such use resulted from plaintiff's failure to sue infringers . . . . Of course, if, through failure to prosecute, a mark continually loses "strength" and "distinctiveness", it will eventually hemorrhage so much that it dies as a mark. That would be "abandonment" through acts of omission . . .
>
> In the typical trademark litigation, the relevance of failure to prosecute others is not to "abandonment", but to "strength". The issue is hardly ever "abandonment", because that requires proof *that the mark has lost all significance as an indication of origin.* That is, the mark is completely without signs of life.'

Sweetheart, 743 F.2d at 1047–48 (quoting 1 J. McCarthy, *Trademarks and Unfair Competition* § 17:5 at 779–80 [2d ed. 1984]) (emphasis added).

Defendants' contention that UNC-CH's marks have lost significance as indication of origin because the public can no longer point to a single source of the origin of *goods* bearing the marks does not establish abandonment, for under *Sweetheart* abandonment occurs only when a mark loses all significance as an indication of origin *as to the mark itself.*

Here, it is clear that UNC-CH's marks would still be regarded by the public as having originated with the University. It is also relevant that the University has never discontinued its use of the marks, for continuous use indicates a lack of intent to abandon. Therefore, the court finds that neither UNC's failure to prosecute alleged infringers nor its allowance of uncontrolled use of its marks prior to 1982 establishes that UNC-CH abandoned its marks. Accordingly, UNC-CH has valid trademarks in its name, initials, seal, and Tarheel foot.

2. Likelihood of confusion

While Defendants have failed to show that Plaintiffs do not have a valid property right in their marks, this does not settle the infringement issue, for it is now Plaintiffs' burden to show that Johnny T-Shirt's use of UNC's marks constitutes a "likelihood of confusion." While cases have indicated at one extreme that an alleged infringer's use of a mark with the knowledge that the public will be aware of the mark's origin is enough to establish likelihood of confusion, and at the other that likelihood of confusion occurs only where there would be confusion as to the origin of the goods themselves, the majority of courts have taken the middle ground on this issue. This middle position, which both parties recognize in this case, is that the requisite likelihood of confusion will exist where there is likelihood of confusion as to source, sponsorship or endorsement of the goods.

Plaintiffs' primary contention on likelihood of confusion is that since the marks used by Johnny T-Shirt are not only similar but are identical to UNC-CH's registered marks there is no dispute as to likelihood of confusion. It is true that in the typical trademark case identity of marks establishes an open-and-shut case of infringement. However, this is not the typical trademark case for, as the Third Circuit pointed out with regard to a similar dispute in *University of Pittsburgh v. Champion Products, Inc.*, 686 F.2d 1040, 1047 (3d Cir.), *cert. denied*, 459 U.S. 1087 (1982), "in this case there is no consumer confusion in the traditional sense. No one would seriously assert that a significant segment of the public believes that Pitt actually manufactured the goods involved." Instead, this case involves what Professor McCarthy refers to as " 'non-competitive' goods," *i.e.*, a situation where the supposed infringer puts a mark on an item which is too remote from any item that the owner would be likely to make or sell. In such a case it is not enough that the marks used be identical to those registered; instead, "it is a question of fact as to whether consumers view such indicia . . . as symbols that identify a secondary source of sponsorship."

While both parties cite cases in support of their respective contentions that there is and is not a likelihood of confusion as to sponsorship or endorsement regarding the tee-shirts and other paraphernalia offered by Johnny T-Shirt, this court . . . finds the record insufficient to support a granting of summary judgment for either party. UNC-CH asserts that the case of *University of Georgia Athletic Ass'n v. Laite*, 756 F.2d 1535 (11th Cir. 1985), supports its position that infringement has occurred because the court found likelihood of confusion based upon similarity of marks and the alleged infringer's intent to capitalize on the popularity of the University of Georgia football program. However, as discussed above, the court agrees with Professor McCarthy that similarity or even identity of marks is not sufficient to establish confusion where non-competitive goods are involved, and the court also rejects the position that intent to capitalize on popularity is sufficient to establish infringement.

The court believes that the view expressed in Judge Fletcher's opinion in *International Order of Job's Daughters v. Lindeburg & Co.*, 633 F.2d 912 (9th Cir. 1980), *cert. denied*, 452 U.S. 941(1981), is appropriate in this case:

> Our jewelry, clothing, and cars are emblazoned with inscriptions showing the organizations we belong to, the schools we attend, the landmarks we have visited, the sports teams we support, the beverages we imbibe. Although these inscriptions frequently include names and emblems that are also used as collective marks or trademarks, it would be naive to conclude that the name or emblem is desired because consumers believe

> that the product somehow originated with or was sponsored by the organization the name or emblem signifies.

In essence, the court is skeptical that those individuals who purchase unlicensed tee-shirts bearing UNC-CH's marks care one way or the other whether the University sponsors or endorses such products or whether the products are officially licensed. Instead, as Defendants contend, it is equally likely that individuals buy the shirts to show their support for the University.

Given that there is a distinct possibility that individuals who buy products from Johnny T-Shirt do not base their decision upon whether the product is sponsored or endorsed by UNC-CH and that Plaintiffs bear the burden of establishing likelihood of confusion, the court holds that UNC-CH must meet its burden by showing more than simply the identity of the marks. Instead, it must provide evidence establishing that individuals do make the critical distinction as to sponsorship or endorsement, or direct evidence of actual confusion.

Here, as UNC-CH has relied heavily on the fact that the marks in question are identical, and the court has already noted that this is insufficient to establish likelihood of confusion under the circumstances, UNC-CH's lack of any evidence as to whether there is actual confusion generated by Johnny T-Shirt's goods precludes a grant of summary judgment in Plaintiffs' favor. However, the court cannot conclude as a matter of law that there would be no likelihood of confusion as to Johnny T-Shirt's goods. Therefore, summary judgment will be denied on both the Plaintiffs' and Defendants' motions.

B. Defendants' Counterclaims

1. Violation of N.C. Gen. Stat. § 75-1.1

In their counterclaim to Plaintiffs' complaint, Defendants assert that UNC-CH's efforts to prohibit Defendants' use of the University's insignia constitute restraint of trade in violation of N.C. Gen. Stat. § 75-1.1. In response, the University contends that it is not subject to suit under Section 75-1.1 because of the doctrine of sovereign immunity. . . .

In the present case, Defendants have asserted a state claim against a state agency and its governing body in federal court. In such a situation, the Eleventh Amendment to the United States Constitution bars an award of either monetary or injunctive relief against the state.

. . . .

3. Defendants' claim under the Sherman Act

In their counterclaim, Defendants assert that since Plaintiffs' "acts and activities directly restrain trade in both intrastate and interstate commerce," the University is acting in violation of Section 1 of the Sherman Act, 15 U.S.C. § 1. In response, Plaintiffs contend that they are immune from suit under the Sherman Act because in instituting the trademark licensing program they acted as sovereign representatives. In the alternative, Plaintiffs assert that even if they are not sovereign representatives of the State of North Carolina who acted as the sovereign in implementing the trademark licensing program, they remain entitled to immunity because they are not part of the plurality of actors required to impose liability under the Sherman Act and also because they acted in accordance with a state policy to displace competition with regulation or a public service monopoly. Because the court finds that Plaintiffs are sovereign representatives who were acting as the sovereign in instituting the trademark licensing program, they are immune from suit under the Sherman Act and hence entitled to summary judgment on Defendants' claim.

Under *Parker v. Brown*, 317 U.S. 341 (1943), when a state through a sovereign representative acts as sovereign, the state representative is immune from suit under the Sherman Act. For purposes of this immunity, the state representative may be the legislative, executive, or judicial branch.

While few cases have considered whether universities and their governing boards are immune from suit under the Sherman Act, decisions indicate that such immunity exists. A case particularly relevant is *Reid v. University of Minnesota*, 107 F. Supp. 439 (N.D. Ohio 1952), in which a wholesaler of books brought suit against the University of Minnesota Press under the Sherman Act for alleged price discrimination. Finding the university press immune from such suit, the court noted:

> The 'Regents of the University of Minnesota' is a constitutional corporation created to carry out State purposes and the acts of the Regents are, therefore, the acts of the State of Minnesota. The University of Minnesota Press, being a creature of the Regents . . . , is, therefore, an agency of the State of Minnesota and the acts of the Press are the acts of the State of Minnesota.

Id. at 442.

Likewise, in *Saenz v. University Interscholastic League*, 487 F.2d 1026 (5th Cir. 1973), the court held that defendant was immune from suit under the Sherman Act for allegedly designing a slide rule contest to exclude plaintiff's design and benefit a competitor. The court based its decision on the fact that defendant was part of the extension division of the University of Texas, that its administrative authority was appointed by the president of the university, and that it received funding and space from the university, which was "inarguably" a state agency.

In the present case the University of North Carolina and its governing board are, respectively, a constitutional agency and body created to "carry out State purposes." Thus, the University and its Board are sovereign representatives of the State of North Carolina. Further, as protection of the name and symbols of the State is an inherent power of states, UNC-CH and its governing board were acting as sovereigns in instituting the trademark licensing program. Thus, Plaintiffs are immune from suit for violation of the Sherman Act in this instance, and their motion for summary judgment on Defendants' claim shall be granted.

4. Defendants' claim under the first amendment

Finally, Defendants claim that their use of the names and symbols of the University is a constitutionally protected form of noncommercial speech under the first amendment. Thus, they claim that the actions of the University must be subject to first amendment scrutiny.

However, the case cited by Defendants in support of their contention, *Lucasfilm Ltd. v. High Frontier*, 622 F. Supp. 931 (D.D.C. 1985), does not support the position that Plaintiffs' trademarks infringe on Defendants' first amendment rights. In *Lucasfilm*, owners of the trademark "Star Wars" brought suit under the Lanham Act against interest groups that used the term in their advertisements concerning the Stategic Defense Initiative. The court found that trademark rights did not entitle the holders thereof to quash the public interest groups' use of the terms, for "the defendants have not affixed any trademark to any goods or services. Indeed, they are not engaged in selling anything but ideas." *Id.* at 934. However, the court did note that the trademark would protect against infringement by

> those who seek to attach those words to products or services that compete . . . in the marketplace, against those who dilute the value of [the] mark by engaging in a noncompeting trade or business but utilize the mark in connection with a disreputable or sleazy product or service, and, under some circumstances, even against those who injure [the business of the trademark holder] by offering goods or services that disparage the goodwill value of [the mark].

Id. at 933.

Here, while Defendants claim that those who wear tee-shirts with the University's names and symbols on them are communicating their allegiance with the University, the Defendants themselves have made no claim that by placing such trademarks and logos on shirts they are doing anything but engaging in commercial activity. Such activity clearly falls within the prohibitions of the Lanham Act. Thus, the court finds that in this instance Defendants' first amendment rights are not infringed upon by Plaintiffs' trademarks; consequently, summary judgment will be granted for Plaintiffs on Defendants' first amendment claim.

An order and judgment in accordance with this memorandum opinion shall be entered contemporaneously herewith.

[The court denied Plaintiffs' and Defendants' motions for summary judgment on Plaintiffs' claim of trademark infringement. The court granted Plaintiffs' motion for summary judgment on Defendants' counterclaims.]

WHITE v. BOARD OF REGENTS OF THE UNIVERSITY OF NEBRASKA

614 N.W.2d 330 (Neb. 2000)

STEPHAN, J.

Brent White appeals from a judgment of the district court for Lancaster County, Nebraska, dismissing his claim for damages and injunctive relief against the Board of Regents of the University of Nebraska at Lincoln (University) based upon the alleged wrongful use of a registered trade name. The district court found that White was not entitled to relief because he failed to establish that he actually used the trade name "Husker Authentics" prior to registering it with the Nebraska Secretary of State. The University cross-appeals, contending the district court erred in dismissing its counterclaims for breach of contract and common-law trade name infringement. We affirm, although for reasons different from those articulated by the district court.

I. FACTS

In late 1995, the University of Nebraska-Lincoln Athletic Department (Department) internally proposed the establishment of an "authentic shop" which would sell to the public apparel and equipment used by its teams and staff. The Department thereafter began making plans related to the development of the new store. As part of this process, the Department began test marketing the sale of "authentic goods" with the intent of developing purchasing statistics for the new store.

. . .

The test marketing was conducted through two principal means. Soft goods, such as T-shirts, sweatshirts, and other apparel, were marketed pursuant to an agreement with Eastbay, a mail-order catalog business located in Wausau, Wisconsin. An Eastbay catalog was developed through the joint efforts of Eastbay and the Department.

This catalog, which displayed various styles of Nebraska Cornhusker wearing apparel, manufactured by "adidas," was mailed by the Department directly to season ticket holders, boosters who had donated money to the Department, and approximately 50,000 alumni of the University of Nebraska-Lincoln.

The catalog was also distributed on game day at Memorial Stadium in Lincoln for one football game during the fall 1996 season. The catalog displayed, in the upper right-hand center, a large "N" over which the word "Husker" was written in script, with the word "Authentics" written underneath in italicized and capitalized block letters. This logo was developed generally by the Department. The catalog also displayed a picture of the then University of Nebraska-Lincoln football coach Tom Osborne, who was quoted as stating, "Husker Authentics is your official provider of Nebraska/adidas sideline shoes and apparel." Beneath the quote in small print was the language, "Husker Authentics is brought to you by the University of Nebraska - Athletic Department, adidas & Eastbay." . . . Pursuant to the agreement with

Eastbay, the Department received 4 percent of gross sales generated by the catalog.

During the same . . . period, the Department test marketed "hard goods" pursuant to an agreement with Awards Unlimited, Inc., a Lincoln business. Hard goods are items such as footballs, photographs, posters, and videos. These products were marketed in essentially the same manner as the soft goods in that a catalog or order form containing a list of available items and their description was directly mailed by the Department to season ticket holders, boosters, and 50,000 alumni of the University of Nebraska-Lincoln. The catalog or order form for the hard goods did not contain a "Husker Authentics" logo similar to that displayed on the Eastbay catalog, but did contain a regular "N" with "Huskers" written over it in script in the lower left-hand corner. The top of the catalog or order form was entitled "Authentic Nebraska Athletic Department Products" . . . . Pursuant to the agreement between the parties, Awards Unlimited operated as a fulfillment house for processing orders and storing inventory, and the Department received revenues from merchandise sold. In addition to this catalog or order form . . . the Department also ran advertisements in the magazine, Huskers Illustrated, and a Lincoln newspaper for the "hard goods." . . .

On July 11, 1996, the "Board of Regents of the University of Nebraska d/b/a UNL Department of Athletics" filed an application with the Nebraska Secretary of State to register the trade name "Husker Authentics." The application stated that the first use of the name in Nebraska was in June 1996 and that the nature of the business was "Sales of University of Nebraska-Lincoln licensed goods." Because the University did not file the requisite proof of publication of the name with the Secretary of State and the county clerk as required by Neb. Rev. Stat. § 87-219, the Secretary of State subsequently canceled the registration. The Department was not aware of the cancellation until June 30, 1997, and, after registering the trade name, continued making plans to open its new retail store.

From 1989 to 1998, White owned and operated two Lincoln businesses named "Nebraska Spirit" and "Team Spirit Industries." Both businesses were engaged in screen printing, embroidering, and selling clothing and novelty items related to a theme of the University of Nebraska-Lincoln athletics. White was aware of the Department's plan to open a retail outlet store to sell authentic goods in February 1997.

He opposed the opening of the store, fearing competition with his businesses. Upon inquiry, White was informed by the Secretary of State on June 26, 1997, that the Department's registration of the trade name "Husker Authentics" was canceled due to improper publication. That same day, White filed an application for registration of the trade name "Husker Authentics." The application indicated that the trade name was first used in Nebraska on the date of the application and that the general nature of the business was a retail sportswear store. White completed all of the requirements for registration and was granted registration of the trade name "Husker Authentics." At trial, White testified that he wanted to use the trade name for a new business, as a name for a department in his store, or to identify his products. He specifically acknowledged that the registration was motivated in part by his desire to prevent the Department from opening its retail store. White further testified that he did not actually use the trade name "Husker Authentics" for his business . . . .

The Board of Regents is the governing body for the University and, as such, is the owner of a number of trademarks, service marks, and trade names associated with the University. The University is a "Member University" represented by The Collegiate Licensing Company (CLC), its exclusive licensing agent. CLC is authorized to grant licenses to third parties, which licenses allow specified use of the indicia that are associated with the University. A license is required for persons who produce or manufacture any of the indicia which the University owns, although a license is not required to simply sell such products in a retail business. White obtained such a license to produce and manufacture the University's indicia for the period January 27, 1995, to January 31, 1998. Approximately 3 weeks after registering the trade name "Husker Authentics," White received a letter dated July 16, 1997, from CLC's counsel informing him that his registration was in violation of the license agreement and that failure to transfer his registration to the University within 15 days would subject his license agreement to "immediate termination." . . . White responded to the July 16 letter on August 8 . . . and informed CLC that he was "canceling [his] license agreement." White testified that after sending his August 8 letter, he never received confirmation that his license was canceled, but he did not after that date manufacture or produce products subject to the license agreement.

After learning of White's registration of the trade name "Husker Authentics" from a published notice, the Department inquired of the Secretary of State and learned that its prior application for registration had been canceled because the process had not been completed, as noted above. On June 30, 1997, the "Board of Regents of the University of Nebraska d/b/a "UNL Department of Athletics" attempted to register the trade name "Huskers Authentic," but the Secretary of State refused to register the name due to the similarity with the name previously registered by White.

On July 28, 1997, the University filed a trademark application with the Secretary of State. The mark sought to be registered was described as an "oval shaped logo with a block 'N' with a script 'Huskers' through it (on the left side of logo) followed by a block lettered 'Authentic.' " The application stated that the mark was first used in June 1996 and was used by applying it directly to goods and to tags or labels affixed to goods. The record does not indicate whether the trademark application for registration was accepted and does not indicate whether the mark was actually used in June 1996.

. . . The store officially opened August 27, 1997, under the name "Huskers Authentic." On September 3, White filed a petition requesting that the University be enjoined from using the trade name "Huskers Authentic."

An amended petition was filed September 15, seeking both an injunction and damages. The University filed an answer generally denying White's claims.

The University also counterclaimed, asserting a right to injunctive relief and damages based upon breach of contract, violation of common-law and statutory trade name and trademark rights, contravention of the dilution statute, and common-law unfair competition.

In an order filed December 1, 1998, the district court found that White's registration was improperly granted because he had not actually used the trade name prior to registration.

The court further found that the University's subsequent trade name application could not be registered due to a similar failure of proof of use prior to registration. The court found that there was no merit to the University's contention that White breached his licensing agreement by registering the trade name. The court also found that the University failed to establish common-law rights to the name "Husker Authentics" because any proof of prior use related only to use as a trademark, and not as a trade name.

In addition, the district court refused to issue an injunction against White's use of the trade name, finding that because White never used the name, there was no likelihood of confusion. White timely appealed, and the University cross-appealed.

II. ASSIGNMENTS OF ERROR

White assigns, summarized and restated, that the district court erred in finding that White had failed to meet his burden of proof and in dismissing his petition.

The University assigns, summarized and restated, that the district court erred in (1) failing to find White breached the license agreement, (2) failing to find a threatened violation of its common-law rights, (3) failing to find a threatened violation of its statutory rights, (4) failing to permanently enjoin White, and (5) denying an award of costs.

. . . .

IV. ANALYSIS

1. White's Appeal

The district court found that White's registration of the trade name "Husker Authentics" was improperly granted and ordered that it be canceled. The court reasoned that actual use and adoption of the trade name is required pursuant to Neb. Rev. Stat. §§ 87-208 to 87-220 before a registration can be enforced and that White failed to meet this requirement because he admitted in his testimony that he never used the trade name at any time other than on his application for registration. Thus, the issue before us is one of statutory interpretation.

On appeal, White contends that the district court misinterpreted the statute. He argues that the Nebraska statutes do not require actual use prior to registration and that his registration established a prima facie case of ownership of the trade name which the University could overcome only by demonstrating its prior use of the name.

The University contends that White's registration was improperly granted because he never used "Husker Authentics" as a trade name or, alternatively, was invalid because the University had acquired a prior common-law right in the name through its use of the name "Husker Authentics" on products during 1996 and its decision in January 1997 to use the name "Huskers Authentic" for its retail outlet.

At the time of the operative facts in this action, Nebraska law applicable to protection of trade names was codified at §§ 87-208 to 87-220. Section 87-208(4) defined "trade name" as "every name under which any person does or transacts any business in this state other than the true name of such person." Section 87-210 set forth the requirements for an application for registration of a trade name, providing:

> Any person who adopts a trade name for use in this state may file in the office of the Secretary of State on a form furnished by the Secretary of State an application, in duplicate, for registration of the trade name setting forth, but not limited to, the following information:
>
> (a) The name and street address of the applicant for registration; and, if a corporation, the state of incorporation;
>
> (b) The trade name sought to be registered;
>
> (c) The general nature of the business in fact conducted by the applicant;
>
> (d) The length of time during which the trade name has been used in this state;
>
> (e) The signature of the applicant, which must be acknowledged before a notary public; and
>
> (f) A filing fee of one hundred dollars.

Section 87-211 provided procedures for renewing a registration, and specifically stated "all applications for renewals . . . shall include a statement that the trade name is still in use in this state." Section 87-216 provided that one who wrongfully used a registered trade name was civilly liable to the registrant. Section 87-217 provided that "any registrant of a trade name" may sue to enjoin its wrongful use by another and recover damages attributable to such use. Section 87-218 provided that "Sections 87-208 to 87-219 shall not adversely affect rights in trade names, or the enforcement of rights in trade names, acquired at any time in good faith at common law."

The district court reasoned that the requirement in § 87-210(1)(d) that the applicant for registration must state the length of time during which the trade name has been used in Nebraska supported its conclusion that there must be actual use of the trade name in connection with a business before it can be registered. Examined in isolation, this statutory language can reasonably be interpreted to require that actual use of the name must be made prior to registration. In addition, the language requiring that the business be "in fact conducted" at the time of registration also supports this interpretation, as does the renewal provision which requires continuing use of the name. §§ 87-210(1)(c) and 87-211. Such an interpretation is consistent with common law, which requires actual use before substantive rights in a designation can be obtained because it is only such use that creates goodwill and the possibility that subsequent use will lead to confusion as to the source of the goods. See Restatement (Third) of Unfair Competition § 18, comment *a.* (1995).

However, whereas the Legislature provided in Neb. Rev. Stat. § 87-113 that a trademark may be registered by "any person who adopts and uses" it, different language was used in § 87-210 with respect to registration of a trade name.

There, the Legislature provided that registration may be accomplished by "any person *who adopts a trade name for use* in this state" (emphasis supplied) § 87-210, which could be interpreted as meaning that adoption and registration may occur before actual use of the trade name. According to the Restatement, registration under a state trade name registration act creates no substantive rights in the name. Rights can be acquired in a designation "only when the designation has been actually used" as a trademark or trade name or "when an applicable statutory provision recognizes a protectable interest in the designation prior to actual use." However, the Restatement notes that trade name acts in several states specifically recognize a right in the *registrant* of a trade name to proceed under the statute against other users of the same or similar name.

We have never addressed the specific issue of whether an enforceable right is created by the registration of a trade name which has never been used by the registrant, and we need not resolve it in this case. Assuming without deciding that actual use of a trade name is not a prerequisite to its valid registration under § 87-210, we conclude on de novo review that the University had prior common-law rights superior to those of White in the trade name "Husker Authentics" and that therefore the district court properly canceled White's registration.

In *Chadron Opera House Co. v. Loomer*, 99 N.W. 649, 650 (Neb. 1904), we stated that in order to establish a legally protectable common law interest in a trade name, a party

> must make it appear, with at least reasonable certainty, that his adoption of the name was prior in time to that of his adversary; that he adopted and made use of it in such manner as would reasonably apprise the public that he intended it as a distinctive appellation for his trade, commodity, or place of business, and that it was not, at the time of his attempted appropriation of it, in common or general use in connection with like businesses, commodities, buildings, or localities.

This is consistent with Restatement (Third) of Unfair Competition § 18 at 184 (1995), which provides that "[a] designation is 'used' as a trademark, trade name, collective trademark, or certification mark when the designation is displayed or otherwise made known to prospective purchasers in the ordinary course of business in a manner that associates the designation with the goods, services, or business of the user . . . ." The Restatement further provides:

> One who has used a designation as a trademark, trade name, collective mark, or certification mark under the rule stated in § 18 has priority in the use of the designation over another user:

> (a) in any geographic area in which the actor has used the designation in good faith or in which the designation has become associated with the actor as a result of good faith use before the designation is used in good faith by, or becomes associated with, the other; and (b) in any additional geographic area in which the actor has priority over the other under an applicable statutory provision.

Id., § 19 at 194–95. We adopt the common-law definition for "use" of a trade name or other designation set forth in § 18 of the Restatement and the rule with respect to priority of use set forth in § 19.

At common law, the use of a trade name may be established by its appearance on signs, documents employed in conducting business, mail solicitations, or advertising. The record reveals that "Husker Authentics" was used by the Department on both mail solicitations and advertising. Specifically, the record reveals that the Department engaged in test marketing pursuant to agreements with both Eastbay and Awards Unlimited. . . .

Although the name was admittedly not used in marketing directed at the general public, [because it was marketed primarily to known university supporters,] the name "Husker Authentics" was used in the ordinary course of business by the Department. The question thus becomes whether it was used in a manner that would associate it with the products and business of the Department.

The Eastbay catalog clearly used the logo "Husker Authentics" and contained a quote from Osborne stating that "Husker Authentics" was the provider of Nebraska apparel. The Department's agreement with Eastbay provided that it would receive 4 percent of the gross sales of the products in the catalog. This evidence establishes that the Department did conduct mail-order business under the name "Husker Authentics," which was a name other than its true name and could reasonably apprise the public of its business. Similarly, the Awards Unlimited test marketing also involved the Department conducting mail-order business as "Husker Authentics." The Department engaged Awards Unlimited to be its fulfillment house, and the order form distributed by the Department listed the name of the business as "Husker Authentics," although it was actually the Department engaged in the business of selling the products. This evidence further demonstrates the Department's prior use of "Husker Authentics" as a trade name.

. . . [W]e disagree with the district court's determination that the University used "Husker Authentics" only in association with products and not with its conduct of business. The district court reasoned that the University utilized the name "Husker Authentics" as a trademark rather than as a trade name. However, the evidence summarized above demonstrates that the Department engaged in the business of selling such products using the name "Husker Authentics," which was not its true name, and thus used the name as a trade name. Persons ordering merchandise from either catalog could reasonably assume that they were purchasing products from a business named "Husker Authentics."

In addition, we note that the Eastbay catalog clearly reveals that the Department used a logo with a large block "N" with "Husker" written over it in script and the capitalized block letters "Authentics" underneath. At common law, "rights in a trade name can also be infringed by its unauthorized use as a trademark, just as a trademark can be infringed by unauthorized adoption as a trade name." Restatement (Third) of Unfair Competition § 12, comment *b.* at 98 (1995). We therefore disagree with the district court's focus on the distinction between use of "Husker Authentics" as a trademark versus use as a trade name.

As noted above, § 87-218 specifically provides that the statutes pertaining to registration of trade names "shall not adversely affect rights in trade names, or the enforcement of rights in trade names, acquired at any time in good faith at common law." . . . Accordingly, we hold that where one has acquired a common-law right in a trade name by its use, the subsequent registration of the trade name by the Secretary of State upon the application of another is invalid and subject to cancellation pursuant to § 87-214.

In summary, we conclude on the basis of our de novo review that the University had a common-law right in the trade name "Husker Authentics" prior to White's registration of that name, and the registration was therefore invalid and must be cancelled.

Where the record demonstrates that the decision of the trial court is correct, although such correctness is based on a different ground from that assigned by the trial court, the appellate court will affirm. We therefore affirm the judgment of the district court canceling White's trade name registration and dismissing his petition.

2. Cross-Appeal

(a) Contract Claim

The University contends that the district court erred in finding that the licensing agreement was rescinded by mutual consent, and in not determining that White's registration of "Husker Authentics" was in breach of the licensing agreement, thereby entitling the University to an order requiring White to transfer the registered trade name to the University pursuant to the remedial provisions of the licensing agreement. We find it unnecessary to resolve this issue because we affirm the district court's finding that the registration should be canceled. Pursuant to § 87-214(4)(b) and (5), the Secretary of State is required to cancel a trade name registration when the registrant is not the owner of the name or when a court of competent jurisdiction orders cancellation on any ground. . . .

(b) Statutory and Common-Law Claims

The University contends that the district court erred in not awarding injunctive relief against White based upon alternative theories of common-law infringement and unfair competition, and violation of Nebraska's Uniform Deceptive Trade Practices Act, Neb. Rev. Stat. §§ 87-301 to 87-306. An injunction is an extraordinary remedy and ordinarily should not be granted except in a clear case where there is actual and substantial injury. Such a remedy should not be granted unless the right is clear, the damage is irreparable, and the remedy at law is inadequate to prevent a failure of justice. The only wrongful act alleged by the University as the basis for its claims was White's registration of the trade name "Husker Authentics," which has been held to be invalid and thus subject to cancellation. It is undisputed that White has never used or attempted to use the trade name "Husker Authentics," and he testified under oath that he had no intention of doing so until the ownership of the name was determined by a court. That determination has now been made in favor of the University, and there is no basis on this record to conclude that it will not be honored by White. Under these circumstances, we conclude that the University's claim for injunctive relief is without merit.

V. CONCLUSION

We conclude that because the University had a prior common-law right to the trade name "Husker Authentics," the district court did not err in determining that White's registration of the trade name pursuant to § 87-209 was invalid and should be canceled.

For the reasons stated above, we conclude that the University would not be entitled to transfer of the improperly registered trade name or injunctive relief under any of its alternative theories of recovery, and the district court therefore did not err in not granting such relief. The judgment of the district court is therefore affirmed.

TRUSTEES OF COLUMBIA UNIVERSITY v. COLUMBIA/HCA HEALTHCARE CORP.

964 F. Supp. 733 (S.D.N.Y. 1997)

John G. Koeltl, District Judge:

This case concerns a dispute over the right to use the mark "Columbia," alone and in combination with other words or phrases, in connection with the provision of medical and healthcare services. The plaintiff, The Trustees of Columbia University in the City of New York, alleges that the use of the name "Columbia" by the defendant, Columbia/HCA Healthcare Corporation, in connection with the provision of medical and healthcare services is likely to cause confusion, or to cause mistake, or to deceive the public as to the source or sponsorship of the defendant's services and the services of its affiliated physicians and to mislead the public into believing that the defendant's services emanate from, are approved or sponsored by, or are in some way associated or connected with the plaintiff. The plaintiff asserts claims under the Lanham Act, as amended, 15 U.S.C. § 1051 *et seq.*, for false designation of origin, infringement of a registered trademark, and dilution of a famous mark, under New York's anti-dilution statute, and under the common law for trademark infringement and unfair competition. The plaintiff seeks injunctive relief, damages, an accounting for profits, treble damages, prejudgment interest, attorneys' fees, and the costs and disbursements of the action. The plaintiff also asks that the defendant be required to run a program of corrective advertising.

Following an eight-day non-jury trial and after reviewing all of the submissions of the parties and having assessed the credibility of all of the witnesses, the Court makes the following findings of fact and conclusions of law:

FINDINGS OF FACT

. . . .

2. The plaintiff is a non-profit corporation organized and existing under the laws of the State of New York, having its principal place of business in the City of New York within this judicial district.

3. The defendant is a for-profit corporation organized and existing under the laws of the State of Delaware, having its principal place of business in Nashville, Tennessee. The defendant, through numerous subsidiaries, joint ventures and/or partnerships, owns and operates proprietary hospitals and ambulatory health care facilities throughout the United States, which it advertises and promotes in television and print advertising that is broadcast or circulated throughout the United States, including New York.

4. The plaintiff has long been one of the world's leading research and teaching universities that offers post-secondary and post-graduate education in a wide variety of intellectual and professional disciplines, including medicine.

. . . .

6. The plaintiff uses the name "Columbia University" in connection with various educational services. It is the owner of a federal registration for the service mark "Columbia University" in connection with "educational services."

7. The plaintiff has over a period of 200 years established itself as one of the preeminent names in medical education. The Columbia University College of Physicians and Surgeons, known generally as Columbia Medical School (the "Medical School"), as well as the School of Dental and Oral Surgery, the School of Nursing, and the School of Public Health, are regarded as among the most distinguished centers for medical education in the United States. . . .

. . . .

9. As an institution, the plaintiff is not engaged in the practice of medicine and is not licensed to provide medical services. The plaintiff permits the members of the faculty of its medical school to engage in the private clinical practice of medicine through its physician practice plans. Patients treated under the practice plans are billed directly by the plaintiff, and all monies paid by these patients are deposited into accounts owned by the plaintiff. After payment of the medical staff salaries, the plaintiff and its medical departments receive approximately five to ten percent of the total income from the practice plans.

10. In 1921, the plaintiff entered into an alliance with The Presbyterian Hospital in the City of New York, a nonprofit hospital, to form the world's first academic medical center. . . . The medical center uses the name "Columbia-Presbyterian Medical Center."

12. . . . Notwithstanding their affiliation, the Presbyterian Hospital and the plaintiff are separate entities that maintain separate trustees, officers, and public relations offices. . . .

13. Pursuant to the alliance, the plaintiff has orally authorized and licensed the

use of the Columbia name to be combined with the name of the Presbyterian Hospital as part of the joint mark "Columbia-Presbyterian Medical Center" that is used by both parties for the services provided by the center. The terms and restrictions of the license are reflected and confirmed in the 1994 Public Relations/ Media Guidelines for the Columbia-Presbyterian Medical Center. . . .

14. Pursuant to the alliance, the plaintiff has also orally consented to the use of the "Columbia" name by the Columbia-Presbyterian Medical Center Fund, Inc. ("the Fund"), which owns a federal service mark registration for the "Columbia-Presbyterian Medical Center" mark for "medical care services." The Fund has granted the plaintiff and the Presbyterian Hospital an irrevocable license to use the "Columbia-Presbyterian Medical Center" logo. . . .

. . . .

16. In connection with recent merger talks between the Presbyterian Hospital and New York Hospital, which is affiliated with Cornell University's medical school, faculty physicians from the plaintiff and Cornell University have formed an alliance designated "Columbia-Cornell Care." . . .

19. The plaintiff publishes and distributes promotional materials aimed at public consumers, primarily under the names "Columbia University," "Columbia-Presbyterian," and "Columbia-Presbyterian Medical Center." It has sponsored only one print advertisement relating to medical services in *The New York Times* entitled "Columbia University Doctors Are New York's Best." The plaintiff has never advertised any healthcare services on television or radio. The hospitals that are affiliated with the plaintiff and/or the Presbyterian Hospital advertise and promote this affiliation in print and on radio. . . .

20. In early 1996, the plaintiff and the Presbyterian Hospital retained the advertising firm, Bozell Worldwide, to prepare a coordinated advertising campaign to promote the services of the Columbia-Presbyterian Medical Center. . . .

21. The plaintiff maintains an Internet Web page at "Columbia.edu" with a well-known and highly regarded medical information service under the name "Go Ask Alice." The Columbia-Presbyterian Medical Center similarly maintains a "CPMC" Web site that is linked to the plaintiff's site.

22. The plaintiff does not own, nor has it attempted to secure, any United States Registration for the mark "Columbia University" or any other variation of the "Columbia" name in connection with medical, hospital, or healthcare services.

23. The word "Columbia" is a term with historic, patriotic, and geographic connotations. . . .

24. The defendant is the largest provider of healthcare services in the United States, operating approximately 340 hospitals, 130 surgery centers, and over 200 home healthcare agencies, all of which use some variation of the "Columbia" name. Since its founding in 1987, the defendant has grown to become the ninth largest private employer in the United States with over 285,000 employees.

25. The defendant's CEO, Richard Scott, who was trained as a lawyer rather than a doctor, initially selected the name "Columbia" because it sounded positive and

national in scope, which was consistent with his vision for the company. In selecting the name, Mr. Scott was not aware of any potential conflicts with any entities in the healthcare industry that use the name. Although he had heard of the plaintiff and its law school, he was not aware at that time that the plaintiff had a medical school and was not aware of the Columbia-Presbyterian Medical Center. The defendant has continuously used the word "Columbia" as part of its corporate name since 1987.

. . . .

28. Prior to 1995, the use of the "Columbia" name and logo by the defendant's hospitals was optional. At its Spring 1995 Leadership Conference, the defendant discussed "the process of moving to one identity," including putting the "Columbia" name on all facilities. The defendant developed and began to use its Diamond <C> logo with its name. . . . By August 1995, there were at least 45 facilities that were officially reported to be using "Columbia" as part of their name and in signage on their facilities.

29. In August 1995, the defendant conducted a trademark search to make sure that the Diamond <C> Columbia, without the HCA, did not conflict with any other uses of "Columbia." The defendant then published particular graphics standards for use of the Diamond <C> Columbia on all its facilities in a uniform way and on November 22, 1995, sent them to all division presidents and facility CEOs.

30. . . . . By August 1996, ninety-eight percent of the new signage was up on the defendant's facilities.

31. The defendant and its activities have been the subject of extensive media coverage, both local and national, particularly since 1992.

32. In late 1994, the defendant established an information and physician referral service using the telephone number 1-800-Columbia, and acquired exclusive rights to the number by January, 1995. . . .

33. In January 1995, the defendant began to publish its *Columbia One Source* quarterly magazine. Distribution has risen from 800,000 households to approximately 5 million households.

34. Beginning in May 1995, the defendant put up its "home page" on the Internet at "Columbia.net." It appears under a banner bearing the word Columbia along with the defendant's design and logo style for the Columbia name. Using hypertext links, the defendant's web page is linked to a "Columbia Physicians Corner," which provides transcripts of real time online conversations with "Columbia Physicians" on a variety of medical topics of interest to the general public. . . . Currently, the defendant's Internet site receives about one million hits per month.

35. In August 1995, defendant entered into an agreement with America Online, a major online computer and Internet service provider, to provide a variety of medical information and referral services "online" to America Online customers and other Internet users using the Internet domain name "Columbia.net." . . .

36. In September 1995, the defendant introduced a "Columbia" Visa card, which uses the Diamond <C> Columbia logo.

. . . .

39. In December 1994 and January 1995, the defendant sponsored its first national television advertising. Between May and December 1995, the defendant also ran a series of national full page print ads featuring the Columbia name and Diamond <C> logo in *USA Today*.

40. In the fall of 1995, the defendant set in motion the process of selecting an advertising agency to conduct a "brand" campaign. In contrast to a mark, which consists of a company's name and/or logo, a brand is a set of values, attitudes, and perceptions about the company that are associated with the company's mark.

. . . .

43. In August 1996, the defendant commenced its nationwide television and print brand advertising campaign. Each print and television ad uses the defendant's distinctive version of Columbia with the Diamond <C> logo in a particular type style and in a particular color.

44. The plaintiff has been aware of the defendant, its history of growth and expansion, and its press coverage for several years.

45. In February, 1993, the plaintiff appointed Richard Scott, the founder of Columbia Hospital Corporation and now the Chief Executive Officer of the defendant, to the plaintiff's Health Sciences Advisory Council. In Mr. Scott's letter of acceptance to the Health Sciences Advisory Council, the letterhead displayed a prominent use of the word Columbia independent of the formal name of the company in the upper left hand corner. In announcing Mr. Scott's appointment in its 1993–1994 brochure, the plaintiff described the defendant as follows: "Columbia was recently identified as the fourth fastest growing company in the United States." Mr. Scott was reappointed to the Health Sciences Advisory Council in 1994 and in 1995.

46. In September 1995, the plaintiff's School of Nursing gave Mr. Scott its "Second Century Award." . . .

47. Prior to September 13, 1996, the day this action was filed, the plaintiff did not express any objection to the defendant regarding the defendant's use of the word "Columbia."

CONCLUSIONS OF LAW

1. The plaintiff's first and second claims for relief are for trademark infringement and false designation of origin under Section 32(1) and Section 43(a) of the Lanham Act, 15 U.S.C. §§ 1114(1) and 1125(a). Section 32(1) provides protection against the "reproduction, counterfeit, copy, or colorable imitation of a registered mark" and its application to "labels, signs, prints, packages, wrappers, receptacles or advertisements" where "such use is likely to cause confusion, or to cause mistake, or to deceive." Section 43(a) protects both registered and unregistered marks against the use of any symbol or mark that "is likely to cause confusion, or to cause mistake, or to deceive as to the affiliation, connection, or association of such person with another person, or as to the origin, sponsorship, or approval of his or her goods, services, or commercial activities by another person. . . ."

2. To succeed on its claims, the plaintiff must, as a preliminary matter, show that it has a valid mark that is entitled to protection. The plaintiff claims that its use of the mark "Columbia," alone and in combination with other words and phrases, is entitled to protection in the field of medical or healthcare services.

3. The plaintiff is not entitled to a presumption of an exclusive right to use the Columbia mark in connection with medical or healthcare services. According to Section 7(b) of the Lanham Act, a certificate of registration of a trade or service mark issued by the United States Patent and Trademark Office is "prima facie evidence of the validity of the registered mark and of the registration of the mark, of the registrant's ownership of the mark, and of registrant's exclusive right to use the registered mark in commerce on or in connection with the goods or services specified in the certificate. . . ." Although the plaintiff has obtained federal service mark protection for the name "Columbia University" for educational services, "the presumption of an exclusive right to use a registered mark extends only to the goods and services noted in a registration certificate." The plaintiff does not own any federal trademark registrations for Columbia, Columbia-Presbyterian, Columbia University, or any other mark in connection with medical or healthcare services.

4. Where a mark is not registered, the plaintiff has the burden of proving that its mark is a valid trademark. The strength of a trademark in the marketplace and the degree of protection to which it is entitled are analyzed under four categories of marks that indicate increasing distinctiveness and protectability: (1) generic; (2) descriptive; (3) suggestive; (4) arbitrary or fanciful. Arbitrary or fanciful are sometimes described as separate categories. Generic marks are not protectable. Descriptive terms are protectable only with evidence of secondary meaning. Suggestive, arbitrary, and fanciful marks are eligible for protection without proof of secondary meaning.

5. The mark "Columbia," used alone and in combination with other words and phrases, is arbitrary. It has a dictionary meaning — "the United States" — that bears no relationship to medical or healthcare services. The mark "Columbia" is therefore eligible for protection without proof of secondary meaning.

6. Once a mark is found to be entitled to protection under the Lanham Act, the central question is whether "numerous ordinary prudent purchasers are likely to be misled or confused as to the source of the product in question because of the entrance in the marketplace of the defendant's mark," "or that there may be confusion as to [the] plaintiff's sponsorship or endorsement of the junior mark." [citations omitted]. Proof of actual confusion is not necessary. However, proof of actual confusion is probative of a likelihood of confusion.

7. The plaintiff alleges that there is a likelihood of both forward confusion and reverse confusion. Forward confusion is the traditional form of confusion in which the junior user uses the mark to sell goods or services based on the misperception that they originate with the senior user. "Reverse confusion exists when a subsequent user selects a trademark that is likely to cause consumers to believe, erroneously, that the goods marketed by the prior user are produced by the subsequent user." [citations omitted].

8. In *Polaroid Corp. v. Polarad Elecs. Corp.*, 287 F.2d 492 (2d Cir.), *cert. denied*,

368 U.S. 820 (1961), the Court of Appeals for the Second Circuit set forth eight non-exclusive factors that courts are to consider when determining whether a likelihood of confusion exists. In *Polaroid*, the court declared that:

> The prior owner's chance of success is a function of many variables: the strength of his mark, the degree of similarity between the two marks, the proximity of the products, the likelihood that the prior owner will bridge the gap, actual confusion, and the reciprocal of defendant's good faith in adopting its own mark, the quality of defendant's product, and the sophistication of the buyers. Even this extensive catalogue does not exhaust the possibilities — the court may have to take still other variables into account.

The decision as to whether a mark infringes requires a "comprehensive analysis of all the relevant facts and circumstances." [citation omitted]. . . .

When the likelihood of confusion is in doubt, the question will be resolved in favor of the senior user.

9. First, the Columbia mark, used alone and in combination with other words and phrases, is not a strong mark entitled to a wide scope of protection in the medical or healthcare field. The "strength" of a mark is a measure of " 'its tendency to identify the goods [or services] sold under the mark as emanating from a particular, although possibly anonymous, source.' " [citation omitted]. As discussed above, the plaintiff is not entitled to the presumption of an exclusive right to use its registered mark "Columbia University" for medical or healthcare services because its registration is for "educational services." Furthermore, although the plaintiff's Columbia mark, used alone and in combination with other phrases, is arbitrary and therefore "among the strongest and most highly protected class of trademarks," it does not signify an exclusive source of medical or healthcare services. [citation omitted]. The Court of Appeals for the Second Circuit has explained:

> Although denominating a mark "arbitrary" can be useful in focusing the inquiry, the strength of a mark "depends ultimately on its distinctiveness, or its 'origin-indicating' quality, in the eyes of the purchasing public." Just as an invented, even bizarre term can lose a measure of trademark protection if it has "become merely descriptive of the product," so too can the distinctiveness of an arbitrary mark be diluted by third party use.

Lever Bros. Co. v. American Bakeries Co., 693 F.2d 251, 256 (2d Cir. 1982). In this case, third party use and registrations of the name Columbia, including in the healthcare field, have diluted the strength of the Columbia mark. The defendant presented substantial evidence of third party use of the name Columbia in connection with a variety of businesses, including hospitals, healthcare services, and institutions. Aside from hospitals associated with or licensed by the plaintiff or the defendant, there are eight hospitals in the United States that incorporate the word "Columbia" in their title including Columbia-Greene Medical Center, Inc. in Catskill, New York and Columbia Memorial Hospital in Hudson, New York. There are at least seven healthcare-related service companies that use the Columbia name including Columbia Medical Plan, an HMO headquartered in Maryland. Even in the field of education in which the plaintiff has a registered mark, there are eighteen colleges, not associated with the plaintiff or the defendant, that use the name "Columbia," including Columbia College, which has approximately twenty locations nationwide. Moreover, the origin-indicating quality of the plaintiff's mark is further undercut by the fact that, as of August 1995, there were over one hundred federal trademark registrations that incorporated the Columbia name in medical, healthcare, and other fields. The plaintiff tries to minimize the significance of these third party uses of "Columbia" by pointing out that some of the hospitals, colleges, and companies are located in cities or counties or on rivers named Columbia and therefore should be disregarded. This argument is not persuasive.

There are many third party uses of "Columbia" that do not appear to have a specific geographic basis including Columbia Medical Center in Milwaukee, Wisconsin, and Columbia College of Nursing in Waukesha, Wisconsin. Moreover, whether or not there is a geographic reason for the selection of the Columbia name by these third parties, they are still openly using "Columbia" as a name, thereby detracting from the plaintiff's claimed distinctiveness or exclusivity. As the Vice Dean of the Columbia Faculty of Medicine and Senior Vice President for the Health Sciences Division of Columbia University acknowledged, the plaintiff does not have the exclusive right to use the Columbia mark for healthcare or educational services. The weakness of the mark therefore weighs strongly against a finding of likelihood of confusion.

10. Second, the marks used by the plaintiff and the defendant are similar to the extent that they both use the Columbia name, although they become more distinguishable when used in conjunction with other words or phrases and distinctive logos. In considering the degree of similarity between the marks, a court should address "two key questions: (1) whether the similarity between the two marks is likely to cause confusion and 2) what effect the similarity has upon prospective purchasers. In deciding whether the marks are similar as used, [a court does] not look just at the typewritten and aural similarity of the marks, but how they are presented in the marketplace." [citation omitted]. Here, the plaintiff uses the names "Columbia University," "Columbia University College of Physicians and Surgeons," "Columbia-Presbyterian Medical Center," and "Columbia-Presbyterian" . . . . The plaintiff generally does not use the name "Columbia" per se to conduct business or in its advertising except in isolated instances. Although the defendant uses the stylized Diamond <C> Columbia name and logo, "Columbia/HCA Healthcare Corporation," or "Columbia/HCA," the defendant more recently has focused on creating a national brand identity under the Diamond <C> Columbia mark alone. The likelihood of confusion between the plaintiff's and the defendant's marks decreases the more that they are used in conjunction with other words or phrases and distinctive logos as they most frequently are. However, the similarity of the names does weigh in favor of finding a likelihood of confusion.

11. Third, the services rendered by the parties are distinguishable. In considering the proximity of the products, a court should "consider whether the two products compete with each other." [citation omitted]. The focus of the product proximity inquiry is "the likelihood that customers may be confused as to the source of the products, rather than as to the products themselves. . . ." [citation omitted]. The plaintiff provides educational services through the operation of a number of graduate and undergraduate schools. One of those schools is a medical school. The

plaintiff's affiliation with hospitals such as the Presbyterian Hospital and with the Columbia-Presbyterian Medical Center does not change the nature of the plaintiff's services. Through the affiliation, the plaintiff's students receive medical training at the affiliated hospitals. This does not mean that the plaintiff provides healthcare services. . . . [T]he fact that faculty members of the plaintiff's medical school practice medicine as either individual practitioners or with a non-party hospital and engage in medical research does not mean that the plaintiff is a provider of medical services. The hospital with which the plaintiff is most closely affiliated — the Presbyterian Hospital — is not a party to this lawsuit and is not disputing the defendant's use of the name Columbia in connection with the provision of healthcare services. The plaintiff did not introduce any evidence that suggests that consumers perceive the medical services offered by doctors who are members of the plaintiff's faculty as originating from the plaintiff or that consumers associate any of the faculty practice plans with the plaintiff as opposed to the Presbyterian Hospital. In contrast, the defendant is a licensed provider of medical and healthcare services and is not an educational institution.

12. Fourth, "bridging the gap refers to the 'senior user's interest in preserving avenues of expansion and entering into related fields.' " [citation omitted]. This factor involves a determination of the likelihood that the plaintiff will enter the defendant's business or of the average customer's perception that the plaintiff would enter the defendant's market. The plaintiff's present and future alliances and affiliations with medical and healthcare providers does not change the fact that the plaintiff has not demonstrated a likelihood that it will become a provider of medical or healthcare services.

13. Fifth, the plaintiff has presented little evidence of actual forward or reverse confusion. . . . No actual consumer confusion need be shown to justify a finding of a likelihood of confusion, although the presence of actual confusion obviously supports such a finding. . . . The plaintiff's proffered evidence of actual confusion is de minimis. Several of the plaintiff's doctors testified that a few third parties had told them that they thought that the defendant's advertisements were connected with the plaintiff. However, the relevance of this type of evidence is lessened by the small number of people who allegedly expressed confusion and the absence of a valid statistical sample. Moreover, there is a difference between isolated expressions of momentary confusion and confusion that leads to actual purchasing decisions. The plaintiff presented no evidence of any patients or doctors who made decisions about which hospital to select based upon confusion between the plaintiff and the defendant. . . .

14. Sixth, the plaintiff has not established that the defendant acted in bad faith in adopting its mark. Bad faith is shown by demonstrating that the "defendant adopted its mark with the intention of capitalizing on [the] plaintiff's reputation and goodwill and any confusion between his and the senior user's product." [citation omitted]. . . .

In this case, there is no evidence to suggest that the defendant acted in bad faith or with the intention of misappropriating any good will built up by the plaintiff in names incorporating the word "Columbia." The defendant's CEO, Richard Scott, testified credibly that he selected the name "Columbia" because it sounded positive and national in scope, which was consistent with his vision for the company. Mr. Scott wanted to imitate other companies that had been successful with "national" or "big" sounding names such as American Medical International, National Medical Enterprises, Republic Health, and Community Health System. . . . Moreover, he was not aware of any potential conflicts with any entities in the healthcare business using the name.

15. Seventh, the quality of the defendant's product does not favor the plaintiff. The analysis of the quality of the defendants' product "is primarily concerned with whether the senior user's reputation could be jeopardized by virtue of the fact that the junior user's product is of inferior quality." [citation omitted]. Although the plaintiff has presented evidence that its educational programs, faculty, doctors, and students are of the highest quality, it has failed to introduce any concrete evidence that the defendant's hospitals, medical services, doctors, and staff would taint the plaintiff. Indeed, many of the defendant's hospitals have been listed among the outstanding hospitals in the country. . . .

16. Eighth, in considering the sophistication of consumers, a court must evaluate "the general impression of the ordinary purchaser, buying under the normally prevalent conditions of the market and giving the attention such purchasers usually give in buying that class of goods. . . ." [citations omitted]. In this case, although members of the general public are the technical purchasers of medical and healthcare services provided by hospitals, the real purchasers for the purposes of trademark analysis are the doctors who choose the hospitals to which they send their patients. The doctors generally are a very sophisticated group of consumers who use great care in deciding which hospitals with which to affiliate themselves and to which they send their patients. There may also be a second possible group of purchasers made up of patients who choose their doctors based on the doctors' affiliations with certain hospitals, but no evidence of this group was presented at trial.

17. The *Polaroid* factors must be weighed as a whole and this process is not a "mechanical process." [citation omitted]. In this case, the great majority of the factors point decidedly to a lack of confusion. More specifically, given the weakness of the plaintiff's mark, particularly in view of the widespread use of the name Columbia, the distinctive services rendered by each of the parties, the lack of actual confusion, the good faith over a long period of time shown by the defendant, and the sophistication of the consumers, the balance of the *Polaroid* factors shows that there is little likelihood of confusion. Although the names are certainly similar, it is unlikely that that similarity will cause either forward or reverse confusion between the plaintiff's and the defendant's marks.

18. The plaintiff's third claim for relief is for federal trademark dilution pursuant to Section 43(c) of the Lanham Act. Section 43(c) entitles the owner of a famous mark "to an injunction against another person's commercial use in commerce of a mark or trade name, if such use begins after the mark has become famous and causes dilution of the distinctive quality of the mark. . . ." 15 U.S.C. § 1125(c). To prevail on a dilution claim, a plaintiff must show (1) ownership of a famous mark; and (2) dilution. . . .

The determination whether a mark is famous and distinctive under Section 43(c) is similar to the analysis for strength of the mark for trademark infringement purposes. Dilution is defined as "the lessening of the capacity of a famous mark to identify and distinguish goods or services, regardless of the presence or absence of-(1) competition between the owner of the famous mark and other parties, or (2) likelihood of confusion, mistake, or deception." Dilution may be shown either through blurring or tarnishment. Dilution by tarnishment occurs where the defendant uses the plaintiff's mark in association with unwholesome or shoddy goods or services. Dilution by blurring occurs " 'where the defendant uses or modifies the plaintiff's trademark to identify the defendant's goods and services, raising the possibility that the mark will lose its ability to serve as a unique identifier of the plaintiff's product.' " [citation omitted].

19. As discussed above, any acquired distinctiveness of the plaintiff's mark in connection with medical or healthcare services has been seriously undermined by third party use of the same or similar marks within New York and across the United States. Even the Vice Dean of the Columbia Faculty of Medicine and Senior Vice President for the Health Sciences Division of Columbia University conceded that the plaintiff does not have the exclusive right to use the Columbia name for healthcare or educational services. Moreover, the plaintiff has also failed to demonstrate how the defendant has used the Columbia mark to tarnish, blur, or dilute the plaintiff's service. . . .

20. The plaintiff's fourth claim for relief is for trademark dilution under N.Y. General Business Law § 368-d . . . .

. . . Similar to Section 43(c) of the Lanham Act, § 368-d requires that a plaintiff show: (1) ownership of a distinctive mark, and (2) a likelihood of dilution. As discussed above, the plaintiff has failed to establish either ownership of a distinctive mark or a likelihood of dilution from the defendant's activities.

21. The plaintiff's fifth claim for relief is for common law trademark infringement and unfair competition. To prevail on a claim of common law trademark infringement, a plaintiff must show "that the symbols for which it seeks trademark protection are valid, legally protectable marks and that another's subsequent use of a similar mark is likely to create confusion as to the origin of the product." [citation omitted]. The plaintiff's claim for common law trademark infringement fails. As discussed above, although the plaintiff's Columbia mark, used alone and in combination with other words and phrases, is a valid, legally protectable mark, the defendant's use of a similar mark is not likely to create confusion. With regard to the plaintiff's unfair competition claim, under New York law, "the essence of unfair competition . . . is 'the bad faith misappropriation of the labors and expenditures of another, likely to cause confusion or to deceive purchasers as to the origin of the goods.' " [citation omitted]. The plaintiff's unfair competition claim must also fail. As explained above, there is no evidence to suggest that the defendant acted in bad faith or with the intention of misappropriating any good will built up by the plaintiff in names incorporating the word "Columbia."

22. The defendant also argues that the plaintiff's causes of action are barred by estoppel by laches. In order to prevail on a laches defense, a defendant must demonstrate (1) the plaintiff had knowledge of the infringing activities; (2) the plaintiff inexcusably delayed in taking action; and (3) the defendant would be

prejudiced if the plaintiff belatedly asserted its rights to the mark. . . . The issue of laches is left to the discretion of the district court.

23. The plaintiff had knowledge of the defendant's infringing activities for at least three and a half years before it took any action. At the very latest, the plaintiff became aware that the defendant was using the Columbia name in 1993. In February 1993, the plaintiff appointed the defendant's CEO, Mr. Scott, to serve on its Health Sciences Advisory Council. In Mr. Scott's letter of acceptance to the Health Sciences Advisory Council, the word Columbia, independent of the defendant's formal name, was displayed prominently in the upper left hand corner. In announcing the appointment of Mr. Scott in its 1993–1994 brochure, the plaintiff stated: "Columbia was recently identified as the fourth fastest growing company in the United States." All of the physicians who testified on the plaintiff's behalf admitted that they have been aware of the defendant and its history of growth and expansion for several years. Several of these physicians acknowledged that they have been "concerned" or "troubled" by the defendant's use of the Columbia name for several years. However, the plaintiff did not do anything to stop the alleged infringement until September 1996, when it filed this action.

24. The plaintiff asserts that its delay in taking action is excusable because the defendant's conduct followed a course of progressive encroachment. The plaintiff argues that the defendant's use of the Columbia name changed qualitatively, quantitatively, and precipitously just weeks prior to commencement of this action when the defendant announced the launch of its branding campaign and intention to rename its growing list of hospitals. . . . In this case, however, the defendant's use of the Columbia name has been both prominent and national in scope for years. . . . The defendant's recent brand campaign was different from the defendant's prior advertising in the sense that it was a centralized effort coordinated by the corporate office. . . . But it did not significantly change the total amount of money spent on advertising by the defendant. . . .

25. The defendant has also demonstrated that the plaintiff's delay in asserting its rights prejudiced it. . . . From the beginning of 1993 until September 1996, the plaintiff was aware of the defendant but did not express any objection to the defendant regarding its use of the "Columbia" name. During this period, the defendant spent millions of dollars developing programs that prominently feature the Columbia name including its Internet site, the 1-800-Columbia telephone number, *Columbia One Source*, and the Columbia Visa card, advertising and promoting its facilities, changing the names of its hospitals, and developing its new unified design and brand campaign. By waiting over three and a half years to assert its present claims, the plaintiff precluded the possibility that the defendant could effectively adopt an alternative marketing position. Accordingly, the plaintiff's claims are also barred by estoppel by laches.

CONCLUSION

For the reasons explained above, all of the plaintiff's claims are dismissed . . . .

NOTE

As is set forth in the cases above, "distinctiveness" is often the most important requirement for trademark protection. It is this qualification that aptly serves to identify the respective goods and protects the product or brand from confusion, deception, or mistake. Additionally, there are usually four types of trademarks: generic, descriptive, suggestive, and arbitrary or fanciful. Which of these four were at issue in the cases above? Can there be situations where more than one of these, if not all, can be called into question? Which of the four categories of trademarks do you think would be easiest to register, that is, easiest to satisfy the "distinctive" requirement?

B. COMMERCIALIZATION ISSUES

1. Technology Transfer Operations

Mark L. Gordon, *University Controlled or Owned Technologies: The State of Commercialization and Recommendations*, 30 J.C. & U.L. 641 (2004)*

University technology transfer is the process by which a university commercializes inventions and innovations developed by university faculty and researchers. Technology transfer takes many forms, from patent licensing to forming start-up ventures on campus. University technology transfer programs are growing exponentially. Universities have long reflected upon, studied, and implemented transfer and commercialization programs. Due to current economic and legal realities, however, an intense, if not completely new, era has emerged. Universities are increasing their commitment to, and support of, commercialization programs. Policies and missions have been revisited and reshaped. Campus research is exploding with applied innovation. Faculty and students are being recruited by the strength and virtue of commercialization programs. Economic pressures and competition are intense. Opportunities, as well as pitfalls, abound in this complex field. Universities that proceed with the proper balance of aggressiveness, creativity, and prudence will realize the many benefits of university technology transfer.

I. HISTORY — THE OPENING OF THE ERA

University technology transfer did not gain real momentum in the United States until the early 1980s. Several forces have coalesced to raise the prominence and expansion of university technology transfer, not the least of which are the Bayh-Dole Act, the changing economy of the United States, and financial pressures on universities coupled with the potential for pay-offs from transfer programs.

A. The Numbers

The statistics clearly illustrate the explosive growth of university technology transfer activities over the past few decades. In 1980, universities generated about $1 million in licensing revenue. According to the most recent Association of University Technology Managers ("AUTM") survey for the year 2002, licensing revenue for survey respondents was $1.267 billion. In 1985, 589 new patents were awarded to academia. AUTM survey respondents filed 7,741 new patent applications and were issued 3,673 new patents in 2002. During the ten-year period from 1974 through 1984, universities granted about one thousand licenses total. In 2002 alone, AUTM survey respondents reported the execution of 4,673 licenses and options. From 1980 through 1993, AUTM survey respondents were involved in the formation of a total of 1,169 start-up companies. In 2002 alone, survey respondents formed 450 start-up companies.

B. The Bayh-Dole Act

The Bayh-Dole Act (the "Act") governs the commercialization of inventions and innovations resulting from research funded by the federal government. The Act was signed into law on December 12, 1980, and became effective in July 1981. It was a response to an increase in global competition in technology-related fields, and was also seen as a way for taxpayers to enjoy the benefits of the investment they made in university-based research. Prior to the passage of the Act, governmental policies regarding ownership of inventions and innovations developed by entities with federal government funding lacked uniformity. Different federal agencies applied different rules. One common element of all of these government agencies' policies was that title to the inventions and innovations funded by the government was presumed to rest with the government. This presumption proved difficult and costly to overcome, meaning that universities rarely retained ownership of inventions and innovations developed by their researchers with federal government money.

In passing the Act, Congress stated that it wanted to promote the commercialization and public availability of federally-funded inventions and innovations. n order to meet this objective, the Act, in most cases, allows recipients of federal funding to retain title to inventions developed with federal funding. Thus, universities that develop inventions and innovations with federal government funding may license them to third parties and keep the proceeds. However, the university is required to grant the government a nonexclusive, irrevocable, paid-up license to utilize the invention throughout the world. The government is also given "march-in rights" to help ensure that the public receives the benefit of the invention. This right allows the government to revoke a university's title to any invention or innovation if the federal agency that funded the research determines that the university's commercialization efforts have been inadequate.

The Bayh-Dole Act is essential to universities' ability to commercialize inventions and innovations developed by their researchers because the majority of university research was, and is, funded by the federal government. AUTM survey respondents reported that 68.2% of their research expenditures for 2002 came from the federal government. Thus, without the Act, universities would have substantial difficulties reaping the financial benefits of a great deal of their research. Likewise, the public did not receive the full benefit of this research prior to passage of the Act, because much of it was not made commercially available. The Bayh-Dole Act opened the door to a new era in which both universities and the general public are able to enjoy the fruits of research funded by the federal government.

C. The Changing U.S. Economy

For much of the twentieth century, the United States had an industrial economy based on large-scale production and manufacturing, such as automobile manufacturing. In 1960, manufacturing output was 27% of U.S. GDP and manufacturing jobs accounted for 31% of total employment in the United States. As the twentieth century came to a close, however, some manufacturing activity had moved overseas and the manufacturing firms that remain in this country have become increasingly dependent on technology to increase productivity and remain competitive. By 1997, manufacturing output was 17% of GDP and, in 1998, manufacturing jobs accounted for 14.9% of total employment. A new type of American economy has emerged. The industries that have remained in the United State are more reliant and focused on scientific and technological innovation in fields such as biomedical and computer technology. With this shift, the type of scientific and technology-related research conducted at universities has become more directly relevant and important to the U.S. economy. The passage of the Bayh-Dole Act represented (among other things) recognition of this shift. Private industry also recognized this trend and has significantly increased its financial support of university research. Many universities have responded by embracing technology transfer and pushing for the commercialization of university-developed inventions and innovations.

D. Economic Pay-offs/Economic Pressures

University technology transfer is "hot." Most universities are involved, and some generate a great deal of revenue from it. This fact, combined with the reality of budget cuts and economic pressures faced by many universities, has made success in technology transfer very important to many universities. Clearly, the pay-off for such success is potentially very significant. This potential has proven attractive to many universities.

The reasons for the growth of university technology transfer, whether it be the Bayh-Dole Act, the changing economy of the United States, economic realities at universities, or a combination of these factors, may be debatable, but it is hard to deny that university technology transfer has grown at an amazing rate over the past two decades. A question remains passionately debated: Is this a good thing?

II. TENSION OF TECHNOLOGY TRANSFER WITH MISSION

Traditionally, it has been understood that universities have a two-fold mission. First, universities are charged with educating their students, and second, universities are expected to conduct research for the benefit of the public. Some argue that these missions can be, and in some cases are, compromised when private interests become involved in the research process and commercialization becomes the goal of research endeavors. Both universities and researchers stand to profit from the successful commercialization of inventions and innovations. Is the traditional mission of universities and their faculty members compromised by this fact?

A. Compromised Faculty?

Prior to the explosion in university technology transfer, it was generally presumed that university researchers toiled for the welfare of the general public, without regard to the commercial potential of their discoveries. More recently, however, it has become clear that this is not always the case. A consequence of increased university commercialization is that the professor/entrepreneur is becoming more and more common, and for good reason. Responsible faculty members now usually receive a portion of any revenue generated by their inventions or innovations. The Bayh-Dole Act requires that the inventors receive some share, albeit an indeterminate one, of the revenue generated from their invention or innovation developed with federal funding. A study from 2000 found that 28% of life sciences faculty at universities received private sponsor funding, 15% held equity in the private sponsor, 33% were engaged in paid consulting arrangements, and 32% held board positions. University researchers often have a direct financial stake in the outcome of their research. Some critics argue that this fact creates conflicts of interest that can compromise their research. Some critics even argue that university researchers sometimes choose their research topics based on the short-term commercial potential of the subject and that, because of this, important areas of research with less commercial appeal are often ignored. On the other hand, a study by Professor David Blumenthal suggests that, instead of having a corrupting influence on faculty members, university commercialization actually has a positive impact. The study concluded that biomedical faculty who were involved in technology commercialization taught no less, published more, produced more patented discoveries, and served in more administrative capacities than faculty not involved in technology transfer activities.

Another matter of concern commonly raised by critics of university technology transfer is that the free flow of ideas in the academic world is stifled by the focus on commercialization of inventions and innovations. Many in the academic community insist that it is imperative that discoveries are published immediately and that information is shared openly. Companies that work with university researchers, on the other hand, often demand delays in the publication and sharing of discoveries and ideas. In order to protect the value of proprietary information, it is often necessary to avoid publication, or other forms of sharing of information and data, until proper intellectual property protection is in place. In the United States, a patent cannot be issued for an invention or innovation if it has been described in a printed publication more than one year before a patent application is filed with the Patent and Trademark Office. This one-year grace period is not even available in some foreign countries, meaning that any sort of publication can lead to the loss of intellectual property rights if steps are not taken to protect them. Likewise, any ownership or rights in trade secrets, or "know-how," can be lost if not properly protected before the information is shared with other parties. . . .

Many universities, along with their faculty members, have reacted to these concerns by adopting conflict-of-interest policies. These policies attempt to avoid conflicts of interest as much as possible, and to ensure that those conflicts that do arise do not taint research outcomes.

B. Compromised Universities?

While university-industry partnerships have become quite common, some believe that a serious conflict in mission arises when universities and companies partner for the purposes of research. Critics have suggested that one negative impact of this phenomenon has been a reduction in funding at some universities for departments that do not produce revenue-generating inventions and innovations, such as humanities departments. At the same time, some of these same universities have increased funding for science and technology departments. Critics suggest that this type of resource allocation, where profit is seemingly put ahead of educational opportunities and offerings, conflicts with the mission of the university to educate students and conduct research for the benefit of the public. Conversely, supporters of university technology transfer often point out the benefits of these activities, which can include upgraded facilities and increased funding for all academic departments. Universities with exceptional technology transfer programs are also able to attract top professors and offer unique learning opportunities in technology, business, and entrepreneurism, leading to a better overall academic environment and more educational opportunities for students at those universities.

Whether one is a proponent or opponent of university technology transfer programs, it appears that such programs are here to stay. Those that continue to fight this phenomenon are likely engaged in a losing battle, although some universities have reacted to the criticism by implementing stronger conflict-of-interest policies. It should be noted, however, that these policies are not foolproof. Conflicts will exist and no policy will completely guard against them. This is a risk that universities must take or, alternatively, should avoid by not involving themselves in technology transfer. Universities that are aggressively pursuing technology transfer opportunities are fighting a battle of their own: attempting to succeed in a highly competitive environment.

III. DISTINCTIVE TECHNOLOGY TRANSFER MODELS

University technology transfer takes many different forms. There is no single optimal structure or mode of operation for a university technology transfer program. Universities have developed numerous models and procedures for their technology transfer programs. Some have flourished, while others have not.

A. University of Wisconsin-Madison

The University of Wisconsin-Madison was a pioneer in university technology transfer. The Wisconsin Alumni Research Foundation ("WARF") was established in 1925 when nine University of Wisconsin alumni each donated $100 as capital. WARF granted its first license, for an artificial Vitamin D supplement, to the Quaker Oats Company in 1927. Currently, WARF has about forty employees, as well as a board of eighteen volunteer trustees. . . .

Revenue generated by WARF is distributed to the University of Wisconsin-Madison Graduate School, the inventors, and the department of the inventors. WARF contributes over $30 million each year to the University and has generated about $600 million for the University during its history. WARF received 279 invention disclosures in fiscal year 2002. The University of Wisconsin-Madison has been involved in the development of ninety-eight technology-based companies in Wisconsin since 1995.

WARF sets up a licensing team for each invention that it accepts. The team consists of the inventor(s), an intellectual property manager, one or more licensing managers, WARF's in-house counsel, marketing specialists, and various support staff. Outside counsel is used for patent prosecution. . . .

The Office of University-Industry Relations was established in the early 1960s to facilitate interactions, and develop relationships, between University of Wisconsin research and the business and industrial community. The University Research Park is home to nearly 100 companies. The mission of the Research Park is to encourage partnerships between businesses and university researchers. . . .

B. Stanford University

Stanford University has an established and very successful technology transfer program through its Office of Technology Licensing (the "OTL"), which was established in 1970. In fact, the program is so highly regarded that it is able to charge between $1000 and $2000 per hour for private tours of its technology transfer facilities. For fiscal year 2001–02, the OTL received 315 invention disclosures, executed 112 new licenses, generated $52.7 million in total royalties, had 42 different technologies that each generated over $100,000 in royalties for the year, and generated $405,000 from liquidated equity. Some of the more prominent inventions and innovations that have come through the Stanford OTL are injectable collagen for plastic and cosmetic surgery, optimization software used in the design of yachts for the Americas Cup, the recombinant DNA "gene splicing" techniques that have given rise to the biotechnology industry, and improved FM sound systems for electronic music devices and systems.

The Stanford OTL licensing process focuses on marketing the inventions and innovations under its control. So-called "Licensing Associates," who generally have degrees in science or engineering, experience in marketing, and prior licensing experience, staff the OTL. These associates are given complete responsibility for evaluating, marketing, licensing, protecting, and monitoring the progress of specific technologies. When intellectual property protection is necessary, the OTL seeks and selects outside counsel on a case-by-case basis based on their qualifications for the particular technology. The OTL works with Stanford's Industrial Contracts Offices when negotiating contracts with outside parties. The Research Incentive Fund has been established by the OTL to help turn faculty discoveries into commercially viable products.

The OTL aggressively markets the services that it provides to the university community, which include intellectual property protection, marketing, licensing, and assistance with forming start-up companies. Likewise, the OTL aggressively markets the technologies under its control to potential licensees and other prospective partners. The OTL works closely with private industry in the surrounding Silicon Valley community and with companies from outside the area. . . .

C. University of Illinois

The University of Illinois has a broad and assertive technology transfer program. In fiscal year 2002, the University had 220 invention disclosures, filed for 143 patents, was issued 42 new patents, executed 74 licenses, and generated more than $9 million in licensing revenue. In addition, in the period from 2001–2002, University of Illinois faculty launched eighteen start-up companies.

The Board of Trustees created the position of Vice President for Economic Development and Corporate Relations ("VPEDCR") to oversee and facilitate all aspects of technology commercialization for the University. Under the VPEDCR are two Offices of Technology Management ("OTM") at the Urbana-Champaign and Chicago campuses. The OTMs protect, market, and license University-developed technology and intellectual property, and coordinate their efforts through the VPEDCR. The staff at the OTM at the Urbana-Champaign campus includes a director, an associate director, several technology managers and attorneys, paralegals, a patent coordinator, and various support staff. IllinoisVENTURES, LLC was formed under the direction of the Board of Trustees to facilitate the formation of start-up companies based on University technology. In addition, University of Illinois Research Park, LLC was formed to manage operations of research parks and business incubators run by the University.

In order to market its technologies, the University holds events called "i emerging" every six months. These events showcase its technology and start-up companies and attract venture capitalists, angel investors, researchers, and representatives from industry. Additionally, the OTMs sponsor technology briefings, where industry representatives are invited to hear presentations on a particular new technology. The web sites for the OTMs provide a comprehensive database of University technology that is available for licensing. All of the above-mentioned organizations work closely together, and with private industry, in an attempt to bring University of Illinois technologies to market.

. . . .

IV. COMMERCIALIZATION MISSTEPS

Not everything has gone smoothly for all universities that have thrown their hats into the commercialization ring. Numerous cautionary tales illustrate the need for universities to proceed cautiously and prudently with regard to technology transfer activities.

The University of Florida was not prepared to take full advantage of technology transfer when a University researcher invented Gatorade in 1965. At the time, the University did not have a formal policy in place regarding the ownership of faculty inventions and, initially, had no interest in marketing the new drink. After the inventors independently reached an agreement with Stokley-Van Kamp to produce and sell Gatorade, the school decided that it did, indeed, want to be involved with Gatorade. By this time, in order to receive any of the licensing revenue from Gatorade, the University was forced to go to court and was only granted a 20% share of the profits. Although the University reportedly receives in the neighborhood of $4.5 million each year from Gatorade, it is easy to conclude that it would be receiving substantially more than that if it had formal revenue sharing agreements in place with its researchers at the time of the invention. The University's current revenue sharing agreement with its researchers gives ownership of all inventions and innovations developed by school employees using its resources to the school and calls for the University to receive up to 70% of any licensing revenue.

. . . .

The University of California at Berkeley ("Berkeley") was criticized for the public-relations aspect of a sponsored research and technology transfer agreement entered into with a Swiss company in 1998. The deal called for Novartis to give $25 million to Berkeley's Department of Plant and Microbial Biology in exchange for first rights to negotiate licenses on roughly one-third of the department's discoveries, as well as two of the five seats on the department's research committee. This arrangement led to widespread protest and dissent within the Berkeley community by those who felt that the agreement gave Novartis too much control over Berkeley research and its results. Berkeley faced protests from both faculty and students, as well as outside groups. Petitions against the deal were circulated, a five-part series in the student newspaper decried the deal and the growing privatization of Berkeley in general, and a group of students protested at graduation by wearing the Novartis logo on their caps.

Boston University fell victim to too much optimism and poor investment controls when it took a large equity position in a University start-up. During the 1980s and early 1990s, the University invested $85 million, nearly one-fifth of its endowment, in one company, Seragen, a biotech firm founded by several Boston University professors that focused on cancer research. Seragen eventually failed and was sold, leaving the University with a net loss of almost $60 million. It was later discovered that the University's president, as well as a number of the University's trustees, had personally invested millions of dollars in Seragen.

. . . .

V. SUGGESTED GUIDELINES FOR COMMERCIALIZATION

University commercialization presents vast opportunities, but also daunting challenges. . . . [E]ach program should do no less than carefully analyze and focus on the following nine fundamentals: (1) institutional mission alignment, (2) program structure and resources, (3) funding sources, (4) asset protection and defense, (5) missionary work, (6) asset evaluation and valuation, (7) marketing and distribution channels, (8) documentation, and (9) the re-evaluation process, each as discussed in greater detail below.

1. Institutional Mission Alignment

A university's technology transfer program should not, and does not have to, conflict with the mission of the university. In fact, a properly developed commercialization program will only enhance a university's ability to achieve its mission by increasing financial resources and educational opportunities. A concerted effort should be made to ensure that a conflict with mission does not arise, both during the establishment of a technology transfer program and throughout its life. The participation of stakeholders from throughout the university community in a technology transfer program and the establishment of a conflict-of-interest policy are two important alignment considerations.

. . . .

2. Program Structure and Resources

. . . .

When a university technology transfer program is in its earliest stages, it may be wise to start a small in-house program and outsource many of its functions. As the program matures, an in-house team of professionals and staff can be added. This strategy allows the university to avoid the large initial capital outlay required to set-up a fully functioning in-house technology transfer program. Additionally, this strategy will allow the university to avoid mistakes in the initial structuring of the program and to access the expertise of those with experience. Needs should be accurately identified and addressed slowly and methodically.

3. Funding Sources; Projections

There are many ways to fund a university technology transfer program. Usually, the university provides some level of initial funding — cash or in-kind services. If a university, however, cannot, or will not, budget for an adequate commitment, there are other options. For instance, individuals and private foundations sometimes fund technology transfer programs . . . . Also, corporations may be willing to fund technology transfer operations at a university in exchange for rights or preferences in the technology that comes through the technology transfer office. Nonetheless, a long-term goal of any technology transfer program must be to become financially self-sufficient and, eventually, a source of sustained value for the university.

Financial planning for a technology transfer program is challenging. It is difficult to project a program's income because it is impossible to predict the quantity and quality of new technologies . . . . Nevertheless, just as in any speculative venture, the process of financial planning and projecting is essential. In essence, these technology transfer programs must have a business and financial plan at least as rigorous as such programs require of third parties that commercialize the university's technologies.

4. Identifying, Protecting, and Defending Assets

Without assets (in this case most likely intellectual property), there is no technology transfer program. The fundamentals of identifying, protecting, and defending intellectual property rights are, however, often not initially concentrated on by researchers. At a minimum, it is therefore imperative that university researchers be educated in the basics of intellectual property law so that the university does not unwittingly lose "control" of the inventions or innovations. . . .

Additionally, a comprehensive intellectual property policy should be developed that clearly articulates ownership and control issues, as well as obligations of both the university and the researchers, including graduate students and research assistants. Some of the important topics that should be addressed in an intellectual property policy include: scope, ownership of inventions and innovations, income sharing formulae, disclosure mechanisms, obligations of inventors, and publication policies.

It is also important that a process, through which researchers disclose inventions and innovations, be developed. Generally, universities should create an invention disclosure form and mandate that researchers complete such a form for every invention or innovation they develop. . . .

Technology transfer programs will also need to take the necessary steps to secure protection of assets by contract and by securing appropriate copyright, patent, trademark, and other legal protections. . . .

5. Missionary Work

Identification and protection are essential, but marketing and distribution are synonymous with "commercialization." University researchers need to be made aware of the existence and role of the technology "transfer" program. They need to have a sense of the value of the technology transfer program to themselves, their research, the university, and the community. Thus, another essential mission of technology transfer officials must be to focus on internal marketing. Effective internal marketing educates and communicates the program's value to university administration, alumni, boards of trustees, and any other stakeholders whose support is needed to nurture or grow a program. . . .

6. Evaluation and Valuation of Assets

One of the more difficult aspects of university technology transfer is the assessment and prioritization of the inventions and innovations. Technology transfer offices must weigh answers to important questions as: What assets hold a reasonable chance to be marketable and under what terms? Which inventions should the technology transfer program spend its valuable time and resources developing and marketing? . . .

7. Marketing and Distribution Channels

There are numerous possible ways to derive market value from inventions and innovations, including through direct licensing, ventures, alliances, start-ups, and donation. Finding the right choice or choices (since few formats are mutually exclusive) is no small task. Researchers are often good resources for information on potential partners in their particular areas of expertise. A university's technology transfer office should also develop a network of contacts both in private industry and in the venture capital community. . . . Regardless of which method is chosen, a technology transfer program's marketing plan should be aggressive if it is to succeed in the commercialization arena.

Another consideration is the different types of partners with whom a university technology transfer program may choose to work. Some of these partner types include: licensees, capital sources, investors, joint venture partners, consultants, and counsel. When choosing potential partners, it is important to carefully evaluate their skills and experience in the relevant field or discipline. . . .

Another aspect of the evaluation process is determining the optimal path to market. This determination often leads to a licensing of the technology. In some instances, however, it is advisable to start a new company to develop and market the technology. . . .

When evaluating capital partners and other potential investors, it is important to be both practical and prudent. It can be difficult to attract investment dollars. It is necessary, therefore, to have a realistic outlook regarding potential investors and what to expect. Regardless of the difficulty, it is important to carefully assess the skills and attributes of all potential investors. . . .

8. Documenting Transactions

No part of our commercial marketplace works without documenting understandings and expectations. Experience, knowledge, diligence, and careful planning are especially important. Proper terms and conditions can make the difference between success and failure.

It is a good idea for a technology transfer office to develop a library of basic form contracts for different situations. This library could include exclusive and non-exclusive licensing agreements of various types (i.e., patent license, software license, etc.), sponsored research contracts, joint venture contracts, and non-disclosure agreements. These basic contracts will serve as starting points in various circumstances.

It is also important to have an understanding of industry standard terms and conditions. . . .

9. Consistent, Critical and Continuous Re-evaluation

University technology transfer programs are often very focused on getting inventions or innovations to market. Such a "launch" of a technology does not end the process for a technology transfer office. Continued monitoring and evaluation of both products and partners are necessary to ensure that the commercial potential of an invention or innovation is maximized. Moreover, university personnel can make program assessments and necessary adjustments. In general, a technology transfer office should conduct regular audits of its partners' activities and its own internal processes.

. . . .

2. Questions of Ownership

UNIVERSITY PATENTS, INC. v. KLIGMAN

762 F. Supp. 1212 (E.D. Pa. 1991)

Jay C. Waldman, United States District Judge

Plaintiffs, The Trustees of the University of Pennsylvania (the University) and University Patents, Inc. (UPI), commenced this action to recover royalties allegedly owed to them by defendants for a preparation for photoaged skin invented by Dr. Kligman and marketed under license by Johnson & Johnson (J & J), and to seek a declaration of ownership in the patent rights to this product.

Presently before the court is defendants' Motion for Summary Judgment premised on the absence of any demonstrated enforceable rights of plaintiffs in Dr. Kligman's discovery. The parties have engaged in considerable discovery and have filed voluminous briefs. Oral argument was held on March 27, 1991.

I. PROCEDURAL HISTORY

On May 10, 1989, UPI filed a complaint, claiming that: (1) Dr. Kligman breached his employment contract with the University and also breached its Patent Policy; (2) UPI, by reason of its agreement with the University, is a third-party beneficiary to the Patent Policy and to the employment contract with Dr. Kligman; (3) because of his wrongful concealment of the invention, Dr. Kligman holds the patent in a constructive trust for the benefit of UPI and the University; and, (4) Dr. Kligman's conduct constituted a tortious conversion of UPI and University property. UPI, relying on a service agreement with the University, also seeks a judgment declaring that UPI is the owner of and has the right to license the invention to third parties.

On January 22, 1990, the University filed a separate action, claiming that (1) J & J's conduct constituted a tortious interference with the employment contract between the University and Dr. Kligman; (2) Dr. Kligman breached his employment contract with the University, specifically Patent and Conflict of Interest Policies set forth in employee handbooks in 1977 and 1983; and, (3) Dr. Kligman and J & J conspired to deprive the University of its rights in the photoaging discovery. The University also claims that J & J failed to pay amounts due under the 1967 and 1975 anti-acne licensing contract. The University seeks an accounting to ascertain the amounts due. Furthermore, the University seeks a judgment declaring (1) that the Kligman/J & J licensing agreement is null and void, and (2) that the University owns all rights and interest in the invention and patent in question. Finally, the

University seeks punitive damages from J & J.

. . . .

III. FACTS

The pertinent facts from the uncontroverted evidence and the balance of the record viewed in a light most favorable to plaintiffs are as follow.

On August 11, 1965, the then President of the University of Pennsylvania, Gaylord P. Harnell, appointed a Patent Policy Committee to meet and make recommendations to the Trustees of the University. The committee consisted of five faculty members, one administrator and University counsel. The committee drafted a policy which was approved by the trustees in January 1966.

Under the policy, all inventions and discoveries resulting from work carried out on University time or at University expense were to be the property of the University. Specifically, the policy provides:

> The Trustees have declared it to be the policy of the University of Pennsylvania that any invention or discovery which may result from work carried out on University time or at University expense by special grants or otherwise is the property of the University. Patents on such inventions or discoveries may be applied for in any country by the University in which case the inventor shall assign his interest in the patent application to the University. The University will exercise its ownership of such patent, with or without profit, with due regard for the public interest as well as the interests of all persons concerned. Procedures for implementation of this policy shall be developed and promulgated by the President of the University.

This basic policy has remained unchanged since 1966. The procedures for implementing the policy, however, have been revised on several occasions. The parties have submitted the procedures as revised in 1973.

As revised in 1973, the procedures make it clear that the policy was to apply to "all members of the staff of the University whether fully or partially affiliated." One of the primary features of the implementing procedures is the disclosure requirement which provides: "If a staff member believes he has made an invention or discovery that may be patentable he shall discuss the matter with the Director of Research Administration. The latter will recommend to the Vice Provost for Graduate Studies and Research whether or not the University shall file a patent application."

If after such disclosure the University decides to apply for a patent, two alternatives are to be considered. The University may arrange for a non-profit patent management organization ("PMO") to exploit the patent through the granting of licenses to commercial firms. If it appears more advantageous, the University may make such arrangements directly with a commercial firm. Finally, if the University decides that it is not interested in assuming the costs of the patent application, the inventor may apply in his own name and at his own expense. Under such circumstances the inventor shall grant to the University a royalty-free, irrevocable, non-exclusive license to make or use the invention for its own purposes.

Plaintiffs contend that the policy was first published and mailed to faculty members on February 25, 1966. The policy was *summarized* in the 1969 Faculty and Administration Handbook. The policy was set forth in the 1977 Research Investigators' Handbook which was distributed to faculty members through the University's internal mail system. The policy as well as new implementing procedures were disseminated in a revised Research Investigators' Handbook in 1983.

The University also had a Conflict of Interest Policy. Defendants contend that the policy was not enacted, or at least not disseminated, until 1983 when the revised Research Investigators' Handbook was released. Plaintiffs contend that the policy existed prior to that time but under a different name. It appears that, at least as of 1973, the Patent Policy Implementing Procedures contained a section captioned "Outside Consulting or Employment Agreements." This section directs the faculty member to advise the Dean or Director of any potential conflict between the member's obligation under the University's Patent Policy and any obligation assumed in connection with outside employment. On or about March 8, 1983, the University issued a "Conflict of Interest Policy" for faculty members which restated relevant existing policy and further required its faculty members to disclose to the University, in advance, any research in their respective fields in which they wish to engage for any private enterprise and first to offer such opportunities to the University.

Dr. Kligman is an Emeritus Professor of Dermatology at the University of Pennsylvania and has been affiliated with the University since 1948. Most of Dr. Kligman's scientific research has been funded through consulting agreements with various drug and cosmetic companies, and performed at private research facilities, principally Ivy Laboratories and the Simon Greenberg Foundation. Dr. Kligman established Ivy Laboratories in the 1950's and the Greenberg Foundation in March 1960. Neither have any affiliation with the University.

In the 1960's, while treating inmates at the Holmsburg Prison, Dr. Kligman discovered that Vitamin A Acid was an effective treatment for acne. In an effort to commercialize the invention, Dr. Kligman consulted J & J and later disclosed his discovery to the University.

Dr. Kligman presented his invention to J & J on or about August 3, 1967. Mr. Warner was a patent attorney for Johnson & Johnson from 1957 until February 1, 1976. Mr. Warner states that he discussed the University's Patent Policy with Dr. Kligman and stated that in his mind there was a question as to whether the Policy applied to this invention. Mr. Warner stated that Dr. Kligman maintained that the University had no claim to the invention because the bulk of the work was done on his own time and expense at Holmsburg Prison but that he intended to donate the royalties to the University because he was expected and wanted to help fund the Dermatology Department. Finally, Dr. Kligman agreed to notify the University and resolve any problems.

On August 24, 1967, Dr. Kligman wrote to Encel H. Dodge, who was then the Director of the Office of Project Research and Grants of the University. In the letter, Dr. Kligman states that he wished to bring to the University's attention his development of a new topical preparation for the treatment of acne. Dr. Kligman also stated that the innovation is "probably not patentable since the active ingredient is a Vitamin A derivative." He further stated that the formulation was developed on his own time with personal funds. Dr. Kligman stated that he was negotiating about potential royalties with J & J, and that he had proposed a 3% royalty to be paid to the University for exclusive use by the Dermatology Department. On September 11, 1967, Mr. Dodge responded stating that, in his opinion, University policy did not prohibit such a royalty arrangement. Mr. Dodge also referenced Dr. Kligman's statements that the invention was probably not patentable and was developed entirely on his own time using his own funds.

Mr. Warner then drafted a three-way agreement which makes clear that Dr. Kligman was the sole owner of the acne invention and that the "University has relinquished its rights, if any, to J & J in the 'Kligman Acne Treatment.' " A patent ultimately issued for the acne invention on April 24, 1973. This patent was assigned to J & J which conducted voluminous tests and thereafter secured FDA approval. The drug was introduced into the market under the name Retin-A and proved to be an enormous success. J & J has profited and the University has received millions of dollars in royalties.

Mr. Warner drafted three subsequent agreements in accordance with his understanding that the University had acknowledged that Dr. Kligman could freely license inventions made on his own time and with his own funds. The University was not made a party to these agreements which included an agreement regarding a Vitamin-A Acid/Steroid combination drug and consulting agreements entered into in 1970 and 1972.

During the 1970's and early 1980's, Dr. Kligman invented a second method of using Vitamin A Acid to retard the effects of aging of the skin. . . . During the 1970's, he used Vitamin A Acid to treat acne among residents of the Riverview Home for the Aged. Dr. Kligman states that this work was conducted as part of his work at Ivy Laboratories. The plaintiffs allege that Dr. Kligman discovered and reduced to practice these inventions using University funds, facilities, hospital patients and staff.

In 1971, Dr. Kligman wrote to J & J regarding the new observations and in early 1974 he sent them a manuscript outlining his findings. At this time, J & J filed an Investigational New Drug Application with the FDA and thereafter filed a Clinical Trial Protocol outlining the studies that would be run. Dr. Kligman's wife, Dr. Lorraine Kligman, who is also a member of the University's Department of Dermatology, was involved in the studies.

On June 15, 1978, J & J agreed to sponsor Dr. Lorraine Kligman's studies of the affect of Vitamin A Acid on rhino mice exposed to ultraviolet radiation. The grant from J & J was paid to the Simon Greenberg Foundation. J & J sponsored other research in this project at Ivy Laboratories and the Simon Greenberg Foundation, including grants in 1980 and 1982.

On August 28, 1981, Dr. Kligman filed a patent application for the photoaging preparation in his own name. Plaintiffs allege that this was in violation of the Patent Policy. . . .

At this time, news of the invention was carried in the popular press and was the subject of numerous magazine articles. . . . Anthony Merritt, the University's Director of Research Administration, was aware of this publicity. He believed, however, that the product in question was merely a new adaption of the old preparation and therefore was covered by the 1967 agreement.

On July 18, 1984, with the patent application still pending, Dr. Kligman signed a licensing agreement with J & J. The new agreement declared that Dr. Kligman was the sole owner and was free to license the invention. The agreement gave J & J the exclusive right to make, use and sell the invention and had a favorable royalty rate for Dr. Kligman, which was on a sliding scale of 5%, 3% and 1% of U.S. sales. Again, like all of the agreements which came after the first Retin-A agreement, the University was not made a party to the agreement.

Patent No. 4,603,146 issued in July 1986 for the photoaging discovery. Because Dr. Kligman filed the patent himself, his attorney claimed that small entity status entitled him to reduced filing fees. The patent application had been denied several times when, in May 1984, Dr. Kligman retained the services of another patent attorney, Mr. Schwarze. Because the licensing agreement was not yet signed, Mr. Schwarze prepared another small entity status application. Once the licensing agreement was signed, the small entity status had to be changed. Dr. Kligman waited until September 1986 to do this, and in January 1987, the Patent Office granted the change.

In June 1978, the University entered into an agreement with UPI which was amended and re-executed in August 1983 and again in September 1987. Under these agreements, UPI was required to provide certain licensing services for the University in exchange for a percentage of royalties to which the University became entitled because of rights it might acquire under its Patent Policy. UPI states that during the course of its relationship with the University it received over 322 disclosures from various University faculty members.

Plaintiffs allege that in April 1988, UPI for the first time became aware of the new invention and thereafter notified the University of its existence. Plaintiffs allege that they spent a year trying to get Dr. Kligman to provide evidence that he discovered the invention independently of the University, but that he failed to produce any such evidence. Thereafter, UPI filed its action in this court.

IV. ANALYSIS AND DISCUSSION

Defendants contend that the University can show no contractual obligation upon Dr. Kligman by which he was required to assign his rights in the photoaging invention to the University. Defendants contend that employment policies and handbooks generally are not binding under Pennsylvania law, that the Patent Policy in question is not binding, and that even if it is, it is not applicable in the context of the present dispute. Plaintiffs argue that the patent policy was binding and obligated Dr. Kligman to assign his patentable rights to the University.

Although "ownership" and "inventorship" are not identical for patent law purposes, they are related. Inventorship provides the starting point for determining ownership of patent rights. The true and original inventor must be named in the application for a patent and, absent some effective transfer or obligation to assign the patent rights, the original inventor owns the right to obtain the patent. Patents have the attributes of personal property and both patents and applications for patents are assignable.

Since a patent is a creature of federal statutory law, it may be transferred only in the manner provided by such law. An assignment of a patent must be in writing. The writing must show a clear and unmistakable intent to transfer ownership, and must be executed by the patentee or by the patentee's assigns or legal representatives.

An agreement to assign a patent or an interest therein is an executory contract which may be valid and enforceable. An equitable assignee may sue in law for damages or in equity for specific performance. Since contracts to assign patent rights do not have a statutory basis, but rather have a basis in common law or in equity, they need not be in writing and they may be implied as well as express. . . .

The present case arises in the context of an employment relationship. . . .

The general rule is that an individual owns the patent rights in the subject matter of which he is an inventor even though he conceived of the subject matter or reduced it to practice during the course of employment. The "mere existence of an employer-employee relationship does not of itself entitle the employer to an assignment of any inventions which the employee devises during the employment." [citations omitted]. This is true even where the employee uses the time and facilities of the employer. . . .

To this general rule there are two exceptions and one limitation. First, an employer owns an employee's inventions if the employee is a party to a contract to that effect. Second, where an employee is hired to invent something or solve a particular problem, the property of the inventions of the employee related thereto belongs to the employer.

Where an employee uses the time or facilities of his employer, the employer may have a non-exclusive and non-transferrable royalty-free license (that is, a "shop right") to use the employee's patented invention. *United States v. Dubilier*, 289 U.S. 178 (1933).

These basic principles were discussed by the Supreme Court in 1933 and have remained substantially unchanged:

> One employed to make an invention, who succeeds, during his term of service, in accomplishing that task, is bound to assign to his employer any patent obtained. The reason is that he has only produced that which he was employed to invent. His invention is the precise subject of the contract of employment. A term of the agreement necessarily is that what he is paid to produce belongs to his paymaster. On the other hand, if the employment be general, albeit it covers a field of labor and effort in the performance of which the employee conceived the invention for which he obtained a patent, the contract is not so broadly construed as to require an assignment of the patent. . . .

> Recognition of the nature of the act of invention also defines the limits of the so-called shop right, which, shortly stated, is that, where a servant, during his hours of employment, working with his master's materials and appliances, conceives and perfects an invention for which he obtains a patent, he must accord his master a nonexclusive right to practice the invention. This is an application of equitable principles. Since the servant uses his master's time, facilities, and materials to attain a concrete result, the latter is in equity entitled to use that which embodies his own property and to duplicate it as often as he may find occasion to employ similar appliances in his business. But the employer in such a case has no equity to demand a conveyance of the invention, which is the original conception of the employee alone, in which the employer had no part.

Dubilier, 289 U.S. at 187–89.

The courts of Pennsylvania will enforce express contracts to transfer patent rights which are clear and unambiguous. In this case, there clearly is no express written contract to assign. The University's 1977 Research Investigators' Handbook included a standard "Patent Agreement" form and there was a "policy" that "all personnel who may be involved in research must execute a Patent Agreement." Dr. Kligman, however, never executed such an agreement and it appears that he was not even requested to do so.

Rather, plaintiffs base their contract claim on implied contract and unilateral contract theories, relying on the University's Handbook and policies and the parties' course of dealing.

In the context of patent rights, the courts have been hesitant to "imply" contracts to assign. This reluctance is based on the "nature of invention" — it being the product of original thought:

> The reluctance of courts to imply or infer an agreement by the employee to assign his patent is due to a recognition of the peculiar nature of the act of invention, which consists neither in finding out the laws of nature, nor in fruitful research as to the operation of natural laws, but in discovering how those laws may be utilized or applied for some beneficial purpose, by a process, a device, or a machine. It is the result of an inventive act, the birth of an idea and its reduction to practice; the product of original thought; a concept demonstrated to be true by practical application or embodiment in tangible form.

Dubilier, 289 U.S. at 188 (citations omitted). The law regarding implied contracts to assign patent rights in the employer-employee context has developed primarily in two areas: (1) where the employee is hired for some particular reason, and (2) where the employee holds a position of trust as to the employer.

. . . .

. . . The employee handbook in question clearly was not communicated as a definite offer of employment. The 1977 Research Investigators' Handbook is a fairly detailed 110-page document describing the various policies and procedures involved in research at the University, including the Patent Policy. The first statement in the

Handbook itself suggests that it is a "guide" rather than an enforceable legal document.

In addition to a discussion of the Patent Policy and procedures, the Handbook contains a patent agreement form to be signed by personnel involved in research. The Handbook states: "It is the policy of the University that all personnel who may be involved in research must execute a Patent Agreement at the time of employment." Research Investigators' Handbook at 82. The Patent Agreement provides in pertinent part:

> UNIVERSITY OF PENNSYLVANIA PATENT AGREEMENTIN CONSIDERATION of information and facilities for research made available to me by The Trustees of the University of Pennsylvania under a grant or contract with the Government of the United States, University sponsorship, or other sponsors, I hereby agree:
>
> 1. That I will promptly communicate to the Director, Officer or Research Administration, full information as to each invention, discovery and improvement conceived or first actually reduced to practice by me during my work under such grant, contract, or sponsorship.
>
> 2. That I will, if and when requested, either before or after leaving the employment of the University of Pennsylvania, execute all papers necessary to file application for patents on any such invention, discovery, or improvement, in any country, and will assign such application, invention, discovery, or improvement covered thereby, and the patents that may be issued thereon as directed in accordance with the established patent policy of the University of Pennsylvania and sponsors of research projects on which I may work.

. . . .

The Handbook contained a second agreement form, captioned "Patent Agreement For U.S. Public Health Service Research And Training Grants," which was to be executed by "all persons who perform any part of the work under a grant or award from the Department of Health, Education, and Welfare."

Plaintiffs suggest that both forms were only required when the research was funded by the government. Mr. Merritt acknowledged that even the first form "was used primarily where people had federal funding." These agreement forms were left out of the 1983 Handbook because as Mr. Merritt states: "Federal laws changed. There was a uniform government patent policy implemented, Public Law 96517; and it was felt under the new law that these kinds of sign-offs weren't required for Federal grants."

It is not clear whether the University ever enforced compliance with the policy that all personnel who may be involved in research execute a Patent Agreement, but it is clear that it never did so with any vigor. . . . There is no evidence that Dr. Kligman ever signed a Patent Agreement. Indeed, there is no evidence that he was ever asked to do so.

In addition to these forms, the University had an Invention Disclosure Form which it used after a faculty member had reported an invention to the research office. The invention disclosure form requires such relevant information as the title of the invention, the name of the inventor, the names of any sponsors, and certain key dates. The Instructions for Completing the form made the import of the document clear: "The Invention Disclosure Form is a legal document and requires a reasonable degree of care in its completion. There are parts of it which may be of extreme importance to the patentability of your invention and to the protection of rights under any patent which might issue related to your invention." The faculty member is required to sign a statement which provides in pertinent part:

> To the best of my (our) knowledge, the information set forth above and in the attachments is true, correct and complete. I (we) understand that this information may be relied upon during the preparation, filing and prosecution of a patent application relating to the invention disclosed herein, and that the accuracy of this information may be important to the validity of any patent which may result from such application. I (we) understand that I (we) have a duty to disclose all information which is material to the examination of any application filed on the invention, and I (we) will, from time to time, update and correct this information during the pendency of this application.
>
> I (we) acknowledge that the invention was made pursuant to the University Patent Policy and agree to assign all right, title and interest in the invention to the University pursuant to the terms of the Patent Policy.

As a general rule, the University did not require the completion of Disclosure Forms at any time prior to actual disclosure. *See* Deposition of Anthony Merritt, at 12–14. In the case of Dr. Kligman even this was not done. The University never requested that Dr. Kligman sign a patent agreement or disclosure form with regard to the acne or photoaging inventions.

In 1967, even after Dr. Kligman wrote to the Director of the Office of Project Research disclosing the acne invention, he was not required to sign a disclosure form. In the letter, Dr. Kligman had stated that the invention was probably not patentable and was developed on his own time. The University's Patent Policy, however, did not strictly turn on "patentability." The agreement which was ultimately executed by J & J, the University and Dr. Kligman clearly evidences the possibility that a patent would emerge.

The language of the Patent Agreement and Disclosure forms make clear that they were intended to be enforceable contracts. It cannot be said, however, that any reasonable person receiving the handbook, without more, would have understood himself to be bound by the terms of a form agreement he never executed.

Plaintiffs also cite Dr. Kligman's first letter to Mr. Dodge and his responses to deposition questions as evidence of his intention to be bound by the policy. Dr. Kligman testified that before Mr. Warner read the patent policy to him, he had no knowledge that this document existed. He testified that he sought a clarification of his position from Mr. Dodge who responded that the University had no rights in the initial discovery since it was not made on University time or at its expense. He understood the policy not to apply to him because his modus operandi was to obtain independent funding and to conduct research at private facilities, principally at Ivy.

A fair reading of Kligman's letter to Dodge of August 24, 1967 suggests that Dr. Kligman decided gratuitously to assign any royalties to the University. Since he states in the letter that he developed the anti-acne preparation "on my own time using personal funds" at a non-University facility, it is not reasonable to infer that Dr. Kligman proposed an assignment pursuant to the Patent Policy.

Dr. Kligman, however, also testified that he would be bound by the Patent Policy if he "came up with some patentable invention which arose out of work done on University time or using University resources" had he been "fully affiliated." Based at least in part on Mr. Dodge's response of September 11, 1967 to Dr. Kligman's letter, he contends that he reasonably believed he was exempt from the Patent Policy as a non-fully affiliated employee. No reasonable person reading that letter could conclude that Dodge was advising Kligman that he was exempt from the Policy. Dodge specifically referenced Dr. Kligman's assurance that no University time or resources were expended on the discovery. Further, the Patent Policy makes clear on its face that it applies "to all members of the staff of the University whether fully or partially affiliated."

Even if there may have been an offer and acceptance, however, it is not clear that there was any consideration. *See Harsco Corp. v. Zlotnicki*, 779 F.2d 906, 910–911 (3d Cir. 1985), *cert. denied*, 476 U.S. 1171 (1986) (agreement to employ defendant for reasonable period of time provided adequate consideration for express agreement to assign patent rights).

In *Harsco*, as in most of the other handbook cases, a handbook provision was used in an attempt to recast the terms of an at-will employment arrangement. In such circumstances, the retention of the employee for a term and his continued performance of services may constitute adequate consideration. Here, although the parties cannot agree on Dr. Kligman's exact status, it is clear that he was and is a tenured professor and thus not subject to the at-will rule. When a college grants a professor tenure, it is giving away its right to terminate the professor at will. "The respective rights and obligations of employer and employee, touching an invention conceived by the latter, spring from the contract of employment." *Dubilier*, U.S. at 187. Thus, the respective patent rights of the parties regarding Dr. Kligman's discoveries during his affiliation with the University must be analyzed in the context of a tenured employment relationship.

The unilateral conferral of a benefit on a tenured employee is not enforceable without additional consideration. It logically would appear therefrom that the unilateral imposition of a new obligation on such an employee would not be enforceable without such consideration. Even courts which have taken a liberal view of the applicability of handbook provisions have held that a handbook issued after the existence of an express or implied contract of employment is not binding in the absence of additional consideration. . . .

The distinction between an express and an implied contract is merely the manner of expressing one's assent. Consideration is required in either context.

Plaintiffs contend that by allowing Dr. Kligman to use the University's facilities and staff, the University provided consideration for his adherence to the Patent Policy. . . . There is no evidence of record to show that unqualified access to the

University's staff and facilities was available to Dr. Kligman as a condition of his employment with the University as a tenured professor. Indeed, the record contains virtually no explanation of the meaning of Dr. Kligman's employment designation or evidence of the terms and conditions of his employment.

Whether a contract was formed generally is a question of fact to be resolved by a jury. Like most jury questions, however, it can be answered by the court when the meaning is so clear that a jury's verdict to the contrary would be set aside.

This is a close case, particularly in view of the manner in which the University conveyed its Patent Policy and its lax enforcement thereof. On the current record, however, the court cannot conclude that no jury reasonably could find that an implied contract to assign the patent in question was formed between Dr. Kligman and the University. There is evidence, however scant, from which one could find that Dr. Kligman was aware of the Patent Policy since August 1967 and manifested an intent to be bound by it. By emphasizing that the initial discovery was on his own time and at his own expense in his letter to Mr. Dodge, Dr. Kligman may have led the University reasonably to conclude that he recognized the applicability of the Policy to any discovery achieved with the use of University resources. There is evidence that such resources were used with regard to the photoaging discovery and no evidence to refute the University's position that the placement of these resources at Dr. Kligman's disposal constituted consideration.

Accordingly, defendants' motion for summary judgment premised on the absence of a binding agreement as a matter of law will be denied at this time.

As noted, the question of whether UPI may have enforceable rights under an agreement to assign as a third-party beneficiary has been reserved. The court notes, however, that since 1950, it has been the law in Pennsylvania that to have standing to recover on a contract as a third-party beneficiary, the actual parties to the contract must express an intention that the third party be a beneficiary to whom the promisor's obligation runs in the contract itself. . . .

That a third party is not expressly named as a beneficiary is not preclusive if the intent of the parties that certain third parties would be benefitted was otherwise clear from the language of the agreement.

An appropriate order will be entered.

ORDER

AND NOW, this 17th day of April, 1991, upon consideration of defendants' Motion to Dismiss for Failure to State a Claim or Alternatively for Summary Judgment and plaintiffs' response thereto and following argument thereon, IT IS HEREBY ORDERED that said Motion is DENIED.

NOTES

1. The general rule for copyright and patent ownership is that it rests with the author or creator of the protected work. However, as can be seen in *University Patents, Inc.*, the analysis is almost never that simple — especially regarding the interplay of faculty work or research and their institutional employer. The "work made for hire" doctrine, codified in 17 U.S.C. § 101 of the Copyright Act, is often invoked in this kind of situation. In a nutshell, the doctrine holds that the employer (for our purposes, the university or college) is considered the author and owner of all copyrights in the employee's work if made within the scope of his or her employment unless expressly agreed otherwise. Not surprisingly, most university faculty handbooks or charters directly address this issue in some regard. For example, in *Fenn v. Yale University*, 283 F. Supp. 2d 615 (D. Conn. 2003), the court addressed an alleged violation of a university patent policy, where a faculty member failed to notify Yale of an invention, as was required. Under the policy, Yale works with a research corporation to carry out the commercialization, and unless the parties agree otherwise, Yale retains ownership of the invention, the research company gets the titles to the patents, and the inventors share in the royalties. Due to long-standing disagreements with the policy itself, the faculty member in *Fenn* refused to disclose the invention. When he presented his research nationally, Yale discovered the work and filed suit. The court found in favor of Yale.

2. Many academics and some courts have championed and created a "teacher exception" to the "work made for hire" doctrine rooted in three main justifications: (1) tradition in the field, (2) lack of congressional refute in light of courts adopting the exception, and (3) the disruption and outrage in the educational setting if this exception were neglected. *See Hays v. Sony Corporation of America*, 847 F.2d 412 (7th Cir. 1988); and *Williams v. Weisser*, 273 Cal. App. 2d 726, 78 Cal. Rptr. 542 (1969). Can you think of any other arguments that would support this "teacher exception?" *See* Sunil Kulkarni, *All Professors Create Equally: Why Faculty Should Have Complete Control over the Intellectual Property Rights in their Creations*, 47 Hastings L. J. 221 (1995). Despite the strong arguments posed by advocates of the exception, it remains in more-or-less direct contradiction of the statutory language: if you created your work in the scope of employment, it belongs to the employer. Is this a battle between good policy and strict interpretation?

3. Lately there has been much controversy over the cost of education (e.g., tuition, room and board, etc.). What about the cost of knowledge? What role does intellectual property law (copyright, patent, trademark) play in the cost and accessibility of knowledge? Think about the costs of textbooks, journals, online database licenses, etc. Think also about fair use, its purpose, and its advantages and disadvantages.

4. In his article excerpt above, Mark Gordon asks whether the commercialization and technology transfer era has led to a conflict of mission. On one hand, faculty is to educate students. On the other hand, they are to engage in research to advance knowledge. Conceptually and traditionally, these two are exceedingly compatible. But with economies as they are — and people as they are — commercialization is not only an expectation, but also a requirement and a rather lucrative proposition, with licensing agreements and royalties to follow. What do you think? Have traditional academics been transformed into entrepreneurs? By necessity? By desire? By requirement? By nature? For the betterment of education and the advancement of knowledge?

5. In his article, Gordon describes the Bayh-Dole Act as one of the forces that have contributed to the expansion of technology transfer in institutions of higher education. The Bayh-Dole Act regulates the commercialization of discoveries resulting from federally sponsored research. According to Gordon, "[t]he Bayh-Dole Act opened the door to a new era in which both universities and the general public are able to enjoy the fruits of research funded by the federal government." Of course, much public good can come from such discoveries when the research that generates them is funded by the government. However, questions of ownership in those discoveries also arise. In *Board of Trustees of the Leland Stanford Jr. University v. Roche Molecular Systems, Inc.*, 131 S. Ct. 2188 (2011), the Supreme Court asked whether the Bayh-Dole Act automatically vested title in federally funded inventions to federal contractors. The Court answered that it did not. Patent law, dating back to the 1700s, has held that inventions belong, first, to the inventor. The Court in *Stanford* held that the Bayh-Dole Act does not alter this history. Instead, the Act provides that federal contractors "may . . . elect to retain title to any subject invention", with "subject invention" defined as "any invention of the contractor conceived or first actually reduced to practice in the performance of work under a funding agreement." *See* 35 U.S.C. § 201(e). This language, according to the Court, is not enough to *automatically* vest title in the federal contractor. Contract language must be clearer.

In *Stanford*, a faculty researcher at Stanford University had agreed to the University's Copyright and Patent Agreement, which held that he "agree[d] to assign" to Stanford his "right, title and interest in" inventions resulting from his employment at Stanford. At Stanford's request, the faculty researcher began working with a research company named Cetus (later renamed Roche). He signed an agreement with Cetus, as well, this one stating that he "will assign and do[es] hereby assign" to Cetus the "right, title and interest in each of the ideas, inventions and improvements" made "as a consequence of [his] access" to Cetus. After some Nobel prize-winning techniques for AIDS treatments were developed at Cetus, Stanford filed suit against Cetus (by then, Roche), claiming it was the rightful owner. However, because of the steep history of assigning rights in inventions to the inventor, the Court must find unambiguous language in Bayh-Dole to automatically assign rights to the inventor's employer (Stanford). The Court found no such language, merely finding that the contractor "may elect to retain" title. According to the Court, the language of the Cetus agreement assigned the researcher's rights to Cetus, preventing Stanford from "retaining" a title it never had. The practical lesson from *Stanford* is that clearly written intellectual property contracts and policies are a must.

Chapter XIII

INSTITUTIONAL TREATMENT OF INDIVIDUALS WITH DISABILITIES

A. THE REHABILITATION ACT OF 1973

Federal legislation calling for nondiscrimination against persons with disabilities began with Title V of the Rehabilitation Act of 1973, 29 U.S.C. § 701 *et seq.* The Act is regarded as the first civil rights statute for special needs individuals, extending the same kind of statutory protection provided to those discriminated against on the basis of race or gender. Originally intended to protect individuals within the employment sector, the definition of an "individual" was expanded to include impairments that substantially limit other major activities. Thus, the legislation mandates nondiscrimination in both employment and education.

Employment falls under the aegis of Section 503 of the Act for any entity receiving federal financial assistance. 29 U.S.C. § 791. This section encourages covered entities to consider the applications of disabled candidates. Section 504 explicitly prohibits the exclusion and discrimination of any qualified individual based on his or her disability:

> No otherwise qualified individual with a disability . . . shall, solely by reasons of his or her disability, be excluded from participation in, be denied the benefits of, or be subjected to discrimination under any program or activity receiving Federal financial assistance.

29 U.S.C. § 794

Initial litigation attempted to construe the definition of "program or activity" narrowly, urging the Act's application to be limited to specific programs or activities within an individual entity or agency. The United States Supreme Court promoted this position, finding that discrimination in one federal grant program should not enable termination of all federal funding in the recipient's other programs. *Grove City College v. Bell*, 465 U.S. 555 (1984). The U.S. Congress objected to this interpretation and added a provision to Section 504 making explicit its intent that the definition of a program or activity extended to *all* operations of the funding recipient. Hence, any program, policy, practice, or department within a postsecondary institution where disability discrimination occurs subjects that institution to the withdrawal of *all* federal funds.

The scope of the nondiscrimination requirement is broad and extends to many areas of operation including social services, health care, facilities, and transportation. The definition of "program or activity" under the statute includes any college, university or other postsecondary institution. 29 U.S.C. § 794 (b)(2)(A). The plain language of the Act does not require that public or private institutions prepare special programs for disabled students or employees; it does, however, require that a college or university be prepared to make appropriate academic adjustments and "reasonable accommodations" so that disabled students may participate in the same way as non-disabled persons. As to the Act's requirements concerning treatment of disabled employees, the main nondiscrimination standard is that such persons must be able to fulfill essential functions of the position with or without reasonable accommodations. Undue hardship may be used as a defense to any requested accommodations that the employer contends to be unreasonable.

B. THE AMERICANS WITH DISABILITIES ACT (ADA)

The Americans with Disabilities Act follows the Rehabilitation Act in protecting disabled persons from discrimination. The ADA expands coverage such that, in addition to public institutions, private educational institutions and private employers and commercial enterprises serving the public are also obligated to engage in nondiscrimination. 42 U.S.C. §§ 12101–12213. Through the Commerce Clause of the United States Constitution, U.S. Const. Art. I, § 8, cl. 3, Congress used its authority to regulate interstate commerce as an avenue to extend the reach of the Rehabilitation Act to both the public and the private sectors.

The ADA is broken down into four categories of regulation. These categories govern disability discrimination in: (1) employment (Title I); (2) state and local government services (Title II); (3) public accommodations (Title III); and (4) telecommunications services (Title IV). 42 U.S.C. §§ 12111–12189; 47 U.S.C. § 225.

The definition of a person with a disability under the ADA is one who:

1. has a physical or mental impairment that substantially limits one or more major life activities;
2. has a record of such an impairment; or
3. is regarded as having such impairment.

42 U.S.C. § 12102(1)(A–C).

The terms "substantially limits" and a "major life activity" have been the subject of heated debate and litigation since the inception of the ADA. *See Sutton v. United Airlines*, 527 U.S. 471 (1999). To correct judicial interpretations defining these terms narrowly, Congress enacted amendments to the ADA in 2008 making clear that "disability" under any of these categories should be defined as broadly and inclusively as possible within the limits of the Act. ADA Amendments Act of 2008, Pub. L. 110-325. Title II adds one more requirement to the definition of a qualifying disabled individual for purposes of analyzing access to public services (like state universities). 42 U.S.C. § 12131(2). For Title II, a qualifying disabled individual is someone with a disability who "with or without reasonable modifications . . . meets the essential eligibility requirements for the receipt of services or the participation in programs or activities provided by a public entity." *Id.* Any service, program, or good offered by the state or local form of government is prevented from discriminating against eligible disabled individuals. 42 U.S.C. § 12131.

For Title III, a "public accommodation" is broadly defined as any private entity which has operations that effect commerce. 42 U.S.C. § 12181(7). Private entities that provide these public accommodations are prohibited from discriminating against any disabled individuals, unless providing modifications or accommodations would substantially alter the nature of the goods, services, or facilities being offered. 42 U.S.C. § 12182(2)(A). Similarly, Title II prohibits employers from discriminating against disabled employees or job applicants. However, as in the Rehabilitation Act, an employer is not required to provide a reasonable accommodation to a disabled employee/applicant if the employer can show that doing so would cause "undue hardship." 42 U.S.C. § 12112(b)(5)(A). The ADA also sets out specific guidelines for new construction and modifications on existing buildings that fall into each category. 42 U.S.C. §§ 12101–12213.

Procedurally, a complaint under Title I of the ADA must first be filed with Equal Employment Opportunity Commission, while complaints under Title II or III must be filed with the Department of Justice. 42 U.S.C.A. § 12188. Either a disabled individual or the U.S. Attorney General may sue to enforce the requirements of the ADA. *Id.* The ADA further requires that the Attorney General investigate complaints and monitor compliance with ADA regulations. Remedies available under the ADA vary based on which title applies and what type of discrimination occurred. On the subject of remedies, it is important to note that the ADA explicitly states that its remedies shall be the same ones available under the Rehabilitation Act. 42 U.S.C.A. § 12133; 42 U.S.C.A. § 12117.

The ADA was designed to reinforce and expand the rights already created under Section 504. H.R. Rep. No. 101–485, at 23 (1990), *reprinted in* 1990 U.S.C.C.A.N. 303, 304. The three-pronged definition of disability in the ADA described above mirrors the definition already established in Section 504. 29 U.S.C. § 701. Accordingly, complaints under the ADA and Section 504 can be joined together in suit, standards of evaluation, procedures, and remedies. 42 U.S.C. §§ 12101–12213. The 2008 amendments to the ADA were designed, in part, to correct the gap in standards of evaluation between ADA claims and Section 504 claims as applied by the Supreme Court in *Sutton v. United Airlines* and *Toyota v. Williams.* 527 U.S. 471 (1999); 534 U.S. 184 (2002).

C. *SUTTON, TOYOTA,* AND THE 2008 ADA AMENDMENTS

JENKINS v. NATIONAL BOARD OF MEDICAL EXAMINERS

No. 3:07-CV-698-H, 2008 U.S. Dist. LEXIS 10905 (W.D. Ky. 2008)

John G. Heyburn, II, Chief Judge.

Plaintiff Kirk Jenkins brought this action against Defendant National Board of Medical Examiners ("NBME"), requesting injunctive relief in the form of an order directing NBME to grant him time and a half to complete Step One of the U.S. Medical Licensing Examination ("USMLE"). Jenkins argues that under the Americans with Disabilities Act ("ADA"), he is entitled to such accommodation because he suffers from a condition that impairs his ability to read. . . .

I.

As is clear from the record, Jenkins does not read at the same rate as many, if not most people. Dr. John Lacy, a clinical psychologist who evaluated Jenkins in 2007, diagnosed Jenkins as suffering from a "reading disorder." This conclusion is generally in line with those reached by other doctors and examiners who have evaluated Jenkins throughout his life, including Drs. Michael Gontarz and David Holmes. The Court had the opportunity to hear extensive testimony from Jenkins, who also made it clear, more particularly, that he processed the written word at a slower rate than most. This condition has unquestionably made it more difficult for Jenkins to keep up with a rigorous medical school curriculum and to succeed on written tests where he is under time constraints, and it is a testament to Jenkins' effort and determination that he has done as well as he has in the demanding field he has chosen. Yet all of these observations are not dispositive for the particular purposes of the ADA.

A.

The ADA requires those subject to its terms, such as the NBME, to provide "reasonable accommodations to the known physical or mental limitations of an otherwise qualified individual with a disability." 42 U.S.C. § 12112(b)(5)(A). A "disability" is:

> (A) a physical or mental impairment that substantially limits one or more of the major life activities of such individual;
>
> (B) a record of such impairment; or
>
> (C) being regarded as having such an impairment.

Id. at § 12102(2). Therefore once a person proves he is impaired in some way, he must then prove that the impairment limits a major life activity, and does so substantially. *Toyota Motor Mfg. Kentucky, Inc. v. Williams*, 534 U.S. 184, 194–95 (2002). "Substantially" means considerably or to a large degree, and "major life activities" are those that are "of central importance to daily life." *Id.* at 196–97. In keeping with its admonition that "these terms need to be interpreted strictly to create a demanding standard for qualifying as disabled," *id.* at 197, the Court emphasized that the relevant standard for determining whether an activity is "of central importance to daily life" is whether it is "central to *most people's* daily lives." *Id.* at 201 (emphasis added).

Courts that have applied this standard to similar facts in the wake of *Toyota's* unanimous decision have determined that test-taking is not a "major life activity," and have emphasized the narrow definition of a "disability" imposed by the terms of the ADA and *Toyota.* Furthermore, the relevant comparison for purposes of determining disability is to "most people," not to one's own hypothetical unimpaired condition or to a chosen subset of one's peers, e.g. medical students. *Singh*, 508 F.3d at 1102-04; *see also Toyota*, 534 U.S. at 201.

Thus, Plaintiff did not seriously contest the Court's view that reading, not test-taking, was the relevant "major life activity," and that the significance of any impairment is measured in the context of an average person's life, rather than that of a medical student's life.

B.

Jenkins has presented substantial evidence that he is impaired in his ability to process the written word. Dr. Lacy testified at length on the subject, noting that Jenkins had performed below the mean (often well below the mean) on a variety of tests designed to ascertain a subject's reading abilities. Jenkins himself described the ways in which his condition affects his ability to import and comprehend words presented to him visually. But as stated in *Toyota*, "*[i]t* is insufficient for individuals attempting to prove disability status . . . to merely submit evidence of a medical diagnosis of an impairment." 534 U.S. at 199. Rather, such individuals must prove that "the extent of the limitation [caused by their impairment] in terms of their own experience . . . is substantial." *Id.* (internal citations omitted).

Thus counsel and the Court questioned Lacy and Jenkins on the issue of what "tasks central to most people's daily lives," *id.* at 200, Jenkins was unable or effectively unable to perform due to his condition. Jenkins told the Court he would have trouble reading street signs with similar names if forced to do so quickly, but offered no evidence that this precluded him from driving. Jenkins also noted his inability to read aloud in church at the same pace as other congregants and his inability to watch movies with subtitles and most of the text scrolled at the bottom of television broadcasts. Yet when asked about activities seemingly more "central to most people's daily lives" such as reading the newspaper, reading a label on a food container, reading a menu in a restaurant, or reading correspondence from his attorney, Jenkins indicated that he was amply capable of doing so, albeit more slowly than others. Perhaps mindful of the remedy he seeks, Jenkins indicated that it might take him fifty percent longer to read those items that might confront him in daily life. However, he emphasized that when reading such things as medical texts, his pace slowed further given his lack of familiarity with many of the words used therein. . . .

II.

Jenkins' ability to read is simply not "substantially limited" on the record before the Court, and indeed to some extent the very accommodation Jenkins requests reinforces this conclusion, since one who was truly "substantially limited" in his ability to read seemingly would need significantly more than time and a half to successfully process the undoubtedly complex and technical information on the USMLE.

As the D.C. Circuit noted, "[t]here is something poignant, in some cases even tragic, in the plight of a person cut off from exceptional achievement by some accident of birth or history. But the ADA is not addressed to that plight." *Singh*, 508 F.3d at 1101; see also *Gonzales*, 225 F.3d at 630 (noting that Congress intended the ADA to apply to a "severely disadvantaged group"). Here, Jenkins' impairment, however characterized, does not appear to substantially limit any major life activities, making it impossible to conclude that Jenkins is disabled for purposes of the ADA or entitled to the relief he seeks. The Court might add that based upon past experience, there seems a reasonable likelihood that Jenkins can overcome this obstacle as he has others.

Being otherwise sufficiently advised,

IT IS HEREBY ORDERED that Plaintiff's Motion for Preliminary Injunctive Relief, Plaintiff's Motion for a Temporary Restraining Order, and Plaintiff's Complaint are DISMISSED WITH PREJUDICE.

JENKINS v. NATIONAL BOARD OF MEDICAL EXAMINERS

No. 08-5371, 2009 U.S. App. LEXIS 2660;
2009 FED App. 0117N (6th Cir. 2009)

Rogers, Circuit Judge.

Kirk Jenkins is a third-year medical student who seeks additional time on the United States Medical Licensing Examination ("USMLE") as an ADA accommodation for a diagnosed reading disorder. Relying on *Toyota Motor Manufacturing, Kentucky, Inc. v. Williams*, 534 U.S. 184 (2002), the district court found that Jenkins did not qualify as disabled under the Americans with Disabilities Act. On September 25, 2008, Congress passed a law repudiating *Toyota*'s strict standard for finding a disability under the ADA and expressing its intent that the ADA be construed in favor of broad coverage, effective January 1, 2009. ADA Amendments Act of 2008, Pub.L. No. 110-325, 122 Stat. 3553 (2008). Because this suit for injunctive relief was pending on appeal when the amendments became effective, the amendments apply to this case. We therefore remand the case to the district court for further consideration in light of the ADA Amendments Act. . . .

II.

A.

Because this case involves prospective relief and was pending when the amendments became effective, the ADA must be applied as amended. The ADA Amendments Act took effect on January 1, 2009. Pub.L. No. 110-325, § 8. Rather than seeking damages for some past act of discrimination by NBME, Jenkins seeks the right to receive an accommodation on a test that will occur in the future, well after this effective date. It is well settled that a court applies "the law in effect at the time it renders its decision, unless doing so would result in manifest injustice or there is statutory direction or legislative history to the contrary." *Bradley v. School Bd. of City of Richmond*, 416 U.S. 696, 711 (1974); *accord Republic Steel Corp. v. Costle*, 581 F.2d 1228, 1233 (6th Cir.1978). Because Jenkins seeks prospective relief, no injustice would result from applying the amended law. Nor does the statute direct that the amendments should not apply to a pending case for prospective relief. In a case parallel to this one, the Supreme Court applied the newly-passed Civil Rights Act of 1960 to a voting rights suit for declaratory and injunctive relief, where the district court had dismissed the case under the then-operative Civil Rights Act of

1957. *United States v. Alabama*, 362 U.S. 602, 604 (1960). The Court held that such a case "must be decided on the basis of law now controlling." *Id.* . . .

B.

Because the district court relied on the Supreme Court's now-repudiated decision in *Toyota Motor Manufacturing, Kentucky, Inc. v. Williams*, 534 U.S. 184 (2002), the district court's legal conclusions require reconsideration. The district court found that the record contained evidence that Jenkins reads written language in a slow and labored fashion when compared to the general public. According to the ADA, an individual is disabled if he has "a physical or mental impairment that *substantially limits* one or more of the major life activities of such individual." 42 U.S.C. § 12102 (2006) (amended 2009) (emphasis supplied). Reading is a major life activity under the existing precedent of this circuit and the amended ADA. *See Gonzales v. Nat'l Bd. of Med. Examiners*, 225 F.3d 620, 626 (6th Cir.2000); 42 U.S.C. § 12102(2)(A) (2006) (amended 2009). Jenkins's status under the ADA therefore turns on the definition of "substantial limitation."

Congress's recent amendments contain operative language governing the definition of "substantial limitation." In the ADA Amendments Act, Congress made clear that it intends for the ADA to give broad protection to persons with disabilities and that the Supreme Court's holding in *Toyota* is at odds with Congress's intent. Congress stated in the findings of the Act that various Supreme Court holdings "have narrowed the broad scope of protection intended to be afforded by the ADA, thus eliminating protection for many individuals whom Congress intended to protect" with the result that "lower courts have incorrectly found in individual cases that people with a range of substantially limiting impairments are not people with disabilities." Pub. L. No. 110-325, § 2(a)(4), (6). Congress stated that one purpose of the Act was:

> to reject the standards enunciated by the Supreme Court in *Toyota Motor Manufacturing, Kentucky, Inc. v. Williams*, 534 U.S. 184 (2002), that the terms "substantially" and "major" in the definition of disability under the ADA "need to be interpreted strictly to create a demanding standard for qualifying as disabled," and that to be substantially limited in performing a major life activity under the ADA "an individual must have an impairment that prevents or severely restricts the individual from doing activities that are of central importance to most people's daily lives[.]"

Pub. L. No. 110-325, § 2(b)(4). Moreover, Congress amended the portion of the ADA governing construction of the term "disability," such that "[t]he definition of disability in this Act shall be construed in favor of broad coverage of individuals under this Act, to the maximum extent permitted by the terms of this Act" and "[t]he term 'substantially limits' shall be interpreted consistently with the findings and purposes of the [Act]." 42 U.S.C. § 12102(4)(A), (B) (2006) (amended 2009). In so stating, Congress overturned the definition of "substantially limits" put forward in *Toyota* and directed the courts to interpret the term in a more inclusive manner.

Without the benefit of these amendments, the district court relied on the Supreme Court's analysis in *Toyota*, which was controlling precedent at the time the district rendered its decision. The district court concluded that Jenkins would only qualify for protection under the ADA if his disability "precluded" him from performing reading tasks that were "central to most people's daily lives." 2008 U.S. Dist. LEXIS 10905, at *4-8. In holding that Jenkins was not substantially limited in his ability to read, the district court relied on the very language from *Toyota* that Congress repudiated in the ADA Amendments Act. *Compare* 2008 U.S. Dist. LEXIS 10905, at *4-5, *with* Pub. L. 110-325, § 2(b)(4). The change in the law has therefore undermined the district court's holding, and the resolution of this case will require the district court to make a fresh application of the law to the facts in light of the amendments to the ADA. The fact-bound nature of the question whether Jenkins is disabled under the revised Act counsels a remand without an appellate attempt to give more precise definition in the abstract to the revised Congressional language.

It can be said, though, that the categorical threshold scope of the ADA's coverage has been broadened. This breadth heightens the importance of the district courts' responsibility to fashion appropriate accommodations. If the district court in this case finds that Jenkins is disabled under the more inclusive terms of the amended ADA, the court must still determine specifically what NBME must do to comply with the requirement that a professional licensing board offer its examination "in a place and manner accessible to persons with disabilities." 42 U.S.C. § 12189. This nuanced determination is not governed by previous, voluntarily provided accommodations that Jenkins has received, nor necessarily by what accommodations were required under the narrower previous definition of disability.

III.

Because this case is governed by the amended ADA and because the district court has yet to review the facts of Jenkins's case under that law, we vacate the judgment and remand the case to the district court for further findings in light of the ADA Amendments Act.

NOTES

1. *Jenkins* gives us the rare opportunity to analyze just how dramatic an impact the 2008 ADA Amendments Act can have on the area of disability law in the higher education arena. Because of the timing of the decision and appeal, the Sixth Circuit confronted the same set of facts as the lower court; however, the reviewing court was bound to analyze the issue through a statutory lens instead of the *Sutton-Toyota* common law test.

Because part of the motivation behind the 2008 ADA Amendments was to statutorily override the Court's decisions in *Sutton* and *Toyota*, a basic understanding of the former precedents are still valuable — especially since some state courts are still grappling with the old common law standards. *See Goff v. Salazar Roofing & Construction, Inc.*, 242 P.3d 604 (Ok. Civ. App. Div. 4); *Medlin v. Springfield Metro. Hous. Auth.*, 2010 Ohio 3654, 2010 Ohio App. LEXIS 3105 (Ohio App. 2 Dist. 2010); *Bennett v. Nissan North America, Inc.*, 315 S.W.3d 832 (Tenn. Ct. App. 2009).

In *Sutton v. United Air Lines*, 527 U.S. 471 (1999), the Supreme Court faced the issue of whether corrective and mitigating measures should be considered in determining whether an individual is "substantially limited in a major life activity," and thus disabled under the pre-amended ADA. After sifting through legislative history and the plain language of the statute, the Court held that petitioners, who were severely myopic, were not "disabled" under the Act, and could not pursue a claim against the airline after being denied positions as global airline pilots. The Court reasoned that the petitioners' alleged "disability" (myopia) could be easily corrected by corrective lenses, and was not the kind of "disability" Congress intended to include. Further, the Court explained that though petitioners' poor eyesight precluded them from becoming a "global airline pilot," the airline still allowed them to apply for other positions such as a "regional pilot" or "pilot instructor"; thus, the Court concluded, petitioners were not "substantially limited in a major life activity" — they were just precluded from pursuing one specialized, particular career option.

In 2002, the Court reaffirmed *Sutton* and narrowed the definition of "disability" even further. *Toyota Motor Mfg., Ky. v. Williams*, 534 U.S. 184 (2002). The Court emphasized that the burden for claims made under the ADA rested on the shoulders of the plaintiff, reiterating that "[m]erely having an impairment does not make one disabled for purposes of the ADA." The Court went on to clarify the degree of impairment necessary to qualify as a "disability" under the ADA: " 'Substantially,' [as used in the ADA provision defining disability as an impairment that substantially limits one or more major life activities], suggests 'considerable' or 'to a large degree.' " Hence, the common law continued to lessen the number of individuals protected under the ADA.

2. At least one legal commentator contends that *Sutton* is the Supreme Court's largest effort to exclude those with mild impairment from the definition of disabled under the ADA. Ruth Colker, *The Mythic 43 Million Americans with Disabilities*, 49 Wm. & Mary L. Rev. 1, 10–11 (2007). Rather than expand the definition of disability broadly in accordance with the legislative history of the ADA, the Court chose to limit the definition of disability in all three contexts to essentially exclude any individual with a mild impairment who uses a device or medication to completely mitigate their impairment. *Id.* at 11–12.

3. If you share in Professor Colker's lamentation and think the Court's decisions in *Sutton* and *Toyota* did not adhere to the spirit of the ADA, Congress agreed. In 2008, Congress enacted, and President Bush signed into law, the Americans with Disabilities Act Amendments Act of 2008 (codified as amended at 42 U.S.C. § 12101). In modifying the definitions of "disability," "impairment," and "major life activities," Congress overturned both *Sutton* and *Toyota*. William R. Corbett, *Fixing Employment Discrimination Law*, 62 SMU L. Rev. 81, n.130 (2009). Specifically,

> [t]he Act emphasizes that the definition of disability should be construed in favor of broad coverage of individuals to the maximum extent permitted by the terms of the ADA and generally shall not require extensive analysis.
>
> The Act makes important changes to the definition of the term "disability" by rejecting the holdings in several Supreme Court decisions and

portions of EEOC's ADA regulations. The effect of these changes is to make it easier for an individual seeking protection under the ADA to establish that he or she has a disability within the meaning of the ADA.

The Act retains the ADA's basic definition of "disability" as an impairment that substantially limits one or more major life activities, a record of such an impairment, or being regarded as having such an impairment. However, it changes the way that these statutory terms should be interpreted in several ways. Most significantly, the Act:

- directs EEOC to revise that portion of its regulations defining the term "substantially limits";
- expands the definition of "major life activities" by including two non-exhaustive lists:
  - the first list includes many activities that the EEOC has recognized (e.g., walking) as well as activities that EEOC has not specifically recognized (e.g., reading, bending, and communicating);
  - the second list includes major bodily functions (e.g., "functions of the immune system, normal cell growth, digestive, bowel, bladder, neurological, brain, respiratory, circulatory, endocrine, and reproductive functions");
- states that mitigating measures other than "ordinary eyeglasses or contact lenses" shall not be considered in assessing whether an individual has a disability;
- clarifies that an impairment that is episodic or in remission is a disability if it would substantially limit a major life activity when active;
- changes the definition of "regarded as" so that it no longer requires a showing that the employer perceived the individual to be substantially limited in a major life activity, and instead says that an applicant or employee is "regarded as" disabled if he or she is subject to an action prohibited by the ADA (e.g., failure to hire or termination) based on an impairment that is not transitory and minor;
- provides that individuals covered only under the "regarded as" prong are not entitled to reasonable accommodation.

U.S. EQUAL EMPLOYMENT OPPORTUNITY COMMISSION, NOTICE CONCERNING THE AMERICANS WITH DISABILITIES ACT (ADA) AMENDMENTS ACT OF 2008, *available at* http://www.eeoc.gov/ada/amendments_notice.html.

The law went into effect on January 1, 2009. For more information regarding the 2008 ADA Amendments, see Kimberly S. Adams et al., *Health Care Law: Survey of Recent Developments in Health Care Law*, 42 IND. L. REV. 1003, 1050–51 (2009); Lauren Siber, *ADA Amendments Act of 2008: New Hope for Individuals with Disabilities*, 33 RUTGERS L. REC. 65 (2009); Chai R. Feldblum, Kevin Barry & Emily

A. Benfer, 13 TEX. J. C.L. & C.R. 187 (2008).

4. The prevailing theory among legal scholars was that the Supreme Court's narrow interpretation of the ADA, enacted in 1990, was a kind of judicial backlash accompanying the Court's increasingly conservative makeup. *See, e.g.*, Robert L. Burgdorf Jr., *"Substantially Limited" Protection from Disability Discrimination: The Special Treatment Model and Misconstructions of the Definition of Disability*, 42 VILL. L. REV. 409, 539–46 (1997); Chai R. Feldblum, *Definition of Disability Under Federal Anti-Discrimination Law: What Happened? Why? And What We Can Do About It?*, 21 BERKELEY J. EMP. & LAB. L. 91, 139–60 (2000); Aviam Soifer, *The Disability Term: Dignity, Default, and Negative Capability*, 47 UCLA L. REV. 1279, 1304–06 (2000); Michael Ashley Stein, *Same Struggle, Different Difference: ADA Accommodations as Antidiscrimination*, 153 U. PENN. L. REV. 579, 631–36 (2004); Rebecca Hanner White, *Deference and Disability Discrimination*, 99 MICH. L. REV. 532, 537–38 (2000).

An alternative theory, however, makes a compelling case that the Court's narrow interpretation of the ADA was caused by much more than a particular kind of judicial philosophy.

> [T]he passage of the ADA . . . occurred through rather curious means. The statute was shepherded through Congress by Members who had personal experience with disabilities either in their own lives or with relatives, and the statute was enacted without the presence or aid of a substantial social movement. As a result, Congress passed an extremely broad statute, modeled after the Rehab Act, and then turned over its particulars to agencies and interest groups. And here is where the problems began: rather than push for narrow legislation that would have protected the individuals Congress principally desired to protect, the interest groups, along with interested congressional staff, opted for broad statutory language that could have brought a much larger group of individuals into the statute's scope - most of whom no one would have considered disabled prior to the passage of the Act. It could be argued that this is what legislation is intended to do, create protections for those who were otherwise invisible; but the individuals I am referring to - those who wear glasses, sustain workplace injuries, or are allergic to perfume - were never intended to be the subject of the legislation. Moreover, there appears to be little public support for extending statutory protections to those individuals. Significantly, most of the restrictive statutory interpretations have arisen in cases involving these sorts of nontraditional disabilities.
>
> One result of the Supreme Court's narrow approach to the statute - which was principally designed to eliminate those unintended, and often frivolous claims - is that the Court carved out a whole class of individuals who were intended to be covered by the statute, namely those whose disabilities can be controlled with medication, including those with epilepsy and depression, among others. Although these decisions are problematic and contrary to the intent of the statute, I do not agree that they are the result of a backlash against those with disabilities. In fact, both the Supreme Court and lower courts have been reasonably protective of

> individuals with traditional disabilities - it is only the attempted expansion of the disability definition that has been rejected. But that rejection was entirely predictable. Without broad public support or a strong social movement pushing to expand our notion of disabilities, it was simply too much to expect the Supreme Court to interpret the ADA expansively, or even to construe the statute consistent with congressional intent so long as the statute provided interpretive room for judicial discretion, which it did.

Michael Selmi, *Interpreting the Americans with Disabilities Act: Why the Supreme Court Rewrote the Statute, and Why Congress Did Not Care*, 76 GEO. WASH. L. REV. 522, 526–28 (2008).* Did the ADA Amendments Act of 2008 expand its protective coverage to individuals whom Congress did not intend to protect when the original law was enacted in 1990? Or did the Act merely extend coverage to individuals with serious conditions — such as epilepsy and depression — who were swept up with others filing "frivolous" claims?

5. What are the policy implications for colleges and universities in states whose courts have interpreted *state* statutes similar to the ADA consistent with the interpretation Congress rejected in 2008? *See generally* Sandra F. Sperino, *Diminishing Deference: Learning Lessons from Recent Congressional Rejection of the Supreme Court's Interpretation of Discrimination Statutes*, 33 RUTGERS L. REC. 40 (2009). Should they stick with the former federal interpretation until their state legislatures or courts respond to the ADA Amendments Act of 2008? Or should they revamp their employment policies to comply with the new federal interpretation? Are the liability risks the same, regardless of which avenue a school chooses? From a best practices standpoint, what should colleges and universities do?

6. Private intercollegiate associations can also be liable for disability discrimination. *See Bowers v. Nat'l Collegiate Athletic Ass'n*, 9 F. Supp. 2d 460, 474 (D. N.J. 1998). The court found that Title III, but not Title II, of the Americans with Disabilities Act applies to the NCAA as a "public accommodation." *Id.* at 474. Further, the court found that there was enough evidence to proceed to trial on the issue of whether the NCAA had discriminated against Bowers on the basis that he was learning disabled. *Id.* at 487–90. Additionally, the NCAA, as an intercollegiate association, also qualifies as a "program or activity" for purposes of liability under Section 504 of the Rehabilitation Act. *Id.* at 492; *see Cureton v. Nat'l Collegiate Athletic Ass'n*, 1997 U.S. Dist. LEXIS 15529 (E.D. Pa.1997). Do eligibility and testing requirements set by the NCAA discriminate against the learning disabled? What effects might "reasonable accommodations" for the learning disabled within NCAA regulations have on collegiate athletics?

7. If after reading the excerpt of the *Sutton* case you wondered why the court didn't just carve out an exception for ordinary eyeglasses, Congress must have explored the same inquiry, as the 2008 amendments to the ADA did just that. Under Section 12102(4)(E), whether or not an impairment "substantially limits a major life activity" should be decided without regard to mitigating measures except for ordinary eyeglasses or contact lenses. 42 U.S.C. § 12102(4)(E).

8. Any individual can lose disability eligibility under the ADA for use or possession of a controlled substance under federal guidelines. Further, drug tests are not considered a "medical examination" for purposes of Title I which means that an employer can require a drug test prior to employment without violating the ADA. 42 U.S.C. § 12114(d)(1).

D. DISABILITY LAW AND SOVEREIGN IMMUNITY

BOARD OF TRUSTEES OF THE UNIVERSITY OF ALABAMA v. GARRETT
531 U.S. 356 (2001)

Chief Justice Rehnquist delivered the opinion of the Court.

We decide here whether employees of the State of Alabama may recover money damages by reason of the State's failure to comply with the provisions of Title I of the Americans with Disabilities Act of 1990 (ADA or Act), 104 Stat. 330, 42 U.S.C. §§ 12111–12117. We hold that such suits are barred by the Eleventh Amendment.

The ADA prohibits certain employers, including the States, from "discriminating against a qualified individual with a disability because of the disability of such individual in regard to job application procedures, the hiring, advancement, or discharge of employees, employee compensation, job training, and other terms, conditions, and privileges of employment." §§ 12112(a), 12111(2), (5), (7). To this end, the Act requires employers to "make reasonable accommodations to the known physical or mental limitations of an otherwise qualified individual with a disability who is an applicant or employee, unless [the employer] can demonstrate that the accommodation would impose an undue hardship on the operation of the [employer's] business." § 12112(b)(5)(A).

Reasonable accommodation' may include —

> "(A) making existing facilities used by employees readily accessible to and usable by individuals with disabilities; and (B) job restructuring, part-time or modified work schedules, reassignment to a vacant position, acquisition or modification of equipment or devices, appropriate adjustment or modifications of examinations, training materials or policies, the provision of qualified readers or interpreters, and other similar accommodations for individuals with disabilities." § 12111(9).

The Act also prohibits employers from "utilizing standards, criteria, or methods of administration . . . that have the effect of discrimination on the basis of disability." § 12112(b)(3)(A).

The Act defines "disability" to include "(A) a physical or mental impairment that substantially limits one or more of the major life activities of such individual; (B) a record of such an impairment; or (C) being regarded as having such an impairment." § 12102(2). A disabled individual is otherwise "qualified" if he or she, "with or without reasonable accommodation, can perform the essential functions of the employment position that such individual holds or desires." § 12111(8).

Respondent Patricia Garrett, a registered nurse, was employed as the Director of Nursing, OB/Gyn/Neonatal Services, for the University of Alabama in Birmingham Hospital. In 1994, Garrett was diagnosed with breast cancer and subsequently underwent a lumpectomy, radiation treatment, and chemotherapy. Garrett's treatments required her to take substantial leave from work. Upon returning to work in July 1995, Garrett's supervisor informed Garrett that she would have to give up her Director position. Garrett then applied for and received a transfer to another, lower paying position as a nurse manager.

Respondent Milton Ash worked as a security officer for the Alabama Department of Youth Services (Department). Upon commencing this employment, Ash informed the Department that he suffered from chronic asthma and that his doctor recommended he avoid carbon monoxide and cigarette smoke, and Ash requested that the Department modify his duties to minimize his exposure to these substances. Ash was later diagnosed with sleep apnea and requested, again pursuant to his doctor's recommendation, that he be reassigned to daytime shifts to accommodate his condition. Ultimately, the Department granted none of the requested relief. Shortly after Ash filed a discrimination claim with the Equal Employment Opportunity Commission, he noticed that his performance evaluations were lower than those he had received on previous occasions.

Garrett and Ash filed separate lawsuits in the District Court, both seeking money damages under the ADA. Petitioners moved for summary judgment, claiming that the ADA exceeds Congress' authority to abrogate the State's Eleventh Amendment immunity. In a single opinion disposing of both cases, the District Court agreed with petitioners' position and granted their motions for summary judgment. The cases were consolidated on appeal to the Eleventh Circuit. The Court of Appeals reversed . . . [holding] that the ADA validly abrogates the States' Eleventh Amendment immunity.

We granted certiorari to resolve a split among the Courts of Appeals on the question whether an individual may sue a State for money damages in federal court under the ADA.

I

The Eleventh Amendment provides:

> The Judicial power of the United States shall not be construed to extend to any suit in law or equity, commenced or prosecuted against one of the United States by Citizens of another State, or by Citizens or Subjects of any Foreign State.

Although by its terms the Amendment applies only to suits against a State by citizens of another State, our cases have extended the Amendment's applicability to suits by citizens against their own States. The ultimate guarantee of the Eleventh Amendment is that nonconsenting States may not be sued by private individuals in federal court.

We have recognized, however, that Congress may abrogate the States' Eleventh Amendment immunity when it both unequivocally intends to do so and "acts pursuant to a valid grant of constitutional authority." The first of these requirements is not in dispute here. *See* 42 U.S.C. § 12202 ("A State shall not be immune under the eleventh amendment to the Constitution of the United States from an action in [a] Federal or State court of competent jurisdiction for a violation of this chapter"). The question, then, is whether Congress acted within its constitutional authority by subjecting the States to suits in federal court for money damages under the ADA.

Congress may not, of course, base its abrogation of the States' Eleventh Amendment immunity upon the powers enumerated in Article I. In *Fitzpatrick v. Bitzer*, 427 U.S. 445 (1976), however, we held that "the Eleventh Amendment, and the principle of state sovereignty which it embodies, are necessarily limited by the enforcement provisions of § 5 of the Fourteenth Amendment." As a result, we concluded, Congress may subject nonconsenting States to suit in federal court when it does so pursuant to a valid exercise of its § 5 power. Our cases have adhered to this proposition. Accordingly, the ADA can apply to the States only to the extent that the statute is appropriate § 5 legislation.

Section 1 of the Fourteenth Amendment provides, in relevant part:

> No State shall make or enforce any law which shall abridge the privileges or immunities of citizens of the United States; nor shall any State deprive any person of life, liberty, or property, without due process of law; nor deny to any person within its jurisdiction the equal protection of the laws.

Section 5 of the Fourteenth Amendment grants Congress the power to enforce the substantive guarantees contained in § 1 by enacting "appropriate legislation." *See City of Boerne v. Flores*, 521 U.S. 507, 536 (1997). Congress is not limited to mere legislative repetition of this Court's constitutional jurisprudence. "Rather, Congress' power 'to enforce' the Amendment includes the authority both to remedy and to deter violation of rights guaranteed thereunder by prohibiting a somewhat broader swath of conduct, including that which is not itself forbidden by the Amendment's text."

City of Boerne also confirmed, however, the long-settled principle that it is the responsibility of this Court, not Congress, to define the substance of constitutional guarantees. Accordingly, § 5 legislation reaching beyond the scope of § 1's actual guarantees must exhibit "congruence and proportionality between the injury to be prevented or remedied and the means adopted to that end."

II

The first step in applying these now familiar principles is to identify with some precision the scope of the constitutional right at issue. Here, that inquiry requires us to examine the limitations § 1 of the Fourteenth Amendment places upon States' treatment of the disabled. . . . [W]e look to our prior decisions under the Equal Protection Clause dealing with this issue.

In *Cleburne v. Cleburne Living Center, Inc.*, 473 U.S. 432 (1985), we considered an equal protection challenge to a city ordinance requiring a special use permit for the operation of a group home for the mentally retarded. The specific question before us was whether the Court of Appeals had erred by holding that mental retardation qualified as a "quasi-suspect" classification under our equal protection jurisprudence. We answered that question in the affirmative, concluding instead that such legislation incurs only the minimum "rational-basis" review applicable to general social and economic legislation. In a statement that today seems quite prescient, we explained that

> if the large and amorphous class of the mentally retarded were deemed quasi-suspect for the reasons given by the Court of Appeals, it would be difficult to find a principled way to distinguish a variety of other groups who have perhaps immutable disabilities setting them off from others, who cannot themselves mandate the desired legislative responses, and who can claim some degree of prejudice from at least part of the public at large. One need mention in this respect only the aging, the disabled, the mentally ill, and the infirm. We are reluctant to set out on that course, and we decline to do so.

Under rational-basis review, where a group possesses "distinguishing characteristics relevant to interests the State has the authority to implement," a State's decision to act on the basis of those differences does not give rise to a constitutional violation. "Such a classification cannot run afoul of the Equal Protection Clause if there is a rational relationship between the disparity of treatment and some legitimate governmental purpose." [citations omitted]. Moreover, the State need not articulate its reasoning at the moment a particular decision is made. Rather, the burden is upon the challenging party to negative " 'any reasonably conceivable state of facts that could provide a rational basis for the classification.' " [citation omitted].

JUSTICE BREYER [writing in dissent] suggests that *Cleburne* stands for the broad proposition that state decisionmaking reflecting "negative attitudes" or "fear" necessarily runs afoul of the Fourteenth Amendment. As we noted in *Cleburne*: "Mere negative attitudes, or fear, *unsubstantiated by factors which are properly cognizable* in a zoning proceeding, are not permissible bases for treating a home for the mentally retarded differently . . . ." This language, read in context, simply states the unremarkable and widely acknowledged tenet of this Court's equal protection jurisprudence that state action subject to rational-basis scrutiny does not violate the Fourteenth Amendment when it "rationally furthers the purpose identified by the State."

Thus, the result of *Cleburne* is that States are not required by the Fourteenth Amendment to make special accommodations for the disabled, so long as their actions towards such individuals are rational. They could quite hard headedly — and perhaps hardheartedly — hold to job-qualification requirements which do not make allowance for the disabled. If special accommodations for the disabled are to be required, they have to come from positive law and not through the Equal Protection Clause.

III

Once we have determined the metes and bounds of the constitutional right in question, we examine whether Congress identified a history and pattern of unconstitutional employment discrimination by the States against the disabled. Just as § 1 of the Fourteenth Amendment applies only to actions committed "under color of state law," Congress' § 5 authority is appropriately exercised only in response to state transgressions. The legislative record of the ADA, however, simply fails to show that Congress did in fact identify a pattern of irrational state discrimination in employment against the disabled.

Respondents contend that the inquiry as to unconstitutional discrimination should extend not only to States themselves, but to units of local governments, such as cities and counties. All of these, they say, are "state actors" for purposes of the Fourteenth Amendment. This is quite true, but the Eleventh Amendment does not extend its immunity to units of local government. These entities are subject to private claims for damages under the ADA without Congress' ever having to rely on § 5 of the Fourteenth Amendment to render them so. It would make no sense to consider constitutional violations on their part, as well as by the States themselves, when only the States are the beneficiaries of the Eleventh Amendment.

Congress made a general finding in the ADA that "historically, society has tended to isolate and segregate individuals with disabilities, and, despite some improvements, such forms of discrimination against individuals with disabilities continue to be a serious and pervasive social problem." 42 U.S.C. § 12101(a)(2). The record assembled by Congress includes many instances to support such a finding. But the great majority of these incidents do not deal with the activities of States.

Respondents in their brief cite half a dozen examples from the record that did involve States. A department head at the University of North Carolina refused to hire an applicant for the position of health administrator because he was blind; similarly, a student at a state university in South Dakota was denied an opportunity to practice teach because the dean at that time was convinced that blind people could not teach in public schools. A microfilmer at the Kansas Department of Transportation was fired because he had epilepsy; deaf workers at the University of Oklahoma were paid a lower salary than those who could hear. The Indiana State Personnel Office informed a woman with a concealed disability that she should not disclose it if she wished to obtain employment.

Several of these incidents undoubtedly evidence an unwillingness on the part of state officials to make the sort of accommodations for the disabled required by the ADA. Whether they were irrational under our decision in *Cleburne* is more debatable, particularly when the incident is described out of context. But even if it were to be determined that each incident upon fuller examination showed unconstitutional action on the part of the State, these incidents taken together fall far short of even suggesting the pattern of unconstitutional discrimination on which § 5 legislation must be based. Congress, in enacting the ADA, found that "some 43,000,000 Americans have one or more physical or mental disabilities." 42 U.S.C. § 12101(a)(1). In 1990, the States alone employed more than 4.5 million people. It is telling, we think, that given these large numbers, Congress assembled only such minimal evidence of unconstitutional state discrimination in employment against the disabled.

Justice Breyer maintains that Congress applied Title I of the ADA to the States in response to a host of incidents representing unconstitutional state discrimination in employment against persons with disabilities. A close review of the relevant materials, however, undercuts that conclusion. JUSTICE BREYER's Appendix C consists not of legislative findings, but of unexamined, anecdotal accounts of "adverse, disparate treatment by state officials." Of course, as we have already explained, "adverse, disparate treatment" often does not amount to a constitutional violation where rational-basis scrutiny applies. These accounts, moreover, were submitted not directly to Congress but to the Task Force on the Rights and Empowerment of Americans with Disabilities, which made no findings on the subject of state discrimination in employment. And, had Congress truly understood this information as reflecting a pattern of unconstitutional behavior by the States, one would expect some mention of that conclusion in the Act's legislative findings. There is none. . . .

Even were it possible to squeeze out of these examples a pattern of unconstitutional discrimination by the States, the rights and remedies created by the ADA against the States would raise the same sort of concerns as to congruence and proportionality as were found in *City of Boerne.* For example, whereas it would be entirely rational (and therefore constitutional) for a state employer to conserve scarce financial resources by hiring employees who are able to use existing facilities, the ADA requires employers to "make existing facilities used by employees readily accessible to and usable by individuals with disabilities." 42 U.S.C. § 12111(9). The ADA does except employers from the "reasonable accommodation" requirement where the employer "can demonstrate that the accommodation would impose an undue hardship on the operation of the business of such covered entity." § 121119. However, even with this exception, the accommodation duty far exceeds what is constitutionally required in that it makes unlawful a range of alternate responses that would be reasonable but would fall short of imposing an "undue burden" upon the employer. The Act also makes it the employer's duty to prove that it would suffer such a burden, instead of requiring (as the Constitution does) that the complaining party negate reasonable bases for the employer's decision.

The ADA also forbids "utilizing standards, criteria, or methods of administration" that disparately impact the disabled, without regard to whether such conduct has a rational basis. § 12112(b)(3)(A). Although disparate impact may be relevant evidence of racial discrimination, such evidence alone is insufficient even where the Fourteenth Amendment subjects state action to strict scrutiny.

The ADA's constitutional shortcomings are apparent when the Act is compared to Congress' efforts in the Voting Rights Act of 1965 to respond to a serious pattern of constitutional violations. In *South Carolina v. Katzenbach,* 383 U.S. 301 (1966), we considered whether the Voting Rights Act was "appropriate" legislation to enforce the Fifteenth Amendment's protection against racial discrimination in voting. Concluding that it was a valid exercise of Congress' enforcement power under § 2 of the Fifteenth Amendment, we noted that "before enacting the measure, Congress explored with great care the problem of racial discrimination in voting."

In that Act, Congress documented a marked pattern of unconstitutional action by the States. State officials, Congress found, routinely applied voting tests in order to exclude African-American citizens from registering to vote. Congress also determined that litigation had proved ineffective and that there persisted an otherwise inexplicable 50-percentage-point gap in the registration of white and African-American voters in some States. Congress' response was to promulgate in the Voting Rights Act a detailed but limited remedial scheme designed to guarantee meaningful enforcement of the Fifteenth Amendment in those areas of the Nation where abundant evidence of States' systematic denial of those rights was identified.

The contrast between this kind of evidence, and the evidence that Congress considered in the present case, is stark. Congressional enactment of the ADA represents its judgment that there should be a "comprehensive national mandate for the elimination of discrimination against individuals with disabilities." 42 U.S.C. § 12101(b)(1). Congress is the final authority as to desirable public policy, but in order to authorize private individuals to recover money damages against the States, there must be a pattern of discrimination by the States which violates the Fourteenth Amendment, and the remedy imposed by Congress must be congruent and proportional to the targeted violation. Those requirements are not met here, and to uphold the Act's application to the States would allow Congress to rewrite the Fourteenth Amendment law laid down by this Court in *Cleburne*. Section 5 does not so broadly enlarge congressional authority. The judgment of the Court of Appeals is therefore

Reversed.

TENNESSEE v. LANE
541 U.S. 509 (2004)

JUSTICE STEVENS delivered the opinion of the Court.

Title II of the Americans with Disabilities Act of 1990 (ADA or Act), 104 Stat 337, 42 U.S.C. §§ 12131–12165, provides that "no qualified individual with a disability shall, by reason of such disability, be excluded from participation in or be denied the benefits of the services, programs or activities of a public entity, or be subjected to discrimination by any such entity." § 12132. The question presented in this case is whether Title II exceeds Congress' power under § 5 of the Fourteenth Amendment.

I

In August 1998, respondents George Lane and Beverly Jones filed this action against the State of Tennessee and a number of Tennessee counties, alleging past and ongoing violations of Title II. Respondents, both of whom are paraplegics who use wheelchairs for mobility, claimed that they were denied access to, and the services of, the state court system by reason of their disabilities. Lane alleged that he was compelled to appear to answer a set of criminal charges on the second floor of a county courthouse that had no elevator. At his first appearance, Lane crawled up two flights of stairs to get to the courtroom. When Lane returned to the courthouse for a hearing, he refused to crawl again or to be carried by officers to the courtroom; he consequently was arrested and jailed for failure to appear. Jones, a certified court reporter, alleged that she has not been able to gain access to a number of county courthouses, and, as a result, has lost both work and an opportunity to participate in the judicial process. Respondents sought damages and equitable relief.

The State moved to dismiss the suit on the ground that it was barred by the Eleventh Amendment. The District Court denied the motion without opinion, and the State appealed. The United States intervened to defend Title II's abrogation of the States' Eleventh Amendment immunity. On April 28, 2000, after the appeal had been briefed and argued, the Court of Appeals for the Sixth Circuit entered an order holding the case in abeyance pending our decision in *Board of Trustees v. Garrett*, 531 U.S. 356 (2001).

In *Garrett*, we concluded that the Eleventh Amendment bars private suits seeking money damages for state violations of Title I of the ADA. We left open, however, the question whether the Eleventh Amendment permits suits for money damages under Title II. Following the *Garrett* decision, the Court of Appeals, sitting en banc, heard argument in a Title II suit brought by a hearing-impaired litigant who sought money damages for the State's failure to accommodate his disability in a child custody proceeding. A divided court permitted the suit to proceed despite the State's assertion of Eleventh Amendment immunity. The majority interpreted *Garrett* to bar private ADA suits against States based on equal protection principles, but not those that rely on due process principles. The minority concluded that Congress had not validly abrogated the States' Eleventh Amendment immunity for any Title II claims, while the concurring opinion concluded that Title II validly abrogated state sovereign immunity with respect to both equal protection and due process claims.

. . . [A] panel of the Court of Appeals entered an order affirming the District Court's denial of the State's motion to dismiss in this case. . . . The panel did not, however, categorically reject the State's submission. It instead noted that the case presented difficult questions that "cannot be clarified absent a factual record," and remanded for further proceedings. We granted certiorari, and now affirm.

II

The ADA was passed by large majorities in both Houses of Congress after decades of deliberation and investigation into the need for comprehensive legislation to address discrimination against persons with disabilities. . . .

Invoking "the sweep of congressional authority, including the power to enforce the fourteenth amendment and to regulate commerce," the ADA is designed "to provide a clear and comprehensive national mandate for the elimination of discrimination against individuals with disabilities." §§ 12101(b)(1), (b)(4). It forbids discrimination against persons with disabilities in three major areas of public life: employment, which is covered by Title I of the statute; public services, programs, and activities, which are the subject of Title II; and public accommodations, which are covered by Title III.

Title II, §§ 12131–12134, prohibits any public entity from discriminating against "qualified" persons with disabilities in the provision or operation of public services, programs, or activities. The Act defines the term "public entity" to include state and local governments, as well as their agencies and instrumentalities. § 12131(1).

Persons with disabilities are "qualified" if they, "with or without reasonable modifications to rules, policies, or practices, the removal of architectural, communication, or transportation barriers, or the provision of auxiliary aids and services, mee[t] the essential eligibility requirements for the receipt of services or the participation in programs or activities provided by a public entity." § 12131(2). Title II's enforcement provision incorporates by reference § 505 of the Rehabilitation Act of 1973, which authorizes private citizens to bring suits for money damages. 42 U.S.C. § 12133.

III

The Eleventh Amendment renders the States immune from "any suit in law or equity, commenced or prosecuted . . . by Citizens of another State, or by Citizens or Subjects of any Foreign State." Even though the Amendment "by its terms . . . applies only to suits against a State by citizens of another State," our cases have repeatedly held that this immunity also applies to unconsented suits brought by a State's own citizens. Our cases have also held that Congress may abrogate the State's Eleventh Amendment immunity. To determine whether it has done so in any given case, we "must resolve two predicate questions: first, whether Congress unequivocally expressed its intent to abrogate that immunity; and second, if it did, whether Congress acted pursuant to a valid grant of constitutional authority."

The first question is easily answered in this case. The Act specifically provides: "A State shall not be immune under the eleventh amendment to the Constitution of the United States from an action in Federal or State court of competent jurisdiction for a violation of this chapter." 42 U.S.C. § 12202. As in *Garrett*, no party disputes the adequacy of that expression of Congress' intent to abrogate the States' Eleventh Amendment immunity. The question, then, is whether Congress had the power to give effect to its intent.

In *Fitzpatrick v. Bitzer*, 427 U.S. 445 (1976), we held that Congress can abrogate a State's sovereign immunity when it does so pursuant to a valid exercise of its power under § 5 of the Fourteenth Amendment to enforce the substantive guarantees of that Amendment. This enforcement power, as we have often acknowledged, is a "broad power indeed." It includes "the authority both to remedy and to deter violation of rights guaranteed [by the Fourteenth Amendment] by prohibiting a somewhat broader swath of conduct, including that which is not itself forbidden by the Amendment's text." [citation omitted]. We have thus repeatedly affirmed that "Congress may enact so-called prophylactic legislation that proscribes facially constitutional conduct, in order to prevent and deter unconstitutional conduct." *Nev. Dep't of Human Res. v. Hibbs*, 538 U.S. 721, 727–728 (2003). The most recent affirmation of the breadth of Congress' § 5 power came in *Hibbs*, in which we considered whether a male state employee could recover money damages against the State for its failure to comply with the family-care leave provision of the Family and Medical Leave Act of 1993 (FMLA). We upheld the FMLA as a valid exercise of Congress' § 5 power to combat unconstitutional sex discrimination, even though there was no suggestion that the State's leave policy was adopted or applied with a discriminatory purpose that would render it unconstitutional . . . . When Congress seeks to remedy or prevent unconstitutional discrimination, § 5 authorizes it to enact prophylactic legislation proscribing practices that are discriminatory in effect, if not in intent, to carry out the basic objectives of the Equal Protection Clause.

Congress' § 5 power is not, however, unlimited. While Congress must have a wide berth in devising appropriate remedial and preventative measures for unconstitutional actions, those measures may not work a "substantive change in the governing law." [citation omitted]. . . . [T]he line between remedial legislation and substantive redefinition is "not easy to discern" . . . . But . . . "the distinction exists and must be observed," [pursuant to this test]: Section 5 legislation is valid if it exhibits "a congruence and proportionality between the injury to be prevented or remedied and the means adopted to that end." [citation omitted].

. . . .

This Court further defined the contours of [the] "congruence and proportionality" test in *Florida Prepaid Postsecondary Educ. Expense Bd. v. College Sav. Bank*, 527 U.S. 627 (1999). At issue in that case was the validity of the Patent and Plant Variety Protection Remedy Clarification Act (hereinafter Patent Remedy Act), a statutory amendment Congress enacted . . . to clarify its intent to abrogate state sovereign immunity from patent infringement suits. Noting the virtually complete absence of a history of unconstitutional patent infringement on the part of the States, as well as the Act's expansive coverage, the Court concluded that the Patent Remedy Act's apparent aim was to serve the Article I concerns of "provid[ing] a uniform remedy for patent infringement and . . . plac[ing] States on the same footing as private parties under that regime," and not to enforce the guarantees of the Fourteenth Amendment.

. . . [I]n *Garrett*, we concluded that Title I of the ADA was not a valid exercise of Congress' § 5 power to enforce the Fourteenth Amendment's prohibition on unconstitutional disability discrimination in public employment. As in *Florida Prepaid*, we concluded Congress' exercise of its prophylactic § 5 power was unsupported by a relevant history and pattern of constitutional violations. . . .

In view of the significant differences between Titles I and II, however, *Garrett* left open the question whether Title II is a valid exercise of Congress' § 5 enforcement power. It is to that question that we now turn.

IV

The first step of the . . . inquiry requires us to identify the constitutional right or rights that Congress sought to enforce when it enacted Title II. In *Garrett* we identified Title I's purpose as enforcement of the Fourteenth Amendment's command that "all persons similarly situated should be treated alike." As we observed, classifications based on disability violate that constitutional command if they lack a rational relationship to a legitimate governmental purpose.

Title II, like Title I, seeks to enforce this prohibition on irrational disability discrimination. But it also seeks to enforce a variety of other basic constitutional guarantees, infringements of which are subject to more searching judicial review. These rights include some, like the right of access to the courts at issue in this case, that are protected by the Due Process Clause of the Fourteenth Amendment. The Due Process Clause and the Confrontation Clause of the Sixth Amendment, as applied to the States via the Fourteenth Amendment, both guarantee to a criminal defendant such as respondent Lane the "right to be present at all stages of the trial where his absence might frustrate the fairness of the proceedings." The Due Process Clause also requires the States to afford certain civil litigants a "meaningful opportunity to be heard" by removing obstacles to their full participation in judicial proceedings. We have held that the Sixth Amendment guarantees to criminal defendants the right to trial by a jury composed of a fair cross section of the community, noting that the exclusion of "identifiable segments playing major roles in the community cannot be squared with the constitutional concept of jury trial." [citation omitted]. And, finally, we have recognized that members of the public have a right of access to criminal proceedings secured by the First Amendment.

Whether Title II validly enforces these constitutional rights is a question that "must be judged with reference to the historical experience which it reflects." [citation omitted]. While § 5 authorizes Congress to enact reasonably prophylactic remedial legislation, the appropriateness of the remedy depends on the gravity of the harm it seeks to prevent. "Difficult and intractable problems often require powerful remedies," but it is also true that "[s]trong measures appropriate to address one harm may be an unwarranted response to another, lesser one." [citation omitted].

It is not difficult to perceive the harm that Title II is designed to address. Congress enacted Title II against a backdrop of pervasive unequal treatment in the administration of state services and programs, including systematic deprivations of fundamental rights. For example, "[a]s of 1979, most States . . . categorically disqualified 'idiots' from voting, without regard to individual capacity." The majority of these laws remain on the books, and have been the subject of legal challenge as recently as 2001. Similarly, a number of States have prohibited and continue to prohibit persons with disabilities from engaging in activities such as marrying and serving as jurors. The historical experience that Title II reflects is also documented in this Court's cases, which have identified unconstitutional treatment of disabled persons by state agencies in a variety of settings, including unjustified commitment; the abuse and neglect of persons committed to state mental health hospitals; and irrational discrimination in zoning decisions. The decisions of other courts, too, document a pattern of unequal treatment in the administration of a wide range of public services, programs, and activities, including the penal system, public education, and voting. Notably, these decisions also demonstrate a pattern of unconstitutional treatment in the administration of justice.

. . . .

With respect to the particular services at issue in this case, Congress learned that many individuals, in many States across the country, were being excluded from courthouses and court proceedings by reason of their disabilities. A report before Congress showed that some 76% of public services and programs housed in state-owned buildings were inaccessible to and unusable by persons with disabilities, even taking into account the possibility that the services and programs might be restructured or relocated to other parts of the buildings. Congress itself heard testimony from persons with disabilities who described the physical inaccessibility of local courthouses. And its appointed task force heard numerous examples of the exclusion of persons with disabilities from state judicial services and programs, including exclusion of persons with visual impairments and hearing impairments from jury service, failure of state and local governments to provide interpretive services for the hearing impaired, failure to permit the testimony of adults with developmental disabilities in abuse cases, and failure to make courtrooms accessible to witnesses with physical disabilities.

Given the sheer volume of evidence demonstrating the nature and extent of unconstitutional discrimination against persons with disabilities in the provision of public services, the dissent's contention that the record is insufficient to justify Congress' exercise of its prophylactic power is puzzling, to say the least. . . .

The conclusion that Congress drew from this body of evidence is set forth in the text of the ADA itself: "[D]iscrimination against individuals with disabilities persists in such critical areas as . . . education, transportation, communication, recreation, institutionalization, health services, voting, and *access to public services*." 42 U.S.C. § 12101(a)(3) (emphasis added). This finding, together with the extensive record of disability discrimination that underlies it, makes clear beyond peradventure that inadequate provision of public services and access to public facilities was an appropriate subject for prophylactic legislation.

V

The only question that remains is whether Title II is an appropriate response to this history and pattern of unequal treatment. At the outset, we must determine the scope of that inquiry. Title II . . . reaches a wide array of official conduct in an effort to enforce an equally wide array of constitutional guarantees. Petitioner urges us both to examine the broad range of Title II's applications all at once, and to treat that breadth as a mark of the law's invalidity. According to petitioner, the fact that Title II applies not only to public education and voting-booth access but also to seating at state-owned hockey rinks indicates that Title II is not appropriately tailored to serve its objectives. But nothing in our case law requires us to consider Title II, with its wide variety of applications, as an undifferentiated whole. Whatever might be said about Title II's other applications, the question presented in this case is not whether Congress can validly subject the States to private suits for money damages for failing to provide reasonable access to hockey rinks, or even to voting booths, but whether Congress had the power under § 5 to enforce the constitutional right of access to the courts. Because we find that Title II unquestionably is valid § 5 legislation as it applies to the class of cases implicating the accessibility of judicial services, we need go no further.

Congress' chosen remedy for the pattern of exclusion and discrimination described above, Title II's requirement of program accessibility, is congruent and proportional to its object of enforcing the right of access to the courts. The unequal treatment of disabled persons in the administration of judicial services has a long history, and has persisted despite several legislative efforts to remedy the problem of disability discrimination. Faced with considerable evidence of the shortcomings of previous legislative responses, Congress was justified in concluding that this "difficult and intractable proble[m]" warranted "added prophylactic measures in response." [citation omitted].

The remedy Congress chose is nevertheless a limited one. Recognizing that failure to accommodate persons with disabilities will often have the same practical effect as outright exclusion, Congress required the States to take reasonable measures to remove architectural and other barriers to accessibility. But Title II does not require States to employ any and all means to make judicial services accessible to persons with disabilities, and it does not require States to compromise their essential eligibility criteria for public programs. It requires only "reasonable modifications" that would not fundamentally alter the nature of the service provided, and only when the individual seeking modification is otherwise eligible for the service. As Title II's implementing regulations make clear, the reasonable modification requirement can be satisfied in a number of ways. In the case of facilities built or altered after 1992, the regulations require compliance with specific architectural accessibility standards. But in the case of older facilities, for which structural change is likely to be more difficult, a public entity may comply with Title II by adopting a variety of less costly measures, including relocating services to alternative, accessible sites and assigning aides to assist persons with disabilities in accessing services. Only if these measures are ineffective in achieving accessibility is the public entity required to make reasonable structural changes. And in no event is the entity required to undertake measures that would impose an undue financial or administrative burden, threaten historic preservation interests, or effect a fundamental alteration in the nature of the service.

This duty to accommodate is perfectly consistent with the well-established due process principle that, "within the limits of practicability, a State must afford to all individuals a meaningful opportunity to be heard" in its courts. [citation omitted]. Our cases have recognized a number of affirmative obligations that flow from this principle: the duty to waive filing fees in certain family-law and criminal cases, the duty to provide transcripts to criminal defendants seeking review of their convictions, and the duty to provide counsel to certain criminal defendants. Each of these cases makes clear that ordinary considerations of cost and convenience alone cannot justify a State's failure to provide individuals with a meaningful right of access to the courts. Judged against this backdrop, Title II's affirmative obligation to accommodate persons with disabilities in the administration of justice cannot be said to be "so out of proportion to a supposed remedial or preventive object that it cannot be understood as responsive to, or designed to prevent, unconstitutional behavior." [citation omitted]. It is, rather, a reasonable prophylactic measure, reasonably targeted to a legitimate end.

For these reasons, we conclude that Title II, as it applies to the class of cases implicating the fundamental right of access to the courts, constitutes a valid exercise of Congress' § 5 authority to enforce the guarantees of the Fourteenth Amendment. The judgment of the Court of Appeals is therefore affirmed.

UNITED STATES v. GEORGIA

546 U.S. 151 (2006)

JUSTICE SCALIA delivered the opinion of the Court.

We consider whether a disabled inmate in a state prison may sue the State for money damages under Title II of the Americans with Disabilities Act of 1990 (ADA, or Act).

I

A

Title II of the ADA provides that "no qualified individual with a disability shall, by reason of such disability, be excluded from participation in or be denied the benefits of the services, programs, or activities of a public entity, or be subjected to discrimination by any such entity." 42 U.S.C. § 12132 (2000 ed.). A " 'qualified individual with a disability' " is defined as "an individual with a disability who, with or without reasonable modifications to rules, policies, or practices, the removal of architectural, communication, or transportation barriers, or the provision of auxiliary aids and services, meets the essential eligibility requirements for the receipt of services or the participation in programs or activities provided by a public entity." § 12131(2). The Act defines " 'public entity' " to include "any State or local government" and "any department, agency, . . . or other instrumentality of a State," § 12131(1). We have previously held that this term includes state prisons. Title II authorizes suits by private citizens for money damages against public entities that violate § 12132. *See* 42 U.S.C. § 12133.

In enacting the ADA, Congress "invoke[d] the sweep of congressional authority, including the power to enforce the fourteenth amendment . . . ." 42 U.S.C. § 12101(b)(4). Moreover, the Act provides that "[a] State shall not be immune under the eleventh amendment to the Constitution of the United States from an action in [a] Federal or State court of competent jurisdiction for a violation of this chapter." § 12202. We have accepted this latter statement as an unequivocal expression of Congress's intent to abrogate state sovereign immunity. *See Board of Trustees of Univ. of Ala. v. Garrett*, 531 U.S. 356, 363–364 (2001).

B

Petitioner in No. 04-1236, Tony Goodman, is a paraplegic inmate in the Georgia prison system who, at all relevant times, was housed at the Georgia State Prison in Reidsville. After filing numerous administrative grievances in the state prison system, Goodman filed a *pro se* complaint in the United States District Court for the Southern District of Georgia challenging the conditions of his confinement. He named as defendants the State of Georgia and the Georgia Department of Corrections (state defendants) and several individual prison officials. He brought claims under Rev. Stat. § 1979, 42 U.S.C. § 1983, Title II of the ADA, and other provisions not relevant here, seeking both injunctive relief and money damages against all defendants.

Goodman's *pro se* complaint and subsequent filings in the District Court included many allegations, both grave and trivial, regarding the conditions of his confinement in the Reidsville prison. Among his more serious allegations, he claimed that he was confined for 23-to-24 hours per day in a 12-by-3-foot cell in which he could not turn his wheelchair around. He alleged that the lack of accessible facilities rendered him unable to use the toilet and shower without assistance, which was often denied. On multiple occasions, he asserted, he had injured himself in attempting to transfer from his wheelchair to the shower or toilet on his own, and, on several other occasions, he had been forced to sit in his own feces and urine while prison officials refused to assist him in cleaning up the waste. He also claimed that he had been denied physical therapy and medical treatment, and denied access to virtually all prison programs and services on account of his disability.

The District Court adopted the Magistrate Judge's recommendation that the allegations in the complaint were vague and constituted insufficient notice pleading as to Goodman's § 1983 claims. It therefore dismissed the § 1983 claims against all defendants without providing Goodman an opportunity to amend his complaint. The District Court also dismissed his Title II claims against all individual defendants. Later, after our decision in *Garrett*, the District Court granted summary judgment to the state defendants on Goodman's Title II claims for money damages, holding that those claims were barred by state sovereign immunity.

Goodman appealed to the United States Court of Appeals for the Eleventh Circuit. The United States, intervened to defend the constitutionality of Title II's abrogation of state sovereign immunity. The Eleventh Circuit determined that the District Court had erred in dismissing all of Goodman's § 1983 claims, because Goodman's multiple *pro se* filings in the District Court alleged facts sufficient to support "a limited number of Eighth-Amendment claims under § 1983" against certain individual defendants. . . .

The Eleventh Circuit did not address the sufficiency of Goodman's allegations under Title II. Instead, relying on [one of] its prior decision[s] . . . the Court of Appeals affirmed the District Court's holding that Goodman's Title II claims for money damages against the State were barred by sovereign immunity. We granted certiorari to consider whether Title II of the ADA validly abrogates state sovereign immunity with respect to the claims at issue here.

II

In reversing the dismissal of Goodman's § 1983 claims, the Eleventh Circuit held that Goodman had alleged actual violations of the Eighth Amendment by state agents on the grounds set forth above. The State does not contest this holding, and we did not grant certiorari to consider the merits of Goodman's Eighth Amendment claims; we assume without deciding, therefore, that the Eleventh Circuit's treatment of these claims was correct. Moreover, Goodman urges, and the State does not dispute, that this same conduct that violated the Eighth Amendment also violated Title II of the ADA. In fact, it is quite plausible that the alleged deliberate refusal of prison officials to accommodate Goodman's disability-related needs in such fundamentals as mobility, hygiene, medical care, and virtually all other prison programs constituted "exclu[sion] from participation in or . . . deni[al of] the benefits of" the prison's "services, programs, or activities." 42 U.S.C. § 12132. Therefore, Goodman's claims for money damages against the State under Title II were evidently based, at least in large part, on conduct that independently violated the provisions of § 1 of the Fourteenth Amendment. *See Louisiana ex rel. Francis v. Resweber*, 329 U.S. 459, 463 (1947) (plurality opinion) (the Due Process Clause of the Fourteenth Amendment incorporates the Eighth Amendment's guarantee against cruel and unusual punishment). In this respect, Goodman differs from the claimants in our other cases addressing Congress's ability to abrogate sovereign immunity pursuant to its § 5 powers.

While the Members of this Court have disagreed regarding the scope of Congress's "prophylactic" enforcement powers under § 5 of the Fourteenth Amendment, no one doubts that § 5 grants Congress the power to "enforce . . . the provisions" of the Amendment by creating private remedies against the States for *actual* violations of those provisions. . . . This enforcement power includes the power to abrogate state sovereign immunity by authorizing private suits for damages against the States. Thus, insofar as Title II creates a private cause of action for damages against the States for conduct that *actually* violates the Fourteenth Amendment, Title II validly abrogates state sovereign immunity. The Eleventh Circuit erred in dismissing those of Goodman's Title II claims that were based on such unconstitutional conduct.

From the many allegations in Goodman's *pro se* complaint and his subsequent filings in the District Court, it is not clear precisely what conduct he intended to allege in support of his Title II claims. Because the Eleventh Circuit did not address the issue, it is likewise unclear to what extent the conduct underlying Goodman's constitutional claims also violated Title II. Moreover, the Eleventh Circuit ordered that the suit be remanded to the District Court to permit Goodman to amend his complaint, but instructed him to revise his factual allegations to exclude his "frivolous" claims — some of which are quite far afield from actual constitutional violations . . . or even from Title II violations. It is therefore unclear whether Goodman's amended complaint will assert Title II claims premised on conduct that does *not* independently violate the Fourteenth Amendment. Once Goodman's complaint is amended, the lower courts will be best situated to determine in the first instance, on a claim-by-claim basis, (1) which aspects of the State's alleged conduct violated Title II; (2) to what extent such misconduct also violated the Fourteenth Amendment; and (3) insofar as such misconduct violated Title II but did not violate the Fourteenth Amendment, whether Congress's purported abrogation of sovereign immunity as to that class of conduct is nevertheless valid.

The judgment of the Eleventh Circuit is reversed, and the suit is remanded for further proceedings consistent with this opinion.

NOTES

1. In his dissent, Justice Breyer — joined by Justices Stevens, Souter, and Ginsburg — criticized the majority for subjecting congressional evidentiary findings in the ADA to the type of scrutiny normally applied to administrative agencies. *Bd. of Tr. of the Univ. of Ala. v. Garrett*, 531 U.S. 356, 376–77 (2001) (Breyer, J., dissenting). In the view of the dissenters, Congress was well within its right under § 5 to abrogate state judicial immunity based on the body of congressional evidence showing a systemic pattern of discrimination in *all* facets of society — including private persons, local and state governments — by providing an *array* of basic services to the disabled, and *not* just in the employment arena.

> The Court's harsh review of Congress' use of its § 5 power is reminiscent of the similar (now-discredited) limitation that it once imposed upon Congress' Commerce Clause power. I could understand the legal basis for such review were we judging a statute that discriminated against those of a particular race or gender, or a statute that threatened a basic constitutionally protected liberty such as free speech. The legislation before us, however, does not discriminate against anyone, nor does it pose any threat to basic liberty. And it is difficult to understand why the Court, which applies "minimum 'rational-basis' review" to statutes that *burden* persons with disabilities subjects to far stricter scrutiny a statute that seeks to *help* those same individuals.
>
> I recognize nonetheless that this statute imposes a burden upon States in that it removes their Eleventh Amendment protection from suit, thereby subjecting them to potential monetary liability. Rules for interpreting § 5 that would provide States with special protection, however, run counter to the very object of the Fourteenth Amendment. By its terms, that Amendment prohibits *States* from denying their citizens equal protection of the laws. Hence "principles of federalism that might otherwise be an obstacle to congressional authority are necessarily overridden by the power to enforce the Civil War Amendments 'by appropriate legislation.' Those Amendments were specifically designed as an expansion of federal power and an intrusion on state sovereignty." [citations omitted]. And, ironically, the greater the obstacle the Eleventh Amendment poses to the creation by Congress of the kind of remedy at issue here — the decentralized remedy of private damage actions — the more Congress, seeking to cure important national problems, such as the problem of disability discrimination before us, will have to rely on more uniform remedies, such as federal standards and court injunctions which are sometimes draconian and typically more intrusive. For these reasons, I doubt that today's decision serves any constitutionally based federalism interest.
>
> The Court, through its evidentiary demands, its non-deferential review, and its failure to distinguish between judicial and legislative constitutional competencies, improperly invades a power that the Constitution assigns to Congress. Its decision saps § 5 of independent force, effectively "confining the legislative power . . . to the insignificant role of abrogating only those state laws that the judicial branch [is] prepared to adjudge unconstitu-

tional." [citation omitted]. Whether the Commerce Clause does or does not enable Congress to enact this provision, in my view, § 5 gives Congress the necessary authority. For the reasons stated, I respectfully dissent.

Garrett, 531 U.S. at 387–89 (Breyer, J., dissenting).

As one commentator put it:

> *Garrett* leaves unanswered the most interesting and important issue the case presented: Why is Congress without authority to abrogate state judicial immunity regarding employment policies that harm persons with disabilities 1) when there are legislative facts showing a pervasive pattern of unconstitutional disability-based discrimination (if one includes the totality of state and local governments' behavior) and 2) when Congress concludes, based on those facts, that integration of the disabled into society is the key to deterring and remedying the prejudice causing this pervasive pattern of unconstitutional discrimination, and 3) when the only efficacious way to integrate the disabled into society is to integrate them into all segments of society, including all aspects of public sector employment?
>
> This is the central question that Title I's abrogation provisions pose and it is unfortunate that *Garrett* avoids it. If there is no principled basis to deny Congress' Section 5 power to abrogate state judicial immunity when the legislative record supports each of the three conditions stated above - and one is at a loss to imagine what that basis might be - then *Garrett* was decided incorrectly. If, notwithstanding the pattern of unconstitutionality that Congress did document and notwithstanding the need to integrate the disabled that Congress did demonstrate, there still is no Section 5 power, one would think that we deserve to know why. *Garrett* provides not a clue.

Roger C. Hartley, *Enforcing Federal Civil Rights Against Public Entities After* Garrett, 28 J.C. & U.L. 41, 57–58 (2001).* How specific do congressional findings have to be? Is establishing a pervasive pattern of discrimination in society *at large* enough to justify abrogating States' sovereign immunity to enforce an antidiscrimination *employment* provision?

2. In his opinion for the majority, Justice Rehnquist noted that

> [o]ur holding here that Congress did not validly abrogate the States' sovereign immunity from suit by private individuals for money damages under Title I does not mean that persons with disabilities have no federal recourse against discrimination. Title I of the ADA still prescribes standards applicable to the States. Those standards can be enforced by the United States in actions for money damages, as well as by private individuals in actions for injunctive relief . . . . In addition, state laws protecting the rights of persons with disabilities in employment and other aspects of life provide independent avenues of redress.

Board of Tr. of the Univ. of Ala. v. Garrett, 531 U.S. 356, 374 n.9 (2001). If a disabled employee suffers discrimination at the hands of her employer, how likely is it that the United States will sue the employer for money damages? Would a successful suit for injunctive relief properly redress the effects of employment discrimination, particularly income loss?

For other potential alternatives for disabled employees — including employing Congress's Spending Power under Section 504 of The Rehabilitation Act of 1973 to sue for money damages — see Roger C. Hartley, *Enforcing Federal Civil Rights Against Public Entities After* Garrett, 28 J.C. & U.L. 41 (2001); Joseph J. Shelton, *In the Wake of* Garrett, *State Law Alternatives to the Americans With Disabilities Act*, 52 Cath. U.L. Rev. 837 (2003); Elizabeth A. Pendo, *Substantially Limited Justice?: The Possibilities and Limits of a New Rawlsian Analysis of Disability-Based Discrimination*, 77 St. John's L. Rev. 225 (2003).

3. Predictably, *Tennessee v. Lane*, 541 U.S. 509 (2004) was a 5-4 decision, with Justice O'Connor breaking from the conservative wing of the party to cast the tie-breaking vote. Chief Justice Rehnquist, joined by Justices Kennedy and Thomas, dissented because he believed the *Lane* decision was irreconcilable with the decision in *Garrett. Id.* at 538. Justice Scalia, dissenting on his own, rejected the "congruence and proportionality" test that the Court uses in § 5 cases, calling it "flabby" and an example of the types of tests that "have a way of turning into vehicles for the implementation of individual judges' policy preferences." *Id.* at 556, 557. And Justice Thomas, also writing his own separate dissent, noted that "Congress fail[ed] to identify any evidence of" States "denying disabled people access to the courts." *Id.* at 566.

Whatever else can be said about the rationales of the dissenting Justices in *Lane*, it is likely, given the Court's more conservative tendencies since that case was decided, that future ADA cases will face even stiffer resistance.

E. STUDENTS WITH DISABILITIES

SOUTHEASTERN COMMUNITY COLLEGE v. DAVIS
442 U.S. 397 (1979)

Mr. Justice Powell delivered the opinion of the Court.

This case presents a matter of first impression for this Court: Whether § 504 of the Rehabilitation Act of 1973, which prohibits discrimination against an "otherwise qualified handicapped individual" in federally funded programs "solely by reason of his handicap," forbids professional schools from imposing physical qualifications for admission to their clinical training programs.

I

Respondent, who suffers from a serious hearing disability, seeks to be trained as a registered nurse. During the 1973–1974 academic year she was enrolled in the College Parallel program of Southeastern Community College, a state institution that receives federal funds. Respondent hoped to progress to Southeastern's Associate Degree Nursing program, completion of which would make her eligible for state certification as a registered nurse. In the course of her application to the nursing program, she was interviewed by a member of the nursing faculty. It became apparent that respondent had difficulty understanding questions asked, and on inquiry she acknowledged a history of hearing problems and dependence on a hearing aid. She was advised to consult an audiologist.

On the basis of an examination at Duke University Medical Center, respondent was diagnosed as having a "bilateral, sensori-neural hearing loss." A change in her hearing aid was recommended, as a result of which it was expected that she would be able to detect sounds "almost as well as a person would who has normal hearing." But this improvement would not mean that she could discriminate among sounds sufficiently to understand normal spoken speech. Her lipreading skills would remain necessary for effective communication: "While wearing the hearing aid, she is well aware of gross sounds occurring in the listening environment. However, she can only be responsible for speech spoken to her, when the talker gets her attention and allows her to look directly at the talker."

Southeastern next consulted Mary McRee, Executive Director of the North Carolina Board of Nursing. On the basis of the audiologist's report, McRee recommended that respondent not be admitted to the nursing program. In McRee's view, respondent's hearing disability made it unsafe for her to practice as a nurse. In addition, it would be impossible for respondent to participate safely in the normal clinical training program, and those modifications that would be necessary to enable safe participation would prevent her from realizing the benefits of the program: "To adjust patient learning experiences in keeping with [respondent's] hearing limitations could, in fact, be the same as denying her full learning to meet the objectives of your nursing programs."

After respondent was notified that she was not qualified for nursing study because of her hearing disability, she requested reconsideration of the decision. The entire nursing staff of Southeastern was assembled, and McRee again was consulted. McRee repeated her conclusion that on the basis of the available evidence, respondent "has hearing limitations which could interfere with her safely caring for patients." Upon further deliberation, the staff voted to deny respondent admission.

Respondent then filed suit in the United States District Court for the Eastern District of North Carolina, alleging both a violation of § 504 of the Rehabilitation Act of 1973, 29 U. S. C. § 794 (1976 ed., Supp. III), and a denial of equal protection and due process. After a bench trial, the District Court entered judgment in favor of Southeastern. It confirmed the findings of the audiologist that even with a hearing aid respondent cannot understand speech directed to her except through lipreading, and further found:

"[In] many situations such as an operation room intensive care unit, or post-natal care unit, all doctors and nurses wear surgical masks which would make lipreading impossible. Additionally, in many situations a Registered Nurse would be required to instantly follow the physician's instructions concerning procurement of various types of instruments and drugs where the physician would be unable to get the nurse's attention by other than vocal means."

Accordingly, the court concluded:

> "[Respondent's] handicap actually prevents her from safely performing in both her training program and her proposed profession. The trial testimony indicated numerous situations where [respondent's] particular disability would render her unable to function properly. Of particular concern to the court in this case is the potential of danger to future patients in such situations."

Based on these findings, the District Court concluded that respondent was not an "otherwise qualified handicapped individual" protected against discrimination by § 504. In its view, "[otherwise] qualified, can only be read to mean otherwise able to function sufficiently in the position sought in spite of the handicap, if proper training and facilities are suitable and available." Because respondent's disability would prevent her from functioning "sufficiently" in Southeastern's nursing program, the court held that the decision to exclude her was not discriminatory within the meaning of § 504.

On appeal, the Court of Appeals for the Fourth Circuit reversed. It did not dispute the District Court's findings of fact, but held that the court had misconstrued § 504. In light of administrative regulations that had been promulgated while the appeal was pending, the appellate court believed that § 504 required Southeastern to "reconsider plaintiff's application for admission to the nursing program without regard to her hearing ability." It concluded that the District Court had erred in taking respondent's handicap into account in determining whether she was "otherwise qualified" for the program, rather than confining its inquiry to her "academic and technical qualifications." The Court of Appeals also suggested that § 504 required "affirmative conduct" on the part of Southeastern to modify its program to accommodate the disabilities of applicants, "even when such modifications become expensive."

Because of the importance of this issue to the many institutions covered by § 504, we granted certiorari. 439 U.S. 1065 (1979). We now reverse.

II

As previously noted, this is the first case in which this Court has been called upon to interpret § 504. It is elementary that "[the] starting point in every case involving construction of a statute is the language itself." [citations omitted]. Section 504 by its terms does not compel educational institutions to disregard the disabilities of handicapped individuals or to make substantial modifications in their programs to allow disabled persons to participate. Instead, it requires only that an "otherwise qualified handicapped individual" not be excluded from participation in a federally funded program "solely by reason of his handicap," indicating only that mere possession of a handicap is not a permissible ground for assuming an inability to function in a particular context.

The court below, however, believed that the "otherwise qualified" persons protected by § 504 include those who would be able to meet the requirements of a particular program in every respect except as to limitations imposed by their handicap. Taken literally, this holding would prevent an institution from taking into account any limitation resulting from the handicap, however disabling. It assumes, in effect, that a person need not meet legitimate physical requirements in order to be "otherwise qualified." We think the understanding of the District Court is closer to the plain meaning of the statutory language. An otherwise qualified person is one who is able to meet all of a program's requirements in spite of his handicap.

The regulations promulgated by the Department of HEW to interpret § 504 reinforce, rather than contradict, this conclusion. According to these regulations, a "[qualified] handicapped person" is, "[with] respect to postsecondary and vocational education services, a handicapped person who meets the academic and technical standards requisite to admission or participation in the [school's] education program or activity . . . ." 45 CFR § 84.3 (k)(3) (1978). An explanatory note states:

"The term 'technical standards' refers to *all* nonacademic admissions criteria that are essential to participation in the program in question." 45 CFR pt. 84, App. A, p. 405 (1978) (emphasis supplied).

A further note emphasizes that legitimate physical qualifications may be essential to participation in particular programs. We think it clear, therefore, that HEW interprets the "other" qualifications which a handicapped person may be required to meet as including necessary physical qualifications.

III

The remaining question is whether the physical qualifications Southeastern demanded of respondent might not be necessary for participation in its nursing program. It is not open to dispute that, as Southeastern's Associate Degree Nursing program currently is constituted, the ability to understand speech without reliance on lipreading is necessary for patient safety during the clinical phase of the program. As the District Court found, this ability also is indispensable for many of the functions that a registered nurse performs.

Respondent contends nevertheless that § 504, properly interpreted, compels Southeastern to undertake affirmative action that would dispense with the need for effective oral communication. First, it is suggested that respondent can be given individual supervision by faculty members whenever she attends patients directly. Moreover, certain required courses might be dispensed with altogether for respondent. It is not necessary, she argues, that Southeastern train her to undertake all the tasks a registered nurse is licensed to perform. Rather, it is sufficient to make § 504 applicable if respondent might be able to perform satisfactorily some of the duties of a registered nurse or to hold some of the positions available to a registered nurse.

Respondent finds support for this argument in portions of the HEW regulations discussed above. In particular, a provision applicable to postsecondary educational programs requires covered institutions to make "modifications" in their programs to accommodate handicapped persons, and to provide "auxiliary aids" such as sign-language interpreters. Respondent argues that this regulation imposes an obligation to ensure full participation in covered programs by handicapped individuals and, in particular, requires Southeastern to make the kind of adjustments that would be necessary to permit her safe participation in the nursing program.

We note first that on the present record it appears unlikely respondent could benefit from any affirmative action that the regulation reasonably could be interpreted as requiring. Section 84.44 (d)(2), for example, explicitly excludes "devices or services of a personal nature" from the kinds of auxiliary aids a school must provide a handicapped individual. Yet the only evidence in the record indicates that nothing less than close, individual attention by a nursing instructor would be sufficient to ensure patient safety if respondent took part in the clinical phase of the nursing program. Furthermore, it also is reasonably clear that § 84.44 (a) does not encompass the kind of curricular changes that would be necessary to accommodate respondent in the nursing program. In light of respondent's inability to function in clinical courses without close supervision, Southeastern, with prudence, could allow her to take only academic classes. Whatever benefits respondent might realize from such a course of study, she would not receive even a rough equivalent of the training a nursing program normally gives. Such a fundamental alteration in the nature of a program is far more than the "modification" the regulation requires.

Moreover, an interpretation of the regulations that required the extensive modifications necessary to include respondent in the nursing program would raise grave doubts about their validity. If these regulations were to require substantial adjustments in existing programs beyond those necessary to eliminate discrimination against otherwise qualified individuals, they would do more than clarify the meaning of § 504. Instead, they would constitute an unauthorized extension of the obligations imposed by that statute.

The language and structure of the Rehabilitation Act of 1973 reflect a recognition by Congress of the distinction between the evenhanded treatment of qualified handicapped persons and affirmative efforts to overcome the disabilities caused by handicaps. Section 501 (b), governing the employment of handicapped individuals by the Federal Government, requires each federal agency to submit "an affirmative action program plan for the hiring, placement, and advancement of handicapped individuals . . . ." These plans "shall include a description of the extent to which and methods whereby the special needs of handicapped employees are being met." Similarly, § 503 (a), governing hiring by federal contractors, requires employers to "take affirmative action to employ and advance in employment qualified handicapped individuals . . . ." The President is required to promulgate regulations to enforce this section.

Under § 501 (c) of the Act, by contrast, state agencies such as Southeastern are only "[encouraged] . . . to adopt and implement such policies and procedures." Section 504 does not refer at all to affirmative action, and except as it applies to federal employers it does not provide for implementation by administrative action. A comparison of these provisions demonstrates that Congress understood accommodation of the needs of handicapped individuals may require affirmative action and knew how to provide for it in those instances where it wished to do so.

Although an agency's interpretation of the statute under which it operates is entitled to some deference, "this deference is constrained by our obligation to honor the clear meaning of a statute, as revealed by its language, purpose, and history." [citation omitted]. Here, neither the language, purpose, nor history of § 504 reveals an intent to impose an affirmative-action obligation on all recipients of federal funds.

Accordingly, we hold that even if HEW has attempted to create such an obligation itself, it lacks the authority to do so.

IV

We do not suggest that the line between a lawful refusal to extend affirmative action and illegal discrimination against handicapped persons always will be clear. It is possible to envision situations where an insistence on continuing past requirements and practices might arbitrarily deprive genuinely qualified handicapped persons of the opportunity to participate in a covered program. Technological advances can be expected to enhance opportunities to rehabilitate the handicapped or otherwise to qualify them for some useful employment. Such advances also may enable attainment of these goals without imposing undue financial and administrative burdens upon a State. Thus, situations may arise where a refusal to modify an existing program might become unreasonable and discriminatory. Identification of those instances where a refusal to accommodate the needs of a disabled person amounts to discrimination against the handicapped continues to be an important responsibility of HEW.

In this case, however, it is clear that Southeastern's unwillingness to make major adjustments in its nursing program does not constitute such discrimination. The uncontroverted testimony of several members of Southeastern's staff and faculty established that the purpose of its program was to train persons who could serve the nursing profession in all customary ways. This type of purpose, far from reflecting any animus against handicapped individuals, is shared by many if not most of the institutions that train persons to render professional service. It is undisputed that respondent could not participate in Southeastern's nursing program unless the standards were substantially lowered. Section 504 imposes no requirement upon an educational institution to lower or to effect substantial modifications of standards to accommodate a handicapped person.

One may admire respondent's desire and determination to overcome her handicap, and there well may be various other types of service for which she can qualify. In this case, however, we hold that there was no violation of § 504 when Southeastern concluded that respondent did not qualify for admission to its program. Nothing in the language or history of § 504 reflects an intention to limit the freedom of an educational institution to require reasonable physical qualifications for admission to a clinical training program. Nor has there been any showing in this case that any action short of a substantial change in Southeastern's program would render unreasonable the qualifications it imposed.

V

Accordingly, we reverse the judgment of the court below, and remand for proceedings consistent with this opinion.

PGA TOUR, INC. v. MARTIN

532 U.S. 661 (2001)

JUSTICE STEVENS delivered the opinion of the Court.

This case raises two questions concerning the application of the Americans with Disabilities Act of 1990, 42 U.S.C. § 12101 *et seq.*, to a gifted athlete: first, whether the Act protects access to professional golf tournaments by a qualified entrant with a disability; and second, whether a disabled contestant may be denied the use of a golf cart because it would "fundamentally alter the nature" of the tournaments, § 12182(b)(2)(A)(ii), to allow him to ride when all other contestants must walk.

I

Petitioner PGA TOUR, Inc., a nonprofit entity formed in 1968, sponsors and cosponsors professional golf tournaments conducted on three annual tours. About 200 golfers participate in the PGA TOUR; about 170 in the NIKE TOUR; and about 100 in the SENIOR PGA TOUR. PGA TOUR and NIKE TOUR tournaments typically are 4-day events, played on courses leased and operated by petitioner. The entire field usually competes in two 18-hole rounds played on Thursday and Friday; those who survive the "cut" play on Saturday and Sunday and receive prize money in amounts determined by their aggregate scores for all four rounds. The revenues generated by television, admissions, concessions, and contributions from cosponsors amount to about $300 million a year, much of which is distributed in prize money.

There are various ways of gaining entry into particular tours. For example, a player who wins three NIKE TOUR events in the same year, or is among the top-15 money winners on that tour, earns the right to play in the PGA TOUR. Additionally, a golfer may obtain a spot in an official tournament through successfully competing in "open" qualifying rounds, which are conducted the week before each tournament. Most participants, however, earn playing privileges in the PGA TOUR or NIKE TOUR by way of a three-stage qualifying tournament known as the "Q-School."

Any member of the public may enter the Q-School by paying a $3,000 entry fee and submitting two letters of reference from, among others, PGA TOUR or NIKE TOUR members. The $3,000 entry fee covers the players' greens fees and the cost of golf carts, which are permitted during the first two stages, but which have been prohibited during the third stage since 1997. Each year, over a thousand contestants compete in the first stage, which consists of four 18-hole rounds at different locations. Approximately half of them make it to the second stage, which also includes 72 holes. Around 168 players survive the second stage and advance to the final one, where they compete over 108 holes. Of those finalists, about a fourth qualify for membership in the PGA TOUR, and the rest gain membership in the NIKE TOUR. The significance of making it into either tour is illuminated by the fact that there are about 25 million golfers in the country.

Three sets of rules govern competition in tour events. First, the "Rules of Golf," jointly written by the United States Golf Association (USGA) and the Royal and Ancient Golf Club of Scotland, apply to the game as it is played, not only by millions of amateurs on public courses and in private country clubs throughout the United States and worldwide, but also by the professionals in the tournaments conducted by petitioner, the USGA, the Ladies' Professional Golf Association, and the Senior Women's Golf Association. Those rules do not prohibit the use of golf carts at any time.

Second, the "Conditions of Competition and Local Rules," often described as the "hard card," apply specifically to petitioner's professional tours. The hard cards for the PGA TOUR and NIKE TOUR require players to walk the golf course during tournaments, but not during open qualifying rounds. On the SENIOR PGA TOUR, which is limited to golfers age 50 and older, the contestants may use golf carts. Most seniors, however, prefer to walk.

Third, "Notices to Competitors" are issued for particular tournaments and cover conditions for that specific event. Such a notice may, for example, explain how the Rules of Golf should be applied to a particular water hazard or man-made obstruction. It might also authorize the use of carts to speed up play when there is an unusual distance between one green and the next tee.

The basic Rules of Golf, the hard cards, and the weekly notices apply equally to all players in tour competitions. As one of petitioner's witnesses explained with reference to "the Masters Tournament, which is golf at its very highest level . . . the key is to have everyone tee off on the first hole under exactly the same conditions and all of them be tested over that 72-hole event under the conditions that exist during those four days of the event."

II

Casey Martin is a talented golfer. As an amateur, he won 17 Oregon Golf Association junior events before he was 15, and won the state championship as a high school senior. He played on the Stanford University golf team that won the 1994 National Collegiate Athletic Association (NCAA) championship. As a professional, Martin qualified for the NIKE TOUR in 1998 and 1999, and based on his 1999 performance, qualified for the PGA TOUR in 2000. In the 1999 season, he entered 24 events, made the cut 13 times, and had 6 top-10 finishes, coming in second twice and third once.

Martin is also an individual with a disability as defined in the Americans with Disabilities Act of 1990 (ADA or Act). Since birth he has been afflicted with Klippel-Trenaunay-Weber Syndrome, a degenerative circulatory disorder that obstructs the flow of blood from his right leg back to his heart. The disease is progressive; it causes severe pain and has atrophied his right leg. During the latter part of his college career, because of the progress of the disease, Martin could no longer walk an 18-hole golf course. Walking not only caused him pain, fatigue, and anxiety, but also created a significant risk of hemorrhaging, developing blood clots, and fracturing his tibia so badly that an amputation might be required. For these reasons, Stanford made written requests to the Pacific 10 Conference and the NCAA to waive for Martin their rules requiring players to walk and carry their own clubs. The requests were granted.

When Martin turned pro and entered petitioner's Q-School, the hard card permitted him to use a cart during his successful progress through the first two stages. He made a request, supported by detailed medical records, for permission to use a golf cart during the third stage. Petitioner refused to review those records or to waive its walking rule for the third stage. Martin therefore filed this action. A preliminary injunction entered by the District Court made it possible for him to use a cart in the final stage of the Q-School and as a competitor in the NIKE TOUR and PGA TOUR. Although not bound by the injunction, and despite its support for petitioner's position in this litigation, the USGA voluntarily granted Martin a similar waiver in events that it sponsors, including the U.S. Open.

III

In the District Court, petitioner moved for summary judgment on the ground that it is exempt from coverage under Title III of the ADA as a "private club or establishment," or alternatively, that the play areas of its tour competitions do not constitute places of "public accommodation" within the scope of that Title. The Magistrate Judge concluded that petitioner should be viewed as a commercial enterprise operating in the entertainment industry for the economic benefit of its members rather than as a private club. Furthermore, after noting that the statutory definition of public accommodation included a "golf course," he rejected petitioner's argument that its competitions are only places of public accommodation in the areas open to spectators. The operator of a public accommodation could not, in his view, "create private enclaves within the facility . . . and thus relegate the ADA to hop-scotch areas." Accordingly, he denied petitioner's motion for summary judgment.

At trial, petitioner did not contest the conclusion that Martin has a disability covered by the ADA, or the fact "that his disability prevents him from walking the course during a round of golf." Rather, petitioner asserted that the condition of walking is a substantive rule of competition, and that waiving it as to any individual for any reason would fundamentally alter the nature of the competition. Petitioner's evidence included the testimony of a number of experts, among them some of the greatest golfers in history. Arnold Palmer, Jack Nicklaus, and Ken Venturi explained that fatigue can be a critical factor in a tournament, particularly on the last day when psychological pressure is at a maximum. Their testimony makes it clear that, in their view, permission to use a cart might well give some players a competitive advantage over other players who must walk. They did not, however, express any opinion on whether a cart would give Martin such an advantage.

Rejecting petitioner's argument that an individualized inquiry into the necessity of the walking rule in Martin's case would be inappropriate, the District Court stated that it had "the independent duty to inquire into the purpose of the rule at issue, and to ascertain whether there can be a reasonable modification made to accommodate plaintiff without frustrating the purpose of the rule" and thereby fundamentally altering the nature of petitioner's tournaments. The judge found that the purpose of the rule was to inject fatigue into the skill of shot-making, but that the fatigue injected "by walking the course cannot be deemed significant under normal circumstances." Furthermore, Martin presented evidence, and the judge found, that even with the use of a cart, Martin must walk over a mile during an

18-hole round, and that the fatigue he suffers from coping with his disability is "undeniably greater" than the fatigue his able-bodied competitors endure from walking the course. . . .

As a result, the judge concluded that it would "not fundamentally alter the nature of the PGA Tour's game to accommodate him with a cart." The judge accordingly entered a permanent injunction requiring petitioner to permit Martin to use a cart in tour and qualifying events.

On appeal to the Ninth Circuit, petitioner did not challenge the District Court's rejection of its claim that it was exempt as a "private club," but it renewed the contention that during a tournament the portion of the golf course " 'behind the ropes' is not a public accommodation because the public has no right to enter it." The Court of Appeals viewed that contention as resting on the incorrect assumption that the competition among participants was not itself public. The court first pointed out that, as with a private university, "the fact that users of a facility are highly selected does not mean that the facility cannot be a public accommodation." In its opinion, the competition to enter the select circle of PGA TOUR and NIKE TOUR golfers was comparable because "any member of the public who pays a $3000 entry fee and supplies two letters of recommendation may try out in the qualifying school." The court saw "no justification in reason or in the statute to draw a line beyond which the performance of athletes becomes so excellent that a competition restricted to their level deprives its situs of the character of a public accommodation." Nor did it find a basis for distinguishing between "use of a place of public accommodation for pleasure and use in the pursuit of a living." Consequently, the Court of Appeals concluded that golf courses remain places of public accommodation during PGA tournaments.

On the merits, because there was no serious dispute about the fact that permitting Martin to use a golf cart was both a reasonable and a necessary solution to the problem of providing him access to the tournaments, the Court of Appeals regarded the central dispute as whether such permission would "fundamentally alter" the nature of the PGA TOUR or NIKE TOUR. Like the District Court, the Court of Appeals viewed the issue not as "whether use of carts generally would fundamentally alter the competition, but whether the use of a cart by Martin would do so." That issue turned on "an intensively fact-based inquiry," and, the court concluded, had been correctly resolved by the trial judge. In its words, "all that the cart does is permit Martin access to a type of competition in which he otherwise could not engage because of his disability."

The day after the Ninth Circuit ruled in Martin's favor, the Seventh Circuit came to a contrary conclusion in a case brought against the USGA by a disabled golfer who failed to qualify for "America's greatest — and most democratic — golf tournament, the United States Open." The Seventh Circuit endorsed the conclusion of the District Court in that case that "the nature of the competition would be fundamentally altered if the walking rule were eliminated because it would remove stamina (at least a particular type of stamina) from the set of qualities designed to be tested in this competition." . . . As an alternative basis for its holding, the court also concluded that the ADA does not require the USGA to bear "the administrative burdens of evaluating requests to waive the walking rule and permit the use of a golf cart."

Although the Seventh Circuit merely assumed that the ADA applies to professional golf tournaments, and therefore did not disagree with the Ninth on the threshold coverage issue, our grant of certiorari, 530 U.S. 1306 (2000), encompasses that question as well as the conflict between those courts.

IV

Congress enacted the ADA in 1990 to remedy widespread discrimination against disabled individuals. In studying the need for such legislation, Congress found that "historically, society has tended to isolate and segregate individuals with disabilities, and, despite some improvements, such forms of discrimination against individuals with disabilities continue to be a serious and pervasive social problem." 42 U.S.C. § 12101(a)(2). . . . After thoroughly investigating the problem, Congress concluded that there was a "compelling need" for a "clear and comprehensive national mandate" to eliminate discrimination against disabled individuals, and to integrate them "into the economic and social mainstream of American life."

In the ADA, Congress provided that broad mandate. . . . To effectuate its sweeping purpose, the ADA forbids discrimination against disabled individuals in major areas of public life, among them employment (Title I of the Act), public services (Title II), and public accommodations (Title III). At issue now, as a threshold matter, is the applicability of Title III to petitioner's golf tours and qualifying rounds, in particular to petitioner's treatment of a qualified disabled golfer wishing to compete in those events.

Title III of the ADA prescribes, as a "general rule":

> "No individual shall be discriminated against on the basis of disability in the full and equal enjoyment of the goods, services, facilities, privileges, advantages, or accommodations of any place of public accommodation by any person who owns, leases (or leases to), or operates a place of public accommodation." 42 U.S.C. § 12182(a).

The phrase "public accommodation" is defined in terms of 12 extensive categories, which the legislative history indicates "should be construed liberally" to afford people with disabilities "equal access" to the wide variety of establishments available to the nondisabled.

It seems apparent, from both the general rule and the comprehensive definition of "public accommodation," that petitioner's golf tours and their qualifying rounds fit comfortably within the coverage of Title III, and Martin within its protection. The events occur on "golf courses," a type of place specifically identified by the Act as a public accommodation. § 12181(7)(L). In addition, at all relevant times, petitioner "leases" and "operates" golf courses to conduct its Q-School and tours. § 12182(a). As a lessor and operator of golf courses, then, petitioner must not discriminate against any "individual" in the "full and equal enjoyment of the goods, services, facilities, privileges, advantages, or accommodations" of those courses. Certainly, among the "privileges" offered by petitioner on the courses are those of competing in the Q-School and playing in the tours; indeed, the former is a privilege for which thousands of individuals from the general public pay, and the latter is one for which they vie. Martin, of course, is one of those individuals. It would therefore appear that Title III of the ADA, by its plain terms, prohibits petitioner from denying Martin equal access to its tours on the basis of his disability.

Petitioner argues otherwise. To be clear about its position, it does not assert (as it did in the District Court) that it is a private club altogether exempt from Title III's coverage. In fact, petitioner admits that its tournaments are conducted at places of public accommodation. Nor does petitioner contend (as it did in both the District Court and the Court of Appeals) that the competitors' area "behind the ropes" is not a public accommodation, notwithstanding the status of the rest of the golf course. Rather, petitioner reframes the coverage issue by arguing that the competing golfers are not members of the class protected by Title III of the ADA.

According to petitioner, Title III is concerned with discrimination against "clients and customers" seeking to obtain "goods and services" at places of public accommodation, whereas it is Title I that protects persons who work at such places. As the argument goes, petitioner operates not a "golf course" during its tournaments but a "place of exhibition or entertainment," 42 U.S.C. § 12181(7)(C), and a professional golfer such as Martin, like an actor in a theater production, is a provider rather than a consumer of the entertainment that petitioner sells to the public. Martin therefore cannot bring a claim under Title III because he is not one of the "*clients or customers* of the covered public accommodation." Rather, Martin's claim of discrimination is "job-related" and could only be brought under Title I — but that Title does not apply because he is an independent contractor (as the District Court found) rather than an employee.

The reference to "clients or customers" that petitioner quotes appears in 42 U.S.C. § 12182(b)(1)(A)(iv), which states: "For purposes of clauses (i) through (iii) of this subparagraph, the term 'individual or class of individuals' refers to the clients or customers of the covered public accommodation that enters into the contractual, licensing or other arrangement." Clauses (i) through (iii) of the subparagraph prohibit public accommodations from discriminating against a disabled "individual or class of individuals" in certain ways either directly or indirectly through contractual arrangements with other entities. Those clauses make clear on the one hand that their prohibitions cannot be avoided by means of contract, while clause (iv) makes clear on the other hand that contractual relationships will not expand a public accommodation's obligations under the subparagraph beyond its own clients or customers.

As petitioner recognizes, clause (iv) is not literally applicable to Title III's general rule prohibiting discrimination against disabled individuals. Title III's broad general rule contains no express "clients or customers" limitation, § 12182(a), and § 12182(b)(1)(A)(iv) provides that its limitation is only "for purposes of" the clauses in that separate subparagraph. Nevertheless, petitioner contends that clause (iv)'s restriction of the subparagraph's coverage to the clients or customers of public accommodations fairly describes the scope of Title III's protection as a whole.

We need not decide whether petitioner's construction of the statute is correct, because petitioner's argument falters even on its own terms. If Title III's protected class were limited to "clients or customers," it would be entirely appropriate to classify the golfers who pay petitioner $3,000 for the chance to compete in the Q-School and, if successful, in the subsequent tour events, as petitioner's clients or customers. In our view, petitioner's tournaments (whether situated at a "golf course" or at a "place of exhibition or entertainment") simultaneously offer at least two "privileges" to the public — that of watching the golf competition and that of competing in it. Although the latter is more difficult and more expensive to obtain than the former, it is nonetheless a privilege that petitioner makes available to members of the general public. In consideration of the entry fee, any golfer with the requisite letters of recommendation acquires the opportunity to qualify for and compete in petitioner's tours. Additionally, any golfer who succeeds in the open qualifying rounds for a tournament may play in the event. That petitioner identifies one set of clients or customers that it serves (spectators at tournaments) does not preclude it from having another set (players in tournaments) against whom it may not discriminate. It would be inconsistent with the literal text of the statute as well as its expansive purpose to read Title III's coverage, even given petitioner's suggested limitation, any less broadly.

Our conclusion is consistent with case law in the analogous context of Title II of the Civil Rights Act of 1964, 78 Stat. 243, 42 U.S.C. § 2000a *et seq*. Title II of that Act prohibits public accommodations from discriminating on the basis of race, color, religion, or national origin. § 2000a(a). In *Daniel v. Paul*, 395 U.S. 298, 306 (1969), applying Title II to the Lake Nixon Club in Little Rock, Arkansas, we held that the definition of a "place of exhibition or entertainment," as a public accommodation, covered participants "in some sport or activity" as well as "spectators or listeners." We find equally persuasive two lower court opinions applying Title II specifically to golfers and golf tournaments. In *Evans v. Laurel Links, Inc.*, 261 F. Supp. 474, 477 (E.D. Va. 1966), a class action brought to require a commercial golf establishment to permit black golfers to play on its course, the District Court held that Title II "is not limited to spectators if the place of exhibition or entertainment provides facilities for the public to participate in the entertainment." And in *Wesley v. Savannah*, 294 F. Supp. 698 (S.D. Ga. 1969), the District Court found that a private association violated Title II when it limited entry in a golf tournament on a municipal course to its own members but permitted all (and only) white golfers who paid the membership and entry fees to compete. These cases support our conclusion that, as a public accommodation during its tours and qualifying rounds, petitioner may not discriminate against either spectators or competitors on the basis of disability.

V

As we have noted, 42 U.S.C. § 12182(a) sets forth Title III's general rule prohibiting public accommodations from discriminating against individuals because of their disabilities. The question whether petitioner has violated that rule depends on a proper construction of the term "discrimination," which is defined by Title III to include:

> "a failure to make reasonable modifications in policies, practices, or procedures, when such modifications are necessary to afford such goods, services, facilities, privileges, advantages, or accommodations to individuals with disabilities, *unless the entity can demonstrate that making such modifications would fundamentally alter the nature* of such goods, services, facilities, privileges, advantages, or accommodations." § 12182(b)(2)(A)(ii) (emphasis added).

Petitioner does not contest that a golf cart is a reasonable modification that is necessary if Martin is to play in its tournaments. Martin's claim thus differs from one that might be asserted by players with less serious afflictions that make walking the course uncomfortable or difficult, but not beyond their capacity. In such cases, an accommodation might be reasonable but not necessary. In this case, however, the narrow dispute is whether allowing Martin to use a golf cart, despite the walking requirement that applies to the PGA TOUR, the NIKE TOUR, and the third stage of the Q-School, is a modification that would "fundamentally alter the nature" of those events.

In theory, a modification of petitioner's golf tournaments might constitute a fundamental alteration in two different ways. It might alter such an essential aspect of the game of golf that it would be unacceptable even if it affected all competitors equally; changing the diameter of the hole from three to six inches might be such a modification. Alternatively, a less significant change that has only a peripheral impact on the game itself might nevertheless give a disabled player, in addition to access to the competition as required by Title III, an advantage over others and, for that reason, fundamentally alter the character of the competition. We are not persuaded that a waiver of the walking rule for Martin would work a fundamental alteration in either sense.

As an initial matter, we observe that the use of carts is not itself inconsistent with the fundamental character of the game of golf. From early on, the essence of the game has been shot-making — using clubs to cause a ball to progress from the teeing ground to a hole some distance away with as few strokes as possible. That essential aspect of the game is still reflected in the very first of the Rules of Golf, which declares: "The Game of Golf consists in playing a ball from the *teeing ground* into the hole by a *stroke* or successive strokes in accordance with the rules." Rule 1-1, Rules of Golf, App. 104 (italics in original). Over the years, there have been many changes in the players' equipment, in golf course design, in the Rules of Golf, and in the method of transporting clubs from hole to hole. Originally, so few clubs were used that each player could carry them without a bag. Then came golf bags, caddies, carts that were pulled by hand, and eventually motorized carts that carried players as well as clubs. "Golf carts started appearing with increasing regularity on American golf courses in the 1950's. Today they are everywhere. And they are encouraged. For one thing, they often speed up play, and for another, they are great revenue producers." There is nothing in the Rules of Golf that either forbids the use of carts, or penalizes a player for using a cart. That set of rules, as we have observed, is widely accepted in both the amateur and professional golf world as the rules of the game. The walking rule that is contained in petitioner's hard cards, based on an optional condition buried in an appendix to the Rules of Golf, is not an essential attribute of the game itself.

Indeed, the walking rule is not an indispensable feature of tournament golf either. As already mentioned, petitioner permits golf carts to be used in the SENIOR PGA TOUR, the open qualifying events for petitioner's tournaments, the first two stages of the Q-School, and, until 1997, the third stage of the Q-School as well. Moreover, petitioner allows the use of carts during certain tournament rounds in both the PGA TOUR and the NIKE TOUR. In addition, although the USGA enforces a walking rule in most of the tournaments that it sponsors, it permits carts in the Senior Amateur and the Senior Women's Amateur championships.

Petitioner, however, distinguishes the game of golf as it is generally played from the game that it sponsors in the PGA TOUR, NIKE TOUR, and (at least recently) the last stage of the Q-School — golf at the "highest level." According to petitioner, "the goal of the highest-level competitive athletics is to assess and compare the performance of different competitors, a task that is meaningful only if the competitors are subject to identical substantive rules." The waiver of any possibly "outcome-affecting" rule for a contestant would violate this principle and therefore, in petitioner's view, fundamentally alter the nature of the highest level athletic event. The walking rule is one such rule, petitioner submits, because its purpose is "to inject the element of fatigue into the skill of shot-making," and thus its effect may be the critical loss of a stroke. As a consequence, the reasonable modification Martin seeks would fundamentally alter the nature of petitioner's highest level tournaments even if he were the only person in the world who has both the talent to compete in those elite events and a disability sufficiently serious that he cannot do so without using a cart.

The force of petitioner's argument is, first of all, mitigated by the fact that golf is a game in which it is impossible to guarantee that all competitors will play under exactly the same conditions or that an individual's ability will be the sole determinant of the outcome. For example, changes in the weather may produce harder greens and more head winds for the tournament leader than for his closest pursuers. A lucky bounce may save a shot or two. Whether such happenstance events are more or less probable than the likelihood that a golfer afflicted with Klippel-Trenaunay-Weber Syndrome would one day qualify for the NIKE TOUR and PGA TOUR, they at least demonstrate that pure chance may have a greater impact on the outcome of elite golf tournaments than the fatigue resulting from the enforcement of the walking rule.

Further, the factual basis of petitioner's argument is undermined by the District Court's finding that the fatigue from walking during one of petitioner's 4-day tournaments cannot be deemed significant. The District Court credited the testimony of a professor in physiology and expert on fatigue, who calculated the calories expended in walking a golf course (about five miles) to be approximately 500 calories — "nutritionally . . . less than a Big Mac." What is more, that energy is expended over a 5-hour period, during which golfers have numerous intervals for rest and refreshment. In fact, the expert concluded, because golf is a low intensity activity, fatigue from the game is primarily a psychological phenomenon in which stress and motivation are the key ingredients. And even under conditions of severe heat and humidity, the critical factor in fatigue is fluid loss rather than exercise from walking.

. . . .

Even if we accept the factual predicate for petitioner's argument — that the walking rule is "outcome affecting" because fatigue may adversely affect performance — its legal position is fatally flawed. Petitioner's refusal to consider Martin's personal circumstances in deciding whether to accommodate his disability runs counter to the clear language and purpose of the ADA. As previously stated, the ADA was enacted to eliminate discrimination against "individuals" with disabilities, and to that end Title III of the Act requires without exception that any "policies, practices, or procedures" of a public accommodation be reasonably modified for disabled "individuals" as necessary to afford access unless doing so would fundamentally alter what is offered. To comply with this command, an individualized inquiry must be made to determine whether a specific modification for a particular person's disability would be reasonable under the circumstances as well as necessary for that person, and yet at the same time not work a fundamental alteration.

To be sure, the waiver of an essential rule of competition for anyone would fundamentally alter the nature of petitioner's tournaments. As we have demonstrated, however, the walking rule is at best peripheral to the nature of petitioner's athletic events, and thus it might be waived in individual cases without working a fundamental alteration. Therefore, petitioner's claim that all the substantive rules for its "highest-level" competitions are sacrosanct and cannot be modified under any circumstances is effectively a contention that it is exempt from Title III's reasonable modification requirement. But that provision carves out no exemption for elite athletics, and given Title III's coverage not only of places of "exhibition or entertainment" but also of "golf courses," 42 U.S.C. §§ 12181(7)(C), (L), its application to petitioner's tournaments cannot be said to be unintended or unexpected. . . .

Under the ADA's basic requirement that the need of a disabled person be evaluated on an individual basis, we have no doubt that allowing Martin to use a golf cart would not fundamentally alter the nature of petitioner's tournaments. As we have discussed, the purpose of the walking rule is to subject players to fatigue, which in turn may influence the outcome of tournaments. Even if the rule does serve that purpose, it is an uncontested finding of the District Court that Martin "easily endures greater fatigue even with a cart than his able-bodied competitors do by walking." The purpose of the walking rule is therefore not compromised in the slightest by allowing Martin to use a cart. A modification that provides an exception to a peripheral tournament rule without impairing its purpose cannot be said to "fundamentally alter" the tournament. What it can be said to do, on the other hand, is to allow Martin the chance to qualify for and compete in the athletic events petitioner offers to those members of the public who have the skill and desire to enter. That is exactly what the ADA requires. As a result, Martin's request for a waiver of the walking rule should have been granted.

The ADA admittedly imposes some administrative burdens on the operators of places of public accommodation that could be avoided by strictly adhering to general rules and policies that are entirely fair with respect to the able-bodied but that may indiscriminately preclude access by qualified persons with disabilities. But surely, in a case of this kind, Congress intended that an entity like the PGA not only give individualized attention to the handful of requests that it might receive from talented but disabled athletes for a modification or waiver of a rule to allow them access to the competition, but also carefully weigh the purpose, as well as the letter, of the rule before determining that no accommodation would be tolerable.

The judgment of the Court of Appeals is affirmed.

WYNNE v. TUFTS UNIVERSITY SCHOOL OF MEDICINE

976 F.2d 791 (1st Cir. 1992)

SELYA, *CIRCUIT JUDGE.*

This appeal requires us to revisit a longstanding dispute between Tufts University School of Medicine and Steven Wynne, a former student. On a previous occasion, we vacated the district court's entry of summary judgment in Tufts' favor. After further proceedings, the district court again entered summary judgment for the defendant. This time around, on an augmented record, we affirm.

Background

. . . .

Wynne matriculated at Tufts in 1983. He failed eight of fifteen first-year courses. Although academic guidelines provided for dismissal after five course failures, the dean granted Wynne a special dispensation and allowed him to repeat the first year of medical school. Over the summer of 1984, Wynne underwent neuropsychological testing at Tufts' instance and expense. The results . . . showed cognitive deficits and weaknesses in processing discrete units of information. However, no differential diagnosis of dyslexia or any other particularized learning disability was made at this time.

During Wynne's second tour of the first-year curriculum, Tufts arranged to supply him with tutors, counsellors, note-takers, and other aids. This time, he passed all but two courses: pharmacology and biochemistry. Tufts still did not expel Wynne. Instead, it permitted him to take make-up examinations in these two subjects. He passed pharmacology but failed biochemistry. That ended the matter. Wynne was dismissed in September, 1985.

Prior Proceedings

In his court case, Wynne alleged that he was learning-disabled and that Tufts had discriminated against him on the basis of his handicap. In short order, Wynne refined his claim to allege that his disability placed him at an unfair disadvantage in taking written multiple-choice examinations and that Tufts, for no good reason, had stubbornly refused to test his proficiency in biochemistry by some other means. Eventually, the district court granted summary judgment in Tufts' favor on the ground that Wynne, because of his inability to pass biochemistry, was not an "otherwise qualified" handicapped person within the meaning of section 504 of the

Rehabilitation Act of 1973, 29 U.S.C. § 794 (1988), as explicated by the relevant caselaw.

On appeal, a panel of this court reversed. That opinion was withdrawn, however, and the full court reheard Wynne's appeal. We concluded that, in determining whether an aspiring medical student meets section 504's "otherwise qualified" prong, it is necessary to take into account the extent to which reasonable accommodations that will satisfy the legitimate interests of both the school and the student are (or are not) available and, if such accommodations exist, the extent to which the institution explored those alternatives. Recognizing the unique considerations that come into play when the parties to a Rehabilitation Act case are a student and an academic institution, particularly a medical school training apprentice physicians, we formulated a test for determining whether the academic institution adequately explored the availability of reasonable accommodations:

> If the institution submits undisputed facts demonstrating that the relevant officials within the institution considered alternative means, their feasibility, cost and effect on the academic program, and came to a rationally justifiable conclusion that the available alternatives would result either in lowering academic standards or requiring substantial program alteration, the court could rule as a matter of law that the institution had met its duty of seeking reasonable accommodation. In most cases, we believe that, as in the qualified immunity context, the issue of whether the facts alleged by a university support its claim that it has met its duty of reasonable accommodation will be a purely legal one. Only if essential facts were genuinely disputed or if there were significantly probative evidence of bad faith or pretext would further fact finding be necessary.

Because the summary judgment record did not satisfactorily address this issue, we vacated the judgment and remanded for further proceedings, leaving the district court "free to consider other submissions [and] to enter summary judgment thereon if [an expanded record] meets the standard we have set forth."

Following remand, Tufts filed a renewed motion for summary judgment accompanied by six new affidavits. The plaintiff filed a comprehensive opposition supported, *inter alia*, by his own supplemental affidavit. The court below read the briefs, heard oral argument, reviewed the parties' updated submissions, and determined that Tufts had met its burden . . . . In the lower court's view, the expanded record clearly showed that Tufts had evaluated the available alternatives to its current testing format and had reasonably concluded that it was not practicable in this instance to depart from the standard multiple-choice format. Accordingly, the court again entered summary judgment in Tufts' favor. This appeal ensued.

Issues

The principal issue on appeal is whether, given those facts not genuinely in dispute, Tufts can be said, as a matter of law, either to have provided reasonable accommodations for plaintiff's handicapping condition or to have demonstrated that it reached a rationally justifiable conclusion that accommodating plaintiff would lower academic standards or otherwise unduly affect its program. There is also a secondary issue: whether plaintiff has advanced significantly probative evidence sufficient to ground a finding that Tufts' reasons for not making further accommodations were pretextual or asserted in bad faith.

Discussion

We have carefully reviewed the amplitudinous record and are fully satisfied that the district court did not err in granting summary judgment. Fairly read, the record presents no genuine issue as to any material fact. Because this case has consumed so many hours of judicial time, we resist the temptation to wax longiloquent. Instead, we add only a few decurtate observations embellishing what the en banc court previously wrote and remarking the significance of the new materials adduced below.

First: Following remand, Tufts satisfactorily filled the gaps that wrecked its initial effort at summary judgment. The expanded record contains undisputed facts demonstrating, in considerable detail, that Tufts' hierarchy "considered alternative means" and "came to a rationally justifiable conclusion" regarding the adverse effects of such putative accommodations. Tufts not only documented the importance of biochemistry in a medical school curriculum, but explained why, in the departmental chair's words, "the multiple choice format provides the fairest way to test the students' mastery of the subject matter of biochemistry." Tufts likewise explained what thought it had given to different methods of testing proficiency in biochemistry and why it eschewed alternatives to multiple-choice testing, particularly with respect to make-up examinations. In so doing, Tufts elaborated upon the unique qualities of multiple-choice examinations as they apply to biochemistry and offered an exposition of the historical record to show the background against which such tests were administered to Wynne. In short, Tufts demythologized the institutional thought processes leading to its determination that it could not deviate from its wonted format to accommodate Wynne's professed disability. It concluded that to do so would require substantial program alterations, result in lowering academic standards, and devalue Tufts' end product — highly trained physicians carrying the prized credential of a Tufts degree.

To be sure, Tufts' explanations, though plausible, are not necessarily ironclad. For instance, Wynne has offered evidence that at least one other medical school and a national testing service occasionally allow oral renderings of multiple-choice examinations in respect to dyslexic students. But, the point is not whether a medical school is "right" or "wrong" in making program-related decisions. Such absolutes rarely apply in the context of subjective decisionmaking, particularly in a scholastic setting. The point is that Tufts, after undertaking a diligent assessment of the available options, felt itself obliged to make "a professional, academic judgment that [a] reasonable accommodation [was] simply not available." [citation omitted]. Phrased another way, Tufts decided, rationally if not inevitably, that no further accommodation could be made without imposing an undue (and injurious) hardship on the academic program. With the diligence of its assessment and the justification for its judgment clearly shown in the augmented record, and with the fact of the judgment uncontroverted, the deficiency that spoiled Tufts' original effort at *brevis* disposition has been cured.

Second: The undisputed facts show that Tufts neither ignored Wynne nor turned a deaf ear to his plight. To the contrary, the defendant (a) warned Wynne in 1983 that he was failing biochemistry and suggested he defer his examination (a suggestion that Wynne scotched); (b) arranged for a complete battery of neuropsychological tests after Wynne failed eight courses in his freshman year; (c) waived the rules and permitted Wynne to repeat the first-year curriculum; (d) furnished Wynne access to tutoring, taped lectures, and the like; (e) allowed him to take untimed examinations; and (f) gave him make-up examinations in pharmacology and biochemistry after he again failed both courses. Given the other circumstances extant in this case, we do not think that a reasonable factfinder could conclude that Tufts, having volunteered such an array of remedial measures, was guilty of failing to make a reasonable accommodation merely because it did not *also* offer Wynne, unsolicited, an oral rendering of the biochemistry examination.

Third: Reasonableness is not a constant. To the contrary, what is reasonable in a particular situation may not be reasonable in a different situation — even if the situational differences are relatively slight. Ultimately, what is reasonable depends on a variable mix of factors.

In the section 504 milieu, an academic institution can be expected to respond only to what it knows (or is chargeable with knowing). This means, as the Third Circuit has recently observed, that for a medical school "to be liable under the Rehabilitation Act, [it] must know or be reasonably expected to know of [a student's] handicap." [citation omitted]. A relevant aspect of this inquiry is whether the student ever put the medical school on notice of his handicap by making "a sufficiently direct and specific request for special accommodations." [citation omitted]. Thus, we must view the reasonableness of Tufts' accommodations against the backdrop of what Tufts knew about Wynne's needs while he was enrolled there.

Several factors are entitled to weight in this equation, including the following: (a) Wynne was never diagnosed as dyslexic while enrolled at Tufts; (b) the school gave him a number of special dispensations and "second chances" — including virtually every accommodation that he seasonably suggested; (c) Wynne had taken, and passed, multiple-choice examinations in several courses; and (d) he never requested, at any time prior to taking and failing the third biochemistry exam, that an oral rendering be substituted for the standard version of the multiple-choice test. Under these circumstances, we do not believe a rational factfinder could conclude that Tufts' efforts at accommodation fell short of the reasonableness standard.

Fourth: Wynne's allegations of pretext do not raise prohibitory doubts about the reasonableness of Tufts' attempted accommodations or about the honesty of its assessment of alternatives to multiple-choice examinations vis-a-vis the school's educational plan. When pretext is at issue in a discrimination case, it is a plaintiff's duty to produce specific facts which, reasonably viewed, tend logically to undercut the defendant's position. The plaintiff may neither "rest[] merely upon conclusory allegations, improbable inferences, and unsupported speculation," nor measurably bolster his cause by hurling rancorous epithets and espousing tenuous insinuations. [citations omitted].

Here, Wynne's charges comprise more cry than wool. They consist of unsubstantiated conclusions, backed only by a few uncoordinated evidentiary fragments. More is required to forestall summary judgment.

Conclusion

We need go no further. In our earlier opinion, we recognized the existence of a statutory obligation on the part of an academic institution such as Tufts to consider available ways of accommodating a handicapped student and, when seeking summary judgment, to produce a factual record documenting its scrupulous attention to this obligation. Of course, the effort requires more than lip service; it must be sincerely conceived and conscientiously implemented. We think that Tufts, the second time around, has cleared the hurdle that we envisioned: the undisputed facts contained in the expanded record, when considered in the deferential light that academic decisionmaking deserves, meet the required standard.

We add a final note of caution. Although both parties to this litigation invite us to paint with a broad brush, we decline their joint invitation. The issue before us is not whether a medical student, authoritatively diagnosed as a dyslexic and known to the school to be so afflicted, is ever entitled, upon timely request, to an opportunity to take an examination orally. Rather, we are limited to the idiosyncratic facts of Wynne's case. The resulting record presents a narrower, easier issue — and we believe that the district court resolved that issue correctly.

Affirmed.

NOTES

1. What would the outcome have been in *Southeastern Community College v. Davis*, if the applicant had been seeking admission into a standard liberal arts program, rather than a professional program? What if she had applied to law school instead of nursing school?

2. While there is a great deal of overlap between Section 504 and the ADA, there is also one important difference as regards eligibility protection. A major question in *Davis* was whether the student's disability was the major cause of the alleged discrimination, an important feature of the Rehabilitation Act, 29 U.S.C. § 794. The remedies available under the ADA, however, also feature the question of whether the unlawful discrimination "was a motivating cause." As a result, "the causation standards applicable in Title VII actions, and not the 'solely because of' disability standard applicable under the Rehabilitation Act, are applicable to violations of the ADA." *Baird v. Rose*, 192 F.3d 462 (4th Cir. 1999). In other words, if a plaintiff claiming discrimination under the ADA shows that "his or her disability played a **motivating** role in the adverse decision, the plaintiff is entitled to relief." *Id.*

3. In his dissent in *PGA Tour, Inc. v. Martin*, Justice Scalia, joined by Justice Thomas, wrote:

> [I]t should not be assumed that today's decent, tolerant, and progressive judgment will, in the long run, accrue to the benefit of sports competitors

> with disabilities. Now that it is clear courts will review the rules of sports for "fundamentalness," organizations that value their autonomy have every incentive to defend vigorously the necessity of every regulation. They may still be second-guessed in the end as to the Platonic requirements of the sport, but they will *assuredly* lose if they have at all wavered in their enforcement. The lesson the PGA TOUR and other sports organizations should take from this case is to make sure that the same written rules are set forth for all levels of play, and never voluntarily to grant any modifications. The second lesson is to end open tryouts. I doubt that, in the long run, even disabled athletes will be well served by these incentives that the Court has created.
>
> Complaints about this case are not "properly directed to Congress." They are properly directed to this Court's Kafkaesque determination that professional sports organizations, and the fields they rent for their exhibitions, are "places of public accommodation" to the competing athletes, and the athletes themselves "customers" of the organization that pays them; its Alice in Wonderland determination that there are such things as judicially determinable "essential" and "nonessential" rules of a made-up game; and its Animal Farm determination that fairness and the ADA mean that everyone gets to play by individualized rules which will assure that no one's lack of ability (or at least no one's lack of ability so pronounced that it amounts to a disability) will be a handicap. The year was 2001, and "everybody was finally equal." K. Vonnegut, *Harrison Bergeron, in* ANIMAL FARM AND RELATED READINGS 129 (1997).

PGA Tour, Inc. v. Martin, 532 U.S. 661, 704–05 (2001) (Scalia, J., dissenting). Should the Supreme Court be the final arbiter of the rules of a professional sports tournament? Is the field of play in that type of tournament the kind of "public accommodation" Congress had in mind when it passed the ADA?

How would the analysis have differed if it had been a collegiate golf tournament? Would it have mattered if it was a tournament between public colleges or private colleges? Whether it occurred on a public or private golf course? What would Justice Scalia have to say about it?

4. As the *Wynne* case demonstrates, courts provide much more deference to schools that can affirmatively document procedural fairness in cases involving disabled or allegedly disabled students. It's a theme that surfaces repeatedly in the litigation in this area. In *Wong v. Regents of the University of California*, the Ninth Circuit refused to defer to a medical school that failed to offer sufficient evidence of inquiry into the condition of a disabled student and the accommodations he was seeking. The court noted:

> The deference to which academic institutions are entitled when it comes to the ADA is a double-edged sword. It allows them a significant amount of leeway in making decisions about their curricular requirements and their ability to structure their programs to accommodate disabled students. On the other hand, it places on an institution the weighty responsibility of carefully considering each disabled student's particular limitations and analyzing whether and how it might accommodate that student in a way

> that would allow the student to complete the school's program without lowering academic standards or otherwise unduly burdening the institution.

192 F.3d 807, 826 (9th Cir. 1999). *See also Guckenberger v. Boston Univ.*, 974 F. Supp. 106 (D. Mass. 1997); *Gill v. Franklin Pierce L. Center*, 899 F. Supp. 850 (D. N.H. 1995).

5. At the same time, to enjoy all of the protections of the law, disabled students have the burden of providing colleges and universities with sufficient evidence of a disability:

> To receive the full benefits of section 504, learning disabled students should provide the documentation as early as possible in their academic careers. The documentation should also be as complete as possible, including physicians' reports, past history of the disability, if available, and possible accommodations that would benefit the handicapped student. Although the law is not clear on how much documentation is sufficient to trigger section 504 coverage, the more information that the student provides about the disability, the more likely the school will be subject to section 504. Moreover, a court will more likely examine reasonable accommodations in deciding whether the school violated section 504 if documentation is provided.

Brigid Hurley, Note, *Accommodating Learning Disabled Students in Higher Education: Schools Legal Obligations Under Section 504 of the Rehabilitation Act*, 32 B.C. L. Rev. 1051, 1102 (1991).*

6. As indicated, the ADA applies to public and private educational institutions. 28 C.F.R. § 36.102. The ADA's breadth and detail to ensure equality and meaningful access to disabled students demand close attention. Universities must make certain that their physical facilities, policies and procedures, and assistive services meet the ADA requirements and allow disabled students to fully participate in scholastic activities. Additionally, the ADA is not dormant; Congress amends and updates the ADA to keep pace with evolving standards and technologies. The most recent changes went into effect on March 15, 2011. *Americans with Disabilities Act Title III Regulations: Nondiscrimination on the Basis of Disability by Public Accommodations and in Commercial Facilities*, Dept. of Just. (Sept. 15, 2010) http://www.ada.gov/regs2010/titleIII_2010/titleIII_2010_regulations.pdf. Many of these amendments were directed specifically at postsecondary institutions and some of the more interesting changes are described below.

- Congress added "Housing at a place of education" to the ADA's definition section to expressly include:

  > [H]ousing operated by or on behalf of an elementary, secondary, undergraduate, or postgraduate school, or other place of education, including dormitories, suites, apartments, or other places of

residence.

28 C.F.R. § 36.104 (2010). Can you recall improvements or alterations in any of your school-sponsored housing to make them more accessible to the disabled (e.g., ramps, disabled shower and bathroom stalls, and elevators)? What about improvements to classrooms or other facilities at your school?

- Disabled students are entitled to auxiliary aids and services to ensure that:

> "[N]o individual with a disability is excluded, denied services, segregated or otherwise treated differently than other individuals because of the absence of auxiliary aids and services, unless the public accommodation can demonstrate that taking those steps would fundamentally alter the nature of the goods, services, facilities, privileges, advantages, or accommodations being offered or would result in an undue burden, *i.e.*, significant difficulty or expense."

28 C.F.R. § 36.303. One common way for schools to assist students with disabilities is by providing them with interpreters or notetakers. You may have been asked or offered a position to take notes for disabled students at your own school. Congress amended the ADA to keep pace with evolving technology. Now, disabled students can receive interpretation in real time or through video remote interpreting (video conference technology). *Id.* Disabled students may also now receive services through text messaging, video phones, or other "effective" methods of communication. *Id.*

- The ADA also makes sure that students are not discriminated against in examinations. An examination must be given in such a way as to:

> [E]nsure that, when the examination is administered to an individual with a disability that impairs sensory, manual, or speaking skills, the examination results accurately reflect the individual's aptitude or achievement level or whatever other factor the examination purports to measure, rather than reflecting the individual's impaired sensory, manual, or speaking skills (except where those skills are the factors that the examination purports to measure).

28 C.F.R. § 36.309. Congress added, in 2010, that any request for documentation must be reasonable and "limited to the need for the modification . . . or service requested." *Id.* Congress also instructed schools and entities to consider previous modifications and services provided to the student in similar testing situations, or consider modifications or services provided to the student within his or her individualized education program (IEP) under the Individuals with Disabilities Education Act. *Id.* Do you think these changes are made in the same spirit as Congress's amendments to

broaden the definition and scope of disability?

- Finally, you probably know that public accommodations shall modify their policies in order to accommodate service animals. Traditionally, people tend to think of dogs as service animals, but Congress amended the ADA to expressly include miniature horses "if the miniature horse has been individually trained to do the work or perform tasks for the benefit of the individual with a disability." 28 C.F.R. § 36.302(c)(9). This is not an absolute right however: public accommodations can show that a modification is overly burdensome. Accordingly, public accommodations must perform an assessment considering the size of the horse, whether the handler has sufficient control over the horse, whether the horse's presence compromises safety requirements, and whether or not the horse is housebroken. *Id.*

F. RETALIATION PROTECTION UNDER THE ADA

The following statutory and regulatory provisions serve to protect discrimination victims, who file a claim under the ADA, from retaliation. As can be seen from the following case law and notes, courts have struggled between applying the plain language of the statute and adhering to the policy reasons behind the enactment of the ADA.

Statute:

42 U.S.C. § 12203 — Prohibition against retaliation and coercion

(a) Retaliation — No person shall discriminate against any individual because such individual has opposed any act or practice made unlawful by this chapter or because such individual made a charge, testified, assisted, or participated in any manner in an investigation, proceeding, or hearing under this chapter.

(b) Interference, coercion, or intimidation — It shall be unlawful to coerce, intimidate, threaten, or interfere with any individual in the exercise or enjoyment of, or on account of his or her having exercised or enjoyed, or on account of his or her having aided or encouraged any other individual in the exercise or enjoyment of, any right granted or protected by this chapter.

(c) Remedies and procedures — The remedies and procedures available under sections 12117, 12133, and 12188 of this title shall be available to aggrieved persons for violations of subsections (a) and (b) of this section, with respect to subchapter I, subchapter II and subchapter III of this chapter, respectively.

Regulations:

28 C.F.R. § 35.134 [Nondiscrimination on the Basis of Disability in State and Local Government Services] — Retaliation or coercion

(a) No private or public entity shall discriminate against any individual because that individual has opposed any act or practice made unlawful by this part, or because that individual made a charge, testified, assisted, or participated in any manner in an investigation, proceeding, or hearing under the Act or this part.

(b) No private or public entity shall coerce, intimidate, threaten, or interfere with any individual in the exercise or enjoyment of, or on account of his or her having exercised or enjoyed, or on account of his or her having aided or encouraged any other individual in the exercise or enjoyment of, any right granted or protected by the Act or this part.

28 C.F.R. § 36.206 [Nondiscrimination on the Basis of Disability by Public Accommodations and in Commercial Facilities] — Retaliation or coercion

(a) No private or public entity shall discriminate against any individual because that individual has opposed any act or practice made unlawful by this part, or because that individual made a charge, testified, assisted, or participated in any manner in an investigation, proceeding, or hearing under the Act or this part.

(b) No private or public entity shall coerce, intimidate, threaten, or interfere with any individual in the exercise or enjoyment of, or on account of his or her having exercised or enjoyed, or on account of his or her having aided or encouraged any other individual in the exercise or enjoyment of, any right granted or protected by the Act or this part.

(c) Illustrations of conduct prohibited by this section include, but are not limited to:

(1) Coercing an individual to deny or limit the benefits, services, or advantages to which he or she is entitled under the Act or this part;

(2) Threatening, intimidating, or interfering with an individual with a disability who is seeking to obtain or use the goods, services, facilities, privileges, advantages, or accommodations of a public accommodation;

(3) Intimidating or threatening any person because that person is assisting or encouraging an individual or group entitled to claim the rights granted or protected by the Act or this part to exercise those rights; or

(4) Retaliating against any person because that person has participated in any investigation or action to enforce the Act or this part.

29 C.F.R. § 1630.12 [Regulations to Implement the Equal Employment Provisions of the Americans with Disabilities Act] — Retaliation or coercion

(a) Retaliation — It is unlawful to discriminate against any individual because that individual has opposed any act or practice made unlawful by this part or because that individual made a charge, testified, assisted, or participated in any manner in an investigation, proceeding, or hearing to enforce any provision contained in this part.

(b) Coercion, interference or intimidation — It is unlawful to coerce, intimidate, threaten, harass or interfere with any individual in the exercise or enjoyment of, or because that individual aided or encouraged any other individual in the exercise of, any right granted or protected by this part.

SHAVER v. INDEPENDENT STAVE COMPANY

350 F.3d 716 (8th Cir. 2003)

Before MORRIS SHEPPARD ARNOLD, BOWMAN, and MELLOY, CIRCUIT JUDGES.

This is a harassment and retaliation case brought under the Americans with Disabilities Act (ADA), *see* 42 U.S.C. §§ 12101–12213, and the Missouri Human Rights Act (MHRA), *see* Mo.Rev.Stat. §§ 213.010–213.137, that comes to us on appeal from an order dismissing the plaintiff's claims on summary judgment. We affirm the judgment of the district court in part and reverse it in part.

Christopher Shaver has suffered from nocturnal epilepsy since he was a teenager. After an operation in which part of his brain was removed and replaced by a metal plate, he was able to get a job working at the timber mill of Salem Wood Products Company. After being fired, allegedly for insubordination, Mr. Shaver sued Salem under various theories. By the time that Salem moved for summary judgment, Mr. Shaver had abandoned most of his claims, but he continued to maintain that he had been unlawfully harassed as a result of his epilepsy and his cranial operation, that Salem had violated the anti-retaliation provisions of the ADA and the MHRA, and that Salem was liable to him under Missouri workers' compensation law. The district court ruled against Mr. Shaver on his ADA and MHRA claims and declined to exercise supplemental jurisdiction over the workers' compensation claim.

We review a district court's summary judgment order de novo. *See Darby v. Bratch*, 287 F.3d 673, 678 (8th Cir.2002). We resolve Mr. Shaver's MHRA claims on the same basis as his federal claims. *See id.* at 682.

I.

We have suggested in dicta that it might be possible to bring a claim for a hostile work environment under the ADA, *see, e.g., Jeseritz v. Potter*, 282 F.3d 542, 547 (8th Cir.2002), but we have never ruled directly on the matter. Today, for the reasons that follow, we join the other circuits that have decided the issue by holding that such claims are in fact actionable. *Cf. Flowers v. Southern Reg'l Physician Servs., Inc.*, 247 F.3d 229, 232–35 (5th Cir.2001), *Fox v. General Motors Corp.*, 247 F.3d 169, 175–77 (4th Cir.2001).

Even broad, remedial statutes such as the ADA do not give federal courts a license to create causes of action after the manner of the common law. *See Alexander v. Sandoval*, 532 U.S. 275, 286–87, 121 S.Ct. 1511, 149 L.Ed.2d 517 (2001). Rather, our rulings must be disciplined by the text of the statute itself. The ADA states that "[n]o covered entity shall discriminate against a qualified individual with a disability because of the disability of such individual in regard to terms, conditions, and privileges of employment." 42 U.S.C. § 12112(a). While the statute does not specifically mention hostile work environment, in construing a statute we must look at how its text was understood at the time that it was passed.

The drafters of the ADA borrowed the phrase "terms, conditions, and privileges of employment" directly from Title VII of the Civil Rights Act of 1964. *Compare* 42

U.S.C. § 12112(a) with 42 U.S.C. § 2000e-2(a)(1). As early as 1971, courts had construed the phrase in Title VII to create an action based on a hostile work environment . . . and by the time that the ADA was passed in 1991, this interpretation was clearly established as the controlling federal law on the subject. . . . Thus, when Congress included the phrase "terms, conditions, and privileges of employment" in the ADA, it was using a legal term of art that prohibited a broad range of employment practices, including workplace harassment. [citation omitted]

In determining whether a hostile work environment claim has been made out under the ADA, we think it proper to turn to standards developed elsewhere in our anti-discrimination law, adapting them to the unique requirements of the ADA. To be entitled to relief, it seems to us that Mr. Shaver must show that he is a member of the class of people protected by the statute, that he was subject to unwelcome harassment, that the harassment resulted from his membership in the protected class, and that the harassment was severe enough to affect the terms, conditions, or privileges of his employment. *Cf. Reedy v. Quebecor Printing Eagle, Inc.*, 333 F.3d 906, 907–08 (8th Cir.2003).

The ADA's employment provisions protect people who are "qualified individual [s] with a disability." 42 U.S.C. §§ 12111(8), 12112(a). In this case, neither party disputes that Mr. Shaver was qualified for his job at Salem's lumber mill. Salem does argue, however, that Mr. Shaver is not "disabled" within the meaning of the statute. A disability is an "impairment that substantially limits one or more major life activities." *See* 42 U.S.C. § 12102(2)(A). Furthermore, one can be within the statute if one is regarded (accurately or inaccurately) as having such an impairment or if one has a record of such an impairment in the past. *See* 42 U.S.C. § 12102(2)(B)-(C).

Before his operation, it is undisputed that Mr. Shaver's epilepsy caused severe seizures of the kind and frequency that this court has held impair "major life activities" such as speaking, walking, or seeing. *See Otting v. J.C. Penney Co.*, 223 F.3d 704, 710–11 (8th Cir.2000). He thus has a record of impairment. Our review of the record also persuades us that at least some of his co-workers regarded Mr. Shaver as "stupid" and "not playing with a full deck" because of his epilepsy and resulting operation. And, since thinking is a major life activity, *see Brown v. Lester E. Cox Med. Ctrs.*, 286 F.3d 1040, 1044–45 (8th Cir.2002), we conclude as well that a jury could find that Mr. Shaver qualifies as disabled because he was regarded as disabled.

Our review of the record indicates that there is no real factual dispute about whether Mr. Shaver was harassed. (The severity and legal consequence of that harassment are separate questions that we deal with below.) There is ample evidence, for instance, that he was routinely referred to as "platehead." Salem argues that the harassment was not the result of his disability, claiming that the name "platehead" was linked to the physical fact that Mr. Shaver has a plate in his skull, rather than with any impairment as such. We think that this distinction may be too fine for us, but in any case the meaning of the statements (that is, what inference to draw from the words used) is properly a matter for the jury. There is certainly nothing in the record to suggest that those who called Mr. Shaver "platehead" made the distinction suggested by Salem. The distinction itself, moreover, may well be meaningless: Even if one calls a person "pegleg" because he has a peg leg rather than because he has trouble walking, it is nevertheless the case that the nickname was chosen because the person was disabled.

With the question of the effect of the harassment on the "terms, conditions, and privileges" of Mr. Shaver's employment we come to the heart of this case. In order to be actionable, harassment must be both subjectively hostile or abusive to the victim and "severe and pervasive enough to create an objectively hostile or abusive work environment-an environment that a reasonable person would find hostile or abusive." *Harris v. Forklift Sys., Inc.*, 510 U.S. 17, 21–22, 114 S.Ct. 367, 126 L.Ed.2d 295 (1993). On the other hand, we have repeatedly emphasized that anti-discrimination laws do not create a general civility code. . . . Conduct that is merely rude, abrasive, unkind, or insensitive does not come within the scope of the law.

Taking the evidence in the light most favorable to Mr. Shaver, we have little difficulty concluding that a jury could find that he found the harassment by his co-workers hostile or abusive. The more difficult question is whether the behavior fell within the elusive category of "objectively offensive[.]". . . . Mr. Shaver's co-workers referred to him as "platehead" over a period of about two years. Some of the co-workers were supervisors, and some were not. Some of the co-workers stopped using the name when Mr. Shaver asked them to, and others did not. Use of nicknames is widespread at the mill, and while this fact does not render the name applied to Mr. Shaver inoffensive, it might reduce its offensiveness. Several co-workers suggested that Mr. Shaver was stupid. On one occasion, a co-worker said that Mr. Shaver "pissed in his pants when the microwave was on," but this uglier statement seems to have occurred outside of Mr. Shaver's presence, a fact that lessens but does not undo its offensiveness.

Taken as a whole, we conclude that the verbal harassment here does not rise to the same level as that in cases where we have granted relief. For example, in *Smith v. St. Louis Univ.*, 109 F.3d 1261, 1264–65 (8th Cir.1997), we allowed a suit to continue where the plaintiff had been subject to verbal abuse, but in that case there was evidence that a supervisor had repeatedly singled the plaintiff out and that she had been hospitalized twice as a result of the psychological trauma that she suffered. Showing some tangible psychological condition is not necessary to make out a hostile work environment claim, but it may be taken into account. *Harris*, 510 U.S. at 22–23, 114 S.Ct. 367. While Mr. Shaver was upset about the harassment at work, it was not so severe as to result in any psychological treatment. . . . Nor does this case involve harassing conduct of a physical nature as was found actionable in many of the cases that Mr. Shaver cites. . . .

Mr. Shaver advances two other arguments in an effort to transform the verbal harassment to which he was subjected into an actionable hostile work environment. First, he asserts that the harassment resulted from the unauthorized disclosure of his medical condition by his supervisor. Viewing the evidence in the light most favorable to Mr. Shaver, we conclude that it would support a finding that the supervisor did disclose Mr. Shaver's medical condition without his authorization. Shortly before the name "platehead" came into use, Mr. Shaver was injured on the job and taken to the hospital by his supervisor, who there learned for the first time about Mr. Shaver's epilepsy and the plate in his skull. Before then, no one at the mill seems to have been aware of Mr. Shaver's condition. Immediately thereafter, co-workers learned of the plate from the supervisor and began calling Mr. Shaver "platehead." We are uncertain as to whether this disclosure of Mr. Shaver's medical records was actionable under the ADA. . . . But Mr. Shaver does not in any case raise this as an independent claim for recovery on appeal (he is procedurally barred from doing so), and so we do not consider whether the facts here would support such a claim. Instead Mr. Shaver argues that because the harassment we have described resulted from the disclosure, it somehow makes the harassment more severe.

Even if the disclosure violated 42 U.S.C. § 12112(d), we note that workplace harassment and the unauthorized disclosure of medical records are different wrongs, involving different interests. Workplace harassment is forbidden in order to ensure that the "terms, conditions, and privileges of employment" are not altered for a legally impermissible reason. *See* 42 U.S.C. § 12112(a). Thus, it is a claim that can be raised under the ADA only by a "qualified individual with a disability." . . . . In contrast, the prohibition on disclosing medical information protects a person's privacy, and one need not even be disabled in order to raise that matter. . . . Harassment resulting from such a disclosure would be relevant to the measure of damages on a claim for such disclosure, but because the wrong is the disclosure itself harassment need not even rise to the level of affecting the "terms, conditions, and privileges of employment" before it can furnish the basis for an award of damages.

Mr. Shaver in effect asks us to stand this last principle on its head and hold that harassment that by itself is not actionable can rise to the level of illegality by being the result of an unauthorized disclosure. We decline to do so. Medical privacy is not a "term, condition, or privilege" of Mr. Shaver's employment. In the absence of a statute, there is nothing to forbid an at-will employer from conditioning employment on the ability to disclose otherwise private information. This is precisely the reason that a separate section of the ADA deals with this issue. . . .

. . . .

II.

Mr. Shaver also challenges the district court's dismissal of his retaliation claim. Salem fired Mr. Shaver after he had an argument with his supervisor, Charles Bacon. After he had commenced his suit for harassment, Mr. Shaver contacted several acquaintances for job interviews and gave them Mr. Bacon's name as a job reference. When contacted by Mr. Shaver's acquaintances, Mr. Bacon told them that he could not recommend Mr. Shaver because he had "a get rich quick scheme involving suing companies." None of the acquaintances with whom Mr. Shaver interviewed offered him a job, and he was subsequently able to find employment when he gave the name of a different former supervisor at Salem as a reference. On the basis of these facts, the district court concluded that Mr. Shaver was attempting to manufacture a retaliation claim against Salem by baiting Mr. Bacon into giving negative references because of Mr. Shaver's suit. In reaching this conclusion, the district court also relied on the fact that no one was hired by any of the acquaintances in lieu of Mr. Shaver and that Mr. Shaver intentionally gave the prospective employers the name of the supervisor with whom he had argued.

We are unable to agree with the district court's view that claims that are "manufactured" in the sense that the court used the word are not actionable. The ADA states that "[n]o person shall discriminate against any individual because such individual made a charge under this chapter." 42 U.S.C. § 12203(a). A prima facie case under this provision consists of proof of protected activity by the employee, adverse action taken by the employer against the employee, and a causal connection between the protected activity and the adverse action. *Cossette*, 188 F.3d at 972. The district court seems to have added an additional requirement, namely, that the party asserting the claim did not purposefully seek the adverse action. Nothing in the words of the statute or in our cases, however, suggests that the conduct of the aggrieved party, other than the party's initial protected activity, is relevant. Rather, the law focuses exclusively on the conduct of the alleged retaliator in determining whether the aggrieved plaintiff has a claim.

. . . .

Our view of the matter finds support in the so-called "tester" cases, where minority applicants apply for jobs or housing that they have no intention of accepting for the sole purpose of determining whether the employer or landlord is unlawfully discriminating. . . . In those cases, defendants have objected that there was no real substance to the plaintiffs' claims since those claims were created solely for the purpose of litigation. The courts, however, have advanced two different reasons for allowing such suits to proceed.

First, the mere fact of discrimination offends the dignitary interest that the statutes are designed to protect, regardless of whether the discrimination worked any direct economic harm to the plaintiffs. *See Kyles*, 222 F.3d at 297. In enacting the ADA, Congress found that "discrimination against individuals with disabilities continue[s] to be a serious and pervasive problem," 42 U.S.C. § 12101(a)(2), and that "individuals with disabilities have been subjected to a history of purposeful unequal treatment, and relegated to a position of political powerlessness in our society, based on characteristics that are beyond the control of such individuals," 42 U.S.C. § 12101(a)(7). This language suggests that Congress was trying to protect a dignitary interest with the ADA. Second, tester cases have been allowed to proceed on a "private attorney general" theory. . . . By giving litigants an incentive to attack illegal activity by employers, Congress enlisted private self-interest in the enforcement of public policy.

In any case, there are many reasons why a person might seek a job interview even though he or she has no intention of taking the job. People may be "testing the waters" to find out what kind of reference they would get, practicing their interviewing skills, investigating a new line of work, or they may have any one of a whole host of other benign reasons for "manufacturing" a job application. . . . For these reasons, we disagree with the district court's holding that a "manufactured" claim that meets the statutory requirements cannot proceed. The issue of whether Mr. Shaver actually failed to get a job remains relevant on the question of the extent of his damages, but even if the whole situation was "manufactured," he would still have a claim for nominal damages, and in the proper circumstances, for attorneys' fees, exemplary damages, and injunctive relief.

Having dealt with the district court's legal holding, the question remains whether the evidence here, taken in the light most favorable to Mr. Shaver, presents a triable issue for a jury. We conclude that it does. Contrary to Salem's arguments, negative job references can constitute adverse, retaliatory action as a matter of law. *See Smith*, 109 F.3d at 1266. In his deposition, Mr. Bacon denied that his words constituted a negative recommendation, and also denied that he was retaliating against Mr. Shaver. But it is for a jury to decide whether Mr. Bacon is to be believed, whether his interpretation of events is consistent with the rest of the evidence, and whether his recommendations caused prospective employers to reject Mr. Shaver's applications. Furthermore, the district court's conclusion that Mr. Shaver had no real intention of seeking a job with his acquaintances rests on contestable inferences from circumstantial evidence. The same is true of the district court's suggestion that the acquaintances were somehow involved in this alleged scheme. Both of these issues are relevant to the extent of the damages that Mr. Shaver suffered and on the present record are matters for the jury to decide.

. . . .

IV.

For the reasons set forth above, the district court's judgment is affirmed in part and reversed in part. We remand the case for further proceedings consistent with this opinion.

NOTES

1. Consider a few additional facts that the *Shaver* court omitted in its opinion:

> The following year [after his initial hiring], Shaver injured his right index finger at work. This began a nearly year-long series of absences, work restrictions, temporary total disability payments, and reprimands. On September 23, 2000, Shaver was called home in the middle of his shift to deal with a sick child. He claimed that he had permission to leave from his assistant supervisor; however, when he returned an hour and a half later, his shift supervisor, Charles Bacon, gave him a written warning and a three day suspension for leaving work without permission. Shaver shoved the papers back at Bacon and stormed out. When Bacon reported the incident to Michael Transano, the mill manager, Transano fired Shaver for insubordination.
>
> In January 2001, Shaver filed a discrimination complaint with the EEOC claiming harassment, failure to accommodate his hand injury, and discharge due to disability. In May, he applied for work with two small companies, both of which were owned by acquaintances of his. Shaver gave Charles Bacon's name as a reference but when both prospective employers called, Bacon told them that he couldn't recommend Shaver because Shaver had a "get-rich-quick scheme" of suing the companies for whom he had worked. Shaver was not hired by either company. Shaver subsequently filed additional claims against Independent Stave for retaliation resulting from his earlier complaint with the EEOC and his attempt to file for worker's compensation for his hand injury.

J. Andrew Hirth, *We Were Only Teasing: The Eighth Circuit Misses the Quintessence of Hostile Work Environment Claims Under the ADA*, 70 Mo. L. Rev. 253, 253–55 (2005).* Do these facts change your opinion of the court's outcome — or at least make you hesitate as to its fairness? As an employer, would you have given Shaver a positive recommendation after his several absences and arguably poor attitude? Has the court's decision in *Shaver* left employers between a rock and a hard place: either be held liable for retaliation or lose your reputation in the field as an honest business colleague?

2. At the time *Shaver* was decided, the ability to pursue a "hostile work environment" claim under the ADA was relatively unsettled and unexplored. In fact, the Shaver court was only the third Court of Appeals to directly decide the issue. In doing so, the *Shaver* court sets forth four elements that need to be met in order to succeed on a "hostile work environment" claim under the ADA: (1) that he is a member of a protected class, (2) that he was subjected to unwelcome harassment, (3) that the harassment was due to his membership in that class, and (4) that the harassment was severe enough to affect the terms, conditions, or privileges of his employment.

However, the two courts to grapple with the "hostile work environment" claim under the ADA adopted an additional requirement to the four outlined above. *See Flowers v. S. Reg'l Physician Servs., Inc., 247 F.3d 229 (5th Cir. 2001)*; *Fox v. Gen. Motors Corp.*, 247 F.3d 169 (4th Cir. 2001). Both the Fourth and Fifth Circuits held that a claimant must also prove (or have some factual basis) that the "employer knew or should have known of the harassment and failed to take prompt remedial action." *Flowers*, 247 F.3d at 235–36.

Which Circuit do you think has it right? Is the fifth factor important to protect employers or just another unnecessary hurdle for plaintiffs to jump? Which test seems overall more "fair"? Which approach seems more closely aligned with the goals and policies behind the ADA? For a criticism of the *Shaver* decision and its four-part test, see J. Andrew Hirth, *We Were Only Teasing: The Eighth Circuit Misses the Quintessence of Hostile Work Environment Claims Under the ADA*, 70 Mo. L. Rev. 253, 253–55 (2005).

3. Some courts expanded the ADA's reach to not only encompass hostile work environment claims but also "hostile learning environment" claims. *See, e.g., Guckenberger v. Boston Univ.*, 957 F. Supp. 306 (D. Mass. 1997) ("This Court concludes, further, that the flexible Title VII standards for establishing a hostile work environment claim apply to hostile learning environment claims brought under the federal statutes prohibiting discrimination against persons with disabilities."). *Guckenberger* set forth a series of requirements a plaintiff must meet in order to succeed on a "hostile learning environment" claim under the ADA:

> To state a cognizable claim for hostile learning environment harassment under the ADA and Rehabilitation Act, a plaintiff must allege: (1) that she is a member of a protected group, (2) that she has been subject to unwelcome harassment, (3) that the harassment is based on a protected characteristic, her disability, (4) that the harassment is sufficiently severe

> or pervasive that it alters the conditions of her education and creates an abusive educational environment, and (5) that there is a basis for institutional liability.

Id. at 316. Do you find this test to be narrower or more expansive than the "hostile work environment" tests described above? Does it closely resemble the four factors discussed in *Shaver* or the five-factor test adopted by the Fourth and Fifth Circuits? Do you find this test to be more university-friendly or plaintiff-friendly?

4. The court, in explicitly allowing "manufactured" claims to proceed, stated "there are many reasons why a person might seek a job interview even though he or she has no intention of taking the job." Are the court's hypothetical situations convincing? If the intent of the claimant is solely to orchestrate a "get rich quick scheme," suffering no real harm from the discrimination, is he or she deserving of the protections of the ADA?

If you are working in university administration and a professor has filed a discrimination claim simultaneously with an application for tenure (even though you are sure he is not interested in pursuing the application) are you hesitant to deny his application for fear of a subsequent retaliation action — even if you are confident his application is part of a "get rich quick" scheme? Is that fair? Should fear of liability for such "manufactured" claims be a factor in making these kinds of administrative decisions? *See McFadden v. State Univ. of New York, Coll. at Brockport*, 195 F. Supp. 2d 436 (W.D.N.Y. 2002).

FOGLEMAN v. MERCY HOSPITAL, INC.

283 F.3d 561 (3d Cir. 2002)

BECKER, CHIEF JUDGE.

This employment discrimination action is presented as a modern rendition of the age-old parable of a son being punished for the sins of his father. The father, Sterril Fogleman, had been an employee of defendant Mercy Hospital, Inc. ("Mercy") for seventeen years before leaving the hospital in 1993. In an action separate from this case, Sterril sued Mercy claiming that he had been forced out of his job due to age and disability discrimination. Sterril's son Greg Fogleman, who is the plaintiff in the case at bar, also worked for Mercy, being employed as a security guard for eighteen years before his termination in 1996. Although Mercy claims to have fired Greg for valid job-related reasons, Greg asserts that these reasons were pretextual, and that the real reasons for his firing relate to his father's legal action against Mercy.

Greg sued Mercy under the anti-retaliation provisions of three civil rights laws: the Americans with Disabilities Act ("ADA"), 42 U.S.C. §§ 12101–12213; the Age Discrimination in Employment Act ("ADEA"), 29 U.S.C. §§ 621–634; and the Pennsylvania Human Relations Act ("PHRA"), 43 Pa. Cons. Stat. §§ 951–963, alleging three theories of illegal retaliation. Greg's first theory of illegal discrimination is that he was fired in retaliation for his father's having sued Mercy for disability and age discrimination. Second, Greg claims that Mercy violated the anti-discrimination laws by terminating him because it *thought* that he was assisting his father with his lawsuit (even if, in actuality, he was not). Third, Greg alleges that he was fired for refusing to cooperate with Mercy in the investigation of his father's claim. The District Court granted summary judgment to Mercy on all of Greg's claims, concluding that none of his theories of illegal retaliation was supported by the language of the ADA, ADEA or PHRA.

In reviewing the District Court's grant of summary judgment with respect to Greg's first claim, we are called upon to determine whether the anti-retaliation provisions of the ADA, ADEA, and PHRA prohibit an employer from taking adverse employment action against a third party in retaliation for another's protected activity. The ADA, ADEA, and PHRA contain nearly identical anti-retaliation provisions that prohibit discrimination against any individual because "such individual" has engaged in protected activity. 42 U.S.C. § 12203(a); 29 U.S.C. § 623(d); 43 Pa. Cons. Stat. § 955(d). Although we recognize that allowing an employer to retaliate against a third party with impunity can interfere with the overall purpose of the anti-discrimination laws, we believe that by referring to "such individual," the plain text of these statutes clearly prohibits only retaliation against the actual person who engaged in protected activity.

Unlike the ADEA and PHRA, however, the ADA contains an additional anti-retaliation provision that makes it unlawful for an employer "to coerce, intimidate, threaten, or interfere with any individual" exercising rights protected under the Act. 42 U.S.C. § 12203(b). We conclude that under this provision, which contains language similar to that of a section of the National Labor Relations Act ("NLRA"), 29 U.S.C. § 158(a)(1), that we have interpreted as recognizing third-party retaliation claims, Greg's claim that he was retaliated against for his father's protected activity is valid as a matter of law, and we will therefore reverse the grant of summary judgment.

We also believe that Greg's perception theory of illegal retaliation-that he was fired because Mercy *thought* that he was engaged in protected activity, even if he actually was not-presents a valid legal claim. Because the statutes forbid an employer's taking adverse action against an employee for discriminatory reasons, it does not matter whether the factual basis for the employer's discriminatory animus was correct and that, so long as the employer's specific intent was discriminatory, the retaliation is actionable. Accordingly, we will reverse the Court's grant of summary judgment on Greg's perception claim of retaliation. . . .

I. Facts and Procedural History

Members of the Fogleman family have a long history of employment at Mercy Hospital. The plaintiff, Greg Fogleman, began working for Mercy as a security officer in 1978. In 1992 Mercy named him Supervisor of Security, a post he held until his termination in 1996. Greg's wife, Michelle, also worked for Mercy for a few years in the late 1980s and early 1990s, and Greg's mother was an employee at Mercy until her retirement in May 1999. But the story of this litigation begins with Greg's father, Sterril Fogleman, who began working at Mercy in 1976 as an engineer and remained on the staff for 17 years, until 1993, when the hospital offered him a choice between accepting a demotion or leaving the hospital. Sterril chose to leave, and suspected that Mercy had pushed him out due to his advancing age and his recent loss of sight in one eye.

In June 1995, after satisfying the administrative prerequisites, Sterril sued Mercy for illegal discrimination in the District Court for the Middle District of Pennsylvania. Just before trial was to begin, in July 1998, the parties settled and the case was dismissed. Greg asserts that he did not participate in any way in Sterril's complaints or lawsuit.

Shortly after Sterril filed his lawsuit in federal court, Martin Everhart, Mercy's Vice President of Human Resources, circulated a one-page memorandum to top Mercy officials offering a brief explanation of why, in the hospital's opinion, Sterril's claim was meritless. The memo acknowledged that commenting on Sterril's lawsuit during its pendency was "done at some risk as we continue to have relatives of Mr. Fogleman employed by Mercy and open ourselves up to further public exposure particularly through newspapers as this document may be shared that way." Greg submits that this language indicates that Mercy considered him a "risk" because of his father's lawsuit. He also asserts that Everhart was "a bit colder" to him after the circulation of this memo. . . . Greg also avers that a representative of management-namely, Michael Elias-repeatedly questioned him about the status of his father's lawsuit in an attempt to pry information out of him to aid the hospital in its defense.

On September 6, 1996, Greg was involved in an incident at the hospital's gift shop that ultimately provided the official — Greg claims pretextual — basis for Mercy's termination of his employment. Greg claims that he used a spare key to enter the hospital gift shop that morning to check on the well-being of an elderly woman, Audrey Oeller, who worked there as a volunteer. Greg avers that his job description authorized him to enter the shop; additionally, his supervisor testified that before this incident Greg routinely entered the shop to check on Oeller.

The hospital, in contrast, asserts that Greg had no authority to enter the gift shop at any time, and that his entry was in violation of hospital rules. Moreover, the hospital represents that it was troubled by Oeller's conflicting account of Greg's reasons for entering the shop. According to Oeller, Greg told her that he entered the shop to check on the sprinkler system at the request of maintenance supervisor Dave Searfoss. Searfoss, however, related to the hospital that he had never made any such request of Greg. According to Mercy, Greg also violated hospital policy by failing to report the incident to anyone until questioned about it, failing to request assistance, failing to document the incident until directed to do so, and failing to report the taking of the key to the gift shop from a secure Maintenance Department Room.

On September 11, the hospital suspended Greg with pay in the wake of the gift shop incident pending further investigation. Greg claims that he was told that he would not receive a final determination on his employment status until September 17, which was also the same day that his father was to be deposed for his federal lawsuit against Mercy. Although it appears that no actual investigation took place before September 17, Greg was fired on that day, allegedly for reasons related to the gift shop incident. Greg avers that his termination was in violation of the hospital's progressive discipline policy. Other employees, Greg contends, were punished less severely for far more egregious infractions.

Greg sued Mercy in the District Court for the Middle District of Pennsylvania alleging violations of the ADA, the ADEA, and the PHRA. Mercy moved for summary judgment on these claims, and the District Court granted the motion, concluding that the statutes did not allow a plaintiff to sue on the theory that he had suffered a discharge in retaliation for protected activity engaged in by another person, even if that other person was a close relative. . . .

II. The Relevant Anti-Retaliation Provisions

Greg alleges that his termination violated the anti-retaliation provisions of the ADA, the ADEA, and the PHRA. The ADA's anti-retaliation provision states:

> No person shall discriminate against any individual because such individual has opposed any act or practice made unlawful by this chapter or because such individual made a charge, testified, assisted, or participated in any manner in an investigation, proceeding, or hearing under this chapter.

. . . .

Because the anti-retaliation provisions of the ADA and ADEA are nearly identical, as is the anti-retaliation provision of Title VII, we have held that precedent interpreting any one of these statutes is equally relevant to interpretation of the others. *See Krouse v. American Sterilizer Co.*, 126 F.3d 494, 500 (3d Cir.1997). . . . For purposes of this appeal, therefore, we will interpret the anti-retaliation provisions of the ADA, ADEA, and PHRA cited above as applying identically in this case and governed by the same set of precedents.

In addition to the anti-retaliation provision cited above, the ADA has a further anti-retaliation provision not found in the ADEA and the PHRA. That provision reads:

> It shall be unlawful to coerce, intimidate, threaten, or interfere with any individual in the exercise or enjoyment of, or on account of his or her having exercised or enjoyed, or on account of his or her having aided or encouraged any other individual in the exercise or enjoyment of, any right granted or protected by this chapter.

42 USC § 12203(b). As will appear, this provision, in light of its similarity to language in the NLRA, *see* 29 U.S.C. § 158(a)(1), is critical to the outcome of this case.

Before analyzing each of Greg's theories of illegal discrimination, we note that in order to establish a prima facie case of illegal retaliation under the anti-discrimination statutes, a plaintiff must show: "(1) protected employee activity; (2) adverse action by the employer either after or contemporaneous with the employee's protected activity; and (3) a causal connection between the employee's protected activity and the employer's adverse action." *Krouse*, 126 F.3d at 500. Because the District Court concluded that Greg failed to satisfy the first prong with respect to his theories of relief, it never addressed the adverse employment action and causation prongs of his retaliation claims. Consequently, we do not address those issues here on appeal in the first instance. Rather, we consider only the District Court's treatment of the "protected activity" prongs of Greg's anti-discrimination claims.

III. Greg's Third Party Retaliation Claim

In arguing that Mercy unlawfully retaliated against Greg for the protected activity of his father, Greg maintains that as a matter of statutory construction, the anti-retaliation provisions are violated even if the person retaliated against did not himself engage in protected conduct. . . . Mercy responds that the anti-retaliation provisions only prohibit retaliation against a person who himself engaged in protected activity.

A.

In determining whether retaliation against a person who has not himself engaged in protected conduct is actionable, we first consider the ADA, 42 U.S.C. § 12203(a), ADEA, 29 U.S.C. § 623(d), and PHRA, 43 Pa. Cons.Stat. § 955(d), each of which contains similar language prohibiting retaliation. We have yet to decide squarely whether these provisions make actionable retaliation against someone who has not himself engaged in protected conduct. Among the other courts that have addressed the issue no consensus has emerged. Some courts have answered the question definitively in the negative — i.e., a plaintiff may not present an anti-retaliation claim without personally participating in protected activity. *See, e.g., Smith v. Riceland Foods, Inc.*, 151 F.3d 813, 819 (8th Cir.1998); *Holt v. JTM Indus., Inc.*, 89 F.3d 1224, 1227 (5th Cir.1996). But other courts have expressly acknowledged the viability of third-party retaliation claims. *See, e.g., EEOC v. Nalbandian Sales, Inc.*, 36 F.Supp.2d 1206, 1212 (E.D.Cal.1998); *De Medina v. Reinhardt*, 444 F.Supp. 573, 580 (D.D.C.1978).

The plain text of the anti-retaliation provisions requires that the person retaliated against also be the person who engaged in the protected activity: Each statute forbids discrimination against an individual because "such individual" has engaged in protected conduct. By their own terms, then, the statutes do not make actionable discrimination against an employee who has not engaged in protected activity. Read literally, the statutes are unambiguous — indeed, it is hard to imagine a clearer way of specifying that the individual who was discriminated against must also be the individual who engaged in protected activity. . . .

Nevertheless, Greg and the EEOC are correct that a literal reading of the anti-retaliation provisions is at odds with the policies animating those provisions. The anti-retaliation provisions recognize that enforcement of anti-discrimination laws depends in large part on employees to initiate administrative and judicial proceedings. There can be no doubt that an employer who retaliates against the friends and relatives of employees who initiate anti-discrimination proceedings will deter employees from exercising their protected rights. Indeed, as the Seventh Circuit sagely observed, "To retaliate against a man by hurting a member of his family is an ancient method of revenge, and is not unknown in the field of labor relations." *NLRB v. Advertisers Mfg. Co.*, 823 F.2d 1086, 1088 (7th Cir.1987). Allowing employers to retaliate via friends and family, therefore, would appear to be in significant tension with the overall purpose of the anti-retaliation provisions, which are intended to promote the reporting, investigation, and correction of discriminatory conduct in the workplace. [citation omitted]

This case, therefore, presents a conflict between a statute's plain meaning and its general policy objectives. In general, this conflict ought to be resolved in favor of the statute's plain meaning. . . .

To be sure, however, there are cases in which a blind adherence to the literal meaning of a statute would lead to a patently absurd result that no rational legislature could have intended. Following the letter, rather than the spirit, of the law in such cases would go against the court's role of construing statutes to effectuate the legislature's intent. . . . We do not believe, however, that this is such a case. Although we think, as explained above, that recognizing third-party retaliation claims is more consistent with the purpose of the anti-discrimination statutes, we cannot say that prohibiting such claims is an absurd outcome that contravenes the clearly expressed intent of the legislature. . . . Rather, while we do not find them particularly convincing, there are at least plausible policy reasons why Congress might have intended to exclude third-party retaliation claims.

. . . .

B.

As an alternative basis for his third-party claim Greg also relies on the second anti-retaliation provision of the ADA, 42 U.S.C. § 12203(b), which reads:

> It shall be unlawful to coerce, intimidate, threaten, or interfere with any individual in the exercise or enjoyment of, or on account of his or her having exercised or enjoyed, or on account of his or her having aided or encouraged any other individual in the exercise or enjoyment of, any right granted or protected by this chapter.

We have noted that the scope of this second anti-retaliation provision of the ADA "arguably sweeps more broadly" than the first. *Mondzelewski v. Pathmark Stores, Inc.* 162 F.3d 778, 789 (3d Cir.1998). In particular, unlike the first provision, the text of this provision does not expressly limit a cause of action to the particular employee that engaged in protected activity.

This provision contains language similar to that found in section 8(a)(1) of the NLRA, 29 U.S.C. § 158(a)(1), which makes it an unfair labor practice for an employer "to interfere with, restrain, or coerce employees" in exercising their rights guaranteed under the Act. In *Kenrich Petrochemicals, Inc. v. NLRB*, 907 F.2d 400 (3d Cir.1990) (in banc), we enforced an order of the National Labor Relations Board that interpreted section 8(a)(1) to prohibit an employer's retaliation against a supervisory employee (who was otherwise unprotected by the Act) for protected activity engaged in by her close relatives. We noted that the firing of a close relative could have a "coercive" effect on the employees engaging in protected activity, *id.* at 407, instilling "fear that the exercise of their rights will give the company a license to inflict harm on their family." *Id.* at 409. . . .

Our interpretations of the NLRA can serve as a useful guide to interpreting similar language in the ADA, as both are "part of a wider statutory scheme to protect employees in the workplace nationwide." *McKennon v. Nashville Banner Pub'g Co.*, 513 U.S. 352, 357, 115 S.Ct. 879, 130 L.Ed.2d 852 (1995). The texts of section 8(a)(1) of the NLRA and the ADA's second anti-retaliation provision are essentially similar-each makes it illegal for an employer to "coerce" or "interfere with" an employee exercising his rights under the act. In view of this fact, as well as the similar policies underlying the two provisions, it seems sensible to hold, as we now do, that Greg may assert his third-party retaliation claim under this section of the ADA just as he would be able to do under the NLRA. Accordingly, we will reverse the District Court's order granting summary judgment to Mercy to the extent that it was based on the Court's view that Greg's third-party retaliation claim was not cognizable under the ADA's second anti-retaliation provision. . . .

IV. Greg's "Perception Theory" of Retaliation

As a final means of showing illegal retaliation under the anti-discrimination statutes, Greg argues that even if he was not engaged in primary protected activity, Mercy perceived him to be so engaged. Greg contends that Mercy fired him with the subjective intent of retaliating against him for engaging in protected activity, thereby violating the anti-retaliation provisions. The District Court disposed of this claim as a matter of law, concluding that the statutory language did not support a perception theory of retaliation. We disagree.

Unlike the interpretation of "such individual" to allow for third party claims advocated by Greg that we rejected in Section II.A, we do not believe that the perception theory contradicts the plain text of the anti-discrimination statutes. Rather, we read the statutes as directly supporting a perception theory of discrimination due to the fact that they make it illegal for an employer to " *discriminate* against any individual *because* such individual has [engaged in protected activity.]" 42 U.S.C. § 12203(a) (emphases added). "Discriminat[ion]" refers to the practice of making a decision based on a certain criterion, and therefore focuses on the decisionmaker's subjective intent. What follows, the word "because," specifies the criterion that the employer is prohibited from using as a basis for decisionmaking. The laws, therefore, focus on the employer's subjective reasons for taking adverse action against an employee, so it matters not whether the reasons behind the employer's discriminatory animus are actually correct as a factual matter.

As an illustration by analogy, imagine a Title VII discrimination case in which an employer refuses to hire a prospective employee because he thinks that the applicant is a Muslim. The employer is still discriminating on the basis of religion even if the applicant he refuses to hire is not in fact a Muslim. What is relevant is that the applicant, whether Muslim or not, was treated worse than he otherwise would have been for reasons prohibited by the statute. We have adopted this same approach in the labor law context, where we have consistently held that an employer's discharge of an employee for discriminatory reasons amounts to illegal retaliation even if it is based on the employer's mistaken belief that the employee engaged in protected activity. *See Fogarty v. Boles*, 121 F.3d 886, 891 (3d Cir.1997); *Brock v. Richardson*, 812 F.2d 121, 125 (3d Cir.1987). Accordingly, we hold that if Greg can show, as he claims, that adverse action was taken against him because Mercy thought that he was assisting his father and thereby engaging in protected activity, it does not matter whether Mercy's perception was factually correct. . . .

Conclusion

For the foregoing reasons, the order of the District Court granting summary judgment to Mercy will be reversed and the case remanded for further proceedings consistent with this opinion.

NOTES

1. The court reasoned that there were "at least plausible policy reasons" why Congress may have intended to exclude third-party retaliation claims. Can you think of any? *See Fogleman*, 283 F.3d at 569; *Holt v. JTM Indus., Inc.*, 89 F.3d 1224 (5th Cir. 1996).

2. From the perspective of the employer, would you be concerned with the possible implications of the *Fogleman* decision? Did the court leave important questions unanswered? For example, how far does liability reach? Should employers be concerned about firing the fiancé of an ADA plaintiff? A girlfriend? A cousin? A second cousin? A brother-in-law?

3. Does the court's decision convert the at-will employment of any relative or family member of a claimant to something other than at-will?

TABLE OF CASES

[References are to pages]

A

B

[References are to pages]

C

[References are to pages]

[References are to pages]

[References are to pages]

G

[References are to pages]

[References are to pages]

K

L

[References are to pages]

M

[References are to pages]

N

O

P

[References are to pages]

Q

R

[References are to pages]

[References are to pages]

T

U

[References are to pages]

V

W

[References are to pages]

Y

Z

INDEX

[References are to sections.]

A

B

C

[References are to sections.]

[References are to sections.]

[References are to sections.]

[References are to sections.]

[References are to sections.]

T

U

W

Z